the TECHNIQUE of PSYCHOTHERAPY

the TECHNIQUE
of PSYCHOTHERAPY

by LEWIS R. WOLBERG, M.D.

Director, Postgraduate Center for Psychotherapy;
Associate Clinical Professor of Psychiatry, New
York Medical College.

GRUNE & STRATTON   NEW YORK 1954

Library of Congress Catalog Card Number 54-5769

First printing, February, 1954
Second printing, May, 1954
Third printing, Basic Books. January, 1957

Printed and bound in U.S.A.

Preface

AMIDST THE LUSH LITERATURE ON PSYCHIATRY THERE LIES A BARREN territory—writings on psychotherapeutic technique. With rare exceptions, the meager offerings that have been published deal with psychotherapy in general terms, and only minimally consider its techniques. Such a dearth of material is no mystery, for psychotherapy is an extremely difficult topic to discuss, dealing with amorphous dynamic concepts that defy description, let alone analysis. Many psychotherapists have abandoned attempts to delineate their techniques on the basis that interpersonal nuances are so subtle, and variables in therapy so myriad, that they cannot satisfactorily be detailed in a text. Indeed, there are those who claim that psychotherapy is more an art than a science, that psychotherapists are born and not made, and that books on psychiatric treatment are consequently of little or no value.

The futility of writing about psychotherapy is seemingly substantiated by certain facts. Two qualified psychiatrists with equivalent educational backgrounds, studying in the same psychoanalytic or psychotherapeutic school, and exposed to the same teaching materials, will handle similar therapeutic problems in unique ways. Differences will manifest themselves in the amount of activity, the focus of inquiry, the relative emphasis on past and current situations, and therapeutic goals. As many kinds of psychotherapy apparently exist as there are people doing therapy. Elucidating on psychotherapy in a book would, therefore, merely describe the biases of its author.

Yet bias not withstanding, good psychotherapy must depend on a basically sound therapeutic structure, irrespective of the specific "kind" of psychotherapy done and without reference to the individual "style" of the therapist. The purpose of this book is to delineate such a structure. Toward this end, transcribed recordings of hundreds of treatment sessions conducted by a sizeable number of therapists, observation of students in psychoanalytic training with me, and critical examination of tape recordings of my own therapeutic sessions were employed. A unique opportunity was afforded me to study the therapeutic methods and results of a large group of psychiatrists, caseworkers and clinical psychologists through the organization of the Postgraduate Center for Psychotherapy, a psychotherapeutic agency devoted to helping people in low and moderate income groups. The pressing need for therapeutic services resulted in the expansion of the Center until it became one of the largest continuous treatment centers in the country, rendering service to thousands of individuals. Patients with a wide assortment of problems requested therapy, being referred by over fifty sources in the community, including social agencies, courts, hospitals and clinics, schools and colleges, employment and vocational guidance groups, as well as private physicians and psychiatrists.

The diversity of the problems encountered, and the varying motivations and ego resources of the patients seeking help, necessitated employment of short and long-term treatment methods, depending on the needs and limitations of the patient and the therapeutic goal.

As Director of the Center, I was able to screen many patients and to follow their progress during therapy. I was also able to study the work of the therapists employed at the Center through direct supervision of their activities and through conferences with their supervisors.

It was soon apparent that a special kind of training was necessary before the therapist could effectively handle, on a once- or twice-a-week basis, the kinds of cases that were being referred to the Center for treatment. Even where the therapist had had formal analytic training, it was essential to supplement this with further training before he could operate with maximum effectiveness. Lack of facilities where such education could be acquired led to the organization of a training program at the Postgraduate Center, the purpose of which was the exploration of an approach to a therapy which extracted from the different schools of psychiatry, psychology, and the other social sciences, validated techniques and procedures.

Participating in the training program of the Postgraduate Center, I was privileged to give seminars in psychotherapy of both an introductory and advanced nature. These form the basis of the present volume. Intended for students and practicing therapists, the book includes the presentation of a flexible framework within which the individual may develop or augment his therapeutic skills. The combination of methods and techniques described is intended to enhance the constructive use of the self in the therapeutic situation.

Understandably, a number of obstacles impede such an eclectic approach. Yet the hope of developing psychotherapy into a concrete methodology requires a careful integration of the work that is being done by the different disciplines engaged in rendering service to people with emotional problems. In this way, from the experiences of the various schools of psychiatry and the social sciences, there may be distilled principles of psychotherapy that can be translated into effective practice. The present volume constitutes an attempt at such integration. It describes, in the main, a blended utilization of methods from fields of psychoanalysis, psychobiology, psychiatric interviewing, casework, and psychologic counseling, which should vastly increase the effectiveness of the therapist in the handling of a wide variety of emotional disorders.

The seminar material, which was recorded and transcribed, has been edited to eliminate unnecessary repetition, and it has, for purposes of better reading,

been restyled, rearranged and divided into chapters. Where only hasty reference was made to important aspects of method, a more detailed elaboration has
been added. The original informality of the seminars is only partly reflected
because it was not possible to include the complete transcript of student participation.

Acknowledgment is made to the Staff of the Postgraduate Center, which
cooperated with me in every way and helped me, through its work, to evolve the
philosophy of therapy which is expounded in this book. Credit is due to the
Supervisors' Group of the Center, whose discussions of technique enabled me
to crystallize my ideas more succinctly. Thanks are due to the editor of the *New
York State Journal of Medicine* for permission to utilize material from my articles, "Recent Trends in Psychotherapy," "The Problem of Self-Esteem in Psychotherapy," "Resistance to Cure in Psychotherapy," "The Role of Motivation
in Psychotherapy," and "Goals and Objectives in Psychotherapy"; to Grune &
Stratton, Inc., for allowing the use of psychotherapeutic material from my books,
Hypnoanalysis and *Medical Hypnosis;* and to the editors of the *Psychiatric Quarterly, The Nervous Child* and *The American Journal of Psychotherapy* for similar privileges in relation to articles published by myself in these journals.

LEWIS R. WOLBERG, M.D.

New York City
January, 1954

Contents

PREFACE v

I. THE SCOPE, TYPES AND GENERAL PRINCIPLES OF PSYCHOTHERAPY

1. WHAT IS PSYCHOTHERAPY? 3
   A comprehensive definition of psychotherapy. Other definitions.
2. VARIETIES OF PSYCHOTHERAPY 7
   Supportive therapy. Insight therapy with reeducative goals. Insight therapy with reconstructive goals.
3. EDUCATIONAL, CASEWORK AND COUNSELING APPROACHES VERSUS PSYCHOTHERAPY 10
   Therapeutic goals in education. Mental health literature. Traditional and modern concepts of social service. Objectives of personal counseling.
4. THE "SPONTANEOUS" CURE 14
   Reparative mechanisms of mental health. Comparison with results in psychotherapy.
5. SUPPORTIVE THERAPY 17
   Guidance. Environmental manipulation. Externalization of interests. Reassurance. Prestige suggestion. Pressure and coercion. Persuasion. Emotional catharsis and desensitization. Muscular relaxation. Hydrotherapy. Shock and convulsive therapy. Drug therapy. Brain surgery (psychosurgery). Inspirational group therapy. Music therapy. Indications for supportive therapy.
6. INSIGHT THERAPY WITH REEDUCATIVE GOALS (REEDUCATIVE THERAPY) 36
   "Relationship therapy." "Attitude therapy." Distributive analysis and synthesis (psychobiologic therapy). Interview psychotherapy (psychiatric interviewing). Therapeutic counseling (psychologic therapy): non-directive or "client-centered" therapy, directive therapy. Casework therapy: functional casework, diagnostic casework. Reconditioning. Semantic approaches to therapy. Reeducative group therapy.
7. INSIGHT THERAPY WITH RECONSTRUCTIVE GOALS (RECONSTRUCTIVE THERAPY) 53
   Freudian psychoanalysis. Non-Freudian psychoanalysis. The "individual psychology" of Alfred Adler. The "analytical psychology" of Carl Jung. Therapeutic modifications of Sandor Ferenczi. The "will therapy" of Otto Rank. The "active psychoanalysis" of Wilhelm Stekel. The "character analysis" and "or-

gone therapy" of Wilhelm Reich. The biologically-oriented theoretic system of Sandor Rado. The dynamic-cultural school of psychoanalysis: Erich Fromm, Karen Horney, Harry Stack Sullivan. Psychoanalytically-oriented psychotherapy. Adjunctive aids in psychoanalytically oriented psychotherapy: hypnoanalysis, art therapy, play therapy, narcotherapy, analytic group therapy.

8. SIMILARITIES AND DIFFERENCES AMONG THE VARIOUS PSYCHO-
THERAPIES   87
Duration of therapy. Frequency of visits. History-taking. Pre-scribed psychologic examinations. Nature of communications. General activity of therapist. Advice-giving. Handling of trans-ference. Nature of patient-therapist relationship. Physical posi-tion of patient during therapy. Handling of dream material. Use of adjuncts during therapy.

9. THE USE OF SUPPORTIVE, REEDUCATIVE AND RECONSTRUCTIVE AP-
PROACHES   96

10. "BRIEF" OR "SHORT-TERM" PSYCHOTHERAPY   103

11. WHAT IS THE "BEST" KIND OF PSYCHOTHERAPY?   106

12. WHO CAN DO PSYCHOTHERAPY?   111
The physician in psychotherapy. The clinical psychologist in psy-chotherapy. The social worker in psychotherapy. The nurse in psychotherapy. The minister in psychotherapy. The teacher in psychotherapy. The concept of team functioning. Psychiatric supervision.

13. THE EQUIPMENT OF THE PSYCHOTHERAPIST   137
Educational equipment. Personality equipment. Experiential equipment. Personal psychotherapy or psychoanalysis for the therapist.

14. GENERAL PRINCIPLES OF PSYCHOTHERAPY   149
Dynamics of therapeutic change. Mechanics of therapeutic change.

15. THE CONDUCT OF THE PSYCHOTHERAPEUTIC INTERVIEW . . .   157
Rationale of interviewing. The language of the interview. Open-ing the interview. Maintaining the flow of verbalizations. Direct-ing the flow of verbalizations. The principle of selective focus-ing. Inculcating insight. Terminating the interview. Special problems in interviewing. The interpersonal climate of the inter-view.

16. THE PHYSICAL SURROUNDINGS OF PSYCHOTHERAPY   186

17. A PRACTICAL OUTLINE OF PSYCHOTHERAPY   189

II. THE BEGINNING PHASE OF TREATMENT

18. INTRODUCTION   195

19. THE INITIAL INTERVIEW: THE FIRST CONTACT WITH THE PATIENT   198
Handling the first inquiry. Preliminaries to the interview. In-

suring the proper emotional atmosphere. Structuring the purpose
of the interview. Dealing with initial resistances.

20. THE INITIAL INTERVIEW: COLLATING ESSENTIAL DATA . . .   207
Pros and cons of history-taking. The chief complaint. History
and development of the complaint. Statistical data. Other symptoms and clinical findings. Dreams. Family data. Previous emotional upsets. Previous treatment.

21. THE INITIAL INTERVIEW: MAKING A DIAGNOSIS   216
A dynamic interpretation of diagnosis. Recommended nomenclature. Illustrative case.

22. THE INITIAL INTERVIEW: FORMULATING THE TENTATIVE DYNAMICS   227

23. THE INITIAL INTERVIEW: ESTIMATING THE PROGNOSIS   230
Criteria for estimating prognosis. Summary of positive and negative prognostic signs in the patient. Summary of positive and
negative prognostic signs from the standpoint of the therapist.

24. THE INITIAL INTERVIEW: ESTIMATING THE PATIENT'S GENERAL
CONDITION   246
Reciprocal responses of patient and therapist. Physical appearance. Patient's estimate of present physical health. Communicativeness. Insight and motivation.

25. THE INITIAL INTERVIEW: MAKING PRACTICAL ARRANGEMENTS FOR
PSYCHOTHERAPY   249
Choice of therapist. Choice of treatment method. Frequency of
visits. Discussing the fee. Delays in starting therapy. Final arrangements. Referring the patient. Anticipating emergencies and
other difficulties. Essential correspondence.

26. THE INITIAL INTERVIEW: SECURING ESSENTIAL CONSULTATIONS .   266
Medical, neurologic and psychiatric consultations. Casework
consultations. Psychologic and other related consultations.

27. THE INITIAL INTERVIEWS IMPORTANT "DON'TS" DURING THE
INITIAL INTERVIEW   272

28. THE INITIAL INTERVIEW: DEALING WITH INADEQUATE MOTIVATION   275
Recognizing, reflecting and indicating acceptance of negative
feelings. Creating incentives for therapy. Dealing with continued
opposition to treatment. Clarifying misconceptions. Treating the
stubbornly non-motivated patient.

29. THE INITIAL INTERVIEW: ILLUSTRATIVE CASE HISTORY . . .   293

30. ANSWERING QUESTIONS PATIENTS ASK ABOUT THERAPY . . .   303

31. ESTABLISHING A WORKING RELATIONSHIP   317
Multiple roles of the therapist. Resistances to a working relationship. Building the relationship. Communicating an understanding of the patient's problem. Communicating interest. Communicating tolerance and acceptance. Communicating objectivity.
Communicating empathy. Sundry "rules" for the building of the
relationship. Signs of a working relationship.

32. STRUCTURING THE THERAPEUTIC SITUATION 340
Explaining the manner of communication. Explaining general
routines operative in therapy. Delineating the patient's responsibilities. Defining the role of the therapist. Explaining how
psychotherapy works. Signs of acceptance of therapeutic structuring.

III. THE MIDDLE PHASE OF TREATMENT

33. IDENTIFYING IMPORTANT TRENDS AND PATTERNS: INTRODUCTION   361

34. IDENTIFYING IMPORTANT TRENDS AND PATTERNS: THE USE OF
THERAPEUTIC INTERVIEWING 364
Focusing on symptoms. Focusing on feelings. Focusing on environmental dissatisfactions. Focusing on current interpersonal
relations. Focusing on past history. Observation of slips of
speech. Use of intuition.

35. IDENTIFYING IMPORTANT TRENDS AND PATTERNS: THE USE OF
FREE ASSOCIATION 376

36. IDENTIFYING IMPORTANT TRENDS AND PATTERNS: THE USE OF
DREAMS AND FANTASIES 379
The structure of dreams. The content of dreams. The therapeutic
use of dreams. Interpretive activities. Fantasies. Illustrative case
material.

37. IDENTIFYING IMPORTANT TRENDS AND PATTERNS: THE EXAMINA-
TION OF ATTITUDES TOWARD THE THERAPIST, INCLUDING
TRANSFERENCE 398
Projection into therapy of stereotyped patterns. Methods of re-
ducing transference. Methods of stimulating transference. Illus-
trative case material.

38. EXPLORING TRENDS AND PATTERNS 411
Selection of areas for exploration. Illustrative case.

39. THE UNCOVERING OF UNCONSCIOUS MATERIAL 421
The symbolism of the unconscious. Forgotten memories and experiences. Hypnotic recall of forgotten memories. The handling
of unconscious material. Case illustrations.

40. INCULCATING INSIGHT THROUGH INTERPRETATION 439
Varieties of interpretation. Content of interpretations. Interpretive techniques. Responses to interpretation. Illustrative case
material.

41. THE HANDLING OF RESISTANCES TO CURE 463
Forms of resistance: suppression and repression, intensification
of symptoms, self-devaluation, forced "flight into health," intellectual inhibitions, "acting-out," superficial talk, insight as
resistance, dissociating the treatment hour from life, contempt
for normality, reluctance to yield pleasure values of therapy,
transference resistances. Methods of handling resistance: exploring resistance manifestations, indicating its purpose, tangential use of reassurance, focusing on material that fosters re-

sistance, managing "acting-out," handling transference resistances. Working-through of resistance. Illustrative case material.

42. THE MANAGEMENT OF UNTOWARD ATTITUDES IN THE THERAPIST
(COUNTER-TRANSFERENCE) 488

43. TRANSLATING INSIGHT INTO ACTION 494
Modern learning theory and psychotherapy. Building motivation
for activity. Providing a favorable environment for action. Psychodramatic techniques. Conferences with family members. Adjusting the patient's environment. The learning of new patterns
within the therapeutic relationship. Case illustration.

44. THE "WORKING-THROUGH" PROCESS 508

45. SUPPORTIVE AND REEDUCATIVE TECHNIQUES DURING MIDDLE
TREATMENT PHASES 523
Principal and adjunctive uses. Mode of action of supportive
therapy. The therapist-patient relationship in supportive therapy.
Guidance. Environmental manipulation. Externalization of interests. Reassurance. Persuasion. Emotional catharsis and desensitization. Miscellaneous supportive measures. Supportive
measures in insight therapy. Reeducative approaches.

IV. THE TERMINAL PHASE OF TREATMENT

46. GOALS IN TERMINATING TREATMENT 551
Success judgments from the standpoint of the patient. Success
judgments from the standpoint of society. Success judgments
from the standpoint of the therapist. "Ideal" objectives of mental health. A practical goal in therapy.

47. TECHNICAL PROBLEMS IN TERMINATION 557
Terminating therapy upon reaching set goals. Terminating on
basis of incomplete goals. Planned interruption of therapy.
Terminal note. Follow-up.

V. SPECIAL ASPECTS

48. ADJUNCTIVE AIDS IN PSYCHOTHERAPY 569
Group therapy. Hypnotherapy. Narcotherapy. Bibliotherapy.

49. HANDLING EMERGENCIES IN PSYCHOTHERAPY 583
Suicidal attempts. Excitement, over-activity and anti-social behavior. Intense anxiety attacks and panic states. Acute alcoholic
intoxication. Acute barbiturate poisoning. Severe psychosomatic
symptoms. Intercurrent incurable somatic illness.

50. PSYCHOTHERAPY IN SPECIAL CONDITIONS 597
Psychoneurotic disorders: anxiety reactions, conversion and dissociative reactions, phobic reactions, obsessive-compulsive reactions, depressive reactions. Psychophysiologic, autonomic and
visceral disorders. Personality disorders: "inadequate," infantile
and dependency patterns, "schizoid" and detached patterns,
paranoid or "'anal" patterns, power patterns, narcissistic reactions, psychopathic personality, alcoholism, drug addiction,
sexual deviations, speech disorders, borderline cases. Psychotic

disorders: involutional psychotic reactions, manic-depressive reactions, schizophrenic reactions. Stress reactions.

51. SUPERVISION OF THE PSYCHOTHERAPEUTIC PROCESS 641
Functions of supervision. Problems in orientation. Problems in recording and reporting. Problems in technical performance. Problems in learning. Problems in termination of supervision. Technical details of supervision. Supervision as an interpersonal relationship.

52. QUESTIONS THERAPISTS ASK ABOUT PSYCHOTHERAPY . . . 661

53. RECORDING IN PSYCHOTHERAPY 682
Statistical data. Initial interview. Daily progress notes. Monthly progress notes. Terminal note. Summary. Follow-up note. Case folder. Electrical recording.

CASE HISTORY 688

REFERENCES   781

RECOMMENDED READING 801

APPENDICES   807
Statistical data (short form). Statistical data (long form). Initial interview. Personal data sheet. Family data sheet. Daily progress note. Monthly progress summary. Terminal note. Summary. Case folder. Outline for case presentation. Application blank for new staff members. Informational sheet. Personal history sheet. Medical form. Physical, neurologic and laboratory examination. Mental examination. Authorization for release of medical records. Progress report.

AUTHOR INDEX 841

SUBJECT INDEX 845

I

The Scope, Types and
General Principles of Psychotherapy

1

What Is Psychotherapy?

PSYCHOTHERAPY IS A FORM OF TREATMENT FOR PROBLEMS OF AN EMO-
TIONAL NATURE IN WHICH A TRAINED PERSON DELIBERATELY ESTABLISHES A
PROFESSIONAL RELATIONSHIP WITH A PATIENT WITH THE OBJECT OF RE-
MOVING, MODIFYING OR RETARDING EXISTING SYMPTOMS, OF MEDIATING
DISTURBED PATTERNS OF BEHAVIOR, AND OF PROMOTING POSITIVE PERSON-
ALITY GROWTH AND DEVELOPMENT.

This comprehensive definition of psychotherapy requires additional
elaboration.

"PSYCHOTHERAPY IS A FORM OF TREATMENT: No matter how much we
attempt to dilute what we do in psychotherapy, it remains a form of treatment.
Such terms as "reeducation," "helping process" and "guidance" are merely
descriptive of what happens in the course of treatment and do not really
disguise the therapeutic nature of the process.

FOR PROBLEMS OF AN EMOTIONAL NATURE: Emotional problems are
diverse, influencing every facet of human functioning. They manifest themselves in distortions in the individual's psychic, somatic, interpersonal and community life. Manifestations of emotional illness are thus multiple, involving
the total human being. In view of this totality of disturbance, it is arbitrary and
unsound to separate social and interpersonal difficulties from psychic and
psychosomatic disorders which are always concurrent, though not at all times
obvious.

IN WHICH A TRAINED PERSON: In his search for relief, the individual is
apt to involve himself in a relationship with a friend or authority. The motivations that prompt such a relationship are disabling symptoms or a realization
that one's happiness and productivity are being sabotaged by inner forces he is
neither able to understand nor to control. Sometimes the consequences of this
relationship are disastrous to both participants, particularly when an attempt
is made to handle the sufferer's emotional turmoil. Dealing with an emotional
problem requires a high degree of skill that may be acquired only through
extensive postgraduate training and experience.

DELIBERATELY ESTABLISHES A PROFESSIONAL RELATIONSHIP: The relationship, the core of the therapeutic process, is deliberately planned and nurtured by the therapist. Unlike non-professional relationships, which are part of
the social nature of man, the therapeutic relationship is started and maintained
on a professional level toward specific therapeutic objectives.

WITH A PATIENT: Since the individual in psychotherapy is receiving treatment, he is best called a "patient" rather than some other designation such as a "client."

WITH THE OBJECT OF REMOVING, [EXISTING SYMPTOMS]: A prime goal in therapy is to eliminate the patient's suffering, as well as to remove the handicaps imposed on him by his symptoms.

MODIFYING [EXISTING SYMPTOMS]: Despite our wish for complete relief, certain circumstances may militate against this objective. Chief deterrents are inadequate motivation, diminutive ego strength, and limitations in the patient's available time or finances. These will impose restrictions on the extent of help that can be rendered, and make for modification rather than cure of the patient's symptoms.

OR RETARDING EXISTING SYMPTOMS,: There are some malignant forms of emotional illness, such as fulminating schizophrenic disorders, in which psychotherapy, no matter how adroitly applied, serves merely to delay an inevitable deteriorative process. This palliative effect is eminently worthwhile, however, often helping to preserve the patient's contact with reality.

OF MEDIATING DISTURBED PATTERNS OF BEHAVIOR,: The recognition in recent years that many occupational, educational, marital, interpersonal and social problems are emotionally inspired, has extended the use of psychotherapy into fields hitherto considered provinces of the psychologist, teacher, sociologist, religious leader and law-maker. Realization that the character structure is involved in all emotional illness has broadened the objectives of psychotherapy from mere symptom relief or removal to correction of disturbed interpersonal patterns and relationships.

AND OF PROMOTING POSITIVE PERSONALITY GROWTH AND DEVELOPMENT.": The final use of psychotherapy is as a vehicle for personality maturation. This has introduced a new dimension into the field of psychotherapy—a dimension that deals, on the one hand, with problems of immaturity of the so-called "normal" person, and, on the other, with characterologic difficulties associated with inhibited growth previously considered inaccessible to treatment. Here, psychotherapy aims at a resolution of blocks in psychosocial development, in order that the individual may aspire to more complete creative self-fulfillment, more productive attitudes toward life and more gratifying relationships with people.

OTHER DEFINITIONS OF PSYCHOTHERAPY

The comprehensive definition of psychotherapy given above has many advantages. However, other explanations of the meaning of the term "psychotherapy" exist which are more limited in scope. For instance, many psychoanalysts differentiate psychoanalysis from psychotherapy on the basis that psychoanalysis deals with unconscious material and psychotherapy treats of conscious material. Freudian psychoanalysts may classify only Freudian psychoanalysis under the term "psychoanalysis," relegating all other approaches to "psychotherapy." Certain therapists consider that psychotherapy is always "psychoanalytic psychotherapy," while others regard psychotherapy as exclusively composed of supportive and reeducative techniques.

The sundry published definitions of psychotherapy agree on one point; namely, that psychotherapy constitutes a form of approach to many problems of an emotional nature. They do not agree on other aspects, such as the techniques employed, the processes included, the goals approximated or the personnel involved. Typical definitions are these:

1. "For a very simple realistic definition, one could say that psychotherapy is the utilization of psychological measures in the treatment of sick people."*

2. "[Psychotherapy endeavors] to alter the behavior and change the attitudes of a maladjusted person toward a more constructive outcome."

3. "[Psychotherapy alludes] to the entire collection of approaches attempting to influence or assist a patient toward more desirable ways of thinking, feeling, and behaving."

4. "By psychotherapy is meant the use of measures which it is believed will act upon the patient's mind and thereby promote his mental health and aid his adjustment to the particular problems which have disturbed his happiness or adaptation."

5. "Psychotherapy is a form of treatment in psychiatry in which the psychiatrist, by his scientific thinking and understanding, attempts to change the thinking and feeling of people who are suffering from distorted mental or emotional processes."

* The definitions are from the following sources, reprinted by permission of the publishers:
1. ROMANO, JOHN: Psychotherapy. In Teaching Psychotherapeutic Medicine, Ed. Helen L. Witmer. New York, The Commonwealth Fund, and Cambridge, Massachusetts, Harvard University, 1947, p. 122. (Additional credit is due The Commonwealth Fund for permission to reprint this reference.)
2. ROGERS, CARL R.: Counseling and Psychotherapy. New York, Houghton Mifflin Co., 1942, pp. 19–20.
3. THORNER, MELVIN W.: Psychiatry in General Practice. Philadelphia, W. B. Saunders Co., 1948, p. 584.
4. NOYES, ARTHUR P.: Modern Clinical Psychiatry. Philadelphia, W. B. Saunders Co., 1948, p. 476.
5. POLATIN, PHILLIP AND PHILTINE, ELLEN C.: How Psychiatry Helps. New York, Harper & Bros., 1949, p. 43.
6. MASLOW, A. H. AND MITTELMAN, BÉLA: Principles of Abnormal Psychology. New York, Harper & Bros., 1951, p. 179.
7. GROTJAHN, MARTIN AND GABE, SIGMUND: Psychotherapy—Outline of its History and Present Situation. In Modern Abnormal Psychology, Ed. E. H. Mikesell, New York, Philosophical Library, Inc., 1950, p. 25.
8. FISHER, V. E.: The Meaning and Practice of Psychotherapy. New York, MacMillan Co., 1950, p. ix.
9. LEVINE, MAURICE: Psychotherapy in Medical Practice. New York, MacMillan Co., 1942, p. xii.
10. WHITEHORN, J. C.: Psychotherapy. In Modern Trends in Phychological Medicine, Ed. Noel G. Harris, London, Butterworth & Co. Ltd., 1948; New York, Paul B. Hoeber, Inc., 1948, p. 219.
11. LOWREY, LAWSON G.: Psychiatry for Social Workers. New York, Columbia University Press, 1950, p. 347.
12. DIETHELM, OSKAR: Treatment in Psychiatry. Springfield, Illinois, Charles C. Thomas, 1950, p. 54.
13. DEUTSCH, FELIX: Applied Psychoanalysis. New York, Grune & Stratton, 1949, p. 182.

6. "This [psychotherapy] is a method of treatment which aims to help the impaired individual by influencing his emotional processes, his evaluation of himself and of others, his evaluation of and his manner of coping with the problems of life. It may also include, if need be, influencing and changing his environment and thus altering the problems he has to deal with and simultaneously increasing his potentialities of mastery and integration."

7. "[Psychotherapy includes] a multitude of psychological methods, all having one thing in common—the intent to help a suffering individual through psychological means."

8. "Psychotherapy is a planned and systematic application of psychological facts and theories to the alleviation of a large variety of human ailments and disturbances, particularly those of psychogenic origin."

9. "In general, psychotherapy can be defined as the provision by the physician of new life-experiences which can influence the patient in the direction of health."

10. "Psychotherapy is the art of combating disease and promoting health by mental influences."

11. "[Psychotherapy] connotes the use of definitive psychological techniques designed to relieve demonstrable disturbances in psycho-social adjustment."

12. "Psychotherapy includes all kinds and ways of utilizing psychologic means to achieve beneficial psychobiologic changes."

13. "Psychotherapy consists of any considered and competent medical endeavor directed toward the improvement of the emotional health of the individual, based upon the understanding of the psychodynamics involved, and of the needs of the individual under treatment."

Varieties of Psychotherapy

A PERSON SEEKING TREATMENT FOR AN EMOTIONAL PROBLEM IS USUALLY in a quandary as to the best kind of available help. For he is apt to get as many opinions about preferred courses of action as there are people he consults. His family physician may admonish him to "slow down and relax," supplementing this advice with such medications as tonics, vitamins, endocrine substances, benzedrine, sedatives or placebos. His minister may enjoin him to devote himself more assiduously to religion, and to put himself more completely in the hands of God. His lawyer may counsel him to take a long vacation in order to get away from the press of business responsibilities. Friends may urge him to leave his job, or to divorce his wife, or to find an absorbing hobby, or to take up Christian Science, or to see a chiropractor, or to read such books as *Peace of Mind, How to Stop Worrying and Start Living,* and *Dianetics.*

If he decides to get professional help, he will be no less confounded, particularly if he lives in a large city where there are many representative types of therapy. If such is the case, what should he do? Should he choose a therapist who practices the "common sense" method of Adolf Meyer? Should he find an orthodox Freudian psychoanalyst? Or should he get an adherent of a deviant psychoanalytic school; and, if so, of what school—that of Adler, Jung, Stekel, Rank, Horney or Sullivan? Is a therapist to be preferred who knows the techniques of hypnosis or narcosynthesis; or one who employs short-term therapy, such as described by Alexander and French; or psychiatric interviewing, like that elaborated by Finesinger; or the non-directive therapy of Rogers; or psychodrama, such as advocated by Moreno and his group? Should he pay credence to the enthusiastic claims of an acquaintance who is getting inspirational group therapy; or to the one who is being "cured" by sitting in an orgone box; or to the more recent acquaintance who is all agog about "conditioned reflex therapy?"

It is confusing, even for the average professional person, to view the multiform methods of treatment that are promulgated for emotional illness, and to listen to the exaggerated claims of their devotees and to the violent denunciations of their critics. Equally puzzling is the fact that published statistical data, tabulating percentages of cure and improvement and failure, reveal that results obtained by various methods of treatment are strikingly similar. Indeed, people seem to be benefitted by all kinds of therapy, by those that have a scientific stamp of approval, as well as those on the fringe of quackery.

How can we explain such inconsistencies? How can we, for instance, explain the failure of a man to respond to years of intensive and skillful

psychoanalysis, who, succumbing to the blandishments of an untutored charla-
tan, loses his symptoms in a few weeks and takes up life with renewed vigor?
Are there differences in the quality of improvement with varied forms of treatment, or do certain kinds of problems respond better to specific types of treatment methods? Are there differences in the permanency of the results obtained
by the respective procedures? Can we say that there is a "best" treatment for
neurosis? Added to these confusing issues is the fact that in some instances an
individual suffering from a severe emotional problem may experience considerable relief, and even a so-called "cure" without the formality of having
received any kind of treatment whatsoever. How much of a spontaneous reparative element, therefore, is present during the course of any therapy? Answers
to these questions will be considered in the chapters that follow.

Chart I. VARIETIES OF PSYCHOTHERAPY

TYPE OF TREATMENT	OBJECTIVES	APPROACHES
SUPPORTIVE THERAPY	Strengthening of existing de-fenses. Elaboration of new and better mechanisms to maintain control. Restoration to an adaptive equilibrium.	Guidance, environmental manipulation, externalization of interests, reassurance, pressure and coercion, persuasion, emotional catharsis and desensitization, prestige suggestion, suggestive hypnosis, muscular relaxation, hydrotherapy, drug therapy, shock and convulsive therapy, inspirational group therapy, music therapy.
INSIGHT THERAPY WITH RE-EDUCATIVE GOALS	Insight into the more conscious conflicts, with deliberate efforts at readjustment, goal modification and the living up to existing creative potentialities.	"Relationship therapy," "attitude therapy," interview psychotherapy, distributive analysis and synthesis (psychobiologic therapy), therapeutic counseling, casework therapy, reconditioning, reeducative group therapy, semantic therapy.
INSIGHT THERAPY WITH RECONSTRUCTIVE GOALS	Insight into unconscious conflicts, with efforts to achieve extensive alterations of character structure. Expansion of personality growth with development of new adaptive potentialities.	Freudian psychoanalysis. Non-Freudian psychoanalysis. Psychoanalytically oriented psychotherapy. (Adjunctive therapies: hypnoanalysis, narcotherapy, play therapy, art therapy, analytic group therapy)

The varieties of psychotherapy may conveniently be divided into two main
groupings: supportive therapy and insight therapy. Subgroups of the latter are:
(1) insight therapy with reeducative goals (reeducative therapy) and (2)
insight therapy with reconstructive goals (reconstructive therapy). The distinctions among these as they relate to objectives and approaches are outlined
in Chart I, above. The available psychotherapies in supportive, reeducative and
reconstructive categories become more diverse from year to year as increasing

numbers of professionals enter the psychotherapeutic field, introducing into it their unique technical modifications. Schools of psychotherapy have crystallized around the various approaches, each of which has its zealous disciples as well as its staunch critics. Each lays claim to multifarious successes and admits to some failures. Actually, radical divergencies in technique are more apparent than real, many distinctions vanishing as soon as semantic differences are resolved [1–2].*
But some differences do exist which will be taken up in detail in the next chapters.

* Numbers in brackets refer to References, p. 781.

3

Educational, Casework and Counseling
Approaches Versus Psychotherapy

BEFORE CONSIDERING THE BASIC DIFFERENCES AND SIMILARITIES AMONG current psychotherapies, it may be helpful to attempt to distinguish psychotherapy from such techniques as educational, casework and counseling approaches.

EDUCATIONAL APPROACHES AND PSYCHOTHERAPY

Education, throughout the ages, has concerned itself with the development of the intellectual capacities of the individual and with his acquisition of knowledge. In recent years a new direction in education has been fostered by the recognition of the vital significance of human relationships in the learning process. The purpose of education has been extended to include the emotional growth of the individual and his more constructive relationships with people.

Conforming to the latter design, the discipline of education has broadened its goals to include "the inculcation of social attitudes," "the development of social sensitivity," and the evolution of "better personal-social adjustment" [3,4]. Educational objectives have been widened to foster personal security, and to expand assertiveness and self-direction [5]. A principle aim developing in education "is to provide rich and significant experiences in the major aspects of living so directed as to promote the fullest possible realization of personal potentialities" [6]. More and more schools are including in their curricula, material "concerned with the total personality—not merely with the intellect but with emotions, habits, attitudes . . . It [general education] consists of preparation for efficient living, no matter what one's vocation" [7]. Among the most interesting experiments along this line are those of the Bullis, Force, Ojemann and Forrest Hill Village projects [8].

Thus education, in its broader aspects, and psychotherapy have in common the objective of fostering personality adjustment and growth. This objective is most effectively achieved in the medium of an interpersonal relationship between teacher and student in the classroom, and between therapist and patient in the therapeutic situation.

An additional factor has lately been recognized: that emotional blocks may prevent the student from accepting or integrating educational media. The traditional pedagogic techniques are usually unable to handle such impediments. Interviewing and group work methods which are presently evolving in educational circles [9,10] attempt to deal with learning blocks. Both in objectives and techniques, these procedures resemble those in psychotherapy.

Educational approaches aimed at preventive mental health in adults have also come into prominence during the past few decades with the growth of the mental hygiene movement. Books, pamphlets, movies and articles in periodicals attempt to educate persons in more wholesome attitudes toward themselves, their families and the community [11]. Materials are also available which are intended to ameliorate the effects of emotional illness on adjustment. An examination of such materials indicates that they strive for the same goals as in certain types of psychotherapy.

The widespread preoccupation with psychoanalytic concepts has currently introduced a flood of writings and lectures formulating psychoanalytic doctrines. The intent is partly to educate parents into the proper handling of their children, and partly to mediate adult conflict. The effect of such writings and lectures is dubious. Where they do not oppose basic defenses, the person may integrate the teachings with a reeducational result. Where they conflict with basic defenses, they either wield no influence whatsoever or inspire guilt feelings induced by a realization that one is unable to abandon attitudes or patterns of behavior potentially hurtful to oneself or others. Group seminars oriented around discussion and clarification are much more effective than writings, provided they are headed by a skilled group leader. But here, too, positive results may be temporary.

CASEWORK AND PSYCHOTHERAPY

Social casework traditionally has been defined as a process in which a trained worker renders to a client one or more specific social services of which the client is in need. Implied in this definition is the assumption that the focus is on the external problem or social situation and not, as in psychotherapy, on the individual's inner distress or illness. In rendering social services, no deliberate attempt is made to alter the client's basic personality patterns, the object being to handle situational problems on a purely realistic level.

This classic definition of casework has, during the last quarter century, undergone considerable modification. Operationally, caseworkers have found it difficult or impossible to limit their area of work to the client's external life situation. Indeed, a conviction has evolved that, unless certain capacities are mobilized or developed in the client, he will be unable to utilize the social services offered or the community resources made available to him toward a better life adjustment. Consequently, much more extensive goals have developed in the practice of casework than are implicit in the early definition. This broadening of objectives is largely the product of psychiatric influence, particularly that of Freud and Rank.

Thus Towle [12] has described the caseworker as one who handles persons "experiencing some breakdown in their capacity to cope unaided with their own affairs." This breakdown, she adds, may be due to external factors, "or

it may be partially, largely, or entirely due to factors within the individual."
Services may be geared toward reality needs or may be "oriented to feelings and
to ways of responding."

Bowers [13], reviewing definitions of casework, adds this one: "Social
casework is an art in which knowledge of the science of human relations and
skill in relationship are used to mobilize capacities in the individual and resources in the community appropriate for better adjustment between the client
and all or any part of his total environment." Another recent definition is that
"casework is a method of helping a troubled person to understand what is
causing his personal or family problems and to find inside himself, in the home,
or in health and welfare agencies the resources to rebuild his or her family's
life." [14]

When we examine these definitions carefully we find that some of the
goals toward which casework is directed are identical with those in our definition
of psychotherapy. Furthermore, in scrutinizing many casework procedures and
techniques, we see little to distinguish these from psychotherapy. There is considerable overlapping, then, in the goals and techniques of these two disciplines,
unless we adhere to the older definition of casework and assume an invasion of
the field of psychotherapy.

COUNSELING AND PSYCHOTHERAPY

Counseling is a technique practiced by members of certain professions,
particularly those of social work, psychology, education and religion. It is customarily defined as a form of interviewing in which the client is helped to
understand himself more completely, in order that he may correct an environmental or adjustment difficulty. The relationship between client and counselor,
which is considered of prime importance in counseling, is used in different
ways, from the offering of suggestions as to available resources, to the interpretation of the client's attitudes and feelings. The directiveness of the counselor
varies: in directive counseling [15] the counselor assumes the role of an
authority offering the client an evaluation of his problem and defining courses
of action. In non-directive counseling [16] the counselor functions as an agent
who encourages the client's expression of feelings, reflecting these and helping
the client to assume responsibility for them. In this way the client thinks
things out for himself, developing his own goals and planning his own course
of action.

Counseling programs are usually organized around educational, vocational, marital and personal problems. The objectives in such programs may be
superficial, related to the correction of situational difficulties, or they may be
more extensive, influencing the intrapsychic structure. Thus, speaking of personal counseling: "Its fundamental objective is to facilitate development of an
integrated and self-directing personality, although it often concentrates on the
solution of specific personal problems" [17]. Counseling is often described
as a relationship in which the counselor acts as a catalyzer to a growth process

within the client [18,19]. According to Rogers [16,20] the counseling relationship becomes an emotional experience in which positive growth processes are released, the individual becoming able "to consider himself and his situation clearly, including those elements ordinarily denied to conscious awareness."

It is thus difficult to differentiate some forms of counseling from psychotherapy, unless we insist on a definition of counseling as a process exclusively directed toward a circumscribed situational difficulty. Counseling procedures pointed at more extensive goals would then have to be classified as forms of psychotherapy.

4

The "Spontaneous" Cure

THE QUESTION OF HOW MUCH OF THE IMPROVEMENT OR CURE IN psychotherapy is of a spontaneous nature is important in evaluating the effectiveness of any specific therapeutic procedure. "Spontaneous" cures probably occur more frequently than we are wont to admit, for neurotic difficulties are associated with periods of exacerbation and periods of remission and, often, without apparent cause, vanish of their own accord. Even the most pernicious forms of psychoses show a tendency toward spontaneous remission, and any institutional psychiatrist is acquainted with the patient who, having spent years in the hinterlands of a chronic mental ward, suddenly returns to the world of reality and expresses eagerness to take up his place as a member of society [21].

The circumstances surrounding such a "spontaneous cure" are so nebulous that it is customary to look on the phenomenon, when it occurs, as a sort of fortuitous development. Were we, however, able to peer into the complex mechanisms of the psyche, we might be able to discern definite laws of cause and effect relating to the spontaneous recovery.

It is unfortunate that so much emphasis has been placed on the evil consequences of emotional and mental disturbance that we are prone to concern ourselves chiefly with destructive pathologic effects and forget that constructive regenerative influences may be coincidentally present. It is as if in an infection, we were to concentrate on morbid elements of the disease without considering such protective manifestations as the antibody defenses and the activities of the reticulo-endothelial system. Any somatic disease whips into action reparative mechanisms in the direction of health. A mental or emotional disorder, too, will set into action defensive devices to restore the individual to homeostatic equilibrium; indeed, a study of the symptoms of emotional illness, whether the difficulty be a mild behavior problem or a pernicious form of schizophrenia, will always demonstrate a fusion of dynamisms representative both of the conflict and of the defenses the organism elaborates in an attempt at cure.

The exact mechanisms involved in "spontaneous" remissions or cures are not exactly known, but a number of operative factors, singly or in combination, suggest themselves.

First, life circumstances may change and open up opportunities for gratification of important but vitiated needs, normal and neurotic. Thus a man with a passive personality organization may, in fighting against passive impulses, elevate himself to a high political post which enables him to exercise secret cravings for power. The expression of these may neutralize inner fears of weakness and lead to feelings of well-being. A masochistic individual may appease a strong sense of guilt through the incidence of a physical illness, an accident, or a catastrophic life happening. A person with strong dependency strivings may flounder around helplessly until he chances onto a stronger individual, an alliance with whom infuses him with strength and vitality. One with schizoid tendencies may be afforded, through advantageous circumstances, an acceptable opportunity to detach himself in his interpersonal relationships. A shift in the current situation may, therefore, work in the interest of promoting psychic stability.

Second, provocative stress sources may disappear as a result of the removal of the initiating environmental irritant, or because the individual extricates himself from it. A child, selected by a classroom bully as a focus for sadistic attack will, in all probability, lose his tensions and fear with the forceful removal from the class of his disturbed assailant. A young dependent adult over-protected by a neurotic parent may decide to move away from home and be rewarded with an expanding sense of independence. A man, promoted into a highly competitive position that sponsors fears of failure, may, by returning to his previous, more mediocre job, overcome his anxiety and depression. A leave of absence or a vacation may, in a similar manner, remove a person from a disturbing life situation, helping him to stabilize himself.

Third, crumbling or shattered defenses, whose failure promotes adaptive collapse, may be restored to their original strength, or be reinforced by new, more adequate, and less disabling defenses. The return of a sense of mastery in the course of buttressing failing defenses, will help to return the individual to functional equilibrium. One way this is accomplished is by consolidating the mechanism of repression, sealing off disturbing conflicts which have managed to get out of control. For instance, a detached individual who has remained celibate all his life due to deep fears of sexuality, falls in love with a young woman. Her demands for reciprocal affection excite sexual fantasies and impulses which frighten him. Anxiety and psychosomatic symptoms precipitately develop. The man then discovers that he is completely impotent, and that his interest in the young woman abates and dies. Restored repression of his sexual desires, with a return to isolation from women, brings about a recovery from symptoms.

The strengthening of repressive defenses may be associated with escape into bodily satisfactions, such as excess indulgence in eating, sleeping and other physical pleasures; extroverted activities, like recreational, social and hobby pursuits; an over-weening interest in religion; acceptance of certain philosophic credos; and over-indulgence in alcohol or sedatives. Also, ultimately helpful to repression may be a cathartic release of pent-up emotion which has been threatening repressive barriers. Thus, the finding of a sympathetic friend may encourage verbal unburdening, with the unleashing of emotion, especially inner resentment and guilt feelings. In this way, the person may be reassured against irrational fears and anticipated threats for repudiated past experiences and reprehensible present strivings. Sometimes the defenses of the individual undergo modification in the direction of greater adaptability to inner demands and external pressures. A person disposed to outbursts of temper and violence may find, in the course of a good human relationship with a tolerant and accepting companion, that he is neither exploited nor hurt by the emergence and expression of soft, tender feelings. While evolving more adequate defenses, greater capacities for compensation and sublimation may develop.

As a general rule, "spontaneous" remissions or cures are of a palliative nature, with no great change being wrought in the intrapsychic structure. In a few instances, however, rather surprising "spontaneous" structural alterations develop in the personality organization itself. Most recalcitrant to spontaneous resolve are deep-seated neuroses linked to repression of infantile anxieties, which are so split off from access to awareness that they do not lend themselves to dissolution. Nevertheless, even here they may be more readily held at bay by a "spontaneous" strengthening of repressive forces, or by avoiding situations that tend to activate them. Focal conflicts may be isolated sufficiently to enable the individual to function satisfactorily without being aware of their content or even existence.

It will be recognized that some of the undercurrent processes in "spontaneous cure" are similar to those in psychotherapy. Whereas, in "spontaneous cure" the individual inadvertently seeks out the conditions in which he can work out his problems; in psychotherapy, circumstances conducive to relief or recovery are actively manipulated. In contrast to the fortuitous nature of the "spontaneous" development, psychotherapy is a planned effort to establish a psychic equilibrium which, if left to chance, can only rarely occur.

5

Supportive Therapy

SUPPORTIVE MEASURES CONSTITUTE A TRADITIONAL APPROACH TO problems of an emotional nature. They are applied by friends in a more or less haphazard way almost as an automatic response to the individual's pleas for help. They are utilized in a somewhat more planned manner by untrained professionals, like ministers, nurses, teachers, lawyers, correctional workers and general practitioners whom the person may consult. They are deliberately implemented by trained professionals, particularly social workers, psychologists and psychiatrists, sometimes as the principal therapy, and at other times as adjuncts to more extensive reeducative and reconstructive procedures.

The object in supportive therapy is to bring the patient to an emotional equilibrium as rapidly as possible with minimization or absence of symptoms, so that he is capable of functioning at a level approximating his norm. An effort is made to strengthen existing defenses as well as to elaborate better "mechanisms of control." Coordinately, one attempts to remove or to reduce detrimental external factors that act as sources of stress. There is no intent to change personality structure, although constructive personality changes may develop as a consequence of treatment when mastery has been restored to the individual. Supportive approaches are utilized adjunctively in practically all other types of psychotherapy. An understanding of how and when to implement supportive measures, therefore, is indispensible in the training of the psychotherapist.

Therapies with designations of "palliative psychotherapy," "social therapy," "situational therapy" and "milieu therapy" fall into the supportive therapeutic category. Among the techniques and procedures utilized in supportive therapy are guidance, environmental manipulation, externalization of interests, reassurance, prestige suggestion, pressure and coercion, persuasion, emotional catharsis and desensitization, muscular relaxation, hydrotherapy, drug therapy, shock and convulsive therapy, and inspirational group therapy.

The specific things done for the patient in supportive therapy depend on the training and orientation of the therapist.

GUIDANCE

Guidance is the term given to a number of procedures which provide active help for an individual in such matters as education, employment, health and social relationships. Many casework, counseling and educational procedures come under the category of guidance.

The extent to which the patient's life is manipulated varies with his condition and with the system of guidance employed. Among guidance schemes are those outlined by Payot [22], Barrett [23,24], Vitoz [25], Eymiew [26], Walsh [27,28], Erickson [29] and Traxler [30]. The role the therapist plays may be that of a completely directing authority arranging for a planned daily regimen which allows no time for idleness and destructive rumination. A balanced day may be organized for the person relating to the time of arising, bodily care and grooming, working schedule, rest periods, recreation, sleep and other activities in order to account for every hour of the day. Such complete control of the patient's routines, however, is rarely necessary. Usually, guidance is aimed at a specific disturbing problem which interferes with the individual's adjustment.

Guidance is based on an authoritarian relationship established between therapist and patient. One of the problems inherent in such a relationship is that the patient may tend to overvaluate the capacities and abilities of the therapist to a point where he suspends his reasoning abilities and rights to criticize. He may also be dominated by feelings of fear and awe.

It goes without saying that under these circumstances any doubt that crops up relating to the strength or wisdom of the authority invokes strong insecurity. Hostility and guilt feelings, if they develop at all, must be rigidly repressed for fear of invoking counter-hostility or disapproval. One may recognize from such irrational patterns the same attitude the child expresses toward the omnipotent parent. Actually, the emotional helplessness of the neurotic individual resembles, to a strong degree, the helplessness of the immature child, solution for which is sought in dependency on powerful parental figures. The neurotic person thus re-creates, in the therapist, the original authority he invested in his parents, and he will seek from the therapist an equivalent kind of love.

It is perhaps because of this that the individual has to maintain an image of the therapist as infallible. Should the latter display any human frailties or lack invincible qualities, the faith of the patient may be shattered, precipitating helplessness and anxiety. He may then attempt to master his anxiety by again annexing himself to another person who possesses those magical and godlike characteristics he believes to be essential for his security. The life history of such dependent individuals demonstrates a flitting from one therapist to another, from clinic to clinic, from shrine to cult, in a ceaseless search for a parental figure who can guide them to paths of health and accomplishment.

Due to the experience of having been disappointed in their search, some persons will resent guidance, even though they feel too insecure within themselves to direct their own activities. Others will reject guidance because of previous conditionings in relationship to an authority who has been hostile or rejecting or who has made such demands on them for compliance so as to thwart their impulses for self-growth. Acceptance of advice may be tantamount to giving up one's independence or may mark one as inferior.

In spite of its disadvantages, guidance may be the only type of treatment to which some patients will respond. These persons feel desperately helpless in the grip of their neurosis; they have neither the motivation nor the strength to work with a technique that throws the bulk of responsibility on their shoulders. Unfortunately, their personality growth may never develop to a point where they can take over the reins of their own destiny. So strong a resistance to self-assertiveness exists, that they can function only when they lean on a parental figure who can prod them on in their daily tasks.

In some guidance approaches, where it is apparent that lack of motivation and ego strength make a more scientific form of therapy impossible, the patient is guided toward religion [31–33]. An attempt is made to convince him that he will be aided in the gaining of health by kinship with the divine being, since in union with God, the soul need not struggle alone. It can draw sufficient strength from this relationship to conquer evil thoughts and impulses, to crush dread and fear, and to achieve confidence and faith in living. This help is to be gained through faith and prayer. Christian Science [34] and other "faith cures" are based on these principles.

Certain individuals are made immensely more comfortable by this religious type of therapy, which sometimes has advantages over pure guidance in that the patient gets his share of help through his own efforts at prayer, and through participation in church activities. In religious therapy, also, the patient is not in a position to dispute the powers of God as he can those of the therapist, whom he may discover to be possessed of human fallibilities.

Within its limited orbit, therefore, guidance has a utility in therapy. One does not implement it under the illusion that any deep change will occur in the underlying conflicts or in the dynamic structure of the personality. Conflicts are usually whitewashed and the person is encouraged to adjust to his problems rather than to rectify them. The patient may be taught many methods by which he can avoid emotional blind alleys. He may learn to correct certain defects or to adapt himself to circumstances that cannot be changed. However, where guidance is not supplemented by other therapies calculated to render the person self-sufficient and independent, fundamental difficulties in interpersonal relationships will probably not be altered.

ENVIRONMENTAL MANIPULATION

Environmental manipulation is an approach to therapy which attempts to deal with the patient's emotional disturbance by removing or modifying disorganizing elements in his environment. Social work more than any other discipline has evolved the most complete and best organized system of environmental manipulation [35–45]. Among services rendered are mediation of financial, housing, work, recreational, rehabilitative, marital and family problems. Many of the environmental manipulative techniques elaborated in social work may be employed by the therapist when he determines that situational difficulties are so disturbing to the individual that he is unable to live with them. Or the therapist may utilize the services of a social worker as an adjuvant toward this end.

Often the patient is so bound to his life situation, out of a sense of loyalty, or because of a feeling that he has no right to express his demands, that he tolerates environmental distortions as unalterable. He may be unaware that his tension and resentment are generated by specific situations, and he may blame his difficulties on things other than those actually responsible. The therapist may have to interfere actively with environmental aspects that are grossly inimical to the best interests of the patient. This may necessitate work with the patient's family, for it is rare that the patient's difficulties are limited to himself. The various family members may require some kind of help before the patient shows a maximal response to treatment.

One must not assume that environmental correction can help all patients. In many instances, environmental difficulties, while accentuating the patient's problems, are only precipitating factors. The basis for the individual's maladjustment here is his personality structure, which contains so many inharmonious elements that inner conflict is incessant, with little relationship to outside circumstances. As a matter of fact, most people have a tendency to objectify their problems by seeking out conditions in their environment that can justify feelings of rage or tension. For example, if a person has a problem associated with the fear of being taken advantage of by others, he will find evidences of this in any situation in which he is involved.

In relatively large numbers of persons, therefore, environmental correction has little effect on the existing emotional upheaval. Here the difficulty has been structuralized in such widespread character disturbance that problems in interpersonal relationships appear to perpetuate themselves endlessly. Indeed, the individual seems to create situations in which he can react in his customary destructive manner. More confounding is the fact that he may need a disturbed atmosphere for proper functioning. He may, for instance, seek to be victimized by others in order to justify feelings of hostility that could otherwise not be rationalized. In cases such as this, the correction of environmental stress, without a corresponding alleviation of inner conflict, may produce depression or psychosomatic illness due to an internalization of aggression. One of the most discouraging discoveries to the therapist is that in liberating a patient from a grossly distorted environment, the patient may promptly involve himself in another situation, equally as bad as the first. The dynamic need for a disorganizing life circumstance will have to be remedied first, before the patient responds adequately to environmental manipulation.

EXTERNALIZATION OF INTERESTS

While not strictly a therapeutic approach, externalization of the patient's interests is sometimes used as a supportive adjunct in treatment. It is employed particularly where the individual has become so absorbed in his inner problems that external reality has lost its meaning. To offset this, an attempt is made to redirect the patient's interests toward the outside world—toward arts, crafts, music, games, sports, recreations or hobbies. Many interests may be exploited in this effort, such as, woodwork, needlecraft, weaving, metal work, rug-making, gardening, cards, chess, table-tennis, handball, quoits, swimming, golf, riding, dancing, dramatics, drawing, painting and sculpturing. Countless other hobbies and recreations may be utilized to divert attention from inner tension and anxiety. Among organized therapies in this division are occupational therapy [46–49], recreational therapy [50–52] and music therapy [53–54]. Because externalization of interests is perhaps the most superficial of approaches, its effectiveness is increased by combining it with other therapeutic techniques.

REASSURANCE

Reassurance is utilized in some way in all forms of psychotherapy. Coming to therapy in itself constitutes for the patient reassurance that he is not hopeless nor destined to ultimate insanity. The relationship with the therapist provides the patient with feelings of acceptance and security, even though such feelings may not be expressed in words. Verbalized reassurances are often given the patient in supportive therapy, particularly when he voices doubts concerning his ability to get well or to gain relief from suffering. The patient is also reassured whenever he is in the grip of fears conditioned by his own fantasies or by irrational thinking. The therapist discusses such fears openly with the patient, offering explanations of how baseless they are, with the hope of making the patient more comfortable and of alleviating tension and anxiety.

The most common misconceptions nurtured by patients are those that relate to a fear of going insane, a notion of being blemished by a hereditary mental taint, an idea of harboring an undetected malignant disease or abnormality, a feeling of having injured oneself irreparably through early masturbatory excesses, and a concern with present perverse sexual fantasies and impulses. Such fears may drive the patient to distraction and induce much brooding and self-recrimination.

Where the patient is convinced of the sincerity of the therapist and accepts his authority, he may be helped by verbal reassurances to master some misconceptions. Reassurance, however, is practically never successful when applied to basic personality difficulties, particularly to devaluated self-esteem and its derivatives. Judiciously employed, nevertheless, it may prove to be a helpful adjunct in more superficial disturbances [55–56].

PRESTIGE SUGGESTION

Symptom removal by prestige suggestion is one of the oldest of techniques. It is still employed extensively throughout the world. Reported results vary from unbounded enthusiasm to a discrediting of the method as an irrational form of psychotherapy. On the whole it is the least successful of all treatment procedures. Because it deals with effects rather than with causes, the method has many limitations; nevertheless, it may, under certain circumstances, serve a beneficial purpose in carefully selected cases.

Suggestion plays a part in every psychotherapeutic relationship. It is often employed without intent by the therapist as a result of the patient's own needs, the patient choosing from the content of what the therapist says or implies, certain things he wants to hear, to which he will be able to react. Suggestion may be used deliberately by the therapist in the form of injunctions voiced with authoritative emphasis to influence the patient in calculated ways.

Where the therapist occupies an omnipotent position in the mind of the patient, certain symptoms may be dissipated by dictation. Symptoms which are removed by prestige suggestion disappear because the patient has a need to abide by the commands of the therapist. The motivation to comply is usually conditioned by a wish to gratify important security needs through archaic mechanisms of submission to and identification with an omnipotent authority. So long as this motivation is greater than the gains the patient derives from the indulgence of his symptoms, he will abandon his complaints on command; and he will remain comfortable, provided he continues to have faith in the omniscience and strength of the therapist. Results are best where the symptom has minimal defensive purposes, and where the need for symptom-free functioning constitutes a powerful incentive. Certain psychosomatic manifestations, some types of alcoholic addiction, and habit disorders, such as nail-biting, insomnia, excessive eating, inordinate smoking and drinking, are often remarkably susceptible to prestige suggestion, especially when they are incapacitating the person. Results are most pronounced where the patient has no other motivation for therapy than to abandon his symptoms or to bring them under control.

Some writers have emphasized the fact that the effect of symptom removal is not merely palliative, but that it may cause a general reorientation in the patient's attitudes. [57] The removal of a symptom may then, as a by-product, have an important effect on the total functioning of the personality. An individual handicapped by a disturbing symptom often loses self-respect. He withdraws from people and gets more and more involved within himself. The symptom becomes a chief preoccupation, around which he organizes his insecurity and inferiority feelings. Here, the removal of a symptom may alter his whole pattern of adjustment. A man addicted to alcohol, for instance, may suffer more from the social consequences of drinking than from the physical effects of alcohol. Minimizing his desire for alcohol by command may start a process of personality rehabilitation. An individual with an hysterical tic may isolate himself because of the embarrassment caused by his symptom. Abolishing his tic can influence his social adjustment materially. A patient with a paralytic limb may be restored to economic usefulness and emotional well-being, and he may benefit immeasurably from this restoration.

Auto-suggestion is regarded by many as a form of prestige suggestion directed at the self. Here, the individual employs his internalized authoritative image, or super-ego, as an authority who gives commands. Coué [58] has claimed that auto-suggestion is one of the most powerful forces at the disposal of the person. Through auto-suggestion, the proper functioning of organs may be influenced, and a restoration of normal emotional attitudes brought about. These claims are, of course, open to challenge.

Among the techniques employed to reinforce prestige suggestion, hypnosis is paramount [59]. The peculiar powers vested by the subject in the hypnotist, makes the subject abide by suggestions with greater persistence. But even with hypnosis as a reinforcing agent, the permanence of effect of suggestion may be limited. No symptom will be abandoned which serves as a defense against intense anxiety, or as an important way of adjusting the patient to his life situation. For instance, if a man develops a paralyzed arm as a defense against the fear of stabbing his wife, suggested removal of the paralysis will be so threatening to him that he will refuse to follow the commands of the hypnotist.

Another limitation of prestige suggestion is that a sizeable group of patients fail to respond to symptom removal because they are unable to develop the attitude that the therapist as an infallible authority. Where there is any doubt as to the capacities and powers of the therapist, the patient will have no motivation to comply, and he will successfully resist the therapist's commands.

There are, nevertheless, occasional patients (usually hysterics) whose need for an invincible and protective authority is so strong as to invest the therapist with supernormal powers. They faithfully follow his suggestions, even to the yielding up of an important symptom. To compensate for the latter, other symptoms may develop in different parts of the body which have the same dynamic significance to the patient as the original symptom, but are perhaps less incapacitating.

The relapse rate among patients who have had their symptoms removed by suggestion is understandably great. Needless to say, the chances of helping a patient permanently are much greater where one does a reintegrative kind of therapy that treats the source of his problem. The concomitant rebuilding of ego strength and inner security gives the person the best chance of remaining symptom-free, even in the face of a disturbing environment. In suggestive treatment, where no change has developed in the inner psychic structure, there is always the possibility of a relapse. This, however, is not inevitable because the patient's life situation may get less complicated, or the patient may, as a result of therapy, develop more adaptive ways of dealing with conflict and of getting along with people.

Another objection that has been voiced to suggestive therapy is that it is apt to eliminate an important motivation for deeper treatment. The inconvenience and discomfort of symptoms incites the individual to want to inquire into their source. If he is made too comfortable by removing his symptoms, he may lose this incentive. Where the goal in therapy is to achieve alteration in the dynamic structure of the personality, suggestion or any other strongly supportive therapeutic method may act as a deterrent.

In spite of its limitations and disadvantages, there are instances when prestige suggestion has to be resorted to as an expedient measure. First, a symptom may be so disabling and may cause such great suffering, that all psychotherapeutic efforts will be blocked until the person obtains some relief. Second, there are patients, as has been indicated, with deficient motivation and minimal ego strength, in whom psychotherapeutic methods aimed at increasing self-growth are destined to failure. The most that can be expected is that the patient will respond to palliative or supportive procedures, such as prestige suggestion. As therapy proceeds, however, the patient may be prepared to accept a more extensive treatment approach.

PRESSURE AND COERCION

Pressure and coercion are authoritative measures which are calculated to bring to bear on the patient rewards or punishments in order to stimulate him towards certain actions. Thorne [60] has indicated that these measures have a value in some dependent personalities who refuse to face life under any other circumstances than to be forced into situations by an authority. They are said to have a use also in immature individuals who tend to "act-out" their problems; in persons who habitually shy away from reality; in emergency situations where the individual is endangering himself or others; in uncontrolled emotionality where other methods fail; and in instances when the patient will not take decisive actions by himself, or where he manifests discouraging indecisive wavering. Only where permissive measures fail are coercive devices said to be justified.

Pressure may be exerted in the form of assigned tasks. Thus Herzberg [61] advises that tasks be assigned the patient which are directed against (1) impulses that maintain the neurosis, attempting to remove them or lower their intensity below the critical threshold, (2) obstacles towards satisfaction of impulses, (3) "essential predispositions," (4) neurotic gains and (5) "delaying factors" which operate to prevent impulse fulfillment.

Threats, prohibitions, exhortations, reproaches and authoritative firmness lend weight to repressive defenses. However, because pressure and coercion reduplicate the disciplinary strictures of the parent-child relationship, the patient is apt to react with hostility, obstinacy, masochistic self-punishment and other responses characteristic of the ways he adjusted to parental commands and injunctions. It is rare that a good therapeutic effect will be forthcoming with the use of such authoritative procedures, since the patient will resent being treated like a child, and he will tend to defy the therapist, even to the point of leaving therapy. Accordingly, pressure and coercion, if they are ever used, should be employed only as temporary emergency measures.

PERSUASION

Persuasion is a technique based upon the belief that the patient has within himself the power to modify his pathologic emotional processes by force of sheer will or by the utilization of "common sense." In persuasive therapy, appeals are made to the patient's reason and intelligence, in order to convince him to abandon neurotic aims and symptoms, and to help him gain self-respect. He is enlightened as to the false nature of his own concepts regarding his illness, as well as the bad mental habits he has formed. By presenting him with all the facts in his case, he is shown that there is no reason for him to be ill. He is urged to ignore his symptoms by assuming a stoical attitude, by cultivating a new philosophy of life aimed at facing his weaknesses, and by adopting an attitude of self-tolerance. An attempt is made to bring him into harmony with his environment, and to induce him to think of the welfare of others.

A number of psychotherapists, in utilizing persuasion, attempt to indoctrinate their patients with their own particular philosophies of life. The therapist establishes a directive relationship with his patient who seeks the therapist's approval on the basis that the therapeutic authority must know what is best for him. The approach is a somewhat more mature one than that of guidance, since it presupposes active participation of the patient in his own cure, and aims for an expansion of his personal powers and resources. The majority of popular books on mental therapy are modified forms of persuasion.

The use of persuasion was first advocated by Paul DuBois [62–63] of Switzerland who held conversations with his patients and taught them a philosophy of life whereby they substituted in their minds thoughts of health for their customary preoccupations with disease and suffering. Much of the success that DuBois achieved by his persuasive methods was due to his own vigorous personality which exuded confidence and cheer.

DuBois recognized the importance of the interpersonal relationship and he insisted that the physician treat the patient not merely as an interesting case, but as a friend. He declared that the doctor must be inspired by a real sense of sympathy and affection for the patient, and should manifest these sentiments so openly that the patient "would really be very ungrateful not to get well." The physician must be sincere in this conviction that the patient would get well, because if he had any doubts, he could not help imparting them to the patient.

The aim of "mental persuasion," according to DuBois, was to build up in the patient a feeling of self-confidence, to make him his own master. This was done by imbuing the patient with a belief in himself by "education of the will, or, more exactly the reason." The physician was enjoined to hammer the truth into the patient's mind with the ardor of a barrister convinced of the justice of his plea.

In order to approach the patient's problem rationally, it was first necessary to understand clearly the nature and sources of the disorder. The physician had to distinguish those symptoms of a physical nature from those of psychic origin. The analysis with the patient of his symptoms, and the understanding by the patient of how these debilitated and inconvenienced him were important, particularly because they made the person feel that the physician was interested in him and was sympathetic to his suffering. The patient had to be shown how he utilized his symptoms to escape responsibilities in life. He had to be convinced that his nervousness had crushed his morale, that, even though he believed his trouble to be physical, it was really mental. The patient was urged to "chase his troubles from his mind," and he was promised that his discomforts then would all vanish. He needed no medicine, DuBois insisted, "for there is none to turn a pessimist into an optimist."

DuBois recommended prolonged discussions, during which it was necessary to convince the patient of his errors in reasoning. He had to be shown that his symptoms were the product of emotional stress. Though annoying, they were not serious in themselves. The less one concentrated on symptoms, the less disturbing these would become. If the heart palpitated, let it pound; if the intestines were active, let them grumble. If one had insomnia, he had best say: "If I sleep, all the better; if I don't sleep, no matter." Undue attention aggravated the difficulty. The best way to overcome symptoms was to stop thinking about them. Fatigue, tension and fear were all exaggerated by attention. It was necessary to stop thinking of pain and suffering and to dismiss petty ailments with a smile. "The proper philosophy," he said, "easily learned, can restore the mental balance."

DuBois contended that healthy people disregarded their bodily sensations. The emotionally upset person, on the other hand, concentrated on them until they became his chief preoccupation. For this reason, he was upset by improper thinking habits. Notions of happiness and health must then replace ideas of disease and suffering. Happiness depended less on external circumstances than upon one's inner state of mind. One might be ill, or have some financial misfortunes, or have lost dear friends; but the intensity of his suffering depended upon the spirit with which he accepted these calamities.

The education of the "self" was the first step in securing real happiness. The patient had to cultivate the thought in his mind that he was going to get well. So long as he was convinced he would experience pain, fatigue or other symptoms, he would feel them vividly. If he obliterated these thoughts from his mind, he would overcome his problem.

Every sign of progress was to be held up to the patient and even exaggerated. Improvement was to be stressed as proof of the patient's tenacity to get well. As soon as ideas of health entered the mind, ideas of disease would vanish. The patient was to be shown that he was not alone in his trouble, that everyone had difficulties that varied only in their manifestations. While he might be concerned with his symptoms, his problem was deeper, involving attitudes which were very significant. Improvement in his attitudes toward life held forth the greatest chances for cure. Above all, he must not be hopeless about the outcome, even though it required a long time to secure real improvement. The patient's nervousness existed a long time before the present difficulty. Relapses might occur as improper thinking habits returned, but these would be easier and easier to combat as one stopped thinking about himself. He had to bear his discomforts cheerfully and make it his ambition to lead a bold and active life. He had to develop confidence in his own powers of resistance.

A questioning of the patient about his conceptions of life and his philosophy was important. False views were to be criticized, and those viewpoints that were logical and helpful were to be encouraged. The physician had to make an effort, also, to discover in the patient qualities of superiority that would elevate the patient in his own mind. It might even be necessary to teach him to make an optimistic inventory of his good qualities. If the patient's condition was brought about by tragic events, one had to soothe his suffering by reassuring him and sympathizing with him. If his difficulties involved irritability and emotional instability, he had to be taught the spirit of forbearance. Therapeutic efforts were not confined to the patient, but also extended to those with whom he lived.

Among the proper philosophic ideas to be imbibed by the patient were moral notions which could guide one's life and make for good relationships with others. The best way to forget oneself was to devote more thought to other people. The best road to happiness was altruism and making others happy. Tolerance, sympathy, kindness, and forbearance were the keynotes of a serene life. Religious sentiments were to be awakened and turned to good account.

Dejerine, [54] using the methods of DuBois, also emphasized the "re-education of the reason," but he stressed emotion rather than the weakened will as the basis for neurosis. He speculated that the emotions under certain conditions might overwhelm the intellect and cause illness. Dejerine believed that therapy must, therefore, aim for a liberation of the personality from the effects of harmful emotions. The emphasis in therapy was to get the patient to talk about traumatic incidents in his life, especially fears and sorrows in the present. Unlike DuBois, Dejerine did not try to impose his philosophy on the patient, but strove to permit the patient to develop an emotional relationship with him until a state of confidence developed. When this was obtained, Dejerine practiced persuasion to encourage the patient to correct his "bad habits." He contended that to cure nervous illness, one had to fight the deceptive systems of monism, fatalism, skepticism and determinism. Reason could overcome obsession once emotions were given a proper outlet. It was necessary to keep an idea before the patient's mind. He had to think thoughts of the noble, the just and the beautiful. He had to learn to gain satisfactions by the fulfillment of duty, yet the brain had "always to be guided by the heart."

Modern persuasive methods draw largely, for their inspiration, on the works of DuBois and Dejerine. Stress is laid on cultivation of the proper mental attitude toward life, on the facing of adversity, and on the accepting of environmental difficulties and the tolerance of self-limitations one is unable to change. There is an accenting of the patient's assets and expansion of his positive personality qualities. The patient is taught to control overemotionality, to live with anxiety, to accept and to tolerate deprivation, frustration and tension, acquiring proper controls for them.

The dynamic basis of many persuasive cures lies in the reinforcing of repression of symptoms by appealing to the patient's sentiments of patriotism, family pride, altruism and self-respect. The therapist builds up in the patient a desire to get well in order to indulge in pleasures inherent in being constructive and sociable. The patient is reminded constantly that if he regards himself as a better person, others too will have a better opinion of him. Furthermore, his duties and responsibilities to get well are continuously emphasized.

Most forms of persuasive therapy are, at best, very superficial, and are often based on the acceptance by the patient of banalities uttered by the therapist who utilizes aphorisms and examples from the lives of the great to reinforce ideas that are scientifically unsound.

Persuasive therapy, nevertheless, has some justification in that it provides some people with a mental crutch where a psychologic analysis of their problem is impossible. The substitution of persuasive philosophic precepts for destructive habit patterns is probably the lesser of two evils. Some obsessive-compulsive personalities do remarkably well with persuasive methods. Indeed they respond better to persuasion than to psychoanalysis.

The greatest fallacy in persuasive therapy lies in the exaggerated value attached to the reasoning powers as potentially capable of diverting inner emotional processes. There is, furthermore, an assumption that the patient is conscious of his basic defects and is therefore capable of mastering them through concentrative effort. Unconscious conflicts and emotions are the most important determinants of neurotic behavior, and this explains why reason, knowledge and will power often fail to bring about the mastery of symptoms. The same effort should, therefore, be made in persuasion as in guidance, to bring about a change in the relationship with the therapist from directiveness to nondirectiveness, and to motivate the patient to work with the dynamic sources of his problem in a manner that will give him as much insight as he can absorb and utilize.

EMOTIONAL CATHARSIS AND DESENSITIZATION

"Confession," "talking things out" and "getting things off one's chest," in relation to a friend or a professional person, like a physician, minister, or teacher, are common methods of relieving emotional tension. Beneficial effects are due to the release of pent-up feelings and emotions and the subjection of inner painful elements to objective reappraisal. The mere verbalization of aspects of the self of which the individual is ashamed or fearful helps him to develop a more constructive attitude toward them.

Ventilation by the person of his fears, hopes, ambitions and demands often gives him relief, particularly when his verbalizations are subjected to the uncritical and sympathetic appraisal of the listener. Hitherto, the patient has retained memories, conflicts and impulses that he has dared not admit to himself, let alone others. A growing confidence in the therapist makes him feel that he has an ally who will help him bear fearful inner secrets. The ability to share his secrets with an understanding person robs the experiences of much of their frightening quality. In addition, the patient finds that his judgment as to the viciousness of his experiences may have been distorted. The very act of translating his fears into words lessens their terrifying hold on him. The fact that he has not been rejected by the therapist, even though he has revealed his shortcomings, encourages him to reevaluate the sinister nature of his experiences or desires.

Many of the patient's disturbing fears and ideas have their origin in fantasies or misinterpretations of early childhood. As the patient expresses his ideas, he gives the therapist an opportunity to correct misconceptions he has hitherto accepted without question. The patient may need clarification on phases of life relating to his physical functions or interpersonal relationships. Often he believes many of his fears and impulses to be unique to himself. When he receives the assurance that his fears are more or less universal, he may become convinced that it is his attitude toward his fears that has been abnormal.

Discussion of the patient's problem is continued until he no longer reacts emotionally to it. Repeated verbalization of unpleasant and disagreeable attitudes and experiences permits him to face his past fears and conflicts with diminished inner turmoil.

Much of the value that comes about from emotional catharsis is based upon the fact that the patient becomes desensitized to those situations and conflicts that disturb him, but which reality demands that he endure. The tolerance of pain, disappointment and frustration are inordinately low in neurotic persons, and it is necessary to build up the ability to deal with difficulties and painful experiences without collapse.

Because the individual conceives of certain memories, feelings, attitudes and impulses as damaging to himself and others, he subjects them to suppression and repression. Particularly traumatic are sexual incidents and impulses, hostile strivings of various types, as well as attitudes which indicate that the person is inferior, evil or contemptible. Some of these elements are fully known to the person; yet he will not acknowledge or express them. Others are so frightening that they have been totally shunted out of awareness by the mechanism of repression.

The pathologic consequences of suppression and repression are legion. The individual over-reacts to incidents that threaten to bring the hidden material to his attention. He may elaborate symptoms such as phobias, compulsions, paralysis, amnesia and other hysterical manifestations in an effort to give vicarious expression to the repressed material, as well as to shield it from awareness. Only by facing the forbidden experiences, impulses or conflicts, by dissociating them from past misinterpretations, and by reevaluating them in the light of present-day reality, is it possible for the person to gain any real relief.

Methods by which desensitization is implemented during therapy vary with the extent of repression. Conscious conflicts may be handled, as has been indicated, by discussion, confession and ventilation. Less conscious material, however, will require techniques discussed under reeducative and reconstruction therapy. Hypnosis is extremely helpful in encouraging emotional catharsis and in bringing about desensitization. [65]

In recent years, the use of hypnotic drugs by intravenous injection has been employed as a means of facilitating catharsis and desensitization. This method (termed narcoanalysis by Horsley [66] and narcosynthesis by Grinker [67]) produces in itself a hypnotic-like state which resembles, but is not similar to hypnosis. Barbiturates, especially sodium amytal and sodium pentothal, and somnifen are the most commonly used drugs. With hypnotic drugs the patient may relieve himself in a relatively short time of painful material that would require weeks or months of interviewing. Repressed conflicts and traumatic memories are released with a cathartic effect. For this reason, narcosynthesis is particularly applicable to the acute neuroses of war, especially in dealing with functional amnesic states and conversion symptoms. The released material is sometimes worked through in a waking state in order to insure more permanent results. Where this happens the techniques employed are no longer in a supportive category, but rather are reeducative or reconstructive in nature.

One may classify under emotional catharsis the procedure that has been named "dianetic processing." Beneficial effects, if any, of "dianetic processing" are probably the product of a cathartic effect with the recounting, remembering and the reliving of past traumatic experiences or fantasies. Originally introduced by L. Ron Hubbard, an American engineer, dianetics has attracted a group of practitioners who function as "auditors." According to the theory of dianetics [68], painful, traumatic memories and experiences are recorded in the subconscious mind as "engrams." These engrams invade the conscious mind, producing a variety of emotional ailments. In dianetics an attempt is made to restore the memory of subconscious experiences, thereby eliminating the effect of engrams.

The subject, reclining on a couch, permits himself to associate freely, probing past incidents which may have a painful import. This is called "taking the patient back along the time track." In the accepting atmosphere provided by the auditor, the patient often finds himself dealing with material in his early past, or speculating about his past in an elaborate system of fantasies. Although these fantasies are claimed to be actual memories, there is little question that a recounting of experiences prior to the age of two, and particularly in the prenatal stage, draws upon the vivid imagination of the person. The subject is encouraged to "relive" painful past events, and to reexperience sensations in the same form he had them originally. The determining effect of prenatal impressions is an important aspect of dianetic theory. Repetition of past traumatic events or fantasies is said to "take the charge out of an engram." With its exaggerated claims, pseudoscientific theory, and theatrical methods, dianetics does not belong among the accredited scientific therapies.

The method of emotional catharsis and desensitization has certain serious limitations. Inasmuch as the most important sources of conflict are usually unconscious, it is impossible to verbalize the basic causes of anxiety. Nevertheless, there are many conscious conflicts that plague a person, ventilation of which may have a beneficial effect. The ability to express fearful memories, strivings and emotions helps to rebuild self-respect and removes the damaging effects of hostility, tension and anxiety.

MUSCULAR RELAXATION

Muscle tension often accompanies emotional problems and contributes to the patient's symptoms. Ensuing spasms that may develop are extremely embarrassing to the patient. Among syndromes created by spasms of the skeletal musculature are severe band-like headaches, painful contractures of the neck, choking sensations in the throat, backache, hand trembling, and abdominal "tightness." Tensions reflect themselves also in spasms of the smooth muscula-ture, influencing various internal organs. Muscle tensions thus may exaggerate the patient's problems by operating as foci for new anxieties.

Muscle relaxation exercises to relieve tension have been used for many years. Many of these are founded on the system of the nurse, Annie Payson Call [69] which combines muscle relaxation, rest and "mind-training" for purposes of repose. The best known modern exercises are those of Jacobson [70] and Rippon and Fletcher [71]. Yates [72] and Neufeld [73] have described a series of exercises which enable the individual to gain voluntary control over his tension. Muscular relaxation is also induced by massage. This enhances muscle tone in addition to encouraging relaxation [74,75]. Enforced rest also has a relaxing effect on the individual's muscular system. In part this was an objective of the old Weir-Mitchell [76] "rest cure" which combined measures of rest, isolation, diet, massage and electrical stimulation. These were often reinforced by prescribed isolation from relatives. Weir-Mitchell's method gained wide repute, although beneficial effects were probably as much induced by psychologic as by physiologic factors.

The influence of muscular relaxation on the individual's tension is purely palliative and always has to be accompanied by some form of psychotherapy.

HYDROTHERAPY

Hydrotherapy, once a favorite treatment process in mental institutions [77], has largely been abandoned with the advent of convulsive therapy. How-ever, it still may be used in the treatment of mental illness as an adjunct to other forms of therapy. The continuous bath, by relaxing the individual, lower-ing muscle tonus, and inducing sleep is helpful in the handling of excited states. Cold wet packs in the form of cold sheets applied to the body stimulate the cutaneous circulation and then act as a sedative. They are employed in states of excitement as well as in sleep disturbances. Cold and hot water sprays under high pressure applied to the body may have a markedly tonic affect on the in-dividual, and are sometimes employed in atonic, listless patients. Cold sitz baths are said to have great value in reducing sexual tension [78], especially in women, relieving premenstrual unrest, and soothing intense sexual impulses that are aroused during the involutional period and that threaten to get out of con-trol in various neurotic conditions.

SHOCK AND CONVULSIVE THERAPY

Insulin shock treatment is often employed in schizophrenia [79–81]. The coma that is induced by injection of insulin may be light or deep, brief or pro-longed, and may or may not be accompanied by electrically induced convulsive seizures. Hospitalization is usually required for insulin shock. Sub-coma insulin treatment is sometimes employed in severe acute anxiety states, toxic confusional conditions, and delirium tremens. The patient quiets down with insulin, often to a point where psychotherapy, previously ineffective, may be expediently applied.

Electric convulsive therapy, originally introduced by Cerletti and Bini [82], is used chiefly in depressive states, namely manic-depressive depression, involutional depression, very severe psychoneurotic depression, and senile depression. Improvement or cure is usually achieved after approximately four convulsive seizures, although more convulsions than this may be required. Treatments are given approximately every other day, but after improvement occurs, may be spaced one week apart. Convulsive therapy is used also in manic phases of manic-depressive psychosis in which one convulsion is prescribed daily. In very disturbed patients, as many as two or three seizures daily may be needed. Involutional psychoses of a paranoid nature are sometimes treated with convulsive therapy, but results are not as good as in involutional depressions. Twenty seizures or more may be required here. Some types of schizophrenia are also treated with convulsive therapy, and in such cases thirty or forty seizures are commonly needed. Except for catatonic excitement in which good results are reported, the outcome in most schizophrenic states is dubious. Psychoneuroses, apart from severe reactive depressions, do not respond well to convulsive therapy.

The effect of shock and convulsive therapy is to restore the individual's contact with reality. Psychotherapy is usually indispensible afterwards to handle the individual's basic conflictual problems.

DRUG THERAPY

Drugs are utilized by some therapists in the treatment of emotional problems. Common medicaments are sedatives and stimulants. To control excitement, tension and anxiety, cortical depressants, like barbiturates, bromides, paraldehyde and chloral hydrate are employed. Most useful of these drugs are phenobarbitol (taken in doses of $\frac{1}{4}$ to 2 grains daily as a long-acting sedative) and sodium amytal (taken in doses of 1 to 2 grains as a short-acting sedative during the day, and in doses of 3 to 6 grains at night as a hypnotic). Because of the dangers of barbiturate addiction, the use of barbiturates must be carefully regulated. Paraldehyde is, for many reasons, an ideal hypnotic, although the disadvantages inherent in its taste and residual odor have not given it the popularity it deserves. Barbiturates are sometimes employed intravenously as an emergency measure in quelling intense excitement, sodium amytal most often being prescribed for this purpose in doses of from 3 to $7\frac{1}{2}$ grains.

Perhaps the most common stimulant employed is benzedrine (amphetamine sulfate) [83] in doses of from 5 to 10 milligrams twice daily, to relieve mild depression, and to produce a sense of well-being and vitality in patients who complain of lack of energy and a sense of exhaustion. It is used also as a palliative in the treatment of alcoholism and drug addiction.

Continuous sleep treatment with barbiturates and somnifen [84–86] is sometimes employed in excited manic and schizophrenic states, although insulin shock and convulsive therapy have largely displaced continuous sleep because of the better results obtained.

Antabuse, originally introduced in Denmark [87], is widely used as a means of controlling alcoholism [88]. Although the drug is generally non-toxic, symptoms of a frightening nature occur when a patient under antabuse medication imbibes alcohol. The reaction is so disagreeable that the individual willingly abstains from drink. His self-confidence soon is restored and his self-esteem increases as a result of his ability to remain sober. Psychotherapy should always be administered jointly with antabuse [89] to help prevent a relapse.

Tonics and vitamins are indicated in instances of dietary deficiency. Where there is evidence of glandular impairment, hormones may be employed. The most commonly utilized products are thyroid, and estrogenic and androgenic hormones. During physiologic upsets, and in the involutional period, oestrins, like stilboesterol and other synthetic estrogenic hormones, have been found useful. Androgens, such as testosterone, are prescribed in males who show a deficiency in this hormonal substance, manifested in waning libido, muscular weakness and atony.

A number of drugs have been advocated for the therapy of emotional problems, although their values have not yet been thoroughly investigated. These include histamine, myanesin and adrenocorticotropic hormone. Good results were claimed for histamine therapy by Sackler and his group [90] in the treatment of psychoses. Myanesin (tolserol), a muscle depressant, has been employed for the relief of tension and anxiety [91]. Adrenocorticotropic hormone of the pituitary gland (ACTH) and cortisone have been found by some observers [92,93] to produce a euphorizing effect in certain emotional problems.

Carbon dioxide inhalations are advanced by a number of psychiatrists as a convenient method of treating neurotic problems. According to Meduna [435] 50 to 80 per cent of neurotic conditions respond favorably to this treatment. Carbon dioxide, in the opinion of Meduna, produces certain morphologic changes in the brain cells, lowering electrical activity and excitability, and increasing the threshold of stimulation. This puts the brain in a state of "temporary hibernation" and balances more equitably the energy output. There is experimental evidence that carbon dioxide increases the function of the pituitary and adrenal glands, and decreases the function of the thyroid gland. Because the neurotic has a "hyper-irritable brain" and some disturbance in glandular activity, carbon dioxide is said to exert an almost specific curative effect. Some observers claim that many of the beneficial influences of carbon dioxide are due as much to the associated abreaction and emotional catharsis, as to the presumed chemical change in the brain cells. Other observers including Hargrove, Bennett and Steele [436] challenge the findings of Meduna and present evidence that most patients subjected to carbon dioxide show no improvement in their emotional condition.

BRAIN SURGERY (PSYCHOSURGERY)

Brain surgery is sometimes utilized in the treatment of severe mental problems [94,95]. The most common forms of surgery are transorbital lobotomy, which consists of a sectioning of the white matter in both frontal lobes in the plane of the coronal suture; topectomy, which involves a partial ablation of the frontal cortex; and a cortical undercutting of certain areas of the frontal cortex. While intelligence is not affected by these operations, imagination and intuition are impaired. Self-criticism is lowered with development of untoward reactions in tolerating frustration, and tendencies toward acting-out and tactless behavior. Brain surgery is restricted generally to patients suffering from schizophrenia, chronic disabling obsessive-compulsive neuroses and hypochondriases, who have not responded to psychotherapy, shock and convulsive therapy.

INSPIRATIONAL GROUP THERAPY

Inspirational group therapy is usually oriented around a leader who establishes himself as an omniscient personage whom the patient is expected to obey. To a large extent, the group exists as an appendage of this leader, and beneficial results are maintained so long as the patient is capable of supporting an image of the leader as powerful and protective. Symptom relief is brought about as the result of repression of conflict and a desire on the part of the patient to gain status in the eyes of the leader. Inspirational group therapy is particularly tempting to dependent persons whose inner will to develop is diminutive, and who flourish in a setting in which they are able to establish a submissive relationship to another individual. Such persons become interminably attached to a leader, a group, or to the individuals within the group. The therapeutic group, nevertheless, exerts an important independent effect on the individual, by virtue of the fact that it is composed of members suffering from problems as severe as or more severe than those of the patient. In a group of normal persons, the patient often feels handicapped and inferior, and he may succumb to defenses of justifying himself or building himself up, or of striking out aggressively in order to avoid fancied hurt. In a therapeutic group, the patient is not subjected to the same pressures, and he cannot help but feel a sense of unity in the course of identification with his companions.

Inspirational group therapy is employed by some therapists who claim beneficial effects for it, including the mastery of symptoms, the institution of self-discipline, the tolerance of anxiety and tension, and the repression of inexpressible impulses and drives [96–100]. The patient feels an acceptance in the group such as he could not experience elsewhere. He finds that he can be self-expressive, and that his impulses and drives do not make him bad or worthless in the eyes of others. He eventually discovers that he can gain status within the group.

Many persons benefit through the social contacts they make in such a group setting, particularly when they find other persons with whom they can share experiences. The relationships established in the group help to ease social tensions and to promote self-confidence.

MUSIC THERAPY

Music has been credited with a potential for releasing psychic energy, for stimulating pleasure feelings, for exciting daydreams and fantasies, for overcoming tension, for bringing the withdrawn individual back to reality, and for diminishing fatigue. These effects have not yet been studied systematically and require research validation. While music undoubtedly has some use as a treatment adjunct, considerable research is required before it can be considered a reliable therapeutic tool [437].

INDICATIONS FOR SUPPORTIVE THERAPY

Individuals responsive to supportive therapy are those with good ego strength who have, up to the present illness, made a satisfactory adjustment, but have broken down under the impact of excessively severe environmental pressures and stresses. Such persons are often enabled, with supportive measures, to restore themselves to the equilibrium that existed prior to their upset. Supportive therapy is also indicated in persons with weak ego structures whose capacities for real change are minimal, and who are unable to endure the anxieties inevitably associated with insight therapy. While the treatment objectives are partial, and do not allow for complete personality rehabilitation, adjustment to the existing neurosis, with utilization of one's available resources to the full and minimization of one's liabilities, may be all the patient wants or all he needs at the time.

It must be recognized that there are persons whose ego structures are so weak, and whose motivations are so inadequate, that they are unable to participate in a treatment process where they might achieve a more or less complete rehabilitation. The aim in therapy, here, may have to be a modest one, toward enabling the individual to live with his neurotic defenses as comfortably as possible.

In certain instances supportive therapy does not work. This occurs principally when the patient has problems with authority which are so severe that he automatically goes into competition with an authoritative person, depreciating, seeking to control, acting aggressive and hostile, detaching himself or becoming inordinately helpless. These reactions, appearing during therapy, may act as insurmountable resistances to the acceptance of help.

In all patients receiving supportive therapy, an effort should be made to motivate them toward accepting some kind of insight therapy in order to insure greater permanence of results.

6

Insight Therapy with Reeducative Goals (Reeducative Therapy)

THE RELATIONSHIP BETWEEN PATIENT AND THERAPIST MAY BE EMPLOYED with the object of achieving more extensive goals than those of supportive therapy; namely, an actual modification of the patient's attitudes and behavior in line with more adaptive life integration. The therapist here attempts to initiate in the patient an examination of his interpersonal processes, with the aim of giving him insight into how he participates in fostering his own emotional disturbance. Disorganizing attitudes and behavior, and some of the conflicts that inspire them, are explored to determine how and why they initiate and sustain maladjustment. With such understanding, the individual is best able to reorganize his values and behavioral patterns. The depth of insight varies. In some cases, a mere awareness of his interpersonal difficulties enables the individual to avoid habitual pitfalls, and to manage his life more constructively. Here, no extensive modification of his basic conflicts occurs, even though latent capacities may be liberated. This approach is, more or less, reeducative, and therefore may be designated as "insight therapy with reeducative goals," or "reeducative therapy."

The objectives in reeducative therapy are the gaining of insight into the more conscious attitudes, conflicts and interpersonal relationships with deliberate efforts, once ample insight has been achieved, at environmental readjustment, goal modification, and the living up to existing creative potentialities. The insight gained is rarely of sufficient depth to permit of a real dissolution of unconscious conflict. Nevertheless, the individual achieves sufficient understanding of his problem to check acting-out tendencies; to modify remediable environmental distortions or to adjust to irremediable ones; to organize his life goals more rationally and to execute them in a facile manner; to consolidate some adaptive defenses and to alter others that are less adaptive. Superficial as these objectives may seem, they are eminently worthwhile, and for reasons that will be considered later, are often as far as many patients can progress, even with the most intensive reconstructive approaches. Indeed, in many instances, reeducative therapy is the treatment of choice.

Reeducative therapy is conducted through an examination by the patient and the therapist of the ways the patient relates to people and to himself. Sources of tension and anxiety are explored, and the patient is helped to recognize certain aspects of his behavior that are destructive to his adjustment. He is then encouraged to experiment with new interpersonal attitudes. Additionally, he is stimulated to utilize his assets to best advantage, and to expand positive qualities within himself. While interview procedures are employed, little or no use is made of dream material, transference manifestations and free association. Sometimes reconstructive changes occur as a consequence of reeducative therapy, although these are not specifically the goals toward which treatment is being directed.

The application of reeducative therapy requires specialized training which sensitizes the therapist to interpersonal nuances and teaches him how to handle or minimize some aspects of transference and resistance. While personal psychoanalysis or personal reconstructive therapy is helpful, it is not absolutely essential in executing this approach, provided the therapist does not have too severe neurotic difficulties, and provided that he is aware of and can control his interpersonal problems as these are projected into the relationship with the patient. Among reeducative therapeutic approaches are "relationship therapy," "attitude therapy," distributive analysis and synthesis, interview psychotherapy, therapeutic counseling, therapeutic casework, reconditioning, reeducative group therapy, semantic therapy and bibliotherapy.

"RELATIONSHIP THERAPY"

Relationship therapy was the name given by John Levy [101] to a process in which the patient-therapist relationship was the focus of treatment. While it was acknowledged that the patient projected into the relationship many attitudes and feelings related to the past, interpretations were given to him in terms of feelings he experienced in the present. Allen [102] has described a system of relationship psychotherapy with children which acts as a positive growth experience, releasing forces that make for more complete development. The work of Taft [103] on the relationship aspects of casework may also be considered in this category.

As the name "relationship therapy" implies, the relationship is the vehicle that both promotes change and serves as a target for an inquiry into basic interpersonal patterns. The therapeutic relationship constitutes for the patient a new experience with a human being, which permits a full expression of habitual strivings without retaliatory injury or rejection, such as he is wont to anticipate in customary relationships. The insight gained in the unique therapeutic relationship helps the patient to readapt himself to his life situation, and to aspire to some of his developmental potentials. Actually, what is described as "relationship therapy," has been recognized as constituting a vital aspect of all therapies.

"ATTITUDE THERAPY"

The term "attitude therapy" was used originally by David Levy [104] to describe a process of treating children by working with the disturbed attitudes of their parents. At present, the term is sometimes employed to describe a reeducative procedure focused on the current attitudes of the patient. Distortions in attitudes are examined, their origins discussed, and their present purpose appraised. Following this, attitudes that make for harmonious relationships are introduced as topics for discussion, and the patient is helped to incorporate these as substitutes for his maladaptive attitudes. Thorne [105], for example, suggests a reeducative method that identifies "core attitudes" which cause varied secondary traits and characteristics. The "core attitudes," once identified, are neutralized by presenting opposite healthy attitudes to promote a reorganization of attitudinal constellations. Since the patient will not yield his old attitudes readily, repeated emphasis of new attitudes is essential to achieve desired results. A systematic reconstruction of the patient's attitudes in various areas of life is attempted. Reinforcement of new attitudes is achieved by providing the patient with corrective emotional experiences.

DISTRIBUTIVE ANALYSIS AND SYNTHESIS (PSYCHOBIOLOGIC THERAPY)

Adolf Meyer [106,107], founder of the psychobiologic school, emphasized that the human being was an "experiment in nature," the result of the integrated activity of his somatic, neurologic and psychologic make-up, blending with his social conditionings. It was impossible, he claimed, to isolate any one of the many structures that made up the totality of man. They all had to be considered in relation to the living individual and not regarded as detached units. Furthermore, Meyer urged an empiric viewpoint, utilizing the contributions of any of the various branches of science that could shed light on the total activity of the person. Man was to be studied as a functioning unit in society and as a part of nature by means of the scientific method of observation which was to be applied on various levels of integration. Because man evolved from lower forms, it was necessary to study his physics, chemistry, biology, embryology, anatomy and anthropology. Because man differed from lower forms, it was essential to study his more highly developed functions which distinguished him from the lower species. The most intricate function was that of his mental activity, which Meyer termed "mentation" or "the minding function." This included the ability to sense, imagine, discriminate, communicate ideas, learn, recall, think and reason.

In studying man's behavior, it was necessary to take into account everything significant in the life history of the person; including his heredity, body build, temperament, developmental history, illnesses, traumatic experiences and the interaction of the individual with his parents, siblings and other significant personages. It was necessary to consider his intellectual, spiritual and sexual development; his school, vocational, marital and community adjustments; as well as his interests, ambitions, moods, habits and life goals. Toward this end, the therapist was enjoined to exploit all methods of diagnosis and to utilize various physical and psychologic tests. In examining and recommending treatment for a person, it was important to understand that each individual had a different capacity for bearing stress. Hence, it was necessary to evaluate the strength of his personality through an investigation of his assets and his liabilities.

The psychobiologic approach, with its emphasis on eclecticism, and its consideration of every facet of the individual's functioning as material for inquiry, had a most important influence on the Mental Hygiene movement in this country. It gave rise also to an eclectic therapy known as "distributive analysis and synthesis," or "psychobiologic therapy."

In psychobiologic therapy [108–110] there is a systematic examination of all forces that go into the shaping of the human being; namely, hereditary and constitutional elements, early childhood conditionings, and later experiential influences, including educational, economic, work, marital, interpersonal and social factors. An initial work-up consists of a thorough investigation of both the patient's problem and his personality. This usually involves an inquiry into the individual's life history, a physical examination, and psychologic testing. A psychiatric social worker, clinical psychologist, internist and psychiatrist can function together as a team here in making a proper study.

The character of the complaint, the history of its development, and the patient's past and current attitudes toward it are discussed thoroughly. All available sources are explored, with the help of a psychiatric case worker if necessary, to determine hereditary, constitutional and experiential elements of importance in explaining the patient's reactions. The patient's social, sexual, work, educational and recreational adjustments are investigated, as are his interests, ambitions, habits, cravings and conflicts. Since the therapeutic objective is the retraining of unhealthful attitudes, and the elimination of immature reaction patterns, it is essential to obtain as clear an idea of the patient's personality in operation as is possible.

A physical examination is important not only in detecting existing organic conditions, but also to reassure the patient, and to inspire confidence in the competence of the therapist. X-ray and laboratory facilities are utilized where indicated. Psychologic testing, particularly projection tests, yield data as to personality resources and liabilities, existing anxieties and conflicts, and the nature of the patient's defenses against anxiety.

The initial work-up is invaluable in estimating the best type of therapy to utilize at the start, the prognosis, and the possible duration of treatment. It allows for a much more scientific approach to the patient's problems.

Factors divulged in the initial study, which have operated to mold the individual's personality and to produce the present disorder, are examined systematically in a series of interviews. The therapist then directs the patient's explorations into important areas of the past and current disturbance. Analysis of the past is considered important in providing the therapist with an understanding of the make-up of the individual. However, the past is translated in terms of the patient's present attitudes. Formulation of his difficulties is couched in concepts consonant with the patient's current capacities for understanding. The therapist always attempts to avoid leading the patient into material he is unable to face, and he tries to circumvent the stirring up of guilt or resentment which may interfere with progress. The manner of thinking displayed by the patient, and his general reaction tendencies, are carefully collated. A life history chart may be constructed, detailing the important facts in the patient's case, including family background, socio-economic influences, and significant childhood and adult experiences.

Once a blueprint is obtained of the formative and presently operating influences in the patient's neurosis, the therapist strives to help the patient make constructive use of what has been discovered. This is done by discussions in great detail covering those facts which have influenced the patient and his problems. The patient is enabled, through these discussions, to gain insight into his difficulty. During each interview, positive and constructive elements are accented, successes are emphasized and hopeful elements are brought to the fore. This is to counterbalance and to counteract negative, destructive forces and liabilities. The patient's assets are constantly weighted against his liabilities. A "synthesis" is then made of those factors that can help in his adjustment, and the patient is encouraged to deal with life from a healthier vantage point. He is enjoined to correct disturbing environmental situations, and to avoid or control traits which influence his adjustment adversely. He is also helped to develop adequate compensations. As treatment goes on, and more material becomes available, the therapist may have to reformulate his initial hypothesis.

A number of supportive techniques, like suggestion, guidance, reassurance, persuasion, and confession and ventilation, may be used jointly in effectuating the goal of a more constructive adaptation. Where the therapist is analytically trained, he may deal with the more deeply repressed material, utilizing psychoanalytic techniques, such as free association and dream interpretation. While the clinical material of psychoanalysis is accepted in psychobiology, psychoanalytic theoretic explanations are considered intuitive and metapsychologic rather than scientific. Therefore, a broader bio-psycho-sociologic explanation is attempted, for which there is experimental evidence or reasonably assured probability.

Even though the therapist maintains a benevolent authoritative relationship with the patient, dependence on the therapist is not encouraged. Pointed questions are asked and areas of discussion are delineated, but the patient is stimulated to think things through for himself. The focus in therapy is on present situations and symptoms, of which the patient is aware, rather than upon unconscious attitudes and mechanisms. The relationship between the patient and therapist is not analyzed, and no attempt is made to induce the patient to relive past experiences, although an understanding of present reactions in the light of past conditionings may be stressed.

The techniques that have been outlined may, in an incredibly short time, help to restore a patient to an emotional equilibrium, symptom-free and capable, because of the knowledge he has gained, of avoiding pitfalls that have hitherto created anxiety. Additionally, the patient may learn to utilize his assets to best advantage and to get along in life far better than he ever did before. By showing him how to avoid difficulties in his relationships with people, it may relieve him of much anxiety, tension and hostility. Acquainting him with his character weaknesses, and guiding him to organize his activities around them, may make his life more tolerable. Helping the person to discover positive qualities within himself, may raise, to some extent, his pathologically low estimate of himself. While the dynamic sources of the individual's emotional problem are not tackled directly, as in reconstructive therapy, the relationship with the therapist may inspire curative forces that influence personality growth.

INTERVIEW PSYCHOTHERAPY (PSYCHIATRIC INTERVIEWING)

Psychiatric interviewing is the name given to certain interview procedures which attempt to bring the patient to an awareness of himself by focusing the interview on pertinent problems. Most types of psychiatric interviewing are forms of insight therapy with limited goals, since deeply repressed elements of personality are not brought to awareness. Transference material and dreams are not generally employed.

Finesinger [111] describes a form of interview psychotherapy which is based on the following four factors: an effective doctor-patient relationship, the employment of goal-directed planning and management, the focusing of content on specific aspects of behavior, and the use of minimal activity.

The ultimate goals in treatment are formulated in advance, considering the preliminary diagnosis, the patient's needs and the therapist's clinical experience. Intermediate goals are determined by what is happening in the doctor-patient relationship, and by the kind of material that is brought up during discussions. Focusing of the interview is generally, at first, along lines of an inquiry into existing symptoms, attitudes and problems. Next, there is a search for repetitive patterns in the patient's behavior. Then, the effect of habitual patterns of current behavior is explored with an investigation of the meaning and function of such patterns, as well as their historical origin. Flexibility must be observed in intermediate goals, and there is usually a shift from one to another, determined by the needs of the situation. Interpretations are made for the patient, as required, and, from time to time, there are summarizing interpretations.

A focusing of the patient's attention on relevant topics is essential to avoid rambling. This may be achieved by exhibiting interest or by displaying disinterest in specific topics brought up by the patient. The therapist employs as minimal amounts of activity as are consistent with his therapeutic plans and goals. Only when the patient fails to respond, does the therapist become more active. A careful regulation of the relationship is essential, being balanced between emotional support and the stimulation of tension to activate therapeutic progress.

Interviewing procedures consist of studied non-verbal and verbal responses. Included in the former are facial expressions, nodding, glances, gestures, postural changes, vocal inflections and intonations. Low activity verbal responses are preferred, and consist of articulate syllables with rising inflection, repetition of the patient's last uttered word, elaboration of the last word, mild commands, and questions of a general or specific nature aimed at exploring a certain topic.

Greater activity is required only where material is not readily obtained. Technical procedures here include a repetition of the patient's statements with special emphasis, rearrangement or juxtaposition; statements of a descriptive, elaborative or summarizing nature; and direct questions in relation to associations. Difficulties in communication may be handled by questions related to the difficulty, and by mild or more active encouragement to talk. Methods of marked activity are used only when absolutely essential. These consist of suggesting reasons for reticence, interpreting the reasons, provoking emotional reactions through rapid probing, focusing on transference, forcing the patient to verbalize material, or displaying affect. Extreme active measures are rarely indicated, such as active reassurance, shared experiences, gratifying the demands made by the patient, and shifting the relationship in the direction of a social experience. The learning of this interview method is said by Finesinger to be achieved readily with some supervision.

A less structured method of therapeutic interviewing, directed toward goals of insight, has been described by Stanley Law [112] which he believes can be learned and practiced by general practitioners.

THERAPEUTIC COUNSELING (PSYCHOLOGIC THERAPY)

Modern counseling methods often utilize psychotherapeutic procedures of a reeducative nature [113–120]. A number of systems of psychologic interviewing have been described. Perhaps the most widely discussed of these are "nondirective therapy" and "directive therapy."

1. Non-directive or "Client-centered" Therapy

The "non-directive or "client-centered" approach of Carl Rogers and his colleagues [121–126] is predicated on the principle that the client or patient is the one who is responsible for his own destiny, in that he has a right of choice of solution for his own problems irrespective of the choice of the therapist. Residual in each individual, it is contended by Rogers, are resources for growth which need merely to be released to enable the person to achieve maturity. The therapist strives to unleash growth forces by refraining from imposing patterns and values on the patient, and by promoting in the relationship the free expression of feeling.

The feelings of the individual are always accepted in a tolerant, nonjudgmental way, and are reflected back to the person in order to bring to his consciousness the full pattern of his emotional attitudes. At times the rephrasing of the patient's utterances helps the patient to clarify facts for himself. The catharsis involved in the process, as well as the therapist's activity in reflecting feeling, are believed to lead to genuine self-understanding and insight in the individual's own terms. The release of normal growth potentials helps the patient to gain control over discordant forces in himself. The role of the therapist, thus, is to act as a catalyst of growth, not to impose growth on the patient.

Treatment, accordingly, is oriented around the idea that the individual himself has the capacity to deal effectively with those aspects of his personality of which he becomes conscious during the relationship with the therapist. It is assumed that the patient can achieve insight in the relationship and that he can accept and make constructive use of responsibility. Because efforts to interpret, evaluate or guide the individual are felt to hamper the emerging sense of self-direction and self-growth, a passive role on the part of the therapist is mandatory. Rogers insists that a non-directive approach is not to be confused with a *laissez-faire* policy, which the patient is apt to regard as evidence of rejection or indifference. A truly non-directive attitude avoids clarification of the individual's attitudes, since this is a form of subtle directiveness. The function of the therapist is to perceive empathically the feelings of the patient and to communicate this understanding to him. It is essential for the therapist to discard his preoccupation with diagnosis, to stop making professional evaluations, to eliminate estimates of accurate prognosis, to abandon all attempts to guide the individual, and to concentrate solely on accepting and understanding the attitudes of which the patient permits himself to become conscious.

During therapy, there is a gradual shift in the content of the material discussed—from symptoms to explorations involving the self. Changes develop in the perception of and attitude toward the self, with more positive appraisals and a more realistic consideration of oneself and one's environment. Judgments are recognized as originating in values residing within, rather than outside of the self. Perceptions shift from wide generalizations to more limited ones rooted in primary experiences. Symbolizations become more adequate and highly differentiated. Movement becomes more and more pronounced toward awareness of denied or repressed experiences and feelings. Changes occur in personality structure and organization, toward increased unification and integration. There is a lessening of neurotic tendencies, a decreased amount of anxiety, a greater acceptance of oneself, a heightened objectivity in the handling of reality, a more constructive way of mediating stress, a more harmonious expression of attitudes and feelings, and an increased intellectual functioning. Developing changes in behavior are in line with improved adjustment and maturity. Decreased tension, lessening of defensive tendencies, and greater tolerance of frustration are concomitant.

As has been indicated, diagnosis in non-directive therapy is not felt to be essential to the treatment process. Indeed it is conceived of as a hindrance. Making a diagnosis is also felt to involve dangers of subordinating the individual to an evaluation by authority, putting the therapist in a godlike role. This opposes the atmosphere of equality essential to the non-directive approach.

Rogers has revised upward his original idea of non-directive therapy as being most useful in essentially normal people who have sufficient personality integrity to solve their problems with a minimum of help from the therapist. His more recent contention is that his method is universally applicable, ranging from mild adjustment difficulties to severe psychoses, from "normal" to deeply neurotic situations, from immature dependent people to those with strong ego development, from lower class to upper class individuals, from lowly to highly intelligent persons, from physically healthy individuals to those with psychosomatic ailments. While in each of these groupings failures are said to occur, non-directive therapy is believed by Rogers to be widely applicable to all people from the ages of two to sixty-five years.

It is claimed that transference does not develop often in non-directive therapy, since the individual is not evaluated or held subject to specific rules. His self-esteem consequently is prevented from crumbling, avoiding thereby a dependent relationship. Where transference occurs, it is more or less disregarded, the other material brought up being considered more important than transference material. Transference is thus simply accepted and not explored or interpreted; and where the individual feels understood, tranference attitudes are said to disappear or to express themselves so minimally as not to interfere with progress.

The popularity of non-directive methods is due to the fact that they are relatively simple for the therapist to master, requiring little clinical experience to get results and involving few dangers to the patient who works out his own problems. Many experienced psychotherapists agree with Thorne [127] that non-directive approaches have serious limitations, both in terms of accomplished goals and in the kinds of problems that respond to the method.

A probable reason for the relative absence of transference in non-directive therapy is that it is circumvented. The focus is on the present rather than the past. Specific discussion of the therapeutic relationship is not encouraged. Concentration is on reality rather than on derivatives of the unconscious. Dreams, fantasies, slips of speech, and the immediate feelings of the patient toward the therapist are not emphasized.

Non-directive methods are most helpful in individuals of relatively sound personality structure who require aid in clarifying their ideas about a current life difficulty or situational impasse. They are definitely much less effective in serious emotional problems in which anxiety elements are present. Anxiety is the greatest motivant of all human behavior. In most emotional ailments, anxiety impedes and even blocks the emergence of positive growth potentials in the patient, no matter how tolerant and permissive the therapist may be. Anxiety nurtures resistance which can effectively prevent the patient from thinking about, or spontaneously focusing on, significant conflictual patterns. Left to his own devices, the patient will usually avoid coming to grips with deep anxieties. He will even choose to retain neurotic defenses, warding off, in this way, inherent impulses for growth. It is essential, then, that the therapist enter actively, at times, into this neurotic cycle. Resistances may have to be dealt with in a direct and even forceful way. Similarly, even though the patient may acquire self-understanding, anxiety may prevent his utilizing insight in the direction of change. Here directive measures may be required before the patient yields up his inertia. Thus choice or rejection of non-directive therapy will depend on whether or not the individual is deeply disturbed emotionally, his existing ego strength and the nature of the problem for which he seeks help.

The field of non-directive therapy has, nevertheless, made an important contribution to psychotherapy by pointing out processes involved in interviewing and in the management of certain phases of treatment, especially termination.

2. Directive Therapy

Directive approaches put the therapist in the authoritative role of making positive suggestions to the patient, supplying him with information and urging him on toward certain courses of action. Goals are more or less vested in the therapist who disects, tears down, rebuilds and resynthesizes the personality.

Thorne [128] describes a number of techniques helpful in achieving these goals. For instance, the patient may be given information along educational lines, with the object of reorienting his *Weltanschauung*. The patient is here confronted with factual information about himself in an effort to get him to re-evaluate his attitudes [129]. The case history is used by Thorne both as a diagnostic and as a therapeutic aid, helping in establishing rapport, promoting catharsis, giving reassurance and fostering insight [130]. A more active technique is the therapeutic use of conflict [131]. On the basis that certain maladjustments are sponsored by a pathologic lack of conflict, certain conflicts may be induced in the patient as a therapeutic method. Here, the patient is confronted with situations or with information that provokes him to reevaluate attitudes in the direction of reality. The patient is thus forced to work through some of his problems toward a more satisfactory solution by being presented with his inconsistent or conflicting attitudes in so forceful a way that he is motivated to resolve them. A number of other procedures may be employed, the extent of directiveness varying from forceful coerciveness to a relatively participating relationship.

Criticisms of directive psychotherapy are voiced in terms of the imposition on the patient of the therapist's goals and sense of values, and the repetition of the disciplinary atmosphere of the child-parent relationship. Under these circumstances, liberation from the yoke of one's authoritarian conscience is impeded, and there is an interference with growth potentials toward assertiveness and independence. A great disadvantage claimed is that the patient is apt to be kept on a dependency level longer than is necessary. Where the aim in therapy is to make the patient self-sufficient and capable of finding security within himself, directiveness may inhibit this aim. In looking for security or support from the outside, from another individual who will impose it or who will present it to him as a gift, the patient never develops the ability to take a stand in life and to become a stronger and more independent being through his own resources. Another criticism of directive therapy relates to the fact that hostility is often said to be mobilized by the very nature of the authoritarian relationship. This prevents the patient from liberating himself from a punitive and severe conscience fostered by an irrational attitude toward authority. While the new ways of conduct that are developed may be better than those the patient has followed most of his life, they do not alter his self-structure. In relation to the therapist, the patient remains still a child who has incorporated the mandates of the parent. He has not been given a real opportunity to grow and develop adult ego strength.

The value of directive therapy is in the techniques that have been evolved, which may be adapted to some aspects of a therapeutic program, particularly during the phase of translating insight into action.

CASEWORK THERAPY

In rendering help to people with social difficulties, the handling of their personality problems has been found to be an essential and often inevitable part of the service given. This expanded kind of service has been designated "casework." Many of the procedures developed and used in casework are psychotherapeutic in nature [132–136]. In recent years the casework field has been divided into two main groupings: "functional casework," and "diagnostic casework," each of which has evolved a special methodology.

1. "Functional Casework"

The school of "functional casework" [137] is oriented around the teachings of Otto Rank. It attempts to help people seeking specific services in social agencies, in such a way that the use of the services becomes psychologically constructive for the individual. The relationship with the caseworker therapist is considered a "helping process" in which the individual experiences a new, constructive way of observing himself and of relating to another person. The relationship serves as a kind of laboratory in which the individual acts out, with a representative of authority (the therapist), the full range of attitudes and patterns that he habitually cherishes toward authoritative persons; such as, belligerency, detachment, ingratiation, and the need to control or be controlled. The therapist handles these projections as a necessary part of the client's accepting help, and, in tolerant acceptance, reflects back to the individual the differentiation between his projections and the existing realities. This enables the individual to become aware of his characteristic ways of relating, and permits him to accept in a realistic manner the kind of help offered him by the therapist. The individual assumes direction for his own processes of change; his choices and goals are conceived of as his right and responsibility. Within the limitations of the structure of the agency, the individual is free to move toward self-responsibility and self-acceptance. The relationship between therapist and individual is thus believed to serve both as a means of solution of a specific problem, and as a genuine growth experience. While some of the aims of functional casework are reconstructive, the average worker is not trained to deal with the more unconscious aspects of experience. Therapy is thus geared to reeducative goals.

2. "Diagnostic Casework"

The school of "diagnostic casework" [138], drawing largely from the teachings of Freud and his contemporaries, tries to provide a corrective emotional experience for the individual, through the medium of a positive relationship with the caseworker therapist. The relationship is not the central core of treatment as in "functional casework," but is rather used as a vehicle toward increasing the individual's ability to solve his problems on a more mature level. The attitudes of the individual and the kind of relationship he seeks with the therapist are used diagnostically, but do not determine the direction of therapy. Treatment is goal-directed toward dissipating inner conflict and expanding ego strength, as well as reducing, by social planning, existing environmental pressures. Objectives are variably graded to meet requirements of the diagnosis and the specific needs of the individual. Techniques, which include emotional catharsis, reassurance, guidance, clarification and interpretation, are used in whatever ways best serve to increase the capacities of the ego. The focus of discussion is on the individual's problems, on ways of resolving these, and on obstacles from the standpoint of inner feelings and social reality. There is a continued evaluation and reevaluation of the problem from cues supplied by behavior patterns and attitudes, from the individual's responses to the therapeutic situation, and from reactions to interpretations and suggestions made by the therapist. Projected irrational feelings and attitudes are recognized and discussed, leading to greater awareness of current patterns of behavior and of their origins in earlier relationships. The individual gradually sees connections between his present attitudes and conflicts and those that he harbored toward parental and other past personages. The result is a strengthening of ego capacities, a reappraising of reality issues divorced from anachronistic expectations, a developing of a sense of being valued, and an incorporating of acceptable social concepts and standards. As in functional casework, dreams and other derivatives of the unconscious are accepted, but are not handled or interpreted unless the caseworker is trained to do reconstructive therapy.

RECONDITIONING

Reconditioning may be described under reeducative therapy, since it has as its aim a substitution of new patterns for old. The fact that neurotic patterns of behavior are the product of faulty conditionings suggests that normal behavior patterns may be substituted for neurotic ones by a process of reconditioning.

Among the earliest work reported along this line is that of Jones [139] who experimented with a child who, bitten by a rabbit, had developed great fear of the animal and of rabbits in general. Jones believed that if he could get the child to associate the rabbit with a pleasant emotion, fear of the creature might be lost. He decided to feed the child appetizing foods when the child became hungry; at the same time exposing the child to the sight of the rabbit held at a distance; then, gradually diminishing the distance. The experiment was successful, and the child no longer experienced fear of the rabbit.

Other reconditioning experiments have been performed by Yates [140], Max [141] and Mowrer and Mowrer [142]. Yates, treating a girl who was upset emotionally by the presence of men, had her repeat the word "calm," while associating with it at the same time, ideas of security, well-being and peace. She gradually learned that constant repetition of the word in the presence of men sufficed to maintain her emotional composure. Max treated a homosexual patient who was obsessed with homosexual thoughts whenever he came into contact with a certain inanimate object. Presenting this object to the patient, and giving him an electric shock at the same time, sufficed to terminate the power of the object to excite homosexual thoughts. Mowrer and Mowrer treated enuresis by constructing an apparatus that was placed in the bed of the enuretic child. The bed, when wet, caused a circuit in the apparatus to close and to ring a bell, thus awakening the child. They discovered that after three or four such experiences, the impulse to urinate in itself sufficed to arouse the child.

The reconditioning of phobias is sometimes effective, particularly those phobias that have been established on the basis of fortuitous conditionings. Habits which the patient finds difficult to break; such as excessive smoking, nail-biting, over-eating, alcoholic indulgence, and some forms of addiction to medicaments, respond to this method, particularly when there is reinforcement by hypnosis [143].

Thorne [144] describes a method whereby fear reactions may be dissipated through a conditioning process of verbally admitting the presence of fear, of appreciating that it is a common reaction, of anticipating its arousal, and of training oneself to avoid inappropriate responses. Tasks may be assigned which enhance emotion-control and self-control, and the patient is reminded that many months will be required before success is complete.

In this category may be classified Salter's "Conditioned Reflex Therapy" [145] in which, through authoritarian direction, the patient is enjoined to abandon destructive patterns of behavior and to practice new habits that will be of value to him. Postulated is the theory that healthy biologic organisms are in a state of free emotional expressiveness (excitatory state). On the other hand, unhealthy organisms, with emotional illness, are said to be in a state of pathologic inhibition, which has become a conditioned response and which blocks normal excitation. Therapy must be directed toward unlearning conditioned inhibitory reflexes, and replacing them with conditioned excitatory reflexes. This is accomplished by deliberately practicing excitatory emotional reactions until they become established as conditioned reflexes. Thus, the patient is encouraged to express his feelings openly, accompanying these by appropriate or exaggerated motor reactions. Whenever he is in a situation where he disagrees with others, he must deliberately and forcefully express himself instead of inhibiting his feelings. Spontaneous reactions to new situations are preferred to practiced or conventionalized behavior. Expressing self-praise and promulgating one's own opinions and values are urged as a means of increasing self-confidence. By practicing such "positive" and "excitatory" acts, the patient is said to be liberated from the harmful effects of inhibition. The hypothesis on which Salter bases his therapy has been attacked as highly speculative, and his claims of success are regarded as over-optimistic.

SEMANTIC APPROACHES TO THERAPY

Semantics deals with systems of symbols; including language structures, and the uses made of these systems by individuals and social groups, as well as the influence on the systems by the existing social values and individual behavior tendencies [146]. Therapeutically employed, semantics tries to teach the individual the principles of scientific thinking through a more valid use of communication.

The employment of semantics as a therapeutic method necessitates a high degree of intelligence in the patient and requires special semantic training for the therapist. During treatment a mutual examination of verbal forms used by both therapist and patient is made, to see whether exact meanings are being communicated. There follows a detailed evaluation of the patient in relation to his language efficiency and the prevalence of semantic problems. Finally, semantic retraining is employed, to teach the patient the more exact use of symbols and terms. Adequate problem-solving presupposes a sufficient mastery of language and use of symbols to enable the person to state his difficulties, differentiate them, make inferences, and draw conclusions from facts. The person must know something about the uses and abuses of symbols. These are the foci of investigation in semantic therapy.

Johnson [147] has outlined the effect of semantic difficulties on adjustment. One syndrome of maladjustment is the product of unrealistic ideals in life which bring about disappointment and frustration. Part of the problem is due to the doubt which governs the individual's ideas, making it impossible for him to conceptualize clearly what he wants from life. He is, therefore, inevitably disappointed in his efforts to gain pleasure in living. Another source of maladjustment is the fact that he cannot identify or even state his problems coherently because his language is poorly organized and lacking in clarity. This vagueness in thinking, embracing faulty notions about himself and fallacious concepts of the meaning of life, interferes with the formulation of realistic goals.

Semantic distortions include over-verbalization, which may serve the function of avoiding silence, of concealing the truth or of searching frantically for meanings. Under-verbalization is another response, which is often motivated by a fear of failure, demoralization or perfectionistic strivings. There may be great verbal rigidity involving content, modes of phrasing and moods. There may also be a defect in the capacity to discriminate levels of verbal and non-verbal abstracting. Other disturbances of communication occur that require careful analysis and diagnosis.

In therapy, once a good relationship with the therapist is established, semantic training and reorganization is practiced. Interpretations are given the patient as his semantic defects become apparent. Training proceeds as rapidly as the patient's resistances will permit. As the patient becomes capable of formulating his problem cogently, he gains confidence in his ability to communicate with freedom and clarity. His verbal rigidities relaxing, he becomes more conscious of his real problems, his feelings about himself and his life goals. By being able to put his problem into meaningful words, the person is helped to achieve greater volitional control over his emotional processes.

When we evaluate the semantic approach to therapy, we have to consider that all emotional ailments are associated with problems in communication. These involve, among other things, vagueness in phrasing and defects in conceptualization. So long as there is an unclearness in the use of symbols, the individual is unable to define, differentiate, or to think critically about his attitudes, values and life goals. It is likely that a good part of the existing communication difficulty in emotional illness is the product of repression—a purposive attempt to cloud issues in order to keep painful aspects of the personality outside the range of awareness. During any kind of psychotherapy, the patient, as he masters anxiety, becomes capable of expressing himself more and more clearly, and of verbalizing in increasingly explicit terms that which he has hitherto merely been able to feel. This restores to the patient a measure of volitional control over his impulses, and enables him to deal more adequately with the sources of his problem.

In summary, semantic approaches to therapy put the emphasis on the patient's difficulties in communication. Emotional illness is regarded as essentially involving problems of symbolic functioning, and the focus of therapeutic effort is on defining and clarifying symbols, making the patient's use of them more precise. It is obvious that the successful achievement of the latter goal presupposes the establishment of a good relationship with the therapist and the working-through of transference and content resistances, as is the case in any other kind of psychotherapy. Thus, while the focus may be different, many of the processes involved are probably the same as in other therapies.

REEDUCATIVE GROUP THERAPY

Group therapy may be conducted toward the reeducative goals of altering attitudinal and behavioral patterns [148–153]. The group offers the therapist a splendid opportunity both to observe the manner in which the individual relates to others, and to bring distortions in his relating to the awareness of the individual. Benefits accrue also by virtue of the real experience of functioning with others within the group setting. A medium is provided whereby cooperative attitudes may grow, expand and eventually replace neurotic strivings.

Practitioners of group therapy contend that groups can liberate and give direction to what is significant, in a social sense, in the individual. Man is a group creature who needs to relate himself to others in order to function adequately as a human being. Unfortunately, emotionally ill persons suffer from disturbances in interpersonal relationships which eventually alienate them from the group. The therapeutic group offers an opportunity to resolve some of these disturbances by providing an atmosphere in which the person is neither rejected nor ridiculed for his neurotic impulses. He becomes, in the group, more tolerant toward himself and less defensive toward others. As the patient interacts with other group members, and his behavior is discussed in a frank and unemotional way, he gains greater self-understanding while experiencing feelings in an acceptable setting. Although the group stimulates destructive patterns in interpersonal relationships, the hope is that eventually the patient will be able to adjust to the group without exploiting his neurotic character drives. For instance, a power-driven person may learn that he can submit to the group without being controlled or hurt. A negativistic individual may discover that yielding to others does not presuppose abandoning his personal rights and freedom. A detached patient may derive positive pleasures by infiltrating slowly into group activities. As the members of the group relate to each other freely, they learn to compromise, to give as well as to receive. This may encourage cooperative participation, helpfulness and friendliness, which may undermine and eventually replace destructive interpersonal feelings.

Moreno [154,155] has devised an elaborate group therapeutic technique of "psychodrama." In this method, the patient is encouraged to dramatize situations spontaneously, and, in the role of actor, to relive many of his conflicts, wishes, fears and attitudes. By acting-out his problem and giving vent to feelings and fantasies, the person is said to desensitize himself to inner terrors, to achieve hidden wishes, to prepare himself for future contingencies, and otherwise to resolve many of his deeper problems and conflicts. Sometimes the therapist, upon reviewing the patient's history, decides on which life situations to reenact, in order to work out important conflictual foci. A device often employed is that of the "auxiliary ego" assumed by a trained worker who both mimics the patient and reacts spontaneously by uttering ideas and thoughts he believes the patient may not be able to verbalize. In reenacting situations, the patient may play the role, not only of himself, but also of a significant person in his life, such as a parent or sibling. While observing the patient's activities, the therapist may remain silent or he may inject questions or suggestions. The material elicited during psychodrama is utilized in discussions with the therapist at later sessions. Though psychodrama usually has an emotionally cathartic value for the patient, it is possible in some circumstances, for the patient to be helped in understanding his problems as they reveal themselves in his expressed acts and thoughts, and as they are reflected back to him by the "auxiliary ego." With coordinate individual psychotherapy, the patient will be better enabled to gain insight into his disturbed behavioral patterns.

A form of reeducative therapy termed "relationship group therapy" is described by Glatzer and Pederson-Krag [156]. In the course of group treatment with this method personality patterns emerge. The group therapeutic relationship becomes a living experience into which the patient projects his impulses and strivings. These are interpreted to the patient by the therapist. Immediate emotions are dealt with and handled, particularly those the patient can face without too much anxiety. In this way, he gradually becomes aware of some repressed feelings and learns the origins of many of his neurotic conflicts. The object is to help the person come to terms with himself.

Slavson [157] describes a type of reeducative therapy under the name "activity group therapy." This is used with children in the medium of a "social club." Complete permissiveness prevails and there is freedom in the expression of all types of behavior. Cathartic ventilation of feelings usually occurs freely. Materials such as arts and crafts are supplied, refreshments are served, and outings made possible. The group functions as a secondary family with the therapist becoming a substitute parent. Relationships, established with the therapist and with other children in the group, lead to a more realistic conception of the world and of the self. Insight is gained by the child within the action setting, and not through interpretation.

Insight Therapy with Reconstructive Goals (Reconstructive Therapy)

A CHIEF DIFFERENTIAL FEATURE IN SUPPORTIVE, REEDUCATIVE AND reconstructive psychotherapy relates to the degree of insight achieved. In supportive therapy, the amount of insight is minimal; in reeducative therapy, it is more extensive, but focused on relatively conscious problems. The objective in reconstructive therapy is to bring the individual to an awareness of his unconscious conflicts and their derivatives, which produce difficulties in interpersonal relationships and a breakdown of defenses and modes of adjustment. This is deemed important in expediting extensive alterations in character structure. Reconstructive psychotherapy aims not only at restoration of the individual to effective life functioning, through resolution of disabling symptoms and disturbed interpersonal relationships, but it strives also to bring about a maturation of emotional development with the creation of new adaptive potentialities.

The methods employed in bringing unconscious material to awareness were originally developed by Sigmund Freud. They include such techniques as those of free association, dream interpretation and the analysis of the transference. Included also are the use of strategically timed interpretations, and the dealing with resistances to the content of unconscious material and to the relationship with the therapist. An understanding of the genetic determinants of the individual's personality, and of the relationship of these determinants to his present-day character structure is helpful in the therapeutic process.

To do this type of therapy, the therapist must preferably have undergone a personal psychoanalysis, and must have treated a number of patients successfully, under the supervision of an experienced psychoanalyst.

As has been indicated previously, reconstructive personality changes sometimes occur spontaneously during the course of supportive and reeducative therapies, or upon completion of these treatments as a consequence of more congenial relationships with people. For instance, the individual may work out, in the medium of the relationship with the therapist, or with a person outside of therapy, such archaic strivings as persisting dependency needs, fears of rejection or overprotection, detachment and untoward aggression. He may even connect the origin of such impulses with unfortunate childhood conditionings and experiences. Reconstructive changes occurring in this way, however, are the exception rather than the rule. In reconstructive psychotherapy, the treatment situation is deliberately planned to promote, inside or outside of therapy, a living through, with insight, of the deepest fears and conflicts of the individual.

If we accept the statement of Freud [158] that psychoanalysis includes "any line of investigation, no matter what its direction, which recognizes the two facts of transference and resistance," we must concede that all reconstructive therapy is psychoanalytic in essence. There are three main "types" of insight therapy with reconstructive goals: "Freudian psychoanalysis," "non-Freudian psychoanalysis" and "psychoanalytically oriented psychotherapy." All of these therapies aim at a reconstructive change in the personality. However, they differ as to the method by which this objective is realized. Freudian psychoanalysis is more or less the original technique of Sigmund Freud. Non-Freudian psychoanalysis, which includes the approaches of Horney, Sullivan, Rank, Jung, Adler and Stekel, is a modified, more active technique. Psychoanalytically oriented psychotherapy, in which category belong some of the techniques described by Alexander and French, is the most active of the reconstructive therapies.

FREUDIAN PSYCHOANALYSIS

Reconstructive psychotherapy owes a debt of monumental proportions to Sigmund Freud who introduced the substructure upon which present dynamic psychiatry is based. While many of his original theoretic assumptions have undergone modification, the clinical observations of Freud remain as fundamental foundations for the scientific method in psychiatry.

In 1880, Joseph Breuer discovered that when an hysterical girl under hypnosis was induced to speak freely, she expressed profound emotion and experienced relief from her symptoms. Under the impression that her hysteria originated in certain painful experiences while caring for her sick father, Breuer enjoined her, while she was in an hypnotic state, to remember and to relive the traumatic scenes. This seemed to produce a cure in her hysteria.

Ten years later, in conjunction with Freud, Breuer continued his research, and, in 1895, the two men published their observations in a book, *Studien Über Hysteria* [159]. Their conclusions were that hysterical symptoms developed as a result of experiences so traumatic to the individual that they were repressed. The mental energy associated with the experiences was blocked off, and not being able to reach consciousness was converted into bodily innervations. The discharge of strangulated emotions (abreaction), through its normal channels during hypnosis, would relieve the necessity of diverting the energy into symptoms. This method was termed "catharsis."

Freud soon found that equally good therapeutic results could be obtained without hypnosis by permitting the patient to talk freely, expressing whatever ideas came to his mind. Freud invented the term "psychoanalysis" for the process of uncovering and permitting the verbal expression of hidden traumatic experiences. Freud found that there were forces that kept memories from invading consciousness, and he discovered that it was necessary to neutralize the repressing forces before recall was possible. An effective way to overcome resistances was to permit the patient to relax and to talk freely about any idea or fantasy that entered his mind no matter how trivial or absurd. Freud could observe in this "free association" a sequential theme that gave clues to the nature of the repressed material.

Mainly through an introspective analysis of his own dreams [160] Freud was able to show how dreams were expressions of unconscious wishes and fears, evading the barriers of repression through the assumption of symbolic disguises. He perfected a technique of arriving at the meaning of the unconscious material through translation of symbols.

Freud also observed that when the patient was encouraged to say whatever came to his mind, he verbalized irrational attitudes toward the therapist; such as, deep love, fear, hate, overvaluation, expectancy, disappointment and other strivings that were not justified by the reality situation. He noted too that the patient identified the therapist with significant personages in his past, particularly with his parents, and that this identification motivated the transfer over to the therapist of attitudes similar to those he originally had toward his parents. This phenomenon Freud called "transference." For example, a patient with a phobia of being subject to imminent, but indefinable injury might, at a certain phase in his analysis, begin to develop an aversion and dread of the analyst, expressed in fears of being mutilated. At the same time, incestuous wishes for the mother might appear in dreams. Analysis of the relationship with the analyst (transference) would then possibly reveal an identification of the analyst with the patient's father. It would then become apparent that the patient secretly feared injury by the father for his forbidden wish to possess the mother, and that his phobia was an expression of this fear of mutilation which had been dissociated from awareness by repression. The bringing of the patient's attention to the sources of his fear, and his realization of its irrational nature, would result in an amelioration or cure of his neurosis.

The material uncovered by Freud from his studies of free association, dream interpretation and analysis of the transference, suggested to him that there was a dynamic portion of the psyche, closely associated with the emotional disorder, that did not follow the normal laws of mental functioning. Freud called this aspect of the mind the "unconscious," and he set about to determine the unique laws which dominated the repressed psychic component. In studying the symbols issuing from the unconscious, Freud noted that they were concerned chiefly with sexual material, and he concluded from this that the unconscious was preoccupied for the most part with sexual wishes and fears. Consequently, he assumed that the most important traumatic events which had been repressed were sexual in nature. It was largely on this evidence that he evolved his "theory of instincts" or the "libido theory."

In his theory of instincts, Freud postulated the fact that all energy had its origin in instincts which persistently expressed themselves (repetition compulsion) and were represented mentally as ideas with an emotional charge (cathexis). A fundamental instinct was that of *eros,* the sexual or life instinct, manifesting itself in a force called "libido." Freud hypothesized a permeation of the body by this vital instinctual force, the "libido," which powered the individual's development toward mature sexuality. Libido was, however, subject to many developmental vicissitudes in its destined course to adult genitality. During the first year of life, it concentrated itself around the oral zone, the mouth and lips, the child gaining a kind of erotic pleasure by sucking and later by biting. At the end of the first year, there was a partial shift in libido to the anal zone, and intense pleasures were derived from the retention and expulsion of feces. During this period, the child's interests were more or less concentrated on himself (narcissism), and satisfactions were primarily localized within his own body (auto-erotism). Relationships with people were primitive, being circumscribed to only part of the parent (part-object relationships), like the nipple or breast instead of the entire parent.

Around the age of three, libido was centered around the phallic zone—the penis or clitoris. "Object relationships" were less primitive and were extended to a more complete relatedness with the parent. Yet, fundamentally, the child was ambivalent, responding to his parents and other people with a mixture of love and hate.

This stage of psychosexual growth continued into the Oedipal period, during which the little boy developed toward his mother a profound interest, with strong sexual overtones and desires for exclusive ownership. The little girl, envying men for their possession of a penis, created in part by a desire to repudiate her femininity and to become a male (penis envy), and resenting the fact that she had no penis, accused the mother of responsibility for this deprivation and turned to the father with an intensified sexual interest. In the case of the boy, hostility toward the father, due to a desire to eliminate him as a rival, generated a fear of counter-hostility, and particularly a fear of castration, which inspired such anxiety as to induce him to give up his interest in the mother and to make friends with his father. The intensity of fear became so overwhelming and so unendurable that the boy was forced to yield to his more powerful competitor by renouncing, repudiating and repressing sexual feelings toward the maternal love-object. He was obliged also to repress concomitant hostile impulses toward the father. The little girl similarly resolved her enmity toward her mother, as well as her sexual interest in her father. This drama, known as the Oedipus complex, was to Freud the crucial nuclear conflict in the development of the personality contributing to both character formation and neurotic symptoms.

The incorporation of parental injunctions and prohibitions, and the repudiation of sexual and hostile aims as related to the parents, resulted in the crystallization of an aspect of the psyche which took over the judging, prohibiting and punitive functions hitherto vested in the parents. This aspect became the conscience or super-ego. The adequate resolution of the Oedipus complex was associated with channelization of libido into the genital zone, with capacities for complete, mature, unambivalent, "whole-object" relationships.

Following upon the Oedipal period, there was an era characterized by the neutralization of sexual impulses. This Freud called the "latency period." With the advent of puberty, however, increased libido, due to the heightened activity of the genital glands, reactivated the old Oedipal interests. The person then lived through the revived early Oedipal conflict, and his capacity to solve this anew was determined by the extent of previous vicissitudes and the adequacy with which his conflict had formerly been resolved. In "normal" solutions, the child transferred his or her sexual interest to extra-familial persons of the opposite sex. The little girl renounced her boyish interests and accepted a passive female role.

Under certain conditions, normal psychosexual development was impeded by a "fixation" of libido onto oral, anal and phallic zones. The libido, bound down in this way, was unable to participate in the development of full genitality. Freud believed that both constitutional and experiential factors were responsible for this. Most prominent were excessive gratifications or inordinate frustrations experienced at an early stage of growth. Not only did libidinal fixations interfere with the development of mature sexuality, but they constituted stations to which the individual might return when confronted with overwhelming stress or frustration. Under these circumstances, the libidinal stream was said to undergo "regression" to pregenital fixation points. When this happened, there were revived attitudes and interests characteristic of childhood, with immature sexual strivings, interest in "part-objects" and narcissism. Infantile conflicts and patterns were also revivified in this process. Sexual perversions constituted the positive expression of pregenital libidinal fixations, while neurotic symptoms were a negative or converted expression [161].

Freud conceived of the mental apparatus as an organ that prevented the damming up of energy. Pain was related to an increase of energy, and pleasure to a decrease. In order to help understand the operations of the mental apparatus, Freud elaborated a topographic structure of the psyche, as involving a reservoir of instinctual energy, the *id;* a supervisory area serving a censoring and sanctioning function, the *super-ego;* and a structure that mediated internal and external adjustments, the *ego.* These sub-divisions, although recognized by Freud as arbitrary, empiric and metapsychologic, were retained by him as a conceptual necessity [162].

Freud classified the id as the original undifferentiated mind, the repository of inherited urges and instinctual energy. It contained the instincts of Eros—the life or sexual instinct, and Thanatos—the death instinct. It provided the individual with dynamic energy (libido), which vitalized every organ and tissue and sought expression in response to a "pleasure principle," along whatever channels were available for it. Through impressions received by the perceptual organs, the id underwent modifications immediately after birth. Differentiation by the child of himself as an entity apart from the world was in keeping with the evolution of the ego, which increasingly assumed the function of an executive organ, harnessing the id to the demands of reality (reality principle). Important impressions, particularly those related to experiences with parents or their surrogates, and frustrations created by prohibitions of pleasure strivings, registered themselves on the child's psyche and stimulated primitive mechanisms of projection and introjection. In projection, aggression was discharged outward and directed toward parents; in introjection, the frustrating parental agencies were "incorporated" within the child's psychic apparatus. Through these mechanisms, rudiments of a super-ego developed which later, with the resolution of the Oedipus complex, crystallized and took over the guiding and prohibitive functions of the parents. One aspect of the super-ego contained constructive ideals toward which the individual felt driven (ego ideal).

Under the lash of the super-ego, the ego created repressions against libidinal strivings and their ideational representatives. Such repressions served to avoid conflict. When, however, for any reason, repression relaxed or proved insufficient, the ego was invaded with some of the content of the repressed. This threat to the individual's security inspired anxiety, a danger signal that indicated a break-through of the repressed material.

As Freud continued his work, he laid less and less stress on strangulated emotions due to early traumatic experiences as the primary cause of neurosis. More and more he became cognizant of the purposeful nature of symptoms, and, in 1926, he revised his theory of neurosis drastically, claiming that symptoms were not only manifestations of repressed instinctive strivings, but also represented defenses against these strivings [163].

Freud contended, however, that the essence of a neurosis was a repression of infantile fears and experiences which continually forced the individual to act in the present as if he were living in the past. The neurotic seemed to be dominated by past anxieties that, split off, operated autonomously and served no further function in reality.

Internal dangers were constantly threatened by the efforts of the id to discharge accumulated tension. Such discharge was opposed by the mental force of the super-ego in the form of repression to prevent the release of tension. Repression was a dynamic force which attempted to seal off internal dangers. However, the maintenance of repression required an enormous expenditure of energy. The ego derived this energy from the id in a subversive manner. Thus, an idea or tendency invested with libido (cathexis) would be stripped of libido and this energy used to oppose the idea or tendency (anti-cathexis).

Subtle mechanisms such as symbolization, condensation, distortion and displacement were employed to evade repressive forces and to provide a substitutive discharge of repressed energy, and a consequent relief of tension. Fantasies, dreams and symptoms were expressions of such mechanisms. Where the substitutive expression was in harmony with social values and super-ego ideals, it provided a suitable means of relief (sublimation). Where it was not in harmony, conflict resulted and repressive mechanisms were again invoked. If repression proved ineffective in mediating tension, a regression to earlier modes of adaptation was possible. This happened particularly where the individual was confronted by experiences similar to, or representative of, those which initiated anxiety in childhood. The ego reacted automatically to these experiences, as if the reality conditionings of later years had had no corrective effect on the original danger situation. It responded with essentially the same defenses of childhood, even though these were now inappropriate.

A retention of a relationship to reality at the expense of an intrapsychic balance, produced a psychoneurotic disturbance. The existing conflict here was between the ego and the id. If an intrapsychic balance developed at the expense of reality relationships, the consequence was psychosis. The latter resulted when the ego was overwhelmed by id forces, the conflict being between the ego and the environment.

In addition to the libido theory described above, Freud elaborated the theory of the death instinct to account for phenomena not explicable in terms of libido. He postulated that an instinct existed in the id which prompted aggressive and destructive drives. This instinct manifested itself in a "repetition compulsion" to undo the forward evolutionary development of the organism, and to return it to its primordial inorganic state. The death instinct, though sometimes libidinized (sadism) was totally different from the sexual instinct.

Freudian psychoanalytic therapy is based on the libido theory described above. It rests on the hypothesis that neurotic illness is nurtured by the repression of vital aspects of the self and its experiences; particularly oral, anal and sexual (including Oedipal) experiences in relation to important parental agencies. This repression is sponsored by fear of the loss of love or of punishment from the parents, which has been internalized in the super-ego. Repressed feelings, attitudes and fears, and the early experiences associated with them, continue to strive for conscious recognition, but are kept from awareness by dread of repetition of parental loss of love or punishment now invested in the super-ego. The removal from the mainstream of consciousness makes it impossible for the individual to come to grips with basic conflicts. These remain in their pristine state, uncorrected by reality and by later experiences. The energy required to maintain repression, as well as to sustain other defenses against anxiety, robs the individual of energy that could be utilized to nurture psychosexual development.

Therapy, of necessity, consists of restoring to consciousness that which was removed by repression, and which has been draining off energies needed to foster personality growth. In therapy, the relationship with the therapist helps strengthen the ego to a point where it can eventually cope with anxiety, mobilized by the return of the repressed to awareness. It is essential that the patient recognize the derivatives of the repressed, since these represent in an attenuated form, the warded-off material. To minimize the distortion of these derivatives, the obtrusion of current situations and other reality influences must be kept at a minimum. This is fostered by certain technical procedures, such as "free association," the assumption of the couch position, passivity of the therapist, encouragement of transference, the use of dreams, and the focusing of the interview away from reality considerations.

The basis of Freudian psychoanalysis lies in what is perhaps Freud's most vital discovery, that of transference. As has previously been indicated, Freud found that the patient, if not interfered with, inevitably projected into the therapeutic situation, feelings and attitudes that were parcels of his past. Sometimes transference manifestations became so intense that the patient actually reproduced and reenacted with the therapist important conflictual situations and traumatic experiences (transference neurosis) which had been subject to infantile amnesia. By recovering and recognizing these repressed experiences and conflictual situations that had never been resolved, and by living them through with a new, less neurotic and non-punitive parental agency, the super-ego was believed to undergo modification. The individual became tolerant of his id, and more capable of altering ego defenses that had crippled his adaptation. There occurred, finally, a mastery of his early conflicts and a liberation of fixated libido which could then enter into the development of a mature personality.

Since the Oedipus complex is considered by Freud to be the nucleus of every neurosis, its analysis and resolution in transference constitutes a primary focus. Where the Oedipus complex is not revealed, where its pathologic manifestations are not thoroughly analyzed and worked through, and where forgotten memories of early childhood experiences are not restored, treatment is considered incomplete.

Because Freudian psychoanalysis *is* transference analysis, all means of facilitating transference are employed. These include the assumption by the therapist of an extremely passive role, the verbalization by the patient of a special kind of communication—"free association"—the analysis of dream material, the maintenance of an intense contact with the patient on the basis of no less than five visits weekly, and the employment of the recumbent couch position.

Passivity on the part of the therapist is judiciously maintained even through long periods of silence. The therapist also refrains from reacting emotionally, or responding positively or negatively to any verbalized or non-verbalized attitude or feeling expressed by the patient. Strict anonymity is observed, no personal information being supplied to the patient irrespective of how importunate he may become. A non-judgmental, non-punitive, non-condoning attitude by the therapist is adhered to, dogmatic utterances of any kind being forbidden.

The only "rule" the patient is asked to obey is the "basic rule" or "fundamental rule" of verbalizing whatever comes to his mind, however fleeting, repulsive or seemingly inconsequential it may seem (free association). This undirected kind of thinking is a most important means of tapping the unconscious, and of reviving unconscious conflicts and the memories that are related to their origin. Most importantly, free association, like passivity, enhances the evolution of transference. So long as the patient continues to associate freely, the therapist keeps silent, even though entire sessions may pass without a comment. The therapist fights off all temptations toward "small talk" or impulses to expound on theory. Only when resistances to free association develop, does he interfere, and only until the patient proceeds with his verbalizations.

Dream analysis is utilized constantly as another means of penetrating the unconscious. By activating repressed material and working on defenses as they are revealed in dream structure, the therapist aids the development of transference.

The frequency of visits in Freudian psychoanalysis is important. To encourage transference, no fewer than five visits weekly are required. In some cases four visits may suffice. Fewer visits than this encourage "acting-out" and other resistances to transference.

The use of the recumbent couch position enables the patient to concentrate on the task of free association with as few encumbrances of reality as possible. It helps the therapist, also, to focus on the unconscious content underlying the patient's verbalizations without having to adjust himself to the demands such as would exist in a face-to-face position. Concentrating on his inner life rather than on external reality, helps to bring on the phenomenon of transference.

During the early stages of analysis, the main task is to observe—from his free associations and dreams—unconscious conflicts, and the types of defenses employed by the patient, which form a kind of blueprint of the unconscious problems of the patient. This blueprint is utilized later at the stage of transference. Since repression is threatened by the operation of exploring the unconscious, anxiety is apt to appear, stimulating defensive mechanisms. These function as resistances to productivity, and even to verbalization. Free association may consequently cease, and the patient may exhibit other manifestations that oppose cooperation with the treatment endeavor. Such resistances are dealt with by interpretation. Through interpretation the patient is brought to an awareness of how and why he is resisting, and the conflicts that make resistance necessary.

Sooner or later the patient will "transfer" past attitudes and feelings into the present relationship with the analyst. Observance of the "basic rule," the attack on his resistances through interpretation, and the consideration of unconscious material in dreams and free associations, remove habitual protective devices and façades that permit the patient to maintain a conventional relationship. Toward the therapist he is most apt to express strivings rooted in past experiences, perhaps even reproducing his past in the present. Thus, a revival of pathogenic past conflicts develops. Unlike supportive and reeducative therapy, in which transference may be utilized as a therapeutic vehicle, the transference is interpreted to the patient in order to expose its nature. This is the chief means of resolving resistance, of bringing the individual to an awareness of the warded off content, and of realizing the historical origin of his conflicts.

The development of transference may occur insidiously and manifest itself indirectly, or it may suddenly break out in stark form. It often shows itself in changes in the content of free associations, from inner feelings and past relationships with parents, to more innocuous topics, like current events and situations. This shift is evidence of resistance to deeper material activated by the erupting transference feelings. Sometimes free association may cease entirely, with long stubborn silences prevailing which are engendered by an inability to talk about feelings in relation to the therapist. The purpose of superficial talk or silence is to keep from awareness repressed emotions and forgotten memories associated with early childhood, particularly the Oedipus complex. Until these can be brought out into the open, the emotions relating to them discharged, and the associated memories revived, the conflictual base of neurosis will remain.

The transference neurosis offers an opportunity for this revival, since, in the relationship with the therapist, the patient will "act-out" his loves, fears and hates, which were characteristic of his own experiences during the Oedipal period.

Transference, however, acts as a source of powerful resistances that impede therapeutic progress. Once the patient is in the grip of such resistances, he is usually determined to cling to them at the expense of any other motivation, including that of getting well. On the positive side, transference is important diagnostically, since it reveals a most accurate picture of the patient's inner conflicts. Additionally, it induces a coming to grips with and a working-through in a much more favorable setting of those unresolved conflicts that have blocked maturation. The resolution of transference is felt by Freudian psychoanalysts to be the most powerful vehicle known today for producing structural alterations in the personality.

Active interpretations of the transference are essential to its resolution. These include the interpretation of its manifestations, its origin, and its original and present purposes. The working-through of transference is accompanied by a recollection of forgotten infantile and childhood experiences—a recounting of distortions in relationships with parents or parental surrogates. Interpretations will usually be denied at first as part of the resistance manifestation. Acknowledgment of the unreal nature of transference is usually opposed by the patient, because this either constitutes too great a threat for him, or because he does not want to relinquish transference gratifications which are deemed essential to life itself. So long as he continues to accept transference as factual, the analysis will remain interminable, unless forcefully terminated by either participant. With persistence on the part of the therapist, interpretations usually take hold, and the patient is rewarded with greater insight, an increased sense of mastery, liberation from neurotic symptoms, and a genuine growth in maturity.

The therapist must also constantly guard against manifestations of counter-transference, which may be both disguised and varied, and which are mobilized by unresolved problems and pressing needs within the therapist himself. Common forms of counter-transference are subtle sadistic attacks on the patient, impulses to be pompous and omnipotent, or desires to reject the patient or to detach oneself from the relationship. Because of counter-transference, a personal analysis is considered essential for the analyst in order that he can deal with his own unconscious tendencies and resistances precipitated by his contact with his patients.

As the ego of the patient is strengthened by an alliance with the therapist, it becomes more and more capable of tolerating less and less distorted derivatives of unconscious conflict. The continued interpretation by the therapist of the patient's unconscious feelings and attitudes, as well as the defensive devices that he employs against them, enables the patient to work-through his problems by seeing how they condition every aspect of his life. In the medium of the therapeutic relationship, the individual is helped to come to grips with early fears and misconceptions, resolving these by living them through in the transference. The patient is finally able to resolve libidinal fixations, and to liberate energy that should originally have gone into the formation of a mature sexual organization [164–185].

Disagreement with certain psychoanalytic concepts is legion. Even those analysts who consider themselves to be "orthodox" Freudians are not in complete accord with Freud in theory and method. For instance, there are many analysts who challenge the death instinct hypothesis. Insofar as technique is concerned, practically every analyst implements psychoanalytic methods in his own specific way. An extensive questionnaire distributed by Glover [186] to a representative group of practicing psychoanalysts demonstrated that deviations from orthodox techniques were extensive. There were differences in the form, timing, amount and depth of interpretation. The degree of adherence to free association varied, as did the assumption of passivity and anonymity, the use of reassurance, and the management of transference. Variation in methods of doing psychoanalysis was indicated by the fact that out of eighty-two questions, there was general agreement on only six, and even here there was not complete conformity.

Criticism of Freudian psychoanalysis is voiced both by those who have had no intimate contact with the psychoanalytic technique, as well as by well-trained psychoanalysts who have been thoroughly schooled in Freudian principles. Lines of disagreement will be discussed in the next section on non-Freudian psychoanalysis. One commonly voiced criticism of the Freudian method is that some analysts insist upon wedging their patients into a preconceived theoretic structure. When the patient does not produce appropriate material that substantiates accepted notions of dynamics, or when he refuses to accept interpretations, he is credited as being in an obstinate state of resistance. Another criticism expressed by non-Freudians is that, in their eagerness to smuggle "deep" insights into patients, certain "orthodox" analysts make dogmatic interpretations which the patient feels obliged to accept. These may mobilize intense anxiety, which disorganizes patients with weak ego structures. A third criticism is that many Freudian analysts are intolerant toward those who practice any therapies other than Freudian psychoanalysis, considering these to be superficial and of little real value. Accordingly, they are inclined to depreciate the results of treatment by non-analysts, as well as by analysts of non-Freudian orientation.

Freudian psychoanalysis is taught extensively in this country, being sponsored by the American Psychoanalytic Association and by most of the current schools of psychoanalytic training.

NON-FREUDIAN PSYCHOANALYSIS

Deviations from Freudian psychoanalysis vary from minor divergences related to one aspect of theory to major disagreements in which substitute hypotheses or therapeutic methods appear to depart radically from commonly accepted definitions of psychoanalysis.

Areas of dissension include doubts concerning the existence of the death instinct; the validity of the libido theory; the importance of infantile sexuality; the conceptualization of stages of development in oral, anal, phallic and genital terms; the primacy of the Oedipus complex as a neurotic source; the existence of such phenomena as libidinal fixation and regression; and the compartmentalization of the psyche into super-ego, ego and id. Furthermore, deviations have been inspired by a belief that founts of conflict are not exclusively, nor most importantly, repressed sexual or hostile impulses. It has also been felt that many conflicts inspiring neurosis need not be completely or even partly unconscious. Difficulties are credited to the effect on the individual of current environmental stresses and immediate interpersonal relationships, rather than past traumatic happenings. The therapeutic situation is not considered principally as an arena of transference phenomena, but equally as a setting which has values in itself as an experience in relationship. Expressed also is the belief that intense transference feelings and transference analysis are not absolutely essential to the achievement of insight.

Deviations from the "orthodox" technique have been many, practiced even by those who adhere to the basic theoretic principles of Freudian psychoanalysis. These variations have been occasioned by the observation that the problems of many patients are not influenced favorably by adherence to the "basic rule," the practice by the therapist of anonymity and passivity, the use of free association, the assumption of the recumbent position, the minimization of the importance of reality stresses and current interpersonal problems, and the setting up of a transference neurosis.

Consequently, therapeutic efforts are directed toward increasing repression, facilitating better compensations and sublimations, and encouraging release of fixated emotion by more active techniques than those of "orthodox" psychoanalysis. Since the focus is more on the current defenses of the individual than on the original vicissitudes that forced him to adopt inadequate defenses, the transference neurosis is not considered a primary objective. Demonstrated constantly to the individual are the contradictions inherent in his present defensive structure and the ineptness of his responses in terms of the existing reality situation. The patient is then helped in evolving more adequate defenses in line with social reality. Stressed in this approach is the idea that the Oedipus complex and the formative experiences contributing to its improper resolution, may not become conscious. Yet, even though it is not recognized and dealt with directly, the unresolved Oedipus complex may better be handled and controlled by more mature defenses issuing from therapy, defenses approximating the adjustment of the "normal" person.

The technical modifications employed by those who have deviated from orthodox Freudian theory and method include the following:

1. Passivity in the relationship is superseded by activity, in order to deal more adequately with resistance and to subdue the development of neurotic transference. Anonymity of the therapist is, for the same reason, not completely observed.

2. Free association is abandoned as a "fundamental rule," the interview being of a focused variety.

3. The couch position is replaced completely or partly by a sitting-up, face-to-face position.

4. The frequency of visits may be reduced to as few as three sessions weekly, and sometimes even two or one.

5. The therapeutic relationship is handled in a manner so as to resolve transference as soon as it begins to operate as resistance. An attempt is made to minimize the development of a transference neurosis. Positive elements in the relationship may be encouraged as a catalyst to therapy. The relationship is regarded not only as a mirror that reflects unconscious strivings, but also as a vehicle which has values in itself as a growth experience.

6. The focus in therapy is on both unconscious and conscious aspects of personality. Current problems and situations are stressed as much as experiences in the past.

7. There is a blending of analytic techniques with methods derived from supportive and reeducative approaches.

The most notable non-Freudian contributions to dynamic pscychiatry have been made by Adler, Jung, Ferenczi, Rank, Stekel, Reich, Rado, and members of the "dynamic-cultural school," including Fromm, Horney and Sullivan.

1. The "Individual Psychology" of Alfred Adler

Adler broke with Freud over the importance of infantile sexuality and the validity of the libido theory. He insisted that man's development was conditioned by social environment rather than by biologic forces. Because each person was unique, his psychology was an "individual psychology." Adler propounded a theory of neurosis based on the idea that behavior must be examined, not historically from the viewpoint of past causes, but teleologically from the standpoint of goals.

According to Adler's theory [187–191], the basic helplessness of the human infant, magnified by existing body or organ defects, by an inadvantageous ordinal position of the child in the family, or by parental neglect or rejection, creates feelings of inferiority. Since inferiority feelings oppose security and a sense of well-being, the individual attempts to cope with them by elaborating compensatory attitudes and patterns of behavior. Among these is a "will to power" characterized by strivings for power, dominance and superiority. This, the "aggressive" way of dealing with inferiority, is, in the minds of both males and females, equated with "masculinity." A "submissive" way of handling inferiority is to conceal, deny or escape from it through such psychologic processes as fantasy and rationalization. Unable to gain self-esteem or power through other means, the individual may attempt to achieve his objectives by a "flight from reality" and the development of neurotic symptoms. Since the feminine role is associated with inferiority, both men and women exhibit a "masculine protest" to compensate for their feminine characteristics.

The constellation of impulses, attitudes and strivings marshalled to overcome inferiority and to achieve power, are organized into an elaborate "life style" or "life plan" which influences the individual in every aspect of his functioning. In accordance with the "concept of unity and purpose" there is a total involvement in pursuit of one's "life style." The improper operation of his "life style" may interfere with the healthy growth of the person and with good social and community relationships.

The technique of Adlerian therapy is organized around the exploration and detection of the "life style" of the individual, including his aims, motivations and compensatory drives that operate in both negative and positive ways. The past, while considered of historical interest, is relegated to a position less important than the present or the future. Once the "life style" is identified, the patient is guided into more effective ways of functioning in order to aspire to greater potentialities through "normal" psychologic means. In the course of this educational process, strivings for power diminish and are replaced by social feelings and interests which lead to healthier attitudes toward oneself and the community.

The relationship between therapist and patient is kept on a positive level, with the avoidance, if possible, of a transference neurosis. Transference is analyzed only when it acts as resistance to the therapeutic effort. The relationship is assumed to possess values in itself as the first real social relationship the patient establishes that can serve as a bridge to other relationhips. The therapist assumes an active role, constantly pointing out self-deceptive tendencies and other resistances in order to introduce reality into the situation. The past life and early memories are stressed only because of their formative influence on the "life style." Sexuality, however, is not considered the basic problem as in Freudian psychoanalysis. The focused interview is generally employed rather than free association. Dreams are utilized, but are interpreted in terms of the present "life style" and future strivings. Patients are seen three or four times weekly, and the face-to-face sitting-up position is usually preferred.

Criticisms of Adler's theory and method are organized around the following contentions: first, that only one of manifold human strivings is stressed—that of feelings of inferiority; second, that not enough credence is given to deep unconscious forces; and, third, that goals in therapy tend to be reeducative rather than reconstructive in nature.

At the present time "individual psychology" is practiced by a multi-disciplinary group strongly loyal to the founder, Alfred Adler. Adlerian Consultation Centers operate in New York, Chicago and Los Angeles, as well as in the principal cities of Europe. An "Individual Psychology Association" exists in New York City with which Adler's children, Dr. Alexandra Adler and Dr. Kurt Adler, are affiliated. Many present-day Adlerians, while adopting the basic theoretic and methodologic premises of "Individual Psychology," have incorporated and utilize findings of other schools.

2. The "Analytical Psychology" of Carl Jung

Jung [192,193] also rejected Freud's biologic and genetic approach for a teleologic point of view. Although he acknowledged the existence of bodily libido, he contended that it issued, not from the sexual instinct, but from a universal force or "life urge." He recognized that neurotic parents promoted neurosis in their offspring, but he minimized the effect of sexual intimidation as well as the general importance of infantile sexuality.

Observing that the symbolic productions of neurotics and psychotics bore a resemblance to those of primitive people, Jung speculated the existence of a collective unconscious—a hereditary portion of the mind that contained the imprints of ancestral experience. A study by Jung of associations, dreams, fantasies and drawings seemed to substantiate the presence of instinctive thought processes. These appeared in the form of primordial images which Jung called "archetypes." Prominent, for instance, was the quadruple "mandala" symbolism, which was represented in ancient civilizations as the "four directions of heaven," and a circular form of symbolism, signifying the "circle" of existence.

Jung compartmentalized the psyche in different terms than Freud. He divided it into a superficial part, the *persona,* which was a social mask assumed by the individual, made up of his social interests and sanctions; a less superficial aspect, the *ego,* which was only to some extent conscious and reflected past personal experiences; and a deeply unconscious part which had within it the *collective unconscious* and contained "archetypes." Among the more common archetypes were the Animus, the mate ideal of the female psyche, and the Anima, the mate ideal of the male psyche.

Difficulties developed where an improper balance of masculine Animus elements and feminine Anima elements prevailed. Difficulties also occurred when there was a lack of harmony between the persona, the ego and the collective unconscious. Jung conceived of the idea that baser elements of the soul were present in the collective unconscious, and he characterized these as "the Shadow." He believed also that the collective unconscious contained creative founts of energy. Primitive fears and other untoward manifestations of the unconscious invaded the patient's conscious mind and created tensions and various neurotic symptoms which were attempts at self-cure. Thus the collective unconscious, unleashed, constituted a source of danger for the person.

Another area of conflict was residual in the way personality structure functioned. Jung evolved a theory of character, dividing people into two types: introverts and extroverts. The introvert had his interests centered on himself; the extrovert's interests were on the external world. Each type was further subdivided into feeling, thinking, intuition and sensation subtypes. Problems developed when an individual pursued his own personality type or subtype with an extreme inhibition of other reactions.

Jungian psychoanalytic therapy involves an exploration, with the help of dream interpretation and art analysis, of various aspects of the psyche, including elements of the personal and collective unconscious. Particularly, an effort is made to explore "archetypes" in order to determine how these imprints contaminate the patient's present life and interfere with his self-development and self-realization (individuation). Bringing the individual into contact with his collective unconscious is said to help liberate creative forces that will have a constructive effect on adjustment. Once non-conscious elements are recognized, an attempt is made actively to guide the patient into a productive relationship with his unconscious. In this way, a balance of masculine and feminine components is restored within the personality. Regressive impulses, such as desires for return to the womb and impulses for rebirth, become dissipated.

Emphasis in treatment is not only on the unconscious, but also on current difficulties. Dreams, for instance, are regarded as reflecting present strivings as well as future plans of action. Activity is the keynote in therapy, and the relationship is kept on a positive level, transference neurosis being avoided as much as possible. Free association is secondary to a focusing of the interview along specific lines. The therapeutic approach varies with the personality type, the introvert being presumed to need elaborate coherent interpretations, while the extrovert is said to achieve adjustment on a much more pragmatic basis. The development of an intellectually satisfying religion is often considered an essential part of therapy, since religion is believed capable of reconciling existing "archetypes" with an ethical system.

Criticisms of the Jungian approach relate to its metaphysical content, to the religious-like elements with which therapy is imbued, and to a tendency for some patients to become preoccupied with a mystic philosophy toward life, and with speculations of "archetypes" and other manifestations of their racial past. Jungian principles have not gained too great a popularity in the United States.

3. Therapeutic Modifications of Sandor Ferenczi

Ferenczi, while remaining loyal to Freud's theories, introduced certain modifications of method. Finding that transference did not develop readily in many patients, Ferenczi advocated "active" therapy in the form of an embargo on physical and sexual gratifications [194]. He believed that this restriction would block libido and make it available for projection into the transference. The patient was consequently enjoined to abstain from sexual satisfactions of all kinds, and even to limit his toilet activities. The release of resentment and aggression directed toward the therapist was felt to be of therapeutic importance. However, experience soon proved the method to be of little value, and Ferenczi himself abandoned it. Instead, he substituted a completely permissive atmosphere by acting as a tolerant, "good" parental figure who acceded to many of the patient's wishes and demands. He urged that the therapist admit his own faults and shortcomings to the patient in order to convince the latter that all authority was not harsh, nor intolerant, nor incapable of admitting to faults. A mutual analysis often resulted.

In order to help the patient to an awareness of his past, Ferenczi also encouraged him to relive it by dramatizing childhood situations, while he remained tolerant to the patient's "acting-out." Ferenczi recognized that the analyst's personal feelings about the patient, and his attitudes toward the patient, often determined the nature of the reactions. He advocated that the therapist consider the patient's reactions to be conditioned both by transference and by responses to definite provocations for which the therapist should admit responsibility. Collaborating with Rank [195], Ferenczi advised setting a time limit to analysis as a means of accelerating the end of the treatment.

Ferenczi's technical innovations are still employed by some therapists, with varying results.

4. The "Will Therapy" of Otto Rank

To Rank [196,197] the process of birth, with forceful separation of the child from the mother, constituted a trauma from which the individual never recovered. Two sets of strivings resulted from the "birth trauma": the first, an impulse to return to the womb in order to restore prenatal conditions of security; the second, an impulse for rebirth or separation from a maternal object. The first group of impulses expressed itself in a need to establish with people relationships of a dependent, infantile and clinging nature. The second group appeared as a "will" to grow, to achieve "individuation," and to separate oneself from confining relationships. The life of the person was governed by these contradictory strivings to unite and to separate.

The primordial anxiety of separation from the mother, rooted in the original birth trauma, was revived at all subsequent experiences of separation; such as, weaning, castration threats, and removal from close relationships with people. The need to restore unity with the maternal figure was contained in a desire to submit oneself in human relationships, including sexual relationships; while the need for assertive individuality was residual in an impulse to fight off the desire to unite with another person.

Rank classified personality into "normal," "neurotic" and "creative artist" types. The normal person was one who had yielded his own will to that of the group. The neurotic retained his will, refusing to sacrifice it to the group. He was unable to assert his will to become a creative artist. He was thus incapable of living up to his creative aspirations and the "will" to be himself.

Rank emphasized the fact that the analytic hour offered the patient a unique opportunity to live through with the therapist his past experiences, particularly the birth trauma. In Rankian analysis, the process of therapy is consequently centered in the patient-therapist relationship, the focus being on the patient's feelings toward the therapist. The analysis is considered an experience from which the patient will eventually separate and then go on to a new experience. The reactions of the patient to the inevitable circumstance of separation are studied carefully with the object of working through fear of, and guilt toward, the separation, as well as needs to control and to be controlled. The struggle of the will is also studied as it is reflected in the desire to continue therapy and to be dependent, as well as to discontinue treatment and to separate oneself from a dependent relationship.

The emphasis in therapy is thus on the present rather than the past. Ac-

tivity in treatment is the keynote, the patient being encouraged to assert himself in order to develop and strengthen his own will. An effort is made to
mobilize constructive elements in the personality and to transfer the negative
expression of will into positive and creative will. A time limit to therapy is
usually set. This is believed to act as a catalyst to the union-separation conflict.
No effort is made to bring out sexual material. Resistance is accepted as an
inevitable expression of the will. It is not met with counter-resistance or interpretation. Transference is also accepted as an aspect of the growth process in
which there is a strengthening of the "will" to be oneself.

Guilt and fear are gradually resolved through this experience in relationship, which liberates the will from its one-sided expression and results in a
"utilization of its own contrariness." The acceptance of responsibility for one's
ambivalence reduces guilt and fear to a point compatible with living. The
patient eventually learns to tolerate separation from the therapist and with
strengthened will achieves independence and growth.

Criticisms of Rankian analysis are expressed by those who object to the
activity involved, and to the focus on union and separation to the neglect of
other personality aspects. The abrupt insistence that the patient stand on his
own feet under any circumstances is said to have an unfortunate effect on persons
with weak ego structures who may require a great deal of support in early
phases of treatment.

Certain Rankian principles have been incorporated into a number of
psychotherapeutic approaches including psychobiologic therapy, non-directive
therapy and functional casework. The theory of the birth trauma is not as generally accepted as are Rank's concepts of therapy, particularly those that deal
with the importance of the patient-therapist relationship as a positive growth
experience.

5. The "Active Psychoanalysis" of Wilhelm Stekel

While Stekel [198] retained Freud's basic concepts of unconscious conflict, transference and resistance, he believed that the libido theory did not explain the multiform conflicts of the human mind, and he felt that the castration complex was not nearly so ubiquitous as Freud had assumed. He believed,
too, that current life conflicts were as important as past conflicts. He contended
that absolute unconscious elements were not the only foci of neurosis; rather,
aspects of the conscious mind might be repressed and transformed by a wide
variety of symbols. Stekel emphasized certain formulations such as the "central
idea of the neurosis" which varied in each person, and the inevitable anchoring
of mental conflict in the immediate life situation of the person. Emotional disturbance was often a product of competition of inharmonious "motives."
Glimpses of these might be captured from dreams and free associations.
Anticipating present-day characterologic approaches, Stekel remarked that the
future of analysis was residual in an analysis of character.

The chief contributions of Stekel, however, were in the field of technique.

The general therapeutic formula propounded was this: "Recall what originated your trouble, recognize your morbid attitude, and surmount it." Stekel alleged that resistance prevented the patient from recognizing his morbid attitudes, from recalling their origins, and above all, from surmounting his difficulty. Resistance, however, could not be resolved by the orthodox analyst's manner of remaining a passive spectator to the patient's free associations and dreams. This was the fallacy of passive psychoanalysis. The therapist must actively interfere in breaking up repression. He must actively collaborate with the patient in the interpretation of his free associations and dreams. Through "sympathy" and "imaginative insight" (qualities Stekel subsumed under the term "intuition") the therapist must alert himself to repressed complexes, and he must intervene actively to make the patient aware of them. The intuitive facility with which the symbolic meaning of the neurosis was determined, and the skill with which interpretation was offered, influenced the speed of therapy. The therapist's main function, then, was as an intuitive artist probing his way into the psyche. Stekel admitted that active analysis presupposes that the analyst be endowed with an intuitive faculty, but he avowed that this faculty was more widespread than had been presumed.

Abandonment of the analyst's passive role was associated with activity and directiveness, even to the point of advice-giving and exhortation. While free association was utilized, the patient must not be permitted to ramble along into blind channels; instead, selection of pertinent topics for discussion was in order. The use of the face-to-face, sitting-up position was also advocated. Emphasis was put on the interpretation of dreams, but the therapist's intuition had to be relied on in order to divine what eluded free associations to the dream structure. The use of adjuvants in therapy was also indicated. Stekel insisted that it was essential to adopt methods to the particular case, rather than to force the patient to abide by a particular method. With active methods Stekel believed that it was rare for more than six months to be required for analysis. This short period avoided interminable analyses, and prevented the development of untoward, unmanageable reactions.

The importance of transference was recognized by Stekel as an essential part of every analysis. Indeed, he felt that analysis was impossible without transference. Transference, however, could serve two functions—that of expediting therapy, and that of acting as resistance to therapy. Only where transference functioned as resistance was its handling justified.

A frequently heard criticism of Stekel's system of psychotherapy is that the activity of the therapist may sponsor an excessively disciplinary, prohibitive and punitive attitude toward the patient. Objections are also expressed in regard to the maximal six-month time limit to therapy on the basis that character reconstruction usually requires a long-term approach. Followers of Stekel have revised his temporal limitation and often do long-term therapy. The "intuitive" aspects of active analysis may also come in for questioning. Many observers would contend that what makes a therapist intuitive is a high degree of sensitivity that enables him rapidly to perceive nuances in the interpersonal process, and, on the basis of extensive experience, to translate these into valid deductions. Not all persons, however, would be capable of doing this, irrespective of the extent of training and experience. The intuitive aspects of the Stekelian system, therefore, would be limited to a restricted number of "intuitive" analysts, who could hypothesize constructs with a high degree of probability. A less intuitive analyst who tried this would indulge in guesswork that might be disastrous to the therapeutic objective, due to the foisting of faulty interpretations on the patient. In order to utilize Stekel's system effectively, then, the therapist would require an extremely high degree of analytic training, an extraordinary flexibility in personality, a deep sensitivity that would enable him to perceive nuances, and above all, good judgment that would permit of the judicious employment of active procedures.

At the present time, Stekelian analysts are not organized into a special analytic school. Some of the students and colleagues of Stekel train psychiatrists individually in the Stekelian method. Modifications of this method, however, have been many, as Stekelian analysts have introduced into their work recent contributions from various other psychiatric groups.

6. The "Character Analysis" and "Orgone Therapy" of Wilhelm Reich

Until relatively recently the basic theoretic orientation of Reich followed along lines of Freud's earliest formulation of the libido theory. This contended that neurosis was due to a conflict between repressed instinctual desires—usually infantile sexual desires—and ego repressing forces. The resulting conflict produced a stagnation of libido which was converted into anxiety, and which subsequently engendered neurotic symptoms or neurotic character traits. Therapy involved the making conscious of unconscious conflict in an effort to liberate strangulated libido. Defensive forces of the ego, however, acted as resistance to the return of the repressed. Before unconscious elements could be restored to awareness, it was essential to eliminate resistances. Through interpretation the patient was helped to see how his resistances operated, their nature, their purpose and their *modus operandi*.

Character formation was conceived of by Reich as a kind of psychic armor which protected the individual from the disturbing stimuli of the outside world, and from inner libidinal strivings [199,200]. During psychoanalysis, the patient's character served the interests of resistance against the repressed. Before one could tap the unconscious, therefore, it was essential to break down "character resistances" until the individual was denuded of defenses that barricaded repressed material. Character resistance revealed itself in attitudes and behavior toward the analyst and the analytic situation. Reich, in his book, *Character Analysis* [201], described the analysis of resistance including character resistance, and he insisted that this was necessary before the content of the unconscious could be accepted and integrated by the patient.

While the theoretic basis for Reich's method has been discounted by many analysts, the techniques of character analysis have proven themselves to be invaluable. Followers of the "dynamic-cultural" school, particularly, find the analysis of character vital, apart from its resistance-disintegrating virtues. Emphasis is placed on the neurotic nature of character trends, analysis of which constitutes a chief objective rather than a means to deeper repressed material.

Reich, however, coincident with his reported discovery of a "cosmic substance orgone" has tended to depreciate his contributions on character in favor of a newer "physiological" orientation to therapy [202]. The establishment of orgastic potency was felt by Reich to be the most important goal in therapy. He described the therapeutic process as a consecutive loosening of the character armor, a break-through of repressed and affect-laden material released by activation of infantile sexual conflicts, a working-through of infantile genital anxieties, a dealing with orgasm anxiety, and, finally, a developing of full orgastic potency. Character analysis in itself, however, he claimed was incapable of achieving the desired goal of orgastic potency. This was because another form of armor besides character armor shielded the unconscious. This was "muscular armor" which, in the form of chronically fixed muscular attitudes, increased tonus and rigidity, and shielded elements of sexuality and aggression from awareness. Therapy, to be effective, had to provide for a loosening of the muscular armor.

These new ideas made necessary a reformulation of his hypothesis. Character was developed from a binding of "bio-energy." Therapy remobilized "bio-energy" from character armor through character analysis, and from muscular armor through "vegetotherapy." The resulting liberation of emotions produced a mobilization of "orgone energy" which vitalized orgastic potency. This was "orgone therapy," and it reached the biologic depths of the human being, bringing him to an awareness of both organ sensations and muscular armoring, with an eventual destruction of the armor, a reestablishment of "plasma motility," and an appearance of "orgasm reflex."

In orgone therapy, the muscles of the patient's back, chest, jaw, abdomen and extremities are pressed firmly by the therapist to elicit emotional reactions and to liberate associations and memories. The patient's reactions are then interpreted to him. Sometimes the therapist imitates the patient's mannerisms or behavior, or encourages "acting-out" tendencies. Verbalization of fantasies, memories and feelings associated with the "muscular armor," is said to dissipate the armor and to permit of the dealing with direct impulses, of which the muscular manifestations are defenses and resistances.

While character analysis has gained wide acceptance among many analysts, the validity of the theory and technique of orgone therapy is generally considered controversial.

7. The Biologically Oriented Theoretic System of Sandor Rado

Rado, in an attempt to apply the scientific method to psychoanalytic thinking, has evolved a psychodynamic system which is biologically based [203–205]. According to Rado, neurosis is the product of faulty responses of the organism to danger registered as "failures in emergency adjustment." A hierarchical organization exists on various psychodynamic levels: "hedonic," "emotional," "low intellectual (emotional thought)," and "self-attributive," corresponding with physiologic activity at the cortical level.

A signaling arrangement, evoked by any kind of pain threatening the organism, or by the anticipation of pain, is the basis for the development of "emergency behavior." Of all motivations, emergency behavior is the strongest; it takes precedence over any other motivation. However, in disturbed emotional states, this rule may be violated.

On the "hedonic" level of organization, pain evokes the "riddance response" in the form of physiologic reactions to rid oneself of offensive agents. Vomiting, diarrhea, spitting, sneezing and coughing are manifestations of these reactions. The psychic correlate of the "riddance principle" is the mechanism of repression. Fear and rage are conditioned by an anticipation of pain. They warn of impending damage, and they inspire protective responses of flight (in fear) and of fight (in rage). On a social level, flight may be into dependency relationships with, and submission to authority; fight may be expressed in terms of defiance of authority. On the level of "emotional thought," emotions are tempered to some degree with ensuing apprehensive and angry thought patterns. Discrimination and analysis promote greater flexibility of performance. However, the person is still subject to escape and combat mechanisms in response to painful stimuli. Basic emergency reactions on the level of "unemotional thought" are controlled to some extent by the intellect. There is an advance detection of threats to the organism with an appraisal of its powers to cope with the threats. On the highest or "self-attributive" level, heightened pride accompanies rage responses or awareness of self-strength, while diminished pride follows fear reactions or awareness of self-weakness.

The development of the individual's conscience issues out of disciplinary rewards and punishments in relationship to parents. Fear of punishment, and the restraints it inspires, become automatized, and, in adult life, continue in force. Obedience, and the moral pride consequent to it, also persist as adaptive patterns. Fear of one's conscience is a residue of fear of parental punishment.

However, temptation may release rage and defiance which, by overwhelming the fear of one's conscience, may drive the individual to disobedience. A fear of condign punishment may then eventuate for such defiance. This may lead to a desire to reinstate oneself. Defiant rage, consequently, may be turned inward with self-reproach, confession, remorse and pleas for forgiveness. The hope is to be restored to the good graces of the parents. This expiatory pattern may become fixed, the individual seeking forgiveness by self-punishment. More pernicious are the phenomena of self-punishment for imagined guilt, and of advance painful punishment as a release for gratification of forbidden desires. Sometimes rage breaks loose with an abandonment of self-reproach and an attack on the person who is feared.

Failures of emergency control may be caused by an overproduction of fear, rage and pain. Resultant are overreactions to existing danger, and emergency responses in the absence of real danger. An overproduction of emergency emotions may express itself in an outflow of emotions. To stop the overproduction, the organism may have to resort to repression and other automatic "riddance" mechanisms. All disordered behavior is the consequence of such failures in emergency adjustment.

The theoretic concepts of Rado are at present taught at the Psychoanalytic Clinic for Training and Research at Columbia University.

8. The "Dynamic-Cultural" School of Psychoanalysis

Freud's theoretic speculations were originally based on the investigation of symptoms and other "ego-alien" phenomena. During psychoanalytic treatment, the consideration of resistances and the mechanisms of defense focused investigations on certain "ego-syntonic" occurrences such as character manifestations. Concentration on dynamisms employed by the ego in its adjustment led to the development of "ego psychology." The contributions of Reich [201], Fromm [206–207] and Anna Freud [208] have been utilized by sociologically minded psychiatrists, who, forming what has come to be known as the "dynamic-cultural" school, have made a significant contribution to ego psychology.

This school is characterized by a shift in theoretic emphasis from biologic to sociologic events, from concern with past experiences to the patient's present-day contacts with people, from consideration of the vicissitudes in sexual development to character patterns which, though of early origin, influence current interpersonal relationships, from concentration on fixations of libido to the thwarting of ego growth and maturation.

It is the contention of the "dynamic-cultural" school that Freud confused cultural phenomena with biologic instinctual manifestations [211]. Challenged also is the sexual nature of infantile urges. Orally-centered activities of the new-born infant, for instance, are believed to stem not from an urge for erotic satisfaction, but rather from the fact that the mouth and the cortical area governing the mouth are more highly developed at birth than any of the other bodily areas. The oral zone, consequently, serves as a primary means of contact with the world. The shift of interest to the anal area, is considered not as a biologic transfer of libido to this locality, but as a pattern characteristic of the emphasis put on toilet training in western civilization. Instead of the emphasis being placed on pleasures in fecal retention or excretion, it is put on the struggle with parental disciplines. The phenomena of the latency period are also said to be culturally determined, field studies of anthropologists demonstrating the absence of a latency period in some societies. The Oedipus complex is regarded as a neurotic reaction, a consequence of certain elements operating in our peculiar monogamous patriarchal society. Sexual feelings in the child for the parent are said to be brought about when neurotic needs cause the parents to over-stimulate and over-fondle the child. The child's reactions are determined by the attitudes of the parents, punitive or disapproving reactions producing fear of the loss of love and fear of castration. Penis envy is explained not by a craving on the part of the girl for a penis, but rather by the desire for the privileges that masculinity brings the individual in our culture. The child's reactions during puberty are also determined by cultural factors. For example, homosexual interests need not occur where boys and girls are given freedom in seeing each other. The resentment a girl feels at accepting her femininity is believed produced not by a need to renounce interest in being a boy, or in transfering clitoral to vaginal pleasures, but rather by pressures and demands put on her by the environment because she is a girl. Experiential and sociologic factors, rather than biologic influences, are thus regarded of prime etiologic importance in conflict formation.

The "dynamic-cultural" school puts an emphasis on character structure. Character is considered the product of interaction of the environment with the constitutional make-up of the individual. It is organized in the form of complex behavior tendencies which regulate the individual's relationships with the environment. Character strivings are patterned around the demands of the culture as vested in the disciplines, prohibitions and commands of the parents. Their aim is to help the individual propitiate his needs for security and self-esteem. Tension and anxiety may result whenever a character drive fails to function, or when one important drive is in conflict with another. Distorted character drives make for defects in interpersonal relationships and oppose normal biologic and social needs. In this way they are considered the core of the neurotic process.

According to Erich Fromm [210,211], social forces encourage irrational mechanisms in man's relationships with the group and promote the isolation of the person from others. A primary need is a desire for closeness with, and approval from, a significant individual. Fear of disapproval from this person, as originally was the case with the parental agency, causes the individual to deny or to repress any feeling, impulse, attitude or reaction that inspires disapproval, no matter how constructive or important it may be. A number of character strivings are elaborated to cope with the reactions of the significant parental figure. Fromm conceives of character types as rooted in certain fundamental attitudes, such as receptive, exploitative, hoarding, "marketing" and productive attitudes, conditioned by experiences with parents who exerted a specific influence over the child that led him to develop these attitudes as security mechanisms. Basic anxiety issues from a conflict between a need for approval from a parental figure and a need for independence. Fromm emphasizes the value in therapy of discovering what healthy aspects of self have been eliminated as a result of environmental restriction or condemnation. The therapist helps the patient to understand and to rectify his need to cling to irrational authority, and to evolve a character organization that permits him to relate to the group in a healthy and productive manner.

The two chief "schools" of "dynamic-cultural" thinking are those of Karen Horney and Harry Stack Sullivan.

The school of Karen Horney. According to Horney [212–214], the forces of neurosis stem from compulsive neurotic drives which are a means, elaborated by the individual, of coping with feelings of helplessness, isolation, fear and hostility. The original source of such drives is residual in "basic anxiety" aroused in the child when he feels isolated and helpless in a potentially hostile world. This "basic anxiety" forces the child to develop coping mechanisms in the form of character traits that become a lasting part of his personality.

There are three lines along which character drives are organized: (1) drives that enable the individual to move toward people, (2) drives against people, and (3) drives away from people. All three of these action tendencies exist in different people in varying degrees, the most prominent set of drives determining the prevailing behavior tendency. However, if one set of drives predominates, it indicates an overdevelopment along one line. A number of sub-drives issue from the philosophy of life involved with moving toward, moving away from, and moving against people. Included here are an inordinate need for affection, compulsive impulses toward modesty, an impelling desire for a partner, and drives for power, prestige, ambition and perfectionism.

Neurosis is a consequence of conflicts between contradictory sets of neurotic trends, as well as between incompatible attitudes towards others and towards the self. The individual is torn by these inner contradictions, and usually refuses to recognize them since an awareness of his tendencies produces great anxiety. The need to deny the existence of such tendencies consumes much energy in the person. Four major attempts are usually made to solve conflict in all neuroses. The individual first blots out a part of the conflict, and then attempts to detach himself from people in order to avoid hurt. Next he tries to move away from himself with a resulting unreality of the self-image and finally with the creation of an idealized image of himself. Thus the need for perfection may be an effort to measure up to the idealized image of the self; while a craving for admiration may be due to a desire to feel that the idealized image has been achieved. Horney believes that of all attempts at solution, the idealized image is perhaps the most important, due to its far reaching influence on the total personality. The last attempt at solution of conflict is through the process of "externalization," in which inner processes are experienced as going on outside of the self. This augments the conflict between the self and the world.

In addition to the four major attempts at solving conflict, there may be lesser attempts, such as a tendency toward "arbitrary rightness" in order to quell all inner doubts, a rigid self-control which serves the purpose of holding the individual together by sheer will power, and a relapse into cynicism which augments all values and eliminates conflict in regard to ideals. The hopelessness of being inextricably entangled in conflict may end in sadism, which, according to Horney, is an attempt at restitution by means of vicarious living on the part of the person who despairs of "ever being himself." Sadism, then, is the outcome of an insatiable need for vindictive triumph. A potent source of conflict lies in the neurotic's loss of capacity to wish for anything wholeheartedly because his wishes are divided.

Therapy must involve itself with a thorough understanding of the character structure of the individual and of the conflicts that are raging within him as a result of fundamentally contradictory attitudes within himself. While character distortions were acquired as a result of past experiences, they are manifesting themselves in the present, and the therapeutic effort of necessity must involve a thorough exploration of present difficulties, and an understanding of the interplay of forces in the existing personality. Examination of the functions of the character trends and their consequences for the patient may reduce anxiety and allow the patient to become discriminatingly friendly toward others, with a gain in inner strength and activity. Free associations are employed to lift unconscious elements into awareness. However, the therapist exercises an influence on the direction of the associations. As in Freudian analysis, the relationship of the patient and therapist is subjected to a detailed study, although there is greater activity and a minimization of genetic factors. Interpretations involve a clarification of problems as well as the making of suggestions as to possible solutions.

The training division of the Karen Horney school is called the "American Institute for Psychoanalysis" and is located in New York City.

The school of Harry Stack Sullivan. Sullivan [215–217] stresses the fact that emotional illness is both nurtured by and manifested in disturbances in interpersonal relationships. These develop out of early experiences and conditionings with parents and other significant adults. Their effect is an interference with the proper assessment of reality and effective communication with the outer world. The patterns of reaction (parataxic distortions) that are elaborated to maintain security bear upon all later reactions and lead to other accumulated distortions. Rejecting the libido theory, Sullivan tends to regard sexual disturbances as one aspect of interpersonal disorganization. Therapy involves an analysis of the relationship between patient and therapist in order to explore the distortions that extend themselves into this and other relationships. The therapeutic relationship is conceived of not only as a repository of archaic attitudes, but also as a reality relationship that has within it many growth potentials.

More specifically, Sullivan contends that the personality of the child is evolved from relationships with parents and other important persons with whom he is in intimate contact. A basic factor that molds personality is a need to maintain a sense of well-being or "euphoria," a loss of which is associated with tension and anxiety. Early in life the maintenance or loss of "euphoria" becomes conditioned to approval or disapproval from parental agencies. Consequently, in order to preserve his well-being, the child imbibes the attitudes, values and standards dictated by the parental sanctions, and there is an inhibition and dissociation of traits and tendencies that meet with parental disapproval and punishment. Demands on the child for social conformity cause him to respond automatically to avoid hurt even though the child is confused as to the meaning of such demands. The self-system of the child thus is established and developed along lines approved by significant adults, and any impulses or attitudes not so approved are apt to produce anxiety. The latter are repudiated as alien to the self and are either tentatively suppressed or are actually blocked off from awareness by repression.

Interpersonal relationships are determined by the many characterologic traits the individual has elaborated as consonant with or alien to his self. These "parataxic distortions," reflecting attitudes toward significant past personages, are automatically projected into all interpersonal relationships.

In the therapeutic situation, as in any other situation, the patient acts out his "parataxic distortions." Bringing these to the awareness of the patient helps him to separate the present from the past, and to appreciate the attitudes and values that are a part of himself which he tends to repudiate. The patient experiences emotionally what has been dissociated, and in this way is enabled to evaluate and to accept aspects of himself that had been split off from awareness. While the current situation is actively considered, childhood experiences and conditioning are also constantly explored in order to expedite insight into the origins of the patient's problems, and to separate the past from the present. In these ways, new and healthier interpersonal relationships may be reconstructed.

The management of a patient in therapy is more flexible and active than in Freudian psychoanalysis. Thus, the patient may assume a sitting or recumbent position; he may use free associations or deal with specific aspects of his experience; he may work with present reality problems as well as early childhood memories and productions from the unconscious, such as dreams. The emphasis is on the character structure and problems in interpersonal relationships, although genetic origins are not neglected. Relaxation of the "basic rule" permits of a focusing of the interview on significant material. The therapeutic situation is considered a real relationship that has values in itself in addition to serving as an arena for transference. Much of the theory and method of Sullivan are at present adopted by the William Alanson White School for Psychiatry, Psychoanalysis and Psychology, which is located in New York City.

Criticism of the "Dynamic-Cultural" School. Criticism of the "dynamic-cultural" school stems mostly from Freudian psychoanalysts who regard the diversion into the sociological field a form of resistance against the biologic-sexual hypothesis of Freud. Franz Alexander has questioned Horney's attack on the libido theory on the basis that it strives to substitute for the mystic biologic substance of libido, an equally empty sociologic slogan of culture [218]. There is a general feeling among Freudians that sociological-cultural approaches deal with only one facet of human experience, and do not consider the basic infantile sexual conflicts which are the nuclei of neuroses. While analysis of character is said to be helpful, it does not eradicate the deepest sources of conflict. Some observers have even gone so far as to say that therapy conducted in accordance with principles of the dynamic-cultural school is "superficial" and has a reeducative rather than a reconstructive influence.

PSYCHOANALYTICALLY ORIENTED PSYCHOTHERAPY

Psychoanalytically oriented psychotherapy is the most active of all analytic therapies maintaining the greatest flexibility in the techniques employed. By focusing on pertinent data and by using active means of dealing with resistance, and of bringing unconscious conflicts to awareness, much unnecessary time is claimed to be saved. The relationship is also actively manipulated, transference being controlled and certain aspects of the relationship stimulated.

Perhaps the best known system of psychoanalytically oriented psychotherapy is set forth by Alexander, French and other members of the Chicago Institute for Psychoanalysis [219]. The therapy described, though of a short-term nature, is believed by the authors to yield results comparable to long-term standard psychoanalysis. Alexander and French stress the fact that they utilize the therapeutic situation as a corrective experience. It provides a new and more favorable medium in which the patient is exposed to, relives, and finally masters the conflicts and emotional problems he was unable to handle as a child. This is achieved either in the transference relationship or outside of therapy in real life. Not only does the patient overcome unresolved childhood conflicts by reliving them—which makes them less acute—but the therapist also responds to the patient and to his behavior in a manner totally different from that of the parent. This gives the patient an opportunity to revive his past and to face his conflicts over and over again under the guiding aegis of the therapist. Activity in the therapeutic situation is said to accentuate the corrective experience.

The authors recommend such modifications in technique as direct interviewing, in addition to free association; the regulating of the number of sessions each week; the offering to the patient of advice and suggestions about certain aspects of his life; the interrupting of therapy for a variable period prior to ending treatment; the manipulating of the transference in each patient in accordance with the needs of the patient; and the employing of real life experiences as a part of the treatment process. Flexibility in method is advocated with a change of technique to suit the patient's personality, as well as his problems. While the transference relationship is believed to be important, the consideration of extratherapeutic experiences is considered of equal importance. Positive transference attitudes are encouraged to establish rapport and to enhance therapeutic progress. Negative attitudes are analyzed when they block the process of therapy. Emphasis is more on the relationship than it is on the transference neurosis. The experience of mutual frankness and sincerity in relationship to the therapist is believed to make it possible for the patient to reorient himself to other human contacts.

While their techniques are not claimed to be applicable to all cases, in many instances the goals achieved are said to approximate those previously considered possible only with "orthodox" techniques. Indeed, the authors are inclined to press the advantages, in certain patients, of their modification of formal psychoanalysis.

The "sector therapy" of Felix Deutsch [220] falls into the category of psychoanalytically oriented psychotherapy. While he admits that psychoanalytic treatment cannot be shortened to achieve extensive goals, limited goals are possible with psychotherapy employing psychoanalytic techniques. Deutsch advocates the use of the "associative anamnesis" [221]. Here the technique essentially involves a focusing of the interview on symptoms and conflicts by accenting key words and phrases which the patient himself has used and which reflect basic problems. The therapist picks a few of the most frequently employed words or expressions, incorporates them into his own conversation, and observes the reactions of the patient. The key words and phrases uttered by the therapist usually stimulate associative ramifications in the form of free associations. However, the associations are guided, and their continuity maintained. Through this means, manifest symptoms or present problems are linked with underlying conflicts. The constant confrontations by the therapist serve some of the purposes of interpretation. Memories are revived, associative chains are broken up and replaced with new ones. By this form of interviewing, the patient learns to discriminate the past from the present, and his ego is induced to alter its defensive attitudes.

Illustrative of the many innovations that are introduced into psychoanalytically oriented psychotherapy is the "objective psychotherapy" described by Karpman [222]. Karpman assigns to the patient a series of written questions dealing with the patient's history, attitudes and feelings. The patient is requested to write out detailed answers to these questions. After reading them, the therapist picks out pertinent points, and formulates new questions to which the patient is expected to reply. Reading material may be given the patient which is related to his problem, and the patient's reactions in writing are requested. Dreams are written by the patient and interpretations to these are handed in written form back to the patient for his leisurely study. Formulations of the dynamics in writing are made from time to time by the therapist, and the patient is requested to study these and to turn in his written comments.

Criticism of psychoanalytically oriented psychotherapy is often expressed to the effect that transference is watered down by the active techniques employed. The consequence of avoidance of a transference neurosis is said to be a limitation of the extent of insight achieved. The inevitability of circumscribed goals in treatment is also presented as an objection. Additionally, the concentrated short-term techniques employed are believed to be dangerous in the hands of any other than the most highly trained and experienced psychoanalysts. Because psychoanalytically oriented therapy is often a rapid procedure, it is unfortunately apt to appeal to therapists who may not be trained in psychoanalysis, but who are searching for dramatic unrealistic short-cuts.

ADJUNCTIVE AIDS IN PSYCHOANALYTICALLY ORIENTED PSYCHOTHERAPY

1. Hypnoanalysis

Work by Erickson [222-225], Erickson and Hill [226], Erickson and Kubie [227,228], Eisenbud [229], Kubie [230], Lindner [231,232], Gill and Brenman [233], Fisher [234] and Wolberg [235,236] has indicated that hypnosis lends itself to a facilitation of the psychoanalytic process. A most important effect of hypnosis is its power to remove those resistances that prevent awareness of unconscious material. Whereas months may be consumed in an attempt to remove such resistances during psychoanalysis, hypnosis is often able to achieve an almost surgical removal of barriers to the conscious appreciation of repressed elements of the personality.

Hypnoanalysis presupposes an aptitude on the part of the patient to enter a trance sufficiently deep to make possible the employment of the various hypnoanalytic procedures. The ability to verbalize during hypnosis without awakening is mandatory. A somnambulistic trance is essential where such techniques as drawing, play therapy, dramatics, mirror gazing, regression and revivification, and the creation of experimental conflicts are to be used. Free association, dream induction and automatic writing often require no more than a medium or light trance.

The mere induction of hypnosis may eliminate many resistances to free association. The material flows freely, and the results of one session are often equivalent to weeks of waking free association. It is often helpful to have the patient visualize scenes in his mind as they appear. Hypnosis may also be used to analyze resistances that prevent waking free association. The hypnotic state, however, cannot in itself dissolve all resistances to free association, and, in some cases, the patient will be unable to verbalize his thoughts even in the deepest somnambulism with the most persistent urging. Occasionally, material may be brought up by instructing the patient that, at a certain count, he will have a thought, or visualize an image.

The ability to dream under hypnosis must be inculcated in the patient by training. A medium trance is usually required. Unconscious ideational processes of a purposeful nature may be stimulated by dream activity, and, frequently, the patient may work out an insight through dreaming when it is suggested that he do so. Dreaming under hypnosis or posthypnotically may also be used as a means of understanding attitudes and feelings that are not yet conscious and which cannot be verbalized. In this way attitudes may be divulged which reveal trends in the transference. Dream activity may also aid in the dissolution of resistance. An important use of hypnotic dreaming is in the recovery of dreams which have been forgotten, as well as specific portions of dreams which have either been repressed or have been subjected to secondary elaboration. Dreaming under hypnosis may also be used to help the recovery of forgotten memories and experiences.

The techniques of regression and revivification are sometimes useful in bringing the individual back to a period in his life during which he had experienced important traumatic happenings. Regression increases the hypermnesic effect of hypnosis to a marked degree, opening up pathways to forgotten memories and experiences which would not be available to the individual at an adult level.

The induction of experimental conflict is another means of demonstrating to the patient the workings of his unconscious. Often it may produce insight where other techniques fail. Many resistances prevent the acknowledgment by the patient of certain unconscious drives. Only by experiencing them in actual operation can the patient realize how they are influencing his behavioral and attitudinal patterns. By means of hypnosis, experimental conflicts may be induced which involve significant incidents in the patient's life, or significant attitudes and relationships with people [237].

Hypnosis is also often effective in promoting recall of traumatic memories and experiences which have been repressed.

Limitations of hypnoanalysis center around the following: first, not all patients are hypnotizable to the depth necessary for use of the various hypnoanalytic techniques; second, since fantasies are easily elicited in the trance, the validity of the evoked material must be scrupulously tested; third, the regressive state associated with hypnosis may introduce elements into the transference that must be analyzed carefully; and fourth, material elicited and experiences encountered in the trance must be integrated into the more conscious layers of the psyche, working through a number of resistances before they are effectively incorporated. Many patients and some therapists regard hypnosis as a miracle cure—a concept for which there is no basis, since there are many problems which do not respond to the hypnotic method, failures occurring here as with any other technique. While hypnoanalysis is useful as a therapy in some conditions, particularly where repression is the favored defense, as in traumatic neurosis and hysteria, it is no more effective than other reconstructive therapies in conditions like personality disorders.

2. Art Therapy

The use of artistic media, such as drawing, painting and finger painting, as ways of exploring unconscious conflict, has been advocated by some observers [238–247]. The productions, whatever their nature, serve as means of emotional catharsis and as vehicles for revealing inner problems, wishes and fears. The aim of insight is attainable since many art productions provide symbolic ways of representing unconscious phenomena [248–253]. The patient projects into his creations significant emotional meanings. This is very much similar to what happens in the Rorschach test [254]. Furthermore, the symbolized content permits of an expression of inner impulses without too much guilt feeling. The art therapist accepts the patient's projections without punitive or judgmental retaliation. Interpretations are offered to the patient at strategic times. Interpretation of art symbols has been described by Pfister [481], Jung [255], Appel [256], Liss [257], Harms [258,259], Reitman [260], Baynes [261], Mira [262], Naumburg [263,264], and Kris [265]. Other informative articles are those of Levy [266], Curran [267], Despert [268], Bychowski [269], and Mosse [270].

Criticism of art therapy relates to the tendency among some art therapists to overvalue the medium of communication—the art production—and to confuse the latter with the therapeutic process itself. While therapy may thus be regarded as a constant uncovering phenomenon that brings up interesting material, there may be a denial or minimization of the true therapeutic vehicle—the relationship between patient and therapist. The use of art as an adjunct to therapy is, nevertheless, considered by some analysts as helpful to patients who express themselves better in drawing and in other artistic ways, than in free association or dreams. While the content of therapy may be focused on art expression, the therapeutic process goes through the usual phases of transference and resistance as in any reconstructive form of psychotherapy.

3. Play Therapy

Play therapy provides the individual with a means of giving vent to feelings, ideas and fantasies he cannot ordinarily verbalize [271–278]. The beneficial effects of play therapy are based ultimately on insight the patient gains into his unconscious problems. More immediately, he acts out in play, hostile, sexual, excretory and other fantasies, as well as anxiety-provoking life situations. The cathartic effect of play therapy temporarily alleviates tension. This is not as important as the gradual insight that develops into the nature and effects of unconscious conflicts. The non-condemning attitude of the therapist, who neither criticizes nor restricts the patient, but accords him freedom in expressing overtly impulses and fantasies of a dreaded nature, alleviates guilt feelings and eventually makes it possible for the patient to acknowledge and to tolerate repressed drives. As these are repeatedly acted out in play, the patient becomes desensitized to their influence. Carefully timed interpretations aid him in developing insight.

Play therapy appears to be particularly suited to the expression of unconscious aggression and to the acting-out of jealousies in relation to a parent or sibling. It is also an excellent medium for exploration of sexual and excretory fantasies. It is of greatest value in children. Merely instructing the child to play as he wants, sometimes suffices to get him interested in the play materials. In this reference the free play technique of Gitelson [279] is useful, or, if the therapist prefers, the methods of Anna Freud [280] and Melanie Klein [281] may be employed. In many cases, however, it is difficult to create in the patient an attitude that is conducive to spontaneous play, and here a more active approach will be necessary, such as represented in the methods described by Conn [282], Levy [283] and Solomon [284,285]. Criticism of play as a therapeutic medium revolves about the age limitations for its use. While play is a normal form of expression in childhood, adults are usually not amenable to play methods.

4. Narcotherapy (Narcosynthesis, Narcoanalysis)

The intravenous injection of sodium amytal or sodium pentothal produces a lessening of inhibition with verbal outflow and, occasionally, motor discharge.

This emotionally cathartic influence has been utilized advantageously in the war neuroses, the patient being induced to verbalize fantasies and to relive experiences associated with traumatic battle incidents [66,67]. The patient's associations are interrupted by pointed questions whenever the therapist believes these to be indicated. Repeated barbiturate interviews gradually restore to the patient a sense of mastery and, when coupled with interviews on a waking level, help the individual to gain insight into his untoward reactions to the traumatic scene.

In the civilian neuroses, intravenous sodium amytal is utilized to facilitate free associations. Transference and resistance are dealt with and interpretations are given. Interviews in the waking state are coordinately employed. The exact effects of this combined therapy, and its advantage over traditional psychotherapy have not yet been accurately evaluated. Results are most notable in anxiety states, hysteria and certain psychosomatic conditions. Sometimes narcotherapy is used as an adjunct in reconstructive psychotherapy where the patient is unable to verbalize readily, or where resistances to unconscious content are especially high. It is used also in panic states which develop during the course of regular psychotherapy.

Because much anxiety is liberated in narcotherapy, ego-supportive techniques like suggestion and reassurance are more frequently employed than in ordinary analytic psychotherapy. Hoch and Polatin emphasize that narcosis in psychotherapy will require further experimentation and evaluation [286].

5. Analytic Group Therapy

Group therapy with reconstructive goals has come into prominence in recent years. In 1939, Schilder [287] described a method which combined autobiographic material with free association and dream interpretation. Wender [288] employed an analytic type of group procedure in a hospital setting. Sarlin and Berezin [289] reported an uncovering approach in group therapy.

Sutherland [290] stresses that the psychoneurotic can be helped adequately in group therapy only if a change is brought about in him through resolution of his unconscious conflicts. He contends that group therapy can be conducted along strictly analytic lines in order to achieve this purpose. Somewhat similar points of view are emphasized by Foulkes [291], Slavson [292] and Ackerman [293].

Ezriel [294,295] lists three hypotheses related to a method of applying psychoanalytic theory to group therapy. The first is that unconscious feelings toward past authoritative personages are projected onto figures in the social environment. The group provides an opportunity for such multiple transferences. The second is that a common group tension develops which involves all group members and elicits in each person unconscious fantasies that have a common denominator. Each member assumes a role in a "drama," enacted in the session by the group. This brings out the individual's particular defense mechanisms. The third hypothesis deals with interpretations that are made to the group members. These are given in relation to the unconscious content of the area of common tension and to the specific defenses the patient employs in relation to the latter.

Spotnitz [296] discusses the enhancing of ego-functioning of the individual in the group setting. Where selection of group members includes a scattering of problems and personality types, an opportunity is afforded the patient to experience and to observe a variety of reactions which help him to scrutinize his own reactions more objectively. Individual resistances are handled rapidly by the group and this results in symptomatic improvement. Spotnitz believes that the instinctual forces at work in groups can be understood in terms of the life and death instincts as outlined by Freud.

Wolf [297] describes a form of group therapy that employs psycho-analytic techniques of free association, dream interpretation, and resistance, transference, and counter-transference analysis. The groups, while heterogeneously composed, are confined to persons of approximately the same age. The mixing of sexes, Wolf believes, facilitates resolution of problems on the hetero-sexual gregarious plane. Excluded are psychopaths, alcoholics, stutterers, mental defectives, hallucinating psychotics and hypermanic patients. The groups, composed of eight or ten members with sexes balanced, meet three times weekly for ninety minutes.

A number of individual interviews may be required before the patient is ready to enter the group. This is the first stage of therapy and is diagnostic. The patient is also prepared for group analysis by explanations regarding its theory and practice. The second stage of therapy is conducted in the group setting. It consists of free associations organized around the dreams of the group members. Once good rapport has developed, the third stage of therapy begins. This consists of each patient spontaneously free-associating about the next. This results in a bombardment of the patient's character structure and exposure of conflicts. The patient learns which of his characteristics please the group and which disturb them. In the fourth stage of treatment, resistances mobilized by the free associations of the group members come up for analysis. The fifth stage of treatment is characterized by an analysis of transference—its identification and resolution. Patients here learn how they project parental and sibling images into the group and toward the therapist. Identification and resolution of transference are said to proceed more thoroughly and rapidly in a group setting. The sixth and final stage of treatment is characterized by planned conscious responses in the interests of the group and the self. These replace strivings of an irrational or compulsive nature engendered by the character structure.

Criticism of analytic group therapy revolves about contentions that the method is not yet tested, and that reconstructive changes are not as extensive or as permanent as in individual therapy. Unless the patient is coordinately in individual therapy, it is difficult to work through certain transference resistances which are more easily concealed in group than in individual treatment.

8

Similarities and Differences
Among the Various Psychotherapies

IN ATTEMPTING TO DIFFERENTIATE THE SUNDRY PSYCHOTHERAPEUTIC approaches, two kinds of data are apparent. The first relates to observations of clinical phenomena made by therapists in the course of working diagnostically and therapeutically with patients. The second is concerned with the interpretation of this data along theoretic, speculative lines.

Common theoretic constructs deal with the following: (1) the nature of the predisposing factors in emotional illness, (2) the manner in which childhood experiences and conditionings produce distortions in personality development, (3) the relationship between personality structure and neurosis, (4) the constituents of inner conflict, (5) the meaning, function and manifestations of anxiety, (6) the structure of the psychic apparatus, and (7) the mechanisms of defense. Various schools may place an emphasis, duly or unduly, on some of these constructs, or they may accent certain phases of psychodynamics which may or may not be verifiable.

Techniques of psychotherapy, though diversified, are not nearly so disparate as theoretic formations. Indeed, basic similarities are apparent among all psychotherapeutic schools which include the following: (1) they are all goal-directed toward specific objectives, (2) they are organized around a relationship between therapist and patient, (3) they require some kind of interviewing procedure, and (4) they evoke emotional responses in the patient which must be therapeutically handled.

The goals in treatment with supportive, reeducative and reconstructive therapies have already been described. Briefly, they consist of a relief of symptoms and better adaptation in areas of living in which the patient has failed (supportive therapy); a reorganization of attitudes and values with expansion of personality assets and minimization of liabilities (reeducative therapy); and an alteration of the basic structure of the character with creation of potentialities that were thwarted in the course of the individual's development (reconstructive therapy). The setting of goals may be determined in some psychotherapeutic systems by the patient, in others by the therapist.

The type of relationship between therapist and patient varies among the different psychotherapies. There are some relationships deliberately set up by the therapist in which he assumes an authoritarian, domineering, directive and disciplinary role. There are others that are non-authoritarian, permissive, non-directive and non-disciplinary, sometimes to a point where the therapist seems detached. There are still others in between these two extremes in which the therapist attempts to relate himself to the patient as a cooperative partner. The degree of activity or passivity the therapist assumes with the patient will vary with the relationship sought; it may remain consistent throughout the course of therapy or may shift at different stages of the treatment process. The kinds of attitudes displayed by the therapist will similarly range from moralistic to tolerant, from judgmental to non-judgmental.

The kinds of verbalization obtained from the patient may be spontaneous and rambling to the point of "free association," or they may be focused by the therapist on selected topics. Similarly, the responses of the therapist may range from spontaneous comments and conversations to controlled utterances and pointed interpretations.

The interview focus will depend on the approach employed. For example, in guidance, it is usually on existent work, marital, social and interpersonal difficulties with the object of correcting these as expediently as possible. In persuasion, the focus is on faulty attitudes and values with the idea of inculcating in the patient a correct philosophy toward life. In emotional catharsis, it is on suppressed and repressed feelings and experiences, with the aim of releasing pent-up emotions. In reassurance, it is on irrational fears and attitudes with the idea of correcting misconceptions and mistaken attitudes. In many reeducative therapies, it is on distortions in interpersonal operations with the object of enhancing character assets and of minimizing liabilities. In semantic approaches, it is on language and communication disturbances for the purpose of clarifying concepts, values and goals. In non-directive therapy, it is on the feelings behind verbalizations in the hope of releasing spontaneous growth forces. In Freudian psychoanalysis, it is on past life experiences with an attempt to resolve the Oedipus complex toward development of mature genitality. In Adlerian analysis, it is on the present "life-style" with attempts to resolve feelings of inferiority and compensatory power mechanisms. In Jungian analysis, it is on the exploration of elements in the collective unconscious with the aim of releasing the individual from the crippling influences of "archetypes." In Rankian analysis, it is on the union and separation strivings of the patient with the ultimate objective of resolving the ubiquitous birth trauma. In Horney analysis, the focus in on the contradictions of character structure with dissipation of character disturbances and of the unrealistic, idealized self-image. In Sullivan analysis, it is on the individual's relationships with people, with the aim of restoring self-esteem and good interpersonal relationships.

It will be seen that the focus of inquiry is on selected aspects of the total functioning. Because the individual projects himself as a whole into the most minute area of living, exhibiting in this area basic patterns of relatedness and basic defensive operations, the working through of problems in one area may result in a restructuring of the personality in other, apparently unrelated areas. Thus, if the focus chosen is inferiority feelings in relation to an employer, the limited resolution of the patient's attitudes toward the employer and toward himself may result in more harmonious attitudes toward other authorities, in greater self-esteem and feelings of mastery, in greater acceptance of himself and his impulses, including sexual and hostile impulses. If the focus is on sexuality and problems in relating sexually to others, or the resolution of fears of mutilation, the capacity to separate the paralyzing archaic prohibitions of childhood from the present will probably eventuate in more constructive attitudes in the patient toward authority, toward his colleagues and toward himself. Consequently, even though our field of inquiry dealt practically exclusively with sexual problems, the total integrative function will have been influenced in successful therapy. These facts perhaps explain why the individual may be helped equally well by many different approaches which selectively consider only a circumscribed aspect of functioning. Readjustment in one area starts a chain reaction that can involve the person as a whole.

The attitudes of the patient toward the therapist show extreme variations in all therapies, the patient reacting to him, first, as a real person, and, second, as a symbol of authority. Attitudes will consequently be molded by the actual role the therapist plays with the patient, as well as by habitual attitudes and feelings residual in the patient's previous dealings with authority (transference). The attitudes of the therapist to the patient are also diverse. First, there are feelings toward the patient as a human being who needs help and services that the therapist renders for a fee; second, impulses are mobilized toward the patient that are neurotically nurtured and are parcels of disturbances in the therapist's own character structure (counter-transference). The methods of handling transference and counter-transference, such as by encouragement, avoidance, control or interpretation, will differ according to the goals in therapy, the specific techniques being followed, and the level of the therapist's understanding of psychodynamic processes in both the patient and in himself.

A private survey among a sizeable number of psychotherapists practicing supportive, reeducative and reconstructive therapies yielded some interesting facts that have been detailed in Chart II, page 90. Outlined is a comparison of technical procedures in the three main psychotherapeutic groups, according to the duration of therapy, frequency of visits, the taking of detailed histories, routine psychologic examinations, the kinds of communications obtained from the patient, the general activity of the therapist, the frequency of advice-giving to the patient, the handling of transference, the general relationship of the patient to the therapist, the physical position of the patient during therapy, the handling of dream material, and adjuncts utilized during treatment.

1. Duration of Therapy

No exact estimate of the time required to achieve therapeutic goals is possible in supportive, reeducative and reconstructive psychotherapies. In some instances, satisfactory goals are achieved in several sessions; in others, treatment requires several hundred sessions. However, the tendency is toward relatively short-term intervals, averaging ten to fifty sessions in supportive, reeducative

Chart II. TECHNICAL PSYCHOTHERAPEUTIC SIMILARITIES AND DIFFERENCES

	SUPPORTIVE THERAPY	INSIGHT THERAPY with REEDUCATIVE GOALS	INSIGHT THERAPY with RECONSTRUCTIVE GOALS		
			Freudian Psychoanalysis	Non-Freudian Psychoanalysis	Psychoanalytically oriented Psychotherapy
Duration of Therapy	One to several hundred sessions	Several sessions to several hundred sessions	2–5 years	2–5 years	Several sessions to several hundred sessions
Frequency of Visits	1–3 times weekly	1–2 times weekly	4–5 times weekly	2–4 times weekly	1–3 times weekly
Detailed History-Taking	Usually	Often	Rarely	Occasionally	Occasionally
Psychologic Examinations	Intelligence Testing Vocational Battery	Intelligence Testing Vocational Battery Projective Testing	Projective Testing often employed	Projective Testing often employed	Projective Testing often employed
Patient's Communications	Interviews focused on symptoms and environmental disturbances	Interviews focused on daily events and interpersonal relationships	Unguided free associations	Interviews focused on current situations, interpersonal relationships, and other conflictual sources Free associations sometimes used	Interviews focused on current situations, interpersonal relationships and other conflictual sources
General Activity of Therapist	Toward strengthening of existing defenses	Challenging of existing defenses Activity—directiveness to non-directiveness	Challenging of existing defenses Passivity, anonymity, non-directiveness Constant analysis of transference and resistance	Challenging of existing defenses Activity—moderate directiveness to non-directiveness Constant analysis of transference and resistance	Challenging of existing defenses Greater activity—directiveness of moderate sort to non-directiveness Constant analysis of transference and resistance

Advice-giving to Patient	Often	Occasionally	Never	Rarely	Rarely
Transference	Positive transference encouraged and utilized to promote improvement	Positive transference controlled, and, if possible, utilized to promote improvement. Negative transference analyzed in terms of the reality situation	Transference encouraged to point of development of a transference neurosis. Transference analyzed in terms of genetic origins	Transference encouraged to point of awareness of repressed attitudes and feelings. Transference neurosis avoided by some analysts. Transference analyzed in terms of character structure or genetic origins	Transference encouraged to point of awareness of repressed attitudes and feelings. Transference neurosis avoided as a rule. Transference analyzed in terms of character structure, and, occasionally, genetic origins
General Relationship of Patient to Therapist	Positive relationship fostered and utilized	Positive relationship fostered and utilized	Relationship permitted to develop spontaneously	Relationship permitted to develop spontaneously	Relationship permitted to develop spontaneously. Positive relationship occasionally fostered and utilized
Physical Position of Patient during Therapy	Sitting-up, face-to-face	Sitting-up, face-to-face	Recumbent on couch	Sitting-up, face-to-face, or Recumbent on couch	Sitting-up, face-to-face. Occasionally recumbent on couch
Dream Material	Not utilized	Not utilized	Constantly utilized	Constantly utilized	Constantly utilized
Adjuncts Utilized During Therapy	Bibliotherapy, Art Therapy, Group Therapy, Physical Therapy, Drug Therapy, Hypnotherapy, Occupational Therapy	Group Therapy, and Bibliotherapy occasionally used	None	Few or none	Analytic Group Therapy, Hypnoanalysis, Narcotherapy, Play Therapy, and Art Therapy occasionally employed

and psychoanalytically oriented psychotherapy. In both Freudian and non-Freudian psychoanalysis, the time estimate is from two to five years with an average of three years.

2. Frequency of Visits

Under most circumstances the frequency of visits is lowest in the supportive and reeducative therapies, averaging no more than one or two visits weekly. In some instances, however, it is as high as three times weekly. In psychoanalytically oriented psychotherapy, visits average twice weekly, with a low of one and a high of three. Most non-Freudian analysts prefer seeing their patients three times each week, occasionaly lowering this to twice, or raising it to four times weekly. Some Freudian analysts are insistent on visits no less than five times weekly, but others allege that they can handle patients on a four-times-a-week basis.

3. Detailed History-taking

In supportive therapy, a routine detailed history is the rule. It is employed in reeducative therapy in the form of a systematic inquiry into areas of adjustment and maladjustment. In reconstructive therapy, analysts, particularly Freudian analysts, prefer a spontaneous unfolding of historical data, some even condemning the practice of history-taking as prejudicial to good therapy.

4. Psychologic Examinations

Intelligence testing and vocational batteries are often used in supportive and reeducative therapies as a means of assaying intellectual capacities, vocational interests and work potentials. Projective testing, most frequently the Rorschach test, is employed in reeducative and reconstructive therapies mostly as an aid in diagnosis to determine the presence of organic brain conditions, and to ascertain the strength of latent schizophrenic tendencies.

5. Patient's Communications

The kinds of communication encouraged in the different therapies vary to a considerable degree. Free associations are rarely or never employed in non-reconstructive treatment. Guided interviews are organized, in supportive therapy, around symptoms, environmental disturbances and immediate interpersonal problems, and, in reeducative therapy, around daily events and the current life situation. In Freudian psychoanalysis, unguided free associations are considered mandatory in order to circumvent conventional resistances to unconscious content. Concern with every-day problems is felt to be of secondary importance, often serving as a diversion from focal areas of conflict. In non-Freudian psychoanalysis, free associations are believed to be useful, but are not

felt to be absolutely essential. Interviews are often focused on interpersonal relationships and other apparent areas of conflict. Analysts who employ psychoanalytically oriented psychotherapy tend even more toward focused interviews.

6. General Activity of Therapist

As might be expected, activity and directiveness are greatest in those who
do supportive therapy, and least in practitioners who employ non-directive and
Freudian analytic approaches. Irrespective of intent, however, or the kind of
therapy practiced, the degree of activity or passivity is determined largely by the
personality structure of the therapist. Recordings of treatment sessions prove
this point amply, therapists of active temperament finding it difficult to maintain passivity and anonymity even though their brand of therapy calls for these
roles. Often therapists whose recordings show them to be very active and directive have no awareness of their activity or directiveness. In supportive therapy,
an active approach reinforces the authoritarian position of the therapist. This
is felt to be helpful to the therapeutic objective. Moderate directiveness in other
therapies, except perhaps in Freudian psychoanalysis, is not considered prejudicial to the therapeutic aim, provided it is controlled during phases of therapy
where it is essential for the patient to think through his own problems and to
arrive at his own set of goals and values.

The lines along which the therapist actively works are determined in part
by his attitudes toward the patient's defensive structure. In supportive and reeducative therapies, the defenses are resurrected and strengthened with a rebuilding of those that have enabled the individual to function satisfactorily
prior to the present upset. In reconstructive psychotherapy, the defenses are
challenged for the purpose of eliminating those that perpetuate the neurosis
and as a means toward alteration of the character structure itself.

7. Advice-giving to the Patient

The amount of advice offered to the patient correlates positively with the
degree of directiveness and authoritarianism assumed by the therapist in his relationship with the patient. In supportive therapy, accordingly, it is often given;
in reeducational therapy, it is occasionally proffered; while in reconstructive
therapy, it is, more or less, avoided except in emergencies.

8. Transference

In supportive and reeducative therapies, certain aspects of the positive
transference are encouraged and utilized to facilitate therapeutic change. There
is also a constant attack on, and dissipation of, negative transference as soon as
this develops. In Freudian psychoanalysis, the spontaneous feelings and attitudes of the patient are encouraged to a point where he may actually react to
the therapist not as a real person, but as a symbol of authority toward whom

archaic emotions and strivings are directed (transference) This enables the patient to live through with the therapist some of the most important traumatic experiences in his past (transference neurosis), gaining insight through actual revivification of events damaging to personality formation. Interpretation is in terms of genetic origins. In non-Freudian psychoanalysis and psychoanalytically oriented psychotherapy, transference also is considered an essential part of therapy, but the transference neurosis is kept at a minimum by greater therapist activity, less frequent visits and by the immediate handling through interpretation of irrational trends and feelings. Transference is analyzed in terms of character structure as well as of genetic origins.

9. General Relationship of Patient to Therapist

In supportive and reeducative therapies, and occasionally in psychoanalytically oriented psychotherapy, a positive relationship is fostered and sustained as much as possible by appropriate actions and utterances, the relationship itself being utilized to promote therapeutic change. Transference reactions which interfere with a positive relationship are usually dealt with as expediently as possible. In all the reconstructive therapies, the relationship of the patient to the therapist is permitted to develop more or less spontaneously. Transference is encouraged in Freudian psychoanalysis as a vehicle of insight; it is controlled to some extent in non-Freudian psychoanalysis and in psychoanalytically oriented psychotherapy.

10. Physical Position of Patient during Therapy

The sitting-up position is always utilized in supportive and reeducative therapies. In Freudian psychoanalysis, the recumbent couch position is employed as a means of fostering free associations. This requirement is less rigidly followed in non-Freudian psychoanalysis, in which the sitting-up position is alternately or exclusively used with certain patients. In psychoanalytically oriented psychotherapy, the sitting-up position is employed, though occasionally, at certain phases of treatment, the recumbent position may be used.

11. Dream Material

Dream material is generally disregarded in supportive and reeducative therapies, although analytically trained therapists, who use such therapies, study dreams without interpreting them to the patient, in order to observe the defensive reactions of the patient, including transference and resistance manifestations. In all of the reconstructive therapies, dream material is employed as a principal means of access to unconscious conflict. The manner in which dreams are handled will vary according to the theoretic training and orientation of the therapist.

12. Adjuncts Utilized during Therapy

Bibliotherapy, art therapy, group therapy, physical therapy, occupational therapy, drug therapy, and hypnotherapy are often employed by therapists practicing supportive therapy. In reeducative approaches and in psychoanalytically oriented psychotherapy, group therapy, bibliotherapy, play therapy, art therapy, narcotherapy and hypnotherapy are sometimes coordinately used. Few or no adjuncts are utilized in non-Freudian psychoanalysis, while in Freudian psychoanalysis, most therapists avoid all adjunctive devices.

9

The Use of Supportive, Reeducative and Reconstructive Approaches

A NUMBER OF DIFFERENT OBJECTIVES ARE POSSIBLE IN ANY CASE UNDER treatment. First, we may try, by supportive techniques, to restore to the individual a shattered sense of mastery so that he integrates on a more adaptive level. We would expect to achieve here an alleviation of symptoms nurtured by a collapse in adaptation, such as anxiety, depression, and psychosomatic complaints; as well as dissipation of neurotic defenses, like phobias, compulsions and conversion phenomena. Second, we may aim, with reeducative therapy, for a correction of disturbed patterns of behavior, with the object of helping the patient utilize the resources that he has to the full in quest of a more satisfactory work, interpersonal and social adjustment. Finally, we may, by employing reconstructive measures, strive for the development of new resources through resolution of personality blocks that have impeded the acquisition of maturity.

To illustrate how supportive, reeducative and reconstructive approaches may be employed in practice, we may consider the case of a patient who applies for therapy after the onset of an emotional illness characterized by tension, depression, anxiety and psychosomatic symptoms. The patient in explaining his upset, attributes it to challenging work pressures brought about by a shift in his position from a relatively routine one to that involving considerable responsibility.

RESTORATION OF MASTERY THROUGH SUPPORTIVE SYMPTOM RELIEF OR REMOVAL

In going over his history, it appears that the patient has, up to the onset of his work problem, made a satisfactory adjustment. He seems to have a good home life; he enjoys his children and respects his wife; he is an excellent provider who conscientiously performs his work duties; he belongs to a number of organizations, and has the usual quota of friends. According to this record, it would seem reasonable to scale our goals toward bringing him back to where he was prior to his collapse. We might calculate that once his symptoms were eliminated or under control, he would have the best chance of recovering his equilibrium. With this in mind, we might attack his symptoms along several different lines. First, we might attempt to subdue them by the administration of medicaments, such as antacids for hyperacidity, atropine for spasm, tonics for anorexia, sedatives and hypnotics for tension, drugs like "tolserol" for anxiety, and benzedrine for depression. Where his depression is so intense as to constitute a suicidal hazard, electric shock therapy might be considered. The patient might also be trained in progressive muscular relaxation in an attempt to relieve his taut muscular state. He may be reassured, in the event he is frightened by his condition, to the effect that his problem is not irremediable, and he may be urged to utilize his will power to get well. He may also be removed from his environmental situation. By absenting himself from existing arenas of stress, there may be an assuaging of tension.

The therapist may, instead of making these efforts, focus attention on the patient's work difficulty, reasoning as follows: "Here is a man who has problems in assertiveness, yet who is involved in a work situation that is too hard for him to handle. Competitiveness demanded by his present job is not for one with this kind of personality. Prior to the unhappy job change, he was getting along adequately. The treatment objective, then, is to return him to his previous job to which he was able to adjust satisfactorily."

Assuming that his vocational situation is the primary source of his difficulty, the patient may be urged to find a different position. He would be helped here to an awareness that the competitive stresses in his present job are those to which he cannot and should not adjust, and he may be encouraged to seek a type of work that avoids competition. Where the patient is willing to give up his present position and to occupy a less burdensome one, he may manage to regain his customary equilibrium.

Environmental difficulties may exist in addition to the work problem that upset the patient, rendering it additionally impossible for him to make an adequate adjustment. For example, were our patient to suffer from a family difficulty in conjunction with his work problem, our focus in therapy would of necessity also occupy the former area. The therapist would help the patient extricate himself from his disturbing plight by bringing him to a realization of both constructive and destructive aspects of his situation, or by more active measures which might involve contact with his family.

If our patient were the victim of a family disturbance that was insoluble, to which he is unable to adjust himself, it might be necessary to advise him to take up residence elsewhere. Temporary or permanent placement in a foster family or rest home might help stabilize the person, provided he had not yet sustained structural damage to his personality. Placement in an institution or hospital might also sometimes be necessary, especially where the patient had become addicted to alcohol or drugs, where he displayed a hypomanic condition or "acted out" his problems in a destructive manner, where he was severely depressed or suicidally inclined, or where he evidenced drastic hysterical or psychosomatic symptoms.

These measures are obviously all aimed at symptom relief or removal. The philosophy behind such approaches is that symptoms impair the functional efficiency of the psyche like a diseased gall bladder upsets the entire digestive system. Suggestion, persuasion, "thought control," progressive relaxation, purposeful forgetting, and the plunging of the self into extroverted activities are among the devices aimed at the symptom, as if it were a foreign body whose presence obstructed an otherwise intact psychic mechanism.

No issue is taken with the successes scored by this type of therapy. Successes do occur and there are certain personalities who are able to forestall complete emotional collapse by practicing such devices as "riding their symptoms," substituting innocuous for painful thoughts, engaging in frenzied pursuit of social activities, and observing a punctilious performance of ritual and prayer. In justification of these methods it must be said that many persons refuse to accept more intensive treatment or are so intellectually or financially handicapped that a more exhaustive analysis of their problems is beyond their means. In these cases, the mastery of symptoms helps the individual gain freedom from excruciating distress and, in some instances, permits him to attain to a more useful existence.

However, one must not minimize the superficiality of goals of this approach, for the dynamic sources of tension and anxiety go untreated. Thus, while the manipulation of the patient's environment toward alleviation or removal of inimical circumstances, or the encouragement of healthy interests and outlets, might be helpful in some cases, in others results would be singularly barren. This is particularly the case where the individual is victimized by deep inner conflicts that are projected onto the environment, and in themselves help to create the environmental distortion. Results are poor also when the environmental difficulty has overwhelmed the resources of the ego to a point where the individual has lost his sense of mastery, the resulting anxiety precipitating old repressed fears and conflicts. Here, infantile defenses are revived which cripple the adaptive resources of the ego to a point where, even though the environmental disturbance has abated, the individual is burdened with a residual neurosis.

We may compare this with the situation of a man suffering from a minor heart ailment which does not incapacitate him so long as no great strain is imposed on his circulation. Should a severe shock or catastrophic happening supervene, or should physical work which is beyond his endurance be foisted on the individual, the resources of the heart will fail, producing cardiac damage with symptoms of circulatory failure that remain long after the initiating stress has disappeared. And so it is with a personality disorder around which the individual has managed to organize his life. When circumstances remove his erected safeguards, and he is propelled into a situation he cannot handle, severe disorganization may result which persists long after the initiating disturbance has passed.

Environmental adjustment may also fail because the patient feels tied to his life situation no matter how inimical it may be, considering it as an inevitable consequence of living, one he has no right to challenge, let alone change. Any tension and anxiety that accompany this acceptance are usually credited by him to sources outside of himself.

MODIFICATION OF DISTURBED ATTITUDES THROUGH REEDUCATIVE THERAPY

An investigation may disclose that our patient's inability to endure competition at his place of work may not be due so much to an environmental peculiarity, as it is to the fact that unique ideas and attitudes possessed by the patient make competition an inacceptable or dangerous circumstance.

When we examine the exact nature of his disturbed attitudes, we may find that the patient is being victimized by a tangle of contradictory character trends that inspire personal insecurity, promote devaluated self-esteem, and impair his relationships with people. For example, we may observe that a basic character trend he possesses is that of dependency which operates insidiously, causing him to ally himself with some other person who is a symbol of strength and omniscience. He relates to this person as if the latter were a powerful and providing parental agency. Accordingly, he may assume a passive role, exhibiting little spontaneity and initiative, anticipating that his needs and demands will automatically be satisfied. Competition poses a threat to his dependency need, for it puts the responsibility on his own shoulders which he believes are too weak to bear the burden of spontaneous enterprise. Other character trends may exist which both reinforce and oppose his dependency. While he has managed to keep a tenuous emotional balance up to the time of the present crisis, the alteration of his vocational situation has disrupted his equilibrium, threatening his sense of mastery and precipitating catastrophic fears and anticipations of injury. He may be aware of how dependent he is, and he may even resent his dependency as opposed to his best interests; yet his security is so bound to this trend that he may be unable to subdue its operation.

When we inquire further into the circumstances underlying the presumably good adjustment prior to the outbreak of his illness, we find that the patient's security has always been maintained by the satisfaction of his dependency. So long as this has been gratified, he has been able to get along splendidly. Ungratified, he has been riddled with disquieting fears and threatened with an ill-defined sense of catastrophe. Investigating the conditions prevailing at the onset of the patient's illness, we discover that for some time prior to the onset, the wife has been withdrawing her attention from the patient and transferring it to her brother and his wife who have, because of financial pressures, moved into the patient's home. As her interest became increasingly diverted from the patient, his feelings of insecurity and resentment expanded. The more importunate his demands, the less she responded, until finally he reacted like an abandoned child in a rejecting world. His helplessness and fears of aggression mounted, until the very act of going to work constituted a challenge which taxed his capacities. Promotion to a more responsible position was the last straw that precipitated a breakdown in adaptation.

As a consequence of this discovery, we may attempt as a goal to inculcate in the patient some insight into his dependency as well as into other disorganizing attitudes and strivings. The object of insight here is the retraining of reaction patterns. Thus, we would try to bring our patient to an awareness of the attitudes and patterns he habitually exploits, and we would demonstrate to him which of these facilitate and which obstruct his adjustment. Next we would help him to apply this knowledge toward modifying or changing his reactions. We would also evaluate his assets and his liabilities to see how much he had minimized the former and exaggerated the latter.

In the course of exploring his dependency, the patient might achieve some insight into himself. He might become cognizant of how compliant he is to authority, over-estimating the virtues of others to the minimization of his own abilities and capacities. He might recognize that his fear of competition is actually associated with anticipating hostilities from people, or with the belief that in pitting himself against others, he would come out second best, thus exposing himself to ridicule. He might discover also that he harbors ambitions that are totally beyond possibilities of fulfillment, contributing to his sense of defeat.

The patient would probably be surprised to learn that his character patterns are regarded as problems, since he has accepted them as normal for himself. As soon as he realizes that his patterns are responsible for much of his turmoil, he might be supplied with a valid motivation to alter his scheme of life. While this motivation in itself would not be enough to produce the desired change, his patterns constituting the only routes he knows to security and self-esteem, it might help him to approach his problems from a different point of view. Faced with his usual difficulties, the patient would, as a rule, be unable at first to give up his destructive drives. Knowledge that frustration or pain was inevitable to their pursuit, would not be enough to get him to relinquish whatever gratifications followed their exploitation. However, even the mere knowledge that his attitudes were responsible for his plight would be healthier from a therapeutic viewpoint than the conviction, existing previously, that sources of misery lay outside oneself. Eventually, when he realizes that his suffering does not compensate for the dubious gratifications accruing from indulgence of immature drives, and when he understands that his reactions interfere with important life goals, the patient might begin experimenting with new attitudes and behavior.

Once convinced that more creative substitutive reactions were possible, a long period of experiment and training would be necessary before habitual attitudes were abandoned. Generally, habits that have persisted over a long time do not vanish within a few weeks or a few months. In spite of good resolutions, automatic responses operate in line with established patterns. Struggle is inevitable until control is won over old patterns, and new ones take their place.

PERSONALITY GROWTH AND MATURITY THROUGH RECONSTRUCTIVE THERAPY

The most ambitious objective we could achieve in therapy would be a replacement of neurotic character strivings with those which will enable the person to relate himself creatively to his environment. This objective would most advantageously be reinforced by liberation of the individual from anxieties and fears that were rooted in past experiences and conditionings. Important also would be the development of the ego to a point where it could cope realistically with inner strivings and environmental pressures. The individual would evolve into a free agent with the willingness to make his own decisions and to take the consequences of his acts. There would be an adaptive choice of ends and means and an ability to act without undue restraint from others. Capacities to plan one's life and to develop goals and ideals in harmony with the disciplines of society would be vital. A sense of inner freedom, independence, assertiveness and self-reliance would, furthermore, add to a well-balanced personality.

To achieve these objectives in our patient with the work difficulty, it would be necessary to eliminate the source of the patient's problem rather than to control its effects. This would necessitate an understanding of the conflictual roots of his disorder with an analysis of factors that have produced a collapse in adaptation. We would strive to expand our patient's sense of self so that he might outgrow the need to fasten himself to a parental figure for purposes of emotional support.

The theoretic basis of the approach we would have to employ to achieve our ambitious goal involves the following propositions: (1) Past inimical experiences and conditionings have retarded the normal psychosocial growth process, and are now promoting in the individual immature strivings and emotions that come into conflict with reality on the one hand, and, on the other, with the person's own incorporated system of ideals and standards. (2) Resultant are tensions, catastrophic feelings of helplessness and expectations of injury that in turn invoke protective devices. Most common of these is repression, a sealing-off process which blankets offending impulses, attitudes and memories from awareness. (3) However noble the attempt, repression of inacceptable strivings rarely succeeds in annihilating them, for their expression is sought from time to time by powerful motivations of impelling need. Their filtering into conscious life promotes bouts of anxiety and whips up the defenses of the ego which, while ameliorating anxiety, may be destructive to adjustment. Additionally, repressed strivings may express themselves subversively as symptoms. (4) The direct or disguised operation of repudiated strivings, and the defenses that are mobilized against them, promote attitudes and values that disorganize interpersonal relationships. Reactions develop that are opposed to good judgment and common sense. While the individual may assume that he is acting like an adult, emotionally he is reacting like a child, projecting into his present life the same kinds of fears and misinterpretations that confronted him in his early years, as if neither time nor reality considerations have altered materially the patterns learned in his past. So long as he protects himself from fancied hurt by circumscribing his activities, he may manage to get along, but should he venture beyond his habitual zone of safety, the precarious balances he has erected will crumble.

Were we to treat our patient with the work problem according to this hy-

pothesis, we would become involved in a more or less extensive therapeutic procedure which would have to go beyond the mere correction of his work difficulty. Indeed, we would consider the vocational disorder as but one aspect of
the problem, and our therapeutic effort would be directed toward mediating
disorganizing drives that are destructive to his total adjustment.

The patient, by becoming aware, during therapy, of the conflictual forces
within him would gradually realize that he was harboring attitudes that were a
carry-over of early conditionings. For instance, our exploratory process might
reveal the patient's mother as a woman who had prevented him from achieving
that type of independent assertiveness that enables a child to resolve his dependent ties. It would demonstrate how the mother's own neurotic needs sponsored
a cloying overprotectiveness that kept the patient infantilized and helpless.
It would bring out how his efforts at aggressive defiance were met with uncompromising harshness, until he gave up in his attempts at independence and
shielded himself by complying with his mother's demands. It would uncover
passive wishes, fears of mutilation in the assumption of a desired masculine role,
and a host of other unconscious conflicts that were engendered by his early
experiences. It would finally expose his infantile impulses as living on in his
adult life, transferring themselves to those with whom the patient became intimately involved. His wife would be revealed as a figure toward whom the
patient reacted as if she were a reincarnation of his mother. Partly because of
her own impulses and partly because the patient had maneuvered her into a
parental role, the wife might be shown as having responded by mothering him.
In this protective atmosphere, the patient had made a tolerable adaptation even
while he repressed desires for freedom and growth. Interpreting the wife's
withdrawal as rejection, the patient had reacted with intense hostility. This he
needed to smother for fear of losing every vestige of his wife's affection. His
increasing helplessness soon reached an intensity where he could no longer
carry on. At this point he was faced with a greater work challenge in the form
of added responsibility, and continuing at work meant coping with further stress.
The patient reacted to this threat as a child would react—by screaming for help.
Reconstructive psychotherapy would bring the patient to an awareness of these
facts, and help him overcome the crippling drives sponsored by his past.

10

"Brief" or "Short-Term" Psychotherapy

THE PLAN TO SHORTEN THE PERIOD REQUIRED FOR PSYCHOTHERAPY is an intriguing proposition from the standpoint of time and financial saving. A number of articles have appeared which deal with theoretic and practical aspects of this idea [298–315]. There is little agreement regarding the dynamics, techniques and results of short-term therapy. Nor is there any conformity as to how few or how many sessions are necessary to make psychotherapy "brief." Some therapists consider twenty-five sessions a maximum, preferably condensed into a period of less than four months; others regard therapy "short-term" even if it has gone on for a year provided that the total number of sessions does not exceed fifty.

As to the utility of short-term therapy, there are those who zealously advocate the practice as an effective substitute for long-term therapy; there are others who depreciate its influence, considering it superficial, futile, and even dangerous in that it may raise false hopes in the patient.

The most serious and perhaps most valid objection offered to short-term therapy is that sufficient time is not provided within the brief therapeutic period to permit of a "working-through" of insight so that it is utilized by the total personality for the establishing of new integrative patterns. Time itself is the essence of those therapies that have for their objective a real alteration of the personality structure.

There are, however, some exceptions to this rule. First, the individual may already have, as a result of a previous therapeutic effort, or by dint of fortunate life experiences, solved significant aspects of this problem. Here, a brief period of treatment may carry him through toward change. Second, the short therapeutic interval may have brought the patient to a sufficient awareness of his problem, resolving some of his defenses, so that he questions his later reactions and explores his relationships in a forthright manner. There are certain individuals who, possessed of an introspectiveness and capacity to tolerate anxiety, may, after having got a start in short-term therapy, proceed on to considerable personality change through their own spontaneous efforts.

Despite these exceptions, one must not overemphasize the extent of change induced by short-term approaches, even though the quantity of insight achieved and the symptomatic relief obtained evokes great optimism in both patient and therapist. The neurotic founts of conflict are many and powerful, and will continue to plague the patient, attempting to force him into defenses which have already proven futile. Indeed, the very insights that are liberated during the treatment period may be utilized to reinforce habitual defenses consolidating them into the neurotic scheme of life in a seemingly innocuous way.

With these cautions in mind, short-term therapy may be used with considerable benefit in selected patients, and, even where the final effect of therapy has been a mere consolidation of defenses with repression of destructive elements in the personality, the effort will often definitely have been worthwhile.

Problems that respond especially well to short-term therapy are those in which the treatment goal is an abbreviated one. For instance, certain aspects of a total problem may often be rectified in a few therapeutic sessions. Here, a brief period of treatment suffices to restore the patient to emotional equilibrium, leaving him symptom-free and capable of eluding certain pitfalls previously unavoidable. Additionally, he may learn how to utilize his assets to best advantage, how to minimize his liabilities, how to avoid crises in relationships with people, how to organize his activities around his characterologic weaknesses, and how to discover and release some positive qualities within himself. These therapeutic aims, as will be noted, are not too extensive. Basically, the objective is to stabilize the individual by restoring defenses that had, prior to his upset, enabled him to function satisfactorily, or to provide him with a somewhat better means of interpersonal relatedness.

Persons who respond well to short-term approaches are those who have, prior to coming to therapy, already worked out many of their difficulties on a non-verbal or partially verbal level. Such individuals merely need a helping hand in the form of clarification, a little more support, or a slight challenge in order to think through their problems toward a satisfactory solution. Other susceptible patients are those with flexibility of character structure, who are capable of relating easily to others without undue dependency, hostility or detachment. Where the motivation for treatment is strong, where ego strength is good, and where concurrent environmental distortions are easily remediable, success is more readily insured. A fairly keen intelligence and the ability to work on one's problems between sessions are also of positive value.

The shortening of therapy depends to a considerable degree on the therapist himself. Unfortunately there is a tendency to think about brief psychotherapy in terms of utilizing one or another special technique or frill. Actually, the most important factor in shortening psychotherapy is not the method that is used, nor the specific syndrome treated, but the therapist himself, his understanding of dynamics and of how to use himself most constructively in the therapeutic interpersonal relationship. What this means is that an incompetent therapist's techniques are not particularly enhanced through the utilization of short-term approaches. Indeed, he may discover that his psychotherapy actually becomes briefer in the wrong sense, in that his patients become dissatisfied earlier and terminate therapy much more quickly than if he had utilized traditional long-term methods.

The therapist must, in short-term therapy, be capable of establishing a rapid rapport with the patient. He must be sensitive, perceptive and capable of focusing on important conflictual areas without undue delay. It goes without saying that he must understand how to utilize with skill the specialized techniques that are part of the therapeutic process. A knowledge of hypnotherapy and narcotherapy are also of great advantage.

Problems which do not yield to short-term measures are those that have persisted a long time and perhaps date back to early childhood. An example of the latter are serious personality disturbances caused by destructive conditionings in the formative years of life. Obdurate attitudinal and behavioral patterns usually cannot be resolved except by a prolonged therapeutic experience. Here, time itself is important since extensive reconditioning is required. Time is an essential part of treatment in instances where emotional growth has been thwarted by unfortunate traumas in early life, and where the therapeutic goal is a maturation of the personality structure.

This does not mean that brief psychotherapy precludes extensive personality change; it does mean that the change to take place will require an extensive time interval following treatment in the medium of life experience itself. What is accomplished in therapy here is that seeds of insight are planted which slowly germinate in the course of living long after therapy has ceased. Resistances are gradually resolved, sometimes with surprising changes in the character structure. This happy result, however, is fortuitous, and where the individual's difficulty has been deeply structuralized, he will usually require long-term treatment before any permanent change is discernible.

11

What Is the "Best" Kind of Psychotherapy?

OF BIAS IN THE PSYCHOLOGIC OR PSYCHIATRIC FIELD THERE IS NO LACK. It usually takes the form of a flaunting of one's special brand of therapy as superior or "best." This is confounding when one considers that the practice of psychotherapy is rooted in empiricism. Nevertheless, there are those who, wedded to a specific school of psychiatric thinking, espouse their theories with as great vehemence as they denounce and depreciate those of other schools. Such dogmatism certainly is not unique to psychotherapy. It is found in many disciplines whose practitioners exhibit rigid sectarianism and a tenacious defense of cherished beliefs, with violent antagonism toward colleagues who dare to countenance deviant opinions.

Since human knowledge is ever in a state of flux and is qualified by the limited methods, instruments and knowledge of the times, no true scientist can ever brand his discoveries as absolute. Indeed, lack of decadence in scientific thinking is mirrored in the ability to tolerate and then to challenge or absorb new ideas. Current rifts are thus present in any virile and expanding science, eventuating in a synthesis of varied thinking—a synthesis that can best survive the tests of time. This is the basis of the interdisciplinary and eclectic approach to science which more and more is filtering into the mental health field. An eclectic viewpoint in psychotherapy is more than justified by the fact that the various schools of psychiatry, psychology and the other social sciences have made significant contributions to the field.

Psychoanalysis, for instance, has contributed theories of personality development and dynamics of the therapeutic process which are fundamental structures around which good psychotherapeutic method is organized. Psychobiology has introduced the philosophy of considering the human being an integrate of a variety of functions, and has stressed the need for a practical assay of his assets and liabilities in working out a treatment plan. The casework field has evolved a whole body of supportive approaches, along with carefully fomulated interviewing and supervisory processes. The field of psychology, complementing its investigations of learning theory and research methodology, has contributed certain non-directive and directive counseling techniques, along with a number of procedures in play therapy, art therapy, group therapy, speech therapy, vocational guidance and rehabilitation. From anthropology there has been gained an understanding of the need to evaluate character structure in terms of family and cultural patterns, and to gauge goals in therapy along lines of anticipated social pressures. Finally, from the field of medicine, there has come the consideration of the reciprocal relationship that exists in physical and psychic illness. Tolerance, then, for the points of view of the various people in the mental health field is conducive to healthy growth.

Eclecticism in method is also justified by the fact that a number of things can be done for a person with an emotional problem which will make him feel better, temporarily or permanently. These include: (1) alleviating or removing his symptoms, (2) adjusting his life situation so that it imposes a minimal burden on him, (3) inducing him to change his disorganizing attitudes and life goals, and (4) investigating what conflicts are at the bottom of his difficulty and dealing with them on various corrective levels.

All psychotherapies approach one or more of these aims, being adapted to some better than to others. Different therapists, by virtue of their unique personalities and specialized training, apply themselves to one or another technical procedure with greater or lesser facility. And patients selectively respond to some therapeutic methods and not to others.

There is, therefore, no "best" kind of therapy except that which happens to suit the patient's needs most at the time he applies for treatment. When we consider the preferred type of psychotherapy to employ—supportive, reeducative or reconstructive—we must keep in mind exactly what we are trying to accomplish. A patient with even a sound and well-organized personality structure may go to pieces in the face of severely traumatizing environmental circumstances. The only help he may require is a short interval of supportive therapy which will suffice to bring him back to the adjustment level he enjoyed prior to his upset. To embark on a long and costly course of reconstructive psychotherapy would be ill-advised, unless he failed to show improvement after the immediate stress source was resolved. A second person may suffer from problems in adjustment that interfere with his ability to get along with people; yet he may be sufficiently flexible to alter his patterns of living once his distorted attitudes are brought to light. The preferred treatment here would be some kind of insight therapy with reeducative goals. A third person may come to treatment with what seems to be a minor work or marital problem. Our examination may reveal that his complaint factor is merely the superficial manifestation of a serious personality disorder, and that we will be unable to remedy his complaint until we have produced a drastic reorganization of his character structure. This will require perhaps years of reconstructive therapy.

The matter of selective response to the different techniques in the supportive, reeducative and reconstructive psychotherapies is of significance. Some patients, for instance, do better with guidance than with persuasive techniques; some are susceptible to emotional catharsis and desensitization; others respond best to inspirational group therapy. Where reeducative therapy is needed, some persons react favorably to directive approaches while others are helped more by those of a non-directive nature. In the realm of reconstructive psychotherapy, certain patients are influenced most effectively by Freudian psychoanalysis, others by non-Freudian psychoanalysis, and still others are best handled by psychoanalytically oriented psychotherapy.

Since psychotherapy is an interpersonal relationship, the personality of the therapist, as reflected in his capacity to relate to patients, is fully as important, if not more important, than the method he employs. Indeed, the personality of the therapist influences the choice of method as well as the modifications he introduces in implementing any set technique. Thus, some therapists, by virtue of basic characterologic passivity, do better with "passive" techniques, such as non-directive therapy or Freudian psychoanalysis. Other therapists, possessing more active character structures, are unable to play a passive role in therapy, and are inspired toward executing supportive approaches, directive reeducative therapies, non-Freudian psychoanalysis or psychoanalytically oriented psychotherapy. Patients seem to do well with all methods of treatment provided the therapist is skilled in his particular approach, and is capable of setting up and maintaining a good working relationship with his patient. This does not mean that goals are interchangeable in supportive, reeducative and reconstructive therapies, because, as has been indicated, there are definite limitations in the extent to which the patient's personality structure may be influenced by the technical methods employed. Yet, within each of these three large groupings, considerable flexibility in method may be displayed consistent with the training of the therapist and with his personality set.

The beneficial effects wielded by psychotherapy, irrespective of type, are to a large extent due to a restoration of the patient's sense of mastery. This results from a constructive use of the therapeutic relationship in a number of ways. First, the patient may gain from therapy sufficient emotional support, sympathy and understanding to help him to endure and to conquer inner tensions and external demands. The relationship, while supportive, is spontaneously utilized by him in such a manner that it does not inhibit, too drastically, impulses for assertiveness and independence. Second, the relationship facilitates the cathartic release of disturbing feelings, with alleviation of guilt and fear. Third, the patient is helped to mediate an external or internal stress source or to adjust himself to it. Fourth, shattered repressions are rebuilt and habitual defenses restored, with alteration of those defenses which are destructive to adjustment. Fifth, a reevaluation of the self develops with modification of certain unrealistic attitudes and strivings and substitution for them of productive patterns that lead to more congenial relationships with people.

Where the therapist's personality and technical skills facilitate the above effects, the results of therapy are usually good. Where his personality or methods block such effects, results will be poor no matter what school of thought the therapist espouses or how thoroughly conversant he is with theory.

In instances where the patient achieves a good therapeutic result, the therapist may deceive himself into believing that what has effectuated the cure or improvement was his focus on a specific theoretic orientation rather than because of important processes evolving out of the patient's constructive use of the relationship in the indicated ways.

Much misunderstanding has developed among the different psychologic schools due to the flaunting by some schools of their superiority to others. Perhaps the most burning question relates to the virtues of Freudian psychoanalysis over other therapies. Current among both professional and lay persons is the idea that Freudian psychoanalysis is the aristocrat of all therapies and that any other type of treatment is a substitute made necessary by financial limitations and the absence of trained personnel. This assumption was probably nurtured by the successes of Freudian psychoanalysis in certain cases, and by the widespread publicity given the method through books and current publications. Resultant is a general feeling that Freudian psychoanalysis is the treatment of choice and that other treatment methods are to be suspected if not condemned.

Actually, Freudian psychoanalysis was never intended as treatment for all types of emotional illness. Freud himself recognized this in circumscribing its application to a group of conditions he called the "transference neuroses" [316,317]. Since transference was the main tool of psychoanalysis, Freud contended that only those individuals who were capable of establishing a transference were susceptible to the psychoanalytic method. According to this hypothesis, the most susceptible syndromes to psychoanalysis were conversion hysteria, anxiety hysteria, anxiety neurosis, certain types of compulsion neurosis and some neurotic depressions. Problems least susceptible were character disturbances, perversions, addictions and psychoses.

Fenichel [318] outlines a number of relative indications and contraindications to psychoanalysis. Included are the following:

1. The age of the patient should ideally be between fifteen and forty. Younger children are considered lacking in "reasonableness," and older persons in flexibility.

2. Since an adequate intellectual capacity is important, a low intelligence is a contraindication.

3. Unfavorable and irremediable life situations which provoke compensatory neurotic defenses may militate against psychoanalysis.

4. Since psychoanalysis is a prolonged and exhaustive procedure, it should not be utilized in mild neuroses which do not justify an extensive expenditure of time, money and energy.

5. Neuroses accompanied by severe or dangerous symptoms are usually best handled by approaches that work more rapidly than psychoanalysis, since in the latter, symptomatic suffering continues for a considerable period.

6. Certain speech disorders may contraindicate psychoanalysis.

7. The method may not be possible in the absence of a kind of "reasonable" ego. This is lacking in psychotic and psychopathic states, and is inoperative where the patient is not motivated to cooperate or to accept therapy.

8. Where secondary gains are intense, psychoanalysis may fail.

9. Character structures of a schizoid nature often do not withstand the rigors of psychoanalysis, sometimes breaking down into psychotic states as a result of treatment.

Stone [319], reviewing the work of various writers, presents the following conditions as prejudicing the use of formal psychoanalysis, in favor of another psychotherapeutic technique: (1) individuals whose mental problems are so severe that extensive personality alteration would expose them to greater difficulties than they now have; (2) those who possess mental problems so slight that an ambitious procedure such as psychoanalysis would not be justified; (3) those whose life circumstances are so unpropitious that extreme personality change might promote greater disasters than now exist; (4) acute reactive disorders in individuals who have in the past shown the capacity to overcome unfavorable conditions; (5) transitional changes involved in adapting oneself to different environmental circumstances or to the inevitable processes of growth, such as difficulties in adolescence; (6) persons who have failed to respond to long or multiple analyses; (7) persons whose neuroses are associated with an extreme degree of secondary gain; and (8) miscellaneous conditions, such as "certain masochistic marital problems, monosymptomatic impotence, 'psychosomatic' illnesses, certain mild chronic neuroses, and certain schizoid personalities."

It will be seen from this that instances are indeed extensive in which some therapy other than Freudian psychoanalysis is to be preferred. It is possible that the poor results reported in Freudian psychoanalysis in certain cases [320–325] are products of improper selection of cases.

Enthusiasm with the Freudian psychoanalytic method has resulted in the wholesale application of the technique to conditions for which it never was intended. The inevitable failures have caused many analysts to introduce modifications in the orthodox technique in the form of greater activity and directiveness, substitution of focused interviews for free association, circumscription of pathologic areas in which to work, concentration on immediate life problems and current interpersonal relationships, abandonment of the couch for the sitting up position, and the occasional use of such supportive techniques as suggestion, guidance, reassurance, environmental manipulation and persuasion. These modifications have given rise to the idea in the minds of some therapists that they were creating new and revolutionary techniques, whereas actually they were merely incorporating in their technical armamentarium procedures which had been in use for many years.

The appreciation of the limitations of Freudian psychoanalysis is a healthy step which can result in a better selection of cases for the method. Employed conservatively, Freudian psychoanalysis remains the treatment of choice in certain problems. In other conditions, modified analytic therapy, or reeducative and supportive approaches are to be preferred.

What is apparent from the results obtained by diverse theoretic and methodologic approaches is that no one person nor school of psychologic thinking has a monopoly on the total truth. It would seem, in fact, as if each variant were dealing with a partial truth, one aspect of a total truth. When we examine critically what successful psychotherapists do, we find that irrespective of the school to which they belong, and in spite of what they say they do, methods are modified to suit the needs of particular patients and situations. The more experienced the therapist, the more flexible he becomes in the kinds of techniques he utilizes. This eclecticism in approach is of the greatest significance if the therapist really wants to help each patient achieve effective relief from symptoms and as extensive a personality growth and development as is within his potential.

12

Who Can Do Psychotherapy?

AN EMOTIONALLY DISTURBED PERSON OFTEN ATTEMPTS TO ASSUAGE his turmoil by seeking out a relationship, not only with a qualified psychiatrist, but with another professional, like a physician, nurse, teacher, psychologic counselor, lawyer or social worker, particularly where his complaint is focused on physical, educational, marital, interpersonal or social difficulties. The urgency of the problems imposed on such professionals, has forced many of them to evolve ways of handling people in distress, largely oriented around advice-giving and active interference in manifest environmental disorders.

There is little question, no matter how deftly we employ semantics or how we distort words, that these techniques are psychotherapeutic in essence, since they involve the setting up of a relationship with the goal of modifying symptoms or correcting personality blocks. The exigency of community need, coupled with the lack of any other resource to which people in trouble might turn for help, has thus maneuvered many professionals into a therapeutic role. As Galdston [326] has commented: "Parent, priest, minister, teacher, faculty adviser, social worker, marriage counselor, vocational adviser: all of them in different ways, indulge in psychotherapeutic gestures. They are in effect lay psychotherapists; have been such for centuries past and are bound to continue as such for a long time to come."

This situation, unfortunately, has proved itself to be not an unmixed blessing, for the great majority of even trained professionals are not equipped by education, disposition or experience to do psychotherapy. While they may be able to function in an advisory or friendship role, they do not have the basic knowledge or the skill to handle the patient on a therapeutic footing, dealing with such requirements as the degree of support to be extended, the manner of inducing and of controlling emotional catharsis, the strategy of timed interpretations, the handling of resistance, and the management of transference.

This is not to say that individuals with emotional problems do not improve in the course of professional relationships with people untrained in therapeutic techniques. There are some persons—usually those with not too severe neurotic problems—who seem to gain great benefit from a reasonably permissive and non-punitive atmosphere. The depth of therapeutic change, however, is usually quite shallow. Moreover, where the partner in the relationship is not trained to do psychotherapy, he will often get involved in serious difficulty with a neurotic person, the relationship becoming explosive in charges of transference and counter-transference. He may even find his own neurosis interlocking with that of the person, until he is unable to extricate himself from the relationship without creating a dangerous crisis in the life of the individual with whom he has become hopelessly involved.

The realization that emotional difficulties are ubiquitous has lent force to an educational movement among professionals whose task it is to handle people in trouble. The aim of such training is helping the professional to differentiate emotional from other problems, and to manage the former on some kind of correctional level. The chief professionals involved have been non-psychiatric physicians, psychologists, social workers, nurses, ministers and educators.

THE PHYSICIAN IN PSYCHOTHERAPY

Because more than half of the patients seeking medical relief suffer from functional instead of, or in combination with, organic ailments, and because there is scarcely a single bodily organ or tissue that may not be influenced by emotional forces, much attention has been centered in recent years on "psychosomatic" factors in physical disease. A virtual plethora of articles on emotionally determined somatic syndromes has appeared in medical journals which have stressed an organismic concept of the human being [327]. An interrelationship between physical medicine and psychiatry has been emphasized [328] as has been the concept that every physician must to some extent be a psychiatrist [329]. It has even been alleged that the internist or general practitioner has an advantage over the psychiatrist in dealing with the common psychogenic ailments of his patients, because he sees them at an early stage when they are more susceptible to treatment and because he is more capable of relating symptoms to the somatic status. Indeed, Groom [330] believes that "Only a small percentage of neurotic patients can be or need to be seen by the psychiatrist."

The curriculum of practically every medical school contains a sizable number of psychiatric courses. The aim of such courses is to prepare the medical student so that he can deal intelligently and skillfully with patients as persons, and to give him a basic understanding of psychologic and social problems in relation to health and disease. These goals are accented in the *Report of the 1951 Conference on Psychiatric Education* organized and conducted by the American Psychiatric Association and the Association of American Medical Colleges [331]. At this conference it was generally agreed that instruction in psychiatry be started during the first and second years of medical school. Among the objectives of psychiatric training are these: (1) the ability to interview, (2) the ability to diagnose the condition of patients who are emotionally disturbed and who express their problems in physical, psychologic or social symptoms, (3) the understanding of what the physician who is not a psychiatrist can do and should do in the management and treatment of emotionally sick persons who may or may not have physical symptoms, (4) the emergency management of disturbed patients, (5) the understanding of what the physician cannot do and should not do in the treatment of the mentally sick, (6) methods of referral to specialists, hospitals and clinics, (7) knowledge of the interrelationships between psychiatrist, social case worker, psychologist, nurse, occupational therapist and others caring for the mentally sick, and (8) an appreciation of the scope and limitations of present methods of psychiatric therapy. Four special topics in the teaching program have been emphasized. The first deals with social influences on the development of personality and the creation of disturbances in personality; the second topic treats the intricacies of the patient-physician relationship, which is considered to be the very core of psychiatry; the third topic undertakes to teach interviewing and history-taking; while the fourth concerns itself with general problems in growth and development.

Once the student has graduated, there are those who believe that he has a responsibility to learn how to do certain kinds of psychotherapy. The role that the physician plays in the community and the prestige he enjoys in the eyes of his patients lay a groundwork for psychotherapy. Indeed, all physicians, whether they know it or not, practice psychotherapy, since a psychotherapeutic influence is inevitable in the doctor-patient relationship [332]. How the physician may function therapeutically in his relationship with the patient has been detailed in a number of writings, including those of Whitehorn [333], Bartemeier [334], Ebaugh [335], Watts and Wilbur [336], Smith [337] and Rennie [338]. Perhaps the most useful books for physicians on therapy are those on general psychotherapeutic techniques by Levine [339], and interview psychotherapy by Law [340]. A very good account of the role the physician plays in mental health is included in the volume by Rennie and Woodward [341]. An excellent quarterly psychiatric bulletin [342] for physicians has been published by the University of Texas which covers the areas in medicine that merge with those of psychiatry. The book on "office psychiatry" by Moench [344] is recommended, as are the articles by Hulse [480].

Recognizing that readings, while helpful, are not in themselves sufficient to inculcate adequate skills in psychotherapy, a number of postgraduate courses for physicians have been organized that rely on the case method of teaching. Perhaps the most noteworthy experiment here is that of the "Minnesota Experiment" set up by the Commonwealth Fund [344] in which an attempt was made to introduce the most pertinent parts of basic psychiatric thinking into general medicine, and which included clinical practice under supervision. More recently, Ziskind [345] described the training program introduced at the Cedars of Lebanon Hospital, a general hospital in Los Angeles, in which volunteer practitioners examine and treat patients with psychogenic problems under supervision of a staff psychiatrist. Ziskind holds that the uncovering of psychogenic conflicts is within the sphere of the practitioner, although the latter is not qualified to do character reconstruction which, an objective of long-term therapy, is reserved for the psychiatrist.

This qualification is important since the great majority of physicians, with the training that has been described above, are unable, unless they are unusually gifted and intuitive individuals, and unless they have ample time in their practices for lengthy interviewing, to do more than to make a diagnosis, to motivate the patient to accept psychiatric treatment, and to do supportive and possibly some reeducative psychotherapy.

It has been said that the background of the physician and the kind of training to which he has been subjected may support traits that are detrimental to
good psychotherapy. For instance, he may possess a certain amount of arrogance
and a tendency toward authoritarianism that interfere with an empathic, non-
judgmental, non-punitive attitude. His background in pathology may cause him
to be more interested in the patient's illness, than in the patient himself as an
individual. He may have a tendency to overestimate the importance of organic
factors and to underestimate sociologic influences. These defects, if present, may
possibly be tempered where the physician gets psychiatric supervision.

If the physician expects to specialize in psychiatry, he will require an
elaborate training. What goes into the making of the psychiatrist varies with
the opportunities available to the physician who seeks to enter this specialty.
After his medical internship and residency, the physician usually associates himself with a mental institution or with the psychiatric division of a large general
hospital. To qualify for certification in psychiatry, three years of institutional
experience are required, as well as an additional two years of practice in the
psychiatric field. Having given evidence of varied experience in adult and
child psychiatry, he is examined in the areas of psychiatric and neurologic
diagnosis, neuroanatomy, neurophysiology, neuropathology, psychodynamics and
the various psychiatric therapies. If the examination is successful, the candidate
is awarded a certificate of specialization in psychotherapy which makes him a
Diplomate of the American Board of Psychiatry and Neurology.

As a general rule, skilled as he is in diagnosis, administration, the use
of shock and physical therapies, and the handling on a supportive level of the
severer forms of mental illness, epilepsy, mental deficiency, alcoholism and drug
addiction, the Diplomate is not trained to do intensive psychotherapy. Should
he, during or after his institutional training, have worked in a community outpatient clinic, he will have had the opportunity to see less malignant mental
illnesses, psychoneuroses, psychosomatic problems and personality disorders. He
will have had the opportunity to work in a team framework with social workers
and psychologists and to consult with correctional workers, educators, ministers
and other professionals. Doing psychotherapy under the intensive supervision
of a seasoned psychotherapist will, more than anything else, train him in
psychotherapeutic methods.

Many psychiatrists seek further training in the specialty of psychoanalysis.
This involves application to and acceptance by a psychoanalytic school. The content of this instruction consists of several years of didactic lectures and seminars
in dynamic psychiatry, clinical conferences and case discussions; a personal
psychoanalysis; and the handling of several psychoanalytic cases under supervision. Some psychiatrists attempt to learn the technique of psychoanalytic therapy
in a less formal way without matriculating, by taking open courses in psychoanalytic theory; by reading of the psychoanalytic literature, by entering into
personal psychoanalysis or psychoanalytic psychotherapy with a trained psychoanalyst, and by carrying one or more cases under supervision of an analyst. How
successful this less disciplined form of training will turn out to be is largely

dependent on the calibre of the psychiatrist. Understandably he is under a greater handicap than a psychiatrist who is enrolled in a regular analytic school and is exposed to a formal course of instruction.

THE CLINICAL PSYCHOLOGIST IN PSYCHOTHERAPY

Since World War II there has been a concerted movement toward psychotherapy on the part of clinical psychologists. Encouraged by their work as therapeutic adjuncts to psychiatrists in Army and veterans' clinical units, many psychologists have added psychotherapy to their traditional domains of testing, research, vocational guidance, remedial reading, speech correction, educational and marital counseling, and personnel selection. Psychologists have been functioning increasingly as therapists in schools, child care institutions, guidance centers, community clinics, courts and correctional agencies. Indeed, the Committee on Training in Clinical Psychology of the American Psychological Association has stated "that no clinical psychologist can be considered adequately trained unless he has sound training in psychotherapy" [346]. Harrower [347] furthermore contends that what makes a psychologist a "clinical psychologist" is his ability to take a responsible and unemotional stand on the subject of therapy.

The surge of interest of certain clinical psychologists in psychotherapy has resulted in the publication of a number of important books on psychologic therapy, perhaps foremost of which are those of Rogers [348,349] and Thorne [350]. Other contributions of the psychologist to mental health have been comprehensively reviewed by Rennie and Woodward [351].

To help the clinical psychologist gain an understanding of what is involved in psychotherapy, many graduate training programs of four years' duration have been evolved which lead to a doctoral degree and include instruction in general psychology, abnormal psychology, the dynamics of behavior, diagnostic techniques, research, guidance and therapy. The candidate is expected to work in a field center under supervision and to engage in interdisciplinary clinical seminars. A curriculum outlined by Jacobsen [352] includes, on an undergraduate level, courses in biology, zoology, general physiology, physics, chemistry and mathematics. Also considered necessary is knowledge of the basic materials in sociology, anthropology, economics, political science, statistics and social, experimental and physiologic psychology. On a graduate level, the first year of study contains courses in the current theories of personality structure and development, problems related to social adaptation, the theory of measurement, the design of experiment, learning theory, testing, team functioning and introductory social case work. During the second year, there are courses in advanced psychologic measurements and projective techniques, and some practical clinical experience in a psychiatric service, neurologic unit, school, vocational counseling division, or social agency for the purpose of gaining experience in the handling of reading disabilities, speech problems, vocational difficulties, and, ideally, in the fundamentals of psychotherapy. A year of internship under supervision is recommended during the third year of training. The fourth year is devoted to the preparation of the thesis and to advanced seminars in psychology, education, vocational guidance, sociology, anthropology, psychiatry and other medical disciplines. Cross-discipline seminars are indicated for an exchange of points of view between members working in different areas of study. After receiving his doctoral degree, the student is then considered capable of doing clinical work under supervision in a mental hospital, or outpatient clinic.

The completion of this course of study by no means qualifies the individual to do psychotherapy. Gifted clinical psychologists working under qualified supervision may, in a hospital, clinic or therapeutic agency, learn the intricacies of therapeutic technique. Apart from Carl Rogers' school at Chicago in nondirective therapy and Theodor Reik's "National Psychological Association for Psychoanalysis" in New York, which offers training in psychoanalysis, few other postgraduate training courses in therapy for clinical psychologists are existent. Some psychologists attempt to get training in dynamic therapy, by entering into a personal psychoanalysis and working under supervision of an analytically trained psychotherapist.

In the face of the tremendous demand that prevails among clinical psychologists for additional training, one may expect within the next few years an expansion of postgraduate training facilities. This possibility has aroused great consternation in medical circles. Alarm has especially been voiced at the development of psychotherapeutic training programs in universities. The absence of proper screening of candidates, the concentration on didactic instruction, and the minimal amount of competent, intensive supervision threaten to turn out unqualified and inadequately trained individuals, not instilled, due to lack of experience, with the judicious caution and conservatism essential in psychotherapeutic work. Such persons constitute a potential public health menace of which they themselves are completely unaware.

Psychologists reply by stating that it is essential to take a realistic view of the existing serious lack of psychiatric facilities and personnel. This lack accounts largely for the alarming activities of untrained and unqualified therapists in the field of psychotherapy. These individuals not only mulct millions of dollars annually from the emotionally ill, but also inflict irreparable damage upon those who, having no other recourse, turn to charlatans and to relatively unskilled practitioners in an effort to alleviate suffering. Until sufficient numbers of skilled psychotherapists are available we will always be plagued by the menace of charlatanry in the area of mental health. It is unrealistic to assume that the medical profession can ever supply from its ranks sufficient numbers of people to satisfy the ever-expanding demand for mental hygiene services.

While physicians agree that not enough trained medical psychotherapists are available to cope with the current need, the oft prescribed remedy of supplementing the supply of therapists from non-medical sources is believed to be ill-advised. Apart from the fact that it is not possible, at the present stage of our knowledge, to mass produce therapists, it has been indicated by Binger [353] that an increase in the number of therapists, even to hundreds of thousands could not meet the current demand for therapeutic services. The more services that were rendered, the more aware individuals would be of the existence of such services, with consequent greater demands for services.

Opposition to non-medical psychotherapy goes back at least to 1916 according to Galdston [354]. At that time the New York Psychiatric Society recommended "that the sick, whether in mind or body, should be cared for only by those with medical training who are authorized by the state to assume responsibility for diagnoses and treatment." It furthermore disapproved "of the application of psychology to responsible clinical work, except when made by or under the direct supervision of physicians qualified to deal with abnormal mental conditions." Galdston concludes that while "the clinical psychologist has a valuable function in and significant contribution to make to the practice of medicine" the psychologist should confine himself exclusively to the treatment of the normal individual or serve in an ancillary capacity to the medical psychotherapist.

More or less, there has been an acceptance of the principle that the psychiatrist transfer some of his functions to ancillary workers within a supervised medical setting [355]. Supervision of the non-medical worker with the sharing of responsibilities is said to dispel anxiety in the worker and to facilitate better psychotherapy [356]. This principle is contested on the medical side by some who absolutely oppose any kind of psychotherapy by non-medical persons irrespective of supervision. It is contested also by certain psychologists who challenge the right of the medical profession to impose on them any kind of restrictions in therapeutic work.

An attempt has been made by some to reconcile the training differences of psychologists and physicians. Thus Kubie [357], acknowledging the shortage of existing clinical services and of training facilities for psychiatrists, and commenting on the fact that it requires from ten to twelve years to train one to be a mature psychiatrist and psychotherapist, advocates the setting up of a paramedical discipline of medical psychology with a condensed, concentrated training program of five to six years to be conducted in medical schools and teaching hospitals. Among the courses there would be included basic training in anatomy, clinical physiology and clinical pathology of the normal and abnormal organic processes. Certain aspects of medical education would be omitted, such as most gross and microscopic pathology, clinical pathology, laboratory techniques and bacteriology. Clinical clerkship would involve history taking, nursing care of patients and administration of psychologic test batteries. Personal psychoanalysis could begin at any time after work on organic wards is started. Such a program would lead first to an understanding of how organic factors and ailments influence the person psychologically; second, to a special sense of responsibility toward the patient as a sick individual; third, to an objectivity in one's clinical evaluations; and fourth, to self-criticism. With two or three years of supervised psychotherapy, candidates should become fairly seasoned therapists.

Miller [358] foresees a future blending of medical and psychologic curricula in an extensive kind of training. Undergraduate instruction leading to a bachelor's degree would consist of two years of liberal arts college, one year of advanced clinical psychology, sociology and cultural anthropology, and one year of preclinical medical subjects comparable to the first year of medical school. After this, the candidate would enter the second and third years of medical school, and then do medical and psychiatric clinical work for a year at a general hospital, mental hygiene clinic or neuropsychiatric hospital. The granting of an M.D. degree in the psychologic sciences would be followed by one year of a rotating psychologic-psychiatric internship, which would include experience in psychologic diagnostic methods and the performance of different psychiatric duties. After this, there would be one year of independent research leading to a dissertation. Seminars and a personal psychoanalysis would also be included. Successful completion of these requirements would result in an award of a doctoral degree in clinical psychology. From this time on the candidate would work for his boards in psychiatry, clinical psychology, or both.

Gardner [359] stresses the need for contact with seriously ill mental patients as part of the training program for psychologists, and he indicates that unless there is a prolonged exposure to the problems of such sick patients, the candidate is handicapped in developing a proper "clinical attitude." For this reason, at least one year of work in a state hospital in close contact with mental patients is recommended as a minimum for all non-medical therapists, including psychologists.

One may suspect that some of the devised plans for the training of psychologists in therapy are motivated by desires to temper the current medical opposition to non-medical psychotherapy. This opposition is organized around one or more of the following arguments:

1. Psychotherapy is part of the practice of medicine. In doing independent psychotherapy, the psychologist is assuming an unauthorized medical responsibility.

2. Only a medical background prepares the professional for an understanding of the human mind, in both its normal and pathologic reactions. Emotional illness, being an organismic disturbance, requires a thorough grounding in the biologic sciences which non-medical people do not receive.

3. Only a medical background enables the professional to make a proper diagnosis. A non-medical person is incapable of differentiating organic from psychologic disease. Because symptoms of emotional illness may mask organic and especially neurologic conditions, non-medical people may not recognize an early treatable condition until after it has become irremediable. Such instances have been reported in the literature [360,361].

4. Only medically trained psychiatrists have had sufficient experience with severe mental disorders to be able to deal with psychotic-like reactions and to differentiate these from milder disorders.

5. The physician, by virtue of the unique position of prestige he traditionally enjoys in the mind of the patient operates in the most effective medium. The psychologist is handicapped in this respect.

6. A strong sense of therapeutic responsibility for the patient is inculcated in the physician as part of his training. It is not so often possessed by the psychologist.

7. Society acknowledges that therapy belongs to the medical profession, and it sanctions the licensing of the latter. In obtaining a license, the medical therapist is subjected to a screening process and to measures of control to which the psychologist is at present immune.

8. Non-medical persons offer the medical profession unfair competition usually operating on the basis of lower fees.

A number of prominent psychologists agree with some of these contentions. For instance, published writings recognize certain limitations in the background and training of the clinical psychologist. Thus, Harrower [362] states that there is nothing in the regular Ph.D. course in academic psychology per se which remotely equips the individual for therapeutic work. To do therapy, he must, among other things, have been grounded in theory and experimental techniques, have exposed himself to dynamic psychiatry, have immersed himself in some kind of medical atmosphere, and have had a personal psychoanalysis. Young [363] contends that the absence of blanket approval for the practice by psychologists of psychotherapy is not only understandable, but more or less desirable for the development of clinical psychology, placing a healthy check on the turning out of inadequately trained persons. Miller [364] lists the following lacks in the training of the clinical psychologist: (1) the creation of a feeling of responsibility for human beings that is in medicine considered a parcel of the patient-physician relationship, (2) an understanding of what people are like in a clinical situation, (3) a recognition of one's own failings and limitations, (4) an understanding of the complexity of clinical problems, (5) cognizance of the utility of empirical methods which cannot at present be scientifically validated, and (6) a realization that research and the clinical situation can be compatible. It has been pointed out by psychologists sophisticated in therapeutic procedures that among the problems in the psychologist that are destructive to his doing psychotherapy is a tendency to a detached, rigid, mechanical approach to patients, nurtured perhaps by his training in research. Psychologists who have been reared in the techniques of non-directive therapy have also been criticized for their fear of allowing patients to become dependent on them. This produces detachment and acts to the detriment of the therapeutic relationship.

On the other hand, many psychologists resent violently the attitudes and allegations of the medical profession. To the arguments presented by psychiatrists, they make counter-claims that their background in learning theory, in counseling, in research, and in educational, vocational, and rehabilitative procedures equips them better to do psychotherapy than the physician. Having had access to the lush field of therapy, many psychologists resist continuing in a role of a technician restricted to psychometrics. They insist that psychotherapy is not a form of medical practice, but rather an art in the management of interpersonal relationships. Lindner [365] has even contended that the orientation required by the medical sciences is totally unsuitable to the problems faced by the psychotherapist. He alleges that emotional illness is not a disease which falls in the province of medicine. A medical education, therefore, in no way trains the individual to do psychotherapy better than a psychologic education. Clinical psychology, furthermore, can diagnose the presence of incipient organic disease as well as can clinical medicine.

To buttress their claims to psychotherapy, psychologists point out that some of the most significant contributions to psychotherapy have been made by non-medical people; for instance, Anna Freud in the field of child psychoanalysis, Erich Fromm in character analysis, Ernst Kris and Theodor Reik in formal psychoanalysis, Otto Rank in modified psychoanalytic therapy, S. R. Slavson in group therapy, Robert Lindner in hypnoanalysis, and Carl Rogers in non-directive therapy. Indeed, some of the best psychotherapists are said to be non-medical people. The latter are possessed of the highest integrity and are said to function with a keen sense of responsibility for their patients.

The upshot of these negative and positive comments, claims and counterclaims is that opinion is sharply divided among medical and psychologic camps as to the role the psychologist may best serve in psychotherapy. There are those responsible medical and non-medical authorities who are unalterably opposed to the practice of psychotherapy by non-medical persons under any conditions. Others believe that such practice may be allowed in organized clinics or hospitals under circumstances of adequate psychiatric supervision. Still others do not object to the private practice of well-trained non-medical persons provided that they operate in close consultation with physicians and psychiatrists. Some non-medical people accept psychiatry as the parent body and recognize that treatment should be carried out under competent medical auspices. However, they do so with a feeling that this is a temporary expedient which will change as soon as enough trained psychologist-psychotherapist teachers are available to start training programs and to undertake supervision independent of medicine.

According to the Committee on Clinical Psychology of the Group for the Advancement of Psychiatry [366], the encouragement of individual psychotherapy by clinical psychologists is consistent with accepted medical and psychiatric practice. However, the Committee is opposed to the independent private practice of psychotherapy by clinical psychologists. Moreover it feels that "psychotherapy done by clinical psychologists should be carried out in a setting where adequate psychiatric safeguards are provided." Absence of such safeguards may lead to diagnostic errors, blundering in the detection in their early stages of serious psychiatric conditions, and failure to recognize a physical disorder that causes the maladjustment. The psychiatrist with whom the psychologist works should assume professional and legal responsibility, and can handle emergencies when they arise. Association of clinical psychologists with physicians who are not psychiatrists is not recommended since sufficient psychiatric safeguards would not be provided.

This principle of psychiatric supervision for non-medical therapies is one which has more or less been accepted by representative organizations. It has, however, been subjected to varied interpretations. In 1949 the following resolution was adopted by the American Psychological Association:

We are opposed to the practice of psychotherapy (not to include remedial teaching, vocational and educational counseling) by clinical psychologists that does not meet conditions of genuine collaboration with physicians most qualified to deal with the border-line problems which occur (e.g., different diagnosis, intercurrent organic diseases, psychosomatic problems, etc.). [367]

In 1951 the American Psychiatric Association Council approved the report of the Committee on Clinical Psychology as endorsed by the Coordinating Committee on Professional Standards to the effect that psychotherapy "should be done in a setting where adequate psychiatric safeguards are provided," that the supervising psychiatrist is responsible for determining the level of competence of his psychotherapeutic assistants and for providing adequate supervision "including continuous supervision of psychotherapy and the securing of adequate medical examinations and care" [368].

The matter of certification and licensure of clinical psychologists has recently come into prominence. The States of Connecticut, Kentucky, Virginia and Minnesota have enacted laws providing for such certification, while Georgia has passed a licensing bill for psychologists. "Certification" means that an individual is qualified by virtue of possession of adequate requirements to use the title of "Psychologist," "Certified Psychologist" or other specified appelations. Licensure means that the individual is permitted by law to practice as a qualified psychologist.

A semiofficial medical viewpoint on the subject of certification and licensure of clinical psychologists is found in the article by Gerty, Holloway and Mackay, outlining the report made by a committee appointed by the Section on Nervous and Mental Diseases of the American Medical Association [369]. The report contends that even though psychologists and social workers in medically controlled agencies are often entrusted with the conducting of psychotherapy under medical psychiatric supervision, unrestricted licensure for private practice is a violation of fundamental medical principles irrespective of how skilled the non-medical individual may be in the technique of psychotherapy. A psychologic internship in a medical institution is not considered the equivalent of basic medical education. Attempts to differentiate between medical and non-medical types of maladjustment are arbitrary and unsatisfactory. Diagnosis and treatment recommendations are the sole function of a medical person with specialized psychiatric training. This does not mean that well-trained non-medical persons are not capable of doing good psychotherapy; indeed, qualified individuals should be welcome "if they have had adequate preparation for their special field of practice." However, it is neither safe nor morally possible for the psychiatrist to give up assuming responsibility for the treatment of persons with psychiatric disorders. The report concludes with the statement that certification of clinical psychologists should be adopted in contrast to licensure which is not endorsed at this time. Psychologists practicing psychotherapy privately should do so under psychiatric supervision. Finally, it is recommended that the medical practice acts of all states include "the categories of mental therapy for which techniques have been developed within the field of psychiatry."

While there is by no means uniformity of opinion, the general feeling of psychiatrists concerning the role of psychologists in psychotherapy may be stated as follows:

1. The practice of psychotherapy entails prolonged specialized training and supervised clinical experience. With adequate postgraduate training, qualified clinical psychologists are capable of handling psychologic problems on a therapeutic level.

2. Because psychologic disorders may be a reflection of underlying medical and neurologic problems, psychotherapy must be conducted in some sort of a medical framework. All patients entering any kind of a treatment program conducted by a non-medical person should be thoroughly checked by a physician to ascertain the presence of physical illness and neurologic disease. In the course of therapy, a periodic medical check-up is essential. All patients manifesting symptoms of psychoneuroses, borderline or actual psychoses, severe character disorders, severe behavior disorders, severe anxiety, physical complaints of any type, moderate or severe depression, alcoholism, or addiction to any drug, should furthermore be under observation of a well-trained psychiatrist who is responsible for the treatment program.

3. Assuming that safeguards are maintained in regard to the medical and psychiatric status of the patient, a non-medical person who has been trained to do psychotherapy and has had sufficient supervised clinical experience may be able to do supportive and reeducative psychotherapy under such supervision of the psychotherapeutic process as his level of training demands. Where he has had a personal psychoanalysis and has treated patients analytically under competent analytic supervision, the non-medical person may be able to do reconstructive therapy under such further analytic supervision as he may require.

4. No matter how thoroughly trained a non-medical person may be in the technique of psychotherapy, his educational and experiential background does not qualify him to make diagnoses or to assay the extent of organic involvement in any patient. Psychologic diagnostic testing is no substitute for clinical diagnosis; these complement rather than substitute for each other.

It will be apparent from the diverse arguments and opinions that have been presented that no easy solution of the suspicions and hostilities between medical and psychologic professionals is in sight. Yet, if psychotherapy is ever to develop into a scientific discipline, and if we are ever to bring therapeutic facilities within the bounds of community needs, it is mandatory that a solution be found to the differences that exist between physicians and psychologists in the field of mental health. Reciprocal respect and tolerance are essential before we can even begin to approach the problem constructively.

THE SOCIAL WORKER IN PSYCHOTHERAPY

Originally, the activities of the social worker were concerned with individualizing the needs of the client and aiding him in utilizing those social services best suited to meet his needs. These limited goals were expanded in later years, and were replaced by objectives of dealing with problems of a social nature which produced personality maladjustment, and with problems of personality adjustment which were responsible for social malfunctioning. The focus was the family. Caseworkers, especially in medical social service departments, and family and child agencies, attempted not only to help their clients utilize social services more effectively, but also to achieve personal and social rehabilitation.

Where the caseworker functioned in a psychiatric hospital, or child or adult psychiatric clinic, the interests of the patient demanded that the caseworker operate in a team relationship with the psychiatrist and clinical psychologist in a collaborative effort toward expediting the patient's recovery. The background of the caseworker made him the team member of choice to interpret the function of the clinic to the referral source, patient and his family; to refer the patient to other more suitable resources if necessary; to coordinate the work of the clinic with other community agencies; and to handle the clinic's relations with the community. Trained in understanding the dynamics of family relationships, the caseworker was chosen as the most logical team member for the intake process. He contributed the orientation as well as the preparation of the patient for therapy, and he made a systematic inquiry into the patient's problems including social, environmental and familial factors which were related to the patient's current disturbance. This data was communicated at the "intake team conference" in planning the treatment program.

These traditional functions of the caseworker have continued throughout the years, but, as the clinic case loads have increased, and as agencies devoted to social services have extended their functions to include the helping of the client with his emotional problems, the caseworker has inevitably been drawn into the psychotherapeutic treatment program itself. In child guidance clinics, for instance, the social worker was designated to handle the child's family on a casework level, while the psychiatrist worked psychotherapeutically with the child. However, the emotional ailments of family members often required psychotherapy, and psychiatric consultants who were called in to help the caseworker observed that no matter how much the caseworker attempted to avoid doing psychotherapy, or how painstakingly he tried to restrict his activity to casework, he often could not help being drawn into a psychotherapeutic relationship.

In addition to contributing to the psychiatrist's diagnostic and treatment efforts by mediating social factors connected with the patient's illness, before, during or after the psychiatric treatment, or by helping the patient and his family to make maximum use of the psychiatrist's services, the caseworker has increasingly, in recent years, been called on to do psychotherapy. Indeed, therapy has gradually become accepted as a function of the caseworker at clinics [370–[373] and there has been some recognition of this new role by the social work profession itself [374,375].

While acceding to the practical necessity for the extension of the caseworker's function in clinics, psychiatrists have insisted that a medical person must assume sole responsibility for the diagnostic, medical and legal aspects of the case. This principle of psychiatric supervision, however, has not been possible in some instances of psychiatric understaffing. Here the psychiatric caseworker carries the treatment responsibility under supervision of a senior caseworker and in consultation with the psychiatrist.

The preclinical training of psychiatric social workers is being designed more and more to include a dynamic understanding of personality in order to enable the worker to operate more effectively in his work with patients [376,377]. In addition to the usual courses in community organization and planning, sociologic processes, anthropology, abnormal and social psychology, statistics, economics, government, medical information, social casework, social research, public welfare, social insurance, and economic and social legislation, the average training of the social worker includes courses in psychosocial development, psychopathology, psychodynamics and principles of clinical psychiatry. Additionally, there is supervised field work in a family agency and psychiatric clinic (child guidance or adult). An understanding of the principles of interviewing, of the confidential nature of the professional relationship, and of the dynamics of therapy are objectives of this supervised work.

In evaluating the aptitudes of caseworkers in therapy, psychiatrists who have worked closely with them observe that some problems are inspired by the caseworker's background and training. For instance, there is a tendency toward overprotectiveness of the patient, toward too great interference in existing environmental difficulties, and toward a minimization of inner psychopathologic elements with overemphasis on external stresses. Ackerman [378] asserts that in his experience he has found caseworkers to be both fearful and fascinated by unconscious phenomena, as well as anxious about going "too deep" with their patients. They are also apt to feel menaced by any psychotic phenomena that emerge in the treatment process.

Ackerman emphasizes, however, that caseworkers with proper professional equipment have an important role to play as psychotherapists within the framework of a clinical team. He recommends that a selection of cases to be treated by caseworkers include personality disturbances "in which the etiology and manifestations are predominantly social." Where the pathology is chiefly biologic, he recommends treatment by physicians. The latter would manage psychoses, borderline psychoses, psychosomatic disorders and, possibly, severe psychoneuroses, especially where ego integration is frail. Ackermann also believes that adequately trained caseworkers may practice psychotherapy privately within a clinical team framework. The team shares responsibility for comprehensive diagnostic study and planning of treatment. The dynamics of therapy are supervised and periodically checked in team conferences. Systematic psychiatric supervision of therapy should, he states, be provided.

A number of psychiatric caseworkers, working in child guidance centers and adult psychiatric clinics, and having gained considerable supervised psychotherapeutic experience, have set themselves up in private practice as child and adult psychotherapists. Where the training has been primarily psychoanalytic, they have designated themselves as "lay psychoanalysts." Some caseworkers have even sought to give up their identity with the social work field on the basis that they have established themselves in a new professional role. The reactions of the medical profession to this development have been identical with reactions to psychologists operating in private practice, although the precipitated feelings have not been quite so intense, perhaps because only a relatively small number of caseworkers have been involved.

OTHER PROFESSIONALS IN PSYCHOTHERAPY

As has been previously indicated, a number of professionals other than physicians, clinical psychologists and social workers come into contact with emotionally disturbed persons. Chief among these are nurses, ministers and teachers. Where they possess the proper training and skill, such professionals are in a strategic position to detect incipient neuroses or psychoses, to educate individuals in the principles of mental health and the meaning of emotional disturbance, and to refer those in need of psychiatric services to available resources. The kind of therapeutic help these professionals are capable of rendering is generally of a supportive nature contingent on the warm relationship that is established, the opportunities for verbalization and emotional catharsis that are offered, and the employment of such measures as reassurance and persuasion. In a few instances, a gifted professional who has received extensive postgraduate training may be able to do a limited type of reeducative therapy. An enlightened and trained professional may thus be capable of influencing personality forces at a time when the neurosis is relatively reversible and before obdurate accretions of neurotic defense have accumulated.

The entry of professionals of varied disciplines into the psychotherapeutic field is, nevertheless, not without its dangers, for there are always aggressive and overenthusiastic participants who do not recognize or accept their limitations of function, and the need for close lines of communication with psychiatrists. Plunging recklessly into the psyche of the patient, they may harm the patient as well as endanger their own professional stature.

1. The Nurse in Psychotherapy

Whether she be associated with a psychiatric institution, a school, an industrial organization or a public health unit, the nurse enters into intimate relationships with sick people and thus has unusual opportunities to practice principles of mental hygiene. This fact has been increasingly emphasized by those who have had the opportunity of utilizing nursing services. Lemkau [379,380] contends that the public health nurse can play a most significant role in early emotional illness, since she sees people in their homes interacting with their families and manifesting subclinical symptoms of neurosis. The nurse easily establishes rapport with the family and is readily taken into the confidence of the various members. By careful listening, she may permit the emotionally distraught individual to ventilate his feelings; she may also reassure, impart knowledge and educate. Her contact with mothers at well-baby clinics, and with prospective mothers at prenatal clinics, enables her to handle misconceptions, anxieties and other potential founts of neurosis. The psychiatric nurse is also equipped to enter into a patient's psychiatric therapy as a member of the therapeutic team [381–383]. In insulin shock therapy [384,385], electroshock therapy [386] and brain surgery [387,388] her role can be most constructive to the total treatment effort.

Cameron [389] has indicated ways that the nurse serving in a mental institution may act as a psychotherapeutic adjunct to the psychiatrist. Indoctrination in psychiatry and psychotherapy enables the nurse to assume some therapeutic responsibility. On the wards, for instance, she may organize patients into a group and hold group discussions on a variety of impersonal and personal topics. These discussion groups, in goal and mode of operation, parallel therapeutic groups. Cameron also describes the possibility of employing the nurse in a psychotherapeutic unit of three, consisting of patient, nurse and psychiatrist. Here the nurse functions as a passive counselor, discussing and clarifying with the patient material that has been brought out by the psychiatrist. The nurse may also "role-play" with the patient, either acting-out a role accorded her by the patient, or gradually shifting her role, so that the patterns of behavior the therapist is seeking to change in the patient will be less and less satisfying to the patient. It is obvious that with the expansion of the nurse's part in psychotherapy, a revision of undergraduate nursing instruction will be necessary, including more concentrated teaching of the dynamics of human behavior, of group relationships, and of the principles of psychotherapy.

Rennie and Woodward [390] emphasize that the nurse should be able to manage in an intelligent way the more common psychiatric and emotional problems evidenced by the general medical patient. They state, however, that in expanding the nurse's role in therapy, a reorientation is needed in our concepts of the nurse's function. Required, furthermore, are better psychiatric educational opportunities for nurses. Bennett and Eaton [391] also contend that basic instruction for nurses in psychotherapy is indicated inasmuch as all nurses who work on psychiatric wards, whether this is acknowledged or not, do psychotherapy of one kind or another. Participation by the nurse in group psychotherapy is also endorsed by these authors.

2. The Minister in Psychotherapy

Traditionally the minister has served as a resource to which the individual may turn whenever he is encountering difficult problems in living. The solace the sufferer receives from such consultation may be great, due in part to the unique prestige the minister occupies in the mind of the average individual. Worship and prayer have served the minister as spiritual aids in this helping objective.

In recent years, it has been recognized by clergymen of all denominations that while religion often serves as a source of strength for people who are confronted with situations of crisis, it may require supplementation, even in the devout, in the face of anxiety and other manifestations of neurosis [392–395]. Accordingly, many ministers have become interested in getting a scientific understanding of the nature of human conflict, and of the ways of managing a relationship so as to increase their effectiveness in dealing with people in trouble. That no real disparity need exist between psychiatric knowledge and religious belief is often pointed out. It is said that the goals of psychiatry and of religion are similar, both striving to help people to achieve satisfactory and meaningful lives [396–398].

Recognition that many of the problems brought to the minister's attention are nurtured by emotional illness has led to the institution, in the training of divinity students, of psychiatric orientation courses as well as of supervised clinical experience in hospitals and agencies [399,400]. In 1923, clinical training for ministers in hospitals and social casework agencies was started, and has been since carried on by the Council for the Clinical Training of Theological Students in New York and the Institute of Pastoral Care, Massachusetts General Hospital in Boston [401]. Courses in mental health have been added to the curricula of many theologic schools.

Some of the training programs offer the student-clergyman opportunities for understanding problems in interpersonal relationships, the forces that enter into personality formation, the difficulties people encounter in adjustment, and the manifold reactions to stress. The student is taught methods of working with people in trouble, and the ways he can cooperate with other workers, such as physicians, psychiatrists, nurses, social workers and psychologists, toward helping the emotionally disturbed individual. Awareness of problems in counseling, of the limitations of the minister in counseling, of resources to which persons may be referred, and of ways of handling the more common types of counseling situations are among the objectives in training.

The term "pastoral counseling" has been given to the new therapeutic role the minister serves with his parishioners, and a few books [402,403] have appeared detailing principles and techniques. Most of the methods taught are of a supportive nature, although the interviewing process, as described in the books and articles on pastoral counseling, draws a good deal from Carl Rogers' nondirective therapy and aims for goals of personality modification [402–405]. With rare exceptions, however, ministers are not equipped to enter into any kind of therapeutic program, and should refer individuals in need of treatment.

The problems brought to the attention of the minister are legion, and offer him an opportunity to help through proper referral. Rennie and Woodward [406] list the following problems as those commonly encountered by the minister: (1) marital problems, (2) parent-child problems and behavior difficulties in children, (3) emotional instabilities, especially in young adults, and middle-aged men and women, (4) disturbing love affairs, (5) conflicts in adolescence, (6) desire for information and help on problems involving education, social health and mental hygiene.

The minister is thus in the strategic position to practice preventive mental health when such problems are brought to his attention.

3. The Teacher in Psychotherapy

One of the fundamental aims of education is to prepare the individual for the business of life and to equip him to play a role as a functioning unit of society. By and large, educational procedures have been successful in broadening intellectual horizons, but have not been so successful in expanding the individual's capacities for productive human relationships. The concept that a healthy life adaptation is dependent upon a healthy personality evolved through a healthy millieu during early years, has given rise to a movement in education whereby the school assumes a responsibility in providing for the student experiences that may reinforce constructive factors in the home and modify destructive factors.

The most significant aspects of school experience toward mental health are, as Rennie and Woodward [407] have pointed out, determined by the personality of the teacher, his skill in managing human relationships, and his understanding of children; by the techniques of instruction; and by the content of the curriculum. Where the teacher has personal emotional difficulties or is victimized by current stresses related to status or economic insecurity, these cannot help but influence adversely the stability of the teacher's relationships with pupils. While little may be done, other than perhaps personal psychotherapy, to alter severe emotional problems in the teacher, the difficulties contingent on status and economic factors may be remedied by better school conditions. The techniques of teaching and the content of the curriculum may be changed in line with mental health needs by setting tasks and goals that are comprehensible and challenging to the child, by helping him to clarify perplexing problems and feelings that are parcels of everyday living, and by inculcating in him some understanding of the complexities of human relationships.

The skill of the teacher in the handling of human relationships may be enhanced where the teacher has a genuine interest in teaching and in children, and is not burdened by too severe neurotic problems. Furthermore, it is essential that the teacher acquire a greater understanding of the child and his needs in undergraduate or postgraduate mental hygiene instruction. Courses for teachers on human development, psychopathology and psychodynamics, principles of counseling and interviewing, and group dynamics, are important here. In a few instances, group therapy has been instituted for teachers headed by a trained group worker, in order to bring the teacher to an awareness of undercurrent attitudes toward children that may be inimical to the establishing of good relationships with them. Additional training of the teacher is considered necessary by all authorities who advocate adding mental health goals to the educational design [408–416].

In the main, this new mental health dimension in education has been introduced on an experimental basis. In nursery schools [417–419] public schools [420–424], and colleges [425–428] programs are operative which incorporate in their content and method principles of mental health calculated to meet the emotional needs of the student and to add to his social development. A number of conclusions have already evolved from these experiments which are gradually being incorporated into school programs [429].

The recognition that emotional disturbances may sabotage learning and school adjustment has created a movement in some schools toward the diagnosis of emotional illness through observation of the child's behavior, attitudes and performance. The average teacher is usually able to discern the more gross symptoms of emotional disorder in such manifestations as hyperactivity, under-activity, emotional outbursts, undue restlessness, irritability, temper tantrums, violent rages, tremors, tics, nail-biting, apprehensiveness, pervasive phobias, compulsive acts and rituals, speech disorders, reading disabilities and writing difficulties. With special training, the teacher may be able to recognize the less obvious signs of neurosis.

Where the child exhibits patterns of emotional illness, and where these patterns have become so structuralized that they cannot be modified through a better school environment, therapy of some kind will be required. In a few instances, a conscious effort has been made by the teacher to apply therapy to students who have been blocked in learning, or who manifest conduct disorders and other problems in school adjustment. Thus Hans Zulliger [430] utilized psychoanalytic formulations in treating conduct disorders. Axline [431] believes that a teacher trained in non-directive therapy may be able to reflect back to the child feelings and attitudes the latter is attempting to express, and in this way inculcate in the child insights into his behavior. She also believes that non-directive methods may be applied to teacher-administrator relationships.

Most authorities, however, contend that the role the teacher can play in therapy is extremely limited. Baron [432] has pointed out that insurmountable difficulties present themselves to the functioning in a dual teacher-therapist capacity in the average class. While the pupil may establish a relationship with an understanding teacher which is therapeutic for the child, the teacher is usually unable to enter into a systematic therapeutic program. Nor does the teacher, even with special training, possess skills that would make more than a supportive approach possible. Therapy of emotionally disturbed children necessitates the services of specialists more highly skilled than is the teacher in diagnostic and treatment procedures.

Consequently, where a child requires therapy, it is recommended that he be referred to the guidance department of the school, to the school psychologist, or to a consulting clinic outside of the school setting. Guidance and counseling services at schools are most efficient where a professionally trained counselor is available in the school, and where there exists an organized pupil-personnel program. The latter should ideally offer such services as educational counseling, vocational guidance, and work placement, as well as health, social and psychologic services. The counselor may supervise the guidance activities of those teachers who are capable of functioning in guidance with students. The most effective way of dealing with the emotional problems of students within the school framework is generally felt to be through a clinical team approach of psychiatrist, social worker and clinical psychologist.

As parents, school administrators and governmental authorities become more enlightened and convinced of the advantages of a mental health approach in education, we may expect expansion of school guidance programs, an increase of diagnostic clinical teams within schools, and more clinics outside of schools which can carry on whatever extensive therapeutic work is required. In the course of this expansion, the teacher's preventive and therapeutic roles will undoubtedly become more clearly defined.

THE CONCEPT OF TEAM FUNCTIONING

In psychiatric clinics, the traditional Mental Hygiene Team, consisting of psychiatrist, clinical psychologist and psychiatric caseworker, is considered the preferred therapeutic framework. In this, the professional responsibility of each team member is clearly defined, and there is provided a basis for mutual interaction and the pooling of skills. The team is regarded as a group of specialists or consultants, each playing a specialized role as well as having some sort of therapeutic function. In addition to the three professions mentioned, other professionals are sometimes employed, according to the specific needs of the clinic and the kinds of case material handled. Thus teachers may be utilized for reading and writing disabilities, speech therapists for stuttering, and rehabilitation workers for special losses of function. The various specialized operations of team members in a community psychiatric clinic are delineated in Chart III.

The background training of the psychiatrist, and his affiliation with the discipline of medicine, puts him in the best position for the assumption of responsibility for the total treatment of the patient. It is generally accepted, nevertheless, that the psychiatrist may utilize ancillary workers, usually clinical psychologists and psychiatric caseworkers, while retaining medical responsibility. The value of the contribution of the psychiatrist, while accepted in principle, does not always lead to his employment. Some agencies, not having a psychiatrist as a regular staff member, merely utilize the services of a psychiatrist for consultative purposes. This is an unfortunate deficiency, since non-medical professionals are not equipped to detect or to evaluate signs of early physical illness, which, if overlooked, may lead to dangerous consequences. Moreover, the significance of organic signs may be misinterpreted by non-physicians.

In some psychiatric clinics, a routine social history is taken by the social worker. The social worker, during this process, observes the motivations of the patient for therapy, not in a deep dynamic sense, but in terms of what the patient says on a surface level. This enables the worker to evaluate why the patient comes for help and what he expects from the clinic. The very process of giving information in the social history enables the patient to relieve himself of certain immediate anxieties. In discerning the motivations of the patient and the misconceptions he may have, the worker has a good opportunity to explain to the patient how treatment can help in his specific problem.

The particular aspect of the case history stressed by the social worker is the patient's social situation, especially the interpersonal relationships within the

Chart III. FUNCTIONS OF VARIOUS TEAM MEMBERS IN A COMMUNITY PSYCHIATRIC CLINIC

PSYCHIATRIST

1. Establishing a psychologic or psychiatric diagnosis.

2. Physical examination.

3. Neurologic examination.

4. Prescription of medications.

5. Administration of narcosynthesis, hypnosis, conditioned reflex therapy, insulin, and electric shock treatments where necessary.

6. Arranging for commitment and hospitalization when necessary.

7. Handling routine physical and neurologic check-ups on patients with physical and psychosomatic problems.

8. Handling of psychiatric emergencies, such as severe depression, suicidal tendencies, excitement, psychotic manifestations, etc.

CASEWORKER

1. Intake interviewing (clarification of services to prospective patients and determining if services are consonant with the needs of the patient).

2. Preparation of patients for psychotherapy, dealing with resistances to treatment and establishing the proper motivation for treatment.

3. Exclusive handling of, or acting as a consultant for problems in patients relating to finance, health, employment, recreation, housing, exercise, companionship, and special training. Acquainting patients with, and aiding them to utilize most effectively, available community resources.

4. Acting as a casework consultant to other team members where environmental manipulation in their patients is essential in addition to psychotherapy.

5. Acting as a liaison between the patient and his family, employer, teacher, etc. when it is essential to interpret patient's illness to them, to give them reassurance, or to enlist their interest and cooperation.

6. Handling of parents, mate or children of patients who are being treated by team members and who require counseling or psychotherapy as an aid to the treatment of the patient.

7. Handling of children with primary behavior disorders.

8. Organizing and handling administrative details of educational projects of team. Interpreting the work of the clinic to the community; securing cooperation of the community in the work of the clinic. Acting as a liaison between the clinic and community organizations which are implementing community programs related to health, welfare and social security.

PSYCHOLOGIST

1. Diagnostic testing: intelligence, educational achievement, vocational, projective personality tests.

2. Exclusive handling of, or acting as consultant for:

   a. Problems of school adjustment, maladjustment and placement.

   b. Corrective work in educational field; therapy of reading or other educational disabilities.

   c. Career planning, vocational guidance.

   d. Rehabilitative work for physical and sensory defects particularly in educational and vocational areas.

   e. Speech disturbances.

3. Organizing and handling administrative details of research projects of team.

family, and disturbing aspects in the home. In the event the patient decides to accept treatment, the social worker will be able to utilize this information in helping to relieve environmental pressures provided the therapist decides that the adjunctive services of a social worker are required.

Another thing the social worker does in a clinic set-up is to help prepare the patient for psychotherapy, where, for various reasons, the patient is not yet ready to enter into a treatment process. In instances where the patient has already started therapy, but does not have adequate motivation, the therapist sometimes sends the patient back to the social worker for further preparation. The procedure the social worker employs is, more or less, on a conversational level, operating in a friendly supportive way with the idea of further clarifying the situation, and perhaps helping the patient to see what it is he actually wants from the clinic. Another basis for referral of the case to the social worker is where the therapist believes that all that can be done for the patient is a supportive kind of therapy. Here there is a differentiation of psychotherapeutic function, the social worker doing supportive therapy where needed, and the psychiatrist doing deeper insight therapy.

In carrying out supportive therapy, the social worker may not insist on regular appointments, but rather will see the patient at any time he can come. If personal visits are not made, a relationship may be attempted either by telephone or by letter. Contacts of this type may eventually develop in the patient a desire for a real therapeutic experience. If the social worker is not equipped to carry the patient in therapy, and the latter requires further help, the social worker may send the patient back to the psychiatrist.

In clinics where no intensive supervision is provided for the psychiatrist, the latter may refer the patient to the social worker should blocks develop in therapy. The social worker here attempts to evaluate with the patient what has been going on, with the object of making a reassignment of the case to another therapist should this be necessary. If the patient stops treatments with the psychiatrist, the social worker may ask the patient to come in and then begin to work out with him the problems that have developed between the patient and the psychiatrist. The psychiatrist may also refer to the social worker patients who require some kind of environmental manipulation in addition to psychotherapy.

The social worker, furthermore, helps in any necessary referral of the patient to other agencies. Where members of the patient's family require clarification about the patient's problems, or where they need help themselves, the social worker enters into the situation, sometimes taking over the management of the disturbed relative.

The clinical psychologist is employed in a psychiatric clinic to administer diagnostic batteries like intelligence, educational achievement, vocational and projective personality tests. He is used as a consultant for difficulties in school adjustment and placement, for corrective work in educational disabilities, for vocational guidance and rehabilitation, and for research designing and administration.

Often the psychiatrist, the psychologist and the social worker have conferences related to the problems of a single patient. The psychiatrist contributes what he feels to be the dynamics of the situation; the psychologist brings up an evaluation of the patient from a psychologic point of view, including projective testing; and the social worker helps round out the picture with an account of social problems in the environment and the family structure. Sometimes the three team members operate jointly on the case, as, for instance, where the patient requires vocational placement and rehabilitation. The psychiatrist here attempts to identify the dynamics of the patient's difficulty as related to the work area. The clinical psychologist administers a battery of tests, including vocational interest and aptitude tests. The social worker helps with social problems that are linked to the work area. In work placement, the psychologist continues to do vocational guidance; while the psychiatrist treats the general emotional difficulties of the patient.

This type of teamwork is also employed in child guidance clinics where the treatment involves not only dealing with the child's personality, but a manipulation of his environment. Interviews with the child's parents and other members of the family are indicated, since the child's disturbance is often provoked by his interaction with those around him. The child is treated by one of the team members, usually the psychiatrist, while the parent is handled by a non-medical therapist; for instance, the caseworker. Consultations between the two therapists, and with the psychologist who does the necessary testing, result in a coordination of the therapeutic program. Efforts to classify the management of a parent by a non-medical worker as "casework" or "counseling" in order to get around the word "psychotherapy" are arbitrary, inasmuch as an examination of what happens in the relationship of the parents with the non-medical worker will clearly demonstrate that the process involved is that of psychotherapy, in spite of any attempt on the part of the worker to limit his therapeutic role. In some clinics, non-medical therapists carry the bulk of the therapy with both parents and children.

Teamwork, such as has been described, may not be employed in psychiatric clinics where the function is primarily insight therapy with adults. This is because the interference of another team member in the treatment program may adversely influence the therapeutic relationship. If psychologic testing is required, nevertheless, the patient is referred to the clinical psychologist. However, when environmental difficulties arise, the therapist may attempt to work out with the patient adequate ways of dealing with his environmental difficulty. He may perhaps consult with the social worker in order to apprise himself of available resources in relation to a specific social lack. Having this information at hand, he may then attempt to help the patient utilize essential resources by working out resistances to a particular plan of action.

In some clinics, following a general screening by the intake social worker, the psychiatrist does the initial interview and provides answers to the following questions:

1. Are there any medical problems that should be referred to a medical practitioner or specialist?

2. Are there any neurologic problems that should be treated by the psychiatrist or referred to a neurologist?
3. Are there any existing psychiatric problems; such as, suicidal tendencies, severe depression, excitement, antisocial proclivities, alcoholism, drug addiction, psychoses, or emergencies that require sedation, medication, hospitalization, or shock therapy?
4. Are there potential psychiatric problems that will need constant observation?
5. What is the diagnosis?

Thereafter the case may be assigned to the team member best qualified to treat the patient. The psychiatrist is selected where psychiatric problems prevail. Non-medical therapists are chosen where there are disturbances in vocational, educational, social, marital and personal adjustment. Sometimes an attempt is made in case assignment to differentiate between "social" and "medical" psychologic problems. Non-medical therapists are assigned to simple situational maladjustments, personality disorders, and behavior disorders. Medical therapists are assigned to syndromes characterized by a breakdown in defenses and adaptation with symptom formation. The syndromes here are anxiety neurosis, conversion hysteria, anxiety hysteria, compulsion neurosis, acute alcoholism, drug addiction, psychosomatic ailments, active psychoses, neurotic and psychotic disorders in organic and neurologic conditions, and traumatic neurosis. This differentiation of social and medical psychologic disorders is, however, artificial inasmuch as the individual is involved as a totality, and every one of his functions—somatic, psychic, and behavioral—are influenced in any emotional illness. Consequently, except for severe psychiatric problems, all types of emotional ailments are assigned in some clinics to non-medical therapists provided they are sufficiently experienced and operate under psychiatric supervision.

Once a case has been assigned, psychiatric supervision of the non-medical therapist is provided. Ideally this supervision is routine and constant. In clinic practice, the psychiatrist customarily designates the intensity of supervision, its frequency and the mode of checking on existing or potential medical, neurologic or psychiatric problems. No satisfactory system of reporting has ever been devised that can result in constant and complete psychiatric supervision of all patients in psychotherapy.

When one examines the practices of representative clinics in relation to the matter of psychiatric supervision, one finds great variation. In some instances, the non-medical therapist spends at least one hour weekly with the psychiatrist, bringing up problems that occur in the total case load. This presupposes sufficient training on the part of the therapist to make him aware of cases which show signs of impending somatic, neurologic or psychiatric difficulties. Where a psychiatric caseworker and clinical psychologist have had an adequate amount of training, this type of psychiatric supervision seems to work out satisfactorily. Where training has been insufficient, supervision of this kind leaves much to be desired. In many clinics, the lack of psychiatrists has resulted in a spotty kind of psychiatric supervision, in that the psychiatrist is called in for consultations, whenever, in the opinion of the non-medical worker, a psychiatric consultation is required.

The subject of supervision in psychotherapy is complex and often befogged in semantic confusion. Actually, several forms of supervision are employed. There is, first, the general supervision of medical problems (*medical supervision*). Second, there is supervision for psychiatric conditions, functional and organic (*psychiatric supervision*). Third, there is supervision of the psychotherapeutic process itself, the relationship between patient and therapist (*psychotherapeutic supervision*). The first type of supervision may be rendered by a good internist. A psychiatrist, while qualified for the second type of supervision, may have neither the inclination nor the skill to look after the medical problems of the patient. Nor may he be qualified to supervise the psychotherapeutic process. The individual who supervises psychotherapy may not be the best person for medical and psychiatric supervision. In some clinics, a highly skilled non-medical therapist may be used for psychotherapeutic supervision. In certain analytic schools, too, prominent non-medical analysts do both training analysis and psychotherapeutic supervision of medical trainees.

In many clinics, hiring policies are such that social workers and clinical psychologists who are employed are without adequate training that would qualify them to do any other than supportive psychotherapy. However, where the therapist has had sufficient training, it may be possible to expand his function to that of reeducational psychotherapy, and, in the event of extensive psychoanalytic training, to reconstructive psychotherapy, under appropriate psychiatric and psychotherapeutic supervision. These rules should also apply to the psychiatrist whose training may qualify him merely to do supportive therapy. Where the psychiatrist has had further training, he may be able to do reeducational and reconstructive therapy under whatever psychotherapeutic supervision is indicated by his experience.

Inevitably, people working with individuals under emotional stress are drawn into some kind of a psychotherapeutic relationship. Because of this, many clinics have set up inservice training programs calculated to help develop the skills of their clinic personnel. One of the problems that has occurred here is that the specialized training in psychotherapy of the various team members tends to divorce them from the roles usually identified with their profession. Thus, the physician doing psychotherapy may give up his interest in general medicine; he may lose his diagnostic medical skills, and he eventually feels himself unqualified to do a good physical and neurologic examination. Many psychiatrists for this reason refer their patients who require medical attention to internists. The clinical psychologist tends to remove himself from testing, often on the basis that being a psychotherapist puts him on a different level of functioning. He, too, may lose his testing skills and refer patients requiring testing to another clinical psychologist. The psychiatric social worker also resents doing casework, and, like the psychologist, may want to give up his identification with his profession. In some instances, the psychologist and caseworker may even attempt to drop

their professional titles and insist on being called "psychotherapists." Another
problem is that many therapists, as soon as they have become sufficiently skilled,
are lured by motives of economic betterment into private practice. This creates
quite a difficult situation for the clinic. The position of the medical profession
here is to tend to regard with disfavor the influx of non-medical workers into
private practice, particularly those who operate without adequate medical and
psychiatric supervision.

13

The Equipment of the Psychotherapist

FOR CONVENIENCE, THE EQUIPMENT OF THE PSYCHOTHERAPIST MAY BE classified as follows: (1) educational equipment, (2) personality equipment, and (3) experiential equipment.

EDUCATIONAL EQUIPMENT

Let us assume that the prospective therapist has been thoroughly grounded in the biologic and social sciences, and that he has had at least one year of intimate clinical contact with severe mental disorders at a mental institution. To do psychotherapy he will require further extensive postgraduate didactic and clinical instruction. Unfortunately there are no short-cuts to the achievement of therapeutic competency. Estimates of the length of time it takes to turn out a fairly seasoned therapist vary. In most instances it requires five or six years of intensive postgraduate work. Among the essential courses are the following:

1. History of Psychiatry

History of psychiatry up to the period of Sigmund Freud, including contributions of Mesmer, Braid, Bernheim, Charcot, Watson, Pavlov, Cannon, Janet, Baudouin, DuBois, Kretschmer, Kraepelin and Bleuler. History of the Mental Hygiene Movement. The psychobiology of Adolf Meyer.

2. The Development of Psychoanalytic Thinking

Readings in psychoanalysis and allied fields. (1) Selected writings of Sigmund Freud. (2) Writings of contemporaries of Freud including Abraham, Ferenczi, Adler, Jung, Stekel, Rank, Reich, Reik, Fromm, Sullivan and Horney. (3) Selected writings in the social sciences related to psychiatry, especially sociology, social psychology (including topologic psychology), clinical psychology (including the psychology of learning) and anthropology.

Psychosocial development. The various forces that enter into the molding of human personality. The roles of heredity, constitution and environment in character formation. Experiences and conditionings in infancy, childhood, adolescence and adult life that enter into conflict formation. The various methods of conflict solution.

Psychopathology and psychodynamics. Anxiety and its manifestations.

Mechanisms of defense. Symptomatology, psychopathology and psychodynamics of the principal neurotic and psychotic syndromes.

3. Basic Neuropsychiatry

Review of neuroanatomy, neurophysiology and neuropathology. Descriptive psychiatry of schizophrenia, manic-depressive psychosis, involutional psychosis, psychosis with cerebral arteriosclerosis, senile psychosis, other organic psychoses, paranoia and paranoid conditions, mental deficiency and epilepsy. Recent statistical surveys of mental illness. Classification of mental and emotional illness. Causes of mental disease. History-taking (anamnesis) and the conduct of the psychiatric examination.

4. Function of Clinical Team Members

The professional responsibility of the psychiatrist, caseworker and clinical psychologist in terms of specialized role and psychotherapeutic function. The uses and misuses of teamwork. The psychiatric consultant and the psychiatric supervisor. Survey of testing procedures used for diagnosis and treatment planning, including the Stanford-Binet, Wechsler-Bellevue, Rorschach, Thematic Apperception, figure-drawing, Szondi, vocational and aptitude tests. The place of casework in a psychotherapeutic program.

5. Techniques in Psychotherapy

Introduction to psychotherapy. Scientific foundations upon which a psychotherapeutic program is based. Prognosis and goals in psychotherapy. General outline of psychotherapy.

A comparative study of psychotherapeutic approaches. Similarities and differences in theory and technique of the various psychotherapeutic approaches, including: (1) supportive therapy; such as, environmental therapy, reassurance, guidance, persuasion, emotional catharsis and desensitization, drug therapy, physical therapy and occupational therapy; (2) reeducative therapy; such as, casework approaches, directive and non-directive counseling, distributive analysis and synthesis, and interview psychotherapy; and (3) reconstructive therapy; such as, Freudian psychoanalysis, non-Freudian psychoanalysis, with modifications of Adler, Jung, Rank, Stekel, Fromm, Horney, Reich, Sullivan, and psychoanalytically oriented psychotherapy.

The technique of interviewing. Basic interview approaches, with methods of opening the session, maintaining the flow of verbalizations, directing the flow of verbalizations, selective focusing, and terminating the interview.

The initial interview. Problems involved in the initial interview. Motivating the patient for psychotherapy. Correcting misconceptions. Structuring the therapeutic situation.

Technical procedures in psychotherapy. The conduct of psychotherapy including such aspects as the establishment of a working relationship with the patient, the determining of the dynamics of the neurosis, the promotion of activity toward therapeutic change, and the termination of therapy.

The handling of special problems in therapy. Coping with severe reactions of panic, suicidal ideas, threats of violence, "acting-out" and other acute reactions of the patient. Somatic complications during psychotherapy and their management.

The handling of borderline patients. Special techniques and modification of methods in dealing with borderline schizophrenic patients.

The technique of dream interpretation. Understanding, utilizing and interpreting dreams in reconstructive psychotherapy.

6. Clinical Seminars

Diagnostic conference. Presentation of a variety of cases for purposes of discussing the diagnosis, psychopathology and psychodynamics.

Clinical conferences. Problems in the conduct of therapy through presentation of a variety of cases.

Continuous case seminars. One case is presented throughout the course period, preferably by process recording or tape recording. Discussions deal with the handling of the therapeutic situation as it develops over an extended period of time.

7. Group Psychotherapy

History of group therapy. Group therapy with parents of children who are in treatment. Inspirational, educational, activity and analytic group therapy. Psychodrama. Group therapy in private practice. Group therapy with unselected groups as in families and institutions. The organizing and working with groups. The significance of group constellations, the reexperiencing of historic nuclear relationships, and the use of dreams and other means of self-expression in a group setting.

8. Child Psychiatry

Principles of child psychiatry and psychotherapy. The most common behavioral, neurotic, psychosomatic and psychotic illnesses of childhood. Problems of adolescence with emphasis on the impact of sociocultural influences, the effects of physical change, and the role of childhood experiences. Therapeutic problems conditioned by the specific adolescent personality structure. Detection of early emotional difficulties in children. Techniques of diagnosing emotional problems prior to their structuralization.

9. Preventive Mental Health Courses

Community organization in mental health. Structure of the community and organized health and welfare services developed to foster mental health; such as, schools, hospitals, social agencies, industry, leisure time agencies, rehabilitation agencies and convalescent agencies. Typical administrative and supervisory set-ups. Federal, state and community health plans in present operation. The roles of the physician, social worker, psychologist, nurse, teacher, minister and correctional worker in various agencies.

Techniques in preventive mental health. (1) Methods of organizing mental health programs. (2) Identification and treatment of community health problems. (3) The role of the professional worker, stressing methods of communicating and working with community agencies and the ancillary professions. Principles of psychiatric consultation. (4) The use of educational media in preventive mental health. Methods of conducting discussion groups; the use of films, recordings and sociodramatic techniques; an evaluation of current books and pamphlets on mental health written for the public; the mental health lecture; writing on mental health topics for the public and for ancillary professions.

10. Organization and Operation of a Mental Hygiene Clinic

Organization, operation and routines employed in a mental hygiene clinic, with analysis of the processes of reception, intake, history-taking, initial interviewing, cooperation with outside agencies, the keeping of case records, the taking of progress notes, and methods of case presentation. Socioprofessional role of the clinical team member in relation to community agencies and organizations which can supplement his individual skills as a therapist and his team role in relation to other team members. Needs for psychiatric services in agencies like social agencies, hospitals, out-patient clinics, schools, public health services, industry, unions, courts, civic organizations, etc. Methods of maximizing cooperative working relations with community organizations.

11. The Treatment of Special Conditions

Treatment of the alcoholic. Hereditary, constitutional, and experiential factors associated with alcoholism. Treatment of the acute and chronic alcoholic patient from various viewpoints, including drug treatment (especially antabuse), institutionalization, individual and group psychotherapy.

Treatment of the criminal. The role of psychiatry in the prevention, control and treatment of criminals.

Treatment of the drug addict. Background material and techniques for the treatment of narcotic and barbiturate addiction.

Treatment of speech and voice disorders. Physiology of speech and the symptomatology of the most frequent disturbances in this area. Therapeutic methods in speech disorders with special emphasis on stuttering.

Management of family problems. Premarital, postmarital and parent-child problems and their handling. Problems of aging and aged parents in the development of the family in its beginning, expanding and declining phases.

The treatment of schizophrenia. Essential psychodynamics of schizophrenia. Techniques and problems in treatment with psychotherapy alone and in combination with physiologic methods.

The treatment of severe depression. Main clinical forms of depressed states and their psychodynamics. Techniques and problems in treatment with psychotherapy alone and in combination with physiologic methods.

The treatment of sexual problems. Psychopathology, psychodynamics and treatment problems in sexual disorders, particularly impotence, priapism, frigidity, vaginospasm, fetishism, sadism, masochism and homosexuality.

12. Adjunctive Aids in Psychotherapy

Hypnotherapy. Techniques of hypnotic induction. Uses and misuses of hypnosis as a therapeutic catalyst.

Narcotherapy. Technique, indications and contraindications of narcotherapy.

Shock therapy and psychosurgery. Uses and misuses of shock therapy, convulsive therapy and psychosurgery. Principles of selection of patients, and way of integrating somatic therapies with psychotherapy.

Miscellaneous adjuncts. Art therapy, music therapy, occupational therapy, bibliotherapy, diet therapy, drug therapy and physiotherapy.

13. Culture and Personality

Influence of superimposition of cultures on divergent national groups. Effect of sociologic and anthropologic data on therapeutic techniques.

14. Industrial Psychiatry

Problems in industry of a normal and psychopathologic nature as they affect employers and employees. Application of psychologic and psychiatric techniques to situations of hiring, job placement, training, problems of staying on the job (including transferring), and discharge. Techniques of interviewing, testing and psychodramatic training.

15. Compensation and Other Medicolegal Problems in Psychiatry

Common compensation and other medicolegal problems in neuropsychiatric practice with tactical approaches to these problems.

PERSONALITY EQUIPMENT

The practice of psychotherapy requires that the therapist possess special personality characteristics that will enable him to establish and to maintain the proper kind of relationship with his patient. These characteristics may roughly be classified into five categories; namely, those of sensitivity, flexibility, objectivity, empathy and relative freedom from serious emotional or characterologic disturbance.

1. Sensitivity

Essential in the therapist is the capacity to perceive what is happening in the treatment process from the verbal and non-verbal behavior of the patient. Not only must the therapist be attuned to the content of the patient's communications, but he must be sensitive to the moods and conflicts that underlie the content. He must be aware also of his own feelings and attitudes, particularly those nurtured by his personal neurosis that are inspired by contact with the patient. These qualities presuppose a superior intelligence and judgment with the ability to utilize one's intelligence in practical life problems.

2. Objectivity

Awareness of his own feelings and neurotic projections helps the therapist to remain tolerant and objective in the face of irrational, controversial and provocative attitudes and behavior manifested by the patient. No matter what the patient thinks or says, it is urgent that the therapist have sufficient control over his feelings so as not to become judgmental and, in this way, inspire guilt in the patient. Objectivity tends to neutralize untoward emotions in the therapist, particularly overidentification, which may stifle the therapeutic process; and hostility, which can destroy it. Objectivity enables the therapist to endure attitudes, impulses and actions at variance with accepted norms. It permits the therapist to respect the patient and to realize his essential integrity, no matter how disturbed or ill he may be.

Among the most common projections and attitudes toward which objectivity is mandatory are infantile demands by the patient for protection, love, gifts and favors; insistence that the therapist be omniscient at all times; desires to be preferred by the therapist above all other persons; demands for sexual responsiveness; expressions of resentment, hostility and aggression; and complaints of being exploited, deceived and victimized. In the face of such projections, it is essential that the therapist be able to recognize and handle his own fears, prejudices, intolerance and other neurotic attitudes as they develop, and to deal with such feelings as impatience, disgust, resentment, boredom, and disinterest whenever these appear. This will necessitate self-understanding and awareness on the part of the therapist of his own conflicts and problems in interpersonal relationships.

3. Flexibility

Rigidity in the therapist is a destructive force in psychotherapy. Unfortunately it is a common occurrence whenever there is tenacious adherence to any one "system" of psychotherapy. Rigidity prevents the therapist from coordinating his approach with the exigencies of the therapeutic situation. Too zealous regard for the sanctity of any system must of necessity reduce his therapeutic effectiveness; for, the requirements of the therapeutic interpersonal relationship call forth promptings that defy methodologic bounds. Flexibility is not only essential in the execution of technical procedures, but in other aspects of therapy; such as, the defining of goals and the setting of standards. Flexibility is also necessary in interpreting the value system of the culture, in order to permit of the relaxation of certain austere demands in the face of which a change in the patient's severity of conscience may be thwarted.

4. Empathy

Perhaps the most important characteristic of the good therapist is his capacity for empathy. This quality enables the therapist to appreciate the turmoil the patient experiences in his illness and the inevitable resistances he will manifest toward change. It presupposes that the therapist is not characterologically detached, a trait most destructive to a proper relationship with the patient. Lack of empathy interferes with the respect the therapist needs to display toward the patient, with the interest to be shown in his welfare, with the ability to give him warmth and support when needed, with the capacity to concentrate on his productions and to respond appropriately to these. Empathy must not be confused with maudlin sympathy or tendencies to overprotect the patient. Empathy means tolerance of the patient's making mistakes, of using his own judgments, and of developing his individual sense of values. This means that the therapist must harbor no preconceived notions as to the kind of person he wants the patient to be.

5. Relative Absence of Serious Emotional Problems

Certain traits in the therapist have been shown by experience to be damaging to good psychotherapy. Among these are the following:

Tendencies to be domineering, pompous and authoritarian. Such tendencies, while tolerable in supportive therapy, are not too helpful in reeducative therapy, and are definitely harmful in reconstructive therapy. They prevent the patient from working things out for himself in order to evolve his own growth patterns. They reinforce his fears of authority and cause him to overvalue the powers of people in high positions. They inhibit self-growth and the development of assertiveness, while reinforcing traits of dependency, submissiveness, ingratiation and detachment. Sometimes they release rebellious and hostile tendencies that interfere with therapeutic gains. Domineering tendencies in the therapist may mask strong fears of people, and here constitute a way of maintaining control by putting the patient in a subordinate or inferior role. They may also be a means of expressing not fully conscious feelings of omniscience, grandiosity, and a need to play God. This does not imply that the therapist must shy away from assuming the role of an authority; it indicates that he must have the capacity of acting as an authority without being authoritarian.

Tendencies toward passivity and submissiveness. These may inspire insecurity and hopelessness in the patient. They stimulate latent hostile and sadistic traits, as well as reactive defenses against such traits. Passivity may manifest itself in a fear of offending the patient, in an inability to be firm, on occasion, and to take a positive stand when it is essential that the therapist do so.

Detachment. Whereas the patient may manage to establish some kind of a relationship with a domineering or passive therapist, he is totally blocked from making essential contact because of detachment in the therapist. This trait may be rationalized by the therapist as a designed attempt to act neutral or to assume a scientific and structured attitude toward the patient. Detachment interferes with the capacity to empathize with the patient and to feel sympathetic with his problems. It thwarts the giving of therapeutic doses of reassurance and support whenever these are required.

Need to utilize the patient for the gratification of repressed or suppressed impulses. The therapist may attempt to gain vicarious gratification of impulses by living them through in the experiences of the patient. Where he does this, he will tend to lose his objectivity and fail in his effort to help the patient. It is vitally important that the therapist be sufficiently well adjusted and possessed of basic satisfactions in living, or else compensating adequately for any lack in vital satisfactions, so as to avoid using the patient to gratify his own frustrated needs. Among the most common frustrated impulses are those related to sexuality, the expression of hostility, and the gaining of prestige. Unpropitiated sexual needs of a normal or perverse nature may be stimulated in the therapist by the patient's recital of his past erotic behavior. His present sexuality may also receive an unwarranted concentration and emphasis. Where the therapist harbors an excess amount of hostility, he may unduly encourage its expression in the patient, directing it toward those agencies with whom the therapist himself is neurotically concerned. Thus, he may sanction a hostile defiance of authority or aggressive acts toward parental figures, with a resultant involvement of the patient in activities that may not be to his best interests. Finally, an over-ambitious therapist may, under press of this impulse, goad the patient into working for success, power and fame, much as a parent dissatisfied with his own mediocrity will try to fulfill himself through his offspring. Such efforts tend to arouse defiance in the patient and interfere with the proper patient-therapist relationship. Ambitiousness may additionally cause the therapist to react with resentment to the patient's resistances, and to the absence of what the therapist considers to be appropriate progress, the therapist feeling here that his own reputation is at stake.

Inability to tolerate the expression of certain impulses. Reaction formations and other defenses in the therapist against important inner drives may mobilize antitherapeutic tendencies. Thus, anxieties investing the therapist's sexuality, hostility and assertiveness may cause him to minimize the importance of such impulses in the patient. The therapist may divert the patient from talking about these topics whenever they are brought up, or he may adopt subtle punitive tactics that cause the patient to repress such impulses or their derivatives, driving them deeper away from awareness, and preventing a coming to grips with them. In the same way the therapist, sensitive to anxiety in himself, may be unable to tolerate it in others. He may therefore tend to dissipate anxiety with reassurance and other supportive measures when even minimal quantities of this emotion arise during treatment, in this way obstructing an examination of its source. A therapist with this kind of problem may do excellent supportive therapy, but will fail in the more extensive reeducative and reconstructive approaches.

Neurotic attitudes toward money. The therapist's insecurity may reflect itself in anxiety about fees and payments. Such concerns will stimulate in many patients feelings of being exploited, and hostile attitudes toward the therapist on the basis that he is more interested in the patient's money than in the patient.

Sundry destructive traits. Many neurotic character traits in the therapist are detrimental to good functioning. Included are these:

1. The therapist may be unable to tolerate blows to his own self-esteem by the patient's acting out tendencies, by manifestations of resistance and transference, and by the inevitable failures and frustrations in treatment.

2. A neurotic need to be liked, and desires for admiration and homage may prevent the therapist from making interpretations that are offensive to the patient or may stop him from otherwise challenging the patient's defenses.

3. Compulsive tendencies toward perfectionism may make less ambitious goals than complete character reconstruction inacceptable to the therapist, and may cause him to drive the patient obstinately toward such goals even when there is little chance of achieving them. Perfectionism may also produce a fear in the therapist of making mistakes.

4. Perhaps the most destructive traits present in the therapist are those which create a relationship that specifically duplicates and perpetuates the early defeating, frustrating and traumatizing experiences in the patient's childhood. The patient will, of course, always try to maneuver the therapist into such a relationship, but an observant and objective therapist will tend to block this design. However, where the therapist's personal needs play into the patient's demands, he may lose his perspective and enthusiastically enact the kind of role that must inevitably end in defeat.

5. Any character traits in the therapist that interfere with his ability to understand, to accept and to deal constructively with the verbal and non-verbal behavior of the patient without feelings of threat or counter-hostility, are damaging to the treatment relationship.

6. Hostility toward the patient, open or disguised, justified by reality or inspired by prejudices and counter-transference, brings about in the therapist

rejection, lack of empathy, loss of objectivity and other manifestations destructive to therapeutic objectives.

7. Militating against good therapy are a number of other characteristics; such as, little creativity, a poor sense of humor, an inability to take criticism, low personal integrity, diminished respect for people, failure to acknowledge self-limitations, low energy level and poor physical health.

EXPERIENTIAL EQUIPMENT

Without extensive experience in the therapeutic handling of a variety of cases, no therapist can be considered well-trained. Preferably the therapist should have treated the common clinical syndromes, including anxiety neurosis, anxiety hysteria, conversion hysteria, obsessive-compulsive neurosis, psychosomatic problems, personality disorders, behavior problems, alcoholism, drug addiction, pre-schizophrenia, schizophrenia, manic-depressive psychosis, involutional psychosis and paranoid states. His experience should have included varied emotional problems in children. It should have given the therapist an opportunity to observe and to do group therapy. The therapist also ideally should learn how to operate in the kind of teamwork with caseworkers and clinical psychologists in which the professional responsibility of each team member is defined, providing a basis for mutual interaction and the pooling of skills. He should be capable of playing a specialized role within the team and of functioning ably as a psychotherapist. He should understand the principles of preventive mental health, and how to utilize educational media in a skilled way. He should finally be able to act as a consultant to those community agencies and auxiliary professions which are in contact with people suffering from emotional ailments.

Such training obviously will take a long time. Indeed, as has been previously mentioned, it is rare for any student to become a seasoned therapist without a backlog of at least five or six years experience under competent psychiatric and psychotherapeutic guidance. Each therapist must be "custom-tailored," serving an apprenticeship under careful supervision which is specifically designed to take into account his various personality problems and characteristics. Sharing experiences in the actual practice of psychotherapy with a highly trained supervisor is the greatest catalyst to the learning of psychotherapy. By bringing the student to an awareness of his blind spots, and his personality and learning blocks, one can most effectively help him toward matureness as a psychotherapist. Supervision of the psychotherapeutic process is so important and essential an experience, that an entire chapter in this book will later be devoted to it.

IS PERSONAL PSYCHOTHERAPY OR PSYCHOANALYSIS NECESSARY FOR THE THERAPIST?

It is obviously impossible for any one person to possess a totality of positive personality features or to be devoid of every negative characteristic that makes for an ideal psychotherapist. These deficiencies do not obstruct good psychotherapy, provided the therapist is not too seriously handicapped by personality disturbances. The therapist, like any other person, will undoubtedly be possessed of a certain amount of neurotic illness. This may manifest itself in difficulties in personal adjustment outside of the therapeutic situation. The fact that he exhibits evidences of personal problems in everyday life does not always mean that he may not be able to manage therapy in the unique setting of the patient-therapist relationship. For, in this relationship the therapist plays a different role than he does in his usual dealings with people. The position he occupies with the patient generally makes him feel more secure and permits him to divest himself of many of his customary neurotic defense mechanisms. A mild neurosis need not necessarily interfere with the effective conduct of therapy if the therapist is aware of his interpersonal problems and is capable of inhibiting their operation in his relationship with his patient.

Mandatory, then, in all individuals doing any kind of psychotherapy, is some awareness of and control over their stereotyped interpersonal reactions. There are some individuals who are sufficiently healthy by virtue of a sound upbringing and a spontaneously mature development, so as to be able to avoid untoward reactions in therapy. Additionally, they possess values and attitudes that are consonant with mental health objectives. Admittedly, such persons are in the minority, since most of us are not so bountifully blessed by a fortunate upbringing and wholesome childhood experiences to make us well-integrated human beings.

The burdens imposed on the average therapist, particularly in doing reconstructive therapy, the fact that his own unconscious conflicts may be mobilized, and the need for him to function simultaneously in multiple roles, require that he have greater freedom from neurosis than the average person. Categorically, it may be stated that all therapists will require some personal psychotherapy if they plan to do reconstructive therapeutic work. Such personal therapy provides the individual with an opportunity to study psychodynamics through self-observation, in watching minutely his own emotional conflicts, their genetic origin and their projection in his present-day functioning. It helps, also, to liberate him from those problems and character disturbances that interfere with the establishing and maintaining of a therapeutic interpersonal relationship.

Personal therapy is not always necessary where the psychotherapist confines his work to supportive and reeducative approaches, provided, of course, that he does not possess too many therapeutically destructive personality handicaps. However, a period of personal treatment may eventually prove itself to be one of the soundest investments the therapist can make. In addition to helping the therapist with his own problems, personal reconstructive therapy or analysis contributes to his sophistication in understanding what is happening, even in supportive treatment. For instance, by observing (without interpreting) the patient's dreams, fantasies and "acting-out," one may follow more effectively resistance to change, the development and vicissitudes of transference, the building of more adaptive defenses and the general trend of progress.

There are many variables in assaying how much more effective the therapist will be with and without personal therapy. Some therapists, never having received personal analysis, are remarkably flexible, sensitive, empathic and intuitive. They recognize and are capable of dealing with their own and their patient's unconscious mental processes, and they are able to do better psychotherapy than many therapists who have undergone treatment. It does not, however, follow from this that they could not have developed themselves even further with personal therapy.

Exposing oneself to therapy does not necessarily guarantee the success of the effort. Over and over again we observe well-qualified individuals who, exposed to prolonged personal analyses, characterologically seem to be little influenced by the process. There are many reasons for this failure. Perhaps of greatest import is the tendency for the student-therapist to consider personal therapy a "didactic" requirement rather than a therapeutic necessity. Unlike the average patient who is driven to treatment by anxiety and the discomfort of disabling symptoms, the student-therapist enters therapy because it is something he is "supposed to go through" as a requirement in his training. The latter motivation is not strong enough to induce him to tolerate the anxieties necessary for the yielding of the protective and pleasure values of his neurosis. His resistance to deep change is consequently greater than that of the patient, since he is not enjoined by suffering to revise his personality patterns.

Currently, there is a tendency to shy away from a labeling of personal therapy or analysis as "didactic," and to accept the principle that every student-therapist possesses a neurosis that requires treatment. Accepted, also, is the premise that even where symptoms are lacking, the alteration of character patterns, with removal of therapeutically destructive traits and the expansion of therapeutically constructive tendencies, will be a long-term proposition. It is recognized that failure in his personal therapy to achieve goals of character change, does not cast a slur on the therapist's integrity, or his ability to engage in successful supportive and reeducative approaches. These are to be regarded not as methods substitutive for, or inferior to, reconstructive therapy, but rather as processes that have a preferred validity in the specific instances where they are employed.

14

General Principles of Psychotherapy

PSYCHOTHERAPY CONTAINS MANY HYPOTHETIC ASSUMPTIONS THAT have never been subjected to experimental validation. This is largely because the therapeutic interpersonal relationship on which psychotherapy is based embraces sundry variables that do not lend themselves to measurement. It is difficult, consequently, to apply to an evaluative study of psychotherapy the precise principles on which scientific method is based; namely, an unprejudiced compilation of facts and information, the formulation of reasonable hypotheses, the retention of objectivity in observation, and the retesting of findings with an attempt to reduplicate results. For the most part, descriptions of psychotherapeutic technique reflect the personal values and convictions of the observer. The clinical attitudes expressed are more pragmatic and empiric than they are scientific.

It is perhaps for these reasons that psychotherapy has been regarded by many as an art rather than a science. One may justifiably consider the ability to establish and to maintain a relationship with a patient a form of artistry, since it is dependent on certain personality factors with which some therapists are more highly endowed than others. Yet conceding that psychotherapy, at our present state of knowledge, is less a science than an art, certain basic principles must apply—as in any other art—of which an understanding is crucial to its effective practice. Without a disciplined application of these principles, no amount of artistic endowment can make for good psychotherapy.

Another factor that makes a study of the psychotherapeutic method difficult is the confusion of broad basic techniques with the unique personal ways in which they are implemented. In psychotherapy as in any other art or part-art, we are confronted with the phenomenon of a highly personalized style that is employed in the medium of a particular method.

An analogy may illustrate this point. A student learning to paint will be aided greatly by studying fundamental techniques of painting and general principles of composition. He will also derive much in observing the methods of painters who have achieved proficiency in their work. His art instructor will help him to master blocks and ineptitudes in putting the fundamental techniques into practice. As he gains confidence in himself, his training will blend itself with individual personality forces such as his creativity, sensitivity, and originality, and out of this amalgam, he will develop his own "style" of painting—a preferential mode of symbolic representation, and a unique use of color and texture. He will still operate within the broad framework of the fundamental techniques, but his finished products will be his own, different from those of his teachers and colleagues, different from those who have been exposed to the same kind of instruction.

In psychotherapy, a student will also be helped by studying general principles and techniques, such as the conduct of an initial interview, the establishment of a working relationship with the patient, the determination of the dynamics of a neurosis, the promotion of activity toward therapeutic change, and the termination of therapy. He will be benefited by observing how trained psychotherapists execute these procedures. Like the artist, he will need to function under supervision, in this way becoming aware of his deficiencies which interfere with the putting into practice of what he has learned. As his experience grows, he will fuse his method with his personality, introducing new elements and modifying others, until he develops his own "style" of therapy. He will still follow the broad principles of technique, but in a manner that is uniquely his own.

A broad structure of therapy must take into account this factor of uniqueness of style in the psychotherapist, in order to preserve spontaneity. For without spontaneity the therapist is truly handicapped in relating to his patients, and in allowing his intuition to help him grasp the dynamic forces that are operative in the treatment process.

DYNAMICS OF THERAPEUTIC CHANGE

Before describing a structure of psychotherapy that provides for this kind of flexible framework, it may be helpful to consider the dynamics of psychotherapy in terms of an example of what happens to the average individual who is exposed to a reconstructive psychotherapeutic approach. Modifications consonant with reeducative and supportive therapies will be considered later.

When the average patient enters into therapy, he is usually bewildered, confused and upset by what is happening to him. His symptoms seem more or less dissociated from the mainstream of his life. He is confounded, therefore, by attempts to investigate in detail aspects of his experience that he considers irrelevant to his complaint factor. Not realizing that his symptoms stem from deep conflicts of long standing, that are reflected in present disturbances in his relationships with people, he expects rapid results. In this respect he is rather like the obese patient who wants the physician to remove, in two weeks, the overweight which has taken ten years to accumulate, while at the same time refusing to exercise or diet. The patient seeks to retain fixed ways of dealing with people and situations, which are responsible for his symptoms, while demanding that the products of his disturbed way of living be quickly eliminated.

With this in mind, the patient desires to relate to the therapist in the traditional way a patient utilizes a physician. He demands some kind of immediate dramatic help, or, in his helplessness, the performance of a miracle by means of mysterious medical powers. He hopefully believes that the therapist will prove to be an omniscient authority upon whom he can collapse, and who will bring health and personal success to him expeditiously. The sicker the patient the more likely he is to consider therapy a conjuring trick.

It may require a great deal of perseverence on the part of the therapist to demonstrate to the patient that his symptoms do not occur at random, but are exacerbated by definite life situations which involve his attitudes toward people and his estimate of himself. Before progress can be made, however, it will be necessary for the patient to realize that his symptoms are not independent manifestations, but rather are the surface warnings of inner problems of which he is only partially aware. Once the patient accepts the principle of continuity between his symptoms and his conflicts, he is more capable of abandoning hopes for immediate symptom relief by some spectacular performance on the part of the therapist. Motivated by the discomfort of his symptoms and the desire for a more fulfilling life, he will enter into a deeper inquiry into himself.

Soon the patient will comprehend that his symptoms vary depending on the happenings of his daily life and on difficulties encountered in interpersonal relations. Awareness of these facts will tend to divert the emphasis from his symptoms. As soon as this occurs, the first basic step in therapy will have been taken.

To bring the patient to such an understanding, however, may prove to be an ambitious undertaking. The patient is used to himself and his character traits and attitudes. He can scarcely accept the fact that these are not a normal part of life. The possibility that his attitudes and behavior are disturbed may seem unbelievable to him. Nearly all neurotic people assume that their own particular pattern for living is not only most acceptable, but probably universal. If they do recognize themselves to be unique, then that in itself is regarded as a special attribute, contingent upon the possession of a constitution that offers them no other course than the one they are pursuing.

It is this attitude which makes for an obstinate resistance to change. The patient cannot readily be made to see that he projects his attitudes and his fears without actual basis. However, in the course of therapy he may gain an understanding that what he has assumed to be normal may actually be unusual. Clues to his fundamental difficulties will be pieced together for him by the therapist. The unique relationship that has developed between the patient and the therapist will help him to accept interpretations of his behavior and his symbolic life as revealed in his verbalizations, his dreams and fantasies.

No better way exists of bringing the patient to an awareness of his problems than by actually living them through in the therapeutic situation. Sometimes the patient will develop and show the same kind of unreasonable impulses toward the psychotherapist that he has displayed in all his previous relationships. The long period of conditioning that makes the individual's personality a part of himself encourages him to respond repetitively and compulsively. He is usually unaware of reasons for his irrational responses, such as, development of attitudes of hostility, disappointment and rejection toward the therapist which he is unable to suppress. Thus, the therapist becomes the target of the patient's neurotic tendencies. The patient may, for instance submit himself, render himself defenseless, or become a martyr. He may struggle with a need to victimize himself so that he can criticize the therapist. He may identify himself with the therapist, or tear the latter down in fantasy or verbally or by an aggressive act. He may strive to cash in on submissiveness by toadying to the therapist while at the same time he burns inwardly with indignation. He may be paralyzed in his relationship and take a thousand precautions before he expresses himself, so as not to offend. He may compete with the therapist or try to outshine him. He may strive to crush whatever atom of individuality he has left, if he feels the therapist will be good to him and protect him. He may resent intrusion into his private ambitions and fantasies and express disguised or open hostility. These and countless other attitudes will unfold themselves as the therapeutic process proceeds.

These attitudes are important clues to the conflicts of the patient, and when they are brought to his attention they permit him to understand his problems while reexperiencing them. This enables him to work through the dynamics of his reaction patterns in his relationship with the therapist. Under these circumstances, the various defense reactions and resistances which are directed against inner fears and strivings become apparent to the patient not as theories, but as real experiences, and he is gradually enabled to gain insight into his unconscious impulses and motivations—the source of his symptoms.

Identifying significant patterns may surprise the patient greatly and be countered with resistance, for basic adaptational patterns are being challenged which, though unsatisfying and productive of anxiety, constitute for the patient the only way of life he knows. Moreover, there are many hidden spurious gains and benefits the patient derives from his neurosis that he will resist abandoning. Debilitating as they are, neurotic symptoms serve a protective purpose in the mind of the patient. To give them up threatens an exposure to inconveniences far greater than anything the patient already suffers. He will therefore exhibit resistances to change that may prove exasperating to the therapist.

The exact form of his resistances will depend to a large degree on the kinds of defenses the patient customarily employs to avert danger. He may feel helpless or hopeless or hostile. He may get discouraged, inhibited, fatigued, or listless. He may succumb to irritability or contempt for the therapist. He may develop feelings of being misunderstood. He may become forgetful and fail to show up for his appointments. He may become depressed and complain incessantly about his health, presenting a vast assortment of physical symptoms. He may express suspicions regarding the therapist's intentions or training or political convictions as a possible justification for halting therapy. He may try to disarm the therapist with strong professions of praise or devotion. He may even evince a forced and artificial "flight into health."

Thus it seems, during therapy, that the patient does not entirely want to get well. He wants a magic recipe from the therapist whereby he may retain his neurosis, but a neurosis stripped of suffering. He wants to be dependent, yet secure and strong within himself. Or he wishes to detach himself, to keep his freedom, yet at the same time to form successful and gratifying relations with people. He will resent the therapist's attempt to change his way of life, and, in order to hinder the therapist, he will erect many impediments to the treatment process.

Counterbalancing resistance, however, are the values the patient injects into the therapeutic relationship and the respect he has for the therapist's opinions and judgments. A powerful ally is also operative in the spontaneous urge that exists in all persons for health, development and creative growth. Utilizing these advantages, the therapist attempts to dissipate resistances by constantly interpreting them to the patient in relation to their content, their manifestations and function. The interpretation of his defensive operations leads the patient into a gradual understanding of his conflicts and character drives, and of the vicarious satisfactions he derives from his neurosis. In this way he learns to appreciate his unconscious fears and to master the anxieties that have made his defenses necessary.

Insight into the fact that his responses are not justified by present-day reality, and that they are residual in misconceptions, is an important step in the process of getting well. It creates a desire to explore more thoroughly the meaning and origin of his various impulses and attitudes. The patient will become increasingly aware of the fact that his patterns have a history, that they go back to crucial formative experiences in early life in relation to important intimate figures, particularly his parents and siblings. Traumatic conditions centered around feeding, toilet training, sexual curiosities, desires for approval and status, and other important biologic and social needs are discovered as provocative of current defenses. The patient becomes aware of the fact that his attitudes toward the world are built up from his early experiences with the world. Such needs as sexuality and assertiveness have become, as a consequence, inhibited or distorted in expression. Impulses, like hostility, have been rendered incapable of gaining acceptable and adaptive outlets. The patient learns that he carries within him expectations of the same kind of frustration and injury that he experienced in his early years. He realizes that his present patterns are understandable in the light of his archaic expectations. Through the medium of interpreted fantasies, dreams, verbalizations and behavioral tendencies, the patient may be able to remember or to reconstruct the experiences and conditionings in his early childhood which actually promoted his insecurities and generated his conflicts.

Sometimes the patient will repeat, in his relationship with the therapist, his most traumatic early experiences or archaic attitudes and feelings that were engendered in his dealings with parental or sibling figures. Such transference manifestations usually reflect experiences the patient failed to master as a child, and which were responsible for his deepest anxieties and deviations in character formation. Because the relationship with the therapist is unique in its protectiveness, this recapitulation of fear-inspiring situations, once too great for his adaptive capacities, may now be reexperienced and faced with not too great anxiety. With this help the patient is now able to re-create early traumatic situations symbolically and to face them with realism.

Each effort that is successful, even though in a minor way, will have the result of awakening the patient to the realization of the manner in which his early difficulties and later conflicts handicap him in the present, necessitating disturbed attitudes toward people and himself. The wish to meet life on new terms grows from this insight. The crippling anxieties which conditioned the former reaction patterns are mastered, and, in the light of existing reality, situations and relationships are reevaluated.

When at last the patient is able to free himself from the ghosts of the past, the world becomes a much safer place for him. His sense of security grows. His interpersonal relationships are easier, unhampered by dependency, aggression, detachment. His basic needs and demands can be freed from the anxiety which has constantly impeded their materialization.

Roughly, this process may be divided into two phases. The first aspect involves an uncovering process, during which the patient becomes aware of impulses, fears, attitudes and memories, which have interfered with constructive relationships with the world and people. The second aspect is reeducative and consists of an elaboration of new and adaptive interpersonal patterns. Social reintegration does not occur automatically. It is a slow reconditioning process necessitating the establishing of new habit and reaction patterns to displace old destructive ones.

The uncovering period of treatment proceeds as rapidly as the individual is capable of tolerating anxiety. This makes possible the gradual yielding of repressions. During therapy, ego strength increases as the positive relationship with the therapist develops. But the patient constantly strives to ward off a close relationship because of fear of the arousal of strivings that he has hitherto kept from awareness. He displays resistances to the therapist, as a defense against his impulses. These resistances must be dealt with constantly before the patient begins to appreciate conflicting feelings and attitudes.

The reeducative phase of therapy is usually even more prolonged than the uncovering phase. Established patterns of behavior are changed with great reluctance—the revelation of the unconscious conflicts that initiated them is only the first step in this change. The patient fights desperately to hang on to habitual attitudes and goals. He continues to show resistances even when he has become aware of the extent to which he is at the mercy of disabling unconscious fears and strivings. He continues to reject insight as an alien force, although it finally comes into its own as he gains a glimmer of understanding of his drives and tendencies. However, intellectual insight alone does not divert him from his customary reactions. It does permit him to gain a foothold on new interpersonal pathways. This foothold is tenuous, and he retreats constantly before the onslaught of his neurotic demands, which, though known to him, continue to function with great persistence and vigor.

Slowly, against great resistance, a remarkable change is wrought in the nature of the patient's behavior. Less and less it is motivated by irrational needs; more and more it is relegated to mere fulfillment in fantasy. Yet, even though blatant neurotic patterns vanish, shadows of them persist and come to life from time to time. It is as if the balance of power keeps shifting from established old ways of life to the as yet undeveloped new.

A further development in the maturative process is recognition on the part of the patient of the incongruity of his old drives. He comes to regard them as irrational elements that he would like to eliminate from his life. A battle then ensues between his desire for change and the dynamic forces that compel him to resume his old neurotic actions. After a period of strife, more or less prolonged, a remarkable change occurs in the inner dynamics of the personality. The customary impulses, which have up to now functioned compulsively, or which he has accepted as an inevitable part of life, are alienated from his ego. Even though they continue to emerge, the ego responds to them with more and more reluctance, refusing them their original hold. Coordinately there is a reorganization of interpersonal relationships, a reintegration with reality, with the self, and with its past experiences. Signs of the abandonment of compulsive patterns are found in a sense of inner peace, happiness, security, and the absence of neurotic suffering. These positive gains serve also as factors in raising resistance to old neurotic attitudes whenever these tend to force the individual into his previous maladaptive actions.

With the patient's expanding insight, he begins to become more self-confident, assertive and expressive. He finds that he has the right to make choices and decisions, to establish his own values and goals. As the ego of the patient expands, the super-ego loses its force and tyranny. The patient becomes stronger, and in time he appreciates real joy in living and in the experiencing of normal productivity and assertiveness. Finally, he no longer requires help from the therapist, and life itself becomes an arena where he can gratify his fundamental needs, which, prior to therapy, he felt were utterly beyond his reach.

MECHANICS OF THERAPEUTIC CHANGE

The therapeutic changes that have been elaborated are brought about in the treatment situation. Through verbalization the patient becomes aware of the forces within himself which produce his symptoms and interfere with a successful life adaptation. On the basis of this understanding he then proceeds to challenge those patterns that interfere with his adjustment, and to substitute for them mature patterns that will gratify basic biologic and social needs. As he abandons archaic fears and liberates himself from paralyzing past forces, he achieves a progressive mastery of his environment, the ability to relate to people, and the capacity to express his impulses in a culturally accepted manner. The function of the therapist during these developments is as an agent who catalyzes change, helping the patient to resolve resistances that block him from his goal of emotional health.

Breaking the treatment process down into component parts, the following sequences are usually encountered:

1. The patient, concerned with his symptoms and complaints, elaborates on these.

2. He discusses feelings which disturb him and which are associated with his symptoms.

3. He realizes that his feelings are related to certain dissatisfactions with his environment, and that they are somehow conditioned by a mysterious turmoil that rages within him.

4. Along with his feelings, he recognizes patterns of behavior which frustrate him and which are repetitive, compulsive and even automatic. Soon he starts to appreciate that some of these patterns are responsible for his disturbed feelings. This causes him to doubt their value.

5. As he becomes aware of how dissatisfied he is with his impulses and behavior, he begins to try to stop their operation; yet he finds that they persist in spite of himself.

6. He slowly realizes, then, that his behavior serves a function of some sort, and that he cannot give it up easily. Indeed, his patterns repeat themselves in various settings, perhaps even with the therapist.

7. If he has the incentive to explore his patterns, he finds that they have a long history, issuing from attitudes originating in his early relationships with people, particularly his parents.

8. Gradually he recognizes that he is governed by impulses and feelings such as were present in him as a child. He sees that by carrying over certain attitudes into his present life, he is reacting to people as if they were facsimiles of his parents, siblings and other significant persons.

9. With great trepidation, he begins to challenge his early attitudes; progressively, he inhibits automatic and repetitive behavior patterns, slowly mastering his anxieties as he realizes that fantasied dangers and expectations of injury do not come to pass. In the therapeutic relationship, particularly, he begins to change, especially in his attitudes toward the therapist.

10. He begins to entertain hopes that he is not the weak and contemptible person who has constituted his inner self-image, that he actually has value and integrity, that he need not be frustrated in the expression of his needs, and that he can relate himself happily to people.

11. This causes him to resent all the more the patterns of living he customarily employs, which are products of devaluated feelings toward himself and devastating fears of his environment.

12. Slowly he begins to experiment with new modes of behavior which are motivated by a different conception of himself as a person.

13. Finding gratifications in these new patterns, he becomes more and more capable of liberating himself from his old goals and styles of action.

14. Growing strengths within himself contribute to a sense of mastery and produce healthy changes in his feelings of security, his self-esteem and his attitudes toward others.

15. He liberates himself more and more from attitudes and anxieties related to past experiences and misconceptions. He approaches life as a biologic being, capable of gaining satisfactions for his personal impulses and demands, and as a social being who participates in community living and contributes to the group welfare.

15

The Conduct of the Psychotherapeutic Interview

MANDATORY FOR PSYCHOTHERAPY IS A THOROUGH UNDERSTANDING OF the process of interviewing. This is because communication is the channel that vitalizes the therapist-patient relationship. Its structured manipulation through interviewing is a studied attempt to influence the mental processes of the patient toward therapeutic gain.

The very act of verbalizing has certain releasing values for the person. It provides for a kind of emotional catharsis in which the individual relieves himself of pent-up tensions and feelings. The benefits of "talking things over" with a sympathetic person and of "getting off one's chest" burdensome thoughts and painful feelings are well-known. Irrespective of any advice received, the mere ventilation of attitudes and emotions helps the individual to evaluate his situation better, and to approach his problems in a more constructive manner.

These beneficial effects unfortunately are short-lived. While the person may quiet down for a while, and perhaps approach life with renewed vigor, the conflicts provocative of his tensions usually continue in force. When sufficient tension accumulates, he will find himself in precisely the same position as before, requiring further cathartic release to appease his unrest.

Instead of permitting a discursive rambling, as in emotional catharsis, the organized interview promotes a selective scrutiny of verbalizations. Focusing the patient's attention on certain aspects of his experience, and the deft choice of the therapist's comments, facilitates an understanding of his feelings.

Each interview necessitates a number of activities on the part of the therapist. These include the following:

     I. Opening the Interview
    II. Maintaining the Flow of Verbalizations
        A. Managing pauses
        B. Managing silence
   III. Directing the Flow of Verbalizations: The principle of selective focusing
        A. Identifying an important theme
        B. Guiding the theme into a goal-directed channel
        C. Circumscribing the area of subject coverage

IV. Inculcating Insight
    A. Accenting
    B. Summarizing
    C. Restating
    D. Reflecting
    E. Establishing connections
    F. Maintaining tension in the interview
    G. Extending measured support
    H. Making interpretations
V. Terminating the Interview

An elaboration of these and other items will constitute the subject matter of the chapter.

THE RATIONALE OF INTERVIEWING

Ontogenetically, feelings antedate symbolic or verbal operations. Present at birth, they condition many of the automatic reactions of the child. With the development of the symbolic functions of the ego, feeling experiences become affiliated with verbal responses. The child then becomes capable of identifying feelings. Coordinately, there develops an ability to exercise some voluntary control over his emotions, as if the very linkage of thoughts with feelings encourages the capacity for such inhibition.

In neurosis, a condition seems to prevail that is similar to that of childhood. The significance of many of the patient's emotionally-determined symptoms and behavioral patterns is unknown to him, the symbolic correlates themselves having been subjected to repression. As a result, the patient is bewildered by his symptoms and by his compulsive behavior. He finds it difficult or impossible to find words that lend meaning to his feelings or actions.

One of the aims of psychotherapy is to restore to the patient a control over his emotions. Before this can be done, he must be able to make the proper symbolic connections with his emotions. Therapeutic interviewing helps to accomplish this, and enables him to scrutinize, identify and elaborate on his feelings and their sources. He then no longer feels helpless; he becomes capable of gaining some mastery over his emotions which have hitherto operated autonomously.

This process was described by one patient in a note to the writer following a session during which she tried to verbalize her feelings of tension:

As I talked, I just didn't know what was happening to me. I felt, at first, as if I was groping in mist, and then I started feeling better. I felt that I was not helpless, that there might be something behind the tension. When I left, I realized what some of my difficulties were, and that realization brings releases from a great many tensions. I noticed I had greater physical energy (still far from its peak), improved memory for small details of organization of work and of every-day living, and Saturday night I approached the vitality which I had three years ago. I must go further into my sympathies for the underdog and into my feelings that I am a second class citizen because I am a woman.

THE LANGUAGE OF THE INTERVIEW

1. Verbal Communications

A common language is essential for the conduct of the interview. Problems arise where the therapist and the patient do not understand or speak the same language.

Problems may also develop where there is a marked disparity in education, cultural background and socioeconomic level, or where the patient comes from an area of the country in which a local dialect contains unusual colloquialisms. Here, the flexibility of the therapist will be put to test, for it is he who will have to make the adjustment, not the patient. This will necessitate an inquiry, from time to time, into the meanings of the words and concepts used by the patient, with adoption of these in the vocabulary of the therapist.

The use of vocabulary similar to that employed by the patient helps interviewing. Many patients lack the sophistication necessary for the understanding of complex psychologic ideas. It is essential to recast these into simple words and phrases which are readily comprehensible to the patient. Even well-educated persons may not grasp the meaning of certain interpretations and comments of the therapist, although these apparently have been clearly stated. A definition of terms may be essential here. Additionally, after the therapist has offered interpretations, it may be necessary to check the patient's understanding by asking him to formulate what has been said, in his own words. In the event there is a lack of understanding, a reformulation may be made by the therapist, and another check then executed of the patient's comprehension.

The therapist should judiciously watch his own need to impress the patient with complex words and high-sounding phrases. The use of as unadorned and straightforward language as is possible will guarantee best results in interviewing.

2. Non-verbal Communications

Non-verbal communications during interviewing reveal aspects of the self that evade verbal expression. The patient is as much aware of the therapist's moods through the latter's non-verbal behavior as the therapist is of the patient's emotions. Thus, the patient often picks up attitudes of disinterest and annoyance on the part of the therapist through his facial expressions, mannerisms and behavior that belie verbal pronouncements of interest and concern.

Since the individual projects himself into every situation with his total personality, one may gain important clues to some of his underlying conflicts and his less conscious attitudes by observing his behavior in the therapeutic setting. His gait, posture, facial expression, gestures and mannerisms all reveal patterns, defenses and façades which are either part of his habitual character structure or specifically reflect the role he is playing with the therapist. One must make these observations casually so as not to give the patient the impression he is being watched like a specimen under a microscope.

It is usually easy to discern tension and anxiety in the patient by noting muscular spasms which communicate themselves in gait peculiarities, fidgetiness while sitting in the chair, wringing of the hands, picking of the skin and lips, flushing, and lapses of attention conveyed by facial blankness. Anger is apparent in a stiffening of posture, clenching of the fists, tapping of the toes and grimness in facial expression. Enthusiasm and excitement are similarly evidenced by appropriate behavioral attitudes.

A check of his own non-verbal expressions may be necessary periodically on the part of the therapist to ascertain that he is not conveying disapproval, boredom and irritation. Ideally, his facial expression should be pleasant, relaxed and non-critical. Scowling, frowning and angry expressions are destructive to good therapy, as are such acts as yawning, skin picking, wriggling in one's chair, and tapping of the extremities.

Head nodding is advantageously employed as a sign that the therapist is paying rapt attention and is following the reasoning of the patient. This is often accompanied by such vocalizations as "uh huh," "mm hmm," "yes," and "I see." Head shaking is used only occasionally as a sign of sympathetic understanding when the patient discusses his suffering, or when the therapist wishes to communicate that he does not like what is going on. In the latter case it may be accompanied by a slight frown and the expostulations "mm mm!" or "hmm!" sharply expressed. A smiling facial expression is often employed to indicate acceptance and approval.

Subvocal utterances are also tremendously important during interviewing. How the patient says things may be as important as what he says. Inflections, intonations, accents, emphasis, pauses, gaps in statements, slurring of speech, and varied sound expostulations may reveal to the therapist emotionally charged areas which the patient cannot put into words. By the same token, subvocal expressions and intonations influence the patient significantly. The therapist must therefore judiciously observe the manner in which he presents his remarks to the patient to avoid an untoward effect. Voice training for therapists, while not practiced at present, may in the future prove indispensable where needed.

OPENING THE INTERVIEW

1. The First Interview

During the first interview, it is highly desirable that the patient be put at ease and that the purpose of the interview be understood as clearly as possible. Consequently, the therapist is more active than at later interviews when the patient recognizes the need for greater responsibility on his part.

As the patient enters the therapist's office the latter may greet him with a smile, introduce himself, gesture to the chair, invite the patient to be seated, and briefly introduce the general purpose of the interview. For instance, a man, referred by his family physician for treatment, walks through the door:

Therapist. (*smiling*) My name is Dr._____. Won't you sit down in that chair over there so that we can talk things over.

Patient. (*smiles, walks to chair and seats himself*) Thank you, doctor. As you know, Dr. T. sent me here. He thought I needed psychiatric help. I've been going to him with a stomach condition for several years.

Th. Yes, he told me a little about your condition. I thought it might be helpful to talk things over in order to see whether you do need psychiatric help, and, if so, the kind of help that would be best for you. Would you like to tell me about your condition?

Pt. Yes, I have had this stomach trouble for some time. (*Patient continues to elaborate on his complaint factor.*)

The conduct of the first interview will be described in great detail in a later chapter, in which variations of approach will be considered, conditioned by special problems.

2. Subsequent Interviews

Later interviews are managed by briefly but pleasantly greeting the patient and waiting for him to make an opening remark. The reason for this is that one must avoid diverting the patient from material that is disturbing or otherwise significant to him. In the event the therapist starts talking at the beginning, the patient may avoid discussing things that concern him most intensely. He may then either try to please the therapist by pursuing topics he imagines the therapist wants to explore, or he may welcome and take advantage of the opportunity to evade anxiety-provoking material. The therapist should avoid conventional pleasantries when he greets the patient, and he should refrain from the temptation to make "small-talk."

Sometimes it is impossible for the therapist to avoid talking about a reality problem at the beginning of the session. This naturally tends to divert the patient. Where the therapist starts a conversation he may attempt to retrieve the situation by saying: "Now would you like to talk about yourself?" and then remaining silent until a trend is defined.

Where the patient starts a session by sitting quietly without comment, he may merely be gathering his thoughts. If silence continues, this may indicate resistance. In the former case, he will soon start verbalizing; in the latter, silence may be maintained. If, after a moment or so, this silence remains unbroken, the therapist may say pleasantly, "Well, what's on your mind?" An example of this is illustrated in the following excerpt of an interview. Because of an unavoidably prolonged telephone call, the writer had to keep the patient waiting for several minutes. When the patient entered the room, he showed no sign of annoyance or anger. He sat in the chair, slowly removed a cigarette from a pack, lit it and kept staring at the window. After a short interval he was interrupted.

Th. I wonder what's on your mind?
Pt. (*pause*) Oh, nothing. I just don't seem to have anything to say.

Th. Any reason for that?

Pt. I do . . . I don't know. I guess I was a little upset and irritated at having to wait.

Th. I'd be mad myself if I were kept waiting without reason. [*This comment is an attempt to support the patient, alleviate his guilt and show him that he is not dealing with an arbitrary authority.*]

Pt. I suppose I'm too sensitive.

Th. After all, this time *is* yours. Whenever I do encroach on your time because of emergencies like this phone call, I try to make the time up by extending the session, or at a later one.

Pt. Thank you. (*smiling*) What I really wanted to talk about today was my reactions to being criticized. (*Patient continues exploring this trend.*)

In the event silence continues after the therapist's initial attempt to break it, the therapist may employ the techniques dealing with silence described in the following section of this chapter.

MAINTAINING THE FLOW OF VERBALIZATIONS

The encouragement of verbalizations is a prime task during interviewing. This is done by listening attentively to the patient, signaling that the therapist is following him by nodding of the head, by controlled facial expressions, by such utterances as "yes," "I see," and "mm hmm," and by carefully selected questions that indicate interest and understanding. So long as a patient continues on an important trend, fulfilling the specific goal toward which therapy is directed at the time, one does not interrupt. However, when there are too prolonged pauses, where the patient shifts his concentration from the pertinent focus, or where one wishes to reflect feeling or to make interpretations, the therapist makes added verbal comments. There are some patients who need little encouragement apart from a few non-verbal interpolations. There are other patients with whom the therapist will have to manifest much more activity, perhaps even after every sentence.

1. Managing Pauses

Pauses in the verbal stream are to be expected, and, in themselves, do not merit interruption. They are advantageously used by the patient to think through some of his ideas. However, when pauses continue for more than a moment or so, the therapist may do one of the following:

a. Repeat the last word or the last few words the patient has used, with the same intonation as that of the patient, with a rising inflection, or with rephrasing as a question. The following part of an interview illustrates these:

Pt. I would say that there is a certain amount of tranquility now, but a lack of direction. A lack in the sense of what I expect. (*pause*)

Th. Expect? [*repetition of the last word*]

Pt. Yes, what I expect out of life. I did used to enjoy some of the activities I indulged in—drawing, painting, music—but I think those activities were enjoyed for their effect on other people.

Th. I see. (*nodding*) [*encouraging the patient to continue*]

Pt. I'm not interested in impressing people any more. Before this, if we went out, we saw people, and I was very particular about the way I dressed and shaved. Every little thing had to be just right. But now I don't care.

Th. Mm hmm. (*nodding*) [*encouraging his expression*]

Pt. I can come home late and rush and shave quickly. I don't particularly care how I look as much as before. Things are looking up. What I did before, something seemed to be lacking. (*pause*)

Th. Something seemed to be lacking. [*repetition of the last few words*]

Pt. I feel somehow that there was lack of pleasure. I'm not clear about it, but it has to do with sexuality. (*pause*)

b. Rephrase what the patient has said either as a plain statement of fact or as a question. Continuing with the above interview:

Th. What do you mean that this lack has something to do with sexuality?

Pt. I feel that if such a thing is psychologically possible, that I was getting substitute satisfaction for sexuality. Careful how I looked, if there were attractive women around. By showing people how smart I was, or how cultured I was, or how rounded I was would show me as a great person, as though to cover up various lacks that I had, one of which was sexuality, my sexual performance, sexual craving and that sort of thing. Now that I can find sexual pleasures, it's different. (*pause*)

Th. Now that you can find sexual pleasures all the substitute pleasure outlets have lost their driving force. (*pause*) [*rephrasing what the patient has said*]

Pt. That's exactly it. I would put all my energies into these things, and now that I can find sexual pleasure, I don't have to keep going in those other directions to find pleasure. But I miss it. (*pause*)

c. Ask a question related to the material under discussion to stimulate associations. Continuing the above interview:

Th. You miss something that still has value for you. I wonder if there were any other benefits you got out of some of the things you did? [*asking a question related to material under discussion*]

Pt. I miss the feeling that I'm not doing something constructive, something that adds to my stature.

Th. Mm hmm.

Pt. I would like to develop myself in as many directions as I can, feasibly. I don't know if it's completely neurotic. If it's partially neurotic, life to be lived and enjoyed for the moment it affords is not enough for me. As though I have to be building toward something, building something up, building myself up, growing, increasing in stature and accomplishment.

2. Managing Silence

Long periods of silence are rare in good therapy. Where silence persists, it is usually a sign of resistance. It may reflect a fear of revealing oneself, or of countenancing anxiety by activating repressed conflictual material. It may be a self-defeating masochistic maneuver, or a hostile act against the therapist. When silence continues, the therapist may try the following in order:

a. Say "mm hmm" or "I see" and then wait for a moment.

b. Repeat and emphasize the last word or the last few words of the patient.

c. Repeat and emphasize the entire last sentence or recast it as a question.

d. If this is unsuccessful, summarize or rephrase the last thoughts of the patient.

e. Say, "and" or "but" with a questioning emphasis as if something else is to follow.

f. If the patient still remains silent, the therapist may say, "You find it difficult to talk" or "It's hard to talk." This focuses the patient's attention on his block.

g. In the event of no reply, the following remark may be made: "I wonder why you are silent?"

h. This may be succeeded by, "There are reasons why you are silent."

i. Thereafter the therapist may remark, "Perhaps you do not know what to say?"

j. Then: "Maybe you're trying to figure out what to say next?"

k. This may be followed by: "Perhaps you are upset?"

l. If still no response is forthcoming, a direct attack on the resistance may be made with "Perhaps you are afraid to say what is on your mind?"

m. The next comment might be: "Perhaps you are afraid of my reaction, if you say what is on your mind?"

n. Finally, if silence continues, the therapist may remark, "I wonder if you are thinking about me?"

o. In the extremely rare instances where the patient continues to remain mute, the therapist should respect the patient's silence and sit it out with him. Under no circumstances should he evidence anger with the patient by scolding or rejecting him.

A patient who had been manifesting greater and greater difficulty in talking, finally became completely silent.

Th. I see . . . (*silence*) . . . when he went away? [*repeating last few words*] (*silence*) . . . You were talking about how little you miss your husband when he is away. [*repeating last sentence*] (*Patient remains silent.*) Perhaps you don't know what to say? (*silence*) Maybe you're trying to figure out what to say next. (*silence*) Perhaps you're upset. (*silence*) You find it difficult to talk. (*Patient is still silent.*) I wonder why you are silent? (*more silence*) There are reasons why you are silent. (*Silence continues.*) Perhaps you are afraid to say what is on your mind? (*no interruption of silence*) I wonder if you are thinking about me?

Pt. I know this is . . . sounds silly. But you *are* on my mind. I mean I keep thinking about you, sex and all. Isn't that terrible?

Th. You feel ashamed of some of the things you think about me?

Pt. (*obviously agitated*) Yes, it is so frustrating and it makes me mad. I imagine how you would be as a husband or a lover. I know one is supposed to react to their doctor, but this is so difficult. I've never really felt this way about any man.

DIRECTING THE FLOW OF VERBALIZATIONS

In formal psychoanalysis the verbal stream is undirected. The patient is enjoined to say whatever comes to his mind without concentrating on any specific topic. Complete spontaneity is the keynote, and the absolute license in verbalization enables the patient to evade repressive barriers and to liberate derivatives of the unconscious, not ordinarily available to awareness. This process of "free association" is helpful to the mobilization of the transference neurosis, which becomes the fount of insight into the most significant unconscious conflicts.

Free association is not employed in supportive and reeducative therapies. This is because one is not too much concerned with the content of the unconscious in these treatment methods. Free association may be used in non-Freudian analysis, but rarely in analytically oriented psychotherapy due to the infrequent weekly visits, and because the setting up of a transference neurosis is not an objective in this form of treatment. Where free association is employed in the latter therapies, it often is used by the patient as resistance, for instance, as a means of diverting attention, of concealing the content of disturbing everyday problems, of seducing the therapist with words, of flaying himself masochistically with recriminations, or of parading his virtues in a narcissistic recital. If the patient is left to his own devices, he will frequently ramble along in his verbalizations, veering away from anxiety-provoking material when crucial subjects are touched on. To allow the patient to follow such a circuitous thought channel may result in endless circumstantiality which serves as a defense against important verbalizations.

Instead of free association, the kinds of communication generally used in psychotherapy center around the focused interview.

THE PRINCIPLE OF SELECTIVE FOCUSING

In general, the process of selective focusing consists of initially identifying an important theme in the patient's verbalizations, of guiding this theme into a goal-directed channel, and of circumscribing the area of subject coverage.

1. Identifying an Important Theme

If one has followed the suggestions outlined in opening the interview—namely, not interfering with the thought content of the patient—the therapist will become aware of certain immediate preoccupations. Irrespective of how unimportant the therapist considers these to be, it is urgent to heed them carefully. They may be far removed from the material the therapist wants to discuss, but to neglect or circumvent them, or to substitute other topics, constitutes a fatal error in interviewing.

Studies of the learning process show that the most effective learning occurs when the individual is concerned with things of strong emotional significance. Discussing material of no immediate interest to the patient interferes with learning; dealing with important moods and attitudes, facilitates learning. This is why the therapist must sensitize himself to current emotions and trends and not throw the patient off by introducing irrelevant topics or asking unrelated questions.

Sometimes it is difficult to select a dominant theme from the content of what the patient says. One may have to reach for feelings that lie behind verbalizations. Sometimes a great number of trends coexist and the therapist may have trouble selecting one as more significant than the others. Focusing on certain themes by asking pointed questions may be helpful here.

For instance, a patient talks about how hard things are for him because of the high cost of living. He is unable to afford luxuries any more. He needs new clothes; his wife wants a Florida vacation; his children are insistent on a new television set. Demands are being made on him to contribute a sum to a necessary charitable cause with which he is identified. He senses pressure from all sides, and this makes him feel disheartened and depressed. As he talks, the patient elaborates on each of the above items justifying the reasonableness of the demands made on him.

It may be hard at first to discern what it is that preoccupies the patient most. Is it that he is complaining about the unjust demands made by his family or by the world? Is he expressing a hidden wish to receive rather than to give? Does he consider his inability to supply luxuries a sign of his failure to live up to responsibilities or to an idealized image of himself? Is he criticizing the therapist subtly for depleting his funds? Is he projecting dissatisfactions from some other source onto immediate tangible foci?

Indicated in these questions are a number of themes which we might pursue, some of which would be productive and others not. One might easily go off on a tangent by focusing on the virtues of new clothes, vacations or television sets, or by talking about the high cost of living. Expressing anger toward his family would be presumptive on the part of the therapist and perhaps too reassuring. Interpreting a hidden wish to receive on the basis of the material presented would be making a judgment without adequate evidence. At least some pre-conscious awareness by the patient of this wish would be necessary. There is similarly not enough evidence to warrant the interpretation that the patient is subtly criticizing the therapist for exploiting him. However, focusing on his feeling that he is a failure in not being able to supply luxuries or make charitable contributions may be one way of starting a more intensive inquiry into his feelings. The comment, "Do you think that there is something wrong with you for not being able to do these things?" may then be expedient.

On the other hand, the therapist may not desire yet to explore the area of the patient's self-depreciation, and he may want to obtain more associations from the patient before focusing. Accordingly, he might remark, "You seem to be dissatisfied with things as they are." The latter statement may center the patient's attentions around his most provocative problems. This was the remark actually utilized during the session with the patient. A recorded fragment of the interview follows:

Th. You seem to be dissatisfied with things as they are.

Pt. Yes, I am. (*pause*) I sometimes wonder if I would do what I did if I lived my life through again. You see I really didn't want to quit school so early. But I had to get married. Sometimes I think it's a mistake to marry so young. You really don't have any idea about things.

Th. Do you feel *you* made a mistake in getting married so early?

Pt. Well, I do, in ways I really do. I could have waited, but she, my wife, insisted that we go ahead. And you know, doctor, when you have a family to support, well you pass up opportunities you could snap up.

Th. For instance? [*The patient then elaborates on his frustrated ambition and verbalizes resentment at his wife for exploiting him. This provides a basis for examining his dependency needs and his inability to stand up for his own rights.*]

It is seen in this interview that the actual content of what the patient brings into the session may be merely a reflection of deeper feelings. These may be elicited through careful interviewing.

While the comment made to the patient elicited satisfactory associations, it might not have done so at some other time. Thus, the patient might have responded with an outburst, elaborating on what he already had said in a frantic attempt to justify his feeling. He might have reacted also by commiserating with himself more intensely.

Other statements by the therapist may have been made rather than the one utilized; for example, "A lot of demands are being made on you these days. How do you feel about this?" or "Things do seem to be different. In what ways are they different?" Actually there is no "right" or "wrong" about the comments made, and the therapist must be guided by his own feelings as to which are the most important aspects to accent. The more experience he has had in interviewing, and the more skill he develops in doing therapy, the more satisfactory will be his selection.

The choosing of themes is complicated by the fact that the individual's verbalizations deal simultaneously with a number of different psychic levels. Most importantly the patient is concerned with three aspects: (1) current environmental distortions, (2) manifestations of his own characterologic strivings and façades, and (3) derivatives of unconscious impulses and strivings.

1. Existing environmental difficulties constitute a bulk of the individual's preoccupations. This is natural since the person is influenced by his environment in both positive and negative ways. During therapy he may discuss factors in his environment which facilitate gratification of needs, which produce satisfactory repression of destructive impulses, and which permit of a reasonably good relationship with others. More likely he will be prompted to talk about inadequacies in his environment that provoke inharmonious strivings, inspire conflict, create disturbances in interpersonal relations, and vitiate the satisfaction of basic needs.

2. The patient's characterologic manifestations will always reveal themselves in his account of current happenings. Involved in his daily life are the specific ways he relates to people, the distortions that contaminate his habitual

adjustments. These display themselves in attitudes and behavior tendencies toward authority figures, toward subordinates, as well as toward himself. Such patterns as dependency, aggression, detachment, perfectionism, masochism, sadism, and compulsive ambition may be interwoven into the fabric of his adjustment. The patient may be unaware of some of these destructive character traits, or of their compulsive nature; he may assume that they are quite normal, or he may accept them as an unusual though constitutional part of himself. The patient may verbalize circumstances that have thrown his character strivings out of adaptive balance.

3. The third and most repressed level involves the deepest conflicts that have survived the passage of time. These were initiated in the formative experiences of early childhood, and consist chiefly of unresolved fears, guilt feelings, and manifestations of shattered security and undermined self-esteem. Such conflicts reflect stages of development—oral, anal, phallic and genital—in which important traumata occurred. They exhibit themselves in such ways as incorporative tendencies; fears of starvation, oral injury, anal damage, contamination, hostility, murderous impulses and castration; incestuous desires and penis envy. Many repressive defenses shield unresolved infantile impulses and additionally contribute to the crippling of personality maturity. Because of repression, only distorted and highly symbolized derivatives of unconscious conflicts are available to awareness. These are sufficiently disguised to evade repressive barriers.

The following account of a session illustrates the simultaneous operation of the three main psychic levels described above. A patient started the session by reciting an incident that had happened two days previously during which he had experienced a brief attack of anxiety. While listening to a friend talk about golf, the patient began to feel uncomfortable and tense. He was filled with a sense of helplessness and with an expectation of impending but indefinable disaster. The attack passed, but he was left shaken. He could not understand why he had had such an attack, since there was nothing to account for it. As the patient continued talking, he revealed having been perturbed at receiving a letter from his employer in Boston inviting him to a house party at the employer's home to be given in a fortnight. His employer, a tycoon whom he admired, seemed to have an overweening amount of confidence in him, constantly commending him as the best man in the firm. He even had hinted at making the patient a director of his organization. Flattered, the patient developed misgivings at having duped his employer into thinking he was stronger than he was. While conceding that he had done a good job, he was aware of how frightened he was inside, how inferior and weak he felt most of the time—characteristics which contradicted the strength and masculinity his employer had imputed in him. The patient sought to avoid too intimate contact with his employer, lest the latter discover his weaknesses. On a business basis he was able to assume a sufficiently detached attitude to maintain what he considered to be a facade. His self-confident pose, however, was severely challenged whenever he socialized with his employer. Particularly upsetting were contacts with employer's friends. He felt vastly inferior in their company, especially when they paraded before him their wealth and other material signs of success. The last social visit he had paid to his employer had been like a nightmare. During the party, attended by important men in the business field, he had felt dizzy and upset. By sheer will power he had forced himself to stay. The next morning he had concocted a false emergency at home, and with vociferous regrets, had cut his visit short. He resolved never to return if he could possibly help it.

When the patient was asked, in the session, to talk about his employer, it was apparent that he both admired and envied the latter's great success and forcefulness, but resented his employer's curt, abrupt manner. He never had dared challenge the authority of his employer, since this would not have been discreet. Moreover, he had no desire to vent his resentment, since, in his opinion, his employer was a great man who had climbed to the top of his profession with little or no help. In his employer's presence he experienced a feeling like that of a small boy who was on his "good" behavior. That his employer reminded him of his father had become more and more apparent to him since he had started therapy. His feelings toward his father paralleled those toward his employer in an astonishing way. He had loved, admired and respected his father; he had feared and resented him too.

Questioned regarding his last bout of anxiety, the patient related having received an invitation from his employer to spend several weeks in the country. As an inducement, the employer promised to take the patient golfing daily. No novice at golf, the patient played a game far inferior to that of his employer. He realized now that he had tried to put out of his mind the invitation of his employer, in the ardent hope that something would eventually come up to prevent him from making the trip. He could see that the mention of golf, at the time immediately preceding his anxiety attack had reminded him then of the visit from which there seemed no escape.

The patient then recalled a dream he had had the evening of his attack. He was in a large barn-like structure that resembled the house of his grandfather. A large man walked into the room balancing an egg on a bloody stick. Then he saw himself drowning in a body of water. He awoke with a feeling of strangulation. Associating to the dream, the patient recalled the talks his father had with him during childhood on the subject of sex. His parent had warned of the dangers of masturbation and of sex play before marriage. He recollected how he had, in spite of these warnings, experimented with masturbation and with sex play, constantly anticipating an indefinable punishment. Even as an adult sex had seemed wrong.

Reviewing the content of this material, one may detect: (1) an assortment of provocative environmental circumstances (invitation to the home of the employer and the golf incident), (2) characterologic distortions (attitudes toward authority in general and toward his employer in particular), and (3) deep inner conflicts historically rooted in the past (fear of mutilation for sexual desires).

The selection of the material to be discussed will depend on what we are trying to achieve in the interview. Because flexibility is the keynote, the focus of concern may have to shift from one level to another—as from problems residual in unconscious conflict to those of an immediate situational nature. We may have to deal with certain levels to the exclusion of others. Thus in some patients, or in doing supportive therapy, it may be necessary to avoid stirring up inner conflict by keeping the interview on everyday situational problems. In other patients, we may purposefully avoid reality discussions, maintaining silences and encouraging the exploration of deeper emotional problems. The kind of content selected must at all times be that which would be most helpful to our immediate therapeutic objective.

2. Guiding the Theme into a Goal-Directed Channel

While the dominant theme may be the vehicle of the interview, it is essential to direct the theme toward a fruitful goal. Of his own accord the patient may not be interested in moving toward this goal. He may even resist violently attempts to shift the topic of discussion away from the goal that is dominant in his mind. It will be necessary, therefore, to accept the patient's choice of topic, and then try, in as subtle a way as possible, to influence the content of thought toward an important goal.

We may illustrate this, perhaps, by the example of a mule who is hopefully surveying a barn loaded with oats which is in a direction other than that toward which the driver of the mule seeks to head. This clash of motives results in an obstinate stalemate, the mule refusing to heed the injunctions of the driver. However, once allowed his freedom, the mule will start for the barn, and it may then be possible to take advantage of his momentum to divert him into a different direction. Our patient often acts very much like a mule when we try to push him toward an area of discussion in which he is not interested. Instead, if he is allowed full liberty of verbalization, it may be possible to swing him, by careful focusing, toward goals we consider of vital importance. This is done by establishing a relationship between the subject of the patient's preoccupations and the area the therapist considers to be important.

For instance, a patient who has recently started therapy comes to a session perturbed at the indifference of her husband. She has wanted a coat for some months and, after dropping several subtle unrewarded hints, has made an open demand. A vague promise has resulted in no action. Moreover, her husband has been acting bored with family life and has taken advantage of every opportunity to remain away from home, giving such reasons as union meetings and American Legion "get-togethers." The evening before the present session she felt emotionally excited and wanted to make love, but her husband informed her he was fatigued. He then retired early and she felt frustrated.

At the previous therapeutic session, the patient had professed curiosity about how mere talking could help her complaints of backaches and migraine. She seemed to show some distrust of the therapist. Since her distrust would interfere with a working relationship, we would be tempted to continue exploring it during the present session. To do this, however, would mean cutting her off from her desire to talk about her trouble with her husband.

Following the principles outlined above, she is encouraged to verbalize her feelings about her husband and an attempt was made to communicate empathy. At the same time her thinking is directed toward her feelings about the therapist. An excerpt of the interview follows:

Th. Was your husband always as indifferent as he seems to be now?

Pt. No, at the beginning of our marriage, things were different, more exciting I mean. But it didn't last more than a short time.

Th. Mm hmm.

Pt. He found more interest in other things than he did me. (*pause*)

Th. What about your relationships with other men besides your husband? Have you ever noticed how they react to you? [*The attempt here is to delineate a larger problem with men into which the pattern of her relationship with her husband fits.*]

Pt. (*pause*) Well, I never thought of it. I never got along too well, that is got too close. That is before my husband, I mean.

Th. What about *our* relationship? How do you feel *we* are getting along? [*Here an attempt is made to focus on the therapeutic relationship.*]

Pt. (*flustered*) Why I just didn't, don't know. I keep wondering if this is what will help me.

Th. Whether it's the sort of thing that will make you well?

Pt. Yes, I just don't know what you expect me to do.

Th. What do you think I expect you to do?

Pt. That's it, I just don't know if I will do what is right, that you will think I'm doing well.

Th. I see. I wonder if you don't have ideas about how I must feel about you.

Pt. Why, *should* I?

Th. It would be rather strange if you didn't have *some* ideas about me, and perhaps have wondered about how I feel about you.

Pt. Yes, as a matter of fact, I did wonder. But why should you feel anything about me?

Th. Perhaps you feel I am indifferent to you?

Pt. Why should you feel any other way?

Th. In what way have I acted indifferently? [*From this point on there is an exploration of her expectations of rejection in the therapeutic relationship.*]

Were the patient in the middle phases of therapy, and were the relationship with the therapist a good one, the focus of therapy would be on exploring the broader dynamics of her feelings that men reject her, on the role she plays in bringing on rejection, and on the genetic origins of this trend. The interview would be directed into channels that would point toward these goals.

The goals pursued are also related to the kinds of therapy done. In supportive therapy, the ultimate goal may be the correction of a situational disturbance. The therapist here organizes his interviewing around the following aims:

1. The establishing of a working relationship with the patient.

2. The understanding of all factors in the environment which provoke stress.

3. The evolution of a plan for coping with the stress situation, and the execution of this plan once the individual is brought to a realization of his potentialities and aptitudes.

4. The termination of therapy.

In reeducative therapy, the general goal is a reorganization of the individual's destructive attitudes and behavior patterns. Interviewing is pursued along these lines:

1. The establishing of a working relationship with the patient.

2. The understanding of the more conscious irrational attitudes and patterns which interfere with a good adjustment.

3. After evaluating positive assets and liabilities, the mobilization of activity toward a reintegration of attitudes.

4. The termination of therapy.

In reconstructive psychotherapy, the successive goals are these:

1. The establishing of a working relationship with the patient.

2. The understanding of unconscious conflicts, through exploration of verbal associations, dreams, fantasies, slips of speech and behavioral irrationalities, both inside and outside of therapy.

3. The utilization of the gained insight toward the freeing of oneself from the effects of unconscious conflict, with resolution of blocks in self-development and maturity.

4. The termination of therapy.

All activity during a session, including the selection of content for focusing, is organized around the goals that dominate an existing phase of therapy.

The general area of inquiry around which the interview is focused will, furthermore, vary with the kind of therapy performed. Thus, the prime focus may be on the environmental distortions that surround the person, and on the symptomatic disturbances that immobilize him. This is the case in supportive therapy where the aims are: first, to reduce environmental pressures to a point where the patient can deal with them with his existing personality resources, and, second, to restore homeostasis within the person which was unbalanced by his illness. No concentrated attempt is made here to modify character strivings or to deal with deep inner conflicts. The focus in reeducative therapy may involve examining how the individual relates to people, and the contradictions of his disturbed drives. An inquiry into the more conscious character drives may have to be made, with the hopes of enabling the patient to suppress those drives that disorganize adjustment, and of encouraging others that expedite adjustment. An inquiry into the more unconscious drives is the object of reconstructive therapy. Here the understanding of the more repressed strivings is facilitated by the examination and analysis of dreams, fantasies and transference manifestations. There may be an exploration of infantile and childhood experiences and fears, as well as the immature strivings they embrace.

3. Circumscribing the Area of Subject Coverage

Studies of the learning process show that only a relatively limited number of things can be mentally absorbed and integrated at the same time. For this reason, once a dominant theme has been guided into a goal-directed channel, it is essential to focus on as concentrated an area as possible during any one session. Taking up one subject at a time, and exploring as many facets of it as possible, will result in the most effective use of the interview.

A patient, in the middle phases of reconstructive therapy, for example, presents in one session the dominant theme of how, since her marriage, she has tended to give up her own creative activities for family responsibilities. The exploration of her attitudes toward married life, and the sacrifices entailed therein, are believed by the therapist to be in line with the goal of understanding the dynamics of her psychosomatic complaints. By verbal and non-verbal means, he therefore encourages the flow of verbalizations along these lines. The patient responds by recounting the events of the past day. Her child dawdled at breakfast. This irritated her so much that she felt like pushing his face into the cereal. Things at home have continued to be "in a mess." Her part-time maid is on a rampage, and may have to be discharged. She fears getting another maid with problems as serious or more serious than those of her present maid. Because her maid had come to work late yesterday, she was delayed in attending a meeting of the parent-teacher association. She anticipates getting out of the house, but she does not get too much pleasure from parent-teacher meetings. Indeed, she has been having some difficulty with an aggressive, argumentative member of the parent-teacher organization who is opposing a resolution for a new school building. She is considering giving up her post as secretary of the organization in order to spend her time studying Spanish. Some day she would like to visit South America because she has been told it is a romantic country. This reminds her of a book she has been reading about Brazil. The book is about the Amazon River. It was sent to her by the Book-of-the-Month Club. She wonders if she would really be happy in South America because of all the insects and diseases that must infest this continent. The United States is the healthiest of all places to live. If only she could be happier. She had hoped that therapy would be able to do this for her. Perhaps she should explore the possibilities of getting an outside part-time job. She might in this way make herself more useful.

This type of rambling achieves very little unless we can confine it to a limited, but significant area. Possibilities are:

(1) Exploration of her feelings about her child and his dawdling. A question such as: "Your child, does he dawdle much at meals?" may open up the subject of her attitudes toward her child and his rebellious behavior. This may lead us into the field of her relationships to other members of the family, and her feelings about herself as a wife and mother.

(2) Exploration of her activities away from home; for instance, the teacher-parent association and the possibilities of her getting an outside job. We may ask: "You put in a good deal of work there. What do you get out of it?" This may encourage an elaboration of her ambitions.

(3) Exploration of her feelings about the recalcitrant member of the association. The comment: "This woman must stir things up in you" may help her

verbalize her feelings of competitiveness and her attitudes toward this woman as well as toward the other members.

(4) Exploration of the general subject that things are not entirely satisfactory at home. One may remark: "There are things that go on in your life right now that bother you. What bothers you most right ~ow?" This may center the patient's attention around her current unhappiness.

(5) Exploration of her feelings about therapy. A comment may thus be phrased: "You seem to be disappointed that therapy has not done for you what you had anticipated it would do for you." This would open up an inquiry into her resistances to therapy and the therapist.

Which of the above aspects to stress would be difficult to say, since this would be determined by the needs of the immediate situation. However, there are certain general rules of priority in content selection. Sensitizing himself to the trends in the patient's verbalizations, the therapist may select topics in the following order:

1. Negative feelings toward the therapist.

2. Negative feelings toward therapy.

3. Unwarranted or unrealistic attitudes toward the therapist; such as, sexual demands or fantasies, aggressive impulses, overwhelming dependency, and serious detachment.

4. Resistances to exploring attitudes or feelings that could give the patient insight into his problem.

5. Resistances to translating insight into action where the patient has gained an understanding of his problems.

6. Feelings of any sort that are verbalized.

7. Feelings that are not openly expressed, but seem to underlie the content of thought.

8. Dreams, fantasies and slips of speech (except in supportive therapy).

9. Observations of the relationship of his symptoms to certain environmental happenings.

10. Pressing environmental concerns and interpersonal relationships with attempts to differentiate realistic problems from projections.

11. Important past experiences and relationships.

Returning to our patient, it will be seen that on the basis of priority items, the second possibility listed (negative feelings toward therapy) would be the best. The interview would be focused as much as possible on her feelings about therapy and why she seems to be discouraged at her progress. This does not imply that the other possibilities are unimportant. However, in order for the patient to benefit most from the interview, dealing with her resistances to therapy would be strategically more important than exploring a character trait at a time when she is in an emotionally discouraged mood. Later, the other possibilities might be considered appropriate items for discussion.

In order to help circumscribe the areas explored, the therapist may apply the principles already outlined for maintenance of the flow of verbalizations, so long as the patient is talking about a selected trend. If he veers off into an irrelevant area, the therapist may focus on pertinent material by quickly summarizing what the patient has said and then asking a question related to the selected area. Resistance to exploring this area, in the form of blocking, evasions, fatigue and other reactions will have to be dealt with by further questions or by interpretations. If the patient persists in dealing with an unimportant subject as a defensive manifestation against handling important material—for instance, if he insists on talking about his car or a current television program at a time when he should be exploring important relationships with people—the therapist may employ certain discouraging tactics. Thus, he may attempt to divert the patient with certain comments, such as: "Now that's very interesting, but I'd like to get back to what we were just talking about." He may then ask a question dealing with this material. If the patient again resists, he may have to handle the patient's resistance directly.

A patient who had been discussing his feelings of discouragement because of his impotence mentioned an impending date with a young woman who was a musician. He then veered off into a prolonged account of the virtues of "Dixieland jazz" over "Bebop." A fragment of the recorded interview follows:

Th. That's very interesting, but I'd like to go back to this young woman and the date with her. How do you feel about it?

Pt. (*pause*) Well, all right, she's a very interesting sort and we have a lot in common. I expect that she doesn't approve too much of my views about music, because she has some ideas of her own. She likes jazz all right, but not the way I do. Now we happened to be together at Eddie Condon's place one night, and his orchestra played a whole series of old numbers, reorchestrated for his band. He . . .

Th. (*interrupting*) Yes, there may be a number of differences of opinion that you have with this girl, but what do you expect will happen when you have your next date with her? [*bringing patient back to the subject*]

Pt. Well, I don't know exactly. I suppose we'll end up in bed.

Th. How do you feel about that?

Pt. I don't know. It sort of scares me in a way. If I could only have an erection and get started.

Th. Perhaps what concerns you is that you may have a repeat failure on your record, that is, that you won't be able to perform. That must upset you.

Pt. It sure does, I hardly feel like talking about it. In fact I wanted to call the whole thing off.

Th. Maybe that's why you find it so hard to talk on this subject. It upsets you.

Pt. Yes, yes, it does, and then I feel like chucking the whole thing up. [*The remainder of the session is concerned with dealing with the patient's resistances to exploring his impotency problem.*]

INCULCATING INSIGHT

The act of verbalization often suffices to help the individual convert vague feelings and undeveloped convictions into concrete explicit formulations. The therapist helps the process of insight by getting the patient to focus on significant areas of his life. Before this can be done, however, the therapist must himself know which aspects are important enough to accent at any given time.

By observing the patient's verbal and non-verbal behavior within the session, by listening to his account of what has happened in his relations with people outside of therapy, by scrutinizing his dreams and fantasies, the therapist will gain an understanding of driving motivational forces. Everything the patient says or does during the treatment session must be carefully noted. This includes how he walks into the room; his posture as he sits in the chair, his bodily movements, gestures and facial expressions; random muscle spasms and tensions; how he gets out of the chair; and how he leaves the room. In the patient's verbal behavior, the therapist must note not only the content of what is said, but the inflections, intonations, evasions, silences, blocks and other evidences of emotion. Listening intently to *what* the patient says, the therapist concentrates on *why* certain verbalizations occur—the underlying feelings and conflicts that evade the awareness of the patient. The therapist must alert himself to the meaning behind the content, by observing the patient's associational processes, shifts in emphasis, omissions, denials, inconsistencies, undue underscorings, inappropriate attitudes or emotions, and slips of speech. He sensitizes himself to the existence of trends in the content of thought, and to underlying emotions. The more experience the therapist has had, the more "intuitive" he will be in perceiving significant areas.

The therapist has at his disposal a number of maneuvers he can use to help the patient achieve insight. Among these are accenting, summarizing, restating, reflecting, establishing connections, maintaining tension, extending support, and making interpretations.

1. Accenting

Where the therapist observes an important trend in the patient's verbalizations, he may ask a number of questions related to this trend, or he may repeat again and again what the patient has said. By bringing it to the patient's attention constantly, and getting him to think about it in a concentrated way, the trend is highlighted in the awareness of the patient. This encourages him to explore its purpose and origin. Accenting is also useful in getting the patient to accept certain facts about himself and his situation. These may have escaped verbalization for the following reasons: (1) a lack of incentive to reveal facts, (2) a conscious fear of such revelations, (3) unconscious fear of the factual implications, (4) a confusion as to which facts are important, and (5) complete ignorance of what the facts are, due to repression. Pointed questions help the patient break through his resistances. Repetition serves the added purposes of questioning the validity of the patient's comments and of obtaining more information about specific topics.

2. Summarizing

The patient is often rambling in his verbal account. He may become so engrossed in details, that he loses sight of the interrelationship of the various topics he discusses. He may fail to connect casual happenings with basic themes. A rapid summarization, from time to time, is therefore helpful in pulling together material which seems to be uncoordinated. It is useful also as a measure preliminary to a pertinent question intended for purposes of focusing.

3. Restating

Recasting certain statements of the patient into different words brings out related aspects of the material that may have escaped the patient's attention. It also verbalizes what may be difficult for the patient to say. The repetitive reformulations involved in restating, emphasize important trends in the patient's mind and help him to rephrase his problems in more cogent terms.

4. Reflecting

Reading between the lines of what the patient says, the therapist attunes himself to feelings affiliated with verbalizations, to emotional undercurrents of the content of thought, as well as to attitudes that have not been expressed. He reflects these back to the patient, putting them into terms the patient will be able to accept without stirring up too much anxiety. For instance, a patient launches into great praise of his employer and the possessions of the employer: Cadillac car, country estate and important friends. The therapist senses jealousy and restrained contempt in the patient's tone. He reflects these feelings by saying: "Yet some of the things your employer does may irritate you." The patient responds by cautiously criticizing, then openly attacking his employer. The exposure of the patient's feelings and acceptance of these by the therapist relieve guilt and encourage a deeper exploration of emotions and conflicts.

5. Establishing Connections

Due to the factor of repression, even obvious connections between symptoms, feelings and inner conflicts may not be seen by the patient. The association of daily happenings in the patient's life with tension and anxiety states that are constantly being mobilized also continues to remain vague. The patient will, therefore, require help from the therapist who establishes the connections for him. For instance, a female patient, suffering from attacks of migraine, manifests such attacks following contact with strong, aggressive women. For a long time, the patient has no idea that there is any association between her attitudes toward aggressive women and her headaches. In recounting her experiences, she presents these two situations as isolated and unrelated events. Whenever this happens, the therapist attempts to fuse the two by saying: "Now here is a situation where you get in a tangle with an aggressive woman and following this you get a headache." The patient may not respond with insight to this connection at first, but repeated comments along the same line, whenever the facts justify them, bring the patient around to seeing a causal relationship of the one to the other.

6. Maintaining Tension in the Interview

The maintenance of a certain amount of tension in the interview is essential in getting the patient to think things through for himself. Tension acts as a driving force by creating in the patient an incentive for change through active participation in the therapeutic process. On the other hand, a relaxed, tensionless state tends to diminish activity. Tension may be created in a number of ways, particularly by focusing on provocative topics, by asking challenging questions related to painful or avoided subjects, by giving the patient interpretations of his disturbed attitudes or behavior, and by the strategic use of silence.

By maintaining silence, the therapist initiates a state of discomfort in the patient. Discomfort deepens into tension which may promote a spontaneous exploration of feeling. Unfortunately, the patient may react adversely to silence, interpreting it as evidence of the therapist's rejection or hostility. For this reason, silence must be employed discreetly and not too frequently, the other indicated measures being more often utilized to promote tension.

Where tension is created in the interview, it must never be permitted to grow to a point where it overwhelms the coping resources of the individual, producing destructive or infantile reactions, such as "acting-out" tendencies and other strong resistances to the therapeutic process. In the event such contingencies occur, the therapist will have to step in with supportive measures to alleviate the tension state.

7. Extending Measured Support

Measured support is given the patient whenever the ego resources crumble and the patient shows symptoms of collapse. This temporary prop may help the patient retain the insights he has developed, since it prevents the ego from employing repressive and regressive defenses elaborated to preserve its integrity. An ego threatened by too great anxiety may protect itself by repudiating the insights it should integrate. Among the measures practiced to give the patient support are reassurance, avoidance of conflictual topics, and direct advice and guidance. For example, reassuring comments may involve statements like, "In spite of all your difficulties, you have achieved a good deal in life." Following this one may enumerate positive achievements of the patient, or the patient may be told, "All people make mistakes and go through periods of misery." Such techniques must be employed sparingly and only where absolutely necessary, particularly in reconstructive therapy.

8. Making Interpretations

The making of interpretations is an important step in promoting insight, since it constitutes a frontal attack on existing blocks in the patient and enables him to come to grips with anxiety. Anxiety is at the root of practically all psychopathologic problems. Defenses against anxiety cripple the adjustment capacities of the patient, causing him to react in an inappropriate way to casual happenings. Interpretations, directed at bringing the patient to an awareness of his anxiety, show him how he is reacting to this emotion and the defenses he utilizes in warding it off. Interpretations also help to dissolve resistances which constantly interfere with the patient's capacities to think for himself. Interpreting blocks which prevent the patient from becoming aware of his problems is a prime task in interviewing.

While interpretation is one of the chief tools of the psychotherapist, it is not without its dangers. Confronting the patient with repudiated aspects of his psyche may promote greater anxiety and stimulate more obdurate resistances toward the warded-off content. Consequently, it is important to interpret to the patient only material of which he has at least pre-conscious awareness. For instance, a patient came late for a session. By observing his behavior and verbalizations, the writer got the impression that the patient felt hostile toward him. This seemed to be substantiated by a dream in which the patient fled from a monster who turned into a doctor. There was a temptation to confront the patient with his hostility. However, therapeutic conservatism necessitated biding one's time, until the patient came out with a statement of how he felt. The following is a recorded fragment of the interview:

Th. I wonder how you have been feeling?

Pt. All right, I guess. (*pause*)

Th. All right? (*pause*)

Pt. Well, yes and no. I felt upset a little when I found I was late.

Th. Mm hmm.

Pt. I just can't seem to remember the exact time of my appointment.

Th. I wonder why? [*focusing on the causes of the patient's lateness*]

Pt. I guess so many things are going on that I just don't think of it. (*pause*)

Th. I wonder if there might be other reasons? [*again focusing on causes*]

Pt. Are there, I mean do you think there are?

Th. I don't know, but often when a person comes late, he does so because of certain feelings about therapy or the therapist. (*long pause*)

Pt. Well, to tell you the truth coming here does upset me, that is, lately.

Th. I wonder why?

Pt. I keep getting feelings as if you've done something, or haven't done something, like as if you want to spite me.

Th. Mm hmm.

Pt. Yes, that's what it is. You know this is silly because I can't figure out why I feel this way.

Th. Is there anything I have done that has upset you? [*attempting to differentiate reality from projection*]

Pt. Honestly, doctor, you haven't.

Th. Then you must be resentful toward me for some other reason.

Pt. I feel flashes of resentment, but I don't know why. That's probably why I've had trouble coming here, on time I mean.

It will seem from the above that the patient has been led to make his own interpretations. Dangers are minimal where this is done. The therapist helps the patient by giving him cues, by arranging material in a sequence, and by asking him pointed questions. The patient is encouraged to feel that he is in a position to refuse to see what is going on if insight is unacceptable to him. Figuring things out for himself facilitates therapeutic progress immeasurably.

From time to time, however, it will be necessary to give the patient direct interpretations, especially when the patient's resistances prevent him from making his own interpretations. The kind of relationship the therapist has with the patient, and the manner in which interpretations are presented, are important here. If the relationship is a good one, and if interpretations are made in a non-judgmental way, they can have a beneficial effect. Interpretations must always be given in such a manner that the patient feels free to reject them if he wishes. To insist that the patient accept interpretations is a poor tactic.

Instead of presenting an interpretation as an authoritative dictum, one may precede it with such phrases as "Perhaps" or "It would seem as if." This gives the patient a feeling that the therapist is not being arbitrary. Where the therapist has good reason for feeling an interpretation to be true, and where it has been offered to the patient and rejected by him, he may say, "Well, maybe it doesn't appear plausible right now. Suppose you think about it, and observe yourself, and see if later it makes more sense." If the patient tries to force the therapist into being absolute in his declaration, the therapist may reply, "I get the *impression* that the situation as I have indicated it *may* be true. But it's important for *you* to test it out for yourself, and see if you feel it really applies to you." Eventually the patient may come around to accepting the validity of the therapist's impression.

Interpretations may be made in relation to any unconscious or partly conscious aspect of behavior or psychic life. Of particular importance is the use of interpretation in dealing with resistance and in uncovering repressed material.

Interpretation of resistance helps the patient make progress in therapy. For instance, a patient with the problem of impotence comes into a session in a distraught state. He rambles along on inconsequential topics and keeps looking at his watch every few minutes as if he is anxious for the session to end. The recorded fragment follows:

Th. I wonder why you have been checking the time so often. [*bringing the patient to an awareness of an unusual aspect of behavior*]

Pt. Oh, I've been wondering what time it is.

Th. I see. (*gazing at his own watch*) It's 10:24. (*pause*)

Pt. Time seems to go so slow today.

Th. I wonder why?

Pt. I just don't seem to have anything to talk about.

Th. Nothing?

Pt. I can't think of anything.

Th. I wonder if there is anything that bothers you, that you don't like to talk about? [*focusing on possible resistance*]

Pt. Like what?

Th. Well, what would be unpleasant to talk about? (*pause*)

Pt. (*smiles*) You know what flashed through my mind?

Th. What?

Pt. I almost forgot the date I made with Helen tonight.

Th. Mm hmm.

Pt. It's something I feel I've got to do, but I don't feel up to it. Maybe I'll call it off.

Th. Any reason for calling it off?

Pt. It's nothing too important. I thought I might go to the Met tonight.

Th. I wonder if you just don't want to avoid seeing Helen because of the fear of the sex business. [*interpreting*]

Pt. I suppose I should go through with it, but I'm afraid of disappointing her again.

Th. Mm hmm. And suppose she was disappointed?

Pt. I'd be disappointed and upset.

Th. You feel you want to be successful and don't want to face any disappointments. [*further interpretation*]

Pt. (*laughs*) I guess that's why I didn't want to talk, to tell you I was going to break the date. I guess I shouldn't really break the date, because it's silly to feel I'll be rejected. I must be really scared of failure.

Interpretation of the content of the repressed is less frequently practiced, and is utilized only in reconstructive therapy where the therapist has a very good relationship with the patient. A woman dating a man for the first time, experienced faintness, heart palpitations and overwhelming fear in his presence. She talks of this experience during the session. The recorded fragment follows:

Th. What do you think this is all about?

Pt. I don't know.

Th. Here you meet this man and then you get this attack.

Pt. Yes, it sounds funny.

Th. Do you think there is any connection between seeing this man and your attack?

Pt. There must be, but what?

Th. Well what? (*pause*) What do *you* think?

Pt. I . . . I don't know, doctor, I really don't.

Th. Well, perhaps the man stirred up feelings in you, upset you, scared you? [*interpreting deep fear of men*]

Pt. (*blushes, stammers, pauses*) Yes, I feel upset. This kind of man makes me feel funny.

Th. What kind of a man is he?

Pt. Well, his eyes and build. He reminds me of my father when he was drinking, which was most of the time.

In interpreting the content, it is important to remember that material from dreams, slips of speech, and transference manifestations should not be directly interpreted until the patient gives evidence of having some conscious or preconscious awareness of the material.

Interpretations must be made repeatedly to be effective. The first interpretation may be resisted violently. If the patient has an untoward reaction, the therapist must respect the patient's resistance, and perhaps make allowance for the fact that his interpretation may be wrong. He may say: "Perhaps we can explore this further to see what the real situation may be." As the core of resistance is resolved, the patient may himself later acknowledge the accuracy of the therapist's observation.

Interpretation is so vital a technique in interviewing that a special chapter is devoted to it in a later section of the book.

TERMINATING THE INTERVIEW

The proper termination of the interview is extremely important. There are some therapists who mismanage this phase of the interview due to a fear that they may offend the patient. Thus they are unable to interrupt a patient at the end of a session for many minutes after the interview time has terminated. The invasion of the next patient's hour complicates the schedule of the therapist, and creates resentment in the succeeding patients.

No matter how lenient the therapist may be in other respects, strict adherence to a time schedule is important. If the therapist allows at least five minutes' interval between patients, he will be able to extend several minutes' time to a patient who is upset, or to one who is dealing with highly charged material. The only exceptions to a rigid time schedule are treatment sessions with very sick schizophrenic patients. Here, at least fifteen minutes of leeway between sessions should be arranged in advance to allow for an extension of the interview if necessary.

In terminating a session, one may take the opportunity in a pause in the patient's conversation to say: "All right," (mentioning the patient's name), or "All right, we meet again on ———," (mentioning the next appointment date). This interruption becomes a signal to which the patient will respond automatically after it has been used several times. In the event the patient is discoursing on an important topic, the therapist may add: "We'll continue with this next time." If the patient, on occasion, continues to talk for too long after interruption, he may simply be told: "I'm afraid we'll have to stop. We'll talk about that next session." By his manner, the therapist should convey an interest in the patient right to the moment he leaves the room. It is important not to dismiss the patient arbitrarily nor to engage in other tasks, like reading one's mail, before the patient goes.

Some patients linger at the door talking on and on. The therapist here may simply remark: "That's very interesting. Suppose you think about it and we'll discuss it next time." If the patient asks the therapist a question that requires time to answer, the therapist may say: "That's a good question, suppose you think about it, and we'll talk it over next time you come."

SPECIAL PROBLEMS IN INTERVIEWING

A number of special conditions may occur that will call for certain responses on the part of the therapist. Among these are the following situations:

1. Occasions will arise when the patient will bring up names and events he

has mentioned in the past which the therapist does not remember. Here the therapist may remark: "I don't distinctly remember. I wonder if you would mind repeating what you had said about (mentioning the person or the event) to refresh my memory."

2. If the patient asks the therapist a personal question, it is important to find out why the question is asked. Thus if the patient asks: "Doctor, are you married?" the therapist may reply: "You're curious about me." After the patient has responded, the therapist may ask: "Do you think I'm married?" As a general rule, it is best to be truthful with a patient, and, once the reasons behind the patient's questions are discerned, they should be answered as directly as possible.

3. If the patient indulges in self-devaluation, by making such statements as: "I'm a queer, peculiar person," or "I really am terrible," or "I'm a hopeless mess," the therapist must never agree. He may ask: "What makes you think you are?"

4. If the patient continues to engage in intellectual discussions, or talks about topics like the weather, sports and current events, one may interrupt in a manner illustrated by the following excerpt:

Pt. What do you think about Truman's seizure of the steel industry? Isn't it something for the books? When I heard about it, it made me feel we were living on top of a bomb. Cholly Knickerbocker says . . .

Th. Yes, now what about you? [*The focus may also be brought back to the patient with such questions as "How does that affect you?"*]

5. There will be times when the therapist feels restless, and when he manifests discomfort by shifting around in the chair or moving his hands or feet. These movements may be interpreted by the patient as evidence of the therapist's disinterest or even maladjustment. If the patient comments on the therapist's fidgetiness, the therapist may ask the patient what he believes this signifies. If an answer is not easily forthcoming, the therapist may ask the patient if he believes the therapist's movements indicate disinterest. The therapist may, if the facts warrant it, give the patient a plausible explanation for his own restlessness, such as that sitting all day in a chair makes one want to stretch his muscles a little. This does not indicate disinterest in the patient.

6. Tempting as it may be, the therapist should resist the urge to give the patient direct suggestions which he insists must be followed; to engage in talk about himself, his accomplishments, and his problems; or to chastise the patient irrespective of the provocation.

THE INTERPERSONAL CLIMATE OF THE INTERVIEW

Without a congenial working relationship with the patient, there will be little progress even with the most expert interviewing techniques. Such an atmosphere will be present where the therapist possesses personality qualities of sensitivity, objectivity, flexibility and empathy; where he accepts the patient uncritically, refraining from arbitrary, moralistic and punitive responses; and where he shows sincere respect for the patient's growth potentials. The maintenance of a tolerant, accepting, permissive attitude will eventually convince the patient that the therapist's role is to help the patient to understand himself, not to hold him in judgment. This unqualified, sympathetic acceptance enables the patient to explore further within himself and his environment for sources of his trouble, and helps him to bring up material he has found difficult to verbalize even to himself. The calm scrutiny of his productions, with absence of praise, surprise, blame or shock, cuts deeply into the defenses of the patient with exposure of the most disturbing and painful conflicts.

Were we to enumerate rules for maintaining the proper interpersonal climate during interviewing, we might list the following:

1. Try to put oneself in the patient's position in order to see things from his point of view. It is obviously impossible to feel exactly what the patient feels because his reactions are habitually different from the therapist's reactions. Nevertheless, approximating his situation as closely as possible, and considering his background and experience, are important.

2. Appreciate the impossibility of understanding the patient's reaction patterns from the standpoint of common sense. Realistically viewed, the patient's symptoms and behavior seem futile and destructive. Yet they are compelling, and persist in the face of the most intense exercise of will power. It is necessary to realize that the years of conditioning responsible for symptoms will not yield themselves to a few months of therapy.

3. Recognize that one is, willy-nilly, going to be prejudiced in relation to some aspect of the patient's problem. One cannot escape being disturbed and perhaps even shocked by certain past experiences or present impulses of the patient. The fact that they conflict with one's sense of "right" and "good" does not necessarily make them "wrong" and "bad." Cognizance of this will make for greater tolerance of values and attitudes that do not coincide with those of the therapist.

4. The reactions of the patient toward the therapist—such as of awe, reverence or hostility—often have little to do with the therapist as a real person. They may be carry-overs of attitudes toward past authorities, or they may be dramatized feelings toward idealized authorities. It is, consequently, important not to react to unpleasant, seductive, insulting or provocative responses as if they were personal assaults or favors.

5. The therapist's reactions to the patient may also be determined by projections from his own past. It is essential to examine responses toward the patient like anger, boredom, sexual feeling, and over-concern. Not only must the expression of such responses be controlled, but they must be thoroughly analyzed by the therapist as to source and meaning. While personal biases and blind spots may be recognized, they may still be hard to control. But recognition of them will be of great help in preventing a too harsh judging of the patient and a blocking of his rights to self-determination.

6. Flexible and tolerant leadership is the ideal matrix of the therapist-patient relationship. No matter how passive or non-directive the therapist may wish to be, he remains the leader in the therapeutic relationship. The manner in which leadership is applied will help determine treatment results. If the leadership is arbitrary, intolerant and punitive, this will merely repeat the reactions of past traumatizing authorities. The patient will respond with compliance and defiance, and there will be an absence of constructive growth. If the leadership is minimally arbitrary, the patient will have an opportunity to work through his feelings toward authority, gaining a new concept of himself in the direction of personality maturity. Accordingly, the therapist must refrain from dominating the interview, allowing the patient to talk even with tendencies to ramble. He must never cross-examine, ridicule, laugh at, or belittle the patient, nor should he argue with the patient, or engage in extensive polemics with him. Contraindicated are open disagreements with the patient over his religion and politics. The therapist must respect the patient's rights to his own ideas and convictions, even though these are neurotic. There will be times when the therapist must be firm, as when the patient is neurotically disposed to hurt himself. There are other times when the tolerance of Job will be required, even while the patient is making what seem to be unnecessary mistakes.

7. There is a need for faith in the basic goodness of human beings, in the potentialities that all people possess for personality growth and maturity. The therapist must view disturbed reactions as responses of illness, and he must respect the essential integrity of the patient in the face of any abnormalities he may display.

16

The Physical Surroundings of Psychotherapy

THE PHYSICAL SURROUNDINGS ARE THE LEAST IMPORTANT FACTORS THAT enter into psychotherapy. If the therapist has the proper didactic, personality and experiential equipment, he will be able to do good psychotherapy in almost any kind of setting. Once psychotherapy is under way, and the working relationship has developed, the surroundings do not seem to make much difference, provided they are not too uncomfortable.

A poor kind of physical set-up, nevertheless, may create certain complications. Due to the inevitable projections that occur in psychotherapy, the physical surroundings should be made as minimally provocative of frustration and hostility as is possible.

PHYSICAL PLAN

It goes without saying that the therapist's office should be reasonably warm, properly ventilated without drafts, and free from disturbing extraneous noises. Obvious comforts need to be provided. These include a conveniently accessible bathroom and a mirror for grooming on leaving the therapist's office. The lights should be as soft as possible, while making provision for accessory illumination for note-taking on the part of the therapist, and for reading written material by the patient.

Because the material discussed with the therapist is highly confidential, the patient should be assured that others will not listen in on his conversations. Arrangements will have to be made to prevent what is being said in the therapist's office from being overheard by people in the waiting room. This may mean hanging draperies on the walls adjoining the waiting room, or it may necessitate an extensive alteration job employing sound-proofing materials. Where sound-proofing or sound-deadening arrangements cannot be practically made, a good arrangement is a separation of the waiting room from the office by at least one intermediate room. Where this is not possible, some therapists have found it convenient to operate a small fan or an air-conditioning unit in the office or waiting room, the distracting adventitious sounds of the motors serving to make indistinguishable the conversations going on in the therapist's office.

A system of separate exits and entrances so that patients will not meet each other is sometimes advised. In the opinion of the writer this precaution is not necessary and merely plays into the patient's idea that it is shameful to possess an emotional problem. There is no reason why the patient should not accept as part of the reality situation the fact that the therapist treats people other than himself. Any anxieties, hostilities or jealousies that are engendered by meeting other patients who may be regarded as rivals may be handled in a therapeutic way.

Practical circumstances sometimes require that a psychiatrist's home and office be together. This fact need not be harmful to the therapeutic objective, provided that no distracting influences obtrude themselves into the therapeutic situation. Interruptions by tradespeople, the presence of children playing in the waiting room, engaging in such activities as would be normal in any home, and other influences related to problems of maintaining a household, understandably may impose hardships on both the patient and the therapist. Where such interferences cannot be controlled, a separation of home and office is mandatory.

DECORATIVE SCHEME

The decorative schemes of the office and waiting room are not too important. Disturbing pictures, gaudy draperies and embellishments should be avoided. In the early phases of therapy, the patient may extract cues from the surroundings to help him in his estimate of the kind of human being he is dealing with in the therapist. At the same time, he may project into the surroundings his own emotional attitudes, and he may try to find evidences for his prejudices in the decorative tastes and furniture preferences of the therapist. The decorative plan, hence, is of not too great consequence, so long as it is not too outlandish.

FURNISHINGS

The furnishings of the waiting room should be simple, consisting of a few chairs, coffee table, ash trays, and selected magazines. It is to be expected that the patient will tend to judge the therapist by the kinds of reading material he finds in the waiting room. A clothes rack and umbrella stand are important conveniences.

The furnishings of the office are also simple. Absolute requirements are two comfortable chairs facing each other. These should neither be too hard nor too soft. Massive, lounge-like chairs are orthopedically bad for the therapist, since they do not give him the proper back support in the long periods of sitting to which he will be exposed. They also tend to frighten some patients who feel trapped within the confines of their embrace. There is some advantage in having the chairs as closely similar to each other as is possible, in terms of size and height of seat. Since one of the goals in therapy is to bring the patient to a point where he feels himself to be on an equal plane with other human beings, some therapists believe that the seating arrangement should not emphasize the difference between therapist and patient. A huge chair in which the therapist towers above the patient imposes an artificial barrier to the cooperative, "give-and-take" atmosphere that should prevail in treatment.

In addition to the chairs that are employed in interviewing, one may have an additional side chair or two for use in conferences with members of the patient's family on the rare occasions when these are necessary. One may also have a desk for writing up reports and records. A comfortable couch in the room is also helpful, where the therapist wishes to employ the technique of free association, or where the patient is dealing with painful material of a transference nature, which might be diluted through observation of the facial expressions of the therapist. Accessories such as conveniently placed end tables, ash trays and matches are necessities. Folding chairs may be stored in a closet and used for conferences or for group therapy.

PETS

Some therapists enjoy having a pet, such as a dog or cat, in their offices on the basis that this creates a homey atmosphere. However, the presence of a pet in the room creates turmoil in some patients, who may regard the pet as a rival, and then, realizing that their resentment is unreasonable, suppress or repress feelings of hostility. The behavior of the pet, whether it is quiet, noisy or seeking of attention, may influence the character of the patient's responses. In general, then, the presence of a pet in the office, is distracting although the patient may manage to adjust himself to its presence.

TELEPHONE

The matter of the telephone is important in any description of the physical surroundings of therapy. Arrangements are best made so that the phone bell may be disconnected during sessions, since telephone calls constitute a serious interruption in the continuity of the therapeutic hour. They are naturally resented by the patient, and if they occur frequently enough, may disturb the therapeutic relationship. Except for extreme emergencies, then, telephone conversations should be restricted to times between sessions. This is no problem in clinics where a switchboard is used. There may, however, be a problem in private practice. In most communities, telephone answering services are available, so that important messages may be communicated to the therapist without cutting into the patient's time.

17

A Practical Outline of Psychotherapy

AS A CATALYST TO PERSONALITY GROWTH, THE THERAPIST MUST OPERATE within the framework of a disciplined therapeutic plan that is geared toward resolution of the patient's resistances to change. Such a plan ideally should be sufficiently pliant to allow for the functioning within its structure of therapists of varied orientations and different kinds of training.

The design of psychotherapy in Chart IV, founded on psychoanalytic doctrines, experimental psychology and modern sociology, is pointed in this direction. It strives to correlate the positive factors of the various systems of psychotherapy into a flexible framework in which therapeutic skills may be developed. The framework is intended to be sufficiently broad so as not to interfere with a spontaneous utilization of the self in the dynamic interpersonal relationship which is the essence of psychotherapy.

The framework may rightfully be termed eclectic, since it utilizes concepts derived from various schools of psychiatry, psychology and the social sciences. The objectives of this framework are aimed at a reconstruction of personality, although there is recognition of, and allowance for, the fact that this goal may, for practical reasons, have to be scaled down.

The principles of therapy delineated are fashioned for the therapist whose training enables him to do psychoanalytically oriented psychotherapy; however, they will also be helpful to the therapist who has not been analytically trained and who confines himself to supportive and reeducative methods. The principles are equally applicable to short-term and long term approaches.

The four phases of treatment described in the present outline have been schematized for purposes of convenience. In actual practice, considerable overlapping occurs among the various phases. Nevertheless a definite sequence will be observed in successful therapy that generally follows the outline.

Chart IV. AN OUTLINE OF PSYCHOTHERAPY

PHASES	I	II	III	IV
OBJECTIVES	Establishing a working relationship with patient.	Determining the causes and dynamics of the patient's disorder.	Translating insight and understanding into action.	Terminating therapy.
THERAPEUTIC TASKS	1. Motivating patient to accept therapy. 2. Clarifying misconceptions about therapy. 3. Convincing patient that therapist understands his suffering and is capable of helping him. 4. Tentative defining of goals in therapy and of the therapeutic situation.	Determining and exploring environmental frustrations and interpersonal drives through interviewing, and unconscious conflicts which mobilize anxiety and vitiate basic needs through psychoanalytic techniques of free association, dream interpretation, analysis of the transference and the exploration of genetic material.	1. Creating incentives for change. 2. Dealing with forces that block action. 3. Helping patient to master anxieties surrounding normal life goals. 4. Correction of remediable environmental distortions. 5. Helping patient to adjust to irremediable conditions. 6. Symptom removal where immediate correction is urgent. 7. Adjustment to those symptoms and abnormal character patterns which for one reason or another cannot be removed during present therapeutic effort.	1. Analyzing the dependency elements of the therapist-patient relationship. 2. Redefining the treatment situation with the aim of encouraging patient to make his own decisions and to establish his own values and goals. 3. Helping patient to achieve as much independence and assertiveness as possible.

RESISTANCES IN PATIENT	1. No motivation for therapy or inability to accept the fact that he can be helped. 2. Refusal to accept therapist's definition of the treatment situation. 3. Hostility, aggression, detachment, intense dependency, sexual interest and other resistances to a warm working relationship.	1. Guilt in acknowledging environmental disturbance or interpersonal difficulties. 2. Unwillingness and, in the instance of a weak ego, an inability to face and to master anxieties related to unconscious conflicts, strivings and fears.	1. Resistance to abandoning primary and secondary neurotic gains. 2. Resistance to normality. 3. Resistance to activity through own resources.	1. Refusal to yield dependency. 2. Fear of assertiveness.
COUNTER-TRANSFERENCE PROBLEMS IN THERAPIST	1. Inability to sympathize with patient and to communicate in understandable terms with him. 2. Irritability with resistances of patient to accepting therapy and therapist. 3. Inability to extend warmth toward patient and to show him he is accepted and his turmoil understood.	1. Avoidance by therapist of those problems in patient which inspire anxiety in therapist. 2. Desire to probe too deeply and rapidly at the start. 3. Impatience with resistance of patient toward gaining insight into his problems.	1. Frustration, hostility and discouragement in therapist to patient's refusal to utilize insight in the direction of change. 2. Tendency to push patient too hard and too rapidly toward normal objectives. 3. Fear of being too directive with resultant excessive passivity.	1. Tendency to overprotect or to domineer patient. 2. Inability to assume a non-directive therapeutic role.
TECHNICAL PROCESSES	Casework and counseling processes.	Psychoanalytic and psychobiologic processes.	Psychoanalytic, psychobiologic, directive counseling, and casework processes.	Psychoanalytic and non-directive counseling processes.

II

The Beginning Phase of Treatment

18

Introduction

THE BEGINNING STAGE OF THERAPY HAS FOR ITS PRINCIPAL OBJECTIVE
the establishing of a working relationship with the patient. This is the crucible
in which personality change is forged. Without such a mutuality, there will be
no therapeutic progress. Because the working relationship is so vital to success
in therapy, all tasks must be subordinated to the objective of its achievement.
Too frequently the therapist plunges into an exploration of provocative conflicts prematurely, before the working relationship has become solidified. Attitudes of respect, trust and confidence in the therapist, inherent in a good working relationship, enable the patient to endure anxiety and to cope with resistance
inevitable to the challenging of basic adaptational patterns. Where a working
relationship does not exist to absorb the impact of suffering and resistance, the
therapeutic process will be hampered. This, unfortunately, is often the outcome
of therapy that is not carefully planned.

To insure an adequate working relationship a number of therapeutic tasks
are in order. First, the patient must be motivated to accept treatment. Persons
who are inadequately motivated, who come to therapy at the insistance of their
physician, or of a concerned relative or friend; or to forestall punishment when
they have been involved in some legal infraction; or who, for any other reason,
are not convinced that they need psychiatric help, will not respond well to psychotherapy. In such instances, the therapist will have to concentrate his efforts
around creating in the patient the proper incentives for the acceptance of help.
No matter how tempted the therapist may be to work on the operative dynamisms, he will have to inhibit this impulse until the patient is strongly motivated
for therapy.

Equally important is the second task of clarifying and removing misconceptions about therapy. Many persons coming for treatment have been filled with
old wives' tales about psychiatry and psychiatrists. They expect the therapist to
be a miracle-monger who reads minds and who can infallibly conjure up a rapid
cure once the patient has confessed his problems. Current periodicals and popular
books may have depreciated the efficacy of psychotherapy or warned of its potentially harmful effects. Attacks by uninformed speakers or professional people
on psychiatry, psychoanalysis and Freud may have created a pessimistic attitude
that will prove harmful to the effective examination of unconscious conflict.
Countless other misconceptions may burden the therapeutic effort and will require careful handling in order to bring about a proper working relationship.

The third therapeutic task of the first treatment phase is to convince the
patient that the therapist understands his suffering and is capable of helping

him. Heretofore the patient will probably have felt condemned for his impulses and rejected for his complaints. He anticipates the same kind of judgmental and punitive attitudes from the therapist. Guilt-ridden and resentful, he dares not open himself up completely to anyone who will repeat the hurts he has experienced at the hands of society. Obviously it would be futile to tell the patient that the therapist is a different kind of authority, since the patient would not understand how this was possible; he would regard such a statement as a dangerous lure. By respectful listening, by sympathetic reflections, and by accepting, non-condemning verbal and non-verbal responses to the patient's productions, the latter soon learns that he is operating in a new kind of interpersonal relationship that warrants his full cooperation. The therapist must keep himself keenly attuned to this new direction in the patient's feelings, which is the best criterion of progress in the evolution of the working relationship.

The fourth therapeutic task, which follows upon the successful execution of the former three, is the tentative defining of goals in therapy and of the therapeutic situation. This task is one which the patient may not readily accept. Insofar as goals are concerned, the patient himself must be made arbiter of how far he wishes to go in treatment. A brief explanation of the goal possibilities in a factual unprejudiced way is indicated. It may have to be explained to the patient that a complete rehabilitation of the personality is the most desirable goal; that it is indicated in some instances, but not necessary in others; that it will require a greater period of treatment than less ambitious goals which may, nevertheless, bring the patient to a reasonable equilibrium, although he may continue to be handicapped by some problems.

Where the patient is unable to comprehend what therapy is and how interviewing helps, time will have to be spent in structuring the therapeutic situation, expounding on the process in very simple language, illustrating it with examples of how other persons have been helped by psychotherapy. Once the patient accepts the true facts, he will be more amenable to the technical procedures employed by the therapist. He will also be more sympathetic with the need for a relationship based on his own participation, cooperation, activity and responsibility.

Resistances to a working relationship and to the therapeutic tasks during Phase I are to be expected. The patient may withstand all efforts to motivate him for therapy. He may boycott attempts to convince him that he can be helped. The investment he has in his neurosis, the need to perpetuate its gains, may obstruct his reasoning powers. Similarly, the patient may refuse to accept the therapist's definition of the treatment situation. He may have well-defined ideas of how he should be treated, and the conditions under which he will cooperate. These may not be congenial with the requirements of good therapy. He may, for instance, resent the professional nature of the relationship and wish to be handled in a special, more personalized manner, even to hobnobbing socially with the therapist. To yield to the patient's wishes will mean almost certain therapeutic failure.

Of greatest interference in the development of a working relationship are characterologic resistances which crop up as manifestations of the patient's habitual interpersonal activities. The threatened intimacy of close contact with the therapist will kindle customary and conflagrate latent character distortions which prevent the kind of relationship from evolving in treatment which will be most conducive to therapeutic gain. Some of the distortions are unique in that they are inspired by the special kind of relationship that exists in therapy. Thus, transference feelings and attitudes may flare up almost from the start in the form of irrational expectations, sexual desires, protective demands, guilt feelings, fears of injury or mutilation and intense hostility. The triad of dependency, aggression and detachment may become operative alternately or in combination.

Dealing with these manifold resistances to a harmonious working relationship constitutes the primary pursuit in the opening phases of treatment. It is obviously useless to attempt any active analysis of deep conflict while such resistances are operative. Irrespective of how impatient the therapist may be to deal with emerging conflicts, he will have to devote himself exclusively to the resolution of resistance, while observing rules that make for a positive consolidation of the working relationship. Resistances, however, may not yield themselves readily. Character resistances, especially, may persist for months, and, in certain patients, for years. Interpretation of these may meet with constant repudiation. Perseverance, nevertheless, coupled with continued demonstrations of understanding and empathy, should eventually lead to their successful resolution.

Certain problems in the therapist, some of a counter-transference nature, also obstruct the achievement of a working relationship. The patient may arouse hostilities in the therapist that the latter neither recognizes nor can control. He may be unable to extend sympathy toward the patient, or to give him the quality of warmth that leads the patient to realize that he is accepted and that his turmoil is understood. Where the patient is prominent socially, economically or politically, the therapist may be in fear of the patient, or in too great awe of him. The therapist may additionally show irritability with the stubborn fight the patient makes against accepting therapy and the therapist. Discouragement, or any outbursts of vexation displayed by the therapist, will have a disastrous effect on the creation of proper rapport.

19

The Initial Interview:
The First Contact with the Patient

THE INITIAL INTERVIEW IS PROBABLY THE MOST CRUCIAL THERAPEUTIC session of all. Vital hours appear later during treatment when resistance and transference manifestations become rife. However, errors in the handling of a session after the therapeutic process is well under way are not nearly so fatal as mismanagement during the initial interview.

The primary goals of the initial interview are these:

1. *To establish rapport with the patient.*
   a. By supplying the proper emotional climate for the interview.
   b. By structuring the purpose of the interview.
   c. By clarifying misconceptions about psychotherapy.
   d. By dealing with inadequate motivation.
   e. By handling other resistances and preparing the patient for psychotherapy.
2. *To get pertinent information from the patient.*
   a. By listening to his spontaneous account.
   b. By focusing on selective data.
3. *To establish a tentative clinical diagnosis.*
4. *To estimate the tentative dynamics.* (In terms of inner conflicts, characterologic distortions, mechanisms of defense and their genetic origins.)
5. *To determine the tentative etiology.*
6. *To assay tentatively the assets, strengths and weaknesses of the patient, actually and latently.*
   a. By estimating the areas of living in which the patient is succeeding and failing.
   b. By determining the motivations for therapy.
   c. By exploring the level of insight.
   d. By estimating the tentative prognosis.
7. *To make practical arrangements for therapy.*
   a. By tentatively approximating optimal goals.
   b. By tentatively selecting a therapeutic method.
   c. By accepting the patient for treatment or arranging for another therapist.
   d. By making appropriate time arrangements.
   e. By making financial arrangements.
8. *To arrange for essential consultations and psychologic testing.*

HANDLING THE FIRST INQUIRY

The first patient-therapist contact is very important since it provides the patient with notions of the personality qualities and traits possessed by the therapist. Generally the patient will have been referred to the interviewer by a physician, minister, teacher, friend, acquaintance or relative of the patient. Sometimes the patient, learning of the work or reputation of the therapist, will apply for help without an intermediary.

If the therapist is working in a clinic, the intake worker will probably handle the initial contact. Under other conditions, the referral source may communicate directly with the therapist. Where the source is other than the patient himself, it is usually best, once it is ascertained that the therapist has time to see the patient, to have the patient get in touch with the therapist or his secretary directly, in order to arrange for a consultation. This puts the initiative in the hands of the patient, and constitutes one more positive step that he has taken spontaneously in working out his problem. Under some circumstances, however, this will not be feasible, as when the patient is a child, or when the patient is too ill or is intractably non-motivated for treatment.

In the event the patient is very upset, and if it is at all possible to do so, he should be seen the same day he telephones for an appointment, even though this may be for only a few minutes. It usually requires a great deal of courage on the patient's part to get himself to telephone for an appointment. He may have fought off "taking the final plunge" into therapy. If he is sufficiently upset, however, he will swallow his pride and ask for help. Should he be rebuffed by a cold statement that he cannot be seen until some date in the distant future, this may mobilize resentment and resistance. Even though he keeps his appointment, he will feel that the therapist is an unsympathetic person, no matter what the reality situation may have been that necessitated the delay.

Should the therapist have absolutely no time on his schedule the same day, he should try to talk to the patient on the telephone, even for a few minutes, attempting to extend some reassurance. By his tone the therapist should try to convey an interest in the patient. An excerpt of a telephone conversation follows:

Pt. Doctor, I've got to see you today, I feel upset, like I'm going to pieces. Doctor_____told me to call you.

Th. This must be very upsetting to you. How long has this been going on? [*attempting to communicate sympathy*]

Pt. For a long time now, but it's never been so bad.

Th. Well, naturally, I want to help you, but we'll have to arrange for an interview. I'd like to see you today, but I could give you only a minute or two. This might be upsetting to you, and I'd rather see you when we can spend some time together to talk things over. [*conveying interest in the patient, and attributing the delay in appointment time to a desire to help him more fully*]

Pt. Can't you see me today?

Th. Much as I'd like to, the amount of time I could give you wouldn't be helpful to you. Now what about Tuesday at 3:40 p.m.?

Pt. Yes, I can make that, but what shall I do in the meantime?

Th. I'd very much like to help you, but it is hard to do this without spending a little time with you. What have you been doing for this trouble up to this time? [*Instead of rejecting the patient's demand, he is told politely that help given him will be better if he waits a little while.*]

Pt. I've been taking some sedatives, some red capsules the doctor gave me. They don't help much.

Th. Why don't you continue doing what you have been doing that gave you a little relief, and then, when we meet on Tuesday, we'll talk the whole thing over? I'll be of more help to you when we go over all the facts.

Pt. (*slight cough, as if in relief*) All right, doctor, I'll be there.

Th. Fine, see you then. Goodbye.

Pt. Goodbye.

If the therapist has no time on his schedule, and it is apparent that the patient needs help immediately, he may give the patient the names of several other therapists. Better still, he may offer to see if these therapists have available time and then communicate this information to the patient.

PRELIMINARIES TO THE INTERVIEW

When the patient comes in for his appointment, he should be greeted by name by the receptionist and made as comfortable as possible. If the therapist utilizes forms that the patient is to fill out for essential statistical data, these may be given to the patient (see "Personal Data Sheet," Appendix D, page 816). Brief statistical entries may be made by the receptionist in the case record (statistical data sheet forms under Appendices A, B or C, pages 809–12, may be used here). The case folder may be either a plain manilla folder or a special folder, such as Appendix J, page 824. Sometimes simple printed informational material on psychotherapy proves helpful (see Appendix M, page 830) and is handed to the patient by the receptionist. If a personal history form is to be filled out (see Appendix N, page 832) the patient should be asked to come in at least twenty minutes before his interview. Where no forms are employed by the therapist, the receptionist may get the patient's name, address and telephone number and make up a case folder which may include an Initial Interview form (such as Appendix C, page 812) or blank sheets of paper on which to enter the initial interview data.

It goes without saying that the therapist should see the patient promptly at the appointed time. This sets the pattern of precision in appointment times, one of the necessary disciplines in treatment.

INSURING THE PROPER EMOTIONAL ATMOSPHERE

When the patient first meets the therapist, he is bound to have some anxiety. Within himself he harbors many conflicting emotions. He is frightened at the prospect of opening up pockets of guilt, of discovering fearsome secrets, and of exposing himself to the scrutiny and judgment of a strange individual. He is terrorized lest he be hurt in some mysterious way by an authority, of whom he knows little, and with whom he feels helpless. He is resentful that he has finally come to the degradation of consulting a "mind doctor" which may indicate to him that he is weak and contemptible. He is hopeful that this new "healer" will do for him what others have failed to do, and his expectations may know no bounds. He is suspicious that he will be dealt with summarily and that he may become a victim of, unscrupulous practices. This tangle of contradictory attitudes and feelings may mortify him until he tests their reality in his relationship with the therapist.

No better rule can be followed in the therapist's first contact with the patient than to heed the injunction to "be himself." Artificial dignity, practiced pompousness and professional poise will easily be penetrated by most patients. A studied, "dead-pan," coldly analytic attitude and manner, advocated by some schools of psychotherapy, are particularly poisonous to a therapeutic atmosphere that makes for the most effective communication. The patient must sense, from the behavior of the interviewer, that his turmoil is appreciated, and that adequate steps will be taken to help him with his problem. At all times the interviewer must manifest as kindly and sympathetic an attitude as possible. Exhibitions of irritation, disgust, or disinterest, or intimations that the patient's difficulties are hopeless or irremediable may prove to be irreparably destructive.

In his enthusiasm to get information, the initial interviewer is apt to lose sight of the fact that it may be more important to establish rapport with the patient than to make a diagnosis. Many patients are lost during the first session because their emotional resistance to the acceptance of help has not been considered by the interviewer.

A good way of handling the initial contact is to greet the patient with a smile and introduce oneself. The patient is then invited to sit down. This casual way of approaching the patient is generally most reassuring to him.

Th. (*smiling*) Are you Mr. Jones? I am Dr. Smith. [*If the patient extends his hand the therapist shakes hands.*] Won't you sit over there in that chair so we can talk things over.

Pt. [*The usual reaction is a smile and a polite comment of some kind.*]

STRUCTURING THE PURPOSE OF THE INTERVIEW

In structuring the purpose of the interview, the role the therapist will play with the patient in the future must be kept in mind. If the therapist is merely seeing the patient in consultation in order to make a diagnosis and to refer the patient to another therapist, he must somehow get this across to the patient. At the end of a well-conducted initial interview, the patient will have established a feeling of confidence in the interviewer and will want to continue in therapy with him. If he is not clear about the purpose of the interview, he will assume that the interviewer will continue in the role of therapist, and he will be frustrated, upset and resentful when he finds he is being referred to another person with whom he may envisage a realization of the fears that somehow have not come to pass with the present interviewer. The patient may be told: "Now the purpose of this interview is to get an idea about your problem so that I can find the best therapist to help you. It is important that you get treated by the very best available person, and I'll help you find such a person."

If the therapist has available time and may be able to accept the patient, he may simply state: "Now the purpose of this interview is to get an idea about your problem so that we can decide the best thing to do for it." This leaves the door open for the therapist in the event he decides that he is able to work with the patient.

In the event the therapist is interviewing a resentful or non-motivated patient, he must not convey an eagerness to get the patient into therapy. A statement such as this may be appropriate: "Now you've been sent here to talk things over with me. I don't know what I can do to help you, but if you give me an idea of the trouble you've been having, I'll see what I can do for you."

DEALING WITH INITIAL RESISTANCE

Most patients proceed to relate their problems to the interviewer without too great difficulty following the structuring of the interview situation. So long as the patient is talking readily and spontaneously, he is not interrupted. He is encouraged by sympathetic facial expressions, by nodding and subvocal utterances. After the patient's spontaneous account, specific information is obtained by pointed questions.

Some patients, however, may be too upset to proceed with an account of their problems. They may feel helpless and insecure, and believe themselves to be at the mercy of forces they can neither understand nor control. Often they resent the circumstances that forced them to apply for psychotherapeutic help, the efficacy of which they unreservedly doubt. Ashamed at being unable to handle their problems personally, they consider themselves to be weak and stupid. Unsure of the therapist's designs, unsure of whether they will be exploited, humiliated, subjected to hospitalization or to other forceful measures, they may respond with resentment. They are apt to project resentment in the form of open defiance. More likely, they may handle their resentment by detaching themselves, by acting apathetic, or by displaying a kind of braggadocio that conceals their underlying turmoil. They may resort to a clinging dependency, plaintively appealing for succor and support. These attitudes have to be handled carefully. One way of doing this is by calmly and sympathetically verbalizing for the patient how he must feel—if the interviewer perceives, from verbal and non-verbal clues, the nature of the patient's distress. Putting the patient's feelings into words does much to help him accept the fact of the interviewer's understanding, and non-punitive role.

The interviewer will have to display relatively great activity at the start of the interview under the following conditions:

1. If the patient is manifestly upset emotionally.
2. If he talks about attitudes toward therapy and toward the interviewer, rather than about his problem.
3. If he cannot seem to get started talking, or does not know what to say.

4. If he pauses too long or evidences protracted silences.

5. If he shifts his trend of talk from relevant to irrelevant material.

The handling of a patient who is upset emotionally will depend on the kind of emotion involved and on the intensity of reaction. If the patient is depressed, agitated and tearful, a display of warmth and understanding may stabilize the patient sufficiently so that he can verbalize freely. For example, one patient, following a structuring of the interview, broke down into tears after uttering a few words:

Pt. Oh, oh . . . I don't know what to say. . . . I feel lost . . . completely lost . . . (*cries*)

Th. I know how difficult this must be for you. [*communicating sympathy*]

Pt. Oh, oh, oh . . . (*continues crying*)

Th. You have suffered a great deal and understandably are upset. But I am going to do everything I can to help you.

Pt. Thank you, doctor.

Th. Now if you will tell me about your trouble, I will see how I can best help you.

Pt. (*relates problem*)

If a patient is tense and fearful, he may be approached as in this excerpt.

Pt. I just can't think of anything to say. I'm so scared to death.

Th. What do you think is going to happen?

Pt. I don't know. I've read so much about psychology. I'm afraid I'll find out something about myself that will be terrible.

Th. Most people feel this way when they start treatment.

Pt. Yes, but, I'm afraid I'm different than other people are.

Th. I see, in what way?

Pt. I get so keyed up about nothing. (*Patient gets into his problem from this point on.*)

In the event the patient is excessively hostile, one must refrain from responding with counter-hostility. A man referred by a physician arrived for his appointment ten minutes late. While the interview was being structured, he angrily stared at the interviewer. The following conversation took place:

Pt. Dr. B_____ sent me here for these headaches. He thinks it might be mental. I really don't think it was necessary for me to come.

Th. Do you believe it's mental?

Pt. Good Lord, no! I think I need something that will ease this pain. I've been told a million different things of what's wrong.

Th. Perhaps you are right. It may be entirely physical. What examinations have you had?

Pt. (*Patient details the many consultations he has had.*)

Th. Then it perhaps made you mad to come here?

Pt. I *was* mad. Not now though. Do you think you can help this headache?

Th. I'm not sure; but if you tell me about your trouble from the beginning, I might be able to help you with any emotional factors that can stir up a headache.

Pt. How can that do it? I know I have been emotional about it. (*The patient proceeds now with an account of his difficulty.*)

In the event the patient is preoccupied with feelings about the interviewer and does not wish to discuss his problem, it is important to explore his feelings as thoroughly as possible before proceeding with the interview. How the patient was referred to the interviewer is important. He may have been forced into treatment by an actual or implied threat; he may have been told that he is a nuisance and deserves to see a psychiatrist; he may have been promised a cure in a few sessions in view of the presumably rapid strides psychiatry has made in recent years. Under these circumstances, the person will possess a certain mental set that will have to be rectified before the proper therapeutic situation prevails. Misconceptions about psychotherapy are rampant and will require clarification. Examples and methods of handling these are detailed in Chapter 30, Answering Questions Patients Ask About Psychotherapy.

The management of difficulties in verbalization, and of pauses, silences and shifts from pertinent material may be along lines indicated in Chapter 15, The Conduct of the Psychotherapeutic Interview.

A source of great initial resistance is the patient's disappointment in the therapist. Patients usually come to therapy with a stereotype in mind of the kind of individual they want as a therapist. This is generally a kindly and wise middle-aged male psychiatrist. Such an image is partially the product of the universal need for an idealized father figure, and in part the popular movie and magazine conception of the "mental healer." Other notions of an ideal therapist are nurtured by desires to fulfill, through special qualities in the therapist, impelling neurotic needs. For example, masochistic patients may yearn for a powerful and cruel individual, who will deal with them firmly, and they will try to seek out a therapist who possesses punitive potentialities. A frustrated middle-aged woman may have a longing for a virile, handsome, male figure through whom she may sublimate her unpropitiated longings. A passive, dependent male may desire a strong female therapist who can take him over and mother him. Where the patient is aware of and verbalizes his disappointment, this will have to be handled in a therapeutic way. Examples of managing such situations follow:

1. *Questions about the age of the therapist*

    Pt. I expected to see an older person.

    Th. You are disappointed that I'm too young?

    Pt. I really wanted an older man than yourself to treat me.

    Th. I see. Perhaps you feel you could have more confidence in an older man. [*reflecting possible attitudes behind the desire for an older person*]

    Pt. It isn't personal, doctor, it's just that I've had this so long, I wanted a person with lots of experience. Dr. J_____ told me you had a great deal of . . . well, but I thought you'd be at least 55 or 60 years old.

    Th. Yes, it's natural for you to want to get the best kind of help for your problem, and you might feel that an older person has had more experience. If you'd like to tell me what your difficulty is, perhaps I could help you locate such a person [*accepting the patient's desire*]

    Pt. Well, it goes back a long way. (*Patient discusses the problem.*)

2. *Questions about the experience and training of the therapist.*

   a. *The extent of experience.*

   Pt. I'd like to ask you about your training.

   Th. Mm hm. (*smiling*) What would you like to know?

   Pt. Well, how long have you been doing psychiatry?

   Th. You must have some questions about my qualifications. What kind of a therapist do you believe you would be able to work with best? [*reflecting possible attitudes behind the question*]

   Pt. Well I wanted someone, someone who had a lot of experience.

   Th. I don't blame you for that. Certainly you would want someone who would really know how to handle your problem. [*again accepting the patient's wish*]

   Pt. Yes.

   Th. Suppose I tell you that I have had enough training and experience to have helped many people. Now whether I am the best person to help you, I don't know. But why don't you tell me about your problem, and then we'll decide on the best kind of a psychotherapist for you. If I'm not the best person, then I'll help you find someone.

   b. *The kind of experience.* (Sometimes the patient seeks a specific kind of psychotherapy, and questions the orientation of the therapist.)

   Pt. Do you do hypnosis and hypnoanalysis?

   Th. Do you feel you need hypnosis?

   Pt. Well everyone tells me I should get that. I read about it.

   Th. Certainly if you need hypnosis, you should get it. But I'd like to go into your problem and then we can decide whether hypnosis is the best treatment for you. If you need hypnosis, then we can decide on the best person for you.

   c. *The kind of training.*

   Pt. Could I ask you a question? Where did you get your training?

   Th. You must be wondering whether I'm adequately trained enough to help you. [*reflecting possible attitudes behind question*]

   Pt. I'm wondering what kind of therapy you do.

   Th. I see. Do you have an idea of the kind of therapy you feel you need?

   Pt. Well, no, but I know training is important.

   Th. I think you have a right to know that the person treating you is adequately trained. [*At this point, the therapist may outline his training, and, if the patient is not satisfied, he may be told that after going over his problems, referral will be discussed.*]

3. *Questions about the sex of the therapist.*

   Pt. Somehow I pictured being treated by a woman.

   Th. Do you have any feelings about working with a man?

   Pt. No, but I think a woman would be better for me. I could talk easier.

   Th. I see, well perhaps what we might do is talk about your problem, and then we can decide on the best person to treat you.

4. *Questions about the religion of the therapist.*

   Pt. Are you Catholic?

   Th. No. Do you feel that makes a difference?

   Pt. I think a Catholic doctor might understand my problem better. You see, I'm Catholic.

   Th. Yes, it's possible that a therapist with a background similar to yours might do better with certain kinds of problems. But suppose you describe your problem and then we'll decide on the best person who can treat you.

5. *Questions about the professional identification of the therapist.*

    Pt. I was told to see a psychologist because I'm failing in my studies.

    Th. Does it make a difference to you if I'm not a psychologist?

    Pt. Well I don't know. You see, my sister called you about me when I told her I should see a psychologist because of how I was doing in college.

    Th. It's true that psychologists do deal with educational problems, but other trained persons can do that too. Now, I'm a psychiatrist and I think I can help you, but suppose we talk about your problem and then we will discuss whether a psychologist would be better for you.

    Once these questions are answered, the patient will, as a rule, talk freely about his problem. It is rare, in a properly conducted interview, for the patient to desire to change therapists. He will usually have found the interviewer sufficiently discerning and empathic to want to continue in therapy with him.

20

The Initial Interview:
Collating Essential Data

ESSENTIAL DATA WILL BE NEEDED TO ENABLE THE THERAPIST TO FULFILL the purpose of the initial interview. The data must be obtained in an atmosphere of understanding and empathy in order to pierce the many resistances the patient has to treatment. In collating data one must remember that the patient may withhold significant information for a number of reasons; such as: (1) He may not know which items are most important, and thus he may stress the less important details. (2) He may accept as "normal," certain neurotic aspects of himself, and, as inevitable, environmental stress situations—not considering them worthy of mention. (3) He may have emotional blocks to revealing some information. Anxiety here invokes suppressive and repressive mechanisms. (4) He may mistrust, fear or have no respect for the interviewer.

Because of these facts, it may be necessary to piece together tentatively whatever information can be obtained, and to await resolution of the patient's resistances during therapy, before one can gather sufficient data for a correct evaluation of the problem.

Some interviewers believe a formal case history to be of advantage in getting pertinent data; others challenge the value of history-taking in patients who are to receive psychotherapy. Those in favor of the practice insist that great gaps in information are present where reliance is placed solely on the spontaneous unfolding of historical material. Only a careful inquiry into the various areas of somatic, psychologic, interpersonal and community functioning is said to reveal a complete picture of what has been happening to the patient. Where adequate historical data is lacking, it may be months before the patient gets around to talking about an aspect of his problem which may give the therapist an entirely different perspective of the situation.

On the other hand, there are many reasons why interviewers hesitate to take complete case histories. First, exhaustive histories are not considered absolutely necessary from a diagnostic point of view. Second, they are not believed to be therapeutically valuable. Therapy is regarded as a process, not of collecting information, but of helping the patient to develop a new outlook on life. Background material is felt to be not too important in promoting this goal. Third, it is argued that when the patient is asked to give a schematic account of his history and of himself, he may use this as resistance in concealing the truly significant facts of his problem. Fourth, he may assume that once he has made a report of his history, he can sit back and expect that a solution for his problems will automatically be forthcoming.

Some therapists have attempted to get around the arguments against taking a case history by having the patient fill out a questionnaire form, or by having some other person, like a social worker, do the history-taking. There is an advantage to be gained in this, where the therapist needs as much information as he can get in outlining a treatment plan. However, even here the presentation to the therapist of historical data may not be as helpful as one may imagine, since the eliciting of these data during the therapeutic process tends to bring the patient and therapist more closely together, helping to establish a working relationship.

In clinics, the tendency is toward history-taking, particularly where teamwork is employed. In private practice, the tendency is away from formal history-taking.

Whether or not a case history is taken, desirable data to be obtained from the patient include the following:

1. STATISTICAL DATA: Name, address, telephone number, age, sex, marital status, education, occupation, employment status and income.
2. COMPLAINT FACTOR:
    a. *Chief complaint* (in patient's words)
    b. *History and development of the complaint*
        (1) When did the complaint begin?
        (2) Under what circumstances?
        (3) What does the patient believe produced the complaint?
        (4) What treatment has he had?
    c. *Other complaints or symptoms*
        (1) Physical
        (2) Emotional
        (3) Psychic
        (4) Behavioral
    d. *Previous attacks of emotional illness*
        (1) As a child
        (2) Later attacks
        (3) Any hospitalization?
        (4) At what period does the patient believe himself to have been completely free from emotional illness?
    e. *Effect of emotional illness on present functioning*
        (1) Effect on physical health, appetite, sleep and sexual functions
        (2) Effect on work
        (3) Effect on family and other interpersonal relationships
        (4) Effect on interests and recreations
        (5) Effect on community relations
    f. *Evaluation of complaint factor*
        (1) What evidences are there of adaptational breakdown; such as, anxiety, depression, psychosomatic symptoms?
        (2) Are the defensive elaborations adaptive or maladaptive?

(3) What are the patient's ideas about his problem and his attitude toward it?

3. ETIOLOGIC FACTORS:
   a. History of hereditary family illness
   b. Family data: relationships with parents and siblings
   c. Significant events in the past history
   d. Precipitating factors in present environment: assay of present environment to determine extent of stress on patient
   e. Other factors including inner conflicts as revealed by dreams, symptoms, etc.
4. ASSAY OF PERSONALITY STRENGTHS AND WEAKNESSES:
   a. Level of maturation: physical growth, educational achievement and school progress, resolution of dependence, sexual maturity, marriage, parenthood, social relationships and community participation
   b. Neurotic disturbances in childhood
   c. Interests, hobbies, ambitions
   d. Character structure: security feelings, attitudes toward authority, interpersonal relationships, attitudes toward self, and methods of handling conflict
   e. Motivational factors and level of insight

The above data will obviously not be obtained in full during the initial interview, due to the limited available time. Nor will it be in the order outlined. It will, therefore, have to be pieced together from various fragments of the interview. Some order in the eliciting of data will, however, be helpful in obtaining as complete a picture as possible.

THE CHIEF COMPLAINT

Immediately after structuring the purpose of the initial interview, and handling initial resistances, the therapist may attempt to get into the presenting problem with such a remark as, "Suppose you tell me about your problem," or a question like, "Would you like to tell me about your problem?" Responses to this are many.

1. The patient may proceed to detail the complaint factor.

Th. Suppose you tell me about your problem.
Pt. Yes, it's that I can't eat. My stomach gets upset, and I have to watch my diet. And then I get jittery all over for the slightest reasons.

2. The patient may hesitate on the basis that he is unable to gather his thoughts or because he is unclear as to the nature of his difficulty. Here, a rephrasing of the question may help.

Th. Would you like to tell me about your problem?
Pt. (*pause*) I just don't know where to begin.
Th. Well, what bothers you most? [*rephrasing the question*]

Pt. Well my worst trouble is how I get along with my wife. We've been married now going on ten years, and we've never gotten along well.

3. The patient may be completely blocked in voicing his chief complaint. Asking repeated questions may unblock him.

Th. Suppose you tell me about your problem.
Pt. (*pause*) I just don't know what it is.
Th. Would you rather that I asked you questions?
Pt. Yes, I'd rather you did.
Th. What bothers you most?
Pt. I don't know.
Th. Do you have any special trouble with anything?
Pt. Nothing seems to stand out. I feel upset all over.
Th. Physically upset?
Pt. Yes, I get the shakes and my bowels are upset when I get tense.
Th. Anything else?
Pt. You mean physically?
Th. Yes, or otherwise.
Pt. Well, I can't think clear. My mind is in a fog. I can't remember things.
Th. Mm hmm. (*pause*)
Pt. And I can't work because I just feel so weak I can hardly sit. (*Patient continues to elaborate on his problem.*)

The chief complaint may not be the most important problem for which the patient needs help, even though he may look upon it as most crippling. As a general rule, the patient voices his complaint in terms of manifest disturbing symptoms. Here he may focus on one symptom to the exclusion of others. Thus, the patient may present as a chief complaint the fact that he is depressed. As he describes his problem, it is evident that he is also detaching himself from people, that he has a gastric ulcer, and that his inability to work has jeopardized his economic security.

Statements by the patient of his most important difficulties as he sees them should be recorded verbatim if possible. The initial interview form in Appendix C, page 812, is excellent for this purpose and for the recording of other data during the interview.

HISTORY AND DEVELOPMENT OF THE COMPLAINT

The patient, immediately upon mentioning his complaints, may spontaneously begin discussing how and when they originated. If he does not do so, pointed questions may be asked, such as:

1. Onset: "How long ago did your troubles begin?"
2. Circumstances under which the complaints developed: "At the time your trouble began, what were you doing?" "Were there any changes in your life situation?" "Were you happy or unhappy at the time?"
3. Progression from onset to the beginning of the initial interview: "Once this trouble started, what happened?" "Did your difficulty get worse as time went on?"

In revealing the history and development of his complaint, the patient may elaborate on his present environment, his daily habits and routines. The description of the patient's present life situation involves judgments by the patient that must be carefully scrutinized. Depending on emotional needs, some persons will react catastrophically to even average vicissitudes, while others seem capable of tolerating very severe environmental stress. The patient may consequently exaggerate, distort or minimize his life difficulty. He may have a need to blame his inner turmoil on his environment, and he may actually create the very crises of which he complains. On the other hand, he may be unaware of how disturbed his situation actually is, accepting it as an inevitable consequence of living, yet reacting to it with untoward emotion. The interviewer must, therefore, never accept the patient's statements at their face value, and must later validate the account given.

The unfolding of the historical development of the complaint may be accompanied by the introduction of many tangential and perhaps irrelevant elements. It will be necessary constantly to focus on pertinent aspects of his problem, since many points will have to be covered to fulfill the purpose of the interview. Generally, if more than fifteen minutes or so are consumed in discussing the history and development of the complaint, the patient may be interrupted.

STATISTICAL DATA

Where the patient has not filled out a Personal Data Sheet (see Appendix D, page 816) or where a statistical form has not been made out in advance by a social worker, it is incumbent on the therapist to get essential statistical information (see Appendix A, page 809 or Appendix C, page 812). Assuming that the patient has discussed sufficiently the development of his complaint, the therapist may interrupt this and proceed, as in the following excerpt:

Th. Well now, I'd like to ask you a few questions about yourself, and then we'll go ahead discussing your problem.

Pt. Fine.

Th. Your full name is?

Pt. George Dickens. [*The patient's name and other identifying details have been changed to conceal his identity.*]

Th. Your address is?

Pt. 211 Thorton Street.

Th. Home telephone?

Pt. Furlong 7-4228.

Th. Business telephone?

Pt. Well, I'd rather you didn't call me there.

Th. Yes, of course. If I do call to change an appointment or the like, when can I call you?

Pt. After six.

Th. Would you rather that I wouldn't mention my name if I do call? [*This is to reassure a patient who is fearful that others will find out he is consulting a psychiatrist.*]

Pt. It really doesn't matter. It'll be all right.

Th. What people are living with you at present?

Pt. My wife and child.

Th. How old are you?

Pt. Thirty-two.

Th. You are married you say?

Pt. Yes.

Th. How long have you been married?

Pt. Three years.

Th. I see. Any previous marriages?

Pt. No.

Th. How old is your wife?

Pt. Thirty.

Th. Does she work other than doing housework?

Pt. Yes, she writes copy for an advertising company.

Th. Mm hmm. About what is her salary?

Pt. Well, I don't know. I'd say about three thousand yearly.

Th. What about children; how many do you have?

Pt. Just one; she's two years old.

Th. How far through school did you go?

Pt. Two years of college.

Th. And your occupation?

Pt. I'm a linotype operator.

Th. What do you earn?

Pt. About forty-five hundred dollars a year take-home pay.

Th. Were you in the armed forces?

Pt. Yes, for three years.

Under some circumstances, this statistical data may be obtained at the beginning of the interview before the patient talks about his complaints and symptoms. It is recommended, however, that the procedure outlined be followed, since the average patient is under considerable tension and considers the giving of statistical information about himself a diversion. Where the patient has filled out a Personal Data Sheet (Appendix D, page 816), it is unnecessary to burden him with the above questions, unless there are points that have been omitted or that need clarification.

OTHER SYMPTOMS AND CLINICAL FINDINGS AT PRESENT

It is helpful to get a general idea of other symptoms besides those discussed by the patient in his complaint. Due to the limited time available in the initial interview—forty-five minutes to one hour is the usual time allotted to a session —pointed questions are necessary. Suggested areas of questioning are indicated in item 3 of the Initial Interview Form (Appendix C, page 812). Continuing with the interrupted interview above:

Th. Now, I'd rapidly like to ask you about other symptoms you may have. What about tension; do you feel tense?

Pt. Oh yes, all the time.

Th. Mm hmm. What about depressions; do you get depressed?

Pt. Yes, now and then.

Th. You snap out of it, though?

Pt. Yes, I do.

Th. How about anxiety?

Pt. I don't know what you mean.

Th. Well, spells when your heart palpitates and you get panicky.

Pt. Yes, when I am in the company of people.

Th. Any other time?

Pt. When I'm asked to do something, like make a speech.

Th. I see. What about physical symptoms; do you have those? [*It will be noted that questions are not asked in reference to suicidal tendencies, hallucinations, delusions and dangerous and excited tendencies. The therapist should ask these questions only where the clinical condition of the patient warrants it. To ask them when they are not indicated, may be upsetting to the patient or may be productive of resentment.*]

Pt. (*pause*) I don't know.

Th. Well, for example, what about fatigue and exhaustion?

Pt. Oh, yes, all the time.

Th. How about headaches?

Pt. No.

Th. Dizziness.

Pt. No.

Th. Stomach or bowel trouble?

Pt. Yes, when I get nervous, upset, they come. Butterflies in my stomach.

Th. Diarrhea?

Pt. Sometimes.

Th. Do you have any sexual problems?

Pt. I wouldn't say so.

Th. Your sex life is satisfactory then?

Pt. Yes. [*The patient's evaluation of this and other aspects of his functioning should not be accepted at its face value. As he explores his problem, he may find that what he considers "normal" may not be good functioning. In this patient, for example, sexual frequency was once every three weeks with no true enjoyment.*]

Th. Any phobias or fears?

Pt. Of talking in front of groups, of meeting strange people.

Th. Mm hmm. Any other fears?

Pt. I don't think so.

Th. Any thoughts or obsessions that crowd into your mind and frighten you?

Pt. No.

Th. Any compulsions—the need to do things over and over?

Pt. No.

Th. What about sedatives; do you take sedatives?

Pt. No.

Th. Do you drink alcohol excessively?

Pt. Well, I have an occasional drink.

Th. Get drunk?

Pt. Oh, no.

Th. What about insomnia; how do you sleep?

Pt. I sleep fine.
Th. Any nightmares?
Pt. No.

DREAMS

The recording of a nightmare, of a typical dream and of repetitive dreams are helpful to the analytically trained therapist in gaining clues as to unconscious foci of conflict. Continuing the interview:

Th. Do you dream a lot or a little? [*This question is phrased this way because patients are apt to think, if they are asked merely whether they dream, that dreaming is abnormal.*]
Pt. Oh, a little.
Th. Remember your dreams?
Pt. Sometimes.
Th. Suppose you tell me a dream that you had recently.
Pt. I can't seem to remember any right now.

FAMILY DATA

Briefly recorded family data are valuable to the initial interviewer in appraising the quality of the patient's relationships, and in anticipating his responses to male or female therapists. The interview continues:

Th. Now I'd like to ask you a few brief questions about your parents. Your mother; is she living?
Pt. Yes, very much so.
Th. What kind of a person is she?
Pt. Well, a nice person; she did what she thought was best. She was a nervous person, self-centered, always fighting with my father.
Th. How did that make you feel?
Pt. Well, I don't know. My mother and father were divorced when I was eight. He left. I saw him rarely.
Th. How did you feel about that?
Pt. I don't know, all right, I guess. My mother thought he was a heel.
Th. Did you?
Pt. No, he was all right. I guess he took quite a beating from my mother. She was the smarter of the two.
Th. What sort of a person was your father?
Pt. A quiet fellow. I didn't know him well.
Th. How did you feel about him?
Pt. I liked him.
Th. Any brothers or sisters?
Pt. Only one older brother. He's thirty-six.
Th. What about him; how did you get along with him?
Pt. Well, when we were small we'd fight a lot. He didn't like me. But we see each other now. (*laughs*) I guess we learned to tolerate each other.
Th. How do you feel about him now?

Pt. (*laughs*) O.K., I guess. We like each other.

Th. Now how about your wife; what sort of a person is she?

Pt. Nice, patient with me. She's got her troubles. Her mother hounds her.

Th. How do you feel about her?

Pt. Fine. We get along better than we ever did.

Th. Like her?

Pt. Oh, sure.

Th. What about your daughter; what sort of a youngster is she?

Pt. Oh, she's a devil, all right. Gets into everything.

Th. How do you feel about her?

Pt. Oh, fine; I like her.

The patient's evaluation of his family and his expressed attitudes toward them do not always indicate his true feelings. Guilt may cause him to conceal or to repress important attitudes that may come up later in therapy when he has developed the strength to tolerate the implications of his suppressed or repressed emotions.

PREVIOUS EMOTIONAL UPSETS

The patient should be asked questions about any previous emotional disturbances that he may have had. This will give the interviewer clues as to the severity of the patient's disorder and how far back in his life it goes. The interview continues:

Th. Now, what about nervous problems previously; any previous attacks of the same kind before?

Pt. No, not exactly like this.

Th. Well, any other kind of nervous upsets?

Pt. I've always been nervous.

Th. How far back would you say your nervousness goes?

Pt. As a kid, I was afraid of the other kids. I didn't like to fight.

Th. Did you have any nervous troubles for which you needed help?

Pt. My mother was always concerned. I was a sickly kid, always had one thing wrong with me or another. I had ear trouble a good deal.

PREVIOUS TREATMENT (INCLUDING HOSPITALIZATION)

Any previous therapeutic efforts should be recorded to discern the problem for which help was sought, the progress achieved, and the patient's response to his former therapists. Unless indicated by the severity of the problem, questions need not be asked about hospitalization. Continuing the interview:

Th. Have you ever had treatments for your condition from a psychiatrist or any other person who gave you psychotherapy?

Pt. No. I've read some books, but never got treatments.

21

The Initial Interview:
Making a Diagnosis

WHILE DIAGNOSIS IS, MORE OR LESS, AN ARBITRARY MATTER AND SHOULD not prejudice the therapeutic approach or the goals, it is convenient to attempt classification as soon as possible.

All emotional problems spread themselves over a wide pathologic area and include a combination of intellectual, emotional, behavioral and somatic symptoms. A disturbed character structure will be found in practically every patient, reflecting itself in difficulties in interpersonal and social relationships. Moreover, one may discern, in most instances, manifestations of adaptational collapse; such as, tension, anxiety, depression and psychosomatic symptoms. Finally, multiform defenses appear in combination; such as, phobic, compulsive, conversion and dissociative mechanisms. In some instances, certain symptoms and defenses are so outstanding that they appear to constitute definite syndromes. For example, the patient may complain of an inability to walk outdoors due to intense anxiety. Emphasis on this symptom tempts us to diagnose the condition as a phobic disorder. Yet a search will probably reveal a concomitant personality problem, psychosomatic manifestations, depression and symptoms characteristic of other syndromes.

A diagnosis is frequently made on the basis of the most important complaint factor of the patient. However, the therapist may most advantageously make a diagnosis on the strength of his own evaluation of the total picture, irrespective of the emphasis placed on symptoms by the patient.

A DYNAMIC INTERPRETATION OF DIAGNOSIS

A neurosis consists of a number of component parts, dynamically interrelated, shifting in manifestations and symptoms. Threats to adaptation, whether inspired by external stress or inner conflict, produce tension, anxiety and physiologic reactions associated with a disruption of homeostasis. This may eventuate in a nascent *anxiety reaction* (anxiety state, anxiety neurosis) and/or *psychophysiologic autonomic and visceral disorder* (anxiety equivalent, psychosomatic disorder).

In general, four levels of defense are employed against anxiety: (1) conscious efforts at maintaining control, (2) characterologic (personality) defenses, (3) repressive defenses, and (4) regressive defenses. The individual may stabilize at any of these levels with a disappearance of tension, anxiety and physiologic reactions. Or the elaborated defenses may only partially control symptoms. Finally, the defenses themselves may involve the person in difficulties and may act as further foci of conflict, stirring up additional anxiety and necessitating other defenses. For instance, claustrophobia may interfere with the economic and social adjustment of the individual, and the ensuing anxiety may provoke characterologic defenses; such as, detachment, aggression and dependency.

1. FIRST LINE DEFENSES: CONSCIOUS EFFORTS AT MAINTAINING CONTROL.

All persons employ defenses on this level to lessen tension and to control anxiety. Such defenses may be considered "normal." Among them are the following:

a. *Removing oneself from sources of stress.* A man irritated with work conditions may quit his job and find a less strenuous work situation.

b. *Escaping into bodily satisfactions.* Over-eating and excessive sexual indulgence may be employed as tension-relieving mechanisms.

c. *Extroversion.* Plunging into hobbies, and recreational and social activities may divert the individual's attention from his inner problems.

d. *Wish-fulfilling fantasies.* Indulging in daydreaming may act as a substitute gratification for unfulfilled impulses.

e. *Suppression.* Willfully keeping painful ideas or impulses from awareness.

f. *Rationalization.* Providing reality and social justifications for behavior motivated by inner needs.

g. *Use of philosophic credos.* Adoption of codes of behavior and ethics to reinforce one's conscience, or to justify one's impulse indulgence.

h. *Exercising "self-control."* Forceful conscious inhibition of tension-producing impulses.

i. *Emotional outbursts and impulsive behavior.* Gaining release of tension through emotional catharsis and by "acting-out."

j. *"Thinking things through."* Arriving at a rational solution of one's problems by carefully weighing alternative courses of action.

k. *Alcoholic indulgence.* Alcohol often serves as a means of propitiating tension and of allowing emotional release. Excessive alcoholic intake may occur.

l. *Use of drugs.* Sedatives (barbiturates) may be employed to alleviate anxiety and tension; while stimulants (benzedrine) help to promote energy in situations where the person feels listless and inert. Narcotics (marihuana and opiates) are abnormally employed. Excess drug indulgence leads to many complications.

In the event the first line defenses allay anxiety, adjustment is possible. If anxiety is not relieved, or if the device used to control anxiety creates more anxiety, second line defenses may be implemented, which involve a regulation of one's relationships with other people.

2. SECOND LINE DEFENSES: CHARACTEROLOGIC DEFENSES.
   a. *Strivings of an interpersonal nature.*
      (1) *Exaggerated dependency* (immaturity)
      (2) *Submissive techniques* (passivity)
      (3) *Expiatory techniques* (masochism, asceticism)
      (4) *Dominating techniques*
      (5) *Techniques of aggression* (sadism)
      (6) *Techniques of withdrawal* (detachment)
   b. *Strivings directed at the self-image.*
      (1) *Narcissistic strivings* (grandiosity, perfectionism)
      (2) *Power impulses* (compulsive ambition)

The characterologic defenses, if exaggerated, may make for *personality disorders* which reflect themselves in educational, habit, work, marital, interpersonal and social problems, and in delinquency, criminality, sexual perversions, alcoholism and drug addiction. The individual may manage to regain stability, albeit with disturbed personality manifestations. He may still retain those first line defenses that he finds helpful in subduing anxiety. He may stabilize himself completely, or continue to experience, from time to time, bouts of anxiety. If anxiety cannot be controlled with characterologic defenses, or if the defenses, and the personality disorders they create, produce more anxiety, third line defenses may come into play. These consist of a mobilization of repressive defenses.

3. THIRD LINE DEFENSES: REPRESSIVE DEFENSES.
   a. *General efforts directed at reinforcing repression.*
      (1) *Reaction formations.* Characterologic drives to oppose and repudiate inner drives; for example, ingratiation and passivity to oppose hostile, murderous impulses.
      (2) *Accentuation of intellectual controls* (with compensations and sublimations)
   b. *Inhibition of function.*
      (1) *Blunted apperception, attention, concentration and thinking*
      (2) *Disturbed consciousness* (fainting, increased sleep, stupor)
      (3) *Disturbed memory* (antegrade and retrograde amnesia)
      (4) *Emotional indifference or apathy* (emotional inhibitions)
      (5) *Sensory disorders* (hypoesthesia, anaesthesia, amaurosis, ageusia, etc.)
      (6) *Motor paralysis* (paresis, aphonia)
      (7) *Visceral inhibitions* (impotence, frigidity, etc.) The function of inhibition of the various cognitive, affective, autonomic and visceral aspects is to deaden the appreciation of repressed inner impulses, to keep any symbolic derivatives from awareness, and to prevent the expression in any kind of motor action of a forbidden impulse. The syndromes that are characterized by repressive inhibition of function are *gross stress reactions* (trau-

matic or combat neuroses) *dissociative reactions* and *conversion hysteria.*

c. *Displacement and phobic avoidance.* The impulse here is displaced to an external object and then an attempt is made to repudiate the impulse by avoiding the object. The syndrome resulting from an extension of this mechanism is a *phobic reaction* (anxiety hysteria).

d. *Undoing and isolation.* The mechanism here consists of a kind of magical neutralization of the offending impulse or its derivatives through compulsive acts and rituals. The syndrome eventuating is an *obsessive compulsive reaction.*

The above efforts directed at reinforcing repression are usually associated with a constant failing of repressive barriers with a breakthrough and release of repressed material. This is usually in the symbolic form of obsessions, which, if accentuated, may cause an *obsessive compulsive reaction* (obsessional state, obsessional neurosis, compulsion neurosis, psychasthenia). Excessive revery and dream-like states may also result. An effort may be made by the psyche for an autonomous expression of the repressed impulses by *dissociative reactions* (conversion hysteria) in the form of somnambulism, fugues, dissociated (multiple) personality and depersonalization. The repressed impulses may also gain expression by being converted into physical symptoms, involving the sensory organs (anesthesia, blindness, deafness), motor organs (tics, tremors, posturing, spasms, convulsions, paresis, aphonia), and visceral organs (globus hystericus, vomiting). If sufficiently extensive these may constitute a *conversion reaction* (conversion hysteria). An internalization of hostility and its concentration on the "self" may produce a *depressive reaction* (reactive depression, neurotic depression). A projection of hostility toward outer objects or individuals may assume the proportions of a *paranoidal reaction.* Finally, there may be an impulsive breakthrough of the repressed material with "acting-out" in the form of an excited episode.

Characteristic, then, of the third line defenses are manifestations of failing repression with release of repressed material and desperate pathologic attempts at the reinforcing of repressive barriers. First and second line defenses that are useful may be coordinately retained. Anxiety may be episodically present whenever defenses fail to preserve the equilibrium. Stabilization at the level of third line defenses is possible, but where anxiety cannot be held in check, fourth line defenses may eventuate.

4. FOURTH LINE DEFENSES: REGRESSIVE DEFENSES.

a. *Return to helpless dependency.* Failing to adjust at an adult level, the individual may attempt to invoke the protective parental agencies who ministered to him in his childhood by assuming the attitudes and behavior of a child. This regressive appeal is associated with a renunciation of adult responsibility and the throwing of oneself at the mercy of a parental substitute.

b. *Repudiation of, and withdrawal from, reality.* Characteristic of withdrawal from reality are dereistic thinking; disorders of perception (illusions, hallucinations); disorders of mental content (ideas of reference, delusions); disorders of apperception and comprehension; disorders of the stream of mental activity (increased or diminished speech productivity, irrelevance, incoherence, scattering, verbigeration, neologisms); disturbances in affect (apathy, inappropriate affect, depression, excitement); and defects in memory, personal identification, orientation, retention, recall, thinking capacity, attention, insight, and judgment. The syndromes are in the form of psychotic episodes and *schizophrenic reactions*.

c. *Internalization of hostility*. Resultant may be *psychotic depressive reactions; manic depressive reactions, depressed type;* and *depressed involutional psychotic reactions*. Suicide is common in any of these syndromes.

d. *Excited "acting-out."* Hostile, sexual and other repressed impulses may be expressed openly in the course of a psychotic reaction. Representative syndromes here are *manic depressive reaction, manic type; paranoid reaction and paranoidal involutional psychotic reaction*.

The patient may manage to stabilize with fourth line defenses at the expense of reality, while possibly still retaining some of the other three lines of defense.

Syndromes never occur in isolation; they are always contaminated with manifestations of other defensive levels. As stress is alleviated or exaggerated, or as ego strengthening or weakening occurs, shifts in lines of defense upward or downward may occur, and changes in symptoms and syndromes will develop.

RECOMMENDED NOMENCLATURE

According to the revised nomenclature prepared by the Committee on Nomenclature and Statistics of·the American Psychiatric Association [438] mental disorders are classified into two large groups:

1. *Organic disorders* ("disorders caused by or associated with impairment of brain tissue function").
2. *Psychogenic disorders* ("disorders of psychogenic origin or without clearly defined physical cause or structural change in the brain").

Psychogenic disorders are of greatest interest to the psychotherapist and are classified as follows:

1. *Psychotic disorders* (Involutional psychotic reactions, manic-depressive reactions, psychotic depressive reaction, schizophrenic reactions, paranoid reactions.)
2. *Psychophysiologic autonomic and visceral disorders* (Formerly known as "psychosomatic disorders" and "somatization reactions." They include psychophysiologic skin, musculoskeletal, respiratory, cardiovascular, hemic and lymphatic, gastrointestinal, genito-urinary, endocrine, and

nervous system reactions, as well as reactions of organs of special sense.)

3. *Psychoneurotic disorders* (Anxiety reaction, dissociative reaction, conversion reaction, phobic reaction, obsessive compulsive reaction and depressive reaction.)

4. *Personality disorders* (Formerly known as "character disorders." They include personality pattern disturbances: inadequate, schizoid, cyclothymic and paranoid personalities; personality trait disturbances: emotionally unstable, passive-aggressive, and compulsive personalities; sociopathic personality disturbances: antisocial and dysocial reactions, sexual deviations, alcoholism and drug addiction; and special symptom reactions: learning and speech disturbances, enuresis and somnambulism.)

5. *Transient situational personality disorders* (Gross stress reaction; adult situational reaction; adjustment reaction of infancy; adjustment reaction of childhood—habit disturbance, conduct disturbance and neurotic traits; adjustment reaction of adolescence; adjustment reaction of late life.)

Excellent descriptions of these categories will be found in the diagnostic and statistical manual written by the Committee on Nomenclature [438].

In listing classifications, it is recommended that the lowest sub-classification of the disorder be used without including the broader generic group. The intensity of the reaction—"mild," "moderate," or "severe," as well as conspicuous symptoms may be listed. Where several psychiatric conditions exist, the primary diagnosis to be listed is (a) the chief cause for treatment, (b) the condition first in the chain of etiology, and (c) the most serious condition. A psychoneurotic diagnosis should not be made with a psychotic diagnosis. Only one kind of psychoneurotic reaction should be listed, even though symptoms of another psychoneurotic reaction coexist, in which event the symptoms of the latter are mentioned along with the primary diagnosis. It is recommended that in making a diagnosis, there also should be included a statement of the severity of the *external precipitating stress situation*, the extent of *premorbid personality and predisposition*, and the *degree of psychiatric impairment*.

ILLUSTRATIVE CASE

The following case illustrates the process of making a diagnosis by studying the spontaneous verbalizations of the patient, as well as by asking pointed questions. It consists of a portion of an initial interview with a 34 year old woman, married for 13 years, who has three children, ages 11, 8 and 4.

Pt. I don't know where to begin. I'd rather you ask me a couple of questions.

Th. It's a little difficult for you to pull things together. So suppose I do ask you a few questions.

Pt. Yes, so I can pull things together for myself, I mean. Technically, I'm suffering from an anxiety. I suppose, that goes back a long way.

Th. How far back?

Pt. It's always been the *same* thing, this terrific feeling of insecurity, or the tenseness, or the fear of death and not being able to breathe, and not being able to swallow and having palpitations of the heart, ulcers of the stomach, or fears of brain tumor.

It takes on different forms I suppose, depending on the season of the year. [*The patient describes symptoms of collapse in adaptation that have existed for a long time. These are in the nature of tension, frank anxiety and psychophysiologic phenomena.*]

Th. Mm hmm.

Pt. I rarely ever suffer from any two diseases at the same time.

Th. In other words, there's a whole succession of things.

Pt. Yes, but not all the time. Sometimes I've gone for months without these symptoms, but it's gotten progressively worse as the years go by. [*From time to time her symptoms abate, probably as her defenses are mobilized and restore her to a kind of equilibrium.*]

Th. I see.

Pt. I had it pretty bad about twelve years ago. I learned to fight it off. But in recent years it's just been too much, and I can't fight it off any longer. I used to be able to get relief by going to plays or movies, or by an occasional drink, or by sedatives. I still try these things, but it helps a little only temporarily. [*These first lines of defense were insufficient to control her anxiety. She still uses them nevertheless.*]

Th. Can you give me an idea of when this thing got so bad that you decided to get further help for it?

Pt. You mean recently? Within the last year it crept on me very suddenly—well, not so suddenly. I developed a pain around my heart. It came to a climax one evening about a year and a half ago and I was positive at the moment that I was dying. Everything sort of blacked out. The feeling: "Oh, my God." [*This is an acute anxiety attack brought on perhaps by a crumbling of her defenses or the impact of stress too difficult for her to manage.*]

Th. This was brought on by the pain around the heart?

Pt. No, that's like an aftermath. Just that everything is blurry, and nothing is sharp. Everything closing in. I went to bed and called the doctor. He told me that I should rest up physically, because I was terribly run down. I do work hard and usually I am able to pull myself together with a rest. But this time, in the middle of the rest, it got worse than ever before. I had a lot of worries and things. I was sure it was complete exhaustion and I knew what the doctor was going to say.

Th. What do you think caused this?

Pt. Well, my being overtired. I couldn't relax. I could hardly breathe. I was thoroughly exhausted. I've lost weight. I've gotten to a point where it's just too much for me to handle.

Th. I see.

Pt. It's either physical or it isn't. The doctor told me it wasn't. I know myself. I've read about this in books and I believe in psychiatry. My husband, on the other hand, doesn't believe in it at all. He thinks I'm just about ready for an institution because of these attacks. I try not to have them when he is around. [*Conflict with her husband may somehow be involved in stirring up her difficulties.*]

Th. He doesn't understand this?

Pt. He gets furious. He stomps out, says he can't take it any more. I try to pull myself together. I'm scared of anger and any form of emotion at all. [*Her inability to deal with anger may be indicative of a personality disorder other aspects of which will undoubtedly reveal themselves.*]

Th. Is there anything else that stirs you up?

Pt. The friction and tension in the house. The children are on the go all the time, and me not being able to stand friction or any kind of emotion at all.

Th. You're caught in the middle?

Pt. Yes, and the battles go on, and my husband can't stand it. It is horrible. Everybody gets on everybody else's nerves. I suppose I am responsible for some of it myself. But my husband won't understand. Personally, I think he's suffering from the same thing that I am, but he doesn't know it. He had a hell of a life himself. His mother is a nervous wreck and his father is a tyrant. I think he needs to be built up, but unfortunately I'm so full of so many things myself that I can't do it. I suppose if I did do it things would be better. He's popular outside, he's a lot of fun, jolly. People would be surprised to learn he had the problems he has. He's not mean, or anything like that, it's just that he won't take the time to be with me, understand me. I suppose he inherits that from his father. I don't dare tell him how I feel. I can't get reassurance from him. I have to get it from my mother. [*The patient is complaining here that her husband is not sufficiently kind and understanding and does not give her enough reassurance. She may be expressing frustrated dependency longings, either in response to a residual personality immaturity, or because her adaptational collapse invokes characterologic defenses, among which increased dependency leanings are prominent. These second level defenses are apparently not sufficiently adequate to neutralize anxiety.*]

Th. From your mother?

Pt. Yes, you see my father died when I was little, and my mother had to pursue her career. She was a career woman. She always felt that money was security. She was after me constantly to get out and get a job and earn money. But I suppose I was more secure than the average person. My aunt was wealthy. But I was sickly and always needed doctors. I had pneumonia and eye trouble and stomach trouble even when I was 14 years old. She then started dragging me around to see people, including psychiatrists. She must have been disappointed that I didn't turn out to be the way she wanted me. She was a great fighter, an intellectual, and I'm not. [*Feelings of rejection, of not coming up to her mother's expectations, may be the background of her insecurity and devaluated self-esteem.*]

Th. She was disappointed in you?

Pt. Oh, definitely, I'm sure I don't come up to her standard. For many years we were estranged. She didn't approve of my marriage. I was the only child.

Th. You present the picture of being insecure as a child.

Pt. I'm sure I was. My mother always tried to push me into independency. I can see it now, in the light of looking back, that I didn't want to be independent.

Th. What about your husband when you first met him?

Pt. I was in love with him. But shortly after my marriage, my real trouble began. I was insecure before, but I got along. But after one year of marriage, things really got impossible. I had a terrible period with both our parents. My mother disapproved and so did his parents. He had an awful time at home. He never told his parents we married. I was upset and lost a lot of weight. Well, I suppose I should have seen at the time that he wasn't very strong and that he wanted someone to lean on. He was petrified of his father. He wouldn't set his foot in our house for years. [*One gets the impression that the patient resents her husband's weakness. As a dependent person herself, she would like a strong mate on whom she might lean. The fact that her husband did not provide this for her may have stirred up hostility and insecurity, and, on the bedrock of his personality immaturity, created a collapse in adaptation.*]

Th. I see.

Pt. Well, anyways, things have gotten bad recently.

Th. Can you describe what trouble you have had recently?

Pt. I can't stay alone in the house for fear I'll jump out of the window. I can't take a bus; I have to take a taxi. I can't walk on the street for fear of falling on my face. Just fears of everything, especially of being alone or of walking on the street. [*These phobic symptoms are those of third line defenses, representing a further breakdown in repression.*]

Th. This must really be very difficult for you.

Pt. It is, it is. I have this constant anxiety. Every minute of the day. I don't know whether I'll live or die. I can't breathe deeply, I can't seem to get enough air. I'm afraid of everything. I can't go out. I don't want to drive a car. I don't want to be alone in the house. I can't go to a theater. I can't eat in a restaurant. Eating seems to have something to do with it. [*These are manifestations of anxiety representing a breakdown of defenses.*]

Th. It does?

Pt. Yes. I seem to be worse at meal times. If I'm eating in bed, it's all right. I noticed that I get tense as soon as I sit up at the table to eat. If I eat in bed I'm all right, but I can't eat up. I don't like a restaurant for that reason. [*This may be a further defensive effort toward helpless dependency, perhaps a regressive need to be fed like a child.*]

Th. Are there any other symptoms?

Pt. Well, recently, thoughts come to me that frighten me. It started when first I was listening to the radio. First I listened to a murder program where a man murdered his wife, and then I was listening to the war situation. I don't know if that has anything to do with it or not. These thoughts seem to crowd in on me. If I pick up the papers and see that somebody got killed, or that somebody died of a heart attack I'm finished. I'm afraid to read the obituary. As long as they are over 65 that's all right, but anything under scares me. Two days ago I was driving with a friend, and she told me of a person she knows who had psychosomatic trouble with his heart, and finally got heart trouble and died. This finished me. I couldn't think or anything. I went home to bed. [*These obsessional thoughts are indicative of a break-through of repressed conflicts, perhaps in relation to hostility.*]

Th. I see.

Pt. It's the funniest feeling, even though I tell myself it's all foolish, it doesn't help. Once it comes, there doesn't seem to be much I can do.

Th. Once it starts . . .

Pt. I can't fight it; I can't reason or anything.

Th. Like you're over a bank of snow on skis.

Pt. Yes. I have to let it take its course. I know it will end. I fight it, but I'm a wreck. I've tried sherry, I've tried phenobarbital, nothing helps. I don't even have enough nerve to commit suicide.

Th. What about other symptoms?

Pt. Like what?

Th. What about physical symptoms?

Pt. Well, when I am upset, I notice my stomach is upset. It's upset most of the time. [*This may be a psychophysiologic disorder associated with her anxiety, or it may be a somatic conversion symptom.*] Also from time to time I get a nervous twitch of my eyes, like blinking. I had it also when I was a child. [*This sounds like a conversion symptom.*]

Th. What about sexual problems?

Pt. Oh, that. My husband thinks I'm a mess. I'm very frustrated. I'm not . . . I'm . . . what's the word I want . . . I'm . . . frustrated. I don't seek it. I'm always afraid, I'm always holding back. From the neck down, I could see it might be a wonderful idea; but from here up something says, no. Once I get started it's all right, but I find it hard to get started.

Th. What do you think is involved?

Pt. Well I suppose it applies to all emotions. I don't cry, I don't get angry. I keep everything inside. A piece of music can make me emotional. I'm afraid I'll cry, so I don't do anything. I'm afraid. It scares me to death. [*Inhibition of emotions acts in the interest of maintaining repression.*]

Th. I see.

Pt. My mother had a violent temper and I was scared of it. I'd rather do anything than have her lose her temper. I guess it's the same thing with my husband and his violent temper. [*The patient presents an aspect of the origin of her fear of hostility and its carry-over into her present relationship with her husband.*]

Th. You're afraid of his temper?

Pt. I'm afraid of everybody. I'm one of the weakest people that ever lived. I can't stand up to anybody, which is another one of my mother's pet peeves about me.

Th. What do *you* think about that?

Pt. I think she's right, but I can't do anything about it. I feel guilty about it.

Th. Would you like to be able to emote and to express your feelings?

Pt. I suppose it would make me feel better. I'd like to be able to express myself. When my husband gets mad, I shrink up into a little ball. I can't be assertive with anybody. I feel hopeless.

Th. Hopeless as if you can't get over it?

Pt. That's what's worrying me because I can't go on like this much longer. [*One may suspect that here hopelessness may also be a defense against yielding her dependency need.*]

Th. Now what about dreams, do you dream a lot, or a little?

Pt. A little.

Th. Do you remember a recent dream?

Pt. Yes, I dreamed the Nazis came back and overran the country and it terrified me no end. There I was in a trap about to be annihilated.

Th. That's about how you feel literally.

Pt. Yes, it is.

In review, this is the case of a patient with a personality problem since childhood, consisting of dependency, insecurity and devaluated self-esteem. Symptoms of collapse in adaptation are tension, anxiety and psychosomatic symptoms. First line defenses are extraverted activities, sedation and mild indulgence of alcohol. Submissiveness and heightened dependency may be regarded as manifestations of second line defenses. Third line defenses are in the form of phobias and conversion symptoms. A waning of repressive barriers is indicated by a breakthrough of obsessions. Her defenses are apparently inadequate in mastering her anxiety. Following the principles of classification discussed, we may diagnose her as follows:

DIAGNOSIS: Anxiety reaction, severe, with phobic symptoms of claustrophobia and agoraphobia, obsessive symptoms and minor conversion symptoms.

[*The anxiety reaction is the primary diagnosis since it is the most severe of her reactions and constitutes the reason why she seeks therapy.*]

STRESS: Mild; husband non-accepting and hostile. [*It is hard to say how much of the patient's reaction is due to her husband's attitudes. It is likely that she has projected her difficulty onto her husband and that she might have responded the same way with any person she married. Under these circumstances we might be inclined to overlook the stress factor.*]

PREDISPOSITION: Moderate; emotionally unstable personality since childhood. [*Abnormal personality traits since childhood required medical treatment and resulted in a social maladjustment.*]

IMPAIRMENT: Moderate; able to carry some marital, work and social responsibilities; requires psychotherapy.

22

The Initial Interview:
Formulating the Tentative Dynamics

A TENTATIVE ASSAY OF THE EXISTING DYNAMICS IS HELPFUL TO THE therapist in outlining a temporary treatment plan, and in roughly prognosticating the extent of future change. This assay will need constant revision, in some instances radical revision, due to the emergence of data during the course of therapy not available at the first interview. Nevertheless, it may provide a sort of guide for the initiation of treatment, without which the therapist may flounder about, adding to the patient's helplessness and confusion.

The formulation of the existing dynamics will vary with the therapist's perceptiveness, skill, training and experience, as well as his theoretic bias. The same patient may thus be seen from different points of view. Each viewpoint will stress familiar aspects of data presented by the patient which substantiate a specific theoretic emphasis.

For instance, let us imagine that a therapist who does supportive therapy is consulted by a patient who complains of tension, anxiety, headaches and gastrointestinal distress brought on by an address he must make to members of his industry at a forthcoming convention. Discerning that the patient habitually gets upset whenever he is called on to make a speech, the therapist may formulate the problem as "stage-fright" and correctly estimate that the symptoms will disappear after the patient has fulfilled his assignment. The therapist may then assert that there is nothing physically wrong with the patient and enjoin him to "ride his symptoms" since his reactions are "natural." A therapist who is a physician may prescribe tonics, sedatives or other medicaments to "tide the patient over" his crisis period, or perhaps refer the patient to his family physician for such medications.

Another therapist, seeing the same man, would possibly formulate the problem as one in which the patient has lost faith in himself, and offer him solace through personal reassurance. A third therapist, psychologically trained, might ascertain through testing the intellectual calibre, vocational interests and aptitudes of the man, thereafter arriving at the conclusion that the problem is essentially one of a person involved in an occupation in which he is not really interested, that public speaking is one of his weak points he might best avoid, and that he is ideally suited for another occupation which will remove the man from his present source of stress. A fourth therapist, with experience in social work, may regard the problem as that of a man who is constantly being called on to perform tasks which frighten him because he has never developed confidence in his ability as a speaker. The man may then be advised regarding community resources for training in public speaking, and he may be guided toward entering into groups where he can exercise his skill. A fifth therapist, with a pedagogic bias, may approach the problem somewhat differently, considering that what has been lacking is adequate organization and preparation of his forthcoming talks. The patient may be shown how to outline his subject for presentation, how to arrange the material, and perhaps how to employ certain tricks to avoid fear such as are practiced by public performers.

If the therapist has been trained to do more intensive psychotherapy, say re-educative therapy, the problem may be formulated in a more incisive way. For example, strong perfectionistic traits may be detected which drive the patient toward exorbitant expectations of himself. He may believe that each projected talk constitutes a challenge which must be overcome by an extraordinary performance. The patient may feel unable to live up to merciless expectations he imagines are demanded of him. Or the therapist may find evidence that the patient automatically anticipates criticism or hostility from people, his panic being a reaction to the ill-will others bear toward him. Fear of failure or of living up to expectations may, in the opinion of the therapist, produce such strivings as detachment, dominance, competitiveness, aggression, compulsive ambition, grandiosity and masochism. Many contradictions would, of course, be residual in the simultaneous operation of several of these traits, and the outcome may be conflict, with the result of inhibition of function such as is being experienced by the patient. A formulation in these terms will be helpful in planning reeducative therapy during which the patient is brought to an awareness of how these traits disorganize him in his relations with people and in the achievement of essential goals. The therapeutic effort will then be directed along lines calculated to bring disturbing traits under control, and to replace them with more adaptive ones.

In the event the therapist has had training in reconstructive therapy, he will undoubtedly organize his tentative formulation of dynamics in terms of his training orientation. He may regard the patient's stage-fright as a manifestation of deep feelings of self-devaluation, of self-contempt, of inferiority, of residual dependence, or of castration. Symptoms may be looked upon as an outcome of fears of castration which pursue the patient, threatening him particularly when he competes or exposes himself to the judgment of an audience. His striving to avoid talks and presentations may also be regarded as a cover for exhibitionistic tendencies, a yielding to which may bring fantasied havoc upon him. He may then seek refuge in a passive retiring manner, shrinking from public appearances. Yet this defense is inadequate, since it convinces the patient that he is inept and mutilated. The therapeutic task here would be to bring derivatives of these unconscious tendencies to the patient's awareness until he recognized the raw conflicts that incited his fear. Once he knew his real enemies, he could cope with them in a manner more appropriate than his prevailing ineffectual infantile methods of defense.

No matter how skilled and well-trained the therapist may be, it is not always possible at the beginning of therapy to obtain an understanding or even a perspective of the dynamics of the patient's problem from his verbalized complaints, his past history, and his reported present relationships. This is because many of his patterns are not identifiable to the patient, although he may act them out constantly. For instance, a man struggling with an urge toward homosexuality may have no idea that he fears and despises women toward whom he professes a congenial tolerance and understanding. A woman, fiercely competitive with males, may not realize the depth of her fury at having been born a female, nor the extent of her refusal to give up the hope of eventually becoming a man. Sometimes it is possible at the start to get glimpses of repudiated trends. Yet the exact operation of repressed aspects of personality may escape definition and even detection until the therapeutic process has well begun, and as repressions start lifting while the patient is helped to face himself and his impulses in an honest and resolute way.

Most patients, thus, are incapable, during the initial interview, of verbalizing sufficiently to give the initial interviewer an idea about the operative conflicts and the important mechanisms of defense. As a rule, many sessions of therapy will be required before the dynamics begin to unfold.

Patients who are able to talk freely about themselves and their feelings, however, are often capable of revealing sufficient clues about their deeper problems to enable an astute interviewer to make some hypothetic assumptions about the dynamics. Much will depend on the perceptivity and experience of the interviewer, and upon his ability to pick up nuances from the verbal and non-verbal behavior of the patient.

Generally, little information about dynamics will be obtained from the statistical data, the elaboration of the chief complaint, the history and development of the complaint, and other associated symptoms. However, where the patient reveals one or two dreams that are significantly imprinted on his mind, where he discourses on his feelings about and his relationships with his parents and siblings, it may be possible for the interviewer to make important connections between underlying mental processes and the surface symptomatology.

Projective psychologic tests are often valuable in formulating the tentative dynamics, especially for patients who are not able to verbalize freely and who do not remember their dreams. From the unstructured ink-blots of the Rorschach, we may discern how the patient handles anxiety, how he reacts to emotionally stimulating situations, and how he organizes his defensive façade. Revealed also are the intellectual operations of the individual, his inner psychologic mechanisms and the quality of his fantasy life. From the structured pictures of the Thematic Apperception Test, we may often elicit associations that are most revealing of basic characterologic attitudes and patterns, as well as the interplay of emotion and personal interaction. The Man-Woman Drawing Test often reveals reflections of the patient's body image, the emotional significance of his various bodily parts and organs, and his basic conception of "male" and "female." The Szondi test is said to bring out the dynamics of the patient's basic needs and drives. Dynamics revealed by projective psychologic tests must always be validated by clinical corroboration.

23

The Initial Interview:
Estimating the Prognosis

NO VALID CRITERIA HAVE EVER BEEN DESIGNED THAT CAN SERVE AS A basis of prognosticating the results in psychotherapy. Published material is not too helpful, and even simple studies on recovery rates with different psychotherapies pose more problems than they solve. Thus Knight [439], reporting on results with psychoanalysis, found that 56% of treated patients were "cured" or "improved." When therapeutic procedures were employed along dynamic lines, but short of extensive psychoanalysis, Miles, Barrabee and Finesinger [440] found "improvement" in 58% of the patients. With non-specific therapeutic measures, principally rest, sedation and reassurance, Denker [441] discovered a recovery rate of 70%. Utilizing a non-directive approach, 74% of the persons treated were rated by Bartlett [442] as "improved." Perhaps most surprising is the reporting by Landis [443] of a spontaneous recovery rate of 68% in patients who were not exposed to any therapy. These figures are confusing since they tend to depreciate the value of intensive psychotherapy. However, without a comparative assay of the standards utilized in rating these reported results, and without a precise definition of the technical procedures employed, caution must be expressed in accepting the validity of these and any other statistics on improvement and recovery.

If so seemingly uncomplicated a matter as success or failure in psychotherapy can be estimated with no greater accuracy than the above studies reveal, it is obvious that the myriad intangibles involved make any estimates of prognosis an even more difficult task. One reason for the predicament is that irrespective of syndrome or any characteristics displayed by the patient, success in therapy is predicated on the response of the patient to a therapeutic relationship in which there are two participants, the patient and the therapist. Unless we know how the therapist will comport himself in the relationship, how objective and empathic he will be, we figuratively are aware merely of one part of an equation. The other part, the activity of the therapist, is the imponderable factor about which we know little, but which will significantly influence the results.

However, if we accept the therapist aspect of the equation as a constant, and assume that he can be therapeutically astute in all cases, we find that some kinds of problems and some characteristics displayed by patients will make for a better response to therapy than other problems and characteristics. It is on these qualities that we may make our estimates of prognosis.

In delineating prognostic signs, it is necessary to qualify them in terms of the ultimate treatment goals. This is because some patients may successfully achieve the goal of stabilizing themselves at the level of their optimal functioning prior to the onset of their illness, while they may be unable to reach the goal of personality reconstruction. Prognostic estimates will, therefore, be different with these two different goals. For example, in a patient with marked disintegrative tendencies, who has manifested an acute emotional disturbance, we may prognosticate a recovery from his acute disturbance and restoration to his previous level of functioning. Yet the prognosis for eradication of the disintegrative tendencies, and for reconstruction of the personality, will be less favorable.

Prognosis may be approached by considering such factors as the age of the patient, the duration of his illness, the severity of his symptoms, the diagnosis, the level of his intelligence, his motivations for therapy, the depth of insight, the factor of secondary gain, his ego strength or weakness, the current environmental situation, past therapeutic failures, and the response of the patient to the present therapeutic effort.

AGE OF PATIENT

Flexibility of personality is more important than the age of the patient in determining responsiveness to therapy. Because the average individual becomes more or less rigid as he grows older, his personality patterns and defenses becoming more inflexible, it is less likely that he can achieve extensive changes with therapy after 45 years of age. Response to supportive therapy, however, does not seem to be correlated with age.

DURATION OF ILLNESS

The more chronic the illness, the poorer the prognosis. Some ailments of more than five years' duration may be extremely resistant to therapy. The reason is that the problem has become highly organized over a period of time with defensive balances and counterbalances that tend to neutralize the therapeutic effort.

SEVERITY OF SYMPTOMS

The severity of symptoms seems to bear little relationship to how rapidly or how completely emotional problems are resolved. Thus, a mild phobia in some patients may be more resistant to treatment than a severe phobic condition in other patients. A person with an intense anxiety reaction may react more rapidly to therapy than one with a personality problem without disturbing anxiety manifestations. Indeed, the absence of severe symptoms may influence therapy in a negative way since discomfort and suffering provide many of the strongest incentives for getting well.

DIAGNOSIS

Some types of emotional disorders seem to respond more readily than other types. While certain conditions may rapidly be restored to stability with supportive therapy, they may resist vigorously the deeper changes wrought by insight therapy. Among such conditions are organic brain disorders, schizophrenia, manic-depressive reactions, involutional psychotic reactions, chronic anxiety reactions, chronic obsessive-compulsive reactions, perversions, addictions, and a great many personality disorders, particularly those in which there is characterologic rigidity. The other syndromes, especially stress, anxiety, conversion, phobic and psychophysiologic reactions, are usually more amenable to insight therapy, but coexistent factors of a destructive nature may possibly interfere with good results.

Neurotic symptoms occurring in the medium of a severe personality disorder and initiated, or sustained, by the disorder may not disappear until the personality problem itself is resolved. Thus, what may concern the patient most importantly, promoting his search for psychotherapeutic help, is his inability to enjoy sexual relations. He may ardently wish to get over the symptom. This, however, may not yield until his fundamental problem of detachment from people is corrected. Here the outlook is guarded, since the personality disorder will first have to be resolved before the sexual symptom disappears.

LEVEL OF INTELLIGENCE

High intelligence is not positively correlated with good results in therapy. However, borderline or defective intelligence will make it difficult to use any other technique than that of supportive therapy.

MOTIVATIONS FOR THERAPY

Unless the patient has the proper motivation for therapy, it may either be difficult to treat him, or therapeutic goals may have to be rigidly circumscribed. Thus, an alcoholic may have no motivation for treatment whatsoever, consulting the therapist merely to please his wife. So long as this lack of motivation persists, the prognosis with any kind of therapy will be poor. An individual with a psychophysiologic gastrointestinal ailment may seek rapid, dramatic relief for his symptoms, but he may not be motivated to explore his inner problems and conflicts in order to arrive at the basis for his complaints. It will not be possible, under these circumstances, to employ insight therapy with reasonable success. An individual with a personality disorder associated with aggression may not be motivated toward changing his way of life no matter how skillfully the therapist applies himself. He may, for instance, rationalize his refusal to change on the basis that an alteration in personality will threaten him economically. He may believe his livelihood to be contingent on fierce competitiveness. He will, therefore, resist therapy that is aimed at reconstructive goals:

A patient, furthermore, may be motivated to find in the relationship with the therapist other things than emotional health. He may thus seek in it a means to power, success or perfectionism. He may regard the relationship as a social experience because he is lonesome, or frustrated in his personal life. He may desire to convert the therapist into a parental figure to satisfy a dependency need. Or he may search for an idealized image of himself in the therapist with which he can identify. Until these defective motivations are altered, the prognosis will be poor.

Among factors that support good motivation for therapy are suffering from symptoms, the realization by the patient that he is handicapped by his neurosis, and a desire to be "normal" like other human beings. Among factors that oppose proper motivation are absence of symptomatic suffering, lack of handicap from symptoms, the fear of finding out something despicable about oneself in therapy, the reluctance to yield neurotic gains and values, the fear of exposing oneself to the unknown dangers of health, and the desire to be unique and unlike other persons.

DEPTH OF INSIGHT

The quality and extent of insight may exert some influence on prognosis. The patient may have no conception that his symptoms are in any way related to basic conflicts within himself and his relationships with people. So long as this lack of understanding persists, there can be little progress in reeducative and reconstructive therapy. It is difficult to estimate how long therapy will be required before the patient develops this degree of insight. On the other hand, the presence of such insight at the start of treatment, or its emergence during therapy, does not presuppose that the individual will be able to handle his insight constructively, or to utilize it in the direction of change. The patient will require considerable fortitude to help compensate for the deprivation of spurious values foisted on him by his neurosis, to master the anxieties related to the challenging of basic defenses, and to experiment with normal values and goals that up to this time have been held in contempt or considered dangerous. While it is difficult to predict how long it will take the patient to develop insight or to utilize it, the existence of intelligence, sensitivity, creativity and flexibility are favorable signs.

THE FACTOR OF SECONDARY GAIN

Secondary gain elements include the use of symptoms and disorganizing personality traits as means to security and self-esteem. Every neurosis possesses a certain protective quality for the patient even though it vitiates his productivity and sabotages his happiness. Indeed, the patient may resent abandoning spurious values that accrue to a neurosis. Thus a psychosomatic illness may inspire sympathy from people, absolve the patient from responsibility, and perhaps serve as a means of punishing intimates in his environment, toward whom the patient feels resentful. In stress reactions (traumatic neurosis) the factor of monetary compensation may make sickness a real asset to the individual. Personality distortions may constitute the only means the patient knows of relating to people. He may, therefore, conceive of therapy as a means of exposing himself to dangers he has hitherto managed to avoid.

The stronger the secondary gain, the less favorable the prognosis. During therapy, however, secondary gain elements may be handled and worked through as forms of resistance.

EGO STRENGTH AND EGO WEAKNESS

The concept of ego strength is an empirical construct that is useful in estimating prognosis. The ego may be conceived of as an integrating force that permits of a mobilization of adaptive resources. The ability in insight therapy to face inner conflict, to tolerate the intense emotions and anxieties liberated in the relationship with the therapist, to recognize the irrationality of these emotions, to understand their genetic origin, to abandon the spurious values and secondary gains of a neurosis, and to establish patterns of behavior in line with mature goals, calls for a relatively strong ego structure.

Estimates of ego strength may be made from data in the following areas: (1) hereditary influences, (2) constitutional factors, (3) early environmental conditionings, (4) developmental history, (5) present interpersonal relations, (6) methods of handling stress, (7) ability to gratify vital needs, (8) symptoms, (9) precipitating environmental factors, (10) type of previous adjustment, and (11) prevailing level of social maturity.

1. Hereditary Influences

The significance of heredity in fashioning ego strength is not clear. We may speculate that a "neuropathic predisposition" imposed on the individual by heredity tends to weaken his ego, but how this operates and the extent of its influence cannot be described. A family history of mental illness, especially manic-depressive psychosis and schizophrenia, of alcoholism, of convulsive disorder, and of drug addiction must always be considered seriously; nevertheless, a favorable early environment may neutralize any destructive hereditary factors. On the other hand, absence of hereditary history of mental illness does not mean that ego strength is guaranteed.

2. Constitutional Factors

Like heredity, it is difficult to assign to constitution a definite role in the molding of ego strength. However, a constitutionally abnormal stature, physique or endocrine disorder, may create problems for the person, and, in this way indirectly influence ego functioning.

3. Early Environmental Influences

Severely traumatizing influences in early childhood may have impoverished ego development so drastically as to limit the extent of its potential growth.

Where historical material during early childhood reveals great stress, an attempt should be made to ascertain the effect on the patient's ego. Among traumatizing influences are disharmony in the home; intense conflict between the parents, or their separation or divorce; tendencies in either parent that make him or her markedly authoritarian, domineering, excessively punitive, cruel, intolerant, unstable, immature, cold, neglectful, rejecting, weak, sickly, superstitious, over-protecting, neurotic, psychotic or alcoholic; and great rivalry with, or jealousy and dislike of a sibling. The absence of such influences is not necessarily a favorable prognostic sign.

4. Developmental History

By the same token, certain findings in the developmental history are indicative of a potential stunting of personality growth. They are often insignias of possible extensive and even irreparable damage to the ego. Among important findings are the following:

a. *Birth.* (1) Patient was an unwanted child. (2) Birth was premature. (3) Birth injury.

b. *Feeding problems.* (1) Never breast fed. (2) Bottle fed before 6 months. (3) Bottle fed after 1½ years. (4) Vomiting spells or colic.

c. *Early care.* (1) Mother sickly after patient's birth. (2) Mother did not participate in early care. (3) Patient had a succession of nurses.

d. *Physical development.* (1) Delayed growth. (2) Deformity.

e. *Habits.* (1) Retarded dressing and toilet habits. (2) Enuresis. (3) Improper sleeping habits.

f. *Intellectual development and school adjustment.* (1) Delayed talking. (2) Started school when seven years old or older. (3) Got along poorly with teachers. (4) Repeated grades. (5) Got along poorly with schoolmates. (6) Unhappy at school. (7) Obtained low grades. (8) Quit school before the eighth grade.

g. *Emotional maturity.* (1) Persistent temper tantrums. (2) Continuing dependency. (3) Unresolved sibling jealousy. (4) Lack of assertiveness. (5) Never self-supporting as an adult. (6) No effort to hold a job. (7) Never married. (8) Married, but divorced or separated. (9) No desire for children. (10) No group interests.

h. *Social development.* (1) Excessively selfish, withdrawn, timid or seclusive. (2) No desire for friends, or unable to form friends. (3) Unaffectionate and undemonstrative. (4) Refusal to accept responsibilities.

i. *Sexual development.* (1) No sex education. (2) Slept in parents' bedroom. (3) Observed parents in sexual relations. (4) Sexually stimulated by parent or nurse. (5) Masturbatory intimidation. (6) Intercourse before 16. (7) Sexual seduction before 16.

j. *Illnesses and accidents.* (1) Convulsive disorder as a child. (2) "Sleeping sickness." (3) Poliomyelitis. (4) Asthma. (5) Fainting or dizzy spells.

(6) Migraine. (7) Trouble with sex organs. (8) Endocrine disease. (9) Head injury. (10) Several accidents. (11) Several fractures. (12) Cardiac disturbance. (13) Stomach and intestinal illness.

k. *Neurotic traits.* (1) Peculiar toilet habits. (2) Persistent thumbsucking. (3) Nail biting. (4) Easy crying. (5) Persistent fears. (6) Nightmares. (7) Sleep walking. (8) Speech problem. (9) Tics. (10) Compulsions. (11) Persistent fears. (12) Excessive day dreaming. (13) Cruelty. (14) Excessive aggressiveness. (15) Truancy. (16) Hyperactivity. (17) Runaway tendencies. (18) Stealing. (19) Firesetting. (20) Detachment.

5. Current Interpersonal Relations

The nature of the patient's current interpersonal relations may yield some clues to ego strength. Human beings display an endless variety of interpersonal reactions. The intensity of such reactions rather than their quality is of pathologic consequence. As a general rule, the personality distortions, tabulated below, indicate that long-term reconstructive therapy will be required to influence them significantly. They do not indicate how the patient will respond to treatment. Some of the distortions are more serious than others; for instance, detachment or open aggression. On the other hand, the relative absence of personality distortions is a good prognostic sign. The characteristics listed below must be considered of negative prognostic importance only when they appear in exaggerated form.

a. *Relationship with people in a superior or authoritative position.* (1) Dependency. (2) Submissiveness. (3) Shyness. (4) Ingratiation. (5) Fear. (6) Dislike. (7) Distrust. (8) Aggression. (9) Detachment.

b. *Relationship with friends and colleagues.* (1) Absence of close friends. (2) Feelings of being disliked. (3) Avoidance of people. (4) Lonesomeness even with people. (5) Fears of people. (6) Inability to mix. (7) Fear of rejection. (8) Dependency. (9) Submissiveness. (10) Distrustfulness. (11) Aggression. (12) Dislike of people. (13) Inability to get along with women. (14) Inability to get along with men. (15) Fear of women. (16) Fear of men. (17) Feelings of difference from other people. (18) Feelings of inferiority. (19) Feelings of superiority. (20) Jealousy of others. (21) Suspicion of motives of others. (22) Stubbornness with others. (23) Insistence on having own way. (24) Furiousness when crossed.

c. *Miscellaneous relationships.* (1) Dislike of younger, older, less attractive, or unfamiliar people. (2) Suspiciousness. (3) Self-consciousness.

d. *Group relations.* (1) Dislike, fear, and avoidance of groups. (2) Shyness in groups.

e. *Attitudes toward self.* (1) Shyness. (2) Lack of self-confidence. (3) Avoidance of responsibility. (4) Indecisiveness. (5) Despising of self. (6) Perfectionism. (7) Meticulousness. (8) Parsimony. (9) Obstinacy. (10) Self-dramatization. (11) Narcissism. (12) Grandiosity. (13) Mysticism. (14) Feelings of guilt. (15) Need for punishment. (16) Resentfulness.

6. Methods of Handling Stress

The adequacy or inadequacy of the defensive reactions of the individual may be of significance. Among the less favorable signs in relation to the handling of stress are physical withdrawal, emotional detachment, fantasy, "acting-out," aggression, sadism, alcoholic overindulgence, excess sedation, intense dependency, self-punishment, self-aggrandizement, intellectual confusion, emotional shattering, physical sickness, compulsions, depression, feelings of unreality, and sexual perversions. Unfavorable also is an inability to face pain or to tolerate anxiety which will occur when the patient's resistances are challenged.

7. Ability to Gratify Vital Needs

The ability to gratify, in conformity with the mores, important biologic and social needs, without guilt, aggression or self-punishment, are signs of ego strength.

8. Symptoms

Prognostically unfavorable symptoms are stammering, homosexuality, exhibitionism, fetishism, sexual sadism, sexual masochism, psychomotor retardation, violent rages, euphoria, apathy, fear of blushing, fear of germs, fear of soiling, fear of contamination, fear of poverty, uncontrollable impulses, hand-washing, ritualistic acts, hair-plucking, self-torture, delusions of influence, delusions of persecution, delusion of "thoughts being stolen," grandiose delusions, delusion of "mission to perform," delusion of body organs rotting, delusion of having committed an "unpardonable sin," delusion of "having lost one's soul," ideas of reference, hallucinations, impaired reality sense, depersonalization, impaired judgment, alcoholism, drug addiction, and criminality.

9. Precipitating Environmental Factors

Emotional ailments occurring in the medium of severe environmental stress, and directly related to the stress factor may have a favorable prognosis, provided that the environmental difficulty can be resolved, or that the patient is capable of making an adjustment to irremediable circumstances. Illustrative are catastrophic life happenings; such as, accidents; disasters of nature or those brought on by war; death of parents, mate, or children; abandonment, separation or divorce; and severe losses of prestige, position or economic security. On the other hand, emotional illness developing in the face of a congenial environment has a less favorable prognosis.

An emotional problem brought on by severe environmental stress, does not always indicate a good prognosis, even in the absence of maladjustment prior to the cataclysmic happening. In some instances the stress situation may touch off a residual neurosis by bringing into play repressive and regressive defensive techniques which persist long after the traumatic event has passed. Instead of recovering rapidly with therapy, the individual may exhibit an obstinate reaction of helplessness, as if he no longer trusts the world that has so abruptly shattered his sense of mastery.

10. Previous Adjustment

If the patient has, at any period in his life, made a good adjustment, the prognosis would probably be better than if maladjustment were present from early childhood continually. In appraising the character of the patient's adjustment, the therapist should consider whether this was maintained at the expense of vital aspects of functioning. One should determine what it takes out of the person to make the kind of adjustment he is making even though he makes it successfully. For instance, a schizoid personality disorder may not militate against a social adjustment, provided that the individual is capable of avoiding situations of environmental stress, and is able to detach himself sufficiently from people to prevent close interpersonal involvements. An aggressive obsessive-compulsive individual may be able to carry on satisfactorily, with a modicum of happiness, if he can control his environment and the persons with whom he is intimately associated. Or adjustment may be contingent on the gratification of immature, dependency strivings, maladjustment ensuing upon withdrawal of the host. Thus the quality of one's past adjustment, and the areas of functioning that must be inhibited, will determine whether or not they can be considered evidences of a strong ego.

11. Level of Social Maturity

Estimates of personality maturity in terms of physical growth, educational achievement, resolution of dependence, sexual maturity, marriage, parenthood, quality of social relationships, and group and community participation, are possible indications of ego strength. However, an individual who has achieved a good social adjustment, satisfying accepted criteria of maturity, may still be a seriously sick person emotionally, who, upon succumbing to collapse in adaptation, may offer strong resistances to psychotherapy. Thus, a person may achieve social maturity by repressing powerful anxiety-provoking conflicts, and by evolving a personality structure organized around perfectionism, obstinacy, meticulousness, repression of hostility, and a compulsive need for order and precision in his immediate environment. Therapy may be a prolonged and difficult task, even though the individual may have operated in life on an apparently high level of maturity.

On the other hand, evidences of immaturity (impaired physical growth, low educational achievement, continued dependency ties, sexual infantility or perversions, distorted life goals, inability to accept marriage or parenthood, inability to coordinate ambitions with aptitudes and the existing reality situation, disturbed social relationships, and lack of community participation) may, if prominent, be regarded as direct signs of ego weakness.

THE CURRENT ENVIRONMENTAL SITUATION

Serious lacks and encumbrances in one's environment influence prognosis negatively. Thus, a disturbed environment which the patient cannot alter, and in which he is expected to function, imposes a burden on his capacities for adjustment. Among inordinate environmental influences are economic stress; bad work, housing and neighborhood situations; abnormal cultural standards and pressures; discordant family relationships; and disturbed daily habits and routines.

1. *Economic situation.* (a) The patient is subject to desperate or poor financial circumstances. (b) He is unable to afford adequate food, shelter and clothing. (c) He cannot support dependents, meet his present indebtedness, or provide for appropriate education and recreation.

2. *Work situation.* (a) The patient is unemployed. (b) He has made the wrong selection of an occupation. (c) He is unhappy at work due to inadequate salary, inimical work conditions, and few opportunities for advancement.

3. *Housing situation.* The patient lives in an inadequate dwelling in terms of insufficient space, absence of privacy, and uncleanliness.

4. *Neighborhood situation.* (a) The patient is subject to malicious activities by delinquent or criminal individuals or gangs. (b) He is exposed to racial, class or religious discrimination. (c) There are no neighborhood recreational and social facilities. (d) He lives too far away from work and social activities.

5. *Cultural standards and pressures.* (a) The patient comes from a different background than people with whom he lives and associates. (b) He feels discriminated against because of his race, religion, color or national background. (c) He finds it difficult or impossible to adjust to the standards of the people around him. (d) He refuses to conform with current cultural patterns. (e) His personal standards clash with community standards.

6. *Family relationships.* (a) The patient is unhappy at home. (b) He is "ashamed of," "afraid of" or "hates" certain members of his family. (c) He disagrees violently with people at home. (d) His independence is threatened. (e) There is constant insistence that he "obey." (f) There is interference with his legitimate social life. (g) His personal appearance is criticized. (h) He is subjected to angry displays. (i) Though adult, he is unable or unwilling to live away from his family. (j) He has a difficult problem with his mother, father, sibling or other relatives at home. (k) He is financially dependent on his parents.

7. *Relationship with mate.* (a) If married, he is unable to adjust to married life or to get along with his mate. (b) He is not in love with his mate. (c) He fights constantly with his mate. (d) His sexual relations are unsatisfactory. (e) His mate is adulterous or emotionally ill. (f) He is mistreated by his mate.

8. *Relationship with children.* (a) The patient is having a severe problem with one (or more) of his children who is physically or emotionally ill. (b) He regrets having children. (c) His children "get on his nerves." (d) He dislikes his children or vice versa. (e) His children quarrel constantly and are refractory to reasonable discipline.

9. *Daily habits, recreations and routines.* The patient is guilty of some of the following: (a) Irregular meal times. (b) Unbalanced diet. (c) Excess coffee and tobacco. (d) Improper body care and grooming. (e) Insufficient sleep. (f) Lack of exercise. (g) Absence of interests, hobbies or recreations; few or no social or community activities.

PAST THERAPEUTIC FAILURES

One or more long unsuccessful psychotherapeutic experiences is generally an unfavorable prognostic sign. Exceptions to this rule include treatment by an unskilled therapist, by one who was unable to handle transference or to control counter-transference reactions, or by one whose approach lacked flexibility. Because his previous treatment had failed, the patient may have lost confidence in the efficacy of psychotherapy. This may act as resistance to treatment.

RESPONSE TO THE PRESENT THERAPEUTIC EFFORT

Once therapy has started, it may be possible to prognosticate the outcome with greater accuracy than from the appraisal of the past history. If the patient has or develops strong motivations for therapy, if he enters into a good working relationship with the therapist, if he is capable of understanding and resolving transference reactions, if he masters resistances to therapy, if he exhibits an ability to face anxieties associated with his inner conflicts, if he shows a willingness to abandon the spurious values of his neurosis and to vanquish the secondary gain element, we may reasonably predict a good prognosis.

Summary of Positive and Negative Prognostic Signs in the Patient

POSITIVE	NEGATIVE
1. The age of the patient is not too advanced.	Patient has advanced to an age where learning is not so easy, where his patterns are set, and where considerable rigidity exists.
2. Problems are of recent duration.	Problems date back to childhood or are of a longstanding nature.
3. Patient's symptoms or behavior patterns are incapacitating, inconvenient or arouse resentments in him.	Patient's symptoms or behavior patterns cause him no inconvenience and are not incapacitating. Symptoms are strongly protective in nature, and yield positive dividends, such as support, attention, and monetary compensation. Symptoms satisfy a masochistic need in the patient.

Positive	Negative
4. The patient is suffering from a stress, anxiety, phobic, conversion, or psychophysiologic reaction.	The patient is suffering from an organic brain disorder, schizophrenia, manic-depressive reaction, involutional psychotic reaction, chronic anxiety reaction, chronic obsessive-compulsive reaction, drug addiction, sexual perversion, or severe personality disorder.
5. The patient has a normal or high intelligence.	The patient has a borderline or low intelligence.
6. The patient has a strong motivation for therapy. He applies for therapy through his own efforts. He sees the need for psychotherapy.	The patient has little or no motivation for therapy. He is brought into therapy by another person. He does not see a need for psychotherapy.
7. The patient has insight into the emotional nature of his problem.	The patient has no idea his problem is emotionally inspired.
8. Elements of secondary gain are relatively lacking.	Secondary gain elements are present.
9. There is no hereditary history of mental illness.	There is a hereditary history of mental illness.
10. The patient has no constitutional abnormal stature, physique or endocrine disorder.	A constitutional disturbance is present.
11. The patient was not subject to severely traumatizing influences in his childhood.	Severe traumatic influences existed in the patient's childhood.
12. Few or no distortions existed in the relationship of the parents with the patient.	There was severe disharmony in the home, severe difficulties between patient's mother and father, or severe distortions in his relationship to his parents.
13. The developmental history shows no serious defects in physical development, habits, school adjustment, emotional maturation or sexual development.	The developmental history shows a serious maladjustment during infancy and childhood.
14. Adjustment failures in childhood were minimal; childhood neurotic disturbances were absent.	There was failure of adjustment in childhood; patient had childhood neurotic disturbances.

POSITIVE	NEGATIVE
15. Patient's relationships with people in general are good. There is plasticity in personality traits and defenses. He is able to establish a good relationship with the therapist.	The patient has severe disturbances in interpersonal relations. There is rigidity in personality traits and defenses. Transference elements are disturbing and interfere with a good relationship with the therapist.
16. Assertiveness is present and self-esteem is good.	Assertiveness is lacking and self-esteem is diminutive.
17. The patient's conscience is not too severe or too diminutive.	The patient's conscience is excessively severe, is diminutive, or exerts an uneven pressure on him.
18. The patient is capable of handling reasonable stress or of enduring reasonable anxiety without repressive or regressive reactions.	The patient tends to handle stress or anxiety by reactions of physical withdrawal, emotional detachment, fantasy, "acting-out," aggression, sadism, alcoholic overindulgence, excess sedation, intense dependency, self-punishment, self-aggrandizement, intellectual confusion, emotional shattering, physical sickness, compulsions, depression and feelings of unreality.
19. The patient is capable of gratifying vital biologic and social needs in conformity with the mores of the group.	Patient is unable to gratify his needs or does so in opposition to accepted mores.
20. The patient's symptoms consist of anxiety, tension, mild depression, mild psychophysiologic reactions or phobias.	Symptoms consist of stammering, sexual perversions, deep depression, violent rages, euphoria, apathy, various obsessions, compulsions, ideas of reference, delusions, hallucinations, impaired reality sense, depersonalization, alcoholism, drug addiction, and criminality.
21. Immediate environmental precipitating factors are strong.	Immediate environmental precipitating factors are not intense.
22. The patient's adjustment prior to his illness was good.	Maladjustment was present since early childhood.
23. The patient has achieved social maturity. There are no defects in physical growth, educational achievement and school progress, resolution of dependence, sexual maturity, marriage, parenthood, social relationships and community participation.	The patient has been delayed in achieving social maturity. There are defects present in the patient's physical growth, educational achievement and school progress, resolution of dependence, sexual maturity, marriage, parenthood, social relationships and community participation.

POSITIVE	NEGATIVE
24. The patient has adequate interests, hobbies and recreational pursuits.	Patient has few or no interests, hobbies or recreational activities.
25. The patient's life situation will reward him for the abandonment of symptoms and the development of new patterns.	The abandonment of symptoms or the development of new patterns of behavior bring negative results, or expose the patient to dangers of a strongly threatening nature.
26. Habitual environmental pressures on, and responsibilities of the patient are average.	Habitual environmental pressures on, and responsibilities of the patient to which he must adjust are severe and irremediable. He will have to live in a disturbed or depriving environment (neurotic parents or mate, poor economic circumstances, harsh culture, etc.)
27. Ambitions are in line with aptitudes and the reality situation.	Ambitions are out of line with aptitudes or the reality situation.
28. The patient has had no previous attacks of emotional illness.	The patient has had previous attacks of emotional illness.
29. The patient has received no psychotherapy in the past.	The patient has received psychotherapy in the past which was unsuccessful.
30. Therapy and the therapeutic situation do not impose too great hardships on the patient in terms of expense, time, travel, etc.	Therapy and the therapeutic situation impose great hardships on the patient.
31. Patient has no problems in communication.	Patient has problems in communication.

SUMMARY OF PROGNOSTIC SIGNS FROM THE STANDPOINT OF THE THERAPIST

It may seem odd to include the therapist in a prognostic index. However, since psychotherapy is an interpersonal relationship, the therapist's attitudes to a specific patient, his capacity to understand the patient and to provide a meaningful relationship for him, are important in estimating what will happen in the therapeutic situation. It is difficult to predict from the general responses of the therapist whether he will be able to establish a good relationship with a certain patient. The therapist may be able to relate better to some patients than to others. Furthermore, since an understanding of psychodynamic problems is mandatory in providing success in psychotherapy, the therapist may be able to work better with certain kinds of emotional problems and not so well with others.

POSITIVE	NEGATIVE
1. The therapist is capable of understanding the dynamics of the patient's illness.	The therapist is confused about the existing dynamics.
2. The therapist is sufficiently sensitive to perceive what is happening in the treatment process.	The therapist is insensitive to what is going on within the patient and within himself.
3. The therapist is aware of his own feelings and is capable of remaining objective irrespective of the attitudes and behavior manifested by the patient.	The therapist is incapable of maintaining satisfactory objectivity.
4. The therapist is flexible in his approach to the patient.	The therapist is rigid in his approach to the patient.
5. The therapist has a capacity for empathy with the patient.	The therapist lacks empathy with the patient.
6. The therapist tends to treat the patient in a respectful and cooperative manner.	The therapist is domineering, pompous and authoritarian.
7. The therapist is capable of being firm on occasion.	The therapist is too passive and submissive.
8. The therapist is capable of establishing a working relationship with the patient.	The therapist is detached.
9. The therapist is well-adjusted and is gaining satisfactions for his own basic needs.	The therapist tends to utilize the patient for the vicarious gratification of his own repressed or suppressed impulses; such as, sexuality, the expression of hostility, and the gaining of prestige.
10. The therapist is capable of tolerating the expression of varied impulses in the patient.	The therapist is incapable of tolerating such impulses in the patient as sexuality, hostility, or assertiveness.
11. The therapist has no neurotic attitudes toward money.	The therapist's insecurity reflects itself in anxiety about fees and payments.
12. The therapist is able to tolerate the vicissitudes inevitable to therapy.	The therapist is unable to tolerate blows to his self-esteem by the patient's acting-out tendencies, by manifestations of resistance and transference, and by the inevitable failures and frustrations in treatment.

POSITIVE	NEGATIVE
13. The therapist feels secure within himself.	The therapist has a neurotic need to be liked, a compulsive tendency toward perfectionism, inordinate hostility, poor creativity, no sense of humor, an inability to take criticism, low personal integrity, a diminished respect for people, a failure to acknowledge self-limitations, a low energy level or poor physical health.
14. The therapist is capable of giving the patient support in accordance with the patient's needs without overprotecting or overdomineering the patient.	The therapist rejects the patient, or refuses to, or is unable to extend to the patient measured support.

24

The Initial Interview:
Estimating the Patient's General Condition

IT IS IMPORTANT TO ESTIMATE HOW THOROUGHLY PREPARED THE PATIENT is for psychotherapy prior to making arrangements for his treatment. This necessitates a number of judgments, including the level of insight and the degree of motivation. Such judgments should be recorded in the initial interview form.

RESPONSE OF PATIENT TO THERAPIST AND VICE VERSA

The therapist will have observed by the time he reaches this point in the initial interview that the patient has responded to him in certain ways; such as, by being cooperative, fearful, suspicious or hostile. He will also be aware of his own feelings about the patient—positive or negative. The interviewer will have to handle the patient's fearful, suspicious or hostile responses along lines suggested in chapter 28, Dealing with Inadequate Motivation. He will furthermore have to manage his own overprotecting and rejecting attitudes toward the patient. Observations of reciprocal responses are important in deciding whether the interviewer will continue treating the patient or whether he will make a referral to another therapist.

PHYSICAL APPEARANCE

The patient's physical appearance—meticulous, presentable, untidy or disheveled—and the manner of his dress may give the interviewer some clues of how the patient feels about himself. Thus, a woman with a short haircut, who wears a mannish-like suit, may have homosexual impulses, or may seek to identify with males. An unkempt personal appearance may be a manifestation of disintegrative tendencies. Pretentious apparel may be a surface indication of feelings of deep self-devaluation, or of contemptuous attitudes toward conventionality.

PATIENT'S ESTIMATE OF HIS PRESENT PHYSICAL HEALTH

The degree of the patient's preoccupation with health may be diagnostically important. Thus underconcern about his physical condition, to a point where the patient neglects an illness, may be indicative of masochism. Overconcern about his physical state may reflect fears of mutilation or of death, such as are found in obsessive-compulsive reactions.

COMMUNICATIVENESS

The way the patient communicates is suggestive of how he will relate in therapy, of his emotional status, and of his contact with reality. A non-motivated patient is usually underproductive. Underproductivity to a point of retardation is also often a sign of depression, especially of a depressed manic-depressive state. Garrulousness may be a manifestation of fear, or it may indicate a serious psychomotor condition, as in the organic psychoses. Overproductivity may additionally be part of a manic phase of manic-depressive psychosis. Disjointed, irrelevant and incoherent productions are sometimes found in schizophrenia.

INSIGHT AND MOTIVATION

In order for the patient to qualify for successful therapy, he must satisfy each of the following conditions:

1. He must be aware of the fact that he has a problem.
2. He must desire to correct the problem.
3. He must be aware of the fact that the problem is emotional in nature.
4. He must be willing to accept psychotherapy.
5. He must be willing to accept help from the interviewer or from some other therapist.
6. He must be willing to accept the conditions of psychotherapy.
7. He must be able to arrange time for treatment.
8. He must be able to afford to pay whatever fee is decided on between himself and his therapist.

The interviewing therapist must, therefore, search for answers to the following questions:

1. Is the patient aware of the fact that he has a problem? If not, why has he come for an interview?
2. Assuming that he recognizes that he has a problem, does he want to correct the problem? If not, what does he want from the interviewer? If so, what kind of help does he believe he needs, and what help has he received to date?
3. Is he willing to accept the fact that his problem is emotionally determined? If not, how intense is his resistance? Does he know anything about emotional illness?
4. Assuming that he accepts the fact that he has an emotional problem, is he willing to receive psychotherapy? If not, why not? Does he have misconceptions about psychotherapy? Are these soluble with appropriate clarification?
5. Is he willing to accept treatment from the interviewer or from a therapist to whom he is referred? If not, what resistances does he display? Can these be handled during the initial interview?
6. Is he willing to accept the conditions, the general arrangements and the method of psychotherapy? If not, is it possible to deal with his objections?

7. Can he arrange the necessary time for treatment? If not, are the reasons emotional or realistic? Can a practical means be devised for handling these problems?

8. Can he afford therapy? If not, can he arrange to obtain or to borrow funds?

The management of the patient's resistances to any of the conditions essential for therapy is a responsibility of the initial interviewer. Ways of dealing with such resistance are indicated in this and in later chapters, particularly Chapter 30, Answering Questions Patients Ask about Therapy and Chapter 28, Dealing with Inadequate Motivation.

25

The Initial Interview:
Making Practical Arrangements for
Psychotherapy

BEFORE MAKING ANY ARRANGEMENTS FOR THERAPY, IT IS ADVISABLE TO give the patient a bird's-eye view of his problem in terms that are meaningful to him. The therapist presents a general statement of the problem as he sees it, and of what might be accomplished through psychotherapy. No interpretations are made; no outline of the dynamics are postulated; no promises of cure are extended; no pronouncements are expressed to the effect that the prognosis is bad. The following is an example of a possible statement: "Now I have a general idea of your problem and I should like to give you some broad impressions of what might be done. Due to a number of factors, you have developed difficulties that 'tie you in a knot,' so to speak. You have some bothersome symptoms, and you are prevented from developing your potentialities. I think you need psychotherapy and can benefit from it."

Included in the making of practical arrangements for therapy are the choice of therapist, choice of therapy, frequency of visits, estimating the duration of therapy, arranging the fee, handling delays in starting treatment, and making final arrangements with the patient or referring him to another therapist.

CHOICE OF THERAPIST

By the time the initial interview is completed, the interviewer will usually have been able to evaluate whether or not he can, with his training and skills, handle the patient's problem. He may, by virtue of his training, be equipped to treat the patient. Whether or not he decides to do so will be dependent on his emotional response to the patient, his interest in the specific problem presented, and his ability to make the proper time and financial arrangements with the patient. He will also have to take into account the patient's own wishes.

The interviewer may not be trained to implement the kind of therapeutic approach best suited for the patient's difficulty. Thus if psychoanalysis is decided on as the treatment of choice, and the interviewer is not analytically trained, he will want to transfer the patient to a psychoanalyst. If a dangerous depressive condition necessitates electric shock therapy which the therapist does not utilize in his practice, he will have to find a suitable psychiatrist who can give shock treatments. If hypnotherapy seems indicated, a specialist in this field will be required.

The patient may possess a type of problem which the interviewer does not care to handle. For instance, some therapists do not like to work with adolescents, older patients, borderline cases, schizophrenic patients, alcoholics, drug addicts, obsessive-compulsive neurotics, severe anxiety hysterics, and psychopathic personalities. Moreover, the emotional response of the patient to the interviewer, and of the interviewer to the patient may be such that it is obvious that they cannot work together. Finally, the patient may decide against starting treatment with the initial interviewer, even though the latter is willing to accept the patient for therapy. While this contingency is rare in a properly conducted interview, the therapist should still be prepared to meet with it on occasion.

The question is often asked regarding the preferred sex of a therapist for the handling of certain problems. Experience proves that the personality and skill of the therapist are more important than whether the therapist be male or female. Nevertheless, some patients seem to do better with therapists of one sex than the other. Thus, if the patient has had damaging experiences of rejection, neglect, or harsh treatment from his father, and has later never been able to establish a good relationship with a man, severe problems of a transference nature are apt to develop with a male therapist. If the ego structure of such a patient is furthermore weak, treatment may stir up anxieties that are beyond his coping powers. Under these circumstances, it is probably better to get the patient started in treatment with a female therapist. The opposite would be true if the prime problems were with a mother figure. Here a male therapist would probably be better for the patient. If, however, the ego of the patient seems strong, if reconstructive therapy is to be used, and if a transference neurosis is desired, the opposite choice would be indicated.

Certain kinds of syndromes seem to respond more readily in a relationship with a female therapist. Borderline cases, and some types of schizophrenia, alcoholism and psychopathic personality are often more easily handled by a female therapist, possibly because existing dependency (oral) needs are, in the opinion of the patient, symbolically gratified, and there is no potentially threatening masculine authority figure.

The age of the therapist may also influence the patient. Some patients are insistent upon an older therapist on the basis that age is an insignia of greater experience. An older female therapist is sometimes desired in cases where there is an urgent need for a mother figure, while an older male therapist may be sought by individuals who yearn for a relationship with a father figure.

CHOICE OF TREATMENT METHOD

So many variables are involved in therapy that it is difficult to decide in advance on the choice of treatment method. These variables include: how the patient will respond to the therapist after treatment has started, how the therapist will respond to the patient, the acceptance by the patient of the therapeutic situation, his reactions to the techniques employed, the emergence of resistances

to a working relationship, reactions to interpretations, manifestations of transference, and the capacity to achieve and to utilize insight in the direction of
change.

Most patients are anxious for as quick relief of their symptoms as possible. They see no need for an exhaustive probing of their patterns. Satisfying
the demand for succor through supportive therapy is justified in only a limited
number of situations. Supportive measures may be considered necessary where
the patient's symptoms reflect an alarming collapse of his coping capacities
in the form of excessive anxiety, depression, and disintegrative tendencies
with shattered capacities for reality testing. They may be indicated also in patients whose ego strength is doubtful, and in whom adjustment to the existing
neurosis, with utilization of available assets to the full, and minimization of
liabilities, is all that can be expected. Immature, dependent and psychopathic
personalities, borderline cases, psychotics, alcoholics, drug addicts, and some
compulsion neurotics often fall into this category. The therapist may have no
alternative but to use supportive measures in patients who have no real motive
for self-growth and who extract from their neuroses elements of profound secondary gain. Finally, supportive approaches are helpful in patients with adequate ego strength whose adaptive capacities are habitually good, but who have
crumbled under the impact of extremely severe environmental stresses.

Irrespective of diagnosis and severity of symptoms, however, the therapist
has a responsibility to bring each patient as far along the path of maturity as
possible, resolving his resistance to the accepting of more intensive help. This
means that some form of insight therapy will be indicated in most patients.
The depth of insight and the goals that are reached in therapy will be dependent
upon the needs of the patient and his motivations.

Where the patient has a history of having made an adequate adjustment in
his early life, and, until the onset of his present illness, has gotten along satisfactorily, the chances are that he can be brought back to his previous level of adjustment with an insight approach geared toward reeducative goals. Restoration
of his former status will generally not require a great deal of time. But where the
patient has been seriously maladjusted since early life, and his later adaptation
has never been adequate, therapy will probably have to be reconstructive in nature, to promote in the patient a development of those capacities that have
never previously existed. A less intensive form of therapy would achieve only
abbreviated and unsatisfactory goals.

For instance, a forty-eight year old successful business man is referred for
therapy by his physician because medications have failed to correct a painful
gastrointestinal ailment which has persisted for eight months. During the initial
interview, it is tentatively determined that the patient was severely neurotic
as a child, and that he managed to adjust satisfactorily as an adult only by assuming a detached attitude toward people. A bachelor, the patient's relationships
with women were sporadic, superficial and largely centered around temporary
sexual affairs. Despite the yearning for "a real woman," who would be a "real"
wife and mother, no such personage had ever presented herself. However, one

year previously, following a short affair, the patient, in spite of the fact that his paramour did not completely come up to specifications, decided to experiment with trial marriage. Shortly after the young woman took up residence with him, he began to develop symptoms. His loss of energy and his "stomach upsets" caused him to confine himself periodically to bed, from which he issued orders to his mistress. Violent rages at her incapacity to supply his demands for service and attention were followed by bouts of apologetic self-reproach.

The patient's history revealed that he had been brought up in an atmosphere of relative emotional deprivation. Following the death of his father, his mother was forced to go to work, assigning the care of the three year old boy to an aunt who was not too happy with her charge. The boy grew up as a tough, detached individual with a deep craving for maternal attention, with a distrust of women, and with what seemed to be compulsive needs for self-reliance and independence. As an adult he maintained his detachment and independence, and so long as he limited his relationships with women to superficial contacts, he seemed to get along quite well. He was a successful, respected business man, with many male friends and a reputation of being "quite a lad with the women."

Apparently a deep unpropitiated need for a mother figure, who would perhaps make up for the dearth of love and care he experienced in childhood, drove him toward finding an idealized female love object. The possibility of his paramour fulfilling this role both intrigued and excited him. He related to her as a child might to a mother, demanding bounties of constant affection and attention. In the process, his protective character drive of detachment was discarded. Anticipating the same kind of rejection he experienced as a child, and, no longer capable of marshalling detachment and independence as security props, he became filled with catastrophic feelings of helplessness. He became more and more demanding of attention. His hostility toward, and distrust of, this new mother figure furthermore threatened his security. The anxiety liberated was apparently converted into somatic symptoms.

In speculating on these dynamics for purposes of choosing the proper therapeutic approach, we may additionally theorize on the following:

1. It would be futile to treat the patient's symptoms with a supportive approach, since he was living in a dynamic conflict that was stirring up symptoms. Attempting to remove or ameliorate his symptoms would be like blowing away smoke without smothering the flame.

2. Were it possible to remove the patient forcibly from his entanglement with the young woman, to bring his relationship with her back to what it was before he got so involved, he would probably lose his symptoms. He would still possess his driving need for a mother figure, and maintain his distrust for women and his detachment; but he would feel secure again and be capable of functioning with his habitual character façades. He might be helped to sublimate his need for dependency, perhaps in an affiliation with some group devoted to community betterment. But, by and large, his adjustment would, for better or for worse, parallel that which he possessed prior to his illness. Unfortunately, the helplessness inspired by the abandonment of his customary

characterologic drives of detachment and compulsive independence, would probably preclude a forceful removal of the young woman from his life. Anxiety might precipitate which was so intense that he could not tolerate her absence.

3. A better approach would be reeducative in nature, aimed toward inculcating insight in the patient into his frenzied search for a mother substitute, and into the futility of satisfying his dependency needs in his present relationships. During treatment, he would probably automatically transfer part of his dependency need to the therapist. This would not be challenged. He would, however, be brought to an awareness of how his desperate desire for security had caused him to make an alliance with a woman who could not supply the tenderness and love he demanded. He would be shown how this disappointment had undermined him, filling him with hate and despair. His having isolated himself from his customary friends and removed himself from his pleasure outlets would be revealed as contributing to his insecurity. The patient might even acquire insight into the origins of his dependency need. These measures might suffice to break up the neurotic pattern he had developed during the past year, and help him to return to his former level of adaptation with its attendant satisfactions and dissatisfactions. The time required for this restoration would probably not be too long.

4. In order for the patient to be more completely liberated, it would be essential to inculcate in him a deep feeling of inner security such as he has never had—a security bereft of dependency need, and involving full measures of self-esteem and assertiveness. It would be necessary to promote the ability to establish warm relationships with people without desires to hurt and to enslave, or to be hurt and to be enslaved. These reconstructive goals would necessitate long-term insight therapy which might last as long as three or four years. The patient would have to be motivated to accept this level of help with all the time and financial sacrifices that were entailed. He would also require sufficient ego strength to endure a certain amount of anxiety. Unfortunately, the patient may see no need for an extensive working-out of his problems. He may be satisfied with the mere achieving of the adjustment he had made prior to his collapse, even though he recognized its inadequacies. He may be unable to make the time or to gather sufficient funds for long-term intensive therapy. He may be unable to accept the treatment situation or the responsibilities that he must share in therapy. He may be incapable of tolerating the anxieties of transference, or of withstanding an attack on his neurotic defenses and needs. He may be so rigid as to resist utilizing insight in the direction of change, even though he has gained an intellectual understanding of his problem.

In the actual therapy of this particular patient, he soon came to a realization of the operative dynamics. He then avowed a mere desire to return to his previous level of adjustment. Realizing that his paramour could not possibly supply his dependency need, he separated himself from her and resumed his previous activity. His adaptative equilibrium having been restored, the patient lost his symptoms and achieved as happy an adjustment as was possible with his underlying personality problem. This was considered an optimal goal in therapy, since he had no motivation for more extensive change. Even with prolonged therapy there was no guarantee that personality reconstruction would have occurred in view of his age and the severity of his character problem. The kind of therapy employed was of an insight variety oriented around reeducative goals.

Once we have decided on the category of therapy—supportive, reeducative or reconstructive—we may wonder as to which of the many approaches are most suited in a specific instance. For example, assuming that a patient requires and can utilize a reconstructive type of therapy, the best kind of reconstructive therapy is a questionable point. Should the therapy be Freudian psychoanalysis, organized around the establishment and analysis of a transference neurosis? Should it be a form of non-Freudian psychoanalysis, focused on the character structure and interpersonal relationships? Or should it be an active psychoanalytically oriented type of psychotherapy?

Since psychotherapy is a learning experience, one criterion of choice of therapies is the method best adapted to the learning aptitudes of the patient. Some patients are capable of learning rapidly in the medium of an interpersonal relationship deliberately kept on a positive level by the therapist. In this medium they analyze their dreams and other unconscious productions, and come to grips with their anxiety, without too severe resistances or too intense transference reactions. Here, psychoanalytically oriented psychotherapy may be remarkably effective. Other patients seem to learn better in a more formal analytic relationship, yet one that is not so intense as Freudian psychoanalysis. Such a non-Freudian psychoanalytic approach would concentrate on transference and resistance, but avoid the setting up of a real transference neurosis. In other cases, particularly where repression is extreme, the only way the patient can learn is through involvement in a transference neurosis, living through with the therapist important frustrations, anxieties, impulses and feelings rooted in past conditionings with early authorities. Here, a traditional Freudian psychoanalysis will be required.

Returning to the choice of categories of therapy, a rough index might consist of the following:

Supportive Therapy

(1) Patients who are in states of acute anxiety or depression, or who have very severe disabling psychosomatic symptoms. (2) Schizophrenics showing disintegrative tendencies. (3) Patients with a history that points to good ego strength who have recently become ill and for whom the goal is merely a restoration to the previous adaptative level. (4) Problems in which a perverse environmental disturbance acts as the most significant stress source. (5) Severe character problems with obstinate dependency and immaturity. (6) Severe obsessive-compulsive reactions. (7) Habit disorders, alcoholism and drug addiction.

Reeducative Therapy

Personality problems expressing themselves in difficulties in work, educational, marital, interpersonal and social adjustment—especially in persons who have fairly good ego strength.

Reconstructive Therapy

Problems initiated by severe distortions in the individual's relationship with parents and other significant persons, which have produced blocks in maturation. Difficulties in which repression is the chief defense are most responsive to reconstructive therapy. Included here are anxiety reactions, phobic reactions, conversion hysteria, some obsessive-compulsive reactions, some personality disorders, and certain psychophysiologic reactions.

It is essential to remember that the type of therapy required may shift during treatment. For example, the patient may be extremely upset at the start and require supportive handling. After he has stabilized, he may be able to benefit from reeducative or reconstructive therapy.

Therapeutic Approaches in Different Syndromes

The choice of therapeutic approach opens up the problem of which syndromes are best suited for different therapies. While some tentative statements may be made about the syndromes that are helped most readily by each approach, these must be accepted cautiously. In all syndromes the treatment of choice is some form of reconstructive therapy. However, special circumstances may make reconstructive therapy inexpedient. Acknowledging that there are major exceptions to the outline below, some use may be found for it, especially where referrals are to be made to therapists with different training backgrounds.

1. *Guidance:* Educational and vocational problems where treatment goals are abbreviated.

2. *Environmental manipulation:* Financial, housing, recreational, marital and family problems where goals are abbreviated.

3. *Externalization of interests:* Detached and introspective patients where goals are abbreviated.

4. *Reassurance:* Patients who require rectification primarily of misconceptions related to heredity, physical illness and sexual functions.

5. *Prestige suggestion and prestige hypnosis:* Habit disorders; such as, nail-biting, insomnia, overeating, inordinate smoking. Hysterical paralysis, aphonia and sensory disorders where symptom removal is the only goal in therapy.

6. *Pressure and coercion:* Patients who "act-out" or endanger themselves or others in situations where the treatment goal is limited.

7. *Persuasion:* Obsessive-compulsive personalities, where no extensive treatment goal is intended.

8. *Emotional catharis and desensitization:* Patients who have gone through traumatic experiences that have caused them guilt, fear or suffering, and who have not allowed themselves to emote sufficiently.

9. *Muscular relaxation and massage:* Tension states, and psychosomatic muscular conditions where an adjunctive palliative approach is indicated.

10. *Hydrotherapy:* As a palliative adjunct in excitements and in atonic listless patients.

11. *Shock and convulsive therapy:* Insulin shock in schizophrenia. Sub-coma insulin treatment in severe acute anxiety states, toxic confusional conditions and delirium tremens. Electric convulsive therapy in manic-depressive, depressed and manic states, involutional depression, senile depression and very severe psychoneurotic depression.

12. *Drug therapy:* Used in depression (benzedrine), anxiety (tolserol), tension and insomnia (barbiturates), and alcoholism (antabuse), as adjunctive measures.

13. *Brain surgery:* Restricted to patients with severe schizophrenia, chronic disabling obsessive-compulsive neurosis and hypochondriasis who have not responded to psychotherapy, shock and convulsive therapy.

14. *Inspirational group therapy:* Dependent, immature personalities and chronic alcoholics who need social contacts and a benevolent parental figure to help them to function.

15. *"Relationship therapy:"* Personality disorders (character problems).

16. *"Attitude therapy:"* Personality disorders where distorted attitudes and values are prominent.

17. *Distributive analysis and synthesis:* Various syndromes.

18. *Interview psychotherapy:* Various syndromes.

19. *Non-directive or "client-centered" therapy:* Patients with relatively sound personality structure who require help in clarifying their ideas about a current life difficulty or situational impasse.

20. *Directive counseling:* Patients with personality problems who require a forceful parental figure to goad them on to activity.

21. *Functional casework:* Dependent, hostile and other personality problems which require specific social services.

22. *Diagnostic casework:* Individuals with various personality problems who are in need of specific social services. Borderline patients.

23. *Reconditioning:* Mild phobias and habit disorders in which the treatment objectives are abbreviated.

24. *Semantic therapy:* Personality problems in patients whose difficulties in communication constitute a primary focus.

25. *Reeducative group therapy:* Patients with some degree of insight into their problems, who need emotional catharsis and the experience of interacting with others while learning about themselves.

26. *Freudian psychoanalysis:* Anxiety reactions, phobic reactions, conversion hysteria, obsessive-compulsive reactions and some psychophysiologic reactions are especially helped; but other syndromes may be treated.

27. *Non-Freudian psychoanalysis:* Personality problems are particularly helped; but other syndromes may be treated.

28. *Psychoanalytically oriented psychotherapy:* Various syndromes.

29. *Hypnoanalysis:* Stress reactions, anxiety reactions, phobic reactions, conversion hysteria, and some types of alcoholism, psychopathic personality and psychophysiologic reactions.

30. *Narcotherapy:* Stress reactions, anxiety reactions, phobic reactions, and some psychophysiologic reactions.

31. *Art therapy:* As an adjunct in reconstructive therapy where the patient is capable of symbolizing his problems in art productions.

32. *Play therapy:* As an adjunct in reconstructive therapy with children.

33. *Analytic group therapy:* Personality problems, preferably in conjunction with individual therapy.

Speculation that the patient can best utilize a certain approach does not necessarily mean that he will respond well to this approach. For instance, if a patient shows symptoms of adaptive collapse, like anxiety and depression, and has what we consider to be a weak ego, we may decide to use a supportive technique, at least temporarily, in order to bolster up his strength. The patient, while yearning for a supportive relationship, may, however, rebel against becoming dependent. Indeed, some of his current symptoms may be a product of his fear that the only way he can function is through the agency of dependency. Our utilizing an approach which makes him feel dependent may create more anxiety than it resolves.

Considering the case of another patient—one with impotence—we may decide that only in using a reconstructive approach can we modify essentially destructive attitudes toward sexuality. As he starts treatments, we may discover that we are dealing with a detached, frightened individual who shies away from any form of human contact. A sexual relationship is particularly alarming to him since it is associated with fantasies of being trapped and castrated. His impotency serves the important purpose of protecting him from irreparable injury. So terrified is he of closeness, that even a carefully regulated therapeutic relationship, with the mildest probing of his psyche, sets off fears of mutilation. His ego may not be able to tolerate the rigors of a reconstructive approach. We may, consequently, have to employ a supportive technique which, while reassuring, will not bring him to the goal of adequate sexual functioning.

We must, therefore, adjust our therapeutic approach to the patient's existing capacities. One cannot make a man with crutches run, no matter how earnestly we want him to reach a desired goal without delay. We must first strengthen his legs and not force on him a load that is too great for him to bear. Working within the bounds of his strengths and limitations, we may gradually increase the burdens and responsibilities, and help him to work with a technique that will bring about the desired results.

Most people come to treatment with an incomplete or erroneous idea of the values of different psychotherapies. They may have developed a conviction from newspaper or magazine articles, or from listening to lectures or the accounts of friends, that there is one kind of treatment that has any value; for instance, psychoanalysis, or hypnosis. When the interviewer informs them that he does not practice these specialties, or that he disapproves of such therapies, or that he has something better to offer, the patient may become stubbornly resistant and refuse to enter into treatment.

In the event the patient asks for any specific kind of approach, the therapist may inquire why the patient desires this treatment, and what were his sources of information. The therapist must never depreciate or ridicule the latter sources, even though he may indicate that there are other treatment methods to be considered.

Ways of managing this situation are indicated in chapter 30, Answering Questions Patients Ask about Therapy.

FREQUENCY OF VISITS

The number of sessions conducted weekly will depend on the individual's mode of response to therapy. Some patients do well on a once-a-week basis, others have such strong resistances that they get little benefit out of any therapy that is less frequent than four times weekly.

Sessions on the basis of once or twice weekly are often prescribed in psychoanalytically oriented psychotherapy, reeducative therapy and supportive therapy. Twice-a-week therapy is to be preferred to treatments on a once-a-week basis. At the beginning, it is sometimes advisable to see the patient as often as three times weekly and even oftener, particularly where he is emotionally upset. A short period of such frequency may enable the psychotherapist to establish a working relationship rapidly and to stabilize the patient sufficiently so that the number of visits weekly may be reduced. There is generally little relationship between the frequency of visits and the length of time it takes the patient to get well.

In formal Freudian psychoanalysis, five visits weekly are the rule, although some analysts may reduce this number to four. An interval between visits is believed to water down transference and to interfere with the establishment of a transference neurosis, which is considered an essential prerequisite for therapy. Three visits weekly are considered adequate in non-Freudian psychoanalysis, perhaps because there is not so much emphasis on the transference neurosis.

Some general rules for increasing or decreasing the frequency of treatment sessions are these:

1. A small number of sessions each week (1–2) are indicated:
    a. In most forms of supportive and reeducative therapy.
    b. In many forms of psychoanalytically oriented psychotherapy.
    c. In dependent, infantile patients to prevent a hostile, dependent relationship.
    d. Where a transference neurosis is to be avoided.
    e. In patients who tend to substitute transference reactions for real life experiences.

     f. In patients who are not too disturbed and who seem to be able to discharge their responsibilities and to carry on satisfactory interpersonal relationships.

2. A larger number of sessions (3–5) are indicated:

     a. Where Freudian and non-Freudian psychoanalysis are to be employed, particularly where a transference neurosis is desired.

     b. Where the patient shows signs of severe adaptational collapse—acute anxiety, depression, psychosomatic symptoms and ego disintegrative tendencies requiring constant emotional support.

     c. In patients with rigid character structures who have built a shell around themselves so thick that a concentrated attack on their defenses is essential.

     d. Where the patient has no motivation for psychotherapy and where a consistent demonstration of its value for him is necessary.

     e. In patients who are intensely hostile.

     f. In patients with a diminutive super-ego who need an ever-present authority to check the "acting-out" of impulses.

The difficulty that arises in once-a-week therapy is that intense anxiety may be mobilized as the individual comes to grips with his inner problems. He may then utilize devices such as sedatives, alcohol, acting-out, or escape from therapy to avoid coming to grips with his conflict. The problems inspired by very frequent sessions relate to a perpetuation of dependency and a stimulation of a transference neurosis.

ESTIMATING THE DURATION OF THERAPY

In a sense, all therapy is interminable in that once it is started, the process of self-understanding and growth can continue the remainder of the patient's life. However, the actual time spent in a therapeutic relationship may be relatively short, lasting until symptoms are relieved, abnormal character patterns corrected, or blocks to maturation resolved. The time required to achieve these goals will depend on the nature of the patient's problem, how extensively he has worked through his difficulty by himself, the flexibility of his character organization, the intensity of his resistance, the motivations he has for therapy, the astuteness and skill of the therapist, and the kind of relationship that develops in the therapeutic situation. It is difficult, therefore, at the start, to predict how long it will take for the patient to get well until his response to therapy has been tested. Nevertheless, a number of broad generalizations are possible:

1. Where the patient's history reveals a good adjustment up to the time of his present illness, and where the latter is of relatively short duration, the chances of restoring the patient to his previous level of adjustment in a relatively short time are good.

2. Where there is a long history of maladjustment, and the patient's present condition appears to be an outgrowth of this, therapy will probably be prolonged.

3. As a rule, one is able to achieve with short-term therapy abbreviated goals—such as symptom relief—while more extensive goals, like modification of obdurate character patterns or expansion of personality growth will require an extensive period of treatment, ranging from two to five years.

4. Some patients, such as those with pre-schizophrenic, schizophrenic and dependent personality problems, may require therapy for five years, or even longer. Rarely a patient may need a supportive therapeutic relationship the remainder of his life.

ARRANGING THE FEE

A frank discussion with the patient about his finances and the expenses involved in therapy is very much in order. This is especially necessary where therapy will last for more than several months. The patient may be apprised of the fee per session and then asked whether he will be able to manage paying for treatment in the event it continues as long as is estimated to achieve a desired goal. In the event he is unable to raise the required sum with his present income, it may be possible for him to arrange the supplementing of his income by borrowing. It is important that the sum spent on therapy be available to the patient without too great sacrifice, since severe financial pressures may negate the effects of treatment.

Many therapists have a sliding scale of fees adjusting these to the income of the patient. This practice is a commendable one, but some therapists may not be able to afford reducing their fees to patients of low income. It will be necessary for the prospective therapist to face the fact that the patient may require therapy for a long time. If the therapist is at all resentful about treating the patient at too low a fee, there will be an interference with the best kind of therapeutic relationship. It is consequently better to provide for a referral of the patient to resources where the patient can get help at a fee within his means, than to start with the patient and thereafter have to interrupt treatments due to counter-transference difficulties.

If the patient has a problem that will require long-term treatment, it is important to determine whether he will be able to make the proper time and financial preparations. The patient may be approached as in the following excerpt:

Th. Now in going over your problem, there are several approaches that we might use. In the first place, your present difficulty really goes far back in your life. As a matter of fact it probably had its inception in your childhood. So, if you really want to untangle yourself more or less completely, it will take time. In other words, if you want to eradicate the basis of your trouble, it may take as long as two or three years.

Pt. Does it have to take that long?

Th. Well it took you a long time to get tangled up. It may take you some time to get rid of your trouble.

Pt. I know it goes far back.

Th. Yes, and, therefore, if you want to untangle yourself, it will require time. As I said it may take as long as two years, and maybe even longer.

Pt. How often would I have to come?

Th. That would depend. In your particular case it would require two or perhaps three visits weekly. [*Should the patient have a problem that required more frequent visits he would be so informed.*] But, it may not be necessary to remake you completely. It may be possible to work on one aspect of your problem—the most disturbing aspect, so that you may adjust yourself better to life, making the most of what you have. In other words, if our goals are less extensive, it wouldn't take so long.

Pt. I don't like to do things half-ways. I'd rather do a complete job.

Th. Of course, there is the matter of your being able to budget your finances to cover a long period of treatment.

Pt. How much would it cost?

Th. That would depend on who treated you. For instance, there are people who might be able to treat you for ten dollars a session, and others may charge as much as twenty-five. But suppose you give me an idea of what you can afford to pay, if you did have to come for a long period.

Pt. Well, I could pay the regular fee, but I would like to have someone experienced. What about you?

Th. Do you feel you can work with me?

Pt. Oh yes, I believe I can.

Th. Well, I do have some available time, and I believe I will be able to work with you. As a general rule, a three months' trial period is best, to see how we work together. That is, at the end of three months we would mutually decide how we get on, and whether I am the best person to help you.

Pt. Good, that sounds good.

Th. All right, now when can you come? At what times?

Pt. Generally, doctor, mornings are best for me.

Th. Well, let's see. (*referring to schedule*) I can see you Mondays at 11:40 and Thursdays at 10. If we have to arrange another appointment, we'll do it later.

DELAYS IN STARTING THERAPY

Sometimes the interviewer will have no time on his schedule for the patient. He may, consequently, have to postpone starting treatments until he can make time available. This is possible if the patient does not need therapy immediately. Where treatment is urgently required, or where an emergency exists, it is obviously essential to start therapy without delay, or to refer the patient to a therapist who does have time. It is highly desirable here that the interviewer make provisions for the patient and not send the latter out on a blind mission to interview other therapists who may also have no time for him.

FINAL ARRANGEMENTS

If the interviewer has decided to start therapy with the patient, and an agreement has been reached regarding time and fees, final arrangements may be made with the patient, giving him an appointment date. It is advisable to inform the patient regarding the length of each appointment, the need for promptness in appointment times, the way payments of fees are to be made, and whether or not the patient will have to pay for broken appointments. The following excerpt illustrates these points:

Th. Now I'd like to tell you something about your future appointments. They start promptly at the appointed time and last three-quarters of an hour. I'll send you a bill at the beginning of the month. Now, it's important that visits be consistent, because it may set you back to skip visits. Of course, if emergencies arise, or if you get ill, you can't help cancelling one or more visits. If this happens, try to let me know at least twenty-four hours in advance. The custom is to charge for broken appointments where sufficient notice is not given, let us say twenty-four hours.

There is no standard length of a treatment session; the average time ranges from three-quarters of an hour to one hour. Practices of billing also vary. Arrangements for payment are usually made at the convenience of the patient. Some patients prefer to make payments at the end of each visit; others prefer a monthly billing. The practice of charging for broken appointments also varies among different therapists. Some therapists assume that the patient has a financial responsibility for all appointments irrespective of the reason they are cancelled. Others are more liberal and do not charge for any cancelled and even broken appointments. To forestall the patient's breaking appointments as a manifestation of resistance, the practice of charging for unjustified broken appointments may be advisable.

REFERRING THE PATIENT

It is understandable that most patients will want to continue in therapy with the initial interviewer. Under certain conditions this may not be possible. Such instances occur when:

1. The interviewer may have no time on his schedule, or his available hours may not coincide with those the patient can arrange.

2. The interviewer may not want to work with the patient because of the kind of problem the patient possesses, or because of the patient's personality.

3. The interviewer may believe another therapist can help the patient more.

4. The patient may be unable to afford the interviewer's fee.

5. The patient may want to work with a therapist of a different sex, age, race or orientation.

No matter how well trained and how experienced the interviewer may be, he will be better equipped to handle some kinds of patients than others. With some persons, he will feel very much at ease, and he will be capable of exercising that balance between sympathy and objectivity that makes for good therapy. With other persons, he will feel less comfortable, more defensive and more incapable of exhibiting an adequate amount of interest. After he has acquired a great deal of therapeutic experience, and he has assayed his results, the therapist may come to the conclusion that he does very well with certain kinds of patients and problems. For instance, his experience may lead him to the conclusion that he is unable to treat schizophrenics, or "borderline" patients, or compulsion-neurotics, or individuals with strong phobias. He may get better results with women than with men, with young adults rather than with middle-aged persons. He may be unable to treat children or people in their later years. He may be inclined to select for his patients those individuals to whom he responds positively, and to refer others with whom he does not feel a certain affinity. This selective process is to be encouraged, since his emotional attitude toward the patient, or the conviction that he is unable to do well with the problem presented, may impose barriers on the relationship. This does not mean that the interviewer will not be able to work out his difficulties in functioning; however, therapy will start out with a handicap that may not be warranted if there are other resources to which the patient may be referred.

Another reason for referring the patient is that the specific training or experience of the interviewer does not permit of the kind of therapy the patient could best utilize. Thus, many therapists who do supportive therapy well are not equipped to do reeducative or reconstructive therapy; those who have been trained in reeducative approaches may not know how to implement supportive or reconstructive treatment; while those who are trained to do reconstructive therapy may not know how to handle problems that require supportive or reeducative measures. Certain aspects of the patient's difficulty may be tackled by any of the three approaches; however, where the therapist recognizes that his particular method is not suited for the patient, he should refer the patient to a resource where more appropriate treatment can be obtained.

Where, for any reason, a referral is to be made, the patient is acquainted with the reasons for this in such a way that he does not interpret the referral as a rejection foisted on him by the interviewer. Where the interviewer knows in advance that the patient will have to be referred to another therapist, it is advisable to mention this in the opening statement to the patient, which outlines the purposes of the interview. With this preparation, the patient will usually accept the referral without too much difficulty. Where the referral possibility has not been mentioned, and it is felt the patient should be treated by another therapist, the interviewer must carefully present to the patient positive reasons for the referral. For instance, if the interviewer believes that the problems of the patient can be helped more by a therapist of a different orientation, the following may be said:

It will be important for you to be treated by a specialist who is best capable of handling your problem. I would like to refer you to someone who has had a good deal of experience with problems such as yours. I shall telephone several therapists who I believe can help you in order to make sure they have the time. Then I shall telephone you, and you can make an appointment.

In the event the interviewer simply has no time at present for the patient, he may remark:

Unfortunately I do not have time on my schedule right now, and I do not expect to have time for some period in the future. I believe you need therapy right away and since I know the facts in your case, I shall be glad to refer you to a therapist who can handle your problem adequately.

Referral to a low-cost clinic or psychotherapeutic center may be made where the financial condition of the patient precludes his getting therapy on a private basis. Here it may be necessary to spend a little time preparing the patient for the routines of the clinic, which may otherwise be threatening to him.

In making a referral, the patient should also be told that the most important element in treatment is his relationship with the therapist who is treating him. It is possible that he may not respond completely to the therapist to whom he is being referred. If, for any reason, he does not feel confidence in, or feels a block in working with the therapist, it will be important to discuss his attitudes openly. For, if he cannot remedy his feelings, it might be necessary to find another therapist. The following excerpt illustrates these points:

Th. Now I believe Dr. _____ can help you; but your response to him will be important. Therapy is most successful where you have confidence in your therapist. If, after several sessions, you don't feel you can work with the therapist, it may be necessary to get someone else for you.

Pt. I see.

Th. But before that happens, it will be important to discuss your feelings about Dr. _____ with him. He will understand your feelings, and if you continue to feel that somehow he isn't the person for you to work with, he will help you find another person. Or you can call me and we can discuss this matter further.

Unless one forewarns the patient that he may not "hit it off" with the therapist to whom he is being referred, he may become discouraged and discontinue treatments indefinitely. Moreover, the admonitions voiced may embolden the patient to discuss and to work through with the therapist to whom he has been referred attitudes that are rooted in transference.

ANTICIPATING EMERGENCIES AND OTHER DIFFICULTIES

Plans may have to be made in advance for dealing with emergencies, should these arise. For example, an alcoholic patient may get into various difficulties and require hospitalization. A drug addict may need careful observation to detect a stealthy resumption of his drug habit. A psychopathic personality will constantly tend to "act-out" his problems, and may involve himself in difficulties with people and with the law. A patient who is seriously depressed must be considered a suicidal risk. One who has had a previous psychotic break may relapse into a psychosis. Patients with sexual perversions may get into serious legal and interpersonal conflicts. By anticipating emergencies, the therapist may avoid serious trouble later on. An alarming recrudescence of symptoms is also to be predicted in certain conditions. For example, patients with anxiety, phobic or obsessional reactions will probably have bouts of anxious emotion that will disable them for a time, and that may undermine their faith in therapy. Patients with psychosomatic problems will repeatedly experience an upsurge of symptoms which will tend to divert them from thinking about the dynamic factors that underlie their complaints. It may thus be necessary, in the early states of therapy, to prepare the patient for a possible relapse in symptoms.

ESSENTIAL CORRESPONDENCE

A brief letter to the individual or agency who referred the patient to the initial interviewer, or to the organization he represents, is a courtesy that is usually much appreciated. It is generally unwise to discuss too many details of the case or to outline the tentative dynamics. Nor is a diagnosis indicated, except, perhaps, where the referral source is a physician. The disposition of the patient should, however, always be mentioned. The following are typical letters, the first to a social agency, the second, to a physician.

Dear _____:

I have seen Mr. _____ whom you referred to me for consultation and find him to be suffering from an emotional problem for which psychotherapy is indicated. I believe he would do best with an analytically trained therapist, and, consequently, have referred Mr. _____ to Dr. _____ who has been able to make time available for him at a fee satisfactory to Mr. _____. Mr. _____ responded well to the consultation and there was no reluctance in accepting the referral to Dr. _____. I should like to thank you for sending Mr. _____ to me.

Sincerely yours,

———

Dear Dr. _____:

I have seen Mr. _____ in consultation and agree with you that a strong emotional element is involved in his present somatic complaint. I believe psychotherapy definitely to be indicated, but I am not, at the present time, able to prognosticate the outcome due to the incomplete motivation that exists for treatment. Mr. _____ responded satisfactorily to the interview and expressed a willingness to start therapy with me. I should like to thank you for the referral.

Sincerely yours,

———

Correspondence may also be required where it is necessary to get further information about the patient from therapists previously treating him, from clinical psychologists who have administered tests, from physicians who have rendered recent examinations, and from institutions in which the patient was hospitalized. A "release" form, such as in Appendix R, page 839, signed by the patient, will usually be required when requesting such information.

26

The Initial Interview:
Securing Essential Consultations

DURING THE FIRST INTERVIEW, OR LATER IF NEEDED, CONSULTATIONS with a number of professionals may be a required supplement to the treatment plan. Where the therapist takes the time to explain the reasons for such consultations, little or no difficulty will be encountered.

MEDICAL, NEUROLOGIC AND PSYCHIATRIC CONSULTATIONS

It goes without saying that each patient under psychotherapy requires a thorough physical and neurologic examination to rule out organic somatic illness. If the patient has been referred to the therapist by a physician, the therapist may check with the former as to whether or not physical and neurologic examinations have recently been administered. If not, arrangements for these should be made with, or through the patient's physician. In the event the patient was not referred by a physician, he should be asked to visit his family doctor for a complete physical check-up. A blank such as that in Appendix O, page 834, should be filled out by the physician and filed in the patient's case record. Where a complete neurologic examination is done, a form such as in Appendix P, page 835, may be found helpful.

If organic illness is discovered on examination, the patient must be guided by the advice of his physician as to required medical or surgical treatments. If no organic illness is found, the physician should be used as a consultant whenever physical symptoms of any kind develop during the course of psychotherapy. Insistence that the patient see his own physician is not only good medicine, but makes for good public relations. Even where the therapist is a psychiatrist who has not lost his medical diagnostic skills, the rules outlined will be found helpful. To do his own physical examinations or to prescribe medications for the patient may interfere with the therapeutic relationship, except, perhaps, in supportive therapy and in the more superficial reeducative therapies.

The expediency of psychiatric surveillance of patients being treated by nonmedical therapists has already been discussed. The psychiatrist makes the diagnosis, and, in doing a psychiatric examination, determines the existence of any serious psychiatric problems. The results of the psychiatric examination should be filed in the case record, utilizing an outline or a form such as in Appendix Q, page 837. The psychiatric supervisor, in addition to routine supervision, can handle any emergencies that develop during the course of treatment;

such as severe depression, suicidal attempts, aggression, excitement and psychotic outbreaks. He can, where necessary, administer or refer the patient for narcotherapy; prescribe drug treatments like antabuse, benzedrene, endocrine products and sedatives; and employ insulin shock and electric convulsive therapy. He may also arrange for hospital admission or commitment when required. As has been indicated previously in discussing teamwork in clinics, the psychiatric supervisor is usually the one who determines the nature and intensity of the psychiatric supervisory process.

CASEWORK CONSULTATION

The therapist may desire a consultation with a caseworker from a local social agency when any of the following difficulties exist:

1. Severe financial problems for which supplementary help is required.
2. Need for job placement or relocation.
3. Need for rehabilitative services.
4. Need for special health services.
5. Need for better housing or for neighborhood relocation.
6. Need for recreational facilities.
7. Need for special schooling and training.
8. Social security problems.
9. Need for referral to special clinics or hospitals for the management of physical illness where resources are unknown to the therapist or where financial difficulties prevail.
10. Aid in placement in a foster home or institution.

In supportive and some types of reeducative psychotherapy, the patient may be referred directly to the caseworker who acts as an adjunctive helper. The caseworker, working actively with the patient, acquaints the latter with, and helps him to utilize most effectively, the community resources best suited to meet his needs. In reconstructive therapy, however, the activity of a caseworker as an accessory helper may tend to disrupt the therapeutic relationship. Should the patient require casework services here, the therapist may get the necessary information from the caseworker; such as, the best available resources to satisfy the needs of the situation. The therapist may then acquaint the patient with possible courses of action, encouraging him to make his own plans. The therapist handles therapeutically any delays or other resistances to the effective utilization of the resources.

A caseworker may also be employed to deal with parents, mate or children of a patient when such relatives require placement, hospitalization, counseling or guidance as an aid in the treatment of the patient. Among the services rendered by the caseworker are the dispensing of information related to sexual problems, child-parent relationships, marital relationships, hereditary influences, budgeting, home management, housing difficulties, work problems, difficulties associated with alcoholism, and problems of old age. Premarital and marital counseling are other areas in which the help of the caseworker is often sought. Additionally, the caseworker may be used as a liaison between the patient and his family, employer, teacher and other persons when it is essential to interpret the patient's illness to them, to give them reassurance, or to enlist their active interest and cooperation.

In psychiatric clinics, caseworkers are often utilized for intake interviewing, to clarify the service of the clinic to prospective patients or to the referral source, and to determine if the service offered by the clinic is consonant with the existing needs of the patient. In addition they are employed to take case histories, and to prepare patients for psychotherapy by dealing with resistances to, and establishing the proper motivation for treatment. Where indicated, they help, directly or indirectly, to manipulate the patient's environment. Lastly, they serve to interpret the work of the clinic to the community, and to enlist the cooperation of the community with the clinic. Caseworkers act as a liaison between the clinic and community organizations which are implementing community programs related to health, welfare and social security.

PSYCHOLOGIC AND OTHER RELATED CONSULTATIONS

A consultation with a clinical psychologist may be necessary where the patient requires intelligence tests, vocational batteries, and tests for special aptitudes. These are utilized as an aid in planning a better environmental adjustment for the patient. Projective tests are also used as a rapid means of revealing important traits and tendencies. The test situation serves as a tiny segment of life, a kind of laboratory in which the individual divulges his customary needs, hopes, impulses, and defensive drives. A trained, astute observer may analyze the strivings of the patient as they are projected into the test materials, and he may make remarkably accurate assumptions about the character structure and the unconscious conflicts of the person.

The most important tests employed by the psychologist are the Rorschach, [444,445], the Thematic Apperception [446,447], the Szondi [448] and the Man-Woman Drawing [449] tests. Sometimes there is an examination of handwriting [450,451], art creations [452], manipulated play materials [453] and word associations [454]. Among the items of information revealed are clues to the intelligence, originality, creativity and sensitivity of the person; the severity of his anxiety; the defenses he employs against anxiety, such as inhibition, repression, phobias, compulsive reactions, aggression, "acting out," somatic preoccupations, fantasy and retreat from reality; the intensity of hostility and defenses against hostility; the nature of interpersonal relations and current disturbances of character, like dependency, aggression, sadism, masochism, detachment, and paranoid tendencies; the quality of self-esteem, with its distortions in narcissism, grandiosity and self-devaluation; sexual problems, inhibitions, fears and perversions; masculine and feminine identifications; existing inner conflicts; schizoid and disintegrative tendencies; and ego strengths and weaknesses.

The virtue of psychologic tests is primarily in the diagnostic sphere. Attempts to evaluate ego strength and to predict the outcome of therapy by means of testing are usually speculative. Where the clinical psychologist makes predictions as to the quality of change the patient will achieve in psychotherapy, where he estimates definite goals in treatment and indicates the kinds of techniques to which the patient will best respond, he is straining his test materials, attempting to adapt them to areas for which they were never designed.

Prognostic estimates and predictions of what will happen in therapy on the basis of psychologic tests are often fraught with disappointment. While it is possible to determine customary responses to authority, and the habitual interpersonal reactions that emerge in a relationship situation, it is not always possible to guarantee that these responses will develop with the therapist. For therapy involves a special kind of a relationship, the uniqueness of which may prompt latent or new responses. Much, of course, will depend on the therapist, on whether he falls in line with the role the patient expects him to play. Similarly, it is difficult to anticipate the interpersonal potentials of the patient, since we do not know how the therapist will manage the tentative thrusts of the patient toward a different kind of relationship. Finally, it is not easy to predict what the patient will do with insight, whether he can acquire insight or utilize it, once it is evolved, in the direction of change. For these developments, too, are largely contingent on the nature of the therapeutic relationship and the skill of the therapist.

All psychologic tests are brief samplings of the patient's reactions to a limited test situation, at a special time, with a specific test administrator. The patient may at another time, with a second test administrator, under changed conditions respond differently. Test results must, consequently, always be correlated with clinical findings. The more experienced the therapist, the more he will rely on his clinical judgment, and the less emphasis he will put on psychologic test materials.

Beginning therapists usually feel more confident when they have in front of them a personality survey which describes some of the patient's defenses and conflicts. The contribution the test makes to his feelings of security more than offsets the disadvantage of having a pre-formed opinion about the patient. As the therapist becomes more experienced, he finds that psychologic tests are not accurate in all instances. He then regards them as tentative blue-prints of neuroses which will require more or less extensive alterations as he delves into his patient's problems. Finally, he may, if his experience is sufficiently extensive, rely much more on his clinical judgment than he does on psychologic tests. He may pay credence to certain warnings sounded by the tests, such as the presence of disintegrative tendencies, which will make him gage carefully the interpretive pressures he applies, so as not to overtax the strength of the patient's ego. However, he will still grant priorities to his "intuition" and clinical feeling.

In the hands of an experienced clinical psychologist who is conservative in his test interpretations, psychologic tests are valuable aids to the therapist, provided the latter does not permit the tests to interfere with the spontaneous planning and execution of his therapeutic approach. Therapy is more influenced by the skill of the therapist, and by his capacity to set up a good working relationship with the patient, than it is by the existing clinical syndrome. Thus, psychologic tests may reveal strong schizophrenic tendencies. This revelation may frighten the therapist, and, on the basis of warnings by the psychologist that the patient cannot stand an insight approach, the therapist may smother the patient with supportive props. Were the therapist to gage the "depth" of therapy by the strength and quality of his relationship with the patient, he would have a much more accurate measurement of the extent of stress the patient's ego could tolerate. On the basis of a good relationship, insight therapy would be possible, and the patient would be able to endure and to resolve considerable anxiety.

Some therapists, who have had training in the administration and interpretation of psychologic tests, prefer to test the patient personally rather than to send the patient to a clinical psychologist. By doing this they are able to observe the behavior of the patient, and the manner of his approach to, and execution of the tests, which may give them valuable clues in addition to those revealed by the test responses. Often the therapist does not score the tests, but relies mainly on a qualitative analysis of the responses. Some therapists utilize test administration therapeutically, accenting certain responses to encourage the patient's associations.

Apart from these traditional uses of psychologic tests, there are some psychologists who advocate the employment of projective materials to provide for a more objective measure of therapeutic progress [455]. By taking a test at the start of, during, and at the end of treatment, it is believed possible to validate clinical impressions of changes developing in psychotherapy.

If the initial interviewer decides in favor of psychologic tests, it will be necessary to prepare the patient for referral to a clinical psychologist. An explanation may be given the patient along lines indicated by the following excerpt:

Th. I should like to get a psychologic examination. Would you have any objection to this?

Pt. What is this examination?

Th. Psychologic tests are like x-rays, they enable the therapist to see things about a person that would otherwise require many therapeutic sessions. In this way it helps to cut down the time of therapy.

Pt. Are the tests expensive?

Th. They cost more than a single treatment session, but they may save money in the long run.

Pt. I want to do anything that is necessary, doctor.

Th. All right, I'll make the arrangements for you.

Obviously the fee for testing must be within the financial means of the patient. Some patients may not be able to afford psychologic testing, and the therapist may then have to forego it.

The most common test employed is the Rorschach. Sometimes the Thematic

Apperception, the Szondi and the Man-Woman Drawing tests are utilized. A complete battery of tests, which is the preferred routine, is prohibitive in cost for the average patient, although the therapist may be able to make special financial arrangements for this with the clinical psychologist. Where only isolated tests can be afforded, the therapist should indicate to the clinical psychologist the special area of interest; such as, diagnosis, dynamics, etc., so that a proper selection can be made of the tests administered.

In addition to giving tests, psychologists are also helpful when career planning and vocational and educational guidance are necessary as part of the treatment plan. Some psychologists are trained to do premarital, marital, adolescent, and old age counseling. In clinics, psychologists trained to do psychotherapy help in the treatment program under psychiatric supervision. They also act as research supervisors in organizing and handling administrative details of research projects.

Corrective work in the educational field; such as, the treatment of reading and educational disabilities, may require the consultative services of special professionals, like remedial reading instructors. Rehabilitation workers may help in physical and sensory defects which interfere with the functioning of the patient. Speech disturbances may require the aid of a speech therapist.

The services rendered by such professionals as psychologists, remedial teachers, rehabilitation workers and speech therapists are adjunctive to psychotherapy. Because prolonged contact may be required with the adjunctive worker, it is essential that the worker be a well-integrated individual. It is important, too, that he recognize his limited role and not interfere with the therapist by giving the patient advice and interpretations that have nothing to do with his specific area of function. The therapist will always have to work out with the patient the matter of divided transference when a consultant is employed. This need not constitute too difficult a hazard unless the consultant is himself seriously disturbed emotionally.

27

The Initial Interview:
Important "Don'ts" during the Initial Interview

1. Do not argue with, minimize or challenge the patient. If the patient presents a point of view that is obviously prejudiced or distorted, one may be tempted to argue with or challenge him. These tactics are ill-advised, since the patient probably needs to maintain his distorted point of view to bolster his defenses. Attacking his viewpoint or theory exposes him to anxiety, and, since there is no close relationship with the therapist, the patient will be unable to tolerate an attack on his defensive system. When he presents a fallacious idea upon which he insists, he may be told: "Understandably you may feel this way, but there *may* also be other ways of looking at this situation." Should the patient keep probing this point, the therapist may say that he does not yet know enough about the problem to make positive statements.

2. Do not praise the patient or give him false reassurance. Because the patient's self-esteem is so damaged, he will probably be unable to accept any praise even though it is sincerely offered and realistically justified. Actually there is little reason for praising the patient for any virtues he may possess; such as, appearance, poise, or accomplishments, since he is undoubtedly aware of these, and has calculated them in his balance sheet of virtues and liabilities. To reassure him may also be a futile gesture, although some reassurance may be attempted where he shows symptoms of adaptive collapse, and where he grossly minimizes his chances for health with psychotherapy.

3. Do not make false promises. These will boomerang, and the patient will utilize them deftly as resistance. The interviewer has no way of knowing what the course of therapy will be, and to promise results before observing how the patient works is folly. The same holds true for promises of special privilege. To make these hastily in order to lure the patient into therapy, and then to withdraw them because they cannot possibly be fulfilled, can be greatly damaging to the patient's trust in the therapist.

4. Do not interpret to the patient or speculate on the dynamics of his problem. The patient is obviously unprepared for interpretations until a working relationship has been established with the therapist. To assault the patient with interpretations at the start is like attempting to plant a seed on untilled soil. Not only will interpretation not take, but its effectiveness will have been vitiated when an attempt is made to interpret later. Similarly, to speculate on the dynamics of the patient's problem is to bombard him with concepts that will do little except to mobilize resistance. If the patient asks for interpretations or wants an outline of the involved dynamics, the therapist may say, "It will be necessary to find out more about the problem before I can offer you a really valid opinion of it."

5. Do not offer the patient a diagnosis even if he insists on it. The patient will usually employ a diagnosis as a masochistic weapon with which he tortures himself. If the patient insists on a diagnosis, he may be told that he is suffering from an emotional problem for which he can get help through psychotherapy. The type of problem is not important from a practical standpoint. Actually, it is impossible to make a complete diagnosis without studying him, over a period of time.

6. Do not question the patient on sensitive areas of his life. It is important not to interrogate the patient on points about which he may be sensitive, particularly his appearance, status, sexual difficulties, and failures in life. An opening may be given him to talk about these, but if blocking occurs, it should be respected until some later date when the relationship is sufficiently firm to countenance greater tension and anxiety. It is necessary in the initial interview, and indeed throughout the first phase of therapy, to avoid all comments that are offensive or humiliating to the patient. In fact, this should be the rule throughout therapy.

7. Do not put the patient on a couch for the initial interview. The establishing of rapport and the eliciting of important data are best accomplished in face-to-face interviewing. A great deal of anxiety is apt to be mobilized in a patient if the interviewer insists on the couch position.

8. Do not try to "sell" the patient on his accepting treatment. Once the facts are presented to the patient, the choice of whether he does or does not want therapy must be left to him. To force him into therapy may create insurmountable problems for both patient and therapist.

9. Do not join in attacks the patient launches on his parents, mate, friends or associates. Because the patient feels ambivalently about people he attacks, he may resent the therapist's criticism of these people. He may consider the therapist impulsive, naive or judgmental to join in an attack with as little information as has been revealed. The therapist's best response is sympathetic listening, not defending, condemning nor condoning the person attacked. If the patient complains about a remark that was made to him that was upsetting, or about a bad situation, the therapist may say: "A remark like that would be disturbing to you," or "This situation must have upset you," or "Actions of this sort can be disturbing to a person." Examples of unsuitable and suitable responses follow:

Pt. My wife is impossible. She's always been this way—nagging, yelling, disagreeable. Nothing satisfies her.

Unsuitable responses:

Th. That's terrible. Doesn't she know what it does to you?
Th. That's bad. She's a destructive person.
Th. Maybe you're prejudiced against her.

Suitable responses:

　　Th. This must upset you.

　　Th. It must be difficult for you.

　　Th. A situation like this could be disturbing to any person. Do you think you get unduly upset by it?

10. Do not participate in criticism of another therapist.

Even if the patient presents accounts of unprofessional behavior, it is bad practice to criticize another therapist. No matter how strong the evidence may be, one never knows how much of the patient's story is colored by misinterpretation or transference. In the event the patient complains that he has made no progress with a former therapist, one must also not agree with him. Often, significant inner changes have occurred which are blocked by transference. A resolution of hostility toward the former therapist may bring out the fact that considerably more progress was made than the patient had estimated. One must remember that should the interviewer fail to help the patient, he may become the victim of accusations that are made to the next therapist the patient consults. An example of how criticism may be handled is given in the following excerpt:

　　Pt. When I say that for three years I wondered what the hell went on, it's true. I don't know what—I can't summarize what I learned or what happened for three years with Dr. _____. I just didn't get anywhere, and I'm at a loss to say just what transpired all that time.

　　Th. You feel it was a waste of time?

　　Pt. Yes. I . . . I . . . I do feel that it was mishandled and I do feel that it was time wasted, and in many ways.

　　Th. Perhaps certain problems came up in your relations with Dr. _____.

　　Pt. Yes, I know I'm as slippery as the next patient as far as being treated goes.

　　Th. Slippery?

　　Pt. Dr. _____ always complained I just didn't catch on, didn't do the right kind of associating.

　　Th. Perhaps the situation just didn't progress for many reasons. At any rate we may be able to discuss your feelings about your past treatment in greater detail later on.

28

The Initial Interview:
Dealing with Inadequate Motivation

PATIENTS WHO COME TO THE INITIAL INTERVIEW WITH INADEQUATE, little or no motivation for therapy require special handling, because their mental set makes them refractory to the usual interview procedures. Among such patients are those with psychosomatic problems referred by physicians; delinquents, criminals, psychopathic personalities, sexual perverts, and other individuals involved in legal difficulties sent in by courts or correctional agencies; husbands and wives whose mates threaten divorce unless their partners get treatment; clients of social agencies who have been inadequately prepared for therapy; alcoholics or drug addicts who are shepherded into the therapist's office through cajolery, threats or exhortations; children with behavior and emotional problems brought in by parents or referred by schools; and psychotic persons out of contact with reality.

An inadequately motivated patient may utterly refuse to start therapy in defiance of the therapist and the referring agency. Or he may apathetically accept his plight, reporting as if to a parole officer, with no intention of cooperating or of conceding that he can be helped. Accordingly, it is impossible to establish the kind of working relationship that permits of the achievement of meaningful therapeutic goals. With proper handling, however, it may be possible to deal with defective motivation and to create the incentives essential for effective treatment. A general outline for the management of the poorly motivated patient is as follows:

1. Recognition and reflection of the patient's negative feelings about therapy and the therapist.

2. Indication of an understanding and acceptance of these feelings.

3. Display of a neutral attitude toward the patient's needing or being able to benefit from psychotherapy, until more facts are known about the patient's problem.

4. Expression of the opinion, when sufficient facts are known to the therapist, that the patient requires psychotherapy and may benefit greatly from it. Attempting to establish some incentive for therapy.

5. Sympathy with his feeling, if the patient continues to be negativistic, or refuses to reveal facts about himself; but attempting to handle what is behind his feeling.

6. Dealing with his misconceptions about psychotherapy, answering his questions as directly as possible.

7. Refraining from "selling" the patient on therapy; respecting his verdict should the patient decide against getting therapy.

8. Acceptance of the patient, should he merely decide to resign himself to therapy because of external pressures or for other reasons.

RECOGNIZING AND REFLECTING NEGATIVE FEELINGS

Because the patient is defensive, evasive, inwardly outraged, and perhaps expressively hostile, little will be achieved until these untoward attitudes and feelings are resolved. It is therefore urgent to focus on them as soon as possible. This is relatively easy where the patient verbalizes readily or otherwise reveals himself. Often, however, disturbed feelings are not openly apparent, and must be perceived from how the patient talks rather than from what he says, or from random gestures, mannerisms, and facial expressions.

For instance, a delinquent boy referred for treatment sulks silently in his chair, he fidgets around when asked a question, then answers in an evasive way with apparent disinterest in the proceedings. The therapist may make one of the following remarks:

"Perhaps you feel you ought not to have come here."

"Perhaps you're angry about being sent here."

"I can understand that you'd be annoyed about this situation."

These responses immediately cut into the underlying mood and enable the boy to comprehend that his feelings are recognized. Resultant may be an outburst of hostile emotion toward the referring agency, and an opening up to the therapist.

A woman, suspected of being emotionally disturbed, is sent to the therapist by her assigned social worker after applying to a family welfare organization for help. The only reason she accepts the referral is to please the social worker through whom she expects to secure supplementation of her income. Her lack of motivation causes her to withhold as many facts about herself as possible, and to be as evasive as she can without offending. Under these circumstances, once the therapist has become conscious of her attitudes, he might say: "I can very well see that you would feel resentful or uncomfortable about coming here. You probably do not believe that it is necessary, and might feel that you could very easily do without it. I do not blame you for feeling that way inasmuch as you didn't really come to the agency to seek any emotional help." This may relax the patient considerably, since she senses in the therapist a sympathetic person. She may then begin to express her feelings about the agency and finally to verbalize her problems quite candidly.

A man with a character disorder expressed in petulant, querulous and sadistic tendencies comes in for an interview on the insistence of his wife, who threatens to leave him unless he gets psychiatric treatment. After spending ten minutes or so disarming the therapist with a genteel account of how well adjusted he is, the therapist interrupts:

Th. But there must be some reason why you came to see me?

Pt. I wish I knew why. My wife insists that I'm cracked.

Th. Cracked?

Pt. Yes. (*laughs*)

Th. Why does she make such a claim? (*The patient then irately expostulates on certain incidents in which he was unfairly treated by relatives of his wife. His responses, though retaliatory, were, he claims, tempered out of respect for his spouse. Yet she accused him of being cruel and irrational—tendencies that were not an integral part of his personality.*)

Th. Do *you* think that you have personality problems?

Pt. Not any more than anyone else.

Th. Then it must make you mad to have to come here to see me.

Pt. (*pause*) Well . . . she thinks I should go to you. I'm mad at her, not at you.

Th. Well, I would think you'd be as mad as the blazes to come here when you really don't see the need for it.

Pt. (*laughs*) I guess I am mad, but I don't blame you. Maybe I have been acting unreasonable at times. I suppose I'm hard to get along with sometimes.

Th. Everybody gets upset and acts unreasonable sometimes.

Pt. I don't know that I do any worse than anyone else.

Th. So that you'd resent being sent to a psychiatrist for no real reason.

Pt. Do *you* think there is anything wrong with me?

Th. From what you've told me, you seem to have a problem with your wife.

Pt. It's that she keeps picking and nagging and wanting to make me over. [*From this point on the patient's relationship with his wife is discussed and the patient participates enthusiastically.*]

INDICATING ACCEPTANCE OF NEGATIVE FEELINGS

By reflecting negative feelings, the therapist conveys an acceptance of them. The therapist, furthermore, may elaborate on the patient's right to feel the way he does, demonstrating an understanding of the patient's mode of thinking. This is illustrated in the following excerpt of an initial interview:

(*The patient stomps into the office with a swagger. She is a young woman with a short haircut and a severely tailored tweed suit. She radiates an air of masculinity, and is obviously disturbed and hostile.*)

Th. Would you like to tell me about your problem?

Pt. (*rapidly and angrily*) The first thing I'm going to tell you is that I am against psychiatry completely.

Th. Why?

Pt. Because of past experience. I'm coming here against my will.

Th. I see.

Pt. Definitely against my will.

Th. Can you tell me about that?

Pt. In the year of 1945 I had two psychiatrists working with me. One was a society doctor who got me in and gave me 10-minute sessions, talking about nothing and charged me fifteen bucks; the other was a complete ass, who just sat on a chair, did nothing. He said he would try to work with me twice a week. He didn't help me one single bit and I am against it because of that.

Th. Well it does sound like you had some ungratifying experiences.

Pt. The first doctor wasn't really a psychiatrist, but he posed as one.

Th. How long did you go to him?

Pt. Just went a few times, maybe ten, I don't know offhand, but I felt it wasn't doing me any good.

Th. What was the reason for going to him in the first place?

Pt. I was kicked out of school.

Th. College?

Pt. Yes. They promised to let me come back if I had psychiatric treatment. I used to go to see the guidance woman, and she said that I had to see a psychiatrist. One of the teachers complained—a special narrow-minded, bigoted woman who had the same affliction I did and that they had condemned me for. This was homosexuality, I guess. I don't know till this day. They got me into such a state that I was willing to do anything and everything. I had no psychiatric treatment, then I went to two of them. They were working with me, trying to get me back to school, and then after this year was up, the president talked to these doctors and everybody else. They started messing around, and then said they wouldn't take me back anyway, so that finished me up at college. That was the only reason I went for psychiatric treatment. I went in with an open mind. I said, "OK, if you can cure me and get me back to school," but it didn't work. And ever since then, I mean, I don't particularly care for college; but I want my degree. I know what I want in life as far as a career goes. I am working toward it now. So I got to go back to college.

Th. So if you're anti-psychiatry, why did you come to see me?

Pt. Well, that's not the point. I don't want you to cure me, as far as that's concerned. I talked to the guidance woman about the whole thing. She is a wonderful person and I adore her, except I think she is psychiatry conscious. She has been insisting on this and I am always trying to please her. In fact, it's not the homosexualism that bothers her, it's the way I dress and walk and things. I was a little out of hand at school.

Th. Is that what *they* say?

Pt. Well, no—that's what *I* say.

Th. What sort of trouble did you have?

Pt. Well, I don't smile enough; I look queer, I suppose; my mind is always a mile away, although I did good in school. I have an excellent mind and my marks showed it. I don't dress; I wear men's shirts; and I am always in this kind of an outfit which is a little different from what the typical girl wears at college.

Th. I see.

Pt. Well, it looks different and my walk is terrific.

Th. You mean you walk with a swagger?

Pt. I do definitely.

Th. Is that affected or is that you?

Pt. I tried to calm it down, but it just doesn't work. You see, I was in physical education, and I am very athletically inclined, and the swagger does come, but it's not to the degree that I have. My voice is very gruff, in fact my speech teacher gave me an E because he didn't like the way I spoke. And that's the lowest mark I ever got, and maybe I will be able to fix that up. It's just these little things—the way I smoke a cigarette. My behavior patterns that I have just don't qualify with the normal. I try to keep away from women 'cause I might be tempted, and as yet I haven't been.

Th. What do you mean as yet you haven't been.

Pt. Well I haven't gone after women, to go to bed with me I mean.

Th. You never have had any homosexual relations?

Pt. Oh yes, but not at college.

Th. What they object to is just the fact that you dress in a certain way and talk in a certain way?

Pt. As this guidance woman puts it, they feel that in the state that I am in now, whatever that is—they have given me no definition of it—they feel that I am not a responsible person, and that I may possibly forget myself and commit an act. Therefore they feel I am not a good risk, but they don't know that I work well with children 'cause I have done a lot of field work, and I have done an excellent job. I have a good reputation at home. These college students and the professors, of course, can recognize the fact that I am queer I guess.

Th. Well, the business of working with children—your course is what?

Pt. It's educational sociology in group work.

Th. What would you like to do?

Pt. I thought about going back to physical education. In fact I may start my graduate work in September.

Th. You don't see anything wrong with the things you are doing, do you?

Pt. Certainly I do.

Th. Well what's wrong with them?

Pt. Anything that doesn't conform to society is wrong in their eyes.

Th. But in *your* eyes—I'm talking about yours.

Pt. I got a conflict. I apparently have two personalities—one is the homosexual, the other is heterosexual. I can't make up my mind which personality I want to be. I think it's the homosexual, because my relationships with men have been "snafu." I don't know. The guidance person thinks I hate women really. She has analyzed this thing with me, every time I talked to her. I always give the right answers as far as myself is concerned. I like women. I like to be with them, but I'm a very obvious homosexual and that's what's wrong with me.

Th. Well, when you are with them, how do you act with them, with the girls?

Pt. I'm aggressive naturally.

Th. Do you ever take a passive role with them?

Pt. No.

Th. And what about your relations with men?

Pt. I am very much in love with one now, and he is also a homosexual. My only associations which are very satisfying are with gay boys. (*laughs*) If I talk to you much longer, you'll get my lingo. Isn't it awful?

Th. You seem to be ashamed of it.

Pt. I'm not ashamed of the fact that I'm a homosexual, but I am ashamed of the fact that I'm obvious.

Th. Well, would you like to change your being obvious?

Pt. Yes, that's the point. I don't particularly care about being cured as far as that's concerned, because a lot of great people were homosexual. If *they* could be homosexual, well *I* certainly can. I'm completely indifferent to that.

Th. Would you like to change some of these mannerisms that you talk about?

Pt. That's the point, if I can get out into society and work. In fact, my ultimate goals are to teach in a college.

Th. I see.

Pt. Now, I'm not going to do anything—inflicting my behavior upon my students—but it is obvious, and that's where the drawback is. And ever since I started in this work, it's not the students. The kids love me. In camping experiences too, it was always the counselors or the teachers that jump on me, because they see something.

Th. Maybe you feel that if you expose yourself to therapy, I'm likely to try to change your preference for homosexuality.

Pt. Well, are you?

Th. I naturally won't change anything you don't want changed. As a matter of fact, you're the one that determines how far you want to change. Actually I don't blame you for being mad at psychiatry, if you feel psychiatry is trying to force you to be something you don't want to be. But getting treatment merely to get into college may do *you* absolutely no good.

Pt. They don't exactly demand it, they haven't gotten to that stage. I don't want you to misunderstand. It was the guidance woman's idea, and she has been at me ever since I've known her. She has taken a keen interest in my work, and she feels that I'm good at it and that my future shouldn't be wasted because I am in this conflict. I am unhappy you see.

Th. What conflict are you in?

Pt. Whether I should go this way or whether I should go that way in sex.

Th. Well, maybe you'd like to work out which direction you'd really like to go, either the one or the other, as long as you are clear in your mind and convinced in your heart.

Pt. I think that I would be homosexual, (*pause*) because my whole environment as a child, and ever since I can remember has been one which was conducive to homosexuality.

Th. Let's accept that; at least for the time being. Are there any other conflicts you might want to handle? [*attempting to discover some incentive for therapy*]

Pt. I sort of isolate myself, I'm afraid, and, as soon as I finish a class, I want to run home. Or I run down to the Village to this friend of mine and I stay with him. What bothers me most of all is the way I look and walk and act. It upsets me.

Th. In other words, you feel the mannerisms and the gestures are not approved of?

Pt. That's right.

Th. And that's what bothers you more than anything else?

Pt. Yes.

Th. Would you like me to let us help you with *that* problem?

Pt. If you can; if not I might as well go to the Bowery. Do you think you can? This problem of what I should wear, what I shouldn't wear. My sister is ultra, ultra feminine, and I have the clothes to wear, but I would prefer to be in this attire. [*The patient defines an area on which she wishes to work.*]

Th. I'll do what I can to help you understand yourself better. If you have the desire to work things out, I believe I can help you.

Pt. That's the whole thing except that there is this tremendous fear that I'm not myself. But, I'd like to get started if you can, as soon as possible.

MANIFESTING AN OPEN MIND ABOUT THE PATIENT'S NEED OF THERAPY

Should the patient want to know whether the therapist considers his problem severe enough for psychotherapy, the therapist may say that he will have to postpone a positive statement until he has obtained more information. Such an attitude helps convince the patient that he is not dealing with an arbitrary authority. The therapist may also remark that he is not sure the patient needs or does not need treatment, but that as soon as he has enough facts about the patient, he will be better able to advise him. The following excerpt is an example of this:

Pt. Do you think I need to get these treatments?

Th. I am not sure yet. Suppose we talk more about your problem, then I will give you an idea of whether or not I think you need psychotherapy.

CREATING INCENTIVES FOR THERAPY

When, during the interview, the therapist has gathered enough facts to justify a positive statement to the patient, he may remark: "Now I know enough about the problem to give you one definite statement. I do think you can benefit greatly from therapy. Whether you want therapy is another matter; but it could be of help to you."

Should the patient demand a reason for the therapist's conclusion, the latter may frankly state that the patient is not as happy, or well adjusted, or creative as he might be, or that he is being victimized by certain symptoms that are signs of neurosis. The therapist must respect the fact that only the patient can decide whether or not he wants therapy, no matter how much he needs it.

It is necessary sometimes to attempt the building of incentives for treatment. Illustrative is the following excerpt from the first session with a single woman of twenty-four whose mother was insistent that she see a psychiatrist because of attacks of moodiness and spells of depression. The patient sat forlornly in the chair replying to questions with monosyllabic answers, and denying that her symptoms were bad enough to warrant treatment.

Th. Are you completely satisfied with your present life and adjustment?

Pt. Yes.

Th. It's very gratifying to be well satisfied. Understandably you wouldn't want any treatment if there is nothing wrong.

Pt. No.

Th. Your mother thinks you ought to get treatment. I wonder why?

Pt. I don't know.

Th. Maybe you're angry that she sent you here, if you didn't need treatment.

Pt. I'm not angry.

Th. Mm hmm. (*pause*) But there must be some area in which you aren't completely happy.

Pt. Well . . . (*pause*)

Th. Are you satisfied with the way everything is going in every area of your life?

Pt. (*pause*) No, not exactly.

Th. Mm hmm. (*pause*)

Pt. It's that I don't go out much, not much. I don't go out with boys.

Th. I wonder why?

Pt. I don't know. I don't have a desire to go out, I mean the energy. I get tired.

Th. Would you like to want to go out more? [*attempting to create an incentive for therapy*]

Pt. Oh, yes. I often wonder what I could do to make me want to go out.

Th. Well, if you really would like to work with me on that, maybe I could help you with it.

Pt. But could you do anything to make me want to go out?

Th. I wouldn't make you do anything, but if you were interested, we could explore this area and find out what it was that held you back.

Pt. I think I would like that, if you could do it.

To help promote motivation for therapy the interviewer may alert himself to any of the following manifestations on which he may focus the patient's attention:

1. Distressing symptoms of failure in adaptation; such as, tension, anxiety and psychosomatic symptoms.

2. Incapacitation and inhibition of function produced by anxiety and defenses against anxiety, like phobic, conversion, obsessive and depressive reactions.

3. Recognition by the patient that he is not living up to his capacities, and that basic biologic and social needs are being sabotaged.

4. Fear of the consequences of neurotic aims; such as, retaliation for "acting-out" or detection of homosexuality.

5. A desire to be like other people.

ATTEMPTING TO DEAL WITH CONTINUED OPPOSITION TO TREATMENT

Where the patient shows continued negative attitudes toward therapy and toward the therapist, it may be helpful to point out that many persons can be benefited by psychotherapy even though they do not see the need for it at the start. If the therapist, from his personal experience, is able to relate in detail a case he has treated with problems resembling those of the patient, it may create a spark of incentive. Reciting a detailed history, such as the one described in chapter 32, Structuring the Therapeutic Situation, may give the patient an idea of how psychotherapy works.

Sometimes assigned reading (see page 579) of informational books on psychotherapy may aid in the working out of the patient's blocks to treatment. Another helpful adjunct, available to the therapist who is acquainted with psychologic testing, is to give the patient a projective test and then to discuss carefully and tentatively the test findings. Many patients open up remarkably when their problems are approached in this indirect way. Finally, if the patient is willing to expose himself to an educational group, and if there is one available, the ensuing discussions in the group may resolve his resistance.

CLARIFYING MISCONCEPTIONS

Throughout the interview it is necessary to clarify any misconceptions the patient has about psychotherapy, and to answer, as factually as possible, whatever questions the patient may ask.*

Where the patient accepts psychotherapy, but has spurious goals in mind in regard to what he wants to achieve from treatment, special handling will be required. For instance, a man applies for therapy with the complaint of tension that prevents the development of his singing voice. His ambition is to become an opera singer. As he elaborates on his problem, it becomes apparent that he is really searching for success in terms of his father's conception of achievement. A music teacher himself, the father had trained his son to be a singer. The boy was driven to practice incessantly in order to discipline himself for a great vocal career. His coming to New York at the age of twenty had a two-fold purpose: first, to study with a famous voice teacher, and, second, to get an audition at the Metropolitan Opera Company. Upon leaving home, however, the patient's vocal ambitions began to ebb, and he found himself increasingly engaged in social and intellectual pursuits that diverted him from voice exercises. Whenever he sang before a group, or even practiced singing for any length of time, he became uneasy, tense and anxious. He came to therapy at the advice of a friend who was also receiving psychotherapy.

One might speculate that the patient was evidencing a delayed adolescent rebellion against his father which took the form of a desire for a self-appointed career. A reasonable objective in therapy thus would be the promotion of independence, even though this might mean an abandonment of singing as a profession.

Yet to tell the patient that his goal to be an opera singer was neurotic, and that therapy would bring him to an independent course, might drive him away from treatment. A preferable approach would be to accept the patient's motivation to acquire a better singing voice, but to avoid any intimation that his voice might improve in calibre. He could be told that therapy may help him understand the source of his tension and the basis of any other interferences with his singing ability.

In the actual treatment of this patient, it soon became apparent to him that his value system and self-esteem were dominated by the goals of his father. Attitudes of submissiveness and reverence masked deep resentment and desires for freedom. Breaking away from his father in coming to New York, released his aggression. His refusal to practice singing was one sign of rebellion. Tension and anxiety were the emotions consequent to this conflict. The patient was able to make a conscious choice of a career when he determined, in consulting with

* See chapter 30, Answering Questions Patients Ask About Therapy.

prominent critics, that his voice was not of operatic quality. He was surprised to find that his father accepted his decision benevolently after he had asserted himself and had insisted on giving up music in favor of a business career.

There are many neurotic goals that patients imagine will be realized from therapy; such as, demands for power and perfectionism, a desire to endure hardships without flinching, and a yearning to remain poised under all circumstances. These motivations will not of themselves block entry into therapy, but they must be handled with determination at some point.

Among the most stubborn of inadequately motivated patients are those suffering from psychosomatic problems. Clinging to an organic etiology may be due in part to ignorance of how emotional factors can produce physical illness. In addition to the fear of being classified as a "mental case," the patient may consider that agreeing with a psychologic diagnosis is a sign that his suffering is regarded as "imaginary." When he is afflicted with disabling symptoms like blinding migrainous headaches, or intense gastric pains or diarrhea, he may not be able to countenance any other but an organic cause. Applying to a psychiatrist for help is to him a sign of weakness, an indication of lack of will power, and an insignia of defeat. Deep fears of revealing repulsive secrets about himself, or of being unmasked as a contemptible, perverse creature, reinforce his antagonism. The possibility of embarking on a long and costly therapeutic adventure, the outcome of which is not guaranteed, is additionally unsavory. Because of these resistances, the referring physician has a formidable job on his hands in getting the patient to accept a psychiatric referral. As the general practitioner has become more sophisticated in his understanding of mental health, he has been able to deal more adequately with many of the patient's objections to receiving psychotherapeutic help. A few articles have appeared in medical journals that outline techniques of referring a patient to a psychiatrist [456], and these can benefit the physician considerably.

In spite of good preparation, nevertheless, the patient may cling desperately to a conviction that his ailment is organic in nature, and that he will eventually find a doctor who can locate his lesion and prescribe the proper medicaments. He may insist that the therapist become involved in this search, and, despite his understanding that no medicines will be prescribed in psychotherapy, there is an almost frantic plea in his manner, if not in his verbalizations, for a remedy that will spell the renaissance of a new era of hope.

While he may intellectually be convinced of the fact that emotions can influence bodily processes, the patient may be unable to apply this information to himself. The therapist may have to reiterate the thesis of how being upset can produce widespread disturbance in every part of the body, inducing even greater discomfort and pain than organic illness. The therapist must, however, always leave the door open to the possibility of at least a partial organic factor. To insist on its complete absence is an indication to the patient of the therapist's arbitrariness and prejudice. The fact is that the patient *may* have a concomitant organic condition; indeed, it is hardly conceivable that there is no physiologic correlate in every psychologic disorder. The physical disorder may be completely reversible once the patient's emotional difficulty is ironed out. Yet it may exist in fact, and perhaps be demonstrated by laboratory and clinical tests.

A prolonged physical ailment may undermine the person and bring out associated emotional elements. The resulting turmoil will then accentuate the physical distress. As a matter of fact, a condition which starts out as physical may, after a while, incite emotional elements that persist long after the physical cause has disappeared. In the event the patient seeks to know how "emotions" can cause bodily pains, he may be told that the brain is connected to every organ in the body by nerves. When mental suffering occurs, the effects may be transmitted through nerves to the bodily organs, affecting their function and producing painful spasms. When mental or emotional relief eventuates, the organ may be restored to a resumption of its normal activity.

The patient will probably repeatedly have to be told that a reciprocal relationship exists between his mental and physical processes—that his nerves influence his organs and vice versa. Sometimes a physical ailment touches off worry and other disturbing feelings, and the emotional disturbance then exaggerates the ailment. It would surely be remarkable if suffering from pain and other uncomfortable symptoms did not promote worry. Once anxiety is mobilized, a chain reaction begins, and the physical condition becomes more and more aggravated. Treating the physical condition with medicines or surgery may not remove the nervous component. Treating the nervous component, on the other hand, helps the organ return to its normal condition. This is why the treatment of the emotional part of the patient's trouble may restore his physical health.

Because the patient may require the preservation of his psychic integrity through a psychosomatic symptom, one must always cautiously and tentatively advance the possibility of emotional causation, always respecting the patient's need for refuge in a physical cause.

Where the patient accepts the sincerity and authority of the therapist, he may be willing to give himself an opportunity to explore the emotional aspects of his problem. Sometimes the patient will listen in a polite manner, and then insist that he wants further medical consultations and tests before he submits to psychotherapy. The therapist here should respect the patient's wishes, and refer him back to his physician with the comment that the patient is unwilling at present to accept psychotherapy. Often this tolerant and open-minded attitude evidenced by the therapist will inspire the patient to return, motivated for treatment, when an additional excursion for more diagnosis has proven futile.

These principles may be illustrated by considering the case of a man who, because of a disabling gastric complaint, consults his family physician. A series of laboratory tests, clinical examinations and x-rays reveal no discernible organic lesion. Alkalis, antispasmodics, vitamins and sedatives are to no avail. In desperation the patient consults a number of specialists, and finally he makes the rounds of medical clinics with no abatement of his symptoms. His suffering eventually drives him back to his original family doctor, who had intimated, to the dismay of the patient, that there might be psychologic factors responsible for the patient's trouble. This indicated to the patient that the doctor considered him insincere and somewhat of a faker. But, having exhausted every possible avenue of traditional medical help, he finally is willing to listen to his physician and to consult a psychiatrist.

His approach to the psychiatrist at the initial interview is one of mingled disdain, fear, frustration and hostility. Secretly he hopes the psychiatrist will produce some kind of magic pill that will allay his suffering. He has been willing to try something new, but he comes to see the psychiatrist with his "tongue in his cheek." He is willing to give this strange doctor a chance to do something the other doctors have not been able to do, but naturally he has his doubts. The slightest intimation that there is a psychologic aspect makes him fear that his pain may be considered imaginary.

The following is an excerpt of part of a session with a patient of this type who has no wish for therapy, but whose lack of motivation is dealt with successfully by the therapist. After the patient discourses on his doubts that he has a psychologic problem that requires psychotherapy, the interview proceeds:

Pt. But how can stomach trouble be caused by the mind?

Th. The brain is connected to every organ in the body, and when a person is disturbed, it is understandable that the disturbance or worry or conflict can get into every organ of the body through nerve channels. And then the organ gets upset.

Pt. But there's nothing wrong with my mind. I'm not worried about anything except this pain and how to get rid of it.

Th. Perhaps that's right. As a matter of fact you *may* have something really wrong with your stomach. Have you satisfied yourself that there is nothing wrong? [*Since patients are suspicious that a psychiatrist will bend backwards to label a condition psychologic, this remark is intended to show the patient that the therapist is not eager to come to this conclusion without good evidence.*]

Pt. Well, the doctors all say that there is nothing wrong. They've given me all the tests. But I feel there is something. [*This conviction of the patient against all evidence may be obdurate resistance to his accepting psychotherapy.*]

Th. You've had all the tests?

Pt. Yes, and they all add up to nothing.

Th. Perhaps you wouldn't be satisfied until you find someone who tells you there is something wrong. It certainly seems reasonable to exhaust every possibility to your satisfaction, that is, get the best doctors to look you over, before you get psychiatric help. (*pause*) [*This lack of eagerness on my part to accept the patient until he is convinced he wants psychiatric help may spur him on to accept it.*]

Pt. Do *you* think there is nothing wrong with my stomach.

Th. There *must* be something wrong, otherwise you wouldn't have pain. The question is whether the cause of the pain is emotional or organic or both. Frankly I don't know which it is, since I'm not acquainted too much with your condition. But from your account nothing organic has been found. And you've had good doctors. Dr. _____ is a good doctor; he's conservative, and he sent you to see me, which shows he feels there is at least the possibility of an emotional factor.

Pt. But what could it be, if it isn't my stomach?

Th. You mean what would the emotional factors be if your stomach trouble was not organic?

Pt. Yes.

Th. That's why you were referred to me. Perhaps we might be able to find out. You know emotional trouble can give you a bigger bellyache than physical trouble.

Pt. As bad as mine?

Th. I don't know how bad yours is, but it can be mighty bad, even worse than organic trouble. (*pause*) Apparently you can't accept this fact as applying to you. Maybe you think it's disgraceful to have emotional problems?

Pt. Well, if I were that much out of control . . . Well, maybe it's so, but I don't, can't see how. Wouldn't I know if there is something wrong, with my mind, I mean?

Th. With your emotions, you mean? Well, usually not. But I don't know that there is anything wrong either. We'd have to give ourselves a little time and begin exploring. (*pause*)

Pt. Doctor, do you think *you* can help me?

Th. If you have an emotional problem that is causing this trouble, yes; that is, if you really wanted to be helped.

Pt. But I do want to be helped. I've spent a fortune of money and nothing has been done.

Th. Maybe you'd rather wait, and keep trying other internists until you're convinced the organic factors are the most important ones.

Pt. But I've tried and tried.

Th. Yes, but you are still not convinced. Why don't you think things over, and, if you'd like to give this a try—with an open mind, I mean—call me and we'll get started. [*Throwing the choice squarely on the patient's shoulders.*]

Pt. I get the pain over here. (*points to his abdomen*)

Th. It must be very distressing. [*showing sympathy*]

Pt. Yes, doctor, it drives me practically out of my mind.

Th. You know, a person with even a real organic problem involving his stomach can get very upset. And his emotional tension can in turn stir up trouble for him.

Pt. This pain does upset me and I think it does make my stomach worse.

Th. So you see, emotional trouble, worry and tension can upset your stomach.

Pt. Well, I do know there are some things my wife does that upset me. [*This is the first indication of the patient's desire to work with his emotional problem. He talks about his difficulty at home and then makes arrangements to start therapy.*]

AVOIDING THE "OVER-SELLING" OF THE PATIENT

Lack of motivation may persist no matter how expertly the therapist applies himself. The patient may cling to the notion that he must be self-reliant, believing that it is threatening to have to depend on the therapist. He may harbor a deep masochistic need for suffering, and refuse to relinquish his symptoms. He may possess a contempt for normal values in life which he anticipates will be the outcome of therapy. He may suspect the intentions of the therapist and doubt the latter's integrity. He may imagine that his creativity, talent and uniqueness will be exterminated in treatment. He may fear that therapy will ruin his marriage and lead to separation or divorce. He may anticipate a life bereft of pleasures he now derives from his neurotic indulgences. He may fancy that getting treatment constitutes a hostile act against his family who actively or indirectly opposes his therapy. He may contemplate with dread the overcoming of any ostensible symptomatic handicap, since this has justified his failure in adjustment. There may be many other reasons for his refusal to cooperate that will nullify the therapist's efforts to guide him into therapy.

From a strategic point of view, it may be argued that irrespective of how resistive the patient may be at the start of therapy, the developing relationship will eventually undermine his resistance. This is probably correct, and many patients who are initially non-motivated do eventually accept therapy. The great problem is to convince the patient to continue in treatment in spite of his doubts. This is easier said than done, and the therapist may, in his eagerness to help the patient, try to "over-sell" psychotherapy. The best practice is to present the facts frankly to the patient and then leave the choice of therapy entirely up to him. Under these circumstances, the patient may decide not to start treatment; but later he may return motivated, having spontaneously worked out his resistance in the interim period.

The following case illustrates this. It is part of an initial interview with a patient with physical symptoms who was referred by a physician. An unsuccessful attempt is made to bring him to an awareness of possible emotional sources of his illness. Also unsuccessful is an effort to convince him to accept therapy for a potential psychologic problem. Throwing the choice back at the patient makes him decide to get a further physical check-up. He is encouraged to call the therapist when he is ready to accept treatment.

Pt. I'm here because I've been working very hard, sometimes till eleven o'clock at night. I was so tired that I thought something was physically wrong, but I was told that there was nothing wrong with me. No matter what reassurance I get, I am still depressed. When I was coming to your office, I felt sort of a fear. I can't explain it, but if I was with my wife I know that I wouldn't feel that way. When I walk by myself I get that feeling and I can't reassure myself, but no, I do reassure myself. I say to myself that this is silly and I have no reason to feel this way. I don't tell this to anyone, just you now, doctor. [*The patient has symptoms of somatic disturbance, depression and anxiety—manifestations of a collapse in adaptation.*]

Th. You feel fearful? [*focusing on his anxiety*]

Pt. Yes, fearful; that's it. (*pause*)

Th. How long has this fear been going on?

Pt. Well I guess . . . I get up at night, and, and that's why my wife came here to explain what goes on at night. [*Patient's wife is in the waiting room.*]

Th. What goes on at night?

Pt. Well, I get up at night. I don't know what food I eat the night before that gives me a full night's sleep, but certain days I do get a full night's sleep, and I get up in the morning, and I still feel that jittery fearful condition. But if I get up during the night, and open up my eyes any time during the night, and I feel the taste in my mouth; if I feel that I'm nauseous, I'm nauseous—if I feel that I want to take an Alka Seltzer, first thing I wake her up out of her sleep. First thing I wake her up. Really I shouldn't, shouldn't do it, but I know I shouldn't do it, but, if I do, for some reason I feel reassured if she's up. I tell her I don't feel good, and she says, "All right just forget about it, and just lie down on your stomach and force yourself to go to sleep."

[*Feelings of anxiety and helplessness make him apply to his wife for succor and re-assurance.*]

Th. Do you feel physically sick?

Pt. See, doctor, the trouble is I still feel that I'm physically sick, in spite of the fact that I had an x-ray taken about a year ago. Dr. _____ in the Bronx told me at the time, and he showed me the pictures right in front of me too. He says the x-ray shows that there's nothing wrong physically. However, year, maybe less than a year, I believe you can find out exactly just when it was, I was told by the doctor there was nothing they could find out about my condition, there was nothing there. You could call Dr. _____. You see, he'd probably have pictures and he could explain it better. But that's the way he explained it to me.

Th. Now this has been going on for how long?

Pt. Well, it isn't so very long. I'd say three or four years—I mean on and off; but the conditions, well from medical doctors I got examinations. They never found anything wrong during all those years. I did feel during that time, and I still feel during the present day, that it isn't mental, that it is something physical that I feel. I don't know how. I get reassured and reassured and reassured, and the only thing is that people confide and talk to me in a certain sense, and it immediately disappears. And then it comes back again almost right away.

Th. Anything else wrong?

Pt. No, everything is very, very nice. When I'm at home, we got a television set nine or ten months ago and I feel reassurance—we, we—the recreation, I mean. I feel wonderful at home, too, but I can be looking at the television, and if I distract my attention from the television, I still feel that feeling. I would say that three years ago, three and a half, four years ago my boss says, "Joe"—well, they call me Joe for short, he says instead of Joseph—"Take two weeks this spring, take three weeks" I mean. I felt kind of run down, and I always felt that when I'm run down, you know, from continuous work, I should rest up more.

Th. What do you think this is all about?

Pt. Well I don't know. That's why I don't know whether it's my physical condition or whether it's my mental condition. I still feel that it's my physical condition for the simple reason that no matter how I feel, I always snap out of my mental condition. Because if I feel too depressed to a certain degree, I don't try to fight deeply against it. I try to get the help of people whether it's in the business or anywhere else. Or else I just cry it out and get the tension off my chest. I mean I don't try to fight it to the extent that it should get the best of me. You see, I got—to get it down to brass tacks, doctor, I have everything to live for. I have a wonderful, I've got a wonderful family, a wonderful family from my side, I mean my brother and my sisters, and my wife on her side, her brother, her father-in-law. My father-in-law lives with us, my daughter and her husband live with us. We have a pleasant environment. I enjoy coming home. I got everything to fight in the direction of health. And so it, that's really the root of it. It gives me the power to fight because I know that everybody is with me.

Th. You feel that there is a physical condition that's undermining you, that makes it hard for you to do things, particularly to work?

Pt. Yes, but when I get that mental condition, I do feel that it comes from something, something physically wrong. I don't know what it is. It might be, it might be the smallest thing, but still the smallest thing might be . . . (*pause*)

Th. Do you think there is anything seriously physically wrong with you?

Pt. I never feel that pain as I—I never feel any pain. The only pain is the usual condition.

Th. A physical condition, like you say you have, may still be there and undermine you emotionally. Also on the basis of your worrying, the emotional state may aggravate the physical state. It's a vicious cycle. It may be important for you to get physical treatment, and also important for you to get treatment for your emotional state. [*This is a tentative attempt to soften the patient's resistance to psychiatric treatment.*]

Pt. Well I do feel, doctor, that all this condition is, is because of the continuous years of work I put into a career like. Well, I've been working since 1919. In all the years I feel that fifty percent of that time I put two days in one. Let's see, I've been working since 1917, which is thirty-three years. I put two years in one, probably ten years of it, so that ten years I put in approximately twenty years of work. And I do know I have because I've been working at times thirteen, fourteen, fifteen hours a day. I mean, not these last couple of years, but in this trend before. Because after all your machine is working, and if you put twice as much as you should, you pay for it. [*The patient is trying to justify his condition on the basis of overwork.*]

Th. Now look, do you feel that you want to get psychiatric help for this condition of yours. What do you think?

Pt. Well, I think I feel that when I go to my place of business, I have the desire to go, I have the desire to work, and I know that I have obligations. I've got to work to make a living for the family and to keep the respect of the people I associate with. I know my obligations and all that, and I know that if I don't work here I've got to work somewhere's else.

Th. Would you like to get some sort of help for this trouble of yours? [*Repeating my question which the patient dodged.*]

Pt. Well, the first thing I feel that if I got reassurance as to my physical condition, I'd be all right.

Th. The reason you were sent to me was Dr. _____ felt that there was perhaps an emotional problem in addition to any possible physical problem that existed. Now let's assume that you have a physical problem such as you say you have, there still might be an emotional condition superimposed on it. But you won't be able to benefit by help for an emotional problem unless you really want it. That's why I ask you, do you want help, do you want me to arrange for help for you? What do you think?

Pt. Well, I'd rather think it over a little. (*pause*)

Th. I tell you what I will do then. You think it over a little and I will get in touch with Dr. _____. I will tell him what I feel. And then after you talk it over with him, and you decide you want help, call me.

Pt. You see, I don't know whether it's psychologic or physical. You see I say that because I'm not convinced.

Th. Are you interested in what *I* think?

Pt. But, first, if I can be reassured as to the physical, then probably that can loosen up the tension.

Th. Do you feel that that would be enough once you are reassured?

Pt. Well, I don't know. I just don't know.

Th. You know from your experience you've tried that over and over again, and it hasn't worked.

Pt. I've tried, but I still feel that in the physical, I feel there's so many other things that just an x-ray or that—it's just like a complete check-up as to every extent of the individual—I haven't had a complete check-up for a long time.

Th. Do you think that the best idea is to go ahead and make arrangements for another complete check-up? Then when you are assured through that complete check-up to your satisfaction that there might be a good reason for you to get psychiatric help, give me a ring.

Pt. That's what I'll do.

Th. All right then. You may call me when you decide.

Pt. Yes, goodbye, doctor.

The contact with the patient was terminated at this point. The referring physician was told that the patient undoubtedly could use psychotherapy, but that he was not ready for it, not being convinced that there was a psychologic factor in his ailment. Without a desire for treatment, it was doubtful that the patient could derive any benefit from it.

Six months later I received a telephone call from the patient asking for an appointment. He was ready, he claimed, to start therapy. Treatment was started and carried on with satisfactory results.

TREATING THE NON-MOTIVATED PATIENT

The non-motivated patient who feels obliged to continue in therapy because of external pressure, or who is willing to experiment with treatment against his own judgment, should be accepted without question. The best way to motivate such a patient for therapy is to start a good relationship with him—one of frankness and sincerity. The patient, finding value in this relationship, may eventually accept therapy, using the therapist to bring some objectivity into his life.

This may be illustrated in the following excerpt of the fifteenth session with a woman of thirty whose husband had forced her to accept treatment under threat of divorce. The patient suffered from a phobic reaction that restricted her movements and caused her to cling fearfully to her husband. She resented his insistence on her getting psychiatric help, and the first sessions were spent accepting her resentment and pointing out to her that her disabling symptoms might provide an adequate reason for her personal acceptance of therapy irrespective of the wishes of her husband. Gradually she concurred with this idea.

Pt. Well, I feel that I am learning a lot. I don't know how it happened. It's been very subtle. I just don't know how it happened, but I don't think the way I used to. That's the only obvious thing that I can see. I think that I'm getting my feet on the ground, I'm thinking more realistically. I know that I did come here because somebody else wanted me to. I'd be telling a big lie if I didn't admit that. But I had absolutely nothing to say about coming here in the first place, not a thing. And the only reason that I didn't like to come here, I thought of the stigma of having anything wrong with my mind. I'm reminded of it, and John (*her husband*) reminds me of the fact that I'm neurotic all the time, and I know it myself. I think that that has been my phobia, more than some of the other things.

Th. Don't you think you would have thought the same way about treatment if there was something medically wrong with you?

Pt. No.

Th. In other words, you put a special stigma on being neurotic as compared to having any other ailment.

Pt. Well, any other thing, I don't know. But dad taught us ever since we were children about people being mentally off, and that whenever we got married, that the one thing to be sure of always was that the other person was well-balanced and didn't have any queer strains in him. That idea has kept on so long, that it has always seemed to me there were cures for physical things, but that something wrong with your mind you had with you until you died. If you think that for a long, long time, and then someone starts telling you you're queer, it accumulates like a snowball.

Th. Well, that made it difficult for you. You then came not of your own free will, but because your husband insisted on it. But you are beginning to see that coming here does not imply that you are seriously mentally ill. Many people come to therapy, not because they have symptoms, but because they want to improve on their potentialities.

Pt. I realize that they go because they themselves feel that. (*pause*)

Th. Because they themselves feel that.

Pt. And it isn't because someone else says they are queer.

Th. Precisely. If you continue to come to see me on the basis that somebody thinks you're queer, you won't get much out of coming. If you don't come of your own free will, and feel that this is your project, that there are problems that *you* have, emotional conflicts that *you* want to work out, your treatment will be delayed.

Pt. No, I don't have that attitude, and you have gotten me over that feeling, I guess it's because of you. Well, your attitude isn't the kind that reminds me that I'm queer, nothing like that at all. It's entirely different. I think that I want to do things about myself.

From this point on therapy proceeded satisfactorily.

29

The Initial Interview:
Case History

THE FOLLOWING TRANSCRIBED RECORDING ILLUSTRATES SOME OF THE processes of an initial interview:

(*The patient telephoned for an appointment stating that he had been referred by a psychiatrist in San Francisco. When he appeared, he presented the appearance of a pleasant, poised young man, somewhat timid in manner.*)

Th. Hello, I'm Dr. Wolberg.

Pt. How do you do. (*extends hand*)

Th. Won't you sit down over there, please.

Pt. Yes, mm hmm.

Th. The purpose of this interview is to get a general idea of your problem so that we can decide the best thing to do for it. [*structuring the purpose of the interview*]

Pt. Well, it's a complicated matter, but I feel like I'm not as complete a person as I might be. In my associations with people I mean. [*Chief complaint.*]

Th. How far back does this go?

Pt. Doctor, now the best way I can preface what I want to say is that I went to see Dr. _____ in San Francisco. I did have a problem, sort of an immediate problem which in turn led to other problems. There was a girl with whom I had been going for the past year, and we had just broken off, and I was very upset about that. And, I had, we had been having an affair which seemed to complicate the matter considerably, since I wanted to be married and she in turn had had a previous engagement which had been broken. She was apprehensive about such things. And my first really severe emotional, what I consider a bust-up, was when she broke off the affair, and I, I lost control of myself pretty well. [*beginning elaboration of the history and development of the complaint*]

Th. How long ago was that?

Pt. This was in early 1948. It just seemed that, as I talked this out with Dr. _____ that (*pause*) that she actually symbolized a type of security which, as we talked over my past and my growing up process, I never had before.

Th. Mm hmm.

Pt. I can remember very, very well getting little from my stepmother who raised me with my father since I was four or five. A person who deprecated me and my accomplishments constantly; a person who, of course, took me to the dentist twice a year and performed all of the routine functions of a mother without really letting herself, uh, be a mother, uh . . . (*pause*)

Th. And your own mother?

Pt. No, my own mother was divorced from my father and she remarried, and my stepmother took care of me.

Th. I see. What about your real mother, did you see your own mother?

293

Pt. Oh yes, about once a week. We were living in San Francisco.

Th. Hm hmm.

Pt. Uh, I don't know if I've answered your question.

Th. Yes. (*pause*) Now to get back to the immediate problem.

Pt. That was the first time I had this kind of relationship. I had had various relations with a couple of prostitutes, and also with several girls, but they only lasted for a short time. This girl not only, she was, she was a brilliant girl in addition to being a, a wonderful partner sexually. And, uh, this really was the first experience of that intensity that I ever experienced.

Th. How old a girl was she?

Pt. She was younger than I was. She was nineteen.

Th. I see.

Pt. But very mature, I might add. As I look back on it now it seems to be almost a shadow. Oh, it comes back every so often. I think that my conduct today would be entirely different. I mean I can't visualize myself actually doing some of the incredibly insane things I did at the time. (*pause*)

Th. What did you do?

Pt. Well, I mean I, I persisted, I was jealous, I, I, I, uh, didn't know whether to phone her or not. I put her on the spot. I made things rather miserable for her. I made them miserable for myself. I . . .

Th. When was this?

Pt. Well, you see, there were actually two stages. Four or five months after I met her, we went back to college together where I was. We were both doing undergraduate work. And she decided to break off, and that was the first severe reaction I had. I mean, uh, I couldn't see that I was enjoying it too much, and it seemed to represent something very wonderful, and so, I protested loudly at that. I felt I lost everything, and I was very emotional and very, well, it's just, it's just something that I look back on. It seems totally impossible to reoccur. It never had reoccurred. But we still went on after that, and we resumed the affair after a month, and everything was fine. But, when we finally did break up, it was because she had started going out with another fellow. We had not gone steady during this entire period, and I can remember one Thanksgiving evening. This was at the height of the affair, and she went out with other people. Well, this was absurd to me, since God only knows I couldn't see myself wanting to go out with four different girls for the following nights after Wednesday or Thursday night, whichever it was. I don't know if it was Thanksgiving or Thanksgiving eve. So, it was a pretty insecure relationship for me throughout, and finally when it did break off, it was because she had become interested in someone else, a fellow who had had an article published in a national magazine. She was sort of enthralled by this because she had a creative bug, even though she was a political science major.

Th. You felt inferior to him?

Pt. In terms of, in terms of suaveness, yes. Not in terms, not because he had published something, though I must admit that I imagined off and on that *I* would publish something some day.

Th. But it must have been a *terrific* blow to you.

Pt. Well, yes. This guy was a very . . . he was very tall, slender, good looking guy. He sort of had a uh, uh, worldliness in general, or so it seemed to me, as I imagined, as I noticed him from afar. And I remember being rude to him one day which, which again is inconceivable for me, because it not only is out of character, but I certainly don't have that confidence. Before I go on, I want to tell you something that the doctor in 'Frisco and I found out after a little while. I have a—I see it coming out of me now—I have a knack for glibness, and, sometimes, I talk—I'm able to talk very slick as I do now—as I seem to be able to do, go into a song and dance. And it's sort of tough to probe. He found it tough, because I, I was a little too glib. And I just want to tell you about that ahead of time.

Th. You want to warn me?

Pt. Yeah! I don't think that it's necessary, but—

Th. You kind of suspect yourself.

Pt. Yeah, I definitely suspect myself of talking glibly and of underestimating, or trying to underestimate in terms of the person to whom I'm talking. I suspect that I try to make friends with the psychiatrist, instead of, instead of—well, (*laughs*) giving an objective account of my problems. [*This may be an awareness of certain interpersonal operations and defenses; for instance, of a need to impress, to win people over, to befuddle them. The patient may be warning me not to allow him to fool or beguile me.*]

Th. Well, it's only natural for you to relate yourself to me in a way customary to the way you always relate to people. You might utilize, in talking to me, glibness or any other kinds of attitudes that are so often used. But if you want to be glib, there's no reason why you shouldn't be. If your glibness, however, does make problems for you, that may be something you may want to change. That would be something we could tackle right here in the therapeutic relationship. But let's get on to your problem again, if you'd like to resume the thread. [*accepting his glibness, but pointing out that it might be a focus for exploration*]

Pt. Sure. Uh, it seems that when my girl and I finally did break up, of course, I was, I was pretty crushed for several months, for almost a year. I had planned to go to Europe on one of these student ships. Several friends of mine and I got all the way to New York in the summer, three months after we had broken up, and I had what I call anxiety dreams at night, the dream of Joan, which was the name of the girl.

Th. Do you remember the content of these dreams?

Pt. Yes, I've had them off and on ever since, although they are fading out. I just don't have them too often any more. Uh, yes, uh, dreams in which I would see her marching off with some other guy, not at the altar, especially, but perhaps after they were married, and in which I, I seemed to sense that other people were taking her away. I remember one dream in which my stepmother and she were on the same side, and that was a blow. And, things like that. So I turned in my reservations. I didn't go to Europe, and I turned around and I went back. Meantime, she had split up with this other fellow, who, in turn, had another girl. Circumstances just seemed to create tragedies, at least (*laughs*) temporarily. So, I went back and we went around that summer.

Th. You went back to the same girl?

Pt. Yes, but we could never pick up the thread. It was just passed. I found it very, I found it just in pieces. You just don't pick those things up again. So, it was one of those things, although she had wanted to start all over again. Her parents had thought I was a nice boy, and that was a pressure on her which I think was an unfortunate thing. And when I went back, she became somewhat disillusioned with me. This comes into another issue of—we, together, the two of us, were the officers of a debating society on various issues including political issues. After listening to the talk back and forth, I had undergone a transformation. I thought I was progressive, but I got disgusted with that philosophy, although I suppose I still am somewhat progressive. I don't know whether to bring it up because I always feel it creates bad feelings.

Th. You don't know whether to bring that up with me?

Pt. Yeah.

Th. You may not know how I might react to your political ideas?

Pt. Yeah. That's exactly it. [*The patient seems to be testing me here to find out how tolerant or judgmental I might be.*]

Th. Do you feel that I might perhaps judge you in a certain light, if you were either conservative or radical?

Pt. Yeah, I'm always scared of people who live too near Park Avenue. This is maybe because I come from a very wealthy family, and didn't like it. These people frighten me. I don't mean frighten me in a conventional meaning of the word.

Th. All I can tell you is that whatever your political convictions may be, they may be right for you. You don't have to tell me if you don't want to, just what your political orientation is. It really wouldn't make too much difference to me. [*attempt at reassurance and at creating an atmosphere of tolerance*]

Pt. I believe you. This, uh, probably what I said was to, probably because I was grasping for information from *you*. I, actually I had undergone a transformation.

Th. Uh, huh.

Pt. I heard of a forthcoming convention, and I didn't like it. She asked me to participate, and I told her no, that I was at a former convention and I was a little disgusted at the goings on, and I wasn't going to work in it. Well, that was the last straw. She had imagined me as the sort of person whose beliefs coincided with hers. And they did, actually, pretty much, except politically I suppose.

Th. What happened then?

Pt. Yeah, we broke up. We never started up from then. That was the last straw. We broke up. And that summer, I went to see Dr. _____. (*pause*)

Th. After the second break, you saw Dr. _____.

Pt. It was during that second break. (*pause*)

Th. What was the *reason* you saw Dr. _____?

Pt. Well, because, because of her in two ways. First, she wanted me to. Both my mother, my real mother, and Joan wanted me to see a psychologist. I had been toying with the idea myself, and one of the things that enraged me particularly was the fact that Joan said that the condition for our rapprochement would be seeing a psychologist.

Th. Why did she want you to see a psychologist?

Pt. Because she, because she, well, she felt—and she was probably quite right—that my emotional attitude was so unstable. I, I jumped back and forth so much that she couldn't see herself living in this, this uncertainty.

Th. I see. Did *you* really think you were unstable?

Pt. Oh, definitely.

Th. Well now, what happened since the break-up of your affair with Joan. Perhaps you could bring the situation up to the present. [*Because the patient may cover many minor facets of his relationship with Joan to the sacrifice of other important aspects necessary to cover in the initial interview, I attempt to focus the material.*]

Pt. Yeah, I shall. There has been one other item of major importance and that recently terminated, but I'll give you that very briefly because I think that's quite important. Well, right after that I transferred to a midwestern school. I missed Joan terribly, and I changed my major. So I changed it without any trouble, since I had another year before I took my Bachelor of Arts degree. So I did that, and I really had a fine time. I lived at the fraternity house, and I was active there, and I did some debating there.

Th. This was '49?

Pt. This was '49, yeah, late '48 and mostly '49. Well, soon I met a girl named Philly, she shall be called, since that was her nickname. So Philly and I started seeing one another, and we started having an affair. She seemed to me, well, she again had interests much similar to mine. So we started going around together and had an affair, but she turned into, in the last analysis, possibly a repetition of what happened with Joan. She turned out not to know what she wanted, and we went around all summer and all spring of '49 last year. I went to school in the East last fall, and when I went home in December, I found out that in spite of the fact that we had been engaged since last May, she had gone out with a boy whom she had previously gone with when she was at college. This is getting complicated. He had transferred to the midwest college where she was still a student in her senior year. He had transferred there the same month last September that I had transferred East. And she had started going around with him, and she was wearing my ring, and although we had both been going out, I had been, had not been carrying on any promiscuous activities. It turned out that she became worried right after I left. She went to see a doctor, and it turned out that she was not pregnant, but, like a fool, she told him. Then it had got back to me, since we knew him mutually.

Th. Who told you this?

Pt. Well, you see, look, uh, here I go again, I'm skipping. This, this is getting complicated.

Th. We have so much to cover in the interview that it may perhaps be essential to cover highlights and then we'll be able to go into detail later. [*again attempting to focus on material pertinent to the initial interview*]

Pt. This is a highlight I'm going to have to tell you. I'm sorry to interrupt you, but I have to tell you this. She was pregnant last summer. I got her pregnant. And I was pretty shaken by it, and I brought my mother in who is a woman of the world.

Th. During this period, was there a lot of turmoil in you, or were you more or less placid?

Pt. Placid, placid, surprisingly. You see, as soon as I met Philly, she was really why I seemed to get so secure. Joan faded from the picture, and it was like, it was like something fell off my back. It was like, I was like the man with the hoe. Well, anyhow, so I got her pregnant. Oh, that was a hell of a summer. So mother, who had been circulating with the literati for many years, she knew I was carrying on an affair with Philly. Mother had, we, we, mother and I had talked everything out, and I had felt very close to her, so I brought her in on this. And she went down to Philly —it was probably a mistake—and we got her, well we got there, everything was all right. Then we went back together. It was very difficult after that, and I began losing a little interest. Well, when I left in September, right after I left, I phoned her one night in October, and her landlady said she went to see her aunt.

Th. Mm hmm.

Pt. Well, she has two aunts there, three, so she said. My suspicions grew and when she came back, she told me that she had gone south with this fellow. But it was platonic; he had gone as a friend. I accepted that. When I got home in December, mother told me that she talked with Philly, and she said she didn't know if I was the one who got her pregnant or if it was the other fellow.

Th. Mm hmm.

Pt. And my opinion of her decreased considerably, since she had sort of done this thing without any responsibility. So, we broke up in December. It was a very terrible scene cause my mother got involved in it. My mother got involved, and she became just like every other mother, very possessive and jealous of her son. I had thought that she had a soul above it before this. But she didn't. She said, "She's no better than a whore." I took great offense to that. I got sore as hell.

Th. Did that knock you for a loop, too—the breakup of that situation?

Pt. Yes, yes, it did, for two or three weeks. Well, it really didn't by comparison with the first. I don't know whether it was because basically, because Joan was an unusual, extraordinary, uh, uh . . .

Th. An exceptional person?

Pt. Yeah, or because Philly was just a second. And the second is, didn't bother me so much. So it, so, it's, it's, it's during that time I went to see Dr. _____. Now, why am I here today, I mean why I came to see you?

Th. Yes.

Pt. I know you want to get to that. Well, right now I have actually never felt in a way so confident except maybe when I was in high school or in the Army. But it may be because I think introspectively. I guess introspection isn't too good either.

Th. Well, now, let me ask you this. What problems do you feel you have now that you'd like to modify?

Pt. Well, there are problems. Mostly they're in terms of pers-, my own personality problems.

Th. Do you want to tell me something about these?

Pt. Yeah, yeah, I will. Well, I find myself feeling at times that I do not, oh, have friends with whom I can possibly associate or, or be at ease with. I feel that I should always be making an impression upon them. Uh . . .

Th. Do you have any idea as to what goes on?

Pt. I have an idea why.

Th. Yes.

Pt. Well, I, uh, I think it's probably the fact that I had been deprecated, I had been deprecated by my stepmother throughout life. She had pointed to her own son as *the* one.

Th. What age difference is there between you and her son?

Pt. It was a year and a half. He was younger. Well, he turned out to be a complete dunce. (*laughs*) I say that literally. And it, it turned out that, that my father started looking toward me. And later on dad was, dad was always the most stabilizing influence in this whole set-up.

Th. Did you like him?

Pt. Oh, yes, dad was wonderful.

Th. So, to come back to what we were talking about before, the basic problem you'd like help with is your relations with people.

Pt. Yes, and there are several other things I already mentioned that may be concomitants of this or other problems. [*Since the patient is garrulous, to allow him to explore this idea would divert us from important tasks.*]

Th. Now I'd just like to ask you a few questions rapidly.

Pt. Fire.

Th. Your full name is? [*getting statistical data*]

Pt. (*Patient spells this out.*)

Th. How old are you?

Pt. Twenty-five.

Th. Your address?

Pt. (*Patient gives this.*)

Th. Telephone?

Pt. (*Patient gives this.*)

Th. Is it all right to call you there?

Pt. Oh, yes.

Th. Are you living alone?

Pt. Yes.

Th. Now, you are single and a postgraduate student?

Pt. Right.

Th. What are the sources of your income?

Pt. Well, I was left a small amount of money, well, maybe it isn't small, but it gives me enough to be comfortable with.

Th. You say you were in the Army?

Pt. I was in the Army, uh, twenty-six months between 1944 and 46. I think the Army was intellectually regressive. I don't recall reading more than three or four books during that time.

Th. Now I'd like to ask you about other symptoms. How about tension, do you feel tense? [*inquiring about other complaints and symptoms*]

Pt. Well, now, if you are talking about now, I don't. Only when I am in certain situations.

Th. How about depressions. Do you get depressed?

Pt. Once in a while when I think of the messes I've been in.

Th. But not habitually?

Pt. No.

Th. How about anxiety?

Pt. Oh, yes, I'm anxious, but I get out of it.

Th. What about physical symptoms?

Pt. Well, no.

Th. Any fatigue or exhaustion?

Pt. Yes, often that.

Th. How about headaches?

Pt. No.

Th. Dizziness?

Pt. I don't think so.

Th. Stomach or bowel trouble?

Pt. No.

Th. Any sexual problems?

Pt. Well, now, it's funny, when I first meet a girl, I can't, I mean I have no confidence, but later it's all right.

Th. I see, any other problems?

Pt. I would say not.

Th. Any phobias or fears?

Pt. Just of speaking in public. Stagefright, I guess.

Th. Any other fears?

Pt. No.

Th. Any thoughts that crowd in your mind that frighten you?

Pt. No.

Th. Any compulsions—doing things over and over?

Pt. Well, no.

Th. How about sedatives, do you take them?

Pt. Only rarely when I can't sleep.

Th. How about alcohol, do you drink excessively?

Pt. No, but at parties I may have too much.

Th. You say you sleep well?

Pt. Oh, yes.

Th. Any nightmares?

Pt. No.

Th. You remember your dreams pretty well?

Pt. Generally.

Th. Can you tell me a recent dream?

Pt. I had one last night, but I can't remember the details.

Th. Any repetitive patterns in your dreams?

Pt. I couldn't say.

Th. Now a few items about your family. Your own mother is alive and well. [*obtaining family data*]

Pt. Yes.

Th. You say you feel different ways about her?

Pt. Yes, good and bad. I seem to miss her and get furious, infuriated with her. She is sophisticated as I say, but always gets into my life, interferes.

Th. Your father is in good health?

Pt. Yes, he's a person I always admired.

Th. And your stepmother?

Pt. As I said, we were strained. I don't think she ever liked me. She gave me physical care, but it stopped at that.

Th. Now what about brothers and sisters?

Pt. I have a half-brother three years older than I am. He is a shy fellow. We got along badly, very badly all our lives. I joined in the cruelty kicking him around. It seems I emerged out of all this better than he did. And then I have a younger half-brother who turned into a sort of nonentity. That was fortunate for me because I felt that I had it all over them.

Th. Now previous to the two bust-ups you had with these two girls, were there any previous attacks of the same kind? [*questions as to previous emotional upsets*]

Pt. No, not that way.

Th. How about when you were little, any problems then?

Pt. I suppose I was a nervous kid, but I, uh, I mean, I never had any real trouble.

Th. You have had previous treatments as you said with Dr. _____. Can you tell me a little more about these. [*questions as to previous treatments*]

Pt. Well, you see, I saw him for a month when I got upset, then, and then I had to go back to school. So I used to see him vacations, and never more than a couple of weeks at a time.

Th. I see.

Pt. And I saw him when I was in California in December, and, it's, well it's been a very short period.

Th. Did you get any psychologic tests of any kind?

Pt. I took some intelligence tests when I was in high school.

Th. Any Rorschach test at any time?

Pt. No.

Th. I'd like to get one on you. How do you feel about it. [*securing an essential psychologic consultation*]

Pt. Sure, if you think it's important.

Th. All right, then, my secretary will make the appointment and will call you. Now how would you estimate your present health, physical health?

Pt. I'd say I was all right physically.

Th. Have you had a physical examination during the past year?

Pt. Only three months ago I had an insurance physical. The doctor said I was in good shape then.

Th. So to review, you'd like to get started in therapy for this personality difficulty. How urgent would you say your need for therapy was?

Pt. I'd say it wasn't an emergency, that is, I've lived with it for a time, and I suppose I could survive. But I want to be the sort of individual who can walk around in this complicated world without feeling that I somehow am, well, not apart from it. Now in my studies in school, I, I work in spurts. I find myself unable to study for a week. And, all of a sudden, I'll spurt. I do an enormous amount of work then.

Th. In other words, your efforts aren't consistent. Now, let's look upon the practical issues that are involved. You're up in the country and you have a commuting problem. If you were to come here to see me, we would have to work out some sort of program for you. First, how would you feel about working with *me?* [*making practical arrangements for therapy*]

Pt. Fine, I find it easy to talk to you.

Th. Good. I believe I can make time for you on my schedule.

Pt. Well, now I have a car. It wouldn't be too bad. I have no classes Wednesdays and only one class on Friday from which I can come to and then come in. Those are really my best days.

Th. What I would really like to do is spend several sessions with you attempting to formulate a goal in treatment, and then outline a plan. I am not sure yet how deeply we want to go into your personality problem, or how extensive the process would be in terms of time. You know personality problems go so far back in one's life that it might take time to remove them. Sometimes it takes as long as two or three years. [*Since this is a personality problem it is likely that therapy will take a long time.*]

Pt. Well, I know it must take time, and I suppose I am too anxious about it. But on the financial end, if I don't have to come too often, I think I can handle it.

Th. As far as frequency is concerned, we could try twice a week and see how things go. You may be able to do well on that. If any unusual resistances occur, you might have to come in more often, at least for a while. But we can't really tell without a trial. As a matter of fact, once we decide to go ahead, it might be a good idea to set up a trial period of say three months to see how we get along in therapy as a team. [*Setting the frequency at twice a week is conditioned partly by the fact that he can come in no more frequently, if he is to continue with all of his classes at school.*]

Pt. I think that's a good idea.

Th. Now my secretary told you my fee. I'd like to tell you about our appointments. They start right on time and the sessions last three-quarters of an hour. I'll send you a bill at the end of each month. Once we set our regular sessions you should keep the appointments consistently unless a real emergency comes up. If you have to cancel an appointment please do so at least twenty-four hours in advance, otherwise I may have to charge you for the session since I set it aside for you. [*making final arrangements*]

Pt. All right.

Th. All right, then, how would 3:40 p.m. next Wednesday suit you for your next appointment and 2:50 p.m. the Friday after that?

Pt. That would be good for me.

Th. All right, my secretary will call you about the appointment with the psychologist for testing. So I'll see you Wednesday.

Pt. Goodbye, Doctor.

Th. Goodbye.

Tentative diagnosis. Passive—aggressive personality.

Tentative dynamics. The patient seems to suffer from tendencies to relate in an immature way to women who take over a maternal role with him. Hostility is probably a concomitant of this relationship. Inevitably the patient is rejected, perhaps through his own participation. A rupture of the relationship produces great anxiety with inability to function. The patient may try to avoid deep involvement by a detached relationship with women for whom he has little respect. The origins of his problem are perhaps rooted in childhood insecurities in relation to an alternately rejecting and overprotecting mother, and a rejecting stepmother. Latent homosexual tendencies may exist associated with the dependency pattern.

Tentative prognosis. There are many positive things about this man, and he seems to have been able to adjust to many vicissitudes. For instance, his early childhood was not too tumultuous; he adjusted well to Army life; he has progressed satisfactorily at school. With adequate therapy the prognosis is probably good.

Reciprocal response of patient and interviewer. The patient was cooperative and seemed to respond well to the interviewer. The latter in turn felt positive toward the patient.

Physical appearance. Meticulous, perhaps a little foppish.

Patient's estimate of his present physical health. Good.

Communicativeness. Somewhat garrulous.

Insight and Motivation.

    a. The patient is aware of the fact that he has a problem.
    b. He desires to correct the problem.
    c. He is aware that his problem is emotional in nature.
    d. He is willing to accept psychotherapy.
    e. He is willing to accept help from the interviewer.
    f. He seems to be willing to accept the conditions of psychotherapy.
    g. He is able to afford the fee.

Choice of treatment method. Psychoanalytically oriented psychotherapy.

Frequency of visits. Twice weekly at the start.

30

Answering Questions Patients Ask About Therapy

MOST PATIENTS HARBOR MISCONCEPTIONS ABOUT PSYCHOTHERAPY AND its allied fields. These are the products of ignorance, fear, superstitution, or lack of proper information. The responsibility of the therapist here is to supply the patient with facts. Although he may not believe or be willing to accept such facts at first, putting them at his disposal gives the patient an opportunity to alter his misconceptions.

It is often advisable to probe for the reasons behind certain questions before answering them. For instance, if the patient asks the question, *"Do you think psychotherapy could help me?"* various responses are possible.

1. *Th.* You seem to have doubts about this.
2. *Th.* I wonder why you ask that question?
3. *Th.* Do *you* think psychotherapy can help you?

Once the patient expresses his ideas, the therapist may provide pertinent facts. The following questions are commonly asked by patients, and suggested answers to these are indicated:

1. *Pt. What are symptoms which may be helped by psychotherapy?*

Th. If you have nervous symptoms such as tension, depression, fears, fatigue, and certain physical complaints for which your doctor finds no organic basis; if you find it difficult to get along in your work or in your relations with people; if you have a school, sex, or marital problem; or if you merely feel irritable, unhappy, and believe you are not getting the most out of life, psychotherapy may be able to help you.

2. *Pt. Can't I get over my trouble by myself?*

Th. Even if your problem is not too serious, it is hard for you to work it out without professional help. It is difficult or impossible to be completely objective about oneself, because living so close to one's problems makes it hard to see them. It's like being unable to see the forest for the trees.

3. *Pt. Will not a change in my external life situation produce a cure in my emotional problem?*

Th. Generally, no. A person's problems are part of himself and usually pursue him wherever he goes. Of course, bad external circumstances aggravate one's difficulties or bring them to the surface. Good environmental circumstances minimize them. But one's problems are always there, and have to be dealt with therapeutically, if any real modification or cure is to be brought about.

4. *Pt. Why is it that a person is unaware of factors that cause him emotional trouble?*

Th. The reason a person is unaware of such factors is that they are associated

303

with such hurtful emotions that they are automatically shut out of his mind. The mechanism of keeping painful ideas from the mind is known as "repression."

5. *Pt. What is the real cause of emotional illness?*

Th. Emotional illness is the product of various conflicts which interfere with one's relationships with life and with people. Some of these conflicts are unconscious, that is, the person is only partially aware of them. The mechanism of repression operates to push painful conflicts out of awareness.

6. *Pt. Can't I find out by myself what is causing my emotional trouble?*

Th. You might, but most people can't. Not only do we fail to see important issues, but we tend to distort them. For instance, it is hard to discard an image of one-self that one has maintained and enlarged from early childhood, even though the image is an erroneous one. Because we can't be objective about ourselves, we will need professional help.

7. *Pt. Do emotional problems start in childhood?*

Th. The personality structure is built up during childhood as a result of ex-periences with parents and other significant individuals. Where one's early life has been unpleasant, the personality structure may be damaged. This may create trouble for him later on.

8. *Pt. I know my personality has not been what it should be, but how could this cause my symptoms?*

Th. Personality problems create difficulties in getting along with people. They stir up unhappiness and initiate many conflicts. The upshot is tension, fatigue, depres-sion, fears, as well as other symptoms.

9. *Pt. Doesn't my needing psychotherapy mean that I have a weak will or am on the way to a mental breakdown?*

Th. No! More and more people, even those whose problems are essentially normal ones are seeking help these days because they realize they can better themselves with treatment. The fact that you desire psychotherapy is a compliment to your judgment and is no indication that you are approaching a mental breakdown.

10. *Pt. If I have a nervous problem, doesn't that make me different from other people?*

Th. All people have some neurotic problems. Their ability to live with these problems and to fulfill themselves creatively in spite of these problems constitutes the difference between "normality" and emotional maladjustment. Most persons whom we call "normal" actually have neurotic problems that do not interfere with their life adjustment or happiness. When such interference occurs, the individual will want to do something about himself and his problems.

11. *Pt. Why do so many people have neuroses?*

Th. It is impossible to escape conflicts in the process of living. The very act of growing up involves sacrifices and the yielding up of individual pleasures for the group interest. There are many deprivations and disciplines to which we all have to adjust. The price of such an adjustment is often frustration and tension. Mild neurotic symptoms are present in all of us; indeed, they are more common than the common cold.

12. *Pt. Am I not indulging myself by seeking treatment?*

Th. If you were suffering from a physical ailment, you would not believe that you were indulging yourself by getting help for it. An emotional problem may be equally disabling or more disabling than a physical problem. It will need expert help and should not be regarded as a form of indulgence.

13. *Pt. Can all persons with emotional problems be cured by psychotherapy?*

Th. All people can be helped in some way by psychotherapy. The extent of help will depend largely on how much the person desires help, and how much he resists being helped. Some people do not really wish to be cured of their neurosis because it yields important dividends for them. Those who are willing to exchange health for the spurious pleasures of a neurosis have gone more than half way to a cure.

14. *Pt. Why are there so many different theories about psychiatry?*

Th. The field of psychiatry is relatively new, and, consequently, new findings are constantly being made. Actually there are more areas of agreement in psychiatry than there are differences.

15. *Pt. There is a history of mental illness in my family. Does this mean that I will have a mental breakdown?*

Th. There is scarcely a family in the country that doesn't have some member or progenitor who has suffered from a serious mental illness. There is a great deal of disagreement in scientific circles as to the exact role of heredity in emotional problems. However, it is generally conceded that even though a person has a strong history of hereditary illness, this does not mean that he will develop a mental breakdown.

16. *Pt. Shall I get treatment now or shall I wait?*

Th. The longer you wait the more ingrained your patterns may become. As in physical illness, so in emotional illness—it is prudent to get help as early as possible.

17. *Pt. Can physical symptoms be caused by emotion?*

Th. Many physical symptoms are psychosomatic in nature, which means that they have an emotional or nervous basis. When you come to think of it, it is not really so strange that emotional strains or worry should produce physical symptoms. After all, every organ in your body is connected with your brain by nerve channels; and so it is logical that when your nervous system is upset by some crisis or conflict, you may feel the effects in various organs of the body.

18. *Pt. What is a psychoneurosis?*

Th. A psychoneurosis is a very common form of emotional illness which indicates that the person is not adjusting himself to all phases of life. Among the more common symptoms of psychoneurosis are feelings of panic or anxiety, depression, fears of various sorts, compulsive acts and physical symptoms.

19. *Pt. What is a character disorder?*

Th. Many people have a character disorder that consists of a warping of the personality brought about by early training. Character disorders are associated with feelings of insecurity, devaluated self-esteem, and other traits that prevent the individual from being as happy and productive as he might be.

20. *Pt. Are alcoholism and drug addiction emotional problems?*

Th. Yes.

21. *Pt. What is insanity?*

Th. Insanity is a severe mental illness in which a person loses his capacity to distinguish between what is real from what is imaginary. While most people who are emotionally upset believe they are going insane, they very rarely do so. Insanity, or psychosis as it is more properly called, is treatable even in its end stages with modern methods of therapy.

22. *Pt. How can I get the proper help for my problem?*

Th. It is extremely important that the therapist who treats you be a responsible person with sufficient training. Unfortunately, there are many charlatans who have had little or no real training, and who advertise themselves falsely as "psychotherapists," "hypnotists," "counselors" and "psychoanalysts." It is unwise to consult any person for treatment unless referred to such a person by a physician or by a reputable agency.

23. *Pt. Who is qualified to do psychotherapy?*

Th. Psychotherapy is an extremely complex skill and requires a great deal of specialized training. Psychiatrists, clinical psychologists and psychiatric social workers can do psychotherapy if they have had proper postgraduate training. It is widely believed that psychologists and psychiatric social workers (also known as caseworkers) should work under medical supervision.

24. *Pt. What is a psychiatrist?*

Th. A psychiatrist is a medical doctor who specializes in the handling of nervous and mental illness.

25. *Pt. What is a neurologist?*

Th. A neurologist is a medical doctor who handles organic diseases of the brain and spinal cord, like brain tumors.

26. *Pt. What is a psychoanalyst?*

Th. A psychoanalyst has had special training in the field of psychoanalysis. This involves an extended period of study, and includes a personal psychoanalysis.

27. *Pt. What is a psychiatric caseworker?*

Th. A psychiatric caseworker is a graduate from a school of social work who has specialized in helping persons with certain kinds of emotional difficulties. Because of specialized training, the caseworker is often utilized as a consultant in interpersonal, family, social and community problems.

28. *Pt. What is a clinical psychologist?*

Th. A clinical psychologist is a graduate of an approved school of training in this discipline. The training of the psychologist enables him to handle certain kinds of emotional difficulties. The psychologist is often used as a consultant in diagnostic testing, rehabilitation, vocational guidance and research.

29. *Pt. How does psychotherapy work?*

Th. Nervous symptoms and unwarranted unhappiness are the product of inner emotional conflicts. In psychotherapy you are helped to understand your conflicts. In this way it is possible for you to do something constructive about solving them.

30. *Pt. What kind of treatment will I need?*

Th. Different kinds of treatments are helpful in emotional problems, just as different kinds of medicines and operations are suitable for physical illnesses. But the goal is the same—to get the patient well. It's like the roads that lead to Rome. There are many different routes one can follow, and one can get there by different vehicles, from donkey cart to airplane. The goal, however, is Rome. The kind of treatment best suited for you can be determined only by a careful evaluation of your problem.

31. *Pt. What different types of psychotherapy are there?*

Th. Roughly, psychotherapy falls into two broad categories. First, supportive therapy which aims for the correction of difficulties and problems in adjustment without necessarily producing a reconstruction in the individual himself. Second, insight therapy, which has as its goal some modification of the individual's personality. Needless to say, the latter kind of therapy is much more extensive and difficult.

32. *Pt. What are the most common approaches in psychotherapy?*

Th. The best known psychotherapies are guidance, persuasion, suggestion, reassurance, desensitization, distributive analysis and synthesis (psychobiologic therapy), interview psychotherapy, non-directive therapy, Freudian psychoanalysis, non-Freudian psychoanalysis, psychoanalytically oriented psychotherapy, group therapy, hypnoanalysis and narcotherapy.

33. *Pt. What is the best kind of psychotherapy?*

Th. The best kind of therapy is that which suits the needs of the person best. A good therapist modifies his methods to suit his patient.

34. *Pt. What is psychoanalysis?*

Th. The word psychonalysis has become so popularized that it has lost its original meaning. Psychoanalysis is the name given to a theory and a technique by Sigmund Freud. The original theory and technique has been modified by many of Freud's contemporaries.

35. *Pt. What is involved in a psychoanalysis?*

Th. Formal psychoanalysis is a special treatment procedure which can be conducted only by those who have had specialized training in this particular field, that is, psychoanalysts. A psychoanalysis requires that a patient have at least three and preferably four to five treatment sessions weekly. Whether a patient should undergo a psychoanalysis rather than some other form of psychotherapy has no relation to the seriousness of his case. Some very serious cases respond well to formal psychoanalysis, whereas others do much better with some other form of psychotherapy.

36. *Pt. What is the difference between psychoanalysis and other types of therapy?*

Th. One of the fundamental differences is the emphasis in psychoanalysis on unconscious conflict as the source of emotional problems. The elucidation and understanding of unconscious conflicts, and the tracing back of conflicts to their origins in childhood, are the chief tasks in psychoanalysis.

37. *Pt. Isn't psychoanalysis the best kind of treatment there is for emotional problems?*

Th. The best kind of treatment for an emotional problem is the treatment that is best for the patient. Sometimes the best treatment is psychoanalysis; sometimes the best treatment is another kind of psychotherapy.

38. *Pt. If psychoanalysis goes deeper into a problem than any other kind of psychotherapy, isn't psychoanalysis to be preferred?*

Th. Not necessarily, because other techniques may be better for a person. We can take example from the field of medicine. Most abdominal conditions can be handled with medicinal treatment; some require surgery. Those that need surgery should get surgery. Those that do not need surgical interference should not get surgery. While some emotional problems need psychoanalysis, others definitely do not. They should, therefore, get the kind of treatment that is best suited for them.

39. *Pt. What is the difference between psychotherapy and psychoanalysis?*

Th. Psychotherapy is the general term applied to the over-all treatment of emotional problems. One kind of psychotherapy is psychoanalysis. Psychoanalysis is helpful in certain kinds of emotional problems and not so helpful in others. Because it takes so long (3 to 5 times a week for from 1 to 3 years) and is so expensive, it should be used only where it is definitely required. Not all people can utilize psychoanalysis, nor do they need it.

40. *Pt. What is Freudian psychoanalysis?*

Th. This is the technique originated by Dr. Sigmund Freud. It is helpful in certain kinds of emotional illness.

41. *Pt. What is non-Freudian psychoanalysis?*

Th. This is a modified approach to psychoanalysis, which, in the hands of competent, well-trained therapists yields good results in certain emotional problems.

42. *Pt. Which is superior, Freudian or non-Freudian psychoanalysis?*

Th. More important than the kind of psychoanalysis is the experience and skill of the analyst. A good psychoanalyst can get good results with either procedure, while a poor analyst will probably fail irrespective of the kind of approach he employs. Some psychoanalysts find that a Freudian psychoanalysis works better for them, others hold non-Freudian psychoanalysis in higher esteem.

43. *Pt. What is psychobiologic therapy?*

Th. This is an approach to psychotherapy originated by Dr. Adolf Meyer which utilizes a number of different techniques. It is helpful in certain kinds of emotional illness.

44. *Pt. What do you think about dianetics?*

Th. The principles on which dianetics was founded have been known to psychiatrists for years. Dianetics itself is not considered a scientifically valid procedure.

45. *Pt. Is group therapy helpful?*

Th. Yes, in certain conditions. However, most therapists find individual therapy more helpful, at least at the start of therapy.

46. *Pt. Won't hypnosis shorten my treatments?*

Th. In certain conditions hypnosis is helpful; in others it seems to do no good.

47. *Pt. Will I need hypnosis, narcosynthesis, group therapy or other special treatments?*

Th. That will depend on the nature of your problem. If your therapist believes any of these or other treatments to be indicated, he will tell you about it.

48. *Pt. Will I need shock therapy?*

Th. Very few people need shock therapy. Its use is limited to only special conditions. The probabilities are that you will not require this form of treatment.

49. *Pt. Will I get medicine for relief?*

Th. If your therapist believes that medicine will be of any benefit to you, he will prescribe it or have it prescribed. But most nervous conditions are not helped by pills or tonics. It would be like prescribing aspirin for a fever. The fever may come down, but the causes of the fever would not be influenced.

50. *Pt. Are there any shortcuts to treatment?*

Th. A number of experimental methods are in process to see whether it is possible to cut down the long period of time required for treatment. This work is not entirely complete, but sufficient progress has been made to indicate that it may be possible to cut down on the treatment time in some cases. However, there are many forms of emotional problems in which time itself is the essence in treatment and shortcuts are not possible.

51. *Pt. Can psychotherapy make a person happy no matter how bad his situation may be?*

Th. Psychotherapy will not stop a person from reacting to a bad situation. It should, however, make it easier for him to deal with this situation in a more constructive manner.

52. *Pt. Am I going to be forced during therapy to give up pleasures in my life situation that I find valuable now?*

Th. Nobody is going to force you to do anything. If any of the pleasures that you enjoy at the present time are destructive to you, you have a right to know this.

Once you are aware of all the facts, you will then be in a better position to judge for yourself whether you want to continue or discontinue certain pleasures. Many people have the misconception that psychotherapy will make them terribly serious and prevent them from enjoying themselves. On the contrary, psychotherapy releases inhibitions to enjoyment and pleasure.

53. *Pt. Is treatment likely to make a person immoral?*

Th. This mistaken notion is caused by the fact that in therapy an individual discusses problems of deepest concern to him, including sexual problems. Immorality is never produced by a proper understanding of emotional problems and drives. On the contrary, immorality is usually the product of misunderstanding. Once the individual surveys himself honestly, healthy and constructive attitudes towards himself and toward his basic impulses will develop.

54. *Pt. Will therapy break up my present marriage?*

Th. Therapy actually preserves many marriages. It is interesting that therapeutic changes occur not only in a person getting therapy, but also in his or her mate. This is because a personality alteration in one member of a family always affects the adjustment of people with whom he is in close contact. Where a marriage seems hopeless, the patient will be able to evaluate better its good and bad points.

55. *Pt. Will I lose my creative abilities if I get therapy?*

Th. Such an idea arises from a misconception that creativity comes from neurosis. Actually, creative work is one of the most normal of human drives. It is crippled by neurosis. Experience shows that people are liberated from their blocks and actually become more creative after therapy.

56. *Pt. Are people supposed to fall in love with their therapist?*

Th. This is a notion that most people have from reading the existing literature. Actually, transference feelings, positive or negative, occur in varying intensities. The particular form the transference takes will be dependent upon the individual's unique problems.

57. *Pt. What is transference ?*

Th. Transference is the experiencing of emotions and attitudes in relationship to another person which are inspired not by the reality situation, but by the individual's previous experiences in his former relationships with people.

58. *Pt. Is transference necessary?*

Th. Transference is a part of every human relationship and consists of a carry-over of attitudes and feelings one has had toward people in the past into the present situation. For instance, you may have had initial impressions of people; these impressions are caused by the fact that the persons resemble somewhat those you have known. Sometimes one can get angry at a stranger, or one can like a person, for no apparent reason. Such irrational attitudes and feelings towards others go on all the time. They are caused by transference. Transference may be present in the therapeutic relationship. It enables us to see what unconscious attitudes and feelings are constantly being projected out towards other people, and are stirring up trouble in adjustment.

59. *Pt. Can transference be at the basis of one's emotional problems?*

Th. Transference distorts logic and judgment and causes unfair and destructive attitudes towards people. These may actually interfere with one's ability to relate in a realistic way to people with whom one requires a good contact.

60. *Pt. Do I have to report my dreams in therapy?*

Th. Yes, if your therapist believes you should do so. Dreams may be extremely important. All people dream; but not all people remember their dreams. Dreams are thought processes during your sleep which embody symbols and bizarre language forms which may seem meaningless. But woven into the fabric of dreams are attitudes, feelings, and memories that yield clues, to an experienced observer, regarding the individual's basic difficulties and conflicts.

61. *Pt. Can dreams really be interpreted?*

Th. Dreams are condensed symbols which can be interpreted by an experienced therapist. Do not expect that all your dreams will be interpreted for you by your therapist. This is both impossible and unnecessary. You may learn to understand the meaning of your own dreams, and you will then be able to see how closely related your dream structure is to your emotions and feelings.

62. *Pt. But my dreams seem so bizarre. How can they mean anything?*

Th. The language of the dream, the peculiar symbols that dreams use may seem weird, but these can often be translated by trained therapists, and the significant meanings thereby understood. Freud called dreams the "royal road to the unconscious." The surface story told by dreams (manifest content) is not so important as what underlies the dream (latent content).

63. *Pt. What causes dreams?*

Th. Dreams serve as an outlet of tensions in expressing open and secret hopes, as well as fears and conflicts. Dreams are the mind's attempt to solve problems which disturb the individual, not only in the present-day life, but also those problems which had upset the person as far back as childhood.

64. *Pt. Is it necessary to recline on the couch for treatment?*

Th. Reclining on a couch for treatment is usually desirable in formal psychoanalysis. It permits the person to concentrate much better on his thought processes by minimizing the influence of external stimuli. It is usually unnecessary in most other forms of psychotherapy.

65. *Pt. What is free association?*

Th. Free association is a technique used in formal psychoanalysis to discover certain deep unconscious associative links in the person's thoughts by letting his mind wander at random, verbalizing without restraint. Free association is not used in most forms of psychotherapy.

66. *Pt. Do I need psychologic tests?*

Th. Psychologic tests are often helpful in arriving at a better understanding of the sources of tension and emotional stress. The fees for tests may sound expensive; however, in the long run, tests may prove economical, since by helping in the diagnosis, they may facilitate the treatment process. Among the more common tests are the Rorschach, Thematic Apperception, Szondi, and Man-Woman Drawing tests. Your therapist will decide which of these or other tests may be most helpful to you.

67. *Pt. Do I have to tell my therapist everything, even those thoughts and experiences that make me feel guilty and ashamed?*

Th. Complete frankness and honesty are the keynotes in psychotherapy. While in ordinary relationships you are subject to existing moral and ethical judgments, this does not happen in the unique kind of relationship during psychotherapy. It may take you a while before you realize that the function of the therapist is not to judge or to criticize you, but rather to help you get well. He actually does not regard your attitudes, your impulses and your experiences, as bad or wrong, but rather as items that yield clues about your basic conflicts and difficulties. An example may make this clear. If you were to visit a friend and tell him that you had, prior to seeing him, just murdered a baby, your friend would express horror and then call the police. If you were to say the same thing to your therapist, he would neither condemn nor condone your actions, but merely inquire as to the reasons why you felt inclined to act as you did. This example is grossly exaggerated to indicate to you the difference between a relationship with your therapist and any other relationship you have ever had. It is important to reveal as much about yourself to him as you can, and your confidences will not be betrayed.

68. *Pt. Why does a therapist act so unemotional?*

Th. Psychotherapy involves participation on the part of the patient in arriving at the sources of a problem, as well as in resolving it. In order to inspire the patient toward activity, the therapist may assume a passive role, guiding the patient only when he becomes blocked in his own capacity to think things through for himself. Actually, the therapist is not so much detached as he is purposefully withholding himself from carrying the chief responsibility for therapy, which, while temporarily reassuring to the patient, would ultimately hamper him in his quest for assertiveness and independence.

69. *Pt. Will my therapist tell me what to do and how I can best conduct my life?*

Th. Understandably you would want such guidance, since life now seems to be so frustrating and difficult. Where it is absolutely necessary, your therapist will help you decide on alternative courses of action. However, the primary object in therapy is to help you achieve a level of growth and development where your own choices and decisions will bring happiness to you rather than grief. In order to do this, your therapist will have to help you understand what is behind your problems, and the reasons why it has been difficult for you to conduct your own life. You will also have to achieve a level of development where you can make your own decisions rather than depend on others. In this way you will achieve the most active and satisfying growth.

70. *Pt. Are there any rules I must follow in therapy about making crucial decisions that will alter my life situation?*

Th. There are several rules. It is essential to understand that in the treatment process one's whole life will come up for understanding. It is important, therefore, not to make any crucial decisions or changes until the meaning of such a choice is understood. If you contemplate any significant alteration in your position or life situation, it is essential to talk it over with your therapist first, in order to make sure that you are not being influenced by temporary emotional feelings stirred up during treatment.

71. *Pt. Is it all right for me to see my therapist socially?*

Th. One of the basic rules in therapy is that the relationship between patient and therapist be kept on a professional basis. This is extreme', important inasmuch as you have a specific task to achieve in your treatment, and this task may be watered down by associations such as may occur in a non-professional relationship. Experience shows that treatments proceed most rapidly where the relationship is kept on a purely professional level. A social relationship with your therapist may create many stumbling blocks in your treatment that will actually destroy its effectiveness.

72. *Pt. How many times a week must I come for treatment?*

Th. There are some persons who come once a week and there are others who desire, or find it necessary, to come two or three or four times a week. Sometimes it is better to come more frequently than once a week to cut down the interval between visits and to gain the advantages of more concentrated work. At other times this is unnecessary. The frequency will depend upon the nature of your problems and the kind of therapy that is utilized. In most cases treatments can be administered on the basis of once, twice, or three times weekly. Where Freudian psychoanalysis is utilized (that is, where your problems are such that your therapist believes a formal psychoanalytic technique is indispensible for you), you may have to come as frequently as five times weekly.

73. *Pt. Aren't charges for psychotherapy excessive?*

Th. It takes longer to make a good psychotherapist than a good surgeon. Fees for surgery are so much higher than fees charged for psychotherapy, that we cannot even make a comparison. Although the fees that are charged may seem high, they actually are reasonable considering the extensive training of the therapist.

74. *Pt. After starting therapy, will I be charged for broken or cancelled appointments?*

Th. Since your appointment times are set aside and reserved exclusively for your use, you may be charged for a cancelled or broken appointment, unless illness or a real emergency interferes with your getting to the therapist's office. Most therapists do not charge for cancelled appointments where sufficient notice has been given them in advance so that they can fill in the session with another appointment. Another reason for charging for broken appointments is to overcome resistance to coming for treatment when basic problems are under discussion.

75. *Pt. How long does it take to get well?*

Th. It is hard to estimate this. Much depends on how much you want to get well. Much depends, also, on how deeply we want to influence your personality make-up. If you have a special problem or symptom that is not too complicated, we may be able to help this in not too long a time. If, however, we must make extensive changes in your personality for you to get well, treatment will require more time. I can assure you that no effort will be spared to get you well as quickly as possible.

76. *Pt. Does it usually take a long time to effect a cure?*

Th. Emotional illness associated with personality problems that go far back in one's life, so as to produce habit patterns of a stubborn nature, take a long time to influence, sometimes as long as two or three years or longer. It is impossible to say how long therapy will last since this will depend upon the severity of the problems and upon the goals one wishes to achieve.

77. *Pt. Won't it be possible for me to get well fast?*

Th. I can appreciate your impatience. I wish it were possible to rush matters But your trouble didn't begin last Tuesday. It's been with you most of your life. It took time to develop your problem, and it may take a little time for you to get over it.

78. *Pt. Why does it take so long to get well?*

Th. If you are like the average person who undergoes psychiatric treatment, you will probably be puzzled or upset when, after several weeks of treatment, you are not materially improved. You will wonder why this is so and you may even believe that your treatment is not successful. There are two things you must consider in evaluating your progress. First, all emotional problems go far back in one's life, even as far back as one's childhood. Therefore it takes time to get to the core of a neurosis. Second, even though your symptoms are still with you, progress is being made nevertheless. Before a seed can sprout, it is necessary to prepare the soil. Before your symptoms disappear and you achieve health, it is necessary to get an understanding of yourself and to overcome resistances that block your progress.

79. *Pt. Why do I need an understanding of myself?*

Th. The first step in becoming well is getting insight into what is the matter with you. Your difficulty may be that your environment is bad and you are trying to adjust to an impossible situation; it may be that you are doing the wrong kind of work; or it may be that you have inner conflicts and fears that make for difficulties in your relationships with people. Whatever your problem, your therapist will help you to understand it clearly. Then, you will be better able to do something constructive about it. It is hard to fight an enemy who attacks you from ambush. It is the same with emotional conflicts. So long as these are only partially known to you, you are helpless. Becoming aware of them makes it possible to take a stand to overcome them.

80. *Pt. Is it possible that I may exhibit resistances to understanding myself?*

Th. There is always resistance in tackling the real source of one's difficulties. The reason for this is three-fold. First, a person may have absolutely no inkling that what he is doing is not normal. For instance, an individual who has acted submissive from childhood may do so because it is the only way he knows of getting along with people. It may cause him anxiety, yet it constitutes the only way of life he knows. It may take a long time before he realizes that he does not have to be submissive automatically. Second, a person may be very reluctant to face his inner conflicts because of a fear that he will find out something about himself that is too horrible to face. This fear is universal and it may take a while before he overcomes it. Third, he may actually derive a benefit out of being sick, and for this reason be unwilling to explore his difficulties. It may seem paradoxic, but being sick often yields dividends one may refuse to give up. An example of this is the person who keeps failing in his work or studies and, as a result, becomes extremely insecure. On the surface he wants to stop failing; yet deep down what he desires even more is sympathy from people. And the reason he fails, is that in failing he imagines he gets sympathy from others. Such a person may be resistive to understanding his tendencies toward failure because he will have to give up a technique through which he derives many neurotic benefits.

81. *Pt. After I get an understanding of my problems, what else do I have to do to get well?*

Th. Getting insight is the first step toward getting well. You must use this insight to achieve a more productive and happier life. An example may make this clear. Suppose you desire to fly an airplane; the first thing you need is the vehicle—the airplane itself. But having procured the airplane does not mean that you can fly. You still have to learn how to work the airplane. Insight is the vehicle that can transport you to health. But having insight alone will not give you health. You must learn how to use this insight toward a constructive end.

82. *Pt. What can I do to aid the process of recovery?*

Th. Most people are confused about what is supposed to happen in treatment. In a physical ailment, once the doctor knows your complaint, he can give you a medicine. But emotional complaints are not helped in that way. *You, yourself, must participate in the cure.* Your therapist will help you to help yourself. One of the best ways to cooperate is to tell your therapist about yourself—your fears, your hopes, your fantasies, and your expectations. If you have any dreams, report them to him. You will probably also have certain feelings about your therapist. Bring these to his attention—no matter how irrational they may seem.

83. *Pt. Can I expect to have ups and downs during treatment?*

Th. You can. A feature of all nervous problems is that they try to repeat themselves. Even when you gain insight into them and begin to readjust yourself to life and to people, they will still crop up from time to time. The reason for this is that they are like bad habits. You know how difficult it is to break so simple a habit as excessive smoking. Faulty patterns of living which are part of your neurosis are complicated habits of long standing and will try to cling to you stubbornly. With patience and determination you can overcome these patterns. The important thing is not to regard a recurrence of your symptoms during treatment as a set-back. Take the attitude that temporary flair-ups are to be expected, and that you will learn something valuable about yourself each time they occur.

84. *Pt. Need I have conflicting feelings about my therapist?*

Th. Some persons do, some don't. In a relationship situation, which is the essence of psychotherapy, it is possible that you may run the entire gamut of emotions in response to your therapist. The experiencing of these emotions is an invaluable part of the treatment process. Do not be ashamed to tell your therapist exactly how you feel about him, no matter how irrational your feelings, demands or expectations may seem. At certain stages in treatment, you will be very much tempted to discontinue therapy because of how you feel about your therapist. Sometimes these feelings may not even be conscious. Consequently, whenever you reach a decision to stop treatment before your therapist thinks that treatment should be ended, examine how you feel toward him and, more important, mention these feelings to your therapist. There are times, of course, when you may become angry at your therapist for realistic reasons. It is also possible that your therapist has a personality to which you are unable to respond. In the latter instance, it may be necessary for you to change therapists. Do not hesitate to tell your therapist how you feel about him and to mention any complaints you may have. He will help you analyze whether your feelings are rational or irrational.

85. *Pt. Is it advisable to talk things over with people other than my therapist?*

Th. It is generally not wise to confide your thoughts to other people because it may prevent you from mentioning important things to your therapist.

86. *Pt. Is it all right to talk about what happens in my treatment to other people?*

Th. No, this is not advisable, since an outside confidant may hurt the therapeutic work. You should consider the therapeutic relationship a completely private situation, in which confidences will not be betrayed.

87. *Pt. Doctor, do you really believe I can be helped?* [To tell the patient that he can be helped without doubt is false reassurance. The therapist may reply in the following way.]

Th. The desire to be helped is nine-tenths of the battle. If you really want help, you will probably be able to be helped. [This makes his active participation a condition to his being helped.]

88. *Pt. What do you think it is that has made me sick?* [To speculate on the cause of his problem, or to elucidate on the dynamics prematurely is therapeutically bad. One way of handling this question is illustrated in the following response.]

Th. There are always reasons why you feel upset. Those reasons may not be clear to you because you are living too close to your troubles. We'll discuss your ideas, and particularly your feelings, and in not too long a time we should discover what is behind your difficulty. [The cooperative nature of the exploratory process is stressed here.]

89. *Pt. In psychotherapy how can you get well by mere conversations?* [Since the patient has already talked to many people without being helped, he naturally wonders about the rationale of interviewing.]

Th. In discussing your reactions, your ideas, and your feelings, you will be able to understand what is happening to you, and this understanding will permit you to take definite steps to correct your difficulties. [The factor of insight and the need for activity of the patient are emphasized.]

90. *Pt. What are you going to do to help me, if all I do is talk about myself?* [The patient is naturally puzzled by the role of the therapist.]

Th. I shall, of course, help you with your difficulty by acting as your third eye, or third ear. Since you are living so close to your problem, you may not be able to see the basic difficulty. I can be of help because I can be more objective and more realistic about what is happening to you. [The role of the therapist is defined here as that of being a partner in the treatment endeavor.]

91. *Pt. Are you sure you can help me?* [expressed at the beginning of the initial interview]

Th. I do not know yet if I can help you. I will know better after you tell me about your problem, and after I examine and study your difficulty. Then I'll be able to tell you whether I believe I can help you or not.

92. *Pt. Are you sure I can be cured?* [expressed at the end of the initial interview]

Th. It is hard for me to answer that. Much depends on how much you want to be cured. If you really have the desire to get well, there is no reason why you can't make good progress. Many persons with problems worse than yours have got well. Your progress will depend also on how well we work together as a team. I believe it is definitely worth a trial.

93. *Pt. Won't I lose my independence and get dependent on you?*

Th. One of the aims of treatment is to expand your independence and make you less dependent.

94. *Pt. Won't I find out terrible and loathsome things about myself?*

Th. The fear of finding out contemptible things about oneself is frightening to most people. When we explore your difficulty, you may be surprised to find that things are not so horrible as you imagine. Indeed, you may discover that your guilt feelings are a primary problem.

95. *Pt. How well is a person after he gets psychotherapy?*

Th. If treatment is successful, the person should be relatively free from symptoms and healthier and happier than he has ever been before.

96. *Pt. Why shouldn't treatment always be successful?*

Th. Success depends on many factors, including how much the person wants to get well. If a person really desires health, he will be willing to endure the time and effort required to get well.

97. *Pt. Is it possible to rebuild an undeveloped personality through psychotherapy?*

Th. In reconstructive psychotherapy a prominent goal is resolving blocks to personality development so that the individual may proceed to emotional maturity.

98. *Pt. If a person is cured of his symptoms and is made happier by psychotherapy, does this mean he will never again be nervous?*

Th. No, neurotic problems may develop later, but he will be better able to cope with them and even to solve them without further professional help.

99. *Pt. What happens to the information about me?*

Th. In scientific work, records are necessary, since they permit of a more thorough dealing with one's problems. It is understandable that you might be concerned about what happens to the information about you, because much or all of this information is highly personal. Case records are confidential. *No outsider, not even your closest relative or family physician, is permitted to see your file without your written permission.*

100. *Pt. How can I help to cooperate with the treatment plan?*

Th. The general practitioner has his medications; the surgeon works with his instruments; the heart specialist has his x-rays and delicate recording apparatus. But for the most part, the therapist has only one aid besides his knowledge—YOU. Your cooperation and trust in him are essential. You must feel free to take up with your therapist anything about the treatment process which disturbs you or puzzles you in any way. By doing this you have the best chance of shortening your treatment and of insuring its fullest success.

31

Establishing a Working Relationship

ONE GREAT DISAPPOINTMENT TO THE BEGINNING PSYCHOTHERAPIST is that painstaking and elaborate exploration of a patient's problem, and a most thorough investigation of the underlying dynamics, may sometimes fail to influence the emotional ailment in the least. Even though he seemingly has insight into his illness, and into the underlying conflicts and mechanisms of defense, the patient continues to suffer symptomatically, and there is no abatement in the distorted way he relates to people. The therapist, as a consequence, may become frustrated, and perhaps dismiss the patient from treatment on the basis of his "unanalyzability," or "too severe resistance," or "negative therapeutic reactions," or "latent schizoid tendency."

When we investigate the causes of such treatment failures, we often find that the patient has been unable to absorb, to integrate or to utilize insight due to anxiety. This has prevented the ego from evolving more effective ways of adjusting the person to his inner conflicts and to external demands. Further investigation usually shows that what is basically lacking in the therapeutic situation, and what probably has been missing from the inception of therapy, is the proper kind of working relationship between the patient and the therapist. This relationship is a unique interpersonal experience in which the patient feels a quality of warmth, trust, acceptance and understanding such as he has never before encountered with any human being.

A neurosis imposes on the individual distortions in his sense of values that undermine his security, depreciate his self-esteem, and make the average pursuits of living vapid and meaningless. Before any significant change can occur in the system of neurotic balances and counterbalances that has been erected, it is necessary to win the patient over to a willingness to experiment with a new way of life. The most expedient way of creating this incentive for change is through the instrumentality of rapport with the therapist.

The cultivation of the proper working relationship between patient and therapist is indeed the primary objective of the first treatment phase. For, without a working relationship, the patient will not resolve basic resistance to the meaningful exploration of his problem.

For purposes of illustration, we may introduce an example from the field of salesmanship. In selling a product, the salesman is confronted with the universal phenomenon of sales resistance. Experience has taught him that any attempt to force his product on the customer before this resistance is overcome will be futile. He has learned that the best way of resolving sales resistance is to sell *himself* to the prospect. Once the prospect has developed confidence in the acumen and integrity of the salesman, he is more prone to accept any statements the latter makes about the advantages of the product.

In therapy, the therapist is a kind of salesman who is trying to sell the patient a product in the form of a new way of life. The sales resistance of the patient is his desire to maintain the status quo. The therapist must persuade the patient to accept the commodity of health in the face of his resistance. To do this the therapist must first win the patient's trust, confidence and liking, by establishing a working relationship. The relationship will enable the patient to overcome his resistance and to examine his conflicts and their attendant anxieties. It will eventually help the patient to buttress up his shattered sense of mastery; to rid himself of suppressed and repressed destructive feelings and attitudes; to achieve a more adaptive relatedness with others, shorn of misconceptions, facades, and fears; and to acquire a more wholesome feeling about himself and his past experiences.

Until a working relationship is constituted, the patient will be unable to handle the anxieties associated with unconscious conflict, to investigate their genetic origins, to resolve repression and other archaic defenses against anxiety, to challenge the spurious protective and pleasure values of his neurosis, and to evolve more constructive modes of personal adjustment.

VARYING NEEDS OF THE PATIENT

Militating against the establishing of a working relationship is the fact that the patient always seeks to utilize therapy in a variety of ways, some of which are inimical to good rapport. Thus he may desire to make himself dependent on the therapist in order to receive guidance, reassurance and other bounties. He may search for unqualified sympathy and acceptance. He may seek factual understanding and objectivity to help him evaluate his thinking and behavior. He may want to express feelings that tear at him from within, and to act-out impulses, demands and other strivings he customarily holds in check. Finally, he may yearn for a cooperative give-and-take relationship without domineering or being domineered. Not only must the therapist be equipped, by virtue of his own personality make-up, to accept the patient's varied strivings, but he must be able to react to them in a therapeutic manner. He must provide the patient with an experience that will act as a prototype of a different kind of human relationship—one that inspires new and constructive patterns toward people. To do this, the therapist must first understand the constituents of each of the patient's needs.

1. The Need to Be Dependent

Because the emotionally ill person usually feels helpless, he wants a kindly agency to relieve his distress, to give him support and guidance, and to nurture him back to health. These regressive needs, found in all patients, are most extreme in those who are severely sick. It is impossible to escape the patient's dependency need. While the therapist may not wish to perpetuate the infantilism of the patient by playing the part of a "giving" authority, except perhaps in sup-portive therapy, this may temporarily have to be accepted without resentment, fear, detachment or aggression. Astuteness will be required in diagnosing how much active help the patient needs, grading the support given to the severity of the sickness, and imposing on the patient as much responsibility as can be tolerated. The therapist must know when to resist dependency demands and how to convince the patient that their fulfillment may interfere with his capacities to develop assertiveness, strength and independence.

2. The Need for Unqualified Understanding, Acceptance and Condonation

Such yearnings are part of the social nature of man. They may be especially urgent in the emotionally sick individual who constantly anticipates rejection and condemnation. In response to the patient's need for understanding and ac-ceptance, it is essential that the therapist be capable of empathizing with the patient, of giving him warmth and approval no matter how destructive and disturbed he may be. At the same time, the therapist must avoid over-protecting the patient and smothering him with cloying kindness which will tend to rob him of the ability to do things for himself. Any personality characteristics in the therapist, like detachment or hostility, that interfere with this empathic ability and with the capacity to feel and to communicate warmth will constitute insurmountable handicaps to the establishing of a relationship.

3. The Need to Relieve Himself of Painful Feelings and Ideas

The desire to unburden himself of guilt, fear and anxiety will often be overwhelming. Ventilation of suppressed and repressed feelings, attitudes and past experiences is usually accompanied by immediate but temporary relief. The therapist must be able to endure cathartic outbursts of painful emotion that are delivered by the patient, displaying a non-judgmental, objective attitude, neither condemning nor sanctioning the behavior of the patient. Since some of the material divulged may be of an unmoral or antisocial character, the therapist must be able to handle personal untoward feelings that are inspired by such de-structive and perverse recitations, avoiding rebuke and other culturally accepted responses to the material.

4. The Need for Factual Understanding

The patient always has a need for an understanding of what is happening to him in order to neutralize fears of the unknown. This requires objectivity on the part of the therapist. The ability of the therapist to remain objective helps to inculcate in the patient a factual appreciation of his problem in relation to inner conflict and external reality. Essential is a good understanding in the therapist of human dynamics, of interviewing techniques, of methods of bring-ing to the awareness of the individual the meaning of his behavior, and of how to help him work through resistance to insight and to the translation of insight into action. This knowledge must be coupled in the therapist with intelligent self-awareness in order to avoid contaminating the patient with personal prejudices, and to allow him to develop his own sense of values.

5. The Need for a Transference Relationship

All patients seek media in which they can project and act-out tendencies and feelings that relate to actual or idealized parental personages. The projection of attitudes and feelings that originate in past relationships (transference) requires for its appropriate handling an understanding of this phenomenon by the therapist, as well as the ability to perceive and to manage manifestations of counter-transference. The therapist must be able to survive the intense dependency needs, sexual demands, hostilities and manifold misinterpretations that will be expressed by the patient in the course of therapy. The therapist's capacity to display warmth and to remain tolerant and objective in the face of transference must be coordinated with skill in minimizing the intensity of transference and of working it through toward the objective of insight.

6. The Need for a Cooperative Human Relationship

Irrespective of how distorted his previous relationships with people have been, the individual earnestly desires a wholesome relationship bereft of neurotic encumbrances. The effective management of the myriad demands of the patient will help to fulfill his basic need for a cooperative human relationship.

MULTIPLE ROLES OF THE THERAPIST

The therapist may show different responses to patients with varied personality constellations. For instance, he may be able to express warmth and to remain remarkably objective toward submissive and dependent persons, while being totally unable to express therapeutically constructive feelings when in contact with domineering or hostile patients. Understandably, the more thoroughly the therapist has worked through his own personal problems, and the greater awareness he has of his relationship difficulties, the more flexible he will be in responding to a variety of patients. A therapist who has little awareness of his interpersonal difficulties will find his therapeutic effectiveness circumscribed to those patients with whom he can feel most comfortable.

In order to express his diverse needs, the patient usually strives to force the therapist to fulfill multiple roles; namely, the following:

1. The Therapist as a Helping Authority

This is the traditional patient-doctor relationship. As an expert, the therapist is credited with knowledge and skills that can help the patient out of his dilemma. The therapist succeeds or fails in this role in accordance with how the patient interprets the therapist's activity.

2. The Therapist as an Idealized Parental Image

The patient seeks an idealized parental figure who will grant him bounties without stint. The character of this giving image varies with the personal biases of the patient, and ranges from omniscience and omnipotence to mere kindliness and acceptance. Often there is combined in the fantasy image a fusion of ideal paternal and maternal qualities. Accordingly, the patient may desire paternal firmness, strength, wisdom and power; as well as maternal lovingness, support and protection. The intensity of such attitudes, as well as their specific content, will be determined by the kinds of early frustrations experienced by the patient. These attitudes will be enhanced if the therapist seems to be the sort of individual who fits into the role the patient designs for him. It will be minimized by the therapist's refusal or inability to play this role.

3. The Therapist as an Actual Parental Representative

On the basis of previous experience, the patient may project into the therapeutic situation expectations that he will be treated by the therapist as he had previously been treated by his parents. He will then adopt defenses against the therapist in accordance with these expectations and fears. Under certain circumstances, he will even act-out with the therapist a rather extensive series of situations representative of those he already had experienced as a child. Such "transference" attitudes will be reinforced by a passive attitude on the part of the therapist, or by the therapist's actually playing the kind of role with the patient that parallels the role of the parent. Transference will also be expedited by the utilization of certain techniques; such as, the couch position, concentration on dreams, the use of free association, frequent visits, and a focusing on the past history and on conditionings in childhood. It will be minimized by the therapist's increased activity with the patient, the playing of a role opposite to that anticipated by the patient, infrequent visits, the use of the face-to-face position, the avoidance of dreams, fantasies and free association, and a focusing on the current life situation and present relationships.

4. The Therapist as a Representative of Other Important Past Personages

The therapist may be employed as an object onto whom transference attitudes may be projected related to other important individuals besides the parents. The therapist may, for instance, be identified with a sibling, an important relative, a teacher, or friend who has played a signal part in the early life of the patient. The therapist's manner, behavior, and physical appearance may expedite the display of such attitudes.

5. The Therapist as a Cooperative Partner

Here the therapist is regarded as an individual with whom the patient is able to establish a friendly, unambivalent relationship. The patient probably always desperately seeks such a relationship, but on the basis of previous conditionings, he may feel that it cannot possibly come to fruition. An objective attitude on the part of the therapist sponsors this kind of relationship.

A blend of several of the above attitudes toward the therapist is usually present at the beginning of treatment. Conflict is inevitable by virtue of the mutual contradictory nature of such disparate attitudes. Which attitudes will prevail will depend on how intense they are in the patient, and on the activity of the therapist. It is important that the therapist be equipped by training and ditionings, he may feel that it cannot possibly come to fruition. An objective that a cooperative working relationship may eventually develop.

RESISTANCES TO A WORKING RELATIONSHIP

The length of time required to establish a working relationship will depend upon the skill of the therapist, and on the intensity of resistance exhibited by the patient. Among common resistances are defects in motivation and misconceptions about psychotherapy. Ways of handling such obstacles have been suggested in chapter 28, Dealing with Inadequate Motivation, and chapter 30, Answering Questions Patients Ask About Therapy. Even more important as a source of resistance are character problems that are parcels of the patient's habitually disturbed attitudes toward people.

Perhaps the most obstinate of these characterologic resistances is a clinging, dependent attitude toward the therapist, who is overvalued as the embodiment of all that is good and strong and noble in the universe. This kind of striving is rooted in an intense feeling of helplessness, escape from which is sought in an alliance with a being who can in some magical way lead the person into paths of health, glory and accomplishment. Building this being into a power figure who can satisfy one's magical expectations, and allying oneself with the object of one's creation, gives one a spurious sense of security and of heightened self-esteem.

The patient must be weaned from his attitude toward the therapist as an omniscient personage who can conjure up a fanciful Nirvana in which all needs are gratified. It is important to bring him to the conviction that he has abilities and strengths of his own.

While recognizing and accepting his dependency need, and refraining from insisting on a completely mature relationship, the therapist may give the patient a rational reason for refusing to take the bulk of responsibility and to make decisions for the patient. The therapist, in exhibiting an understanding of the patient's need, may explain that supplying his demands will inhibit his self-growth and that it is out of respect for the patient's growth potentials that the therapist is not more active. Such an explanation may help resolve some of the hostility at what the patient otherwise might consider negligence and rejection.

Another unfavorable form of relationship is fear of the therapist as a potentially destructive or malevolent being who threatens to injure or to engulf the patient. Here the patient retreats whenever he feels that he is getting too close. A "testing period" precedes a final acceptance of the therapist as one who bears only good will toward him. During this period he will be torn between his desire to establish a gratifying relationship and an overpowering fear of injury. The outward manifestation of this struggle may be hostility to the therapist. Some patients may even attempt to provoke the therapist and to incite him into acts of aggression to prove to themselves that all human beings are alike and are not to be trusted. This "testing period" will be especially prolonged in patients with immature personality structures, and it may be many months before the therapist is accepted as a friend.

Because of his hostility, fear and guilt, the patient may automatically expect the therapist to condemn, prohibit or punish him for his past behavior as well as for his present attitudes and impulses. He may, therefore, display fear, distrust or rage toward the therapist, as well as defenses against these emotions. When fragmentary revelations of his inner life fail to bring forth the expected punishment or condemnation, the patient may feel contempt for the therapist for failing to respond as a strong authority should respond, and he may evidence a desire for a more competent, more punitive therapist.

The patient will usually anticipate criticism from the therapist as merciless as that which he imposes on himself. Furthermore, while he has managed to conceal from people the elements about himself that he considers vicious or contemptible, it is difficult to do this with the therapist. He will, therefore, constantly anticipate attack or condemnation, and he will be non-plussed when attack is not forthcoming. He may await the evil day when the expected blow will fall; he may even become resentful at the delay of what he considers inevitable. As he recognizes that he can speak his mind, and that the therapist considers his revelations as neither good nor bad, he may begin to reevaluate his concept of the therapist as an arbitrary authority. A feeling of warmth emerges which is mingled with confidence.

Other strivings in the patient that interfere with a good working relationship are intense sexual feelings, submissiveness, masochistic impulses, perfectionism, fear of closeness, compulsive ambition, distrust and detachment. The handling of a patient's detachment is of particular importance due to its prevalence as a defensive character pattern. With perseverance and tolerance detached individuals may eventually be helped to enter a working relationship.

For instance, a patient with a personality disorder of detachment comes to treatment because of depression, tension and feelings of lonesomeness and isolation. He is aware of the fact that close relationships fill him with a sense of foreboding, and that soon after a relationship has started he becomes anxious and wants to run away. In therapy, as he develops confidence in the therapist, the same kind of anxiety and terror emerges, and the patient is seized with an impulse to stop treatment. His respect for the therapist, however, and his incentive to get well, halt the escape. Manifesting warmth, acceptance and understanding, the therapist interprets what is happening. From a dream in which he crosses a bridge and becomes the target of sharp-shooting snipers, the patient learns of his fears of attack in a confining relationship. He recognizes that this fear has been with him for years—as far back as he can remember—and has created the impulse to escape from entangling alliances, and even from the threat of coming close to a person. This knowledge enables him to reevaluate his feelings in relationship to the new kind of authority he has perceived in the therapist, to test his anachronistic fears of hurt against his knowledge that the therapist does not desire to injure him. He then veers in his struggle between his old conviction and his new. Temptation to break away from treatment is intense; but the therapist forestalls escape by pertinent interpretations. Eventually, perhaps for the first time, the patient is capable of accepting a person, the therapist, as a friend rather than a foe. He takes a bold step toward a working relationship.

In helping a patient master his fears of a working relationship, the therapist must allow him to choose his own pace. He must respect the patient's hesitation and other defensive mechanisms issuing from the patient's terror that he will discover the same destructive potentialities in the therapist that he has found in other human beings. The realization that he is dealing with a different type of authority permits him to abandon compromising facades that have up to this time served unsatisfactorily to keep anxiety in check.

BUILDING THE RELATIONSHIP

Skill as a therapist is measured to a considerable degree by the ability to establish relationships with patients that will be therapeutically meaningful to them. While no therapist is capable of establishing rapport with all people, he should, if he has the proper training and personality equipment, be able to relate to the majority of persons who come to him for help.

Knowledge of interviewing techniques will foster confidence in the therapist and expedite a working relationship. Thus, by appropriate facial expressions, gestures, and sub-vocal utterances, the therapist may convey an attentive and accepting manner. By asking pointed questions, restating, summarizing and other techniques, he may demonstrate to the patient that he is interested and observant. By reflecting feelings and making cautious interpretations geared to the level of the patient's current capacities for understanding, the therapist may exhibit an astuteness and perceptiveness in knowing what is going on in peripheral areas of the patient's awareness.

Specific personality problems of the therapist may, however, inhibit the establishing of a relationship. For instance, an inability to tolerate hostility may make it difficult for the therapist to develop rapport with a patient who displays hostile outbursts. Or personal sexual problems may cause the therapist to respond with anxiety when the patient tells of sexual fears or impulses with which he is preoccupied. The therapist may then fail to show the necessary warmth, objectivity, and empathy.

From time to time, the therapist may experience emotions toward the patient which, if unchecked, may hurt the relationship. Hostility, boredom, apathy, uneasiness, fear or sexual interest may be provoked by the patient's behavior or inspired by counter-transference. Should such emotions emerge, self-searching will be indicated. The following self-directed questions are important:

(1) Is the patient doing anything that causes these emotions? (2) Does the patient resemble or remind the therapist of anyone the therapist knows or has known in the past? (3) What does the therapist really feel about a person like the patient? (4) Does the therapist anticipate that the patient will do anything disturbing or upsetting while in therapy?

Arriving at answers to these questions requires a great deal of self-exploration in an attempt to understand any projections that are operative. For example, a patient talks about his problems of intolerance with people. As the patient relates several episodes illustrating his intolerance, the therapist becomes aware of a personal feeling of boredom and of not wanting to pay attention to what the patient is saying. He asks himself why such attitudes exist toward the patient and he suddenly realizes that he considers the patient an extremely hostile person. He recognizes then that he fears a demonstration by the patient of hostility toward him. Knowing of his own problem in handling hostility, the therapist realizes that his boredom is a defensive means of avoiding closer contact with the patient and thus of circumventing any expressed hostility. Challenging the reality of his fear, he finds that he is able to overcome the response of boredom, and he becomes attentive to the productions of the patient. Another therapist may, in feeling irritable with a patient, examine this emotion. In so doing he realizes that he has had similar feelings of irritability with a brother with whom he was competitive and whom the patient resembles slightly. This insight results in a dissipation of the emotion of irritability. A third therapist may observe that he feels resentful during a session. Thereupon he notices that the patient is talking about material that is stirring up anxiety within him. Under these circumstances, he may be able to handle his anxiety directly and thus to overcome his resentment.

Where the therapist is unable to control disturbed emotions and attitudes by processes of self-observation, he should, in fairness to the patient, refer him to another therapist.

There are a number of things the therapist can do to sponsor a working relationship. Among these are communicating to the patient an understanding of his problem, and expressing toward him unqualified tolerance, empathy and objectivity.

1. Communicating an Understanding of the Problem

Every patient wants his therapist to be intelligent, sagacious and perceptive. It is generally not difficult to convince the patient of the therapist's competence by such simple techniques as reflecting unverbalized feelings and attitudes, putting into words the unexpressed worries and concerns of the patient; and by displaying sensitivity to the patient's moods and conflicts. While the therapist need not present himself as infallible, he must try to avoid expressions of confusion, such as acting bewildered and forgetting important items of information about the patient. Since he is merely mortal, the therapist is bound to make mistakes sometimes, but these are not fatal if they do not occur too frequently, and if he has a fairly good relationship with the patient.

An excellent way of demonstrating an understanding of the patient's turmoil is available to the psychoanalytically trained therapist, through dream interpretation. Dreams during the first phase of therapy are never interpreted deeply. Since dreams are condensations of a variety of items, including early traumatic experiences, basic conflicts, habitual mechanisms of defense, and present characterologic strivings, it is usually easy to select from the dream the kind of content that will satisfy the goals of a particular phase of therapy. In the first phase of treatment important goals relate to a recognition of attitudes and impulses that act as resistance to a working relationship. For instance, a patient presents a dream in which he is traveling in a subway, sitting next to a man who is busily engaged in reading a newspaper. The patient tries to attract the man's attention, but all of his efforts are rebuffed. He finally gets up and leaves the train feeling humiliated.

In examining the dream, we observe the patient attempting to make contact with a man who, detached and disinterested, virtually rebuffs the patient. The dream may reflect a general fear in the patient of being rebuffed by people. We may speculate further that the patient is expressing in the dream a feeling that he is being rebuffed by the therapist. Riding on the subway would then indicate the therapeutic situation. These formulations are, naturally, not communicated to the patient. The method by which they are brought to his attention is illustrated in the fragment of the actual interview that follows:

Th. What thoughts come to your mind as you think about the dream?

Pt. Why nothing. I don't particularly like riding on the subway, but that's nothing. It's the quickest way of getting any place.

Th. Mm hmm.

Pt. And when you're in a hurry it gets you there. (*pause*)

Th. Any other thoughts about a subway?

Pt. No.

Th. Now how about your feelings in the dream; what were your feelings?

Pt. I was anxious to talk with him, make friends, you see, but he was one of these types of people who was busy with his own things.

Th. What type?

Pt. Well, I should say studious type, not interested in me.

Th. Now what about this man; did he resemble anybody you know or knew?

Pt. Yes, he was like an uncle of mine. He is not too much older than I am. When I was a kid he used to bring me things. I called him my second father.

Th. Mm hmm.

Pt. And when I was in boarding school, one of my roommates reminds me of him. That was the one I had that homosexual experience with I told you about.

Th. Was there any sexual feeling in the dream?

Pt. No, just that I wanted to know this person better.

Th. And when he didn't respond, how did this make you feel?

Pt. Terrible. I wanted to get out of the train.

Th. Angry?

Pt. No, just irritated.

Th. Now it's possible that when a person isn't responsive enough and giving enough, this may make you want to get out of the situation.

Pt. Yes.

Th. And that might also apply to me. [*a tentative probing for transference*]

Pt. Why . . . (*pause*) why . . . I don't think I should feel that way.

Th. After all, there is no reason why you shouldn't. But have you felt this way about me?

Pt. As you said, I shouldn't expect you to do everything for me.

Th. But you may resent the fact that I don't take over more responsibility.

Pt. I know I shouldn't feel that way.

Th. But you *might* feel that way. (*pause*)

Pt. (*laughs*) Well I do . . . sometimes.

Th. And even want to leave treatment.

Pt. (*laughs*) I did feel that I wanted to quit.

Th. Like you wanted to get out of the subway train in the dream.

Pt. (*laughs*) Yes, you mean you could be the man on the subway? Come to think of it, I do think it's you.

Th. Do you want to stop therapy?

Pt. Of course not.

Th. Do you feel that I don't want to relate to you, that I don't pay attention to you, or like you?

Pt. Well, as you say, I must think that, but it isn't true.

After several weeks, the patient exhibited evidences of greater security in the relationship. This was accompanied by a dream in which the patient saw himself trying to use a pencil that had no lead. A man nearby offered him a new pencil which he accepted. The patient associated having "no lead in the pencil" to his vitiated masculinity. The man nearby was the therapist who was offering him new masculinity.

2. Communicating Interest

Showing interest in the patient as a person rather than as a laboratory of pathologic phenomena is an important way of helping the relationship. By paying close attention to what the patient is saying about his personal life, ambitions, likes, dislikes and goals, the therapist may indicate non-verbally that he considers the patient a significant individual. Remembering and repeating to the patient details that he has mentioned about himself in previous sessions impresses the patient with the genuineness of the therapist's interest. Sometimes the greater part of a session may profitably be spent talking about the patient's work, hobbies, or other random subjects, not for the purpose of eliciting information, but to show the patient that the therapist wishes to know him better. Making necessary financial and time allowances for the patient, and a demonstrated willingness to do what one can for the patient, within the bounds of therapeutic propriety, are other manifestations of interest.

Damaging to the relationship are evidences of disinterest; such as forgetfulness about important details the patient has previously mentioned, reading of one's mail during a session, telephoning in the patient's presence, and other shifts of attention.

The therapist's attitudes toward the patient will, of course, not be the same from day to day. On some occasions he will feel happy, inspired and active; he will then be responsive, alert and sensitive to what is going on in therapy. At other times, he will feel slightly depressed, dull and inactive; he will find his mind wandering, and he will be somewhat insensitive to nuances in the therapeutic situation. Sometimes he will be pleased with the patient. Occasionally he may be irritated with him, particularly when the patient is hostile, aggressive or accusatory. These ups and downs need not interefere with the setting up of a working relationship, provided that the therapist likes the patient and manages to communicate adequate interest in him.

3. Communicating Tolerance and Acceptance

The average patient comes to therapy at the mercy of a medley of moods and attitudes. He feels helpless in the grip of symptoms he is unable to control. He tries hard, more or less unsuccessfully, to cover up his turmoil. He has arrogant notions about himself and his potentialities which alternate with self-devaluating and contemptuous attitudes. He believes that coming to psychotherapy is an insignia of defeat, yet he is hopeful that the therapist will magically wipe out his trouble. His defenses are mobilized against accepting help by minimizing his condition, by denying that he is ill, by a diffuse and undifferentiated resentment or one that is specifically directed against the therapist, by plaintive self-abasement and masochistic submissiveness.

No matter how mature the patient may seem on the surface, he will always project into therapy some childish demands, needs and misinterpretations. In casual relationships he may have these under control, and he may be able to disguise them with various blinds. But the therapeutic relationship will activate suppressed and repressed emotional foci. His usual stratagems will be revealed for what they are. It is for these reasons that the utmost permissiveness and understanding must prevail in therapy, with absolute avoidance of indignation and moralistic judgment. If the therapist is able to treat the patient as an adult in spite of his immature feelings, respecting his need to display childish emotions and strivings, and accepting them temporarily as inevitable, the patient will best be helped to a more mature expression of feeling.

In dealing with the ambivalent emotions of the patient, the therapist must express as complete tolerance and acceptance as possible, neither condemning nor condoning the patient for his drives and desires, but accepting his right to experience them in their current form. Irrespective of how provocative the patient may act, it is essential that the therapist control his personal feelings. Some patients will subject the therapist to a barrage of hostility, accusations and demands. To respond with counter-hostility may prove fatal to the establishing of a relationship. The therapist must also shun criticizing the patient for his inability to verbalize or to think clearly about himself. He must evade considering the patient's problems as "faults."

Other activities that sponsor convictions in the patient of the therapist's tolerant, non-punitive, non-judgmental attitudes are attentiveness to everything the patient says, a calm and accepting facial expression, absence of irritability and emotional outbursts, and lack of expressed or implied condemnation or reproach. The continuing or stopping of therapy should be regarded as a choice of the patient, and he should be encouraged in the point of view that his coming for treatment is predicated solely on his conviction that he is getting something positive out of his experience. Should he actually decide to discontinue treatment, this must be handled by the therapist as a manifestation of resistance.

Respect for the patient's defenses and resistances is another way of expressing tolerance. The therapist may be tempted to charge the patient's resistance to change to displays of ignorance or stubbornness. But if he realizes that the patient is protecting himself against a flood of anxiety, he may be able to display greater indulgence. He must content himself at the start of therapy with moving at as slow or as rapid a pace as the patient may dictate.

4. Communicating Objectivity

Objectivity is insured by a tolerant, non-punitive manner in the face of any attitudes, demands or ideas expressed by the patient. A sense of humor, the ability to take criticism, and an unflagging respect for the patient are other traits that help establish the therapist's objectivity. In handling his personal feelings, the therapist should keep in mind the fact that the attitudes of the patient are not necessarily permanent ones.

Acknowledging the patient's right to his own opinions, even though they may be faulty, helps to convince the patient he is not dealing with a despot. Other ways of demonstrating one's objectivity are by abstaining from imposing on the patient one's personal opinions, philosophies, judgments and values; and by observing the patient's right to self-determination, once he has become cognizant of the conflicts within himself. At all costs the therapist should avoid situations which make the patient feel that he must yield to the bias of a superior authority.

5. Communicating Empathy

All people have the craving to be liked. Neurotic problems make them feel unloved and incapable of evoking sympathetic responses from others. Yet they long to be appreciated in spite of their convictions of having no worth. By communicating empathy, the therapist attempts to convey to the patient a feeling that his turmoil is understood.

Among the measures that may be employed toward this end are verbalizing for the patient how upset he must feel; elaborating on some of the obvious conscious conflicts that plague the patient explaining why these may be disturbing; recognizing the patient's feelings and seeing things from his point of view; being frank and sincere with the patient, and accepting him in spite of any "bad" qualities he reveals about himself; and expressing warmth, not in words, but by gestures, facial expressions and other types of non-verbal behavior. Nothing is more damaging to the relationship than displaying a stilted, detached and cold attitude toward the patient. Sometimes such an attitude is practiced by certain therapists in an effort to maintain anonymity. Usually this kind of behavior is interpreted by the patient as evidence of the therapist's unfeelingness toward him.

The therapist must be able to extend support and reassurance to the patient when these are needed. Such measures are, of course, graded to the degree of shattering of the patient's adaptive powers, and are not to be confused with domination or over-protection. A strong deterrent to the giving of necessary support is a fear in the therapist of making the patient dependent on him. At the inception of therapy, all patients are dependent to a greater or lesser degree, irrespective of the activity of the therapist. The dependency is not avoided by a detached attitude, nor does it necessarily become hypertrophied by a display of interest or warmth.

Empathy must also be demonstrated when the patient manifests hostility. One way of handling undifferentiated hostile feelings is by accepting them as inevitable. A casual explanation such as the following may be very reassuring to the patient: "People who suffer a great deal may become resentful toward the world and toward themselves. You may be angry at the fact that you are suffering, or that you need help, or that you have to come to see me. You may be angry at me for various reasons. And this is to be expected." Further responses will be determined by the reactions of the patient to this explanation.

Once empathy is communicated to the patient, he may experience considerable relief, or there may be an abatement of his symptoms. This may be due to a certain measure of psychologic appeasement, or to a feeling in the patient that he no longer is alone and helpless. It may be due to a concomitant emotional unburdening, or because of the reassurance gained through contact with the therapist. This improvement, sometimes called a "transference cure," is usually temporary, lasting so long as the relationship with the therapist yields important satisfactions. The improvement may continue indefinitely if coincidentally there is an amelioration of the stress-producing circumstance, or if the patient has been able to master the stress situation in some way. This may be the sole goal in supportive therapy. In reeducative and reconstructive therapies, however, any relief achieved by this means is considered inadequate unless it is accompanied by insight into the provocative conflicts.

SUNDRY "RULES" FOR BUILDING OF THE RELATIONSHIP

It is not necessary to employ special tricks to establish a good working relationship. This will be readily forthcoming if the therapist has the proper training and personality equipment. However, there are a number of rules that may help build a relationship more rapidly. These are illustrated in the following group of "unsuitable" and "suitable" responses to sundry questions asked by patients.

1. *Avoid exclamations of surprise.*
    Pt. I never go out on a date without wanting to scream.
    Unsuitable responses.
        Th. Well, for heaven's sake!
        Th. That's awful!
        Th. Of all things to happen!
    Suitable responses.
        Th. I wonder why?
        Th. Scream?
        Th. There must be a reason for this.

2. *Avoid expressions of over-concern.*
    Pt. I often feel as if I'm going to die.
    Unsuitable responses.
        Th. Well, we'll have to do something about that right away.
        Th. Why, you poor thing!
        Th. Goodness, that's a horrible thing to go through.
    Suitable responses.
        Th. That must be upsetting to you.
        Th. Do you have any idea why?
        Th. What brings on this feeling most commonly?

3. *Avoid moralistic judgments.*
    Pt. I get an uncontrollable impulse to steal.
    Unsuitable responses.
        Th. This can get you into a lot of trouble.
        Th. You're going to have to put a stop to that.
        Th. That's bad.
    Suitable responses.
        Th. Do you have any idea of what's behind this impulse?
        Th. How far back does this impulse go?
        Th. How does that make you feel?

4. *Avoid being punitive under all circumstances.*
    Pt. I don't think you are helping me at all.
    Unsuitable responses.
        Th. Maybe we ought to stop therapy.
        Th. That's because you aren't cooperating.
        Th. If you don't do better, I'll have to stop seeing you.
    Suitable responses.
        Th. Let's talk about that; what do you think is happening?
        Th. Perhaps you feel I can't help you.
        Th. Is there anything I am doing or fail to do that upsets you?

5. *Avoid criticizing the patient.*
    Pt. I just refuse to bathe and get my hair fixed.
    Unsuitable responses.
        Th. Are you aware of how unkempt you look?

Th. You just don't give a darn about yourself, do you?

Th. That's like cutting off your nose to spite your face.

Suitable responses.

Th. There must be a reason why.

Th. Do you have any ideas about that?

Th. How does that make you feel?

6. *Avoid making false promises.*

Pt. Do you think I'll ever be normal?

Unsuitable responses.

Th. Oh, sure, there's no question about that.

Th. In a short while you're going to see a difference.

Th. I have great hopes for you.

Suitable responses.

Th. A good deal will depend on how well we work together.

Th. You seem to have some doubts about that.

Th. Let's talk about what you mean by normal.

7. *Avoid personal references or boasting.*

Pt. My six year old child is balking at going to school. It annoys me.

Unsuitable responses.

Th. I know exactly how you feel; I went through that myself with my youngster.

Th. I'd feel exactly the way you do under the circumstances.

Th. I'm glad you bring that up because I'm kind of an expert on managing problems of this kind.

Suitable responses.

Th. Annoys you?

Th. Do you have any idea why your child is balking?

Th. It must be upsetting to you.

8. *Avoid threatening the patient.*

Pt. I don't think I can keep our next two appointments, because I want to go to a concert on these days.

Unsuitable responses.

Th. You don't seem to take your therapy seriously.

Th. If you think more of concerts than coming here, you might as well not come at all.

Th. Maybe you'd better start treatments with another therapist.

Suitable responses.

Th. I wonder why the concerts seem more important than coming here.

Th. Maybe it's more pleasurable going to the concerts than coming here.

Th. What do you feel about coming here for therapy?

9. *Avoid burdening the patient with your own difficulties.*

Pt. You look very tired today.

Unsuitable responses.

Th. Yes, I've been having plenty of trouble with sickness in my family.

Th. This sinus of mine is killing me.

Th. I just haven't been able to sleep lately.

Suitable responses.

Th. I wouldn't be surprised, since I had to stay up late last night. But that shouldn't interfere with our session.

> *Th.* I've had a touch of sinus, but it's not serious and shouldn't interfere with our session.
>
> *Th.* That comes from keeping late hours with meetings and things. But that shouldn't interfere with our session.

10. *Avoid displays of impatience.*

> *Pt.* I feel helpless and think I ought to end it all.
>
> *Unsuitable responses.*
>
> *Th.* You better "snap out of it" soon.
>
> *Th.* Well, that's a nice attitude, I must say.
>
> *Th.* Maybe we had better end treatment right now.
>
> *Suitable responses.*
>
> *Th.* I wonder what is behind this feeling.
>
> *Th.* Perhaps there's another solution for your problems.
>
> *Th.* You sound as if you think you're at the end of your rope.

11. *Avoid political or religious discussions.*

> *Pt.* Are you going to vote republican or democratic?
>
> *Unsuitable responses.*
>
> *Th.* Republican, of course; the country needs good government.
>
> *Th.* I'm a democrat and would naturally vote democratic.
>
> *Suitable responses.*
>
> *Th.* Which party do you think I will vote for?
>
> *Th.* Have you been wondering about me?
>
> *Th.* I wonder what you'd feel if I told you I was either republican or democrat. Would either make a difference to you?
>
> *Th.* I vote for whoever I think is the best person, irrespective of party, but why do you ask?

12. *Avoid arguing with the patient.*

> *Pt.* I refuse to budge an inch as far as my husband is concerned.
>
> *Unsuitable responses.*
>
> *Th.* It's unreasonable for you to act this way.
>
> *Th.* Don't you think you are acting selfishly?
>
> *Th.* How can you expect your husband to do anything for you if you don't do anything for him?
>
> *Suitable responses.*
>
> *Th.* You feel that there is no purpose in doing anything for him?
>
> *Th.* Perhaps you're afraid to give in to him?
>
> *Th.* How do you actually feel about your husband right now?

13. *Avoid ridiculing the patient.*

> *Pt.* There isn't much I can't do, once I set my mind on it.
>
> *Unsuitable responses.*
>
> *Th.* You don't think much of yourself, do you?
>
> *Th.* Maybe you exaggerate your abilities.
>
> *Th.* It sounds like you're boasting.
>
> *Suitable responses.*
>
> *Th.* That puts kind of a strain on you.
>
> *Th.* Have you set your mind on overcoming this emotional problem?
>
> *Th.* You feel pretty confident once your mind is made up.

14. *Avoid belittling the patient.*

> *Pt.* I am considered very intelligent.

Unsuitable responses.

    Th. An opinion with which you undoubtedly concur.

    Th. The troubles you've gotten into don't sound intelligent to me.

    Th. Even a moron sometimes thinks he's intelligent.

Suitable responses.

    Th. How do *you* feel about that?

    Th. That's all the more reason for working hard at your therapy.

    Th. That sounds as if *you* aren't sure of your intelligence.

15. *Avoid blaming the patient for his failures.*

    Pt. I again forgot to bring my doctor's report with me.

Unsuitable responses.

    Th. Don't you think that's irresponsible?

    Th. There you go again.

    Th. When I tell you the report is important, I mean it.

Suitable responses.

    Th. I wonder why?

    Th. Do you know why?

    Th. Perhaps you don't want to bring it.

16. *Avoid rejecting the patient.*

    Pt. I want you to like me better than any of your other patients.

Unsuitable responses.

    Th. Why should I?

    Th. I don't play favorites.

    Th. I simply don't like a person like you.

Suitable responses.

    Th. I wonder why you'd like to be preferred by me.

    Th. Perhaps you'd feel more secure if I told you I liked you best.

    Th. What *do* you think I feel about you?

17. *Avoid displays of intolerance.*

    Pt. My wife got into another auto accident last week.

Unsuitable responses.

    Th. Those women drivers.

    Th. Women are sometimes tough to live with.

    Th. The female of the species is the most deadly of the two.

Suitable responses.

    Th. How does that make you feel?

    Th. What do you think goes on?

    Th. How did you react when you got this news?

18. *Avoid dogmatic utterances.*

    Pt. I feel cold and detached in the presence of women.

Unsuitable responses.

    Th. That's because you're afraid of women.

    Th. You must want to detach yourself.

    Th. You want to destroy women and have to protect yourself.

Suitable responses.

    Th. That's interesting; why do you think you feel this way?

    Th. How far back does this go?

    Th. What feelings do you have when you are with women?

19. *Avoid premature deep interpretations.*

    Pt. I've told you what bothers me. Now what do you think is behind it all?

    Unsuitable responses.

        Th. Well, you seem to be a dependent person and want to collapse on a parent figure.

        Th. You've got an inferiority complex.

        Th. You never resolved your Oedipus complex.

    Suitable responses.

        Th. It will be necessary to find out more about the problem before I can offer a valid opinion of it.

        Th. We'll continue to discuss your attitudes, ideas and particularly your feelings, and before long we should discover what is behind your trouble.

        Th. That's for us to work on together. If I gave you the answers, it wouldn't be of help to you.

20. *Avoid a dogmatic analysis of dreams.*

    Pt. I had a dream the other day. I was sitting in the kitchen and food was being spilled on the floor by someone. When I tried to pick it up someone kicked me in the face, and then I saw a man standing with a knife ready to stab me in the back.

    Unsuitable responses.

        Th. This dream indicates fear of a homosexual attack.

        Th. You must feel orally deprived.

        Th. Your mother must have been a depriving woman.

    Suitable responses.

        Th. What does this dream seem to indicate to you?

        Th. What associations come to your mind?

        Th. How did the dream make you feel?

21. *Avoid the probing of traumatic material when there is too great resistance.*

    Pt. I just don't want to talk about sex.

    Unsuitable responses.

        Th. You'll get nowhere by avoiding this.

        Th. You must force yourself to talk about unpleasant things.

        Th. What *about* your sex life?

    Suitable responses.

        Th. It must be hard for you to talk about sex.

        Th. All right, you can talk about anything else you feel is important.

        Th. Sex is always a painful subject to talk about.

22. *Avoid flattering and praising the patient.*

    Pt. Do you like this dress?

    Unsuitable responses.

        Th. You always show an excellent taste in clothes.

        Th. I think you make a very excellent appearance.

        Th. Any man would find you attractive.

    Suitable responses.

        Th. Yes, but why do you ask?

        Th. Do *you* like it?

        Th. Perhaps you wonder what I think of you?

23. *Avoid unnecessary reassurance.*

    Pt. I think I'm the most terrible, ugly, weak, most contemptible person in the world.

    Unsuitable responses.

    Th. That's silly. I think you're very good looking and a wonderful person in many ways.

    Th. Take it from me, you are not.

    Th. You are one of the nicest people I know.

    Suitable responses.

    Th. Why do you think you feel that way?

    Th. How does it make you feel to think that of yourself?

    Th. Do others think the same way about you?

24. *Extend reassurance when really necessary.*

    Pt. I feel I am going insane.

    Unsuitable responses.

    Th. Maybe you are.

    Th. Sometimes this happens even with treatment.

    Th. If you do go insane, you still can be treated.

    Suitable responses.

    Th. I find no evidence of insanity in you.

    Th. The feeling of going insane is one of the most common symptoms in neurosis. Fortunately, it rarely happens.

    Th. I wonder if you aren't really worried about what may happen to you in other ways too.

25. *Express open-mindedness, even toward irrational attitudes.*

    Pt. I think that all men are jerks.

    Unsuitable responses.

    Th. That's a prejudiced attitude to hold.

    Th. You ought to be more tolerant.

    Th. With such attitudes you'll get nowhere.

    Suitable responses.

    Th. What makes you feel that way?

    Th. Your experiences with men must have been disagreeable for you to have this feeling.

    Th. Understandably you might feel this way right now, but there may be other ways of looking at the situation that may reveal themselves later on.

26. *Respect the right of the patient to express different values and preferences from yours.*

    Pt. I don't like the pictures on your walls.

    Unsuitable responses.

    Th. Well, that's just too bad.

    Th. They are considered excellent pictures by those who know.

    Th. Maybe your taste will improve as we go on in therapy.

    Suitable responses.

    Th. Why?

    Th. What type of pictures do you like?

    Th. What do you think of me for having such pictures?

27. *Clarify the purpose of the interview as often as necessary.*

    Pt. But what am I supposed to do to get well?

Unsuitable responses.

Th. Well, you just let me take care of that.

Th. Once you get confidence in me, you'll start getting well.

Th. The more cooperative you are, the quicker you will get well.

Suitable responses.

Th. We will talk over your problems, and your ideas about them. Things will then gradually clarify themselves, and you will get a better idea of what to do about your problems.

Th. In discussing your reactions, your ideas, and your feelings, you will be better able to understand what is happening to you, and the understanding will permit you to take definite steps to correct your difficulty.

Th. It may puzzle you as to how talking things over helps; but that is the way to understand yourself and your problems. When all the facts are known to you, the solution to your troubles will become clearer.

28. *Make sympathetic remarks where indicated.*

Pt. My husband keeps drinking and then gets violently abusive in front of the children.

Unsuitable responses.

Th. Why do you continue living with him?

Th. Maybe you do your share in driving him to drink.

Th. He's a no-good scoundrel.

Suitable responses.

Th. This must be very upsetting to you.

Th. It must be very difficult to live with him under these circumstances.

Th. You must find it hard to go on with this kind of threat over you.

SIGNS OF A WORKING RELATIONSHIP

Evidences of a working relationship are, on the part of the therapist, a feeling or conviction that he likes the patient, that he is making contact with the patient, that the patient is responding well in the relationship, and that he can help the patient irrespective of the syndrome or the severity of the condition. On the part of the patient there are verbal and non-verbal evidences of liking, feeling relaxed with, and being confident in the therapist.

The length of time it requires to establish a relationship will vary. With some patients a working relationship can be established in the first session. With many patients a dozen sessions may be needed. Occasionally, with patients who are fearful, detached, hostile or non-motivated, or with therapists who have problems in relating to patients, one or more years may be required before a relationship develops. Where severe transference and counter-transference reactions interfere with the setting up of a working relationship, they will have to be dealt with before any progress can be made.

The following is from a session illustrating the beginning of a working relationship. It is an excerpt from the sixth session with a young divorced woman of thirty-two, who came to therapy because of anxiety, tension and feelings of detachment from people. The first four sessions were spent discussing her problem generally. During the fifth session, she introduced with some anxiety the idea that she believed her problem to be due to traumatic sexual experiences in her childhood, during which she was seduced by her father, her mother and perhaps her sister. She had no recollection of such experiences, but this was, in her opinion, due to amnesia, since her dreams were often about sex with members of her family. Although I was tempted to underplay the possibility of such a situation, I listened attentively to her theories and remarked that a situation about which she felt so strongly must be taken seriously. The attitude I evinced was one of neither indorsement nor rejection of her theory, but of acceptance of her right to entertain the ideas she had, which we were obliged to explore. This attitude seemed to precipitate the working relationship since it apparently meant that I was tolerant and accepting.

Pt. I don't know exactly where to begin because I don't feel as desperate as I did the last few times.

Th. Mm hmm.

Pt. I certainly have a feeling, I'm grateful for the last, the last session. Because you went out of the way, as far as I was concerned. I'm glad you had me speak it out, because if I hadn't done it, I probably wouldn't have mentioned it again, because it was fresh then and it did mean a lot to me.

Th. In what way?

Pt. That you understand what I'm thinking about and how I feel about things, and so on.

Th. I see.

Pt. And you took me seriously. Whether you believed it or not is beside the point, but you did take me seriously, which is very important to me.

Th. Mm hmm.

Pt. And I felt relieved that you understood me. It's so hard to find anybody who really understands. I realized that the fact that you took me seriously was important to me. If you take *me* seriously then I can take *you* seriously. Not that I didn't think that before, but it gave me a certain base. Then I went further and realized something I had, of course, known before, and that is if a person has faith in me, or believes in me, not me, but in me, that's the biggest compliment they can give me. And then I will do anything for them. It must be I want to have that feeling toward you.

Th. Mm hmm.

Pt. And then I can in turn respond. But I can't give it first. I mean I have to see that my basis for exposing myself emotionally, so to speak, is respected.

Th. Yes.

Pt. So that's how it is. (*pause*)

Th. Apparently you had a suspicion when you came here first that I might not understand how you feel, that I might not understand you.

Pt. Yes, I was aware of that, and the reason I felt anxious about it was that I just didn't know if you would reject me. And another thing, when you keep emphasizing that I should tell you about anything I feel about you, whether you do anything in any way to annoy me, I felt, it occurred to me, that maybe you meant that you wondered how I felt about you being Jewish. I don't know if you are or not, but you know it would be a sensible thing to think about. But I wouldn't think two minutes about it. Each time I come it is a good experience. I thought maybe you were referring to whether I had any feelings for, or against or about Jewish people. (*Laughs*)

Th. Do you?

Pt. Why no, of course not.

Th. Actually I didn't have that in mind, but it's important to express whatever thoughts you may have about our relationship.

Pt. That's interesting. I'm very glad.

Th. It is possible that you might have certain prejudices about Jewish people, which are, as you know, common; or, it may be, as you say, that you do not have prejudices.

Pt. Oh, those feelings are non-existent in me.

Th. Do you have other feelings about me?

Pt. My feelings about you are very good. I have come in contact with other people. I am opinionated. But nothing could have set us on firmer ground than by my walking in here; and you took me as I was. You didn't question, you didn't probe about all sorts of things. I mean my seriousness about it; many things that you could have in the best of faith, but you didn't. That could not have made me feel better. I walked in as a stranger and you accepted me. I know you are important in your profession, and you have to be selective in a certain sense. I didn't come here with any recommendations; I didn't write you a letter. I just picked up the phone, feeling I've got to do something, and I got an appointment. I walked in and felt very relaxed and very easy. I know that I can feel that way, and I know that I'm not unselective myself. There were things, many things that were bothering me, but you let me choose my words and didn't interfere.

Th. Your feeling is a good one and will help us work more readily with your problem.

Pt. I feel that if a person has faith and respect for me and I can give it back, that I will really be able to get help. I have a full acceptance of you. There are things within me, but they don't concern you. You, yourself, don't cause me anxiety.

Th. Well, if I ever do, I'd like to have you tell me, so that we can try to iron out our relationship.

Pt. It's very necessary to keep myself straight in all relationships, and I'm sure it would be doubly necessary with you. I feel I can do it with you although maybe things may happen later on in our relationship. [*It is possible that the patient is anticipating transference, which actually developed quite strongly as we began exploring her problem in the second phase of therapy.*]

Th. What do you think may happen?

Pt. I don't know. (*pause*)

Th. Something I may say or do?

Pt. I have no idea except that anything I would tend to take exception to would be something you would say. (*pause*)

Th. Mm hmm. (*pause*) About you?

Pt. No, not necessarily. You seem to be very sensitive, and you seem to have omitted all the little difficulties that could arise from a person being somewhat insensitive and not being aware of the condition the patient is in, being pretty much on the defensive. You never violated anything like that. And what I like about it is that you act natural, as if you're not putting on an act to get along.

Th. All right, now that we seem to have a good understanding, we can talk about what we will do in approaching and understanding this problem of yours. [*The therapeutic situation is structured for the patient at this point.*]

32

Structuring the Therapeutic Situation

DURING THE FIRST PHASE OF THERAPY THE PATIENT BECOMES AWARE OF the routines, requirements and responsibilities of psychotherapy. He relinquishes the idea that things will be done for him and to him, and he accepts his role as an active participant in the therapeutic process.

Some patients assume the obligations of the therapeutic situation with scarcely any direction from the therapist. Other patients balk every inch of the way, resisting the conditions with a doggedness that seems borne of perversity.

So long as the patient is observing the "rules" of therapy, there is no need to emphasize any aspect of procedure. When, however, he seems confused or shows resistance, clarification will be necessary. Among areas that may require structuring are the manner of communication, the general routines of therapy, the responsibilities of the patient, the role of the therapist, and a description of the psychotherapeutic process.

EXPLAINING THE MANNER OF COMMUNICATION

1. The Focused Interview

The kind of communication that is used in psychotherapy is generally that of the focused interview which has been described in chapter 15, The Conduct of the Psychotherapeutic Interview. It is usually unnecessary to instruct the patient on what to say and how to say it, since the therapist will, by skillful focusing, and by the use of other techniques that have been described, manage any problems in this area that develop. In the event the patient specifically asks about the content of the interviews, he may be instructed to report on any thoughts and ideas including those that are fleeting, seemingly insignificant or repulsive, or that one might ordinarily be tempted to suppress. Also, he may be told that it is important to mention any tensions or physical symptoms that occur during the session, as well as anxieties, fears or feelings of resentment. He may be enjoined to observe the relationship between his symptoms and environmental happenings. He may also be asked to indicate if he has ever had thoughts, feelings and anxieties similar to those he has at present, and, if so, under what circumstances these occurred.

The following are excerpts from sessions with patients who require instruction in the manner of communication:

Example 1:

Pt. I don't know what I should say.

Th. It is important to talk about anything that is immediately pressing on your mind no matter what it might be. This refers to your feelings and your ideas. If there is an immediate problem you are facing at your job, with your family or in any other area, talk about that. The best rule to follow is to talk about things that are bothering you most.

Example 2:

Pt. Is there anything special you want me to talk about?

Th. I want you to tell me what is mostly on your mind. You may have to face yourself to tell me things that are painful or shameful. Talking about these things may be hard, but will be most helpful to you.

Pt. But how do I do this?

Th. Try to "think out loud" and not hold anything back. In the process of "thinking out loud," you may want to express what you have been thinking or feeling about me.

Example 3:

Pt. What should I talk about?

Th. Anything that is on your mind is important.

Pt. Like what?

Th. Well, any factual observations that you make as well as irrational ideas or feelings that come to you. For instance, you may go out with your girl, and then get furious with her, or indifferent to her, for little apparent reason. Mention these things to me. If you are emotionally bothered by anything at all, talk about it. If you have fantasies, or day dreams or dreams at night, these are very important. If there is anything good or bad that you feel about your treatments here, or good or bad thoughts about me, bring these up too.

Example 4:

Pt. I just don't know what's causing these feelings. I get so frightened and upset, and I don't know why.

Th. That's why you are coming here, to find out the reasons, so you can do something about your trouble.

Pt. But why is it that I can't sleep and concentrate?

Th. That's what we'll begin to explore.

Pt. But why?

Th. What comes to your mind? What do you think?

Pt. I don't know.

Th. You know, there are reasons for troubles like yours, and one must patiently explore them. It may take a little time. I know you'd like to get rid of this trouble right away, but the only way one can do this is by careful exploring.

Pt. Yes.

Th. And to take your anxiety feelings, for example, you may not be aware of the reasons for them now, but as we talk about you, your ideas, your troubles and your feelings, you should be able to find out what they are.

Pt. How do I do this?

Th. When I ask you to talk about your feelings and thrash things around in your mind, you won't be able to put your finger on what bothers you immediately, but at least you will have started thinking about the sources of the problem. Right now, the only thing you're concerned with is escaping from the emotion. That's why you're just going around in a circle. While you're operating to seal off anxiety, you're doing nothing about finding out what's producing this anxiety.

Pt. It sounds sort of clear when you say it. (*laughs*)

Th. Well, do you think you understand what I mean?

Pt. What you're explaining now?

Th. Yes.

Pt. Yes. (*pause*) The point is that I keep thinking about myself too much. It's that I feel inferior to everyone. I must win at rummy. When I play golf, I practically beat myself red if I don't get the low score. And this is silly.

Th. What happens when someone beats you at golf?

Pt. I get upset and these feelings come.

Th. Now there seems to be some kind of connection here; let's talk some more about that.

2. Free Association

Free association will rarely be employed except in Freudian psychoanalysis. Where the therapist uses it as a means of communication, the patient may be given the following explanation:

The kind of communication that we will use here is different from the ordinary back-and-forth talk. It is called "free association." To do "free association" you just talk about whatever comes to your mind without censoring anything. Try not to hold things back, including any ideas, feelings or impulses, no matter how insignificant or ridiculous they may seem. If you think that something is too trivial to report, it may be doubly important to mention it. If you notice any tension in your muscles, or if you experience fear, happiness, excitement or resentment, tell me about these. In other words, I'd like to explore with you thoughts and feelings that are sort of on the periphery of awareness. In this way we will be able to understand some of the problems and conflicts that are hard to get at by ordinary conversations.

In using "free association," it will be necessary to give the patient a reason why the therapist does not respond constantly to the patient's productions with comments and explanations. The following is an example of how this may be done:

Another important thing for you to know is that I will not interfere with your flow of ideas by interrupting with comments. This may puzzle you, but if I don't keep up a conversation with you and enter into back-and-forth talk, there's a good reason for it. I will, of course, occasionally bring important things to your attention. But don't be upset if I fail to respond to everything you say.

3. Dreams

Where the therapist utilizes dreams, it will be necessary to request that the patient bring in his dreams. The patient may be told:

I should like to have you try to remember your dreams and tell me about them in as full detail as possible.

In the event the patient states that he cannot remember his dreams, he may be asked to keep a pad of paper and a pencil at the head of his bed, and to jot down any dreams the first thing in the morning before they slip out of his mind. Often this safeguard helps the patient to remember dreams he otherwise would forget.

Should the patient ask why dreams are important, the therapist may say:

Dreams are important because the mind asleep thinks thoughts in dreams that tell a story about inner problems and conflicts. Sometimes dreams tell us a clearer story than can be told in ordinary conversations. It's hard to understand this, but the best way you can find out how dreams work is to bring them in so we can talk about them.

It is generally not wise to encourage the patient to write his dreams down in detail unless he has a tendency to forget them. Some patients get so immersed in detailed dreaming which they record painstakingly, that the entire' session may be spent on dream material to the neglect of other aspects of the psychic life. This activity may be a subtle form of resistance which the patient uses to avoid talking about anxiety-provoking reality situations.

EXPLAINING GENERAL ROUTINES IN THERAPY

1. Elucidating on the Time Limits of the Interview

A brief explanation may be given the patient regarding the duration of a treatment session, the fact that sessions begin and end promptly at the appointed time, and the need to keep appointments regularly. Where the patient challenges these limits or defies them, his resistance must be handled.

2. Informing the Patient of Expected Delays in Getting Well

Early in treatment the therapist may inform the patient of expected ups and downs in treatment, and of the possibility of temporary relapses. He may also be told that alleviation of his symptoms may not come immediately, and that there might even be a slight set-back before improvement occurs. This helps to forestall untoward reactions to delays in achieving relief, and to the inevitable suffering associated with the giving up of neurotic patterns.

3. Discussing the Confidential Nature of Communications

It is usually advisable to explain to the patient that any information revealed to the therapist is completely confidential and will, under no circumstances, be divulged. This allays the patient's fear that the therapist will discuss him with others. The same reassurance may be given the patient about his case record, and he may be told that it will not be released, even to the patient's personal physician, without his permission.

4. Explaining the Use of the Couch Where It Is to Be Employed

There are advantages and disadvantages to the recumbent position in psychotherapy. Lying on the couch out of visual range of the therapist enables the patient to delve into aspects of himself without restraining his thought processes. Reality is tempered for the time being, and the patient is less apt to subject his responses to what he believes the therapist demands of him, or to modify his thought content in accordance with the facial responses and non-verbal gestures of the therapist. However, the couch position is not indicated in most forms of psychotherapy because of the very fact that it removes the patient from reality. Lying on a couch may furthermore mobilize anxiety in some patients. It may foster silence or a senseless rambling of fantasy material. Face-to-face interviewing is thus generally preferred, and, since this is the natural conversational position, it will not have to be explained to the patient. In reconstructive therapy, however, where free association is to be employed, the couch position may be desired. Here the patient may be told:

Now in talking about yourself, it is helpful to use the couch. The reason for this is that when you face me you are apt to be distracted by what I say and do, and by my facial expressions. This restricts you and makes it hard for you to concentrate on deeper feelings. We can make faster progress by your reclining while you talk.

5. Planning for Vacations

It is necessary to inform the patient well in advance regarding any vacations or extended absences the therapist plans to take. This enables the patient to handle his emotions in advance and minimizes his feeling of being deserted when the time comes for vacation. "Springing" a vacation or recess on the patient without prior notice is apt to precipitate anxiety and to stimulate conceptions of the therapist as a rejecting or irresponsible person. Most therapists urge their patients to plan for their own vacations at a time that coincides with the therapist's absence.

6. Smoking during the Interview

The presence of ash trays generally invites the patient to smoke, should he so desire. Sometimes the patient asks permission where he notices that the therapist does not smoke. To forbid the patient to smoke imposes on him what he may consider authoritarian pressure. Should the therapist be sensitive or allergic to smoking, a good ventilation system will be helpful. In the rare instance where the therapist is unable to tolerate smoke, he may explain the reasons to the patient and ask how he would feel about not smoking. If the matter is tactfully presented, the patient may willingly forego his indulgence during the treatment session.

7. The Taking of Notes

Some patients object to the taking of notes. If the therapist explains the purpose of note-taking and confines himself to recording only important data such as dreams, the patient will generally accustom himself to this practice. If the patient continues to object, even after his feelings have been discussed, and the reasons for his objections explored, the therapist should confine his entries in the case record to the period following the session.

8. Accounting for the Long Time It Takes to Get Well

Where the patient is insistent on knowing how long it will take to get well, and if long-term therapy is necessary, an explanation is helpful such as was given to the patient in the following excerpt:

Th. Now your problem seems to have originated way back in your life, as far back as childhood. It will, therefore, require a little time to correct.

Pt. How long would I need?

Th. That will depend on your cooperation and desire to get well.

Pt. I do, I mean I want to get well. But could you tell me approximately how long it will be?

Th. Now, because the problem goes so far back it may need two or three years of treatment.

Pt. As long as that?

Th. Unfortunately deep change takes time. Actually it's not so long. It took you all your life to get tangled up in a knot. You know this problem didn't begin last Tuesday. It's been with you for a long time. And a couple of years of treatment is short compared to how long you've had it.

Pt. Aren't there any short cuts like hypnosis?

Th. Yes, there are, and we'll use whatever techniques are best for you to cut down the time. But hypnosis does not shorten the period of treatment in a problem such as yours. Time itself seems to be an element of cure. You know how hard it is to overcome a tobacco habit?

Pt. Yes, I know.

Th. Well, personality habits require even more time, because they are part of a person from childhood on.

Pt. Yes, I see.

9. Handling Consistent Lateness

If the patient is consistently late, this may indicate resistance and will necessitate an inquiry. The therapist may ask, "I wonder if there is any reason why you have come so late the last few times." The patient may possibly then bring up an area of resistance. If he is defensive and insists on explaining his lateness on the basis of a reality factor, it is best not to challenge him. Instead one may say, "Let us see what happens in the future." If lateness persists, he may be more directly challenged.

10. Handling Broken Appointments

Where the patient breaks an appointment without telephoning, this must be considered seriously and discussed thoroughly at the next session. If two successive appointments are broken, the therapist may advantageously telephone the patient and inquire as to the reasons. Should the patient remark that he has decided to terminate therapy, it is advisable to invite the patient to come in to talk things over. Consistent breaking of appointments is a critical matter and calls for active analysis of prevailing resistances.

11. Handling Too Frequent Cancellations

Where the patient calls in advance to cancel his appointment, he is generally not charged for the session provided the reasons for the cancellations are valid emergencies. Should cancellations be too frequent, resistance is probably operative, and the patient may be reminded that interruptions in therapy are not only expensive, but detrimental to his progress.

12. Handling Non-payment of Bills

Most patients pay their bills promptly if, during the initial interview, mention is made of the fact that bills are sent out at the end of the month. Should a considerable time elapse without payment, and without mention by the patient of the reasons for this deficiency, the therapist may discuss the matter frankly in a manner such as this:

Th. I noticed that you haven't paid your bill for the past two months. I wonder if there are material reasons for this or whether you have forgotten.
Pt. Oh, I just don't think of it; haven't gotten around to it.
Th. Do you have any feelings about paying the bill?
Pt. Why no. It's that so many other expenses have come up.
Th. Well, look into it anyway. There may be emotional reasons for your forgetting. Are you at all irritated with me or uncertain about your treatment?
Pt. (*pause*) Maybe, in some ways. I feel we haven't been going fast enough.
Th. Let's talk about that.

The subject of non-payment of bills may open up a pocket of transference. Should there be realistic budgetary problems, it is incumbent on the therapist to make as liberal allowances for the patient as circumstances permit.

DELINEATING THE PATIENT'S RESPONSIBILITIES

Most patients will proceed to work actively in therapy without too much prodding or too extensive a definition of their responsibilities in the treatment situation. In some patients, however, confusion about their role, or resistance to activity, may require that the therapist delineate their obligations.

How best to present the matter of the patient's responsibilities will depend on the kinds of resistances displayed. In addition to dealing with a specific resistance, the patient may be told that comprehending his problem is the first step in its control. It is hard for him to do this by himself because he lives too close to his problems to see them clearly. In treatment, the therapist can help the patient find out the cause of his trouble by guiding him along certain paths of thinking. The patient and therapist act together in a sort of partnership in the project of exploring his patterns. Knowing what is behind his difficulties will help the patient to do what is necessary to rid himself of them. The therapist may say:

Perhaps we can regard therapy as an arrangement in which we both are participants. You will help me understand you by telling me about your thoughts and feelings, and I will help you understand what goes on inside of you that creates your trouble. Together we can work this thing out.

When the therapist informs the patient that the therapeutic situation is one in which he is expected to work out his own problems, resentment, depression or panic may be mobilized. For the patient feels that he has already attempted with his own resources to cope with his trouble, and that he has been unsuccessful. He may then look upon the therapist's refusal to take complete responsibility as a dereliction. Consequently, it is best not to stress too much, at the start, the obligations the patient must assume, and to let the relationship develop along the lines that it will, helping the patient slowly to accept more and more responsibility. It is, of course, essential that eventually the patient come to an understanding within himself that the extent of his participation will determine the ultimate goal. If the therapist makes decisions for the patient and tells him how to conduct his life, this will delay the development of essential inner resources which enable the patient to manage his problems constructively. If we are aiming for goals of assertiveness and independence, it will therefore be necessary for the patient to treat the treatment situation as a medium in which he can develop capacities to make his own choices and decisions.

One way of insuring the patient's cooperation is to present to him the process of working in psychotherapy in terms that will be at least partially cogent to him. For instance, a patient during the third interview expresses confusion about what to say. He then expostulates that he would like the therapist to do something positive for him. An excerpt of the interview follows:

Th. I know how difficult this has been for you. Were it possible to remove your trouble immediately, I would want to do it. But this thing has been with you for some time, and it may require a little time to get at the bottom of it.

Pt. How can I get well, then, how?

Th. There are ways of working in psychotherapy that will help you get well. Let's look at it this way: you've learned patterns of feeling and thinking that have gotten you into trouble. These patterns are part of you. What we'll do is examine these patterns and see why they've failed, and have gotten you into a mess. After that you'll be able to learn new patterns that will make it possible to enjoy life.

Pt. But how do I do this?

Th. Now, learning new patterns is like learning a new language. If you were going to learn a new language, you would have to start talking that language. It would be difficult at first and you would make mistakes, but you would eventually learn it through practice. I'll be like a teacher helping you when you make mistakes. But if I were to do all the talking in this new language, you would never learn how to talk.

Pt. I see, but how do I start?

Th. The best way is to tell me what is on your mind, what you feel, what bothers you. I'll ask you questions from time to time. Now I'm not going to give you the answers, because if I did, it wouldn't help you. But I'll help you find the answers for yourself.

Pt. I see.

Th. It's like doing algebra. To learn algebra it wouldn't help you if I gave you the answers. The important thing is to learn how to get the answers. In problems like yours, learning *how* to arrive at the answers to your disturbing feelings and patterns is as important as getting the answers themselves.

Pt. Yes.

Th. This may sound mysterious, but as we go on, it will become clearer.

1. Assigning Tasks to the Patient

Sometimes it is feasible to assign certain tasks to the patient to work on between sessions, such as to observe his dreams, to watch his attitudes toward· the therapist, and to note which situations exaggerate or alleviate his symptoms. The patient may deny that there is any connection between circumstances in his life and his symptoms, but the therapist must insist that he keep watching for a relationship between the severity of his symptoms and provocative environmental happenings. Whenever the patient brings up the circumstance of exacerbation of his symptoms, it will be important to explore the conditions associated with it.

2. Explaining the Need Not to Make Important Decisions without Discussing These with the Therapist

During therapy the patient's values are in more or less of a transitional state. Extremely important decisions, like changes in occupation or marital status, must be considered very carefully before acting on them. Tragic consequences may follow impulsive decisions. For these reasons the patient may be told that a rule in therapy is that the patient must not spontaneously and impulsively make any radical changes in his life situation; that he must discuss all important actions with the therapist before executing them.

DEFINING THE ROLE OF THE THERAPIST

In supportive therapy, it is usually unnecessary to define the role of the therapist, since the latter consciously functions as a "giving" authority. In insight therapy, on the other hand, as has been explained above, the therapist's role may have to be delimited when the patient protests the apparent lack of direction. He must be apprised of the fact that giving him advice and guidance will block his development and prevent him from achieving strengths essential to his independent functioning.

Insight therapy calls for respectful listening, and a communicating to the patient of an understanding of his turmoil and of a desire to help him in his plight. This process is different from an artificial cultivation of dependence on the therapist. No promises are made to the patient, nor does the therapist hold himself out as a savior. Rather, he indicates that there are ways of getting relief for one's problems contingent on the patient's active cooperation in therapy.

Partly because the patient puts the therapist in the traditional role of magical healer, and partly because his helplessness inspires regressive dependency impulses, he demands or secretly expects immediate and dramatic relief. He is bound to feel resentful and hopeless if this relief is not immediately forthcoming. He may be unable to understand why a rapid cure is not possible, why therapy requires frequent sessions over a prolonged period, and why the therapist displays minimal activity, expecting him to shoulder the brunt of the work.

As soon as possible, the therapist must clarify these doubts and hopes in order to help prevent the experiencing by the patient of too great disappointment, and to thwart the patient's leaving therapy in confusion.

The following excerpts from early sessions illustrate the defining of the therapist's role: ˙

Example 1:

Pt. I'd like to know, doctor, what makes me feel so sick.

Th. There are reasons why you feel the way you do. Those reasons may not be clear to you, because you are living too close to your difficulties. We will discuss your ideas and particularly your feelings, and in not too long a time, we should discover what is behind your problem.

Pt. Yes, but what would you like to know? I mean what do you want me to talk about?

Th. Just anything that bothers you, that's on your mind. In discussing your ideas, reactions and feelings, we will gradually be able to understand what is happening to you, and this understanding will permit you to take definite steps to correct your difficulty.

Pt. And you'll tell me what is wrong?

Th. Not exactly. I'll, of course, help you with your problem, by acting as your third eye, so to speak. You may not be able to do this for yourself, because, as I said, you are living too close to your problem to see the forest for the trees. But I can be more objective, and I shall direct your thinking along certain lines.

Pt. You mean you will not do the work for me; you'll just show me what to do.

Th. Yes. You see, if my doing the work and telling you what to do would really help you, I'd do it. But experience shows that emotional problems are not helped this way. In being told what's wrong with you and what to do, you may never be able to develop as much personality strength as in working things out with my help. Together we can work out a logical and constructive solution for your problem.

Example 2:

Pt. But aren't *you* able to take these fears away from me?

Th. Your fears bother you a great deal and you want to get rid of them as soon as possible, don't you?

Pt. Yes.

Th. Now it would be natural for you to expect me to give you medicines or some other remedy, or to do something forceful to make your troubles disappear. Believe me, I would do this for you if they *would* disappear this way. But experience shows that you *can* get rid of them by first finding out what they mean, how they got started and why they continue to bother you. This will take time and you're likely to get impatient with the slowness of the process.

Pt. (*laughing*) I hope it isn't too slow.

Th. (*smiling*) Well, we'll go as fast as *you* can travel.

Verbalizing the permissive nature of the relationship is not advisable, since the patient may interpret this as a lure. Rather, it is important that the patient, on the basis of his own experiences, spontaneously arrive at the conclusion that the therapeutic situation is unique in its permissiveness, that he can talk about things that are ordinarily censored, that he will not be held in judgment, and that reprimand and punishment will not be forthcoming. The permissiveness of therapy does not presuppose that the patient will receive unmitigated support and reassurance. The patient will not be told what to do; rather he will be helped to decide for himself the best course of action. As has been mentioned previously, it is important to explain to the patient, as soon as he expresses disappointment with the amount of direction he is receiving, the reasons for the seeming passivity of the therapist. To delay this explanation is apt to result in feelings of helplessness, hopelessness and despair. Dependent patients will, of course, be loathe to accept the defined limits in therapist responsibility; but they will be much less hostile if they understand that the role of the therapist is a deliberately cultivated one rather than one of neglect.

1. Limits of Demonstrativeness

Displaying acceptance does not mean that the therapist should behave too demonstratively toward the patient. Such acts as putting one's arm around the patient, comforting him solicitously, helping him with his coat, and other pleasantries are not to be encouraged. Should the patient wait for such attentions, or show by his attitudes or statements that he expects the therapist to act in accordance with certain amenities, the therapist may briefly explain that it is not the custom in psychotherapy to treat the patient in a conventional sense. For example, a female patient, having placed her wrap on a chair in the therapist's office, walks over to it at the end of a session and then waits for the therapist to help her with her coat. To respond by doing this would be a normal thing in the ordinary social atmosphere, or when supportive approaches are employed. However, to act this way in insight therapy may cause the patient to regard the therapist as a person who should act in other conventional ways toward her. Generally, where the therapist, at the end of the session, does not offer to help the patient with her coat, the patient will do this for herself. Should she ask the therapist to help her, the therapist may do so, remarking, "Much as I'd like to do this regularly, it is customary not to do this in therapy. It tends to put the therapist and patient in a sort of conventional relationship that may interfere with your progress. If I don't help you with your coat from now on, you'll know that it's because it isn't wise to do so."

2. Limits in Gift-giving

The same taboo is extended toward giving the patient gifts. There are times in doing supportive therapy where a small gift may be tendered the patient as a demonstration of the therapist's thoughtfulness and his desire to bring comfort to the patient. In insight therapy, gift-giving puts an artificial bias on the relationship and may be harmful. Similarly, accepting gifts from the patient must be handled carefully. Even small gifts must be questioned. Should the patient offer the therapist a small gift, the therapist may accept it appreciatively, but ask why the patient gave it to him. An excerpt from a session illustrates this point:

Pt. I thought you would like this necktie.

Th. Thank you very much. I appreciate your thoughtfulness, but I wonder why you got it for me.

Pt. (*blushes*) Oh, I just thought you'd like it.

Th. (*smiling*) You know in therapy one has to look a gift horse in the mouth, and inquire into the meaning of everything that happens, including bringing gifts. For instance, let's try to figure out why you gave me this tie.

Pt. (*laughing*) I suppose it's because I wanted to. I noticed that you wear drab ties.

Th. You thought I might look better in a snappy tie?

Pt. (*laughing*) Not that you haven't good taste, but . . . (*pause*)

Th. Perhaps you're not quite sure of my taste.

Pt. (*laughing*) Come to think of it, maybe I'm not.

Under no circumstances should the therapist accept a large gift, since this is generally a manifestation of resistance or a way of bribing the therapist. When a patient offers the therapist such a gift, the therapist must refuse it without rejecting the patient. The following excerpt is illustrative:

Pt. I brought you a little something. (*gives therapist a box*)

Th. Thank you, very much, but I wonder why you got it.

Pt. Oh, I know you'll like this. It's a very nice thing.

Th. What is it?

Pt. A fine watch.

Th. Well, now I do appreciate your thoughtfulness, but one of the rules of therapy is not to accept gifts. It may interfere with your treatment. If I don't accept it, it's because of this rule. But tell me, why did you get it for me?

Pt. Well, does there have to be a special reason?

Th. There usually is. You know, in therapy one looks a gift horse in the mouth. Mind you, I think it's very fine of you to bring me a gift, but let's explore this a little. We may learn something important from it.

3. Avoiding Social Contacts

Meeting the patient on a social basis is very destructive to the relationship. The patient may employ his observations of the therapist's behavior as a weapon to reinforce his resistance. He may utilize the social relationship as a means of neutralizing the therapist's effectiveness.

4. Avoiding Physical Contacts

It goes without saying that physical contact with the patient is absolutely taboo. Touching, stroking or kissing the patient may mobilize sexual feelings in the patient and therapist, or bring forth violent outbursts of anger. Should the patient approach the therapist sexually, this must be handled as a manifestation of transference, and the patient should be encouraged to verbalize her feelings. Were the therapist to respond to the patient's gesture, therapy would terminate immediately with perhaps disastrous consequences for both patient and therapist. The utmost care must be exercised to avoid mobilizing guilt in the patient when she makes a physical gesture toward the therapist. Occasionally an enthusiastic patient may throw her arms around the therapist and kiss him. This embarrassing situation will call for the greatest tact. To push the patient away harshly and scold her will cause her to feel rejected and resentful. To respond by embracing the patient may be interpreted as a seductive lure for which the therapist will pay dearly later on. The best way to handle this contingency is to stand one's ground, smile and ask, "Now, I wonder why you did that?" By his facial expression, the therapist must convey no embarrassment, fright, hostility or excitement. If the embrace is during a session, the focus of the session should be on the meaning of the gesture to the patient. If it is at the end of a session, the therapist may add to the statement he has made: "Suppose you think about why you kissed me and we'll talk about it next time."

5. Avoiding Business Dealings

Sometimes the patient will offer the therapist opportunities to enter into business dealings with him. The temptation for the therapist may be great, since he may assume that an investment in the patient's enterprise will be helpful both to him and to the patient. Such business arrangements will usually be very destructive to therapy, and should be resisted unequivocally. Similarly, one must never take advantage of the patient's professional or social contacts, if he happens to be prominent.

EXPLAINING HOW PSYCHOTHERAPY WORKS

A case history explaining how another patient developed an understanding of himself in therapy, and of how he achieved relief or cure, is a dramatic way of persuading the patient to accept the treatment situation where he stubbornly resists it. The following is an example of such a history. Undoubtedly the therapist will be able to present examples from his own experience. These should be sufficiently disguised so that the discussed patient's identity will not be revealed.

I may be able to give you an example of what happens in therapy by telling you of a case I treated.

A patient was referred to me for treatment by a physician for migrainous headaches which did not respond to medications. He wanted me to give him sedatives. I told him: "The prescription that I'm going to give you will be much better than medicine. It is going to be a prescription that may take possibly a little time; but this thing did not develop last week. What I am going to ask you to do is to connect up for me your headache and any fears or conflicts or problems that exist in your life. Once you do this, your headaches will have the best chance of disappearing, because you will then be able to take the steps necessary to correct the cause. If I fail to give you medicine, it is because medicine does not help the kind of problem you have. You must be patient in working this thing out with me. Relief will eventually come."

The patient was somewhat dismayed at my reaction, and he retorted: "But I don't see any real connection between the headache and what I'm doing. Sure, I wish I had a better job, and I wish that I had things that I don't have now, things like that. I don't have anything worse than anybody else. I'd like to have some more money. I'd like to be able to travel more and see the world, but I'm not any more dissatisfied than most people that I know. So even though you say that maybe there is fear or something, I don't see it." I retorted, "Suppose you watch your headache and see if there is a connection between it and your life situation. Are there things that happen to you day by day that upset you inside and give you a headache?"

At the next visit, the patient revealed that he had had a headache. He said, "I can see no reason why I had the headache from the different things that happened during the day. I went to work, and everything went along pretty well. I did a job that was assigned to me with no trouble at all. That night I had a bowling date with a friend. Now this friend called me up, and we were supposed to go out on a date. He said, 'Suppose I meet you at eight o'clock.' Right at that point my wife, who had been coming down with a head cold, says to me, 'Why don't you postpone your going out until later on, after the kids are in bed or tomorrow?' And she did have a terrible cold. So I told my friend we'd go out the next day. I didn't want the youngsters to catch my wife's cold, so I helped them. Then I sat on my wife's bed. She was sniffling, and I began getting an awful headache right at that point. And there was no reason for it." When asked whether he might have resented the fact that he had to stay home and put the children to bed, he remarked, "No, why should I? The kids would have gotten a cold. I could have bowled the next day; there's no reason why I should." The patient was assured that perhaps there was no cause for the headache that we could see at this time, but that it was necessary to continue observing the circumstances under which his headache developed.

One week later the patient reported a severe migrainous attack. "Again I had an awful headache. Things went around. I had a bunch of junk last night, and it was probably what I ate." When asked to talk about the events that had occurred, he said, "We went over to call on some people we know. They are nice people, but I don't care very much for them. But my wife thinks that because he is my superior at work we've got to cultivate them; and I suppose if I really want to go along, get ahead in my job, that I might as well try to be friends with him. So I went over there, and I sat there, and we drank a while and we talked. They're terrible bores. I really don't like being with them. Then it started; an awful headache."

When asked whether he resented making the visit, the patient replied "Sure, I didn't want to be there. I just resented being there." He was then reminded that he had presented two instances in which his wife had asked him to comply and that in each case a headache followed. "Yes," he admitted, "I don't know; maybe you've got something."

That he had made a connection was evidenced by his reaction to his next headache. He said, "By George, you know what happened? My wife asked me to stay at home again and not go bowling, but afterwards I got a bad headache." Almost excitedly he continued, "When I look back, I can see the headache just comes like that. There have been innumerable times when automatically I feel as if I have to do what my wife asks me to do, that I can't say no. I say she is a reasonable person and a nice person, and I get a bad headache every time. Now, why should that be?"

I replied, "So you do see a connection between your life situation and what has happened to you? Now, that's a rather interesting situation, isn't it? Here you notice things happening at home that have a much greater meaning to you than before. A headache seems to occur when your wife suggests something that you resent or that makes some demands on you. Suppose we start inquiring into that, and suppose you, yourself, begin to figure out for yourself, with my help, what goes on here." He retorted, "Well, can't you do that for me? Can't you tell me why?" This explanation was given: "If I told you, it wouldn't do *you* any good, because if you figure things out for yourself, the insight will stick."

I told him then that he could now see that his headache was not mysterious, but that it had an origin in certain attitudes. It would be important for him to figure things out more in detail; his inner strength would increase if he figured things out for himself.

Following this we decided to use the technique of free association which required that he recline on the couch. After several sessions, during which he discussed certain resentments he had toward people which had bothered him, he expostulated in an irritable way that nothing seemed to be happening. "I just can't seem to figure things out. I can't seem to make any sense out of what I'm saying or why I lie down here. I can't possibly arrive at the reasons why these things go on inside of me. Now why don't you tell me? Why don't you tell me what's going on, and why do I get these headaches?"

Emphasis was again placed on the need to work things out for himself. "But I'm trying to," he replied, "and nothing happens. All right, I'll try." At this point he complained of a pounding headache which he insisted had started two days ago. "I can't see how my wife is responsible here because nothing has happened. I've had several awful headaches in the last couple of days, and I can't see the sense in it." As he talked, he became critical of the technique of free association. He then revealed a dream of fleeing from a dangerous man who had plugs in his ears. He

associated the ear plugs with a stethoscope. He remarked, "This man, he had a stethoscope, and he was chasing me, and I didn't want to do what he wanted me to do,
and I felt he was going to hurt me and so I ran." I then inquired, "Is it possible that
you are doing something *now* that you don't want to do?" "No," he retorted, "I
want to get well, I want to do what you say. I want to do everything you say, even
though I do not know the reason for free association. I want to do everything you say."
My reply was this: "Well, it seems apparent that you are developing toward me the
same type of feelings that you have toward your wife. Maybe you feel I'm forcing
you to do something you really don't want to do. Aren't you doing exactly with me
what you do with your wife? Aren't you complying with me, and doing free association, and trying to figure things out for yourself, when you would really like to sit
up and have me tell you what to do?"

At the next session the patient reported a dream. "There is a baby, a tiny baby
in the arms of its mother. The mother is stuffing a nipple of a baby bottle down the
child's throat. The child yowls and screams and shakes his head, and as he shakes
his head, he bangs it against the wall." The patient then exclaimed, "I have a terrible
headache, one of the worst headaches I've had." It was pointed out that the banging
of the baby's head in the dream might symbolize a headache. The patient acquiesced
that his head felt as if he were banging it against a wall.

As we talked, the patient remembered an incident when he was six years of
age. His mother had put him in a baby swing. He had wanted to play in the open with
the other children, but his mother refused to permit him to do so. He screamed with
rage, but he was forced to sit in the swing. He then developed a headache—his first
headache.

For a number of sessions thereafter the patient talked angrily of how his mother
had treated him. She had overprotected him, he insisted, and she demanded compliance as a reward for her love. He felt powerless to resist her demands. He recalled many episodes of having to swallow his pride, and having to conform with
his mother's commands without revolt. The aftermath of each of these episodes was
a violent headache. The patient was then able to connect his past relations with his
wife with this pattern, and he could also see that he had developed the same kind
of attitude toward me in complying with my suggestion that he utilize an analytic
technique and do free association. He could see that he entered automatically into a
type of relatedness with people in which he did what was expected of him without
questioning its propriety. The result was generally a headache.

The next step in therapy was showing him that his compliance and passivity
were products of his own doing. In his relations with people he was always exceedingly formal, even obsequious at times. It was possible that he maneuvered himself
into a role in which he had to act compliantly, perhaps even forcing people to act
in a domineering way toward him.

The patient accepted this interpretation and later reported that he had observed
himself improving with his wife. He made decisions and assumed a more and more
dominant position in the household. He discovered that he could disagree with his
wife, and resist demands he believed to be unreasonable, and that she adjusted to his
new attitude toward her. Indeed, she seemed more contented in many ways. Life began to assume an entirely different aspect. He had tested himself and found he did not
have to be compliant nor submissive. He did not have to sacrifice his integrity and
his sense of self. With this reoriented attitude, his attacks of headache disappeared
completely.

This prolonged description illustrates how psychotherapy works. What happened to this patient naturally does not apply to you. But by examining *your* ideas and feelings, and talking about *your* problems, we should be able to help you too.

SIGNS OF ACCEPTANCE OF THERAPEUTIC STRUCTURING

Signs of acceptance of the structuring of the therapeutic situation are reflected in greater participation and activity. This is illustrated in the following excerpt. The patient is a thirty-five year old married woman with an hysterical symptom of vaginal burning which, since its inception eight years previously, had been increasing in severity until she could no longer tolerate it. It was apparent that she had magical expectancies of my removing her difficulty in a few sessions. When I structured the ideal way of working in psychotherapy, she responded with silence. At the sixth session, she complained of intense burning and remarked that she was thinking of stopping therapy. I attempted to analyze her resentment at my passivity, and tried to justify my stand on the basis that, if I could remove her trouble by waving a wand, I would do so. I explained that emotional problems like hers could be resolved, but that it was necessary for the patient to work hard and to cooperate actively. During the next session, the seventh, she seemed to be resolving her resistance to accepting the way we were supposed to work together. A part of the session follows:

Pt. Today I'm forty years old.

Th. Are congratulations in order?

Pt. No, nor commiserations. But I never thought I'd spend it here in New York getting treatment away from home. (*laughs*)

Th. You never realized ten years ago, or even five, that at your fortieth birthday you'd be sitting opposite a psychiatrist.

Pt. (*laughs*) I finally had a dream. I didn't have that dream until this morning. It was the silliest thing. I was living in this large room. I was living there with a man. He looked like a combination of an old boy friend and a man who works in the same place I do. And we weren't sharing the same bed for some strange reason. And there was a double cot over on one side of the room, and a double cot on the other side. And there was a sink, and there was a bunch of people there having a party for some reason. I was supposed to wash up the dishes, and I was very resentful of the fact that everyone was having a good time and I wasn't. In fact, I had to go out to go to work, and the dirty dishes were going to be left for me to do. And all of a sudden I realized that the man in the room had taken the sink out and put it up so high that I had to stand on my toes to reach it. Then I realized that one of the cots had been taken out. I was shocked, as if I was being eliminated. [*This dream seems to reflect a feeling of rejection and resentment at being made to do "dirty work." The idea occurs to me that this is a transference dream.*]

Th. What does that make you think of? Do you have any associations?

Pt. Why no. I just awoke and was going to go to work.

Th. But the emotion in the dream. What was that like?

Pt. Well there didn't seem to be any love involved.

Th. Here was a man doing peculiar things?

Pt. Well, it didn't seem to be a man I was emotionally involved with, yet I was sharing the room with him. (*pause*)

Th. And what was he trying to make you do?

Pt. The dirty dishes while the others were standing around, talking and having a good time. [*Could this possibly refer to my wanting her to do the "dirty" work in therapy?*]

Th. Mm hmm.

Pt. And I was under strain. I had to stand on my toes to do that, and it was hard. He had put the sink up too high. I could see the bolt holes where the sink had been before. He put it up too high. [*Indicating that I was making the therapeutic task impossibly hard for her?*]

Th. He was making you do the work.

Pt. Yes, and when I noticed the other cot gone, I said, "What the hell does he think he's doing?"

Th. Why would he take the cot away?

Pt. I don't know, maybe so the woman sharing the room would sleep with him.

Th. What kind of a person was he?

Pt. He reminds me of two people I know: one, handsome and charming; the other, boorish and vulgar. He clowns around, but he's a good Joe.

Th. I see.

Pt. And something very peculiar happened last week, something I couldn't quite figure out. First, I realized I wasn't so frightened as I used to be. And I wasn't complaining as much. And I said, "Won't Dr. Wolberg be pleased to hear that," and all of a sudden this vaginal burning that I have went away completely. It made me chuckle. (*laughs*)

Th. All right, how do you make that connection?

Pt. I don't make any connection (*laughs*) except that maybe the treatments are doing me good in spite of myself.

Th. In spite of the fact that you may be a little annoyed at the way the treatments are going. (*pause*) [*It was hoped here that the patient would verbalize her feelings of resentment or disappointment. Because she did not do so, the next comment was made.*] Perhaps you feel disappointed that so much responsibility is being put on you?

Pt. Possibly, possibly. (*laughs*)

Th. Like being made to do the dirty dishes. [*interpreting one aspect of the dream*]

Pt. (*laughs uproariously*) I just hate to do dishes. That's my mother's fault. She wanted me to be a pianist and not spoil my hands. I was always annoyed at doing dishes. What you say is right; I don't want, didn't want the responsibility of figuring things out myself.

Th. Are you annoyed at accepting responsibility?

Pt. Well . . . not exactly, that is, when I am not under tension, I don't mind responsibility. But since this tension started, I have tried to evade responsibility as much as possible, because I felt I couldn't accept it or carry it out.

Th. And how do you feel about accepting responsibility in our therapy here?

Pt. I am a little confused about that. (*laughs*) Less than before though. I just didn't feel as if I was capable.

Th. You see, if it were possible for me to remove these symptoms from you myself, I would do it. I would want to do it. But we find that cures are not accomplished this way. As a matter of fact, the more active a person is in working out the sources of a problem, even though the person has to sweat it through a little, the quicker one gets well. In the long run this is what strengthens the person. The ability to understand the sources of one's problem and to handle the resistance in working things out for himself or herself . . . [*I continue to structure the therapeutic situation.*]

Pt. (*laughs*) It's not conscious resistance I assure you.

Th. I know.

Pt. I want to tell you what happened last night. This symptom that I have had is associated with sex in my mind, for some reason. I started thinking about my husband and all of a sudden this burning began to loosen up and to become a sexual feeling. Ordinarily I would have stopped thinking right there, because in the past, if I started thinking about the person involved and couldn't do anything about it, the burning would keep on, and keep on, and only go away when I slept. So I just decided that I would keep on thinking about it just to see what would happen. [*This is an excellent sign of her beginning to accept responsibility by working on a problem.*]

Th. Good.

Pt. And I didn't get a sexual craving and I started being able to think about something else and I wasn't afraid of what would happen . . . and, for heaven's sake, the burning went away.

Th. It sounds as if you've been afraid to let your mind wander in the past.

Pt. I see. You mean if I'm afraid to think about sex I might get pain there instead.

Th. Yes, perhaps in the future you could let your mind wander and see what you think about.

Pt. I guess I'm afraid to think, because, after all, it's been seven years that I've lived with this thing. If I thought it would clear things up, I wouldn't be afraid to think anything I want. Mother was very moral about sex, and I could never bring it up. Oh, yes, after I left you, I went to the store to get groceries. I wanted to get out so I got in line ahead of other people and the burning started. Then it went away. I went to sleep and had a dream I forgot. When I tried to remember the dream, the burning returned and my mind got hazy.

Th. Now it's important for you to continue thinking about yourself, like making a connection between your symptoms and your thoughts. You may not at first see the connection, but you will, after a while, see a trend developing, a connection. Now one impression I get that I can offer to you is that every time you feel you've done anything that's "bad" the burning comes on you.

Pt. When I ever did anything bad as a child, mother would scream, bang her head against the wall and practically have a breakdown. [*patient continues to associate to her early relations with her mother*]

From this session on the patient seemed to accept the conditions of therapy and to work actively on her problem.

III

The Middle Phase of Treatment

33

Identifying Important Trends and Patterns: Introduction

ONCE THE WORKING RELATIONSHIP IS CONSOLIDATED, AND THE PATIENT has accepted the mode of working in therapy, we enter into the middle stage of treatment. This has as one of its objectives the determination of the causes and dynamics of the patient's disorder. The extent of such determination will depend on the goals of our therapeutic effort. In supportive therapy, we may merely seek to bring the patient to an awareness of discordant elements in his environment that activate his turmoil. Here, an examination of factors that promote the situational disturbance, and study of the effects on the patient of his disturbance, may be all that is attempted. In reeducative therapy, there may be an exploration of his more conscious interpersonal reactions and of the ensuing difficulties that follow expression of his personality patterns. These therapeutic tasks are implemented by the conventional interviewing techniques.

In reconstructive psychotherapy, the task is more ambitious, since the level of exploration is on the unconscious strata of mind. The symbolic extensions of unconscious conflicts are explored through a number of techniques that will presently be described. The contamination of rational behavior with derivatives of the unconscious is investigated and analyzed. There is also an inquiry into the genetic origin of the individual's conflicts, the determining childhood experiences that initiated and produced character distortions and maladaptive mechanisms of defense.

The underlying dynamics as they disclose themselves during the middle phase of therapy will be specific for the individual. While a great deal of variation exists in patterns of psychodynamics, it is possible to make a few generalizations. In the main, the individual who possesses an emotional problem is suffering from a failure or a collapse in adaptation. Signs of adaptational collapse are symptoms which vary in both quality and intensity. Except for situational difficulties which realistically act as inordinate sources of stress, symptoms are the outcome of many inner disturbances which affect the person's feelings of security, his self-esteem, his relationships with people and his capacity to express basic needs and demands. The primary source of these disturbances in personality functioning is disorganizing life experiences, dating back to the very earliest contacts of the child with his parents and other important persons in his past. Distortions in values and attitudes engendered by unfortunate conditionings with parental agencies cling to the individual when he matures, and he usually reacts to life with archaic fears, frustrations and hostilities which singularly are little modified by adult experiences. It is as if he creates out of the epoch of his child-hood, paradigms in his adult life which reflect the very values and contain the same expectations of injury that he had as a child.

The consequence of disturbances in security feelings, self-esteem and inter-personal relationships caused by unfortunate early conditionings is to make the individual vulnerable to even average deprivations and vicissitudes. This is registered in terms of a failing life adaptation, when inner conflicts exert their pressure, and external demands tax the coping capacities of the person. Earliest signs of adaptive disorganization are tension, anxiety, and the psychophysiologic components of anxiety. The latter symptoms, universal phenomena in neuroses, provoke the ego into marshalling all the defensive instrumentalities it has at its disposal to bring the individual to a psychic equilibrium. Anxiety and its at-tendant physiologic reactions are so destructive to the person that attempts to cope with it are always made.

Many symptoms the person displays in response to the stimulus of anxiety serve to defend him against the effects of this emotion. They defend him also against the initiating conflicts themselves. Why different symptoms and syn-dromes are elaborated in different people to cope with essentially the same kinds of conflicts is a challenging question, the answer to which is not entirely clear. However, the species of symptom is, from a therapeutic standpoint, not so im-portant as the conflictual difficulties that create anxiety.

The knowledge that symptoms arise out of failure of the individual in his dynamic dealings with life, has, in recent years, tended to displace the em-phasis in treatment from a consideration of the patient's symptoms to his functional relationships with other people. What one hopes to effect in recon-structive therapy is a building of security in the person so that he no longer feels menaced by fears of the world. In addition, self-esteem must be enhanced to the point of self-confidence, assertiveness and creative self-fulfillment. The individual must gain respect for himself without strivings for perfectionism or superiority. His relationships with people must become harmonious and shorn of such impulses as dependency, detachment and aggression. Finally, he must become capable of satisfying his inner needs and demands without anxiety and in conformity with the standards of the group. Not every patient is capable of achieving the ideal goal in therapy of complete personality rehabilitation; yet the therapist has a responsibility in promoting in each individual as extensive a growth in personality as is reasonably and practically possible.

Personality change is catalyzed by helping the patient in psychotherapy to arrive at an awareness of the operative forces within himself. This process is characterized by progressive stages of self-understanding and steps of adaptive action which, in the main, may be delineated as follows:

1. Elaboration by the patient of his symptoms and complaints.
2. Discussion of feelings associated with symptoms.
3. Relation of feelings to dissatisfactions with his environment.
4. Recognition of repetitive patterns of behavior and appreciation of their responsibility for disturbed feelings.

5. Awareness of dissatisfaction with his patterns, but realization of their compulsive persistence.

6. Cognizance of the functional nature of his behavior patterns.

7. Exploration of his patterns and the determination of their origin in early relationships.

8. Disclosure of the archaic nature of his disturbing life trends and mechanisms of defense.

9. Challenging of his early attitudes.

10. Serious consideration of rights to a more productive life.

11. Intense dissatisfaction with his current patterns, insecurities and devaluated self-esteem.

12. Experimentation with new modes of behavior.

13. Liberation from old values and types of action.

14. Evolution of greater security, assertiveness, self-esteem, and a sense of mastery.

15. Development of a different conception of himself, of more constructive interpersonal relationships, and of greater capacities for the expression of biologic and social needs.

These stages of understanding and adaptive action are never pursued by the patient in as rigidly sequential a manner as has been outlined. There is generally a shifting back and forth, and, as one pattern is discovered and explored, new discoveries are made that call for further elaboration.

The principle techniques by which the therapist helps the patient to the acquisition of insight are: (1) interview procedures, (2) free association, (3) dream analysis, and (4) the examination of attitudes toward the therapist, including transference.

34

Identifying Important Trends and Patterns:
The Use of Therapeutic Interviewing

In all forms of psychotherapy, except freudian psychoanalysis, the focused interview is the chief exploratory vehicle. From material obtained in the initial interview and during the early sessions, the therapist will have some idea of the sources and dynamics of the patient's symptoms. Of these the patient may be fully conscious, partially conscious, or, more rarely, completely unconscious. Underlying causes and dynamics are investigated through such techniques as maintaining the flow of verbalizations, directing their course through selective focusing, and devices like accenting, summarizing, restating, reflecting, establishing connections and maintaining tension in the interview. It is imperative that the therapist become thoroughly conversant with the principles of interviewing which have been described in chapter 15, The Conduct of the Psychotherapeutic Interview. For without a good understanding of interviewing, he will be handicapped in carrying the patient through the middle phases of therapy.

In attempting to identify important patterns during the interview, the therapist may listen carefully for a dominant theme which tinctures the patient's verbalizations. Sometimes unexpressed feelings are as significant or more significant than the verbalizations themselves. The patient's non-verbal behavior also reveals many important clues. Slips of speech, hesitations, blocks, evasions and changes in content may furthermore give the therapist warning of conflictual areas. The therapist must constantly sensitize himself to evidences of conflict in the various concerns of the patient.

The following excerpt is an illustration of how insight may be gained through focused interviewing. The patient, an associate editor on a magazine, interested in music as a possible profession, brings up an incident in her work with an orchestra which arouses in her a destructive neurotic pattern.

Pt. I was getting along fine, but then things started to go wrong. (pause)
Th. Wrong? [repeating the last word to focus on the source of the difficulty]
Pt. Everything went bad. My head hurt and my stomach kicked up badly.
Th. How long did this go on? [attempting to focus the patient's attention away from symptoms]
Pt. It all started vaguely about two days ago. (pause)
Th. Anything happen at that time? [probing for a cause]
Pt. Nothing unusual . . . I've been menstruating, and have a lot more pain than usual. I listened to a recording of our orchestra last Tuesday, and it sounded

very bad, particularly in parts where I came in. [*The patient advances environmental happenings which may or may not be causative.*]

Th. How did this make you feel? [*focusing on feelings*]

Pt. Well, I'm disgusted. I wonder why they have to have a group of inexperienced people with us. It makes me feel no good too. [*What comes to mind at this time is, first, that the patient is resentful and cannot adequately express her resentment; and second, that she is blaming and devaluating herself.*]

Th. This disgusts you. [*repeating the patient's expressed feeling*]

Pt. Yes, I'm furious at them, but it's impossible to say anything. [*This sounds like suppressed or repressed hostility.*]

Th. That must be very frustrating. [*expressing sympathy with how the patient feels*]

Pt. Yes, it is. How can they expect to have a good orchestra if they include beginners? [*The patient apparently seeks approval here for her resentment.*]

Th. It does sound unreasonable. [*backing the patient up in her feeling*]

Pt. I am so mad that I feel like quitting. (*clenches fists*) [*Apparently my encouragement helped to mobilize this aggression.*]

Th. Mm hmm.

Pt. But I know I won't. (*pause*)

Th. You must get something out of wanting to stay in the orchestra in spite of how bad things are. [*inquiring about positive values in her present situation*]

Pt. I don't think anything is worth what I go through.

Th. Then you may have the temptation to give up your place in the orchestra in spite of any possible good it does you.

Pt. But why should I be pushed out of a good thing? [*Apparently there are many positive values in her present situation.*]

Th. Yes, why should you? [*supporting the patient in her determination*]

Pt. (*pause*) You know, I ordinarily would get mad and then quit. I've done this about many things all my life—school, jobs, everything. I'd get mad and then blow everything up. It's awful. [*Patient recognizes a destructive pattern related to how she handles frustration and hostility. This insight should be of great value to her.*]

Th. There must have been a reason why you did this. [*focusing her attention on causes*]

Pt. I'd get so mad, I'd be willing to blow everything up including myself. I'm not going to let myself be maneuvered out of the orchestra though. I'm not going to be that silly.

Th. But your anger may be hard to control. [*warning her of possibilities of repetition of her neurotic behavior*]

Pt. Yes, I know, but I won't let it—at least now I won't. [*Her understanding of her resentment encourages more rational behavior.*]

The focus in interviewing may be on the patient's symptoms, feelings, environmental dissatisfactions, interpersonal relationships, past history, slips of speech, and on the therapist's "intuitive" understanding of the patient's problems.

FOCUSING ON SYMPTOMS

While symptoms are mere surface manifestations of deeper problems, a careful exploration of their content and function, and of the patient's attitudes toward them may reveal important data about repudiated impulses, as well as defenses against the impulses.

Focusing on symptoms is largely for the purpose of demonstrating their relationship to underlying feelings. In order to do this the patient's attention should be brought to undercurrent emotions whenever he mentions his complaints. It is important also to explore the relationship of symptoms to definite life situations. If the therapist knows how to employ dreams, these may advantageously be used to establish the connections of symptoms with feelings and causal life situations.

A patient who had come to therapy because of depression following the rupture of a love affair started a session with the complaint of a skin symptom. Focusing on the symptom brought out the fact that it was a conversion phenomenon, resulting from certain conflicts of which the patient became aware during interviewing.

Pt. Margaret was in my apartment no more than two hours when I noticed my arms itching. I took off my jacket. [*Margaret is the young woman with whom the patient is having an affair, after the violent rupture of a relationship with another young woman.*]

Th. Where was the itch?

Pt. On both arms, the round surface up here just below the elbow, like a band.

Th. I see.

Pt. It started in the left arm and then it spread to this arm in the same place.

Th. Exactly the same kind of band?

Pt. Yes, and several hours after that I noticed a band about the size of six inches over the ankle on both sides. Almost like a wide bracelet.

Th. Mm hmm.

Pt. And immediately I thought, "Jesus Christ I'm itching." Funny I hadn't had it before. And Margaret said, "What are you so nervous about?" And then I started on her. "I don't know," I said, "I don't know what it is." (*pause*)

Th. Now suppose you talk about the things that happened to you just before you got this itch. [*focusing on possible causes*]

Pt. Well, I was coming home from work and I decided to walk on Harriet's street, where she lives. [*Harriet is the young woman with whom the patient was in love and who broke up the relationship.*] I passed Harriet's house and looked up and saw the light on and figured what's going on there. I'm itching like hell now. There must be a direct connection. This proves it. This itching is bad. I scratched so furiously I drew blood. So I said, "Jesus Christ that's stupid." So I put some salve on. Then I went to sleep with Margaret. I went to sleep and I dreamed about Harriet. I dreamed I was back with her and I was suspicious as to what she wanted from me. She seemed to want to screw me, that is, get physically in me. I don't know if she was on my back, on the side, or what. She was bent forward in what I suppose was her driving position. I asked her why she was back, but she gave me no clear-cut answer except that she wanted "to get laid." Then I realized that she wanted to reduce me to impotence. I played along with her even though I didn't trust her. Then, in another room another girl came into sight. I thought I can lay this other dame. Do I owe Harriet anything? No. I don't trust her. I'll do as I want. I felt, the hell with her. (*pause*) That's all. (*pause*)

Th. I see. What are your ideas about that?

Pt. Well, you see, Harriet did make me impotent. That is, I got impotent with her. She kept comparing me with the other guys she screwed. She'd say, "Be a man and fuck me like the others did." It would make me furious. I'd compare myself with them, and ask her about them. She kept telling me that I didn't rate much when it came to fucking.

Th. What do you think this did to you?

Pt. I got so I couldn't function with her and I got impotent.

Th. And then she threw you out.

Pt. That god-damn bitch. I hate her. Margaret is such a better person. Considerate and kind, but . . . (*pause*)

Th. But . . . (*pause*)

Pt. I shouldn't feel so dissatisfied with her.

Th. But you do.

Pt. I must. I keep on thinking about Harriet. The other days when I walked by her house—I do that now a lot—I would look up at her room and feel relieved that the place was dark. Then I'd figure where else is she, and I'd say that she must be screwing in somebody else's apartment, not her own. But I'd push that out of my mind. This time when I saw the light, I felt very upset. I said to myself that she is half undressed or she's all undressed. She's in bed with a guy. He's undressing her or she's undressing him. I don't know who the guy is. He's probably a son-of-a-bitch who doesn't look anything like me.

Th. What emotional effect did it have on you?

Pt. I thought to myself, it's amazing how little it concerns you; you have no reaction.

Th. It astonished you?

Pt. Where is the reaction there, I said. I'm going with Margaret. I've got a better girl. I thought I'd go home and make love to Margaret. So when I got home, there was Margaret, and then I got that god-damned itch.

Th. Mm hmm.

Pt. I kept thinking about what time this man with Harriet went home. Then I began to resent Margaret. I felt why can't Harriet be with me.

Th. In other words, Harriet still has more value to you than Margaret.

Pt. (*scratching his arms*) This itch is awful. I gradually moved into the position of asking Harriet to marry me. Every time I built up to the point she greeted me with complete silence.

Th. How do you feel about being with Margaret now?

Pt. I feel like I've got chains on.

Th. What kind of chains?

Pt. Tying me down. (*touches itching area of arm*) (*pause*) You know I just thought of something. I thought of chains in Egyptian times used to tie down slaves. You've seen pictures of them. I have seen pictures of them.

Th. What do the pictures look like?

Pt. Either there or here—bands of iron with the chain between them and anklets governing the size of the step. And, you know, the bands of irons on the arms and legs are like, in the same position as the areas of my itching!

Th. So the conclusion would be what?

Pt. That I'm wearing chains.

Th. And the scratching?

Pt. (*excitedly*) I want to tear them off.

Th. But these emotional chains you're wearing are what?

Pt. Jesus Christ, I feel a defiance. This thing is building up with Margaret. I was getting to think I was comfortable, but I resented the comfort. She's giving up her job, fluttering around, looking for this, looking for that. Basically she's here to stay because she wants to be with me. I feel as if I'm in chains with her. I don't want to marry her.

Th. So Margaret is your chain and you want to get rid of her. [*interpreting*]

Pt. But I know what is enslaving me. I don't want chains on me so I can go back to Harriet. But, shit, I don't want to go back to her; she's chains for me too. [*We thereafter discuss his masochistic need to be dominated and hurt by women.*]

FOCUSING ON FEELINGS

Feelings that are openly manifested or that lurk unexpressed behind verbalizations are extremely important aspects of the inner life of the person. Feelings cannot be isolated from intellectual and behavioral components, although anxiety may cause a dissociation. By constant focusing on feelings, and encouraging verbalization, a reunion of dissociated elements may be effectuated. Awareness of feelings and their meaning brings the patient to an understanding of his relationships with people and to some of the basic sources of his symptoms.

Thus, a patient may talk about his work situation: sympathizing with his employer, he presents an account of how difficult things must be for his employer. The responsibilities that confront the employer are so pressing that they would make anyone irritable and hard to approach. He feels sorry for his employer on this account, and he forgives the employer's rudeness. The therapist, legitimately suspecting that the patient feels resentment he does not dare to express, or of which he is unaware, may decide to focus on latent hostility by saying, "Doesn't such behavior on the part of your employer irritate you?" or "I should imagine that your employer's attitudes would sometimes make you mad." This may liberate an acknowledgment of resentment, and a more precise investigation of attitudes toward the employer and toward other authorities.

Another patient may be aware of strong sexual feelings in relation to a teacher. Such feelings preoccupy her a large part of the day. She has no idea of why the teacher has made so vivid an impression on her. The therapist, in order to help the patient connect her feelings with attitudes toward the teacher, may say, "The teacher arouses certain feelings in you. Have you had similar feelings toward other people?" A description of previous situations in which sexual feelings were intense may reveal a succession of men with certain qualities. Asking the patient what all the men have in common may bring out the fact that they all resemble her older brother of whom she was enamored as a child, and toward whom she had strong sexual feelings which made her feel guilty.

During the treatment of a patient with a psychophysiologic intestinal disorder, a session was occupied listening to explosive outbursts directed by the patient at her children who were going through a recalcitrant, defiant stage in their development. She brought out several incidents in which one of her children demanded attention and she pushed him away. The patient berated herself for acting so heartlessly. As she spoke, I noticed what seemed to be a frightened expression on her face. Bringing this to her attention, she smiled with relief, and said, "You're right. I just realized that I am afraid, as if I expected you to beat me." She then revealed incidents where her father beat her for doing "wrong things."

In focusing on feelings, it is essential to help the patient to a realization that many of his emotions are not rooted in reality, but derive from misconceptions about life, about people and about himself. The patient's attention may be directed toward a variety of aspects; such as, the relationship of feelings to disturbing symptoms, the environmental situations that stir up untoward emotions, the repetitive patterns of behavior that provoke destructive feelings, and the relationship with the therapist.

In the following fragment, focusing in the session on the patient's feelings of tension and discomfort helps to bring him to an awareness of how disappointed he is in his progress, and how resentful he is toward me. He realizes that his resentment conflicts with the pattern of constant need for approval, and that his inability to express resentment fosters his symptoms.

Pt. I have a funny feeling of uneasiness that's been with me all day, all week, I mean.

Th. Any clues to this feeling?

Pt. No, just my feeling bad. Even yesterday I felt like throwing up.

Th. When did this uneasiness get most uncomfortable?

Pt. Just before coming here. (*pause*)

Th. Just before coming here?

Pt. I think I'm disappointed that I'm not better than I am. I've been coming here two months now. I feel I've accomplished nothing. I can't put it more bluntly.

Th. Well, you have a right to feel disappointed, if you expected an immediate cure. Sometimes, rarely, this happens, but usually it takes a period of time before a person learns about patterns that stir up symptoms.

Pt. This whole week of complete tension made me think. But I could only think of my tension. I can't organize my thoughts. These thoughts are meaningless to me until I get so bad I have to force myself to think and try to solve my problem.

Th. Mm hmm (*pause*)

Pt. I feel insecure and inferior and I need approval. Why do I need this approval? Because I have no security in myself. So I need somebody else's approval. So I don't act on my own motives. I try to be a smiling servant to everybody, to gain their good graces, to gain their approval. I lower myself to kiss everybody's behind to get their approval. Now why haven't I got confidence in myself?

Th. That's a good question. If you need approval from the outside and have no confidence from within, there are reasons for it.

Pt. Why don't I have that self-security or self-approval?

Th. Well, what do *you* think?

Pt. I don't know. (*smiles*) But I do think you are helping me.

Th. But that isn't what you were just telling me.

Pt. Well . . . (*pause*)

Th. Could it be that you tell me this to get *my* approval—right now, I mean?

Pt. I know I told you I was disappointed in therapy. Maybe it doesn't make any difference what you think. I'm coming here and paying my hard-earned money and I have a right to say it.

Th. You have a right to say what you feel.

Pt. Maybe . . . wouldn't it be enough to cause tension for me to want to criticize you if I needed your approval, like I need everybody's approval? [*This sounds like insight.*]

Th. It might be.

Pt. So, if I got mad at you, that would be enough to make me feel that you wouldn't give me approval if I told you. And that could upset me like I was upset. But now that I've told you, I feel relieved and not upset any more.

FOCUSING ON ENVIRONMENTAL DISSATISFACTIONS

Only rarely are reality circumstances entirely responsible for the patient's condition. Catastrophic life happenings occasionally do occur in the form of accidents, inclemencies of nature, disasters of war, death of close relatives and friends, and financial and prestige losses. Operative also are pressures of desperate economic circumstances, unemployment, inimical work conditions, unhappy choice of occupation, bad housing, disturbing neighborhood, abnormal cultural standards and pressures, and exposure to destructive family members and mate. The reactions of the patient to his environment, however, are usually more important than the environmental distortions themselves.

Most persons project their insecurities, expectations, fears, guilt feelings and hostilities onto their environment. The presence of disturbing life circumstances that seem to justify these attitudes may satisfy the individual's needs and expectations; their absence may create a void in the person's life and perhaps incite him toward involvement in some situational difficulty. Thus, an individual who is intensely hostile may manipulate his environment in such a way that he can conveniently vent his hostility. He may entangle himself in relationships with aggressive or domineering people, or get engulfed in situations in which he is exploited. These conditions will tend to justify to himself his own outbursts of hostility, and to support his protestations that he is being misused. He will bitterly protest his plight, little mindful of the fact that he has created the very conditions of which he is so indignant. Indeed, where there are inadequate circumstances to warrant the deep hostility he feels, he will experience depression, tension, anxiety and various psychophysiologic reactions. Environmental manipulation, and other supportive efforts directed at the milieu rather than at the individual may fail utterly in their effectiveness here, or may precipitate neurotic symptoms more incapacitating than those for which therapy was originally sought. Even in severe environmental distortions, the personality of the patient must be taken into account as a primary concern.

The following excerpt brings out how a patient gains an awareness of patterns of aggression through the consideration of her immediate life situation.

Pt. My husband has been acting up constantly. Just doing mean things. I asked him if he would go out with me and he said in a nasty way, "Don't intimidate me."

Then he said, "Goodbye, you bitch." I had no desire to look at that bastard after that. Then I visited some old friends and stayed out until 1 a.m. When I got home, he was waiting up for me. He screamed at me, "What the hell do you think you are doing." The nagging continued. He said, "A fine household I have." I told him to go to the devil. He shook his finger at me. I pushed his hand away and told him to just stop that. I was going to hit him before he hit me. This marriage of mine is what's causing all my trouble. (*pause*)

Th. You must have felt very upset.

Pt. I was. He is so insulting all the time. I called him a son of a bitch, and then told him to go to hell and went to bed. I woke up 4 a.m. crying, and went over to him and woke him up and warned him. I said, "Why should you sleep when I can't." I shook him and told him I'd break his head open if he repeated it.

Th. You didn't want to let him get away with anything?

Pt. You're darned tootin'. And I won't. I won't with anyone. Anybody starts anything, and I finish it.

Th. What usually happens after you finish it?

Pt. That's just it. Nobody seems to understand. I make enemies.

Th. Is it possible that any aggression toward you sets a process into motion where you explode a little too much? [*a tentative interpretation*]

Pt. I have to do what I do to protect myself.

Th. Mm hmm. (*pause*)

Pt. Maybe I *do* go to extremes though. (*pause*)

Th. Perhaps to protect yourself, you feel you have to go to extremes. [*more interpretation*]

Pt. But I do see that it can give people the impression that I'm an attacking bitch. I think I do go to extremes. Maybe I shouldn't explode the way I do. Maybe I cause some of my own troubles.

Th. Is this something you'd consider a pattern?

Pt. I can see that it's been with me many years. I used to be a timid thing, but my marriage made a change. I seem to have gone to the opposite extreme.

FOCUSING ON CURRENT INTERPERSONAL RELATIONS

Identification of basic patterns and conflicts may be achieved through an examination of the patient's relationships with other people. The characterologic strivings of the patient in relation to authority, to compeers and to himself are, in addition to environmental happenings, a dominant theme in the interviews. Such strivings may indicate why the patient's adjustment is being sabotaged. For example, he may anticipate criticism and attack from others. Accordingly, his life will be spent in fearful anticipation, in detaching himself from others or in retaliatory counter-attack. He may, in contemplating exploitation, assiduously avoid intimate contact with people, and then act outraged at his isolation. He may feel forced to assume a submissive and ingratiating role, and then burn inwardly at the indignation of needing to humiliate himself in this way. He may be consumed by a power drive, and want to domineer all persons with whom he has dealings. These drives will become evident as the patient talks about his daily concerns and tribulations.

The relationship disturbances manifested by the patient will usually be vigorously defended by him, and he will attempt to justify them with rationalizations. He may even incite the individuals with whom he relates to provocations that precipitate the very reactions about which he complains. Repeated demonstrations are usually required before the patient recognizes how he distorts reality in line with his expectations.

It may be possible, therefore, by considering his immediate relationships with people, to bring the individual to an awareness of how his patterns influence his adjustment and maladjustment. Sooner or later he will express dissatisfaction with his patterns, but he will recognize the compulsive hold they have on him. He will realize, too, that his patterns serve a spurious and temporary function of enhancing his security and of bolstering his self-esteem.

The following excerpt illustrates how a consideration of current interpersonal relations may bring a patient to cognizance of important strivings. In the session the patient exhibits tension and he relates it to a recent meeting with a woman who had attracted him. He becomes aware of ambivalent attitudes toward certain women.

Pt. I just don't know what it is that upsets me, and I've been having lots of trouble.

Th. Let's talk about it and maybe we'll learn something about it.

Pt. I don't know what it is. My wife is having trouble with the kids. She thinks I'm not sympathetic. It's like I fear she'll attack or criticize me.

Th. Mm hmm.

Pt. And I met this woman and I found myself thinking about going with her, (*pause*) having an affair, I mean.

Th. Mm hmm.

Pt. But I don't want to go out with her. (*pause*)

Th. Why?

Pt. I don't know. She's very attractive, but still . . . (*pause*)

Th. Anything to do with your wife and how she would feel?

Pt. Oh, no. It's more to do with her—the woman. I feel like irritating and teasing her.

Th. What does she mean to you?

Pt. I have a picture of her as a big wheel in the community. I think she is a person who likes to control things with men. I feel she doesn't want to be at home, wants to be a big wheel in the community.

Th. I see. (*pause*)

Pt. I'm a sucker for this kind of woman. Before I know it I'm up to my neck in trouble. I go for them and then I can't get away. I feel like digging at this woman. Not that I'm mad at her personally, but she does something to me.

Th. The fact that you feel she's a big wheel in the community seems to have something to do with it. [*making a connection for the patient*]

Pt. I hate women who try to wear the pants. My first wife was like that. My mother was like that. Never home, always telling you what to do.

Th. But this type of woman seems to attract you.

Pt. Yes, that's the peculiar thing. I smell them out. At any party I make a beeline for certain women, and, by gosh, there I am.

Th. What do you think this means?

Pt. Well, there's only one conclusion. I must be crazy about them and hate them too. I must want to suffer to get involved with them, but that's what I keep doing. [*This is the first inkling of awareness the patient had of this problem.*]

Th. It sounds like a vicious circle.

Pt. But I'm not going to call this woman I met (*laughs*) although I must admit the temptation is great.

Th. Well, that will at least give us an opportunity to investigate this attitude you have toward certain kinds of women.

FOCUSING ON PAST HISTORY

Inimical influences in early childhood, sometimes produced by improper handling by parents, sometimes by unfortunate experiences in relationship with other persons, can be catastrophic even to children who have the most perfect heredity. Where experiences during early life are harmonious, the child is able to evolve a system of security which permits him to regard the world as a bountiful place, and to develop self-esteem that encourages assertiveness and self-confidence. He will be convinced of his capacities to love and to be loved. He will most probably possess character strivings that enable him to relate constructively to other persons, and to express, through culturally condoned outlets, social and biologic needs. On the other hand, where the child has been rejected, overprotected or unduly intimidated, the world will constitute for him a place of menace. He will be devastated by fears and tensions. His self-esteem will be warped to a point where he is overwhelmed by feelings of helplessness, by lack of assertiveness and loss of self-confidence. His relationships with people will be disturbed with the harboring of destructive attitudes toward others. Finally, inner strivings and demands will suffer repression in greater or lesser degree.

It will usually be discerned during interviewing that the patient projects onto others attitudes and impulses derived from relationships with important past personages. Thus, the individual may regard and treat certain people as rejecting mothers, punitive fathers, and jealous or hostile siblings, irrespective of the reality elements in his existing relationships. If his early experiences with his mother had conditioned him to expect that women are overprotecting, there is apt to be an automatic transfer of this attitude toward all women, or specifically toward those persons who symbolize in his mind a mother image. As defensive gestures, one may observe in the relationships of the individual toward others such attitudes as detachment, resentment, aggression, submissiveness and masochism that have no affinity with the reality situation. Where the patient has been unfavorably conditioned by strong sibling rivalry in childhood, he may respond to people as if they were facsimiles of destructive brothers and sisters. The individual's social and work relationships will possess a pervasive competitive tinge that expresses itself in fears of being vanquished, or in triumphing over others.

Other aspects of the past history are also important in understanding the life circumstances under which adjustment is most adept and maladjustment most apparent. Repetitive patterns will clearly be evident as one focuses on different epochs in the patient's past.

Through proper interviewing the patient may be brought to an awareness of his trends and mechanisms of defense as they have manifested themselves in his past life. The tracing of his interpersonal patterns to their origins in his childhood, their disclosure as archaic and destructive to reality functioning, will also enhance a challenging of early attitudes and a new conception of the self.

A patient with a personality problem of detachment which had interfered with her capacity to establish a relationship with men, came to therapy because of a feeling that she would never get married because of her attitudes. Focusing on her past life brought out certain trends that were operating in the present.

Pt. I feel that I have the capacity to feel, but I feel impersonal about everything. I've had this feeling as far back as I can think. With my father I was given the basic necessities of life—food, clothing—but aside from that there was nothing.

Th. Nothing?

Pt. One never dreamed of going close to him for everything. I remember when I was little I would run to him, but he would keep pushing me away. I felt it was wrong to need him. I felt awful when I was little, but then I felt all right. At school I had some friends, but I never felt close to them.

Th. Did you ever feel warm and close to any person in your past?

Pt. Yes, I had a music teacher. I felt he knew me and understood me. I felt that he was like God. But I hated him too. He seduced me. I couldn't resist him. I felt awful about the thing.

Th. Mm hmm.

Pt. I remember once my father came home with a box of candy. He handed it to me, and I was so happy I cried. Father asked me why I was crying and I didn't know.

Th. Do you know why now?

Pt. I believe that meant to me he preferred me. But he didn't. He said, "That's for your mother, bring it to her." I cried and cried and never got over it. I felt it was better not to expect anything.

Th. Not to expect *anything?*

Pt. From people I mean.

Th. Could that account for one of the reasons why you can't feel anything now? [*interpretation*]

Pt. You mean a feeling I might be disappointed. (*cries*) I do expect that all the time.

OBSERVATIONS OF SLIPS OF SPEECH

While slips of speech do not happen frequently, focusing on them when they do occur may reveal significant patterns. A young woman, in a defiant relationship with her father, showed a poor response to therapy during the first few months. During one session, she exhibited a slip of speech which revealed rebellious attitudes toward any type of control.

Pt. I just don't know what I'm getting out of life right now.

Th. What are you getting out of coming *here* right now?

Pt. I come here to get well—that's my *blame.* [*slip of speech*]

Th. That's your *blame?*

Pt. Did I say that? I meant that's my *aim.*

Th. You said "blame." I wonder if you blame yourself.

Pt. (*blushes*) Maybe I'm ashamed of myself.

Th. Ashamed of coming here?

Pt. I just think I don't want to get well to annoy you.

Th. To annoy me?

Pt. You know that I'm capable of doing anything, and I slop around so.

Th. Maybe you are slopping around for my benefit. (*smiles*)

Pt. (*blushes*) I don't want you to get too controlling. I feel if you would only leave me alone.

Th. You feel I control you?

Pt. Yes, I do.

Th. How?

Pt. Not so much control as I need to do things for myself. I don't want you to interfere.

Th. Am I interfering?

Pt. This is what's funny. You don't, but I think I do feel you do. I don't like anybody controlling me.

Th. But why do you come here then if I do these terrible things to you?

Pt. I look on you as my bridge to health. I don't want to be this way. I don't like to slop around. I can see this is something I do all the time. Even good things I throw away, because the goodness spells danger in my standing alone.

Th. So that your "blame" in coming here is in not wanting to do what part of you wants, which is health? [*interpreting the slip of speech*]

Pt. I'm being a horror by fighting everybody, I know. Why do I act so rebellious?

Th. That's a good question. Let's start investigating that.

USE OF INTUITION

Sometimes the therapist has to depend on "hunches" and "intuition" in perceiving what is going on in the patient. By self-observation, the therapist may recognize certain emotions in himself that are evoked by what the patient is saying or not saying. The therapist may use this "intuitive" feeling in various ways, as by questioning, reflecting feeling, focusing and interpreting. Where the therapist is sensitive and has had a great deal of experience, he may be able to perceive nuances through this use of "intuition" that escape the usual observational methods. "Intuition" is probably a misnomer, since the skill alluded to does not just automatically happen; it is acquired by an astute therapist with good clinical judgment who has had extensive clinical experience.

Identifying Important Trends and Patterns: The Use of Free Association

FREE ASSOCIATION IS EMPLOYED EXCLUSIVELY IN RECONSTRUCTIVE psychotherapy, particularly in Freudian psychoanalysis in which it constitutes the primary kind of communication. The use of the couch position, the extreme passivity of the therapist, and his removal from the line of vision of the patient, reduces the influence of reality to a minimum. This encourages internally inspired stimuli. As a result, thought images reflect unconscious dynamic conflicts and impulses which come to the surface in a more or less direct form.

Patients must be trained to associate freely. Verbalization of thoughts without restraint is often very difficult, because obscene ideas, distressing recollections, and offensive notions concerning the therapist may press for expression. As a defensive gesture, the patient may exhibit blocks in his stream of thought, or he may try to protect himself by going off into reverie. Impulses and strivings even at the periphery of awareness may be so repulsive that the person may not dare to permit himself to think of them.

Some resistances to free association are relatively superficial. The patient may believe that the therapist considers his fears and fantasies absurd because he, himself, considers them ridiculous. He may want to analyze his impulses and actions beforehand, since he anticipates censure, or he may feel that the therapist will think more of him if he analyzes his problems without help. There may be a conscious need to maintain control, with resistance extended toward the revelation of significant material. An intense fear of failure may foster an inability to utter what comes to mind.

By far the majority of resistances to free association are unconscious in nature. The patient may want to cooperate, but whenever he attempts to verbalize fantasies and thought images, he experiences, to his consternation, anxiety that blocks his efforts. He may not even be aware of anxiety, because memory of the traumatic material is so fleeting that it never actually occupies the field of attention. In some cases the character structure acts in resistance to free association. The individual's pattern of life, for instance, may be so stereotyped that he will permit nothing spontaneous to intrude itself. He may fear expressing hostile or erotic impulses if he lets himself go, or he may be convinced that releasing his thoughts will uncover the fact that he is inept and contemptible. On this basis, he may exhibit a mental or vocal inertia that can develop into mutism.

The following example of free association demonstrates how a female patient of thirty-eight with a phobic disorder gains an understanding of certain unconscious conflicts.

Pt. So I started walking, and walking, and decided to go behind the museum and walk through Central Park. So I walked and went through a back field and felt very excited and wonderful. I saw a park bench next to a clump of bushes and sat down. There was a rustle behind me and I got frightened. I thought of men concealing themselves in the bushes. I thought of the sex perverts I read about in Central Park. I wondered if there was someone behind me exposing himself. The idea is repulsive, but exciting too. I think of father now and feel excited. I think of an erect penis. This is connected with my father. There is something about this pushing in my mind. I don't know what it is, like on the border of my memory. (*pause*)

Th. Mm hmm. (*pause*) On the border of your memory?

Pt. (*The patient breathes rapidly and seems to be under great tension.*) As a little girl, I slept with my father. I get a funny feeling. I get a funny feeling over my skin, tingly-like. It's a strange feeling, like a blindness, like not seeing something. My mind blurs and spreads over anything I look at. I've had this feeling off and on since I walked in the park. My mind seems to blank off like I can't think or absorb anything. [*This sounds like a manifestation of repression, with inhibiton of intellectual functioning, perhaps as a way of coping with the anxiety produced by a return of the repressed.*]

Th. The blurring of your mind may be a way of pushing something out you don't want there. [*interpreting her symptoms as resistance*]

Pt. I just thought of something. When father died, he was nude. I looked at him, but I couldn't see anything, I couldn't think clearly. I was brought up not to be aware of the difference between a man and a woman. I feared my father, and yet I loved him. I slept with him when I was very little, on Saturdays and Sundays. A wonderful sense of warmth and security. There was nothing warmer or more secure. A lot of pleasure. I tingle all over now. It was a wonderful holiday when I was allowed to sleep with father. I can't seem to remember anything now. There's a blur in my mind. I feel tense and afraid.

Th. That blur contaminates your life. You are afraid of something or afraid of remembering something. [*focusing on her resistance*]

Pt. Yes, yes, but I can't. How can I? How can I?

Th. What comes to your mind?

Pt. Sunday I got stomach pains. I was depressed and frightened. I started crying. I wanted to hold onto mother. What is the use of becoming aware of needs if you can't satisfy them. I had a dream that night. A group of army officers in my sister's room. I felt jealous. They weren't interested in me. Then I was on the water. One man was walking on water with no legs. He walked confidently. I asked him where his legs were, and he said that when he had legs he felt strong and masculine. Then I see flowers and I feel lost. Then I am on a ruined street. I see an old horse, emaciated, waiting to be slaughtered. I'm horrified, sick, upset. I have flowers, but everybody criticizes them. I felt they weren't good. And that's all.

Th. What do you associate to the dream?

Pt. I felt the officers kissed my sister and mother and not me. I feel father gave my sister and mother everything and not me. I wanted to look into the room where the officers were with my sister, but my mother wouldn't let me. I was mad. I remember a part of the dream where I saw condoms in a box. I felt my sister could have it and not I. I feel deprived and helpless, like a mutilated person. That must be me walking on the water. I walk, but like a cripple. I want to be strong and not weak. Men are strong. My father wouldn't let me grow up. My sister has a husband and I don't have one. She has everything. I have nothing. Not anything that is worth while. What I have is not much. I always wanted to be strong. I used to fantasy being a boy and having a penis. I suppose the flowers in the dream are my femininity. I put little value on myself. I realize now how bitter I feel toward father for not devoting himself to me. [*The patient goes on to correlate her incestuous wishes, her castration fears and her penis envy.*]

36

Identifying Important Trends and Patterns: The Use of Dreams and Fantasies

IN ALL FORMS OF PSYCHOTHERAPY, DREAMS GIVE THE THERAPIST important clues, not only about dynamics, but also about the therapeutic process itself. The use that is made of dreams will depend largely on the skills of the therapist. In supportive therapy, dreams help the therapist perceive more accurately the inner responses of the patient; however, the dream material itself is not usually discussed. In reeducative therapy, therapists who are adequately trained may utilize dreams with the object of investigating important patterns. In reconstructive approaches, dream analysis is constantly employed and is considered indispensable for the proper implementation of therapy.

THE STRUCTURE OF DREAMS

Dreams are not random productions of the mind; rather they fulfill a vital purpose in the psychic economy. Freud pointed out that the prime function of dreams was to safeguard sleep by fostering solution in fantasy of powerful needs, fears and conflicts that were too dangerous or repulsive for resolution in reality. Dreams apparently aid in the psychic mastery of seemingly insoluble situations, providing for a discharge of tension, a propitiation of deep wishes and demands, and a working-through to a successful conclusion of destructive experiences that defy the coping capacities of the individual in the waking state. The wish-fulfilling drives represented in dreams are compromised by the demands of the repressing forces. What the dreamer then tends to satisfy is not the raw wish, but a compromise made necessary by the repressing elements. An important effect of dreams is to discharge the emotion that is associated with deep conflicts in the personality.

With the shutting out of sensory receptors and the progressive cortical inhibition induced by sleep, a number of important changes occur in the operative psychic processes. These changes, reflecting themselves in dreams, consist of the following:

1. Visual images rather than words are employed to represent concepts.

2. The mind becomes contaminated with an archaic, prelogical kind of ideation that utilizes perseverations and stereotypes. There is a replacement of abstract conceptual, for concrete thinking, and an abandonment of accepted rules of time and space.

3. Certain distortions prevail in dreams, probably conditioned, first by a need to evade the psychic censorship which continues to operate in sleep, though to a lesser degree than in the waking state, and, second, by a primitive type of thinking that seems to be released by inhibition of the higher cortical centers. Inacceptable and repudiated aspects of the personality are, through distortions, made acceptable to the dreamer's ego.

4. Among the mechanisms serving the interests of distortion are symbolization, displacement, condensation, representation by multiples and opposites, secondary elaboration, and substitution for people of emotionally equated objects.

5. Symbolic representations are unique for the person, although there is some universality of symbols. Because primitive processes permeate the thinking process in sleep, there is a tendency toward a universal language in dreams. The similarity of experiences of the average person within a certain culture also makes for some unity of symbols.

THE CONTENT OF DREAMS

Each dream is a fragment of the total life experience of the individual. Two kinds of content are apparent. The first, the "manifest dream content," is an overlay of situations and events which mask more fundamental latent meanings. The manifest content is constructed out of events in the recent past, usually events of the previous day, blended with remembered situations in the distant past. The second, the "latent dream content," embraces some or all of the following:

1. Early memories or experiences, perhaps long forgotten, that have made a significant imprint on the person.

2. Attitudes and fantasies in relation to parental agencies and siblings.

3. Defenses that were elaborated against early experiences, conditionings and fantasies.

4. Emotionally important immediate life experiences.

5. Current wishes and demands in open or disguised form, as well as defenses against these.

6. Interpersonal strivings and attitudes.

7. Unconscious repudiated impulses and needs.

8. Nascent conflicts that agitate the person and create tensions and anxieties.

9. Patterns of reaction and mechanisms of defense habitually utilized by the person.

10. Latent character strivings and latent mechanisms of defense.

11. Representation of different aspects of the self, as well as disparate interpersonal drives, through such symbols as multiple characters.

12. Attitudes toward therapy, including resistances to the various phases of treatment, and defensive reactions that are marshalled by interpretations.

13. Attitudes toward the therapist including transference manifestations.

THE THERAPEUTIC USE OF DREAMS

In requesting the patient to report his dreams, one may give him an explanation such as in the following excerpt:

Th. I should like to have you try to remember your dreams and bring them to me.

Pt. I never dream. Are dreams important?

Th. Dreams are important because when the mind is asleep problems that bother it are brought up more openly. In the waking state, a person pushes those problems away.

Pt. I suppose I dream, but I can't remember my dreams.

Th. All people dream, but many people don't remember their dreams. If you find it hard to remember your dreams, keep a pad of paper and a pencil at the head of your bed and jot down any dream fragments you remember the minute you get up. Otherwise they are likely to slip out of your mind. If you wake up in the middle of the night and have had a dream, take the time out to write it down.

Simple suggestions along these lines often induce dreaming. Should the patient persist in being unable to remember his dreams, the therapist may remark: "I wonder why it is that you have no dreams. It's possible that certain things are bothering you so much that you just don't remember what you dream." Mention of possible resistance sometimes promotes enough tension in the patient to force a break-through of a dream.

It is, however, generally unnecessary to employ adventitious methods to promote dreaming, for the patient will readily relate his dreams once he is told that the discussion of dream material is helpful in therapy. If the patient refrains from mentioning dreams spontaneously, he may be asked at each session whether he has any dreams to report.

The first dream after therapy has started is frequently of great moment, sometimes containing a cross-section of the patient's problem. It may require many months before the patient and the therapist will appreciate the full importance of the material portrayed in the dream.

During the third therapeutic session, a female patient presented her first dream:

My husband's family took suitcases to the station in a streetcar. I thought this was grubby.

Then, I dreamed of an old woman who invited me to eat roast lamb. It didn't seem good and I wouldn't eat more. I said it was spoiled, and if you kill and eat lamb that's led a lonely life, that makes you sad. And then—this is the horrible part—she prepared to kill another lamb. She got it partly skinned and the skin was up over its head, but it was alive. It kept looking at me for protection, linking its head in my arm and pulling me, as if to say, 'Please get me out of this,' And I thought, oh god, I wish I could help this poor creature, but the only way to help it is to kill it. But I didn't want to tell the lamb that. And I couldn't kill the lamb myself.

Then I dreamed I was on a cloud, high up; but it wasn't a cloud, it was terra firma. I was on the edge and with me on the earth-cloud was a young man. I didn't know what he looked like or who he was. I kept slipping off the cloud with a dreadful fear of falling off. He couldn't support me and I was panicky.

Then I dreamed I was in bed with my husband, Dick. A sex-dream. We just had an affair. He got up, but I stayed in bed and hid back under the bed covers. He came back with his penis erect. I wanted another affair, but he started horseplaying like a frisky kid.

Associations to the dream were barren. Even mention of the similarity between "kid" and "lamb" brought little response. The patient's feelings about her husband were hesitantly expressed, but were on the positive side. It was many months before the patient realized her ambivalent attitudes toward her husband, her pity for him as a "poor lamb" she felt she was destroying, and her murderous rage, mobilized shortly after her marriage, because her husband and his family were "grubby" people. She believed she had demeaned herself by a mismated alliance. Appreciating that she had been "up in the clouds" about her marriage, she realized that she was very much dissatisfied with the sexual aspects of her relationship. Her hostility had been self-directed and had expressed itself in depression and psychosomatic symptoms for which she sought psychotherapy. Her responses to her husband, positive and negative, were shown to be part of a larger pattern in her relationships with men that went back to her relationship as a child with her father. Her dream brought out many aspects of her problem, but her ego needed strengthening in therapy before she could accept the full implications of the dream.

THE TECHNIQUE OF DREAM INTERPRETATION

Once the patient has presented a dream to the therapist, it may be handled in a number of ways. Some therapists ask the patient to associate to the different objects, people and incidents in the dream. Others pick out a general theme from the content and then present this to the patient as a focus on which to concentrate. Still others formulate their impressions of the dream for the patient's benefit.

Inasmuch as every dream is a sampling of the person's total adjustment, and embraces diverse aspects of thinking, feeling and behavior, it is important to approach each dream in a disciplined way. It is also expedient to utilize dreams, at any special phase of therapy, for the purpose of promoting the goals of that particular phase. Thus, the same dream may be employed in different ways at different stages of therapy.

The techniques of dream interpretation include: (1) summarizing for the patient the basic trends in the dream, (2) asking the patient for spontaneous associations, (3) making a tentative, unverbalized formulation of the dynamics, and (4) encouraging further associations through focusing.

1. Summarizing for the Patient the Basic Trends in the Dream

Although this routine is not absolutely nesessary, it may be advantageously employed at the beginning stage of working with a dream. To illustrate this and other routines in dream interpretation, we may consider the following dream of a woman who has been in treatment for ten months:

A person—I don't know who it is—wants to kill me and my child. The room I'm in has a double dormer window, but the furniture is modern. I can't get out. I try to escape and can't. Then the next part is that I am somewhere with two men. One man wants me, but I don't like him and feel contempt for him. I like the other person, but he doesn't want me. I say to him, "I'm sick and going to die in two weeks." He reassures me and tells me he loves me and everything is sad and beautiful.

In summarizing the trends in the dream, the therapist may remark:

Now here is a dream that takes place in a room. A person is there who threatens to kill you and your child. You try to escape and can't. Then you are with two men. One you like, and one you don't. The one you like doesn't want you. You say you are sick and going to die. Then he tells you he loves you and everything is sad and beautiful.

2. Asking the Patient for Spontaneous Associations

Following the summarizing of the dream, or in the event summarizing is not employed as a routine, the patient may be asked to associate to the dream immediately after it has been reported. The following excerpt of the session with the patient whose dream was described above is illustrative:

Th. What are your associations to the incidents and people in the dream?

Pt. I don't know who the person is, but it's a man, like an ogre. I was frightened of him. He was making frightening gestures to us. (*pause*)

Th. What about the room?

Pt. There is something familiar about it. It's like the room I had when I was a girl. This was in North Carolina. The room I shared with my sister. It had a dormer window like the one in my dream. I'm sure this was the room.

Th. What about the furniture?

Pt. We had this curly maple old American furniture. But the furniture in my dream was modern, like (*looks around the room*) in your office. (*pause*)

Th. What about the rest of the dream?

Pt. Yes, this man who didn't like me was a very desirable man, the kind I feel so embarrassed with and uncomfortable. And the last part gives me a quiet, wonderful feeling as if everything is going to be all right.

3. Tentative Unverbalized Formulation of Dynamics

On the basis of what knowledge he has already gained of (a) the patient's problem, history, current life situation and dream symbols he has employed in the past; (b) the patient's associations to the present dreams; (c) what is happening immediately in the therapeutic situation; and (d) the therapist's intuitive feelings, the therapist will be able to make for himself some tentative formulations of the existing dynamics. These are concocted in full recognition of the fact that they may later have to be radically revised.

In organizing the material of the dream for purposes of this formulation, it is often helpful to employ a certain framework that considers the setting of the dream, the characters, the underlying wish, the revealed personality traits, the apparent mechanisms of defense, the ostensible conflicts, the movement, the outcome, and resistance and transference phenomena.

a. The setting of the dream. The therapist may ask himself a number of questions here, such as: What is the locale of the dream—outdoors, indoors, a changing setting? Does the patient recognize the locale? Does the locale have any special signifiance for the patient? Is there an indication as to the temporal setting—past, present or both?

In the dream we are using as an example, the setting seems, according to the associations of the patient, to be a fusion of the past (the room shared with her sister as a child) and the present (the therapist's office). One may speculate that the patient is talking about a situation or about feelings that are equally applicable to the past and to the present, or that, originating in the past, are being projected in the present.

b. The characters in the dream. Who are the characters in the dream? Are they identifiable people, do they resemble in appearance or behavior people the patient knows or has known in the past? What is the relation of the patient to the characters in the dream? How does the patient feel about the various characters? Are they possibly parental or sibling representatives? Are the characters in the dream representative of various aspects of the patient himself? Are any of the characters symbols for the therapist?

Referring to the dream that we are considering, the characters are the patient, her child, a hostile unidentified man, a man who likes the patient whom she rejects, and a man whom she likes but who rejects her. From her past history, there is a suggestion that the hostile man in the dream is representative of her father whom she considered a person one could never approach closely enough to know. She remembered him as one who was disposed to hostile outbursts. There is a possibility also that the man may be representative of the therapist (transference), since the patient had for several weeks manifested resistance in therapy, and had on several occasions mentioned that I seemed distant from her and that it was hard to get to know me. The other two men are probably representations of a dualistic attitude she displays toward men. In response to those men who express a liking for her, she exhibits coldness and contempt. On the other hand, she manifests a keen interest in men who are not approachable.

c. The underlying wish or need. A search will usually reveal one or more deep wishes or hidden demands. These may consist of early repudiated impulses and strivings, or of later wishes, or of current demands. Sometimes the wish is an extremely concealed one that is hard to detect in the dream content. At other times it is very clearly defined.

In the dream under discussion, the wish is perhaps to win the love and approval of a rejecting, aloof man; in this way breaking down the barrier to a warm relationship with a father figure. There is a desire to be accepted for herself and to be the preferred one in any competitive struggle.

d. Personality traits as disclosed in the dream. What personality traits are divulged in the dream? What is the nature of the patient's relationship with other persons in the dream? What are his feelings about himself? What are his attitudes toward authority? Toward subordinate persons?

In the dream that we are reviewing, the patient shows great fear in relation to a hostile male figure; contempt toward a person who likes her; and feelings of rejection when she approaches someone she admires. These tendencies are actually substantiated by studying her real life adjustment. They explain why it is difficult for her to relate well with people. Strong people are overvalued; she fears their hostility and rejection and she tends to detach herself from them. Toward weaker people she feels contempt and hostility, and she removes herself from their presence out of fear of being exploited.

e. Mechanisms of defense. What are the mechanisms of defense that are exhibited in the dream? How do these compare with the defense mechanisms the patient habitually employs in life? Are there any evidences of anachronistic defense mechanisms that issue out of early life experiences and impulses?

In our patient's dream, the defense mechanisms suggested are those of (1) flight from hostility or from a hostile authoritative person, (2) disdainful and perhaps aggressive attitudes toward individuals who are fond of her, and (3) masochism and hypochondriasis in relation to rejecting personages, the latter tendencies perhaps serving as means of winning sympathy and love. These mechanisms are essentially those the patient exhibits in her reality adjustment.

f. Conflicts expressed in the dream. What conflicts are manifested in the dream? Do these result from clashes with, or stress from special situations? Are these a consequence of incompatable relationships with people, or contradictions of various character traits? Are there evidences of deep inner wishes and needs that come into opposition with moral prohibitions.

Returning to our patient's dream, there are a number of conflicts that suggest themselves. The attitudes of flight, contempt, admiration, and masochism are mutually contradictory. Her relationships with people are fertile sources of conflict, since she constantly anticipates attack, or she may desire to attack others. Her need for a close relationship conflicts with a fear of being hurt or of hurting. There are hints of an Oedipal conflict.

g. The movement and outcome of the dream. What is the drama enacted in the dream? What emotions are associated with the actions? Does the dream reveal any important early memories or situations? Does it reflect emotionally significant immediate experiences? What is the outcome of the dream?

In our patient's dream, the drama is, first, a fear of being destroyed and helplessness in escaping destruction. The emotion here is terror. The outcome of this episode is not defined. Second, the patient plays a rejecting role with a man who seeks her companionship, and she is rejected by someone she likes who does not want her. Her protestation that she is sick and about to die incites the man to profess love for her, and she feels emotions of contentment, but also sadness. The outcome, though satisfactory to her, is actually a neurotic masochistic solution to her feelings of being unloved and unworthy in a relationship with a "superior" man.

h. Resistance and transference manifestations. What manifestations in the dream are reactions to therapy and the therapist? Are there any evidences of fear, antagonism, detachment, or sexual interest in relation to the therapist? Are there any responses that seem oppositional to the therapeutic effort?

The fact that our patient associates the furniture in the room in which she is trapped with the furniture in my office suggests a transference situation. She perhaps feels trapped by therapy as she was trapped in an untenable relationship with her father in the past. She may fear attack from me, as she feared attack from her father. It is possible that she exhibits resistance to therapy in the form of fear or helplessness. There is a possibility also that the last part of the dream reflects an impulse to win my affection by displays of illness and depression. Actually, the patient started the session by complaining that she felt physically ill. Emotionally she appeared listless and depressed.

4. Encouraging Further Associations by Focusing

Once the therapist has come to certain tentative conclusions about the dream, he may want to direct the patient's associations toward certain parts of the dream in order to validate his own formulations and to help inculcate insight in the patient. The process of focusing will depend in part on the dream material, and in part on the specific phase of therapy in which we are engaged.

Because the dream is so highly condensed a production, it is possible to extract from it material that will fit in with the objectives of our immediate therapeutic effort. Thus, if we are in the opening phases of therapy, our chief goal is to establish a working relationship. An attempt is made to discover in the dream evidences of resistance to a working relationship, defective motivation for therapy, and transference blocks to the full acceptance of the treatment situation. For instance, were the dream we are studying presented during the first therapeutic phase, we might perhaps consider her fear of the man in the dream and her terror of being trapped, as symbols of a fear of therapy and of me. We may speculate from this that she would, during therapy, try to get me to express my liking for her so that she could reject me; or, that, convinced of my aloofness, she would employ a masochistic reaction in order to get me to profess my fondness for her. With these factors in mind, we would try to focus her attention on her feelings toward me, in order to work through her resistances to a working relationship.

Were the patient in the exploratory phase of therapy, we would utilize her dream as a means of investigating the dynamics of her disorder. Thus we would focus on, and attempt to demonstrate provocative elements in her immediate environment that activated basic conflicts. Actually, the patient was in this treatment phase. An excerpt from the interview follows:

Th. Perhaps, if you tell me about any special things that happened to you the day before, or a few days before the dream, we may learn something important. [*Events of the day before, which had an emotional impact on the patient, consciously or unconsciously, may have detonated the tensions revealed by the dream. Focusing the patient's attention on possible stimuli may enable her to make certain connections.*]

Pt. There were several things that happened. I got a letter from Sally (*her sister*). She rarely, if ever, writes. Since my divorce I don't think I have gotten more than three letters from her. She told me about how wonderfully she and John (*her sister's husband*) were getting on, and how well her two children were doing in school. I felt she was needling me, blaming me for making a mess of my life. [*The resentment evoked by her sister's letter may have touched off early competitive feelings. I decide to explore these.*]

Th. How did you get along with your sister before?

Pt. As I told you, we hated each other when we were little. My father told me I used to admire her when I was a tot. She was three years older and I tried to do everything she did. The only thing I remember is fighting with her. She considered herself wonderful and would tell on me. I'd get spanked plenty. [*Is it possible that unresolved sibling rivalry still continues?*]

Th. How did your father feel about her?

Pt. After mother died, she was the favorite. She used to do everything with dad. I used to get the spankings. They told me I had an awful temper. That amuses me because I'm such a Casper Milquetoast now. (*pause*)

Th. How do you feel about your sister's taking your father away? [*This is a very provocative question, and is actually intended as an interpretation.*]

Pt. I guess I accepted it. There was nothing else I could do. [*The patient is probably unaware of her deep resentment about being rejected, and of her intense desire for a good relationship with her father.*]

Th. But it would seem natural to resent such a situation. [*more interpretation tentatively given*]

Pt. Well, it was a bad situation all around. And I was difficult, I suppose. There were times when dad was very sweet though. When I was sick for instance. [*Could this be a genetic determinant of the masochistic impulse? Her present tendencies toward depression and psychosomatic illness may be a result of a pattern of sickness which in her childhood invoked her father's attention. This is the mechanism that seems so clearly portrayed in the dream.*]

Th. This must have made sickness a premium for you? [*I am attempting here to get her to think about this mechanism.*]

Pt. (*laughs*) I was a sick child they tell me. Even now I don't feel good. I don't think I ever felt like I was all together.

Th. There may *still* be dividends that you get out of your being sick or feeling sick. [*a tentative interpretation of her hypochondriac pattern*]

Pt. (*pause*) Say . . . well, I wonder. Do you think I make myself sick so people can feel sorry for me? [*This sounds like emerging insight.*]

Th. There is *some* reason why you feel sick.

Pt. I did feel like hell yesterday and today. My back is killing me. I dosed myself up with aspirin. [*deviates into talking about her symptoms*]

Th. (*interrupting*) Now let's look into this thing. If you got dividends of love and attention from your dad by being sick, this could have started off a pattern. Do you have any idea whether you get sick with people you want attention from?

Pt. All I know is that I make a nuisance of myself with people. I guess I make them sick. [*The patient is resisting here.*]

Th. Well, now the dream brings out the fact that you tell the man who is hard to get that you are sick and going to die, and then he tells you he likes you, and everything is sad and beautiful. That sounds like the same thing, doesn't it?

Pt. Yes, I see. The night before the dream I went to a party. There was this very attractive man there who was taken over by another girl. I tried to engage his interest. He was polite, but I didn't get too far.

Th. Mm hmm.

Pt. The nice men always are in demand and married, or something.

Th. Sounds like nobody takes any interest in you.

Pt. The men who are attracted, I feel there is, I know they are cast-offs. They are either people who want a mother or are married and want an affair. And that's not for me.

Th. Maybe you undervalue people who like you. [*This is more tentative interpretation.*]

Pt. I don't know, but I must attract the wrong people. [*The patient is apparently not ready for the interpretation.*]

Th. You know, the dream seems to bring out your pattern of disinterest in men who want you, and hopelessness with men you want.

Pt. Yes, it does. (*pause*)

Th. But what do you do in the dream to get the person to tell you he loves you? [*attempting to stimulate thinking about her pattern*]

Pt. (*laughs*) I tell him I'm sick and going to die.

Th. Like you did with *whom* before, as far back as childhood? [*more questioning to promote thinking*]

Pt. With father, of course.

Th. It sounds like you are using this pattern constantly, whenever you are up against a situation where you feel you are second best. It's like you are still living with a sister your father prefers; and you have to use drastic measures to win out. [*interpreting her pattern*]

Pt. It's true, that's what I must be doing. In everything I feel hopeless, in everything. (*cries*)

Th. But is it *really* hopeless or do you *feel* it's inevitably hopeless, because this has been the pattern of your life?

Pt. Just look at how my sister is, and look at me.

Th. You still are pitting yourself against your sister. Let's take the letter she wrote you, which seems to have stirred up the dream and the old conflict of being preferred or not. Now you read into it something she may not at all have intended.

Pt. Of course, that's possible.

Th. Or take your feeling about me. If the pattern we talked about is there, it may come up with me too. Have you felt that I didn't like you, or didn't pay attention to you? [*probing for possible transference reactions*]

Pt. I have felt you were distracted and not interested in what I was saying.

Th. Perhaps I did something that gave you that impression?

Pt. Well, you changed my appointment last week.

Th. What did you think that meant?

Pt. Nothing, I suppose, but (*laughs*) I'll tell you what I thought about.

Th. Yes.

Pt. I thought you were seeing somebody in my place, more important or attractive.

Th. Like your sister? [*accenting the transference element and the possible misinterpretation*]

Pt. (*laughs loudly*) I suppose so. It seems like I keep doing the same thing all over.

Were the patient in a phase of translating insight into action, the focus would be on resistances to activity, normality, and the abandoning of primary and secondary neurotic gains. The dream material would be utilized in such a way that any possible resistances or defenses against utilizing insight constructively would be accented in order to expedite the therapeutic process. If the patient, finally, were in the terminal phase of treatment, the dream would be searched for evidences of resistance to termination, or for refusal to yield her dependency and to exercise assertiveness. In this way the greatest good would be derived from the interview.

FANTASIES

Fantasies or "day dreams" are almost as important as night dreams in reflecting deeper mental trends. While fantasies are influenced more by conscious ideational processes, they follow many of the laws of dreams. They may be handled in a manner similar to that in working with dreams. Of particular importance are masturbatory fantasies which embrace some of the most disturbing conflicts of the person. The individual's emotional reactions to his fantasies may be as significant as their content, and should, therefore, always be taken into account.

ILLUSTRATIVE CASE MATERIAL

Example 1:

A patient with an anxiety reaction came to therapy partly because of distressing symptoms and partly because of a realization that she was unable to get along with people, particularly with those in authority. She felt great envy toward persons who possessed more material things than she had, or who knew more than she knew, or who happened to be in any kind of superior position. She feared expressing her hostility and, in defense, adopted a compulsive ingratiating attitude. Her relationships with men were characterized by an initial period of temporary enthusiasm and passionate involvement, followed by disillusionment, resentment and an inevitable rupture of the friendship. During the thirty-sixth session, she presented the following dream.

I am in a field, but instead of there being grass, the earth is blanketed in a cloth cover with a peculiar design. I see an animal in the distance coming toward me. I don't know if it is a cow or a bull. I somehow have the power to make it either, by looking at it a certain way. I make it a bull and run away as it charges me.
Then I see myself in a room. A woman is about to leave two little children. They are good children and I feel angry that they are left alone.

In her spontaneous associations, the blanketed earth resembled the cover of the couch in my office. During her last visit, as she entered the waiting-room, she ran into my wife who was on the way out. She had a transient fantasy then that my wife was abandoning my two children in protest over my working constantly and, therefore, having no time to devote to my family. Associating to the animal in the dream, the patient described a recurrent fantasy of being caught some day on a field by a bull who charged her while she was completely helpless.

A tentative unverbalized formulation on the basis of what I had learned about her in therapy was that she related in two distinct ways to people. First, she would idolize any person whom she could identify as a powerful authority. She needed to convince herself, however, of the omniscience of this authority. Any flaws or weaknesses she detected in a personage whom she endowed with superior virtues, resulted in her losing respect for the person and then running him down. Second, she would, in association with a weaker person, assume command and insist on the person's complete submission to her. When this happened, she would develop contempt for the individual's weakness and then feel repulsed by any contact with him.

In her relationship with me, the first pattern had prevailed. I was elevated to the position of the invincible authority who knew all and could do no wrong. From time to time I challenged this attitude, attempting to show her that her notions were based on a need for a power figure. While she accepted this idea intellectually, emotionally she clung to the feeling that I was a kind of demigod, possessed of varied virtues, including superb judgment and exquisite intelligence.

Several days prior to the dream, we had, during a session, discussed her relationship with her fiancé, which had followed along the lines of her typical pattern and now was in the final stages of disintegration. I had given her several strong interpretations, her response to which was that I was criticizing her. I had a feeling she resented my intimation that discharging her fiancé might not be the best solution for her present plight.

Focusing on her present dream, I suggested that the blanketed earth on which she stood in the dream and which resembled my couch cover was probably a symbol of the therapeutic situation. Her emotion in the dream then might relate to therapy, or to me. This remark sponsored associations to the effect that she had been angered by my comments of the previous session. She confessed that as she left the office, she had begun, for the first time, to doubt my competence.

The meaning of the dream then became more apparent. She viewed me, first as a cow, tearing me down as an incompetent, weak person over whom she could ride roughshod. Second, she regarded me as a "superior" ferocious bull who could hurt her. In this way she symbolized her conflict between wanting to tear me down as she had torn down other authorities, or making me even more invincible, and hence potentially dangerous. She chose the latter in the dream. Envisaging escape from therapy, she rationalized her contemplated move with the idea that, in providing me with more leisure, I could devote myself to my wife. This would prevent my wife from leaving my children, who did not deserve a broken home. The last part of the dream was a partial expression of this notion. The interpretation of the dream helped the patient to realize that she was expressing in her dream structure a symbolized version of many of her basic life patterns.

Example 2:

Sometimes spontaneous associations to a dream help the patient gain awareness of inner conflict with dramatic force. In the following excerpt a patient achieves insight into fleeting homosexual impulses:

Pt. I dreamt my father was quite ill and I was taking care of him. I don't know what was the matter with him, but he was ill. I guess my sisters were around there somewhere, but I seemed to be feeding him and giving him his medicine. And there's one thing that sticks in my mind—a view of a spoon, an ordinary tablespoon, leaning up against something—in jelly or something along that line, something gelatinous. And I thought I was sort of half awake and I thought: "Well, Jesus Christ what am I doing—what can I say to that dream? It means that I am being my mother; I'm carrying out the functions of my mother, taking care of my father." And this is what I know it means: I have a desire or fear of being homosexual. I'm taking my mother's place. It hit me hard between the eyes and I almost fainted. And the next night I dreamt about a hasp, kind of a lock—you know, the kind where the hasp drops over a part when you drop a padlock into it. And I thought there was something about the hasp, and I thought I'm on this side of it; somebody is on the other side and can't get in, and I can't get over there. It could be turned around the other way. I could be over there, couldn't get in and, *he* could be here and not get out. It was not in any way a menace or anything like that, but it was that I'm here, and the presence of this hasp keeps *him* out and keeps *me* in. I can't get to him and he can't get to me. It's possible that you can turn it around, and the same thing would be true. In other words, it's an equation. (*pause*)

Th. What are your associations to this dream?

Pt. That is, if I were on the other side, the hasp would prevent me from getting inside. He would be inside, and he would be prevented from getting outside. I just remembered that I had another dream. I dreamed about a man I worked for about the time I got married the second time. I had worked for him once before. He was very fond of me, and I of him. Now I suspect there was a funny component in that relationship. He was, himself, in analysis. We had a lot in common for artistic reasons, philosophic and political reasons. However, in the end he turned out to be a heel. In spite of this guy's glowing promises, and so on and so on, I hadn't been married a month before I was fired. It wasn't his fault; he was just going broke. But the slob didn't even buy me a drink when I got married. This was a pal, wept on my shoulder when his wife left him, and I used to go up there to spend all the evenings with him. When he was very bad I'd stay over, you know, that kind of thing. He was going through what I went through with Anna, only I didn't know it then. You know I'd get flashes—now I know what they mean—that maybe he and I would be better off without women.

Example 3:

The following portion of a session with a man suffering from impotence illustrates the value of focusing associations to a dream for the purpose of inculcating insight.

Pt. I have sort of a feeling of frustration at the business of looking around for an appropriate woman. This is partly the result of the fact that it's such a time-consuming operation, and rather unrewarding unless one actually, until one actually, finds the appropriate person. And there is, there was one such futile evening which I spent yesterday. I suppose you may say that this is in the nature of resistance, but it generates feelings of how much more profitably I could have spent my evening yesterday had I not had to waste it looking for some woman. (*pause*)

Th. Some woman?

Pt. Yes, some girl I had never met before. She was a close friend of other close friends of mine. I called her up, you see. I had a fairly elaborate description of her. But the situation produced was that it was not something I could pursue very far because I was not substantially interested in her. I suppose I had a strong negative reaction, that I felt that she was tightly absorbed in her family, which produced a negative reaction. [*This reaction is typical of the patient's responses whenever he attempts to relate to a woman. He finds some objective reason to justify his apathy and disgust. He is not aware of more fundamental fears and conflicts that condition his desires for flight.*]

Th. Could there possibly be more basic reasons why you found her unattractive? [*attempting to focus his attention on deeper conflicts.*]

Pt. Well, I keep thinking that what I want from a woman is to find her substantially attractive, but more than just a sexual relationship. It is one in which there is substantial frankness. She should have a substantial intellectual capacity. Since those don't abound in very large numbers, that reduces the field very much, uh, uh, especially if you, uh, introduce the factor that there is some sort of automatic resistance which would, in any case, reduce the attractiveness of most women on the sexual level. [*The patient dodges my question, but does bring in the factor of his sexual resistance.*]

Th. Well, what about that automatic resistance? [*another attempt to focus on his conflict*]

Pt. Why, there is this impotence problem I came to you for, which is still with me. This substantially reduces my effectiveness with women.

Th. It doesn't seem to have made you unpopular. After all, there are many women after you, in spite of the impotence.

Pt. I suppose so. (*laughs*)

Th. I wonder if all of the specifications that you have for an ideal woman, and the lack of feeling for women, may not be indicative of certain fears? [*focusing still on basic conflicts*]

Pt. I suppose they must be.

Th. Like what for instance? Do you have any ideas or feeling about this?

Pt. Frankly, no. Except that there is this lack of enthusiasm. (*pause*)

Th. What about dreams; have you had any since our last visit?

Pt. Yes, quite a few. On Tuesday night I dreamed I was in some sort of a revolutionary turmoil, and some dictator had his arm torn off. Then I became the dictator, and my arm is attached. As I proceed somewhere, each time someone touches my arm, I feel it's going to be torn off. This is followed by a dream in which I and a girl are going somewhere, and running to catch a bus, and my hand begins to bleed. I'm becoming covered with blood, and she says, "Look what's happening." I say, "It doesn't matter; let's get there in a hurry." Then I exclude from an appointment I had arranged with people, this girl.

Th. Exclude her?

Pt. Yes, she was excluded in some way.

Th. By whom?

Pt. By me.

Th. Mm hmm.

Pt. I was in considerable turmoil. And then I dreamed of my cousin, my young cousin at school. He reports that a number of children at school have succumbed to some epidemic, to some disease. Following this, I help him conceal a knife that he's to use illegally in fights with other boys, and I instruct him how to use it. Then I walk along a dark street alone and see adults discussing something. Then these adults transform into a group of children. I walk along in imminent fear of attack. I pass a boy with a large hound. At first the dog appears planning to attack me, and he does, and the dog jumps on me and seizes me by the arm, and, oh, I had a painful sensation in my arm. (*pause*)

Th. Is that all?

Pt. Yes.

Th. What do you make of it, the dreams, I mean?

Pt. I suppose I am upset and afraid. I must be the dictator whose arm is hurt.

Th. Yes, as if you are in jeopardy of being attacked as a dictator and physically hurt.

Pt. Yes.

Th. What about being a dictator?

Pt. That's what some girls call me, when they fall in love with me and get angry. This dream followed this date with the girl.

Th. I see. Perhaps your feelings about this girl touched off the dreams. It's significant that in the dream you are running with the girl to catch a bus and your arm is bleeding.

Pt. Yes, we are going somewhere and I want to get there in a hurry.

Th. Where do you think you want to go in a hurry?

Pt. (*pause*) To get sex I suppose. I am in a rush to get this thing settled.

Th. But perhaps this dream tells us why it's difficult to get things done in a hurry. After all, your arm is mutilated. Could it be that in rushing into sex you feel you might be mutilated in some way?

Pt. (*emotionally*) There must be something that scares me. I feel anxious as I talk now.

Th. In what way could you be mutilated? Who would mutilate you and why?

Pt. I don't know. In the dream I help my cousin fight off an attack. This must be an aspect of me. Then I am attacked by a boy and dog who jumps me.

Th. And you get a painful sensation in your arm. The arm that bled in the other part of the dream?

Pt. Yes.

Th. But what about the part of the dream where you exclude her?

Pt. I don't know.

Th. Why should she be excluded?

Pt. I might want to exclude her, I suppose, from myself.

Th. That's what you actually did in your feelings toward her during the date.

Pt. Yes.

Th. And is what you do with other women?

Pt. I suppose so.

Th. Is it possible that you exclude her because of feelings, indicated by the dream, of fear, of bloody mutilation?

Pt. If I were to expect attack from this source I can see that.

Th. One way to escape attack is to give up the sex object, remove yourself from her, become impotent and apathetic. [*interpretation*]

Pt. I just remembered. I had a dream the day before I saw the girl.

Th. Mm hmm.

Pt. A series of two dreams, not entirely clear. There's a small girl who demonstrates strong friendship feelings towards me and offers something valuable which, in the dream, is a source of energy which she tells me to take from a series of intangible columns of materials. Later in the dream a small girl is very friendly to me. However, she transforms into a small boy who then picks up my pack of cigarettes and throws it out of the window, despite my protests. Then I'm with a police officer and he hides a pearl necklace in the files. I'm interested in it, but tell him I'm not, and I just want to go to some town. I go to the railway station, check my suitcase and enter the train car. Then some woman rushes out with a suitcase that looks like mine. I follow her, but we investigate and find the suitcase is hers. I return to the car and find my suitcase. The contents are all female articles, and I think to myself it will be difficult to prove that this is my suitcase. (*pause*) And that's all.

Th. I see. What do you think of that?

Pt. (*laughs*) Well, I suppose my impending date got me to dream of this girl. I think of this treasure, the pearl necklace.

Th. The treasure being hidden by a police officer?

Pt. Yes, keeping it from me.

Th. What is the most precious treasure you can think of?

Pt. What I want here. To have sex with a woman. Sex must be locked away from me, if we are to believe the dream, by some authority.

Th. Mm hmm.

Pt. The recognition of that by the woman—the suitcase—is rather more puzzling. It apparently involves some uncertainty in my, uh, virility and masculine qualities, as much as the woman had the same suitcase as I.

Th. As if she's a counterpart of you, as if you don't know your identity—male or female. [*interpretation*]

Pt. Yes, I can see something now; it occurs to me that the arm in the dreams is a symbol of my genitals.

Th. Mm hmm.

Pt. And the dictator, being in the position of dominance like a male, can have his genitals hurt and not be a man. If I try to be a man, I may be hurt—my superiority and power torn off so to speak.

Th. And sexually mutilated.

Pt. Yes, undoubtedly.

Th. And in a sexual role with a woman?

Pt. I'll be sexually hurt, hurt.

Th. Now, if it's true that you could be hurt for trying to be a man, what defense would you use?

Pt. To get away, run away, or to be a woman and not have to face it.

Th. What about fighting back?

Pt. Yes, yes. The aggression. Like in the dream, the attacking with a knife.

Th. Your dreams seem to bring out mechanisms of why you act the way you do.

Pt. I can definitely see that, but it's so peculiar. I know it's true. I feel it. But it's so strange.

Th. It would explain your coldness with women, the impotence. If you expect to be castrated, that's no fun.

Pt. (*laughs*) Gosh, uh, yeah, uh, I had one reaction of this sort, which I became conscious of, and that is that in playing with my girl friend, the old one, she accidentally hurt me very slightly around the genital region, but it was very slight. And nonetheless it, for a while, caused a complete disappearance of sexual desire.

Th. When did this happen?

Pt. A number of days ago.

Th. Before or after the dream?

Pt. Before.

Example 4:

The fragment of a session that follows is an illustration of the active working out by a patient of an anxiety attack with psychosomatic symptoms through an analysis of her dreams:

Pt. After I left you the last time I felt good, but it didn't last. The next day I awoke and felt tense and bad all over, physically sick. I wanted to go to my desk and do that work; I could have made myself do it. So I gave myself the only therapeutic treatment I know of. I just went to bed. I stayed there all afternoon.

Th. Did you feel better?

Pt. I still felt awful when Mark got home last night. Janet, my friend, came in about four o'clock, and I had had nothing to eat all day, you see.

Th. Mm hmm.

Pt. Well, I started to figure out things in bed and I apparently figured out some things, because I had some good results. I didn't order groceries. I didn't do a god-damned thing. But I did get up, and we ordered Chinese food in, last night; and I did get up and fix that and ate dinner. First meal in almost twenty-four hours.

Th. What have you figured out?

Pt. This morning when I awakened, I felt fine. When I say fine, I mean as fine as I can feel. And I've been doing everything in perfectly normal order all day. Almost called you yesterday; then I thought no. It's absolutely ridiculous; this thing is my own doing. I might as well try to figure it out myself.

Th. Did you?

Pt. No, I don't think I have completely, but I think I worked some of it out though.

Th. Well, let's talk about it.

Pt. Well, would you rather hear some dreams first or second?

Th. Whichever you want.

Pt. There was one damn dream that was important that I forgot. All these things happened one on top of the other. For instance, when I went to bed yesterday at twelve o'clock, with the exception of phone call interruptions, which I talked perfectly normally on, I'd go right back to sleep. When things get too tough, I can go to sleep. That's what I did yesterday. Things got too rough to stand it, so I went to sleep, but all that time I had one dream, after the other dream, after the other dream; and the night before, that would be Sunday night, I had a dream about you. It seemed that you must have been visiting me, or else you had taken over my production, I don't know. But anyway it was a big house and we were in one small room of it with a table between us, a regular interview set-up like this. There was a table between us, and on one side was sort of a rack where equipment could be put. And, although I never saw this in my dream, I knew that in the other room, it was a large room, you were helping me prepare a product and you were in charge. And you had something to do with that. Then that room opened off onto several other rooms which we never got into; we were still in this one room. And every so often we could hear the clatter of the girls who were also making the product. Finally, at about four o'clock, quitting time, these girls came in, a couple of them, and rolled this piece of equipment thing used in the product and put it in this rack right next to us. And at that time you were telling me that you didn't think my behavior was very good, that you did not like me to call you by your first name, that you felt that until our relationship was established on a firmer foundation, that I should at least give you the courtesy of calling you by your second name. And about that time I was feeling sort of slapped down about it, Mrs. Wolberg came through. It seemed that she kept the books, and she said to me, "Well, besides that, you won't have much more credit up here." Then yesterday afternoon I dreamed of a marriage. Elsa Maxwell handled all the arrangements for the thing, and so forth. And someone else was going to be the overseer and the participant in the affair to replace me. And I saw all this very clearly, the arrangements and the publicity and the beautiful church and the gown; and I felt very much left out of it, and very resentful of the other woman. That's when I awoke and realized it was nothing but a dream. I guess they're all anxiety dreams, but that was a dream that showed to me at least what my feeling was.

Th. Which was?

Pt. That I feel very rejected by you and left out of things. (*laughs*)

Th. You feel rejected by me?

Pt. Then I dreamed of a room full of little girls, blondes and brunettes of different ages, but all within say, three to six years. Going into this room was like going on the boat that goes to Catalina where they have all these benches. You know what excursion boats are like. That's what the room looked like. The benches were all full of these little girls. I went in with these attendants and I was told that I was to pick out the child that I thought I should have had. The phone rang and I never got to picking her out, and that was that.

Th. What do you think this all means?

Pt. This morning after I awakened I tried to piece this stuff together with what little I know about it. I usually think, well, what's my day going to be, the first thing when I wake up in the morning. How soon do I have to get up? How soon do I have to dress? Who do I have to phone? And so forth and so on. This morning I thought: "What is my day today and what is going to be pleasant in it." And the first thing I thought of being pleasant this morning was to come up here! And I had to have my hair done, and I had a certain amount of desk work to do which to me isn't particularly pleasant or unpleasant. It's something that has to be done, and that's that. It never bothers me too much, but neither do I look forward to it. But I looked forward to coming up here.

Th. It's interesting that in the dreams you put me in a certain role with you.

Pt. As if I want to be in Mrs. Wolberg's place.

Th. Do you?

Pt. Yeah, and very much so. (*laughs*) I'd like to have you take me over, I guess.

Th. So that here you're shoved out, and it's almost as if you tentatively have a place and don't have a place. You just don't know. As long as you pay your bills, you have a place. If you don't, god knows what will happen to you. You may be thrown out on your ear. The role that you play with me is not defined. The corollary of that is that you may want me to play a masterful role with you. [*interpretation*]

Pt. And yet I'm the very person that fights against any authority.

Th. That's the annoying part of it. You may not want an authority, but when it isn't there, you may feel insecure. [*giving her more interpretation*]

Pt. I think . . . I know you're absolutely right. Because right after our last session, I said, "god damn it, why doesn't he do more for me." Then I started getting angry at your wife. I felt like killing her. That made me laugh, because after all, I'm not twenty. Why should I feel this way about you? But I do, and I know damn well that your not telling me what to do, and your not letting me figuratively move in with you, bothers me like hell. I know it's silly, but that's how I felt. And it made me feel guilty.

Th. And crowding these things out of your mind must have brought on some reactions.

Pt. It made me sick, I know it did . . . (*pause*) It's so silly. (*laughs*) I feel better now.

Identifying Important Trends and Patterns: The Examination of Attitudes Toward the Therapist, Including Transference

ALL PEOPLE PROGRESS FROM CHILDHOOD TO ADULT LIFE WITH ATTITUDES, values and behavior tendencies that are parcels of past experience. These persist in the form of fixed patterns that repeat themselves compulsively in certain interpersonal situations. Thus a grown man, intimidated as a child by a punitive father, may respond to all authoritarian men with a cowering, ingratiating set of reactions, as if he virtually still were a little boy awaiting punishment for a misdeed. A grown woman who, as a child, was violently competitive with a younger sister for the attentions of her parents, may carry on a campaign for absolute supremacy in important endeavors or situations, as if she repeatedly had to prove that she was "best" and hence worthy of praise and affection. Such patterns, given the proper stimulus, go on repetitively, forming the very fabric of the individual's way of life. They are stoutly defended irrespective of how irrational they may be, or how inherently contradictory they are in operation. The motivants for these drives, and the early experiences that engendered them, seem to exist in the unconscious of the individual. He is aware merely of an impelling urge that makes him adopt, in certain situations, stereotyped ways of thinking, feeling and behaving.

Obviously such tendencies sooner or later, prove themselves to be disruptive to the individual and involve him in difficulties that disorganize his adjustment. Occasionally he is capable of exercising some measure of control by virtue of wanting to avoid the difficulties that inevitably follow his responses. The defenses he employs may help him to adjust, but in no sense minimize the urgency of his impulses which periodically may express themselves in action.

Fortunately, in addition to immature stereotyped patterns, all persons exhibit reactions that are reality determined. These make up many, perhaps most of the varied responses to people.

Thus, the man described above who behaves like a little boy may respond to certain males in an assertive manner once he has assured himself of their good will, or has ascertained their incapacity to hurt him. Indeed, with selected men, under special conditions, he may even act the part of authority. Or the woman who competes blindly may be content with a secondary role whenever her security and self-esteem are assured.

The individual will, therefore, play varying roles with different people, and, contingent on how secure he feels and the measure of his self-esteem, he will react with infantile past patterns or with more mature ones.

In a previous chapter we have considered the examination, through focused interviewing, of the patient's current interpersonal involvements in order to identify disturbing patterns responsible for his emotional disorder. In the present chapter we shall cover the process of investigating both stereotyped infantile and mature rational responses as they are expressed toward the therapist within the framework of the therapeutic situation.

Before taking up this process, it is necessary to emphasize that in supportive therapy, and in directive forms of reeducative therapy, it is usually unwise to delve into the nature of the relationship with the therapist. Such a move tends to challenge the foundations of faith on which success in treatment may depend. Indeed, one often strives to prepetuate in the patient the illusion of the therapist's protective powers, no effort being made to peer into the irrational sources of the patient's dependency need. The hope is to adjust the individual to his less disturbing unconscious impulses, to increase repression of the more destructive ones, to expand existing assets, and to encourage compensations and sublimations, so that the patient can live as happy a life as is possible with his liabilities.

In many forms of reeducative therapy, however, the more conscious manifestations of stereotyped patterns projected into the therapeutic relationship are explored and discussed in an attempt to modify or to control them. In reconstructive therapy, where an effort is always made to bring infantile patterns and their manifestations to full awareness and to determine their genetic origins, a thorough study of what goes on in the patient's relationship with the therapist is mandatory.

Insight into many of the patient's problems may be gained expediently through examination of his feelings and attitudes toward the therapist. The patient always projects into the relationship strivings that are both reality determined and those that are conditioned by his habitual, unrealistic impulses toward people. The differentiation by the therapist of these two kinds of strivings helps the patient to understand the automatic, compulsive nature of some of his responses.

There is nothing so dramatic to a patient as to realize that he reacts to the therapist, not as a real personage, but as a virtual reincarnation of a parental or sibling figure (transference). The demonstration of how his attitudinal and behavioral reactions are rooted in past relationships, and how they distort the present reality situation, is a living demonstration to the patient of the irrational way he feels and behaves in his everyday contacts with people. This realization may start a process of reevaluation of the self.

One of the important effects of understanding the nature of his impulses and attitudes toward the therapist is that it enables the patient to differentiate rational from irrational authority. Expectations of being treated by the therapist in a manner similar to the way the patient was handled by previous authorities are not fulfilled. Avoiding a punitive, judgmental attitude, the therapist regards the patient's difficulties with sympathy and understanding. Expressions of hostility by the patient are accepted without indignation or retaliation. This allows the patient to display resentment more and more openly. It permits him to investigate its source as well as to understand reasons for its present existence.

Although every patient responds to the therapist with some patterns that are unrealistically determined, these may not be openly expressed. Subjected to reality testing, certain impulses are recognized by the patient as irrational. They may be considered threatening to an idealized relationship with the therapist. Accordingly, they are disassociated, suppressed or repressed. Sometimes they impinge merely on the periphery of awareness, appearing in a symbolized form in dreams and fantasies, or revealing themselves in slips of speech, and random behavior, such as "acting out." Transference may manifest itself in relationships outside of therapy, the patient discharging toward a mate, relative, friend or other person, feelings and attitudes that he dares not express toward the therapist.

Certain activities on the part of the therapist discourage or encourage the revivification in the therapeutic relationship of archaic patterns. Where the therapist considers that he can achieve desired goals in therapy without the stirring up of excess transference, he may decide to deal with emerging irrational attitudes in as immediate and forthright a manner as possible. Thus, hostility, sexual impulses and intense dependency are handled by discussion and clarification as soon as they become apparent, an effort being made to keep reality in the fore. The relationship is maintained constantly on a positive level

Among the techniques utilized to reduce transference are these:

1. Focusing discussions on present relationships and the current life situation.

2. Minimizing the consideration of the past, including relationships with parents.

3. Avoiding dreams, fantasies and free associations.

4. Avoiding the couch position and employing face-to-face interviewing.

5. Spacing interviews no more frequently than twice weekly.

6. Dealing with any unrealistic attitudes or feelings toward the therapist as soon as these are perceived.

7. Playing a role opposite to that which the patient anticipated on the basis of his past relationships with traumatizing authority.

8. Exercising activity rather than passivity in the relationship.

Through the use of these techniques it may be possible to withhold infantile urges from awareness, or to direct them away from the therapeutic relationship toward outside relationships, or to relegate them to a position where they may be held in check by rational controls.

In spite of these activities and precautions, transference may burst forth in full fury, interfering with the treatment plan. When this happens, it will have to be handled like any other kind of resistance, by such techniques as active interpretation.

Transference, may, however, be encouraged in certain patients whose problems are very deeply repressed and who are constantly being upset by unconscious conflicts. Here, no insight may be obtained except through the direct experiencing of their problems in the relationship with the therapist. Among syndromes in which there is such intense repression are anxiety reactions, phobic reactions, conversion reactions, dissociative reactions, stress reactions and certain obsessive-compulsive and psychophysiologic reactions. Here, mobilization of transference as a learning vehicle may be considered advisable.

Transference may become so intense that the patient will actually live through with the therapist some of his early developmental blocks and traumatic experiences which produced the original repressions and other mechanisms of defense. The development of exaggerated transference reactions (transference neurosis) enables the patient to reexperience early deprivations and intimidations, and to master them in another, more favorable setting with a new, more accepting, more permissive, better disciplined authority.

The techniques that may be used to accentuate transference are:

1. Employing passivity and anonymity in the relationship.

2. Focusing discussions away from the present life situation.

3. Encouraging consideration of the past, including relationships with parents.

4. Using free association and the couch position. Removing of oneself from the direct gaze of the patient.

5. Concentrating on dreams and fantasies.

6. Increasing the frequency of sessions to four or five times weekly in order to break down repression.

7. Avoiding answering questions and restricting interpretations.

8. Avoiding dealing with unrealistic attitudes or feelings toward the therapist until these have built up to overwhelming proportions.

9. Acting in a role that coordinates with that assumed by the patient's traumatizing parent.

Patients will respond variably to these techniques, from failure to mobilize transference in certain rigid and detached persons, to explosive reactions that prove traumatic to the individual in "borderline" conditions. Indeed, in some patients intense transference may promote too great a shattering of repression which, not being reestablished, may eventuate in a psychosis. Syndromes such as "borderline" conditions, psychotic states and certain personality disorders, psychophysiologic reactions and obsessive-compulsive reactions do not respond favorably to the deliberate mobilization of transference. Even in cases where it is indicated, the fostering of transference is not to be encouraged by any therapist who has not had extensive analytic training and experience.

ILLUSTRATIVE CASE MATERIAL

Example 1:

A beginning break-through of transference is indicated in the following **excerpt:**

Th. You know sometimes I get the impression that you act with me as if you are walking on eggs. I wonder if you have any feelings toward me you are not talking about.

Pt. I don't, I don't know. This is one of the disturbing things . . . when I'm all tangled up inside and don't know (*weeps*) . . . I don't want to cry . . . I'll wipe my nose . . . I don't know why I'm so upset today, really I don't. I felt so much better yesterday.

Th. Perhaps it's because I bring up the subject of your feelings toward me.

Pt. (*cries*) I feel irritated, just a momentary anger. I haven't been particularly conscious of it. I don't dislike you, just irritated. (*pause*)

Th. Do you want to tell me more about your feelings toward me?

Pt. I don't want to have feelings for you.

Th. You don't want to have feelings for me?

Pt. No. I don't know why.

Th. Perhaps you are afraid of showing emotion?

Pt. I certainly would be afraid of feeling affectionate.

Th. You would?

Pt. I certainly would.

Th. I wonder why?

Pt. I was thinking of it, as a matter of fact, yesterday. I felt . . . well . . . if I behaved well . . . perhaps you would be good to me . . . fatherly like, I mean.

Th. If you behaved affectionately to me you mean?

Pt. Yes, but I'm afraid.

Th. Afraid? Of what?

Pt. That it would not be taken seriously. Would it?

Th. If you felt affectionate toward me, of course I would take your feelings seriously. Perhaps what you're saying is that I might reject you or hurt you in some way?

Pt. What I mean is that I'd be ashamed of my feelings, that this would be a one-sided relationship. I think I feel you'd ridicule me.

Th. Actually, you don't know how I'd act, and yet you behave as if I do ridicule you for your feelings.

Pt. If I had feelings would they be responded to . . . would they?

Th. You mean would I reciprocate with the same kind of feeling?

Pt. That's it.

Th. If I did, this would not be a therapeutic situation for you.

Pt. I suppose not.

Th. But if you allowed yourself to talk about your feelings, I might be of considerable help to you in your problem.

Pt. (*giggles*) Now I feel very silly.

Th. Silly?

Pt. I do like you very much.

Th. (*smiling*) Mm hmm.

Pt. And I did feel about you . . . that you were able to help me. I did feel you were protective, something like I wanted father to be.

Example 2:

The following excerpt is from a session with a patient suffering with a severe anxiety reaction with psychophysiologic components. During the session the patient brings up a transference reaction which she traces to its source and then recognizes the operation of similar reactions in her relationships with people.

Th. I notice that you don't want to look at me today.

Pt. I don't want to like you. I'd rather not like you.

Th. I wonder why?

Pt. I feel I'll be hurt. Liking you will expose me to being hurt.

Th. But how *do* you feel about me?

Pt. I don't know. I have conflicting emotions about you. Sometimes I like you too much and sometimes I get mad at you for no reason. I often can't think of you, even picture you.

Th. Do you feel that you stop yourself in your feelings toward me?

Pt. Yes, I don't want to like you. If I do, I won't be able to stop myself. I'll get hurt. But why do I feel or insist that I'm in love with you.

Th. Are you?

Pt. Yes. And I feel so guilty and upset about it. At night I think of you and get sexual feelings and it frightens me.

Th. Do I remind you of anyone?

Pt. Yes. (*pause*) There are things about you that remind me of my brother. (*laughs*) I realize this is silly.

Th. Mm hmm.

Pt. My brother Harry, the one I had these sex experiences with when I was little. He made me do things I didn't want to. I let him fool with me because he made me feel sorry for him.

Th. Do you have any of the same feelings toward me?

Pt. It's not that I expect that anything will really happen, but I just don't want to have feelings for you. I never liked doctors or dentists, especially dentists. The other day I had to go to a dentist. My mind was filled with crazy thoughts.

Th. Mm hmm.

Pt. These crazy things come into my mind that make no sense. I made this dental appointment and I thought of the drill going into my tooth. Then I thought of the drill being an egg beater. Later I went to the movies and in a cartoon I saw eggs. I then realized my attitude toward eggs has always been wrong. As a child my mother scolded me for frying eggs and burning them. Then the day before I went to the dentist, I got nervous. I then pictured eggs being cooked, and then I had a picture of a raw egg and realized the white of the egg looked like seminal fluid and I got sick. It's like this fluid can kill me. I remember my brother wanted to have sex with me when I was a child. He said he had this fluid in him and it would poison him if he didn't get it out. I let him fool with me. Then he told me about people putting it in their mouth. It disgusted me, made me sick. I have dreams of my mouth being smashed and my teeth falling out. The whole thing seems to be connected with sex.

Th. But what about your feelings for me?

Pt. I know it's the same thing, I'm afraid of you taking advantage of me. If I tell you I like you that means you'll make me do what *you* want.

Th. Just like Harry made you do what he wanted.

Pt. Yes. I didn't want to let him do what he did, but I couldn't stop myself. I hated myself. That's why. I know it now because there is no reason why I should feel you are the same way. That's why I act that way with other people too. It's like what happened not long ago with my art lessons. I went to this art place where I study, and I got very nervous and I had to go home. (*pause*)

Th. Try to connect up what happened.

Pt. It irritates me that I can't paint as well as I should. This woman who runs the art place seems to like me. I don't like that. It's like I'd get too friendly with them. I don't like to have people get too close to me. I think wrong about that. When I was little my sister used to take advantage of me too. But the most of it was my brother. The whole thing is the same as happens with you. It's all so silly and wrong. You aren't my brother and the other people aren't my brother. I never saw the connection until now.

Example 3:

A patient on the verge of experimenting with the expression of aggression brings out transference feelings that help her understand some reasons why she repressed aggression.

Pt. I want to talk about my feelings about you.

Th. Mm hmm.

Pt. You sit here, a permissive person who lets me go on. I want to do something now, but I'm afraid you will be disappointed in me if I upset the apple cart, if I explode. I think we are too nice to each other. I'm ready not to be nice. My greatest fear of you is that you are potentially going to be severe with me if I let loose. Also, I fear I will let you down by not performing well, by not being nice. I feel I will gain your disapproval. And yet I see you don't condemn and don't criticize. It is still important to me to gain a nod from you or a smile. (*pause*)

Th. It sounds as if you would like to let loose with me, but you are afraid of what my response would be. [*summarizing and restating*]

Pt. I get so excited by what is happening here. I feel I'm being held back by needing to be nice. I'd like to blast loose sometimes, but I don't dare.

Th. Because you fear my reaction?

Pt. The worst thing would be that you wouldn't like me. You wouldn't speak to me friendly; you wouldn't smile; you'd feel you can't treat me and discharge me from treatment. But I know this isn't so, I know it.

Th. Where do you think these attitudes come from?

Pt. When I was nine years old, I read a lot about great men in history. I'd quote them and be dramatic. I'd want a sword at my side; I'd dress like an Indian. Mother would scold me. Don't frown, don't talk so much. Sit on your hands, over and over again. I did all kinds of things. I was a naughty child. She told me I'd be hurt. Then at fourteen I fell off a horse and broke my back. I had to be in bed. Mother then told me on the day I went riding not to, that I'd get hurt because the ground was frozen. I was a stubborn, self-willed child. Then I went against her will and suffered an accident that changed my life, a fractured back. Her attitude was, "I told you so." I was put in a cast and kept in bed for months.

Th. You were punished, so to speak, by this accident.

Pt. But I gained attention and love from mother for the first time. I felt so good. I'm ashamed to tell you this. Before I healed I opened the cast and tried to walk to make myself sick again so I could stay in bed longer.

Th. How does that connect up with your impulse to be sick now and stay in bed so much? [*The patient has these tendencies, of which she is ashamed.*]

Pt. Oh . . . (*pause*)

Th. What do you think?

Pt. Oh, my god, how infantile, how ungrown up. (*pause*) It must be so. I want people to love me and be sorry for me. Oh, my god. How completely childish. It is, *is* that. My mother must have ignored me when I was little, and I wanted so' to be loved. [*This sounds like insight.*]

Th. So that it may have been threatening to go back to being self-willed and unloved after you got out of the cast. [*interpretation*]

Pt. It did. My life changed. I became meek and controlled. I couldn't get angry or stubborn afterward.

Th. Perhaps if you go back to being stubborn with *me,* you would be returning to how you were before, that is, active, stubborn but unloved.

Pt. (*excitedly*) And, therefore, losing your love. I need you, but after all you aren't going to reject me. The pattern is so established now that the threat of the loss of love is too overwhelming with everybody, and I've got to keep myself from acting selfish or angry.

Example 4:

A patient with a homosexual problem is brought to an awareness through transference of sexual feelings toward her father which incite anxiety and detachment from men.

Pt. Inwardly I feel like a wreck right now. And yet I just sit here very quietly and calmly as if nothing is wrong.

Th. In other words, you can put on a beautiful front.

Pt. Yeah, I'm doing it right now. You don't know what I look like from the other end. You don't know what I look like, I mean. I wondered what would happen if I came in here and said exactly what I feel. I'm sick of this faking which I still do in here. But in what respect, I don't know. I'm so scared to tell you a lie, I live in a fear of it. And the other day when you asked me—this is an example of it. You were pointing out an example and asked me, did I see, what was it, "Born Yesterday?" I said, "Yes." But I saw the play, not the movie. Now what the heck difference it makes, I don't know, but it bothered me later. Don't you remember it. But a few sentences later I, I corrected myself and said "I saw the play," because it bothered me. The thought of telling you even that much of a lie is intolerable.

Th. Do you feel you've been lying to me in any other way?

Pt. I haven't lied to you about anything that I know of.

Th. Mm hmm.

Pt. But it's just that I feel I'm still not myself. I want to find somebody to give my whole self to.

Th. Mm hmm.

Pt. That's exactly what I want to do, and still I don't do it. (*pause*)

Th. Still you're holding back.

Pt. But, in what way I don't know.

Th. And you feel somehow that maybe I don't know the real you.

Pt. Yes. Like everything that happened to me all day long. I carry on long discussions with you in buses and trains (*laughs*) and, I say, " I must remember to tell him that tomorrow." And then I never bother to tell any of these things.

Th. Are they any specific kinds of things?

Pt. Yes, now I, I could just pick out one.

Th. Mm hmm.

Pt. Yesterday I went to buy some glasses, dark glasses, with the idea of getting some eccentric looking things—things must be eccentric looking with me.

Th. Mm hmm.

Pt. So I asked the saleslady what she would suggest. So she suggested black. So I said, that's idiotic, but I'll get black glasses. And they are a bit eccentric looking, but silly, and, I wanted to go and read you something out of a book that I thought about today. But why? Because I wanted you to see those glasses. You see? And I would have gone right through with it, but I doubled back on myself in the train today and said it's silly to do that. And when I put them on on the train I noticed somebody looking over at me. I'm aware of myself all the time, and of being a fake. I sit down with a book in front of me, one leg over the other. I'm doing it now, and I don't feel this way at all. I don't feel like a blah-blah woman of the world person at all.

Th. What *do* you feel?

Pt. I don't know. I don't know what it is that I feel. All I know is that what I look like—what I believe I look like anyway—I'm not. And I do a billion things during the day which, which are just crazy, which I carry on about.

Th. Do you feel that way right now?

Pt. All the time. And then before I came up here I got weak. By god, I didn't feel I had the strength to walk one block over to the Madison Avenue bus. I took a taxi. Absurd. And then I stopped to have this drink. It's ridiculous.

Th. Maybe you're afraid and tense about coming here.

Pt. No. It, it, it's the idea, it's always been: "If I could only have one person to tell the whole truth to, one person who could see me just nude, period. With nothing on." (*pause*)

Th. Mm hmm. And?

Pt. And that's exactly what I'm not doing. And I try so desperately.

Th. In other words, what you're saying to me is, "Look, I'm putting something over on you. I'm not letting myself be completely exposed to you."

Pt. But why I do it, I don't know. (*pause*) I'm putting up a front with you, or maybe I'm pulling the wool over your eyes, the way I'm pulling the wool over my father's eyes, and my mother's, and over at the school, and with everybody. And I feel maybe you're going to be sucker enough to fall for that.

Th. Perhaps I know you better than you think I know you.

Pt. I have the feeling as though you don't know a darn thing about me.

Th. Mm hmm.

Pt. I mean I've never talked about these things that have meant so much to me, like this morning.

Th. Mm hmm.

Pt. Uh, I go along wearing filthy clothes, underclothes. (*laughs*) I mean what people can't see, I don't care. Nobody sees it, it's so small it couldn't possibly smell, so I don't worry about it. (*laughs*)

Th. Mm hmm.

Pt. And so I didn't bother with it, and I thought about it: "Now here you sit down in the doctor's office, and he sees you look very decent in that. Does he know that you've got filthy underclothes on? There's no button here; there's no button there. Does he know that?"

Th. You feel very guilty about how you are inside, and the kind of person you are. [*interpreting*]

Pt. I want somebody to see it, that's the point of it.

Th. Do you think I'm not observant enough to see it?

Pt. No, but I feel as though I'm putting on an act for you. Oh, I know (*laughs*) it's your business after all, I mean . . .

Th. Maybe you feel I'm not smart enough to know you, all of you?

Pt. That's not it. I feel that I haven't given you a chance to see everything. (*laughs*)

Th. (*laughs*) I see.

Pt. But I don't know why I'm so upset. It has something to do with you.

Th. What do you feel about me?

Pt. (*pause.*) Number one, (*sigh*) the thing I felt very much about you, I mean, uh, uh, as a person I like you very much.

Th. Mm hmm.

Pt. But I have a tremendous curiosity about you.

Th. Have you?

Pt. Yeah.

Th. For instance?

Pt. Marriage, children, everything about you. I'm interested in knowing.

Th. What about your theories about that? What do you think?

Pt. Well, I, it's always my purpose. I'm concerned with that all the time. When I talk to your secretary, I walk out with a smile and joke about something, and I always think, "Oh, I bet she thinks I'm a really happy little kid running around. I bet she likes me. Or maybe she doesn't like me." Always concerned with what people think.

Th. Mm hmm.

Pt. And, and with you, for instance, there were two men I was putting on the young lady act with, always an act. I dressed up to kill every time I saw them, and all that kind of thing. And then, when I found out they had grown daughters, I felt like a fool. I said, "What are you trying to impress them with? They've got one of their own." And that's why I'm interested in you, too. I, I must impress you still.

Th. Mm hmm.

Pt. I want to know what you think of me. How do I strike you, and how I would strike you if you met me on the street.

Th. Do you have any theories about how I might feel about you?

Pt. Well, the only thing you've ever said which stuck in my mind so hard was that you thought it was all right to say what I wanted. But I want to know more. I want to know what strikes you? Every analyst also is, is a casual observer, and I want to know what you think of me.

Th. It's more important for me to get an idea of what *you* think I think of you, than for you to find out what *I* actually think of you at this time. You're not quite sure of what I think of you.

Pt. No, not at all.

Th. You're not sure that I like you?

Pt. Yeah, I believe you like me. I believe you consider me rather intelligent.

Th. Well, how do you know?

Pt. Well, first of all you told my father so.

Th. Mm hmm. Did he tell you that?

Pt. Yeah. I had him repeat it thousands of times (*laughs*) just to make sure. It made me feel like a million dollars that day. In fact I even celebrated. I went downtown.

Th. Is that so?

Pt. This is absurd, but that's, that's just the way I felt. So concerned over what you must think of me.

Th. Now if I told you I liked you and that sort of thing, it would not help you. In fact it would prevent you from feeling spontaneously about me. It's important that you become aware of all of the feelings you have, some of which are justified, and some of which have nothing to do with reality. We can get important clues about things that are happening to you from your feelings.

Pt. Yes.

Th. It may be a little hard on you if I don't come out and tell you exactly how I feel all the time.

Pt. Mm. Yeah.

Th. If I keep saying, "What do you think I feel about you?" . . .

Pt. Yeah.

Th. Or, "What are your theories about this or that?" it might be a little hard on you, but in the long run it will be most helpful to you.

Pt. Yes.

Th. But if you resent this kind of role that I'm playing with you, then tell me about it.

Pt. No, it, it's just pleasantly annoying, you know, that's all; it's tantalizing, so to speak. (*pause*) If you asked me to be truthful and tell you what I would most like to do right now I'd have to say: "I want to sleep with a man, but I want him to have his pants on."

Th. Mm hmm.

Pt. "But no top. Big shoulders. And I would be nude. And I want to inspect his penis, and I want to play with it. And I want him, just, just to sort of annoy me, but I don't want to have to lie back and just take it. I want to be able to just squirm around and let myself go, just be a whole physical thing and no mind at all."

Th. Yes.

Pt. And then I come to think about what would this man have to look like. From his shoulders, right around about here—and that's you. It just came to me. The man is you. I have been thinking these thoughts since I started coming here, sex thoughts.

Th. The man is I?

Pt. Yeah.

Th. Mm hmm.

Pt. I got, I got those feelings of sex now that are driving me crazy. By god, I didn't know I could ever say that.

Th. You couldn't say that to me?

Pt. No, no. Well, but I did. But I thought, "Well, maybe it's not so. Maybe it's just nonsense." But the more I thought about it, the more it was you. I tried to push it out of my mind, but it's true.

Th. Maybe that's why you were upset.

Pt. It's possibly that. But it's a horrible thought that I can think that. I remember seeing daddy without his clothes. His penis seemed enormous. I get a funny feeling. It's repulsive and exciting too. Just like I feel about you. I try not to think about it. [*It is apparent that her feelings toward me are projections of her feelings toward her father.*]

Th. What about your sex feelings about men?

Pt. Zero. That's why it's so funny I feel this way with you. It makes me upset to think about it. [*The need to repress incestuous impulses probably inhibits her sexual feelings toward all men.*]

Th. Perhaps you feel it's wrong to feel sex about men.

Pt. I just have no feeling about it. Maybe it's safer that way.

Th. Maybe it's safer to feel sexy toward women, because it's not safe to feel sexy with men? [*interpreting her homosexuality*]

Pt. Definitely.

Example 5:

The following case illustrates the operation of a transference neurosis in facilitating insight. Sporadic backaches (lumbago) were among the patient's most disturbing symptoms. From time to time, backaches became exaggerated during a treatment session. Observing the content of his conversations when this happened, it was determined that backaches developed whenever the patient bragged or boasted about himself, whenever he voiced comments that might be construed as criticisms of me, whenever he expressed demands which I might possibly reject, or whenever he mentioned circumstances in which he had behaved in a selfish or intolerant manner. On one occasion, when these facts were brought to his attention, the patient stiffened with severe back pain which became so intense that he winced. This was coupled with pain in his scrotum and drawing sensations in the perineum. Asked to tell me what was on his mind, he expostulated that he could never express himself frankly with his father. A stern puritanical man, his father had subjected him to severe discipline whenever the patient deviated in the least from the righteous path of moral, unpretentious living. Even childish pranks were forbidden. When questioned about the form of punishment his father employed, the patient said, "He would beat me across the back with a stick." The area of attack coincided precisely with the zone of his present backaches.

At this point I mentioned that it was rather significant that in talking to me about certain topics, he had symptoms of backache. This sounded as if he were being punished for his thoughts. Seemingly, no impression was made on the patient by the interpretation. However, when he appeared for the next session, he was manifestly disturbed. Hitherto gentle and courteous, he stormed into my office and launched into a verbal attack on me. A fragment of this session follows:

Pt. I haven't wanted to say this, but it's bothered me for some time. Your attitude, I mean. [*The patient is quite anxious as he talks.*]

Th. My attitude?

Pt. You remember when I first came to see you and told you about my flight instruction and taking my instructor's test?

Th. Yes. [*This incident was a minor one that I almost had forgotten.*]

Pt. Well, you acted very flippant and disinterested.

Th. In what way?

Pt. The way you talked and looked.

Th. I wonder. Why didn't you mention this at the time?

Pt. (*pause*) Well, I thought that I was wrong to boast about it. And I felt you resented my boasting, blowing my horn. I know I feel this, and you'll say it's my imagination, but I feel I'm right that you cut me off from talking. I felt you were contemptuous of me.

Th. If this were true, I certainly wouldn't blame you for feeling the way you do. But searching into myself, and trying to recapitulate what happened, I don't remember wanting to cut you off, or feeling flippant, or deriding you in any way or acting contemptuous toward you. Is it possible that you see in what I did or said, something that wasn't there?

Pt. (*angrily*) I don't believe you. I think you're saying that to be therapeutic. I feel that.

Th. As if I'm saying this to reassure you?

Pt. Yes, because I feel this is what you did.

Th. Cut you off and acted contemptuous on the basis that you were boasting?

Pt. Yes. It's confusing to me.

Th. Say, how come you bring that up now? This happened five months ago.

Pt. Something you said last time I was here made me mad. I don't know what it is now. [*Apparently my pointing out the possibilities of a transference reaction, removed his repression and released hostility.*] I still feel you don't want to admit what you did.

Th. Well, I'll try to examine my feelings about you, and see if I really did cut you off and deride you. As far as I know right now, this isn't how I felt. As far as I can see right now, I don't feel at all contemptuous toward you.

Pt. It's hard for me to believe that. I mean it's hard to see why you shouldn't be annoyed.

Th. Why should I be annoyed at you?

Pt. Look at the crazy things I did, I told you about. That episode with that woman and everything else that followed.

Th. Maybe you feel I ought to look down on you for what you've done?

At the next session the patient was again accusatory. He said that I acted detached and unfriendly. I didn't give him an opportunity to attend my lectures or to socialize with me. He recalled that he had recently met me at a restaurant and that I had nodded, but did not offer to share my table with him. Again I assured him that if it were true that I had willfully rejected him, he had a right to be angry. However, the nature of the therapeutic situation was such that any social contact might interfere with an opportunity to work out his problems.

For several sessions, we talked back and forth in this manner. I was aware of the fact that the patient was trying to goad me into acting in an angry, recriminatory way, paralleling his father's reactions. Were I to have responded in this way, he probably would have left therapy, convinced that I was an arbitrary, hostile person. Or he would have submitted himself and then developed a dependent, compliant attitude with a continuance of his symptoms. The upshot of our talks was a recognition of his projection into our relationship of attitudes he had about his father which had conditioned his general feeling toward authority. His ability to challenge my reaction, to vent his hostility, to understand that his reactions were carry-overs of earlier patterns, without encountering counter-hostility enabled him successfully to work through his problem in therapy.

38

Exploring Trends and Patterns

ONCE AN IMPORTANT TREND OR PATTERN IS IDENTIFIED, THE THERAPIST should attempt its exploration in as elaborate detail as possible. The relationship of the trend to other aspects of the psychic life, and a study of the conflicts it engenders, may be investigated by focusing the patient's attention on, and eliciting detailed associations to every trend manifestation. In the course of doing this, the therapist should attempt to circumscribe the subject coverage so as to prevent rambling. Where the patient is permitted to bounce along from topic to topic, he will pursue a course of least opposition, veering away from pockets of anxiety. This, a manifestation of resistance, is partly without conscious design and must be combatted in the interest of making more rapid progress. A certain amount of rambling is, of course, inevitable, but where it takes the patient too far afield from the subject under inquiry, he should be brought back to it.

The immediate preoccupation of the patient may cover such diverse areas as disagreeable symptoms, a general state of unhappiness or boredom, daily happenings and events, obligations, hopes, ambitions, important past incidents, experiments with parents and siblings, current interpersonal relationships, fantasies, dreams, attitudes toward therapy, and feelings about the therapist.

Eventually, each of these areas will be explored in detail; however, the learning process will be enhanced where every session is organized around an important theme. Thus we may, during one session, work on the patient's sexual problems, since these seem all embracing to him. Or, if he is preoccupied with a fear of being exploited or hurt in an interpersonal relationship, this may constitute the area of investigation. Actually, all of the patient's difficulties are interrelated. Consideration of one element will of necessity eventually involve others. For instance, in dealing with his sexual life, our discovery of masochistic impulses will bring out attitudes toward males, females, authority figures, compeers, subordinate persons, parents and children. Working through his sexual problem will of necessity also involve a resolution of interpersonal distortions. Conversely, if we focus on problems with authority, with subordinates, with parents and other persons, the individual's sexual relationships will inevitably come up for inquiry.

Where a number of trends simultaneously occupy the mind of the patient, a more effective use of the session may often be accomplished by a selection of areas according to the priority rating indicated in chapter 15, The Conduct of the Psychotherapeutic Interview.

Generally, however, the matter of selection poses no problems for the therapist because important trends or patterns are sufficiently intense to warrant their consideration as a primary focus for exploration.

Experience will readily confirm the fact that any pattern under exploration has tendrils that permeate many facets of the patient's personality. Constant exploration eventually brings the patient to an awareness of the implications and contradictions of his way of life, and to a recognition of how he fosters the very difficulties of which he is so intolerant. Insight into the fact that his responses to people are not justified by present-day reality is an important step in the process of getting well. As mechanisms of defense are exposed, and resistances are resolved, the patient becomes increasingly motivated toward experimenting with life on new terms; he becomes more and more capable of mastering the anxieties that have conditioned his customary reactions. Life no longer is regarded as a mere arena of past happenings. Situations and relationships are reevaluated in the light of existing reality.

To illustrate, we may consider the case of a married woman of thirty-two, with two children, four and two years of age. The reasons for her coming to therapy were spells of excessive tension, attacks of anxiety, obsessional fears of her children dying, and periodic bouts of violent scrubbing of her hands, which had become progressively worse during the past two years. During the first phase of therapy, the patient readily established a working relationship and accepted without too great resistance the structuring of the therapeutic situation.

A great deal of her concern during the ensuing treatment sessions was with her marriage. From its very onset she had become aware of great boredom in her role as housewife. A successful buyer in a large department store, she had given up her position as soon as she had become pregnant. Whereas previously she had enjoyed considerable standing as a buyer, she now had very little status as a mother. In addition, her husband's salary did not permit of liberties in spending. She was, in fact, forced to conserve in order to budget the family funds. This imposed a great strain on her. Since she had never experienced neurotic symptoms prior to her marriage, she assumed that they were caused by the responsibilities of being a mother, of having no distinction as a wife, and of needing to operate with restricted funds. My comment to these statements was that while hardships undoubtedly had existed, it was likely that she was responding to her situation with certain attitudes and feelings that might bear examination.

Enjoined to observe her reactions to various life happenings, the patient began to make certain connections as illustrated in the following fragment of an interview:

Pt. I had a bad few days last week. Everything got on my nerves. Betty (*the patient's older child*) came down with a bad cold and I was tied down more than ever. The scrubbing returned, and I was more upset than ever.

Th. I see.

Pt. And on Wednesday I began thinking. (*laughs*) The funniest thing happened. I was working in the kitchen and suddenly I got that awful feeling. It came on me like a squirmy wave. I got scared and tense and the muscles back here (*strokes the muscles in the back of her neck*) got tight and my head filled up as if I had a tight bandage around, and queasy feelings in the pit of my stomach.

Th. Mm hmm.

Pt. And there was something else that happened. I knew something was bothering me and I just didn't know what.

Th. Mm hmm.

Pt. Something bothering me. It's like something I had to do, supposed to do. It was such a frustrating feeling. (*pause*)

Th. A frustrating feeling, as if you just couldn't grasp what was going on?

Pt. Yes, just like that. So out of desperation, I guess, I turned on the radio. The first thing was one of those breakfast Mr. and Mrs. programs. They were bantering back and forth, and I detected a snide attitude toward the woman. This made me boil. And all of a sudden the thing flashed in mind. It came to me that I promised my husband that I'd buy him several pairs of socks a week ago. I've been putting it off, and putting it off, and not thinking of it. When I'd go out, it wouldn't occur to me to get the socks until I'd remember when I got home. (*laughs*)

Th. (*smiles*) You suspected something was going on inside of you?

Pt. I knew it. As I was listening to the program, it came to me. I suddenly got mad, furious and said, "Darn him, why doesn't he buy socks for himself? Why should I do *his* dirty work?" (*laughs*)

Th. You resented his making this demand on you?

Pt. (*laughs*) No question about that. My next thought (*laughs*) . . . it was, "Damn him, why doesn't he buy socks for *himself*. Why do I have to do *all* the dirty work around here. He wants and expects me to be a slave, just tidy up the place and get nowheres." I thought of him in his nice comfortable office. Then I thought of how wonderful I felt when I was working. At least I felt appreciated and didn't get the constant criticism I get now.

Th. This must really burn you up.

Pt. I suppose marriage is a sacrifice. I do love the children. I don't know what they'd do if I went back to work. But it's the noise, noise, the howling of the kids and the criticism of my husband.

Th. When you were working, you felt you were doing something significant that gave you status.

Pt. You know, doctor, I sometimes feel as if I was absolutely crazy to give up my job. I don't know what I imagined marriage was going to be like.

Th. And it turned out to be something where you have to take care of howling kids and buy socks for your husband.

Pt. You know, as soon as I had these thoughts I got very mad. I screamed out loud, "Why doesn't he buy the socks himself." I had a picture of him (*laughs*) this is silly . . . slipping on, (*laughs*) slipping on a banana peel and turning a half somersault in the air, I started laughing. Doctor, do I want him to break his neck? When this all happened I noticed that I felt better. My headache went away and the stiffness in the neck. [*Apparently, realization and acknowledgment of her hostility, removed the necessity for its repression and its conversion into symptoms.*]

Th. Now what do you think this was all about? [*testing her insight*]

Pt. I know you have been hinting to me that there must be reasons for the state I'm in. I get very mad at things all the time. Most of the time I'm on fire in here. (*points to stomach*)

Th. But you haven't been too aware of how angry you've been.

Pt. I just began to realize it because after this happened and I still felt mad, I called my husband and asked him to pick the socks he wanted himself. I told him to get them himself. Just like that, I did.

Th. What did he say?

Pt. (*laughs*) He said O.K.

Th. O.K., nothing more?

Pt. No, he wasn't upset or mean or angry.

Th. Did you expect him to be angry?

Pt. Why, of course. You know, doctor, I must be scared to death of my husband to act the way I do.

Th. Maybe you're scared of your own anger too? [*a cautious interpretation*]

Pt. I don't know. I just feel as if this whole thing is mysterious—what happened to me. [*The patient rejects this interpretation temporarily. Later she advances it herself, having accepted its implications.*]

Observation of her responses to varied situations and interpersonal relationships, brought the patient to an awareness of attitudes, and impulses that mobilized anxiety and generated symptoms. Hostility toward her husband and children had been so repressed that she was only tangentially aware of its manifestations. The recited episode of the radio was an indication that she was attempting to understand and to come to grips with her basic problems. The quarrel between the radio breakfast couple had apparently exposed her own unexpressed feelings about her husband. Further exploration of her resentment at being asked to do a menial chore for her husband, opened up a channel to her feelings about the role she played as a woman, a wife and a mother.

In later interviews, the patient brought up more fantasies which included the accidental crushing of her husband by a truck while crossing the street, the untimely death of both of her children with a virulent strain of pneumonia, the winning of a radio prize of fifty thousand dollars with which she purchased a prosperous business, and, upon the demise of her husband, marriage to a gallant, soft-spoken "sweet" man with qualities antithetical to those of her husband. Hitherto she had paid little attention to her fantasies, their connection with deeper conflictual sources being unknown to her. But appreciating that there were reasons for her fantasies as well as symptoms, she alerted herself to possible meanings.

Although she had been, to some extent, aware of her unhappiness as a housewife, she was not cognizant of how deeply she resented this role. Exploring her resistances to the awareness of her hostility, however, enabled her to focus on her right to experience and to express spontaneous feelings. As expected, this constituted an assault on her repressions and mobilized guilt and some anxiety. The patient recited incidents when she was unable to assert herself. However, she also described situations when she was capable of taking a forceful and even aggressive stand. It became apparent that under circumstances when she was in a subordinate position, she became submissive, passive, afraid and unable to express aggression. Under other conditions, where she was dominant, "in charge of things," and "on top of the heap," she could be expressive and even cruel. As a buyer in a prominent store, she had enjoyed prestige, the respect of her associates, and a considerable amount of power. She had felt free and had been able to stand up for her rights whenever crossed. Indeed she had gotten the reputation of being a "strong woman." The obvious delight in her voice as she recalled her exploits as a buyer was in contrast to the hopeless, apathetic manner with which she discussed her present life experiences. When this fact was brought out, she agreed that the discrepancy was indicative of what she secretly might be wishing—a return to the security she had had as a buyer.

The patient recalled her feelings of defeat in the past when, as a girl, she was barred from games by the boys in her neighborhood. She had always wanted to be a boy and she deeply resented being "hemmed in" as a girl. Toward a younger brother she evinced great envy, and she recalled with guilt having been envious of his possession of a penis. Shamefully, she admitted that she had anticipated as a child being changed into a boy, and in her dreams as an adult, she sometimes pictured herself as a man. While working as a buyer, she remarked, she donned attire of mannish style which gave her "a wonderful sense of freedom."

An illustrative dream indicating some of these trends was the following:

I see myself on a veranda. Everything seems shoddy and strange. I am in the house with my mother. I see an animal like a rat in the kitchen on a mirror. It is small like an embryo. It makes me sick. Then I see a manly woman with a man on the veranda and am frightfully jealous.

Associations to the dream made it apparent that she conceived of her life with her mother (and perhaps on a transference level her relationship with me) as shoddy and weakening. The rat embryo was a reflection of her debased infantile feminine self. The manly woman who could appropriate and manage a male was the other aspect of herself that she cherished.

Much of the material during this period of treatment concerned itself with her relationships with her parents and her younger brother. Her mother, she felt, was a cold, rejecting person who gave her little love and acceptance. Her father was a detached, harsh, puritanical individual who spent little time with her, and with whom she never developed a feeling of closeness. Her brother remained, until recent years, a source of envy and concern. On the one hand, she felt resentment toward him; on the other hand, she felt strongly attracted to him physically. She never believed that she was respected as a person by any member of her family. For instance, she recalled with bitterness how all efforts to express aggression or to resist the demands of her parents were met with violence. During her entire childhood she was reminded of her stubborn, recalcitrant nature; she was told that she had uncontrollable rages which had to be dealt with severely.

This information was utilized during interviews to facilitate inquiry into the genetic origin of her resentment at being a woman, and into the defenses she employed against expressing hostility. To show any hostility when she felt herself to be in a subordinate role threatened her with the same feeling of loss of love and punishment that she had experienced as a child in relation to her parents. To stand up for her rights, and to express aggression, meant that she was "bad," unloved and unlovable. She equated this with being a woman. On the other hand, when she was in command of a situation, "on top of things," and dominant, she identified herself with males, she felt invulnerable and capable of expressing aggression.

Gradually, the patient could see how she extended these feelings into her environment, and how she responded to every aspect of her life situation with attitudes rooted in past misinterpretations. For example, some of her dreams reflected a desire to be married to the husband of her best friend. Her associations revealed great envy of her friend for being wedded to a passive man who allowed himself to be domineered by a woman. In her relationship with me, too, she began to express basic patterns. Encouraged to verbalize her feelings, she expostulated attitudes of envy and resentment. On one occasion she remarked angrily: "It makes me furious to come here and see you sit comfortably on your behind all day in a nice soft chair, and collect a nice fat fee. I've got to struggle in the kitchen all day and do scut work for nothing. I catch myself thinking, 'Who does he think he is, telling me, what to do?' But I know you don't order me around." Focusing on our relationship, the patient was able to appreciate her competitiveness with me, which was of a quality similar to that which she had sustained with her father and brother.

Her ability to express hostility toward me without encountering retaliatory punishment, enabled her to bring up more and more undistorted manifestations of her conflict. Murder wishes toward her husband and children, homosexual impulses, desires to repudiate her femininity and to become masculine, prostitution wishes, compulsions to soil and many other impulses were verbalized and explored.

CASE ILLUSTRATION

The process of exploring a trend may be illustrated by a fragment of a session with a patient suffering from a psychophysiologic bladder disorder, who, coming late for the session, exhibited strong tension and anxiety. The ramifications of a compulsive need to please others are investigated.

Th. You appear to be greatly upset by coming late. I wonder why.

Pt. It's that I don't like to come late. I have a feeling you will look down on me and find me out to be an unreliable person. As if you would be displeased with me for not coming on time. [*This suggests a trend related to feelings of being accepted by authority, as well as doubts about his capacity to "please."*]

Th. What might I do if I were displeased? [*exploring the trend by asking questions*]

Pt. You could show your displeasure by acting, say cold, like father did. Even possibly you might not continue treating me. [*introducing one genetic determinant of his reaction and an association of the therapist with his father*]

Th. I see. [*I could focus on his relationship with his father at this point, but decide instead to let him associate at random.*]

Pt. And a feeling of good performance comes into it. I want to be an ideal patient (*laughs*) someone who is on time, someone who cooperates and becomes successfully analyzed. [*This may be another aspect of wanting to be a "good" boy.*]

Th. In other words, you have to please. [*interpreting*]

Pt. Yeah.

Th. Even if it means getting well to please?

Pt. That would be an interesting motive to get well—to please somebody. But I know what you're saying, that I might do it because I have a need to please everybody. (*pause*)

Th. Everybody?

Pt. Yes. You know, when I first started coming here, I didn't know what I was doing, like needing to please every woman that came along, to do things for *them*.

Th. Do you think you still do that?

Pt. (*pause*) Why . . . yes, I find myself doing that automatically, without thinking. It's still a very important thing with me. In that sense I'm getting a satisfaction out of pleasing them. But I find lately that it's more irksome than before. I'm getting a little more selfish than before. I suppose it's good, or isn't it?

Th. You don't sound convinced. [*challenging the patient's conviction that he is doing a "good" thing*]

Pt. (*laughs*) Well, you know I don't realize I'm doing something to please someone until I begin to think what I did. Then I get mad. [*The thought comes to me that hostility generated by his constant need to please may be responsible for his psychosomatic symptoms.*]

Th. There must be a reason why you need to please others. [*focusing the patient's attention on the purpose of his trend*]

Pt. I don't know why I have to do it.

Th. Well, suppose you start thinking about why anybody should want constantly to please and not to offend. [*more focusing*]

Pt. I can see that I feel I have no worth as a person, except in pleasing people. I mean that's what it seems to resolve itself down to. [*While this is probably correct, the patient is not yet aware of the implications of what he is saying, and of the connections of the trend to please with other important aspects of his personality.*]

Th. And if you have no worth as a person, unless you please somebody, what do you think happens when you please somebody?

Pt. I achieve, I get some worth.

Th. And if you do please someone, how would you feel about that person after you please?

Pt. Resentment, I suppose.

Th. Well, how *do* you feel, I mean what *has* your experience been?

Pt. I've noticed that often I kick myself afterward, feel I'm a "heeler" and have to toe the mark. Then I start not wanting to see the person. This holds true with my wife too. A wall falls in between the two of us, I just feel nothing toward her for days afterward. [*The patient is aware of his detachment which, an important part of his character structure, seems to be a defense against further encroachment, as well as a manifestation of hostility.*]

Th. Mm hmm.

Pt. It's a very complex problem because, after all, people do like you for your qualities. They can't just like you really for nothing, and they can't like you for being a bastard unless they're sadistic, I mean masochistic, really. If these women, for example, like me the way I am, they must like me because I am the way I am. People have liked me. I would say that with most of the people I come in contact with, I'm fairly well-liked. It must be because of the way I am. [*The patient seems to be defending his character traits.*]

Th. Which is what?

Pt. Which is a pleasant guy.

Th. You mean they like you because you please? That you go out of your way to please?

Pt. I guess so.

Th. You mentioned that if you don't please, then you might be a bastard. People couldn't like a bastard. Does it follow that, if you don't supposedly please people, you have to be a bastard? Or that you just reject, repudiate, and act sadistic toward people if you don't please?

Pt. No, except that that's easier to do than to reach the happy medium, I suppose.

Th. Do you feel that you might have impulses to be a bastard and not to please and just be sadistic toward people? [*exploring possible sadistic traits*]

Pt. I don't consciously, but Jesus, I must be trying to cover up something. I'll show my resentments in disguised ways. I can be very brusque in the office. If people come in to see me when I'm busy, and I don't want to see them, instead of saying— being pleasant about it—sorry, but I'm busy today, come back another time, I convey a feeling to them, I know it, that I don't want to see them. And I wish to hell they'd get out of there. But it's not done in an open way, it's a compromise, I suppose. I can honestly say that consciously I have no destructive feelings at all, to speak of, unless something occurs and my temper might flare up, I used to have . . . when I was a kid I threw a hammer at my cousin. But I must have had some display of temper at one time, but it's gone. I actually don't like other people trying to please me. If someone wants to do something for me, a favor of some kind, I don't like it, I don't want them to. Now *why*, I don't know. I never examined why. [*The patient is aware of contradictions in his trends.*]

Th. There must be a reason why you don't want people to do favors for you, or to do things for you.

Pt. Maybe it implies that I, I'm not worthy of being done a favor, and that there are strings attached to favors.

Th. What may happen if you accept a favor from a person?

Pt. I feel that I'm putting them out in some way, and I don't want to put them out. "Why are you doing this for me?" I say.

Th. You distrust their motives?

Pt. Well, I know that I never liked to take anything from my father. He used to be pretty generous in a material way, always used to bring me toys when I was young, and presents, usually the best that he could get. Then there was money. From the time I was in high school and college I remember feeling uncomfortable when he gave me the money. So I'm not sure whether it's a feeling that I was unworthy of getting the money. Maybe unconsciously my feelings were so destructive that by taking anything from him I compromised, I don't know.

Th. All right, what might other reasons be for not wanting to accept things from people? For example, have instances occurred where you felt uncomfortable or turned down offers of a person wanting to please you or to do things for you?

Pt. Well, for example, my girl wanted to see me yesterday, and I wanted to see her, but it involved her coming in, making a special trip. And there was a chance that I couldn't see her. I felt that it wasn't fair of me to ask her to come in and she didn't insist on it. I felt under those circumstances it would be unfair and hurtful to her.

Th. That you might hurt her? You didn't want to be hurtful to her. You felt it would be ungracious and aggressive of you?

Pt. It would be an unpleasant experience for her, and she would do all this for me and get nothing out of it. I don't like people to take trouble from me.

Th. Have people taken trouble from you at any time in the past?

Pt. I guess when they took trouble, they let me know that they took trouble. (*pause*)

Th. Who?

Pt. My mother. (*pause*)

Th. What did she do?

Pt. Well, she always would say, for example: "Now be a good boy, because you have such a good father. Your father is so good to you, he gets you all these things."

Th. He pleases you, therefore you have to be good to him?

Pt. Yeah.

Th. And under what circumstances would you be angry at father? [*I decide to explore his relationships with his parents to see if the trend we are working on goes back to his childhood.*]

Pt. They'd be damned scarce.

Th. In other words, did she convey to you the idea that because your father did things for you, you'd better not be mad at him? There was no reason why you should be angry at him?

Pt. Well, I don't know if she particularly conveyed to me that there was no reason, but she implied that even if I had a reason, I wasn't justified. He was my father and he did all these things for me. In fact, she conveyed that *she* did things for me too, and it was trouble for her that she did them for me. She gave the impression that she loved me, but she let me know that she went through a lot of trouble for me. She happens to be a very selfish person, but that was the impression that I had when I was young. So maybe I'm afraid that I don't really want to do anything for anybody, that if they do a favor for me, then I have to do something for them. You have a payment, almost, to make. And paying would be much against what I really feel. And all these years I've been going on pleasing people with, I guess, a very strong resentment against it. But the other extreme of not ever pleasing anybody is just as bad.

Th. Isn't it possible that the problem in your not being able to accept things from people, is that there might be strings tied to the acceptance? They'd be pleasing you, but you would also have to please them back. You wouldn't be able to stand up for your rights; you wouldn't be able to fight with them if necessary, or feel resentment toward them, if it was justified. It's as if they tried to buy you off and you couldn't maintain your independence. [*This is a tentative interpretation.*]

Pt. If I take a favor, yes. And I don't like to ask people to do anything for me.

Th. Is it also possible then, that your not being able to take things from people means to you the ability to maintain your freedom and to express your feelings of resentment? If that's so, you might also try to keep their resentment at bay by doing things for them. Then they won't be angry at you. Is that possible? [*more interpretation*]

Pt. That's very true. Yeah. Particularly exemplified in these women. I don't like scenes. I don't like resentment shown. I don't like anger shown at me, and if I see them, I see them often so that they won't get nasty, and they won't say anything. So it becomes a double-faceted thing, doesn't it. To gain acceptance and also to do away with any resentment or aggressions that they might have. [*The patient shows here a good capacity to make a connection between several important tendencies.*]

Th. What happens when you *are* exposed to aggression or resentment? How do you react then?

Pt. I don't like it at all. It's a feeling that there is no strength inside of me to withstand it. I must be wrong. I guess that's another part of the problem. And, of course, the more significant the people are, the more important it would be to me. I guess with my girl, for example, I don't like it; but I don't get any anxiety feelings. I guess I throw a kind of shield up around myself, separate myself from her when she does get to show resentment. And maybe I feel a little stronger inside, a little more worth while now. I feel that she's wrong in many cases. I never felt really, that *anyone* was wrong, as far as I was concerned. I could always see their side of the picture very clearly. One time, just before I went to California, I'd been working for my uncle. Some people in his business quit and he wanted me to come back, and I didn't want to come back. To me the work had ceased to be important and we had quite a to-do. He was very angry with me and caused me a lot of anxiety. I wanted to go back, but my girl was on the other side. "Don't do it," she said, "take your vacation." That sort of thing. But I disliked intensely the fact that he was angry at me. I couldn't feel that he was right. I think that I might feel a different way today in such a situation. I'm sure I wouldn't have the reaction I had then, but the reaction I had then was a very, very anxious one. I couldn't be right; I should go back to work; he's mad at me, my uncle, and that sort of thing.

39

The Uncovering of Unconscious Material

THE BRINGING OF THE PATIENT TO AWARENESS OF CERTAIN ASPECTS OF his unconscious is an integral part of all insight therapy. Where treatment is geared toward reeducative goals, this uncovering process need not be too ambitious. On the other hand, the achievement of reconstructive goals may require extensive exposure of segments of the inner psychic life which have been isolated from consciousness by repression, and which serve as actual or potential sources of conflict.

The "depth" of exploration of repressed conflictual foci will vary according to the needs of the patient. It is doubtful that a total divulgence of unconscious material is ever required. Nor is it possible, through the use of any of the techniques known today—focused interviewing, free association, dream and fantasy interpretation, exploration of transference, hypnoanalysis, narcoanalysis, art therapy and play therapy—to uncover the unconscious completely. There are some repressions that seem to remain insoluble in the face of the most skilled therapeutic handling. Fortunately, however, most people may be helped sufficiently through the gaining of insight into merely some of their unconscious conflicts.

Among repressed and repudiated aspects of psychic activity are fears and fantasies associated with the various bodily functions, particularly eating, excretion, and sexuality. There are hostile and destructive impulses directed toward other persons and toward the self. There are traumatic memories and experiences too painful to be recalled in consciousness. There are incestuous desires and other unresolved Oedipal elements. There are impulses toward sadism, masochism, voyeurism, exhibitionism and homosexuality. There are such normal strivings as desires for love, companionship, recognition, self-esteem, independence, and creative self-fulfillment, which have developed incompletely, or, for anxiety reasons, been abandoned. There are, in addition, rejected neurotic drives for affection, dependence, superiority, dominance, ambition, power, and detachment, as well as the conflicts that these drives initiate.

The individual, while often partially aware of his unconscious strivings, usually does not understand their meaning or how they act to create his symptoms. For example, he may know that he has had certain damaging experiences, and that he has tried to banish from his mind some painful events in his life; yet he does not fully appreciate the important hold they have on him. He may be aware of murderous aggression or perverse sexual impulses, and he may feel repulsed by these. However, the determining influence that such impulses have on his behavior is outside the range of his understanding. He may, from time to time, realize how his character drives operate; for instance, he may recognize how dependent he is in one or another relationship, but he may not know how dependency acts as a key motif of his life. He does not understand the extent to which it saps his self-esteem and renders him helpless and without energy. Nor does he see how it clashes with such coexistent drives as those for independence and power, generating tension and anxiety.

The specific psychic elements that are repressed are dependent upon the unique experiences of the individual. Any aspect of feeling or thinking or behaving may be subject to repression if it conflicts with social standards, as transmitted to the patient by the parent through disciplines. These injunctions, incorporated into the superego, continue to exert pressure on the person. In our culture such impulses as sexuality, hostility and assertiveness are particularly subject to repression. Also commonly repudiated are impulses toward dependency and passivity, as well as compulsive drives for power and independence.

In spite of deflection from the mainstream of the individual's thinking, repressed material may gain access to awareness in the form of highly symbolized and distorted derivatives. It is through detection and translation of such derivatives that awareness of the deeper content becomes possible.

THE SYMBOLISM OF THE UNCONSCIOUS

Thus, the patient's dreams, fantasies, free associations, symptoms and behavioral tendencies may reflect extremely primitive or childish symbols. Often, expression is couched in terms of various organ functions. Simple activities, such as sucking, eating, excreting, and sexual functioning may represent a host of attitudes and strivings. The form of expression may seem bizarre, senseless, and without rational design. A need for security and dependency may thus appear as a desire to suck the breast, penis or nipple. All parts of the body, including the genital organs, may be implemented in this sucking process. Dependency may also be expressed by fantasies of cannibalistic incorporation of a real or nonexistent person. The amalgamation may be achieved by other means, as by entering the body of the person through any of the various orifices, by sexual intercourse, or by changing into a phallus and being sucked up into the vagina and womb. There may be a peculiar extension in which the person on whom the subject wishes to depend is identified with the fecal mass, with resultant overvaluation of excretory products and activities.

Hostile attitudes toward women may be represented by the biting and destroying of a female figure, or of a woman's body contents, breasts, or nipples, or of a fantasied penis within her abdomen. This attack may be attempted with the mouth, anus, or penis, or with excretory products. Destructive feelings toward males may be symbolized by impulses to castrate, or to devour or incorporate the penis or the body conceived as a penis. Fantasies of eating or of expelling loved or hated persons in the form of feces may occur.

Guilt feelings and fears of retaliation may be symbolized by fantasies of being eaten or castrated by devouring animals, ghouls, monsters, or witches, of being absorbed into a vagina for purposes of destruction, of being attacked by a male sexual organ, a female organ, or an imagined intravaginal penis. There may be fears of being penetrated anally by the penis of a strong man, or of being injured and killed by feces. A loss of aggressiveness and intactness may be designated by a fear of castration; this in males may be accompanied by reparative attempts, and in females by a denial of the fact that there is no penis, or by frenzied attempts to secure one in fantasy from a paternal, fraternal, or maternal person in whose body a penis may be imagined to exist.

Phallic symbolism is extraordinarily common in unconscious ideation. Some persons are more prone than others to use it to express basic needs and attitudes. Sexuality here becomes a magical short cut to close relationships with people and the nucleus around which the individual's thoughts and symptoms are oriented.

Possession of an intact male organ is frequently utilized to represent a sense of aggressiveness and power. It may become the symbol of the chief values and goals in life. Strivings for strength, activity, and dominance may thus be symbolized unconsciously by a desire for a penis in a female, who may believe that possession of a penis would be a magical solution for all her problems, including the fear of functioning as a female. The same impulses may also bring about a wish for a larger and more powerful penis in a male. Submission, passivity, and subordination may be signified in a woman by the lack of a penis, and in a man by desires for breasts, castration and homosexuality. Where security is sought through dependency and subordination, castration may also be a goal which is usually countered by a desire for activity and a fear of castration.

FORGOTTEN MEMORIES AND EXPERIENCES

In the course of exploring the unconscious, the patient is apt to revive experiences in his past that have been traumatic to him. Forgotten memories may be remembered of which the patient may have been relatively or completely unaware. The importance of this material constantly comes up for appraisal.

There are those who believe that the recall of forgotten traumatic incidents in the developmental history is essential for cure in reconstructive therapy, since repressed memories are fountainheads of conflict. A criterion of cure set by Freud was a removal of the amnesia of the third and fourth years, and a recovery of memories during this period that are associated with the patient's neurosis. There are other authorities who tend to disagree with this standard, believing that therapy, focused on immediate interpersonal relationships, can change personality without the need for probing into the past.

The mechanism associated with the repression of early experiences is organized around the need to avoid anxiety. In early childhood, inimical happenings are extremely traumatic. One reason for this is that the child feels relatively helpless in a world, the manifestations of which are a constant source of mystery to him. Relations between cause and effect are indeterminate, and he is menaced by many inscrutable events over which he has no control. One way of coping with childhood anxieties is to project them in the form of phobias. Another way of dealing with anxiety that threatens to overwhelm the immature ego is through processes of repression and dissociation. These phobic and repressive defenses continue to function far beyond the period of childhood, and the ego reacts to the original traumatic events as if it still were too weak and too vulnerable to deal with them. This is possibly the reason why many adults feel that there is something buried deep within themselves so terrifying that they cannot bear to bring it up.

An important question is whether early traumatic experiences are universally damaging. It is difficult to provide a complete answer to this question. All children undergo traumatic experiences of one sort or another during the period of socialization. A cataclysmic happening, however, can bring the effects of minor experiences to a head and can embody the accumulated emotions of all past inimical events.

Traumatic experiences in early childhood thus act upon a sensitized soil at a time when ego resources are relatively limited. Often these experiences, when uncovered, appear so insignificant that one might doubt their potency in evoking such disproportionate emotional responses. Yet, if one considers that the traumatic experience is a condensation of a series of damaging events, and that it comes to stand symbolically for all of them, one may appreciate that it can be greatly overvalued.

As a general rule, early traumatic experiences are of two types. In one type, the events are so devastating or destructive that no child could be expected to cope with them. This occurs where the child is severely injured physically, or witnesses an incident so horrible that the experience takes away his security. The other type of traumatic experience can in no way be considered extraordinary, since it is part of the normal growth process. Growing up involves the capacity to abandon narcissistic and omnipotent strivings, to tolerate frustration, to channelize aggression into socially accepted outlets, to control sexual impulses, and to develop independence and self-assertiveness. In the course of his development, the child is subjected to many frustrations that involve abandonment of selfish strivings in favor of those that will bring him into cooperative relationships with the group. Most children are capable of handling such frustrations without too great difficulty. However, an insecure child, and particularly one who has been rejected and denied legitimate demands for love and support, will be so overwhelmed by feelings of helplessness that he will be unable to tolerate frustration and to withstand traumatic experiences that are a usual component of growing up. Such an individual is likely to react catastrophically to relatively normal hardships as are imposed on every child. In him certain events like the birth of a sibling, the discovery of the genital difference between the sexes, the witnessing of parental intercourse ("primal scene") or exposure to any bloodshed and cruelty, may mobilize inordinate anxiety.

The insecure child may feel so threatened by rejection or punishment that he will find it necessary to repress such impulses as hostility toward his parents and siblings, masturbatory desires, sexual curiosities, and strivings for mastery, independence and self-assertion. The repression of these impulses involves much experiment. The child for a long time defies the parents, even at the risk of incurring retaliatory punishment. Gradually, however, he may yield to parental discipline. Frequently repression occurs dramatically following a particularly traumatic incident that convinces the child that danger can be real. For instance, an insecure child who retains within himself certain rebellious tendencies may witness the flogging of a dog that has done something to offend its master. He may be frightened by this brutal treatment, and he may unconsciously identify himself with the animal, fearing that he will be injured in the same way if he persists in defying his parents. The result may be a phobia in regard to dogs, the dynamic purpose of which is to insulate himself against fear of his own aggressive impulses. The event comes to constitute a traumatic experience that may be repressed in an effort to avoid any reminder of pain. The dog phobia will nevertheless persist, aiding the repressive process.

During later life, too, even in adulthood, intensely traumatic experiences may shock the organism into a revival of the mechanism of repression. This move is motivated by a need to ward off a threat to the ego. There are no better examples of this than those seen in the neuroses of war in which traumatic incidents may be blotted from the mind.

In the course of therapy, the recovery of repressed traumatic experiences may ameliorate or dissipate certain symptoms, especially those that serve the function of keeping these memories repressed. Many compulsions, obsessions, and conversion symptoms fall into this category. The most dramatic results occur in simple conditioned fears and in amnesias of recent origin such as hysterical amnesias, trauma of the skull, and exposure to unbearable stresses like those during disasters and war. Where the personality is relatively intact, and the individual has, prior to the traumatic event, functioned satisfactorily in his interpersonal relationships, the recall of forgotten events may restore the previous status.

Theoretically, all symptoms have an historical origin. It may be argued that were we capable of probing deeply enough into the past, of penetrating the myriad conditionings, of reviewing every stimulus that ever invaded the senses and every idea that entered the mind, of peering into all influences, pleasurable and inimical that have impinged on the patient, we might be able to demonstrate to him how each of his symptoms came into being. This task, however, is impossible, for many vital early experiences that have molded the personality are not accessible to recall, having occurred prior to the phase of mnemonic accessibility, or having been subjected to a practically impenetrable sealing off process of repression. In spite of a most extensive analysis one is able to recapture only a fragment of the total of life experiences. Even where we have not laid out for ourselves so ambitious a task, and are satisfied with reviewing the most important experiences in the patient's development, we find these so numerous as to defy recapitulation.

However, to indulge our imagination, we may conjure up a situation in which we track down the origin of each of the patient's symptoms. Having done this, we should probably find, in most cases, that the symptoms themselves would not vanish. The expectation that recovery of traumatic experiences will invariably produce an amelioration or cure of the patient's neurosis is founded on a faulty theoretic promise. Even though the individual's character structure is in large measure developed from the bedrock of past experiences and conditionings, and even though damage of his personality has resulted from untoward happenings in his early interpersonal relationships, it does not follow that a recall of these experiences will correct the existing condition.

As an analogy, we may consider a focus of infection that operates insidiously over a period of years. The original source of the individual's physical disability is this infective focus, but by the time it is discovered, it has already influenced other bodily structures. It may have produced kidney damage or acted as a stimulus of secondary foci of infection. The removal of the primary focus will leave the body still suffering from the effects of the original infection, and it will be essential to cure these secondary effects before the patient can be pronounced cured. A single catastrophic experience or a series of harmful experiences can likewise act as a focus, engendering in an insecure person the conviction that the world is menacing and that the people in it are not to be trusted. The experience may influence him in forming decisive attitudes and reaction patterns. By the time he enters adulthood, however, his manner of dealing with his conflicts will have been structuralized into behavior so ingrained that the recall of the original trauma will have little effect upon his habitual responses. Therapy will involve tedious reeducation and reconditioning long after the recall of the initial traumatic memories.

Often during therapy a patient may recover the memory of a forgotten traumatic happening, and through this recall he may experience considerable abreaction. He may even liberate himself from certain associated symptoms. However, the essential difficulty will probably remain. The patient will still be insecure. The circumstances that sensitized him to the original traumatic scene will continue to plague him in his daily interpersonal relationships. The essential task in therapy, therefore, would seem to lie not only in recovery of early traumatic experiences, but also in ascertaining the reasons why the experiences became so catastrophic as to necessitate repression.

It must always be remembered that a neurosis is not a fortuitous happening dependent exclusively upon early traumatic events. It is rather a form of adaptation to, and defense against a world that is regarded by the child and later by the adult as potentially hostile and menacing. Current reaction patterns and attitudes, while derived from past experiences, are not an automatic repetition of infantile modes in an adult setting. They are forms of behavior motivated by a desire to escape helplessness, to gratify vital needs, and to allay tension, anxiety and hostility. The individual reacts to the present with characterologic machinery that is rooted in his past experiences; but his present-day problems are the immediate result of conflicts deriving from demands, fears and resentments that arise also from his current interpersonal relationships.

Overemphasis on the part played by the past may produce certain unfortunate effects during therapy. The patient may utilize his inimical childhood experiences as a justification for his neurosis and for resistance to change. His therapy may bog down in a compulsive historical review of his past, a definite cleavage developing to isolate it from the present. Some patients who have familiarized themselves with early theories of psychoanalysis are led to believe that awareness of their past conditionings will magically dissolve their problems and reintegrate them in their dealings with the world. Consequently, the analysis becomes a stereotyped search for an illusory pot of gold at the end of a mnemonic rainbow.

While an exclusive preoccupation with the past imposes definite limitations in therapy, one must not be won over to the fallacious notion that the historical experience can be entirely meaningless. Tendencies in this direction are apparent in certain present-day insight therapies, and foster a concentration on relatively superficial material. There is in this approach a dichotomization of the personality, as though the individual had two parts—an important present, and a past that has little bearing upon prevailing attitudes, values and goals.

Knowledge of the historical roots of a disorder is in itself not sufficient to produce cure, but it is of tremendous value in establishing continuity in the individual's life, from infancy to adulthood. It points to weakness and sensitivity of the ego at the time of a particularly traumatic experience. It demonstrates how repetitive happenings in the present are a reflection of the same problems that existed in childhood. Of particular therapeutic benefit is the ability of the ego to withstand the emotions liberated by the recall of early traumatic incidents. The neurotic individual often has little respect for himself because he has to yield to his fear of the past. To be able to master this fear, and to tolerate the anxiety that previously caused him to cringe, has an enhancing effect on ego strength.

The relationship with the therapist acts as an important tool in the recall of buried memories. In the transference the patient will be stirred up emotionally and will experience attitudes and impulses that have a potent effect in reviving mnemonic prototypes of what he is undergoing in the present. The transference will frequently touch off patterns that cannot be uprooted by any other method.

During therapy the patient may, however, for some reason be incapable of remembering any traumatic experiences. This failure need not necessarily block the therapeutic process, and important changes in the dynamic structure of the personality can occur with little recall of the past. Interpretation of the transference and the establishing of an unambivalent relationship with the therapist may enable the individual to function on better terms with himself and with others. It is possible also that he may give up infantile defenses without recalling the specific traumatic memories or experiences that inspired them.

On the other hand, analysis of the transference, and interpretation of dreams, free associations, and material elicited through interviewing, may, in themselves, fail to produce change. The patient seems to be stymied by a stubborn amnesia relating to vast segments of his childhood or later life. The inability to recall vital situations of the past may represent resistance to accepting the implications of certain drives and defenses as they reveal themselves in the relationship with the therapist.

Obdurate resistance to recall frequently constitutes a means of avoiding anxiety of a sort that initially fostered the repression. In some patients it serves to retain the secondary gain inherent in their neurosis. The amnesia affecting recall may be so stubborn that even the most concerted effort will fail to bring the repressed material to the surface. Where, with extensive probing the patient is unable to recover damaging traumatic experiences—although one is reasonably certain that such experiences have occurred—it is probable that the amnesia protects the ego from anxiety that it would be unable to handle if the experiences were recalled. Here the reasonable ego is still too weak to absorb anxiety and to reconsider the experience in a factual light. The ability to recall early traumatic experiences, and to reevaluate them, requires considerable ego strength. In a number of conditions, for example hysterical disorders, sufficient ego intactness exists so as to make possible the handling of fears and conflicts associated with an inimical past. In these ailments the recovery of repressed experiences may suffice to produce a cure of specific symptoms.

In other conditions, however, such as certain personality disorders and psychoses, the ego is so vulnerable and weak that it cannot tolerate either the repressed memories or their implications. Therapy may fail to break down the resistances to recall, or the traumatic experience may be remembered with a peculiar dissociation of its emotional content. The forgotten event may be remembered as a vague experience without emotional implication, what is recalled being enough to satisfy the rational demands of the individual. The damaging emotions and the significance of the experience itself are, however, repressed. The individual reacts to devastating childhood incidents or fantasies in an apathetic manner, as if they were somehow detached from himself. There is no abreactive process. It is almost as though the patient, by his recall, seeks to fulfill a dual purpose; first, to retain the good will of the therapist by remembering things, and, second, to hold on to his resistance by repressing the emotional meaning of the traumatic event.

Failure to uncover buried memories may be due to the fact that therapy has not bolstered the ego to a point where it can absorb the anxiety liberated by the recall of early experiences.

HYPNOTIC RECALL OF FORGOTTEN MEMORIES

In some cases, hypnosis may uproot unconscious memories. One may question the efficacy of such a process, for it is axiomatic that a premature confrontation of the ego with unconscious material merely serves to create anxiety and to enhance resistance. Yet hypnosis need not have this effect, providing the recall is adroitly handled. Instead of battering down the patient's resistances by forcing him to remember things, it is best to give him full freedom to recall when he feels himself able to handle his memories. During deep hypnosis the patient may be told that there are certain experiences and memories that are quite important, and that, because of their painful nature, they have been forgotten. He may be assured that it is not necessary to remember all details of such memories at once, but that he will be able to reveal and to tolerate isolated fragments of these memories and experiences as time goes on. Under the influence of such suggestions the patient will bring out those elements of a forgotten memory or experience that he can tolerate, and as he becomes stronger and realizes that he is not injured by the recall, more and more material will be available to him, until finally he can reconstruct the fragments into a consistent whole.

Piecemeal recovery of a forgotten memory or conflict may be furthered by employing such techniques as dream induction, automatic writing, regression and revivification, dramatics, drawing and mirror gazing. The evidence elicited by all these procedures may make the meaning of the experience increasingly clear to the patient. As a general rule, the implications of the memory will not be accepted by the patient until he himself realizes its importance and presents the interpretation as a product of his own efforts and conviction. Reconstructing the patient's memory for him in the waking state, from material uncovered during hypnosis, may rob the recall of its therapeutic effect.

One of the best methods of handling material which is recalled in hypnosis is to instruct the patient to forget a revived memory until he feels that he is convinced of the truth of the memory and understands it thoroughly. It may be weeks before the patient is capable of bringing up portions of the material spontaneously, with corresponding insight. Even where the patient recalls in the waking state memories recovered in a recent hypnotic session, he will usually be unable to integrate their meaning until his ego has had time to prepare itself.

THE HANDLING OF UNCONSCIOUS MATERIAL

The actual handling of derivatives of the unconscious depends upon the projected goals in treatment. In supportive therapy, one may totally disregard unconscious outpourings. In reeducative therapy, the more manifest eruptions are selected for exploration. Thus, immediate character distortions and the surface conflicts these initiate may be a chief focus. The less manifest, more repressed aspects of the unconscious, are usually deliberately avoided. In reconstructive therapy, various strata may be explored, from topical spontaneous unconscious manifestations to those that are so deeply repressed that they require mobilization through the dissolution of repressive barriers.

Among the techniques employed to stir up unconscious activity and to remove repression are: employing a passive role in the therapeutic relationship; focusing on dreams, fantasies, past experiences and early relationships with parents; increasing the frequency of sessions; and using the couch position and free association. These activities may lead to a transference neurosis. Sometimes narcoanalysis, hypnoanalysis, art analysis and play analysis are utilized as adjuncts for the probing of unconscious material. Of all measures, the provocation of a transference neurosis is perhaps most effective.

Unless the therapist is trained to do reconstructive psychotherapy, it is unwise and even dangerous to stir up unconscious material. Explosive forces may be liberated by a lifting of repressions with which the untrained therapist may be incapable of coping. Where, in the course of supportive or reeducative therapy, disturbing unconscious material spontaneously appears, the therapist may strive to help repression by avoiding discussion of the material, by dealing with it reassuringly, by focusing the interview on reality matters, and by the use of greater activity in the relationship.

There are a number of ways in which unconscious feelings and attitudes can be expediently brought to the patient's attention. Some activities employed during interviewing are: restating, reflecting and interpreting whenever the therapist recognizes an unconscious trend in the patient's verbalizations, dreams, fantasies, slips of speech, free associations or transference reactions. These activities at first register themselves only minimally on the patient's mind, since acknowledgment of unconscious trends is laden with much anxiety. Incredulity or polite acceptance without conviction may mark the first reactions of the patient to the disclosures.

As has been indicated, a patient may be helped to accept repudiated aspects of his psyche by the recollection of early traumatic experiences and memories. The realization that he has been repressing traumatic memories, and the understanding of their symbolic significance may provide him with a wedge with which he can penetrate into his unconscious conflicts and gain insight into their significance.

In presenting interpretations to the patient, it may be important to recast the wording of early memories or experiences in the very terms utilized by the patient, even though these parallel the expressions used by him as a child.

CASE ILLUSTRATIONS

Example 1:

The following excerpt illustrates the verbalization in transference of unconscious sexual impulses on the part of a male patient toward his father. The material was expressed explosively with great anxiety, following a prolonged period of silence. This is from a session in which free association was employed.

Pt. My God. I feel I'm in love with you. I can't break away from you, but I want to come. I want to come here every day.

Th. Every day?

Pt. I'm afraid of you. You are so high and I am so low. I'm afraid of my feelings for you. Oh, God, as I talk I think of your penis. It's in my mouth. Oh, oh . . . it makes me afraid. It makes me so afraid . . . oh, oh. [*The patient seems to be in a transference neurosis.*]

Th. Why?

Pt. You're so big and I'm so little. I'm down on the floor. Oh God, I'm frightened . . . oh, oh. I'm afraid you'll stick it up. This is awful. Please don't. I have to do what you want me to do. I want you to put me down on the floor. I want you to be powerful like my father. I want you to tell me what to do. I want to love you and I want you to love me. I don't want you to hurt me or kill me.

Th. You feel I may hurt you?

Pt. I know this isn't real, but I have a feeling you are my father. I want to reach out and grab my father. He is sitting there, gentle and strong. I want to scream and cry. I want you to come to me. Father, come to me! Please come to me! I want you to kiss me and hold me close. Everything is whirling around. I can't stand it. I see myself nude. You are standing over me. Oh, God, please give it to me.

Th. What is it that you want?

Pt. Don't get near. Oh God, don't kill me. I'll do anything you say. I feel so little when I talk. I'm afraid to be big. I can't be the same as you. I don't want to, I don't want to. (*cries*) I don't want to . . . no, no, no. (*cries*)

Th. Why don't you want to?

Pt. I don't want to grow up. I can't fight like the other boys. I never could. I love you. I want to wear your suit, but I can't wear it. I can't touch it, anything you wear. (*continues crying and then begins to act more cheerful*)

Th. Well, how do you feel now?

Pt. God, that was a horrible experience. It was like I was a little boy again. I can't understand why I said the things I said. I remember father. He never let me do anything. I always thought I hated him and was afraid to do anything, not even shovel the snow. He acted like he always had to be the boss. Kind of hard on me, I can see it now. I always felt that I never wanted to grow up; I wanted to be a little boy. Maybe I wanted to be punished because I felt guilty about not liking my father. Even now, when I am near him, I am afraid he will hit me. He goes into such a rage. I wonder what would happen if I hit him back. I felt the same way about you, but I never realized these sexual feelings. It scares me to think about that. (*pause*)

Th. It scares you?

Pt. It's funny I never wanted you to touch me. It scares me. It scared me suddenly to realize I want you to treat me like a woman. On the other hand, I want you to touch me. I was afraid for father to touch me. Maybe I felt the same way toward him as toward you. This whole thing must be some way connected with my fear of homosexuality.

Th. And with fantasies about your father.

Pt. I just remembered a dream I had last night. I'm at home, the house we had when I was little. There is a bed against the wall. Father is there in the room. He is undressing. I wonder if he is approaching me. I'm in bed. There is a funny excitement, repulsion and fear. His body is big. It has a nauseating smell. His penis is enormous, enormous, big and red, fearful. I feel repelled by his body. I know he wants to stick his penis up my rectum. This I realize will kill me. I grab a gun and shoot at him, but it doesn't go off. I keep firing, but the bullets shoot out a couple of inches and fall on the floor. Father comes closer. I want to scream and can't. I then woke up screaming and found I had an ejaculation.

Th. What do you think this means?

Pt. It must be connected with what we've been talking about—my fear of women, my fear that they'll reject me. I must be scared of being rejected or even killed for my interest.

Example 2:

The following interview illustrates the use of hypnosis in recovering the memory of a traumatic incident, in the form of a "primal scene," which engendered an hysterical conversion symptom. The patient, a woman of twenty-eight, came to therapy because of anxiety that was so severe that it absorbed all of her attention and energy. It had its inception in a particularly violent quarrel with her boy friend, with whom she had expressed growing dissatisfaction. The imminence of a rupture in her relationship with her friend caused the patient to respond with panic, since she was devoted to the man, and marriage had been contemplated in the near future. She was aware of the fact that she was repeating a pattern, because all of her relationships with men had terminated in the same kind of violent disagreement. During one interview, while working on her sexual attitudes, the patient complained of a blurring of vision. She confided that this symptom had appeared on certain occasions when she looked into a mirror. She then searched the room intently with her eyes, and asked if a mirror were present. The following is an excerpt of the recorded interview, during which the meaning of her eye symptom becomes apparent. The patient is in a waking state at the start of the session.

Pt. (*panic in voice*) I have that funny feeling again about a mirror—looking at it, (*pause*) and everything is blurred.

Th. You act somewhat upset by this.

Pt. Everything is upside down.

Th. Upside down?

Pt. Not really, but it seems like it. (*pause*) Do you have a mirror here? I don't see one, but it feels like it.

Th. What does it feel like?

Pt. I . . . don't . . . know . . . An upside down feeling . . . I'm doing something with a mirror reflection . . . a reflection.

Th. Tell me about it.

Pt. It's like last night. The same thing happened. I was at a friend's house, thinking of coming here. There was a mirror table in front of the sofa, when I was sitting there . . . I looked in the mirror and everything I saw in the mirror began to look more real than the women in the room. And I thought, that's strange, and it looked like I could walk right into the room . . . the mirror room.

Th. Almost as if it were a different world?

Pt. Well . . . well, it didn't seem to be upsetting anyhow. (*pause*) It looked very inviting.

Th. You were not afraid to walk into that mirror room?

Pt. Now, it looks very frightening, but I have been dreaming about a mirror. (*pause*)

Th. Tell me more.

Pt. Upside down, backwards, and all the letters and all . . . (*pause*) everything you say—everything has to be read backwards. I used to do mirror writing when I was little.

Th. What about your writing; you say it was mirror writing?

Pt. Oh! I wrote quite a lot.

Th. What did you write?

Pt. Oh, just the way I felt, and whatever I did when I was a child. I sometimes would doodle something about a mirror. A mirror of some kind seemed to be on my mind.

Th. You did write about a mirror?

Pt. Well, sometimes.

Th. Do you remember seeing anything unusual in a mirror?

Pt. I can't think . . . I can't remember.

Th. Maybe I will put a pen in your hand, and we'll see. Let your hand just do what it wants. [*I try to induce automatic writing in the waking state which may be possible in patients suffering from hysterical reactions. This may reveal repressed material.*]

Pt. I use the typewriter.

Th. You can write freehand pretty well, can't you?

Pt. I guess so.

Th. Just let your hand move along as it wishes. Just let it do as it wishes, and pay no attention to what it writes. Just put the pen right down, and don't look at it as you talk to me; just let your hand travel along as it wishes. You will notice that it will be almost as if an outside force pushes your hand along without paying any attention to what your hand writes. Just talk to me. You acted a little bit nervous when you walked in here today.

Pt. Yes.

Th. Are you any less panicky than you were?

Pt. Well . . . it isn't panic exactly.

Th. What is it then?

Pt. I don't know.

Th. Like something deep down underneath that bothers you?

Pt. Uh huh.

Th. Are you now aware of what that something is?

Pt. Oh! It's disgusting—something I saw, I guess.

Th. Something you saw?

Pt. Uh huh.

Th. What?

Pt. I don't know.

Th. There was something you saw?

Pt. Uh huh.

Th. Put your pen down and maybe your hand will tell us more about what you saw—what it actually was that you saw. (*The patient's hand scribbles a few words.*) Can I see that? I mean the sheet you wrote on. Your hand seemed to scribble something while we talked. Now let's see what your hand wrote. [*The patient responded to the suggestion to write automatically.*]

Pt. It says, "You used to have a mirror to write in when you were a girl."

Th. You used to write in a mirror?

Pt. Yes, it was a mirror with a barricade in front of it, and when you put the paper down, you couldn't see what you were writing, but you had to look in the mirror and then you could see. That was the mirror writing.

Th. I see. How old were you then?

Pt. I guess around eight, seven or eight.

Th. Around seven or eight?

Pt. Uh huh.

Th. It would seem that perhaps around that period of your life something quite significant happened to you.

Pt. Yes, I guess so.

Th. Do you know what that was?

Pt. (*pause*) I can't remember.

Th. Now I would like to have you sit just exactly as you are. [*Hypnosis is induced at this point.*] And I want you today to bring your hands up, this way—clasp them together closely. I want you to watch them—watch your hands. I am going to count from one to five. You are going to notice when I count from one to five that your hands will become pressed together, the muscles will stiffen, your hands will get tighter, tighter and tighter, so that at the count of five, it will be difficult or impossible for you to open them. Keep gazing at them. One, tight; two, tight, tight; three, tighter and tighter; four, as tight as a vise; five, so tight now that when you try to separate them, you cannot. (*pause*)

You notice now that your eyelids will get very heavy, that they close, they shut, they feel as if little steel bands are pulling them together. Your breathing gets deep and automatic, and you go into a deep, deep sleep. You are very, very drowsy; you are very tired—very, very sleepy, you are going to get drowsier, drowsier and drowsier. You are going to fall asleep now, and you will stay asleep until I give you the command to awaken. You'll stay asleep until I give you the command to awaken. You feel very relaxed. Let your breathing become regular and deep. You feel more comfortable and relaxed. You are very, very sleepy. I am going to unclasp your hands now—just like this. I am going to bring them right down to your sides.

I am going to take this arm and stretch it out in front of you now, and as I do this, the arm is going to get very stiff and rigid. The arm will get stiff and heavy and rigid, heavy and stiff like a board. I am going to count from one to five. At the count of five, the arm will have got so firm, stiff and heavy and rigid, that it will be difficult or impossible to bend it. One, firm; two, heavy; three, firmer and firmer; four, just as firm and stiff and rigid as a board; five, just as firm and stiff and rigid as a board. Notice how stiff it is. The harder you try to bend it, the heavier and stiffer it becomes, until I push it back the other way, and then it loosens up. Bring it down, bring your head down this way. Relax yourself and go to sleep. Go to sleep, deeply asleep, very deeply asleep. Just relax all over. (*pause*)

Now I am going to give you a suggestion that you begin to enter into a deep sleep, so deep that you don't keep anything back from me. I am going to help you to a point where you will be able to see what it is that is behind the mirror. (*pause*) I want you to start getting very, very little. I want you to start feeling very, very little. Your head is getting smaller, your arms and legs are getting smaller. You are going back, back, back to the time when you had that mirror. You are going right back to the time of the mirror. Your feet are getting tiny, you are shrinking, you are getting little, you are getting very small, you are shrinking, you are getting very, very small, you are getting very tiny. You are very, very small and tiny as if you are little again, just the way you were then. You are little, you are tiny. How old are you? How old are you?

Pt. Eight.

Th. You are eight years old. (*Patient appears to be trembling with fear.*) Are you afraid? You look afraid. Tell me what you are afraid of. What are you afraid of? Tell me.

Pt. (*panicky*) Of myself.

Th. Anything else?

Pt. I don't know. It's a secret.

Th. You are afraid of yourself, afraid of yourself. Now listen carefully to me. I am going to ask you now to make your mind a blank; I am going to ask you now to make your mind a mirror. You are a little girl and you are looking in a mirror. In your mind, you will see a letter that will appear in the mirror. Every time when I clap my hands together, you will see a letter. It will appear in the mirror. The letters all put together, in whatever order they may come, will spell a word. That word holds the secret of what frightens you. One, two, three, four, five—watch the mirror. (*clap*)

Pt. K.

Th. K—one, two, three, four, five—watch the mirror. (*clap*)

Pt. F.

Th. F—one, two, three, four, five—watch the mirror. (*clap*)

Pt. U.

Th. Now, when I clap my hands together, see the entire word.

Pt. F-U-C-K.

Th. F-U-C-K. Now watch that mirror again—watch that mirror, and when I clap my hands together, you will see that secret, you will see that secret. Don't be afraid now . . . One, two, three, four, five. (*clap*) (*pause*) Tell me about it.

Pt. Woman up on top of a man. (*Patient is panicky as she talks.*)

Th. Who? (*Patient moans in a distressed manner.*) You see a woman on top of a man. All right now, watch that mirror. Watch that mirror. I am going to clap my hands together, and then, all of a sudden, the face of the woman in the mirror becomes clear. As soon as I clap my hands together, it will be as if you see the face, you see the features. Watch carefully. (*clap*)

Pt. Mother.

Th. Your mother! Now watch carefully. I am going to clap my hands together. The minute I do, you will be drawn right into the mirror, and the man's face will become clear.

Pt. (*with fright*) My father.

Th. Your father. Are you afraid? What do you think is happening?

Pt. I'm afraid.

Th. Now listen carefully. If this is an actual scene—an actual memory—you finally will be able to understand it. Your fear is getting less now; you are beginning to get less and less fearful. Don't be afraid, don't be afraid. Good. I want you to sit here for a while, then I'm going to help you start growing up to your present adult age. If you like, you can remember what you saw, remember everything that happened, when you awaken. After that, you can talk to me; we can talk this thing out. You would like to be well, completely well and unafraid, wouldn't you?

Pt. Uh huh.

Th. Good. In a moment I am going to wake you up. (*pause*) Now listen carefully to me. When you awaken, I want you to begin talking. Try not to be afraid even if you remember an actual memory. If you remember all the details, I want you to remember also the reasons you became afraid and had to forget them. I want you, if you can, to remember your fears, whatever they were. When you talk to me, the thing may come back as it happened, just exactly as it happened with all details. If you remember, tell me exactly how it happened. You have spent your life running away—hiding. You may not want to hide now. I am going to count from one to five, and, on the count of five, open your eyes suddenly and talk to me rapidly. One, two, three, four, five. (*patient awakens*) How do you feel?

Pt. (*mumbles*)

Th. I can't hear you.

Pt. Very funny.

Th. Tell me all about it.

Pt. I don't know. What shall I do now?

Th. Do you remember what happened here?

Pt. Yes.

Th. What happened?

Pt. (*somewhat fearful*) The mirror writing happened . . . and then mother and father vanished.

Th. Are you afraid now?

Pt. Yes.

Th. Did you ever see your mother and father together—intimately?

Pt. I know I did. It's all been in the mirror writing.

Th. Do you recall the incident when you saw your mother and father together?

Pt. My father's dresser with the mirror was next to the door, and that was reflected then. I was outside and I saw it all. [*It would seem that the image inspired such anxiety in the patient, that she attempted to repress it. Yet the mirror image also caused great excitement. The consequence of this conflict was mirror writing and blurring of vision.*]

Th. I see. So you stood outside there, and you saw the mirror reflection?

Pt. I saw mother on top of father.

Th. So you saw your mother on top of your father?

Pt. I think so.

Th. A child, when she perceives these things, thinks of them in different terms than an adult. What might you have thought as a child, what could have been going through your mind? What do you think was happening? You must have thought something. (*pause*)

Pt. They keep turning around.

Th. Do you see the two of them now?

Pt. Yes, when I close my eyes.

Th. Do they keep turning around?

Pt. Yes.

Th. Describe to me what they do.

Pt. First father is on top, and then mother is on top now. First mother is on top, and then father is on top. (*There is fear and excitement in the patient's voice.*)

Th. Now what's happening?

Pt. Upside down.

Th. Do you remember the first few weeks when you came to see me? You were so upset, you said everything was upside down.

Pt. Uh huh . . . upside down.

Th. Perhaps you were excited by what you saw?

Pt. Yes, yes.

Th. Do you have any thoughts of upside down?

Pt. I don't like it upside down. (*pause*)

Th. Why?

Pt. I feel as if it's been killing me.

Th. You feel what?

Pt. As if it's been killing me.

Th. What's been killing you?

Pt. It isn't real, like in the mirror.

Th. Now keep your eyes closed, and when I count from one to five, you will be asleep. [*Hypnosis is reintroduced here.*] One, go to sleep; two, sleepier and sleepier; three, go to sleep, deeply; four, deeply asleep; five, deeply asleep. (*pause*) How did you feel about your mother, when you saw that thing? What did you think about your father when you saw a thing like that?

Pt. I don't know. [*It is possible that the patient has repressed some of her feelings in relation to this memory.*]

Th. Now listen carefully. I want you to sit there. I am going to count from one to five, and then clap my hands together. When I do, you are going to have the same emotion that you had when you looked into that mirror, if you actually did look into that mirror. You won't be able to keep it back. Just let it come out spontaneously. As soon as I clap my hands together, tell me the emotions that you feel. One, two, three, four, five, as soon as I clap my hands together, tell me the emotion. (*clap*)

Pt. Anger.

Th. You feel anger? Listen to me now. When I count from one to five, and clap my hands together, you will see who it is that you are angry at. One, two, three, four, five. (*clap*)

Pt. (*pause*) Mother.

Th. Mother. You were angry at mother; at what you saw?

Pt. Yes, but I always try to see backwards.

Th. Why?

Pt. I was angry at father, too. She didn't really want him.

Th. She didn't want him?

Pt. No.

Th. Why?

Pt. Mother didn't seem to want to bother with him, I guess.

Th. Did you love your father?

Pt. Yes.

Th. You did love him?

Pt. Uh huh, very much, but I stopped loving him.

Th. What made you stop loving him? How old were you when you stopped loving him?

Pt. I don't know. Maybe I didn't love father because of mother.

Th. Did you feel that you would eventually like to find a man like your father?

Pt. Oh, I did in my teen age, yes. Father is quick—he used to be very clever and funny. Once he got angry with mother, and he didn't speak to her for a long time. He was very jealous. He was very cross with me.

Th. He was very cross with you?

Pt. Yes, father was, when I started going out with boys.

Th. He did not like to have you go out with boys?

Pt. He was always . . . (*pause*) jealous.

Th. He was jealous.

Pt. Yes, he was.

Th. What was his name?

Pt. Lewis (*laughs*).

Th. Why did you laugh when you said Lewis?

Pt. 'Cause your name is Lewis.

Th. 'Cause my name is Lewis?

Pt. Uh huh.

Th. Do I in some way resemble your father?

Pt. Not very much. I got awfully upset when I saw that mirror thing.

Th. What sort of person was your father?

Pt. He was very determined.

Th. Determined?

Pt. Uh huh. Maybe I liked him too much.

Th. Most little girls love their father. Little girls often get infuriated with their mother for having father; but they finally decide that they will find a man of their own, that they don't have to have father.

Pt. Mother was always like that, telling me that too.

Th. Did she want you to go out with men?

Pt. Yes, she did (*pause*), oh, yes; but I think she turned me against them.

Th. What did she do to turn you against them?

Pt. Oh, always blazed at me; she's always blazed at me. I think she really hated men.

Th. She really hated men?

Pt. Uh huh.

Th. How did you learn that?

Pt. I . . . I . . . I just felt it.

Th. Now I am going to wake you up. When you feel you understand the meaning of what we have been discussing, you will remember what is necessary. I will count from one to five. At the count of five, open your eyes and wake up. One, two, three, start waking up, four, five.

This excerpt has illustrated the use of hypnosis for the recovering of a traumatic memory by employing hypnoanalytic techniques of regression and re-vivification, along with a counting procedure. These adjuncts are of aid in circumventing repression. Because repression is sponsored by anxiety which the patient is yet unable to control in the waking state, she is given a suggestion at the end of the session to remember the incident only when she has worked through its implications. In this particular case she was able to understand in a short while the significance of her mirror fixation and eye symptom, and to integrate her reaction to the traumatic scene of childhood. She was also able, with further therapy, to resolve her difficulty in her relationships with men.

40

Inculcating Insight Through Interpretation

IN CHAPTER 15, THE CONDUCT OF THE PSYCHOTHERAPEUTIC INTERVIEW, a number of techniques have been described by means of which insight may be propagated. Among these are: (1) *accenting* certain verbalizations; (2) *summarizing* what the patient has said in order to coordinate and emphasize specific aspects; (3) *restating* the remarks of the patient to elucidate on situations the patient has overlooked; (4) *reflecting* back to the patient the emotional forces behind his utterances; (5) *establishing connections* between symptoms, feelings and inner conflicts; (6) *maintaining tension* in the interview to stimulate a thinking-through of a problem; (7) *extending measured support* when tension threatens to shatter the cognitive functions; and (8) *making interpretations* by which the more unconscious elements of the psyche are brought to the patient's awareness.

Interpretation as a vehicle for insight is particularly valuable in reconstructive psychotherapy, since there is, in this form of treatment, an emphasis on unconscious aspects of mental activity. In the present chapter we shall deal with the dynamics and methods of interpretation.

VARIETIES OF INTERPRETATION

Interpretation consists of seeing beyond the facade of manifest thinking, feeling and behavior, into less obvious meanings and motivations. Involved in interpretative activities are different degrees of directiveness. The lowest degree consists of waiting for the patient to interpret things for himself, giving him as few cues as possible. Next, the patient is enjoined to attempt the interpretation of representative experiences. Of greater degree, is a piecing together of items of information, and of seemingly unrelated bits, so that certain conclusions become apparent to the patient. Leading questions are asked to guide the patient to meaningful answers. More directive is the making of interpretations in a tentative way, so that the patient feels privileged to accept or reject them as he chooses. Finally, the therapist gives the patient strong authoritative interpretations, couched in challenging, positive terms.

1. Helping the Patient to Make His Own Interpretations

The insights the patient achieves through his own reasoning powers have certain advantages over those that are defined by the therapist. Accordingly, wherever possible, the therapist works toward stimulating the thinking through of problems by restating the material the patient has verbalized, by summarizing, by emphasizing important connections, by focusing on pertinent data, by asking specific questions, and by arranging cues in such a way that inferences will be more easily forthcoming from the patient. Understandably, the patient, bewildered by his neurosis, will want the therapist to give him answers to his questions. He resents the responsibilities the therapist imposes on him. Particularly is he dismayed at the therapist's refusal to make positive pronouncements. He may, therefore, require a reason why the therapist does not act as a detective who uncovers dramatic facts, but rather assumes the role of an objective helper who merely aids the patient to arrive at his own discoveries. As a general rule, self-interpretations are possible only where the patient has become sophisticated in his understanding of dynamics, and where significant material is not too deeply repressed. Interpretations, when they are presented by the therapist, are made to dispel resistances to self-understanding, and to remove blocks to learning, rather than to apprise the patient of the content of the repressed. However, once the patient has made what seems to be a valid interpretation, the therapist may elaborate on this.

In the following excerpt, the patient is helped to an awareness of the projection into his present relationships with women of attitudes that he had toward his mother.

Pt. In the presence of women I find myself wanting to please them. I don't know why that is. It doesn't occur with all women. Where a woman has no physical attraction to me, it makes no difference; but even there, I try to please them to some extent. Physically attractive women I must please. Then I pick up weaknesses in them and then feel contemptuous of them. I look for perfectionism in women. But then I try to please them. I realize that there is something funny about trying to please someone you also have contempt for, but I want them to think I'm a certain kind of person.

Th. A certain *kind* of person?

Pt. Yes, I want them to think of me as attractive. Maybe that's why I have to please them.

Th. How do you feel when women make all the effort in wooing and pleasing you?

Pt. Wonderful, I like that. I get very happy and relaxed.

Th. But when they aren't forward?

Pt. I've got to make the passes.

Th. To get from them something?

Pt. Yes, to get praise and love from them.

Th. But when you have to make the effort to get that, you start finding fault with them. I wonder why?

Pt. I want it to be spontaneous. My mother used to do things for me until my younger brother was born. Then I felt out of things. But I remember the tantrums I had. When I raised hell, I got attention. [*He seems to be aware of the fact that his tantrums were attention getting devices.*]

Th. You had to make an effort there to get praise and love from her. [*emphasizing the association*]

Pt. Yes, yes, yes, just like the feelings I get now when I have to force myself on someone to get praise from them. [*The patient makes a connection with the present.*]

Th. How did you feel when you did this with your mother?

Pt. Angry, disgusted, bitter toward her.

Th. And with these women you try to please? [*presenting cues to the patient so he can come to certain conclusions*]

Pt. Exactly the same.

Th. So the conclusion is what?

Pt. That I'm treating other women as if they are my mother, or I want them to be my mother. But that's nuts. But it must be so that I act that way. [*This seems to be an important insight.*]

2. Making Tentative Interpretations

The presentation to the patient of the therapist's observations, "hunches" and conclusions, prefaced by such phrases as "Perhaps," "It may be," "Possibly," and "Do you think it's possible," is an excellent way of making interpretations. This allows the therapist to confront the patient with facts in a non-authoritarian manner, permitting the patient freedom to accept or to reject the interpretation on the basis of his judgment, and without the feeling of having offended or contradicted the therapist. This makes for a relationship of cooperation, in which the patient feels that he is an active participant and that his voice carries at least as much weight as that of the therapist.

A patient comes in to a session with a headache. Through tentative interpretations she arrives at its source and dynamics.

Pt. I really feel I'm an ungrateful person. In many ways people have done things for me, and I do little in return. At the office, for instance, my boss told me I could have an extra week off for vacation this year, with pay. It made me feel good, but I was left dissatisfied and I've had this headache since. [*The patient recognizes the irrationality of her having responded with a headache to a thoughtful gesture by her employer.*]

Th. What about your feelings about your boss?

Pt. He's a wonderful man, energetic, and he knows what he wants. He's really gotten places.

Th. Mm hmm. How do you get along with him?

Pt. Oh, fine. We get along well. Of course he irritates me sometimes. He acts as if he knows everything. But he's an all right guy.

Th. But it's funny you had this headache after the boss gave you an extra week off. [*exploring the situation that led to her feeling of dissatisfaction*]

Pt. Yes, I did.

Th. Do you have any idea why?

Pt. No.

Th. What does his giving you a week off mean to you?

Pt. Well, I appreciate it, but I shouldn't be like that. I always was independent and liked to be on my own. My father wanted me to go into medicine, but when he died all those plans went out of the window. But I've tried to be on my own. [*This sounds as if the patient interprets her boss's gesture as threatening her independence. If she takes something from him she may put herself in his power.*]

Th. Is it possible that you resented your boss's gesture because it put you more under his power, and threatened your independence? [*tentatively interpreting this "hunch"*]

Pt. (*laughs*) It's more than possible. I don't like to have people do things for me. It makes me feel helpless. I don't want to owe anybody anything. [*She responds favorably to the interpretation.*]

Th. So that you might possibly feel that this gesture by your boss took away from you an important thing—your independence. [*a further tentative interpretation*]

Pt. Well it does, doesn't it? [*This indicates that my "hunch" was correct, since she seems to equate the two.*]

Th. *You* think it does.

Pt. Don't you?

Th. There may be other ways of looking at this thing. Because you may need to maintain a sense of independence for special reasons, any relationship or situation that does anything for you may destroy this security mechanism and arouse resentment.

Pt. But isn't it silly for me to feel that, because I know Mr. Meyers (*her boss*) doesn't want to take me over. [*She recognizes the irrationality of her feelings.*]

Th. Is it possible that *you* might be afraid that you, deep down, want him to take you over, to become dependent on him? [*tentative interpretation of her resistance to possible dependence on anyone on the basis of a deep desire to be dependent*]

Pt. No, I don't. I mean I don't really want to be dependent, (*pauses and laughs*) or maybe I do. (*laughs*) You know my headache is lifting now and is practically gone. [*We seem to have hit an important conflict.*]

Th. Do you see the connection between your impulse toward independence, your possible striving for dependence, your reaction to your boss, and your headache?

Pt. Yes, I believe I do. [*The patient continues to explore the interrelationship.*]

3. Making Authoritative Interpretations

Sometimes the repressions of the patient are so intense that they impair his capacity for critical thinking. Here the patient may be unable to make connections or to arrive at insights through his own efforts, no matter how adroitly clues are presented to him. Even-tentative interpretations may have little impact on the patient. During reconstructive therapy, especially, it is sometimes desirable to employ a bold authoritative approach in offering interpretations. This is a deliberate step, calculated to upset the balance between the repressed and the repressing forces. The released tensions and anxieties mobilize defensive reactions which can then be observed and explored. One of the defensive devices is a denial of the validity of the interpretation. Eventually, however, the patient may work through resistances to its acceptance.

Because of the anxiety that is apt to be stimulated, authoritative interpretations should be made only where there is sufficient frequency of visits to handle any disturbed reactions that may occur. As a rule, interpretations of this type are made only when there is some pre-conscious awareness of a pattern. The stronger the ego of the patient and the better the working relationship between patient and therapist, the more unconscious may the material be with which one deals.

A patient remarked during a session that a peculiar uneasiness came over her recently while in the presence of her husband. This feeling had started two weeks previously and had become increasingly intense since then. Through an authoritative interpretation she was helped to realize that the basis for her reaction was transference toward the therapist, which she had repressed.

Pt. I have this dead feeling toward Tom. (*her husband*) I have a feeling he will hurt me and beat me. I remember his slapping me when he was drunk a time ago. I was badly frightened but furious. I feel I'm wasting my life with him. The whole relationship sounds impossible.

Th. Do you have any positive feelings about Tom?

Pt. Yes, I'm terribly attracted to him sexually. This type of man is charming, but kicks your teeth in.

Th. Under what conditions does he do this?

Pt. Whenever I am in any way critical of him. I feel like half a person. I'm afraid to say anything critical. [*She may feel critical toward her husband and expect counter-hostility.*]

Th. Does this fear of being critical relate to other people? [*exploring for a neurotic pattern*]

Pt. Not everybody.

Th. How about me? [*This is an attempt to see if her critical feeling applies to me.*]

Pt. (*pause, patient's eyes tear*) This is silly. I'm afraid you'll think me silly. (*cries*) [*The fact that this emotional reaction is evoked shows that transference may be operating.*]

Th. You are afraid to be critical of me. [*authoritative interpretation of her reaction to the expression of criticism toward me*]

Pt. (*continues crying*) There have been several things you said that hurt my feelings. (*cries*)

Th. Like what?

Pt. A long time ago, (*cries*) when I first came here. I told you I felt I hadn't grown up. You said I'd have to grow up to be well. You said it as if you were blaming me. I can't help it if I'm this way. I wouldn't be here if I was well. [*The patient has taken something I said out of context, distorted it, and is using it to justify her feeling toward me.*]

Th. Did I give you the impression I was critical of you?

Pt. You sounded like you were. You gave yourself away. I've been afraid to say everything that came to my mind since then. Afraid to stir up your anger. (*cries*) [*This is good evidence that transference is operating.*]

Th. Perhaps I gave you that impression, but I'm not aware of wanting to criticize you in any way.

Pt. But you did.

Th. You *felt* I did.

Pt. Yes, and this is how everybody has been with me. [*Fear of criticism seems to be a basic pattern.*]

Th. All your life?

Pt. Yes, as far back as I can remember. I was never allowed to tell my parents what I felt, my disappointments. They hushed me up when I cried for anything. It happened with my teachers and it happened with my husband. It's still going on.

Th. And it happened with me.

Pt. (*smiles*) I'm being awful, I know, feeling like this. I know you don't intend to be like that, but I can't get confidence to be myself. And if I can't, I'll never get well.

Th. It is important for you to be yourself and tell me everything you think. Actually, I don't feel critical toward you, but I may give you that impression. As a matter of fact, you are injecting feelings in your relations with me that are the same as those you had toward your parents. Suppose you think about that. [*authoritative interpretation*]

Pt. (*smiles*) I feel better talking about it. I expected you to reprimand me. I remember when I was eight and played hooky with a girl. [*The patient goes on to relate an incident for which she was criticized.*]

CONTENT OF INTERPRETATIONS

Interpretation choices are usually in the following order:

1. Resistances of any nature, particularly to insight, to the translation of insight into action, and to a working relationship with the therapist.

2. Defense mechanisms of various types—their nature, purpose, manifestations and origin.

3. Indications of transference, especially those aspects that serve as resistance.

4. Personality traits and patterns—their form, expression, purpose, genetic origin and contradictions.

5. Conflicts, impulses, feelings, attitudes and other repressed aspects of the psyche of which the patient is at least partially aware.

6. Current sources of stress and their interaction with personality needs and defenses.

7. Early experiences as revealed by the patient in relation to conflicts, defense mechanisms, transference and personality patterns.

INTERPRETIVE ACTIVITIES

The manner of presentation of interpretations is as important as the content. The following points may prove helpful:

1. The language in which interpretation is couched should be as simple as possible, employing terms familiar to the patient.

2. Most patients integrate short, pointed interpretations rather than elaborate ones. However, certain patients seem to require long intellectual explanations. Sometimes the use of analogies and illustrations from the problems of other people are helpful. Interpretations should, if possible, be related to a basic theme.

3. Too many interpretations or scattered interpretations should be avoided, since the patient can learn only a little at a time.

4. Tentative and even authoritative interpretations should be tactfully presented in such a way that the patient has a right to reject or accept them without

feeling he is offending the therapist. Under no circumstances should the therapist argue with the patient or act chagrined if his interpretations are not accepted.

5. Before making an interpretation, the therapist must be reasonably convinced of the verity of his assumptions. To advance an opinion in a hit or miss manner, hoping that it will touch something off in the patient, is worse than useless.

6. The timing of interpretation is important. The patient must be prepared sufficiently for an interpretation so that it does not take him too much by surprise. One index of preparation is pre-conscious awareness of a trend or pattern. The dynamics of the patient's problem may soon become known to the therapist. It may require an enormous amount of restraint to withhold interpretations until the patient displays a certain amount of insight, thus indicating a degree of ego strength favorable to understanding. Interpretations prematurely presented to the patient will create resistance, since they act as a warning to the ego that its defenses have been penetrated and that a further attack is impending.

7. Attitudes and beliefs of the patient should never be ridiculed, nor should interpretations be made in such a manner that the patient assumes them to be accusations. Where attitudes and patterns are to be undermined because they wield a pernicious influence on the patient, he may be shown that he has been forced to employ these devices as defenses. For instance, a woman complains that she is never able to keep the interest of men because she is much too eager to make an impression on them. She relates an incident in which she forcefully attempts to establish a relationship with a new male acquaintance. An incorrect interpretation would be: "See what you are doing; you are throwing yourself at the man." This interpretation involves an accusation and a moral judgment. A better interpretation would be: "Perhaps you are acting too anxious here about setting up a relationship." This poses a problem the patient must ponder.

8. Interpretation is most effective where there is good rapport between patient and therapist. Where a patient feels negatively toward the therapist, he will usually be unable to accept interpretations.

9. Some therapists believe that a "terminal interpretation" is useful at the end of each session, summarizing the important material of the session. Other therapists find no need to employ this procedure.

In reconstructive therapy, where interpretation of very deep unconscious needs and defenses is deemed necessary, special handling will be required. Neurotic defenses are elaborated in early life by a weak ego threatened with overwhelming anxiety. The mature accretions that later invest the ego may not destroy the core of helplessness laid down in childhood. The patient, afraid of being overwhelmed by feelings of catastrophic helplessness that once threatened to destroy him, will, when an anxiety experience is imminent, attempt to overcome the threat by employing the same defenses that protected him originally. Logic plays no part in this process.

The rational approach in dealing with an ego that has swathed itself in impenetrable defenses is through an analysis of resistance. Interpretation of the resistance accomplishes the purpose of confronting the patient with the question of what he is defending himself against. This leads to an uncovering of unconscious impulses, fears and conflicts, and opens the way of access to deeper and deeper material. The dangerous nature of the material again stimulates anxiety and mobilizes further resistances, usually of an unconscious nature. It is essential to demonstrate to the individual the manifold disguises that his resistances may assume, for unconscious resistances can crumble only when their conscious derivatives are repeatedly presented to the patient. The interpretation of layers of resistance progressively exposes the deepest drives and impulses and ultimately leads to original resistances. Only through such work is the patient able to appreciate the purpose of his resistance, its historical origin, his active participation in maintaining it, and, finally, the unconscious impulses the resistance is opposing. This permits him to tolerate more and more undisguised derivatives of his impulses and eventuates in a gradual recovery of repressed elements of the personality.

How aggressive the attack on the resistances should be, depends upon the quantity of anxiety that is present, and upon the ability of the ego to withstand the attack. Interpretation of resistances will often produce tension, anxiety and hostility. If the patient is already suffering from as much anxiety as he can stand, the additional emotional burden may be too difficult for him to bear, and he may react with an increase of resistance. In such cases it is essential to proceed more cautiously. On the other hand, if the patient manages to repress his anxiety through the operation of neurotic defenses, a more aggressive attack on the resistance will be necessary. This must be undertaken as early as possible in order to mobilize anxiety for the purpose of increasing self-observation.

The technique by which interpretations are presented is also of vital importance in determining the acceptance of components that the ego is warding off. The patient may present evidences of hostility, erotic strivings, castration fears and penis envy. To interpret these as such to the patient may accomplish little or nothing. As a general rule an interpretation is futile if the patient does not have an idea of what is going on. Interpretation will produce no real change until the unconscious is represented by pre-conscious material familiar to the patient. Consequently, when an unconscious derivative makes its appearance in the field of awareness, the patient's attention may be directed to considering what may be behind the derivative. For instance, one patient, while discussing his relationship to me in glowing terms, became aware, through my calling his attention to it, of the clenching of his fists and the tension of his muscles. At first he denied these facts, but as I repeatedly called his attention to his mannerisms, and as I presented him with the possibility that there might be a reason why he became tense and clenched his fists, he thereupon became aware of hostile feelings.

It is essential to demonstrate to the patient the connection between his symptoms, feelings and attitudes, in order to show him how a purposeful trend runs through his life. He must learn that his behavior is not a series of random events, but that it has continuity and meaning. He must also realize that his symptoms are not fortuitous and that he is actually bringing about what he believes he is experiencing passively. He must become aware of the purpose of his evasions, of how he fallaciously draws the past into the present, of what compromises he makes with life, and of the consequences of these compromises on his functioning. It is also often essential to trace his symptoms back to their historical origins. Here the manner in which interpretations are made is also of the greatest importance. It matters little how accurate our interpretations may be if the patient is unable to understand their meaning and to integrate them within himself in the form of insight.

In tracing genetic origins of drives, defenses and conflicts there is often a tendency to interpret present behavior as if it were a mere stereotyped repetition of earlier patterns in the relationship with the parents. As a practical matter, this type of explanation usually has little effect on the patient. It is true that the individual carries over in his character structure attitudes and patterns molded out of specific conditionings in his early interpersonal relationships. It is true also that he reacts to people as if they were virtually reincarnations of his parents, with attitudes, fears, and demands such as he expressed in his early relationships. However, such a repetitive process does not occur automatically. It is dynamically motivated by needs in the individual which are so intense that no amount of logic can swerve him from his purpose. To say to the patient that he has hostilities or erotic wishes directed toward the therapist, because the latter is a symbol of his mother toward whom he once had an erotic urge that was repressed, is not really a helpful interpretation. What is essential is that he understand what motivations underlie the present emergence of hostile or erotic feelings toward the therapist. Ultimately, of course, we are concerned with why and under what circumstances the patient developed certain attitudes toward his parents that have functioned as nuclei of his later interpersonal strivings. Explaining to the patient that unresolved strivings in relation to his parents must be present, because the therapist is a parental surrogate toward whom he has irrational feelings, arouses merely an intellectual acknowledgment without any deeper understanding.

Once we concede that all behavior serves a dynamic purpose, we must attempt to define the purpose behind the patient's present behavior. For instance, we must discern the reasons why the patient feels erotic in the therapeutic situation. In analyzing the motives behind his erotism, we may find that he is becoming more and more anxious about the therapist and that his erotic feelings constitute a wish to absorb the latter within himself in order to gain exclusive love and support. Or the patient may have become more and more fearful of the therapist, and may wish to disarm him by expressing extreme devotion and sexual love.

If the patient acts in a hostile manner toward the therapist, it is not sufficient to show him that he is using the therapist as a father substitute, creating a new childhood situation in the present. It would be more meaningful to discover the immediate circumstances associated with the hostility. Thus, the patient may feel frustrated by the therapist, for no apparent reason. Upon investigation the therapist may discover that the reason behind the frustrated feeling is a secret desire to engage in an extramarital affair, along with a fear that the therapist will frown on such a venture.

To interpret the patient's strivings as related to something that is happening to him in the present helps provide him with a picture of his interpersonal attitudes in operation. It permits him to see how his drives relate to feelings that actually have no source in present-day reality. He comes to realize that his feelings do not arise out of nowhere and that he is not working with intangibles. Eventually he may be able to appreciate how similar impulses operated also in his relationships with important persons in the past, and that there too they served a vital purpose, of a sort similar to the purpose they serve now. Considerable activity on the part of the therapist may be necessary, since the patient usually has a tremendous amount of resistance to divulging the motives behind his feelings. The patient's drives, neurotic as they are, constitute for him a way of life that he may not desire to relinquish.

One of the tasks of reconstructive psychotherapy may be the recovery of important unconscious memories and experiences. The mere revival of forgotten traumatic events will not in itself correct the damage that has been done to the ego. While it is true that the ego has been rendered weak by inimical childhood happenings, other defensive attitudes have also been elaborated on the basis of experiences relating to persons and circumstances in the patient's later life. Interpersonal reactions are composed of a chain of patterns that show a continuity, each link predisposing the individual to later reactions. If the patient is to understand how his early inimical experiences relate themselves to his present behavior, it is necessary to analyze and to interpret the intermediate links. This does not mean a discarding of important deep material that is brought up during therapy. It means that the patient himself must be given the task of working back from his immediate character patterns and interpersonal attitudes to disclose the connection with the deeper experiences and impulses.

The proper interpretation of the transference makes it possible to establish the connections with these deeper impulses. It must be emphasized again that in interpreting the transference, it is not enough to tell the patient that he is acting out an irrational striving that has its origin in what happened in his early relationships with his father, mother or siblings. Such an explanation is interesting and possibly true, but practically judged it is without therapeutic value. What is important is to demonstrate to the patient the reason why such infantile reactions persist, and what purpose they serve in the present.

In a certain number of patients the therapist will be overwhelmed with unconscious material while no effort is made by the patient to relate this material to the present malfunctioning. In such persons there is probably a dissociation of the past from the present. There may be a minimization of current feelings in the desire to conserve the secondary gain derived from the neurosis. The outpouring of unconscious material here is somewhat in the nature of a confessional. The patient may seek to relieve his sense of guilt and to avoid responsibility for his symptoms through the absolution obtained in divulging his past. It is always essential to get the patient to realize that his current problems cannot be solved merely by revealing unconscious material. The material must be related to what is happening to him in the present. Hidden wishes, conflicts, fears, and early traumatic experiences certainly condition the individual's habitual behavior patterns, but it is essential to work out with him an understanding of how they manifest themselves in every act and thought in his daily life.

The exploratory process is likely to bring out an enormous amount of sexual material, and one may get the impression that the only existing difficulties are of a sexual nature. The therapist will certainly be led into a blind alley if he takes unconscious symbolisms at their face value. Presentation to the patient of raw oral, anal, and phallic material may be very confusing to him, not only because he will want to repress the implications of this material, but also because the language of the unconscious is inscrutable to his conscious mind. Emerging from unconscious strata, it is like foreign speech. The material is, of course, valid, but it must always be translated into constructions that are meaningful to the patient in terms of his relationship to others.

It is not enough to demonstrate to a female patient beyond any vestige of doubt that unconsciously she desires to possess a penis. It is essential to correlate this wish with her envy of men and with her rivalry and destructiveness in relation to them. It is particularly important to understand what the desire for a penis signifies in terms of the current needs of the patient. It may, for example, be a means of refuting a fantasy of being irreparably injured, or it may constitute a striving for superiority that is rooted in a sense of helplessness.

Desire for, or fear of castration must also be explored from the standpoint of what purpose these strivings serve in the psychic economy. It is not sufficient to assume that preoccupation with castration is the mere continuance of an infantile fear or wish that has never been completely resolved. The persistence of such an impulse indicates that it serves some purpose in the present. For example, a castration fear may originate in a current feeling of loss of self, a solution for which is sought in strivings for passivity and dependency, which are equated with femininity and castration. Again it must be emphasized that all conscious and unconscious behavior is dynamically motivated, and has a definite meaning and function.

RESPONSES TO INTERPRETATION

Inexperienced therapists, impressed by readings in dynamic psychology, often operate under the illusion that they need merely to bring the patient to an awareness of his problems for these to come to some kind of dramatic halt. In practice this does not happen. Indeed, the effect may be, not an amelioration of distress, but its exaggeration.

The individual's reaction patterns have already been set up in an almost reflex way. Many values accrue to his manner of life, no matter how disturbed this may be. Knowing that he reacts with certain patterns and appreciating why they exist does not eliminate his need for such patterns. A confronting of the patient with interpretations may do nothing more than to create a sense of hopelessness, because the patient feels powerless to inhibit his customary responses.

The patient's reactions to interpretations will depend on a number of factors, including his intelligence and his capacity to understand the interpretive meanings. They are conditioned by how basic his neurotic patterns are to his security and self-esteem. The manner in which interpretations are presented, and the quality of the existing relationship with the therapist are other important items. Any interpretation may seriously unbalance the equilibrium between the patient's defenses and the repressed conflicts. The responses to interpretation may, therefore, reflect an upset in homeostasis, and contain customary defensive efforts to restore homeostasis as well as experimentation with new and better defensive devices.

1. Acceptance of Interpretations

Possible signs of acceptance of an interpretation are expressions of surprise, enthusiasm, relief, excitement, increased flow of associations, and confirmation of the validity of the interpretation. An immediate acceptance does not necessarily mean that the patient will continue to subscribe to the accuracy of the interpretation or to put it into operation. Indeed, untoward later responses may be the consequence of interpretation due to resistances that are set into motion by the challenging of primary and secondary neurotic gains and the mobilization of anxiety. This is why such phenomena as apathy, depression or defiance may follow a successful session during which the patient accepts and responds well to interpretations. On the other hand, the acceptance of interpretations may sponsor a working-through of the particular pattern under exploration, in the course of which new trends are uncovered, requiring further interpretation and working-through.

The ability of a patient to accept an unpalatable interpretation will be proportionate to his positive response to the therapist. If he trusts the latter, if he is convinced of the therapist's good will, if he realizes he has the right to reject the interpretive offerings, he will usually be able to tolerate the interpretation more readily, without undue transference reactions. Resistance to interpretation is most common in the absence of a good working relationship, and is often caused by a fear of succumbing to the therapist, of being overwhelmed and dominated, and of losing one's independence.

2. Stimulation of Tension and Anxiety

Since interpretation upsets the balance between the repressed and the repressing forces, it is bound to mobilize anxiety which may express itself in nascent form or may release depression, hostility, aggression or psychosomatic symptoms. This effect may be desirable where there is little activity in the therapeutic process. Here, interpretation may provoke anxiety which in turn will stimulate movement. The arousal of anxiety, however, may not be intended, or, if calculated, the quantity of anxiety may be so great that it threatens the working relationship. Here, the therapist will have to stop the investigative process temporarily and attempt to stabilize the patient, perhaps using supportive measures if the integrative capacities of the patient show signs of shattering. Such undue anxiety may be the product of the improper timing of interpretations, of the inaccuracy of the interpretive effort, or of the presentation of the interpretation in an accusatory, belittling or derisive manner.

3. Rejection of the Validity of the Interpretation

The immediate rejection of an interpretation may mean that the patient's capacities for insight are not yet sufficiently developed, that resistance is being mobilized to protect the status quo, or that the interpretation is incorrect. Forms of rejection are many, such as outright denial, shifts in the content of verbalizations, inability to think, evasions, anger or detachment. More deceptive is a surface intellectual acknowledgment of the possible accuracy of the interpretation with no real emotional conviction. The rejection of an interpretation does not preclude its therapeutic effect. There may be an uncalculated absorption of the interpretation and an activation of conflicts with a marshalling of defensive forces. A delayed reaction occurs here, the working-through process operating on an unconscious level, resistance being resolved slowly, with an eventual restructuring of patterns.

4. Handling Untoward Effects of Interpretation

If the patient responds to interpretation with anxiety, rage or other disturbing reactions, he may have to be reassured to offset a deterioration of the working relationship. The following excerpts from treatment sessions are suggestive of how this may be done.

Interpretation to a patient of a pattern of destructive aggression toward persons with whom the patient became friendly brought this response and reply:

Pt. I feel ashamed and hopeless when I realize what I've been doing to people. I can hardly face myself, but I can't stop myself. (*cries*) [*The patient may be utilizing a masochistic defense here to support survival of his pattern.*]

Th. The fact that you see the problem doesn't make you bad, or any worse than you were before. But in seeing your problem more clearly, your guilt is being aroused and you may want to torment yourself. Actually you *can* do something about your problem if you do have a desire to get well. But it will take a little time, and you must try not to be impatient.

Another patient presented the following dream:

My wife left me, I cried uncontrollably and my mother came in to console me and pet me. I wanted consolation and somebody's sympathy. Then my mother's face changed to that of my wife, but her face had a Roman nose. She wanted sex. She wanted to go down on me. I said no, but she insisted and I succumbed. The room was filled with people, and as I looked at her she seemed taller. She said, "Don't forget to get in touch with me. My name is Janet James and I am at the Edison Hotel." Then I overheard a conversation about my wife, Flossie. I heard she was pregnant. I was astonished. I felt it was impossible unless she was unfaithful.

In his associations the patient interpreted the dream as a need for a mother figure in his wife. He expressed disappointment with the mothering his wife had given him. When asked to associate to "Janet James," he remarked that James was the name of a boyhood friend with whom there had been mutual masturbation. This friend, who had a Roman nose, had written to the patient last week saying he planned to visit New York in the fall and requesting that the patient make arrangements to meet him. At this point I made a tentative interpretation that disappointment with his wife might cause the patient to regard with favor an earlier form of relationship with a boy friend. In response to this interpretation the patient blanched and complained of panicky feelings. An excerpt of the interview follows:

Pt. Does this mean I want to be homosexual? My God, if that's true! (*Patient is obviously upset.*)

Th. Of course not. You know the mind thinks in symbols. When a person is disappointed in his wife, the mind may say, "Oh, the hell with women; maybe a man would be better." (*I laugh and the patient rapidly overcomes his panic and laughs with me.*) [*Months later the patient began working on his homosexual impulses.*]

ILLUSTRATIVE CASE MATERIAL

Example 1:

The following session illustrates the technique of helping a patient make her own interpretations. The patient, a young newspaper woman with a homosexual problem, with symptoms of frigidity and vaginospasm whenever she attempted sexual relations with men, translates the meaning of her symptoms from her dream symbols.

Pt. I had a complicated dream last week. The first part concerned a ship in drydock. It was surrounded on either side by land, but was pointed toward the sea. It was being repaired to go out to sea.

Th. Mm hmm.

Pt. And the rear end of the ship was like one of the landing ships that were used for tanks or something like that. It had sort of a drawbridge drawn down to the drydock.

Th. Mm hmm.

Pt. And it opened from the bottom of the ship, not from the deck. It opened actually into a dry river bed. It had a lot of pebbles and stones, and there's no vegetation around any place. (*pause*)

Th. Rather stark and drab.

Pt. Yeah, and the problem was to get this ship repaired before this enemy army arrived and . . .

Th. There was a war going on?

Pt. There was a war of some kind going on. And, they were approaching from the other side of the river. When it became apparent that we wouldn't have time to finish getting the ship ready to go to sea, we decided something had better be done for defense against the enemy. (*pause*)

Th. Mm hmm.

Pt. And I was more or less in charge of the project and decided that the thing to do was to build up the hill on the other side of the dry river.

Th. As a defense?

Pt. As a defense and disguise. So that the enemy might be confused. And I was in the process of doing it when a man came along, an unidentified person, and said, "Well, I think I can do a better job. I have some bulldozers that can build the thing up." So I said, "Fine," and I didn't actually see the bulldozers in operation, but the hill began to build up. And it had a, a series of sort of turrets on it, made out of earth, probably phallic symbols.

Th. Phallic symbols?

Pt. Yeah.

Th. Why do you say that?

Pt. Well, because of the way they just sort of rose out of the ground.

Th. I see. You mean their shape?

Pt. Yeah. And when he got that built up, I saw it was a magnificent job. And then I realized that there was danger of a flood, and asked him what should be done in those circumstances about the ship. And he said "Well, we could close all the doors and windows on the ship and tie it down to the drydock and just let the water flow over it."

Th. You mean a flood was about to happen?

Pt. It was about to happen.

Th. In addition to the invasion.

Pt. Yeah. And I asked him about water on the deck, and he said, "Well, that happens all the time and there wouldn't be any damage there. So we'd be quite secure staying on the inside of the ship." The character of the flood was sort of a flash flood that would be over in a very short time. We knew that the waters were backed up.

Th. Mm hmm.

Pt. And we didn't know whether, whether the flood would hit, but we had to be prepared in case it did. Then we went back to the ship, and I couldn't get the door at the rear end to work properly. It wasn't opened quite far enough. Either someone had, had knocked a lever and it had closed a little bit, or a spring had slipped. But it wasn't wide opened, and there were several levers and I was confused as to which one to use. I asked the man which one to use, and he told me, and I tried it, and the door began to close more, and I said, "Here, I want it opened." And he said that you have to push another lever as well.

Th. Mm hmm.

Pt. So I did and the door came on opened. And in that circumstance I felt a little helpless, as if I didn't quite know what it was that I needed to do.

Th. And this man came along to help you. [*The thought occurs to me that the man may represent the therapist.*]

Pt. Yeah. And it was the same one who helped build the hill.

Th. Oh, yes.

Pt. Then the next dream had to do with a big courtyard, cobblestone courtyard with stone buildings around it, European style, completely deserted. And, again, an army was going to make an invasion. And this dream also was very stark. It was like a drawing rather than like an actual scene. And a woman came into the courtyard and she was sort of an animated cartoon and not a real person. And it could be seen that she'd been drawn with charcoal, actually. She came in to the courtyard, obviously fleeing the armies. I knew that she was hunting a place to hide, and I knew that there was no place really to hide. Well, she went into the ladies room. The door for it was on a flat stone wall, and shaped like a Gothic window with the point at the top, very narrow, so narrow that you had to turn sideways to get into it. And I knew that she was going to be found anyhow, and that when she was found, that all kinds of horrible things would happen. Because it was the Communist army that was coming in, and she was known as a very active anti-Communist.

Th. Mm hmm.

Pt. And it was more as if I were watching a movie that was going on. (*pause*)

Th. Mm hmm. Any other elements to the dreams?

Pt. I think that's all.

Th. Well, now, what associations do you have to those dreams?

Pt. Well, the first one in the ship, my parents are at sea on a, on a ship now. I don't know whether it has anything to do with them or not. But certainly the ship lying in a drydock, again it's sort of like a vaginal canal. (*pause*) And it needed repair and wasn't ready to go to sea. Perhaps going to sea, is sallying forth in a, a sexual light.

Th. Mm hmm.

Pt. And, who the enemy was I don't know. But it was very stark and very cold and, no vegetation of any kind, no real warmth.

Th. It sounds very bleak.

Pt. And, the bleak feelings, I think, are the same bleak feelings that I have about my sexual life.

Th. Uh, huh.

Pt. And about relationships with men. (*pause*)

Th. All right, now, what about the bleak feelings that you have about your sexual life and relationships with men? And what is there that may have inspired the bleak feelings? Do you have any idea?

Pt. It might have been our discussion the other day about Howard. (*Howard is a married man with whom the patient started having a sexual affair.*)

Th. Mm hmm.

Pt. I have feelings of not quite knowing where I stand in the relationship.

Th. Not knowing where you stand in the relationship with him.

Pt. No.

Th. How could that have stirred up the feeling that you were about to be attacked?

Pt. Gee, I don't know.

Th. What else did we talk about the other day?

Pt. We talked about the, the seduction scene in the "Ways of Love," which I feel is, is a matter of an attack. In fact, it probably means that to me very much. I know whenever a pass is made at me, I feel as if it's, it's kind of an assault.

Th. Mm hmm.

Pt. And, less a compliment than the reverse. And I feel that there's an aggression against me rather than, than for me.

Th. Mm hmm.

Pt. And that it's something I have to fight.

Th. You're conscious of a feeling of danger when anybody makes a pass at you?

Pt. Yeah, very much.

Th. Well, now specifically in terms of what we have been talking about in the past couple of weeks, what danger might there be related to facing something you perhaps want to face?

Pt. Yeah. (*laughs*) The going out and making an acquaintance with a man that would come to a satisfactory relationship. [*There was evidence that the patient conceived of a relationship with a married man as safe. Unmarried men frightened her since she feared being trapped by them in marriage.*]

Th. Do you think that that could have stirred up the dream?

Pt. I think it very probably could. I know it could.

Th. So that in the face of our talking about the necessity of not marking time with a safe situation, Howard, and experimenting with unmarried men, there may have been anxiety.

Pt. Yeah.

Th. Now what could those anxieties be in terms of the dream?

Pt. Well, I felt that the ship which is, I think, obviously *me* had to be repaired.

Th. The ship had to be repaired. It wasn't yet completely repaired.

Pt. Yeah.

Th. And?

Pt. And the door at the rear end of the, of the ship, I think is certainly a symbol of the genital area.

Th. Mm hmm.

Pt. And that was where the entrance and exit from the ship were made. It's obvious that it's in a sexual sense the repairs have to be made, and a feeling that the enemy is going to arrive before the repairs are made.

Th. Mm hmm.

Pt. Before the ship is really secure, and ready to sail, on the sea itself.

Th. The enemy being symbolized by the war?

Pt. Yeah.

Th. And the actual invading enemy was what?

Pt. The flood.

Th. The flood, and in previous dreams water had meant what?

Pt. It's a sexual symbol.

Th. The flood is a sexual symbol. Now here you were then in charge of yourself and your own sexual functions, and the feeling was that repairs had not been completely made and, as such, you would be vulnerable to attack?

Pt. Yeah.

Th. Or to drowning. And you go off on to the shore and procure the help of a man. Now what does that bring to your mind?

Pt. Well, he came up to me and volunteered to help. And my feeling about it was one of, uh, I was very happy that he had, because I felt that I needed help. I welcomed it. And then when he built up the defenses against the flood and against the enemy, I felt that he'd done a very adequate job.

Th. Mm hmm.

Pt. And it had given me time, and it had helped to know what to do. You see, the flood came along, but still I felt secure.

Th. But what kind of defenses were they that he had built up?

Pt. The phallic.

Th. Phallic? Now what would that mean in terms of your own defenses?

Pt. Homosexuality.

Th. Homosexuality and also masculinity? [*The patient had assumed masculine attitudes, dress and mannerisms.*]

Pt. Yeah.

Th. So that in the masculine facade that you might have displayed, there was a defensive attitude, wasn't there?

Pt. Yes.

Th. Which might explain perhaps the wearing of the masculine cut clothes, the assumption of a kind of masculine role in life.

Pt. Yeah.

Th. As a defense against what?

Pt. Against a pass. (*laughter*)

Th. Against a sexual approach by men, against war, against invasion. It seems that your mind conceived of masculinity as something behind which you could hide.

Pt. Yeah.

Th. All right. Now in the dream the man assures you that you could seal up.

Pt. Mm hmm.

Th. What does that remind you of?

Pt. Mm, of the conversion hysteria, the tightening of the vaginal canal, the spasm and pain.

Th. The tightening of the vaginal canal. The vaginal spasm. The sealing up, and also other elements of detachment from men.

Pt. Yeah, keeping a distance from men.

Th. That is, keeping a distance, keeping a cloak around yourself, making yourself invincible, a fortified city that no man can approach. Not making dates with men, keeping away from men, all that as a defense against invasion. All right, now let us examine the next part of the dream, that is, the second dream. This involves also a war, and you're in an open court and there are many buildings around. There is this woman who's playing some kind of a role, she's drawn into this thing.

Pt. Mm hmm.

Th. What is going to happen to her?

Pt. She's about to be captured.

Th. Captured, and what are the horrible things that might happen to her if she is captured?

Pt. Probably death.

Th. Death?

Pt. But torture before.

Th. Torture and death. Now, in terms of the previous dream, what is the torture and death equated with?

Pt. With sex.

Th. With sex.

Pt. Yeah.

Th. If there is an emotional attitude toward sexuality that equates it with torture and death, understandably it would have very little pleasure value for you.

Pt. Yeah, that's right, and that's how it's been.

Th. And if your feeling toward sex was that emotionally it was like torture and death, well, nobody could blame you for wanting to run away from it. All right, now, what did this woman in the dream do to escape?

Pt. She went into the ladies room.

Th. The ladies room. She goes into the ladies room thinking this would be her sanctuary?

Pt. That maybe it would be, but knowing that she probably would be caught anyway.

Th. That was escape into femininity? It was like a church, a Gothic structure?

Pt. The door was, but yet I think the door was nearer a phallic symbol than a church.

Th. Like a phallic symbol?

Pt. Yeah, uh huh. It was, it was narrow. She had to go into it sideways, and it was twice as high as she was tall.

Th. I see. What type of symbol would that be?

Pt. I think a male phallic symbol.

Th. Male phallic symbol? So that no matter what escape she tried, the outcome was inevitable, wasn't it?

Pt. Yes. Well, in this dream, I was, I was sort of a spectator and didn't really take part in it. I just watched these things going on. I'd had some fear for my own safety. But I seemed to be separated from the dream. I wasn't really taking part in it. [*Detachment is one of the patient's characterologic defenses.*]

Th. Yes.

Pt. And my concern was for this woman who had really stood up and asserted the things she believed in.

Th. Mm hmm.

Pt. And I felt that she was unjustly going to be caught and tortured.

Th. Yes. Well, now in terms of your own feelings, how did you feel in the dream? Was there anxiety?

Pt. Um, not so much anxiety as a sort of detached feeling, a feeling that the whole thing was going on sort of coldly and relentlessly.

Th. And you had no way of controlling it?

Pt. In the, in the first dream I felt that there were some means of control, and in the second one I really didn't have anything to do with the dream, with what went on in it.

Th. Do you think I'm pushing you too hard in therapy? [*I ask this question to see if the patient feels threatened by what is happening in treatment and to probe for transference.*]

Pt. Uh, I don't feel I'm being pushed too hard.

Th. Because, in the dream the inevitability that you feel about what is going to happen, and the fact that you're helpless in the situation, would seem to indicate that maybe if you did get yourself involved with an unmarried man, it would be to please me. That old pattern of compliance?

Pt. Mm hmm.

Th. The old pattern of not being able to resist. I'm just throwing this out to you because it may complicate your feelings for me if you feel yourself pushed into a relationship without your wanting it.

Pt. No, I don't feel pushed. I think I see the inevitability of it from my own standpoint.

Th. How?

Pt. Well, it comes down to a choice between I guess the boat being overcome by the flood and closing itself off, and going forth and maybe facing it. A choice between having no relationship with a man and having one.

Th. Mm hmm.

Pt. Dissociating myself from what's going on or getting into the swing of it.

Th. In other words, either detaching yourself the way you have previously or facing the dangers you've invested in sex.

Pt. Yeah.

Th. And in running away from men you would be letting all your sexual emotions drain off in a relationship with a woman.

Pt. Yeah.

Th. Well, how do you feel about that? I mean, which of these choices do you feel you want?

Pt. Well, I want to make the heterosexual choice.

Th. You do?

Pt. Yeah.

Th. But it may be awfully hard. [*anticipating resistance*]

Pt. Yeah, and I, I, I feel that it will be. I feel that I'm going into, I think like that second dream, that I'm going into a world that I don't really have any feelings in.

Th. Mm hmm.

Pt. Um, except maybe feelings of torture and fear of death. Um. (*pause*) I feel reluctant to do it. [*The patient has good insight into her resistance.*]

Th. Mm hmm.

Pt. But I feel that, that it has to be done.

Th. Why do you feel it has to be done?

Pt. Well, I don't think I can mature as a person unless I do it.

Th. Yes. And you really feel that you want to make a try at it?

Pt. Yeah.

Th. It may be hard. You may feel as if you're being invaded and may want to run away. The emotions certainly are powerful, as the dreams would seem to indicate. They might impel you to just break off the relationship, break off therapy, return to the old status quo of homosexuality, and all that sort of thing. [*Mention of possible setbacks helps forestall disappointment if setbacks occur.*]

Pt. No, I don't think so. (*laughs*)

Th. Well, what do you think?

Pt. I don't know. I know that I'll, I'll resist making the relationships.

Th. Mm hmm.

Pt. And I anticipate going through anxiety states.

Th. Mm hmm.

Pt. As I try to make the relationships.

Th. Mm hmm.

Pt. I think that I've got enough of a one track mind that I'll stick to it, (*laughs*) until I get it done, by golly. And, I, I feel like I've started something, and I feel the need to finish it.

Th. Wanting to get it done is nine-tenths of the battle. The fears and the panicky feelings which are so vivid inside, and which you've undoubtedly experienced, or have prevented yourself from experiencing by detaching yourself; the hysterical defenses of spasm and frigidity, and all that sort of thing, you feel you can begin to handle?

Pt. Yeah.

Th. Now, the intensity of your feeling will probably still be there. You can anticipate that you're going to get scared, because, after all, this is an emotional thing. You may not even know where the feelings come from. All you'll feel is a vague kind of panicky feeling, or a cold feeling that there's nothing in sexuality. Or another feeling may be that in some inscrutable way you may be damaged or hurt in a sexual role.

Pt. Yeah.

Th. This isn't absolutely definite. You may now have the strength and the motivation to experiment with men and see just what actually does happen, always anticipating the old defenses, which are what? What are your old defenses against heterosexuality?

Pt. Well, homosexuality mainly.

Th. Homosexuality. That's one defense, certainly, because it keeps your sexual energies drained off, and it keeps you in a dependent relationship, as we've seen.

Pt. Yes, and the other defenses are there too, the sealing off, vaginal spasm, the running away and acting masculine.

Th. And the whole assumption of a masculine role. Now all these things you may find operating insidiously as you begin to function in a heterosexual role.

Pt. Mm hmm.

Th. And it may be awfully hard. The temptation to go back to homosexuality may be terribly great, because the starker the fields on this side, the more green the fields seem across the river.

Pt. (*laughs*) Well, I've had sort of flash backs insofar as dreams are concerned, and once in a while in terms of conscious feelings, toward homosexuality. I've always known that, that it was in relationship with Howard, if I felt helpless, or felt that I was being aggressed against, then immediately the homosexual thing would happen. It would just sort of be like pushing a button. (*laughs*) Not only that, but almost as if, whenever there was any kind of heterosexual involvement of any kind, that it was just like pushing a little button and a picture would come on the screen.

Th. And the fields may possibly begin to grow and get greener and even abundant with vegetation, as experimentation proceeds. With Howard, which was really a break in this homosexual pattern, you experienced, at first, pain, and then no pain, but no feeling.

Pt. With Howard I was able to make that break because I felt safe in that relationship. I felt very safe in it.

Th. In what way?

Pt. Well, a lot because of his attitude. I didn't feel that he was overly aggressive. I didn't feel that he was possessive.

Th. Mm hmm.

Pt. And I didn't feel that he'd force himself on me when I didn't want him to.

Th. Mm hmm.

Pt. And often when he would come to see me, he would ask me, "Are you busy?" or "Do you expect someone else?" or "Is there something else that you had planned that I'd be interfering with?" And I always knew that if I said, "Yes, I am busy," or "Yes, I am expecting someone," he'd go away.

Th. I see. So he was not a formidable enemy.

Pt. No. (*laughs*) I felt that he was rather cooperative.

Th. Mm hmm. And that gave you an opportunity to begin to handle some of your anxieties about men. But you may have doubts about other men. You have doubts that they are gentle, or could be handled as easily or that you'd have as many escape routes as with Howard.

Pt. Yeah, well, the escape routes were always there with Howard, and I was always conscious that they were there.

Th. Mm hmm.

Pt. In fact I pretty well had to be conscious that they were there in order to be able to make a relationship with him.

Th. Yes, after all, he was tied down to a wife, if you ever wanted an escape route.

Pt. (*laughs*) Yes, that was true.

Th. Envisaging a relationship with another person, however, who was not tied down, and who would not perhaps be as diffident, and, as he fell in love with you, would be more insistent about seeing you when *he* wanted to see you, this might produce a little more anxiety, mightn't it?

Pt. I imagine it would.

Th. Yes. On the other hand, a relationship need not be entirely made up of anxiety. There may be some positive values there for you, as you begin to work this thing out.

Pt. I find that in my general relationships with, with men, that their personalities come through. Which didn't happen at all before. Before it was sort of like dealing with someone in an animated cartoon. It was a person without personality or life.

Th. Almost as in the last dream, this woman sort of going through motions like an animated cartoon.

Pt. Yeah.

Th. Going through a sexual attack perhaps. It'll be very interesting, when you get a man who's worthwhile, to begin experimenting to see just whether the feelings still duplicate the feelings in the dream. It will be rather interesting to see that.

Pt. Well, I felt in the dream that this woman was an admirable person because she had stood up for her rights.

Th. Mm hmm.

Pt. And my sympathies were with her.

Th. Yes.

Pt. She was very aggressed against and helpless in the situation. And the things she really stood for were going to be killed, which I think is myself in a heterosexual relationship.

Th. And the things she stood for that were likely to be killed in a heterosexual relationship were what?

Pt. Yeah, my own aggressiveness, my own creativeness and my own plans toward my personal life.

Th. Your creativeness, your aggressiveness, your plans, which are symbolized by what?

Pt. By masculinity.

Th. By masculinity. And in a feminine role your masculinity is likely to be taken from you?

Pt. Yeah.

Th. And that which you have cherished so ardently may possibly just be smashed to smithereens if you get into a female role. Now that's a rather dismal concept.

Pt. I should say it is.

Th. That creativeness, aggressiveness, productivity, being worthwhile, are so equated with masculinity is interesting. It is something we may have to work out very,

very carefully, in order to permit you to go on. Because, if it is really true that your creativeness and aggressiveness and productivity will be crushed in a female role, there is no reason why you should want a female role. But this is a misconception and a challenge. Why there has been this equation, what the meaning of it is, are interesting things we may begin to explore.

Example 2:

A man, with a reputable position in the community, allowed himself to be picked up by a prostitute. Falling in love violently with this woman, the man abandoned his wife and his three children, and, to the horror of his friends, took up residence with the prostitute. Of all persons, only his minister was able to make enough of an impression on the patient to get him to seek psychotherapy. After three months of treatment, the patient, realizing how destructive his behavior was to himself and his family, left the prostitute and returned home. This was accomplished without pressure from me. However, I had the feeling that the patient felt resentful that therapy had deprived him of a source of intense sexual excitement. This anger was not openly expressed, but I intuitively sensed it. In the following fragment of a session, the patient presents enough material for me to make both tentative and authoritative interpretations of his resentment.

Pt. I know I shouldn't want Marie (*the prostitute*) as bad as she is. The whole thing is silly, the kind of a person she is, I mean.

Th. But you do seem to want her in spite of her faults. [*Reflecting underlying attitudes.*]

Pt. I know she is bad for me, Rita (*his wife*) is so much more of a real person. But I can't get Marie off my mind. I don't want to go back to her though, because that same mess will happen all over again. I would like to be able to think about Rita all the time, to be thrilled by her. But I can work better now and would like to help Rita get the art training she wants. (*long pause*)

Th. I see. (*pause*) What are you thinking about?

Pt. A flash came to me, a fantasy of my standing on the subway platform. A person in front of me. As the subway approaches, I imagined myself pushing this man off.

Th. What kind of a person is this?

Pt. Unidentified. I couldn't identify the man. I seem to see him with a blue suit. He seems sinister for some reason. Sometimes when I stand on the platform of a subway, I have a fear I may jump off, or that someone may push me off.

Th. But in your fantasy you push this man off. You're angry with him?

Pt. Oh no, I don't feel . . . I didn't feel anything. Just felt like pushing him off. (*yawns*) I'm kind of tired today. I had a hard day at the office, all kinds of pressures. I thought of cancelling my appointment today, because my secretary had forgotten to mark it and I forgot it, and I was supposed to talk to one of the out-of-town advertising people. [*This sounds like resistance.*]

Th. How do you feel about coming here? Do you feel it's an inconvenience to you? [*handling his mention of wanting to cancel his appointment*]

Pt. (*laughs*) It is. I come because I think it's necessary, not because I want it. There isn't anything enjoyable in it.

Th. So maybe you resent coming here. [*a tentative interpretation*]

Pt. No, I don't think I resent it, because I know I *should* come. [*He rejects the interpretation.*]

Th. Mm hmm.

Pt. But it is a lot of work to get here; it does take time. It isn't anything I would do for fun. And then I feel that I have the responsibility to my family to get this thing straightened out.

Th. But how do you feel about doing it for yourself?

Pt. Frankly I'm doing it for my family. Indirectly, I suppose, I benefit from it.

Th. You know, I get the feeling that you really resent coming here. [*an authoritative interpretation*] Let's take that fantasy. Here in fantasy you do an aggressive thing to someone in a blue suit.

Pt. Yes.

Th. What kind of suit do I have on?

Pt. (*startled*) Why *your* suit is blue! [*The patient seems astonished.*]

Th. Maybe I'm the man in the fantasy and you want to get *me* out of the way. If so you do seem to resent me. [*tentative interpretation*]

Pt. Oh, I almost forgot. [*Reaches in his pocket and pulls out a check.*] I've been carrying this around for two weeks and always forget to give it to you when I'm here.

Th. There must be a reason for that.

Pt. (*blushes*) You mean I might not have wanted to pay you?

Th. That's possible. (*pause*)

Pt. But I did have the intention to pay you. I just forgot.

Th. People forget for definite reasons very often. Could you possibly not have given me the check because you felt critical of me? [*a tentative interpretation*] If that's the case, then your giving me the check now is making up with me for being critical.

Pt. (*laughs*) Well, I'll tell you, I have been annoyed having to come here. I've even resented your good intentions. Not that you've ever told me to stay away from Marie, but I've been ashamed to go on the way I did. I've even wanted you to tell me Rita was better than Marie for me. But, damn it, the pull is there, the excitement. I can't go back, but I can't seem to push myself forward either.

Th. You see, there is a contradiction in some of your strivings. Your present stalemate is a result of being wedged in between your desire for Marie and your guilt and sense of responsibility to the family. You want me to make the choice for you and you are angry if I don't. [*authoritative interpretations*]

Pt. Yes, I can see that, and I know that attractive as Marie is, life with her would be poison for me. I don't need you to build up Rita because she's a person with quality.

Th. Now were I to make the choice for you, you'd have trouble. For instance, if I told you to give up Marie, I'd become the repressing authority you've been fighting all your life. As a matter of fact, you may find Marie attractive and want to kick over the traces to defy this authority and to do as you please. Then our relationship would get bad, because you'd probably want to defy me. On the other hand, if I encouraged you to give up Rita and to yield to your desires, you would be contemptuous of me. And if you went back to Marie, you'd blame me for exposing you to something from which you got pleasure, but which was very destructive to you. [*more interpretations*]

41

The Handling of Resistances to Cure

===

THE INTERPRETATION OF THE DEFENSIVE MECHANISMS OF THE PATIENT leads him gradually to an understanding of his neurotic patterns and to a discovery of what vicarious satisfactions he gains from them. In this way he becomes better acquainted with his neurotic tendencies, and he learns to master the anxiety that has made his defenses necessary. However, because neurotic trends serve a protective function and yield intense gratifications, the individual is apt to fight treatment desperately. Inevitably he interprets therapy as an attack on his philosophy of life, as an assault on his secret wishes and expectations.

Destructive as they are, many neurotic symptoms protect the individual from catastrophic helplessness and anxiety. To yield them promises exposure to dangers far greater than the inconveniences the patient already suffers. Furthermore, the ego gains, through neurotic illness, certain advantages of a positive nature, and resistance to cure is often based upon the fear of abandoning these secondary gains.

FORMS OF RESISTANCE

During treatment, consequently, the patient will feel that his secret hopes and expectations are under attack. He will sense danger and almost intuitively he will retreat or rebel. In spite of his better judgment he will throw up smoke screens and camouflages to confuse the therapist and to block his own progress.

In supportive therapy, resistance may be manifested in a refusal to acknowledge environmental disturbance, or in a defensiveness about one's life situation. There may be a greater desire to cope with present known vexations than to chance unknown and perhaps grievous perils. There may be a reluctance to yield inimical conditions that gratify needs for self-punishment and justify one's recriminations against the world. In reeducative therapy, resistance to the changing of modes of relating to people cannot be avoided. New interpersonal relations are, in the mind of the patient, fraught with danger. They can be approached only tentatively and with great hesitation. The patient may accordingly remain oblivious to his interpersonal distortions, no matter how frequently they are brought to his attention, and how thoroughly they are interpreted. He will repeat the same patterns, with continuous bouts of suffering, and seemingly little insight into what is going on. In reconstructive therapy, impediments are even more manifest. A most complex array of resistances may materialize. This is especially the case where a weak ego creates an inability to face and to master anxiety related to unconscious conflicts.

1. Suppression and Repression

Any material which is emotionally disturbing to the patient will be suppressed or repressed by him until he gains enough strength to handle the anxieties evoked by its verbalization. This material may seem, and actually may be, insignificant or innocuous. It is essential to remember, however, that it is not so much the events or ideas that are disturbing, but rather the emotions that are related to them. Thus a patient suffering from feelings of hopelessness and depression, relieved through excessive alcoholic indulgence, could talk about her present homosexual and heterosexual exploits, and her bouts of antisocial behavior which bordered on the criminal, with little disturbance; yet she required one year of therapy before she could relate an experience of removing the clothing of her younger brother, and observing and handling his penis. The excitement of this experience and the guilt engendered by it, were so intense that she had isolated the memory in her mind. Only when I had proved myself to be a non-condemning person, who would not punish or reject her for the desires that produced this incident, was she able to bring it up, and to reevaluate it in the light of her present-day understanding.

2. Intensification of Symptoms

One of the earliest symptoms of resistance to cure is a reenforcement of those neurotic devices that had previously kept the individual free from anxiety. Something to anticipate, consequently, is an acute exacerbation of neurotic symptoms. An explanation that the patient may possibly get worse before he gets better is often a safeguard against interruption of therapy.

3. Self-devaluation

An insidious type of resistance is that of self-devaluation. Here the patient refuses to concede that there is anything about him of an estimable nature or that he has any chance whatsoever of standing on his own feet. To every interpretation, he responds with the allegation that he is lost, that there is no need for him to continue, that he is hopeless, that it is too late in life to expect a change for the better. The inner image of himself is often that of a hideous, contemptible person, and any attempt to show him that this is a distorted picture usually serves to throw him into a panic; his self-contempt is used as a bulwark to progress in therapy. There may be, in addition, a deep wish to be cared for like a child by rendering himself helpless. The desire to depreciate himself may be in the nature of escaping criticism by anticipatory self-punishment. A masochistic indulgence is also a cover for a fear that if one acknowledges himself to be an able person, active and independent efforts will be expected of him. Patients with this misconception will hang on to their self-contempt with a determination that is astonishing, and only painstaking analysis of this resistance can lead them out of their morass.

4. Forced Flight into Health

Another form of resistance is "forced flight into health." Here the individual tries to convince himself and the therapist that he is well and that he no longer needs treatment. Any implication that he is not making a good adjustment is resisted with vigor. Actually the patient may conduct his affairs with a semblance of normality in that he appears to be confident, self-reliant and normally assertive. Yet the trained observer may detect a false note and often can perceive the tremendous effort that is needed to maintain the illusion of health. This form of resistance is usually associated with the need to maintain a rigid watch over everything one says for fear he will lose control.

5. Intellectual Inhibitions

The urge to ward off the therapist may result in an inability to think, to talk, or to feel. The patient, if he yields to this urge, will insist that there is absolutely nothing on his mind, and he will exhibit a singular sterility in his associations and in his ability to think constructively about his problems.

The patient may break appointments, come late, forget to mention significant aspects of his day, block off memory of his dreams and fantasies, manifest inattention, show an inability to concentrate or to remember what has gone on before, relapse into silence during the interview, or display a mental fogging that persists both inside and outside of therapy.

The following excerpt from a session illustrates this phenomenon. The patient, a divorcee of thirty-two, with an hysterical, infantile personality, involved sexually with two men who were supporting her, came to therapy after making a suicidal attempt. After one year of treatment, her recognition of her dependency caused her to decide to get rid of her lovers and to get a productive job. The patient came one-half hour late for the session that follows:

Pt. (*apologetically*) I've been forgetting things lately. Absent-mindedness for about six months. Last week I forgot to go to an important meeting. I will make appointments and completely forget them. I forget things to do.

Th. Let's explore that and see if we can learn something about it.

Pt. I keep forgetting names and telephone numbers. I don't know why. Maybe I'm so preoccupied with what's to become of me.

Th. Are you preoccupied?

Pt. I am. I can't remember anything.

Th. What *is* on your mind?

Pt. I have the constant worry that I better hurry and do what I have to do. I am concerned with dying. I keep thinking I may not be here long. I noticed yesterday that my shoes on the floor were empty. I then said, "What will people do with my shoes when I die? I wonder who'll go over my papers."

Th. What's this all about? Do you feel the life you are now living is not worth living?

Pt. I feel threatened by giving up these people who are supporting me. I wonder if I can live and get along. What will become of me?

Th. Maybe you resent giving up these dependent patterns?

Pt. I must resent it; yet even though I do, I can't tolerate them any longer. I've gotten to the point where I can be casual with my supporters and tell them exactly what I feel. I told Max that I can't go to bed with him; he's too old for me. This is terribly threatening for me because the instant I do that my income is cut off.

Th. Mm hmm.

Pt. And Max told me he would give me money without strings tied to it.

Th. This must be a great temptation.

Pt. It is, and I see myself not wanting to give it up. I've accepted it in my mind to try it out.

Th. You may be in a great conflict between being dependent and being active and independent.

Pt. Yes, I don't know which to do.

Th. That's something that you yourself will have to work through.

Pt. I suppose my mind is in a fog because I don't know what to do, but somehow I feel I'm getting stronger. [*The mental fog and her coming late for the session are apparently signs of resistance.*]

Very frequently, negativistic resistant states develop several weeks or several months after the patient appears to have entered into the spirit of treatment, spontaneously analyzing his difficulties and making what appears to be good progress. Suddenly, without warning, he will go into a blocked, inhibited pattern.

6. "Acting-out"

Along with his unwillingness to verbalize ideas and impulses, the patient may indulge in irrational acts and behavior in his everyday life. This "acting-out" appears to be a way of supporting his inability to talk during treatment. The acts serve to drain off anxiety and leave little energy available for ideational processes during the treatment hour.

7. Superficial Talk

Another form of resistance is a veering around one's problems in superficial talk. Here verbal comments are used as a defense to ward off basic issues. The patient may spend the entire time of treatment in talk that embraces topics of the day, current events, or past experiences portraying personal tragedy and martyrdom. There is little of deep significance in his conversation, and, if he is allowed to, the patient may continue for years to discuss material that is interesting enough, but that actually has little to do with his deeper problems. Often he will want to monopolize the interview, and he will resent the therapist getting a comment or an interpretation in edgewise. Rarely will he talk about his attitudes toward the therapist, who may begin to feel that he is merely an audience for the patient's boasts and diatribes. It is almost as if in superfluous conversation the patient defies the world to make him talk about his innermost self. Associated with this there may be an attempt to intellectualize his problems, to figure out connections, and to present a rigid and logical system of what must have happened to him.

8. Insight as Resistance

A device that is apt to be confusing to the therapist is the use of insight as a form of resistance. Here the patient will routinely go through a detailed accounting of how well he understands himself, using the best accepted terminology, presenting the dynamics and mechanisms of his disorder in approved textbook style. To all appearances he has gained complete insight into the origin of his problems, into his compulsive trends and distorted relationships, and into the consequences and destructive influences of his neurosis. Yet in his daily experiences, he goes right on with his usual neurotic modes of adjustment, manifesting the same symptoms that originally brought him to treatment. It is probable in such cases that the patient's insight is a highly intellectualized affair that he employs to confuse himself and the therapist.

There are many reasons why he utilizes insight as a smoke screen behind which he can indulge his customary neurotic trends. One of the most common reasons is desire to escape criticism and detection. Here, a dissociation exists between how the patient thinks and how he feels. It is often easy for the therapist to minimize the seriousness of the patient's disorder when confronted during treatment with a beautiful recitation of psychopathology. Behind the camouflage of insight, it is apparent that the patient uses his knowledge of mechanisms as an instrument to allay his guilt and to forestall criticism in regard to his daily actions.

This mechanism is often found in the extremely dependent patient who has magical expectations of what therapy will do for him. The chief motivation for his coming to treatment is the feeling that the therapist will bring about those neurotic objectives that he, himself, has failed to obtain through his own efforts. Compliance here is the keynote, and the patient, by reciting his spurious insights, will feel that the therapist must reward his aptitudes in learning with anticipated bounties. This façade is at least partially unconscious, and the patient may really believe that he understands himself thoroughly. The clue to what is going on is usually furnished by the tremendous hostility and aggression that eventually is exhibited toward the therapist when, after months of precise and punctilious performance, the patient does not magically get what he originally set out to achieve.

9. Dissociating the Treatment Hour from Life

Sometimes resistance takes the form of the patient's utilizing the treatment hour as a special event dissociated from life. Regarding it as such, he will go into the mechanisms of his interpersonal relationships with complete freedom, but it is obvious that with the therapist he is operating under a set of standards entirely different from those that he uses with people in general. There seems to be something recondite about the treatment hour, for it is set apart from all other experiences. The special resistance here is that of not seeing how the material that is uncovered in the treatment hour relates to his everyday situation. This isolation of treatment from life is often rationalized by the patient to himself on the basis that the therapist is a scientist who does not condemn him for acts for which he would be punished by others. In this way he will lead a dual existence and seemingly be unable to fill the chasm between what happens in treatment and his experiences outside of treatment.

10. Contempt for Normality

An insidious kind of resistance expresses itself in a fear of, or a contempt for normality. Associated is a refusal to assume responsibility or to make an effort on one's own. By substituting new patterns for old, the patient believes that he is yielding up something valuable, something he may never be able to replace, that he will become a prosaic bore, or that he may be exposing himself to dangers with which he will be unable to cope. This type of resistance appears most intensely after the patient has gained insight and is ready to execute it into action.

A patient with a phobic reaction extended to subway travel made a trip to my office by subway for the first time since treatment had started. She entered the room sullenly and remarked fretfully that she was furious with me. Her anger had started when she discovered that she had no great anxiety riding on the train. A fragment of the session follows:

Pt. I am so angry and resentful toward you. (*pause*)

Th. I wonder why.

Pt. I feel you are gloating over my taking a subway. I feel mother is gloating too. I resent her too. I felt she was pushing me, trying to force me to break away from her. She gloats if I do something that makes me independent. I feel that when I go ahead you gloat too. [*The patient had become so pathologically dependent on her mother that she was scarcely able to let her out of her sight. Mastering some dependency and walking alone was achieved previously in therapy, although the patient was very reluctant to give up this aspect of her dependent relationship.*]

Th. It sounds as if you are angry about being able to travel on the subway.

Pt. Mother seems to be anxious to give up her responsibility for me. I resent that. But I also don't like the idea of my being so close to mother, too.

Th. I see, as if you want to continue being dependent and yet resenting it.

Pt. When I get sick at night, I ask her to make me some tea; and then I resent her patrician attitude when she does this.

Th. But what about your feeling about me?

Pt. It's like giving in to you. But yesterday I felt liberated by the idea that I'm in the middle of a conflict and that coming here offers me hope. I realize that my neurosis is threatened by my getting well. (*laughs*)

Th. What part of your neurosis do you want to hold onto?

Pt. (*laughs*) None. But I have a feeling that I don't want to be normal, that in giving in to you, I'll be like anybody else. Also that you'll expect more things of me.

And (*laughs*) that if I get too well you'll kick me out. [*Here the patient verbalizes a variety of resistances; namely, a desire for uniqueness, a contempt for normality, a fear she will be expected to face more anxiety-provoking situations, a reluctance to give up her dependence on me, a punishing of her mother and of me by refusing to acknowledge improvement, and an unwillingness to yield her masochism and the various secondary gain elements accruing to her neurosis.*]

Occasionally a psychosomatic complaint may be a manifestation of resistance, as illustrated in the following fragment from a session with a male patient:

Pt. Everything was going well until this morning when I got stomach cramps. It has been with me all day.

Th. Mm hmm.

Pt. I find it hard to concentrate because my stomach bothers me so much. Mondays I always have a hard time for some reason. It's happened the last few Mondays.

Th. Seems like an unlucky day for you. (*pause*)

Pt. I was thinking about how long it takes to get well, and I was wondering if others did any better than I do. Of course, things are a lot better now, and I was thinking of taking a course in journalism up at the New School. The only thing is that it comes on Mondays, and that's hard. I . . . uh . . . uh . . . (*Patient brings hand to his abdomen.*) I had something I wanted to say . . . but I can't think of anything but these cramps. (*He takes a cigarette from a pack, reaches into his pocket for matches but cannot find them.*) Do you have a match?

Th. I believe so. Here's one. (*pause*)

Pt. Well . . . (*coughs*)

Th. You were saying that Mondays are pretty tough on you? Perhaps something happens to you on Mondays that upsets you.

Pt. I . . . I . . . I don't know.

Th. You do come *here* on Mondays.

Pt. Why . . . yes . . . yes . . . I mean I do.

Th. Maybe something is upsetting you in coming here?

Pt. I don't know what it might be. (*pause*) Maybe I'm upset that you feel I'm not doing well. [*We discuss his feelings that he is not living up to expectations. This is what has been giving him anxiety. His cramps are manifestations of internalized resentment and act in the service of resistance.*]

11. Reluctance to Yield the Pleasure Values of the Treatment Hour

A form of resistance that is frequently overlooked is one that involves reluctance to yield the positive pleasures the patient gets out of the treatment itself. He may derive such comfort from the therapeutic hour that other gratifications seem dubious, and he may refuse to give up his neurosis because of a desire to continue to see the therapist. This is frequently the case in a very dependent patient who looks forward to the hour to get a "lift," who perhaps pays lip homage to all the dynamic principles uncovered during treatment, but whose chief motive for therapy is to get suggestions and courage to carry on with his daily routines. Unless the therapist watches himself carefully he will fall into a trap laid out for him by the patient, and he may, by the patient's helplessness and apparent inability to do things voluntarily, feel forced to load the patient with advice and admonishments which the patient absorbs as if there were pronouncements from the Diety.

12. Transference Resistances

Perhaps the most common and disturbing of resistances are those that are produced in response to the relationship with the therapist or that take the form of transference. Contact with the therapist is understandably disturbing, when it mobilizes attitudes, impulses and feelings that threaten the repressive forces. The patient will, in the attempt to escape from the associated anxiety, exhibit his usual characterologic defenses to detach himself, to control and overwhelm the therapist, or to render himself invincible. In supportive and some types of re-educative psychotherapy, the patient will manage to restore his equilibrium through the medium of such defenses, and he will, more or less successfully, repress disturbing irrational, unconscious drives. In reconstructive therapy, on the other hand, the therapist constantly interprets the nature and purpose of the various defenses as they arise. This constitutes an assault on the integrity of the repressive system and will precipitate much tension. Eventually the patient cannot help coming to grips with the emotions and drives that he has hitherto succeeded in avoiding. He will then mobilize further protective devices to reinforce his shattered repressions.

One of the earliest manifestations of this struggle is an intensification of symptoms, which seems to serve a desperate function of restoring psychic equilibrium. Soon the struggle becomes more personalized, as the patient realizes that his relationship with the therapist is the womb of his distress. Resistance may be exerted against the original unconscious material or to its projected and animated representations in the transference.

The patient may exhibit a clinging dependent attitude toward the therapist who is regarded as a godlike individual, the embodiment of all that is good and strong and noble in the universe. This kind of resistance is often found in individuals who are characterologically submissive, subordinate and ingratiating, and who strive to adjust to life by clinging parasitically to a more powerful person. It is as if the individual had an amputated self that could be restored only by symbiosis with a stronger individual. There is an associated tendency to overvalue the characteristics and qualities of the therapist. This type of relationship is extremely shaky, because the patient regards therapy as a magical means to security and power. Consequently, the therapist must always live up to the inordinate expectations of the patient, which are so sheerly in the realm of fantasy that they are beyond possibility of fulfillment. The patient will demand more and more of the therapist, and, failing to get what he secretly wants, will be filled with hostility and contempt. It is essential that the therapist recognize a dependency trend, in order that he may point out to the patient the need for activity and the necessity of avoiding acceptance of interpretations on the premise of faith.

Another form of relationship that may develop is based on an intense fear of the therapist as one who is potentially capable of injuring or enslaving the patient. This attitude stems from a hostile image of the parent and is usually applied to all authoritative individuals. Treatment in such cases proceeds only when the patient realizes that the therapist does not desire to punish or condemn him for his ambitions or fantasies, but instead is benevolently neutral toward them. Little progress is possible until the patient accepts the therapist as a friend. Until then resistance will be intense.

Sometimes the patient displays a need to be victimized and unfairly treated. He will maneuver himself into a situation with the therapist in which he feels that the latter is taking advantage of him. He may exhibit various symptoms that he attributes to the harmful effects of therapy. In order to reinforce his waning repressive system, he may seek to transform the therapist into a stern authority who commands and punishes him. Where this happens he will experience severe anxiety if the therapist is tolerant and condones his inner impulses.

Resistance is frequently displayed in the form of hostility. The resulting reaction patterns depend on the extent to which the patient is able to express aggression. Where the character structure makes it mandatory to inhibit rage, the patient may respond with depression and discouragement. He may then want to terminate therapy on the grounds that he has no chance of getting well. He may mask his aggression with slavish conformity, and perhaps evince an interest in the therapist's personal life, assuming an attitude of comradery and good fellowship. There is in such efforts a desire to ally himself with the therapist in order to lessen the danger to himself.

On the other hand, where the patient is able to express hostility, he may exhibit it in many ways. He may become critical, then defiant, challenging the therapist to make him well. Irritability is often transmuted into contempt, and the patient may accuse the therapist of having exploitative or evil designs on him. Feeling misunderstood and humiliated, he will manufacture, out of insignificant happenings in his contact with the therapist, sufficient grounds to justify his notion of being mistreated. He will become suspicious about the therapist's training, experience, political convictions, and social and marital adjustment. He may enter actively into competition with the therapist by analyzing the latter, by reading books on psychoanalysis to enable him to point out the therapist's shortcomings. He may become uncooperative and negativistic to the point of mutism.

Sometimes hostility is handled by attempts at detachment. The need to keep the therapist from getting too close may burn up a great deal of the patient's energy. He may refuse to listen to what the therapist says. He may ridicule in his mind proffered interpretations. He may forget his appointments or seek to discontinue therapy, inventing many rationalizations for this. He may strive to ward the therapist off by discussing irrelevant subjects, or by presenting a detailed inventory of his symptoms. In his effort to keep aloof he may attempt to take over therapy, interpreting in advance his unconscious conflicts, the existence of which he suspects. An insidious type of defense is a preoccupation with childhood experiences. Here the patient will overwhelm the therapist with the most minute details of what must have happened to him when he was little, presenting a fairly consistent and logical survey of how previous inimical experiences must have produced all of his present difficulties.

Occasionally the impulse toward detachment is bolstered by contempt for the therapist's values; the patient will feel that his own values are what really count. Because of this he will be convinced that the therapist cannot like him and will "let him down." He will rationalize these feelings and say to himself that the therapist is no good, or incompetent, or of no importance, or that psychotherapy is nothing but nonsense.

The desire to control the situation may reflect itself in many ways. The patient may seek to shower the therapist with gifts and favors, or he may develop a sentimental attachment that assumes a sexual form. Therapy may be regarded as a seduction, the patient experiencing in it intense erotic feelings. One of the motives involved in falling in love with the therapist is to put him in a position where he will not pry too closely into the patient's deepest secrets. There are often hostile components associated. The incentive may be to devaluate the therapist, to enslave him, to test his convictions, or to fuse with him; in this way taking a short-cut to cure. Progress may suddenly stop as the patient blocks himself in his love experience. The real purpose of this type of attachment is resistance, although the patient will seek other gains; such as the living out of fantasied neurotic gratifications.

Many patients come to treatment, not because they desire to function more adequately in their interpersonal relationships, but rather because they seek to obtain from treatment the fulfillment of neurotic demands they have been unable to gratify through their own efforts. In such cases resentment and resistance develop when the patient does not receive from the therapist the specific type of help that he has expected.

Upon analyzing the evidence as to what the patient seeks from the therapist, it turns out that what he wants is not a cure for his neurosis, but an infallible method of making it work. He particularly desires to achieve his neurotic expectations without having to pay the penalty of suffering. The individual with a power drive may thus insist on a formula whereby he can function in an invincible manner in all activities in which he participates. The perfectionist will want to find a way to do things flawlessly, with as little effort as possible. The dependent individual will expect to amalgamate himself with the therapist and to have all of his whims gratified without activity on his own part. The detached soul will seek the fruits of social intercourse, though he wants at the same time to keep his distance from people. When these drives are not gratified in therapy, when the patient senses that they are instead being challenged, he will become tremendously resistive.

Frequently, resistance is exerted against accepting the idea that it is possible to function adequately without repairing a fantasied injury to the genital organs.

In the female the resistance may be to continuing life without the possibility of ever procuring for herself a penis, which she regards as the bridge to activity and self-fulfillment. In males the assumption of a passive role is often interpreted as equivalent to being castrated, and resistance may be directed against assuming any role that does not involve aggressive fighting. Even accepting help from the therapist may symbolize passivity.

Psychotherapy may produce other unfavorable resistance reactions in patients with immature ego structures. The transference becomes so dramatic and disturbing to the patient that he responds to it in an essentially psychotic manner. He will accuse the therapist of being hostile, destructive and rejecting, and he will refuse to acknowledge that his attitudes may be the product of his own feelings. The reasonable ego here is very diminutive and cannot tolerate the implications of unconscious drives and conflicts. The patient acts-out his inner problems and constantly avoids subjecting them to reason. To him the therapist is actually a cruel or lecherous or destructive being who threatens him with injury or abandonment. Any action or interpretation on the part of the therapist is twisted around to justify his convictions. The entire therapeutic procedure is interpreted in the light of this delusional system. Fear and anxiety issuing from the functioning of his irrational strivings lie like boulders in his path, barring the way to a more congenial therapeutic relationship. In such cases therapy will be prolonged, and the relationship must be worked on actively so as to constitute for the patient a gratifying human experience.

METHODS OF HANDLING RESISTANCE

As soon as the therapist realizes that resistance is interfering with therapy, he must concentrate on it to the exclusion of all other tasks. He may do this in a number of ways:

1. Calling the Patient's Attention to the Resistance Itself and Exploring Its Manifestations

For example, a patient has for the past few sessions arrived five to ten minutes late. The sessions are spent in a discursive account of family events, including the impending marriage of his son, the forthcoming graduation of his daughter, and the attacks of "gall-bladder trouble" suffered by his wife for which she may need an operation. The responsibilities imposed on him by his business and social position also occupy his attention. He mentions having suggested a two-week vacation in Florida, but his wife promptly vetoed the idea. He pauses in his conversation and then remarks that there is nothing on his mind. Sensing resistance, I direct the interview along the following lines:

Th. I wonder if there is something on your mind that bothers you that you are not talking about.

Pt. Why, no, not that I'm aware of.

Th. The reason I bring this up is that you have been coming late to your sessions, and during your sessions you have kind of rambled along, not talking about things that bothered you too much. At least I have that impression. [*pointing out possible resistances*]

Pt. Why no, I mean you want me to talk about anything on my mind. I'm supposed to do that, am I not?

Th. Yes.

Pt. Well, I haven't had anything else bothering me.

Th. Perhaps not, but have you had any symptoms that upset you?

Pt. No. I've noticed though that my jaws tighten up sometimes. And my wife tells me I'm grinding my teeth in my sleep.

Th. Mm hmm. That sounds like tension of some kind.

Pt. I know I feel a little tense.

Th. A little tense?

Pt. I've been upset that I have to do, do, do for other people, give, give, give, and get little in return.

Th. As if people expect things from you and do not want to give anything?

Pt. Yes, I'm getting fed up with my life, the way it's been going.

Th. I see. This could be upsetting.

Pt. I suppose you'd say I feel frustrated.

Th. Well, what do *you* say?

Pt. (*laughs*) It's hard to admit it, but I am. Sometimes I'd like to chuck up the whole thing, and be single again, without responsibilities, to do what I want to do.

Th. I should think you would feel frustrated that you can't.

Pt. Lately I've been getting this way. [*The patient discusses his secret ambition of wanting to be a writer and admits that he was embarrassed to talk about this. He was also, he remarks, afraid to admit that he resents being tied down to a routine family life. His resistance to talk about these things along with his internalized rage at his life situation seemed responsible for his muscular symptoms.*]

2. Pointing Out Possible Reasons for the Resistance

This is done where the patient is cognizant of his resistance, but does not recognize its purpose. The therapist may interpret the defensive objects of the resistance along with the various facades the patient elaborates to block himself. The patient may be shown that his resistance protects him against the threat of change. Thus, a patient blocks repeatedly during a session; the periods of silence are not broken by the usual interview techniques.

Th. I wonder what the long silences mean.

Pt. Nothing comes to my mind, that's all. I kind of wish the time was up.

Th. Perhaps you are afraid to bring up certain things today. [*suggesting that her silence is a resistance to prevent her from bringing up painful material*]

Pt. Like what?

Th. Well, is there any event that happened since I saw you that you have not mentioned to me?

Pt. (*silence*) Yes, there was. I met a man last Wednesday who sent me. I made a big play for him and am going to see him Sunday. [*The patient's infidelity to her husband is one of her symptoms, of which she is ashamed.*]

Th. I see.

Pt. I have wondered why I did this. I realized you wouldn't tell me not to, but I feel guilty about it.

Th. Was that the reason why you were silent?

Pt. (*laughing*) Honestly I thought there wasn't much to talk about. I minimized the importance of this thing. But I realize now that I didn't want to tell you about it.

Th. What did you think my reaction would be?

Pt. (*laughs*) I guess I thought you'd think I was hopeless, or that you'd scold me.

3. Reassuring the Patient in a Tangential Way about That Which He Is Resisting

This necessitates an understanding by the therapist of the warded-off aspects. For instance, a woman with an obsessional neurosis comes into a session with symptoms of exacerbated anxiety. She has no desire to talk about anything but her suffering. This seems to me a sign of resistance. Inquiring about dreams she may have had, the patient reveals one which, in a disguised way, indicates murderous attitudes toward her offspring. The idea occurs to me that she is attempting to suppress and repress thoughts about her children. A significant portion of the session follows:

Th. I wonder if you haven't been overly concerned about thoughts of your children.

Pt. I'm frightened about them, the thoughts.

Th. You know, every mother kind of resents being forced into playing the role of housewife. This is a cramped life to many persons. Most women may resent their children and from time to time wish they weren't around. It's natural for them to feel that. [*reassuring the patient about possible hostility*]

Pt. (*rapidly*) That's how I feel.

Th. They may even get a feeling sometime that if the children pass away, that will liberate them. Not that they really want that, but they look at it as an escape. [*more reassurance*]

Pt. That's what I didn't want to say. I've felt that it was horrible to be like that.

4. Bringing the Patient's Attention to the Material Against Which the Resistance Is Being Directed

This must be done in a very diplomatic way, preferably by helping the patient to make his own interpretation, or by a tentative interpretation. A patient with a problem of dependency complained of an intense headache and a general feeling of disinterest in life. The interview was rather barren, but enough material was available to bring the patient to an understanding of what he was trying to repudiate.

Pt. My wife has been telling me that I just am not like the other husbands. I come home and read the newspaper and don't go grubbing around in the garden.

Th. What does that make you feel like?

Pt. I guess she's right. But as hard as I try, I know I'm being a hypocrite. I just gave that up.

Th. But your wife keeps pounding away at you.

Pt. Well, what are you going to do. I don't help her around the place. She resents my being as I am.

Th. But what do you feel your reaction is to her pounding away at you?

Pt. (*fists clench*) It drives me nuts. I'd like to tell her to stop, but I know she's right.

Th. Is it possible that you resent her attitude nevertheless and would prefer her laying off you when you don't do the chores? [*a tentative interpretation of the material against which there is resistance*]

Pt. God damn it. I think she is being unreasonable when she sails into me. [*The patient takes courage from my interpretation and expresses resentment.*]

Th. Mm hmm.

Pt. After all, I come home tired and I find no interest in planting cucumbers. Besides, it's crazy. My neighbors plant dollar tomatoes. Each tomato costs them a dollar. It's no economy. The whole thing is silly. [*The patient continues in a diatribe, venting his resentment about his wife's attitude. At the end of the session his headache has disappeared.*]

5. Handling "Acting-out"

The appearance of acting-out will require special handling. This resistance is commonly stimulated by the transference situation, energy from the latter being drained off through behavioral manifestations. Because the patient refuses to verbalize prior to acting-out, it is difficult to bring him to an awareness of the sources of his conduct. He may, for instance, engage in random, multiple sexual affairs to the point of satyriasis, or involve himself in dangerous, but exciting aggression-releasing situations that are potentially disastrous to him. One patient, for instance, whenever provoked by hostility toward his therapist, of which he had profound guilt, would get into his car and drive recklessly. Only when he would narrowly escape an accident, would he slow down.

Whenever the therapist recognizes acting-out, it is necessary that he bring this to the attention of the patient. The therapist may suggest that there are reasons why the patient feels forced to engage in certain deeds. Talking about his feelings *prior* to putting them into action will help the therapeutic process. Acting compulsively the way he does tends to interfere with therapy. Should the patient accept these statements and verbalize, he will usually drain off enough energy in the interview to forestall acting-out. Interpretation may also help to dissipate the need for unrestrained behavior.

Should acting-out persist, and should this be potentially dangerous to the patient, the therapist may direct the patient to desist from the acts on the basis of their destructive nature, while enjoining the patient to talk about his impulses. Of course, in some instances, it may be impossible for the patient voluntarily to stop acting-out. Homosexuality, voyeurism and other sexual perversions are examples. However, with persistence it may be possible to get the patient to talk freely about his "temptations" and to help him, through more insight, to gain some voluntary control over them. Increasing the frequency of sessions to five times weekly, and giving the patient the privilege to telephone the therapist whenever the impulse to act-out occurs, are often helpful. As a last resort, if the patient continues dangerous acting-out, the therapist may threaten to withdraw from the therapeutic situation unless the patient exercises control over his impulses.

It goes without saying that acting-out within the therapeutic session, like physical attacks on the therapist and love-making gestures toward him, are to be prohibited. The patient may be told that he can talk about anything he pleases, but that unrestrained actions are not permitted by rule in therapy. Experience has shown that they interfere with the therapeutic process.

6. Handling Transference Resistances

Where transference has developed to the point where it constitutes resistance to treatment, it will have to be resolved. If it is not dissipated, it will seriously interfere with the working relationship. Treatment may become interminable, the patient utilizing the therapeutic relationship solely as a means of gratifying neurotic impulses at the expense of getting well. Frustrated by the absence of what he considers to be the proper response to his reasonable demands, the patient may terminate treatment with feelings of contempt for, or antagonism toward the therapist.

Superficial manifestations of transference may often be adequately handled by maintaining a steadfast attitude and manner, constantly bringing the patient back to reality. Sometimes a studied avoidance of the role the patient wants the therapist to play, or acting in an opposite role, minimizes transference. For instance, if the patient expects the therapist to be directive and controlling, on the basis of a conviction that all authority is this way, the therapist deliberately acts permissive, tolerant, and encouraging of those activities toward assertiveness and freedom the patient himself cherishes, but which he believes his parents wanted him to repress.

A patient, conditioned to expect punishment for infractions by a punitive parent, appears for a session depressed and guilt-ridden. He seems to demand that the therapist scold and punish him for having drunk to excess the evening before and for having acted sexually promiscuous. Not being able to stimulate this reaction in the therapist, the patient launches into an attack, upbraiding the therapist for his passivity. The therapist continues to react in a tolerant and nonjudgmental manner, but interprets the responses of the patient in terms of his desires for punishment and forgiveness to propitiate aroused guilt feelings.

Severe manifestations of transference being rooted in infantile conditionings will usually require prolonged "working-through." Strategically timed interpretations of the sources of transference in childhood experiences and fantasies, and of its present functions, will be required.

Among the most disturbing of transference resistances is that of the sexual transference, which takes the form of insistence that one can be cured only in a sexual relationship. While therapy may set off a temporary sexual attraction toward the patient, this fascination usually disappears as therapy progresses, or upon the simple structuring of the therapeutic situation. However, in some patients, the sexual preoccupation becomes intense and persistent. The patient will pick out from the behavior of the therapist minor evidences that she will enlarge to justify her belief that the therapist must love her. The protestations of the patient may greatly flatter the therapist, and the urgency of the expressed demands may tempt him to respond partially by touching or holding the patient. These advances are most provoking to the patient and incite greater sexual feeling. Should the therapist engage in any kind of sex play with the patient, this can have only the most destructive effect on both participants. Once the patient has even partially seduced the therapist, she will develop contempt for his weakness, and for his abandonment of ethical principles. The therapeutic situation will obviously terminate with any expressed intimacy.

It is important in handling sexual transference not to make the patient feel guilty about her sexual feeling. Rather, the feeling should be accepted and an attempt made to find out what it means in terms of the patient's past sexual attitudes and behavior. For instance, sex may indicate being accepted or preferred by someone. It may perhaps have the connotation of vanquishing or humiliating others. Sometimes reassuring comments are helpful in abating the patient's reactions. Thus the patient may be told: "It is usual for persons to develop such feelings for their therapist," or "It is good that you have these feelings because they will enable you to work out important attitudes and relationships," or "The feeling you have toward me is a step in your ability to feel and to relate to other people," or "This will serve as a means toward better relations with others." Where the patient brings in dreams and fantasies, it may be possible to interpret, with all the precautions already mentioned, the sources of the patient's transference reactions.

Another disturbing resistance is that of the hostile transference. Here the patient will react to the therapist as if he is convinced of the reality of the therapist's unfriendliness, destructiveness, ineptness, seductiveness and maliciousness. He will be importunate, irrascible and insistent that it is the therapist who misinterprets and not he. He may become retaliatory or destructive in response to the therapist's fancied hostility, or he may experience panic, depression or psychosomatic symptoms. A resolution of hostility by the introduction of reality and by interpretation is indicated, following some of the suggestions given for the management of the sexual transference.

Where transference cannot be handled in any other way, active steps will have to be taken to minimize it. Such measures include a focusing in the interview on the current life situation rather than on early childhood experiences, avoidance of dreams and fantasies, discouraging discussion of the patient's relationship to the therapist, abandonment of the couch position and free association if these have been employed, decreasing the frequency of the interviews, presenting interpretations in terms of the character structure and current life situation rather than in terms of genetic determinants, and greater activity in the interview.

THE NEED FOR WORKING-THROUGH OF RESISTANCE

Resistance may burn up the entire energy of the patient, and he may concentrate solely on fighting the therapist, or defending himself, or proving the therapist to be wrong, or winning him over with gestures of helplessness, praise, or love, or seeking various means to escape or to evade treatment. The struggle is an intense one and usually goes on below the level of awareness.

When one appreciates the purpose of resistance, one realizes that patience is a great virtue. The therapist must bear with the neurotic individual as he progresses, and as he takes refuge over and over again in his customary defenses. Resistance is yielded only after a great struggle, for change is a painful affair.

Since resistance has a dynamic function, an effort is made to help the patient to yield it up slowly. Too sudden removal may produce severe anxiety and may provoke a reinforcement of the neurotic defenses intended to protect the individual. Relinquishment of resistance will thus be blocked by a threat of repetition of the anxiety experience.

Resistance is best managed by demonstrating its presence, its purpose, its ramifications, its historical origin, and the manner of its operation in the patient's present relationships with the therapist and with people in general. As resistances are gradually analyzed and resolved, repressed material appears in consciousness in a less and less disguised form. Resistances require a constant working through. A single interpretation of a resistance is hardly effective.

The therapist should allow resistance to evolve fully before he takes it back to its origins. If a second resistance develops, he must handle it by returning to the first one and demonstrating to the patient the interrelationship of the two. Tackling the patient's defensive reactions inevitably causes him to feel threatened, and to resist interpretations of his resistance. This reaction is opposed by a contrary motive, that of retaining the good will of the therapist. Often the patient will attempt to satisfy both of these motivations at the same time by abandoning his defense in the forms recognized by the therapist and changing it to a less obvious type. The understanding of these elaborations and their continued exposure forces the patient to take a real stand against them and, finally, to abandon them entirely.

It is always essential to remember that resistance has a strong protective value. The patient will usually reject any insight that is too traumatic, or he will toy with it for a while, then forget it. However, through careful handling, he may gain insight as to how and why the resistance is operating. First of all he must be made aware of the resistance. Merely calling his attention to it makes him concentrate on a specific task. It prevents him from burning up all his energy in maintaining the resistance; it enables him to use some of his energy in tracing down its meaning.

Once a resistance develops, it is essential to abandon other tasks until it is analyzed, because the patient will not be productive while battling the therapist. It is best at first not to probe too deeply for unconscious material, but rather to work intensively upon the immediate interpersonal relationship. To aid in the process, the patient must be impressed with the fact that there is nothing morally bad about his showing certain defensive attitudes in the form of resistance.

The dealing with transference resistances may be a prolonged affair in the personality disorders. Here, the ego seems blocked in absorbing the full meaning of the unconscious material as it becomes apparent. The patient may acknowledge the presence of certain drives. He may even understand their irrational nature and historical origin, but this pseudo-insight provokes little change in his customary life adjustment. The entire therapeutic process is intellectualized, the patient using his insight to fortify himself against pain. His relationship with the therapist never proceeds to a level of positive feeling, shorn of hostility and inordinate expectations.

In infantile, narcissistic character structures particularly, intellectuality serves as a defense against unconscious impulses. Habitually there is a repression of the feeling aspects of the patient's personality, and mastery is sought through intellectual control. Any experience of feeling is regarded as catastrophic. By a curious transformation, the defense itself may become a vicarious means of gratifying non-permissible drives as represented in hostile and sexual impulses. Another secondary gain hoped for from this façade is that of acceptance by the therapist.

Patients who have a tendency to isolate emotional components from emerging unconscious material may make the latter acceptable to themselves by repressing the affective content. Frequently they strive to neutralize their panic by means of foresight and reason. During therapy they give the impression of being very active, and at first seem to work extraordinarily well. Even though they make a brilliant feat of minutely analyzing their inner mental processes, little change occurs. The patient may involve the therapist in long dialectic arguments that take on the nature of debates. Words replace experiences and constitute a defense against feelings.

Interpretation of this type of defense is bound to create great turmoil in the patient. The patient is prone to feel attacked and criticized by the therapist. "Negative therapeutic reactions" are common, the patient responding to important interpretations not with insight or relief, but with depression and discouragement. Hostility may be directed at the therapist in an effort to annihilate his therapeutic work.

It is essential to remind every patient not to get too distressed if cure is not immediate. Some patients are confounded and depressed when they find, in spite of their own wishes, that they go on reacting to their various trends. It may be necessary to explain that reaction patterns that have become established over a long period cannot be removed in a few sessions. They are habits that call for extended working-through and reeducation.

ILLUSTRATIVE CASE MATERIAL

Example 1:

In this session a female patient with a homosexual problem introduces a number of different resistances which block her progress.

Pt. I keep losing my keys constantly. My mind can't seem to concentrate lately. I notice that the only time I want to think about my problem is when I come here. The minute I get out I feel relieved. When I leave here I notice my hands are very cold. [*This sounds like resistance in the form of intellectual inhibition.*]

Th. I see. Can you tell me more about this?

Pt. When I get out of the office, in waiting for the elevator, I push myself up against the wall pretending the wall to be Helen (*the patient's homosexual love object*). I actually kiss that wall and I say, "Who does he think *he* is, trying to pull me away from my darling Helen. I won't have it, I just won't have it." [*This device seems to be a magical way of neutralizing therapy, which she interprets as a threat to her homosexuality.*]

Th. What does it remind you of when you do that?

Pt. Like being united with my mother. Everything seems to be O.K. again, and I can go on living. [*Having lost her mother in childhood, the patient's homosexuality, in part, is a neurotic attempt to reunite herself with her mother.*]

Th. Mm hmm.

Pt. You see. I do that.

Th. But why do you think I want to take you away from your mother?

Pt. I see that. You see, the information I get here, I feel, is going to get rid of the old regime and bring on a new regime.

Th. And the old regime is what?

Pt. Homosexuality. That's strong. It's easier to live in than the new regime.

Th. And the new regime?

Pt. Is getting rid of the mother fantasy and working it out.

Th. So that you would consider any insights that you get here in a certain way.

Pt. As dangerous to my ability to function (*pause*) for the moment.

Th. So when you come here, I upset the balance and you may want to go to the opposite extreme.

Pt. I shift to the opposite extreme so I can function.

Th. You must perhaps think of me as a terrible person to do this to you. [*probing our relationship*]

Pt. You are a horror. (*said facetiously*) I adore you, you know.

Th. You do? Why?

Pt. You know I do. [*Our relationship, though ambivalent, seems good.*]

Th. In spite of what I do?

Pt. In spite of it. (*coughs*)

Th. Maybe I better stop doing this to you. [*challenging her desire for health*]

Pt. Hell, no. I don't go wild. There is a certain amount of control.

Th. The fact that you know all the reasons that exist for your problem . . .

Pt. (*interrupting defiantly*) Doesn't do me any good.

Th. You are still the arbiter of whether you'll do anything about the situation or not. But at least you have the right to know all the facts. There is no magic about this. The whole thing is *your* choice. Nobody is going to take anything away from you, you don't want to let go of.

Pt. But I don't have the ability to make a choice rationally. (*yawns*)

Th. Right now your choice would be irrational.

Pt. Yes, I'd choose homosexuality. But, not really. You know, my mind is wandering. I'm trying not to listen to you. You know what I'm doing now? I'm trying to figure out my school homework. [*Patient is aware of her resistance.*]

Th. Not paying attention to what I'm saying.

Pt. Isn't that awful. First I yawn and then my mind wanders. And I wasn't even aware of what I was doing. [*Again she recognizes her resistance.*]

Th. But now you've caught yourself.

Pt. I caught myself.

Th. There must be a reason why it's dangerous for you to integrate what we talk about. [*pointing out possible reasons for her resistance*]

Pt. I just won't listen to you. (*coughs*) I'll bet this throat business has something to do with it. Obviously.

Th. You sense your own resistance. Do you want me to leave you alone?

Pt. No, no. But I do want to get well.

Th. It may take time for you to overcome this problem. It started far back in your childhood. And you have been reacting automatically since.

Pt. You know, I didn't hear a word you said. My mind keeps wandering. [*more resistance*]

Th. Do you remember anything we talked about the last session?

Pt. Nothing. My mind's a complete blank. I can't pull myself together at all. (*coughs*) And you know why I can't do this?

Th. Why?

Pt. Because you are sitting back and judging me on my little speeches.

Th. I'm judging you?

Pt. It's not true, but that's how I feel. I sort of feel I'm on trial and that I'm likely to do things wrong. The same thing happens when I get up and speak in class. It's funny that I don't remember a damn word of what you said today.

Th. How about what I said to you last time?

Pt. Oh, I remember that, but I can't put it together.

Th. Suppose you try.

Pt. It's like the only thing that can give me pleasure is my homosexuality, and my torture fantasies with masturbation. I feel that you will take these from me. I say to myself that if I let you take these things away, the time will come when I'll need them and I'll be without them. Take life's last spark away.

Th. No wonder you can't concentrate here, if you think this is what really is going to happen. As if there can't be a good substitute for your present pleasures.

Pt. But it's not entirely what I feel, because I do want to get well. But I can't seem to do it today. When I leave here, I suppose I'll kiss that wall to get my equilibrium back. Or I will get a hopeless desire and sexual attraction for you. I don't want to listen to what you have to say. I just want to be close to you. [*transference resistance*]

Th. In a way that's the same thing as clinging to and kissing the wall?

Pt. It is exactly the same thing. It's the same thing I have about Helen. Intellectually I'm not interested. I want to get into bed with her. So stop talking and let's have sex. That's how I feel about you. Same kind of feeling.

Th. Sex appeases your tension? Is that what you really want exclusively?

Pt. Obviously not, but I can see how this operates. And another crazy thing I do. When I leave here and get onto the street, I imagine you are watching me from the window. I get into my car and roar off.

Th. What does that mean to you?

Pt. It's like I get my masculinity back again.

Th. Which means you feel you lose it when you come here?

Pt. (*laughs*) Yes, I really do. I know that's silly. I say, "I'll show him. I'll roar off. I'll show him he can't make me into a woman." I try to get my feeling of power. (*laughs*) How silly can you get?

Example 2:

A patient comes in with a hoarseness so severe that she can hardly talk. This symptom came on her several hours prior to her session and was not accompanied by any other signs of a head cold. Exploration reveals the symptom to be a manifestation of various resistances.

Th. I wonder if you have been at all emotionally upset prior to this hoarseness. [*focusing on possible emotional sources of the symptom*]

Pt. I don't know what you mean.

Th. Are you aware of anything emotional that is happening right now? (*long pause*) What about your feeling about therapy?

Pt. The only thing I can say now, which is nuts, is that I'm scared to death of you. (*pause*)

Th. The way you look at me is suggestive that you are afraid of me. (*The patient has a frightened expression on her face.*)

Pt. I was always aware that I had a tenseness before, but it never was like this. (*The patient is so hoarse it is difficult to make out what she is saying.*)

Th. What do you think this is all about?

Pt. I don't know. (*pause*)

Th. Have you had any dreams?

Pt. Yes, I had one dream I can hardly remember. It's scrambled. (*pause*) I dreamed I was in some sort of clinic. It was your clinic. (*pause*) And there was a young chap there who was very attracted to me. He was there for treatment too. I liked him and he liked me. But I was a patient at the clinic and I was working there, both. I talked to a group of people on the stairs. You were there as an onlooker in a benevolent way. And I was kidding. I said I want to go to Paris and live a couple of years. But this guy I liked and I decided we would have to take you with us. We have to take Dr. Wolberg with us because we have to finish this treatment. I looked at you and said, "That's involved for you, isn't it?" You laughed. It was all said in fun. Then this young chap and I decided to go home, and we walked and walked. And all of a sudden it occurred to me that I was walking without any trouble at all. (*Among the patient's problems are muscular pains and arthritis complaints in both legs which make it hard for her to walk.*)

Th. Mm hmm.

Pt. (*pause*) And then I was back in the clinic and this young chap said he wanted me to do his analysis. I said that's impossible. And he sort of grinned at me and disappeared out of the door. That's all I can remember. [*The thoughts that come to my mind are that the patient may represent herself in the dream as her feminine component, and the young man as her masculine component. She wants to return to narcissism (loving the man) and feels she can function this way (being able to walk). However, she is unwilling to give up her dependency on me (returns to the clinic) and she relinquishes her masculine component (the man disappears out of the door). Another possibility is that the young man is a disguised symbol for me toward whom the patient feels she can express an erotic feeling. In this way she can dissociate her sexual feeling for me from her therapy.*]

Th. When did this dream occur?

Pt. Last night.

Th. What are your associations to it?

Pt. (*pause*) I'm blocked off on associations, (*pause*) I'm blocked off on thinking. I'm in a complete state of suspension. [*intellectual resistance*]

Th. What in the dream might give you clues about your fear of me? What might you be planning or thinking of that would make you afraid of me?

Pt. Well, when I said I want to go to Paris, I might want to run away.

Th. What does Paris mean?

Pt. If I could do what I want to do, I'd go to Paris for a couple of years. I love it, just adore it. I love the French people, their relaxation and acceptance. It was wonderful.

Th. What does Paris symbolize to you?

Pt. Fun and sex. It's a sexy place.

Th. And here you wanted to go with this young man.

Pt. Yes, he was cute. (*laughs*)

Th. Was there a sexual feeling about that dream?

Pt. Oh, yes, sure. I was all for this guy. I'll tell you who he was. I never thought of it until now. He was a guy I met at Bob's party last Wednesday night. He turned out to be a young psychiatrist and he knew you. Which is connected with you. So there you are.

Th. So you really felt attracted to him.

Pt. Yes, but had to take you along.

Th. Why do you think you had to?

Pt. Obviously you two are the same.

Th. So that you may have sexual feelings for me and project them onto another person, or you have a fear of sex and also fear disappointment. [*tentative interpretation*]

Pt. (*sighs*) Couldn't that be the same thing?

Th. It might. There may also be a desire to leave your therapy and run off and have fun, and wonder about my disapproval of that. There may be many things. What do you think? [*tentative interpretations*]

Pt. Consciously I'm not aware of wanting to run away from therapy. It's very painful to me as you can see. I wouldn't be happy getting out of it; I'd only be happy getting through with it. But the sexual thing troubles me.

Th. What about any sexual feelings toward me?

Pt. I think I've always had that. I block off though and can't talk about it. It's almost impossible. [*She recognizes her resistance.*]

Th. What does talking about the feelings do?

Pt. Make me scared of you. I don't want to talk about it. I'm sure that's what's happening to me now, (*pause*) I'm just preventing talking, that's all. (*pause*) And I feel silly. [*This indicates an awareness that her hoarseness may be a form of resistance against verbalizing sexual feelings toward me.*]

Th. Silly about your feelings?

Pt. Mm hmm. *I* think it does. All my life I've covered up important things, so to let it out is an almost impossible thing. I talk about sex often in a pseudo-sophisticated way. I can make smart cracks faster than anybody I know, but it has nothing to do with me. To talk about my sexual feelings—no, no. The minute it touches me, I clam up.

Th. Yet you haven't been too inhibited in your sex life.

Pt. I think I was a great deal, even though I didn't act it. (*pause*) I just thought of a dream I had in which you kissed me. I told you about it two months ago. From that time on I haven't been able to talk about my sexual feelings for you.

Th. Mm hmm.

Pt. When I'm lonesome I say you are very attractive to me sexually. (*pause*) I feel sexual contact with you is forbidden, like it would be with a father. (*The patient's voice is much clearer now, as if her hoarseness is vanishing.*)

Th. If it's true that you feel extremely guilty about having sexual thoughts about me, that would cause you not to want to tell me your thoughts. [*interpreting her resistance*]

Pt. That comes close to it, I think. It's silly. (*laughs*) I'm beginning to see through you. (*The patient's voice is very clear at this point, her hoarseness having subsided considerably.*)

Th. What do you mean?

Pt. You're trying to make me talk about you. All right. (*laughs*) I have varying emotions about you. First, I say, "To hell with that bastard, I won't go back to see him." Then I say, "That's what he expects me to do, so I shall go back to see him." And then I say you are trying to be my friend, trying to do something decent. Then I get contrite about having had bad thoughts. All of which is a bunch of crap. I know it as well as you know it.

Th. So you must feel resentful toward me sometime.

Pt. I feel, (*long pause*) I feel now and I have for the last few times I've seen you that all of the threads that have bothered me have all come together in one knot, which knot has become *you*. If I can get that knot untied, then I'll be free. All the other things that bothered me are minor. I'm pulling out everything I have to resist you.

Th. Resist me in what reference?

Pt. Horribly enough I'm afraid it's a resistance to getting cured. [*recognition of resistance to normality*]

Th. You sound disgusted with yourself.

Pt. I am.

Th. What might cure do to you?

Pt. Well, it could put me back to work. It could eliminate all my excuses for not doing things. It could make me take an aggressive and active role. It could make me stop drinking and take that fun away from me. It could make me take a decisive action about George (*her husband*). I've come through the labyrinth and I'm up to the door, and I'm just resisting like hell. [*The patient elaborates her many resistances against normality.*]

Th. You must be frightened. Because that door is the door people want to reach.

Pt. That's what I've been coming here to reach.

Th. And now that you're approaching it, you are a little afraid of it.

Pt. I'm scared as hell, but I'm beginning a little to understand it.

The following is an excerpt of the very next session which brings out some interesting points:

Pt. I had a very peculiar reaction. Of course, it is almost impossible for me to say it, a very peculiar reaction last time. And I don't know what it was that was said, whether it was something I said or something you said, I don't know. But it was something in connection with our conversation, our relationship. Then all of a sudden I got a "cat-and-canary" deal, which you knew perfectly well, because you couldn't help but see it on my face. I don't see how you couldn't, and then just as I left, I said, "I feel like you're laughing at me." I knew that you weren't laughing at me in the sense of being nasty, but you knew damned well I wouldn't tell you what was on my mind. And, of course, that's the hell of the "cat-and-mouse" thing, because I'm perfectly aware that you know what's on my mind. Or at least you know very well whether I'm holding something back and won't say it or not. And I know that you know, so therefore I get into one of these, as I say, "cat-and-mouse" deals.

Th. What makes you feel that I can read your mind, that I know what you're holding back?

Pt. I'll bet 99 times out of a hundred you do. It's very difficult and I feel very silly. Whatever it was, whether that was a part of it or something else, I got a reaction of being very silly and ingenue, and very ridiculous, and I couldn't get over that feeling. Now what tossed me into that?

Th. When did you get this feeling?

Pt. Sometime during the last part of our conversation last time. I don't remember very much what we said, only that I think you asked me how I feel about you.

Th. How *do* you feel?

Pt. Giddy.

Th. Giddy?

Pt. Yeah. I think when I use the word "silly" I probably mean that. (*pause*)

Th. How did you feel *I* must have viewed you? Was it that you thought *I* thought you were silly?

Pt. Yeah. I imagine that's it.

Th. Well, why?

Pt. (*pause*) My reaction when I left was that I wanted to put my arms around you and kiss you. Now whether that is a little-girl reaction or not, I don't know. But that was the feeling I had.

Th. You felt affectionate?

Pt. Yeah. And then I think that's probably why I felt embarrassed. I felt I (*laughs*) wanted to go over and sit on your lap, like a little girl, and I'm probably older than you are.

Th. You think I think you're silly if you want to do that?

Pt. Probably because I had the idea that you've been trying to make me grow up. And goddamn it, I don't want to grow up.

Th. If this is what you feel, this is what you feel. Let's try to understand it. Suppose you do feel like putting your arms around me or sitting on my lap, do you think there is something wrong with that?

Pt. Apparently I do. I don't think so, but I *feel* there is. I must or I wouldn't react that way. And when I get the "cat-and-canary," as they say, the "cat-that's-robbed-the-canary-look" on my face, I usually have something in my head, which I entertain, which I think is not in order. (*pause*)

Th. You know it is rather interesting that you find it so hard to mention to me what had happened. [*focusing on resistance*]

Pt. Sometimes I'll go for months and won't mention some things to you. And it isn't because I want to hide something. That's the god-damned mechanism of this thing. I blurted out and told you the last time, but, of course, by the time I get to talking about things, it's just when I'm putting on my coat. Like last time I kicked myself around the block when I got outside. I thought, why that's perfectly silly, why shouldn't I have said that; I've said every other god-damned thing. It's a wonder I came back today and said it. Because sometimes I might go for months and I might talk about every subject in the world. But some little thing like that which apparently has significance for me, I can't talk about.

Th. Perhaps it had such deep significance to you for a special reason?

Pt. Well, I find you attractive. (*laughs*) It's silly, but I have a thought it would be nice . . . last time what I failed to say was that I thought it would be nice to go to bed with you. But it kills me to tell you that. [*sexual transference*]

Th. Perhaps you wonder what my reaction would be.

Pt. I can remember one instance now. I don't suppose it was the type of person. It was probably the way I was feeling at the time. But usually men have approached me and I pretty much took what I wanted and left what I didn't want alone. That's always the case. A few times I thought someone was awfully cute, and I have deliberately gone after it, trying to look undeliberate. The exception was this once, and I can't remember who this man was. I think I'd read it in a novel, and I decided to try to ask a man to sleep with me, and did. And the result was disastrous. He ran like he was hit by a poisoned arrow.

Th. I see.

Pt. This guy ran. I don't think I ever did see him again. I remember now. Yeah. To show you that I'm embarrassed about it, I can't remember his name. Anyway, he was a guy that I went to Virginia with. I was going on my business. He was going on his business. He was trying to make a business deal with me. He was very good looking and he was my type. He was dark and not too damned tall and big, and I thought he was very attractive. I had lunch with him several times. And so I was going to Richmond. And I said at lunch one day that I was going to go to Richmond on such and such a day. And he said, "What are you taking?" And I told him the train number. And I got on the train, and he had the compartment right next to me. That I've never figured out. Maybe it was just luck. So anyway, he started making love to me. He came in to my compartment, and we were having a couple of drinks, and we were talking. And he started making love to me and all in a roundabout way, an inch at a time, an inch at a time. He put his arms around me first, and all the pow-wow they go through. So I thought this is going to be silly. I'd been thinking about it for weeks. That looks good. I'd like to have that when I can get a hold of it. So I just turned and looked at him. I said, "You don't have to go through all this, because I *want* to sleep with you." And it scared the hell out of him.

Th. Do you feel that maybe you're afraid of being outspoken with me too?

Pt. God damn it, yes. (*laughs*) I see it now. I must be afraid. You will run off and leave me if I'm too outspoken. My parents never let me speak my mind. Everything I learned I got out of being on the go with the other kids on the street. [*We continue to explore her sexual feelings toward me.*]

42

The Management of Untoward Attitudes in the Therapist (Counter-transference)

AMONG THE MOST CONFOUNDING DETERRENTS TO TREATMENT ARE transference responses in the therapist that are directed toward the patient (counter-transference). Here the therapist projects onto the patient revived elements of attitudes, misconceptions, fears and impulses derived from his own emotionally significant past relationships. The patient's appearance, gestures, manner, age, sex, personality structure and symptoms are apt to excite promptings in the therapist, some of which are unrealistically determined. Never static, these reactions vary with different patients. Toward some, the therapist may display affectionate feelings. Toward others, he may manifest irritation and even hostility. He may be impressed by certain patients, and he may be bored by others. Such responses are usually more or less automatic, being nurtured by motives that operate outside the awareness of the therapist.

Where the therapist is disciplined in self-observation, he may become cognizant of troublesome attitudes and feelings toward his patients before he expresses them in behavior. The more insight he has into his interpersonal operations, the more capable he is of exercising any necessary control. Where the therapist has little understanding of his unconscious dynamisms, he is most apt to respond with unmanageable counter-transference.

An illustration of how counter-transference may act to the detriment of therapeutic competence may be cited by the case of the therapist who, well-trained and endowed with more than the usual warmth toward people, was able to achieve good results in psychotherapy with most patients. Notably defective, however, were his results with male patients who had serious difficulties with women. The therapist himself was involved in conflict with his wife, the details of which he was not at all loath to verbalize. This was undoubtedly a manifestation of his unresolved problems with women. Whenever his male patients divulged their difficulties with their wives, the therapist would immediately respond with rancor, and vehemently denounce the chicanery of scheming females. This attitude, while temporarily comforting to some patients, ultimately resulted in their distrust of the therapist, engendered by a realization that they could never work through with him some of their basic life problems.

It is rare indeed that a therapist, irrespective of how free from personality blemish he may be, can respond with completely therapeutic attitudes towards all patients. With some, he may display an adequate degree of sensitivity, flexibility, objectivity and empathy, so helpful to good psychotherapy. With other patients he may manifest a lack of these qualities and an inability to perceive what is happening in the treatment process. There will be a failure to recognize neurotic projections in the relationship, and to remain tolerant in the face of the patient's irrational and provocative behavior. Thus, infantile requests by the patient for exclusive preference or sexual responsiveness, or expressions of resentment and hostility, or unfounded complaints of being exploited, may bring out in the therapist attitudes that interfere with a working relationship.

The specific display of counter-transference will vary with the problems of the therapist. Thus a need in the therapist to be directive and authoritarian, while advantageous in supportive approaches, tends, in insight therapy, to interfere with the individual's growing sense of self, with his expanding assertiveness and with his independence. Authoritarian attitudes also pander to dependency strivings in the patient, and coordinately nurture rebellious tendencies in him. Some therapists are driven by pompousness to make too early and too deep interpretations, which they hope will impress the patient with their erudition and perceptiveness. They may also attempt to force the patient into actions before the latter is ready for them. However, this playing of a directive role with the patient to satisfy certain emotional needs in the therapist must not be confused with a deliberate extension to the patient of emotional support when this is therapeutically indicated. The former is usually based on the motivation to parade one's power and omniscience; the latter is a studied, measured giving of help that is inspired by the needs of the patient.

Tendencies toward passivity and submissiveness in the therapist may also have a detrimental effect on treatment, since it is sometimes necessary to be firm with the patient, as in helping him to avoid retreat, in enjoining him to execute insight into action, and in offering him essential guidance and reassurance. Submissive traits in the therapist furthermore operate to bring out sadistic, hostile attitudes in the patient.

Impulses toward detachment may develop in the therapist as a defense against entering into close contact with some patients. This trait is particularly destructive to the therapeutic relationship. The patient may be able to establish some sort of relatedness with a domineering or a passive therapist, but he is totally unable to relate to one who is detached.

A therapist who, because of personal anxiety or a depriving life situation, is thwarted in the expression of certain basic drives may attempt to live them through vicariously in the experiences of the patient. He may, therefore, tend to overemphasize certain aspects of the patient's behavior. Thus, if the patient is in a position of fame, or is financially successful, or is expressing sexual or hostile impulses, the therapist, if he has the unconscious need to satisfy such strivings, will focus unduly on these perhaps to the exclusion of other vital psychic aspects. This loss of perspective is particularly pronounced where there is any overidentification with the patient.

Neurotic ambitiousness may cause the therapist to glory in the patient's accomplishments and to push him inexorably into areas that are calculated to lead to success and renown. Overambitiousness may also be extended toward seeking rapid results in treatment. Here the therapist will be unable to wait for the gradual resolution of resistance. Accordingly, he will promote the exploratory process too hurriedly at the beginning of therapy. Perturbed by the slowness with which the patient acquires insight, the therapist may interpret prematurely, and then respond with resentment at the oppositional tendencies of the patient. The therapist may also propel the patient too vigorously toward normal objectives, and then become frustrated at the patient's refusal to utilize insight in the direction of change.

Due to anxiety or guilt, it may be difficult for the therapist to countenance certain needs within himself. When such needs appear in the patient, the therapist may exercise attempts to inhibit their expression. Difficulties here especially relate to impulses toward sexuality, hostility and assertiveness. Should the patient introduce these topics, the therapist may act disinterested, or he may deliberately focus on another area. The therapist may be unaware of these personal psychic blind spots which prevent him from exploring anxiety-inspiring conflicts in the patient. Thus, if he himself has problems in dealing with hostility, he may, upon encountering hostile expressions, reassure the patient compulsively or channelize verbalizations toward a less threatening topic. Fear of hostility may also cause the therapist to tarry, to lose initiative, and to evidence paralysis on occasions when the patient attempts to act in an aggressive or assertive way. Fear of other aspects of the patient's unconscious may cause the therapist to circumvent the discussion of pertinent material to the detriment of reconstructive therapeutic goals.

Other counter-transference manifestations may reflect themselves in neurotic attitudes toward money with an overemphasis of fees and payments, in an inability to tolerate acting-out tendencies in the patient, and in a tremendous desire for admiration and homage. Perfectionistic impulses may cause the therapist to drive the patient compulsively toward goals in treatment that are beyond the patient's capacities. Sometimes the therapist, under pressure of his own neurotic drives, may set up a situation in treatment that parallels closely the traumatizing environment of the patient's childhood. When this happens, transference may become extreme and perhaps insoluble. Certain patients may mobilize in the therapist strong feelings of rejection and intolerance, which will destroy the emotional climate that is so important for personality development. Other therapists, burdened with narcissism, and needing to impress the patient constantly with their brilliance, may utilize interpretation too freely and water down the therapeutic process with intellectualizations.

At certain phases in therapy, counter-transference may become more openly pronounced than at others. For instance, during periods of resistance, the therapist may respond with aggressive or rejecting behavior. Some actions of the patient may also stimulate counter-transference. A patient who is frankly seductive may stimulate sexual feelings in the therapist; one who is openly antagonistic may precipitate counter-hostile attitudes. The patient may be sensitive to the moods of the therapist and work on these for his own specific gains, the most insidious effect of which is a sabotaging of the treatment effort.

Because counter-transference may result in therapeutic failure, it must be handled as soon as possible. Where recognized, the therapist may be able to exercise some control over it. There are therapists, who, though unanalyzed themselves, have an excellent capacity for self-analysis and an ability to restrain annoying expressions of counter-transference. This permits the therapeutic process to advance unimpeded. A therapist who has undergone successful personal psychotherapy or psychoanalysis will still be subject to counter-transference from time to time. Nevertheless, he should, by virtue of his training, be capable of detecting and of managing troublesome reactions as soon as they develop.

Detection of counter-transference, unfortunately, is not always possible, especially where deep unconscious needs are pressing. It is this unawareness of his inner drives that so frequently causes the therapist to rationalize them. Indeed, the very selection of certain methodologies and kinds of therapeutic practice may be determined by unconscious motivations. Thus a therapist, basically passive, who fears human contacts and has evolved a detached manner as a defense, may be attuned to schools in which extreme passivity and non-directiveness are the accepted modes. Or, if he is by personality domineering and aggressive, he may be inclined toward endorsing the doctrines of those schools that advocate directive or coercive techniques.

In order to sensitize himself to manifestations of counter-transference, the therapist may advantageously subject himself to self-examination throughout the course of therapy. Such questions as the following are appropriate:

1. How do I feel about the patient?
2. Do I anticipate seeing the patient?
3. Do I overidentify with, or feel sorry for the patient?
4. Do I feel any resentment or jealousy toward the patient?
5. Do I get extreme pleasure out of seeing the patient?
6. Do I feel bored with the patient?
7. Am I fearful of the patient?
8. Do I want to protect, reject, or punish the patient?
9. Am I impressed by the patient?

Should answers to any of the above point to problems, the therapist may ask himself why such attitudes and feelings exist. Is the patient doing anything to stir up such feelings? Does the patient resemble anybody the therapist knows or has known, and, if so, are any attitudes being transferred to the patient that are related to another person? What other impulses are being mobilized in the therapist that account for his feelings? What role does the therapist want to play with the patient? Mere verbalization to himself of answers to these queries, permits of a better control of unreasonable feelings. Cognizance of the fact that he feels angry, displeased, disgusted, irritated, provoked, uninterested, unduly attentive, upset or overly attracted, may suffice to bring these emotions under control. In the event untoward attitudes continue, more self-searching is indicated. Of course, it may be difficult to act accepting, non-critical and non-judgmental toward a patient who is provocatively hostile and destructive in his attitudes toward people, and who possesses disagreeable traits which the therapist in his everyday life would criticize.

The ability to maintain an objective attitude toward the patient does not mean that the therapist will not, on occasion, temporarily dislike many of the things the patient does or says. Indeed, he may become somewhat irritated with any patient on certain occasions, especially when he is being subjected to a barrage of unjust accusations, criticisms and demands. The stubborn resistances of the patient to acquiring insight and to translating insight into action, and the clinging of the patient to attitudes and action patterns that are maladaptive and destructive, will tax the endurance of any therapist, no matter how well-integrated his personality may be. But the capacity of the therapist to understand his feelings will help him better to tolerate the neurotic strivings of the patient and to maintain a working relationship.

To illustrate how a therapist may control counter-transference, we may consider the case of a patient who is having an affair with the wife of his best friend, and feels exultant about this situation. The therapist is repulsed by the enthusiasm and sexual abandon displayed by the patient. He may, therefore, have a temptation to interpret the situation as a disgraceful one, with the object of putting pressure on the patient to give up his paramour. With this in mind, he may enjoin, order or suggest that the patient stop seeing the woman in question, or desist from having sexual relations with her. Should the therapist step in boldly in this way, his interference will probably be resented by the patient. Indeed, transference may be mobilized, the patient regarding the therapist as a cruel, depriving, dangerous father who prohibits him from having sex or freedom. An artificial note will thus be injected into the relationship, the patient utilizing his affair as a means of defying the therapist. Not only will the patient continue in his infatuation, but the therapeutic situation may deteriorate. Or the patient may yield to the therapist's suggestion and give up the relationship with the woman, and then become depressed and detached, as if he has been forced to relinquish something precious. He will feel that his independence has been violated.

In attempting to control his responses, the therapist may indulge in self-searching. Realizing that he feels moralistic, the therapist is better capable of keeping in the forefront the general principle that, right or wrong, the patient is the one who must make the decision about continuing in the affair or giving it up. Accordingly, instead of suggesting to the patient that he stop the illicit relationship, the therapist may say:

"Now here is a situation that seems to have a good deal of value for you. You get fun out of seeing your friend's wife, but you also see that there are difficulties in the situation. Now suppose we discuss the good and bad sides of your predicament." The patient then will verbalize his feelings about the virtues as opposed to the liabilities of his intrigue. Thereupon the therapist may remark: "Here, you see, there are values as well as liabilities in the situation. It is important for you to consider all the facts and then decide the course of action you want to take." In this way the therapist strives to keep his own feelings from influencing the patient. The patient is then better equipped to evaluate what is happening and to plan his own course of action.

It is unnecessary for the therapist to feel that he must strap himself into an emotional strait-jacket to avoid upsetting the patient. Nor is it essential that he be a paragon of personality virtues to do good psychotherapy. So long as he is reasonably flexible, objective and empathic, and provided that a working relationship exists, he may indulge a variety of spontaneous emotional responses, even some that are neurotically nurtured, without hurting the patient or the therapeutic situation. Actually the patient will adjust to the therapist's specific personality, if he senses that the therapist is a capable, honest, non-hostile person who is interested in helping him get well.

For example, a therapist may be inclined to be active and somewhat domineering. The patient may then exhibit toward the therapist his usual attitudes toward domineering and authoritative people: he may become fearful, or hostile, or submissive or detached. As the therapist interprets these reactions without rancor, the patient may challenge the therapist's overbearing manner. The therapist, if not threatened by this stand, will acknowledge the operation of some domineering tendencies. The very fact that the therapist admits responsibility, may give the patient a feeling that he is not dealing with the same kind of imperious authority with whom he has always involved himself. He may then question the façades and defenses he automatically employs with authority, and he may countenance a new kind of relationship. In working out this aspect of his problem, he will undoubtedly see connections with other personality facets and begin working on these also.

If, on the other hand, the therapist is a quiet, non-domineering person, basic attitudes toward passive people may emerge. Thus, the same patient may become disappointed, sadistic or depressed. The therapist, observing such reactions, will be able to bring the patient to an awareness of why he is manifesting these tendencies. The patient will learn by this that the therapist is really not an inconsequential person, in spite of a quiet manner. Indeed, the patient may discover that he seeks a godlike authority, and that he has contempt for any lesser kind of human being. The patient will learn then that he can respect the therapist, and the therapist's personality, even though this happens to be passive. He will then have resolved one important part of his problem. With this resolution other aspects will come in for consideration; such as his attitudes toward domineering people. Thus, even though the patient deals with two entirely different people in the two distinct therapists, he will have been able to work out basic difficulties with each.

The important thing therefore is not whether the therapist has an impeccable personality, but rather that counter-transference reactions can be sufficiently reduced or controlled to provide the patient with a suitable medium in which to work through his neurotic patterns.

43

Translating Insight into Action

IMPROVEMENT OR CURE IN PSYCHOTHERAPY IS POSITED ON THE FOLLOW-ING PROPOSITIONS:

1. The patient successfully acquires an understanding of the nature of his problem by developing the capacity to conceive of it in terms that are meaningful to him.

2. On the basis of his understanding, he begins to execute his insight into positive action. He acquires symbolic controls, replaces destructive with adaptive goals, and propitiates these in accordance with the mores of society.

Insight is, therefore, a liberating and an enabling force; it upsets the balance between the repressed and repressive psychic elements; it creates motivations to test the reality of one's attitudes and values; it gives the person an opportunity to challenge the very philosophies with which he governs his life. But insight is not equivalent to cure; by itself it is insufficient in arresting the neurotic process and in promoting new and constructive patterns.

Indeed, the development of insight may surprisingly produce not relief from distress, but an accentuation of anxiety. For the ensuing challenge to change his *modus operandi,* and the sloughing off of neurotic protective devices, make the possibility of exposure to hurt all the more real. No longer is he capable of hiding behind his defense mechanisms. He must face his façades, and he must proceed to tackle life on new assertive terms. Prior to his acquisition of insight, he may have envisaged "normality" in fantasy as a desirable quality, but the approaching "showdown" fills him with a sense of impending doom.

Thus a man with an impotency problem may learn in therapy that his impotence is a defense against a fear of being mutilated by destructive, castrating women. Realizing that his defense is realistically unfounded, he must still expose himself to intercourse. This will continue to be extremely frightening to him until he convinces himself through action that the imagined dangers will not come to pass. A woman, working in an advertising agency, may discover that a fear of competition with men is due to her repudiation, on the basis of anxiety, of a desire for masculinity. Her knowledge then opens up the possibility of her being able to stand up to men. Specifically, she may practice her new insight on a man in her office who has advanced himself professionally over her because she had assumed a retiring and passive attitude. The understanding that she is playing a role with men akin to the subordinate role she had assumed as a child with her brother, does not ameliorate the anxiety she feels at having to compete with her office associate.

To protect himself from facing the threatened perils of action, a patient may throw up a smokescreen of resistance. He may reinforce old and employ new defensive mechanisms. He may devaluate strivings for health even though these had constituted strong incentives for starting therapy. The original motivations may be submerged under the anxiety of impending fulfillment and the patient may then interrupt treatment.

MODERN LEARNING THEORY AND PSYCHOTHERAPY

The difficulties that invest the resolution of old patterns and the elaboration of new ones, make it necessary for the therapist to use every stratagem at his disposal. Since psychotherapy involves a learning process in which the patient acquires abilities to abandon his neurotic adjustment in favor of an adaptation consonant with reality, it may be interesting to consider the therapeutic situation in the light of the theory of learning. A number of attempts have been made to coordinate psychotherapy with the principles of modern learning theory. None of these has proven successful, since the various propounded theories—including the stimulus-response and cognitive theories—are unable to account for the complexities of ego functioning, both normal and pathological. The ego seems to operate under laws of its own which have scarcely been embraced by any of the learning theories. Furthermore there are various kinds of learning to which different postulates may be applied. The unsolved problems of learning would seem too diffuse to permit of any real application of learning theory to the phenomena of psychotherapy.

Yet it is interesting to consider certain aspects of learning theory in relationship to what happens in the yielding of abnormal patterns and their replacement by adaptive behavior. From a purely speculative point of view, therefore, the following premises may be pertinent:

1. The basis for acquisition of new patterns is generally a strong need or drive that motivates the individual toward responses of a goal-directed nature.

2. Multiform actions are exploited which are meaningful to the individual in that they are calculated to satisfy the need. A successful response which reduces the motivation tends to be repeated whenever the original need recurs. Continued satisfaction of needs that follow the same response may lead to fixation of the specific response and to a suppression of other responses. Eventually this results in the establishment of a habit. Mere repetition of a response without adequate reward does not encourage continuance of action; conversely it may minimize the response. However, reinforcement is not always necessary to maintain a "good" response, nor will lack of reinforcement extinguish the response. The meaning of the response to the individual is what determines its continuance.

3. Associated stimuli and cues often become linked with the goal-attaining response. These incidental stimuli may eventually elicit the response through conditioning. Such conditioned responses make it possible for the individual to react in anticipation of a real need. Established responses thus do not confine

themselves to a specific stimulus; they are evoked by a wide variety of stimuli, symbolically similar to the rewarded stimulus. Learning may eventually produce anticipatory responses to mere hints of stimuli.

4. Anxiety is one of the strongest motivants to learning. It stimulates responses intended to reduce or eliminate its force. Great problems in learning develop when new habits that are being evolved stimulate anxiety. The latter emotion will evoke strivings that inhibit the new responses (resistance). Eventually, resistance may cause habits to undergo extinction. Since anxiety is present in most forms of learning, its proper handling constitutes an important pedagogic principle.

5. Each person exhibits a unique learning pattern, in both method and speed of learning, in relation to the understanding and integration of stimuli, and in regard to the pursuit of goal-directed actions.

BUILDING MOTIVATION FOR ACTIVITY

If empirically we are to pay credence to these concepts of learning, we have to abide by the rule that the first step in helping a patient to translate insight into action is to build adequate incentives toward the abandoning of old patterns of living. A constant analysis of the individual's habitual drives—their purpose, their origin, their contradictions, and the conflicts they inevitably inspire—enables the patient to doubt their values. Gradually he realizes that his strivings do him more harm than they do him good, that they are responsible for much of his maladjustment and promote many of his symptoms. Eventually he understands that the pleasures he derives from the fulfillment of his patterns are minute indeed compared to the devastation they produce in his life. He then becomes willing to challenge the validity of his customary modes of adjustment.

For example, a woman with a strong dependency drive discovers that her need for dependence dominates every aspect of her thinking and feeling. Finding an omnipotent person on whom to lean fills her with a sense of "goodness" and security. Life then becomes a bountiful place; she is suffused with vitality, imagination and creativeness. But not long after this metamorphosis, a curious change takes place in the way she feels. Fear and panic begin to overwhelm her; she becomes sleepless and she feels depressed; headaches, dyspepsia and muscle tension develop. To her consternation she seems to invite suffering, masochistically assuming the manner of a martyr, and then undermining the person who acts as her host. She appears also to want to capitalize on her plight, by holding forth physical weakness and infirmity as reasons for her avoidance of responsibility.

These patterns become apparent to her during psychotherapy. She learns that while she is driven to submit herself to a powerful parental agency, this crushes her assertiveness and fosters feelings of helplessness. Exploration of the genesis of her patterns may show her how her dependency resulted from subjugation by an overprotecting mother who stifled her independent emotional growth. This knowledge gives impetus to her desires for freedom. She sees how continued pursuit of dependency since childhood, causes reflex helplessness and crushing of independence. Such insights are fostered in a non-judgmental and tolerant treatment atmosphere, the therapist never holding himself out as an authority who orders the patient to change her way of life.

On the basis of her new understanding, much dissatisfaction may be created in the patient with her present life situation. She will also be motivated to experiment with different modes of adjustment. The desire to give up dependency as a primary adaptive technique, may, however, be blocked by a fear of, and a contempt for normal life goals. Anxiety here may mask itself as anhedonia—an indifference to, or boredom with pleasures and impulses accepted as valuable by the average person. For, compared with the ecstatic, albeit spurious, joys of neurotic fulfillment, customary routines seem uninspiring indeed. The therapist accordingly engages himself in a constant analysis of misconceptions about normality in terms of their anxiety-avoidance components.

When our patient, for instance, manifests disinterest in certain people, it may be possible to show her that she harbors contempt for any individual who does not possess a glamorous omniscience. She may actually classify people into two categories: those who are "superior" and who potentially can serve as parental substitutes; and those who are "inferior" and therefore are "utter bores." The immense narcissism and grandiosity inherent in her attitudes about herself may become apparent to the patient as she realizes how she strives to gain omnipotence through passive identification with a godlike figure. At this point the patient may become aware of why she refuses to have children. She realizes that she does not want to be replaced as the favorite child of her husband. She does not want to "give" and be a parent to a child, since she herself wants to be that child. She conceives it her right to take from others.

This analysis of anxieties and expectations, and the continued verbalization by the patient of fears and anticipated pleasures, provides increased motivation to attempt a different life expression. But no new patterns can be learned unless the motivation to acquire them is greater than the motivation that promotes the survival of the existing neurotic habits. Therapist activities, therefore, must embrace encouragement of any desires the patient voices for mental health, emotional growth and freedom from suffering. The therapist must attempt to undermine the pleasure and security values the patient seeks from the prosecution of her neurosis. Thus, the therapist may show the patient that the rationale of her dependency need is inescapable if one accepts the premise that she is incorrigibly helpless. While it is true that conditions in her childhood made dependency and related patterns necessary, she now continues to operate under assumptions that are no longer true. Her expectations of injury approximate those of a child. If she analyzes her situation today, she will see that conditions no longer necessitate anachronistic reactions that are so destructive to her adjustment. She is challenged to revise her assumption of life as a repetitive phenomenon that is blackened by shadows of her past.

PROVIDING A FAVORABLE ENVIRONMENT FOR ACTION

With expanding insights, neurotic strivings become linked in the mind of the patient with his suffering and maladjustment. Their operation and even their appearance begin to evoke discomfort. This provides motivation for their inhibition. Involved in the inhibitory response are incidental stimuli or cues which are associated with the neurotic patterns and which once could initiate them. More and more the patient becomes capable of controlling his reactions and of engaging in productive responses.

It may be necessary for the therapist to prepare the patient in advance for any foreseen disappointments that may occur in the course of executing a new response. Thus, if our dependent patient decides that she must assert herself with her husband, she may resolve to do this by asking him for a regular allowance weekly, from which she can budget her household expenses, purchase her clothing and provide for certain luxuries. Hitherto her husband has doled out funds whenever she needed to make a purchase, requesting an itemized accounting in order to check on her spending. He has considered his wife irresponsible —an attitude the patient has sponsored, partly out of ignorance and partly out of hostility—because she has made many unnecessary purchases. He has for this reason restricted her spending. We may, therefore, anticipate that he will react negatively to her suggestion that he provide her with a weekly sum, and that she be entrusted with the family purchasing. Because she has chosen this area as a test for her assertiveness, a negative or violent reception of her assertive gesture will probably mobilize anxiety and result in defeat. She may then suffer a decisive setback in her therapy, and perhaps never again dare to approach her husband assertively.

To forestall this contingency, the therapist may, when the patient presents her plan, ask her to anticipate her husband's reaction. In her reply, the patient may be fully expectant that her husband's response will be negative. She may then be asked to anticipate her own reaction should he refuse to cooperate. The therapist may even predict for the patient a violent response on the part of her husband, and get her to verbalize how she would feel if he became recalcitrant and punitive. Once the patient accepts the possibility that her request may bring forth hostility, and once she recognizes that her husband may, on the basis of her past performance, perhaps be justified in his refusal to trust her management, the therapist may encourage her to approach her husband on a different basis. Discussing with him the need for practice in making herself more independent, she may suggest that he allow her to assume greater responsibility in the handling of finances. However, since even this prudent method of presentation may be rejected, the patient should be prepared for a disappointment. What is accomplished by this tactic is that the patient is desensitized to failure and musters the strength to cope with an absence of rewards for her new responses.

In most patients insight is translated into action without too great activity on the part of the therapist. In some patients, however, considerable activity may be required before therapeutic movement becomes perceptible.

1. Psychodramatic Techniques

In occasional instances, role-playing may be efficacious, the therapist taking the role of the individual with whom the patient seeks to relate on different terms. Or the therapist may suggest that the patient assume the role of the person, while the therapist himself takes the part of the patient. The patient, in addition to building up immunity to rebuffs, enjoys in this technique an opportunity for emotional catharsis. The therapist is in turn availed of a means of bringing the patient's undercurrent feelings and responses to his awareness.

2. Conferences with Family Members

Where a patient lives in a close relationship with another person, like a mate, parent or family member, and his security is bound up with this person, his ability to respond with different patterns toward this person will be circumscribed by the permissiveness extended to the patient by the person. In the event the person has problems that interlock with those of the patient, and if the person utilizes the patient as a means of insuring his own neurotic adjustment, the person is bound to react with anxiety when the patient threatens to upset his routines. Thus the mate of our patient with the dependency problem will probably regard any change in the patient in her striving for freedom as an assault on his own rights. He may then attempt to undermine the patient's treatment.

Surmising such a contingency, it may be expedient to arrange for a talk with the person in question. The consultation will have to be arranged with the knowledge and even cooperation of the patient. One or several conferences with the person can often make the difference between success or failure in the patient's initial effort at a new response. Once the person sees the rationale of the new plan of action, and senses that he is not being blamed by the therapist; once he realizes that his own problems and needs are being taken into account, he may voluntarily cooperate. Even hostile reactions of the patient may be tolerated by him, if the person is alerted to the possibilities of such reactions. In our dependent patient, for example, an interview may be geared around the discussion with the husband of what he has noticed about his wife. Any troublesome attitudes and behavior mentioned may then be pointed out as manifestations of her problem of lack of assertiveness. In order for her to overcome this problem, which is so crippling to her adjustment, including her marital adjustment, it will be necessary to give her an opportunity to grow. Even though she may make mistakes, the husband is enjoined to exercise tolerance, since this is how people learn and grow. It would be better for her to make a few mistakes, for instance, in the way she budgets her allowance, and to help her to learn through her mistakes, than to let her continue in her present state of turmoil.

Obviously, in order for the husband to adjust to the patient's assertiveness, it will be necessary for him to master some of his own needs that are being satisfied by the patient's passivity and dependence. A fear for his own masculinity, a compulsive striving for superiority and power, may demand that his wife relate to him as a subordinate. Consequently, the husband may have to experience a therapeutic change himself in order to allow his wife to exercise assertiveness in the relationship. He may go through an emotional crisis before this happens, even though he appreciates the purpose behind the plan as explained to him by the therapist.

The following excerpt from a session with a woman whose dependency problem resembled that of the hypothetic patient we are considering as an example illustrates this point:

Pt. And Sunday morning I was in church and I got a little nervous. Then when I came home my husband started acting funny, wanting to go here, wanting to go there. I told him I thought he didn't really want to go anywhere. He brought up a lot of things. All of a sudden I looked at him and saw hatred on his face and my mind stopped working. He said, "You care more about the doctor than you do me." He acted very jealous and I got upset.

Th. I see.

Pt. And in the last few months we had been getting along so well. You know I just am never going to go back again to what I was. I got upset at his attitude and wanted to throw something at him, but instead I turned it on me. I cried and tore my hair. He got me so angry, I lost control. I don't want to live with a man I have to appease. I told him he is a mean man and that I would leave him.

Th. And then what happened?

Pt. He got upset and cried. He told me it was his fault. He said he always was this way and that he could see he was wrong. Then I started feeling sorry for him. Then I got mad at him. I don't think I can stand him. He's brutal and mean. He isn't happy until he sees me groveling on my knees. Then he's happy. Maybe I'm not the woman for him. (*pause*)

Th. But you *could* assert your rights. You *could* define what you feel your rights to be.

Pt. But I have. I don't see what I did to aggravate him. I know he has a problem in wanting to treat me like a slave. Maybe someone else could stand it, but I can't. And I told him and threatened to walk out. (*pause*)

Th. So what happened then?

Pt. Surprising. He broke down and cried. Then he said it was all his fault. He said he could see how he treated me, that it was all his fault. He said he didn't know how I could stand it so long. He said he would try to treat me more like an equal.

There are many instances in which improvement in therapy of one marital partner results in increasing emotional disturbance of the mate. Indeed a disturbed adaption of the patient may be a condition necessary for the equilibrium of the mate. Thus a man, domineered by a power-driven wife, may satisfy masochistic needs under a domain of tyranny. He may be unable to adjust to an atmosphere of cooperative equality brought about by the wife's improvement through psychotherapy. Or a frigid woman, receiving treatment, may make sexual demands on her impotent husband who will then develop strong anxiety. Where the mate of a patient has good ego strength he may possibly be able to progress spontaneously on the basis of new demands made on him by the patient toward a healthier adjustment. The outcome of psychotherapy in one partner then will be emotional improvement in both members. However, it may be necessary for the mate of the patient to receive psychotherapy also where spontaneous improvement does not occur.

3. Adjusting the Patient's Environment

Where the patient's environment is disturbed, it may have to be altered before insight can adequately be translated into action. Thus, if there is undernourishment, shabby physical attire, bad housing and other consequences of a subminimal budget standard, which are outside of the patient's control, a community or private agency may have to render assistance. An individual who is living with a brutal or neurotic parent or marital partner may be unable to achieve mental health until an actual separation from the home is brought about. Domineering parents who resent their offspring's self-sufficiency may cause a patient to feel hopeless, since compliance seems to be a condition for his security.

The majority of patients are capable of modifying their environment through their own actions, once the disturbance is clearly identified and the proper resources are made available to them. Occasionally the adjunctive services of a trained social worker may be required, especially with children and patients with weak ego structures. The therapist, with the help of a social worker, may materially alleviate certain problems by simple environmental manipulation. This is particularly the case where the people with whom the patient lives are capable of gaining insight into existing defects in the family relationship. Such factors as favoritism displayed toward another sibling, lack of appropriate disciplines and proper habit routines, the competitive pitting of the child against older siblings, overprotective and domineering influences of the patient's parents or mate, may sometimes be eliminated by inculcating proper insights. The correction of sources of discord and tension frequently is rewarded by disappearance of anxiety.

Such situational treatment, while admittedly superficial, can have a definite therapeutic value, and may permit an individual to proceed to a more favorable development. Often family members become so subjectively involved with the problems of the patient, so defensive and indignant about them that they are unable to see many destructive influences that exist in the household. An honest and frank presentation of the facts may permit intelligent people to alter the situation sufficiently to take the strain off the patient.

It must not be assumed, however, that all situational therapy will be successful, even when gross disturbances exist in the household. Frequently the family is unable or unwilling to alter inimical conditions because of severe neurotic problems in other members, or because of physical factors in the home over which they have no control. Here the social worker, through repeated home visits, may start interpersonal therapy which may bring the family around toward accepting the recommendations of the therapist. The worker may, in specific instances, render material aid to the family, or may assist in the planning of a budget or a home routine. Direct contact of the social worker with the family may reveal that others need attention or therapy.

Another function that the social worker can fulfill is to make available to the individual the various church, school and neighborhood recreational facilities. Persons with emotional problems frequently become so rooted to their homes, out of a sense of insecurity, that they fear outside contacts. Establishing a relationship with the patient and introducing him to groups outside the home may start a social experience that becomes increasingly meaningful for him, helping to release forces that make for self development.

In cases where the destructive elements within the family are irremediable or where the individual is rejected with little chance of his eventual acceptance, it may be necessary to encourage him to take up residence elsewhere. Temporary or permanent placement in a foster family or rest home may be essential. Although there is evidence that such change of environment rarely has an effect on deeper problems, residence in a home with kindly and sympathetic adults may serve to stabilize the individual and to give him an opportunity to execute in action the insight he has learned. The most significant factor in changes of residence is the meaning that it has to the patient himself. If he regards it as another evidence of rejection, it can have an undermining rather than a constructive influence. Instead of getting better, he may regress to more immature patterns of behavior. Above all, the patient must be adequately prepared for residence change or placement and should look forward to it as a therapeutic experience rather than as a form of punishment.

Caution must, however, be exercised in effecting drastic and permanent changes in the work or home situation, and thorough study of the patient is essential before one is justified in advising anything that may recast his entire life. This applies particularly to problems of divorce and separation.

Many patients seek therapeutic help while on the crest of a wave of resentment which compels them to desire separation or divorce. Mere encouragement on the part of the therapist serves to translate these desires into action. The therapist should therefore always be chary of giving advice that will break up a marriage unless he is completely convinced that there is nothing in the marital situation that is worthy of saving, or until he is sure that the relationship is dangerously destructive to the patient and that there is no hope of abatement. This precaution is essential because the patient may completely bury, under the tide of anger, positive qualities of his mate to win sympathy from the therapist or to justify his own resentment.

Where the therapist lets himself be swept away by the patient's emotion, and encourages a breakup of the home, many patients will be plunged into despair and anxiety. They will blame the therapist for having taken them so seriously as to destroy their hopes for a reconciliation. It is advisable in all cases, even when the home situation appears hopeless, to enjoin the patient to attempt the working through of his problems in his present setting, pointing out that his mate may also suffer from emotional difficulties for which treatment will be required. The patient will, in this way, not only help himself, but also his mate; and constructive features of the relationship will be preserved. It is wise to get the patient to talk about positive qualities possessed by his spouse instead of completely absorbing himself with the latter's negative characteristics.

4. The Learning of New Patterns within the Therapeutic Relationship

The reexperiencing by the patient, within the therapeutic situation, of his early unresolved fears, attitudes and needs, and the proper management by the therapist of these strivings, are important means of learning. The patient has an opportunity to work out, in a more favorable setting, problems he was unable to resolve in his relationship with early authorities. The new patterns resulting are gradually absorbed into the ego and become a part of the patient's personality.

For this to happen, the therapeutic situation must serve as a corrective experience, and must not repeat early disappointments and mishandlings. While the patient is motivated to grow and to develop within the relationship, he is hampered by anxiety, residual in expectations of hurt from domineering, rejecting, overprotecting and punitive authorities, which he may project toward the therapist. The therapist may be tempted by the patient's unprovoked attitudes and behavior to repeat the prohibitions, penalties and retribution of authoritative figures in the patient's past. Should the therapist respond in this way, the patient's convictions that authority is not to be trusted will be reinforced. No modifications of his attitudes can occur under these circumstances.

Realizing that the patient must verbalize or act-out unreasonable strivings in order to get well, the therapist will have an opportunity to react to these in an entirely different way from that anticipated by the patient. The therapist acts in a warm, accepting and non-judgmental manner. These attitudes inspire the patient to retest the original traumatic situation. He does this anticipating hurt. If the therapist, by virtue of understanding and the ability to remain objective, can avoid repeating the punitive and rejecting threats, the patient may be permitted to live through in a new setting crucial experiences that he should have resolved as a child. The therapist will constantly have to interpret to the patient the latter's expectation of hurt, and to help him to realize that the circumstances under which he failed to develop security and self-esteem were peculiar to his disturbed childhood.

This will call for a high degree of mental health on the part of the therapist, who is bound to incorporate in his own value system many of the judgments and arbitrary attitudes residual in the culture, which, incorporated in the parent's attitudes, have crushed the patient's growth.

Within the therapeutic relationship itself, therefore, the patient is helped to find a new and healthier means of adjustment. A virtue of the working relationship is that it acts as a prototype of better interpersonal relationships. It fosters the patient's faith in other people and ultimately in himself.

One way the working relationship is utilized is to resolve resistances to action. It is sometimes necessary to encourage the patient to face certain situations that have paralyzed him with fear. Utilizing the relationship as a fulcrum, the patient may be urged to experiment with new patterns while observing his responses. A program sometimes may be planned cooperatively with the patient, the therapist occasionally making positive suggestions. While advice-giving is best eschewed, the advantages and disadvantages of alternative courses of action may be presented, the patient being encouraged to make a final choice for himself. Thus, if the patient wants the therapist to decide something for him, the therapist may ask, "What do *you* feel about this?" Possibilities of failure, as well as anticipated reactions to entering into new situations may be explored. The patient may be cautioned by such statements as: "It isn't easy to do this," or "This may be hard for you." A method of stimulating action is to confront the patient with the question: "What are you doing about this situation?" whenever he expresses dissatisfaction with his progress.

Even with these promptings the patient may shy away from executing actions that threaten to promote old anxieties. If the initiative is put in the patient's hands, a stalemate may result. Although an analysis of resistances may encourage him to take a cautious step into dangerous territory, he may need gentle but firm pushing by the therapist before he boldly approaches a new activity. In phobias, for instance, the patient may have to be strongly urged to face the phobic situation, on the basis that he will have to learn to master a certain amount of anxiety before he can get well. Where the relationship with the therapist is a good one, the patient will be motivated to approach the danger situation with greater courage.

Success and pleasure in constructive action constitute the greatest possible rewards for the patient. Occasionally the therapist may indicate approval in nonverbal or in cautiously phrased verbal terms. Conversely, whenever the patient fails in an attempted action, sympathy, reassurance, encouragement and active analysis of the reasons for the failure are indicated. The patient may be reminded that his difficulty has been with him a long time, and that he need not be discouraged if he does not conquer his trouble abruptly. The patient may be given an explanation such as the following: "You know, an emotional problem is often like a hard rock. You can pound on it with a hammer one hundred times without making any visible impression. The hundred-and-first time, however, it may crumble to pieces. The same thing happens in therapy. For months no visible change is present, but the neurotic structure is constantly being altered under the surface. Eventually in therapy, and even after therapy, signs of crumbling of the neurosis occur."

Eventually the rewards of positive achievement and enjoyment issue out of the new and healthy patterns themselves. Surcease from suffering, reinforced by joys of productive interpersonal relationships, enable the patient to consolidate his gains.

CASE ILLUSTRATION

The following is a portion of a session in which a man with a personality problem of dependency, submissiveness, passivity and detachment, indicates how he has put his insight into action and asserted himself.

Pt. There has been a great change in me. I haven't felt this way in my whole life. And it has been going on for weeks.

Th. Is that so?

Pt. Yes. Of course, I used to have spurts of good feeling for different reasons. Once I felt as happy as a lark when I was about thirteen. I had had eczema for years and x-ray treatments took it away. I felt grand for a short time. And then I felt wonderful when I met my wife; but it lasted only a short while. But all these things came from external causes. The way I feel now seems to be coming from inside of me. All my life I seem to have been a zombie, really dead. Because I carried inside of me all sorts of standards of other people. I was like an automaton. If you would press a button, I would react in a certain way. I never had a sense of myself.

Th. Mm hmm.

Pt. Things have happened these weeks, which I think I handled well, and my reactions were good too. I have never had a prolonged period like this. Several times I'd say to myself, "I wonder if I can keep this up?" People mean different things to me now, you know. They are not powerful and threatening. My daughter was operated on at the hospital, for example. I regarded it in a sensible way. I said, "It's a minor operation. I'm concerned about her, but it's a simple thing and nothing to be upset about." I used to have a whole string of emotional responses that go along with illness. Now my wife has this worrying bug that was instilled in her by her mother. So I had to go along handling various things with her feelings which used to suck me into a trap before, and arouse guilt feelings in me.

Th. I see.

Pt. So she started to hammer at me a few days before the operation to see to it that the room in the hospital was a good one, that there was a television set there, and so on. Now this is a good hospital, I know, but their policy is annoying. I know they have a program and you could stand on your ear and get nowhere by ordering them around. So I said to my wife: "I'm not going to follow out your directions and do this and do that because I don't think it's right. Everything will go smoothly." So I did it my way and everything went smoothly.

Th. Previously how would you have done it?

Pt. To tell you this is a revolution is an understatement. I'd always appease my wife like I did my mother. I'd do what she said without questioning it. This time I did what *I* wanted and I felt no guilt. I had a sense of power. Everything went smoothly. When I got to the hospital my wife was frantic because they gave my daughter a rectal sedative and she expelled it. The nurse was all confused and didn't know what to do. Then they called for her to go to the operation. I said, "I won't let her out of the room until she is properly sedated. I don't care if they get the whole hospital on my head, I'm just not going to do it." And I did this with ease. There was nothing to it. Before this I would say, "Look, I'm making these people wait, and so forth, and so forth." So the interne came up and gave her a sedative. They called the surgeon who agreed that the child shouldn't come down until she was sedated. (*laughs*) Everyone was chewing their nails, but I stuck to my guns. Not that I was unreasonable, but I did stick to what I felt was right.

Th. And things came out well?

Pt. Better than well. It's like a miracle. To think how fearful I was, before therapy, to take a stand with anybody. Especially, I wasn't able to be firm with my wife. When I got home, though, my wife started on me and said that I should have acted more cooperative. That burned me up because that questioned my stand. I told her calmly (*laughs*) that I had sized up the situation and felt this is what had to be done, and the proof was that things turned out well. Even if they didn't, I was sure I was doing the right thing.

Th. I see.

Pt. I then realized that my wife was under a strain, and I told her I was sorry if I talked rough to her. And then she said, "Yes, you're sorry," sarcastically. I said to her, "Look, I said I was sorry. I'm not going to crawl; I'm not going to stand on my head or any god damn thing." And I didn't feel any anxiety or any guilt or anything. This morning my wife was as happy as a lark, as if nothing had happened.

Th. That made you feel you could take a stand, and nothing bad would happen.

Pt. I just brought that up to show that I wasn't drawn in; I felt I was right and I wasn't going to try to dope out my wife's neurotic reactions to things and turn myself inside out trying to please her. I felt wonderful about this. So that was that.

Th. Yes.

Pt. I get a lot of resentment now at certain women mostly, and say, "Why did I have to knock myself out for years? What's so great about them? They are just people, and there are plenty of them around. Why were women so important to me?" I know what it springs from and it seems so crazy to me now. (*laughs*)

Th. What *did* it spring from actually? [*testing his insight*]

Pt. Well, I would say that there were many factors involved and the picture becomes clearer; my whole life becomes clearer all the time. I would say it all started out, leaving psychologic terms out, with getting a terrible deal with my mother—she killed me. She must have acted in such a way that I was terribly uncertain of her love, and I must have gotten the feeling that if I didn't do exactly as she wanted me to do, she wouldn't love me any more. And there was no approbation given to me as a person. I became a thing. I became something that was used as a ground for other people's neurotic problems. My mother, on the one hand, being defeated in her life, used me to a point of smothering me with affection, which, I have a feeling now, covered a lot of repressed hostility, and a lot of rebellion against being a mother. My father, on the other hand, showered on me his own lack of confidence as a man. He impressed me with what a man should be, that when he was with people, he wouldn't let them get away with anything. If a cab driver said anything to him, he'd beat him up. He had a tremendous temper. He'd say, "You got to fight, don't take anything from anybody." He never gave me any affection. He couldn't. I think he has a lot more qualities than my mother, but he is very compulsive in the matter, as shown by the fact that he couldn't be warm. He was compulsive about his own work and emphasized to me not to procrastinate or put off to tomorrow what could be done today. The approbation came from getting good marks in school. That was the big thing.

Th. Yes.

Pt. So, I grew up with two big areas that were involved—the love area with my mother and the work area with my father. And then, in addition to that, my mother presenting the picture of what a bastard an aggressive man is. My father was a bastard, she said, "I love you," she said, "so don't be a bastard to me. If you do certain things that I don't like, then you are a bastard to me." So I grew up that way with no confidence in myself, no feeling about myself as having worth. The only worth I had was getting good marks to please my father, and giving in to please my mother. So with one thing and another I started to crack up.

Th. What happened with your wife?

Pt. She became a mother, and the same thing would have happened with every woman. No matter what the woman was, she was irreplaceable, because I had no confidence I could get another woman.

Th. How would you say your attitudes are now in that respect?

Pt. Well I would say, number one, I know they are not irreplaceable. I think I use sex in an abnormal way. First, it was to prove being a man and to get this feeling of being approved and accepted by a woman like my wife, which after a while stopped working because it proved nothing. So I feel now they are not irreplaceable. I know they have problems, and I don't have to get involved in their problems. I don't have to be sucked in again into being an automaton who is prey to their whims. Pleasing a woman, no matter what her problems, is good as long as it is a reciprocal thing; but doing it just to please her becomes detrimental to the relationship. I suppose in our culture women are more insecure than men and have problems; but I don't have to get involved in their problems. I also have learned that making a woman insecure by making her feel uncertain about you is not the answer. Because, while it works temporarily to incite her interest, it breaks up the relationship after a while.

Th. So that you feel your attitudes are altogether more wholesome.

Pt. My, yes. I realize that my feelings and my needs are just as important as the woman's. All this time I've been making an intellectual exercise about resolving conflict. Instead, the drives I feel now are healthy and good. After all, if it's a fifty-fifty proposition; you can't be too submissive and you can't be too aggressive. I feel a lot more strength within myself. I feel more alive and more vital. The reactions of other people don't matter as much as my own, or I'd say better that my reactions are equally important as the opinions of other people.

44

The "Working-through" Process

MENTAL HEALTH IS WON ONLY AFTER A LONG AND PAINFUL FIGHT. Even in supportive therapy, where goals are minimal, the person clings to his symptoms with a surprising tenacity. In reeducative therapy, the patient returns repetitively to his old modes of living while making tentative thrusts in a new and more adaptive direction. In reconstructive therapy, the struggle is even more intense, the patient shuttling back and forth, for what seems to be an interminable period, between sick and healthy strivings.

The initial chink in the patient's neurotic armor is made by penetrations of insight. The patient tries stubbornly to resist these onslaughts. He resists even more vigorously the implementation of any acquired insight in the direction of change. Only gradually, as he masters his anxieties, does he begin to divest himself of his neurotic encumbrances.

Change is never in a consistently forward direction. An insight takes hold and the patient improves. This improvement is momentary, and the patient goes backward with an intensified resistance. He reintrenches himself with all his previous defenses as he delves deeper into his problem. Anxiety forces a reverse swing toward familiar modes of coping with fear and danger. This is not a setback in the true sense, because new insights emerge, and the individual integrates what has happened to him into the framework of his rational understanding. Usually he will gain from this experience and take another step forward. Again, however, as he experiences anxiety, he will return to his old methods of dealing with stress or will resort to disguised adaptations of his defenses. In association with this there may be discouragement and a feeling of helplessness. But this time, the reintrenchment is more easily overcome. With the development of greater insight there is further progress; and there may again be a regression to old defenses. The curve of improvement is jerky, but with each relapse the patient learns an important lesson. The neurotic way of adaptation is used less and less, and as the patient gains cognizance of what is happening to him, he is rewarded with greater and greater progress.

It is discouraging to some therapists to encounter such curious reluctances in their patients toward moving ahead in treatment. The therapist is bound to respond with discouragement or resentment when, after having made an estimable gain, the patient experiences a recrudescence of his symptoms. Should the therapist communicate dismay to the patient, the latter is apt to regard this as a sign that he is hopeless, or that he has somehow failed the therapist. Actually there is no need for despondency or pessimism should the patient fumble along, repeat the same mistakes, or backslide when logic dictates that he forge ahead.

One way the therapist may maintain control of his feelings is to anticipate setbacks in all of his patients. He must decide that no patient will be able to acquire new patterns overnight. He must also recognize that each patient has his own rate of learning, which may not be accelerated by any technical tricks.

Before structural psychic change can take place, it is necessary for the patient to amalgamate an insight he has achieved in one area with other areas of his personality. Analogically, it is as if in a business institution that is failing, specific enlightenment comes to one department of the organization. After a new policy is accepted and incorporated by this department, it is presented to the other organizational divisions for consideration. Resistance against changing the status quo will inevitably be encountered, with eventual painful yielding by department heads, executives and other administrative personnel. Many months may go by before the recommended reforms are generally accepted and put into practice. Not until then will the influence on the business be felt. In emotional illness, too, enlightenment produced by understanding of one facet of the individual's behavior will have little effect on the total behavior until it is reconciled with the various aspects of the patient's personality.

This process of "working-through" is usually extremely slow, particularly where basic character patterns are being challenged. One may painstakingly work at a problem with little surface change. Then, after a number of months something seems to "give," and the patient begins responding in a different way to his environment. Gaining satisfaction from the new response, he integrates it within his personality. The old patterns continue to appear from time to time, but he becomes increasingly capable of controlling them, and of replacing them with new reactions. Having achieved a partial goal, he is motivated to tackle more ambitious aims. The investigative operation is extended toward these new objectives, and the "working-through" exercise then goes on with retreats and advances until constructive and established action eventuates.

Thus, a patient with a disturbing personality problem came to therapy because of the symptom of impotence. Understanding of his sexual misconception with a "working-through" of his fear of performance, opened up the possibility of more advanced objectives. A portion of an important session with this patient follows:

Pt. I saw Jane after I spoke to you. Sexually we got along better than we ever had. She had a good orgasm, and it was really the first time. We've been seeing each other for about five months, so it was sort of a milestone as far as I was concerned. And yet I wasn't, I didn't feel as though I'd done a great thing, as though I'd "arrived" or anything like that.

Th. Previously you had felt—I can even recapture your own words—that if an occasion ever occurred with a person like Jane where you could really function to your own satisfaction and to hers, it would really mean you had achieved your goal. Now that it's come about, it hasn't proved to be anything like you anticipated.

Pt. I said to myself that something seems to be stopping me almost from thinking about it. I said, "Now, let's think about this thing because this is supposedly very important." And I just didn't grasp it, as though there's something you want so much, and you get it, and it doesn't mean anything. I said this ought to give you a wonderful feeling; this should be good for you, that this happened. It was good, but it didn't solve all my problems like I imagined it would. And I don't know whether it's because it's become less important to me. It continually demonstrates this business of I could do such-and-such, if only this were the case. How foolish that is because I thought to myself, "Well, really it's just once. Maybe it should be another time. Maybe I should prove myself again. Once really isn't enough." But I feel I could do it three or four times, or a hundred, and it still wouldn't be enough. [*The patient is apparently aware of the fact that sexual success will not solve all his problems.*]

Th. As a matter of fact, it is possible that the reason you weren't functioning well sexually with her is that you weren't permitting yourself to enjoy sex for the pleasure value, but rather for its value in building you up. [*interpreting his neurotic use of sex*]

Pt. I would guess that I have certainly changed in that respect. It bothered me though that it didn't mean more to me than it did. I thought, well maybe that's why it happened, because it didn't mean so much to me. So that we're still really on the same basis, as far as this business is concerned.

Th. Mm hmm.

Pt. I say to myself, "Well, there's three women, Barbara, Martha and Jane, that I'm sleeping with. I have now reached a point where I, they've all been able to have orgasms. It made me feel comfortable, but not . . . maybe I could be better off if I could think, "Jesus, I'm terrific, or what a great man I am now." But I don't feel that way.

Th. It would be a very neurotic thing to build up your self-esteem solely and completely, or largely, on the basis of how you function sexually. That's a facade that will cross you up.

Pt. It would be like evaluating a man on the basis of his appetite. If I would be with a woman and I could only have one orgasm I would think to myself, well, you're not as much of a man as if you had two or three orgasms. And yet, it would be like saying, if a man eats a plate of oysters, if he eats only one plate, he's not as much a man as if he'd eaten two or three plates. I realize my attitude is ridiculous.

Th. But still you seem to think one way and feel the other way.

Pt. It really is a tough situation. This sort of thing seems to be pretty much the kernel of my difficulty. It radiates in all actions and all spheres. I mean the sexual element now seems to, right now, this week anyhow, seems to be receding somewhat into the background, and other aspects becoming important. I see where it's necessary to do more, to alter your personality and your attitudes. A whole new set of values have to be evolved, what's good and what's bad, what's right and what's wrong, the sort of life you want to live and what you want to do about it, which, I presume most people never really figure out. I have toyed with the idea before, but now I want to get into myself more.

Another patient with sexual fears and problems in his marital life was, with continued "working-through," able to make good progress. His relationship with his wife improved. Sexuality became less compulsive a function; he began to achieve greater assertiveness and a feeling of increased self-esteem. These changes are illustrated in the following fragment of the session that follows:

Pt. Tuesday night I decided to bring some flowers home. It was like a miracle, a tremendous response. In fact my wife's face was so overjoyed that I really felt a little sorry that—well, she'd been so miserable—it just required little things like that, not much to make her happy. I talked to her last night about my work, and she interpreted my actions as rejection. But it wasn't so, I told her. I said the things you really want are the important ones. She said that it's true. I explained to her about my work and eventually I thought I'd be able to spend more time with the children, and I was working toward that end. I feel much more comfortable in the situation. I was afraid that I'd have a compulsion to want to do as many things as possible along these lines, so that she'd know I was thinking of her. And the result would be that I'd have a conflict between wanting to do those things and other things like my work. But I find it's not so. I feel very comfortable, much more comfortable in the situation. I feel that I can do those things if I want to. If I think of something to make her know that I'm thinking of her, it's not an effort really on my part. I don't feel a compulsion to want to do them. In fact, when I got the flowers, I really enjoyed getting them. I would say right now that my situation, therefore, on the whole is a little better. These other things aren't important to me. My wife is enjoyable. I'm more in control of the situation.

Th. You'll be able to make even further progress if you can think objectively about your situation and not act impulsively as you once did.

Pt. Yes, I guess so. I guess being tied up in a situation makes you lose your perspective, but I was so interested in the things that she was actually finding fault with me for, I felt that I concentrated on those, taking them as a personal affront, instead of realizing what they were. I suppose that the situation will change again in some way, but right now I guess things are fairly peaceful, considering everything. I have a great deal of work to do, but I think I'm less neurotic about it; for the first time, I would say, since I've been in business, I am willing and eager to strip myself of as much detail work as possible. Before I was just holding on to it. I made up my mind that this work has to be done and that until I do it, I won't be able to take it easy. The work has to be done before I can take it easy. So I said to myself, "Well, it's really awful because if I had three days like Saturday, where no one bothered me, in a row, I could do it all." So I told my wife that I'm going to have to work a few nights and she said O.K. In fact, last night, I did one of the things that she complained about, I came home late again. But it was wonderful, she didn't complain about it, she greeted me with a smile and said nothing about it. So I could see that that wasn't the important thing. I would say that I feel on the whole that I sort of climbed a little and reached a little plateau, if such a thing is possible.

Th. Well, let us examine that plateau, and see what incentives there are to move ahead. Because virtually, in terms of your goals that you came to see me for originally, you've pretty much achieved those, haven't you?

Pt. I suppose so. The physical symptoms that I had, I don't have them any more. I assume they'll just fade away, because I never think of them. Sexually, I'm functioning much better than I ever did before. So I guess on those two counts I've come a long way. That's true.

Th. In your assertiveness, in your capacity to stand up for your own rights, what about that?

Pt. Well, I'd say there is probably less progress made on that score. We haven't been working on it as much as the other thing.

Th. Well, do you feel that it's been a problem? Do you feel that that constitutes a problem for you?

Pt. Yes, definitely, but now I feel more like a person with rights and things like that, more of an individual than I felt before. But I think I still have a long way to go to feel really an assertive person, I would say. And this may be just a temporary peace that I've achieved. All the elements that caused me anxiety for the past few months have reached the point of equilibrium.

Therapeutic progress is gaged by the ability of the patient to apply what he has learned toward a more constructive life adaptation. The recognition of disturbing drives, and the realization that they are operating compulsively do not guarantee that any modification will occur. Nor do they mean that the patient has the capacity for change. The ability to progress depends upon many factors. Foremost is the desire for change. Among the motivating influences here, are a sense of frustration induced by an inability to fulfill normal needs, and growing awareness that neurotic strivings are associated with suffering far in excess of compensatory gratifications.

The detection of contradictions in the personality structure also acts as a powerful incentive to change. It is, however merely the first step in the reintegrative process. Thus, if a patient exhibits a pattern of compulsive dependency, the mere recognition of his dependency and its consequences will not alter his need to cling tenaciously to others. While it may point the way to the more basic problem of his inner helplessness and devaluated self-esteem, there is still a need to examine the meaning of his impaired self-esteem, as well as to determine its source. There is furthermore required an appreciation of the motivating factors in the individual's present life that perpetuate feelings of helplessness. Understanding the origins of his dependency trend, and tracing it to determining experiences with early authorities, are important steps, but these too are usually insufficient for cure. So long as basic helplessness continues, dependency has subjective values the individual cannot and will not relinquish. While he may recognize the irrationality of his drive or its unfortunate consequences, he will desperately cling to it, at the same time rationalizing his motives. He may even have partial insight regarding his dependency, but deep down he feels that he must become reconciled to it the remainder of his life.

"Working-through," as has been previously indicated, is especially difficult in reconstructive therapy. The releasing of the self from the restraint and tyranny of an archaic conscience, freeing it from paralyzing threats of inner fears and conflicts, is an extremely slow process. Ego growth gradually emerges, with the development of self-respect, assertiveness, self-esteem and self-confidence. It is associated with liberation of the individual from a sense of helplessness and from fears of imminent rejection and hurt from a hostile world.

To encourage such growth it is necessary to cajole the ego into yielding some of its defenses. Within himself the individual feels too weak to do this, and too terrified to face his inner conflicts. Unconscious material is invested with such anxiety that its very acknowledgment is more than the patient can bear. Rooted in past conditionings, this anxiety possesses a fantastic quality, since it is usually unmodified by later experiences. It is as if the anxiety had been split off and were functioning outside the domain of the ego. In therapy it is essential to reunite the conscious ego with the repressed material and its attendant anxiety, but resistance constantly hampers this process. Promoting resistance is the hypertrophied set of standards and prohibitions that developed out of the individual's relationships with early authorities. These standards oppose not only the uncovering of unconscious material, but also the expression of the most legitimate biologic and social needs.

"Working-through" in reconstructive therapy is accompanied by a strengthening of the ego to a point where it can recognize the disparity between what is felt and what is actually true, where it can divest the present of unconscious fears and injuries related to the past, where it can dissociate present relationships with people from attitudes rooted in early interpersonal experiences and conditionings. Ego growth is nurtured chiefly through a gratifying relationship with the therapist. The exact mechanism that produces change is not entirely clear. However, the therapist-patient relationship acts to upset the balance of power between the patient's ego, his conscience, and his repressed inner drives. The ultimate result is an expansion of the ego and a replacement of the tyrannical conscience by a more tolerant superego patterned around an identification with the therapist.

The relationship with the therapist may, however, light up the individual's fears of injury, his inordinate demands and expectations, and his forbidden erotic and hostile desires. Despite the lenity of the therapist, the patient will keep subjecting him to tests in order to justify a returning to his old way of life. If the therapist is too expressive in his tolerance of the patient's deepest impulses, the patient will look upon treatment as a seduction for which he will pay penalties later on. On the other hand, a repressive attitude expressed by the therapist will play in with the patient's residual concept of authority as restrictive, and therefore, deserving of customary evasions and chicaneries. At all times, the patient will exploit his usual characterologic defenses to prevent relating himself too intimately to the therapist. He has been hurt so frequently in his previous interpersonal relationships that he is convinced that danger lurks in the present one. Under the latter circumstance the "working-through" experiences may take place within the transference relationship itself.

Many months may be spent in dealing with resistances that ward off the threat of a close relationship with, and the acknowledgment of certain irrational feelings toward the therapist. The therapist acts to dissolve these facades by direct attack. Perhaps for the first time the patient permits himself to feel, to talk, and to act without restraint. This freedom is encouraged by the therapist's attitude, which neither condones nor condemns destructive impulses. The patient senses that the therapist is benevolently neutral toward his impulses and that he will not retaliate with counter-hostility in response to aggression. Gradually the patient develops reactions to the therapist that are of a unique quality, drawing upon emotions and strivings that he has hitherto repressed. The release of these submerged drives may be extremely distressing to the patient. Because they conflict so strongly with his standards, he is bound to reject them as wholly fantastic or to justify them with rationalizations. There is an almost psychotic quality in projected inner feelings and attitudes, and the patient will fight desperately to vindicate himself by presenting imagined or actual happenings that put the therapist in a bad light.

As the patient experiences hostility toward the therapist, and as he finds that the dreaded counter-hostility does not arise, he feels more and more capable of tolerating the anxiety inevitable to the release of his unconscious drives. He finds that he can bear frustration and discomfort, and that such tolerance is rewarded by many positive gains. Finally, he becomes sufficiently strong to unleash his deepest unconscious drives and feelings, which previously he had never dared to express. Projecting these onto the person of the therapist, the patient may live through infantile traumatic emotional events with the therapist that duplicate the experiences initially responsible for his disorder. The latter phase occurs when the patient has developed sufficient trust and confidence in the therapist to feel that he is protected against the consequences of his inner destructive impulses.

Sexual wishes, perverse strivings, and other drives may also suddenly overwhelm the patient and cause him to react compulsively, against his better judgment. The patient almost always will exhibit behavior patterns both inside and outside the therapeutic situation that serve either to drain off his aroused emotions or to inhibit them. He may, for instance, in response to feelings of rage, have a desire to frustrate and hurt the therapist. Accordingly he will heap imprecations and derisive remarks upon the therapist, minimizing the latter's intelligence, or emphasizing any shortcomings. He may become sullen or mute or negativistic.

These reactions do not always appear openly, and may be manifested only in dreams and fantasies. Sometimes hostility is expressed more surreptitiously in the form of a sexual impulse toward the therapist which has its basis in the desire to undermine or to subdue him. At the same time, the patient realizes that he needs the love and help of the therapist, and he may feel that expression of hostility will eventuate in rejection. He may then try to solve his conflict by maintaining a detached attitude toward the therapist, by refusing to talk, by forgetting his appointments, or by terminating treatment.

A danger during this working-through process is that the patient may act-out his inner impulses and feelings and fail to verbalize them. This is particularly the case where the patient is given no chance to express everything that comes to his mind. Such acting-out has a temporary cathartic effect, but is not conducive to insight. If the patient does not know what he is reliving, he will think that his reactions are completely justified by reality. If acting-out goes on unchecked, it may halt the therapeutic process. The most important task of the therapist here is to demonstrate to the patient what in the therapeutic relationship he is avoiding by acting-out.

As the patient realizes that his emotions and impulses are directly a product of his relationship with the therapist, he will attempt to justify himself by searching for factors in the therapist's manner or approach that may explain his reactions. Inwardly he is in terror lest the therapist call a halt to therapy and thus bring to an end the possibility of ever establishing an unambivalent relationship with another human being. Yet he continues to respond with contradictory attitudes. On the one hand he seeks praise and love from the therapist, and, on the other, he tries to injure and destroy the therapist. He resents the tender emotions that keep cropping up within himself. The battle with the therapist rages back and forth, to the dismay of both participants.

One of the effects of this phase of the therapy is to mobilize ideas and fantasies related to past experiences and conditionings. The interpersonal relationship is the most potent catalyst the therapist can employ to liberate repressed memories and experiences. As the patient expresses irrational impulses toward the therapist, he becomes tremendously productive, verbalizing extremely important material.

Sooner or later, the patient discovers that his attitudes and feelings toward the therapist are rooted in experiences and conditionings that have gone before; he realizes that they have little to do with the therapist as a real person. This has a twofold effect. First, it shows him why exaggerated expectations and resentments develop automatically in his relationships with others. Second, it permits him to see that he is able to approach people from a different point of view.

The transference is a dynamic, living experience that can be intensely meaningful to the patient. Recovery of repressed material is in itself insufficient. The material has to be understood, integrated and accepted. During therapy much material of an unconscious nature may come to the surface, but the patient will, at first, be unable to assimilate this material because it lies outside the scope of his understanding. In the transference relationship the patient is able to feel his unconscious impulses in actual operation. He realizes them not as cold intellectual facts, but as real experiences. The learning process is accelerated under such circumstances.

The transference not only mobilizes the deepest trends and impulses, but also it teaches the patient that he can express these without incurring hurt. This is unlike the ordinary authority-subject relationship, in which the person feels obligated to hold back irrational feelings. Because of the therapist's tolerance, the patient becomes capable of appreciating certain attitudes consciously for the first time. He appreciates that when he expresses destructive attitudes toward the therapist, these do not call forth retaliatory rejection, condemnation or punishment. He gradually develops a more tolerant attitude toward his inner drives, and he learns to reevaluate them in the light of existing reality rather than in terms of unconscious fantasies and traumatic events in the past. As he undergoes the unique experience of expressing his deepest strivings without retaliation, he also begins to permit healthy, congenial social attitudes to filter through his defenses. The therapist becomes an individual who fits into a special category. He is less the authority and more the friend.

The tolerant and understanding attitude of the therapist endows him with a peculiar attribute of protectiveness, for the patient by himself is unable to accept his inner conflicts and impulses, and he uses the therapist as a refuge from danger. The conviction that he has a protector enables him to divulge his most repulsive impulses, emotions, memories and fantasies, with an associated release of affect. Along with growing awareness of his unconscious drives and the recalling of their existence in earliest childhood, the patient sooner or later discovers that there is a difference between what he feels and what is actually going on in reality; he finds that his guilt feeling and anxiety actually have no basis in fact.

The patient may bring up more and more painful material. Encouraged to express himself, he begins to regard the therapist as one who bears only good will toward his repressed drives. He will continue to exhibit all of his customary interpersonal attitudes and defenses in his relationship with the therapist, but he can clarify them to himself under a unique set of conditions—conditions in which he feels accepted and in which there is no condemnation or retaliatory resentment.

The reorientation in his feeling toward the therapist makes it possible for him to regard the therapist as a person toward whom he need not have an ambivalent attitude. His acceptance of the therapist as a real friend has an important effect on his resistances. These are genetically related to the hurt he experienced in his relationships with early authorities. The removal of resistances is dynamically associated with an alteration in his internalized system of restraints, for, if he is to yield his defenses, he must be assured that the old punishments and retributions will not overtake him. It is here that his experience with the therapist plays so vital a role, because in it he has gained an entirely new attitude toward authority. His own conscience is modified by adoption of a more lenient set of standards and injunctions.

One of the chief aims of rational psychotherapy is to render the conscience less tryannical and to modify its values so far as to permit the expression of impulses essential to the mental health of the individual. Perhaps the most important way in which this modification can be achieved is through acceptance of the therapist as a new authority whose standards subdue and ultimately replace the old and intolerable ones. In the course of the therapeutic relationship, the patient tends to identify himself with the therapist and to incorporate his more tolerant values. The ultimate result is a rearrangement of the dynamic forces of the personality and a reduction in the harshness of the superego.

The identification with the therapist also has a remarkable effect on the patient's ego. Progress in reconstructive therapy is registered by the increasing capacity of the reasonable ego to discern the irrationality of its actions, feelings and defenses. The rebuilding of ego strength promotes a review of old repressions, some of which are lifted, while others are accepted but reconstructed with more solid material, so that they will not give way so easily to unconscious drives. Growth in the rational power and judgment of the ego makes it possible to identify these destructive strivings which, rooted in past experiences, are automatically operative in the present.

Ego strength consequently results both from liberation of the self from the repressive and intolerant standards of the tyrannical conscience, and from identification with the accepting, non-hostile figure of the therapist. Ultimately, ego growth involves an identification with a healthy group. This is, of course, the final aim in therapy, and this relation to the group eventually must supplement and partly replace the personal identification.

The undermining of the superego and the strengthening of the ego give the patient courage to face his fearsome impulses, such as of hate. He becomes increasingly more capable of expressing rage openly. The possibility of his being physically attacked by the therapist becomes less and less real to him. As he resolves his hate and fear, he is likely to experience an onrush of loving emotions. Often these burst forth in a violent form, as in a compulsive desire for sexual contact. In this guise they may be so loathsome and terrifying that they are promptly repressed. Sexuality, to the mind of the patient, involves unconditional love or surrender or a desire to attack or to merge with another person. Inextricably bound up with such destructive feelings are healthful ones, but because the patient has been hurt so frequently in expressing tender impulses, he has customarily been forced to keep them under control. In his relationship with the therapist he learns that normal demands for understanding and affection will not be frustrated and that they have nothing to do with hateful and sexual attitudes.

As the therapist comes to be accepted as an understanding person, the unconscious impulses come out in greater force, and the patient discovers that he is better able to tolerate the anxiety that is created by their expression. In contrast to what occurs in real life, resistance to their divulgence is not reinforced by actual or implied threats of retaliation or loss of love. The patient then becomes conscious of the fact that his terror has its source within himself rather than in an implied threat of hurt from the therapist. This insight does not help much at first, but gradually it permits the patient to experiment in tolerating increased doses of anxiety.

The development of the capacity to withstand pain makes it possible for the patient to work out more mature solutions for his problems, instead of taking refuge in repression, a defense hitherto necessitated by his inability to tolerate anxiety. The discovery that he has not been destroyed by his impulses, and the realization he has not destroyed the therapist, whom he both loves and hates, are tremendous revelations to him, lessening the inclination to feel guilty and to need punishment, and contributing to his security and self-respect.

At this stage in therapy, the patient becomes more critical of the therapist and more capable of injecting reality into the relationship. He attempts to test out his new insights in real life. He does this with considerable trepidation, always anticipating the same kind of hurt that initially fostered his repression. As he discovers that he can express himself and take a stand with people, a new era of trust in the therapist is ushered in, with a definite growth of self-confidence. Over and over he works through with the therapist his own characterologic strivings, reexperiencing his unconscious impulses and his reactions of defense against them. Gradually he becomes aware of the meaning of his emotional turmoil, as well as of the futility of his various defenses. The continuous analysis of the transference enables him to understand how his neurotic drives have isolated him from people and have prevented expression of his normal needs.

A new phase in his relationship with the therapist ensues. Realizing that the therapist means more to him than does anyone else, he seeks to claim his new ally for himself. He may wish to continue the relationship indefinitely, and, he may look upon the completion of therapy as a threat. Clinging to his illness may then have positive values. However, he soon begins to understand that there are reality limitations in his present relationship, and that he does not get out of it the things that he is beginning to demand of life, that the outside world is the only milieu in which he can gratify his needs. He finds the relationship with the therapist gratifying, but not gratifying enough; his reality sense becomes stronger and his ability to cope with frustration is enhanced. Finally, he sets out in the world to gain those satisfactions that he has never before felt were available to him.

The working-through process is not always accompanied by the intensive transference manifestations such as have been described. Indeed, the relationship with the therapist may be maintained on a more or less equable level, the working-through of attitudes, feelings and conflicts being accomplished exclusively in relation to persons and situations outside of therapy. This is particularly the case in supportive, reeducative and psychoanalytically oriented psychotherapies in which a transference neurosis is more or less discouraged. But even in the latter therapies, it may not be possible to keep transference from erupting; if this occurs, some of the working-through will have to be focused on the patient-therapist relationship.

CASE ILLUSTRATION

Illustrative of the "working-through" of transference is the case of a young divorcée with a personality problem of detachment, whose marriage had disintegrated because of her general apathy. Sexually frigid, and with little affectionate feeling for people, she had never been able to establish a relationship in which she could feel deep emotion. After a prolonged period of working on her resistances, she began to evince positive transference feelings toward me as manifested in the following fragment of a session:

Pt. I had a dream yesterday. We were dancing together and then you make love to me. Then the scene changes and there is a fellow sitting on a bench, and you kiss me and in jest ask him to leave. And then you sit down and I lie down with my head against you. You put your arms around me. And then the scene shifts again and you and I are in the kitchen. And my daughter, Georgia, is climbing over the sink toward the window, and I pull her in. Then I'm standing there with my son, John, in the hallway and you very professionally ask if there is anyone else I am waiting for. You came to find out about John. You forget the fact that you asked me for dinner, and I'm very let down and wake up with that let down feeling.

Th. What are your associations to this dream?

Pt. I awoke with the feeling that I'm very much in love with you. I want you to love me very much. It's a desperate feeling that I can't control.

Th. How long has this feeling been with you?

Pt. It's been accumulating over a time, but it suddenly hit me last night and when I awoke this morning, I knew. (*pause*) This is a funny thing to ask you, but I feel sexually attracted to you. Is it ever permissible to . . . to . . . I mean (*blushes*)

Th. You mean to have an affair?

Pt. Yes.

Th. Well, I appreciate your feeling very much. It often happens that in therapy the patient falls in love with the therapist. This is understandable because the patient takes the therapist into her confidence and tells him things she wouldn't dare tell herself. But in therapy, for the therapist to respond to the patient by making love would destroy therapy completely.

Pt. I can understand perfectly. But I felt that you responded to me, (*laughs*) that *you* were in love with me. I think you are the most wonderful man in the world.

Th. You may possibly feel I reject you. It is important though to explore your feelings for me, no matter what these may be.

Pt. I agree, agree with you, of course. I can't see how this happened to me though. It never happened before. It's a hell of a note, but as you say, it must inevitably happen.

There ensued a prolonged period of strife in which the patient veered from sexual to hostile and destructive feelings toward me. The following session, for example, reflects negative impulses.

Pt. I'm furious at you. I don't, didn't want to come today.

Th. Can you tell me why?

Pt. Because you've gotten, gotten me to feel like a human being again instead of a piece of wood, and there's nothing to do about it, you know very well there's nothing to do about it.

Th. You mean, now you're able to feel about people and there's nothing you can do about expressing yourself?

Pt. (*angrily*) Oh, please be quiet will you. (*pause*) Here you went and got me all stirred up for absolutely nothing. It's like you want to torture and hurt me.

Th. What makes you think that I want to torture you and hurt you?

Pt. I didn't say you wanted to. I don't believe I've reproached you at all. I never reproach anybody for anything, I never have.

Th. But . . .

Pt. Have I ever implied or said one word of reproach to you? I don't believe I have.

Th. No.

Pt. No. I don't think so. I don't reproach anybody for anything. I don't want you to do anything at all, except just let me walk out of that door.

Th. Do you really want to walk out of that door?

Pt. I'm going to walk out of that door. You see, what you don't know about me yet is that I've a very, very strong will. (*pause*) You sit there in that chair, and I sit here opposite you, and you've got that lovely warm darn way of speaking, and, before I reach that door, you'll freeze like an icicle. And I can do exactly the same thing, exactly the same thing.

Th. You mean just to get even with me?

Pt. Have you ever seen me try to get even with anybody? I don't think you have. I'm not a very vindictive person.

Th. Do you think I really act icy to you?

Pt. But you do.

Th. When?

Pt. I went out of here the last time ashamed of myself. I went down that street crying. I was crying. I felt you rejected me, cold to me.

Th. You felt that I rejected you? You felt that I acted cold toward you? When did I act cold toward you?

Pt. Let's drop that rejection business, shall we? It isn't a question of being rejected. It has nothing to do with it at all. And if we get right down to it, what difference does it make whether you do or you don't?

Th. It makes this difference, that I am very much interested in helping you.

Pt. If I walked out of this room, you'd never think of me again.

Th. You feel that if you walk out of this room I'll never even think of you again.

Pt. That's exactly how I feel! Exactly what I feel. Yes. Suppose you had to do the same thing for every patient. You couldn't last. Any more than any other doctor could last, any more than any trained nurse could last. They can't. (*pause*) Well, I'm feeling a lot better getting that off my chest.

Th. I'm glad you're feeling better.

Pt. Yes. I'm sure. I think you owe me quite a little time. I don't believe I've ever stayed here forty-five minutes, have I? I don't think so. I've always looked at that clock and I've gone. I've gone to the second at forty minutes after I got here. [*This is not exactly correct, but I decide not to challenge it.*]

Th. Why?

Pt. Because I don't want anything from anybody. Because I don't want one minute of anybody's time.

Th. You just want to be completely independent?

Pt. Yes, I do.

Th. I wonder if you trust me?

Pt. I've always trusted you. What do you think I'm coming here for? There isn't anybody that is forcing me to come. Who is it that drags me any place on a chain? If I didn't want to come, there isn't anybody that could make me come.

Th. Indeed. You know, too, that it's good that there's nobody that forces you to be here. It has to be completely a free thing with you, a voluntary thing with you, a thing that you really believe in.

Pt. I don't know what I'm going to do when I have to leave you, when I'm through with this.

Th. Why?

Pt. I can't depend on anybody, see?

Th. You're afraid to get dependent on me?

Pt. I'm afraid to get dependent on any human being, because there isn't a living human being that I can trust. Not even you. I can't trust anybody on earth. And that's the truth.

Th. I can't force you to trust me, but I hope you will. I'll do everything in my power to be worthy of that trust. But I can appreciate the suffering and torment that you must go through as you begin to feel feelings for me.

Pt. But you do torment me.

Th. How do I torment you?

Pt. I think you resent me, even despise me.

Th. Did I ever do anything to give you that impression?

Pt. No, but . . . I guess I must *think* you reject me. But you really don't.

The "working-through" of her feelings toward a more constructive solution is shown in this portion of an interview that occurred several months after the initial onset of transference:

Pt. When I came to you, you were exactly what I needed at that moment, and you comforted me when I came, and for the first few weeks—it was no more than that— then I began to like you. I liked you more and more, and it was interesting to me that I could feel that way about a person, because I had not up to that point. You were the first person that I felt anything for since many, many years ago. So I reasoned it out, and I felt that you were probably . . . I didn't know what you were like as a man. I knew you only from a professional standpoint, what you were like. Maybe I would not feel that way if I did know you, I don't know. I was trying to tell myself I didn't know enough about you to feel that way. It wasn't anything sound. And another thing I felt was that you were probably a symbol of what I would like to have or feel for someone, that you just were a symbol. Actually, I didn't know enough about you to feel that way, and I kept telling myself that, and, during your vacation when I left I thought I didn't know how I was going to get along without seeing you. It was really the high point of my week when I came to see you. I looked forward to it, and I really enjoyed that more than anything else that I did. So, during the summer, I thought, "Well, I am going to miss him. How will I get along?" I sort of leaned on you, and I had gotten so much comfort. Then, something began to happen to me, and I felt that even if I felt that way, maybe you did like me very much, maybe you didn't. I don't know whether what you say is all professional. I felt that as far as you were concerned, even if you did like me, and I liked you as you said, which was what I had figured out for myself, that any sort of very close friendship was not possible and isn't practical. I felt that I needed you much more as a doctor than a man at that point, and that I should forget about it. So it was something that I was putting on. I probably needed something, maybe it wasn't necessarily you. So I sort of started to look around at men. I was aware more of the attention they paid me. I responded more, which I had never done. I found that I was giving them a little more encouragement, because I never radiated any encouragement. I felt that if I were to find someone, I was very happy that I could feel that way about someone. I really was, because I didn't think I could any more, I just didn't. I missed seeing you, which was very unusual for me, because I hadn't felt that way about anyone in many years. So I started to look around, as I say I have responded, but I haven't found anyone that I do feel that way about. Of course, I haven't had the opportunity.

Th. At least you are not running away and are not guilt-ridden. You may feel that if the right sort of person came along, there may be a possibility for a relationship. But what about me right now?

Pt. Well, I'll tell you how I feel about that. When I first came here, not the first few weeks, but a little later, I felt that you did like me personally. I don't know how justified I was, but I did feel that.

Th. You mean that I was in love with you?

Pt. Not that you were in love with me, but that you were attracted to me, that you did like me. But of course, again I said that maybe I was so keyed up, I thought maybe I had sort of colored it, which was unusual for me, because I have never in all my life responded to any man or made the first steps without his feeling a great interest in me. I have never, so that if it was so, it was different than it had ever been, because that was never so before. I have never made the first move or picked someone and said I liked him and want to know him, and I'd like to be in love with him. I never felt that way.

Th. It was always as a result of somebody else's actions first.

Pt. Of somebody radiating more than the usual amount of interest. So that I felt that it was different and I was rarely wrong, I mean, I was always right, but, of course, as I say, I was in a different state of mind than I am today. I am much calmer, probably see things a little clearer. So that I felt that you didn't love me, and I hoped that you didn't. In a way I wanted it, and yet I realized that I hoped you didn't because I might respond. I just felt it was wrong, because you were the wrong person, because you are my doctor. So find somebody else I said to myself. (*laughs*) As a matter of fact a very funny thing happened. I ran into my uncle who referred me to you shortly after first starting with you. I was beginning to feel that way about you, and I was curious about you. I met him in a restaurant. We talked for a few minutes. He asked me how I was getting along. I said I was making progress. He asked me how I liked you, and I said very much indeed, you were grand. He said he thought so too. You were practical, and he recommended you because he thought you would be what I needed. So I said, "Is he married?" And I was blushing. So he said, "He has an awfully nice wife and some lovely children." I realized then that probably I had radiated something that I hadn't intended to. I must have radiated some interest.

Th. Your reaction to me was one that occurs commonly in psychotherapy.

Pt. I realize this.

Th. Sometimes it's necessary to have such a reaction to get well.

Pt. That's the thing, that's the reason I bring it up.

Th. You might never get well if you didn't have a positive attitude toward me. That attitude we can use as a bridge to better relationships with men. There is a possibility that you may not find a man right away. There is a possibility of that, but at least you will know that it's not because of any block in you; it's not because you have no capacity to love.

Pt. Well, it's been, and I'll tell you it's been an amazing thing. I used to wonder at it myself, because I certainly am not cold. I used to wonder at myself because it didn't seem to concern me. I mean sex. That's the truth of it. But I'm getting myself interested now.

45

Supportive and Reeducative Techniques during Middle Treatment Phases

SUPPORTIVE APPROACHES ARE EMPLOYED DURING THE MIDDLE PHASES of treatment under the following conditions:

1. As a Principal Form of Therapy

a. Where the patient possesses a fairly well-integrated personality, but has temporarily collapsed under severe stress, a short period of palliative psychotherapy may suffice to bring the individual back to his habitual stability. Supportive techniques may also be efficacious where the problem has not yet been structuralized, as in behavior disorders in children.

b. Patients who require more intensive psychotherapy, but are temporarily too ill to utilize insight advantageously, may benefit from supportive approaches as emergency measures.

c. Supportive therapy is often mandatory in patients whose symptoms interfere drastically with proper functioning or constitute sources of danger to themselves and to others. Among such symptoms are severe depression, suicidal impulses, homicidal or destructive tendencies, panic reactions, compulsive acting-out of perverse sexual strivings, severe alcoholism, drug addiction, and disabling physical symptoms of psychologic origin.

d. Where motivation for extensive therapeutic goals is lacking, supportive treatment may prove sufficient, or may constitute a preparatory period for insight therapy.

e. Where the personality has been severely damaged during the formative years so that there is little on which to build, the objective may be to stabilize the individual through supportive measures. Some patients with severe infantile, dependent personality disorders, and with borderline and psychotic reactions, may be unable to tolerate the anxieties of insight therapy.

f. Supportive treatment may be indicated where the patient lacks adequate intelligence, or where the available time and finances are limited, or where there is extreme character rigidity, or where the personality is so constituted that the patient can respond only to commanding authoritative injunctions. Even though manifest neurotic difficulties continue in force following therapy, life may become more tolerable and the individual may adopt a more constructive attitude toward reality.

2. As an Adjunctive Form of Treatment During Insight Therapy

a. Where the coping resources of the ego are failing, as evidenced in feelings of extreme helplessness, severe depression, intense anxiety, and disabling psychosomatic symptoms, extension of support is usually necessary.

b. In cases where the environment is grossly disturbed so as to impede progress, supportive techniques like environmental manipulation may be required.

MODE OF ACTION OF SUPPORTIVE THERAPY

Supportive therapy owes its efficacy to a number of factors:

1. A correction or modification of a disturbed environment or other stress source may restore the weakened ego to its former stability.

2. The improved situation that results may permit the individual to exact gratifications essential to his well-being.

3. The patient may fulfill, in the supportive relationship with the therapist, important interpersonal needs, the deprivation of which has created tension. The supplying of emotional needs in the relationship constitutes what is sometimes known as "transference cure." For instance, the patient, feeling helpless, may desire the protection and security of a stronger individual on whom he may become dependent. Finding this with the therapist, he feels the comfort akin to a child who is being cared for by a loving and powerful parental agency. This relieves him of responsibility and fills him with a sense of comfort and security.

4. In the medium of the therapeutic situation, the patient may verbalize freely and gain a cathartic release for his fears, guilt feelings, damaging memories and misconceptions which he has suppressed or repressed, having no opportunity for such discharge in his customary life setting. The draining off of tension, that has been converted into symptoms, produces a surge of relief and usually a temporary abatement of symptomatic complaints.

5. The patient may rebuild shattered old defenses, or erect new ones which serve to repress more effectively his offending conflicts. Supportive therapy is suppressive in nature, helping to keep conflicts from awareness or modifying one's attitudes toward the elements of conflict.

6. Under the protective aegis of the therapist, the patient is enabled to face and to master life problems that have hitherto baffled him. Greater capacity to deal with these problems not only helps to rectify current sources of stress, but also gives the patient confidence in his ability to adjust to other aspects of his environment. The resultant expansion of security may eliminate the patient's need to exploit certain inadequate defense mechanisms.

7. There may be an alleviation of guilt and fear through reassurance, or through prohibitions and restrictions which, imposed by the therapist, are interpreted as necessary disciplines by the patient.

8. Certain measures, like hydrotherapy, drugs, and relaxing exercises may remove tension or moderate its effects.

9. An outlet for excessive energy and tension may be supplied through prescribed physical exercises, hobbies, recreations and occupational therapy.

THE THERAPIST-PATIENT RELATIONSHIP IN SUPPORTIVE THERAPY

The different techniques employed in supportive therapy presuppose a relationship of therapist to patient that varies from strong directiveness, to a more passive permissiveness. In most cases the relationship is essentially authoritarian.

Success in treatment is associated with acceptance of the therapist as a wise or benevolent authority. A consistent effort is made to establish and maintain a positive relationship. Because inimical attitudes oppose the incorporation of therapeutic suggestions, it is essential to try to avoid a negative transference. Hostilities are therefore dissipated as soon as they arise, and an attempt is made to win the patient over to a conviction that the therapist is a helpful friend. Whenever the patient manifests any other irrational attitudes in the relationship, therapy is focused on discussion and clarification of the latter; the patient is brought back to a reality level in an attempt to restore the original rapport. This may be difficult in some cases, since the patient will always try to involve the therapist in his neurotic structure. Much skill may be required to halt transference as soon as it starts developing; but unless this is done, the therapist may find himself in the midst of resistance he is unable to control.

Forcefulness of personality, and an ability to inspire confidence are important qualities in the therapist. The ideal attitude toward the patient is that of a sympathetic, kindly, but firm authority. The therapist must be constituted so as neither to derive sadistic pleasure from the patient's submission, nor to resent the latter's display of aggression or hostility. He must not succumb to blandishments of praise or admiration. A non-condemning, accepting attitude, shorn of blame or contempt, secures best results. The neurotic individual may, of course, display impulses and attitudes which can incite pique; but if the therapist is incapable of controlling his resentment, he will probably be unable to do productive work with the patient. His irritation cannot usually be concealed by a judicious choice of words.

The attitudes of the therapist are important because many of the patient's responses have been conditioned by the reactions of other people. At the start of therapy, the patient will expect the continuance of rejection or condemnation if he has encountered these reactions habitually. When such responses do not appear even with provocation, the patient's attitude toward the therapist will assume a quality significantly different from his other relationships. He will begin to feel accepted as he is, and warmth toward the therapist will develop which paves the way for constructive therapeutic work. The patient may then recognize the therapist as an ally with whom he can identify and whose standards and values he may incorporate. Unity with the therapist gives him strength to abandon some of his customary maladaptive patterns.

There are therapists who attempt, in a supportive framework, to deal boldly with pathogenic conflicts by manipulating the therapeutic relationship. Here the therapist deliberately plays a role with the patient in order to reinforce or subdue the parental image, or to introduce himself as an idealized parental substitute. Transference responses are deliberately cultivated by employing permissiveness or by enforcing prohibitions graded to a desired effect. Thus, acting as a "good" parental figure is considered helpful with patients who need an accepting "giving" situation. Deprived in childhood of a good, understanding maternal relationship, certain patients are presumed to require a living-through with another human being of an experience in which they are protected and loved without stint. Another role assumed by the therapist is that of a commanding, stern authoritarian figure. This is believed to be helpful in patients whose superegos are relatively undeveloped.

Sometimes role-playing procedures are implemented on the theory that it is essential for the patient to live through with the therapist emotional incidents identical in type with the traumatizing experiences of his childhood. Only by dramatizing his problems, it is alleged, can the patient be prodded out of the rigid and circumscribed patterns through which he avoids coming to grips with life. In order to mobilize activity and to release inner drives, the therapist attempts to create a relationship that is charged with tension. The ensuing struggle between patient and therapist is said to catalyze the breaking down of the neurosis.

One may rightfully criticize this technique on the grounds that the patient actually experiences frustration as a direct result of the therapeutic situation. His hostility may thus be justified. The tension and hostility that are mobilized may eventually become sufficiently intense to break through repression, with an acting-out of impulses; however, this may be destructive to the patient and to the therapeutic relationship.

A misdirected positive use of role-playing is also to be impugned. Even though open demonstrations of affection may seem logical in making the patient feel loved and lovable, such gestures are usually ineffective because of the patient's ambivalence. Love is so fused with hate that the patient may completely misinterpret affectionate tokens. This does not mean that the therapist must be cold and withdrawn, for a refrigerated attitude will even more drastically reinforce the patient's feelings of rejection.

GUIDANCE

In the supportive technique of guidance, the therapist acts as a guide or mentor, helping the patient to evolve better ways of adjusting to the reality situation. Therapeutic interviews are focused around immediate situational problems. While the therapist may formulate in his own mind an hypothesis of the operative dynamics, he does not interpret this to the patient unless the dynamics are clearly manifest, and the interpretations stand a chance of being accepted by the patient without too great resistance. The employment of guidance requires that the therapist encourage the patient toward a better understanding and evaluation of his situation, toward a recognition of measures that will correct his difficulty, and toward the taking of active steps in effectuating a proposed plan. Generally, the patient is required to make his own choices, although the therapist may clarify issues, outline the problem more succinctly, present operational possibilities, suggest available resources, and prompt the patient to action. Reassurance is utilized in proportion to the existing need, while as much responsibility is put on the patient as he can take.

Guidance suggestions must always be made in such a manner that the patient accepts them as the most expedient and logical course of action. It may be essential to spend some time explaining the rationale of a tendered plan until the patient develops a conviction that he really wishes to execute it. In this choice the patient should always be led to feel that his wishes and resistances will be respected by the therapist.

There are, however, a few patients whose personalities are so constituted that they resent a kindly and understanding authority. Rather they are inclined to demand a scolding and commanding attitude without which they seem lost. Such patients appear to need a punitive reinforcement of their conscience out of fear of yielding to inner impulses over which they have little control. At the start of therapy, it may sometimes be advisable to respect the needs and demands of such personalities, but an effort must always be made later on to transfer the disciplinary restraints to the individual himself. Unless such an incorporation of prohibitions is achieved and becomes an integral part of the individual's conscience, he will demand a greater and greater display of punitive efforts on the part of the therapist. To complicate this, when he has responded to dictatorial demands, he will burn inwardly with resentment and hate for the therapist, and he will feel a tremendous contempt for himself for being so weak as to need authoritative pressure.

One way of conducting the guidance interview is to try to avoid, as much as possible, the giving of direct advice. Rather, the therapist may couch ideas and suggestions in a way that the patient participates in the making of decisions. Furthermore, advice should be proffered in a non-dictatorial manner, so that the patient feels he may accept or reject it in accordance with his own judgment.

The sicker the individual, the more he will need active guidance and direction. How long the supportive relationship will have to be maintained will depend on the strength of the patient's ego. Usually, as the patient gains security and freedom from symptoms, he will want to take more and more responsibility for his own destiny. Even those persons who offer resistance to assertiveness and independence, may be aided in developing incentive toward greater independence. This may require considerable time and patience, but in most instances such constructive motivation can be achieved.

ENVIRONMENTAL MANIPULATION

There is current a tendency to depreciate the value of environmental manipulation on the basis of its superficiality and its temporary effect. Nevertheless, correction of environmental disturbances is indispensable in certain cases. For one thing, the relief the patient experiences through manipulative measures may bring comfort to him and otherwise positively influence his total adjustment.

Conditions for which environmental manipulation may be required are the following:

1. *Economic situation.*
   a. Location of resources for financial aid.
   b. Budgeting and managing of income.
   c. Home planning and home economics.
2. *Work situation.*
   a. Testing for vocational interests and aptitudes. (Referral to a clinical psychologist may be required.)
   b. Vocational guidance and vocational rehabilitation. (Referral to a clinical psychologist or rehabilitation resource may be required.)
3. *Housing situation.*
   a. Locating new quarters.
   b. Adjusting to present housing situation.
4. *Neighborhood situation.*
   a. Moving to a new neighborhood.
   b. Locating and utilizing neighborhood social, recreational or educational resources.
   c. Adjusting to present neighborhood.
5. *Cultural standards.*
   a. Interpreting meaning of current cultural patterns.
   b. Clarifying personal standards that do not conform with community standards.
   c. Clarifying legality of actions.
6. *Family and other interpersonal relations.*
   a. Consulting with parents, siblings, relatives, mate, child or friend of patient.
   b. Promoting education in such matters as sexual relations, child rearing and parenthood.
   c. Helping in the selection of a nursery school, grade school, camp, or of recreational facilities for the patient's children.
   d. Referring patient to legal resources in critical family or interpersonal situations.
7. *Daily habits, recreations and routines.*
   a. Referring patient to resources for correction of defects in dress, personal hygiene and grooming.
   b. Referring patient to appropriate recreational, social and hobby resources.
8. *Health.*
   a. Clarifying health problems to patient or relative.
   b. Referring patient to hospital or institution.

    c. Referring patient to resources for correction of remediable physical disabilities.

The therapist may have to interfere actively where the environmental situation is grossly inimical to the best interests of the patient. This usually implies work with the patient's family, since it is rare that a patient's difficulties are limited to himself. Various family members may require psychotherapy before the patient shows a maximal response to treatment. Indeed, the cooperation of the family is not only desirable, but in many instances unavoidable. A psychiatric social worker can render invaluable service to the therapist here.

EXTERNALIZATION OF INTERESTS

The turning of the patient's interests away from himself may be considered important as part of a supportive program. Hobbies, occupational therapy and recreational activities may be exploited here.

A most effective hobby is one that provides an acceptable outlet for impulses the person cannot express directly. The need to experience companionship, to give and to receive affection, to be part of a group, to gain recognition, to live up to certain creative abilities, and to develop latent talents may be satisfied by an absorbing hobby interest.

External activities can provide compensations which help the individual to allay some of his inferiority feelings. Instead of concentrating on his failings, he is encouraged to develop whatever talents and abilities he possesses. For instance, if he is proficient as a tennis player, or has a good singing voice, these aptitudes are encouraged so that the patient feels he excels in one particular field. Whatever assets the individual has may thus be promoted.

Some patients harbor within themselves strong hostilities of an unconscious nature, with needs to vanquish, defeat and to overwhelm others. Hostility may have to be repressed as a result of fear of retaliatory rejection or punishment. Sometimes even ordinary forms of self-assertiveness may be regarded as aggression. As a consequence, the person may have to lead a life of detachment in order to avoid giving expression to what he considers forbidden impulses. In such patients, hobbies that do not involve competition will be most acceptable, at first. The ultimate object is to interest the patient in a hobby that has some competitive element. The patient may come around to this himself. For example, one patient chose photography as an outlet principally because it involved no contact with other people. Gradually, as he became more expert, he exhibited his work to his friends, and, finally, he entered his pictures in various photographic contests. Later on, with encouragement, he learned to play bridge, which acted as a spur to an interest in active competitive games and sports.

The ability to express hostility through activities that involve the larger muscle groups permits of a most effective expression of unconscious aggression. Boxing, wrestling, hunting, archery, marksmanship, fencing, and such work as carpentry and stone building can burn up a tremendous amount of energy. In some individuals the mere attendance at games and competitive sports as baseball, football and boxing has an aggression-releasing effect. It must be remembered, however, that this release is merely palliative, because it does not touch upon the dynamic difficulties in the life adjustment of the person that are responsible for the generation of hostility.

Many other impulses may be satisfied through occupational or diversional activities. Hobbies may foster a sense of achievement and can help the individual to satisfy a need for approval. Energy resulting from inhibited sexual strivings may gain expression sometimes in an interest in pets or naturalistic studies. Frustrated parental yearnings may be appeased by work with children at children's clubs or camps.

One must expect that the patient will try to employ his hobbies as a means of reinforcing the neurotic patterns by which he adjusts to life. If he has a character structure of perfectionism, he will pursue his hobby with the goal of mastering intricate details. If he is compulsively ambitious, he will strive to use his interest as a way to fame or fortune. The same holds true for any of the other character traits he may possess.

Most patients gain temporary surcease from neurotic difficulties during the period when they are working at a new interest; however, their illness will become exacerbated when the hobby has failed to come up to their expectations. In spite of this, the diversion may open up avenues for contact with others which will neutralize this tendency.

Neurotic difficulties are often associated with disturbances that cause the individual to isolate himself from the group. The pleasures he derives from social activities do not compensate him for the tensions and anxieties incurred in his mingling with people. Occupational therapy, hobbies and recreations give the person an opportunity to participate with others in a project of mutual enjoyment. Pleasure feelings radiate to those with whom the patient is related, and help lessen his defenses against people. They may even lead him to find values in a group.

Once the patient has established a group contact, he may find sufficient pleasures to sustain his interest. It is to be expected, nevertheless, that he will manifest his customary withdrawal defenses. But the benefits he derives from the group may more than make up for his discomfiture.

In some instances, it may be possible to convince the patient to engage in activities or work that contribute to the general welfare of the community. This can create in him a feeling of active participation with others, and a conviction that he is doing something that is really altruistic.

REASSURANCE

Some reassurance may be necessary at certain phases of psychotherapy. This is sometimes given in verbal form; more commonly it is indicated through non-verbal behavior, as by maintenance of a calm and objective attitude.

Verbal reassurance, when used, should not be started too early, since the patient at first may not have sufficient faith in the therapist to be convinced of his sincerity. He may imagine that the therapist is secretly ridiculing him, that he does not know how serious the situation really is, or that he is merely delivering therapeutic doses of solace without deep conviction.

In practicing reassurance, the therapist must listen to the patient with sincerity and respect, pointing out that his difficulties may perhaps seem overwhelming because they represent much more than appears on the surface. Under no circumstances should the patient be disparaged for illogical fears. He usually appreciates that his worries are senseless, but he is unable to control them.

One of the most common fears expressed by the neurotic person is that of going insane. Panicky feelings, bizarre impulses and a sense of unreality lead him to this assumption. He becomes convinced that he will lose control and perhaps inflict injury on himself or others. He may attempt to justify his fear of insanity by revealing that he has a relative who was insane, from whom he believes he has inherited a taint. It is essential to show him that fear of insanity is a common neurotic symptom, and to acquaint him with the fact that there is scarcely a family in which one cannot find cases of mental illness. A presentation may be made of the facts of heredity, with an explanation that insanity is not inevitable even in families that have a history of mental illness. He may be furthermore reassured that his examination fails to reveal evidence of insanity.

Another ubiquitous fear relates to the possession of a grave physical disease or abnormality. The patient may believe that through masturbation, physical excesses or faulty hygiene, he has procured some irremediable illness. A physical examination with x-ray and laboratory tests should be prescribed, even though negative findings may not convince the patient that his fear is founded on emotional factors. Assurance may be given the patient that anxiety and worry can produce physical symptoms of a reversible nature. Where his fears are not too integral a part of the patient's neurosis, these explanations may suffice. Even where fears are deep, as in obsessional patients, and where he does not accept the results of the physical examination, his more rational self will toy with the idea that he may be wrong. At any rate, the absence of manifest physical illness will give the therapist the opportunity to demonstrate to the patient that his problem is not really just a physical one, and that feelings of being ill or damaged may serve an important psychologic function.

Masturbatory fears are often deep-seated and operate outside the awareness of the person. The patient may, through reading and discussions with enlightened people, rationalize his fears, or he may conceal them under an intellectual coating. Either because of actual threats on the part of early authorities, or through his own faulty deductions, he may believe that his past indulgences have injured him irreparably. He may shy away from masturbatory practices in the present or else engage in them with conscious or unconscious foreboding. Assurance that he has misinterpreted the supposedly evil effects of masturbation, coupled with assigned reading of books which present scientific facts on the subject, have remarkably little effect on the patient's qualms. He is unable to rid himself of childish misapprehensions that seem invulnerable to reason. Nevertheless, the therapist's point of view should be presented in a sincere and forthright manner, with the statement that the patient, for emotional reasons, may not now be able to accept the explanation. Eventually, as he realizes the depth of his fears, he may be able to understand how victimized he has been all his life by faulty ideas about masturbation absorbed during his childhood.

Reassurance may also be needed in regard to other aspects of the individual's sexual life. Frigidity, for instance, is the concern of many women who often expect that it will disappear automatically with marriage. Projecting their disappointment, some women tend to blame their mates for their sexual incompetence. In therapy this misconception will have to be carefully clarified with a focusing on guilt and other provocative conflicts.

In men, reassurance may be required in conditions of temporary impotence. Many males are excessively concerned with their sexual powers, and have exorbitant expectations of themselves in so far as sexual performance is concerned. Discussions may be organized around the theme that episodes of impotence are quite natural in the lives of most men. Temporary feelings of resentment toward a marital partner, or attempts at intercourse during a state of exhaustion, or without any real desire, will normally inhibit the erective ability. On the basis of several such failures in performance, the individual may become panicky, and his sense of tension may then interfere with proper sexual performance thereafter. The patient may be shown the necessity for a different attitude toward sex, treating it less as a means of performance, and more as a pleasure pursuit. Reassurance that his impotence is temporary and will rectify itself with the proper attitude may suffice to restore adequate functioning.

Another concern shown by patients is that of homosexuality. Fears of homosexuality may be overwhelming. It is helpful sometimes to reassure the patient regarding homosexual fears or impulses with which he happens to be concerned. Elucidation that a liking for people of the same sex may occasionally be associated with sexual inclinations toward them, that this impulse is not a sign that one is evil or depraved, and that it need not be yielded to, may be extremely reassuring. An effort may be made to explain how, in the development of a child, sexual curiosities and sex play are universal and may lead to homosexual explorations. Usually this interest is later transferred to members of the opposite sex, but, in some persons, for certain reasons, an arrest in development occurs. The patient may be informed that homosexuality represents a basic attitude toward people as part of a neurotic problem, and that it need not be considered any more significant than any other problem which requires psychiatric treatment.

Reassurance is often necessary in the event of infidelity of one's marital partner. Where a woman is extremely upset because her husband has been unfaithful to her, she may feel not only a threat to her security, but more importantly, she experiences a shattering of self-esteem. The therapist may affirm that infidelity on the part of one's marital partner is indeed hard to bear, but that it is far from a unique experience in our culture. She must be urged not to be stampeded into a rash divorce simply because she feels outraged. It is natural that knowledge of her husband's infidelity should have filled her with indignation, but in her own interest, she must not act precipitously. She may find herself encouraged by friends, family and public opinion to hate her husband and to cut herself off from him. There are few women who can resist acting dramatically and precipitating a divorce over an affair that is in all probability quite insignificant. Such reassurance may convince the woman that she really does not desire a divorce, but that she can work out a better relationship with her husband and perhaps discover why they had drifted apart.

One use of reassurance that is practiced by some therapists is helping the process of ego building. Patients become so preoccupied with their troubles and pain that they are apt to lose sight of the constructive aspects of their personality. They may, consequently, minimize their good points or be unaware of them. The therapist here selects aspects of the individual's life adjustment and personality that the patient may underestimate. Positive qualities of the patient may be indicated with emphasis on how these have been sabotaged by the patient's neurosis.

Direct reassurance in response to inferiority feelings, however, is generally futile. One of the most common symptoms of neurosis is devaluated self-esteem which fosters inhibitions in action, perfectionistic strivings, and feelings of worthlessness, inadequacy and self-condemnation. Any attempt here to inflate the patient's ego by reassurance accomplishes little.

Self-devaluation may be a symptom that serves a useful purpose for the patient, protecting him from having to live up to the expectations of other people or of his own ego ideal. Rebuilding his self-esteem by reassurance, therefore, threatens to remove an important coping mechanism. Many persons who devaluate themselves insidiously do penance for forbidden strivings and desires. Reassurance here may actually plunge the person into anxiety.

Apart from the instances mentioned, reassurance is not too commonly employed even in supportive therapy. It can, however, serve a useful purpose where indicated. Where the patient has sufficient ego resources, reassurance even though necessary should be tempered, the patient being apprised that responsibility for investigating his patterns has to be borne by himself. If this precaution is not taken, the patient will lose initiative in getting at the source of his difficulties, and he will tend to seek more and more reassurance from the therapist.

PERSUASION

Persuasive techniques are sometimes helpful as supportive measures, particularly in obsessive-compulsive personalities. The object is to master conflict by forces of will power, self-control and powers of reasoning.

Persuasive suggestions have arbitrarily been subdivided into several categories. They represent a point of view and a slant on life which may not always be accurate, but which, if accepted by the patient, may help alleviate his distress. In general, suggestions tend toward a redirection of goals, an overcoming of physical suffering and disease, a dissipation of the "worry habit," "thought control" and "emotion control," a correcting of tension and fear, and a facing of adversity. These suggestions are superficial, but their pursuit is considered justified by some therapists as a means of helping the patient control his symptoms. The following suggestions are a summary of a number of different "systems" of persuasion:

1. Redirection of Goals

If the patient's goals in life are obviously distorted, he is instructed that the most important aim in living is inner peace rather than fame, fortune or any other expedient that might be confused with real happiness. In order to gain serenity, he may have to abandon hopes of becoming rich, famous or successful. He may be causing himself much harm by being overambitious. If he is content to give up certain ambitions, and to make his objective in life that of mental serenity and enjoyment, he should try living on a more simple scale. He should give up struggling for success. Health and freedom from suffering are well worth this sacrifice.

One can attain happiness and health by learning to live life as it should be lived, by taking the good with the bad, the moments of joy with the episodes of pain. One must expect hard knocks from life and learn to steel himself against them. It is always best to avoid fearsome anticipations of what might happen in the future. Rather one should strive for a freer, more spontaneous existence in the present. One should take advantage of the experiences of the moment, and live for every bit of pleasure he can get out of each day. The place to enjoy life is here. The time is now. By being happy oneself, one can also make others happy.

It is profitable to concern oneself with the problems of other people. Many persons who have suffered pain, disappointment and frustration have helped themselves by throwing their personal interests aside and living to make others happy. Man is a social creature and needs to give to others, even if he must force himself to do so. Thus, he can take a little time out each day to talk to his neighbors, to do little things for them. He can seek out a person who is in misery and encourage him to face life. In giving he will feel a unity with people.

The person may be enjoined to avoid the acting-out of a sense of despair. One of the pitfalls into which most "nervous" people fall is a hopeless feeling that paralyzes any constructive efforts. One must not permit himself to yield to feelings of hopelessness, for life is always forward-moving. Hopelessness and despair are a negation of life. If a person stops holding himself back, he will automatically go forward; since development and growth are essential parts of the life process.

2. Overcoming Physical Suffering and Disease

The patient, if he is suffering from ailments of a physical nature, may be told that physical symptoms are very frequently caused by emotional distress. Studies have shown that painful thoughts can affect the entire body through the autonomic nervous system. For instance, if we observe an individual's intestines by means of a fluoroscope, we can see that when the person thinks fearful or painful thoughts, the stomach and intestines contract, interfering with digestion. On the other hand, peaceful, happy thoughts produce a relaxation of the intestines and a restoration of peristaltic movements, thus facilitating digestion. The same holds true for other organs.

Understanding the powerful effect that the mind has over the body lucidly demonstrates that physical suffering can be mastered by a change in attitudes. By directing one's thoughts along constructive lines, by keeping before the mind's eye visions of peace and health, a great many persons who have been handicapped by physical ailments, and by even incurable diseases, have conquered their suffering and even have outlived healthy people. This is because a healthy mind fosters a healthy body and can neutralize many effects of a disabling malady.

Physical aches and pains, and even physical disease, may be produced by misguided thoughts and emotions. The body organs and the mind are a unity; they mutually interact. Physical illness can influence the mind, producing depression, confusion and disturbed thought processes. On the other hand, the psyche can also influence the body, causing an assortment of ailments. In the latter instance, the institution of proper thought habits can dispel physical distress.

It is natural for a person who is suffering from physical symptoms to imagine that there is something organically wrong with him. He cannot be blamed if he seeks the traditional kinds of relief. But palliation is not found in medicines or operations. Relief is found in determining the cause of his trouble and correcting the cause. Worry, tension and dissatisfaction are causes for many physical complaints, the treatment here lies in abolishing destructive thoughts.

The first step in getting relief from physical suffering is to convince oneself that one's troubles are not necessarily organic. The difficulties may lie in one's environment, but usually they are due to improper thinking habits. If there is a remediable environmental factor, this must, of course, be remedied. Where it cannot be altered, the person must learn to change himself so that he can live comfortably in his difficult environment. In the latter case, he has to reorganize his patterns of thinking.

Where a patient actually has an organic ailment that is not amenable to medical or surgical correction, an attempt may be made to get the patient to accept the illness, but to change his attitude toward it. It is essential to help the patient reorganize his philosophy so that he can find satisfactions in life consistent with his limited capacities.

In physical conditions of a progressive nature, such as coronary thrombosis, cancer or malignant hypertension, the patient may be in a constant state of anxiety, anticipating death at any moment. Here it is wise to emphasize the fact that death is as much a part of living as is life, and that the horrors attached to it are those that come from a misinterpretation of nature. Life must go on. Babies are born, and people pass on to a peaceful sleep that is death. The chances are that the patient still has a long useful life ahead of him that can be prolonged by adopting a proper attitude toward his condition. If suffering and pain do not exist, this should be pointed out as a fortunate occurrence. The person should think about the present, and avoid dwelling too much on the future. No one can anticipate what the future may bring. Accidents can happen to anyone, and even a young person in the best of health does not know when he will be smitten by an illness or accident. The only rational philosophy is to glean whatever pleasure one can from the moment, and to leave the future to take care of itself.

The patient is encouraged to develop hobbies and to engage in activities that will divert his thinking from himself. A list of diversions that the patient can pursue may be prepared, and the patient guided into adopting new interests.

3. Dissipating the "Worry Habit"

Patients who are obsessed with worrying about themselves may be urged to remember that much energy is expended ruminating about one's problems and fears, instead of doing something positive about a solution. Worry tends to magnify the importance of petty difficulties; it usually paralyzes initiative. The worrier is constantly preoccupied with ideas of fear, dread and morbid unpleasantness. These thoughts have a disastrous effect on the motor system, the glands and the organs.

In order to overcome the "worry habit" it is first necessary to formulate in one's mind the chief problem with which one is concerned. To do this it will be necessary to push apprehensions boldly aside. In a seemingly insurmountable problem, one should attempt to reformulate the situation to bring clearly to mind the existing difficulty. If one is honest with himself, he will realize that he has spent most of his energy in hopeless despair, in anxiety, or in resentful frustration, rather than in logical and unemotional thinking that can bring about tranquility.

First, it is necessary to review all possible answers to the problem at hand. Next, the best solution is chosen, even though this may seem inadequate in coping with all aspects of the problem. A plan of action must then be decided on. It is necessary to proceed with this design immediately, and to abandon all worry until the plan is carried out as completely as possible. Above all the person must stick to his project, even if he finds it distasteful.

If the person himself cannot formulate a scheme, the therapist may help him to do so. The patient should be told that it is better to concern himself with a constructive plan than to get tangled up in the hopelessness of an apparently insoluble problem. Until he can work out something better, it is best to adjust himself to the present situation, striving always to externalize his energy in a constructive way.

The patient may be urged to stop thinking painful thoughts. He may be told that forgetting is a process that goes on of its own accord if one does not interfere with it. Worry is a process that has been learned. One can therefore help himself by controlling his thoughts and avoiding painful ideas. If action is impossible for the moment, one can try to crowd out apprehensions by simply resolving to stop worrying.

Discussing painful topics with other people should also be avoided. If he must ventilate disturbing feelings, he can do so with the therapist. "Blowing off steam" and relating his troubles to friends often does more harm than good because the suggestions offered are usually unsound. It is better to underestimate his difficulties than to become too emotional about them. It is also necessary for him to ask his friends and relatives to stop talking about his personal problems, if such discussions are aggravating. It is understandable that people close to him will be much concerned with his illness, but they must be reminded that their solicitude may aggravate his condition. Often a person can forestall trouble by insisting that he feels "fine" when questioned by others about his health.

4. "Thought Control" and "Emotion Control"

Patients who seem to be at the mercy of painful thoughts and emotions may be enjoined never to permit their minds to wander like flotsam, yielding to every passing thought and emotion. It is necessary to try to choose deliberately the kinds of thoughts to think, and the kinds of emotions to feel. It is essential to eschew ruminating about resentments, hatreds and disappointments, about "aches and pains," and misery in general.

One must think thoughts that nourish the ego and permit it to expand to a better growth. If a person wants to be big in spirit, if he wants to be without pain, he must fill his mind with painless ideas. If he wants to be happy, he must smile. If he wants to be well, he must act as if he *were* well. He must straighten his shoulders, walk more resolutely, talk with energy and verve. He must face the world with confidence. He must look life in the face and never falter. He must stand up to adversity and glory in the struggle. He must never permit himself to sink into the quagmire of helplessness or give himself up to random worries, thus feeling sorry for himself. He must replace thoughts of doubt and fear with those of courage and confidence. He must think firmly of how he can accomplish the most in life, with whatever resources he has. He must feel those emotions that lead to inner harmony.

He must picture himself as above petty recriminations, avoiding the centering of his interest around himself. Even if he suffers from pain and unhappiness, he must stop thinking about his daily discomforts. He must give to others and learn to find comfort in the joys of giving. He must become self-reliant and creative. Emancipation from tension and fear can come by training one's mind to think joyous and peaceful thoughts. But new thought habits do not come immediately. One must show persistence and be steadfast in one's application. One must never permit himself to be discouraged. One must practice, more and more. Only through persistent practice can perfection be obtained, so that the mind shuts out painful thoughts automatically.

It is not necessary to force oneself impetuously to stop worrying or feeling pain. Will power used this way will not crowd out the painful emotions. One must instead substitute different thoughts or more appropriate actions. If one starts feeling unhappy or depressed, he should determine to rise above this emotion. He should talk cheerfully to others, try to do someone a good turn; or he may lie down for a short while, relax his body and then practice thinking about something peaceful and pleasant. As soon as this occurs, unhappy thoughts will be eradicated. A good practice is to think of a period in one's life when one was happiest. This may have been in the immediate past or during childhood. One may think of people he knew, the pleasant times he had with them. This substitution of pleasant for unpleasant thoughts may take several weeks before new thinking habits eventuate.

5. Correcting Tension and Fear

Where undifferentiated tension and fear exist, the patient may be told that difficulties may come from without, but that one's reactions to these difficulties are purely personal and come from within. By changing these reactions, he can avoid many of the consequences of stress. If one is confronted with tension, anxiety or feelings of inner restlessness, it is best to start analyzing the causes. Are these emotions due to disappointment or failure? Or are they the product of a sense of hopelessness? Once the cause is found, it is necessary to face the facts squarely and take corrective steps. It is urgent to plan a course to follow and to execute this immediately. If facts cannot be altered, one must change his attitudes toward them. It is essential to stop thinking about the painful side of things, and to find instead something constructive on which to concentrate.

One may be unable to prevent anxious thoughts from coming into one's mind, but they can be prevented from staying there. The person must stop saying, "I can't," and think in terms of "I can." So long as one says, "I can't," he is defeated. Being resolute and persistent in saying "I can" will eventually bring results.

The first step in overcoming tension is to stop indulging oneself in self-pity. Tension will drag one's life down if not interrupted. It is necessary to learn to love life for the living. One must learn not to exaggerate troubles. One must let other people live *their* lives and one should live one's own.

Many people suffering from tension and fear have helped themselves by saying, "Go ahead and hurt all you want; you will not get me down." Fears are best faced by courageously admitting them. They can be conquered by stopping to fight them or by refraining from trying to master them by sheer will power. Acknowledging that one is afraid is the first step. Thereafter one must determine to rid himself of fear by developing the conviction that he will overcome it. A sense of humor is of unparalleled help here. If one laughs at his fears instead of cringing before them, he will not be helpless and at the mercy of forces he cannot control.

Practicing relaxation sometimes is useful. Each day a person may lie on his back, on the floor, or on a hard surface for twenty minutes, consciously loosening up every muscle from his forehead to his feet, even his fingers and toes. He may then start breathing deeply, with slow, deep exhalations through pursed lips. At the same time he may think of a peaceful scene at the mountains or seashore. Mental and muscular relaxation are of tremendous aid in overcoming states of tension.

6. Facing Adversity

In the event a patient has an irremediable environmental difficulty, he may be reminded that there are many dire conditions in one's environment that cannot be changed no matter how diligently one tries. Poor financial circumstances, an unstable mate, overactive youngsters who make noise and tax one's patience, a physical handicap, or an incurable physical illness can create a great deal of worry, tension and anxiety. It is not so much these difficult conditions that are important as it is the reaction of the person to them. Life is usually full of struggle; but the individual need not permit himself to get embroiled in the turmoil and misery of the world. There are many persons who are deformed, or deprived of sight, hearing, and of vital parts of their body, who live happily and courageously because they have learned to accept their limitations, and to follow the rule to live life as it is right now. There are many persons who, forced to exist under the most miserable conditions of poverty, with no resources or education, are not distressed by worry or nervousness because they have not yielded themselves to their emotions.

It is a human tendency to exaggerate one's plight. If one compares himself with many other people, however, he will discover that he is not so badly off. An individual may not be able to achieve all the ambitions he has in life. He may not be as intellectual as he wants to be, or as strong, or successful, or rich, or famous. He may have to earn a living at work he detests. As bad as he imagines his state to be, if he were to be faced with the possibility of changing places with some other persons, he would probably refuse to do so. He might be dissatisfied with his appearance, and he may long for features that would make him look more handsome and distinguished. If this were possible, he might instead find that his health had become impaired, or his intellect was not up to its present level.

It is necessary to make the most out of the little one has. Every person possesses weaknesses and must learn to live with them. He must pattern his life so as to make his weaknesses as little manifest as possible. He must expand all of his good qualities to the limit. One's facial appearance may not be handsome, but one may have nicer hair and teeth than many other people. These may be emphasized in hair style or proper facial expression. One can appear well-groomed with well-tailored clothing. If one's voice is good, he should cultivate it. In this way one may take advantage of every good feature he possesses.

Instead of resigning oneself to a sense of hopelessness, it is wise to turn one's mind toward creative activities and outlets. It will take much perseverance to conquer feelings of helplessness and frustration, but this can be done, particularly by living honestly and courageously. The wealthiest person is he who has not riches, but strength of spirit. If one is dissatisfied with himself, he may try to imagine himself as the kind of person he would like to be. He may then find that he can do these things that he has hitherto felt were impossible. He must never yield to despair or discouragement. Crippled persons have learned to walk by sheer perseverance of will. On the other hand, one should not set goals for oneself that are impossible of fulfillment. Thwarted ambition can give rise to bitterness and greed.

A sign of character is to change those conditions that can be remedied and to accept those that cannot be changed. To accomplish this one must face the problem squarely. What is to be done about a difficult situation? What can be done? How will one go about accomplishing the change? This calls for a plan of action which, once made, must be pursued diligently without discouragement.

There are always, of course, situations one must accept. Unalterable facts must be faced. If one cannot change things as they are, he can change his own attitude so that he will not overreact to his difficulties. As soon as a person has decided to make the best of things, his condition will improve immediately. If one is unable to possess the whole loaf, he must learn to content himself with part of a loaf. He must disregard minor discomforts, and pay less and less attention to them. His symptoms may be annoying, but they are not fatal. Keeping two written lists, outlining on one side the things that have troubled him, on the other side the things that have gone in his favor, will often convince the person, after a while, that the balance is on the positive side.

It is particularly important to train oneself to overcome the effects of frustration and disappointment. These may be expressed in the form of quarreling, or holding grudges against others, or by depression or physical symptoms. There are many dangers associated with permitting oneself to become too discouraged. It is best here to forestall despair before it develops, by adopting the attitude that one will not allow himself to get too upset if things go wrong. One must force himself to regard all adversity dispassionately, with the idea of modifying the cause if possible, or changing his point of view, if the cause cannot be removed.

The above persuasive suggestions do not represent a scientific point of view. However, their use is believed, especially by non-dynamically oriented therapists, to be consonant with a pragmatic approach to therapy in certain patients who do not respond well to insight approaches.

EMOTIONAL CATHARSIS AND DESENSITIZATION

Release of painful feelings and desensitization to their effects constitutes an important supportive technique. The patient is encouraged to talk about those things in his past life or in his present-day relationships that bother him most. His responsiveness will depend on the confidence and trust he has in the therapist.

The patient may be told that most people have bottled up within themselves memories and experiences which, though seemingly under control, continue to have a disturbing effect on them. The attempt to obliterate emotional experiences by banishing them from the mind is not ordinarily successful. Disturbing ideas keep obtruding themselves into the stream of thought. Even when will power triumphs and suppression succeeds, casual everyday happenings may remind the person of his conflict. In addition to memories, there are also impulses and desires of which the person is thoroughly ashamed, and which he dares not permit himself to think about. Among these are desires for extramarital sexual gratification, homosexual interests, hostile strivings and impulses of a fantastic and infantile nature.

Emotional catharsis must never be foisted on the patient. To force him to reveal inner fears of a traumatic nature prematurely, may cause him such panic that his resistance to further revelations will be increased. Actually, the patient has built up so hard a crust of repression that it keeps him from admitting his deepest fears even to himself. It is essential to let him feel his own way and choose his own pace with casual encouragement.

In continued discussions with the patient, it may be emphasized that every individual has difficulties and problems of which he is ashamed, that the patient probably is no exception and may have had experiences which make him feel he is wicked. Discussing the patient's problem in this roundabout way makes it possible for him to talk about his worries more openly. For instance, where it is obvious that the patient has a suppressed homosexual wish, the therapist may weave into the discussions the fact that every person, at certain times in life, develops friendships with and crushes on people of the same sex. This is by no means abnormal, but is merely a developmental phase in the life of the individual. Some persons, for certain reasons, continue to have ideas which were normal at an earlier phase of growth. As a matter of fact, most people have fears of homosexuality. The patient may be told that it would be unusual if he did not have such ideas at one time. He may then casually be asked whether or not this is so.

The ability of the patient to discuss his impulses, fears and experiences openly, without encountering condemnation, enables him to tolerate the implications of the suppressed material.

In the event the patient confesses to a truly reprehensible incident in his life, the ventilation of these facts may have to be followed by active reassurance. He may be reminded that the incidents he has revealed do not necessarily pollute him, that many persons are compelled, for neurotic reasons, to do things which they regret later, and that their subsequent actions can fully neutralize what they have done. The patient may be urged to spend his energy doing something positive in the present, rather than to wear himself out regretting the past. He may, if he desires, make some restitution to any person who has been injured by his act, or to society in general.

In cases where the individual has irrational feelings that issue out of his relationships with people, or where he has phobias, he may be repeatedly urged, for purposes of desensitization, to expose himself to those situations that incite painful emotions. His experiences are then subjected to discussion, and the patient is trained to face those situations gradually, without quaking. For instance, if the patient has a fear of closed spaces, he may be instructed to lock the door of his room for a brief instance for the first day, to increase the interval to the count of ten the next day, then to one-half minute, extending the time period daily, until he discovers through actual experience that he can tolerate the phobic situation. Other phobias may be treated in a similar way by varying the offered suggestions. The therapist must appreciate, of course, that the patient's fears may be rooted in deep unconscious conflicts and may not yield to such desensitization techniques until the sources of fear are uprooted through insight approaches.

MISCELLANEOUS SUPPORTIVE MEASURES

Relaxation exercises and massage may be prescribed for muscle tension, spasms, contractures and tremors, the patient being referred to a physiotherapist when this is necessary. Enforced rest is sometimes advised for fatigue and exhaustion in the form of a prolonged vacation or a sojourn in a rest home. Hydrotherapy is occasionally utilized for its sedative or stimulating effects. Insulin shock treatment may be necessary in schizophrenia; sub-coma insulin therapy is utilized in acute anxiety states, delirium tremens and confusional syndromes; electrical convulsive therapy is helpful in manic-depressive psychosis, involutional depression, severe psychoneurotic depression, and senile depression. Drug therapy is employed where indicated; for example, sedatives in excitement or insomnia, benzedrine in depression or listlessness, antabuse in alcoholism, and glandular products in endocrine disorders. Brain surgery, especially transorbital lobotomy, is used as a last resort in severe, intractable schizophrenia, chronic disabling obsessive-compulsive neurosis and hypochondriasis. Inspirational or social group therapy is often helpful where patients require a group experience and social contacts.

SUPPORTIVE MEASURES IN INSIGHT THERAPY

Supportive measures during insight therapy must be employed cautiously, because the patient may invest the therapist with directive, authoritarian qualities that interfere with a good working relationship. Moreover, alleviation of symptoms and suffering may remove a most important motivation for continued treatment.

There are, nevertheless, certain circumstances under which support is necessary. The challenging of one's defenses exposes basic conflicts and may revive the early anxieties that inspired them. A period of some instability and turmoil is to be expected during the course of insight therapy, and the therapist may, where the reactions are severe, temporarily have to assume the role of a helping authority.

The specific kinds of supportive measures implemented will vary according to the patient's needs. Where severe environmental disturbance exists, the therapist may suggest available resources that hold forth promise of mediation. He may also aid the patient in resolving resistances toward utilizing the prescribed resources effectively. Active reassurance may be dispensed where the patient harbors gross misconceptions or where there is a threat of a dangerous shattering of the ego. There may be a cautious extension of advice when the patient is thoughtlessly embarking on a potentially destructive course of action. Encouragement may sometimes be voiced when the patient does a significant job in thinking through a problem, or in effectuating insight into action.

The degree of emotional support employed will depend upon the strength of the patient's ego. A withholding of support by the therapist, when the patient actually needs it, may be harmful. On the other hand, excessive support may interfere with assertiveness and activity. The person's reactions to support will depend on its symbolic meaning to him. The most common response is an abatement of symptoms and a cessation of anxiety. Occasionally, however, anxiety breaks out due to fears of being overwhelmed and mutilated in a protective relationship. This emotion will have to be handled promptly, should it emerge.

REEDUCATIVE APPROACHES

In insight therapy with reeducative goals, the investigation of the dynamics of the individual's disturbed patterns of adjustment is conducted by means of the focused interview. Prime consideration is given to present problems and current interpersonal relationships. Dreams, fantasies and early childhood experiences are of secondary importance. The couch is usually avoided; instead, interviewing is conducted in the sitting-up, face-to-face position. The frequency of visits is generally from one to two times weekly. The relationship is maintained on a positive level, transference being minimized as much as possible, or, when it develops, being handled immediately to avoid its operation as resistance.

An attempt is made in reeducative therapy to rehabilitate the individual as rapidly as possible by discovering and modifying factors that provoked the emotional illness, by assaying the patient's assets and liabilities, and by mobilizing all of the available positive forces of his personality. In the medium of a warm relationship with the therapist, the patient is brought to an awareness of interpersonal conflicts that have contaminated his adjustment. Maladaptive attitudes are explored, with a demonstration to the patient of the difficulties they create for him. The individual learns the reasons for their development in his past life and for their persistence in the present. Finally, he is helped to adjust with new, healthful, more adaptive patterns.

In reeducative therapy, less weight is placed on exploring the origins of patterns, while more emphasis is put on reorganization of habits, regardless of their sources in constitution or in specific inimical experiences. During the process of retraining, early difficulties that originally produced disturbing character traits may spontaneously be remembered by the patient. As part of his schooling, the patient must be taught to face his early childhood experiences, and, if necessary, to change his attitudes toward them.

The patient is encouraged to rectify remediable environmental difficulties, to adjust to irremediable handicaps while finding adequate compensations and sublimations, to enhance his personality resources through education and activity, to abandon unrealistic goals, and to coordinate his ambitions with his capacities. The therapist concentrates on all the healthy personality elements, actual and potential, that can mediate pathologic patterns of adjustment.

In dealing with abnormal traits and patterns, the therapist may strive to bring the patient to where he can reason unemotionally, facing facts bravely, adjusting to painful memories and impulses without panic, meeting stresses of life with courage, and forsaking fantasy in thinking. Each trait that the patient exhibits may be taken up in detail, discussing its origin, purpose, value, and the ways it interferes with his happiness and adjustment. More adaptive substitutive patterns may then be explored, and the patient may be urged to execute his insight, suggestions sometimes being given him of positive courses of action.

Thus a discussion of the patient's life history may reveal to the therapist that the patient has insight into his inordinate attachment to a domineering parent who continues to infantalize him. Evidences of how dependency undermines him are brought to his attention, and the patient may be shown how some of his symptoms are produced by his conflict over his dependent need. If the patient evidences a desire to overcome his dependency on his family, the wisdom of visiting his family at increasingly infrequent intervals, of making his own decisions, and of finding outlets for his energy and interests, may be indicated. It is to be expected, because neurotic reaction patterns are so deeply imbedded, that this advice will not be heeded at first; but as the patient constantly experiences untoward emotions associated with the giving up of his independence, he may agree with the therapist's observations and gradually experiment with new modes of adjustment.

Where a patient is too compliant and recognizes his compliance, it may be pointed out that he has probably always felt the need to be over-respectful to authority. His security is perhaps bound up with this reaction. However, he has a right, as a human being, to his own opinions, and he need not accept the wishes or orders of other people unless he wants to do so. He can review in his mind the pros and cons of any advice given him, and he may then accept or reject it as he sees fit. If he does not wish to abide by the orders or judgments of other people, he can try to explain to them why his own plans seem best. Should he decide to conform with the wishes of others, he must be sure that this is what he really wants, and is not what he feels forced to want. Above all, he must be logical rather than emotional in his choices of action. Specific ideas on how to function independently may be advanced. The help of other people with whom the patient lives may be enlisted in this training process.

An individual who is aware of a power drive may be shown how this is a dominating force in his life, preoccupying his thoughts and actions. He may be partly aware of how he strives for power and strength in all of his interpersonal relationships. What he may not realize is how mercilessly his drive rules him, and how it results in his forfeiting normal goals. The person may be alerted to how his power trend brings him into conflict with others and evokes retaliatory hostilities. It is necessary to get the patient to see the need of adopting a more mature attitude, and of readjusting his standards in line with the reality situation. Other outlets than power may then be suggested to satisfy the patient's drive for self-assertiveness and self-esteem.

The same technique may be used in dealing with other compulsive neurotic patterns; such as, detachment, aggression and perfectionism. Their manifestations are repeatedly brought to the patient's attention and he is shown why they stir up difficulties for him. He is challenged in his assumption that they are the only ways of adjusting to life, and substitutive responses are suggested.

The patient may be acquainted with the ways in which his character drives operate insidiously. He may be shown that unknown to himself he lashes out at others, or vanquishes them in actual deeds or in fantasy, or renders himself invulnerable and strong, or retreats from competition, or engages in any number of façades that become for him basic goals in life, making average pursuits meaningless.

Such unhealthy attitudes perhaps might be understandable were we to insist on what is probably not true—that the patient really is an inferior person who has to eliminate adult and realistic methods of dealing with his problems. The patient must be shown the need to stop taking refuge in childhood defenses, and he must be apprised of the wisdom of facing his difficulties with decision and courage. However, because he has utilized his defenses for so many years, he must understand that they will not vanish immediately. Indeed, they will keep cropping up from time to time. If they do, there is no need for discouragement. When he becomes sufficiently strong, his defenses will no longer be required. Yet, he must not abandon his patterns out of a sole conviction that they are wrong, or out of a desire to please the therapist. Rather, as he realizes the implications of his neurotic drives, he will want to substitute creative goals and patterns for those that have resulted in his present unhappiness.

The therapist should, in this way, actively encourage a conscious analysis by the patient of his customary trends, as well as stimulate him to substitute new ways of thinking and acting. In the event the old patterns reappear, it may be necessary for the patient to try to bring them to as complete a halt as possible by deliberate effort. The patient should be encouraged to feel that he has the capacity to change, that others sicker than himself have done so successfully.

Usually the patient will be dismayed to find that his character patterns are regarded as problems because he has accepted them as natural and normal. As he realizes that they constantly bring him into difficulties with people, and are responsible for much of his turmoil, he is supplied with a valid motivation to alter his scheme of life. He is confronted with a choice for which he, himself, will have to assume a measure of responsibility.

Many persons faced with this choice are unwilling or unable to give up their destructive drives. The knowledge that frustration or pain will follow observance of their patterns is not enough to make them give up the gratifications that accrue from the propitiation of neurotic goals. An extreme example of this is the alcoholic who appreciates the physical, social, and moral hardships that inevitably follow his bouts of drinking, but seems unable to do anything about it. In cases where the patient refuses to abandon his immature objectives, the knowledge that he is responsible for his own plight is healthier, from a therapeutic viewpoint, than the conviction that may have existed previously, to the effect that the sources of his misery lay outside of himself.

Where the person is convinced that his adjustment is eminently unsatisfactory, where he realizes that his gratification does not compensate for the suf·fering that comes from indulgence of his immature drives, where he is awar: of how his patterns interfere with biologic and social goals, he will be motivated toward experimenting with new reactions toward people.

Once patterns that are inimical to adjustment are clearly defined, and more adaptive substitutive reactions are suggested, a long period of experiment and training is necessary before unhealthy attitudes are replaced by those of a more mature nature.

Even where the patient has the motivation to change, a struggle will be necessary to achieve reeducative effects. In spite of all good resolutions, the patient, at first, will find himself responding automatically, in line with his customary habits. He will, however, become more and more conscious of his reactions, and, as they occur, he will better be able to subject them to analysis and control. Even though this may fail to stop him from following his usual patterns, he will become more and more aware of their irrational nature, and he will have a greater determination to substitute for them constructive behavior tendencies.

For instance, a perfectionistic person may become conscious of the fact that his impulse to do everything meticulously extends itself into every aspect of his life and poisons his relationships with people. He will see, as the therapist brings it to his attention, that the slightest failure to perform flawlessly suffices to create tension and panic. He may learn that the reason for his disturbance lies in the fact that when he is not perfect, his image of himself is shattered, and he feels unloved and unlovable. Life then becomes a constant series of frustrations, since it is obviously impossible to do things perfectly every minute of the day and still be human. The patient will, as he becomes aware of his inordinate expectations, find himself toying with the philosophy of self-tolerance, which he will not wish to accept at first, probably because being mediocre is equivalent to being no good at all, and because he is unconvinced that perfectionism is not really the keynote of life. As he tests the truth of the therapist's exhortations, and as he realizes the extent to which his perfectionistic strivings dominate him, he may attempt to restrain himself before yielding to perfectionistic impulses. He will review in his mind the reasons why he must be perfect on every occasion. He may eventually even try to substitute for this impulse the attitude that he can do things without needing to be perfect.

In these ways the individual eventually undergoes reeducation of his attitudes, values and customary modes of dealing with people, which encourage the various neurotic symptoms for which he seeks relief.

IV

The Terminal Phase of Treatment

46

Goals in Terminating Treatment

THEORETICALLY, PSYCHOTHERAPY IS NEVER-ENDING, SINCE EMOTIONAL growth can go on as long as one lives. It is consequently necessary to employ some sort of measurement of goals in order to determine when to discontinue treatment.

The problem of goals in psychotherapy is one about which there are differences of opinion. On the one hand, there are those who believe a definition of goals to be vital in any psychotherapeutic program. On the other hand, there are many professionals who consider goals to be an extremely arbitrary matter —a manifestation of the authoritarianism of the therapist who seeks to impose on the patient artificial values and standards.

Irrespective of how one feels about the uses made of them, goals are understandably of concern to the psychotherapist, since success or failure in the treatment effort can be gaged only in the context of set objectives. Before describing goals, however, we must admit that judgments of "success" in psychotherapy are really a matter of definition, and may be viewed differently from the standpoints of the patient, society and the therapist.

1. Success Judgments from the Standpoint of the Patient

Estimates by the patient as to what has been accomplished for him in therapy are in themselves not a reliable index of therapeutic success. Most patients regard symptomatic relief as the best measurement of positive gain. This index, however, is not a completely valid one in assaying the effectiveness of treatment.

Symptomatic improvement may be achieved in several ways. First, it may be associated with the giving up of vital aspects of personality functioning. For example, where anxiety and guilt are aroused by sexual impulses, the abandonment of all forms of sexual expression may relieve symptoms. Or where close interpersonal relations are conceived of as dangerous, the patient may, in the course of therapy, detach himself from people. The bargain that the patient makes with anxiety here cannot be regarded as successful therapy, even though his suffering is relieved. Second, the patient may, during treatment, propitiate certain neurotic drives, gaining thereby a spurious kind of security. Thus he may make himself dependent on the therapist, acquiring a regressive fulfillment of security needs. His symptoms will abate so long as he conceives of the therapist as a bountiful, loving and protecting parent. This happy situation may, nevertheless, be placed in jeopardy whenever the therapist fails to live up to the patient's expectations. Under these circumstances, we cannot consider the surcease of symptoms a sign of cure. Third, symptom relief may be produced by the repression of damaging conflicts. Many annoying but relatively innocuous symptoms may be blotted out of awareness in the course of supportive therapy, only to be replaced by substitutive symptoms of a more serious nature. Thus, the symptom of anxiety may be relieved during therapy by repressive techniques of one sort or another. Anxiety equivalents may, however, appear in the form of psychosomatic complaints. Damage to viscera may later eventuate, of which the patient is not conscious until an irreversible somatic ailment develops, perhaps years after the presumed "success" in therapy had occurred.

The patient's estimates of failure in therapy must also not be accepted at their face value, since he may base his concepts of failure on a false premise. Thus, he may consider his treatment unsuccessful where he has failed to develop traits that identify him with an ideal. For example, he may have secret notions of being a genius, and he may believe that therapy can release potentialities in him that will put him in the genius class. Or he may regard therapy as unsuccessful unless he has developed complete equanimity and the ability to remain tranquil, to endure tension and to vanquish discomfort, even in the face of the most devastating environmental conditions. The failure to develop these and other traits, which are, in the patient's mind, considered indices of health, security and self-esteem, may cast a shadow on even estimable therapeutic results.

2. Success Judgments of Society

Judgments as to success in therapy from the standpoint of social standards must also be held suspect. The patient's family, mate, or friends may have ideas about the kind of individual they want the patient to become that may not correspond with standards of mental health. For instance, parents may expect and even demand that the therapist mold the patient into a creature who is cooperative and pleasant at all times, and who never challenges parental authority. A mate may insist that the patient develop a personality that tolerates his or her own shortcomings and never gives vent to resentment. Friends may have stringent standards of character that might apply to themselves, but not necessarily to the patient.

The culture or sub-culture may also impose arbitrary norms that differ from those of the patient or of the therapist. Political and economic forces in one group may make for a value system that is not accepted by, or acceptable to another group. Thus a "normal" individual in a totalitarian framework would be expected to submit himself willingly to the yoke of dictatorship and to subordinate personal freedom for the welfare of the state. In another cultural framework, the individual's personal rights, and his ability to make his own choices would be paramount; he would not be expected to yield himself completely to authoritative demands. It is, accordingly, important not to regard as goals of normality traits and drives which, though culturally condoned, may prove to be at variance with mental health.

3. Success Judgments from the Standpoint of the Therapist

The therapist may fashion therapeutic goals around certain set standards and values. These may relate to personal concepts of normality, or to a general ideal of mental health.

He may, reflecting cultural concepts, pronounce certain traits as normal, believing that the patient must acquire these before being considered emotionally balanced. The therapist may himself operate under a cherished set of attitudes which constitute for him the highest goal. Thus, if he puts value in ambitiousness, perfectionism, detachment, dependency, narcissism, or power devices, he is apt to consider these real assets toward which he must aim his therapeutic sights. A word of caution must especially be voiced in regard to that group of attitudes collectively embraced under the term of compliance. A reasonable compliance to authority is a necessary thing, but compliance is too often utilized by neurotic persons as a form of security. This is most often the case in those cultures in which the child is considered a relative nonentity who is expected to submit himself without question and to yield without complaint to the dictates and commands of the stronger, more authoritative individuals with whom he lives. Where the therapist, himself, has been reared in an atmosphere that makes compliance tantamount with good breeding, he may expect the patient to adopt a submissive attitude. The patient may sense this trend in the therapist and try hard to please, even at the price of crushing self-strivings and needs for independent thought and action. The therapist may also, because of his own character structure, consider any aggression a sign of recalcitrance and ill-will. He must be careful, therefore, not to try to pattern the patient after his own image, for he, himself, may be the victim of values that are basically faulty.

4. "Ideal" Objectives of Mental Health

Ideal objectives of mental health are many. They require that the person be capable of deriving pleasure from creature comforts in life—from food, rest, relaxation, sex, work and play. He is capable of satisfying these impulses in conformity with the mores of the group. Mobilizing whatever intellectual and experiential resources are required, he is able to plan creatively and realistically, and to execute his plans in accordance with existent opportunities. This involves an appraisal of his aptitudes and limitations, and a scaling down of his ambitions to the level of his true potentialities. It includes the laying down of realistic life goals, an acceptance of his abilities and a tolerance of his shortcomings. Presupposed is a harmonious balance between personal and group standards, and those cultural and individual ideals that contribute both to the welfare of the self and of the group. The individual must be able to function effectively as part of the group, to give and to receive love, and otherwise to relate himself congenially to his fellow creatures. He must be capable of engaging in human relations without indulging neurotic character strivings of detachment, needs to dominate or to be enslaved, or desires to render himself invincible or perfect. He must be able to assume a subordinate relationship to authority without succumbing to fear or rage, and yet, in certain situations, be capable of assuming leadership without designs of control or power. He must be able to withstand a certain amount of disappointment, deprivation and frustration without undue tension or anxiety when he feels these to be reasonable, shared or necessary to the group welfare, or when the consequences of impulse indulgence entail more than their worth in compensatory pain. His capacities for adjustment must be sufficiently plastic to adapt himself to the exigencies of life without taking refuge in childish forms of defense or in fantasy. To achieve a healthy regard for himself as an individual, he must have a good measure of self-respect, the capacity to be comfortable within himself, a willingness to face the past and to isolate from the present anxieties relating to childhood experiences. He must possess self-confidence, assertiveness, a sense of freedom, spontaneity and self-tolerance.

Unfortunately, limitations are imposed by a variety of factors on the achievement through therapy of such ideal goals. Chief among these are obstacles within the patient; such as, lack of incentives for change, diminished ego strength, and practical considerations of insufficient time and money. Additionally, society itself imposes insuperable embargoes on certain aspects of functioning. It supports many neurotic values which necessitate the maintenance of sundry defenses for survival reasons. A personality structure that is ideally integrated might actually serve as a source of conflict where the individual has to operate in the framework of a severely neurotic culture.

TOWARD A PRACTICAL GOAL IN THERAPY

Goals in therapy are always patient-directed, for, no matter how well-trained and skilled the therapist may be, nor how extensively he may desire to reconstruct the patient's personality, the latter is always in a position to veto the therapist's intentions. The patient is particularly strategically placed to thwart the ideal goal of personality maturation—the most difficult of all objectives. Irrespective of how thoroughly conversant the therapist may be with the technique of reconstructive psychotherapy, his efforts may prove unsuccessful.

Even where conditions are most propitious, reconstructive efforts may fail. The patient may be able to afford extensive psychotherapy and to make the necessary time arrangements; he may earnestly desire to achieve deep change. Yet he may gain little or no benefit from therapy. This fact has confounded many therapists as well as their patients who are wont, as a result, to regard reconstructive psychotherapy as ineffectual.

When we investigate failures in reconstructive therapy in patients who are adequately motivated, we find a number of operative factors. The patient may have sustained such damage to his personality during the formative years of his life that the chances for complete growth are remote. The secondary gain factors may be so powerful as to make health a handicap rather than an asset. Environmental conditions may be irremediably destructive and the patient may need some of his neurotic defenses in order to survive them. Disintegrative forces within the personality may be so strong as to threaten to break loose with the employment of uncovering procedures. Finally, neurotic symptoms or character distortions may constitute the only means of adjusting the patient to his conflicts, even though he possesses insight into their nature.

There are some patients who can make an adaptation solely by employing such neurotic façades. While partially debilitating, they help prevent regression and the upsurge of disintegrative tendencies. Thus, a psychosomatic ailment may serve to drain off hostile and masochistic impulses which, deprived of a somatic expression, may shatter the ego and produce a psychosis.

While the ideal goal of absolute resolution of blocks in personality maturation, with achievement of complete functioning in all areas of living, is a cherished aim in every patient, in practice very few people can reach this objective. Lorand [433] recognizes this when he says that in doing psychoanalysis it is sometimes essential to satisfy oneself with "practical" though superficial results which permit the patient to get along more satisfactorily than he did before therapy.

Clara Thompson [434] in an excellent discussion of what constitutes a "cure" in therapy, describes the need for goal modification. She contends that, first of all, the patient must be relieved of neurotic suffering. He must also be able to relate to others with a minimum of unrealistically perpetuated attitudes that have their origins in early significant relationships. He must be capable of achieving as complete a development of his powers as his education and life circumstances will permit. If his life situation and the culture in which he functions are favorable, he will be most capable of relating to the group constructively; if not favorable, he may have to learn to endure relative isolation. So long as the person does not deceive himself through neurotic escape mechanisms, he may remain healthy even under inimical conditions. However, since we live in a sick society, some neurotic compromises are necessary in order to function. An absolute cure is thus not possible. So long as the person is relieved of anxiety, inferiority feelings, and other destructive elements, and is capable of coping effectively with life difficulties as they arise, this may constitute as much as can be done for him in treatment.

A realistic approach in therapy recognizes these principles of goal modification. It acknowledges that we may have to content ourselves with the modest objectives of freedom from disturbing symptoms, the capacity to function reasonably well, and to experience a modicum of happiness in living. The patient may continue to be burdened by outbursts of his neurosis, which escapes control from time to time. He may have to circumscribe his activities and employ certain protective devices that hamper him in certain areas. Yet he will be as well adjusted as most persons with whom he is in contact, which means that he may continue to be neurotic, although better able to live with his neurosis and to approach average life objectives.

In the process of modifying goals, cognizance is paid to the fact that while each person is capable of change, there are various levels of change, from the altering of relatively superficial attitudes to the modification of the deepest strata of personality. The strength of the ego in itself may bear no relationship to the extensiveness of goals approached during therapy. Thus, in many patients with strong egos, who have successfully dealt with infantile conflicts through repression, compensation and sublimation, and whose present illness consists of a breakdown of these defenses, the goals may advantageously be oriented around mediating the stress situation that has provoked collapse, restoring to the person his habitual defenses.

In patients with a weak ego who have dealt with infantile conflicts unsuccessfully, with a serious thwarting of maturation, one may also have to content himself with the goal of restoring repression, and of strengthening defenses to bring the person back to his customary equilibrium.

Were we, in summary, to attempt the definition of a practical goal in therapy, we might say that it is the achievement by the patient of optimal functioning within the limitations of his financial circumstances, his existing motivations, his ego resources and the reality situation. Such a goal would put upon the therapist the responsibility of resolving the patient's resistance in working toward the ideal objective of personality reconstruction. It would, however, admit of the expediency of adopting modified goals, such as dealing with only those aspects of the patient's problem that can be practically handled during the present therapeutic effort.

47

Technical Problems in Termination

THE CONDITIONS UNDER WHICH TERMINATION OF THERAPY IS INDICATED are: (1) Achievement by the patient of planned treatment goals, (2) Decision by the patient or therapist to terminate on the basis of incomplete goals, (3) The reaching of an impasse in therapy or the development of stubborn resistances that cannot be resolved, (4) Counter-transference the therapist is unable to control, and (5) Occurrence of physical reasons, such as moving of the residence of patient or therapist.

TERMINATING THERAPY UPON REACHING SET GOALS

Therapy may be terminated after the patient has achieved planned goals; such as, the disappearance of symptoms, the mediation of environmental stress sources, the acquisition of greater happiness, productivity and self-fulfillment, the resolution of difficulties in interpersonal relationships, or the establishment of creative and productive patterns in living, with the evolution of greater emotional maturity.

With the accomplishment of the purposes of therapy, termination is best effectuated by discussing the possibility of ending treatment with the patient, handling any resistance he displays, warning of the possibility of relapses, and inviting the patient to return after therapy has ended whenever he believes this to be necessary.

1. Discussing Termination with the Patient

In advance of the termination date, it is wise to discuss with the patient the matter of ending therapy. A tapering-off period may be suggested, and a termination date perhaps set. Thereafter the frequency of sessions may be reduced and the intervals between visits steadily increased. The following is an excerpt from a session with a patient with a phobic disorder who has achieved adequate improvement in therapy:

Th. It sounds as if you are reaching the end of treatment. How do you feel about stopping?

Pt. Oh, of course I am glad that I am feeling so well, and I am very thankful to you, doctor.

Th. Actually, you did the bulk of the work. Of course, we could go on with treatment indefinitely, reaching more extensive goals in your personality development, but frankly I don't see the need for that, unless you do.

Pt. Well, I suppose I can benefit, but as you say, I am comfortable and happy now with Jim (*the patient's husband*) being so much better now to live with, and all these fears and things are gone now.

Th. If you agree with me that we should begin to terminate, we can cut down our visits to once weekly for the next month, and then a session every two weeks.

Pt. All right, doctor.

During the tapering-off period, any relapses or resistances are handled, sessions being again increased if the patient's condition demands this. In occasional cases, it may be decided to terminate therapy abruptly without tapering off, in order to expose the patient to a complete break with the therapist. Forced to function on his own, the patient may marshal inner strength more rapidly.

2. Handling Resistances to Termination

If the therapist has conducted the treatment sessions with the full participation of the patient, and if he has avoided playing a directive role, termination will not pose too great a problem in the average patient. In supportive therapy, however, where the patient has accepted the therapist as a guiding authority with whom he has conformed, or in insight therapy where the patient has, on the basis of a residual dependency drive, made the therapist a necessary factor in his adjustment, termination may present great difficulties.

In some patients in whom no manifest dependency operates in the relationship with the therapist, termination may still be troublesome. The patient may be fearful of giving up the protective situation which he enjoys in the therapeutic relationship. Memories of his past suffering and anxiety may cause him to want to hold on to the security he now has, even at the cost of continuing in therapy indefinitely.

The therapeutic tasks in termination with all patients involve analysis of the dependency elements in the relationship, a search for needs in the patient to perpetuate dependency, and a helping of the patient to achieve as much independence and assertiveness as possible. A shift in the character of the relationship may be necessary where the therapist has operated in a directive manner. Here the therapist behaves non-directively with the patient, aiding him in establishing his own values and goals in relation to both minor and major aspects of his life.

Resistances in the average dependent patient are multiform. Some patients bluntly refuse to yield dependency, adopting all kinds of guiles, even to relapse in their illness, in order to demonstrate their helplessness. Other patients exhibit a profound fear of assertiveness, perhaps promoted by a neurotic equation of assertiveness with aggression. Resolution of such resistances may consume a great deal of time, but must be accomplished before the patient can be considered cured.

It may be necessary to interpret to the patient the reasons for his self-paralysis, and to emphasize the need to make his own choices no matter how inappropriate these may seem. The patient may be told that because of the fact that he never has developed full confidence in himself as an individual, he has doubted his right to experience himself as a constructive human being. The insidious operation of his dependency may be demonstrated, and the patient may be shown how dependency has crippled his efforts toward self-growth. In his relationship with the therapist it is natural for him to expect the therapist to give him the answers, and to make his decisions for him. Should the therapist do this, however, the patient will never develop strength within himself. The therapist wants to give the patient the opportunity to grow by encouraging him to take complete responsibility for his own decisions. The patient may be apprised of the fact that he will feel some of his decisions to be wrong; but even though he makes mistakes, the very fact that they are his own mistakes will teach him more than being told what to do at all times. The therapist does not want to withhold support from the patient, but he must do so now out of consideration for the patient's right to develop.

When the patient accuses the therapist of being cold and distant, the therapist may say:

The reason I'm not more demonstrative is that if I were to act like the traditional authority, it would eventually infantilize you; you would have to keep me around as a leaning post the rest of your life. You'd have to come to me for every decision with such queries as, "Am I doing something wrong?" or "Am I doing the right thing?" Rather, it's better for you to make mistakes, bad as they may be, and to feel that these are your own decisions than for me to tell you what to do.

A definition of the non-directive nature of the treatment situation in this way will give the patient an incentive to take responsibility. It will not serve to liberate the patient completely from his dependency demands. His neurotic attitudes and behavior patterns will continue in force. He may still exhibit toward the therapist the same insecurity, submissiveness, fear and aggression he always has manifested toward authority. He will claim the same ineptitudes in dealing with life and people. He will ingratiate himself, or act destructive, or detach himself in his customary manner. But he will do these with a slight difference, with doubts that they are really necessary.

The following excerpt of a treatment session with a patient resisting termination illustrates some of these points:

Th. You want me to tell you exactly what to do, how to do it and when. If you really feel that you just don't have strength to do things for yourself, I will do them for you, provided you understand it isn't going to be of help to you if I make your decisions. I'll leave it up to you to decide. If you really feel as bad as you say you do, and you haven't got the confidence to make your own decisions, I'll let you depend upon me, if you *really* want that. [*This statement is offered as a challenge to the patient. She actually has become quite assertive through therapy, but is evincing a regressive dependency reaction to prevent termination.*]

Pt. I do feel just as badly as I told you, but at the same time I can hang on to various little things, one of which is that I long ago accepted the idea that you know what you're doing and I don't want to go against it. [*She seems to doubt the wisdom of her desire to have me function as a parental image.*]

Th. You don't want to go against what I have outlined as the best for you? What do you feel about making your own choices and your own decisions completely, with absolutely no help from me?

Pt. Oh, I think it's great, except that there doesn't seem to be much I can do about it.

Th. Well, what do you think would happen if I told you what to do, if I took you over and acted like a parent?

Pt. I feel two ways about it. I feel, first of all, that it might be an excellent idea because I'm certainly amenable to letting you take me over. But the other way I feel about it is that all this time I've been trying to, more or less, cooperate with you. I trust your judgment and I can see very well that keeping throwing decisions at me is what will in the end make me self-sufficient. Yes, I can see it, but right now I just can't imagine it ever happening or my being able to stand on my own feet. I feel very much as if I have slipped constantly downward during the last few weeks. [*This is since termination was suggested.*] That's all. I mean it's not as if I don't have lucid moments every now and then, but they're very few and far between.

Th. All right, then would you want me to play the role of telling you what to do on the basis that you can't come to decisions for yourself?

Pt. If it was making decisions, I might be able to do it; but I just can't see any decisions to make. There's nothing clear-cut. I don't know where I am at all.

Th. So that you'd like to just let yourself be taken care of by somebody?

Pt. It sounds nice, but I know perfectly well that it wouldn't be so good for me.

Th. You mean my making the decisions for you wouldn't be so good?

Pt. Well, certainly not.

Th. But some people seem to want that.

Pt. Grown people?

Th. Yes, grown people. Their feeling about themselves is so diminutive, their capacity to function so low that they want a parent watching over them all the time. If you'd like to adjust on this level all your life, you'd need to have me around to make your decisions for you indefinitely.

Pt. And then if I wasn't living here I'd try to find someone else to do it, if I let you go ahead with this plan. [*This is a healthy reluctance to accepting dependency.*]

Th. If you don't develop strengths within yourself so you can figure things out and plan your life and follow it through, right or wrong, then you're going to need somebody around all the time.

Pt. I'd rather not depend on you then.

Because the therapist operates in a more passive role, the patient will be encouraged to act with greater assertiveness, to initiate actions and to follow them through. Increasingly he will make his own plans and express his own choices. He will experience failures, of course, but he will have successes too. And his inner strength will grow on the bedrock of his successes. He will develop new feelings of integrity and a more complete sense of self.

Ego growth will thus be catalyzed during the terminal phase, eventuating in the patient's desire to manage his own life. Such growth is contingent to a large extent on the continued permissiveness of the therapist and his persistent encouragement of the patient's activity and self-expressiveness. The fact that the patient successfully figures things out for himself during the session eventually shows him that he is not at all at the mercy of forces on the outside. Ultimately he comes to the conclusion that he can live his own life, not because he is given permission, but because he has the right to do so. He feels equality with the therapist and a growing sense of self-respect. The self-confidence he develops in therapy promotes an extension of assertive feeling toward the extra-therapeutic environment.

The proper conduct of therapeutic sessions during the terminal phase of insight therapy requires that the therapist be so constituted that he permit the patient to feel equality. The personalities of some therapists are essentially so authoritarian that they will not be able to function on equal terms with the patient. They automatically will set themselves up as leaders making judgments, giving directives, and setting goals for the patient they insist must be followed. They may respond with hostility if challenged or abused by the patient. This is least apt to occur where the therapist has had personal psychotherapy and can analyze and control his counter-transference before it acts to interfere with the treatment situation.

Even where he has had personal therapy, the therapist may manifest attitudes that support the resistances of the patient to termination. He may continue to want to overprotect or domineer the patient, and he may be unable to assume a non-directive role. This may lead to interminable therapy, until the patient forcefully asserts himself through the marshalling of aggression, and in this way violently breaks his ties with the therapist.

In some instances, a complete resolution of the patient's dependence may not be possible, or may not even be attempted, as in supportive and some forms of reeducative therapy. Here the dependency is reduced to as innocuous a level as possible, by encouraging contact with an outside group, or by maintaining a casual therapeutic relationship at prolonged intervals over an indefinite period.

3. Warning of the Possibility of Relapses

No matter how thoroughly the patient's neurotic patterns seem to have been eradicated, shadows of his old reaction persist. One may be incapable of eliminating them completely, as one cannot obliterate entirely other aspects of the patient's past. Under conditions of great insecurity, when the patient's sense of mastery is threatened, or during periods of disappointment, frustration and deprivation, his ego is apt to invoke old defenses and strivings characteristic of past neurotic modes of adaptation.

Symptoms may return insidiously without the patient even being aware of having entered into the old conflictual situations that propagated them. Thus, migrainous attacks may recur in a man who, having learned to channelize hostility constructively and to avoid competitive relationships that create damaging resentment, changes his job to one where he is judged solely on the basis of comparison of his productivity to that of other employees. A woman with a propensity for dependent involvements may experience a return of her helplessness and her symptoms when she falls in love with, and acts submissive toward a power-driven individual who constitutes for her an omnipotent father figure. Unconsciously she has yielded to a childish yearning for complete protection, and she is again paying the price in shattered self-esteem and its attendant symptomatic penalties.

It is essential for the patient to realize that his getting well is no guarantee that he will experience no further return of symptoms. Indeed, at the point where therapy is being discontinued, he may be informed that he will probably undergo several relapses. However, if he investigates himself and analyzes the causes of each relapse, he will realize that the old conflicts that he has explored during therapy have been revived. His ability to understand the circumstances that had revived his trouble will not only help him to overcome the relapse, but will consolidate his insight and solidify his new, healthy patterns. Some therapists find it profitable to tell patients at termination that they do not consider a person cured until he has suffered at least one relapse and has been able to work it out for himself. This practice forestalls the situation of the patient classifying his therapy as a failure, should a return of symptoms ensue. It alerts him to the insidious operation of his inner conflicts and promotes a continuing self-analysis. His ability to recognize the truth of the lessons he has learned in therapy strengthens his newly acquired traits and expands his personality growth.

4. Inviting the Patient to Return for Further Sessions

The therapist may advantageously invite the patient to return for additional interviews in the event he meets with a relapse and is unable to work through the problem by himself. Should the patient take advantage of this invitation, it will be possible for the therapist rapidly to help the patient gain insight into the conflicts and patterns that have been revived, to connect this understanding with what the patient already has learned in therapy, and to analyze why the patient was unable to gain insight through his own efforts. This process will occasion much relief in the patient and send him forth into life with a greater sense of mastery. Relatively few sessions are usually required to effectuate this objective.

The patient may also desire to return to therapy in order to achieve more extensive personality development. Growth is a never-ending process, and the patient may be so dissatisfied with his present status that he insists on inquiring more exhaustively into himself.

For example, a patient in an anxiety state, mobilized by involvement in a love affair he has been unable to control with his habitual character defense of detachment, may utilize the therapeutic situation to break the relationship with the young woman of whom he has become so hopelessly enamored. Restoring his detached defenses and again functioning satisfactorily without anxiety, he may decide that he has accomplished his treatment objective. However, because he has become aware of a conflict that makes close relationships dangerous for him, necessitating his withdrawal, he may develop, after he has stopped treatment, an incentive to return to therapy for more extensive work. He will do this with a new goal in mind; namely, to be able to relate closely to a person without needing to invoke his defense of detachment. With this expanded motivation, a reconstructive approach may be possible.

TERMINATING ON THE BASIS OF INCOMPLETE GOALS

Therapy may have to be terminated prior to the achievement of planned goals. There are a number of reasons for this, most important of which is insoluble resistance. Thus, a patient may, with psychotherapy, lose certain symptoms; but other symptoms may cling to him obstinately. He may relinquish many neurotic patterns, but continue to exploit a few without which he feels himself incapable of functioning. He may develop a number of new potentialities, yet be unable to progress to as complete emotional maturity as either he or the therapist may desire. Working on his resistance accomplishes little, and the therapist may then deem it advisable to interrupt treatment.

Therapeutic objectives may have to be scaled down considerably in certain individuals. Thus we may be dealing with a sick borderline patient who is on the verge of a schizophrenic break and who is insistent that he be brought in therapy to a point where he can be more normal than normal. This wish, while admirable, is not realistic, for the patient does not possess the fortitude to endure the rigours of a reconstructive approach. Because he does not have sufficient ego strength to work out a better adaptation, one may have to make a compromise with projected goals.

Sometimes therapy is started with a patient whose motivations are unalterably defective. For instance, he may have a tremendously arrogant notion of his capacities, and he may seek treatment solely because he has read somewhere that psychotherapy can bring out an individual's buried potentialities. The bloated image of himself which the patient supports may be the only way he has of counteracting feelings of inner devastation, or of rectifying a contemptuous self image. Therapy with such a patient may be extremely difficult and may have to be terminated due to impenetrable resistance.

The therapist may be confronted with a patient whose life situation obstructs his progress. His environmental difficulty is so irremediable that possibilities of correction are remote, and hence the patient must be persuaded to live with it or be desensitized to its effect. Or the patient's symptoms may possess for him so strong a defensive value that their removal will produce a dangerous reaction. Therapy may have to be terminated on the basis of only partial symptomatic relief.

It may be impossible, due to other obstructions, to get some patients to progress beyond a certain point in therapy. To continue treatment may prove discouraging to the therapist and undermining to the patient. It is better here for the patient to retain some of his neurotic drives than to expose him to interminable and frustrating therapy to which, in all probability, he will be unable to respond.

As soon as the therapist decides that maximum improvement has been obtained, or that a stalemate has been reached, he may bring therapy to a halt by utilizing the techniques described above for termination after the achievement of planned goals. The therapist will, however, have to explain the reason for termination in such a way that the patient does not arrive at the conclusion that he is hopeless. Thus, the patient may be told that therapy has alleviated some of his symptoms, has brought him to an awareness of his basic problems, and has pointed the way to a more adaptive life. Because his difficulties have been with him a long time, his resistances to a complete cure may persist for a period. Putting his insight into practice in real life will give him the best opportunity to achieve a more complete development.

The mere mention of termination, and the discussion of resistances that seem to have blocked progress, may stimulate incentives to break through these hindrances. If a termination date has been set, the patient may work through his resistances prior to the expiration date. On the other hand, the termination techniques may not resolve the many impediments to further change. Yet, after the patient has left treatment, he may show spectacular progress. The fact that no headway was made while in therapy may have been due to the operation of a subtle transference situation that acted as resistance. For example, hostility toward the therapist may have expressed itself in a refusal to go forward in personality advance; or dependence on the therapist may have taken the initiative away from the patient. Once the patient is functioning away from therapy under his own power, such resistances no longer operate and a spurt in development is possible.

1. Planned Interruption of Therapy

Instead of outright termination, a vacation from therapy may be suggested. During this period, the patient may experiment with the insight he has gained by attempting productive actions. The interruption may also enable him to experience his neurotic tendencies as they operate in his life situation and to cope with disturbances as they arise without help. Discussing these later with the therapist may prove to be invaluable to the patient. The proposed interruption may be presented to the patient as in the following excerpt:

Th. It seems to me that we have reached a plateau in your therapy and that a vacation from treatment may be indicated. How do you feel about that?

Pt. I just can't seem to get any further. I've been thinking of that. How long would you suggest?

Th. Suppose we plan on a month's vacation. After a month call me and we'll arrange an appointment.

Pt. Do you believe that will be of help?

Th. I do. You might observe yourself during this period and see if you can determine what is happening, what stirs up your symptoms and what alleviates them.

We might learn something important, and the interlude may help pull you out of the plateau.

2. Transferring the Patient

Sending the patient to another therapist may sometimes be preferable to outright termination. Where the therapist believes he is unable to deal with the patient's resistances, where he cannot control destructive counter-transference, or where, for any other reason, he feels that he cannot help the patient any more, he may decide that the patient will do better with a different therapist. Sometimes a transfer is arranged when it is presumed the patient will benefit by a kind of therapeutic experience other than that provided by the present therapist. For instance, a therapist trained mainly in reconstructive approaches may feel that the patient needs reeducative or supportive therapy, and he may consequently want to refer the patient to a professional person who is highly skilled in these techniques. Or a change to a therapist of the opposite sex may be considered advisable. Should a transfer be indicated, the therapist may discuss the matter with the patient as illustrated in this fragment of a session:

Th. For some time I have felt that we haven't been making very much progress.

Pt. Yes, I was worried about this. I wondered if you were getting impatient.

Th. Of course not, except that sometimes a snag like this does happen, and a person may be able to work it out better with another therapist.

Pt. You mean you want me to see somebody else?

Th. My desire is for you to get well. What would you feel about seeing someone I would recommend and who I believe can help you? I have a feeling you may do better with another type of technique, and Dr. _____ is very excellent at this.

Pt. Well, I don't know.

Th. Why don't you talk to Dr. _____ after I determine that he has the time for you? Then, after a couple of sessions you can see how you feel.

Pt. If you think this is best, I'll do it.

Th. I do, and I'll make all the arrangements and call you.

TERMINAL NOTE

At the time of termination, a note should be entered in the patient's case record indicating the reasons for termination, the patient's condition on discharge, the areas of improvement, the patient's attitude toward the therapist, the recommendations made to the patient, and the final diagnosis. A form, such as in Appendix H, page 821, may be found useful.

FOLLOW-UP

Prior to discharging the patient it is advisable to ask him whether he would object to receiving an occasional letter from the therapist regarding his progress. Most patients are delighted to cooperate and consider the therapist's gesture a mark of his interest in their development. Follow-up letters, briefly inquiring into how things have been progressing, may be sent to the patient yearly, preferably for at least five years. This enables the therapist to maintain a good check on what has been happening over a considerable period of time. The patient's replies to the follow-up inquiry may be entered in his case record, and, if necessary, a brief notation may be made of the contents.

V

Special Aspects

48

Adjunctive Aids in Psychotherapy

THE PRINCIPAL ADJUNCTS IN PSYCHOTHERAPY ARE GROUP THERAPY, hypnotherapy, narcotherapy and bibliotherapy.

GROUP THERAPY

Group therapy is a valuable adjunct in all forms of psychotherapy—supportive [96-100], reeducative [148-157], and reconstructive [287-297]. Its theory, principles, and methods have been under investigation during the past years, resulting in a number of published studies, the most notable being the works of Slavson [151-153, 292] and Powdermaker, et al. [457].

While some persons contend that the results of group therapy by itself approximate those of individual therapy, one may reasonably question the validity of this notion. Certain therapists claim advantages for combined therapy, that is, individual therapy combined with group therapy. Here the therapist is able to deal, at an individual session, with the manifold resistances and responses to the group which the patient is unable or unwilling to bring up in the group setting. Greater exploration of vital patterns is also possible during the alternate individual sessions. For these reasons, it is likely that the goals reached in combined therapy are more extensive than in group therapy alone.

In combined therapy, only those patients are introduced into a group who have had sufficient individual therapy to appreciate the nature of their important neurotic patterns. The group acts as a laboratory in which the individual projects and watches the operation of his impulses and strivings in relation to other human beings. He will play specific roles with different group members, often shifting his attitudes as the members assume a modified meaning for him. He will set up nuclear situations with the different members, utilizing one, perhaps, as a maternal object, another as a paternal substitute, and a third possibly as a sibling symbol. By observing the activities and projections of the other patients, the patient gains added insight. He is provided with a constant medium for reality testing and with opportunities to think critically about himself. Personality problems are most responsive to a group approach.

1. Organizing a Group

In organizing a group for combined therapy, the therapist will be limited by the patients he has who are in individual therapy. He should choose those who are sufficiently advanced in their understanding of themselves to be able to identify their patterns as they will appear in the group setting. While the clinical diagnosis is not too important, experience shows that the following conditions and patients do poorly in a group:

a. Psychopathic personalities
b. Acute depressions
c. Aggressive homosexuals
d. Extreme masochistic personality disorders
e. Hallucinating patients
f. Patients with marked paranoidal tendencies
g. Patients who "act-out" too readily
h. Patients with a low intelligence

The age difference should preferably be no greater than fifteen years. Some homogeneity in educational background is desirable. A well-balanced group often contains an "oral-dependent," a "schizoid-withdrawn," a "rigid-compulsive," and perhaps a "provocative" patient, such as one who is in a chronic anxiety state. This variety permits the members to observe a wide assortment of defense mechanisms and to experience tensions they might otherwise evade.

The number of group members is optimally from six to eight. Marital status is relatively unimportant. A mixture of males and females in the group allows for an opportunity to project and to experience feelings in relation to both sexes, although acting-out is more likely in a mixed group.

In introducing the matter of group therapy to a prospective member, the therapist may explain that he is organizing a group of patients for purposes of group therapy. Talking over one's problems or ideas in a group tends to sharpen one's insight and to expedite individual therapy. The patient may then be invited to join the group, with the statement that it will probably facilitate his progress.

The length of a group therapy session is approximately one and one-half hours. The frequency of meetings is one to two sessions weekly, with alternate individual sessions. The best seating arrangement is in a circle.

2. The Opening Sessions

At the first session, the members are introduced by their first names, and the purpose of group discussions is clarified. The therapist may simply state that the group will offer the members an opportunity to talk about their feelings and in this way to understand better their individual patterns. It is not necessary for any person to feel compelled to talk about anything he wants to keep to himself; however, the ability to communicate freely will help the patient to understand his problems more rapidly. For instance, each person in the group must have had certain feelings about coming to the group. He may have been fearful or embarrassed or upset. The therapist then may ask how the members felt and what they had anticipated in coming to the first group session. As one member expresses his feelings, others will join in. This usually leads to the discussion of problems common to all members.

Toward the end of the first session, the confidential nature of the sessions should be stressed and the fact mentioned that each member will be expected to keep to himself the identity of the other members and the content of the subject matter discussed. While no person need divulge any secrets about himself to the group that he wants to hold back, he will have to follow the rule of talking about any accidental or other contacts made with members of the group outside of the session. This qualification is important to prevent acting-out, which is possible especially in mixed groups. Sexual involvements may be forestalled by verbalization by the patients of feelings and impulses in relation to each other.

During early stages of treatment, a certain amount of guidance is usually required from the therapist, but not so much as to inhibit the development of spontaneous neurotic patterns. The therapist may also want to divert the patient from divulging painful material before the group is ready to support his revelations. On the other hand, the therapist encourages free interaction verbally among the members to bring out each patient's customary façades and defenses. At later stages in treatment, the members themselves take over the operation of the session, deciding on the best procedure to follow in eliciting material. Thus the members may agree on some formal arrangement of giving each person an opportunity to express himself at each session. This is followed by informal discussions during which any person may say whatever comes to his mind whenever he so desires. Actually, any rigid structuring of procedure will not be pursued as soon as emotion begins to operate in the group. The content of discussions will vary greatly, covering important current incidents in the life of a member, dreams, attitudes toward other members or toward the therapist, and general subjects such as family relations and sex.

3. Later Sessions

As the group organizes, personal problems of a most intimate nature are brought in by the members for discussion. The relation of his problem to a theme common to other group members enables the patient to achieve insight. Therapist activities should, therefore, be directed toward helping to stimulate thinking around common themes. The therapist's comments and interventions aim toward a bringing of other group members into the discussion, even though one member's problems may constitute the main content of the session.

Examination of repudiated inner feelings is facilitated by the support the patient senses in the group and the leader. If expression of his feelings strikes a resonant note among several of the other members, the ensuing discussion often leads to a lifting of tension and the sharpening of awareness of neurotic patterns. A study of the patient's interactions with the other group members, as, for instance, manifestations of hostility, fear, suspicion, or sexual feeling, and the relationship of these emotions to the basic character structure contributes to the most effective learning. In this reference, difficulties and antagonisms arising between two members may, through an analysis of the operative projections, lead to a constructive end.

The activities of the therapist include comments, interventions, structuring, focusing, interpreting resistance, encouraging group interaction, and clarifying group interrelations. The ability of the therapist to accept hostility or criticism from one or more group members encourages a further examination of, and a working through of many of the patient's damaging emotions. Reactions of the patient occur in complex clusters as the group accelerates the release of feeling. Lack of restraint in one group member results in lack of restraint in the others. The group setting thus tends to remove repression, and to bring the patient to a more rapid understanding of his inner conflicts.

4. Value of Combined Therapy

The value of combined therapy is demonstrated by the following comments of patients who have received this treatment:

It has been revealing to me to see how people react both to me and to my problems. It has been equally revealing to me to see how I react to people and how I invest others with qualities that have little basis in fact.

The group speeded up my individual therapy, since many tensions and anxieties were produced by the interaction process which I might never have looked at.

I was amazed to observe the same problems in others in the group that bothered me. This made me realize others have difficulties as great or greater than my own. I became more tolerant with these problems in other people and this increased my tolerance with myself.

The ability to express myself in any way I wanted with other people, and to say anything on my mind without being rejected or punished, was a turning point for me.

I learned that others throw out unreasonable attitudes like I do. This made it possible for me to be criticized and attacked and to realize the criticism might have nothing to do with me.

The guilt and shame I had in myself were, I discovered, my own doing because nobody felt I was bad or evil for having sexual thoughts or murderous desires. When I didn't feel blamed for them, they stopped being important.

The thing that helped me most was to see how I felt different toward the other people in the group at different times, and to know that this had nothing to do with them, only with the way I felt.

HYPNOTHERAPY

In the main, the trance state influences the individual in two ways. First, it produces a remarkable relationship to the hypnotist, in which the subject accepts suggestions which enable him to experience widespread psychic and somatic effects. Second, it tends to modify or to remove repressions which keep certain aspects of the personality from awareness. The first property of hypnosis is perhaps based on the fact that the trance symbolically represents to the patient a relationship with an idealized parental figure to whom he submits, and whose suggestions he follows in the hopes of winning love, support, and a variety of coveted bounties. This type of relationship expedites certain supportive therapies; such as, reassurance, guidance, persuasion and symptom removal through prestige suggestion. The second property of the trance relates to the deadening effect of hypnosis on repression, which enables the return to awareness of material that has been relegated to unconsciousness. Hypnosis may in this way be useful in uncovering techniques during insight therapy.

The first property of hypnosis permits of the employment of the trance for the following purposes:

1. As a means of removing certain conversion symptoms, like paralysis, aphonia, and some psychophysiologic reactions.

2. As a way of controlling the drinking urge in some alcoholic patients.

3. As a vehicle of establishing the authority of the therapist, which the patient does not dare to defy, thus inhibiting acting-out, especially in psychopathic personalities.

4. As a means of bolstering persuasive therapy in obsessive-compulsive reactions.

5. As treatment for certain habit disorders, like insomnia, over-eating, and nail-biting.

The second property allows for these uses in insight therapy:

1. Removal of amnesia in stress reactions with release of repressed memories and emotions.

2. Lifting of repression in conversion and dissociative reactions.

3. Resolution of repression in the treatment of other conditions, like anxiety reactions and phobic reactions.

4. Dissipation of certain transference and content resistances.

In certain problems and syndromes, where the objective is resolution of deep characterologic distortions and removal of blocks toward emotional maturation, hypnosis does not seem to contribute too much. In other cases, however, hypnosis may be useful where psychotherapy alone fails. For instance, where repression is so intense that it defies all attempts at resolution, free association, dream interpretation and other traditional routes to the unconscious are of little avail. Hypnosis here may be singularly effective. In supportive therapy, where an authoritarian relationship cannot be set up with facility, hypnosis may put the therapist in a sufficiently omnipotent position to produce better results.

There is another use of hypnosis that has not received the attention it deserves, that is, as an experience in relationship. All therapy requires the establishing of a working relationship between therapist and patient. It is impossible to help the patient to an understanding of his problem and to the resolution of the manifold resistances in utilizing insight in the direction of change, without good rapport. The mere induction of a trance produces a feel-

ing of closeness and trust in a remarkably short time resolving certain transference resistances, and enabling the patient to proceed toward the exploration
of anxiety-provoking inner conflicts. In some patients, one may employ hypnosis
at the start of therapy, and, once a relationship has crystallized, one may go on
to implement the traditional psychotherapies without hypnosis. This may cut
down on the time required for the establishing of a working relationship.

Another technique utilized occasionally during the exploratory phase of
therapy is the training of the patient in self-hypnosis, suggesting to him that
he will investigate spontaneously, through dreams and fantasies in the self-
induced trance state, puzzling aspects of his problem, and also that he will
work out various resistances that may arise. In this way, the patient actively
participates in the investigative process, and time may be saved.

The Induction of the Trance State

The induction of hypnosis is a relatively simple procedure in most
patients. The factor of greatest importance is the confidence of the therapist in
himself, and his capacity to communicate this confidence to the patient.

Elsewhere, a detailed account of trance induction has been elaborated
[458]. In brief, the required steps are these: (1) promoting motivations that
will lead to hypnosis by associating the desire to get well with cooperation
in the hypnotic process, (2) removing misconceptions and fears about hypnosis by explanation and clarification, (3) introducing a suggestibility test,
like the hand clasp test, to demonstrate that the patient can follow directions,
(4) giving the patient a short preparatory talk to the effect that he will not
really go to sleep, even though sleep suggestions will help him relax, and
that he will not be asked embarrassing questions or forced to do anything
he does not want to do, (5) inducing a trance by any chosen method, (6)
deepening the trance by suggesting more and more complex hypnotic phenomena, (7) making therapeutic suggestions, (8) awakening the patient, and (9)
discussing with him his trance experiences.

In giving suggestions that lead to a trance, the therapist must couch these
in a positive way. Any hesitance or faltering, or any communication to the
patient that the therapist anticipates failure, will interfere with the proper
atmosphere conducive to hypnosis. The therapist must adopt a persuasive, calm,
reassuring tone of voice, droning suggestions rhythmically, repetitively and
monotonously.

One of the easiest ways of inducing hypnosis is by means of the suggestibility test of the hand clasp. To do this, the patient is made comfortable
in an armchair, and asked to relax his body progressively starting with the
muscles in his forehead, then his face, neck, shoulders, arms, back, thighs and
legs. Following this, the patient is enjoined to clasp his hands in front
of him, a foot or so away from his eyes. With his eyes fixed on his hands, he
is asked to clasp his hands together more and more firmly as the therapist
counts from one to five. At the count of five, he is told his hands will be so

firmly clamped together that it will be difficult or impossible to separate them. After the patient has cooperated with this suggestion, he is told that his hands will relax a little, but his eyes will begin to feel tired and his eyelids heavy as he stares at his hands. They will get heavier and heavier, and he will get drowsier and drowsier until his eyelids feel like lead. He will then let his eyelids close, and he will feel a pleasant sense of tiredness and relaxation sweeping over him. These suggestions are repeated over and over, in a monotonous cadence, and in a firm, reassuring tone until the eyes close.

In my experience the best way to induce a trance is by means of hand levitation. This method is more difficult to master than the other techniques and calls for greater effort and persistence on the part of the therapist. With the patient's hands resting lightly on his thighs, he is asked to concentrate his attention on everything his hands do. As he notices sensations, such as the warmth of the palms of his hands against his thighs, the texture of his clothing, and perhaps the weight of his hands, he will observe one of the fingers wiggle a little. As soon as he notices this, he is to raise the finger that moved first. Thereafter, he will gaze at his right hand and will notice that the fingers will fan out, the spaces between the fingers getting wider and wider. When this happens, suggestions are made that the fingers will slowly lift from the thigh; then the hand will rise as the arm becomes lighter and lighter; the eyes will become tired and the lids heavy. However, much as he wants to, the patient is not to fall asleep until his arm rises and his hand touches his face. As he gets more and more tired, and his lids get heavier and heavier, his arm and hand will get lighter and rise higher until it touches his face. When it touches his face, he will be relaxed and drowsy and his eyes will be firmly shut. Suggestions are repeated constantly until they are acted on by the patient.

The traditional method of hypnosis through staring at a fixation object continues to be useful. Here a coin, pencil or shiny object is held above the head, the patient being asked to stare at it while suggestions are made to the effect that he is tired, that his eyes begin to water, and his lids blink until he no longer can keep his eyes open.

Hypnosis through sleep suggestions is often an effective method. Here the patient, sitting in a comfortable chair or lying on a couch, is asked to close his eyes and to visualize a relaxing scene. He is then asked to breathe deeply and regularly while relaxing muscle groups from forehead to lower extremities. He is told that he will visualize himself or another person resting comfortably, observing the eyelids of this person closing as the person falls asleep. He will get sleepier and sleepier until he dozes off or goes into a completely relaxed state.

As soon as the eyelids close by the use of any of the above methods, the trance is deepened by suggesting, progressively, heaviness and stiffness of the left arm (limb catalepsy), heaviness of the lids until the patient cannot open them (lid catalepsy), inability to move his extremities or to get out of the chair (inhibition of voluntary movements), hyperesthesia of the hand, anaesthesia of the hand, and, perhaps, auditory and visual hallucinations.

When the patient is in as deep a trance as can be induced, therapeutic suggestions may be made. These are either of a supportive nature, in the form of palliative commands and persuasive comments, or of a probing nature, the patient being enjoined to explore memories or feelings for the purpose of acquiring a better understanding of personality patterns and inner conflicts. Facilitating the latter task are hypnotically induced fantasies, the training of the patient to regress to significant periods in his childhood, and the induction of experimental conflicts. An illustration of how hypnosis may aid the uncovering process may be found in the excerpt of the session on pages 431–438.

NARCOTHERAPY

The difficulty of inducing hypnosis in certain subjects, the relatively long time required to produce a trance even in susceptible persons, and the inability on the part of some therapists to acquire skill in trance induction, has brought into prominence a simple technique of promoting hypnosis by the intravenous injection of a hypnotic drug, such as, sodium amytal or sodium pentothal [66,67,286].

These substances produce a cortical depression with relaxation and heightened susceptibility to suggestion, reassurance and persuasion. The name given to this combined use of narcosis and supportive therapy is "narcosuggestion." The psychologic regression in narcosis, as in hypnosis, incites archaic dependency feelings toward the therapist and expedites authoritative supportive procedures. Acute anxiety reactions may sometimes be effectively treated by narcosuggestion as may other conditions that call for supportive measures.

In some instances, narcosis, by releasing cortical inhibition, liberates charges of pent up emotion that have been kept from awareness by repression. Resultant is an emotional catharsis. This effect may also sometimes be facilitated in narcosis by suggestion, by persistent questioning and probing, and by encouraging the patient to explore painful areas of his life. Recollection of repudiated traumatic memories and experiences may remove mental blocks, flurries of anxiety, depression, and psychosomatic symptoms associated with the repression of such harassing foci. These effects have been found helpful in the treatment of certain emotional problems, particularly acute stress reactions (traumatic neuroses, war neuroses), and some anxiety and hysterical reactions. In the war neuroses particularly, beneficial results are possible especially in cases of recent origin treated before rigid defenses have organized themselves. The working-through of the repressed or suppressed material in both narcotic and waking states helps to insure the permanency of the "cure." In chronic war and civilian neuroses, however, the patient does not seem to benefit so readily, since the illness has structuralized itself, and stubborn resistances block progress. The "cathartic" or "analytic" use of narcosis has been referred to by various observers as "narcoanalysis," "narcosynthesis" and "narcocatharsis."

While narcotherapy is principally employed for purposes of short-term therapy, it is sometimes introduced during the course of long-term insight psychotherapy where little material is forthcoming or obdurate resistance blocks the exploratory effort. Here one may frequently save a treatment situation that has come to a stalemate by inducing narcosis and liberating repressive forces through concerted probing. Transference phenomena which have evaded both patient and therapist sometimes become dramatically operative as emotionally charged material is released. An emergency use of narcotherapy is in the dealing with acute anxiety and panic states that occur during the course of long-term therapy. These symptoms may be so severe that they threaten the therapeutic relationship. In obsessional neurosis, for instance, occasional sessions devoted to narcosis may prevent alarming reactions at phases when defensive forces subside too rapidly.

Another use of narcosis is to expedite the induction of hypnosis in resistant subjects. During narcosis, it may be possible to give the patient suggestions to the effect that he will be susceptible to hypnosis. Suggestions must be detailed and specific, covering every aspect of the induction process. For example, the patient may be told that when he is shown a fixation object, he will gaze at it, and as he does, he will notice that his eyes will water, his lids will get heavy, his breathing will deepen, and he will fall asleep. He will sleep deeper and deeper until he is as deeply asleep as at present. These suggestions should be repeated and the patient may be asked if he understands thoroughly what he is to do. If he seems confused, the suggestions should be repeated when the drug effect is not so pronounced. As soon as the patient understands what is expected of him, he is asked to repeat what will happen at the next session. After the narcotic session, and before the patient is fully awake, he may be shown the fixation object and sleep suggestions given to him with the added suggestion, when he closes his eyes, that the next time he is shown the object, he will go to sleep faster and more deeply. Again, before leaving the room, this procedure is repeated. The technique works best when positive transference phenomena are operative in the narcotic state. It may not succeed in the event the patient does not understand what he is to do, or if he is in a state of hostile resistance.

Induction of Narcosis

The actual technique of inducing narcosis is simple. Most observers consider sodium amytal the drug of choice. There are various techniques of administration. One method is to dissolve one gram of sodium amytal in thirty or forty cubic centimeters of sterilized distilled water. A small gage intravenous needle attached to a large syringe is used for the administration which is made slowly at the rate of about one to two cubic centimeters per minute. Caffeine with sodium benzoate, or a solution of benzedrine, should be kept at hand and used in the event of respiratory embarrassment. At the termination of the interview, seven and one-half grains of caffeine may be injected subcutaneously to facilitate awaking. Sodium pentothal may be used instead of sodium amytal, dissolving seven and one-half grains in twenty cubic centimeters of sterilized distilled water. In the course of administration, a conversation is carried on with the patient, and drug injections should be halted temporarily in the event the patient gets too incoherent. Should the patient become too alert, more drug is introduced. It goes without saying that adequate preparations must be made for the patient so that he can sleep off the effects of the drug.

In the technique of narcosuggestion, commands, suggestions, reassuring comments or persuasive utterances are given when the patient achieves ample relaxation. In narcoanalysis, the patient is asked questions and the therapist attempts in other ways to stimulate the flow of associations. The release of repressed material fosters insight as the material is accepted and integrated by the waking ego. Later interviews in the waking state deal with whatever aspects of the material the patient wishes to explore. Over and over again the patient is questioned in the narcotized state about material to which he has reacted emotionally. This is continued until desensitization occurs, and preferably until good insight is achieved into the conflictual material as well as into reasons for its psychic repudiation. The depth of interpretation may be adjusted to the level of understanding of the patient.

In the event psychotic material is brought up during narcosis, giving evidence of a potential disintegrative tendency, this will call for the reappraisal of therapeutic goals and methods. Where the patient becomes too upset through release of traumatic material, it is best not to let the excitement mount to the point of overtaxing the ego. More drug is injected to put the patient to sleep, which will enable him to overcome the cathartic effects of the narcosis.

BIBLIOTHERAPY

Attempts are sometimes made by therapists to change faulty attitudes and to influence poor motivation in certain patients through the assigned reading of articles, pamphlets and books. By these measures, the patient is helped to understand how personality is evolved, why adaptation breaks down, the manifestations of collapse in adaptation, and how psychotherapy may help repair the damage. Advice on the handling of specific problems in adjustment, marriage and child-rearing may also be obtained from some reading materials. This therapeutic use of reading has been designated as "bibliotherapy."

Bibliotherapy is of value chiefly to persons who are not yet motivated for psychotherapy and who require more information about emotional illness before they can admit of its existence in themselves or can recognize that beneficial results may be obtained from treatment. It may correct misconceptions about mental health, psychiatry and psychotherapy. It is sometimes effective in bolstering repression through acceptance of written authoritative statements and directives which help the person to suppress inner fears, to gain reassurance, and to adopt socially acceptable attitudes and values. The latter influence makes bibliotherapy a useful adjunctive device in certain patients receiving supportive therapy. The patient may gain from readings a number of methods by means of which he may regulate his life, inspirational formulas that help in the achievement of happiness and success, and devices that permit of a regulation of those conflicts and strivings that are more or less under volitional control.

On the whole, reading adjuncts will not prove themselves to be too valuable for the patient who is receiving insight therapy. This is because no intellectual approach is of great service in modifying deeply repressed conflicts or in ameliorating symptoms that have strong defensive virtues for the individual. Indeed, the educational materials may be utilized by the patient as resistance, items being extracted out of context to justify neurotic patterns. The relative ineffectuality of reading materials in severe neurotic difficulties is attested to by the fact that scores of patients come to psychotherapy after having read more extensively from the psychiatric literature than has the therapist himself.

Nevertheless, bibliotherapy may help certain individuals to break through specific resistances and to gain limited insight, as for instance, those patients who, unconvinced of the value of psychotherapy, require examples from the experiences of others of how therapy helps. Resistance to working with dreams may sometimes be handled by asking the patient to read books in which the rationale of dream interpretation is explained. A patient who has in therapy resolved crippling sexual inhibitions may be aided in achieving a more complete sexual life by reading appropriate materials dealing with marriage. Or a patient having problems with her children may benefit greatly from books on child psychology.

The following is a list of recommended books, should the therapist decide that bibliotherapy is indicated:

1. Books on General Psychology and Psychiatry

ZILBOORG, GREGORY: Mind, Medicine and Man. New York, Harcourt Brace, 1943.

BINGER, CARL: The Doctor's Job. New York, W. W. Norton & Co., 1945.

PLANT, JAMES S.: Personality and the Cultural Pattern. Cambridge, Harvard University Press, 1937.

PRESTON, GEORGE H.: The Substance of Mental Health. New York, Rinehart, 1943.

MEAD, MARGARET: From the South Seas. New York, Wm. Morrow, 1939.

MENNINGER, KARL A.: The Human Mind. New York, Knopf, 1945.

MENNINGER, WILLIAM C.: Psychiatry in a Troubled World. New York, Macmillan, 1948.

DEUTSCH, ALBERT: The Mentally Ill in America. New York, Columbia University Press, 1949.

THOMPSON, CLARA: Psychoanalysis: Evolution and Development. New York, Hermitage House, 1950.

FREUD, SIGMUND: A General Introduction to Psychoanalysis. Garden City, New York, Garden City Publishing Co., 1943.

——: New Introductory Lectures on Psychoanalysis. New York, W. W. Norton & Co., 1933.

FROMM, ERICH: Escape From Freedom. New York, Farrar & Rinehart, Inc., 1941.

DUNBAR, H. FLANDERS: Mind and Body. New York, Random House, 1947.

2. Books Explaining How Personality Problems Operate.

TRAVIS, LEE E. and BARUCH, DOROTHY: Personal Problems of Everyday Life. New York, Appleton-Century, 1941.

ENGLISH, O. SPURGEON and PEARSON, GERALD H. J.: Emotional Problems of Living. New York, W. W. Norton & Co., 1945.

HORNEY, KAREN: The Neurotic Personality of Our Time. New York, W. W. Norton & Co., 1937.

3. Books Explaining How Psychiatry and Psychotherapy Help

PRESTON, GEORGE H.: Psychiatry for the Curious. New York, Rinehart, 1940.

REES, JOHN R.: The Health of the Mind. New York, W. W. Norton & Co., 1951.

SAUL, LEON J.: Emotional Maturity. Philadelphia, Lippincott, 1947.

FREEMAN, LUCY: Fight Against Fears. New York, Crown, 1951.

HINSIE, LELAND E.: Understandable Psychiatry. New York, Macmillan, 1948.

POLATIN, PHILLIP, and PHILTINE, ELLEN C.: How Psychiatry Helps. New York, Harper & Bros., 1949.

4. Books on Marriage and Sex

DUVALL, EVELYN M. and HILL, REUBEN: When You Marry. New York, Association Press, 1945.

McHUGH, GELOLO: Training for Parenthood. Durham, N.C., Family Life Publications, 1950.

DUVALL, EVELYN M.: Facts of Life and Love. New York, Association Press, 1950.

EASTMAN, NICOLAS JR.: Expectant Motherhood. Boston, Little, Brown & Co., 1940.

STOKES, WALTER R.: Modern Pattern for Marriage. New York, Rinehart & Co., Inc., 1948.

LEWIN, S. A., and GILMORE, JOHN: Sex Without Fear. New York, Lear Publishing, 1950.

———: Sex After Forty. New York, Grosset & Dunlap, 1952.

VAN DE VELDE, TH. H.: Ideal Marriage. New York, Random House, 1930.

STONE, ABRAHAM and STONE, HANNAH: A Marriage Manual. New York, Simon & Schuster, 1952.

WHITMAN, HOWARD: Let's Tell the Truth About Sex. New York, Pellegrini & Cudahy, 1948.

5. Books on Family Living and Adjustment

LEVY, JOHN, and MUNROE, RUTH: The Happy Family. New York, Knopf, 1938.

BENEDICT, AGNES and FRANKLIN, ADELE: The Happy Home. New York, Appleton-Century-Crofts, 1948.

DUVALL, EVELYN M.: Family Living. New York, Macmillan, 1950.

GROSSMAN, JEAN S.: Life With Family. New York, Appleton-Century-Crofts, 1948.

HARWOOD, E. C., and FOWLE, HELEN: How to Make Your Budget Balance. Great Barrington, Mass., Am. Inst. for Economic Research, 1941.

6. Books on Child Care and Guidance

SPOCK, BENJAMIN: Pocketbook of Baby and Child Care. New York, Pocketbooks, Inc., 1946.

WOLF, ANNA W. M.: Parents' Manual. New York, Simon & Schuster, 1941.

ALDRICH, C. A., and ALDRICH, W. M.: Babies are Human Beings. New York, Macmillan, 1938.

JENKINS, G. G., SCHACTER, H. and BAUER, W. W.: These Are Your Children. Chicago, Scott, Foresman, 1949.

MACKENZIE, CATHERINE: Parent and Child. New York, William Sloane Associates, 1949.

GESELL, ARNOLD and ILG, F. L.: Infant and Child in the Culture of Today. New York, Harper, 1943.

GRUENBERG, SIDONIE M.: We, the Parents. New York, Harper & Bros., 1948.

Child Study Association of America: Parents' Questions. New York, Harper & Bros., 1947.

BARUCH, DOROTHY W.: Parents Can Be People. New York, Appleton-Century, 1944.

FRANK, MARY and FRANK, LAWRENCE K.: How to Help Your Child in School. New York, Viking, 1950.

WHIPPLE, DOROTHY V.: Our American Babies. New York, M. Barrows & Co., Inc., 1944.

7. Books on How to Explain Sex to Children

BECK, LESTER F.: Human Growth. New York, Harcourt Brace, 1949.

DE SCHWEINITZ, KARL: Growing Up. New York, Macmillan, 2nd ed., 1935.

GRUENBERG, SIDONIE M.: The Wonderful Story of How You Were Born. Garden City, N.Y., Hanover House, 1952.

8. Books on How to Understand and Handle the Adolescent

TAYLOR, KATHERINE W.: Understanding and Guiding the Adolescent. New York, Grosset & Dunlap, 1948.

ZACHRY, CAROLINE B. and LIGHTY, MARGARET: Emotion and Conduct in Adolescence. New York, Appleton-Century, 1940.

9. Books to Be Read by Adolescents

McKOWN, HARRY C.: A Boy Grows Up. New York, Whittlesey House, 1940.

FEDDER, RUTH: A Girl Grows Up. New York, Whittlesey House, 1948.

LAWTON, GEORGE: How to Be Happy Though Young: Real Problems of Real Young People. New York, Vanguard Press, 1949.

BIBBY, CYRIL: How Life Is Handed On. New York, Emerson Books, 1947.

10. Inspirational Self-Help Books

LIEBMAN, JOSHUA L.: Peace of Mind. New York, Simon & Schuster, 1946.

HOGUE, HELEN G.: Bringing Up Ourselves. New York, Scribner, 1943.

OVERSTREET, HARRY A.: The Mature Mind. New York, W. W. Norton & Co., 1949.

11. For Patients with a Mentally Ill Relative

STERN, EDITH M. and HAMILTON, SAMUEL W.: Mental Illness: A Guide for the Family. New York, National Association for Mental Health, 1951.

12. Books on Problems of Old Age

LAWTON, GEORGE, ed.: New Goals for Old Age. New York, Columbia University Press, 1943.
LAWTON, GEORGE: Aging Successfully. New York, Columbia University Press, 1946.

13. Advanced Books for the Semi-Professional

MASLOW, A. H. and MITTLEMAN, B.: Principles of Abnormal Psychology. New York, Harper, 1951.
MURPHY, GARDNER: Personality: A Biosocial Approach to Origins and Structure. New York, Harper, 1947.
FREUD, SIGMUND: An Outline of Psychoanalysis. New York, W. W. Norton & Co., 1949.
BARKER, ROGER G., et al., eds.: Child Behavior and Development. New York, McGraw-Hill, 1943.
BULLIS, H. EDMUND and O'MALLEY, E. E.: Human Relations in the Classroom. Delaware State Society for Mental Hygiene. Courses I, II, and III.
KILPATRICK, WILLIAM H. and WILLIAMS, VAN TIL, eds.: Intercultural Attitudes in the Making. New York, Harper, 1947.

49

Handling Emergencies in Psychotherapy

EMERGENCIES SOMETIMES DEVELOP DURING PSYCHOTHERAPY WHICH require prompt and cautious handling. Among such emergencies are suicidal attempts; psychotic attacks; excitement, over-activity and antisocial behavior; panic states; acute alcoholic intoxication; acute barbiturate poisoning; severe psychosomatic symptoms; and intercurrent incurable somatic illness.

SUICIDAL ATTEMPTS

In well-conducted psychotherapy, suicidal attempts are rare. Vague suicidal threats may be expressed at the start of treatment, the patient making such comments as that he might be better off dead, but that he is "too much of a coward" to try suicide. Where such statements lack the tone of conviction, it is best for the therapist not to subject the patient to concentrated interrogation around the matter of suicide. The therapist's expressed concern may frighten the patient badly and rob him of faith in himself.

The following signs, symptoms and situations, however, do point to a potential suicidal risk: (1) depressions of a psychoneurotic or psychotic nature, (2) irrespective of diagnosis, any patient who has made a suicidal attempt in the past or who has a history of a severe depression, (3) a patient who, during therapy, insistently threatens suicide, (4) loss of appetite, severe weight loss, insomnia, listlessness, apathy, persistent expressions of discouragement and hopelessness, loss of sexual desire, extreme constipation, hypochondriac ideas, continuous weeping and general motor retardation which are present at the start or appear in the course of therapy, and (5) dreams of death, mutilation and funerals.

Where, during treatment, the patient talks openly and seriously about a desire to "end it all," it is important not to change the subject or to reassure the patient unduly. Rather, a frank talk about the reasons why he feels that suicide is the best recourse for him may permit the patient to investigate his feelings. This will enable the therapist to determine whether the threat is real, whether it is casually made as a dramatic gesture, whether it is a hostile stab at the therapist, or whether it constitutes an appeal for reassurance. Under no circumstances should the therapist minimize the importance of the threat, cajole the patient or subject him to verbal attack. Where the threat seems serious, the therapist might make helpful statements to the effect that suicide *seems* to be a way out of his difficulty, but that it actually accomplishes nothing; that there may be other solutions than suicide which are not now apparent; and that suicide is a final act which cannot be undone, and which could always be resorted to later on if the patient so wishes. The attitudes conveyed to the patient in such statements are respect for his right to self-determination, and a reminder that he is not giving himself an opportunity to explore more constructive actions. Talking openly about suicide often serves to rob it of its awesome or appealing quality.

1. Hysterical Personalities

Suicidal attempts in hysterical personalities are common and consist of histrionic gestures calculated to impress, frighten or force persons with whom the patient is in contact to yield attention and favors. Such attempts are incited by motives for display rather than by genuine desires to take one's life. Dramatic performances of an ingenious nature are indulged, during which there is a superficial slashing of the wrists, or feigned unconsciousness with stertorous breathing while placing an empty bottle of sleeping pills alongside the bed, or the gulping of tincture of iodine, or the impetuous opening of gas jets. Feverish demonstrations of suffering and martyrdom continue after the patient is restrained or "revived," until he is convinced that he has emphasized his protests sufficiently. The danger of these pseudo-suicidal maneuvers is that the patient's judgment may not be too good during dramatic overacting and he may accidentally go too far and commit suicide even though this was not his original intent.

In treating hysterical cases with suicidal tendencies, it is necessary that the therapist demonstrate to the patient that he is neither intimidated by, nor angry at the actions of the patient. Interpretation of the purpose of the patient's frenzied behavior should be made in terms of the broader neurotic patterns.

2. Psychopathic Personality

Of a related but more serious nature are the suicidal attempts of the psychopathic personality. During episodes of excitement, violence, deep remorse, excessive drinking or temporary psychotic outbreaks, the psychopath may slash his wrists or take an overdose of sleeping pills. The desire for self-punishment and death are genuine though temporary. Hospitalized, such patients, their attempt having been aborted, recover rapidly, evidence no further suicidal impulses, and express great remorse at their folly. Yet, a short time later, under propitious circumstances, the attempt will be repeated, with further contrition and promises of abstention. Interpretation of the episode is essential, but it usually fails to act as a deterrent to the patient's actions. Because the suicidal episodes are motivated by disturbed interpersonal relationships, as, for instance, a broken love affair or rejection by a love object, the continued exploration of the patient's feelings and patterns is indicated. In addition, the therapist may have to increase the frequency of visits, and insist that he be telephoned when the patient is tempted to indulge in suicide. Where the patient persists in his impulsive suicidal behavior, after seeming to have acquired insight into his patterns, the therapist may have no other alternative than to tell the patient that treatments will have to be discontinued. It may be suggested that the patient may perhaps want to start treatment with another therapist. This may give the patient enough of a jolt so that he will insist on the therapist's continuing to treat him, on the condition that he will abandon all further suicidal attempts. Whether or not the therapist concedes to the patient's wishes to continue treating him will depend on how he feels about the patient. Unfortunately, with some psychopaths the threat of discontinuance of therapy may be the only force that can control their explosive conduct. Even here the effect may be temporary.

3. Schizophrenia

In some types of schizophrenia suicide is a grave possibility. It is most common in acute, excited catatonic states, particularly those associated with panic. Hallucinations may drive certain patients to mutilate or kill themselves. Fear of homosexual attack or of being persecuted may also force some paranoidal individuals to suicide. The methods of self-destruction employed in schizophrenia may be bizarre, including such mutilations as disembowelment and genital amputation.

The handling of the suicidally inclined schizophrenic patient is organized around administering ample sedation, communicating with his family so that they may assume some responsibility, and arranging for transportation and admission to a mental hospital. Insulin shock therapy or electric convulsive therapy is often indicated.

4. Pathologic Depressions

Depressed states may appear in all people, due to loss of security, status or a love object; however, the depression is rarely of such depth as to inspire a desire to take one's life. Where the depressed state is extreme, suicide is always a possibility. Among the pathologic depressive conditions are psychoneurotic depression, manic-depressive depressed psychosis, involutional depression, senile depression, and depressions in organic brain disease.

In managing a patient with a pathologic depression, certain palliative measures are helpful. The watching of his diet with the inclusion of stimulating and appetizing foods, and the prescription of tonics and vitamins, may be indicated in anorexia. Benzedrine or dexedrine may be useful to stimulate the patient during the day, while sedation may be required at night for insomnia. The patient's family, or a reliable friend, should be interviewed and acquainted with the potential dangers. Where the patient remains at home, a trustworthy adult person should be in constant attendance, the patient not being permitted to lock himself in any room, including the bathroom. Sleeping pills, poisonous drugs, razor blades, rope, sharp knives and instruments should be removed. Window guards are necessary if there is a chance the patient may hurt himself by leaping through a window. Hospitalization on a closed ward with constant supervision by efficient nurses or attendants may be essential. The treatment of choice is electric convulsive therapy which may prove to be a life-saving measure. Psychotherapy during severe depression is generally confined to supportive measures, insight approaches tending to stir up too much anxiety.

Suicide is especially possible during the spontaneous resolution of a depression, when the patient begins to recover from a depressive attack after a few electric convulsive treatments, or when, after having started to recover, he suffers a relapse. The patient must consequently be watched carefully during these periods, since he is apt to put into practice a suicidal desire he was previously unable to execute due to retardation.

5. Miscellaneous Suicidal Conditions

Sometimes a therapist is consulted by the parents or friends of a child who has made a suicidal attempt. Examination may fail to reveal hysteria, depression or schizophrenia, especially when the child is non-communicative to the point of mutism. It is possible here that the child is internalizing destructive feelings. Because he is non-motivated for therapy, and resents having been taken to a psychiatrist, it may be difficult to treat the patient. By following the rules outlined in chapter 28, Dealing with Inadequate Motivation, and by indicating to the patient that he seems to be angry at someone, it may be possible to establish rapport.

A girl of fourteen, who had made a suicidal attempt by swallowing fifty aspirin tablets, was brought in for a consultation. Refusing to talk except in monosyllables, it was difficult to carry on an interview. The therapist finally remarked: "You must have been awfully angry at someone to have done this to yourself." The patient blanched, then brought her hands to her face and started compulsive sobbing which went on for fifteen minutes. Intermittent were outbursts in the form of protestations of how "bad" she was for feeling the way she did about her mother. Ventilation of her resentment produced immediate emotional relief and established sufficient contact with the therapist to start psychotherapy.

PSYCHOTIC ATTACKS

In the process of doing insight therapy, certain patients may be unable to tolerate the anxiety that is liberated by an attack on their resistances and defenses, or that is mobilized by transference. Ego shattering may develop which can eventuate in a psychotic episode. This phenomenon does not imply that persons with weak egos or with disintegrative tendencies should not receive reeducative or reconstructive therapy. They may indeed do well with such therapies. The crucial factor is the quality of the working relationship. Much here is dependent on the therapist—his skill, personality and flexibility. Some therapists are so equipped that they can do good reconstructive work with potentially psychotic and even outright psychotic patients. Other therapists, particularly those who are unable to manage their counter-transference, may be unable to treat patients whose ego organizations are unstable. Such therapists may refuse to work with infantile dependent personality disorders or with borderline and psychotic patients unless the approach is to be exclusively supportive in nature. They may also have to transfer patients who show tendencies toward psychotic outbursts, once the treatment process is under way.

Symptoms that lead one to suspect beginning ego disintegration during psychotherapy are feelings of unreality, depersonalization, excessive day-dreaming, ideas of reference, paranoidal ideas, bizarre somatic sensations, motor excitement, uncontrollable sexual and hostile impulses, propensity for perversions, heightened interest in toilet activities, compulsive talking, fears of castration, and fleeting hallucinations and delusions. These symptoms may appear individually or in combination. For a while the patient may maintain a good grasp on reality, recognizing the unusual or irrational nature of his ideas, impulses and acts. Later on, distortions of reality may occur in the form of fixed delusions and hallucinations, perhaps accompanied by panic reactions, suicidal tendencies and violent aggression.

Psychotic attacks may be handled within the therapeutic situation by a therapist who has a warm feeling for the patient, who is not disturbed by the existing symptoms, and who is capable of modifying his approach so as to bring about the restoration of repressive barriers. The fact that a psychosis has precipitated is indicative of something having gone amiss in the therapeutic relationship. If the therapist can admit to himself the possibility of errors in handling, and if he is able to restore the patient's feelings of trust and confidence, he may be capable of bringing the retreat from reality to a halt. In line with this objective, it is best to discontinue probing for deep conflictual areas and to keep the content of the interview focused on current reality problems. The relationship with the therapist should be kept on as positive a level as possible, the therapist assuming a helpful active role. Under no circumstances should the therapist express alarm at, and condemnation toward any of the patient's misconceptions. Listening attentively to the patient's productions, the therapist counters with reality, suggesting that perhaps things seem to be as they are because the patient has been so upset. If disturbing transference is at the basis of the patient's turmoil, measures to lessen transference, described in chapters 37 and 41, may be invoked. Should the patient require more support, the frequency of interviews may be increased.

Where these practices fail to bring relief to the patient, it is likely that the therapeutic relationship has deteriorated, and that the patient will have to be referred to another therapist. The referral may be upsetting to the patient, and he is apt to consider it a further manifestation of rejection or an indication of his failure. The therapist may explain that the patient's specific problem will probably be helped more by another therapist with a slightly different approach. If the patient is incapable of thinking rationally, and if his difficulties are potentially dangerous to himself and others, a reliable family member should be asked to assume some responsibility in the matter of referral. Should the patient object to the therapist's making contact with his family, the therapist may, if the situation is sufficiently dangerous, have to communicate with the family irrespective of the patient's wishes.

Where self-injury, suicide, homicide, violent aggression, ruinous spending, criminality, or other disasters are possible, hospitalization will be mandatory. Discussion with the patient may convince him that he should enter an institution voluntarily. Hospitalization will, however, have to be accomplished against the wishes of the patient where he sees no need for confinement. In the event he is actively resistant, intravenous sodium amytal to the point of deep sleep will permit of his transport to an institution without the need for physical restraint. A physician should be in attendance in the ambulance that transports the patient in order to handle such emergencies as respiratory paralysis.

The therapist may have to arrange the details of hospital admission in cooperation with the patient's family, and he may have to explain the reasons for hospitalization to them in a reassuring way. In doing this, he may experience some guilt and anxiety, as if he is accountable for the patient's collapse. It is important, however, not to castigate himself for what has happened, nor to confess to failure; rather, the family may be informed that the patient's personality structure has been unable to stand his inner tensions and that he has temporarily broken down. A period of hospitalization is necessary to restore his equilibrium.

The specific treatment rendered in the hospital will depend on the severity and type of psychosis. In acute excitement or depression with exhaustion, it will be necessary to sedate the patient adequately, to correct dehydration by injecting fluids and salts parenterally, and to administer electric convulsive therapy or insulin shock therapy, whichever is indicated. In milder excitements or depressions, sedatives and hospitalization alone may suffice to restore the patient's stability.

EXCITEMENT, OVERACTIVITY AND ANTI-SOCIAL BEHAVIOR

States of excitement and overactivity developing during psychotherapy are signs of "acting-out" or manifestations of ego shattering.

During acting-out the patient may engage in destructive, anti-social, or perverse sexual behavior. In attempting to understand acting-out, our first suspicion is that the patient is protecting himself from awareness of transference by projecting it away from the therapist. Hostile or aggressive outbursts, delinquency, criminality, homosexuality and marked promiscuity are often products of hostile and sexual impulses toward the therapist which the patient is unable to acknowledge.

The only way to resolve such acting-out is to explore the patient's feelings and attitudes toward the therapist, to determine which of these are rooted in realities and which are irrational carry-overs of the past. So long as he is unaware of, and cannot verbalize his strivings toward the therapist, the patient will continue to "blow off steam" outside of therapy. Skillful use of the interviewing process that brings out verbalizations related to the transference, may put a halt to the patient's destructive patterns.

Sometimes it is difficult or impossible to get the patient to analyze transference, and in this way to terminate acting-out. The therapist here may attempt to deal with this obstruction by: (1) stimulating transference through devices already described, in order to make its manifestations so obvious that the patient cannot help but talk about his feelings, or (2) controlling acting-out by increasing visits to as many as daily sessions, and by the assumption of a prohibitive, authoritative role. If these measures fail to help the situation, therapy will have to be terminated with transfer to another therapist.

Excitement and anti-social behavior which occur as a result of ego shattering may be dealt with after identifying the cause of the present difficulties. Supportive techniques are generally indicated. If the decline continues, the therapist had best transfer the patient to another therapist, since he, himself, is probably unable to control the situation. Where a dangerous psychotic condition develops, the patient's family will have to be apprised of it, since hospitalization will in all likelihood be necessary.

INTENSE ANXIETY ATTACKS AND PANIC STATES

Severe anxiety sometimes breaks out in the course of psychotherapy. It may become so overwhelming that the patient feels helpless in its grip. His coping resources, seemingly having come to an end, can no longer crush the fear of imminent disintegration. His demands on the therapist then may become insistent, and he will bid for protection and comfort.

The handling of intense anxiety reactions will require much fortitude on the part of the therapist. By assuming a calm, reassuring manner, the therapist provides the patient with the best medium in which to achieve stability. Accordingly, the therapist must be able to tolerate the emotions of the patient. He must be able to convey to the patient a constant feeling of warmth, understanding and protectiveness, while respecting the patient's latent strengths that have been smothered by his turmoil. Upbraiding the patient for exhibiting foolish fears, and attempting to argue away anxiety, serve to stimulate rather than to reduce tension.

The best means of handling acute anxiety is to permit the patient to verbalize freely in an empathic atmosphere. One or more sodium amytal interviews (narcotherapy) may prove useful in promoting adequate relaxation or mental catharsis. Helping the patient to arrive at an understanding of the source of his anxiety, whether it be rooted in unconscious conflict, transference, resistance, or the too abrupt removal of existing defenses, promises the quickest possibility of relief. The triad of emotional catharsis, insight and reassurance operates together to permit of a reconstitution of defenses against anxiety.

Where anxiety is intense, it is usually impossible to work with the patient on an insight level. Here, supportive measures will be necessary to restore the habitual defenses. If the patient is living under intolerable environmental circumstances, a change of environment may be indicated to lessen pressures on him. In the event anxiety has followed intensive mental probing, a holiday from exploration may be necessary, with a focusing on casual or seemingly inconsequential topics. A patient who has spent many sleepless nights tossing about restlessly, or, once asleep, has awakened periodically with frightening dreams, may benefit from a dose of three grains of sodium amytal which can alleviate his tension remarkably and restore his stability. The use of sedatives during the day is to be avoided, if possible, to forestall the sedative habit. If anxiety continues, the frequency of sessions may be increased and the patient may be assured that he can reach the therapist at any time in the event of a real emergency. Several sessions devoted to "narcosuggestion," that is, reassurance and suggestion applied under sodium amytal narcosis, may be tried. Where these measures do not control anxiety, which threatens to get out of hand, a short period of hospitalization is occasionally prescribed. During this period sub-coma insulin may be administered.

The treatment of panic states is more difficult than the management of anxiety. Here, the patient is victimized by a wild, unreasoning fear that drives him into disorganized thinking and behavior, or to the point of immobilization. Suicide is always a grave possibility. Strong sedation is often given in panic states in sufficient dosage so that the patient goes into narcosis; and prolonged narcotic sleep may be helpful where the patient has exhausted himself. Because of the dangerous consequences of severe panic attacks, hospitalization on a closed ward is often necessary.

ACUTE ALCOHOLIC INTOXICATION

Pathologic intoxication occasionally presents itself as a psychiatric emergency, especially in psychopathic personalities and alcoholics. Excited, destructive, combative, homicidal or suicidal behavior may occur here which will require immediate management. While sedation is generally given to a patient who is acutely intoxicated, morphine and barbiturates are not suitable for this purpose. Paraldehyde is a most effective drug, given orally in doses of one to two teaspoonsful, or intravenously in doses up to one cubic centimeter. Useful also are metrazol, injected intravenously very slowly in doses of five to six cubic centimeters of a ten per cent solution; and apomorphine, hypodermically, in doses of four to six milligrams. Detoxification therapy consists of an intravenous infusion of twenty-five grams of glucose, twenty to forty units of insulin, one hundred milligrams of niacin, one hundred milligrams of thiamine, and one hundred milligrams of vitamin C. This is repeated every four hours for four doses, gradually reducing the quantity of niacin. With this treatment, recovery from pathologic intoxication is generally rapid.

ACUTE BARBITURATE POISONING

The popularity of barbiturates as sedatives has resulted in a relatively large incidence of barbiturate poisoning. Patients who have developed a sedative habit may accidentally take an overdose of barbiturates, or the drugs may be purposefully imbibed with suicidal intent. Sometimes the patient, having swallowed a lethal dose, will telephone the therapist informing him of his act. At other times relatives or friends will chance on the patient before respiratory paralysis has set in.

Therapy consists of immediate hospitalization, if possible, and the institution of the following measures: (1) establishing an airway, such as with an endotracheal tube, (2) administration of oxygen or artificial respiration, using a mechanical resuscitator, (3) gastric lavage, (4) fluids given parenterally, and, in extreme hypotension, plasma injected intravenously, (5) stimulants, such as amphetamine sulfate, in doses of forty milligrams intravenously; or caffeine one-half gram intravenously, injected at frequent intervals; or electro-stimulation, where the apparatus is available. (6) Metrazol is recommended as the pharmaceutic agent of choice. Five cubic centimeters of a ten per cent solution are injected intravenously. If there is no response in fifteen minutes, another ten cubic centimeters are injected. Thereafter twenty cubic centimeters of the solution are very slowly injected at intervals of thirty minutes. Some physicians prefer picrotoxin to metrazol, in repeated intravenous doses of ten milligrams.

SEVERE PSYCHOSOMATIC SYMPTOMS

There are a number of psychosomatic symptoms for which the patient initially seeks treatment, or that develop suddenly in therapy, which may be regarded as emergencies. Most of these are hysterical conversion or dissociative reactions, such as blindness, seizures, fugues, vomiting, aphonia, amnesia, paralysis, astasia-abasia, violent contractures and anorexia nervosa. The patient may be so disabled by his symptom that he will be unable to cooperate with any attempted psychotherapeutic endeavor. Immediate removal of the symptom may thus be indicated. Such removal need not block the later use of more ambitious therapeutic measures. In the course of symptom removal, efforts may be made to show the patient that his symptoms are rooted in deeper personality problems, the correction of which will necessitate exploration of conflictual sources.

Hypnosis is an ideal adjunctive technique to expedite the emergency relief of hysterical symptoms. Once symptom removal has been decided upon, it is necessary to determine whether to attempt the removal at one session, or whether to extend therapy over a period of several weeks. The severity of the symptom, its duration, the nature of the patient's personality, and his aptitude for hypnosis have to be considered. The approach is an individual one, and suggestions must be so framed that they will conform with the patient's personality, the type of symptom, and its symbolic significance. It is essential to adapt one's language to the patient's intelligence and to his education. Many failures in symptom removal are due to the fact that the patient does not clearly comprehend what the hypnotist is trying to convey to him.

If hypnotic removal of the symptom at one session is decided upon, sufficient time must be set aside to devote oneself exclusively to the problem. As many as two to three hours may be necessary. At first the patient is encouraged

to discuss his past history and his symptom in order for the therapist to determine his reaction to his illness, as well as to gain clues to the patient's attitudes,
motivations and character strivings. It is essential to get the patient to verbalize
how uncomfortable he is, and to get him to see that his life is being hampered
by his symptom. Once the therapist is convinced that the patient has an intense
desire to gain relief from suffering, he may proceed with a further elaboration
of what is required to get well.

An optimistic attitude on the part of the therapist is important because
many patients are terrified by their illness and have convinced themselves of the
impossibility of cure. However, a cure should not be promised, and the therapist
must insist that relief will depend upon how well the person cooperates. An
attempt must be made to inculcate in the patient's mind a firm conviction that
he will get well. He may be told that hypnosis has helped other people recover
and can help him, too, if he will let it.

The patient may then be informed that it is necessary to determine how he
will respond to suggestions. He is instructed that he need not try to concentrate
too hard on what is said, because, even though his attention wanders, suggestions
will get to his subconscious mind and he will find himself reacting to them. If
he has the desire to rid himself of suffering, he will have the desire to relax
and to follow suggestions. No indication is given the patient at this time that
his symptom will be removed in its entirety since the symptom may have
unconscious values for him, and he may show resistance if he feels he will be
deprived of it immediately.

Hypnosis is then induced, and confidence in his ability to follow suggestions is built up by conducting the patient through light, medium and, finally,
deep trance states. In the event the patient has a symptom which consists of loss
of a physical function, it may be expedient to suggest that he is unable to use
the part. This is done in order to associate malfunction with the hypnotist's
command instead of with a personal inadequacy.

The next step in treatment is to get the patient, if he so desires, to discuss
under hypnosis his immediate life situation and his reaction to his illness. A
persuasive talk may be given to the patient, avoiding, for the time being,
reference to his symptom.

In some patients active participation is encouraged. A reasonable explanation is given the patient for suggestions that are advanced. In some instances he
may even be encouraged to veto suggestions, if he does not wish to follow them
or if he believes them to be against his best interests. Active participation is
utilized in patients with relatively good ego strength who shy away from too
authoritarian an approach.

Symptom removal by suggestion is far more effective where it is demonstrated to the patient that he has not lost control over his functions, and hence
is not the helpless victim of symptoms which cannot be altered or removed.
This is achieved by showing the patient, while he is in a trance, that it is
possible to create on command such symptoms as paralysis, spasticity and
anesthesia. Once the patient responds to these suggestions, he is informed
about the important influence that the mind has over the body. Then a symptom

identical with the patient's chief complaint is produced in some other part of the body. Should the patient respond successfully, a partial removal of his own symptom is attempted. For instance, if he has a paralyzed arm, he is told that his fingers will move ever so little. Then paralysis of the other arm, which has been artifically produced, is increased in intensity, while a strong suggestion is made that the patient will find that function is restored to his ailing part. In the case of a paralyzed arm, it is suggested that his hand will move, then his arm, and, finally, that the paralysis will disappear altogether.

The fact that symptoms can be produced and removed so readily on suggestion may influence the patient to accept the fact that he is not powerless, and that he can exercise control over his body.

In order to protect the patient, should his symptom have a defensive function, he may be left with some residual symptom which is less disabling than the original complaint, but which, it is hoped, will absorb its dynamic significance. For instance, in the case of a paralyzed arm, paralysis of the little finger may be induced, and a suggestion may be given the patient that the finger paralysis will have the same meaning for him as the arm paralysis, and that the finger paralysis will remain until he understands fully the reasons for the original paralysis and no longer needs the paralysis. In the event of an extensive anesthesia, numbness of a limited area may be suggested as a substitute.

Posthypnotic suggestions are next given the patient to the effect that his restored functions will continue in the waking state, except for the induced residual symptom. An activity may then be suggested which brings into use the ailing part; and the patient may then be awakened in the midst of this action.

These suggestions are repeated at subsequent visits, and, if desired, the patient is taught the technique of self-hypnosis so that suggestive influences may continue through his own efforts.

Although removal of the patient's symptom at one sitting may be possible and desirable in certain hysterical and psychosomatic conditions, it is usually best to extend therapy over a longer period. Suggestions are carried out very much better where the patient is convinced that he has been hypnotized and that hypnosis can have a potent influence on his functions. It may therefore be advisable to delay giving therapeutic suggestions until the patient achieves as deep a trance as possible, and gains confidence in his ability to experience the phenomena suggested to him. The employment of therapeutic suggestions at a time when the patient is skeptical about his ability to comply, and before he has achieved sufficient faith in himself and in the therapist, may end in failure and add discouragement and panic to the patient's difficulties.

A deep trance seems to increase therapeutic effectiveness in most patients. Where only a light trance is possible, the patient may not be able to get to a point where he becomes assured of his capacity to control his symptom.

All suggestions must be as specific as possible and should be repeated several times. The therapist should build, as completely as possible, a picture of what he wants the patient to feel or to do.

The lighter the trance, the less emphatic should the suggestions be. In extremely superficial hypnotic states, the patient may be instructed that he need not concentrate too closely on the suggestions of the therapist, but rather should fixate his attention on a restful train of thought. This technique is based on the idea that the patient's resistances can be circumvented in this manner. A logical explanation may be presented of why suggestions will work, along such lines as that the unconscious mind is capable of absorbing and utilizing suggestions even though the conscious mind may resist them.

If the patient is in a medium or deep trance, suggestions should be framed in as simple a manner as possible. The patient, especially when he is in deep hypnosis, should repeat what is expected of him. Otherwise he may be so lethargic that he may not understand clearly the nature of the commands. If he is a somnambule, he may be instructed to carry out instructions even though he does not remember that they were formulated by the therapist. It is also a good idea in somnambulistic patients to give them a posthypnotic suggestion to the effect that-they will be unresponsive to hypnotic induction by any person except the therapist. This will prevent the patient from being victimized by an amateur hypnotist who may very well undo therapeutic benefits.

If facts important in the understanding of the patient's condition are uncovered in hypnosis, these may or may not be brought to the patient's attention, depending upon their significance and upon the ability of the patient to tolerate their implications. It is best to make interpretations as superficial as possible, utilizing knowledge one has gained in working with the patient to guide him into activities of a creative nature which do not stir up too much conflict.

Termination of hypnosis by having the patient sleep for a few minutes before interruption is advantageous. The patient is simply instructed that he will continue to sleep for a designated number of minutes, following which he will be awakened. The period of sleep may range from two to fifteen minutes. Where the patient is able to dream on suggestion, this period may profitably be utilized to induce dreams either of a spontaneous sort or of a nature relevant to the particular trends elicited during the trance.

There is no set rule as to how much time to devote to hypnosis during each session. Except for the initial induction period, the trance need not exceed one-half hour. Ample time should be allowed to take up with the patient his problems both before and after hypnosis. His reaction to the trance may also be discussed.

INTERCURRENT INCURABLE SOMATIC ILLNESS

The incidence of an intercurrent incurable physical illness constitutes an emergency in some patients. Development of such conditions as multiple sclerosis, brain tumor, Hodgkins disease, cancer, cerebral hemorrhage or thrombosis, or of a coronary attack, will make it necessary for the therapist to take stock of the reality situation and perhaps to revise therapeutic goals. Essential also is a dealing with the emotional impact of the intercurrent illness on the individual. Insight therapy may have to be halted, and supportive approaches implemented.

Where the person is suffering from a non-fatal illness, and where there is a possibility of a residual disability, as in coronary disease, apoplexy, tuberculosis and various neurologic disorders, an effort must be made to get the patient to accept his illness. A desensitization technique may be utilized, encouraging the patient to discuss his illness and to ventilate his fears concerning it. The need to recognize that his illness does not make him different from others, that all people have problems, some of which are more serious than his own, that it is not disgraceful to be sick, may be repeatedly emphasized.

Persuasive talks may be given the patient to the effect that the most important thing in his achievement of health is to admit and to accept the limitations imposed on him by his illness. This need not cause him to retire in defeat. He will still be able to gain sufficient recognition and success if he operates within the framework of his handicap. It is most important for his self-respect that he continue to utilize his remaining capacities and aptitudes, expanding them in a realistic and reasonable way. Many people suffering from a physical handicap have been able to compensate for a disability in one area by becoming proficient in another.

In patients who tend to regard their disability as justifying a completely passive attitude toward life, an effort must be made to stimulate activity and productiveness. The dangers of passivity and dependency, in terms of what these do to self-respect, are stressed. The person is encouraged to become as self-assertive and independent as his handicap will allow.

Where it is important for the patient to relax and to give up competitive efforts, persuasive therapy may be combined with a reassuring, guidance approach aimed at externalizing his interests along lines that will be engaging, but not too stimulating. The cultivation of a different philosophy toward life, directed at enjoying leisure, and looking with disdain on fierce ambitious striving, will often help the patient to accept this new role.

Severe intractable pain which does not respond to the usual non-narcotic analgesics, and which is extremely disturbing to the patient, may require psychosurgery (lobotomy).

In progressive, incurable and fatal ailments there may be a temptation to stop therapy on the basis that nothing more can be done for the patient. Actually, the patient may need the therapist more now than before the ailment had developed. Where the patient has no knowledge of the seriousness of his condition, as, for instance, inoperable cancer, the decision of whether or not to inform him of his calamity is a grave one which will influence the degree of his suffering in the remaining days of his life. In some cases it is unwise to burden him with the full seriousness of his condition. Statements may be made to the effect that he has a condition which his physician has classified as one that will get worse before it gets better. Many persons cling to a straw extended to them by an authority and maintain a positive attitude to the end. Where this ruse is considered advisable, the patient's family will have to cooperate.

In other patients, it may be more practical to inform them, if they do not already know, of the fact that they have a progressive ailment. They may be told that everything will be done to reduce pain and suffering and to keep the patient in as good health as possible. Persuasive suggestions to face his remaining months with calmness and courage may be very reassuring to the patient. The patient may be told that while his life span is limited, he may extend and enjoy it by the proper mental attitude. A guidance approach helps reduce the disturbing effect of environmental factors, and permits the patient to divert his interests toward outlets of an enjoyable nature. Where the patient is so disposed, he may be encouraged to cultivate religious interests in which he may find much solace.

Psychotherapy in Special Conditions

THE PRINCIPLES OF PSYCHOTHERAPY THAT HAVE BEEN OUTLINED, AND the technical procedures that have been delineated, apply to all emotional problems and conditions irrespective of clinical diagnosis. It is possible, with the proper kind of working relationship and the adroit use of appropriate techniques, to approach goals of personality reconstruction in any syndrome. Experience, however, has shown that certain kinds of conditions make extensive therapeutic objectives difficult to achieve, and that they seem to respond favorably to specific techniques or combinations of methods. In this chapter, we shall consider the problems and modifications often encountered in the treatment of the different neurotic, psychophysiologic, personality and psychotic disorders.

PSYCHONEUROTIC DISORDERS

1. Anxiety Reactions (Anxiety States, Anxiety Neuroses)

The average patient with an anxiety reaction is so upset by his symptoms that relief from suffering constitutes his prime motivation. Because he feels helpless and frightened, he is apt to demand an authoritative, directive relationship in which he is protected and through which he obtains immediate symptomatic relief. To abide by these demands will mean that the therapist will have to employ supportive measures which may or may not be successful in abating anxiety. Where successful, the patient may lose his incentive for further therapy and be contented with his symptom-free state, even though this may be temporary. Where unsuccessful, he may lose confidence in the therapist and then go off elsewhere in search of relief.

It is important, therefore, to work on the motivation of the patient in order to get him to accept insight therapy. This may prove to be a more formidable task than the therapist had calculated. Because repression is a chief defense against the conflicts which inspire anxiety, the patient may be reluctant to challenge any coping mechanism he has elaborated, though it be inadequate in dealing with his difficulty. Resistances against insight are manifold and ingenious. Sometimes repression is so powerful that only a transference neurosis is capable of breaking it down and of revealing the underlying sources of conflict.

Where anxiety interferes with treatment, temporary mild sedation may be helpful, during which period it may be possible to set up a working relationship and to begin active therapy. One must recognize, however, that sedatives are props the patient may be reluctant to give up. Under circumstances of especially intense anxiety, narcotherapy may be useful; and where anxiety mounts to panic, sub-coma insulin therapy is of possible value.

2. Conversion and Dissociative Reactions (Conversion Hysteria)

The basic defense employed in conversion and dissociative reactions is repression. Therapeutic techniques must be organized to resolve repression and to deal with inner conflicts. Transference analysis, especially with the working-through of a transference neurosis, is ideally suited to the cure of this disorder. From the viewpoint of mere handling and removal of symptoms, hypnosis is classically of value. However, while hysterical symptoms can often be eliminated in relatively few hypnotic sessions, the dramatic, infantile and self-dramatizing personality constellation associated with this reaction will require prolonged psychotherapy, preferably along reconstructive lines. Unfortunately, even though insight therapy is accepted by the patient, a great many impediments will become manifest during the course of treatment in the form of intellectual inhibitions and other devices to reinforce repression.

Whereas insight therapy is the best treatment for this condition, circumstances of obstinate resistance, of faulty motivation, and of profound secondary gain may prevent any other but a supportive approach.

Symptom removal by authoritative suggestion, with or without hypnosis, is occasionally indicated, particularly where the symptom produces great physical discomfort and interferes with the individual's social and economic adjustment. There are some symptoms which serve a minimal defensive purpose in binding anxiety. The inconvenience to the patient of such symptoms is an important incentive toward their abandonment. Where the symptom constitutes a plea for help, love and reassurance on the basis of helplessness, the therapist, by ordering cessation of symptoms, virtually assures the patient of support and love without his needing to utilize symptoms for this purpose.

Such symptoms as paralysis, aphonia, visual disorders, anesthesia, astasia-abasia and hysterical contractures may often be removed in relatively few sessions with a strong authoritarian approach. One must not overestimate the permanency of the cure, however, since the original motivations which sponsored the symptom are not altered in the least, and a relapse is always possible. Consequently, wherever the therapist can do so, the patient should be prepared for further therapy by explaining the purposeful nature of his symptom and its source in unconscious conflict.

Since hysteria often represents a reaction to unpleasant circumstances which stimulate inner conflicts, a guidance approach is sometimes utilized in appropriate cases to adjust the patient to environmental demands from which he cannot escape, and to help him to modify existing remediable situational difficulties. It may be possible to get an hysterical individual to make compromises with his environment so that he will not be inclined to overreact to current stresses. Here, too, an attempt must be made to acquaint the person with the fact that his symptoms, though inspired by external difficulties, are actually internally sponsored. Once the patient accepts this fact, therapy along insight lines may be possible.

The treatment of hysteria through hypnotic symptom removal and by guidance therapy are least successful where the symptom serves the purpose of providing intense substitutive gratification for sexual and hostile impulses.

Difficulty will also be encountered where the symptom tends to reinforce the repression of a traumatic memory or conflict, as in amnesia. The extent of amnesia varies. It may involve a single painful experience in the past, or it may include a fairly wide segment of life. It may actually spread to a point where the person loses his identity and forgets his past completely. Amnesia serves the defensive purpose of shielding the individual from anxiety. The intractibility of an amnesia, consequently, is related to the amount of anxiety bound down, and to the ego resources that are available for coping with the liberated anxiety. The fear of being overcome by anxiety may be so great that an impenetrable block to recall will exist despite all efforts to reintegrate the person to his past memories. Indeed, the fear of uncovering a memory may be so strong that the person will resist trance induction.

Where resistance to hypnosis is encountered, a light barbiturate narcosis, either oral or intravenous, may remove the block. A trance, once induced, is deepened, and a posthypnotic suggestion is given the patient that he will henceforth be responsive to hypnosis without narcosis.

It must again be emphasized that while certain hysterical symptoms may be treated rapidly through short-term treatment, the basic personality problems which are associated with the hysterical disorder will necessitate a considerable period of insight therapy.

3. Phobic Reactions (Anxiety Hysteria)

Anxiety may be controlled by displacement of inner dangers onto external objects or situations. Due to its apparent protective quality, the phobia may become fixed, the patient manifesting the greatest obstinacy in facing it. The treatment of phobic reactions may consequently be very difficult. The residual repressions frequently require the creation of a transference neurosis before they can be resolved. Because the individual feels helpless in dealing with his anxiety, he is apt to regress to a childlike kind of relationship with some person, usually a parent or mate, who becomes a parental substitute toward whom he evidences a hostile, dependent attitude. This "blind alley" may consume a great deal of the therapist's attention, diverting him from dealing with the original conflictual sources.

The only satisfactory way of treating phobic reactions is by insight therapy, preferably with reconstructive goals. In the process of treatment, the therapist will constantly have to handle the patient's discouragement at the persistence of his phobias and his tremulous anticipation of bouts of anxiety.

Where the patient is not motivated for an insight approach, very little can be done for him therapeutically. In isolated cases, persuasion, reconditioning, and desensitization may partially alleviate the phobia. Through persuasive methods an attempt is made to build up the individual's self-confidence and self-esteem, encouraging him to engage in activities which will overcome his phobia. Unfortunately, although the patient is apt to make a better adjustment, and may learn to control his fears on the basis of positive benefits he derives from their conquest, he will still experience panic reactions, and he will have to force himself over and over again to face fear-provoking situations.

Associated with persuasive techniques, techniques of self-mastery through autosuggestion are advocated by some therapists as a supportive device. The person fortifies himself to face a phobic situation by minimizing its fearful aspects, and by concentrating on the pleasure values incidental to the phobic pursuit. Persistent suggestions to gather courage and to master his fears may inspire sufficient fortitude to pull the person successfully through a situation he ordinarily would be unable to face. Needless to say, such techniques are palliative and results are temporary at best.

Another means of supportively treating phobias is by desensitization. The aim in desensitization is to get the patient to master his fears by actually facing them. It is essential for the individual to expose himself repeatedly to the phobic situation, in order that he may finally learn to conquer it. For example, if a person fears open spaces, or going outdoors, he can, on the first day, walk several steps from his house, and then return. On the second day, he may increase the distance between himself and his house, and similarly on each day thereafter until he is able to walk a considerable distance from his home. The hope is that triumph over deliberately stimulated fear will desensitize him to its influence, although this is the exception rather than the rule.

In the event an insight approach is employed, some therapists find hypnoanalysis adjunctively helpful in tracing the origin of a phobia. In cases where a fear has been produced by an incident so terror-inspiring that it has been repressed, it may be possible to get the person to recall the original emotional experience under hypnosis and then to reevaluate the situation in terms of his present-day understanding. A helpful technique is to regress the person to a period prior to the development of the phobia, and then gradually to reorient him in his age level to later and later periods of life, until the original situation associated with the development of the phobia has been uncovered. Where the phobia is complicated by a character disturbance that originated early in life, it will be necessary to produce a more or less drastic reorganization of the personality through further therapy after the phobia has been analyzed and its sources determined.

4. Obsessive-compulsive Reactions (Obsessive Neurosis, Compulsion Neurosis)

The treatment of obsessive-compulsive reactions is notoriously difficult. Not only is it necessary to deal with nascent anxiety, which becomes particularly pronounced when obsessional ideas break loose, but more significantly one must manage the hostile, distrusting, dependent character structure that is a component part of the disorder.

Attitudes toward the therapist are so ambivalent that a working relationship may never develop. On the one hand, the patient desires to be dependent on the therapist, and toward this end he will employ varied techniques like making himself obsequious, ingratiating and submissive. On the other hand, in spite of the fact that he desires to be dependent, he will resent dependency. He will express hostility toward the therapist, either openly or covertly. While on the surface he may exhibit a great deal of deference, inwardly he is rebellious and he is fired with much resentment. The dreams he displays, related to the transference, demonstrate the intense hostility he feels toward the therapist. The patient looks upon his impulses for dependency and compliance as threats to his independence and to his capacity to function by himself.

The battle with the therapist can go on for a long time without the patient's being aware of how he seeks to make himself dependent, and at the same time to detach himself. While he asks the therapist for help, he will stubbornly oppose accepting the therapist's interpretations or suggestions. He may become tremendously demanding and insist on being relieved of his symptoms; yet, when attempts are made to help him in a positive way, he will resist these, and then act hostile toward the therapist for not helping him more. The rigidity he displays during therapy is manifested in intellectualizing what is going on. This serves as a defense against his feelings. Many compulsive persons are capable of learning the mechanisms of their illness, but this seems to have not the slightest effect upon the intensity and severity of their symptoms. Their tendencies to doubt make interpretations difficult. When they do accept interpretations, evincing interest in what goes on in their psyche, it is quite apparent that they do not feel what they intellectually accept. The "isolation" of the intellectual processes from the emotional content makes therapy extremely difficult.

The compulsive individual may attempt to disarm the therapist by obeying punctiliously every suggestion or command expressed or implied. While he may be responsive on the surface, inwardly he maintains a tremendous amount of scepticism about what goes on. One may attempt to change the patient's way of life by pointing out prevailing contradictions. Though the patient seems to have accepted and understood thoroughly the implications of his difficulties, and though he voices a desire for change, the way he acts outside the therapeutic situation indicates that he has not really absorbed the insight he had verbalized. Sometimes the behavior of the patient is in a direction opposite to his intellectual understanding. Partly responsible is the fact that the patient seeks to ridicule the therapist by contradicting his suggestions.

Compulsion neurosis does not respond to insight therapy as well as do other neurotic syndromes. It can be treated, of course, but the therapist must be extremely skilled in the handling of the transference, and he must have much fortitude to tolerate the vicissitudes that will come up in the course of treatment.

Frequently, the most that can be done is to fortify the patient's failing defenses, and to get him to function with the personality makeup he had prior to the development of disabling symptoms. The complicating element is that detachment, which is one of his primary defenses, may be the symptom the patient desires most to abandon. He seeks to live a better life, and he is thoroughly disgusted with his detachment. He understands that he is missing many of life's pleasures. But he cannot stop being detached. When the patient realizes that yielding his detachment creates in him anxiety and turmoil, and when he appreciates that he cannot help being isolated from people, he may become depressed. In some instances desperation can even drive him to suicide.

Whenever possible, therefore, the therapist must attempt not only to control the patient's symptoms, but to promote sufficient alteration in the character structure to permit of a reasonable functioning with people in a close relationship situation. Where the patient has a motivation to gain normal satisfactions in life, and where he realizes that his detachment, obsequiousness, perfectionism, meticulousness, obstinacy and other character traits create difficulties with people and prevent enjoyment in living, he may then have the incentive to tolerate and to work through the anxieties incumbent upon giving up these traits.

The therapy of compulsion neurosis or compulsive-obsessive personality disorders must take into account the patient's dependency, the profoundly hostile impulses he has toward people, his need for detachment, the tendency to "isolate" intellect from feeling, and the magical frame of reference in which his ideas operate.

Among the most important tasks to be achieved in therapy are: demonstrating to the patient that his symptoms have a definite cause and that they stem from no magical source, that aggression is a common impulse originating in hostile attitudes, that he can express a certain amount of hostility without destroying other people or injuring himself, and that he can relate to a person without needing to make himself dependent or compliant.

Some therapists find a combination of insight and supportive therapy the best treatment for obsessive-compulsive reactions A transference neurosis is avoided and techniques like guidance, persuasion and reassurance are used whenever necessary.

At the start of therapy, the patient is often bewildered, tense, and torn by ambivalent strivings. He pleads for relief and often assumes that the therapist is delinquent in his responsibility by failing to annihilate his symptoms. He may furiously insist that he feels no better, that he has uncontrollable impulses to do damage to himself and others, that he is impelled to engage in sexual activities which repel him, that he is helpless in coping with his tension and panicky feelings. It is essential to explain to him that his symptoms and feelings have a meaning, and that it is necessary to understand some of the factors creating his difficulties before they can be corrected. As a general rule, the patient will be skeptical about this explanation, since inwardly he believes that his trouble is caused by some sort of evil magic. Only when he establishes a feeling of confidence in the therapist is it possible to influence his superstitious nature.

Where the patient is very upset, he may be given reassuring and persuasive suggestions to the effect that he can get well, that others sicker than himself have been able to experience relief from their symptoms, and that, if he has the desire to recover, he will want to do what is essential in overcoming his difficulties.

One of the most important things he must realize is that his symptoms are not the product of supernatural forces, but rather follow scientific laws of cause and effect. Understandably, because he is victimized by fear, tension and panicky feelings, which seemingly come from unknown sources, he has been unable hitherto to ascertain the meaning of his symptoms. However, the reasons he suffers will become known to him as he begins to connect events in his environment with how he feels. Nothing in the universe happens by chance. If he hears a sound, he knows very well something has created the sound. Science has definitely shown that a causal relationship exists in the world.

The patient is usually reassured by such a talk, since he does not want to be at the mercy of wicked, inscrutable forces over which he has no control. These forces are nightmarish in quality and give him the feeling of being manipulated by demons. It must be remembered that the compulsion neurotic often thinks in terms akin to witchcraft. To be advised by a person he respects that a matter-of-fact cause is responsible for his agony, gives him much solace. Accepting this explanation on faith, however, is not enough. It is essential to point out to him how, when he gets involved in specific environmental difficulties, his symptoms become exacerbated.

A persuasive technique is sometimes expedient. The patient is first reassured about his obsessive fears and impulses. He is told that, were he actually going to execute them into action, he would not now be tormenting himself so. The chances are that he will not perpetrate any of the wicked deeds of which he is so frightened.

For instance, if he fears he may become violently dangerous and kill people, he may be shown that actually he expresses aggression far less freely than the average person. As a matter of fact, he probably fails to exhibit even ordinary amounts of assertive aggressiveness. He is encouraged to observe himself in his daily reactions with people, to see whether he is not restricting a show of aggressive feeling.

One of the tendencies of the compulsive neurotic is to keep tormenting himself with his fears and anxieties. A masochistic element undoubtedly exists here. It is sometimes helpful to point out to the patient that occupying his mind with frightening ideas stirs up tension and physical symptoms. The patient may be reminded that the mind is closely linked to all the organs in his body. Upsetting ideas can thus upset all of the bodily organs. More perniciously, irritating the mind with frightening and uncomfortable thoughts may delay mental healing.

The patient may be asked to practice changing the type of thinking that preoccupies him. This may not be successful at first, but it will begin to work after a while. What is necessary is that he begin to direct thoughts away from concern with his obsessions to some other group of ideas. This could be some activity, or hobby, or some period in life when his happiness was greatest. The patient is warned about the difficulty of controlling his thinking at first. He will be tempted to tease and torture himself with his fears, just like picking at an irritating sore. Surely the sore may be provoking. It itches, and the person wants to scratch it; but as long as he does, healing will be delayed. It is the same with irritating ideas. Even though these are provoking, it is necessary purposefully to divert thoughts into some other channel. This persuasive approach, though superficial, often helps the patient to exercise some control over his obsessions which otherwise would tend to preoccupy him to distraction.

A word is necessary concerning dependency in the compulsion neurotic. Because of the patient's desires for dependency, and because of the difficulty in controlling a neurotic transference, it may be best not to permit the patient to come too frequently for treatments. Should treatment sessions be too concentrated, the patient may become inordinate in his demands on the therapist on the basis that he cannot function by himself. Therapy once or twice weekly is ample in most cases.

It is helpful to give a Rorschach test to compulsion neurotics to see whether any elements of schizophrenia are present. Some compulsion neurotics are very close to schizophrenia, and in such individuals the therapist will have to be careful in offering authoritative interpretations. Rather, one should be reassuring, manipulating the individual's environment so that he can function as effectively as possible with his existing personality equipment. The prognosis for extensive goals here may not be too favorable; nevertheless, a great deal can be done for the patient when therapy is oriented along lines such as are used in schizophrenia. Should a reconstructive approach be attempted, the chances are that the therapist will be rewarded with a therapeutic failure. The ego is usually too weak to handle the anxiety that will be released. Compulsion neurotics with this type of weak ego structure may develop psychotic-like excited episodes irrespective of the kind of therapy employed. Convulsive therapy may be expedient here.

The prognosis for goals of restoration of equilibrium will depend upon the severity of the condition and the amount of ego strength that exists. It will also depend upon the length of time the patient has been ill. In some instances, compulsive-obsessive patterns appear to be of relatively recent duration, the compulsive difficulty having developed as a result of external pressures and problems to which the patient could not adjust. Under these circumstances, the prognosis is much more favorable than where the compulsive illness has been with the individual ever since puberty. Patients who do not respond to psychotherapy, and whose anxiety and suffering become unendurable may ultimately require transorbital lobotomy, which, in some cases, will control symptoms where everything else fails.

5. Depressive Reactions (Reactive Depression, Psychoneurotic Depression)

Depressive reactions are symptomatic of basic conflictual problems and constitute a special way of dealing with anxiety. They require an insight form of therapy. The therapist must always be on the alert to prevent suicide should the depression become too deep. This is a possibility in all cases, but especially in those patients who have already made a suicidal attempt. Sometimes benzedrine or dexedrine help to lift the apathy and sluggishness that are symptomatic of this condition. Mild hypnotics at night may be required for insomnia. Where the depression becomes too deep, electric convulsive therapy will be necessary.

PSYCHOPHYSIOLOGIC AUTONOMIC AND VISCERAL DISORDERS

Psychophysiologic (psychosomatic) disorders are often rooted in deep disturbances in the personality organization engendered by defects in the earliest contacts of the infant with the mother. The personality structure of the patient consequently contains dependent, hostile and masochistic elements which tend to obstruct a good working relationship. Because the ego is more or less fragile, anxiety, mobilized by the transference and by interpretation, may be intolerable. Insight therapy may, therefore, have to be delayed in favor of preparatory supportive techniques, during which the patient is permitted to transfer his dependency to the therapist.

The negative elements of the relationship with the therapist must constantly be worked on, the therapist alerting himself to hostile manifestations which the patient will tend to repress. Once a good working relationship is established, exploration of repressed strivings, needs and conflicts with cautious interpretations may be attempted. Exaggeration of the patient's physical symptoms is a common sign of resistance. When symptoms increase in intensity, the patient may be tempted to leave therapy. Treatment is generally a long-term proposition, since the deep personality problem associated with the symptoms resolves itself slowly.

A constant danger during insight therapy is the unleashing of excessive quantities of anxiety, usually the result of too speedy symptom removal or too rapid dissipation of defenses. Often the somatic disturbance represents the most acceptable avenue available to the patient for the discharge of anxiety and hostility. Because the ego has been unable to handle these emotions on a conscious level, the mechanism of repression is invoked. Where this mechanism is threatened without a coordinate strengthening of the ego, where the person becomes prematurely aware of unacceptable conflicts and strivings, there is definite danger of precipitating a crisis. The patient may exhibit such intense anxiety that he will employ certain neurotic mechanisms to bind this emotion. He may, for instance, develop hysterical or compulsive symptoms, or he may display characterologic defenses. Anxiety may nevertheless get out of hand and shatter the ego, precipitating a psychosis.

In some cases it may be impossible to do more for the patient than to give him supportive therapy. For instance, persuasion and guidance may enable the patient to organize his life around his defects and liabilities, to avoid situations that arouse conflict and hostility, and to attain, at least in part, a sublimation of his basic needs. The object here is to bolster the ego to a point where it can handle damaging emotions more rationally, as well as to improve interpersonal relationships so that hostility and other disturbing emotions are not constantly being generated. In some instances, such therapies help to liberate the individual from the vicious cycle of his neurosis, facilitating externalization of interests, increasing self-confidence, and indicating ways of discharging emotions.

The therapeutic relationship is kept on as positive a level as possible, an attempt being made to show the patient that his symptoms are not fortuitous, a causal relation existing between his symptoms and his difficulties in dealing with life. The circumstances under which symptoms become exaggerated are investigated with the object of determining areas of failure in interpersonal functioning. Once a pattern is discerned, its significance and origin are explored. Finally, the patient is encouraged to put into action his retrained attitudes toward life and people.

Where the patient is coordinately under the care of an internist, cooperation between the therapist and internist will insure the best results.

PERSONALITY DISORDERS

The therapy of many personality (character) disorders is difficult because of what has been called the "negative therapeutic reaction." The patient almost always utilizes his relationship with the therapist as a focus for his various character drives. He may subject the therapist to attitudes of contempt and ridicule. He may seek to vanquish, provoke, and to hurt him in subtle ways. He may slavishly subject himself to ingratiating or masochistic tactics to win the tribute, affection and support he believes he deserves. Feelings of self-devaluation and hopelessness often permeate his outlook and lead him to anticipate failure in therapy. In spite of the fact that the individual may be talented and outwardly successful, the inner image of himself is depleted and contemptible. Self-devaluation acts as a potent block to treatment. The patient seems to utilize the façade of helplessness to avoid making any effort to get well.

Because of the vulnerability of the relationship with the therapist, interpretations are apt to be regarded by the patient as a blow to his self-esteem, initiating depression, rage or anxiety. They are evidences that the therapist does not approve of him. The patient is apt to intellectualize the entire therapeutic process, using his knowledge either as resistance or as a means of fortifying himself against change. Despite all logic, the patient strives to wedge therapy into the framework of his distorted attitudes toward life. He exhibits feelings of rejection and of distrust, and at the slightest challenge from the therapist his defenses crumble, leaving him in a state of collapse and despair. He may then show a psychic rigidity that refuses to yield to reason or entreaty.

The initial aim in therapy in personality disorders must be toward a solidification of the working relationship. This process is expedited where the patient does not feel forced to comply with demands he believes are against his interests. Analytic probing and exploration of unconscious material should be in the most tentative terms.

Until the patient is capable of understanding that many of his attitudes toward the therapist have no basis in reality, but are rather an outgrowth of personal difficulties, interpretations must be delayed. Attempts are first made to establish a positive relationship without analyzing its source. Hostile feelings toward the therapist and other irrational impulses which interfere with a good relationship must be dealt with actively. It may be necessary to confine the entire treatment hour to current problems, shying away from historical material. Only when the patient's relationship with the therapist becomes more congenial will it be possible for him to benefit from attempts to connect historical data with his present difficulties.

During the course of treatment, the patient will seemingly modify his attitudes toward the therapist, but in this alteration the therapist must search for areas of resistance. For instance, a submissive, ingratiating attitude, which is a cover for a fear of abandonment, may, upon interpretation, be replaced by an apparently sincere attempt to search for and to analyze inner problems. The therapist may, if the patient is observed closely, detect in this attitude a fraudulent attempt to gain security by complying with what the patient feels is expected of him. While the patient appears to be analyzing his problem, his real motive is to gain security by adjusting himself to what he considers are the demands of the therapist. In this way, the process of therapy itself becomes a means of indulging his neurosis.

In analyzing resistances, their sources in infantile attitudes and conditionings usually become apparent. Eventually it is essential to bring the patient to a realization of how the machinery with which he reacts to the world now is rooted in early conceptions and misconceptions about life. The interpretation of character strivings does not suffice to change their nature, for they are the only way the patient knows of adjusting; they are to him "ego-syntonic."

A breakdown of character strivings often brings out in sharp focus the repressed needs and impulses from which the strivings issue. When the patient becomes cognizant of the conflicts which produce his destructive interpersonal attitudes, he has the best chance of taking active steps toward their modification.

In certain cases, particularly where there are time limitations, the only thing that can be accomplished is to adjust the person to his neurosis in as expedient a manner as possible. Environmental manipulation may be necessary to take pressures off the patient. He may be shown how to adjust himself to the reality situation. For instance, if the patient has a strong striving for perfectionism which drives him incessantly into positions he cannot handle with his intellectual and physical equipment, he may be shown how he can confine himself to a project which he can master proficiently. Whereas the scope of his operations may be limited, he can indulge his perfectionistic strivings in a circumscribed way, gaining some measure of gratification in this. If he is inordinately dependent, it may be pointed out that he can maintain a certain freedom of action in spite of the fact that he has to lean on authority. If he has a power impulse, avenues for its exercise through competition may be suggested. This approach, of course, merely panders to the patient's neurosis, but it may be the only practical thing that can be done for the time being; in many cases, it will make the patient's life immeasurably more tolerable.

Whenever possible, the patient should be brought to an awareness of the nature, genesis and dynamic significance of his character trends. He should be encouraged to observe how his strivings and defenses operate in everyday life, and to scrutinize ways in which he can change his attitudes toward people.

While character trends can be classified in such categories as dependency, power strivings and detachment, they are always interrelated and the fusion makes for a picture that is unique for each individual. Behavior is not the static product of a group of isolated trends, but rather is a complex integrate of a number of drives. The product of this intermingling differs from any of the component strivings. That is, if the person is compulsively modest, is fired by perfectionism, is unconsciously arrogant and aggressive, some of these traits will tend to neutralize and some to reinforce each other. Nevertheless, for treatment purposes, character disorders may be regarded in terms of the most dominant trend.

1. "Inadequate," Infantile and Dependency Patterns

The treatment of extreme "inadequacy" and dependency reactions poses special problems. Dependent persons are often brought to the therapist for treatment not because they feel a need for change, but rather because parents, marital partners, or friends insist that something be done for them. Visits to the therapist, in such cases, are kept merely as a formality. The patient expects that no change will occur, and he will be resistant to any effort to get him to participate in the treatment process. The limit of his cooperativeness is to expose himself to the therapist during the allotted hour.

With a defective motivation such as this, little progress can be expected. The patient will particularly resent interpretations which he may regard as criticisms of himself. He will be antagonistic to any implication that there is something wrong with him. He may respond with bewilderment, aggression, or pseudo-conformity. Months and even years of therapy may effect little alteration in the inner dynamics of the personality.

So long as the patient has no real incentive for therapy, no change will be possible. The sole hope lies in convincing the patient that in the therapist he has a friend who will not influence him against his will, and who understands and sympathizes with the way he feels. The struggle with the therapist will stop only when the patient senses that the therapist is a person who does not challenge his scheme of life, but rather seeks to participate in it.

The only real way of aiding the patient is to help him to establish a contact with the therapist which will assume a more mature form than his previous interpersonal relationships. Unfortunately, this is easier said than done, because the dependent individual, if he is not fighting the therapist, will utilize him in the same way that he uses all authorities—as a prop to security.

The patient seeks to establish himself with the therapist in ways which resemble the infant's strivings toward the parents. He does not seem to be interested in developing resources within himself. Rather, he desires to maneuver the therapist into a position where constant favors will be forthcoming. He will abide by any rules of therapy in order to obtain this objective, even to the apparent absorption of insight. It is most disconcerting, however, to learn that assimilated insights are extremely superficial, and that the patient is less interested in knowing what is wrong with him than he is in perpetuating the child-parent relationship. He actually seems incapable of reasoning logically, and there is an almost psychotic quality to the persistence of his demands for support and direction.

Interpretations of the patient's dependency are usually regarded by him as chastisement. He will assume that any attempt to put responsibility on his shoulders is a form of ill will expressed toward him by the therapist. He will demonstrate reactions of disappointment, rage, anxiety and depression, and he will repeat these reactions in spite of lip service to the effect that he wants to get well.

In treating a dependency reaction, it is essential to recognize that hostility is inevitable in the course of therapy. The demands of dependent people are so insatiable that it is impossible to live up to their expectations. Only when the patient begins to experience himself as a person with aggressiveness, assertiveness and independence, will he be able to function with any degree of well-being. This goal, unfortunately, may in some instances never be achieved.

Supportive therapy, based on propitiation of the patient's dependency needs, is of extremely temporary effect. It is advisable to strive for a therapeutic approach in which the individual learns to accept responsibility for his own development.

There are some individuals, however, whose self-structure has been so crushed that they will resist any attempt to make the therapeutic situation a participating one. Here the treatment program will have to be organized around a partial therapeutic goal. The therapist will need to resign himself to creating a modicum of security within the patient, and to educating him to function with his dependency strivings with as little detriment to himself as possible.

When it is apparent that one cannot work along participating lines, and that the patient's only objective is to make himself dependent on the therapist, visits may be cut down to once weekly, the patient being encouraged to engage himself in various outside activities. He may be urged also to affiliate himself with a group to which he can make some contribution.

As much pressure as the patient can bear must be imposed upon him so that he will engage in his own choices and decisions. It is to be expected that the patient will resent this vigorously, accusing the therapist of refusing to accept responsibility in the therapeutic situation. Should this occur, the therapist may explain to the patient that were he to pander to the patient's demands for support and make decisions for him, this would tend to infantilize the patient. It would make him more dependent and more unable to develop to a point where he could fulfill himself productively and creatively. He must earnestly be instructed that the therapist does not wish to shirk responsibility, but actually withholds directiveness out of respect for the patient's right to develop. Although the patient may still resent the therapist's intent, he will understand more and more that unless he begins to make his own decisions, he will never get to a point where he is strong within himself. He will realize that security will be fostered in proportion to his ability to develop resources capable of mediating his needs through his own positive efforts. He will accept the fact that, should the therapist be too supportive of him, he will never be able to take those steps which will enable him to grow.

Many patients who seemingly are fixated on a dependent level may, with repeated interpretations and injunctions, finally begin to accept themselves as having the right to make their own choices and to develop their own values. Persistence, however, is the keynote. In therapy, the patient will exploit every opportunity to force the therapist to assume a directive role. Nevertheless when the patient sees that the therapist has his welfare at heart, he may be able to develop more independence and assertiveness. The shift in therapy from a directive to a non-directive role calls for considerable skill, and must be tempered to the patient's insight and ego strength. Unless such a shift is made at some time, psychotherapy will probably be interminable, and the patient will continue on a dependent level requiring the ever-presence of the therapist or some other giving person as a condition to his security.

2. "Schizoid" and Detached Patterns

The treatment of a patient with a personality problem of detachment also presents many difficulties. Such a patient is usually motivated to seek therapy because detachment interferes with his livelihood or capacity to achieve social or sexual gratification. Often anxiety, which has developed from the individual's effort to emerge from his detachment, is the complaint for which the patient wants help.

The type of therapy employed will depend upon the function of detachment in the life adjustment of the individual. It will also depend on the ego strength of the patient and his capacity to tolerate the anxieties incumbent upon relating himself intimately to other persons.

Detachment may be a means elaborated by the individual to protect himself from intense dependency strivings. A close relationship poses dangers of being overwhelmed, for in it the patient may envisage a complete giving up of his independence. Detachment may also be a technique of avoiding injury or mutilation which the patient believes will occur when he comes close to a person. Finally, it may be a method by which the patient protects himself from fears of attacking and destroying others. In treating the patient, therefore, the dynamic significance of detachment must be kept in mind and efforts must be made to modify the cause if possible.

One way of estimating the capacity of the patient's existing ego to tolerate interpersonal relationships is through the Rorschach test, especially noting his reaction to the color cards. The best way of estimating ego strength is, of course, the patient's actual response to the therapeutic situation, and a study of his dreams, fantasies and feelings mobilized by the transference.

Where the patient's ego is so weak that it must fortify itself against shattering, and where there is little practical possibility of modifying its strength, therapy along supportive lines may help the patient to reinforce his character defenses and to modify his detachment to some extent in line with a more comfortable adaptation. Where the ego strength will permit of close interpersonal relationships, insight therapy may result in a real alteration in the character structure.

In treating a detached patient, one must anticipate that there will be difficulty for a long time in establishing a close relationship, since this tends to mobilize his fears of injury and inspires detachment. Much active work will be required in detecting and dissolving resistances to insight. The detached patient often has a tendency to intellectualize the entire therapeutic process. He will particularly shy away from expressing his feelings, because he will conceive of them as dangerous.

Great hostility is bound to arise, which may be disconcerting; but the therapist must realize that hostility is a defense against interpersonal closeness. It is extremely important that the therapist be as tolerant toward the patient's outbursts as possible. The patient will probably attempt to provoke the therapist into expressions of counter-aggression to justify attitudes toward people as untrustworthy, and his withdrawal from the world as potentially menacing.

Sometimes the patient may be encouraged to participate in social activities, competitive games and sports. Commanding, restrictive directions should, however, be avoided. With encouragement, detached people may begin to relate themselves with others. In groups they drift cautiously from the periphery to the center as they realize that they will not be injured in a close interpersonal relationship. Group therapy may sometimes be most rewarding in certain detached, schizoid individuals, where no pressure is put on them to participate.

A common reaction in the therapy of detached persons is anxiety, which is manifested by disturbing nightmarish dreams or by actual anxiety attacks. The reaction will usually be found when the patient experiences for the first time real closeness or love toward the therapist. The emotions terrorize him and cause him to fear injury or destruction of an indefinable nature. It is essential to deal with this reaction when it occurs by giving him as much interpretation as is necessary. Detached patients whose defenses have crumbled may go into a clinging dependent attitude when they realize the full weight of their helplessness. Supportive therapy may have to be given here, in an effort to provide the patient with an experience in which he receives help without being domineered or smothered with cloying affection.

3. Paranoid or "Anal" Patterns

A type of personality disorder often found in our culture, characterized by a self-entrenched attitude, is one commonly called an "anal" or "paranoid" personality. The core of this personality is one of great distrust. This motivates the fear of being overwhelmed, and produces great suspiciousness and a desire to preserve oneself by warding off all intrusions through the building up of an impenetrable wall between oneself and others. The individual seems to want to take things in, but to give up little. Associated are impulses of stinginess, orderliness, cleanliness, obstinacy and sadism.

The function of most of these traits is to preserve the wall that protects the person from others. Cleanliness becomes a means of warding off contacts with the outside world. Orderliness is a technique that keeps things in place so that the individual may not be caught unaware. Obstinacy is a technique of fighting off overwhelming power by negativism. Sadism stems from a feeling of weakness within oneself, and from the necessity to deal with others in kind through domination and force. One of the motivants of homosexuality, which often appears in this type of personality, is a fear of people of the opposite sex, who are not to be trusted because they are different from oneself and hence potentially evil. Intimacy with persons who are more familiar because they have the same sexual organs is less threatening. Homosexuality also represents a means of destroying others, of making oneself passive and dependent, and of gaining power. Love is conceived of as dangerous; indeed, any outgoing feelings are dangerous.

There is much to indicate, in this personality disorder, that difficulties in relationships to parents occurred at the stage of social and toilet training, at which time intolerable frustrations were imposed on the child. During this period of development, the ego expands, and the child experiences a desire for mastery and dominance. He is exposed, however, to parental disciplines which challenge his claims for mastery. The child may strive to cling to his sense of·power by conforming as little as possible to demands made on him. Toilet training usually becomes the arena in which he proves he can gain mastery over his parents. An ambivalent attitude exists in that he also realizes that by conforming to the demands of his parents in establishing habits of cleanliness, he will obtain their love and support. Nevertheless, his desires for power and mastery conflict with this aim and create impulses to retain fecal material or to soil. It is probably for this reason that excretory activities become so overvalued and constitute symbols of danger and destructiveness in dream and fantasy life.

Punishment inflicted by others and self-punishment may actually be symbolized by anal punishment. The intense hostility that is generated in this condition may be projected outward in a paranoid reaction. An obsessive-compulsive neurosis is also common when the character façade fails. Understandably, the patient, for a long while, will regard therapy as a personal encroachment.

Patients with this type of problem tend to intellectualize the therapeutic process. This serves as a defense against feeling. Sometimes all that can be done for the patient is to give him as much insight as he can tolerate, in this way cooperating with his need to intellectualize therapy. Interpretations should deal with the more superficial character defenses rather than with the deep hostile and sexual content. They must be made in a reassuring manner. A persuasive approach as outlined for compulsion neurosis is usually best, although in some cases insight therapy is possible.

4. Power Patterns

Another type of personality disorder is one in which power impulses predominate. In this condition all that seems to matter in life is forcefulness and strength. The feelings and rights of other people are disregarded. There is a blind admiration for everything invincible. The person is contemptuous of softness and tenderness, and self-esteem is seemingly dependent on the ability to be dominant. As in dependency, the dynamic force behind the power impulse is a profound sense of helplessness and an inability to cope with life with the individual's available resources. A motive behind the power drive is to coerce people to yield to one's will, which provides bounties of various sorts.

The treatment of the power driven individual is oriented around a building up of frustration tolerance, an increasing of his capacity to withstand tension, and a gaining of security through his own resources. A reeducative approach may be effective in permitting the individual to develop inner restraints capable of exercising control of his impulses. It is essential to be firmer in this type of disorder than in either dependency or detached reactions. The patient must be shown that there are limits beyond which he cannot go, and that he must face responsibility. Whenever possible, the patient should be acquainted with the dynamic significance of his power drive, and he should be encouraged to make efforts toward the expansion of his inner resources.

Where dependency and power drives are fused, the effort must be directed toward correcting through insight therapy the core of selflessness which makes for trends of compulsive submissiveness and dominancy. The individual here functions in a dual manner, seeking security from stronger people by clinging to them helplessly, or wresting security from them by force and aggression.

5. Narcissistic Reactions

In treating the character disorder of excessive narcissism, much difficulty will be experienced. Persons with this problem seem to have such a need for personal admiration that they conceive of therapy as a means of making themselves more worthy of praise.

Unlike the mature person who gains security from cooperative endeavors in attitudes of altruism and sympathy, the narcissistic individual concentrates most of his interest on himself. His self-love may actually become structured into grandiose strivings, omnipotent impulses and megalomania. Although the image of the individual appears to be bloated, analysis readily reveals how helpless and impoverished he actually feels. There is danger here of precipitating psychotic depression or excitement in presenting insights prematurely. The shock-absorbing capacity of the ego must always be weighed, and interpretations must be given in proportion to the available ego strength. In markedly immature individuals, little development may be expected other than a somewhat better environmental adaptation through guidance techniques.

6. Psychopathic Personality

Most authorities agree that the treatment of psychopathic personality is most difficult. All therapies have yielded meager results. In many cases the only thing that can be accomplished is manipulation of the environment to eliminate as many temptations as possible which stimulate the psychopath into expressing his vicarious impulses.

If a psychopathic individual can establish a relationship to a person, the latter may be able, as a kind but firm authority, to supervise the patient's actions. Hypnosis can reinforce this authoritative relationship. The therapist may, by adroit suggestions, act as a repressive moral force and as a pillar of support. The patient may get to the point where he will turn to the therapist for guidance when temptation threatens him. Suggestions may be couched in such terms as to convince the patient that he is actually wiser and happier for resisting certain activities which, as he knows from past experience, are bound to result disastrously. On the basis of a guidance relationship, the patient may be instructed in the wisdom of postponing immediate gratifications for those which, in the long run, will prove more lasting and wholesome. He is taught the prudence of tolerating frustration, and the need to feel a sense of responsibility and consideration for the rights of others. Not that these lessons will be immediately accepted or acted on, but constant repetition sometimes helps the patient to realize that it is to his best interest, ultimately, to observe social amenities and to exercise more self-control.

Experience demonstrates that it is possible to modify to some extent the immature explosive reactions of the psychopath by an extensive training program, particularly in cooperative group work where the individual participates as a member toward a common objective. Adequate group identifications are lacking in the psychopath, and the realization that ego satisfactions can accrue from group experiences, may create a chink in the defensive armor. In cases where the psychopath comes into conflict with the law, and where incarceration is necessary, a program organized around building up whatever assets the individual possesses, particularly in a group setting, may, in some instances, bring success. In young psychopaths, vocational schools that teach the individual a trade may contribute to his self-esteem and provide him with a means of diverting his energies into a profitable channel.

7. Alcoholism

When the average alcoholic applies for therapy, the therapist is usually confronted with the expressed or secret hope that the patient will learn to drink normally and to "hold his liquor like anyone else." While this may be possible in the anxiety drinker following abatement of his neurosis, it is not true in the case of the real alcoholic.

Although there are some persons who believe that the alcoholic can be cured by weaning him gradually from the bottle, and who are of the opinion he may learn to engage in social drinking without exceeding his capacity, experience has shown that success is possible only where alcohol is completely and absolutely eliminated from the individual's regime. The object in therapy is complete elimination of all alcoholic beverages, including wine and beer.

The treatment of alcoholism not only embraces the removal of the desire for alcohol; it also involves restoration of the patient to some kind of adaptational equilibrium. Without such restoration, the person will become pathologically depressed, and his tension will drive him to drink no matter what pressures are put on him.

In the anxiety drinker, any attempt to force or to shame the person into sobriety will interfere with the therapeutic relationship. The patient should be made to feel that he need not apologize for his drinking desires. He should be shown that alcohol provides him with an escape, and that he may require liquor so long as his fundamental problems remain. The danger of his continued drinking may be pointed out to him. However, while the therapist does not approve of the patient's drinking, the patient will not be ordered to stop. When the patient believes he is ready to give up alcohol, the therapist will help him to do so. The therapeutic program should be organized around the treatment of the underlying neurotic or character problem. A sympathetic attitude toward the patient's need for alcohol is always appreciated by the patient. Nevertheless, the therapist must insist that the patient come in sober for his sessions.

While a reconstructive approach is useful in the anxiety drinker, it is usually futile in the real alcoholic. The ego of the alcoholic is immature, and his capacity to integrate and to utilize insight in a constructive manner is impaired. The alcoholic patient will dig out fascinating dynamic structures during psychotherapy, but this effort will have little influence on his drinking. In many cases the therapist must be satisfied with the partial therapeutic objective of weaning the patient from alcohol, thus permitting him to adjust to life with his immature character organization in as adaptive and non-destructive a manner as possible.

The greatest difficulty will be experienced in the handling of those alcoholics who do not wish to stop drinking, and who apply for treatment under coercion of parents, mate or friends. Exposure to therapy is merely a device to retain the good will of the people close to the patient. Treatment here will usually be unsuccessful, the patient utilizing the therapist as a referee who is expected to arbitrate between himself and his family. Sessions are spent lamenting his plight or presenting himself as a misunderstood and abused person who is completely justified in his drinking.

Such alcoholics are best treated in an institution where they cannot obtain drink. The usual reaction to hospitalization is indignation and promises to refrain from alcohol if released. When such release is not forthcoming, the patient will make an exemplary adjustment, creating such an appearance of normality that one may be tempted to discharge him prematurely. One difficulty is the attitude of relatives who will be goaded by the patient to secure his release. In the hospital, psychotherapy may be started and an attempt may be made to get the patient interested in hobbies, crafts or an occupation which will engage his energies. Supportive therapy of a guidance and persuasive type is useful to help the patient discover and utilize his assets and talents. Insight therapy is, of course, the method of choice. A period of one to two years of hospitalization may be required, and before the patient is discharged, his environment should be manipulated to assure a minimum of stress.

Where hospitalization is impossible, certain forceful measures may be required, particularly in the alcoholic who has no motivation whatsoever to abandon liquor. The best time to start therapy is when the patient is in an acute alcoholic episode. At this time, he is given the usual detoxification therapy of insulin, sugar and vitamins. The contact with the patient here will serve a psychotherapeutic purpose in promoting a close relationship. The therapist, utilizing the remorse and self-condemnation of the patient during the "hangover" period, may enjoin him to seek psychotherapy. To offset depression and to give the patient a sense of well-being, benzedrine sulfate may be utilized. Ten milligrams are taken by mouth twice daily, after breakfast and after lunch. A good diet supplemented with vitamin B is essential, and a sedative, like seconal, may be prescribed at nighttime in the event of insomnia.

The next phase of therapy is a coercive one in which an attempt is made to bring the patient to a point where he refuses to drink or is unable to drink. Cajolery and appeals to reason are usually futile. Sometimes a belittling and challenging manner mobilize in the patient a need to prove that he has the "guts" to master the craving for alcohol. This, however, cannot be depended on. Once the patient verbalizes a desire to stop drinking, conditioned reflex therapy or antabuse therapy may be started. The patient should be under close supervision during this period.

An attempt must always be made to establish a rapid relationship with the patient. Should the patient become dependent on the therapist, the latter may utilize the dependency situation to reinforce the patient's desire to abstain from drink, and to motivate him towards utilizing his assets to best advantage. Interest in hobbies and recreations should be stimulated. The patient should also be urged to join a group like Alcoholics Anonymous.

The approach utilized by the Alcoholics Anonymous organization is a most effective one. Here the person is forced to admit that he is an alcoholic, that he needs help and that he wishes to do something about his condition. He is enjoined to realize that because of his own powerlessness in managing his drinking, his life has got out of control. He is encouraged to feel that a Power greater than himself can restore him to health, and he is advised to turn himself over to this Power in his quest for security. He is furthermore encouraged to make a searching moral inventory of himself, admitting his faults to others in the group, as well as to God. He must be willing to make amends to those persons whom he has in any way harmed. At the same time he is shown that he may have overemphasized his bad points.

The alcoholic is never actually urged to say he will stop drinking entirely. Rather, he is informed that each day he will tell himself that he will remain dry, with God's help, for twenty-four hours. At the end of the day he may take an inventory of himself to see if he did anything which was not constructive or was intolerant, resentful, jealous, spiteful or unkind.

The group meetings are extremely useful, since the patient finds companionship with others who share similar emotional problems. Furthermore, when the patient feels tempted to drink, he is able to telephone one of his friends and make an appointment to talk things over. An important part of the program is the patient's participation in helping other alcoholics who are in the grip of their drinking habit. The fact that the workers in the movement are ex-alcoholics enables them to display an enormous amount of tolerance, and to convince the patient that he, too, can do what others have done. It goes without saying that only an alcoholic really understands the drinker. An identification is thus expedited.

Many alcoholics stop drinking when they feel that their dependency is appeased by an alliance with God. The religious cure of alcoholism is often dynamically based on the drinker's conviction that if he lives up to God's expectations and stays sober, he will be given bounties, if not now, then in the hereafter. God becomes the ideal parent who is all-wise, all-supporting and all-forgiving. The alcoholic is unable to challenge this new parental figure, or to test his omnipotence or weakness, as he can a flesh and blood person. His hostility is consequently held in check. When a drinker "gets religion," he may overcome his alcoholic habit.

The treatment of the alcoholic who spontaneously applies to the therapist for help, while difficult, does not present as many problems as that of the person who is maneuvered into therapy through the agency of another concerned individual. In treating such a patient, the following steps may be kept in mind. First, a relationship is started with the patient with the object of developing positive rapport. Second, an effort is made to build up the patient's self-esteem. Third, his interests are externalized and outlets are provided for his aggression. Fourth, he is taught to handle frustration and deprivation. Fifth, he is en-

couraged to stop drinking. Sixth, he is urged to make social contacts with individuals and groups.

The first aim is to get the patient to substitute a dependency relationship
on the therapist for his alcoholic habit. The alcoholic seeks and needs this
type of relationship. When he accepts the therapist and has confidence in him,
the latter will then be able to utilize this to help break the drinking habit. It is
essential, therefore, to make the alcoholic feel that he is accepted on his own
level, drunk or sober. The patient may be told that the therapist wants to help
him, but that the therapist is not going to act as a policeman and force him
to give up drink if he believes it is so vital for his adjustment. He is informed
that the therapist realizes that alcohol plays a major role in his life. Drinking
does not make him a bad person. If he has the desire for alcohol, it is because
of a sequence of conditionings and experiences that have happened to him
which he can now overcome.

It may be difficult to convince the patient that the therapist is interested in
him, and he will often test the therapist's good faith by indulging in repeated
heavy bouts of drinking. Should the therapist fall into this trap and become
embittered with the patient, the relationship will terminate. One must remember
that the patient habitually tries to wring out of the environment a good parental
figure who will supply him with unqualified love and support. It is essential
at first, then, to get the patient to accept the therapist in this role.

Any existing remediable elements in the patient's environment which may
be creating conflict for the patient should be straightened out, with the aid of a
social worker if necessary. In spite of his expressed optimism, the patient is
unable to handle frustration, and any objective source of difficulty may suffice
to promote tension which will produce a craving for drink. An inquiry into the
patient's daily routine and habits may be expedient. Often one finds a gross
defect in the person's diet. Alcoholic overindulgence is coincident with a de-
pletion in dietary intake and with vitamin deficiency. The prescription of a
well-balanced diet with sufficient calories and with supplementary vitamin B is
of great help. The patient should also be encouraged to appease his hunger
whenever he feels a need for food. Hitherto he has propitiated hunger pains by
drinking alcohol. He may be surprised to observe that eating three square meals
a day can remove much of his craving for liquor.

The numerous difficulties a patient has experienced through his inability to
control drinking, the general condemnation of society, and the disdain of his
family, all contribute toward a depreciation of his self-esteem. It is difficult
to rebuild self-esteem by reassurance, but an effort must be made to demonstrate
to the patient that he has many residual assets which he can expand. Because
alcoholics become negligent about their appearance, it is essential to rebuild
interest in their personal care. Appearing neat and well-groomed usually
has a bolstering effect upon the person. Alcoholic women may be directed
toward taking care of their complexions and hair by going to a beauty parlor.
Whatever interest the patient shows in hobbies or external recreations should be
encouraged. He must be reminded that he is not a hopeless case and that he has
many good qualities which he has neglected. His guilt may be appeased by

showing him that he is not solely responsible for his alcoholic craving. It will be possible to substitute for it something much more constructive. The therapist will help him make a proper substitution. In discussing his work situation, a battery of vocational tests may disclose that the patient's interests and aptitudes are in a direction other than his existing work. He may be helped to develop along the lines indicated by his tests. The ultimate aim of these efforts is to get the patient to accept himself as a person with value and dignity.

Because the alcoholic often is inwardly hostile, an outlet should be provided for his aggressive tendencies. Joining a Y. M. C. A. or athletic club, engaging in competitive games and sports, in swimming, archery or boxing, may be of value here. As release is provided for the patient's aggression, he will become much less tense.

Teaching the alcoholic to handle frustration will require considerable effort. The patient must be brought around to a realization that everyone has frustrated feelings, and that an important job in life is to exercise control. Because of what has happened to him, he is apt to misinterpret any disappointment as a sign of his own personal failure. It is mandatory that he build up a tolerance of frustration, even though he has to extend willful effort in this direction.

Since frustration is usually accompanied by gastric distress, it may stimulate a desire for drink. The patient may therefore be advised to carry with him, at all times, a piece of chocolate or candy. Whenever he feels frustrated, or, under any circumstances where a craving for drink develops, he can partake of this nourishment. Hot coffee, cocoa, and malted milk are also good for the same purpose and can act as substitutes for alcohol. As the patient gains more respect for himself, it will be possible for him to tolerate greater and greater amounts of frustration.

At some stage in therapy, the patient must be encouraged to stop drinking. He may be told that while the therapist does not condemn him for alcoholic indulgence, because liquor has a destructive effect, he must try to control its intake. The close relationship with the therapist, the increased self-esteem that comes from positive achievements, the correction of difficulties in his life situation, and the heightened ability to handle frustration, all help to reduce his thirst for alcohol.

When the propitious time arrives, an explanation may be given the patient of how alcohol is poisonous to him because he has built up an allergy to it. It must be stressed that physiologically he is different from other persons, and for this reason he is unable to tolerate alcohol. Many alcoholics regard their inability to "hold liquor" as a sign of weakness. An organic reason for their intolerance usually has a soothing influence on them. The patient may be told that because of his allergic condition, alcohol is as much a poison to him in the long run as cyanide. While he has needed alcohol to appease his tension, he will find that he can utilize other methods now and can, therefore, reduce the amount of his alcoholic intake. Gradually, he will want to give up alcohol entirely.

The patient must abandon the prevailing idea, so current among alcoholics, that eventually he will get to a point where he can drink like anyone else. He must be assured that one drink is equivalent to a thousand, and that because of his inability to drink due to allergy, he must make up his mind to forsake alcohol completely. One way to do this is to live his life and make resolutions for only twenty-four hours in advance.

An important phase of therapy is encouraging the patient to make social contacts and to affiliate himself with groups. If a branch of Alcoholics Anonymous exists in the community, the patient will find that he can make many friends there, and that he can involve himself in numerous constructive activities that will engage his energies and consolidate the gains he has made in therapy.

In recent years, the use of the drug antabuse has come into prominence. The administration of antabuse creates an intense sensitivity to alcohol, with such violent reactions upon any consumption of liquor that the pleasure values of drinking are no longer possible. This serves to protect the patient against his uncontrollable urge to imbibe alcohol and gives him a sense of security. In order to employ antabuse therapy, the patient's cooperation is necessary. Should the patient refuse to take antabuse, it will be impossible to force him to do so. With proper medical supervision, antabuse therapy is not dangerous, although disagreeable side effects are possible. Accidents, however, sometimes do happen, as where a patient unintentionally or defiantly swallows an alcoholic beverage. This may result in death, if a large amount of drink has been consumed.

Once the patient is reasonably alcohol free, antabuse therapy may be started by a competent physician. The initial dose is 2 grams; on the second day 1.5 grams are given; on the third day 1 gram; and on the fourth day, 0.75 gram. During the fourth day, a test reaction is administered with approximately 12 to 14 cc. of alcohol in the form of the patient's favorite beverage. Provision for emergencies during the test reaction must be made in the form of available oxygen, and cardiac and respiratory stimulants. After the test reaction, 0.5 gram of antabuse is given daily as a maintenance dose. Occasional test reactions with alcohol are given for reinforcement. This routine, described by Mann, et al. [459] is commonly employed although Fox [460] considers it to be too drastic. She recommends 0.5 gram daily for two weeks before the test reaction, which is made with three-fourths to one ounce of whiskey. The latter is repeated if no response occurs in twenty to thirty minutes. The maintenance dose is cut to 0.25 grams daily. Antabuse therapy must always be combined with psychotherapy in order to insure the best possible results.

8. Drug Addiction

The treatment of addiction to narcotic drugs, such as opium, morphine, heroin, dilaudid, demerol, methadone, marihuana, and cocaine is best achieved in a specialized institution where withdrawal symptoms can be handled and where the person is kept under close supervision to prevent him from obtaining drugs. The treatment plan should be organized so that total abstinence is achieved within ten days. Supplementary barbiturate sedation, a high caloric diet with vitamins, hydrotherapy, massage and glucose infusions are most easily administered in an institution. Hospitalization is best planned for a period of at least six months, during which period psychotherapy should be utilized. Unless sources of conflict are mediated and faulty attitudes toward life altered, relapse of the addiction is almost inevitable.

The patient cannot be considered cured until all craving for drugs has disappeared, and until he is able to resist taking them even though they are available.

Where the patient's financial condition forbids hospitalization in a private institution, it is advisable to ask the patient to apply for voluntary admisson or commitment to the U. S. Public Health Service Hospitals at Lexington, Kentucky or Fort Worth, Texas [461].

Following discharge from the institution, intensive psychotherapy provides the best opportunity for helping the addict remain drug free. The psychotherapeutic principles outlined for the treatment of the alcoholic may be found helpful in dealing with the addict. At all times, the therapist must be wary of signs of relapse in the use of narcotic drugs. He should make arrangements for further hospitalization where this occurs. Under no circumstances should narcotics be prescribed in the office management of addicted patients.

The treatment of the barbiturate addict is also difficult and will require that he be hospitalized except where the person has stabilized his intake and does not require excessive amounts of the drug. Barbiturates in large doses are destructive to brain tissue. Withdrawal must be gradual to avoid convulsions or the precipitation of a psychosis. As in the treatment of narcotic addiction, abstinence must be complete before the patient can be pronounced cured. Such abstinence should be complete within fourteen days. Generally, the drug is reduced at the rate of 0.1 gram daily. In the event great weakness, tremors or insomnia occurs, the reduction of the drug is stopped until these symptoms disappear. As with narcotic addiction, psychotherapy should be administered during and following the withdrawal of the drug.

9. Sexual Deviations

The sexual function in the human being is often employed as a vehicle for the expression of varied strivings, interpersonal attitudes and needs. Thus, sexual behavior may embrace, among other things, impulses to hurt or to be hurt, to humiliate or to be humiliated, and to display or to mutilate oneself.

The common kinds of sexual perversion encountered by the therapist are homosexuality, sexual masochism, sexual sadism, exhibitionism and voyeurism. These conditions are among the most difficult of all syndromes to treat. Because of the intense pleasure values inherent in the exercise of the perversions, and the fact that they serve as avenues of discharge of deep needs other than sexual, the patient is usually reluctant to give them up. Although he may have a desire to correct certain disagreeable symptoms, like anxiety or tension, he may not have the motivation to abandon his specific kind of sexual expression. Due to this lack of incentive, resistance often becomes so intense as to interfere with the therapeutic process.

The treatment of sexual perversions must be organized around removing blocks to personality development in order to correct the immature strivings that are being expressed through the sexual perversion. Fears of adult genitality and of relating intimately and lovingly to persons of the opposite sex must be resolved before adequate sexual functioning is possible. The only rational approach is, therefore, reconstructive in nature. Unfortunately, lack of motivation may inhibit the patient from entering into reconstructive treatment. Additionally, ego weakness and disintegrative tendencies are often present in sexual perversions and act as further blocks to deep therapy. For these reasons, the therapeutic objective may have to be confined to the mere control of the perversion and to its possible sublimation. The therapist here may have to function as a supportive, guiding authority who helps the patient to lead a more restrained life.

In treating perversions, the therapist must prepare himself for a long struggle. Resistances are, as has been mentioned, usually intense, and the patient will repeatedly relapse into the sexual deviation. The patient should not be blamed, reproved or made to feel guilty for this. Rather, he must be helped to see the purposes served by his perversion, and to appreciate why the need to express it becomes more overwhelming at some times than at others. While the ultimate outlook is not as favorable as in some other problems, there is no reason why patients who become motivated for, and who can tolerate reconstructive therapy, cannot achieve a good result.

10. Speech Disorders

Functional speech problems, which are sometimes arbitrarily called "stuttering," are the consequence of incoordination of various parts of speech wherein the speech rhythm becomes inhibited or interrupted. Associated are vasomotor disturbances, spasm and incoordination of muscle groups involving other parts of the body. The speech difficulty is initiated and exaggerated by certain social situations, the individual being capable of articulating better under some circumstances than under others. This is confirmed by the fact that the person is usually able to sing, and to talk without difficulty to himself and to animals.

The treatment of stuttering should proceed on two different levels: correction of the improper speech habit, and the handling of the deeper emotional problem which originally initiated and now sustains the difficulty. A guidance approach is of help in achieving the first objective. The second goal is obtained through a persuasive, reeducative, and, where possible, a reconstructive approach. Therapy involves correction of patent difficulties in the environment that stir up the person's insecurity, and a dealing with disturbing inner conflicts. Since the character disturbance in stutterers is extensive, therapy is bound to be difficult, prolonged, and, in many cases, unsuccessful insofar as alteration of the underlying personality disorder is concerned. The most that can be done for many stutterers is symptomatic relief in the form of speech correction.

Speech training may do as much harm as it does good. It is valuable only as a means of building up confidence in the individual's powers to articulate. Unfortunately, it may psychologically have the opposite effect, since it over-emphasizes will power and control, and concentrates the stutterer's attention on the mechanics of his speech rather than upon what he says. Instead of becoming less conscious about his speech difficulty, he becomes more involved with it, thus intensifying his problem. This is not to say that proper exercises in diaphragmatic breathing, phonetics and articulation are of no value in certain patients. Sometimes, with these methods, a symptomatic recovery may take place in mild cases. However, in severe cases, they are relatively ineffectual, and, especially where the person makes a voluntary effort to put his stuttering to a halt, the severity of his speech problem may increase. There is one method, known as the "chewing method," which has advantages over others, since it diverts attention from the speech mechanism. Rhythmics and eukinetics are also sometimes helpful. Training methods, when utilized, should be employed by a therapist experienced in speech techniques.

There are certain evasions and defenses that the stutterer may learn in order to tide over situations where he must talk. Drawling, speaking in a rhythmic manner or in a sing-song tone, utilizing distracting sounds like "ah" or a sigh prior to articulation, employing a gesture or engaging in some motor act like pacing or rubbing a watch chain, purposeful pauses, and a variety of other tricks may be taught the stutterer by the speech teacher. These are entirely palliative and must be considered escapes rather than therapeutic devices.

Since stuttering is essentially a symptom of a deep personality disturbance, the most rational form of treatment is that of reconstructive therapy. This is associated with many vicissitudes, such as have been described by Glauber [462].

Where reconstructive therapy cannot be done, a persuasive approach is sometimes helpful. The first step in therapy consists of convincing the patient that because of his experience and disappointments, he has come to over-emphasize the speech function. To him it constitutes an insignia of aggrandizement and defamation. His self-esteem has become linked with how he performs in his speech. Because of this, he concentrates his attention on the way he talks more than on what he says. It is essential to remember that while his speech problem is important in his mind, it is probably not regarded with the same emphasis by others. He must understand also that he will overcome his stuttering more easily when he stops running away from acknowledging it. He must face the situation and even admit his speech problem to others. When he does this, he will be more at ease and his speech will improve.

A talk such as the following may be indicated:

There is nothing disgraceful about stuttering. Avoiding social situations because of fear of ridicule merely serves to exaggerate the sense of defeat. It is necessary to regard stuttering in the same light as any other physical problem. If you stop being ashamed of it, and do not concern yourself with embarrassing others, people will notice your speech less and less. As you become more unconcerned about *how* you talk, you will concentrate on *what* you say. Keep concentrating on what you say, and pay no attention to how it sounds. Fear and embarrassment exaggerate your speech difficulty, so make yourself act calm and you will feel calm, and your speech will improve.

The next stage of therapy draws on some reeducative techniques and consists of demonstrating to the patient how he becomes upset and loses his sense of calmness in some situations. There will be no lack of material, since the patient will bring to the therapist's attention many instances in which his stuttering becomes exaggerated. Examining his emotional reactions to these situations as well as his dreams will give the therapist clues as to the dynamic elements involved in the patient's speech disorder. These may be pointed out to the patient in terms that conform with his existing capacities for understanding. The aim is to show the patient that his speech difficulty appears when he loses his capacity to remain relaxed, and when, for any reason whatsoever, emotional instability develops.

The patient is encouraged to cultivate a calm, unemotional tone of voice. He may practice this with a friend or with members of his family. One half hour each day devoted to reading aloud from a book, jotting down those words that are difficult to pronounce, is helpful. He may then practice enunciating words several times during the day. Some persons find it helpful to talk for a short time daily in front of a mirror, watching their facial movements as they utter sounds. Other individuals find such autosuggestions as the following useful:

I am able to talk and to pronounce each word. I shall be able to do this better and better, under all conditions. I will make myself calm and unemotional when I am with people. I will concentrate on what I say rather than how I say it. Under no circumstances will I get discouraged. If my speech gets bad on any occasion, I will do better next time.

Two important adjuncts in speech therapy are self-hypnosis and group therapy. Persuasive autosuggestions in a self-induced trance reinforce the patient's desires for self-confidence and assertiveness. Group therapy, in which the patient comes into contact with other persons suffering from speech problems, removes his sense of isolation. The fact that his companions experience the same trepidations as he does helps him to reevaluate his reaction. An opportunity is provided him to speak and to recite in a permissive setting. The identification with the group, along with the growing confidence in his ability to express himself, may have a most positive effect on his speech performance.

As the patient begins to experience improvement in his interpersonal relationships, his speech problem will plague him less and less. Utilizing the speech group as a bridge, he may be able to integrate himself with other groups and to consider himself on an equal plane with its constituent members.

11. Borderline Cases (Latent Schizophrenia, Pseudoneurotic Schizophrenia)

Patients who diagnostically hover between neuroses and psychoses are very commonly encountered in practice. These patients possess a personality disorder characterized by dependency, immaturity, detachment, tendencies toward autistic thinking, disintegrative ego proclivities, faulty reality testing, transient psychotic episodes, and shifts in defenses from neurotic to psychotic-like processes.

Therapy is best conducted on a once- or twice-a-week basis. The modifications in method that are necessary include several points: (a) Establishing a warm supportive relationship is of paramount importance, the therapist doing the giving, being careful not to offend the patient. (b) Time restrictions in the session must be elastic. (c) A long testing period is to be expected. It may often be very difficult for the patient to make a relationship with the therapist. (d) Environmental manipulation may be necessary. (e) Working with the patient's family to reduce pressure on the patient is frequently indicated. (f) The interview focus is on reality, the patient's relapse into daydreaming or delusion being interpreted as a reaction to fear or guilt. (g) Avoiding the probing of psychotic-like material is advisable. (h) Active reassurance and advice-giving may be necessary. (i) Directive encouragement is given to the patient to participate in occupational therapy, hobbies, and recreations. (j) Neurotic defenses are supported and strengthened. (k) Challenging or disagreeing with the patient's distorted ideas is delayed until a good relationship exists. (l) Therapy may last a long time, perhaps the rest of the patient's life.

Excellent accounts of the therapy of borderline cases may be found in the articles by A. Wolberg, [463], Eisenstein, [464], Federn, [465], and Bychowski [466].

Some of the techniques for the treatment of schizophrenia described in the following section of this chapter may be valuable in the borderline patient.

PSYCHOTIC DISORDERS

In the treatment of a psychosis the chief aim is to bring the ego back to a realistic level of integration, even though one has to restore habitual character traits and neurotic symptoms that have maintained the person in a sort of functional relationship with life. For instance, the individual, responding to a feeling of inner paralysis and helplessness, may have mastered his anxiety on the basis of a strong dependency drive. However, the death of the person on whom he has depended may suddenly confront him with feelings of isolation and despair so profound that his integrative capacities shatter, with a resulting psychosis. In therapy an attempt may be made to restore equilibrium by providing the patient with a compensatory dependency relationship. Active guidance, manipulation of the environment, and other supportive therapies may be useful in achieving this goal. Where the hold on reality is minimal, hospitalization, sedation, electric convulsive therapy and insulin shock therapy may be required to bring the ego back to a more realistic stature. A most important element in the treatment program is establishing a relationship with the patient of an accepting nature, tolerating any psychotic projections he may display.

1. Involutional Psychotic Reactions

In the treatment of involutional psychosis, both good results and poor results have been reported following the use of estrogenic hormones in females and testosterone in males. As a general rule, endocrine therapy is indicated where there are such evidences of endocrine insufficiency as vasomotor instability, flushes, sweats, headaches and tension. In certain cases, an estrogenic deficiency, as determined by accurate tests, seems to be coincident with the psychosis. Here, substitution therapy produces dramatic results. In other cases tests may show an estrogenic deficiency in which injection of estrogen has little effect. In most patients, however, the psychosis is a product of more complicated factors than endocrine substances.

Milder cases of involutional psychosis may be cared for at home, or better still in a nursing home under the constant supervision of a nurse or attendant. At all times it is essential to keep in mind the great risk of suicide, and to make plans to forestall any suicidal attempt. In some cases treatment is best started by complete bed rest for a few weeks. Attention must be paid to the patient's diet and to his insomnia. Many patients refuse to eat and tonics prove of little avail. Forced feedings may have to be utilized to avoid emaciation. Insulin and barbiturates in small doses are often helpful.

In disturbed, agitated, acutely paranoid, and suicidally inclined patients, hospitalization is mandatory. Some type of sedative therapy is advisable, at least at first, and in occasional cases prolonged narcosis therapy appears to have a real value. Continuous baths and wet packs may reduce the need for sedatives. However, massage is contraindicated. Occupational therapy may be of some help in diverting the interest of the patient from himself.

By far the most effective therapy in involutional melancholia is convulsive treatment. Electric convulsive therapy has a definite advantage over other types and is to be preferred from the standpoint of safety. The results of convulsive therapy are often dramatic, and experience has shown that physical contraindications to treatment need not be too stringent.

Involutional psychotics are largely inaccessible to psychotherapy. All psychic probing in an analytic sense is to be avoided, and efforts must be directed at increasing repression rather than stimulating and interpreting the material that emerges from the unconscious. Persuasion and reassurance sometimes have the effect of tiding a patient over a crisis. Many patients confide that they have been immeasurably cheered by the physician who reassured them during their acute disorder, even though they were unable at the time to acknowledge the beneficial effect.

In mild cases of involutional melancholia, hypnosis may have a beneficial influence. Hypnosis may be used to induce relaxation and to reinforce reassurance and persuasive suggestions. These suggestions attempt to help the individual adjust to his life situation and to the limited capacities induced by his advancing years. If hypnosis cannot be induced, psychotherapeutic talks may be conducted on a waking level. If possible the patient should be diverted from concentrating on his various symptoms, and his attention should be directed to his daily activities, hobbies, recreations and occupational therapy.

Psychotherapy is particularly indicated following convulsive therapy. The patient may be shown that advancing years inevitably bring with them convictions that one's views are considered old fashioned and intolerable, along with feelings that one may be unable to gain praiseworthy recognition. There are numerous other blows to self-esteem at this time of life. Some persons attempt to compensate for this by becoming markedly egotistic or bigoted in their opinions, by clinging to their convictions stubbornly against logic, hoping thereby to regain their self-respect. Others react by depression, hopelessness, inferiority feelings, hostility and rage directed at the world at large. One must always recognize the limitations inherent in the process of aging. He should also realize that many creative capacities are unimpaired and that some are actually increased.

It is important for the patient to appreciate and to accept the fact that as a person grows older, he does have modified physical and working powers. If he is so constituted that he considers an inability to compete physically with younger and stronger persons a blow to his self-esteem, he is apt to respond disastrously. He may become sullen, irritable, and defiant, or else he may evolve expansive notions regarding his own capacities, projecting his inability to function perfectly on the basis that he is misunderstood by others. He will then become more and more unable to withstand frustration, and he will be victimized by his own emotion of rage. He may even withdraw from social contacts and encrust himself in a bitter vituperative shell, isolating himself from relations with other people.

The patient may be shown that some persons attempt to adjust to the problem of their advancing years by a vicarious display of aggressiveness and energy, resenting any curtailment of activities. There is in this a frenzied attempt to regain one's lost youth by proving to the world that one is still physically virile. Yet it is most essential that the patient be able to tolerate certain frailties within himself. If the person persists in refusing to recognize self-limitations, he may continue to operate under exorbitant expectations of what he must accomplish in life. The realization that the most active period in his life span is over, that he does not have as strong sexual feelings as he once had, may arouse considerable anxiety. It is thus necessary to appraise honestly one's impulses and demands in relation to expected goals in life. It may be difficult at first to admit weaknesses in oneself; but the gradual understanding that later years bring mellowness and measures of contentment that cannot be approached in the impetuosities of the early decades, can lead to self-tolerance and acceptance. It is essential to remember that in this self-acceptance there is no element of "giving-up," that reasonable physical activity is still essential to health, and that mental activity can continue in a vital manner. It is urgent also to increase one's social contacts and interests so as not to be upset with the spectre of "aloneness."

2. Manic-Depressive Reactions

Psychotherapy is usually ineffective in manic phases of this disorder. The patient's attention is too easily diverted; acting-out is too unrestrained; and emotion is too explosive. Because of this, hypomanic and manic patients are extremely difficult to manage in the office. They will seek to involve the therapist in all of their fantastic plans. They will make demands of him which, when unfulfilled, will release great hostility or aggression. They will try to overwhelm and dominate those around them, and they may become uncontrollable when their wishes are not ratified.

One of the chief reasons for hospitalizing the manic patient is to prevent him from involving himself and other people in projects which issue out of his overconfidence. Because he is inclined to be erotic, he must be protected from sexual indiscretions and from a hasty marriage, which he may contract on the crest of an ecstatic wave. Another reason for early hospitalization is that some manic cases will go into a state of delirium when they are not treated intensively at the start. These delirious attacks may be fatal due to exhaustion, dehydration and hypochloremia. Sedation, hydrotherapy and electric convulsive therapy are the usual treatments for a manic attack in a hospital set-up.

Psychotherapy is also very difficult in depressed patients because their demands for help and love are insatiable. No matter how painstaking the therapist may be in supplying their demands, they will respond with rage and aggression, often accusing the therapist of incompetence or ill-will. The patient should be shown, nevertheless, that the therapist understands and sympathizes with his suffering. Such measures as active guidance and externalization of interests may be attempted. As in schizophrenic patients, the basis of treatment is a warm relationship between the patient and the therapist. The relationship that the patient establishes with the therapist will, however, be extremely vulnerable, because of the existing infantile ego. Much lenity and tolerance is needed and an attempt must be made to show the patient that the therapist realizes the depth of his fears and misgivings. This however is more easily said than done, since the depressed patient has a distrustful nature.

Distrust springs from the fusion of hate with love. Hostile feelings generate guilt which may be so disabling that the person will want to discontinue treatment. The slightest frustration during therapy, such as the unavoidable changing or cancelling of an appointment, may be equivalent to rejection and will mobilize a tremendous amount of anxiety. Under the surface there is always fear of abandonment, and the patient will tend to misinterpret casual actions. He has a tendency to seek reassurance, but he resents its being called psychotherapy.

The aim in treatment is to develop and to reinforce all positive elements in the relationship. This will involve much work, since the attitudes of the patient are so ambivalent that he will feel rejected spontaneously, no matter what the therapist does. It is best to let the positive relationship take root without attempting to analyze its sources.

One of the ways of maintaining the relationship on a positive level is by communicating empathy, by avoiding differences in opinion, by trying to see his point of view and sympathizing with it. It is essential to convey to the patient by non-verbal means the idea that he is liked and that the therapist is his friend in spite of anything that happens. An attitude of belittling, harshness, ridicule or irritation must be avoided. Treatment is bound to be prolonged, and is always punctuated with relapses corresponding to the cyclic phases of the disorder.

Hypnosis can aid some of the milder depressions. The trance state is used primarily as a means of inducing relaxation and as a vehicle for persuasion in the attempt to stabilize the person. A number of depressed patients appear to thrive under hypnotic therapy, probably because it appeals to their dependency need.

Mild depressions may be treated at home under supervision of a psychiatrically trained attendant or nurse, or, better still, the patient should be admitted to a rest home. Isolation from parents and friends, bed rest and constant care by a motherly attendant may prove very beneficial. Massage and hydrotherapy should not be neglected except in agitated patients who may become acutely upset by such treatment. Because of anorexia, efforts should be made to bolster the diet with high caloric and high vitamin intake in the form of small but frequent feedings. In severe cases of malnutrition a few units of insulin before meals may be helpful. If sedatives are needed, phenobarbital one-quarter of a grain at 3 p.m., 7 p.m. and 10 p.m. may suffice in allaying tension, and also in producing sleep at night-time. In extreme insomnia, three grains of seconal or one dram of paraldehyde may be necessary. Rest is important and a midday nap or rest period can be prescribed. Where it is essential for the depressed patient to continue work, dexedrine or benzedrine sulphate, five to ten milligrams after arising and before lunch, may be helpful as a stimulant. In the event these efforts fail to control the depression, electric convulsive therapy should be used.

Where the depression is more than mild, hospitalization is advisable. Suicidal attempts in depression occur in almost one-third of cases, and deaths resulting from these attempts occur with great frequency. The patient's complete loss of interest in himself makes mandatory the establishment of definite daily routines, such as a hospital can best supply. Electric convulsive therapy is the treatment of choice and often dramatically arouses the patient from the depths of his depression.

Psychotherapy is usually ineffective during extremely depressed phases. The only thing that can be done is to keep up the patient's morale. He should not be forced to engage in activities that he resists because this may merely convince him of his helplessness and of his inability to do anything constructive.

Where there is little suicidal risk, he should be encouraged to continue his work, if he feels at all capable of managing it, since inactivity merely directs his thinking on his own misery. In many cases contact should be established with the patient's family and environment. This is necessary since the family of the patient often chides him for "not snapping out of it," and constantly reminds him that he must make up his mind to get well. The family members may be told that recovery is more than a matter of will power, and they must be urged to avoid a nagging and critical attitude.

The material elicited during the periods of active psychosis, both as to mental content and as to the character of the relationship with the therapist, may yield important clues to the inner conflicts of the patient. Notes may be made for later reference, but all interpretations during the active period must be suspended. Only during a remission can interpretive work be helpful. Many patients spontaneously express a desire to know more about their illness. Here, a modified insight approach may be used. The majority of patients, however, show an unwillingness to go into their difficulties, and resist insight therapy. Having recovered, they are convinced they are well, and they desire no further contact with the therapist. Without the "wish" to get well, little can be accomplished in the way of deep psychotherapy.

Once the patient has emerged from his depression, either spontaneously, as a result of convulsive therapy, or through psychotherapy, an attempt may be made to work with his character strivings, analyzing the relationship to the therapist actively, in an effort to help the patient become more assertive and self-sufficient. Whether or not psychotherapy can prevent the onset of, or ameliorate an endogenous manic-depressive reaction is difficult to say, since one cannot validate results where a tendency to spontaneous recovery exists, as in this illness. Development to a point where the individual is capable of tolerating frustration, and where he is able to achieve greater self-sufficiency and independence, will probably require a period of years, during which a number of relapses are to be expected.

3. Schizophrenic Reactions

The treatment of schizophrenia depends upon the stage of the disease, the depth of regression, the grasp on reality that remains, the desire of the patient for therapy, and his ability to establish some sort of relationship with the therapist. The first objective in therapy is to bring the patient from his inner regressed state to a more realistic level of integration. Once this is achieved, the second stage in therapy may be attempted, which is to determine the cause of the patient's anxiety, which has forced the ego to shatter in schizophrenic illness.

Where the patient's psychosis has been precipitated by an overwhelming external traumatic situation, simple environmental manipulation may suffice to bring the patient back to his prepsychotic level of adaptation. For example, a man inducted into the Armed Forces may develop an acute schizophrenic reaction as a result of an inability to adjust himself to the demands and disciplines of army life. The personality resources of the individual, while adequate for satisfactory functioning in civilian life, are not now sufficient to cope with the added burdens imposed on them. In such a case the discharge of the man from the Army, and his return to his previous civilian capacity, may achieve a complete cure of the psychosis.

Most schizophrenic reactions, however, are associated with such great weakness of the ego that the person is unable to withstand even average stresses. Ordinary processes of living and relating to people are much more than his ego can mediate. Environmental manipulation does not suffice to restore the patient to reality here, because he senses menace everywhere, even in the most obviously congenial atmosphere.

Fears rooted in past inimical conditionings and damaging conflicts generate anxiety continuously and prevent the ego from emerging from its regressed level of integration. The patient erects a wall of detachment and isolation to protect himself from further hurt; it is this wall which interferes so drastically with any attempted therapy.

The key to the treatment of schizophrenia lies in the ability to establish some sort of contact with the patient. Most schizophrenics fear relationships with people desperately, and they erect all kinds of obstacles to any interpersonal threat. The withdrawal from reality, and the archaic type of thinking and symbolism, enhance the individual's isolation from people, since there is no common means of communication. Yet beneath the surface the patient yearns with all his might for a friendly and loving relationship. He wards it off, however, because he has been injured by past interpersonal contacts. He does not wish to encounter further rebuffs. His apathy, his detachment, and his expressed hostility and aggression are means of protecting him from his desire for a closer union with people. Establishing rapport with the patient is in line with two objectives: first, to reintegrate the patient in his relationships with people to where he can obtain at least partial gratification of personal needs without fear of abandonment or injury; and second, to bring him back to the realistic world by proving to him that reality can be a source of pleasure rather than of pain.

The technique of developing rapport varies with the patient. A great deal of activity is essential. In very sick patients whose productions are seemingly irrelevant and incoherent, a careful analysis of the productions will disclose a language that is very meaningful to the patient. The ability to show the patient that his words and gestures are understood may be the first constructive step. Sullivan [467] has stressed the need to communicate understanding of the patient's language and gestures as a means of solidifying the interpersonal relationship. In order to do this it may be necessary to talk to the patient on his own regressed level. Rosen [468] interprets the utterances of the patient in terms of their symbolic meaning, and he has been able to develop a remarkable relationship with his patients through this method.

In mute patients, therapy may consist of nothing more than sitting with the patient without prodding him to express himself. The very fact that the therapist refrains from probing his trends, and avoids discussing the causes of his breakdown, but accepts him as he is, may help the patient to regard the therapist as a less threatening force than he regards other people. In many cases, therapy may consist of working with the patient at occupational projects and playing games with him; such as, cards, checkers or chess. Sometimes a more positive approach is made to the patient by giving him food, like milk, candy and cake. For a long time it may seem that these gratuities are the only reason the patient desires to see the therapist. In querying the patient after his recovery, however, one becomes convinced that the patient actually had a desire for closeness and was testing the therapist constantly.

Any relationship that the patient is able to establish with the therapist is at first bound to be extremely unstable. The schizophrenic individual feels very vulnerable and helpless within himself. His level of frustration tolerance is inordinately low. He is distrustful, suspicious and inclined to misinterpret the motives of the therapist in accordance with his inner fears and prejudices. He feels incapable of coping with life, and he resents the intentions of the therapist to return him to reality, which holds for him unbounded terrors. He fears injury and frustration from people, and it may be months, sometimes years, before he is willing to accept the therapist as a friend. Even then he will sense rejection and neglect in the most casual attitude of the therapist. Anxiety with a temporary return to regression will interrupt therapy repeatedly, and it must be handled by a consistently reassuring and friendly attitude. Violent hostile reactions may punctuate treatment from time to time, especially when the patient senses that his liking for the therapist is forcing him to leave the relative security of his reality retreat.

Fromm-Reichman [469] has commented on the unpredictable nature of the schizophrenic's relationship to the therapist. A sympathetic, understanding and skillful handling by the therapist of the relationship is far more important than an intellectual comprehension of the patient's illness. She ascribes difficulties in therapy to the fact that the therapist is unable to understand the primitive logic and magical reasoning which governs schizophrenic thinking.

Unless the therapist analyzes his own reactions repeatedly, his sense of frustration may arouse aggression that will interfere with treatment, because it is manifestly impossible to treat any psychotic person where there is no genuine liking for him. If the therapist is able to regard the patient as essentially a child or an infant, emotionally speaking, he will best be able to understand the patient's vagaries. Cold logic fails miserably in explaining the reactions of the schizophrene. Despite his age, the patient seeks a childish relationship to the therapist, and he desires unlimited warmth, understanding, protection and help. He seeks a mothering rather than a give-and-take relationship between two equals.

Therapy in schizophrenia must, therefore, be oriented around the fact that the ego of the patient is extremely immature. As a result the individual is as helpless as an infant in his dealings with life. He requires the aid of a stronger person upon whom he can depend. Like an infant, furthermore, his emotional reactions to people are unstable and ambivalent. He is easily frustrated, and he feels rejection for insufficient reasons. He is unreasonable and demanding. His concept of reality is wholly unreliable. He often confuses inner mental processes with outside reality. He may believe that the person on whom he depends is omniscient and will supply his every demand, expressed or unexpressed. He will react with hostility if he is not granted what he believes he deserves. Alone, his ego is so weak that he is unable to tolerate the impact of the world. He needs help and support.

Because of this, it is usually advisable to enlist the aid of a relative or friend, preferably a motherly person who can take upon herself the responsibility for the patient. Federn [470] stresses that no schizophrene should be allowed to depend on his own resources. He should at all times be surrounded by an atmosphere of love and warmth. His stability and his strength grow as a result of positive identifications with loved ones. If he is at all able to develop to self-sufficiency, his independence will grow best in the soil of this positive identification. The hope is to bring him to a point where his own ego can function satisfactorily without the aid of a parental figure. In many cases, the latter stage of self-sufficiency is never attained, and all one can do is adapt the individual to reasonable social functioning, while attached to some kindly person.

The need to surround the patient with a favorable atmosphere necessitates work with his family or with people with whom he lives. This is essential to relieve the burden on the patient induced by demands and responsibilities he is incapable of fulfilling. Often the inertia and apathy of the patient stir up resentment in his family, and when the patient is aware of their hostility, he may retreat further from reality. Considerable work with the patient's relatives may be required before they are sufficiently aware of the dynamics of the patient's reactions and before they are willing to aid the therapist in the treatment plan.

The chief emphasis in treatment must be on the creation of a human relationship with the patient that has pleasure values for him. Only by this means will he relinquish the safety and gratification of regression, and, utilizing the relationship with the therapist as a bridge, return to reality. The handling of treatment, however, requires considerable tact. No matter how detached the patient is, he is extremely sensitive to everything the therapist says or does. An avoidance of situations that evoke anxiety in the patient is essential. This is often a very difficult task because the most casual remark may stir up powerful emotions in him.

The patient may choose to remain silent throughout the treatment hour, and he will appreciate the therapist's refraining from forcing him to talk. It is expedient with such a mute patient to point out occasionally that he perhaps abstains from talking because he believes that the therapist is interfering with him, or because he is afraid of what he might say. The patient may feel more at ease due to such remarks, and he may finally break through his silence.

In most cases, the patient at first will feel alone, helpless and misunderstood. He resents the intrusion of the therapist into his private life, and he believes that the therapist, like everyone else, is unable to understand him. The initial task is to show the patient that his impulses and wishes are respected, and that he is not required to comply with demands that are unreasonable. Usually in all of his previous interviews he has been bombarded with questions about his breakdown, and, even when he has responded to these questions in a more or less frank manner, he has sensed disapproval. The fact that the therapist accepts him as he is, may eventually build up his own self-respect and strengthen his desire to return to reality.

Constantly, during treatment, the patient will react by detachment or withdrawal, or he may subject the therapist to a testing period during which he is recalcitrant and hostile. His purpose is to determine whether the therapist is the kind of person who can be trusted, or whether the therapist is like all other people in his experience, who make unfair demands or react to his hostility with counter-hostility. The patient may believe that what the therapist demands of him is to be "good." This "goodness" means to the patient that he must comply with standards that all other people impose on him. At first he will act as if the therapist actually expects him to abide by these standards, threatening him with rejection or aggression if he resists. The testing period may be a trying one for the therapist, since it may continue for many months during which the patient constantly rejects the therapist's friendship. When the patient realizes that the therapist does not expect him to do certain things, that the therapist sides with him against his family, he will begin to reevaluate the therapist in a new light.

The beginning of a feeling of closeness may precipitate panic; the patient may try to run away from therapy, or he will exhibit aggression toward the therapist. The ability to see the patient through this stage may finally succeed in breaking down his reserve and in establishing for the first time an identification with a person based upon love. There exists within every schizophrene a psychic tug of war between the spontaneous forces of mental health that drive him to seek gratifying relationships with people, and the security of his regressed state that harbors him from the imagined dangers of a hostile world. The therapist's attitudes will determine which of these impulses will triumph.

The method of handling the treatment hour is of signal importance. It is best not to cross-examine the patient because he may interpret this as censure. He must be convinced that the therapist does not want to invade and to remove him from his private world, but rather seeks to participate in it with him. This does not mean assuming a cloying sweetness during sessions, because the patient will be able to see through this. It must be expected that the patient's attitudes will be ambivalent. He may profess little interest in the interview, yet resent its termination at the designated time. He may attempt to defy or to provoke the therapist, or he may refuse to cooperate. If the therapist becomes ill and cannot keep an appointment, the patient may react with rage and refuse to continue treatments. If the therapist is unavoidably late for an appointment, the same thing can occur. The patient may resent the therapist's taking any vacation or assigning another person to care for him. Where customary routines have to be interrupted, it is best to prepare the patient far in advance, and if necessary, to enlist the help of those members of his family with whom he has an attachment. If the patient becomes hostile toward the therapist, every attempt must be made to explore why he believes the therapist has failed him. Should he persist with his hostility and insist on seeing some other therapist, his wishes should be respected, because it is futile to do any work with a patient while he is governed by feelings of resentment.

Once a positive relationship has been established, it is necessary to cherish it carefully. Nothing must jeopardize the relationship. For example, the patient must never be led to feel that his delusions are ridiculous. His feelings and attitudes must be respected at all times. It is unnecessary to reinforce these attitudes by agreeing with them; but they should be accepted as something the patient believes in sincerely. However, it may be impressed on the patient that there might possibly be another explanation for his experiences than the one he supports. All probing for dynamic material must assiduously be avoided. This is one of the most frequent errors in the handling of psychotic patients. It is also an error to cross-examine the patient regarding previous mental upsets.

Because the aim is to increase repression, because the ego is already too weak and permits the filtering through of disturbing unconscious material, such techniques as free association are to be discouraged. Rather, the patient should be enjoined to talk about everyday reality happenings. In general, the past had best be avoided and the patient may be aided in any expressed desire to regard it as a "bad dream" or something that should be forgotten. Under no circumstances should a positive relationship with the therapist be analyzed. Where the patient exhibits inhibitions or phobias, these too should be respected, since they probably have protective values. All resistances he uses to repress psychotic material must be reinforced, although the symbolisms he employs may sometimes be interpreted to him. Unlike neurosis, analysis of resistances should be avoided to prevent the release of the unconscious content which will upset the patient more. When the patient himself brings up delusional material or symptoms, and spontaneously talks about the connection with traumatizing circumstances in his past, an effort may be made to explain in uncomplicated terms how these manifestations originated. The rule never to dissolve resistance does not apply to resistances to getting well or to integrating himself more closely with the therapist and with reality. These impediments should be analyzed and removed if possible. Guilt feelings may be met by reassurance, and hostilities dealt with in a manner that does not put responsibility or blame on the patient.

One of the ways in which a positive relationship with the therapist may be used is to try to show the patient that his thoughts and ideas often appear to be realistic, but that it is necessary always to differentiate between what seems to be real and what actually is real. In the patient's case too, he may confuse both, even though there is no question of doubt in his mind that the two states are identical. An excellent sign of restoration of ego strength is the ability of the patient to recognize the irrational nature of his ideas while he was in an upset condition.

Hospitalization is frequently necessary. It may be essential for the safety of the patient and the protection of his relatives to hospitalize him. Occasionally it may be advisable to admit the patient to an institution even though he manages to get along well on the outside.

Insulin shock therapy is administered best in the protective atmosphere of a hospital, and such treatment may dramatically bring the patient to a more realistic level of integration. Whatever the psychologic effect of shock, regressed patients are often enabled through it to establish contact with reality. This can materially shorten the period of therapy. Along with shock treatments, psychotherapy is essential. All the general rules expounded above for the handling of schizophrenic patients are applicable to patients in a state of remission brought about as a result of shock therapy. If possible, the psychiatrist who administers psychotherapy should be the one who carries out shock treatments. A very close relationship to the therapist is often established during the administration of shock.

On the other hand, there are certain disadvantages to hospitalization. The most insidious feature of "institutionalization" is that the patient's tendencies to regress will be reinforced enormously by any lack of stimulation in the hospital. As one of a large group of patients, the individual may lose his identity. He becomes dilapidated in his appearance and oblivious to customary habit routines. There may be little in his environment to encourage his latent desires for growth and development. This unfortunate feature is due, to a large extent, to the overcrowding of institutions, and to the lack of enlightenment and education of the personnel. The motives governing an employe's choice in working in an institution may not be those helpful to the patient in restoring him as an active unit of society.

That hospitalization can prove itself to be a stimulating rather than a retarding influence is illustrated in institutions with a progressive administration and well-trained personnel. Selected occupational therapy and craftsmanship, carefully applied to the patient's interests and aptitudes, can help prevent the abandonment of reality. Exercises, games, entertainment, dancing, music, social affairs and group discussions can also be of estimable benefit. The physical aspects of treatment should not be neglected. Correction of remedial physical defects, the use of glandular therapy where necessary, and the employment of hydrotherapy and sedatives, where indicated, may be helpful. Many of the benefits from such therapies are psychologic. They help convince the patient that he is not considered hopeless, in this way building up a feeling of confidence in the therapist and in himself. It is probable that the so-called Aschner treatment for schizophrenia with its stress on detoxification, stimulation, exercise, baths, sweats, venesection, catharsis, emesis and hormone therapy was really psychotherapeutic in effect. Where psychotherapy, drug therapy, rehabilitative procedures, or shock therapy fail to retard the deteriorative process, lobotomy is sometimes found helpful.

While many patients retain a fairly good grasp on reality and tend to return to their customary occupations, and even to tolerable relationships with other people on the basis of the close attachment they establish with the therapist, it may be necessary to do further work with the patient to prevent a relapse. Some of the patient's problems may be rooted in the fact that he harbors bloated ambitions of what he should accomplish in life. His grandiose expectations may have resulted in constant frustration. Under such circumstances it is essential to modify the patient's goals through the careful use of the therapeutic relationship. It may be possible, for instance, to convince him that it is better to devote his life to the attainment of happiness in the immediate present than to strive for things in the unknown future. Character disturbances may exist that make relationships with people fraught with anxiety. An active manipulation of the patient's environment through consultation with his family may enable him to function more comfortably. Attempts should also be made to introduce him gradually into social contacts with other people.

In spite of such corrective measures, hostility, tension and anxiety may constantly be created by unconscious inner conflict. The intensity of these emotions may again tend to shatter the patient's ego. The danger of another schizophrenic collapse may therefore be imminent. As a preventive measure, the cautious use of an insight approach may be indicated. It is best here not to attempt probing for conflicts until the patient evinces an interest in understanding his own problems. Schizophrenic persons are remarkably intuitive and can grasp the dynamics of their disorder better than most neurotics. This is probably because they live closer to their unconscious, and because ego barriers to deep impulses and fears are not so strong. It is for this reason that one must proceed very carefully in analyzing the patient's deepest impulses. Bychowski [471] and Fromm-Reichmann [472] give some excellent suggestions for the analytic handling of schizophrenics.

The realization of unconscious guilt, hostility and erotism through analysis has a dual effect on the psychic apparatus. On the one hand, it floods the ego with destructive emotion; on the other, by forcing a more realistic adaptation, it serves to liberate the psyche from incessant conflict. In this way the dynamic probing is like a two-edged sword; the ego has to be traumatized by the liberated emotions before it is able to mobilize defenses less destructive to the person than regression. The ego, however, may still be so weak that it collapses under the impact of emotion before it can adapt itself in a more adequate manner. This is always a danger in psychotic and prepsychotic conditions. All interpretations must, therefore, be very cautiously applied. Reconstructive techniques should be abandoned temporarily if excitement or great hostility develop. For only when the patient is positively attached to the therapist is he able to bear the suffering brought out by a realization of his unconscious trends.

STRESS REACTIONS

Except for transportation and industrial accidents, and the rare catastrophes of hurricane, flood and famine, stress reactions (traumatic neuroses) are mainly consequent to the disasters of war. Especially prominent is combat fatigue among the soldiers of the participating armies.

Knowledge of the dynamics of war neurosis made certain preventive measures possible in World War II. Where the soldier had had effective training that made him feel he could defend himself under all circumstances, where he was shown that he had adequate weapons of attack, where he had confidence in his leaders, and where he had obtained sufficient indoctrination and morale building, he was best prepared to resist a breakdown. An important element in prevention was group identification. Cooperation with others was essential, and the individual had to be made to feel that he was part of a team, with enough of an idea of the battle situation and the planned strategy so that he would not be caught by surprise.

The incidence of war neuroses is proportionate to shattered morale and to feelings of isolation from fellow soldiers. An organized body of men fighting for a cause they consider just can best overcome war stress and hardship.

The treatment of the soldier with acute battle exhaustion depends upon whether he is or is not to be returned to duty. The sequel of all battles are reactions of fear and great fatigue. Only later are these reactions organized into actual neuroses. Experience in previous wars has shown that evacuation and a too reassuring attitude encourage collapse. Unless the individual anticipates going back to the front in spite of his reactions, he may develop neurotic illness to avoid duty.

Combat exhaustion, if treated early, does not necessarily result in neurosis. Early therapy consists of sedation, rest, good food and assignment to non-combat duty at the clearing station. It is assumed that the soldier will be returned to the front. Where there is reluctance to return to battle duty, appeals to patriotism, courage, and "not letting one's buddies down" often build up the person's morale and determination. Encouragement to verbalize fear and disgust is vital, since the soldier in this way releases tension, and discovers that others share in his anxieties. The value of respecting the soldier's "gripes" in building morale has long been recognized. The role of the leader is important, too, and an intrepid commanding officer has always been of great service. It is amazing how often a change of attitude on the part of the individual can prevent neurotic collapse.

Treatment of stress reactions in peace as in war should be started as soon as possible, since delay permits the neurosis to become more highly organized and allows the secondary gain element to take hold.

In treating war neurosis in the incipient stages, where sleep disturbances and states of tension exist, a breakdown may often be averted by adequate periods of rest during the daytime, by the use of hypnotics, such as seconal and veronal, and by the person's being permitted to sleep in a dimly lit room. Many soldiers in the incipient stages show terror of the dark and of being alone. They may, therefore, be given some assurance on this account.

In World War II, if sedation therapy failed to resolve the disorder, the soldier was confined to an evacuation hospital, from where, if his condition warranted it, he was sent to the rear echelon hospital. The immediate treatment consisted of rest, good food and quiet. The soldier continued under military discipline. Psychotherapy was in the form of persuasion, suggestion and appeals to go back and try again. A simple explanation of anxiety was given to the patient along with assurances about the universality of fear reactions. The soldier was made to feel that there was nothing unusual in his breakdown and that he could learn to control his fear. Individuals who had not developed too severe reactions could occasionally be helped to return to combat. In some instances, pressure was exerted by stressing the fact that release from the fight was dishonorable, that it was the soldier's duty to finish the job for the sake of his loved ones and companions.

Where a patient has a well-defined stress reaction, narcotherapy and hypnotherapy are often remarkably effective for purposes of symptom removal and as a means of controlling insomnia and tension. Being palliative, these measures often reassure the patient and restore to him a sense of control and mastery.

In instances where anxiety is extreme, one may utilize an "uncovering" type of technique. Here hypnosis and narcotherapy are also of signal help. The recovery of amnesias, and the reliving of the traumatic scene in action or verbalization, have markedly ameliorative or curative effects on acute stress reactions.

While hypnotherapy and narcotherapy accomplish approximately the same results, the emotions accompanying hypnotherapy are often much more vivid, and the carthartic effect consequently greater, than with narcotherapy. There are other advantages to hypnosis. The induction of a trance-like state, once the patient has been hypnotized, is brought about easily without the complication of injections and without post-therapeutic somnolence. Additionally, hypnotic suggestions are capable of demonstrating to the patient more readily his ability to gain mastery of his functions. On the other hand, narcotherapy is easier to employ and does not call for any special skills.

Where it is essential to remove an amnesia, the patient is encouraged under hypnosis or narcosis to talk about the events immediately preceding the traumatic episode, and to lead into the episode slowly, reliving the scene as if it were happening again. Frequently the patient will approach the scene and then block, or he may actually awaken. Repeated trance inductions often break through this resistance. Also, it will be noted that the abreactive effect will increase as the patient describes the episode repeatedly. Apparently the powerful emotions which are bound down are subject to greater repression that the actual memories of the event.

In the treating of postwar neuroses of traumatic origin, Hadfield's original technique is still useful [473]. The patient is hypnotized and instructed that when the therapist places his fingers on the patient's forehead, the latter will picture before him the experiences that caused his breakdown. This usually produces a vivid recollection of the traumatic event with emotions of fear, rage, despair and helplessness. The patient often spontaneously relives the traumatic scene with a tremendous cathartic effect. If he hesitates, he must be encouraged to describe the scenes before him in detail. This is the first step in therapy and must be repeated for a number of sessions until the restored memory is complete. The second step is the utilization of hypnosis to readjust the patient to the traumatic experience. The experience must be worked through, over and over again, until the patient accepts it during hypnosis and remembers it upon awakening. Persuasive suggestions are furthermore given him, directed at increasing assurance and self-confidence. After this, the emotional relationship to the therapist is analyzed at a conscious level to prevent continuance of the dependency tie.

Horsley [474] mentions that where the ordinary injunctions to recall a traumatic scene fail, several reinforcing methods can be tried. The first has to do with commanding the patient to remember, insisting that he will not leave the room until his memory is complete. The second method is that of soothing, coaxing and encouraging the patient, telling him he is about to remember battle scenes that will remind him of his experiences. The patient may, if this is un-successful, be told that although he does not remember the experience during hypnosis, he will remember it upon awakening. He may also be instructed to recall it in a dream the next night.

Various hypnoanalytic procedures, such as dramatization, regression and re-vivification, play therapy, automatic writing and mirror gazing, may be utilized to recover an obstinate amnesia. The reaction of patients to the recall of re-pressed experiences varies. Some patients act out the traumatic scene, getting out of bed, charging about the room, ducking to avoid mortar shells and ap-proaching tanks. Other patients live through the traumatic episode without getting out of bed. Some individuals collapse with anxiety, and they should be reassured and encouraged to go on. Where the patient voices hostility, he should be given an opportunity to express his grievances and dislikes. Clarification of his feelings of injustice may afford him considerable relief.

It must be remembered that the object in therapy is to dissipate feelings of helplessness and of being menaced by a world the patient no longer trusts. The sense of mastery and the ability to readjust oneself to life must be restored. It is necessary to proceed with therapy as rapidly as possible to prevent organiza-tion of the condition into a chronic psychoneurosis. Follow-up therapy is essential with integration on a waking level of the material brought up during the trance. Where anxieties relating to war stress have precipitated hysterical, phobic, com-pulsive and other reactions characteristic of the ways the patient has dealt with anxiety in civilian life, long-term insight therapy will usually be required.

In chronic stress reactions, treatment is difficult, due to the high degree of organization that has taken place, and because of the strong secondary gain element involving monetary compensation and dependency. The recovery of amnesias should always be attempted, but even where successful, this may not at all influence the outcome. An incentive must be created in the patient to function free of symptoms, even at the expense of forfeiting disability com-pensations, which in comparison to emotional health may be shown to be diminutive indeed.

51

Supervision of the Psychotherapeutic Process

THE AVERAGE STUDENT LEARNING TO DO PSYCHOTHERAPY IS POSSESSED of a zeal generated by his didactic training in the psychotherapeutic method. He believes sincerely that he can help people with emotional problems by providing for them an accepting, non-judgmental, non-punitive relationship, in which the patient can verbalize his innermost fears and then gather strength to liberate himself from the shackles of his neurosis. His own personal psychotherapy, and the experiences of his colleagues and teachers in clinical conferences and continuous case seminars, point out to the student that the course of treatment never runs smoothly; instead, that the dual saboteurs, resistance and transference, always interfere with progress. Nevertheless, he is confident that once given the opportunity to do psychotherapy, important things will happen to his patients.

In actual practice, things do happen to his patients, but not always the things he imagines. There is the initial enthusiasm of establishing a contact with the patient, of listening to dreams, fantasies, free associations, and other verbalizations, of appraising behavior both inside and outside of therapy, and finally, of elucidating and bringing the dynamics of the disturbance to the patient's awareness. Both patient and therapist then bask in the glow of this achievement, and often there develops a dramatic alleviation of the patient's symptoms. But shortly thereafter, to the dismay of the therapist, a peculiar inertia strangles the therapeutic situation. The momentary lift the patient had got out of treatment disappears; dynamic revelations no longer become inspirational; they serve merely as sources of depression for the patient. Clinging desperately to the therapist for relief which does not seem to be forthcoming, the patient then becomes enveloped in a miasma of frustration, hopelessness and rage. And the therapist stops looking forward to the treatment sessions; he finds his mind wandering while the patient talks; he feels himself to be on the defensive. More and more he becomes embittered, until finally he loses his therapeutic perspective. He chides the patient for his stubborn resistance or lack of motivation, and he looks forward with relief to forthcoming vacations, to the termination of treatment, or to a transfer to another unsuspecting therapist.

When this experience repeats itself with other patients, the therapist undergoes a kind of crisis associated with a battering of his self-confidence. He may doubt his choice of profession, and regard himself as a sort of fraud. He may become critical of the therapeutic system he has learned, and search for an answer in schools of a different theoretic bias. Or he may take refuge in a peculiar grandiosity, crediting himself, his therapeutic skills, and the psychotherapeutic school to which he belongs, with virtues of a totally unrealistic nature.

In most instances, the reason for this unhappy turn of events is lack of adequate preparation for actual functioning in the psychotherapeutic process. Psychotherapy is probably the most complex of all human relationships. During its course the therapist participates in a variety of roles both spontaneous and studied. Additionally, the therapist is burdened with responsibilities, and is subjected to an assault by the patient's neurotic strivings from which there is no retreat, and toward which he is expected to react in a manner that will be of therapeutic value for the patient. No matter how extensive his training, the beginning therapist will find it difficult, without support and expert guidance, to stand up under the unreasonable demands and violent projections of the patient. He will need a skilled objective person to aid him in clarifying the dynamics of the therapeutic relationship. The most effective help of this type can be rendered by an experienced psychotherapist, who, in an atmosphere of warmth and sympathy, provides for the student a learning and growth experience [475–479].

FUNCTIONS OF SUPERVISION

Supervision of the work of the young therapist is an essential requirement in his learning. Without supervision it will be difficult or impossible for the therapist to translate his theoretic knowledge into effective practice, to work through blocks in understanding, and to develop his skills to a point where he can help his patients achieve the most extensive goals. Supervision, then, is essentially a teaching procedure in which an experienced psychotherapist helps a less experienced individual acquire a body of knowledge aimed at a more dexterous handling of the therapeutic situation.

The traditional type of supervision, unfortunately, has become so contaminated with overseeing, directorial and inspective functions, that it has frequently been diverted from its teaching objective. This has particularly been the case in agency work, where the supervisor, as part of the administrative body, is responsible for the quality of service rendered to clients. Many difficulties arise here because the supervisor serves in a dual role—as an overseer and a teacher.

As overseer, the supervisor may be so concerned with maintaining the standards of the agency, that he may not be able to exercise the kind of tolerance and patience required in a teacher. For instance, under press of responsibility, he is likely to "jump in" and interfere with the treatment plan set up by the supervisee, the execution of which, while perhaps less expert than a plan devised by the supervisor, would prove of greatest learning value to the supervisee. Because the student's status is dependent on evaluations by the supervisor, the process of supervision in agencies is apt to become extremely trying. This is less frequently the case in psychotherapeutic supervision, although a parallel situation does develop where the supervisee is in training at a psychotherapeutic or psychoanalytic school, and his career is dependent on the evaluation by his supervisor. Similarly, where the supervisee is a staff member of a clinic, the supervisor as part of the administration may subordinate his teaching role to a meticulous concern with the total case load. This shift in emphasis cannot help but influence adversely the quality of training received; this is inevitable whenever the training is oriented around circumscribed goals set up in relation to specific kinds of service for which the clinic is responsible. Much less complicated is the supervision of the psychotherapist in private practice, who chooses a supervisor principally to expand his technical skills, not being dependent on the supervisor for an evaluation which may destroy his career or eliminate his means of livelihood.

As teacher, in instances where the supervisor is attached to a school or clinic, he will usually operate along the following lines:

1. Teaching

The first responsibility of the supervisor is observation of the total functioning of the therapist, in order to help him in his educational growth. Toward this end, it may be essential to bring the supervisee to an awareness of how he fails to live up to his therapeutic potentialities, either because of insufficient knowledge or because of his own neurotic character problems that inject themselves into the psychotherapeutic relationship. It is incumbent on the supervisor, among other things, to help the supervisee (a) to gain knowledge he is lacking, (b) to achieve an awareness of his own character problems which may interfere with the establishment and maintenance of a therapeutic relationship, and (c) to overcome resistances to learning.

2. Evaluating

A second responsibility of the supervisor is an evaluation of the capacities and progress of the supervisee, for the purposes of determining his professional development and current skills as a therapist. Evaluation involves a number of areas including theoretic understanding, therapeutic aptitudes, and the kinds of relationships that are established with patients and the supervisor.

3. Administration and Policy-making

The third responsibility of the supervisor lies in the administration and policy of the school or clinic under whose aegis he functions. The supervisor here recommends modifications of the therapeutic and teaching programs in order to accomplish a better cooperation between the therapist and the agency. He helps also in an analysis of administrative, intake and pedagogic policies which may influence adversely the training and the work of the therapist, as well as the patient's responses to treatment.

To summarize, supervision in psychotherapy is fundamentally a teaching process in which a more experienced participant, the supervisor, observes the work of the less experienced participant, the supervisee, with the aim of helping the supervisee acquire certain essential therapeutic skills through better understanding of the dynamics involved in mental illness, and through resolution of personality factors which block performance of effective psychotherapy. Supervision embraces a sharing of experiences; not only those gathered in the relations between therapist and patient, but also those occurring in the relationship between the supervisor and supervisee.

Qualifications of a good supervisor are:

1. Ability to function expertly as a psychotherapist.

2. Ability to function effectively as a teacher.

3. Ability to accept the supervisee unconditionally, without contempt, hostility, possessiveness and other unwarranted attitudes and feelings.

Supervisory problems may roughly be divided into five categories: (1) problems in orientation, (2) problems in recording, (3) problems in technical performance, (4) problems in learning, and (5) problems in termination of supervision.

PROBLEMS IN ORIENTATION

1. Differences in Theoretic Orientation

Important and often irreconcilable differences occur in the theoretic background and orientation of the supervisor and the therapist whom he is supervising, a product usually of varying kinds of preclinical training. Illustrative of such differences are the following:

a. The relative weight to be placed on constitutional as compared with experiential factors in the genesis of neurosis.

b. The importance of biologic, as contrasted with sociologic factors.

c. The respective emphasis on past childhood experiences and on current environmental hardships.

d. The degree of stress placed on unconscious conflict as the focus of neurotic difficulties.

e. The extent of acceptance of the Oedipus complex, castration fears and penis envy as universal phenomena.

f. The primacy of sexual over other drives.

g. The significance of character structure in creating and sustaining neurotic disturbance.

The most effective supervisor is one who respects the right of the therapist to his own ideas and opinions, yet who insists on the acceptance of a broadly conceived dynamic orientation which, discussed in chapter 14, is along the following lines:

a. Emotional difficulties are sponsored by a variety of conflicts operating on different levels of awareness.

b. The most intense conflicts originate in early childhood, issuing from unfavorable experiences with and conditionings by important authoritative personages, particularly the parents.

c. Resultant are blocks in psychosocial development and distortions in the character structure with impairment of the individual's capacity for adaptation.

d. Disturbances in interpersonal relationships and in the expression of basic biologic and social needs inspire threats to mastery and expectations of injury which, in turn, alter the individual's emotional homeostasis and provoke anxiety.

e. Symptoms of neurosis consist of manifestations of anxiety, as well as defenses against anxiety and its causative conflicts.

A dynamic formulation of the treatment of neurosis, agreed on by supervisor and therapist, would conceive of therapy as taking place in a unique relationship that is established between the therapist and the patient. This relationship serves as a corrective experience for the patient, restoring his shattered sense of mastery to a point where he can deal effectively with his inner tensions, as well as with the demands of the outside world. The relationship supports the patient in the vicissitudes he undergoes while gaining an understanding of the conflictual sources of his difficulty. It helps him to reevaluate himself, and to discard some of his archaic fears, attitudes, and patterns of behavior, substituting for them strivings that enable him to relate congenially to life and people. Finally, through the resolution of developmental blocks, it enables him to achieve an optimal level of emotional growth and personality maturity.

Formulations such as these will provide considerable latitude for the merging of the views of both supervisor and supervisee.

2. Differences in Communication

Since communication is the basis of the supervisory relationship, it is important that verbalizations and concepts be understood by both supervisor and supervisee. Assuming that there are no important language differences, problems in communication are usually related to differences in terminology.

One of the most poignant objections to psychiatry voiced by scientists in other fields is that it is so partial to neologisms. The worst offenders in this direction are followers of the Freudian and Meyerian schools, and to a lesser extent, those of the Rank, Horney and Sullivan schools. Tendencies to utilize neologisms and complex language forms have acted as one of the strongest barriers toward a rapprochement of the varying orientations.

Both supervisor and supervisee may be victimized by an esoteric terminology. Translation of complex language forms into concepts with which both participants are conversant is vital to a mutual understanding, and to the establishment of a common frame of reference.

3. Differences in Method

Another problem in supervision relates to differences in method; that practiced by the supervisor, and that accepted or practiced by the supervisee. Such differences may involve various matters, such as the most desirable number of treatment sessions per week, whether or not to employ routine history-taking and psychologic work-ups, the use of free association, the emphasis on dream material and the manner of its employment, the use of the couch, the extent to which a transference neurosis is permitted to develop, and the adjuncts to be utilized during therapy. Resolution of serious differences in method is to be expected in the course of good supervision.

Considerable flexibility will be required in methodologic approaches, particularly where the therapist is expected to handle, in the practice for which he is being trained, a wide assortment of clinical problems. Supportive of the principle of technical eclecticism is the fact that no single approach is applicable to all types of emotional difficulties. Some problems seem to respond better to certain kinds of therapeutic method than to others.

4. Differences in Goals

Problems may arise between supervisee and supervisor on the basis of varying concepts of what makes for success in psychotherapy. Is success in therapy the achievement of complete resolution of all blocks in personality maturation with effective functioning in all areas of living? Or is success to be graded in terms of optimal development within the practical limitations imposed on the individual by his existing motivations, his ego strength and environmental pressures from which he cannot reasonably escape?

While the therapist has a responsibility to the patient in bringing him to the most extensive personality reconstruction possible, he must realize that many circumstances may interfere with extensive goal achievement. A modified treatment objective may be the only possible alternative, at least temporarily. However, a therapist, having been trained in the tradition that any therapeutic change falling short of complete reconstruction is spurious, may look askance at the supervisor who considers goals in terms of optimal functioning within the limitations of the reality situation. Or the supervisor may be unwilling to accept goal modification and may regard with contempt changes that fall short of absolute psychosocial maturity with complete performance in all areas of living.

PROBLEMS IN RECORDING AND REPORTING

Data on functioning are supplied by the therapist's reporting of his activities with patients. Careful listening to the content of the report, to the manner of reporting, to the evasions and points of emphasis, to slips of speech, and to casual off-the-record references to his feelings about his patients help the supervisor to evaluate the therapeutic work of the therapist.

In making this appraisal, it is important to remember that the role the therapist plays with the supervisor, and his attitudes toward the supervisor, are no reliable index of what he does with his patients. For with his patients he is operating in an entirely different setting than with the supervisor, with whom he is in a more subordinate status—more vulnerable, and more capable of being challenged or criticized. He may respond to the supervisor with fear, detachment, resentment and other character patterns related to his feelings about authority. He will therefore not be able to communicate to the supervisor his capacity to be spontaneous, empathic and responsive, which he may show in the relatively secure atmosphere in which he operates with his patients. His activity in the supervisory session may be contaminated by defenses against the supervisor, and his struggle with his supervisor may reflect itself in the content of his report.

For instance, one therapist presented material to his supervisor in a cocky, superior manner, containing a somewhat contemptuous attitude toward the patient about whom he talked. However, it soon became obvious to the supervisor, in listening to tape recordings of actual treatment sessions, that hostile feelings were not manifest in the therapist's responses nor in the manner of their presentation. A further inquiry revealed that hostility, marshaled by transference feelings toward the supervisor, was seeping into the supervisory session and was influencing the nature of the reporting.

Neurotic feelings toward the supervisor may thus distort the therapist's presentation of material. Pertinent data may be deleted, irrelevant items may be introduced, and secondary elaboration may destroy totally, or in part, the value of the presentation. Fear of exposing deficiencies, of appearing ridiculous, of incurring the displeasure and contempt of the supervisor are among the more common causes of poor reporting.

Some of the difficulties in reporting may be obviated by insisting on process recording in which there is a verbatim account of both the patient's and the therapist's verbalizations. Process recording has the advantage of presenting a reasonably cogent picture of what is going on, since the tendency toward distortion or deletion will be minimized. However, there are certain objections to this method, in that the therapist may be unable to record simultaneously with the performing of good therapy, or because of other personal blocks or due to the protests of the patient. Furthermore, no matter how carefully he attempts to record, he will be unable to include everything that is said. There will then be a tendency to curtail the material, consciously or unconsciously eliminating elements which cause him to feel that he is revealing himself unfavorably. In intensive supervision, in which one case is being presented over a long period of time, the supervisor may nevertheless have to insist on process recording until he has convinced himself of the therapist's ability to report correctly in a more abbreviated way. (See Appendix K, page 825, for a case outline.)

Perhaps the most effective type of recording is done with a recording machine. Recording on plastic discs is cheap, but it lends itself only to typewritten transcription rather than to playback, because of the poor quality of reproduction. Tape recordings are excellent for playback, and, if desired, a typewritten transcription can always be made from them. Few patients object to the use of machine recorders, and, once the therapist has overcome his fears about revealing himself, he can function freely.

The value of this kind of recording cannot be overestimated, since one has a most factual report of what has gone on in the session, not only in terms of content, but also in terms of intonations and sub-vocal utterances which cannot be communicated in written types of recording. The method enables the supervisor to observe aspects of the interviewing process that are handled well or poorly. It helps him to understand how the therapist deals with different kinds of content, whether he exaggerates, minimizes, or negates the importance of certain types of material. It permits of observation of how he responds to unreasonable demands of the patient, to hostilities and other transference attitudes that are developing in the relationship. It enables the supervisor to study techniques in interviewing, the handling of dream material, and skill in interpretation in terms of timing and presentation. The difference between the written or verbal account and what actually went on, which is revealed in listening to a playback, is often so astonishing as to leave little question about the value of this kind of recording.

For instance, one therapist's verbal account made no mention of hostile feelings in the patient, to which the therapist was responding by shifting the topic of discussion and by complacent, reassuring utterances whenever the patient introduced a slightly antagonistic remark. The therapist was totally unaware of his responses, but in the playback he could not escape what had happened. The educational value of listening to recordings of one's own treatment sessions is enormous, as the above experience illustrates.

Understandably, it will be impossible to utilize recordings at every supervisory session, due to lack of time. Several recorded sessions presented during each six months of supervision will usually suffice to measure the therapist's progress, and in themselves will merit the training of the therapist in the use of the recording machine.

PROBLEMS IN TECHNICAL PERFORMANCE

The supervisee will experience trouble in various areas in the process of doing psychotherapy. These difficulties are the consequence either of lack of understanding, experience and skill, or of counter-transference. They will have to be handled by the supervisor in relation to their origin and function. Most common are the following problems:

1. Difficulties in the conduct of the initial interview.
2. Inability to deal with inadequate motivation.
3. Inability to clarify for the patient misconceptions about psychotherapy.
4. Inability to extend warmth and support to the patient or to establish an initial contact with him.
5. Inability to define for the patient goals in therapy.
6. Inability to structure the therapeutic situation adequately for the patient.
7. Inability to recognize and to handle manifestations of transference in the therapeutic relationship; specifically, dependence, sexual feelings, detachment, hostility and aggression.
8. Lack of knowledge of how to explore and to bring to awareness conflicts which mobilize anxiety in the patient.
9. Lack of sensitivity and perceptiveness to what is going on in therapy.

10. Lack of technical skill in the implementation of free association, dream interpretation and analysis of the transference.

11. Inability to deal with resistances in the patient towards verbal exploration of his conflicts.

12. Tendencies to avoid problems of the patient which inspire anxiety in the therapist.

13. Tendency to probe too deeply and too rapidly at the start.

14. Impatience with resistances toward the acquisition of insight.

15. Faulty techniques of presenting interpretations.

16. Frustration and discouragement at the patient's refusal to utilize insight in the direction of change.

17. Tendency to push the patient too hard or too rapidly toward normal objectives.

18. Fear of being too directive with resultant excessive passivity.

19. Lack of understanding of how to create incentives for change.

20. Lack of understanding in dealing with forces that block action.

21. Lack of understanding of how to help the patient master anxieties surrounding normal life goals.

22. Inability to scale down therapeutic goals when modification of objectives is mandatory.

23. Lack of understanding of how to implement the translation of insight and understanding into action.

24. Inability to deal with resistance toward abandoning primary and secondary neurotic aims.

25. Inability to deal with resistance toward normality.

26. Inability to deal with resistance in the patient toward activity through his own resources.

27. Tendencies to overprotect or to domineer the patient.

28. Inability to assume a non-directive therapeutic role.

29. Lack of understanding of how to deal with the refusal on the part of the patient to yield his dependency.

30. Lack of understanding of how to handle the patient's fear of assertiveness.

31. Lack of understanding of how to analyze dependency elements in the therapist-patient relationship.

32. Lack of understanding of how to terminate therapy.

In observing his functioning, the supervisor must exercise great tolerance for the specific style of activity of the therapist. He must remember that irrespective of training and exposure to specific schools of psychiatric thinking, basic personality patterns of the therapist will infiltrate into the treatment situation and cannot help but influence the techniques that are learned. Some modification of techniques will always occur, particularly of those that do not coordinate with the therapist's personality structure. The therapist will probably never be able to duplicate the exact style of the supervisor, nor vice versa, since they are two different people and relate to patients in their own unique ways.

Yet certain basic principles in psychotherapy must not be violated, no matter what kinds of relationships one establishes and what types of techniques one employs. By defining the broad bounds of psychotherapy, and by elucidating on the fundamental principles to which every therapist must adhere, the supervisor may help the supervisee perfect his skills, yet maintain his spontaneity, which is a most cherished characteristic in the psychotherapist.

PROBLEMS IN LEARNING

A number of propositions are involved in the learning of psychotherapy that may be expressed as follows:

1. All learning necessitates a substitution of new patterns for old. This requires a working-through of blocks which constantly invest the acquisition of new patterns. Sometimes the struggle is a minimal one; sometimes it is intense.

2. The manner in which learning proceeds is unique for the individual both in relationship to the rate of learning, as well as the methods by which material is absorbed and integrated. Some persons learn by leaps and bounds, others by cautious precarious crawling. Many variants expedite or interfere with learning in different people. What is taught an individual has to be accepted by him in his own terms.

3. Learning involves both an understanding of theory as well as its integration and translation into effective action. The responsibility for understanding theory is vested in the instructors and teachers with whom the therapist has had preclinical training. The responsibility for execution of theory into practice is vested in the supervisor.

4. No learning is possible without a motivation to learn. This motivation must be sufficiently intense to overcome the difficulties that inevitably envelop all learning. It is assumed that the therapist has sufficient motivation—in terms of a desire to be a psychotherapist—to expose himself to the ordeals of the learning process.

5. Anxiety is present in all learning. Its sources are related to fear of change and the desire to cling to familiar patterns, as well as to resistance in altering basic accepted attitudes and behavior tendencies.

6. Resistances to learning are present in all people in response to anxiety. The kind and the degree of resistance will vary with the individual. Most common are lack of attention, lack of retention, amnesia and simulated stupidity. In addition, resistance may take the form of patterns of dependence, submissiveness, self-depreciation, ingratiation, arrogance, grandiosity, resentment, aggression and detachment. These are products of specific neurotic character problems; but there may be a universality of expression of such trends in certain cultures, reflecting accepted attitudes toward education and toward the authorities that are responsible for education.

7. Resistances to learning must be overcome before learning can proceed. The attitudes of the supervisor are crucial here. His tolerance, flexibility, and capacity to extend warmth, support and acceptance toward the therapist, irre-

spective of the errors the latter makes, promotes the most effective medium for the handling of resistance.

8. Learning is thus facilitated by a warm working relationship between supervisor and therapist. It is impeded by hostility that develops in this relationship. A primary focus, then, in the supervisory process, is the existing relationship between student and teacher, with thorough ventilation of negative feelings before these exert a corrosive influence on the learning process. The therapist must be encouraged to express disagreements, criticisms or feelings in relation to the supervisor. He must be able also to accept criticism, and this will be possible where there is good rapport with the supervisor.

9. As a general rule, learning blocks are resolved during the first few months of supervision. An inability to master such blocks after several months indicates a severe problem that necessitates incisive investigation.

10. In learning, the therapist has a backlog of past experiences on which to build. He cannot be expected to progress any faster than would be warranted by the degree of his experience, no matter how hard the supervisor may push him. As a matter of fact, too severe demands will be of greater hindrance than of help.

11. As a rule, the therapist will in the early stages of learning feel resentful, unsure, and certain that he will fail. He will want to be told how to function; indeed, he will demand that the supervisor show him exactly what to do. The supervisor must accept the therapist's dependency, and yet treat him as an equal. The setting of supervision is best permissive, the therapist being given the feeling that he is free to act, experiment and to make mistakes. Emphasis is on the sharing of experiences and responsibilities.

12. Learning is a tedious process enhanced by the active participation of the student in his own growth. It is facilitated also by selected cases which serve a specific purpose in filling in gaps in the therapist's experience, as well as by assigned reading and by recommended courses. At all times, critical thinking is to be encouraged, even at the expense of inflicting narcissistic slights on the supervisor.

13. Learning is more an educational than a therapeutic process, and the focus in psychotherapy is on the therapist's work rather than on his problems. It is essential that the therapist be treated as an adult, and not as a problem child.

14. Learning is expedited by successes, and it is impaired by failures. Provision should be made for some successes which will reinforce learning. Where the therapist encounters repeated failures, damage will be done to the learning process.

PROBLEMS IN TERMINATION OF SUPERVISION

The relationship the therapist establishes with the supervisor will, in general, proceed through various phases, including the establishing of rapport with the supervisor, the understanding of problems that occur in relationship to the supervisor, the translation of this understanding into corrective action, and finally, the ending phase in which the therapist develops the capacity to carry on, on his own, the working-through of his dependence on the supervisor.

Where the supervisor has an authoritarian personality structure, it may be difficult for him to operate on equal terms with the therapist. He will want to continue to make decisions, to utter judgments and to offer interpretations, consciously or unconsciously resenting the therapist's right to self-determination. Under these circumstances the ending of supervision may impose great hardships on both supervisor and therapist.

On the other hand, the greater the dependency needs in the therapist, the more difficult it will be for him to countenance termination. An inability to resolve dependence on the supervisor indicates a severe characterologic problem for which the therapist may require further therapeutic help.

During the terminal phases of supervision, the supervisor, in anticipation of the trauma of separation, may assume a non-directive role, insisting that the therapist be active and figure things out entirely for himself. One may expect that the therapist will respond to such non-directiveness with anxiety and hostility, and that he will attempt to force the supervisor to abandon this role. If the supervisor is persistent, however, justifying the passivity displayed on the basis of a respect for the therapist's growth process, the therapist will eventually be convinced of the rationale of the supervisor's behavior.

TECHNICAL DETAILS OF SUPERVISION

1. Preclinical Training of the Therapist

Before supervision begins, the supervisor will desire information about the preclinical training of his prospective supervisee. Questions he may have in his mind may include these: Is the theoretic background of the supervisee adequate for functioning in psychotherapeutic practice? Has he had the required courses and done essential reading? Has he integrated this theoretic material satisfactorily? Does the supervisee have the personality qualities that will make for a good therapist? How profound an understanding does the supervisee have of his own emotional and interpersonal processes? Will he be able to resolve or to control the expression of hostility, detachment, sexual interest, overprotection, rejection, and other strivings that will be inimical to the psychotherapeutic relationship? Can we reasonably assume that the supervisee is sufficiently adjusted to life now, so that he will not use the therapeutic situation and the experiences of the patient to live through vicariously his own frustrated ambitions, dependencies and hostilities? Does the supervisee have a capacity to empathize with people, to feel and to communicate warmth to them? Does he have the capacity to be resolute and firm on occasion, capable of insisting on certain essential actions during the therapeutic process? How much experience has the supervisee had in doing psychotherapy? What kinds of cases has he treated, and with what results? Has he had previous supervision, and if so, with whom and for how long? Does he believe he has benefited by such supervision?

There is general agreement that the prospective psychotherapist requires an extensive amount of preclinical training. A review of training which is being given in most of the recognized schools reveals a close similarity in prescribed courses and requirements. These include the following:

a. Courses in basic neuropsychiatry, normal psychosocial development, psychopathology, psychodynamics, techniques of interviewing, techniques of psychotherapy, dream interpretation, child psychiatry and group psychotherapy.

b. Clinical conferences and continuous case seminars which have been attended regularly.

c. Readings in psychiatric literature of sufficient scope to provide the student with a good background in history, theory and practice.

d. Enough personal psychotherapy or psychoanalysis to provide the student, first, with an opportunity to study psychodynamics, through self-observation by observing his own emotional conflicts, their genesis and their projection into his present day functioning; and, second, to liberate him from personal problems and character disturbances that interfere with the establishment and maintenance of a therapeutic interpersonal relationship.

Should the supervisee be lacking in any of these basic requirements, the supervisor must help him find ways of making up his deficiencies. (See Appendix L, page 827, for application blank for staff members.)

2. The Beginning Stages of Supervision

The first contact of the supervisor with the therapist is in the nature of an exploratory talk. At this time there may be a discussion of the therapist's preclinical training, and arrangements may be made as to the hours, frequency of visits, and the method of recording and presentation. The therapist may be given preliminary orientation as to what will be involved in supervision, and how supervisory sessions may best be utilized. Arrangements may furthermore be made for the handling with the supervisor of any emergency situations which may occur during the course of supervision.

In the early months of supervision, a period of disillusionment is to be anticipated. The therapist will be brought face to face with practical problems in implementing therapy which may be at variance with what he has learned from books. He may also be upset by the fact that the specific kinds of problems that provoke his patients may be precisely those that are disturbing to himself. He may be exposed to certain situations that develop in treatment with a violent impact, that tax his own capacities for adjustment. It is incumbent on the supervisor to extend to the therapist, during this period, a good deal of warmth and understanding. The primary focus in early supervision is the relationship between supervisor and supervisee, since little progress will be possible until good rapport exists.

3. Later Phases of Supervision

In supervision, the supervisor seeks to ascertain whether or not the therapist is living up to his potentialities. If not, the sources of this lack must be diagnosed. For instance, the problem may relate to deficiencies in the kind of preclinical training received, or in the assimilation of educational materials presented to him in his training. It may be due to an absence of perceptiveness, or to insensitivity about what is going on in the therapeutic situation. It may be the product of personality problems that prevent the therapist from establishing a meaningful contact with the patient.

The areas in which the therapist needs help most will soon become apparent. In the main, technical problems break down into difficulties in diagnosis, the conduct of the initial interview, the use of interviewing techniques, the understanding of the operative dynamics, the use of dreams, the detection and handling of transference, the awareness and mastery of counter-transference, the dealing with resistance, the use of interpretations, and the termination of therapy.

The task of the supervisor here is not to tell the therapist what to do, but rather to teach him how to think through solutions for himself. Toward this end, it will be essential to ask questions and to structure problems so that the therapist can come to his own conclusions. Learning problems are to be diagnosed and handled along lines indicated previously.

In the course of supervision, the therapist is bound to show transference manifestations. The supervisor will also have emotional attitudes toward the therapist. Both positive and negative feelings will have to be subjected to close scrutiny, in order to permit of the development of the proper kind of empathic yet objective attitudes. Furthermore, the supervisor will have to maintain a certain amount of tension in the supervisory sessions, to expedite activity.

The beginning supervisor, particularly, may respond to supervision with untoward feelings. He may evidence a tendency to be pompous and over-bearing, and to overwhelm his supervisees with material. He is apt to feel irritable when a supervisee does not learn rapidly, when he defies suggestions and criticisms, even though these are offered in a constructive way. He may be provoked when there is persistence in errors that are so obvious that they scarcely need identification. Such attitudes on the part of the supervisor will, of course, interfere with learning. An honest search for feelings within himself will often reveal tendencies that stifle the development of his supervisee. One must emphasize again that counter-transference is always present, and that it need not be destructive to the teaching objective, provided the supervisor is capable of understanding his feelings, and of modifying and correcting them before they get out of control.

Disagreements between supervisor and therapist are inevitable, even desirable. All learning inspires resistance. The therapist will voice protests in changing his habitual patterns. He is bound to be critical. Actually, he cannot change unless he is given an opportunity to voice and to work through his criticisms. The supervisor may be offended by the reactions of the therapist who presumably challenges his judgment with little provocation. The supervisor will best be able to respect the therapist's right to his own opinions when he realizes the unavoidable learning struggle that is involved.

4. "Intensive" versus "Technical" Supervision

In practice, two general types of psychotherapeutic supervision may be defined. The first type, "intensive" supervision, consists of the "continuous case" type of reporting with a single patient, preferably from the initial interview to termination, utilizing process recording. This enables the supervisor to help the therapist in all phases of treatment, by observing his operations with one patient over a long-term period. "Intensive" supervision is the most effective kind of teaching for beginning therapists.

The second type of supervision, arbitrarily called "technical" supervision, may be further divided into two sub-types. The first, or "case load" supervision, which is usually prescribed especially for the beginning therapist in a clinic, covers the general progress and specific difficulties being encountered in the entire case load of the therapist. One might consider this a kind of administrative supervision. The second sub-type, which we may, for want of a better name, call "special problem" supervision, is handled in a manner similar to a clinical conference. Any pressing problem in diagnosis, psychodynamics, or technical management may be presented, and the discussion centers around the specific difficulty encountered by the therapist.

The latter kind of supervision is more highly advanced than other types, and presupposes more experience on the part of the therapist. It may also be effectively practiced in a group of no more than three or four therapists, who participate in the discussion with the supervisor. Each therapist may be given the privilege of presenting material on successive sessions. In practice, this proves to be a highly provocative teaching device, provided all the supervisees are approximately on the same level.

5. The Evaluation of the Supervisee

Evaluation is a means of helping the therapist develop his skills through a continuous assay of his strengths and weaknesses. As such, it becomes part of the teaching method, pointing to areas in which more development is needed, and helping in a positive way to promote such development. Criteria of evaluation may be along the following lines:

a. Method of presentation, and recording ability.

b. Theoretic understanding.

c. Diagnostic ability.

d. Integration of theory into practice.

e. General therapeutic aptitudes, sensitivity and capacity for critical thinking.

f. Kinds of relationships therapist establishes with his patients, and his skill in handling these relationships.

g. Type of relationship therapist has with supervisor, and the use he makes of the sessions.

h. Types of relationships therapist establishes with colleagues and personnel of the clinic, if any, to which he is attached.

i. Therapist's good points and his special skills.

j. Therapist's lacks and deficiencies.

k. General learning ability, and the progress that has been made in learning.

l. Positive recommendations for increasing learning, including recommended readings, prescribed courses, and preferred kinds of cases to be assigned to him.

Yardsticks of expected progress have never been set. Arbitrarily, a rough gage such as the following may be useful to indicate minimal levels of achievement:

End of first six months of supervision: ability to make diagnoses; ability to keep patients in therapy.

End of first year: ability to understand dynamics; capacity to establish good rapport with patients.

End of one and one-half years: recognition of personal problems in therapeutic functioning.

End of second year: ability to overcome most personal problems in therapeutic functioning.

End of two and one-half years: ability to function without serious mistakes.

End of three years: ability to do good psychotherapy.

Evaluation imposes burdens on both supervisor and therapist. The supervisor may not want to criticize the therapist out of fear of hurting or offending him. The therapist in turn may feel humiliated at having his weak points exposed. The manner in which evaluation is presented, and the purpose for which it is used, will largely determine the reactions of the therapist. If the understanding is clear that there will be periodic evaluations, let us say every six months, to point out the areas in which the greatest or least development has been made, the experience can prove to be in the interests of learning.

The evaluation conference may be set up in advance and both therapist and supervisor may prepare their observations for mutual discussion and consideration. At the conference a common understanding must be reached, and if a written evaluation must be sent to the head of a clinic or school, agreement on as many points as possible is best achieved in advance of sending the report.

6. Administrative Responsibilities

Where the supervisor and therapist are both associated with a clinic, the supervisor will have further responsibilities. For instance, he may participate in an analysis of administrative or intake policies, making recommendations of alteration of old or the devising of new policies. The object here is that of eliminating influences which are destructive to the patient's therapy or to the therapist's functioning. He will also, if supervision is part of a school training program, probably be engaged in an analysis of administrative and pedagogic procedures in the program. This will include methods of choice of students, modification of curricula, introduction of new courses, and proposed changes in instructors or instructional methods. Routine meetings among the supervisors, or between supervisors and the supervisory head, will cover discussion of such problems in detail, with the introduction of whatever current difficulties the supervisor is having with supervision, and routine evaluations of the progress shown by the different therapists.

SUPERVISION AS AN INTERPERSONAL RELATIONSHIP

The supervisory relationship is one to which the supervisee reacts with mingled attitudes of admiration, jealousy, fear and hostility. Admiration and jealousy are usually inspired by the supervisor's superior knowledge, training and status. Fear of the supervisor is often the product of the therapist's helplessness in the face of an authority, who, he feels, may judge him unfairly and destroy his career and livelihood in the event he fails to live up to expectations. Hostility issues from many sources. On the one hand, it is the product of dependency on the supervisor, which is especially inevitable at the beginning of supervision. Dependency yearnings which are mobilized are usually accompanied by convictions that these yearnings will be frustrated. Feelings of being victimized by his own dependency needs, and the threats imposed by these needs on his independence and assertiveness, inspire further resentment. The very acceptance of supervision implies to some therapists a kind of subordination which imposes burdens on adjustment, particularly where independence has become the keynote in the person's life struggle. The therapist, in addition, resents demands he believes the supervisor makes on him. The restrictions imposed on the therapist, the criticisms directed at his functioning, deliver vital blows to his narcissism and contribute to further fears of loss of self.

Supervision will thus produce feelings in the therapist that are related to neurotic attitudes toward authority. Difficulties in relationships to authority may come out toward the supervisor in the nascent state, in the form of verbalizations or behavioral acting-out. They may also be concealed behind a barrage of defenses which reflect the therapist's habitual patterns in his dealings with authority.

The supervisor will, in his turn, respond in supervision with feelings toward the therapist, many of which are the product of neurotic attitudes toward subordinates. He may, in a flush of omnipotence, assume a patronizing attitude toward the therapist, presenting his ideas as if they were irrevocable pronouncements. He may feel contempt for the relatively inferior knowledge, skill or status of the therapist. He may develop hostility toward the therapist when the latter challenges his opinions or theories. He may resent the growth or advance of the therapist, seeking to keep him on a subordinate level, in an effort to preserve his own superiority. Accordingly, he may minimize successes the therapist achieves, being chary of any praise or admiration he accords him. He may express his feelings directly toward the therapist, or, more likely, he may respond with defenses against his feelings which are intended to conceal them. For instance, he may cloak aggression in a solicitous, ingratiating attitude, with overkindliness and overattentiveness. Or he may show disinterest in the productions of the therapist, offering him little help or reassurance.

The supervisory process will thus arouse feelings and attitudes in both supervisor and therapist. The readiness of dissolution of these attitudes will depend upon their severity, the level of insight possessed, the strength of existing provocative factors, and their functional utility or destructiveness.

Sufficient resolution of transference and counter-transference feelings must occur before real learning is possible, since the emotions that contaminate the relationship are apt to divert it from the goals for which it is intended. Neurotic feelings, along the lines indicated above, will always exist to some degree, although the intensity should not ordinarily be so great as to interfere with learning, nor so obdurate so as not to be resolved in the ordinary process of supervision. As a general rule, assuming that both participants are integrated people, capable of facing inimical attitudes and feelings, the initial resistances, fears and distrustful attitudes will be dissipated by the development of positive identification and rapport.

Transference and counter-transference, however, may persist, blocking the therapist in his development and progress. Certain attitudes the supervisor displays, for instance, may militate against learning. Among these are tentativeness, indecisiveness, minimization of himself, his knowledge and skill, irritability with the therapist, overprotectiveness, and a benign patronizing attitude which puts a damper on the therapist's need to express critcism and to verbalize his doubts and indecisions. Lack of interest in the therapist and in his growth, and absence of praise when he has made an important gain, also act as dampers to learning.

The therapist, undergoing a more violent struggle than the supervisor, is bound to show many resistances, some of which will persisit with an amazing tenacity. Among these are attitudes of conformity, and a seeming absorption of every utterance of the supervisor. This spurious kind of complacency is accompanied by a constant repetition of mistakes, as if the therapist sheds his knowledge immediately after leaving the supervisor's office. A pattern of this kind is often the product of a continuing fear of losing one's independence by yielding to the supervisor's dictates and demands. Clinging to his old attitudes then becomes for the therapist a means of retaining his identity.

Another kind of resistance is the need to dominate and to take control by outsupervising the supervisor. Here the therapist overwhelms the supervisor with material, editing his reports, even falsifying material, in order to impress the supervisor. Belittling and derisive attitudes and feelings may exist toward the supervisor which are only indirectly expressed, and which serve to protect the therapist from fancied exploitation and injury.

On the other hand, the therapist may become so terrified about what is happening in his relationship with the supervisor as to seek reassurance, affection and support in sundry ways. He may become helpless and hopeless, and assume a defenseless attitude. He may seek from the supervisor various panaceas for his difficulties, and insist that something positive be done for him that will help him in his conduct of therapy. In making such demands, he may express refusal to work out his own problems, attempting to force the supervisor to take decisive steps for him. Self-devaluation may follow in the wake of this attitude, much of which is an effort to avoid criticism and to forestall any responsibilities being put on the therapist. Where there is a strong masochistic bent, there may be attempts to flay himself, to undermine his intelligence and adjustment, and then to protest his being victimized or unfairly treated.

Resistance to learning may also be expressed in the form of hostility. The patterns which hostility takes are legion, depending upon the individual's habitual modes of dealing with this emotion. Where the person finds it difficult to express rage, he may respond with depression and discouragement. He may seek to terminate supervision on the basis that he is completely incapable of learning. He may mask his hostility with dependence, with feigned amiability and with strong gestures to force the relationship with the supervisor into social channels. In instances where the therapist is capable of expressing his hostility openly, he may become defiant, challenging and overcritical. He may develop feelings of being exploited, misunderstood and humiliated, and he may attempt to find evidence for these feelings by misinterpreting what goes on between himself and the supervisor. He may become suspicious about the supervisor's abilities, training and personal adjustment. He may enter into active competition with the supervisor, bringing in materials, quotations and references from authoritative works in order to challenge the supervisor or to nullify suggestions the latter has made. In some instances, the therapist may actually become uncooperative, negativistic and even mute. In other instances, hostility is masked by apathy and detachment. Here one will get the impression that the therapist, while presenting material and listening to the comments of the supervisor, is mentally "off in the clouds."

The therapist may try to ward off the supervisor by discursive talk about superficial topics, or by self-interpretations that are expressed with great vehemence. This attempt to disarm the supervisor by spurts of productivity has little corrective value for the therapist, since it is motivated by an effort to hurt the supervisor, rather than to learn.

Other resistances take the form of an inability to think clearly and an incapacity to express one's ideas. There may be an insistence that the therapist has achieved great development which is not supported by facts, and while self-confidence and assertiveness may be expressed, these will be found to be without substance. Another defense against the supervisor is an attempt to seduce him with gifts, lavish praise and compliments. The overvaluation of the abilities of the supervisor may know few bounds, and unless the supervisor watches himself carefully, he is apt to respond to these devices with happy and omnipotent feelings.

Assuming that the supervisor is capable of controlling or of resolving counter-transference, can he help the therapist to overcome such varied resistances to the supervisory relationship?

One must remember that supervision is a student-teacher relationship rather than a patient-therapist relationship. Emotional problems stirred up in the therapist in his work with his patients cannot entirely be handled by the supervisor in the setting of supervision. While often the outcome of supervision is definitely therapeutic for the supervisee, the goal is toward more adequate functioning in psychotherapy rather than the helping of the therapist with his own neurotic difficulties. Naturally, the supervisor does point out neurotic problems of the therapist that express themselves in the latter's counter-transference, in order to bring the therapist to an awareness of blocks in his functioning. It is assumed that the therapist has had sufficient personal psychotherapy, or is sufficiently integrated emotionally, to be able to work through these blocks with his own resources in the supervisory setting. In the event this is not possible by virtue of the depth of disturbance, it may be necessary to refer the therapist for more personal psychotherapy, or to enjoin the therapist, if the latter is in the process of receiving psychotherapy, to report to his own psychotherapist the problems that have developed in supervision.

However, the supervisor will have to handle those aspects of feeling and attitude which impede the therapist in his acquisition of therapeutic skills. This experience may prove itself to be therapeutic for the supervisee, but, if this occurs, it is a by-product of the chief objective—the learning of psychotherapy. Should the supervisor's effort to help the therapist to resolve his difficulties in supervision fail, referral for more personal psychotherapy may be necessary, a contingency the supervisor himself may want to seek where he realizes that he cannot work through his own problems in the existing relationship with his supervisee. In the event mutual trust and respect do not develop between supervisor and therapist after these devices have been exploited, transfer to another supervisor may be necessary.

52

Questions Therapists Ask about Psychotherapy

SUNDRY QUESTIONS PLAGUE THE INDIVIDUAL DOING PSYCHOTHERAPY. Answers to these questions are not easily provided, since there are many ways of accomplishing the same task in psychotherapy, some of which are suitable for one therapist, and wholly inappropriate for another. In this chapter, a number of common questions, posed by therapists participating in case seminars conducted by the writer, and not answered completely in the text of this book, are considered. The answers given to these questions are, of course, not absolute and will require modification in terms of the individual's unique experience and specific style of working.

Q. If a patient attacks you verbally at the initial interview, how would you handle the situation?

A. An aggressive outburst in the first interview is clearly an indication of great insecurity or fear in the patient. The patient will generally rationalize his hostility on one basis or another. A way of handling the situation is to accept the patient's hostility and to inform him that under the circumstances you do not blame him for being angry. As a matter of fact, it would be difficult for him to feel any other way. If possible, an effort should be made to bring the meaning of the aggressive outburst to the awareness of the patient. If this can be done, it may alleviate his tension and initiate more positive feelings toward the therapist.

Q. How do you handle a patient who comes to see you while he is being treated by another therapist?

A. This situation occasionally happens and will have to be managed diplomatically. There are a number of reasons why a patient finds it necessary to consult a second therapist. He may be in a state of resistance, and his visit constitutes an attempt at escape from, or a gesture of hostility toward his therapist. Or the patient may sense that he is unable to relate to his therapist, or that his therapist is unable to relate to him, and he is reaching out for a new, better therapeutic relationship. In either instance, one must respectfully listen to the patient, and focus particularly on the specific meaning of his consultation with you. Under no circumstances should one participate in criticism of the other therapist, no matter what outlandish activities are ascribed to him by the patient. On the contrary, one should alert himself to transference manifestations, and attempt to clarify any misconceptions or irrational attitudes about the patient's therapist that present themselves. The ultimate result of the interview may be emotionally cathartic for the patient, and he may return to his therapist with insight into his resistance. Should there be reason for your considering treating the patient, and if he has not informed his therapist about his prospective consultation with you, it will be important to emphasize the need to discuss the situation with his therapist. The patient may be told that for ethical reasons it will be impossible to start treatments with him unless both he and his therapist agree that a transfer is indicated. In the event the patient has, when he consults you, discontinued treatment with his therapist, the visit may, of course, be conducted as an initial interview.

Q. Is it permissible to treat one's friends?

A. It is extremely difficult to be therapeutically objective with friends. Nor will they be able to establish the proper kind of relationship with you. For these reasons friends who consult you about starting treatment are best referred to another therapist.

Q. How far can the therapist go in making interpretations at the beginning of therapy?

A. An experienced therapist may discern in the first interview or shortly thereafter, from verbal or non-verbal communications, important dynamics underlying the patient's neurosis. To interpret these to the patient may be fatal. One must bide his time and wait for a strategic moment—which may come many months later—before revealing to the patient what the therapist already knows. New therapists, in their enthusiasm, frequently violate this rule, as do experienced therapists with strong narcissistic leanings who attempt to demonstrate to the patient how much they know about him.

Q. What causes violent feelings which are stirred up in the patient after the first interview?

A. These may be caused by transference or by something the therapist has done in error.

Q. Are mistakes that a therapist makes in doing psychotherapy irretrievably destructive?

A. Even the most experienced psychotherapist makes mistakes in the conduct of therapy. There are many reasons for this, including the fact that the interpersonal relationship is so complex that the therapist cannot see all of its facets. Such mistakes are not too important if the working relationship with the patient is a good one.

Q. Are the various psychotherapeutic approaches ever used together?

A. Practically all forms of psychotherapy purposefully or inadvertently employ a combination of approaches. Even in formal psychoanalysis, one may, at times, be unable to avoid suggestion and reassurance. Persuasive and other supportive influences may by design enter into insight therapy from time to time, and disturbing environmental factors may deliberately have to be handled in order to promote maximal progress. Wittingly or unwittingly then, no approach exists in a pristine form. Rather, it is blended with other approaches, made necessary on occasion by the exigencies of the therapeutic situation.

Q. Does one ever start off using one approach and then, in the course of treatment, switch over to another approach?

A. This is very frequently the case. One may start off with an approach aimed at a supportive or palliative goal. In the course of treatment, it may become apparent that no real improvement will be possible unless one deals with underlying causative factors. One will consequently have to motivate the patient toward accepting therapy aimed at reconstructive goals. On the other hand, one may begin reconstructive treatment and, in the course of administering this, discover that circumstances, such as inadequate motivation or diminutive ego strength, make less extensive goals desirable. A supportive approach may therefore become necessary.

Q. Should the patient be required to pay for his own treatment?

A. As a general rule, the patient will get more out of therapy if he feels in some way responsible for its payment.

Q. How is the matter of fees best handled?

A. The matter of setting a fee satisfactory to both therapist and patient, and of agreeing on the manner in which payments are to be made, is part of the reality situation which therapy imposes on the patient. Most therapists gage their fees according to the patient's ability to pay. In setting a fee, it is important that the therapist consider the patient's capacity to carry the financial responsibility over the estimated treatment period. Unless this is done, both therapist and patient will find themselves in a difficult situation later on. Though grading the patient's fee according to his ability to pay over the estimated time period of his treatment, the therapist must be assured that he is setting a fee acceptable to himself. Should he enter into an agreement whereby he accepts a fee so low that he is hampered in meeting his own obligations, he will feel insecure. Resentment or anxiety may occur that will impose a destructive influence on the therapeutic relationship. Once a fee is set, it is difficult and unfair to raise it unless the financial situation of the patient has changed for the better. Often a neurotic problem interferes with the work capacity and productiveness of the patient. At the start of therapy, the earning ability of the patient will therefore be minimal. Once therapy gets under way, the patient may be able to earn a great deal more money. Under such circumstances, discussing with the patient the raising of a fee is justifiable, and an adjustment of fees upward usually will be acceptable to the patient. On the other hand, financial reverses may occur during the course of therapy. In such instances a reduction of fee may be required.

Q. What do you do when a patient neglects payments of fees?

A. Lack of punctuality in the payment of fees may be a manifestation of temporary financial shortage, a problem in the patient related to money or to giving, or an indication of resentment toward the therapist and of a desire to frustrate him. Should the patient disregard the payment of the bill for a considerable period, the matter may merit inquiry and therapeutic handling. Where the therapist himself has neurotic problems in relation to money, he may evidence marked anxiety when payments are not being made on time. He may consequently tend to overemphasize the importance of punctuality in payments, and he may introduce the matter of finances completely out of context with the material that concerns the patient. On the other hand, the therapist may be negligent as to the matter of payments, and he may fail to bring to the patient's awareness possible avoidance of a responsibility which is part of the reality situation. Unless justified by financial reverses, the accumulation of a debt creates hardships for the patient which may be harmful to his relationship with the therapist.

Q. If you discover that the patient's finances are greater than those he reported at the beginning of therapy, would you boost the fee?

A. Financial arrangements with a patient may have been made on the basis of a reported low income. If the patient has purposefully concealed his finances from the therapist, this deception will, in all probability, later create guilt and tension. The therapist may assure the patient that there must have been reasons why he felt he had to falsify his income. Understandably, careful handling is necessary to avoid mobilizing further guilt. In the event the set fees require adjustment because of the patient's larger income, this matter must be discussed thoroughly with the patient, no change of fees being made except on mutual agreement. If the patient's fees are arbitrarily raised without his complete cooperation, grave difficulties may be anticipated in the therapeutic relationship.

Q. Should the therapist ever visit a patient in his home?

A. Only in the event of a serious incapacitating illness or accident where it is impossible for the patient to come to the therapist's office and where it is urgent to administer psychotherapy.

Q. What do you do when a patient talks too much and doesn't allow the therapist to speak?

A. If the patient is focused on an important area and is doing good therapeutic work, one does not interrupt. If he is talking about irrelevant things, or his rambling seems to be resistance, one interrupts and focuses on pertinent topics. If this does not help, one may question the reason for rambling, or perhaps attempt its interpretation.

Q. What do you do if the patient has been in negative transference for a long time and this continues no matter what the therapist does?

A. First the therapist might examine his own feelings and behavior to see if he is provoking these feelings. If he is sure there is nothing in the therapeutic situation that is stirring up the patient, he may attempt to analyze possible projections by the patient into the present relationship of negative attitudes toward important past personages. If this does not help, he may go back to the first phase of therapy and actively try again to establish a working relationship with the patient.

Q. What is the relative merit of focusing on past as compared with present life difficulties in reconstructive therapy?

A. In reconstructive psychotherapy, some controversy exists as to the relative importance of material that deals with the past, and material relating to the present. Extremists of both points of view argue the merits of their particular emphasis. On the one hand, there are those who regard the present problems of the individual as a superficial product of personality disturbances arising out of insecurities in childhood. These insecurities have undermined the self-esteem and blanketed sexual and aggressive drives with a mantle of anxiety. Environmental difficulties and current situational distortions stir up hardships for the individual by agitating past problems. Dealing with provocative current situations may restore the equilibrium of the individual. This stability is, however, precarious due to the continued operation of immature strivings. While harmony may be reconstituted, the recurrence of environmental stress will promote a new breakdown in adaptation. It is fruitless, therefore, to concentrate on the present, since the roots of the difficulty, imbedded in the past history, will remain firmly entrenched. On the other hand, there are therapists who are opposed to an emphasis on the past. It is claimed that the individual repeats in present-day patterns his important childhood disturbances. A concern with the present must of necessity involve a consideration of the past. To discuss the past in detail results in a mere raking over of dead historical ashes; while interesting material may be exposed, it may bear little relationship to current happenings. A dichotomy may then be set up between the past and the present, with lacking unity of the two. As irreconcilable as these two viewpoints appear, they are not so disparate as the proposed arguments would seem to indicate. In psychotherapeutic practice, one constantly utilizes current life experiences as vehicles for discussion, for it is in the present that the individual lives and feels. Yet, a consideration of the past is mandatory in understanding what is happening in the present. Current life experiences may be regarded as reflecting a patterning from the past through the use of present-day symbols. It is therefore necessary to blend the past and the present, and to focus on whichever element is of immediate importance.

Q. Is it ever permissible to assign "homework" to the patient?

A. Where the patient is not too productive and does not work industriously at therapy, asking him to keep a kind of diary, writing out his reactions, observations, and dreams between sessions, may get him to approach treatment more seriously. Each interview may be organized around discerning and exploring basic patterns which are revealed in the patient's notes or observations. The patient should leave every session with a general problem to focus on up to the time of the next session. He may then work on this problem, observing himself and his reactions, noting which environmental or interpersonal situations tend to aggravate or moderate it. This "homework" may catalyze the patient's thinking, and get him to assume more responsibility for his treatment.

Q. If a patient wants information about a subject like sex, do you give it to him?

A. Yes, but only after ascertaining why the patient asked for this data.

Q. Isn't a routine physical examination for all patients a wasteful practice?

A. Every patient about to get psychotherapy should have a good physical examination and preferably a thorough neurologic examination performed by a competent neurologist. The findings will be negative in the vast majority of patients, but the occasional case of early cancer, brain tumor, or other operable maladies that may be detected will justify the precaution of routine physicals.

Q. How would you handle a patient who appears to have read just about everything on the subject of psychiatry and keeps citing the opinions of different authorities which may or may not agree with your point of view?

A. The patient may have read more on psychiatry than you, but this does not mean that he has integrated what he has read. As a matter of fact, he will probably tend to utilize the knowledge he has gained as resistance, by intellectualizing what goes on, or by criticizing the technique or formulations of the therapist. At some point in therapy, it may be necessary to mention to the patient that, while his reading has given him a good deal of information, this information may be a hindrance to his therapy rather than a help. No two problems of an emotional nature are alike, and things he has read applying to other people surely do not exactly apply to himself. He can be fair to himself only by observing his feelings and his attitudes, without speculating what they must be like on the basis of his readings. Sometimes it may be necessary to be very blunt and to tell a patient that it is important for him to forget everything that he has read, since this seems to interfere with his spontaneity.

Q. What do you do when the patient asks a question the therapist is unable to answer?

A. The therapist may say that he cannot answer the question at this time, but will do so later when the answer becomes more clear.

Q. Is it ever justifiable to lie to a patient?

A. Lies eventually reveal themselves and shatter the patient's trust and confidence in the therapist. Truthfulness is, consequently, the keynote in therapy. In an effort to be truthful, however, one should not reveal things to the patient that may be harmful to him. It may be essential, therefore, where his security and health are menaced, to avoid answering certain questions directly. If, for instance, the patient shows symptoms of an impending psychosis, and is dangerously tottering between sanity and mental illness, and if he is frightened by the upsurge of archaic unconscious material to a point where he believes himself to be insane, it may be harmful to tell him that he is approaching a psychosis. Rather, he may, if he questions the therapist, be told that his preoccupation with becoming insane is more important than the symptoms he manifests. These are evidences of great insecurity. Whenever the patient asks a direct question, an honest answer to which may be upsetting to the patient in view of existing ego weaknesses, he may be asked why he asks this question, and his concern may be handled without upsetting him with a straight reply. It is important to remember that truthfulness must not be confused with necessary caution in divulging information and interpreting prematurely. Where a patient is insistent on a complete answer to his question, it may be helpful to point out to him that therapy involves a mutual inquiry into a problem, and an avoidance of premature judgments. One must patiently wait until enough evidence is available before being certain of one's observations. The answer to questions will soon become evident, both to the patient and to the therapist. If for any reason the patient cannot perceive the truth, the therapist will point out to him why it is difficult for him to understand what is happening. The patient will eventually develop confidence in the fact that the truth will not be kept from him, but that ideas must be checked and double-checked for their validity before they can be communicated.

Q. Sometimes it is necessary to break an appointment with a patient. How can this best be done?

A. Appointments should, if possible, never be broken without adequate notice being given to the patient. Unless this is done, the relationship may be injured and a great deal of work may be necessary to undo the damage. Where circumstances make it necessary to break an appointment, the therapist or his secretary should telephone the patient, explain that an emergency has developed that necessitates a revision of the therapist's schedule, and that, consequently, it will be necessary to make a new appointment for the patient, or to skip the present appointment. In instances where the therapist is ill, or expects to be away from his practice for an indefinite period, the patient may be informed that the therapist will get in touch with him shortly to give him a new appointment. If a reasonable explanation is given to the patient to account for a broken appointment, there will be no interference with the working relationship.

Q. How would you handle a patient's resentment because you do not keep appointments on time?

A. The patient's resentment may be justified. Because of ambivalent feelings, the patient usually has difficulties trusting any human being completely. The therapist must therefore give the patient as little reality basis for his distrust as possible, always explaining to the patient the reasons for unavoidable irregularities in appointment times, so the patient will not assume that the therapist is irresponsible. Giving the patient an allotted amount of time is part of the reality situation to which both the patient and therapist must adjust. Where appointments are forgotten by the therapist, or where the patient has to sit around and wait for the therapist because the therapist has not finished with a preceding patient, resentments will develop which may interfere with therapy. Of course, there will be occasions when the therapist cannot help being late for a session. Emergencies with a preceding patient may develop, and the therapist may have to run over in time into the next session. Under such circumstances, an explanation must be given the patient to the effect that an emergency occurred which could not be avoided and which necessitated a delay in starting his session. In order to impress on the patient the fact that he is not being exploited, he may be told also that time taken from his session will be made up. In the event a mistake has been made in the patient's appointment, and the patient appears for his session at a time allotted to another patient, he must be taken aside and given an explanation to the effect that an unfortunate error in scheduling has occurred which resulted in the patient's being given the wrong appointment time. Another appointment should then be given the patient during which any resentment resulting from the error may be handled.

Q. If you are unable to understand what is going on dynamically in a case you are treating, what do you do?

A. Occasions will arise when the therapist may be unable to discern exactly what is happening in his relationship with a patient. When this occurs, it may be indicative of such blocks as unyielding resistance in the patient, or of counter-transference. In either instance, where the therapist is disturbed by what is happening, or where progress is blocked, several supervisory sessions with an experienced psychotherapeutic supervisor may be helpful in resolving the difficulty.

Q. When do you increase the frequency of sessions?

A. During the course of therapy it may be necessary to increase the number of sessions weekly for the following reasons: (1) an upsurge of intense anxiety, depression, or hostility which the patient cannot himself control; (2) violent intensification of symptoms; (3) severe resistance that interferes with progress; (4) negative transference; (5) unrestrained acting-out that requires checking; (6) threats of shattering of the ego unless constant support is given the patient; and (7) where one wishes to stimulate transference to the point of creating a transference neurosis.

Q. When would you decrease the number of sessions weekly?

A. A decrease in the number of weekly sessions is indicated: (1) where a patient is becoming too dependent on the therapist; (2) where alarming transference reactions are developing which one wishes to subdue; (3) where the patient has a tendency to substitute transference reactions for real life experiences; and (4) where the patient has progressed sufficiently in therapy so that he can carry on with a diminished number of visits.

Q. Is advice-giving taboo in reconstructive therapy?

A. Generally. One must keep working on the patient's resistances to the solving of his own problems. The ultimate aim is self-assertiveness rather than reliance on the therapist.

Q. Should the therapist ever insist on the patient's engaging in a specific course of action?

A. Only when it is absolutely necessary that the patient execute it, and its rationale is fully explained to, and accepted by the patient.

Q. Should the therapist ever try to forbid the patient from making crucial decisions during therapy?

A. While important changes in his life status, like divorce or marriage, may best be delayed until the patient has achieved stability and greater personality maturity, it is obviously difficult for the therapist to "forbid" the patient to make any decisions. The patient may be reminded that it is important not to take any drastic steps in altering his life situation without discussing these thoroughly with the therapist. If the therapist believes the decisions to be neurotic, he may question them, presenting interpretations if necessary. In the event the patient decides nevertheless to go through with a move that is obviously impetuous, it means that he is still at the mercy of neurotic forces he cannot control, that his insight is not yet sufficiently developed, or that he has to defy or challenge the therapist. The therapist may have no other alternative than to let the patient make a mistake, provided the patient realizes that he has acted on his own impulse. It is important not to reject the patient or to communicate resentment towards him for having made a move against advice. Only when the patient is about to take a really destructive or dangerous step is the therapist justified in actively opposing it.

Q. What do you do if the patient brings in written material for you to discuss?

A. Occasional written material may be important, but if large quantities are brought in, this practice should be discouraged.

Q. What would you do if the patient refuses to talk session after session but offers to write out his ideas?

A. If this is the only way the patient will communicate, it should be accepted. However, an attempt must be made to handle the patient's resistance to talk at the same time that he is encouraged to bring in written comments.

Q. What do you do if a patient says he fears he will kill someone?

A. One should not reassure the patient nor minimize what he says. Rather, he may be told that there are reasons why he feels so upset that he believes that he will kill someone. He may then be encouraged to explore his impulses and fears. If the patient is psychotic or destructively dangerous, hospitalization may be required.

Q. Should the therapist permit the patient to express hostility or aggression openly in the therapeutic situation?

A. Any overt behavioral expressions of hostility or aggression are forbidden, although verbalization of these emotions or impulses is permissible, even indispensible.

Q. Do you ever reassure the patient during insight therapy?

A. Reassurance should be kept at a minimum. However, gross misconceptions will require reassuring correction; or the patient may be in an emotional crisis which needs mitigation. Reassurance should never be given the patient when he is in a negativistic state, since this may produce an effect opposite to what is intended.

Q. Are fleeting suicidal thoughts arising in the patient during treatment important?

A. Suicidal thoughts are not uncommon during therapy. They often serve a defensive purpose, acting as a kind of safety valve. Vague ideas of suicide may be entertained as a way of ultimate escape from suffering in the event life should become too intolerable. In most instances, such ideas are fleeting and are never put into practice no matter how bad conditions become. They are handled therapeutically in the same way that any fantasy or idea might be managed. It is important not to convey undue alarm when the patient talks about escape fantasies in taking his life. To do so will frighten the patient or cause him to use suicidal threats against the therapist as a form of resistance. Rather, the therapist may listen respectfully to the patient and then state simply that there may be other ways out of his situation than suicide. Suicide is an irrevocable act. More suitable ways of coping with the situation will present themselves as he explores his difficulty. Where, however, the patient has, in the past, made an attempt at suicide, fleeting suicidal thoughts must be taken very seriously. A careful watch is indicated, since the attempt may be repeated. Any evidence of hopelessness or resentment that cannot be expressed as such, must be explored and resolved if it is possible to do so. Should resolution be impossible, and should the danger of suicide continue to lurk, hospitalization may be required. Suicidal thoughts in patients who are deeply depressed must be considered as dangerous, and the patient must be handled accordingly.

Q. What do you do if a patient you are treating telephones and insists on seeing you that very day?

A. If possible, this request should be respected, provided the situation upsetting the patient is an emergent one. Should the therapist be unable to arrange for an appointment, or for a partial appointment, he may promise to telephone the patient at a specified time that day to discuss the situation with him. As early an appointment as possible should be made for the patient.

Q. What would you say to a patient who asks whether he may telephone or write to you whenever he desires?

A. Lack of time will obviously make it difficult for the therapist to answer telephone calls or to read all the material that the patient wishes to communicate in writing. The therapist may handle a request on the part of the patient to telephone by saying simply that it is much better to take up matters during a session, since the limited time available during telephone conversations may create more problems than are solved. In response to excessive written communications, the therapist may remark that verbalization is to be preferred to writing. The patient may be informed that where emergencies occur, he may feel free to telephone the therapist. Where a crisis has developed, the patient may be given specific times at which he may call, or he may be told that the therapist will telephone him at a certain hour. It is usually best to keep such telephone calls at a minimum, and to increase the sessions of the patient should a more intensive contact be required.

Q. How would you handle a patient who is insistent that you inform him of your whereabouts at all times, so that he can get in touch with you?

A. One would deal with this the way any other symptom in a neurosis would be handled. The patient may be told that it is important to find out why he needs to know the therapist's whereabouts. It may be that he feels so helpless and insecure within himself that he must be convinced that the therapist will not desert him or deny him help in the event of a catastrophe. The patient may be assured that the therapist will, in the instance of an emergency, always be happy to talk with him, but that it is important to understand what is behind the patient's insecurity in order that he be able to overcome his feelings of helplessness.

Q. In the event a patient who has been using the couch position manifests anxiety and asks to sit up, would you encourage this?

A. Anxiety may be the product of penetration of unconscious material into preconsciousness, or it may indicate a feeling of isolation from, or a fear of the therapist. Encouraging the patient to continue his verbal associations on the couch, may enable him to gain awareness of important feelings or conflicts. However, if anxiety becomes too great, his request to assume the sitting-up, face-to-face position should be granted. This will generally permit of a restoration of stability, especially if supportive measures are coordinately employed.

Q. What do you do when a patient has reached a stalemate in therapy? He is completely unproductive, and any attempts of the therapist to mobilize transference and to resolve resistance fail.

A. Group therapy with alternate individual sessions often stimulates activity, as may several sessions of hypnosis or narcotherapy. Continued resistance may justify a vacation from therapy, or, as a last resort, transfer to another therapist.

Q. When is psychotherapy likely to become interminable?

A. A patient whose personality has been so damaged in early childhood that it has never allowed for a satisfactory gratification of needs or for an adequate defense against stress may feel he requires a continuing dependent relationship in order to function. Transference here is organized around maneuvering the therapist into a parental role. There is strong resistance to a more mature relationship. Where the therapist enters into the patient's design, due to his own needs to play parent, therapy is apt to become interminable.

Q. What does dreaming indicate when it becomes so excessive that it takes up the entire session?

A. Where the patient deluges the therapist with dreams, the therapist should suspect that they are being used as resistance, perhaps to divert the therapist from other important material.

Q. Which dreams that the patient presents should one consider of great importance?

A. Repetitive dreams and those with an anxiety content may be of great importance.

Q. What do you do when a patient constantly brings up important material several minutes before the end of a session, leaving no time to discuss it?

A. This is usually a manifestation of anxiety. It may be handled by mentioning to the patient the fact that the material he has brought up sounds important and should be discussed at the next session. If the patient does not spontaneously bring it up, the therapist may do so, handling whatever resistances arise.

Q. How would you handle a parent who brings a child to you for therapy, and you are impressed by the fact that the parent needs treatment more than does the child?

A. It may be important to determine how much motivation the parent has for therapy, and his level of understanding. Should the parent be unaware of how he participates in the child's neurosis, it may be necessary to inform him that the treatment of his child will require seeing the parent also, both to determine what is going on at home and to help the parent understand how to handle developing problems. In this way, the parent himself may be brought into a treatment situation.

Q. Are interviews with the patient's family or with other persons important to the adult patient of any value?

A. The therapist may frequently get information from persons close to the patient that the patient himself has been unable to convey. Often a conference reveals distortions in the patient's attitudes and behavior that are not based on reality. One or more interviews with important family members may thus serve as a constructive experience. Furthermore, where the patient is unable to correct a disturbed environmental situation by himself, the cooperation of a related person as an accessory may be helpful. Where the patient is reacting destructively to a relative who then responds in a counter-destructive manner, where demands on the patient by a relative are stirring up problems in the patient, where a related person is opposing the patient's therapy—and his help, financial and other, is needed—an interview with the relative, aimed at the clarification of these issues, may yield many dividends. The relative may require reassurance to neutralize his guilt about the patient. Sometimes relatives can be prepared for contingencies that may arise in therapy, such as rebelliousness and hostility directed at them by the patient. An explanation that such occurrences are inevitable in treatment, and that they are part of the process of getting well, may forestall retaliatory gestures. The patient's need for independence and assertiveness may be explained for the benefit of relatives who unwittingly overprotect the patient. Statements to the effect that the patient will get worse before he gets better, and that it will require time before results are apparent, often prevent discouragement and feelings of hopelessness among concerned relatives. Because a therapeutically induced change in the patient's attitudes brought about by therapy may impose new and unaccustomed burdens on persons with whom the patient associates, preparing these persons for the change may avoid a crisis. An interpretation of the patient's actions in dynamic terms will often relieve a related person's guilt and lessen his resentment. For instance, if an adolescent is beginning to act cantankerous and resistive, an explanation to the parent that this behavior is to be expected at the patient's time of life, that all adolescents are often difficult to live with, and that parents are bound to feel resentful at the behavior of their offspring, may foster greater tolerance. Or a wife distraught at her husband's inattentiveness may be helped to realize that her spouse is responding not specifically to her as a person, but rather to her as a symbol of some actual past or fantasied personage against whom the patient had to build a wall of detachment. This insight may help avoid the creation of the very situations that would drive her husband deeper into isolation.

Q. How would you approach a patient should you decide a conference with a relative is necessary?

A. The patient may be told that in psychotherapy the therapist may want to have an occasional conference with a relative or other person close to the patient. The purpose is to get to know the relatives and their attitudes. Following this, the therapist may say, "I wonder how you would feel if I thought it necessary to talk with _____ (*mentioning name of person*)?" The patient may acquiesce; he may question the need for such a conference; or he may refuse indignantly to permit it. If the patient is insistent that no contact be made, his desire should be respected. Important material concerning the relative will undoubtedly be forthcoming and may constitute the material of later interviews.

Q. If an interview with a family member or other significant person is decided on, are there any rules one should follow?

A. Experience has shown that a number of precautions are necessary when it is decided to contact the family. First, the patient's consent should always be obtained, the only exception being where he is dangerously psychotic. Second, confidential material revealed by the patient must never be divulged, since the breach of confidence will usually be flaunted at the patient even where the relative promises to keep the revelations to himself. Third, in talking to the related person, the therapist will often have a temptation to blame, to scold or to enjoin the person to change his ways or attitudes toward the patient. Distraught, confused, frustrated, and filled with guilt and indignation, the related person will expect the therapist to accuse him of delinquencies toward the patient. Permitting the person to talk freely, sympathizing with his feelings, and encouraging him to express his ideas about the situation, will tend to alleviate his tension. It is important to try to establish a rapid working relationship with the person, if this is at all possible. Once the person realizes that the therapist is sympathetic with him, he will be more amenable toward accepting interpretations of the patient's reactions, and he will be more cooperative in the treatment plan. Indeed he may, if he has been hostile to the patient's therapy or to the therapist, become a helpful accessory. Fourth, should the person telephone the therapist, he must be told that it is best that the patient be informed about the call, although the specific details need not be revealed. Fifth, if the patient is insistent on knowing what went on in the conference or conversation with the therapist, he may be told that the conversation was general and dealt with many of the person's own problems, as well as his relationship with the patient. Sixth, it may be necessary to see the person more than once, perhaps even periodically. Seventh, the therapist should not participate with the patient in "tearing down" a family member, nor should the member be defended when the patient launches an attack. A sympathetic, impartial attitude is best.

Q. Under what conditions would you advise a relative of a patient to get psychotherapy?

A. Where the patient is in close contact with a neurotic relative, and he is being traumatized by the relative, psychotherapy may be advised, provided the therapist has a sufficiently good relationship with the relative to make this recommendation. Therapy may also be advised when a change in the patient's condition makes a new adjustment by the relative necessary. For instance, a frigid wife, living with an impotent husband, may, as a result of psychotherapy, on the basis of experiencing sexual feelings, make sexual demands on her husband that the latter will be unable to fulfill. In order for the husband to make an adjustment, he may require psychotherapy.

Q. Is it permissible to treat several members of the same family?

A. The situation often becomes complicated, but it can be done. Whether or not simultaneous treatment is practiced will depend on the goals. Where one wishes to achieve goals of personality reconstruction, simultaneous treatment is usually not advisable. On the other hand, effecting a better adjustment in such difficulties as marital problems may permit of therapy of both partners. Whether or not members of the same family are treated by the same therapist will also depend on the therapist, and his ability to handle inevitable complications, like being used as a referee.

Q. How should one act when one meets a patient on the street or at a social affair?

A. The character of the therapeutic relationship is such as to make it essential to reduce social contacts to a minimum. Occasions will, however, arise where the therapist will run into the patient on the street, in public places or at private social affairs. This may prove embarrassing to both therapist and patient. One cannot handle such situations by running away from them. Once the therapist is recognized by the patient, the former may greet him cordially and then proceed with his activities as usual. Understandably, at private gatherings, one's spontaneity will have to be curtailed to some extent. The patient's reactions to seeing the therapist in a different role may have to be handled with him during the ensuing sessions.

Q. Should you expect all your patients to like you?

A. Except for very sick patients, a satisfactory resolution of prejudices, suspicions and resentments will occur relatively early in therapy, leading to a good working relationship. Periodically, however, the patient's feeling about the therapist will be punctuated by hostility, issuing either out of transference or out of an inadvertent error in the therapist's handling of the patient. Analysis and resolution of hostilities as they develop should bring the relationship back to a working level.

Q. If a patient continues to dislike you no matter what you do, should you discontinue therapy?

A. A continued dislike is usually indicative of either errors in therapeutic management or of transference which the patient cannot resolve. So long as the dislike persists, little progress can be expected in treatment. Should the therapist be unable to correct the patient's feeling, he may have to suggest the possibility of transfer to a different therapist. This must be done in such a way that the patient realizes that the transfer is being recommended out of consideration of his welfare and not because the therapist rejects him. As a general rule, very few patients will need to be transferred because of persistent negative feelings. Where a therapist encounters this problem frequently, the chances are that he is doing something in the therapeutic situation that is inspiring the dislike of his patients. He should, therefore, seek supervision with an experienced psychotherapist who may be able to help him to understand what is happening.

Q. How should you act to displays of crying or rage on the part of the patient?

A. One generally permits these to go on without reassurance until the meaning of the reaction is explored and determined. If the reaction is dangerous to the patient or to others, it should be controlled by supportive measures.

Q. Should the therapist engage in a confessional, confiding his past or present life to the patient in an effort to show the patient that he too has frailties?

A. This can be very destructive to the relationship, especially at the beginning of therapy. The patient may use any revelations made as a confession of the therapist's weakness and ineptness, and he may then decide to discontinue treatment.

Q. Should you ever admit to the patient that you may be wrong about certain things?

A. Except in prestige suggestion, it is important to admit of an error when this is obvious to the patient and he questions the therapist about it.

Q. If a patient asks you if you are ill or tired, would you admit it?

A. If it is true, it may be important to confirm the patient's observation, adding that you do not believe this will interfere with your ability to work with the patient.

Q. What happens in insight therapy if the therapist's personality is authoritarian?

A. If the authoritarianism of the therapist interferes with the patient's ability to express hostility, and with his assertiveness, it will probably limit therapeutic goals.

Q. Is it possible that a therapist may develop a deep hate for a patient?

A. If a circumstance like this develops in therapy, there is something seriously wrong with the therapist or with his technique. It is not possible for the therapist to like all patients to the same degree, nor is it possible to avoid disliking some of his patients temporarily in certain phases of treatment. When this happens, the therapist must resolve the untoward feeling before it interferes with therapeutic progress. If he cannot do this, he should transfer the patient to another therapist, and perhaps seek psychotherapy for himself.

Q. Does a therapist ever fall in love with a patient?

A. If such a situation develops, it is a manifestation of counter-transference which will seriously interfere with the therapist's essential objectivity. Failure to analyze his feeling and to resolve it will make it necessary to transfer the patient to another therapist.

Q. Does a therapist ever develop sexual feelings for a patient?

A. It is possible that certain patients may arouse sexual feelings in the therapist. If this happens, such feelings must be subjected to self-analysis and resolved.

Q. Should not the conduct and attitudes of the psychotherapist be as passive and noncommittal as possible?

A. The idea that the therapist should remain detached and completely passive stems from the notion that this attitude will best demonstrate to the patient how he automatically projects onto the therapist attitudes and feelings that are rooted in past relationships. Not having done anything to incite his attitudes, the therapist is in a better position to interpret transference. The passive, detached attitude also is believed to avoid dependency and to throw the patient on his own resources. Experience shows, however, that the projections of the patient, which are sparked by past distortions in interpersonal relationships, will develop whether the therapist be passive or active. A patient with hostile problems will thus develop hostility toward the therapist who acts detached, as well as toward one who acts accepting. If the patient has a problem of dependency, he will get dependent on the most passive therapist. Rather than cripple the spontaneity of the therapist in the dubious quest of interpreting transference phenomena, or of mobilizing assertiveness, it is best for the therapist to act himself, and not to assume artificial passivity, if he is not normally a passive person. Such an assumption may signify rejection to the patient, and, in mobilizing hostility, may interfere with the working relationship.

Q. *Are not warmth and emotional support necessary for some patients?*

A. Yes, especially when the patient's adaptive resources are at a minimum. Unfortunately, some therapists have been reared in the tradition of passivity and non-directiveness to a point where they provide for the patient a sterile, refrigerated atmosphere which, in seriously sick patients, is anathema to a working relationship.

Q. *Is the assumption of a studied role by the therapist of any help in insight therapy?*

A. It has been recommended by some authorities that the therapist play a deliberate role in insight psychotherapy that is at variance with his usual neutral, though empathic, position. Such role-playing, however, may inspire intense transference that the therapist may be unable to control. As a general rule, the therapist should not transgress his defined role of a professional person who seeks to enable the patient to help himself through understanding. An exception to this rule is an extremely experienced and skilled therapist who is thoroughly acquainted with the existing dynamics operative in a patient, and who, by dramatizing a part and injecting himself actively into the patient's life, strives to expedite change. Such activity is not without risks, but it may, in some cases, produce brilliant results. On the whole, role-playing is not to be recommended. Most patients quickly perceive the artificiality in the assumed part played by the therapist.

Q. *If the therapist acts consistently permissive and accepting, will this not in itself eventually reduce the patient's irrational responses to authority?*

A. The behavior of the therapist, no matter how well-controlled will, to some degree, always be subject to distortion in terms of the patient's conceptual framework, which, in turn, is based on his previous experiences with authority. This is not to say that gross deviations of behavior on the part of the therapist will not bring about appropriate reality-determined responses. A brusque, disinterested, detached or hostile manner will produce untoward reactions in most patients. However, one must not delude himself into thinking that absolutely correct activity and behavior will always bring about good responses, since the patient may interpret the therapist's actions as a hypocritically conceived lure.

Q. *Should deprivations ever be imposed on the patient?*

A. Occasionally it is necessary to enjoin the patient to deprive himself of certain sources of gratification to help the exploratory process. Thus, a homosexual patient may be urged to control his sexual impulse so that tensions may accumulate which will facilitate an analysis of his problem. Where the patient is shown the reason for his need to give up certain pleasure promptings, he will be less inclined to resent the therapist.

Q. *How would you handle the overanxious and completely unreasonable patient who acts more like a child than an adult?*

A. It is essential to remember that while the patient may be chronologically an adult, emotionally he may not have progressed beyond a childhood level. One may expect, therefore, childish tantrums, ambivalent feelings, unrestrained enthusiasms and other reactions. If one can respect the patient despite his unreasonableness, one will best be able to help him.

Q. What do you do when your relationship with the patient starts getting bad?

A. All other tasks cease, and one must concentrate on bringing the relationship back to a satisfactory level. It is useless to explore patterns, to interpret and to engage in any other interviewing tasks so long as good rapport is absent. Essentially, one must go back to the first phase of therapy and focus on reestablishing a working relationship.

Q. Why is the handling of transference important in reconstructive therapy?

A. Since much of the suffering of the patient is produced by destructive transference involvements with people, part of the therapeutic task in reconstructive therapy is to put a halt to such reactions and to replace them with those that have a foothold in reality. If, for instance, the patient responds automatically to authority with violent hate, as a result of an unresolved hatred toward a parent or sibling, his reaction may have a disorganizing effect on his total adjustment. The patient usually does not appreciate that this response to all authority is undifferentiated. He may not even be aware of his hate, which, considered to be dangerous in expression, becomes internalized with psychosomatic or depressive consequences. Liberation from such reactions is essential before the patient can get well. This can best be insured in therapy by bringing him to an awareness of his projections. Several means are available to the therapist in executing this goal. First, on the basis of functioning in the role of an objective and impartial observer, one may help the patient realize how many of his reactions outside of therapy have no reality base. Second, by watching for instances of transference toward the therapist, one may demonstrate to the patient, often quite dramatically, the nature of those projections which constitute basic patterns.

Q. What is the difference between "transference," "transference neurosis," "parataxic distortions," and "positive relationship?"

A. Stereotyped early patterns, projected into the relationship with the therapist, were called by Freud "transference reactions." When these became so intense that the patient acted out important past situations, this was known as a "transference neurosis." No satisfactory name was given to repetitive early patterns occurring with persons outside of the therapeutic situation until Sullivan invented the term "parataxic distortions" which included all stereotyped patterns that developed inside or outside of therapy. A "positive relationship" usually refers to a good working relationship with minimal transference contamination.

Q. Isn't the accepted idea of transference as a manifestation of purely infantile or childish attitudes or feelings a restricted one?

A. Probably. A broader concept of transference would consider it to be a blend of projections onto the therapist of attitudes and feelings that date back to infancy and childhood, as well as more current attitudes that have had a formative influence on, and have been incorporated into, the character structure.

Q. Does every patient have to go through a transference neurosis in order to achieve very deep, structural personality changes?

A. There is much controversy on this point, but experience shows that some patients can achieve extensive personality growth without needing to live through a transference neurosis.

Q. What activities on the part of the therapist encourage neurotic transference responses?

A. Dependency may be stimulated in the patient by such therapist activities as overprotecting the patient, making decisions for him and exhibiting directiveness in the relationship. Sexual feelings in the patient may be provoked by seductive behavior displayed toward the patient, by socializing with the patient and by physical contact of any kind. Fearful attitudes and hostile impulses may be mobilized where the therapist acts excessively passive, detached, authoritarian, overprotective, hostile, pompous or belligerent. It must, however, be remembered that transference may arise without any provocation whatsoever on the part of the therapist. This is the case where needs are intense and can be voiced and expressed in transference due to the permissiveness of the therapeutic relationship.

Q. What is the best way of handling transference?

A. There is no best way; methods depend on the kind of therapy done and the therapeutic goals. Transference may not be explored or handled in supportive therapy. In reeducative therapy, it may be immediately interpreted in an effort at resolution whenever it becomes apparent as resistance. In some types of reconstructive therapy, it may be allowed to develop until it becomes so disturbing that the patient himself achieves awareness of its irrational nature. In Freudian analysis, it may be encouraged to the point of evolution of a transference neurosis.

Q. Are so-called "transference cures" ever permanently effective?

A. Structural personality changes rarely occur. However, a "transference cure" may permit a patient to relate better to his life situation. This facilitates the development of more adaptive patterns that can become permanent.

Q. How does counter-transference lead to an improper assessment of neurotic traits in the patient?

A. Counter-transference may cause the therapist to make incorrect interpretations of the patterns exhibited by the patient. Thus he may, if he welcomes hostile outbursts, regard these as manifestations of assertiveness rather than as destructive responses. If he relishes a submissive, passive attitude on the part of the patient, he may credit this to cooperation and to the abatement of neurotic aggression, rather than to a neurotic need for compliance.

Q. Should you ever emphasize positive aspects of the patient's adjustment?

A. Therapists too often tend to regard the patient as a repository of pathologic strivings, emphasizing these to a neglect of constructive traits, mention of which is very important in the reality assessment.

Q. Is acting-out always a bad sign?

A. No. It may be a transitional phase in therapy indicative of a shift in the psychic equilibrium. Thus a repressed, timid individual, realizing that he has been intimidated by an archaic fear of physical hurt for assertiveness, may become overly aggressive and act-out his defiance of authority as a way of combating his terror. Proving himself to be capable of this expression without experiencing the dreaded punishment, may enable him to temper his outbursts. In the same way, a sexually inhibited person may become temporarily promiscuous, almost as if liberation from fear is tantamount with indulgence in sexual excesses. Incorporated also in the acting-out process are unresolved impulses and conflicts, in relation to early authorities, that have been mobilized by the transference. When the therapist becomes aware of acting-out, it is important for him to discourage it in favor of verbalization. As verbalizations replace impetuous acts, and as understanding progresses, a more rational solution is found for neurotic drives and impulses.

Q. How do the value prejudices of the therapist interfere with treatment?

A. Whether he wants to or not, the therapist will accent in the interview, attitudes and feelings that are in line with his value system, and he will minimize those that are opposed to it. Where, for instance, the therapist has a problem in his own relationships with authority, manifesting submission and ingratiation, he may overvalue these traits. He may then tend to discourage assertiveness or aggressiveness when the patient seeks to take a stand with authority. He may credit his philosophy to "good common sense" and to justify it in terms of the benefits that accrue to ingratiation. This may seriously inhibit the patient from working through neurotic feelings toward authority. On the other hand, where the therapist himself reacts to authority with aggression and hostility, he may inspire defiance or promote aggressive attitudes toward authoritative persons which may seriously endanger the patient's security.

Q. What value standards should the therapist have?

A. The values of the therapist should reflect the constructive values of the culture. However, the therapist should be able to tolerate those biologic needs that do not entirely conform exactly with the existing mores, recognizing that cultural values and folkways may inhibit the spontaneous expression of some biologic and social needs. The therapist should also be sensitive to neurotic distortions that are culturally nurtured, and help bring the patient to an awareness of these distortions in order that the patient be able to take a more rational stand with life. Respect for the patient's right to autonomy and self-determination must be blended with a realistic appraisal of social disciplines to which the patient will have to make an adjustment.

Q. Shouldn't the therapist be trained in all therapeutic approaches?

A. The most effective therapist is one who can implement whatever therapies are indicated, whether these are of a supportive, reeducative or reconstructive nature. If the therapist has a broad understanding of various therapeutic procedures, if he knows how to execute them, and if he is sufficiently flexible in personality so as not to be tied to a single treatment process, he will score the greatest therapeutic successes. This, however, is an idealistic situation. Most therapists learn only one kind of technique, which enables them to handle only a certain number of problems—those which are amenable to their technique. They may also be limited by their character structure so as to be unable to utilize certain techniques. For instance, a therapist may be an essentially passive person, and, on this account be unable to employ the directiveness and authoritarianism of approach essential for symptom removal, reassurance, guidance, persuasion, environmental manipulation and other supportive therapies. On the other hand, the therapist may be so extremely authoritarian and dogmatic that he may not be able to allow his patient to make mistakes, to work out his own problems and to establish his own sense of values, so essential in reconstructive therapy.

Q. When is supportive therapy justified?

A. Supportive psychotherapy is aimed at a rapid relieving of the symptoms of the patient, enabling him to function as effectively as possible within the limitations of his neurotic difficulties which cannot or should not, for one reason or another, be dealt with in the present therapeutic effort.

Q. Is not insight a basic factor in all therapies?

A. Insight on some level is fundamental in all therapies. Even in supportive therapy, an understanding of the existing environmental encumbrances eventually leads to a correction of remediable difficulties, or to an adjustment to irremediable conditions. In reeducative therapy, knowledge of the troublesome consequences of existing behavioral patterns is ultimately accompanied by substitution with more wholesome interpersonal relationships. In reconstructive therapy, insight into unconscious conflicts and their projected manifestations into his everyday life, leads the patient to attempt reactions motivated more by the demands of reality than by the archaic needs and fears of his childhood.

Q. What is the difference between the level of insight effectuated in reeducative therapy and the kind in reconstructive therapy?

A. In reeducative therapy an inquiry is conducted into conscious and preconscious drives, impulses, feelings and conflicts with the object of suppressing or changing those that disorganize adjustment, and of encouraging others that expedite adjustment. In reconstructive therapy, the exploratory process deals with the more unconscious drives and conflicts. Due to the intensity of repression, one must implement the inquiry through examination of, and the inculcation of insight into, derivatives from the unconscious as revealed in verbal associations, dreams, fantasies, slips of speech, and the transference. The object in reconstructive therapy is to liberate the individual as completely as possible from anachronistic values, attitudes, strivings and defenses, and to remove blocks to personality growth.

Q. What is the best kind of therapy to use when the sole object is symptom relief or mere control of certain obnoxious personality traits?

A. The objective in the treatment effort may practically be limited to the restoration of habitual controls to the individual, to the mediation of any continuing environmental stress, and to the modification of strivings and goals that are inimical to the person's well-being or that are beyond his existing potentialities. Through the use of supportive techniques, and by bringing the patient to an awareness of some of his character distortions and strivings, we may accomplish these objectives in a satisfactory way. There are, however, some conditions where the character structure is so disturbed, and where elaborated crippling mechanisms of defense are so tenacious, that even the objective of mere symptom relief presupposes an extensive exploration of aspects of the personality that have been repressed. This will necessitate reconstructive approaches.

Q. Is it possible to do reconstructive therapy on the basis of once-a-week sessions?

A. The effectiveness of therapy is dependent upon factors more important than the number of times each week the patient is seen. Reconstructive therapy is possible in some patients on the basis of sessions once weekly; it is not possible in others. Great skill is required to bring about reconstructive changes where there are long intervals between visits. Serious developmental blocks usually necessitate frequent visits, and where a transference neurosis is to be created, four to five sessions weekly will be needed.

Q. What is the difference between an apparent and a permanent recovery as related to reconstructive therapy?

A. An apparent recovery is mere restoration to the pre-morbid level with the strengthening of the defensive techniques that have served, prior to illness, to maintain the ego free from anxiety. A permanent cure involves a real alteration of the ego to a point where those compromising defensive attitudes and mechanisms are no longer necessary to keep it free from anxiety. Under these circumstances, the individual is capable of gratifying his basic needs and strivings without undue conflict. Recovery in psychotherapy is permanent only insofar as it produces a real change in the character structure of the individual, and a reorientation of his relationships with others and with himself. Due to the operation of resistances which blanket offending impulses, and because of repressions which keep from awareness the most important problems of the individual, reconstructive psychotherapy offers the person the greatest chance of overcoming a severe emotional difficulty.

Q. What would you consider an acceptable minimal goal in reeducative therapy?

A. The least we can do for a patient is to bring him to as great an awareness of his problems as is reasonably possible; to enable him to lead as useful, happy and constructive a life as he can with his personality and environmental handicaps; to help him to overcome remediable life difficulties, and to adapt to irremediable ones; and to adjust his ambitions to his existent capacities.

Q. What is the difference between a "normal" and "neurotic" person?

A. "Normality" is a social designation that embraces characteristics not entirely consonant with a definition of mental health. The average "normal" person in a culture possesses many neurotic drives that are sanctioned and perhaps encouraged by society. While these drives nurture some anxieties, the "normal" individual is still capable of functioning and of making a satisfactory social adjustment. Where the person is no longer able to adjust himself, and he begins to manifest excessive anxiety and maladaptive mechanisms of defense, we may classify him as "neurotic." In therapy, our objective may be to restore the person's social adjustment and his "normal" neurotic tendencies. However, a more extensive objective would be a correction of all neurotic traits, even those condoned as "normal."

Q. If ideal goals of complete reconstruction are impossible, what would be reasonably good goals in reconstructive therapy?

A. It is manifestly impossible for any one individual to reach the acme of emotional maturity in every psychic and interpersonal area. One may decide that a satisfactory result has been achieved when the patient loses his symptoms, abandons his disturbing neurotic patterns, deals with his difficulties spontaneously without needing help from the therapist, manifests productivity and self-confidence, shows absence of fear following expression of assertiveness, and exhibits an improvement in his interpersonal relationships with increased friendliness and respect, and lessened suspiciousness, detachment, aggression and dependency.

Q. What is the chief use of "short-term" or "brief" psychotherapy?

A. In "brief" psychotherapy the whole object is to achieve as rapid change as possible in a limited period of time. This entails a circumscription of goals. We may achieve symptomatic relief, or the facing of one's problems more constructively, but we will usually not effectuate deep character change which will require a long period of treatment. Nevertheless, with all of its limitations, "brief" therapy has an important utility in selected patients.

Q. How does the therapist's personality influence his techniques?

A. Each therapist eventually evolves his own therapeutic method which is a composite of the methods he has learned, the experiences he has had, and his specific personality traits. For instance, an analytically trained therapist, inclined by personality to be authoritarian, may be unable to maintain the traditional silence and passivity demanded by psychoanalysis. To do so robs him of spontaneity; it provokes tension and prevents him from exhibiting the kind of relaxed objectivity that is most helpful in treatment. He may find it necessary to abandon passivity and to permit himself to participate more actively in the treatment process. His patients will perhaps respond to this change in a gratifying way and react more positively than when he was behaving in a stultified manner. This success may encourage the therapist to be himself, and he will probably find that his results continue to justify his alteration of technique. For him, then, the shift is justified since it liberates him from acting in an artificial, inhibited way. Yet another therapist may not be able to do the same thing; for instance, one who by personality is more retiring, quiet and unobtrusive. For him, the passive technique will probably work well; to attempt to force activity would be as artificial as to expect the former therapist to assume a feigned passivity.

Q. How do you explain the misunderstanding that exists among the different schools of psychiatry and psychology?

A. In so virgin a territory as the uncharted psyche, a diversity of theories, interpretations and methods may be expected. A great deal of animosity has, however, unfortunately come to the surface among groups with divergent points of view. Splinter societies have erupted, justifying their break with the parent body on the basis of discrimination and lack of academic freedom in the older organization. Sparked at first by the impulse to create groups possessed of scientific liberalism, a number of the splinter organizations have, upon achieving stability, fallen victim to the same intolerant forces that initiated their secession, developing their own dogmas and rejecting original thinking among the members. Such entrenched and reactionary attitudes are to be condemned in any scientific group.

Q. Should a good therapist be able to cure or help all patients?

A. No matter how highly trained the therapist may be, he will be able to help some patients more than others. There will be certain patients he will not be able to treat—patients which other therapists may successfully manage. On the other hand, he will probably be able to cure some patients with whom other therapists have failed. He will make some mistakes during the course of therapy with all of his patients, but these mistakes need not interfere with ultimate beneficial results. Finally, he will be rewarded by a large number of successes, but he will also have his quota of failures.

Q. Does it follow that a psychoanalytically trained therapist will do better therapy than one who has not been analytically trained?

A. It is fallacious to assume that a non-analytically trained therapist is incapable of doing many kinds of psychotherapy as well as one who has been analytically trained. However, where the therapist plans to do reconstructive psychotherapy, utilizing dream interpretation, transference and resistance, he will require sound training in reconstructive therapy including a personal analysis.

Q. Must the therapist be completely free from neurosis?

A. It is doubtful that any person in our culture is entirely free from neurosis, no matter how much personal psychotherapy he has had. In order to do psychotherapy, however, the therapist must be sufficiently free from neurosis so that his own personal problems do not divert the relationship from therapeutic goals.

Q. Will personal psychotherapy or psychoanalysis guarantee good functioning on the part of an adequately trained therapist?

A. In most instances it will. However, serious personality difficulties may not be resolved to a point where the individual will be able to function as a therapist, although he might work satisfactorily in some other field. In other words, where his ego has been so damaged through a combination of constitutional predisposition and traumatic life experiences, he may not, even with extensive psychotherapeutic help, be able to achieve that kind of personality flexibility, objectivity, sensitivity and empathy that are prerequisite for functioning as a psychotherapist.

Q. Why should not psychotherapy or psychoanalysis be able to resolve the neurotic problems of the psychotherapist, since he actually is not as sick as most patients and should benefit greatly from psychotherapeutic help?

A. The motivation to do psychotherapy, which is what inspires many therapists to seek personal therapy, may not be sufficient to enable the therapist to endure and to work through the anxieties underlying his character distortions. For instance, the individual may, prior to his determination to become a therapist, have been functioning in a more or less detached manner, removing himself from disturbing interpersonal situations periodically when these had become too difficult for him to handle. Under ordinary circumstances, and in average relationships, he would be able to function quite effectively with this kind of a defensive attitude. However, his detachment may seriously affect his capacity to operate in a therapeutic interpersonal relationship, in which he will constantly be brought into contact with critically disturbed people who will seek to extract from him responses he may be unable to give. A tremendous amount of personal psychotherapeutic work may be required before the therapist will be able to give up his detachment as an interpersonal defense. However, where he does not have sufficient anxiety to incite him to seek new modes of adjustment, he may not have the incentive to tolerate the great amount of work and suffering that will be involved in effecting a reconstructive change in his own personality. Consequently, in his personal therapy, he will keep warding off the deepest character change, and he may go through his total treatment without significant modification of his detachment. The fact that many therapists have exposed themselves to extensive personal therapy or psychoanalysis, and have emerged from it without any basic character changes, is no indictment of psychotherapy. Rather, it is an indication of how difficult it is to treat certain kinds of emotional disturbance without adequate motivation. In other words, the desire to become a psychotherapist is not in itself sufficient motivation to promote deep character change.

Q. What can the therapist do whose personality problems interfere with his executing good psychotherapy even after he has gotten extensive personal therapy and supervision?

A. If a qualified supervisor finds that the therapist's problems are interfering with his therapeutic effectiveness, the therapist may be advised to seek further personal psychotherapy. Should no change occur, it may be necessary for the therapist completely to give up psychotherapy as a career. He should not regard this as a personal defeat or as a sign of devaluated status, since he will probably be able to function very effectively in another role. For example, a psychiatrist may decide to do diagnostic, institutional, or other kinds of work that do not bring him into an intimate therapeutic relationship with patients. A caseworker can confine his activities to an agency organized around other areas than therapeutic services. A psychologist can restrict his functions to diagnostic testing, research, vocational guidance and counseling.

Q. Don't you believe that every therapist should know the principles of preventive mental health in addition to knowing how to do psychotherapy?

A. Mental health needs are only partially served by an exclusive program of psychotherapy. This is because the impact of emotional problems on the lives of people so often reflect themselves in disturbances in work, family, marital, interpersonal and social relations without causing collapse in adaptation characteristic of neuroses. The providing of help for these pre-clinical problems requires an ability to consult with, and to supervise community workers and professionals like social workers, teachers, nurses, physicians, psychologists, correctional workers and ministers, who are unable to handle such problems alone. It is advisable that every therapist be acquainted with the principles of preventive mental health and know how to communicate himself to community agencies and the ancillary professions.

53

Recording in Psychotherapy

SATISFACTORY RECORDING IS CONDUCIVE TO GOOD PSYCHOTHERAPY. It acts as a kind of discipline to the beginning therapist. It is helpful even to experienced therapists, facilitating the following of the progress of a case, and helping in the rendering of a report. It is indispensible for purposes of research.

Except in those clinics where an ample budget provides dictating facilities and secretarial services, records of patients receiving psychotherapy are apt to be pitifully sparse. To some extent this is due to the absence of an organized routine recording system. Additionally, note-taking during the treatment session is distracting to the therapist and annoying to some patients. Of utmost value, therefore, would be a recording system that is both simple to follow and not too disturbing to the patient.

Most patients expect that some kind of record will be kept. They usually accept note-taking during the initial interview, and do not object to occasional notes being written during later sessions. Where objections are voiced, these may be dealt with by an explanation to the effect that the keeping of a record is helpful in following the progress of the patient. If fear is expressed that confidential material may be read by another person, the patient may be informed that under no circumstances will the record be released, nor any information divulged, even to the patient's family physician, unless the patient gives written permission for this.

The case record should minimally contain the following data: (1) Statistical data sheet, (2) Initial interview, (3) Daily progress notes, (4) Monthly progress notes, (5) Terminal note, (6) Summary, and (7) Follow-up note.

1. Statistical Data

Basic statistical data include the following:

a. Patient's name
b. Address, home and business telephone
c. Age
d. Sex
e. Marital status, how long married, previous marriages, ages and sex of children
f. Age and occupation of mate
g. Education

    h. Occupation, salary, sources of income if unemployed
    i. Military record
    j. Referral source

This data may be entered on a separate sheet or on a form (see Appendix A, page 809), or the first sheet of the initial interview form (see Appendix C, page 812). A more complete statistical form, which is useful in clinics, is illustrated in Appendix B, page 810.

Sometimes the patient may be asked to fill out certain questionnaires to help get statistical data without taking up too much of the therapist's time. Short forms are included under Appendix D, page 816, which is a Personal Data Sheet, and Appendix E, page 818, which is a Family Data Sheet. In using these forms, the Personal Data Sheet is given to the patient to fill out immediately prior to the initial interview. The Family Data Sheet is filled out after the therapist has accepted the patient for treatment.

2. Initial Interview

The data to be included in the recording of the initial interview are the following:

    a. Chief complaint
    b. History and development of complaint
    c. Other symptoms and clinical findings
    d. Patient's attitudes toward his family
    e. Previous emotional upsets
    f. Previous treatment
    g. Estimate of existing insight and motivation
    h. Tentative diagnosis
    i. Tentative dynamics
    j. Disposition of the case

A convenient initial interview form is included under Appendix C, page 812, the first sheet of which is for statistical data.

3. Daily Progress Notes

At the end of each session, the date and a brief note, which may consist of no more than one sentence, should be entered on a progress note sheet. This should contain the dominant theme of the session. Other entries may be:

    a. Present state of symptoms or complaints (absent, improved, the same, worse)
    b. How the patient feels (anxious, placid, depressed, happy)
    c. Important life situations and developments since last visit and how they were handled
    d. Content of the session

    e. Significant transference and resistance reactions
    f. Dreams

Since the wording of the patient's dreams is important, it is best to write dreams down during the session while they are related by the patient.

Appendix F, page 819, is a convenient form for progress notes.

4. Monthly Progress Notes

A summarizing monthly progress note is of value in pulling together the events of the month. This may be a succinct recapitulation of what has been going on in treatment. In clinic set-ups where supervision of the total case-load is essential, a monthly progress summary, such as illustrated under Appendix G, page 819, which is routinely reviewed by the supervisor, may make for a more efficient kind of reporting.

5. Terminal Note

A terminal note is important containing the following:

    a. Date of initial interview
    b. Date of terminal interview
    c. Reason for termination
    d. Condition at discharge (recovered, markedly improved, moderately improved, slightly improved, unimproved, worse)
    e. Areas of improvement (symptoms, adjustment to environment, physical functions, relations with people)
    f. Patient's attitude toward therapist at discharge
    g. Recommendations to patient
    h. Diagnosis

A terminal note form will be found under Appendix H, page 821.

6. Summary

The summary should contain the following information:

    a. Chief complaint (in patient's own words)
    b. History and development of complaint (date of onset, circumstances under which complaint developed, progression from the onset to the time of the initial interview)
    c. Other complaints and symptoms (physical, emotional, psychic and behavior symptoms other than those of the complaint factor)
    d. Medical, surgical, and, in women, gynecologic history
    e. Environmental disturbances at onset of therapy (economic, work, housing, neighborhood and family difficulties)

    f. Relationship difficulties at onset of therapy (disturbances in relationships with people, attitudes toward the world, toward authority and toward the self)

    g. Hereditary, constitutional and early developmental influences (significant physical and psychiatric disorders in patient's family, socioeconomic status of family, important early traumatic experiences and relationships, neurotic traits in childhood and adolescence)

    h. Family data (mother, father, siblings, spouse, children—ages, state of health, personality adjustment, and patient's attitude toward each)

    i. Previous attacks of emotional illness (as a child and later). When did patient feel himself to be completely free from emotional illness?

    j. Initial interview (brief description of condition of patient at initial interview, including clinical findings)

    k. Level of insight and motivation at onset of therapy (How long ago did the patient feel that he needed treatment? For what? Awareness of emotional nature of problem. Willingness to accept psychotherapy.)

    l. Previous treatments (When did the patient first seek treatment? What treatment did he get? Any hospitalization?)

    m. Clinical examination (significant findings in physical, neurologic, psychiatric and psychologic examinations)

    n. Differential diagnosis (at time of initial interview)

    o. Estimate of prognosis (at time of initial interview)

    p. Psychodynamics and psychopathology

    q. Course of treatment:

        (1) Type of therapy employed, frequency, total number of sessions, response to therapist

        (2) Significant events during therapy, dynamics that were revealed, verbatim report of important dreams, nature of transference and resistance

        (3) Progress in therapy, insight acquired, translation of insight into action, change in symptoms, attitudes and relationships with people

    r. Condition on discharge (areas of improvement, remaining problems)

    s. Recommendations to patient

    t. Statistical classification

A summary form with spaces for the above items will be found under Appendix I, page 822.

7. Follow-up Note

A note on follow-up visits, or the inclusion of follow-up letters from patients, helps the therapist to evaluate the effectiveness of treatment. A follow-up letter may be mailed out one, two and five years after therapy. A form letter such as the following may be used:

"Dear _____:

In the past year I have wondered how things were progressing with you. Would you drop me a note telling me how you feel, and indicating any new developments. You may perhaps want to comment on your experience in treatment and how this was of help to you.

                                                                    Sincerely yours,

                                                                    _____

8. Case Folder

A manila folder is advisable to hold the case record of the patient. The name of the patient is written on the flap, and, if the patient is being treated in a clinic, the case number is also entered. Some therapists prefer a folder which has several pockets that may be used for correspondence in relationship to the patient, as well as for detailed notes. Under Appendix J, page 824, there is a folder the writer has found useful in private practice as well as in clinic practice. Printed on the front of an ordinary folder are spaces for entry of the date of each visit, payments made, and certain items that are pertinent to the treatment of the patient. It is a simple matter of only a few seconds to check on the total number of visits, the number of broken or cancelled appointments, the payments that have been made and the dates of completion of the statistical data sheet, initial interview, monthly progress notes, consultations (psychiatric, medical, psychologic and casework) if these were obtained, tests administered by the therapist, terminal note, summary and follow-up notes. There is space also for entry of supervisory sessions if these were obtained in relation to the patient. Printed on the back of the folder are lines for entry of dates for more visits if the space on the front of the folder is not sufficient.

9. Miscellaneous Enclosures

Included in the case record, in addition to the above data, are other notations and forms used by the therapist, such as psychologic test results, notes on medical and other consultations, detailed notes made by the therapist, written comments of the patient (see Appendix S, page 840), and correspondence in relation to the patient.

ELECTRICAL RECORDING

Recording the treatment session on wire, tape or plastic disc has become popular in recent years. Such recordings are valuable to the beginning therapist who may play certain sessions back to his supervisor to study how he functions in an interview situation. It is amazing to observe how rapidly a therapist can learn from listening to his own recordings, provided he has the capacity to be objective and he is not too defensive about his techniques. Recordings may sometimes be played back to a patient who has progressed in therapy, and who has forgotten how upset he was in the early stages of treatment. This is a most impressive demonstration to the patient of his progress, and it tends to evoke further insight.

From a practical point of view, it is impossible to record all of the treatment sessions of any single patient. Apart from the expense of the recording materials, and the problem of storage of the recordings, transcription of even a single recorded session is an item of considerable, and in many instances prohibitive, cost. Occasional recordings that are saved until they have served their purpose will, however, be found valuable. The best kind of recording apparatus is that which uses plastic tapes, and which operates continuously for the entire treatment session. Such a machine may be purchased at a reasonable price.

Where the therapist is not afraid of recording the session, he will experience relatively little difficulty in gaining the patient's permission and cooperation. The microphone is placed unobtrusively (it must not be concealed) midway between the patient and the therapist. When the patient enters the room (usually when recordings are to be made, it is best to introduce this fact to the patient at the initial interview) he may be approached in a way somewhat similar to this:

Th. Hello, I'm Dr. _____.

Pt. Hello.

Th. Won't you sit down in this chair so we can talk things over?

Pt. Yes, thank you.

Th. (*pointing to the tape recorder*) Don't mind this machine. Sometimes I record an important session during therapy. It saves me the need to write everything down, so I can pay attention better to what is said.

Pt. I see.

Th. (*smiling*) Does this scare you?

Pt. Oh, no, if it's useful, I've never been recorded.

Th. Of course, what is recorded is completely confidential between us, but if you object for any reason, we don't really have to record.

Pt. No, I don't mind.

Th. If, for any reason, it interferes in any way or bothers you, tell me and I'll turn it off.

Pt. All right, I really don't mind.

Th. All right then, would you like to tell me about your problem so we can decide the best thing to do for you?

The recorder may be turned on at this point, or, if it has been on, no further attention should be paid to it. During later sessions, it may be started prior to the patient's entering the room, so that the first comments may be recorded. If the recording is to be used for teaching purposes or transcribed for publication, it is important to remove all comments that may identify the patient. If, for any reason, the patient objects to the machine, it should immediately be turned off and not used again unless the patient's permission has been obtained.

Case History

The case history presented here illustrates many of the techniques described in previous chapters. The case was chosen, not for its dramatic interest—since there was nothing spectacular about the involved dynamics—but because it delineates within the nine sessions that comprised the total treatment period, important processes observed in the opening, middle and terminal phases of therapy. A five year follow-up was obtained to see how many of the gains in therapy continued.

The treatment sessions, which had been recorded on tape, were then typed and minor changes were made to conceal the identity of the patient. The original transcription was read at a seminar of psychiatrists in training, and interpolations were made by me during the reading. The seminar sessions were additionally recorded on plastic discs, and the recordings, which contained the treatment sessions as well as my comments, were transcribed and then minimally edited for purposes of inclusion in this chapter. The complete transcription follows:

In preparing this course I was somewhat in a dilemma as to the best kind of case material to present. The goals I had in mind were, first, to demonstrate the actual process of therapy from the first contact with the patient to the terminal interview; second, to illustrate the procedure of interviewing; and third, to try to give you an idea of the thinking that went into the total handling of the case. I felt I might do this by reading to you a full transcription of the tape recordings of a patient whom I had treated, interpolating comments as to what I believed was going on in the patient's mind, what conscious thoughts were in my mind, and the reasons I employed the methods I used.

To do this it was necessary to select a case that illustrated typical situations encountered in psychotherapy. Because I wanted to cover beginning, middle and terminal phases of treatment, it was essential to describe a patient who had been handled on a short-term basis. One should not interpret from this that all patients will respond to short-term measures as well as did the patient chosen. Even in this patient, while some personality changes occurred, many more would undoubtedly have eventuated had the patient remained longer in treatment. Nevertheless, for the purposes outlined, the case presented will suffice.

The type of treatment employed was insight therapy with reeducative goals. The problem for which therapy was sought was a "run-of-the-mill" type of situation often encountered in practice. I was happy that the psychopathologic material elicited in this case was not so startling as to excite concentration on psychodynamics. In teaching therapy there is so often a temptation to focus on the spectacular, to wallow so in symbolic representations of conflict and in the manifold defenses that the human mind employs in seeking surcease from turmoil, that one may fail to emphasize what is really important in treatment: the study of the relationship that develops between the patient and the therapist. I felt that the case I chose would permit us to explore such aspects as the conduct of an initial interview, the establishment of a working relationship with the patient, the techniques for arriving at the dynamics of a neurosis, the promotion of activity toward therapeutic change, and the termination of therapy.

In the course of my presentation I expect that you will, from time to time, be puzzled and perhaps even critical of some of the things I said and did. Psychotherapy, after all, is essentially a blend of the personality of the therapist and the method he has learned. Since no two personalities are exactly alike, the blend must always be different no matter how similar the training may have been. Your personalities will make you see things differently from the way I see them, and perhaps to emphasize and to focus on different areas. Your specific character traits will enable you to employ varying degrees of directiveness and non-directiveness in therapy, and, even, to some extent, to strive for divergent objectives. This need not disturb you, because your results will be good, provided you do not violate certain basic principles in therapy. As I present the material, I shall try to show you how I personally function within the bounds of these basic principles. But I do not expect that you will be able to accept or to follow my techniques precisely as I present them to you. These techniques are germaine to my own personality structure; all may not be germaine to yours. Indeed, it would be remarkable if you saw things exactly the same way as I see them. Yet you should be able to derive out of the material presented a method through which you can fulfill the basic principles of a good psychotherapeutic program. Appreciating your own personality assets and limitations, you may then be able to work out means by which you can reach satisfactory goals in therapy in ways that coordinate with your unique personality traits.

It may be proper at this time to say something about the interview process utilized in this case. The fact that I made certain responses and focused on special problems does not mean that they were the only responses that could have been offered the patient. Other comments and different areas of focus may have been chosen, and the therapeutic result would probably have turned out equally satisfactorily. But there were special reasons why I selected the responses I did; and I shall point out the reasons to you. Again, you may have seen things in another light, and, if you conducted yourself within the bounds of good therapeutic procedure, your personal selection of responses would probably have ensured success in treatment.

In going over the transcription, I can see certain things that I did, and that I failed to do, that I shall point out to you as mistakes. Mistakes are commonly made in the conduct of therapy; understandably they are more frequently perpetrated by inexperienced than by experienced therapists. You are bound to make many mistakes in the course of learning psychotherapy. These will probably wound your ego, but without mistakes you will probably be unable to develop into good therapists. Even experienced psychotherapists sometimes make mistakes. The process of treatment is so complex that one cannot always be right. As a matter of fact, mistakes need not hurt the patient nor interfere with the relationship, provided the therapist has a good feeling for the patient and does not violate the general principles of a good psychotherapeutic structure.

Now a word of warning. While case presentations such as this, and other didactic teaching aids, are important in learning psychotherapy, supervised clinical experience is indispensible. Without supervision, the person seeking to do psychotherapy is truly handicapped, because he will be unable to develop himself to his full potential. The psychotherapist is, after all, merely a human being, and he may react to his patients with an array of prejudices, likes and dislikes of which he may be partially or completely unaware. Even though he has been psychoanalyzed, he may be unable to control feelings which will interfere with the execution of sound therapeutic procedures. In supervision, the supervisor may be able to detect and to help the therapist to overcome blocks which strangle the therapist's effectiveness.

With this brief introduction I should like to tell you something about the patient in the case. I received a telephone call from a former patient who asked if I could see a friend of hers in consultation. Her friend, a retired business woman, had, during the past two years, become progressively more depressed, and in the past six months had retreated from her customary social contacts. An attractive widow, and comfortably situated financially, there was no objective reason why she should act in this manner. She had tried to convince her friend to seek therapy six months previously, but the reaction to this suggestion was a bad one. However, her friend had telephoned her this morning and had asked to be referred. My comment was that I would want to see her friend in consultation before I could decide whether I was the best person to treat her particular problem. If she would ask her friend to call me, I would be pleased to give her an appointment. That afternoon the patient telephoned me and I set up an appointment for an initial interview.

FIRST SESSION

The goals of this interview are: (1) to establish rapport with the patient, (2) to make a tentative diagnosis, (3) to get an idea of some of the involved psychodynamics, (4) to determine the extent of motivation for therapy, and to help motivate the patient if this is necessary, (5) to elicit and correct misconceptions about therapy, (6) to test the existing level of insight, (7) to determine if the therapist is capable, with his skills, of treating the patient, (8) to make the essential time and financial arrangements for therapy, (9) to refer the patient to another therapist if necessary, (10) to prepare the patient for psychologic testing if testing is required, and (11) to make any other disposition of the case that is necessary.

Because so much data must be collected, the therapist is inclined to be very much more active during the first interview than during later interviews.

*   *   *

(The patient enters the office with a depressed worried expression on her face. She is an attractive, well-groomed middle-aged woman.)

Th. Hello. I'm Dr. Wolberg. [*Most patients are frightened at the first session, anticipating censure or rejection. The mysteries of psychiatry both intrigue and terrify them. They expect to have their minds dissected by a cold, detached, scientific wizard. A friendly greeting may help put them at their ease.*]

Pt. How do you do. [*This conventional remark may conceal various feelings. In some patients there is deep despair and hopelessness. In others there is tension or panic related to expectations of injury. Some patients are quite resentful that they have been finally forced to seek help. By listening closely, the therapist may detect the feeling behind the content of the patient's verbalizations.*]

Th. Won't you sit here in this chair opposite me so we can talk things over? [*Sitting in a chair opposite the patient sets the stage for a more cooperative relationship. Interviewing from behind a desk in the traditional doctor-patient position helps maintain the authoritative station of the therapist which is best minimized in insight therapy.*]

Pt. Thank you. (*pause*) [*There are many reasons why the patient may pause here. She may be waiting for the therapist to ask her questions. She may be fearful, hostile or frustrated. These emotions may block her speech or ideation.*]

Th. Would you like to tell me something about your problem? [*This question is necessary only because the patient hesitates. Most patients are only too eager to talk about their problems.*]

Pt. Well, doctor. I don't know what's wrong, but there is something seriously the matter with me. I am upset, and depressed, and I have pains around my heart. I'm frightened that I have a heart condition. (*pause*) [*These symptoms indicate that the patient is experiencing adaptational collapse. Her defenses apparently are no longer capable of protecting her or of mediating a satisfactory adjustment. She is concerned with her symptoms, and she realizes that something is wrong.*]

Th. I see. (*pause*) Have you had your heart checked by your physician? [*Whether her heart complaint is organic, psychosomatic or hypochondriac is not known and this question attempts to probe further into this.*]

Pt. Yes, I have. He gave me an electrocardiograph.

Th. Uh huh. (*nodding*) [*non-verbal encouraging responses to signal the patient to keep on talking*]

Pt. He said that I had a heart condition. (*pause*) [*It seems probable to me that this patient will need much activity in interviewing to keep her talking. Most patients are only too willing to tell their story, and therefore few responses from the therapist will be required. Some patients, like this one, do not communicate well, and need constant responses by the therapist to keep them verbalizing.*]

Th. What was your reaction to this? [*This question was asked to determine the patient's reactions to a potentially serious condition.*]

Pt. I was upset, but he reassured me it wasn't serious. (*pause*)

Th. Do *you* feel that your heart condition is a serious one? [*Even though reassured by her physician, the patient may still worry about the seriousness of her heart condition. This question is to test her own evaluation of the condition.*]

Pt. No, I don't. I don't think about it as being serious. You know doctor, I don't feel very good. I don't feel strong. I don't . . . (*pause*) well, maybe it's nerves. [*She returns to her provocative symptoms and acknowledges at least a possibility of their being emotional in origin.*]

Th. Nerves? [*focusing on the word "nerves" to explore the depth of her insight*]

Pt. That's right. I have a good doctor and I trust him as far as my physical condition is concerned. (*pause*)

Th. But?

Pt. Well, doctor, I know that there's something wrong. And I don't know what it is. There is something wrong with me. I can't seem to get interested in anything.

Th. I see. (*nodding*)

Pt. I don't have any interests . . . of course, I have the theater, but I haven't been going. I've had no desire to go. I just don't feel like it. I've been going to bed every night about 9 o'clock 'cause I guess I think I'm sick and I should go to bed and rest. I mean, I mean I don't do anything that would be pleasant. I just sit home and read, and I can do those things, but that isn't the way to live. [*It would seem from this that her insight is not too extensive. A profound dissatisfaction with her symptoms is, however, apparent, which is good in the sense that it can provide strong motivation to get well.*]

Th. It must be very frustrating. [*communicating sympathy*]

Pt. I have a feeling that life makes no sense. I suppose I worry too much about things like my heart. [*This sounds as if she recognizes her worry about her heart as emotionally determined.*]

Th. And you get little real pleasure out of life. [*I feel that it would be of little avail to talk any more about her heart condition.*]

Pt. That's right. And I tell myself it's because of the heart, but I know it isn't a heart condition.

Th. I see. (*pause*) You're sure it's not a heart condition? [*testing her conviction*]

Pt. I haven't had a pain in two months. I used to get a pain across here, in my back. But that really doesn't bother me.

Th. I see. (*nodding*)

Pt. Yes. And I was talking to an old friend of mine. She's the one that recommended you. She said you helped her a lot and she was sure you could help me.

Th. You would really like to get rid of this trouble?

Pt. Doctor, there is nothing I wouldn't do to get rid of it. Life doesn't mean anything, you know, the way things are going. (*pause*)

Th. How did you come to the conclusion that it was your nerves that were at fault? [*again probing the extent of her insight*]

Pt. Well doctor, you know Mrs. Henshaw, and I'm very fond of her, and I've seen how she's come along so nicely that I thought that maybe I could get something out of it too. [*Mrs. Henshaw is the friend who referred her to me.*]

Th. Mm hmm. (*nodding*) [*encouraging her verbalizations along this line*]

Pt. I said to her, "You know, really I should do something for myself. This is awful what's happening to me, now." This was only last week, because, really, I said I don't do anything, but just sit at home. I don't want to see anyone, and I get into bed and can't wait to get into bed. I just look at my bed, and it looks so good that . . . but I guess, I don't know whether it's health or what it is doctor, whether it's mental or . . . I don't know. (*pause*)

Th. Well, let's see. You do seem to have a problem and perhaps I can help you with it. First, however, I should like to get a little more information, and then we'll talk things over and see what can be done. [*We seem to have reached a dead-end in her talking about her difficulties. Direct questioning seems necessary to gather essential information.*]

Pt. Anything that I can tell you, doctor, that will be of help, I wouldn't hesitate.

Th. Do you have any ideas about what is causing this trouble? [*more probings for insight*]

Pt. I really do not, except that I find that nothing really matters. It's so discouraging, you know. I don't feel as if I'm living. You know that . . . you know about that song "Old Man River?" Scared of living and afraid of dying? Well, that's it.

Th. Mm hmm. (*nodding*)

Pt. It goes back further than I think, because while I was in business my mind was occupied and I didn't think about myself so much. You know, we had a book business, my husband and I. We built it up into something very substantial. And then when he died I was left with the business. That was six years ago. (*pause*)

Th. I see. (*pause*) Perhaps if I ask you a few pointed questions, it may make it unnecessary to come back to preliminary things later on. [*To permit the patient to ramble on in this interview would result in a failure to obtain essential data.*]

Pt. All right, anything you say, doctor.

Th. How old are you? [*questioning for essential statistical data*]

Pt. Fifty.

Th. Your husband died six years ago you say?

Pt. Yes.

Th. How long were you married?

Pt. About twenty-three years.

Th. Any children?

Pt. No.

Th. And you were in the book business. When did you give that up?

Pt. About a year ago.

Th. Have you been doing any work since?

Pt. No, doctor, I've been retired and haven't wanted to do anything. I gave up my business because I felt I couldn't stand working any more.

Th. Now briefly, what other symptoms do you have besides those you told me about? [*The patient is questioned as to symptoms other than the complaint factor.*]

Pt. I don't know what you mean.

Th. Do you feel depressed?

Pt. Very much so—most of the time.

Th. Any panicky feelings that scare you?

Pt. (*pause*) No, not anything like that.

Th. Any fears?

Pt. No.

Th. Any thoughts that crowd into your mind that you can't get out of your mind?

Pt. I don't think so.

Th. How about compulsions? Do you feel compelled to do anything over and over?

Pt. No.

Th. What about headaches and dizziness?

Pt. I do get dizzy feelings from time to time.

Th. Any stomach trouble?

Pt. No.

Th. Any sexual problems?

Pt. Well . . . there just is no sex, and I don't seem to miss it.

Th. Upset by that?

Pt. I don't think so.

Th. Any tension?

Pt. I am tense most of the time.

Th. How do you sleep?

Pt. Very poorly. I average 4 to 5 hours of sleep a night.

Th. Any nightmares?

Pt. No.

Th. Do you dream a lot or a little? [*This question is better phrased this way rather than asking the patient if she ever dreams. Many patients will answer the latter in the negative who might respond positively to the former phrasing.*]

Pt. I rarely remember any dreams.

Th. Can you recall a dream that seems vivid in your mind? [*A therapist trained in dream interpretation can sometimes get the essential dynamics of the patient's problem from a vivid dream.*]

Pt. (*pause*) No, not a single one.

Th. How about drinking? I mean alcohol.

Pt. Just an occasional drink.

Th. How about sedatives?

Pt. I take none.

Th. Do you feel fatigued or exhausted?

Pt. A good deal of the time.

Th. In other words, the chief problems are this lack of energy, the exhaustion and depressed feelings. [*summarizing*]

Pt. Yes, if I could get rid of those, I would be happy.

Th. You have no financial worries? [*Information as to the financial status is important in planning a psychotherapeutic program the patient can afford.*]

Pt. I don't have to worry. I mean, of course, I can't go crazy, do a lot of stupid things with money, but I can get along nicely with what I got for the business. And there's another thing, I like to do things. If I can get things for someone else, I break my neck to go out and get it. For myself I just haven't any interest. I'd walk miles to find the right thing for a friend or any one that I'd want to do something for, but I haven't . . . I don't even want to go out and get anything for myself. I need a hat, and one night I should go out and buy a hat. This hat is about five years old. I should go out and buy a couple of hats. You see what I mean? [*Why the patient does not buy things for herself is of interest. Does she value herself minimally, does her guilt prevent her from getting nice things she can enjoy, or is she masochistically punishing herself?*]

Th. I believe I do. You find this very annoying? [*reflecting feeling*]

Pt. I do very much. It's about time I did do something for this trouble.

Th. To get back to the origin of this trouble, was there ever a period when you felt happy? [*This question is asked to determine whether the patient ever experienced a period of good adjustment, and whether the present complaint is an outgrowth of earlier maladjustment.*]

Pt. That's hard to say. I suppose there were times.

Th. How about your childhood? [*questioning to elicit family data*]

Pt. Well, that was bad. We had a tough time. My father died when I was five years of age.

Th. Do you remember him?

Pt. No, but I do remember going to live with my mother's cousin. I saw my mother though, occasionally. [*This remark is significant. A child wrested from its mother is one whose security mechanism is damaged and whose self-esteem is apt to be undermined.*]

Th. What sort of a person was she?

Pt. She was a sweet person. I was very close to her, a wonderful mother, and understanding. She lived with my sister and I before I was married, and with my husband and I after my marriage. She passed away five years ago. [*One wonders how she could both have been separated from and have been close to her mother. This should be explored later.*]

Th. I see.

Pt. My husband liked my mother too.

Th. What about your husband?

Pt. Well doctor, that's where a lot of my trouble was. He was a playboy type, and didn't pay enough attention to me. Well, it hurt, my pride was hurt, but then I thought he's probably seen so much of me, he's tired of me, you know. You work with someone all day long, and you have all the troubles together. You know, doctor, we've been through so much, through the depression, and through so many problems we had to work out. And I thought maybe he was just tired of the whole thing. I don't know whether I resented it or not. I don't know. [*This area is undoubtedly a painful one that should also be explored later.*]

Th. You were attached to him?

Pt. Well, I was crazy about him. And, of course, he was very good, he was very good to my mother, see, and I appreciated that. And after all, I got along with him.

Th. And then he passed away, and after that your mother died. Were you alone then?

Pt. Well, I had my sister, and I, we, have a great deal in common; and besides being a sister she's a good friend. I can talk to her.

Th. Do you see her?

Pt. Every week, she comes in to see me once a week and we have lunch at my home together and we visit. She stays a few hours and that's about all. I haven't anyone else. I mean not anyone else to confide in or go over anything else that I might feel.

Th. How old is your sister?

Pt. A few years older than I am.

Th. Any other children in the family?

Pt. Yes, an older brother who I don't see often.

Th. How do you get along with him?

Pt. Very well, but we don't see each other often.

Th. I see.

Pt. You see, doctor, while I was working I wasn't thinking about how bad things were, but I haven't regretted getting out of my business, doctor, not for one minute—that I haven't, because it was too much for me. (*pause*)

Th. It was too much? [*helping to maintain the flow of verbalizations*]

Pt. And I wasn't too happy in there because I was forcing myself, see. It was evening work too, and I'd find myself, oh so depressed going in there every night from my home, and then going home alone from there, and tired and everything, don't you know? And I have not regretted that for one minute in spite of the fact that I am very lonely. But I haven't regretted selling it, not once. But, I don't know, maybe I should get a little something to do. Get out into something different again. I don't know.

Th. You've been very lonesome. [*accenting her expressed feeling of lonesomeness*]

Pt. Yes, as far back as I can remember. You see, my husband was a playboy type, as I said, and he didn't pay enough attention to me. Up until he had his kidney condition he was a very strong fellow, but he got a condition, and he had that for eight years, and, of course, I worried about that, and I never knew but that when I'd come home that I'd, well, that he wouldn't be there. You know what I mean. His doctor told me he might pass away any time.

Th. You worried a great deal about him? [*accenting her expressed feeling of worry*]

Pt. Well, he was a wonderful man, but he was a playboy—a lot of fun for himself, and toward the end I really was neglected, in a sexual sense, and, and that went on a long time. [*Her emphasis of unhappiness in her relations with her husband points to one of her past conflictual concerns.*]

Th. How come you stuck to him for so long? Did you feel a loyalty to him?

Pt. Well, I did, and I felt that he needed me, doctor, that he was ill; and I felt that being with him I would probably see that he would take better care of himself than if I wasn't there. You know how it is, and I was married to him for a good many years by that time. [*One may ask himself if the patient is describing a character trait of abnegating herself for the benefit of others.*]

Th. You were in love with him? [*Since the patient is focusing on her husband, I decide to explore this relationship more completely.*]

Pt. Oh yes, definitely.

Th. How did his not paying attention to you affect you?

Pt. Well, I felt very hurt about it naturally, because we had been together so long, and we had worked so long together.

Th. And did you bring to his attention the fact that he paid no attention to you?

Pt. Oh, yes, of course I did.

Th. How did he react?

Pt. Well, he said that he felt that we were together too much, and that had something to do with it, because we worked together in the business, you see. (*pause*)

Th. And he tried to explain the fact that he was detaching himself from you because you had been together so much?

Pt. Well, that's the way he explained it, yes, and we took vacations separately, which isn't bad. That isn't anything, a lot of people do that.

Th. What about your own personal life? Had you become interested in anybody else?

Pt. No.

Th. During the period when you were sexually active with your husband, were there any sexual problems?

Pt. Perfectly normal. I enjoyed it.

Th. After he stopped having relations with you, didn't you feel that you wanted to continue?

Pt. Well, yes, I did doctor, but you see, it was just about that time, it was about in 1938 that I had had this operation, and that also did something to me.

Th. What operation was that?

Pt. A hysterectomy, removal of the womb because of fibroids.

Th. I see.

Pt. After that I felt I was out of things because it made me feel there was something lacking. I was ashamed of it, or something. [*another possible conflictual focus*]

Th. You were ashamed of this operation?

Pt. Yes, and then it took me a long time to recover from it. It's quite a shock, it's quite an operation. And, of course, that started during that time. From that time on, doctor, that we weren't . . . ah . . . that I, that we, ah weren't . . .

Th. Together?

Pt. It's just that I had been ill, you see. I was in the French Hospital for about five weeks with this thing. And then when I came home, things seemed changed for me, because my husband started withdrawing from me more than ever.

Th. There were no other people you could be close to as friends?

Pt. Yes, I'll tell you, doctor. In that business you meet a lot of people. It's all a part of the whole work. You know what I mean. And my having, well my working with my husband there, and all the help that had been with us for so many years, I mean, that I felt that there was a certain amount of dignity along with my position there. And I didn't at any time give anyone any encouragement, and even after I was a widow I just did what I should, and I don't know why I just thought it should be that way.

Th. You mean for six years you have been leading a solitary life?

Pt. Yes, isn't that awful?

Th. You feel that's pretty bad. [*To agree with the patient might substantiate her feelings that she is "awful" rather than she feels what she has done is "awful."*]

Pt. Well, I guess it's myself doctor. [*indulging in self-recriminations*]

Th. Do you think that you could be very attractive to men? [*This question is related to one aspect of her feelings about herself.*]

Pt. I don't know . . . (*pause*) I suppose if I had a child things would be different. [*Could this possibly be another source of conflict?*]

Th. Did you want children?

Pt. Yes, but I suppose I couldn't have them. I never used contraceptives, but just couldn't have them, and then, of course, after the operation it was impossible.

Th. And now there doesn't seem to be any person with whom you are close?

Pt. No.

Th. Is it possible that a block exists in you that prevents a relationship from starting? Is it possible that such a block made you more and more discouraged toward your getting intimate with any person? [*attempting to bring the patient to an awareness of a problem more fundamental than her isolation*]

Pt. Well, you see, now even in this present time, when I've so much time on my hands, time to think, which I didn't have before, that is to think about myself—I didn't have any time before to think about myself—now I can't imagine myself being married again, which would be the logical thing to think about now when I haven't any other responsibilities or problems that I had had in the past. I can't imagine it, that I would meet someone now, someone that I could care for, which would be a wonderful thing, but I just can't conceive it. I can't imagine how I could do it, doctor.

Th. You can't find within yourself any possibility of this?

Pt. I've met many men, but can't get interested.

Th. You've met a lot of men—probably many of them that would want to take you out?

Pt. Yes, yes.

Th. But could you warm up to them?

Pt. No, no. I didn't believe it, and I don't know what it was.

Th. What is it about a man that would appeal to you, what type of man particularly?

Pt. Someone that would be understanding and sympathetic, a nice person.

Th. A nice person. And haven't you met any such people?

Pt. No. Well, I don't know, it seems to me that . . . well, I know some married men—and I resent that sort of thing, and, I mean, that someone would think as little of you as to think that, you know, that you'd go out with them, and they were married.

Th. Primarily your desire is not to have a pure sexual affair.

Pt. No.

Th. Companionship and understanding.

Pt. Someone you know that you could be with. I'm absolutely alone, because my sister is married, my brother is married, and he has his daughters, and they all have their lives, and I understand that, and I don't expect them to give me their time, because they have their interests. But I should have mine too.

Th. You would like to be able to have your interests too.

Pt. Yes, yes.

Th. So it seems that you have been frustrated a good deal. You were a loving wife and were rejected. You wanted love and companionship and these were not forthcoming. You had your business on your mind to divert your attention; but after you gave that up all your frustrations piled up on you. And now nothing seems worth while. [*An attempt is made here to summarize as succinctly as possible the various points brought out by the patient.*]

Pt. That's it exactly, doctor; that's exactly how it is.

Th. The important thing is doing something about it.

Pt. If there is anything you can do to help me, doctor, I do need help. You can see that. [*The patient is obviously well motivated, and it will not be necessary to spend any time creating an incentive for therapy.*]

Th. Do you have any ideas about psychiatry or psychotherapy? [*This is to determine any misconceptions she may have about therapy.*]

Pt. No, nothing other than I've read in the papers, and what Mrs. Henshaw told me. I think it's a wonderful thing to be able to help these problems.

Th. Well, then we can get started. We will meet once weekly. How would Tuesdays at 4:30 p.m. suit you? [*Apparently the patient is quite naive about psychotherapy, but has no misconceptions about therapy. For a number of reasons I was unable to see her more frequently during the next few weeks. I somehow felt she would do well on a twice-a-week, or three-times-a-week basis; but I decided to observe her progress with one session weekly, and then to increase the visits if necessary. This was no arbitrary decision, but was conditioned by practical necessity.*]

Pt. That's fine, doctor.

Th. You say there is no financial problem?

Pt. No, not really.

Th. I should like to obtain a psychologic examination. Often this can be of help in expediting treatments. If you agree, my secretary will give you the name and address of a good psychologist.

Pt. Anything that you say will help, doctor. Do you think I can really be helped? [*The patient is so well motivated that it is unnecessary to go into a detailed explanation of why a psychologic test would be helpful.*]

Th. All people can be helped. The extent to which they can be helped, however, varies. The most important item is the desire for help, which enables a person to do what is necessary in the treatment process to get well. [*No false promises are given the patient with this explanation.*]

Pt. I know—I do want to do all I can because things are no good the way they are.

Th. All right, then, we will meet next week. One thing more, in the event you have any dreams, try to remember them and mention them to me next week. [*A better way to have approached the patient would have been to tell her that sometimes dreams reveal a story about one's fears and wishes that could be helpful, and that it might be important for her to try to remember any dreams she may have so that she can discuss them with me.*]

Pt. All right, doctor, I'll try.

Th. Good. So I'll see you next week. Goodbye.

Pt. Goodbye, doctor.

*   *   *

If, at the end of the first session, we attempt to see how many of the goals enumerated for the initial interview have been fulfilled, we would say: (1) rapport seemed to be satisfactorily established, (2) the tentative diagnosis is psychoneurotic depression engrafted on a personality disorder, (3) the involved psychodynamics were unclear, but a number of elements were suggested, namely, the possibility of having experienced shattered security and self-esteem due to maternal neglect, the need to submit herself to exploitation as evidenced in her relationship with her husband, the low estimation of herself along with self-neglect, and the blocking of her ability to relate to people, (4) she seemed well motivated for therapy, (5) ideas about psychotherapy were few, but no misconceptions were apparent, (6) the existing level of insight was minor, (7) I felt I could adequately treat the patient with my skills, (8) we were able to make agreeable time and financial arrangements, (9) no outside referral was necessary, and (10) I prepared the patient for psychological testing and my secretary gave her the address of the psychologist.

SECOND SESSION

Most patients, except perhaps those who have had psychiatric treatments in the past are somewhat bewildered at the techniques employed in psychotherapy. Reassured by the first interview, they question more openly the value of "mere talking." Since they expect some mysterious remedy or device, they are disappointed at the relative passivity of the therapist. It is, therefore, usually essential to clarify the therapeutic situation for the patient in order to give him an idea of why "talking things out" helps, and why his active participation is necessary. This we may have to do as soon as the patient begins to display any doubts about treatment.

A word about psychological testing may be helpful at this point. Projective testing is useful as an aid to diagnosis, and as a means of providing brief glimpses into dynamics. It is no substitute for a clinical appraisal. Its value, for the inexperienced psychotherapist, is to give him a feeling of confidence by providing him with a rough blueprint of the involved dynamics. This blueprint is usually revised and perhaps even discarded as the therapist gets deeper into the clinical material. As the therapist grows more experienced, he relies less and less on projective testing and more and more on his clinical judgment. But even a seasoned therapist can get something of value out of psychological testing, provided he does not go "overboard" on its virtues and ascribe to it properties it does not possess. Some clinical psychologists attempt to give the therapist too much data about the patient. It is difficult or impossible to determine such things as the prognosis or the best kind of therapy to employ from psychological tests alone, since the most crucial determining factor here is the therapist himself and how skillful he is in his conduct of therapy. Psychological tests cannot give one too accurate predictions about such factors. On the whole, if the tests are regarded as tentative, not absolute, and one's therapeutic spontaneity is not crippled by advance information, some of which may be inaccurate, psychological testing has a place in psychotherapy.

During the last session with our patient we arranged for psychological testing. The patient was referred to a clinical psychologist who did a Rorschach and Thematic Apperception Test which are appended at the end of this session. Of the two tests, the Thematic Apperception Test was the most useful. Some of the interpretations of the tester were not valid in terms of what happened in therapy—others were remarkably accurate.

*   *   *

Pt. Doctor, I saw the psychologist and she showed me some ink blots. [*The fact that the patient brings this matter up in her first sentence indicates some concern about the test or its meaning.*]

Th. Yes.

Pt. What does this show? [*Apparently she is concerned with its meaning. It would be fatal to read the test results to the patient. Whenever a patient insists on getting test results, a brief watered-down version indicating the good points revealed, and merely stating that there are certain problems that have to be substantiated by clinical findings, are all that should be told to the patient.*]

Th. The interpretation is a rather technical one and it would mean little to you at this point. As you know these tests are merely sign posts of problems and must be correlated with clinical observation.

Pt. Did it show anything? [*She is pressing for some answer.*]

Th. Yes, of course. It shows that you have many potentials that are being hindered by an emotional problem. That's what we're going to work at so that you can be unblocked.

Pt. I have not been feeling too well, doctor. I feel like staying in all the time. I am wondering if there is any medicine I can take. [*The fact that the patient wants medicine brings out her feeling that I should do something immediate and dramatic. She may be puzzled about how psychologic measures can be of help to her.*]

Th. It's natural that you want medicines. However, problems of this kind cannot be treated by medicines or injections. They require understanding through conversations together, such as we are having now. [*If the patient has already been taking medicines to no avail, this fact can be brought out. Yet the patient may believe a new, more powerful, medicine to be indicated.*]

Pt. But how can just talking help? [*My prediction seems to be borne out in this question.*]

Th. This question puzzles everybody when they are about to start psychotherapy. Certainly it sounds unusual that talk can remedy as powerful feelings of despair, hopelessness and fatigue as you have. But you know there are reasons why these symptoms exist in you. [*Some patients already have gone through the experience of talking at length with people about their problem to no avail. It is important to bring the patient to an understanding that talking about themselves to the therapist is different from the usual kind of conversations.*]

Pt. I know there must be, doctor, you know. It's been there so long.

Th. Do you have any idea what causes these feelings, what is actually behind these symptoms? [*focusing her attention on the fact that there are causes that underlie her symptoms*]

Pt. I have thought about it all week, doctor, and I see what you mean. I know my life was unsatisfactory, you know what I mean, doctor, with the business worries and the worrying about my husband and all. But that's all over now and I can't seem to be myself. [*Obviously the patient has no idea about the sources of her problem. Because she sees no reason for her symptoms, she is puzzled that they persist.*]

Th. This is where psychotherapy comes in—to help you understand the connection between your symptoms and basic causes for the symptoms. This is why talk is important. [*again attempting to bring out that there are causes, and that discovering these through psychotherapy will help her*]

Pt. I see what you mean, doctor. [*This is a cliché. One would justifiably doubt that she really can see what I mean at this point*]

Th. And once we really know what is behind your suffering you can do something constructive about yourself aimed at correcting the sources of your trouble. [*Some patients through reading get the idea that all that is required in psychotherapy is to find out what causes their trouble. Cure then will follow automatically. The statement I made tends to put responsibility on the patient to do something constructive about herself after the causes have been explored.*]

Pt. I would like to do this because I am so miserable. It's been so long since I last felt good at all. [*Her suffering will undoubtedly provide a good incentive to get well, if she can overcome her other resistances.*]

Th. Then it will be important for you to talk to me about your thoughts and your feelings and I will help you clarify what is going on. This will really help you a lot more than medicines. In fact, it's the only way. [*attempting to show her that she can do something positive about her problem in cooperating with me*]

Pt. I don't know what to talk about. Is there anything you want me to talk about? [*Apparently the patient believes she has told me all about herself and that there is nothing more she need tell me. Perhaps she is irritated that I haven't helped her with all the information she has already given me.*]

Th. Any problem that is immediately on your mind is what you might explore, particularly any feelings that are of concern to you. I will help you as you go along. [*I am provided here with an opportunity to structure the therapeutic situation for the patient, to show her how therapy might help her and how she can cooperate with me.*]

Pt. For instance, doctor, what?

Th. Well . . . for instance, you were just bothered about how talk might be of any help to you in mastering your symptoms, so you mentioned your feelings to me. Any other important thoughts or feelings would be topics of conversation.

Pt. Yes, I see what you mean, doctor. So if I can understand why I feel the way I do, everything will be all right? I would like you to tell me what is wrong, doctor, and I'll do anything you say. [*Obviously the patient has not integrated what I said about activity on her own part, she continues to request that I tell her what is wrong, which is what the traditional physician should do in her opinion.*]

Th. Now I'd like to tell you how I feel about this situation. First, I very much want to help you work this problem out. It seems a shame that a person as manifestly gifted as yourself should feel the way you do, where you retreat from practically everybody and everything. And I would like to work with you so that you can get well as soon as possible. [*Expressing sympathy in the attempt to consolidate the relationship. Actually, this is really how I feel.*]

Pt. I am very thankful to you for this.

Th. So that I would like to acquaint you with how we can best make progress in getting you well. [*again preparing her for a recital of how she can cooperate*]

Pt. Yes, I will do anything I can to help.

Th. First, as we begin to talk about your problems, things will become more obvious to me than to you. This is because I can be more objective than you. You live too close to your problems to be objective about them. Second, I'm trained to do psychotherapy and can see the connections better. Now the funny thing we have found is that a therapist's telling a person about what he observes about him does not really help him much in getting well. What really helps is for the person to figure things out for himself, with the therapist's help. This really helps. [*explaining why her role must be an active one*]

Pt. You can help me figure out why I don't feel well, and then things will get better? [*This is an encouraging comment and may indicate the beginnings of an intellectual grasp of her responsibilities.*]

Th. Yes. Because you live so close to your problems, it's difficult to see them for what they are. I might be able to tell you what the problems are very fast, but this wouldn't help you as much as my showing *you* why *you* aren't able to see what is going on in you, so that *you* then can really figure things out. It's like learning French. If I were your French teacher and did all the talking, you'd never learn *how* to talk French.

Pt. Well, that sounds reasonable.

Th. I know all this is a little difficult to understand, but we will clarify matters as we go along.

Pt. You know, doctor, I want to do everything I can, but I don't know how to go about it. You asked me to remember my dreams, but I don't dream much. Sorry to disappoint you. [*Perhaps the patient felt I expected her to dream, and if she didn't dream it meant she was a bad girl who didn't cooperate.*]

Th. You felt that you ought to have dreamt?

Pt. Well, I thought you mentioned that dreams would help.

Th. I see . . . Yes, I did mention that.

Pt. I didn't have them. Does it really have something to do with all of this? [*Not having read anything on the subject, it must have puzzled the patient to have me mention the fact that dreams were important.*]

Th. Well, let's look upon it this way. A person's mind is never absolutely inactive. One often has thoughts in sleep that are very significant, that one won't allow himself to think about when he's awake. The content of these thoughts will sometimes reveal what a person is worried about and what paralyzes him in his daily activity. Thoughts in sleep often take the form of dreams. Now one of the things that is bothering you a great deal is that you used to be very active and mingled with people, and now you do not. You have no idea what caused this change? [*The reason for the shift from dreams to a personal reference is that I later want to tell her that dreams may help tell us why she has retreated from people.*]

Pt. No, not really.

Th. Then it is possible that we might learn something from your exploring your feelings about this. And maybe if you do remember a dream or two, we may get a clue to what is behind this problem.

Pt. It's like a shock, the things that happened. I am not myself at all. I don't like to have people around. (*pause*)

Th. You don't like to have people around. [*repeating what the patient has said in an attempt to stimulate more verbalizations about this point*]

Pt. It's just the opposite to the way it's been. It's a mystery to me. (*pause*) [*Apparently the patient feels blocked in knowing how she can pursue this trend.*]

Th. There's a mystery to it for you that we will try to work out together.

Pt. But I don't know what I'm supposed to do. [*She again expresses her helplessness here. I will have to explain more fully, by giving her an example, of how one works in psychotherapy.*]

Th. Let me give you an example. A young woman I treated came to see me because of unhappiness in marriage. She was on the verge of divorce. It turned out that this was her third marriage, the first two terminating in divorce because she was so unhappy with her husbands. After her second divorce, she got into three or four affairs, and each affair ended with her dismissing the man. She finally married the third time, and the marriage was about to break up when she came to see me, at the insistence of her lawyer. "Well," she said, "this is awfully silly, I know that there's nothing wrong with me. I don't have anything wrong with my mind. I don't see why I should see a psychiatrist." I replied that psychiatric practice these days didn't confine itself to treating very severe mental problems, but also helped people with normal problems. She was quite certain, she answered, that there was nothing wrong with her; there was no reason in the world why anyone should feel that she had any real problems. She could not see that there was anything wrong in any of her relationships with men, except that they turned out to be the wrong kind of people for her. At the second session she reported a dream. She was about to be married. At the altar she was confronted with choosing one of two men. One of them was a small, wiry person; and the other was a tall, rather austere fellow. And she chose the tall austere man. When she got home, he turned out to be a Jack-the-Ripper character who went after her with an ax. She ran away in terror; but he caught her and started hacking her up. She awoke from her sleep in a cold sweat. She thought that was a rather silly dream, but I urged her to talk about the dream and particularly about her associations to the incidents and people in the dream. In her talk she revealed that the only type of man she really respected was one who had great qualities that she could admire and respect. She went on to associate that her father was an unusually wonderful person, even though her mother had a great deal of difficulty with him. Her father treated her mother badly, and on several occasions he had slapped her around. As she talked, she remembered that she had been quite terrified of her father as a child. This seemed to clear up certain doubts in her mind as to why she chose men who bore no resemblance to her father. She liked very passive, suave men who were no threat or challenge to her. But when she began to relate herself to a man like this, she realized that he didn't have the qualities she admired in a man. Then she developed a lot of contempt for his passivity and broke up the relationship. This is what happened in each marriage. Now the dream was the first clue as to what was going on.

Pt. But she didn't know, she didn't recognize it.

Th. She became aware of it by talking. Now, when she was aware of what she was doing to herself, when she became conscious that even her third marriage was to a man she felt no respect for, she was able then to reevaluate the whole situation. [*Examples such as this one, are invaluable in helping to structure the therapeutic situation.*]

Pt. And she's happy?

Th. And she's happy.

Pt. Well, that's wonderful that you could help her just like that.

Th. That's what we want to do with you. Now in your particular case, there are reasons why *you* suddenly got to a point in your life where you don't want to see people.

Pt. Well, I've probably had some disappointments. There's no question about that. I think my husband, John, was a disappointment to me. I mean the way I helped him and went along with him and gave up everything practically. And, of course, that's all right. I think I've benefitted by it. I mean, it's experience. Sometime maybe I'll . . . but it took a lot out of me. It was an awful hurt, you see. I didn't have any children. I took an interest in helping crippled children, and, of course, I don't feel too badly about that because again I feel that I've done something good. I mean, aside from the fact that I could have had a child that was normal and it would have been a nice thing for me, a companion and all, to enjoy—but it didn't happen. So, well, I'm taking that as it was given to me. There must be a reason, I guess. I don't know, I was happy helping crippled children, especially in institutions. They are happy in that little atmosphere over there. They live in their own little world, doctor, you know. They have no worries and, being protected that way, they aren't hurt. Normal children hurt little children, you know, that aren't up, and being able to be as alert as they are. And these little children are protected. So, I mean, that really doesn't hurt me too much. I feel badly about it, but I don't think that has anything to do with it, with what's happened to me, you know. [*The patient is unblocked to some extent. The meaning of her interest in crippled children is not clear.*]

Th. There are other things? [*attempting to get her to explore things more thoroughly*]

Pt. It goes further. (*pause*)

Th. It goes further? It involves your own feelings about yourself? [*I am not sure why I introduced the last statement. Perhaps I had a hunch at the time that this area was important.*]

Pt. Yes, and people. (*pause*)

Th. And people? [*repetition of the last word in the form of a question to maintain the flow of verbalizations*]

Pt. Now, I have some friends, and, of course, they're nice, but they aren't too interesting. They're people I met in business, and John liked them. They're along more on the sporting type, like he was, you see. And I could take a drink or two, but, I mean, it didn't interest me. It isn't everything with me to go out for an evening, and just see how much I can drink, or how drunk I can get. That doesn't mean anything to me. You see, I like to be with people, but I like to be with interesting people. Someone I . . . as you say . . . someone that you can respect. It goes back to the same thing too. Now, these friends of mine now are all carry-overs. They are friends of his that we both used to go out with. And those are the people that I see, and those are the only people that I know. Now the result of that is that when I go away for a winter vacation, I always go where they are, because I don't want to be alone. Now I feel that I want to go somewhere and be alone. Before I was afraid to go without anyone. Now this year I'm thinking differently. I'd like to get away from all that and be alone, you see. I don't know which is the worse of the two, doctor. [*One may ask whether she is bored with these persons specifically, or whether they are being used as an expression of general boredom with people. Is there some-*

thing that happens in her relationships with people that upsets her, and if so, is it with certain kinds of persons or with all people?]

Th. What type of people are they specifically?

Pt. Well, they are business people.

Th. They don't have similar interests to yours?

Pt. Well, I've been going a long time with these people, fifteen or twenty years. You know how it is, doctor. And I feel as if I'm neglecting them if I don't call them and say, "How are you?" You know how it is. Isn't it awful?

Th. It must be kind of tough for you. [*The patient may want to be blamed. I try to avoid expanding her guilt by sympathizing with her suffering.*]

Pt. It is. It really is. You see what I mean. And that's about all there is to it.

Th. Do you think you need a few new interests?

Pt. Well, there's no question about this.

Th. Have you ever done anything—hobbies, art, anything?

Pt. No, all I've ever done, as I've told you, is work at our book business. You see what I mean? And see that the books were in order and then get everything going. People start coming in at all times. You'd have to see that the girls were on the job and everything. And then readying for new customers again. Well, you know, doctor, you do that for twenty-two years, and then I finally got out of it because this thing began working on me that I have now. And I couldn't stand it any more. (*pause*)

Th. Apparently, it was more than you could stand.

Pt. That's why I got out of it. (*cries*)

Th. You suffered a great deal. (*conveying sympathy*)

Pt. You see, that's really why I got out. Because this was coming, and I was forcing myself. Every step that I took to go in there, doctor, was an effort. It was agony, just like a person who didn't know how to say a word, but was always forced to say something. It was the same thing. I was dragging myself, and I did that about two years. That's what I went through, and I was foolish to do it. Well, finally I got out of it and I think it was the best thing that ever happened. I think I might have cracked up very badly. (*pause*)

Th. There wasn't anything in it that was of real value to you, that you enjoyed?

Pt. Suddenly, it all . . . everything took the opposite. When people talked to me, I just could hardly stand it, you see. And everything, the whole picture was just the reverse of what it had been before. Before I loved it, and then it took that sudden turn. It all seems impossible. (*cries*)

Th. Look, we've got to work so you can get out of this thing. It may take a short time, or it may take a long time. Your vitality and creativeness seem to have been snowed under by this hopelessness. [*The patient seems to be in need of some reassurance and support and this was the intention behind these comments.*]

Pt. Whatever it is, the worst part is that I'm being forced to see these old friends who are bores, and who I don't want to see. What can I do? [*The thing that comes to my mind here is why she feels she is forced to see these old friends who are bores.*]

Th. It may be that you have to take a stand with some of your friends. [*I make the assumption here that she feels forced to see them.*]

Pt. Yes, I see, I could tell them that I'm busy. They are things in my past, like the business.

Th. You may feel toward them the same thing that you finally felt toward your business.

Pt. Yes, doctor, that's how I feel. I think a person needs to have something or do something with meaning. Regardless of what it is, you must have something with meaning. Money isn't everything, you know. If it was, I'd have stayed in business. (*pause*)

Th. Your business was a profitable one?

Pt. You see, if I had thought that that was everything to me, I would have stayed in there, because I had a wonderful thing. But I got so, that I knew that that wasn't the thing that I was interested in any more. That had no more interest for me. I knew that I was getting nothing out of life, and I realized that all I was doing was working and sleeping and eating. And there wasn't anything else. You see, so I mean that, doctor, money is not everything. I'd have traded everything for a nice life.

Th. And your life was not too satisfactory. [*focusing on what she seems to consider the basic problem of her life.*]

Pt. No, for several years before my husband died, he had no intercourse with me at all. You know how that is, doctor . . . leave you there, just leave you there, and, I mean, just completely ignore me, that way.

Th. How did you take that?

Pt. How did I take that? Well, as I say, he had a kidney condition, and he blamed it on that. And then, of course, I finally found out that he was running around, you see. And I knew that it really wasn't true that he was so sick that we couldn't do anything that way. So then, of course, I knew that it wasn't true, that he was lying to me about that. And, of course, that went on and on. You know, doctor, there's so many things. And then my sister was on my mind. I had to take care of her. You know, there was that responsibility, which was quite an expense. And it wasn't always all right. We had gone through that last depression in '29, you know, and it took a long time for us to get back again, you know. You have ups and downs. You know how that is, doctor. And it was all, you know, one of those things. And then, you know, that my mother lived with us. So there were some things that I had to think about. The same old thing again. You know, you can't always do what you want to do. And so that was that. And, of course, at that time I had a lot of opportunity to go out with others, but I didn't. Naturally, I wouldn't. [*The patient presents a picture here of having been exploited by others. The question is whether she was really exploited, whether she is complaining without adequate basis, or whether she insisted on being exploited out of some personal need.*]

Th. You felt you didn't want to be unfaithful?

Pt. Well, I wouldn't. Not only for him, but for myself, you see. You see what I mean?

Th. I believe I do.

Pt. I wasn't thinking of whether I was being honest about it for his sake, but just for my own sake, I wouldn't do that, you see. But it took an awful lot out of me, seeing that I was hurt, and I suffered surely. But then he passed away, and I had to take care of the business. (*pause*)

Th. Then you were left with the business. [*repetition of the last phrase to maintain the flow of verbalization*]

Pt. Then I was left with the whole thing which I knew how to take care of, fortunately. Because he, being ill so many years, I was really preparing for that, and didn't know it. I mean gradually taking more and more over, you see. (*pause*)

Th. So you absorbed yourself in business. [*summarizing*]

Pt. What I needed was affection, and understanding and love from people. [*This may be a focal conflict. The lack of affection and understanding may be something she brings on herself in some way.*]

Th. Which you didn't get. You couldn't find another man?

Pt. Well, you see, I suppose I should tell you that I did have an affair with someone for three years. It's just over now, and maybe it was my fault.

Th. How did it terminate? [*It may be important to explore this affair as a reflection of a general pattern.*]

Pt. Well, he's had another sweetheart for about twenty years. I always played second fiddle to her. He didn't tell me about it, and then I found out. It upset me, and I stopped seeing him. Things like that keep happening to me. [*Is her playing "second fiddle" a pattern in which she participates as part of her neurotic problem?*]

Th. That same pattern as with your husband?

Pt. Isn't it awful? And, of course, when we first started going around together, he said that he would absolutely get rid of this other woman, but he didn't. I mean it still exists. This girl works for him, you see. And in the capacity of a buyer. She's been with him; he's had her in business. It's one of those jumbled things. And then I just got fed up with it, see, doctor? (*pause*)

Th. It must have been very difficult.

Pt. Well, you see, he said that this affair with the girl didn't exist any more, you see.

Th. He was just telling you this?

Pt. I suppose so, because she's still around.

Th. And he had very little time for you?

Pt. I'll tell you why I never did see him over week-ends, and it sounds like the same old story. Saturday and Sunday he was always busy. He has three children. They're married, three daughters. And, well, I just got a little tired of the whole thing. I mean, it just didn't seem right, and I guess it wasn't. And I just sort of cooled off, you know, and when he called, I just didn't encourage him. He called again, he called a couple of times. And that was that. That's how it is. I haven't heard from him in three months. [*Is it possible that her difficulties with and her breaking off of her affair with this man precipitated her present serious depression?*]

Th. Do you miss him?

Pt. Well, there is a little . . . well, an interest.

Th. He hasn't pursued you?

Pt. No, he hasn't at all since, but I haven't given him any encouragement to call again.

Th. He hasn't shown any sort of an interest?

Pt. No, and if he was interested, he would call. [*Apparently the patient is still interested.*]

Th. How old a man is he?

Pt. About sixty-two, too old for me.

Th. What else was there about him?

Pt. He was always in a lot of trouble. He always had troubles and always brought them to me. He's involved a lot, and there's an ex-wife. He's divorced, and, oh, I get myself into the worst kinds of things. Just one of those things, just being lonesome, you see. You see, to get someone to pay a little attention to you, have an interest, go to the theater or dinner or something. But there wasn't anything to it. That isn't for me, doctor. You have too many troubles then. He's too involved. He has this girl, which is probably still going on. (*pause*)

Th. If he were a special person, perhaps you wouldn't give him up so easily. [*I test her desire here to continue seeing him.*]

Pt. Well, I feel this way, as you say, if he was interested, he would have tried to see me again, I think.

Th. And he only called you that once, you say.

Pt. Twice.

Th. Twice, and what did he say specifically?

Pt. Well, he was going to Europe, you see, and he said, "I'll call you before I leave," and that was supposed to be the next day, and he didn't call. (*pause*)

Th. And he didn't call.

Pt. And he hasn't called since he came back. So that's that. I'm not, I just . . . I wouldn't, just . . . (*pause*)

Th. He may come back . . .

Pt. Forget it. And even if he doesn't, it's probably the best thing.

Th. It may be hard to give him up. [*testing how much she wants him to pursue her*]

Pt. I can get somebody better than that. (*pause*)

Th. You feel perhaps that it is important for you to be discriminating with people you get mixed up with from now on? [*reflecting an attitude that may be behind her previous statements*]

Pt. Because they do something to me . . . You see, doctor, people do something to me. And I seem to go along in that pattern. Now, I know another girl that's with a doctor, and she isn't married to him. Isn't it funny, and I get involved in those kinds of pictures, and that isn't good and I know it isn't. You know what I mean, you can't respect yourself. (*pause*)

Th. Because it makes for complications that are destructive to you as a person? [*reflecting her feeling of being devalued in being involved with certain men*]

Pt. Yes. (*pause*)

Th. You just get to a point where you don't respect yourself any more, after a while. (*continuing to reflect her feeling devalued*)

Pt. You see what I mean. And I don't need that because, after all, I . . . ah . . . people respect me, and I should really get something, something for myself. Which I haven't been smart enough to, apparently. I don't know. I've missed a lot of opportunities on the way, you see. [*She expresses her feeling here of having been exploited by people.*]

Th. There must have been some reason for this. [*focusing on the motives behind what has been happening to her*]

Pt. You know, maybe I don't put enough of a value on myself, doctor. That's very possible, you see. I always bring myself down to the other person's level instead of trying to bring myself up to a better level, that is, something I could look up to. You know what I mean? Like I feel sorry for other people, you know, and I go along with them. And I find myself with them instead of others that would do me some good. Somehow I avoid the others. [*The patient here is verbalizing what may be insight, that is, a feeling that she is underestimating her value and that she is yielding to the impulse of feeling sorry for other people.*]

Th. What happens when you meet the other kind of people, those that you could look up to?

Pt. I am not interested. (*pause*)

Th. Not interested?

Pt. Why? Because I suppose they haven't all these troubles and complications. I seem to go for that for some reason. [*Does the patient have an awareness of a need to take care of helpless or disturbed people?*]

Th. In other words, you find that your interests are for getting involved with people who are in a lot of trouble, who need your help. And you get involved with them, and then you find that after a while that . . . [*attempting to consolidate insight if it exists*]

Pt. That it isn't any good, it's a nuisance, and then I'm where I started, only worse off, because I have my head filled with that other thing.

Th. So that the type of person who might be able to help you . . .

Pt. I'm not interested in them. [*Again this has the sound of some insight.*]

Th. Perhaps you feel that . . .

Pt. They're above me and . . . (*pause*)

Th. They're above you and that they might not accept you? [*This is merely a guess, and it is presented as a possible interpretation.*]

Pt. I really do, I really do. It's exactly like that. (*pause*) [*The patient apparently accepts the interpretation.*]

Th. Now let's investigate that. How far back does that go? [*If we are on the track of an important trend, it would be helpful to explore how far back it goes in her estimation.*]

Pt. Oh, I didn't have any childhood days, at all. I told you that I was five years old when my father died. My mother was left without anything at all. And she had a furnished-room house. That was the only way she knew how to make a living, in order to take care of us. And then there was, I don't know, some talk about . . . oh . . . I don't know, that the place wasn't right. She wasn't running it right. And we children were taken away from her for a short period. [*This must have been a painful period in her childhood.*]

Th. Oh, is that so, where were you taken?

Pt. Put into an asylum for a little while. Then my mother's cousin took me. I lived with her and she was married to a very nice man, he was in the avocado business. He had a ranch in California. And then my oldest brother was about twelve, and he was all right. And I lived with mother's cousin, oh, until I was about fourteen. [*Her account of her childhood is that of great insecurity. One wonders if she harbors resentment about it. We must ask if her insecure childhood could be linked with her feelings of self-devaluation. Our time is up at this point, which will be indicated in the next remark.*]

Th. All right. We meet again at the same time next week.

Pt. Thank you, doctor, I'll be here.

*   *   *

During this session a structuring of the therapeutic situation has enabled her to open up and to explore several painful areas of her life including that of her childhood. She brings out the inkling of a trend in which she feels exploited by people whom she feels forced to help.

PSYCHOLOGIC TEST INTERPRETATIONS

1. Rorschach Test. The record is that of an intelligent woman whose cognitive and conative processes at this stage are being distorted by her tremendous fear and apprehension. The intensity of her apprehension seems to be related to her inability to adequately suppress her hostility. She is constantly at war with herself and the external reality so that at certain points reality is misperceived and distorted on the basis of her struggle.

This is a woman who cannot conceive of relationships except in terms of aggression. The whole outer environment is a place of hostility—people are aggressive toward one another and, to her mind, this is the source of inter-action. She is sufficiently integrated to be able to doubt her own perception and interpretations, but cannot work out a more positive and constructive approach to living. When she does attempt this, she is most likely to end up with maso-chistic activity. There is some indication that her self-destructiveness is restrain-ing impulsive, aggressive acting-out, upon and in the environment.

This patient seems to function, generally, on the basis of fear, ensuring retreat and withdrawal, rather than on the basis of permitting any overt anxiety.

The record reveals much oral emphasis and suggests strivings to be nurtured, dependent and protected. At the same time (in consideration of what has been mentioned) she is likely to be highly resentful of such a position, since it would inevitably expose her marked aggressiveness, and she would very easily become panicked by the upsurge of hostile attitudes.

She cannot tolerate much external pressure or excitation and has to detach herself. When this occurs, her masochistic fantasies take over and she actually has no "place."

This is a woman who can experience shallow emotionality in her inter-personal relationships, more in the order of sentimentality than warmth and affection (except for explosive, highly immature and intense outbursts).

It is felt that she could not accept deep insight analysis of a probing nature, and will attempt to structure therapy herself on a guidance basis. The possibility of her dealing with aggressive impulses (on herself and towards others), by some indirect means, could be considered (art, needle work, etc.).

At the present time she is sufficiently integrated to be able to detach herself, but the possibility of released anxiety leading to a paranoid process should be considered.

2. Thematic Apperception Test. The record suggests a woman struggling with a deep feeling of inadequacy, isolation and dissatisfaction. She feels herself to be misunderstood and lacking in an understanding of others. Her con-fusion regarding the nature of relationships has led to an interpretation of the total environment as hostile and unsympathetic to her. Her expectation is to be hurt, deprived and maligned. This results in hostile and aggressive attitudes towards others—a constant struggle with environment and her inner impulses.

This woman appears to conceive of relationships in terms of aggression. That is, that the basis of interaction of people is hurting one another. She is sufficiently integrated to be able to doubt her perception; she has a close enough contact with reality for this doubt to occur; and when things do happen that impinge on her illusions and distortion, she can experience much anxiety. At such times she is likely to end up with highly masochistic activity. One gets the impression that self-destructive attitudes restrain acting-out aggressive im-pulses.

The record suggests a striving for nurture and dependence, as though she lives under a sense of loss and, burdened by life's vicissitudes, she seeks protection. However, she is the kind of person who would be highly resentful of a position of dependence; also, it would inevitably expose her aggressiveness and she would be panicked in such a situation. Her difficulties in relationships are marred, too, by her inability to integrate effective stimulae into an emotionally meaningful and rich experience. She tries not to become involved with situations that carry pressure or excitation. When she does, she struggles to detach herself, to remain on the periphery and to become evasive. She is likely to reveal emotional shallowness, to demonstrate much feeling in terms of sentimentality, rather than any depth toward or about people.

It appears as though one of her needs to be detached is in order to avert any open anxiety.

Some of the difficulties she is experiencing at this time seem to be around questions of age, with resentment and bitterness in regard to her present status. This appears to express itself in questions of sexuality, and some doubt and confusion regarding femininity.

It is rather doubtful whether this patient can accept deep insight therapy or analysis of a probing critical nature. She is more likely to structure therapy by herself on a supportive-guidance bases. The possibility of released anxiety leading to a paranoid process should be considered. On the whole, however, the record suggests a neurotic process with an hysteria syndrome.

THIRD SESSION

The structuring of the therapeutic situation during the last session might be expected to provoke certain reactions in the patient. She may respond by greater activity, or she may manifest further hopelessness or discouragement which will have to be worked through.

*   *   *

Pt. I had a dream, doctor.

Th. Good.

Pt. I had a dream. I am in a store buying presents, pocket books and purses, and I have them wrap them into nice little bundles. It is like I get them for . . . I mean . . . like I have to get them home; important like . . . almost as if my life depended on it. Then I am home and my husband and sister are there—waiting. They open up the presents and everything is gone—just empty boxes. I feel awful and my husband laughs at me. You know, doctor, I felt so awful in my sleep that I woke up crying. (*pause*) [*My own associations to this dream—tentative, of course—are that something valuable that she has to offer people close to her, is found to be without content. She feels ridiculed for her gesture and becomes upset. The fact that she awoke crying indicates the intense emotional feeling associated.*]

Th. Does the dream bring any thoughts to your mind?

Pt. Why no, doctor, should it? [*Either the patient is extremely naive or shows resistance to the dream's latent content.*]

Th. You may have certain ideas or associations to the different events or objects in the dream. For instance, what does buying presents in a store bring to your mind?

Pt. We . . . I like to buy presents and really do enjoy giving things.

Th. I see. (*pause*) What about this business of having to get the presents home, as if your life depended on it?

Pt. I don't know about that—that's funny, isn't it? (*pause*)

Th. Any associations to your husband and sister waiting?

Pt. Well . . . they are just waiting for me. (*pause*)

Th. Any feelings about this?

Pt. No. (*pause*)

Th. What about the rest of the dream?

Pt. Well, the last part makes me feel foolish, and as if I failed them. It's like I had been fooled, you see. Buying the presents and then having been given a raw deal.

Th. How do you feel about being given a raw deal?

Pt. Very upsetting. It makes you feel like you are a perfect fool.

Th. Did anything like this ever happen?

Pt. You mean like in the dream?

Th. Yes.

Pt. Why no, that is, I never bought anything and came home with an empty box.

Th. How about feeling like a perfect fool?

Pt. Why, yes. I felt that way a good part of my life. (*pause*)

Th. What other feelings do you have?

Pt. (*pause*) I am tired today, I suppose I get up too early. (*yawning*) [*There seems to be little point in pursuing the dream due to the resistance that is present. It is possible that her feeling tired may be a manifestation of resistance, and I decide to explore it.*]

Th. What time do you get up?

Pt. I get up about 8:30, and I fix my own breakfast. I used to have my girl come in—my maid—come in the morning at 8:30 to fix my breakfast, but I've changed that because I wanted to be alone in the mornings. And I have her come in now at eleven. I fix my own breakfast for myself now, so I'll have a little time alone again in the mornings instead of her being there. This girl that's been with me for twenty-two years, and a lovely girl, I can't even stand her. (*pause*)

Th. She irritates you? [*I decide to explore her feelings about her maid to see if any patterns are apparent.*]

Pt. I even resent her doctor. (*pause*) And she is a wonderful girl. (*pause*)

Th. She gets on your nerves?

Pt. Yes. (*pause*)

Th. What does she do that gets on your nerves?

Pt. Everything. (*pause*)

Th. Just irritating?

Pt. Yes, and I just hate myself for it, because she is a nice girl. (*pause*)

Th. Perhaps you're blaming yourself too much for this, because, after all, you have a problem that disturbs you very much. [*One of the worst blocks the patient can get into is to flagellate herself with her shortcomings. I attempt to point out that her difficulty is a problem, not a personal defect.*]

Pt. (*crying*) It's ridiculous for me to feel this way about people that have been good to me. I miss the nice girl when I don't even want to be around her. [*The patient does not pick up my statement and she continues to blame herself.*]

Th. You blame yourself for your feelings. (*pause*) It upsets you to feel irritated by the girl who actually has been nice to you.

Pt. Yes, I do.

Th. Well, there may be things she does that are very disturbing to you. [*In this comment there is an intent to get the patient to test reality; the opportunity is offered to her to project her difficulties if she wishes to do so.*]

Pt. I don't think so, doctor.

Th. Is there anything that she does that is unusual?

Pt. Oh no, I don't think so. It must be me. [*The patient continues to blame herself, although her recognition of her role may indicate some insight.*]

Th. All right then, we have to determine why your resentment piles up. [*stressing the sources of her feeling*]

Pt. Well, doctor, I don't know. I know that I have nice friends and I just haven't any patience with them. (*pause*)

Th. I see.

Pt. I don't get mad at them, but I lose my interest in them after I've been with them a little while, and . . . oh, I don't know . . . start criticizing them to myself, and there's no reason for it. They're the same as they've ever been. (*pause*)

Th. Is there any person with whom you now feel comfortable? [*This is asked to see what exceptions there may be to the patient's feelings about being critical of people.*]

Pt. No. (*long pause*)

Th. There isn't a single person with whom you feel comfortable?

Pt. No.

Th. You may, in coming to see me, perhaps, not feel comfortable with me either. [*probing for possible transference reactions*]

Pt. No, I think you're wonderful, doctor, I do. I like you very much. [*This may or may not be transference, or it may be a way of expressing her awareness that we have a good working relationship.*]

Th. Why do you like me, why do you think I'm wonderful? [*Inquiring into what "wonderful" means to her to test the extent of transference.*]

Pt. Why I think you're wonderful to be in the profession you're in, helping people.

Th. Look, I'm going to try to help you, but you may happen to get critical of me too sometime. After all, if you feel this toward other people, you're likely to feel it toward me. If you do, it would be helpful to mention this to me so we can see what it means. [*Giving her "permission" to express any irrational feelings she may have toward me as part of the therapeutic process.*]

Pt. No, I mean I think anyone who would do this work is very . . . must be very good and kind, to listen to all these things all day. And I imagine it must take a lot out of you. [*Her concern with what listening to patients does to me may be a projection of her own resentment and fatigue at helping people.*]

Th. Actually, this is my work and I enjoy doing it. And I am going to do what I can to help you solve *your* problem. This thing has got you by the throat, and it's sort of shaking you all over. Now, what I'd like to work out with you is the best approach to the handling of your problem.

Pt. Yes, so that I can enjoy being with people, which is the natural thing. (*pause*)

Th. Now what *we* have to understand is why these feelings of irritation with people occur.

Pt. Doctor, I just don't know why. All I know is that they come. Why should they come? [*The patient's curiosity is understandable, but she still may be trying to force me to give her the answers.*]

Th. Now that's a good question. You realize that they are not natural feelings and that they interfere with your happiness. They are nevertheless significant in that there is a reason for their existence. The reason may not be known to you now. You don't know why these feelings develop; they just creep up and overwhelm you, and you feel guilty about them. Now, what we're going to try to do is understand what these feelings mean and why they develop. [*I am trying to create motivation here to explore her feelings.*]

Pt. Well tell me, doctor, why is it that I don't do the things that I want to do? There's so many things even in my own home that I know that I should do, that I would be very much happier for doing. [*The patient is beginning to question certain things about herself, which is a good sign, but I get the feeling she still wants me to give her the reasons for her behavior.*]

Th. For instance?

Pt. Well there's, for instance, order in my home. I know that there are some things that I should take care of myself. No one can do that for me. I can't get myself to do these things. (*long pause*)

Th. You can't do them. [*restating*]

Pt. Well, why is that? [*apparently trying to force an answer out of me*]

Th. All right now, that's a very good question. [*throwing the question back at her*]

Pt. Well, what is it? [*She is still trying to make me act directive.*]

Th. I wish I could give you the answer right now, but it wouldn't do you any good if I presented you with an answer. We'll have to find out about what it is together. Let's find out what it is that makes you feel that there's nothing you can . . .

Pt. Do.

Th. Yes.

Pt. There isn't anything that I can do. I read a little article the other day about a person who did a great deal with just a little organized knowledge. It is worth so much more than someone that has a fund of knowledge but with no organization behind it. You see what I mean?

Th. You mean that's how you feel?

Pt. Well, I have a lot of ideas, but I can't put one of them across. I can't do a thing. I can't do anything or be well. Why is that? [*Again she tries to put me on the spot.*]

Th. If you really have a desire to get well, you will have the best chance of understanding what causes you to feel the way you do. [*What I am saying here is that if she really wants to overcome her suffering, she will have to figure out the answers for herself with my help.*]

Pt. I do want to get well. I do.

Th. There's no question in your mind about that?

Pt. I certainly do, because this isn't living. I'm willing to do anything to get well. [*If her incentive is strong enough, she will break through her block and start working actively on her problem.*]

Th. So you are willing to do what is absolutely necessary to bring yourself to a point where you can experience yourself as a different person, where you can really start living. [*implying that if the patient works at understanding herself she can achieve the objective of getting well*]

Pt. Yes, of course, of course. This isn't living—I mean it's nothing. You're here and you are not here. (*cries*)

Th. It must have been terribly difficult for you. [*expressing sympathy*]

Pt. Well, I want to be helped, be normal like other people, be able to enjoy life.

Th. This runs through your mind a good deal?

Pt. Yes.

Th. You've suffered terribly haven't you?

Pt. Oh terribly, for an awful long time. Always fighting with myself. There isn't anything that I want to do that I do. (*cries*)

Th. You feel almost as though you're completely defeated. [*reflecting possible feeling*]

Pt. Yes. It's all so futile. I mean, there isn't a thing that I make up my mind to do that I can fulfill. It's just as if I didn't have the, well, the mind or even anything else to do it with, doctor. It's a terrible thing, awful, awful. It's an awful thing. I get up in the morning and I think I'm going to have so much ambition today, and I'm going to take care of these things, one after the other. I have them laid out, and I say I'll do it this way. And I don't do it. Not a thing, not one of them. Isn't that awful, doctor?

Th. Why awful? You mean it's awful in the sense that you have the capacity?

Pt. And I can't do it. (*pause*) But the fact that I think of it doctor, and I have hands and I have legs and I'm breathing and living, and why can't I do it, if I think that I want to do it? [*Again she tries to force me to do something positive for her, or tell her something positive.*]

Th. If you have the desire to do it, I will help you figure out what is wrong. You act and feel almost as if you gave up life years ago, as if your whole life is over. You act almost as if you are as old as Methuselah, and at the end of your rope. (*long pause, using silence to stir up tension*) [*We seem to be having a contest here. She is trying to force me to do something active for her; I side-step this attempt by putting her on the spot to think things through for herself.*]

Pt. Well, I don't know what to do. (*pause*)

Th. There isn't anything?

Pt. Well, yes. You see there's a couple of things that I want to do, and I feel, well, now I'm going to do that, and then I don't care if I die. You know what I mean?

Th. Like what, for instance?

Pt. Well, there's a little girl that I've taken care of, and I want to put a little trust fund aside for her. She's a little paralytic. And I want to adopt her so that there won't be any trouble when I pass on, that she'll get this to help her to grow up. [*This may possibly be an opening wedge into a more unconscious focus of conflict.*]

Th. Who is the little girl?

Pt. A little orphan.

Th. A little orphan—and is she with you?

Pt. No, she's in a boarding school.

Th. In school?

Pt. Yes, for backward children who require special care.

Th. Where is this?

Pt. In Michigan.

Th. How long have you known her?

Pt. About twenty-seven years.

Th. Oh, she's a big girl.

Pt. About twenty-eight or so. You know how it is, they're like babies, I mean.

Th. I see.

Pt. It's partial paralysis, doctor, and she needs special care. (*pause*)

Th. Special care?

Pt. She's utterly dependent. (*pause*)

Th. What sort of a place is she in?

Pt. It's a private school. They have about, they take care of a small number of children. (*pause*)

Th. And you're paying for her.

Pt. Surely.

Th. How'd you get interested in that?

Pt. Well this is a long story doctor. You see I took an interest in the baby when she was an infant. I felt it was what I needed. It was after my divorce. I had been married to this man at sixteen, then two or three years later we separated. I was living in Detroit. Then I got divorced. Afterwards I met someone who got very much interested in me. It was his idea that I get this little girl from an orphanage. You see, he was married and he knew that he could never be to me . . . I mean, well, he thought I ought to have a child that I adopt, and be in the community, established like. [*Now we have opened up a pocket of material that must be very difficult for her to verbalize. One would speculate that the incidents to which she refers casually must create intense conflict and guilt.*]

Th. I see.

Pt. Give me a home environment. When I got the infant, she was about, she was only about four months old. Of course, I didn't know that she had this paralysis, you see.

Th. It wasn't apparent at first, it wasn't noticeable?

Pt. No, no doctor, not at four months.

Th. I see.

Pt. And I only found that out after I had had her about two years, you see, when the time came for her to talk and walk.

Th. You took care of her yourself when she was a baby?

Pt. Of course, myself. And then about two years later, I found out that she had this handicap, see, and along about that time I met John. And we were married. So, about when she was about five years old, we put her in this school. But we had never put a trust away for her, you see. That's one of the things that I want to do. And I can't seem to get around to it. And you know why?

Th. Why?

Pt. Because I'm afraid there might be a lot of embarrassing questions.

Th. What would be embarrassing?

Pt. But I should do it though doctor. [*She avoids my question.*]

Th. Well, maybe you can work out something so that you won't be embarrassed. [*I decide not to press her for an answer at this time.*]

Pt. That would be good. (*pause*)

Th. It means a good deal to you?

Pt. Yes, it does. Because I don't want her to be a public charge. I want her to be looked after, you know, and taken care of.

Th. Were you devoted to this child? [*Unlike most patients who are only too eager to talk, this patient must practically be forced to verbalize by much activity on the part of the interviewer. In this respect she is not typical, but from a teaching standpoint, presenting a case of a passive patient, showing how she is approached in interviewing, is probably advantageous.*]

Pt. Yes, she's a lovely girl. Her mentality is low though.

Th. Does she recognize you?

Pt. Oh yes, surely. (*pause*)

Th. She looks forward to seeing you?

Pt. Sure. (*pause*)

Th. She thinks that you're her mother?

Pt. Oh, yes, certainly, surely. (*pause*)

Th. You'd like to make security provision for her then?

Pt. Yes, I would. That would give me pleasure—I mean it's what I think I should do. (*pause*)

Th. I see. (*pause*) But the big problem is what is behind how you feel about yourself and your inability to do what you'd like. [*This is about as far as the patient seems to want to go in talking about her adopted child. I decide to focus again on the larger problem of how she feels about herself.*]

Pt. Yes, yes. I keep wondering about what has happened to me. It all seems funny, I mean. Because, when I was working—hard like—I could go on and on, could do a thousand things, and now I can hardly drag myself around. I want to do nothing and see nobody. (*pause*) Why is that? [*The patient resumes her effort to force me to give her the answers.*]

Th. There are reasons for it. [*Again I dodge this intent and throw the responsibility back to her.*]

Pt. I surely do not know why. I do feel ashamed of what has happened to me. I mean, doctor, that man I told you about, his having . . . I mean . . . not being frank with me. You see, I can't understand why I let this go on so. [*A great deal of guilt and resentment seem to lurk behind these remarks.*]

Th. Do you possibly resent what has happened? [*reflecting possible feeling*]

Pt. I . . . I . . . I feel that maybe nothing else . . . that is . . . I think maybe I expect him not to want to see me any more. (*pause*) I always felt like I wasn't wanted—just do, do, do for others. (*pause*) With John, I think I felt that I was being used and all that, you see. I never had . . . I mean things as they were, I never felt I was happy except with this middle man. [*The patient expresses again an idea that she is not wanted for herself, that she must do things for other people. It is possible that the patient, feeling little value in herself, believes she must do material things for people to be liked.*]

Th. With him you did feel a sense of happiness. [*I might better have focused on the matter of her feeling she had to do things constantly for other people.*]

Pt. Yes, yes, it was the only thing that I ever had, that meant something. Except, of course, I was in love with John, and he meant everything, until this thing happened, where he didn't . . . well, I mean where he paid no attention to me. (*pause*)

Th. I see. (*pause*)

Pt. So maybe what I feel now, hopeless like, doctor, is no mystery considering what I've been . . . what's happened to me, and my not feeling I am, I amount to anything, you see. [*Her verbalized comment that she feels hopeless because she amounts to nothing may be significant, in that it may be used in later interpretations. Of course, we will want to find out why she feels she amounts to nothing.*]

Th. You mean, except with the man you knew before you married John?

Pt. Yes, he was the one that suggested the little girl, so I could feel settled, and as if I had a place in the community.

Th. Uh huh.

Pt. So I got this little girl, and then it turned out the way it did. Things like that are always happening, I suppose, and I shouldn't regret it, because, after all, how do you know?

Th. Nevertheless, it must have been a blow to you.

Pt. It was, it was. And it made me feel guilty too, because when I married John, he just assumed it was my little girl. [*another guilt pocket opened*]

Th. You didn't tell him?

Pt. Why, no . . . well, I felt that it all would be very hard to explain, so I let him go on thinking that, you see what I mean? After all, there was no sense . . . Oh, it all seems terrible.

Th. You must have felt guilty about that. (*reflecting her guilt*)

Pt. I did, oh, I did. But the poor child. It was not her fault. She is so much better off in boarding school, away from, away from others, where she might be hurt.

Th. Perhaps you feel embarrassed and guilty about this whole situation? (*re-emphasizing her guilt feeling*)

Pt. Oh . . . I . . . I . . . I never told anybody about that before, doctor. And it hurts me when I think how things went. [*Suppression of past experiences and partial repression of her guilt probably have contributed to her emotional illness.*]

Th. Do you blame yourself? [*continuing to encourage her to explore this area*]

Pt. No, I did everything, everything. I didn't stop at expense or anything. She has the best, the poor thing. (*long pause*) The thing that bothers me is that I've always been so unhappy. There seems no way out.

Th. No way out?

Pt. With John, it was all right at first, but then he lost his interest, and I felt sorry for him and did everything I could, doctor, you see. It couldn't be helped. And I tried, but I felt it was all of no use. (*pause*) I kept thinking that with my first husband, you know, the one I married to get away from it all, it was nothing—there was nothing there. I tried and I gave, but there was nothing, nothing. (*pause*) [*again the theme that she gives, gives, gives, and there is no return*]

Th. Hmm. (*shaking head*) [*expressing sympathy*]

Pt. Yes, you see how it went, doctor, I never would have married him had it not been for what happened to me when I was little, you see. No home and being put away, I mean, and all that.

Th. I see.

Pt. And that was only part of it. (*pause*)

Th. You mean there was more?

Pt. Well, I've always been disappointed. Like that man I told you about who I went with after John died, who just . . . just . . . well, who didn't seem to think that my feelings shouldn't be hurt. (*cries*)

Th. So, as a child you were unhappy, and you married to get away from it; but you were still unhappy. Then you met the middle man, and you put everything into that relationship, but it ended. You took care of an orphan and that ended tragically for you, too. You married John and felt exploited and used. And with the last man, too, things ended by your feeling you got little out of it. That's quite a series of depriving incidents. [*summarizing the events the patient discussed to point out that they all add up to the same thing—her feeling deprived*]

Pt. Oh, that's the way it's been. (*cries*)

Th. No matter what you did and gave, it ended as if you had nothing to give. [*The tentative interpretation here is made largely from the cue in the dream that the packages she had to offer were empty. From her verbalizations, too, it would seem that she feels she has little to offer people within herself.*]

Pt. Yes, yes, it all seems so hopeless. [*Should the assumption be true that she has nothing to give, she would be justified in feeling hopeless.*]

Th. Particularly when you give, give, give, and nothing happens. [*implying indirectly that she gives materially to make up for a lack of substance within herself*]

Pt. I always enjoy doing things for people.

Th. I guess you do. (*pause*) [*This is said a little ironically.*]

Pt. Why, is that wrong, doctor? [*The patient picks up the irony from my tone.*]

Th. Why should it be wrong?

Pt. I don't know.

Th. Let me ask you this, do *you* enjoy having people do things for *you*?

Pt. Why, why, when it happens, doctor, it makes me want to cry. When it happens. [*The implication here seems to be that people do little or nothing for her.*]

Th. You mean it happens so rarely? [*reflecting how she may feel*]

Pt. Yes, rarely. (*pause*) It's more the other way. But, don't mistake me, doctor, I don't expect people to return favors. They seldom do anyways, I find. But I do enjoy giving, you know. I like to help people arrange things. Before I felt so terrible I helped a friend fix up her entire apartment. Went shopping for things, seeing that the draperies and things were all done. That's easy for me, you see, because we . . . I . . . being in business, you see, had to do these things all the time. I know about these things, like decorating. [*The positive virtues she finds in doing things for people may be linked to a need for self-exploitation, and to a desire to win the favors of others.*]

Th. I see.

Pt. I noticed, for instance, in your waiting room, doctor, and the landing, why, I can do many things there to help. I would be delighted if you wanted me to, doctor. [*This is the first real projection. She apparently would like to act-out her problem with me. To allow her to do this would foster her feeling exploited by me and her becoming resentful toward me. I will later use this episode to point out the active workings of her problem.*]

Th. Thank you very much. I do appreciate your offer to help, but maybe it's more important that we understand this need to help and to give. [*To allow her to decorate my waiting room would have been a fatal therapeutic mistake, probably involving her immediately in a transference neurosis.*]

Pt. I don't know what you mean, doctor.

Th. Do you think you have an impulse to do things that serves a purpose of some kind? (*pause*) [*Posing a basic question which is probably still far beyond her comprehension. Yet, it should set her thinking.*]

Pt. I don't know. It's all been that way, you see. (*pause*) With everyone . . . why do you think this is so, doctor? [*again trying to force me to give her the answers*]

Th. Why do you think it's so? [*throwing the question back at her*]

Pt. Can't you tell me? [*She persists.*]

Th. I'd really like to do this for you, but *my* doing it really wouldn't help *you.* If you think this thing through for yourself, it will make a tremendous difference. [*I also persist.*]

Pt. Yes, doctor, I see what you mean. (*laughing*) Well, I'd like to have *you* do it for me, but if you can't, you can't.

Th. It isn't that I don't want to help, you know, it's that . . .

Pt. (*laughing*) It will do me good if *I* do it. [*I finally seem to have made my point.*]

Th. (*laughing*) That's right.

Pt. All right, doctor.

*   *   *

During this session we engage in a struggle of her wanting me to be active and to give her the answers to her problems. I bring out the need for her own activity and participation in terms of her finding the answers for herself with my help. As tension accumulates in the interview, she comes out with suppressed and partially repressed material, with some catharsis. She attempts to act-out an impulse to be exploited in the transference, which I circumvent. She continues to try to force me into a directive role, and finally she becomes aware of her intent. At the end she seems to accept my structuring of the therapeutic situation. We seem to be entering into the middle phase of treatment.

FOURTH SESSION

During the following session the patient explores the dynamics of her problem with beginning insight. She may be considered in the middle phase of treatment.

*   *   *

Th. Hello.

Pt. (*laughing*) Well I'm feeling pretty good. I feel very quiet and the same.

Th. (*smiling*) What do you mean very quiet and the same?

Pt. (*still laughing*) Well, I haven't done anything.

Th. How about your own feeling?

Pt. Better, much better—lighter.

Th. Lighter?

Pt. I've been doing a little more around the house. I seem to be able to accomplish a little more anyway. I mean, I have a little more ambition for things that I didn't before, so I'm quite pleased about that.

Th. I see. (*nodding*)

Pt. I do think that you're helping me, so far.

Th. In what way?

Pt. In the first place, I've felt better. My mind has been a little more at ease. And I've been able to pass my time a little in the house, by doing things that I wasn't able to do before.

Th. Why do you think you are feeling better?

Pt. Well, I think talking to you and getting rid of these things that I've held in all these years, without ever having told them to anyone.

Th. Particularly what?

Pt. Well, I think my relationship with John. And I think my first marriage which, I mean, wasn't good. And the little bit of my childhood that I told you the other day. (*pause*)

Th. Mm hmm. (*nodding*) (*pause*) Perhaps there is more about your early childhood you'd like to talk about?

Pt. Well, I think I've really told you about all of it, doctor. I had very little schooling. I went through the lower grades, as I recall, and I went to work just as soon as I was able to. I mean there was a child law at that time. I think I went when I was about fifteen years old. And I had taken up a little business course that my cousin paid for, something like three months or something like that. I'd taken up typewriting and a little shorthand. Then I went to work doing that, and I think I worked for about two years. And, as I've said, then I was married. I was married when I was about sixteen or seventeen, something like that.

Th. I see.

Pt. I was able to support myself. Yes, and I mean I always found time to help the family too, you see.

Th. Uh huh. (*nodding*)

Pt. Well, I mean, well, for instance, my sister wasn't able to; she didn't seem to work. I did. And she wore my things that I was able to buy, and when I was working she wore my clothes, and that sort of thing. I mean, I helped her along that way. (*pause*)

Th. What was the difference in the ages between the two of you?

Pt. Well, she was four years older.

Th. Older? [*It seems unusual for her to have had to care for an older sister.*]

Pt. That's right. I'm the youngest.

Th. She seems to have been more passive than you. [*This comment is to stimulate her to discuss why she believes she had to take care of the sister.*]

Pt. Well, I don't know; well, probably because she had a few more advantages; she went to school longer than I did, and, I don't know, my mother seemed to favor her. Oh, I don't know. Maybe I just thought so. (*pause*) [*This may be a significant remark perhaps pointing to a feeling her mother did not value her sufficiently.*]

Th. Did your mother insist that you go out and work?

Pt. Well, doctor, my mother couldn't do anything for me. You see, as I told you, we were taken away from her. And then my cousin was taking care of me, you see. After she took me out of the asylum. And then I went to work. Naturally I felt that I should.

Th. Mm hmm.

Pt. I felt I had to do it. All my life.

Th. Mm hmm.

Pt. That's right. I felt I had to do things for people.

Th. Why?

Pt. I don't know. That's me, I guess.

Th. If you didn't do things for people, what then?

Pt. I . . . I . . . felt they wouldn't like me. (*long pause*)

Th. You always did things for people then?

Pt. Always, yes.

Th. Why?

Pt. I don't know. I always did things. I don't know why.

Th. Perhaps you felt that if you did things, people would like you. [*Interpretation reemphasizes statement patient has made.*]

Pt. Yes . . . Yes . . . that's so. [*Apparently she accepts this interpretation.*]

Th. Now it would seem then that the way you got approval and understanding and love and recognition was through the ability to demonstrate that you could take care of yourself and do things for others? [*elaborating on the interpretation*]

Pt. Of course.

Th. Did the same thing hold true after your marriage? Who did most of the giving? [*At this point I feel it might be fruitful to explore the theme of her being exploited.*]

Pt. Well, I think I was so happy to be married, you see, and I really was in love with John. I did do most of the giving. You see, John was sick and I felt I had to.

Th. What about your first marriage?

Pt. The first one, well, that was something to get away from, to get away from all that I had been through, and sort of to be free.

Th. Did your husband do anything for you?

Pt. No, no.

Th. You did most of the giving?

Pt. Yes.

Th. Now what about the boy friend you had after you divorced your first husband?

Pt. This man was very wonderful.

Th. Was he warm to you?

Pt. Yes, yes, and very kind, and a very wonderful person in every way.

Th. And what did he do for you?

Pt. Well, he really helped me. He was married; that I knew. He helped me. He suggested that I get established in the community. That's why I thought I would adopt a child, to give me a feeling I was established. (*pause*) [*The fact that the pattern of exploitation has one exception, at least, sounds like a hopeful sign. We must remember, however, that she was being exploited even here, since she was living with a married man who was using her for his own gratification.*]

Th. I see. (*pause*)

Pt. To feel a nicer life, surroundings, in every way, doctor. Do you see what I mean? I got into a nice little community, and people respected me, and then I was able to take my mother with me and get her away from the others, you see. [*The question that crosses my mind is whether she also allowed herself to be exploited by her mother.*]

Th. You felt you had to do something for your mother?

Pt. Well, I do that all the time.

Th. Why do you think you do that all the time?

Pt. Why (*pause*) that's the way I am.

Th. Are other people like this? [*challenging "the way she is"*]

Pt. Why, no. They expect *me* to do things. [*Undoubtedly the patient feels herself to be unique.*]

Th. Do you think *you* are made up differently than others in that *you* have to do things and they do not? [*again challenging her concept of uniqueness*]

Pt. Why, it's always been this way. I feel it's expected. (*pause*)

Th. If you don't do things that are expected, how do you feel? [*I am trying to get the patient to explore a painful area. I attempt to deal with her resistances to verbalizing by challenging her with questions.*]

Pt. Awful and guilty.

Th. So this is why you feel forced to do things?

Pt. (*pause*) I . . . I . . . (*pause*)

Th. Does this needing to do things for others go on all the time?

Pt. Why, of course.

Th. How about with me?

Pt. What do you mean?

Th. Remember last time when you asked me about my waiting room? You wanted to help me fix it all up, to do things for me. [*Nothing has as much impact on a patient as to point out a pattern happening in the relationship with the therapist.*]

Pt. Yes, yes, I remember. I would, too.

Th. Isn't this the same kind of pattern: your putting yourself out to do what you can for me?

Pt. Yes, I understand. (*pause*)

Th. So, whatever the reasons for it, you feel obliged to do things and put yourself out for other people.

Pt. But I've always done this, doctor. (*pause*) [*The patient seems to be resisting even acknowledging the abnormality of her pattern.*]

Th. You've always done this. With John, too?

Pt. Of course.

Th. All right then, the repetitive pattern of this thing seems to have worked out with John too. You were the understanding and giving wife. You had to make allowances for him.

Pt. I did.

Th. You had to make the adjustments. All right. Now, what do you think a pattern of this kind does, first, to your security, and, second, to your feelings about yourself?

Pt. Well, I did find out, doctor, that it didn't help me. With John, he didn't respect me for it.

Th. Uh huh.

Pt. Truly. I mean, you see, at that time I was so happy to be married, you see, and get a position, you know what I mean, to have a husband after all the rest of what happened to me, you see. And I kept living with him all the time because I kept thinking, had to think, he did so much for me. See what I mean?

Th. And did he do much for you?

Pt. Well . . . (*pause*) Yes and no.

Th. I see.

Pt. I kept giving, giving, giving. Like working in the place long hours because I wanted to help him. And then he felt as long as I could do it, he wouldn't. I mean, he was only having fun and I was always working. (*long pause*)

Th. You must have resented this. [*reflecting feeling*]

Pt. I never learn. I keep taking on things on myself all the time. Still get myself in the same messes over and over, no matter who I meet.

Th. No matter where you are and whom you meet the pattern repeats itself. [*restating*]

Pt. Well, I like to do it you see. [*This is an important statement. To acknowledge the values of a neurotic pattern is a sign of insight.*]

Th. You must then get some value out of what you are doing.

Pt. But I'm getting nothing for myself. [*She is not sure about the real value of her pattern.*]

Th. You're getting absolutely nothing for yourself?

Pt. No pleasure, no happiness, not even . . . I like to do things for people, don't misunderstand me, but this isn't compensating me enough within myself doctor, you see.

Th. No?

Pt. And I'm a very unhappy person.

Th. Then why do you have to put yourself out when you get little or nothing in return? (*pause*)

Pt. I guess I do it to be liked. What else do I need to do it for? I was just thinking why do I do it, why do I get into these messes with people. (*pause*)

Th. That's a very good question. Why?

Pt. I *must* have to do it—why, why? (*cries*)

Th. Why do you think?

Pt. I don't know. (*pause*)

Th. Maybe you feel people wouldn't like you unless you did. [*restating what she already has said*]

Pt. Unless I would do something.

Th. If this is so, how do you think this would make you feel?

Pt. Terrible, feeling always they won't like me. (*pause*)

Th. That they'd reject you. And, if this is so, isn't it possible that if you have to keep doing things to keep people liking you, you would either want to run away from the relationship or else continue to have to do things for the person over and over? [*interpreting more deeply*]

Pt. That's the whole thing. Now you see, in this last affair, this man I told you about, you see . . . well the last time we were out to dinner, I don't know, I don't know how he found out these things, but he said to me, "You were married twice." When he said that to me, I never wanted to see him again. He did call me a couple of times, but I just ran away from the whole thing, because the fact that he told me that, I figured that he must know an awful lot more, and I was afraid that he'd tell me more and hurt me, you see. Do you understand? Isn't it the truth?

Th. What do you think he'd know about you or say about you that is so bad?

Pt. Why, he's worse than I am, really. He has someone, and he was absolutely deceitful about the whole thing. (*pause*)

Th. But? (*pause*)

Pt. I feel *I'm* the bad one. Oh, yes, everything, everything bad. (*pause*)

Th. As if you've done something that is terrible?

Pt. I'm afraid to see him again for fear he has found out more about me that's bad, and hurt me by telling me. But that's silly because I haven't done anything. Yet I feel bad. (*pause*)

Th. You seem to be carrying around the feeling that you are no good, the feeling that there's something damaged about yourself.

Pt. Well, there was. I mean, really. (*pause*) Well, what I mean, according to the . . . well, that isn't the normal thing. I've been through so much and everything that . . . that . . . (*pause*)

Th. Like what?

Pt. All in all, I've had to struggle through the whole thing. (*pause*)

Th. You've had to struggle through the whole thing?

Pt. You know, I have absolutely no one to do anything for me, nobody. My mother was sweet, but she didn't know.

Th. So what does this have to do with *you* as a person?

Pt. But look at all that I've had to go through.

Th. You feel that because you had to go through a lot, and had no one to do anything for you, that you are a bad, damaged person?

Pt. It's something like that—like I went through what I went through because I'm bad. [*The thought crosses my mind that the patient may have felt her mother separated from her because she was a bad girl.*]

Th. What you are saying then is this: "Because I am a bad person, and always was bad, I had to go through all this. Because, if I were a good person, then I wouldn't have to go through all this."

Pt. It's terrible how I've had to do this and act as if it didn't matter. Now here I am fifty years old, and I feel as if I am a child, bad, bad; not as good as other people. (*cries*)

Th. Now what material evidences do you have that you are not as good as other people?

Pt. Well, when I was little and mother was away so much, I felt terrible. (*pause*) [*This remark may indicate a source of her feeling "bad."*]

Th. Perhaps you felt she was away because you were bad? Perhaps you felt that if you were good your mother would have spent more time with you?

Pt. I felt as if I were different, almost as if she didn't really like me. (*pause*)

Th. That must have been frightening to you.

Pt. It was. (*cries*) I felt that when anybody was good to me, I could cry, like I didn't deserve it. (*cries*)

Th. What other evidence do you have that you were not as good as other people?

Pt. Well, I didn't have the education.

Th. How does that jibe with the fact that you were able to build up and handle such a good business?

Pt. I know I am intelligent; that's what's so funny about it.

Th. So that what you know and what you feel are two different things. What else is there different about you now, that makes you feel as if you are bad?

Pt. Well, when I had this operation I felt this was because I was different. (*pause*) I know it's silly. (*pause*)

Th. Again the difference between how you think and how you feel. [*reemphasizing the disparity between thinking and feeling*]

Pt. I know my life isn't any worse than a lot of other people. They do worse than I have done.

Th. It is possible for you to find many things in your life that you don't like. All people do things about which they may have shame. You can catalogue all the bad things you have done and make testimony that sounds overwhelming, but when you compare your life to any other person's life, your sins will probably compare to theirs. So far, you haven't told me a thing that would justify your feeling the way you do. [*This reassurance is given the patient to try to counteract the extreme tension evoked by the material discussed up to this time.*]

Pt. I've told you all the important things in my life that I thought were important. [*The patient apparently grasps at this reassurance.*]

Th. There isn't any more?

Pt. I haven't done anything, doctor. I've never hurt anyone. I mean, an injury of any kind, you know; but it's myself that I injure, I guess. Like I crossed myself up with this man. (*pause*) Three and one-half years I went with him, imagine! And he hasn't called me up in three months. But he did call me twice and he . . . (*pause*)

Th. He did call you twice?

Pt. Yes, but after he asked me these questions, I felt things were changed.

Th. You resented the fact that he was prying into your life?

Pt. He was, apparently, wherever he found it out. Maybe someone that he met or some talk maybe around the business, I don't know. You never can tell.

Th. What do you think would be so bad if he knew the truth?

Pt. Then he would be disappointed in me.

Th. Why? What have you done that's so terrible?

Pt. Nothing, except that I didn't tell him everything about myself. I guess I kept a lot of things to myself. I never let anybody into my life . . . except you. [*This may be interpreted as evidence of a good working relationship.*]

Th. Uh huh. (*nodding*)

Pt. I didn't really think it was necessary. You understand, he didn't ask me to marry him or anything like that. You see.

Th. This secretiveness that you kept about yourself, never letting anybody in on your life, could that be a cover for a fear that you will be considered a terrible person?

Pt. Yes, that's it.

Th. But how terrible are you really?

Pt. It's only those things that I told you.

Th. You believe that they make you a terrible person?

Pt. I . . . I don't know.

Th. If you feel you are a terrible person then, you would have to act in a certain way with people, wouldn't you?

Pt. About the way I do now. I have to show them that I'm all right. (*pause*)

Th. In other words by doing what you do—being secretive, buying presents, giving people things, being nice to them—you cover up the fear that you will show yourself as being a terrible person. [*interpreting her defense mechanism*]

Pt. (*pause*) Well, I . . . (*pause*) Well, I find that I do start doing all kinds of things, and I am always fearful that they'll leave me. Like with this man, I kept it up for a long time, but I felt mad about how things were going. (*pause*)

Th. Mad?

Pt. Well, I sort of resented that with him; see, we'd only go out maybe once a week, you see.

Th. Uh huh.

Pt. Yes, and well, that's really the only affair I had, since John died. And so only once a week, and, as I say, I never used to see him over the week-ends, and, of course, that did something to me too. That gave me an inferiority complex, to think he didn't think enough of me to give me more of his time. You see what I mean?

Th. Mm hmm.

Pt. Well, I felt that at least I had someone interested in me, and that's something. You see what I mean? Someone to go to the theater with, even if it was someone that saw me only once a week, instead of nobody at all. Well, and it was something to look forward to, and that was that. But still I knew that it wasn't right. I knew that he wasn't treating me right. That it wasn't the right thing to do. Do you understand?

Th. You must have suffered a great deal because of this conflict.

Pt. Just going along and suffering, and not realizing it until I came to see you, never realizing how I *should* be, and am not. I mean, other people get some happiness out of life. I didn't get any, and I'm not getting any.

Th. Why do you think you aren't getting any happiness from life?

Pt. Because there is no one I can feel close to.

Th. Why do you think that is?

Pt. I'm afraid of being hurt.

Th. You're afraid of being hurt. Rejected?

Pt. That's right, and it takes a lot out of me, you see. When I've been with people, I never say anything or contribute anything to the conversation, as far as myself is concerned, because I'm very much more interested in what *they're* doing—do you know what I mean?—than to tell them anything about what I've been doing. What I do doesn't matter—I mean it's all the other people. With me it's everybody else and I just don't count.

Th. All right, now, there must have been a reason why you minimized yourself so much. Could it be that you just accepted the fact that you were a terrible person?

Pt. Well, certainly, well, I've told you things that I've never told, and never would have told, anyone else, honestly, because I would be ashamed.

Th. Because telling them such things would make them feel about you what you felt about yourself. [*interpreting her tendency toward secretiveness*]

Pt. Maybe that's why I did those things.

Th. Mm hmm.

Pt. Like put on a front, and act dumb and try to please.

Th. Mm hmm.

Pt. Exactly, you see, it's the same way if someone would ask me to go out. For instance, if a man would ask me to go out. It's my own fault that I don't go, because I think that I have to give something to him. Now I'm being very honest with you. Do you see what I mean?

Th. You mean you'd do anything *they* wanted to please them, and you'd feel that was not what *you* wanted to do?

Pt. Do you understand? I mean to sleep with them. If they take me out, I feel, well, why would they otherwise want to take me out? Do you understand? Doctor, that's a terrible thing, so I don't go out.

Th. Isn't that the same thing we've been talking about, that you feel the only reason they want you is so that you can do something for *them*, to give *them* something? [*relating what she has said to a general pattern*]

Pt. Well, that's the thing that hurt me with this other man. To see me just to go out once every week; I felt that that was all that he was interested in. And you know I'm not like that.

Th. If you're not like that what else could you have done?

Pt. Well, all right, what could I do about it?

Th. We could at first find out what this is all about. We're doing that now, and we see a pattern in your life that goes back as far as you can remember.

Pt. It's terrible. That's right.

Th. The same thing, that you feel that you can't be wanted for yourself.

Pt. Unless I could give something, or just please people. (*pause*) [*The patient seems to have achieved some insight.*]

Th. Unless you give something—money, time, your services—or unless you sleep with a man.

Pt. Isn't that terrible, doctor? Truly, I mean I'm not common; I haven't any of those things really in me.

Th. It's just that you feel forced to comply.

Pt. I shouldn't ever see any man unless he is worthy.

Th. Mm hmm.

Pt. Sure, then it would be worth while, you would get something out of it. (*pause*) I want to be respected for myself.

Th. Yes.

Pt. Well, I didn't give anything to this other man. He's very nicely situated, and I wouldn't do that because I . . . (*pause*)

Th. Because you . . .

Pt. Because I felt that he didn't respect me. I felt that he only went out with me once a week just for that, do you understand?

Th. Well, it's going to take a little time for you to think this thing through and see how you've got yourself in a kind of vicious cycle. You may be afraid to break out of that cycle. The next time you get into a situation with a person, you will be tempted to repeat the same pattern, to feel that you aren't liked for yourself, that you aren't going to be respected, that you will be found out for your past. It's going to be hard. [*emphasizing the compulsiveness of the neurotic pattern*]

Pt. I am ashamed of my past.

Th. What really is wrong with your past?

Pt. Well, I just felt it was bad.

Th. What particularly?

Pt. Just that people would think I was common and . . . to do that sort of thing. (*pause*)

Th. What sort of thing?

Pt. What I did. (*pause*)

Th. Which is what?

Pt. Well, having that other married man in between my marriages. [*This is a pocket of guilt that must torture the patient.*]

Th. I see.

Pt. And then the way John treated me, too, that hurt me terribly. And then this last thing that didn't turn out right.

Th. Let's take the thing about John. [*focusing on the situation with John to see how the repetitive pattern operates here*]

Pt. He ignored me.

Th. I see.

Pt. Well, doctor, it's not a nice thing to have it known your husband ignores you.

Th. Were you sure other people knew this?

Pt. Well . . . I thought they must. (*pause*) But I see what you mean, that I go about blaming myself for everything. (*pause*) [*Insight seems to be dawning on her.*]

Th. All right, what about this love affair between your marriages? [*again focusing to explore for a pattern*]

Pt. I felt very guilty about it because he was married.

Th. You had a need for affection and love and understanding. [*This reassuring interpretation is given to help counteract her guilt.*]

Pt. Yes, doctor, and he gave that to me.

Th. Do you have to be ashamed of such needs? Do you think such needs are abnormal?

Pt. You mean all people need this. I see what you mean, doctor, I see that.

Th. Now what about this last man, are you ashamed of what happened there? [*I continue to explore the pattern by focusing on her last affair.*]

Pt. I really couldn't go on with it because it took too much out of me.

Th. Couldn't you have been reaching for the same affection and understanding, and not really have got it with him?

Pt. He couldn't give it; he was too involved. I did everything I could.

Th. But the interesting thing is that you see that you haven't done anything unusual or really bad; yet you turn all of these incidents against yourself.

Pt. Then how can I, doctor, how can I rise above this thing, and get it out of my system, so to speak? How can I get this over?

Th. Well that's what our job is in therapy here. Our job is to get you out of this morass and for you to see if you are as terrible a person as you imagine, or whether you might be mistaken in some ways. [*It will be noted that whenever the patient asks for an answer, she is told that we will have to work the problem out between us.*]

Pt. I see.

Th. What do *you* think the answer is?

Pt. For me to convince myself that I just don't have to please everybody all the time.

Th. In other words, not have to give presents and practically stand on your head to convince people you amount to something.

Pt. (*laughing*) Really, isn't that awful, doctor? And, I mean, I did feel bad about it myself, I mean I did that. This is something I'm going to stop. All this nonsense. You see what I mean? [*Naturally it is too early for the patient to have integrated any insight; yet her verbalization of determination to change is encouraging.*]

Th. You mean you feel it's unnecessary to give, give, give, all the time?

Pt. I felt that the only thing I have to give them is something material. [*more indications of insight*]

Th. Material. How could you ever have a real friendship on this basis?

Pt. Oh, I don't know; it's my own fault. [*Self-recriminations emerge.*]

Th. It's your fault only because you felt there was nothing else for you to give. [*The session time is up, but since my next session is open, due to a cancellation, and because we are dealing with important material, I decide to go on.*]

Pt. I shouldn't do this any more. [*This determination is easier said than done, due to the habit patterns that must have been established.*]

Th. It's going to be very hard to give up the old patterns. You'll automatically find yourself reacting the same way. [*To warn the patient that her old patterns will persist even though she realizes their futility, is a wise move and helps prevent discouragement.*]

Pt. I may lose all my friends, but that's all right. They're no friends of mine, if they're that kind, where they expect me to give all the time and where they just don't take me for myself. [*The warning also serves to bolster the patient's determination to experiment with new ways of life.*]

Th. Uh huh.

Pt. (*laughing*) Isn't that awful doctor? People are funny, you know. Don't you think I'm terrible to be this way? [*more masochism*]

Th. Now you're tearing yourself down in front of me by saying what a terrible person you are. [*interpreting what she is doing*]

Pt. Of course not, doctor; I don't really mean that.

Th. Do you think you have the right to expect people to accept you for yourself, instead of for what you do for them? [*challenging her verbal determination to change her compulsive pattern*]

Pt. I do, sure. I lose all my own self-respect along with it, you see, when it's the other way. I only see that now, not before. Before, I thought it was the thing to do, not because I felt I had nothing else to give, but because I thought I wanted to help everyone, be nice to them in that way, you see. That goes all the way down the line with my family. (*pause*)

Th. Uh huh.

Pt. All the way down the line, you see. Gosh, I've given, I mean, I've given more to my family than, well, than I've ever had for myself really. And for myself, I hate to spend anything on me really, you know.

Th. Really?

Pt. Yes, really.

Th. Why?

Pt. Oh, I don't know. I'd rather do it for somebody else. That's one of those things.

Th. Do you think you should start spending money on yourself?

Pt. I should.

Th. And not for anybody else?

Pt. I should.

Th. Nobody else?

Pt. Well, you see, this man that I was going around with for three years, he used to send me things. He really was very nice that way to me. He was really the nicest that I've met so far. At least . . .

Th. At least he gave you *things*. That's something.

Pt. At least he did. That's something. But that isn't for me doctor, though.

Th. That isn't for you?

Pt. That man isn't for me.

Th. No?

Pt. He was too involved and he isn't for me. There's not the warmth. (*pause*) If he were the sort of a person that really loved me, he'd be a little bit more warm; he'd come around. (*pause*) [*Her protest is a little too vigorous, and points to a wish to resume the relationship. Apparently her break-up with this man was the precipitating factor in her present upset.*]

Th. But he didn't call you?

Pt. Well, he called me twice, I told you.

Th. Mm hmm.

Pt. And I didn't encourage him, that's it, you see.

Th. I see.

Pt. I mean, there's another thing again. That three and one-half years where I should have had really a wonderful time—all in all, I didn't. I suffered through it.

Th. You sat around waiting?

Pt. For him to call. You see what I mean?

Th. And you wonder why you got yourself in this mess?

Pt. Oh, now I see it, little by little as the dawn is coming.

Th. You stood in the dark for many years.

Pt. Yes, but it isn't good. That isn't good, doctor. I mean showing myself how much will-power I have; that isn't good for me, doctor. You don't want to live that way, challenging your own happiness. That's what I've been doing, you see. You understand? Never ever doing what I want to do, always doing what the other person wants to do, you see. And never giving in to a feeling, you understand, and that's a terrible thing. That isn't being strong. You're really killing yourself. You're killing everything that's in you. I only know that now that you've just . . . talking to you about these things. I never thought of it that way before. But I realize now just what it has done to me. It's almost inhuman really. And I don't want to be that way.

Th. You have a right not to.

Pt. I'm really a very unhappy person and have never been happy as far back as I can remember. (*pause*)

Th. If you begin to think into your whole life, things will begin taking shape. As you yourself say, this did not start just yesterday; your difficulty goes back much farther.

Pt. Well, you see, I really didn't have any love in the first place. All I can remember when I was five years old was all commotion. And then my mother was dispossessed from where she lived and all, and didn't have anything, I mean. That's the thing that stood out in my mind. Even the gas stove was taken out, you see, the little house and all. And then I remember going into this other place, and then we were all taken away, see, and that had a, oh, that made a tremendous hurt in me, you see. And I didn't have any childhood really. Like kids have friends and they come in and have a lot of fun and play after school, and all that. I didn't have any of that, see. So then my cousin was very kind. But there wasn't anything there, you see. She was married to this very old man, and it was a very funny relationship there too, you know. And I felt that I was just a relative, you know, and it wasn't my mother, it was my cousin and it was more or less pity that she did it for me. You see what I mean? So as soon as I was able to go out and work, I did. I didn't have any fun at all like other children, anything like other children have. You know how children are brought up in a home and have a lot of little parties and things, you know, doctor. It does something to you. So when that first man came along, I married him to get out of all this. But it didn't work. The one kindness, I mean warmth, that I felt was the man in between. [*The patient is exploring the genetic determinants of her devaluated self-esteem.*]

Th. Perhaps that's why he's so important to you.

Pt. It was the nicest experience, the nicest in my whole life. (*pause*)

Th. How did it terminate?

Pt. He died. Yes, and we were friends to the end. Before he died, I married John, and I didn't have anything more to do with him. He was happy that I was married, of course; he felt that that had been the thing he wanted to happen. He wanted for me to be established in the community. That's really what he had in mind.

Th. It was a good experience. [*attempting to alleviate her guilt*]

Pt. The best thing that's ever happened to me, you see.

Th. Why should you be ashamed of it, then?

Pt. Well, because I'd hidden it so long I feel doubts about it now that it's way in the past.

Th. Perhaps you've been ashamed too much for what has happened?

Pt. You're right; I have nothing to hide. I haven't killed anyone. I haven't hurt anyone.

Th. It was a good experience for you.

Pt. You know, that's true. Oh, it's really terrible, doctor, but that's the situation I'm in. I'm in a very bad way. [*The patient is beginning to realize that she has been ashamed of a relationship that had much meaning for her.*]

Th. Maybe you can begin breaking out of that situation—in little ways with different people.

Pt. Oh, how I'd like to do that.

Th. It may take a lot of courage. [*warning her of the hardships involved*]

Pt. But this, what I've been going through, is so bad. [*This indicates a realization that her patterns cause her much suffering.*]

Th. It might frighten you. [*more warnings*]

Pt. I couldn't be worse off. [*She again responds well.*]

Th. It's going to take time. [*additional cautions*]

Pt. Sure it will. You know what? Tonight I was invited to a big dinner, and these people invited me and I thought I would (*laughs*) send them a present, some nice bottles of Scotch. [*This may be a turning point in that the insight she has gained may be translated into action, at least in her mind.*]

Th. I see.

Pt. The idea occurred to me. (*laughs*)

Th. The idea occurred to you?

Pt. I won't send it. [*If she can follow through on this, and if she discovers that she is not rejected for her failure to give presents, it may begin to undermine her neurotic pattern.*]

Th. Think you can go through with it? [*challenging her determination*]

Pt. But I was going to, though, this afternoon. I mean, I was going to send it before I came here.

Th. Do you think you can go there without sending or bringing anything?

Pt. I think I can all right. Thanks for helping me, and do you think I'm going to be all right?

Th. Having the desire to get well is nine-tenths of the battle. But you mustn't be impatient. You're going to find that you will want to act the way you always have, even though you understand how destructive it is to you. [*again warning her of the possibility of a relapse*]

Pt. Yes, I know. But you do think I will be all right?

Th. You seem to have a doubt about it. [*To tell her that she will get well, which is what she wants to hear, would put me in an omniscient position. Actually I do not know that she will get well; all I know is that she has the best chance of getting well if she is active in therapy. I do not wish to discourage her, so I focus on the doubts that lurk behind her question.*]

Pt. Well, I've had this so long, It's a long time, isn't it doctor? However, I hope that I'm going to be able to get something out of living.

Th. You really want to, don't you?

Pt. Because this is, I mean, I've suffered, and it's been so hard for me.

Th. The important thing is to understand your patterns of living thoroughly, see how they cross you up, why they occurred and are still occurring, and then challenge them.

Pt. Well, I hope I can do this, doctor. Then I'll see you Monday at 11:40.

Th. That's right.

Pt. All right, thank you, 'bye, 'bye.

*   *   *

In this session the patient has arrived at several insights. She sees a pattern weaving through her life and connects it with what happened to her in her childhood.

She realizes the values of her neurotic patterns, but also appreciates their destructive effects. At the end of the session she challenges her need to pursue the pattern of her giving presents to be loved.

FIFTH SESSION

The patient here shows signs of utilizing her insight in the direction of change.

* * *

Pt. Doctor, I bought you a nice pencil. I noticed that you were looking for one the other day.

Th. Thank you. (*not accepting pencil*) But why did you get it? [*Could this be her "giving" pattern coming through again in our relationship?*]

Pt. I felt it would be nice to get it.

Th. All right now, why did you feel that way? Mind you, I appreciate the gesture, but, as you know, we have to inquire into everything that happens here.

Pt. 'Cause I wanted to help you. [*This would seem to corroborate my suspicion.*]

Th. (*laughing*) Isn't that the same thing you've always been doing, helping people, being nice and considerate?

Pt. (*laughing*) I suppose it is and I suppose I tell myself that's because *he* needs it. Well anyway, I've been quite well the past few days. (*puts pencil into bag*)

Th. Uh huh. (*smiling*)

Pt. How have *you* been, doctor?

Th. Quite well, thank you, and you?

Pt. Well, doctor, things have been a lot better for me. I find myself a lot more active. The other day I joined an art class. I had a card on me given me by a friend a long while ago. I put it away and then remembered it. I began to think I should get active. So, well, you know, I took that art class lesson on Friday afternoon, and I enjoyed it. [*Her getting out of her house into outside activities is an encouraging sign.*]

Th. You did.

Pt. It was fun. Yes, and Friday evening, what did I do? Oh, I went up and read to the blind for an hour and a half. And then I went to a movie, saw "Foreign Affair." Have you seen it?

Th. No, I haven't.

Pt. With Marlene Dietrich; it was excellent. And Saturday I didn't do very much. I stayed home, and took a little walk in the afternoon. Yesterday, I went to church in the morning, came back home and read the Sunday papers. In the evening I listened to the radio. I did some things around the apartment, hung some curtains. That's about all. [*This sounds like a break in her neurotic pattern with a lifting of depression.*]

Th. I see. (*pause*)

Pt. I feel better. The depression isn't as depressed as it was.

Th. And you find yourself being a bit more active.

Pt. Yes, and sort of releasing some things. I mean, this is only an instance. I was coming from the movies on Friday evening and I'd been looking for some large serving platters, you know. Well, before I saw you, I wouldn't even cross the street. I saw one in the window across the street, so I crossed over and at least looked at it before I would leave, and had the ambition to do it. Little things like that encourage me.

Th. I see.

Pt. And I had another dream.

Th. Mm hmm.

Pt. I dreamed I was jumping over a creek of water. And had my pocketbook in one arm, and I dropped it in the water because I had to use my two hands to save myself from falling in the water. And then after that I don't know how these people came around, but there were a couple of . . . like nurses or something, and one girl was a tall girl with red hair, and apparently she was queer because she was making advances to me. Said how wonderful it would be if she and I got together, and that's all I remember about it. [*The patient used the symbol of the pocketbook also in her first dream. What the significance of this may be will be explored. In this dream she drops her pocketbook to save herself from falling in water. Following this, a woman makes homosexual advances toward her. The latter, an eruption of deep unconscious wishes and fears, is on a different level from the characterologic conflicts we have been working on so far.*]

Th. Any associations to the dream? [*To give her my associations would have been disastrous.*]

Pt. There were a couple of nurses like, yes, just in white.

Th. I see.

Pt. That's all I can remember, doctor. [*This inability to associate may be the product of repression. If, as I suspect, she is dealing in the dream with deep unconscious fears, she may be expected to show resistance.*]

Th. What about the stream?

Pt. I don't know. I don't recall ever having jumped over a stream.

Th. What does an episode like that suggest? Here you're walking and you're crossing a creek.

Pt. That had some water in between and I had to jump over it, you see, and I thought it would be an easy jump. Instead of that I almost fell in, and then I had the pocketbook in my arm and I had to grab hold of something that was something like a log or some arrangement there. But I didn't fall in and I got up over this trespass, or whatever it was. And then this, this girl, these two girls were there, and I don't know how it happened, but kind of a homely looking girl with red hair approached me. That I remember.

Th. Red hair?

Pt. Yes, I don't know what that is. It reminds me of nothing. (*pause*)

Th. I see.

Pt. She was ugly. (*pause*)

Th. Ugly? [*I hope to stimulate associations by these questions.*]

Pt. Well, she wasn't nice.

Th. But she was making a pass at you.

Pt. Oh, oh yes. Oh, I wouldn't think of it . . . nothing like that.

Th. What about your ideas about homosexuality?

Pt. Well, I . . . it disgusts me. I think it's an awful thing.

Th. Awful?

Pt. Well, I mean, with women particularly, I mean. (*pause*)

Th. Mm hmm.

Pt. Yes, I think it's awful, two women or two men. Because, I mean, anything isn't normal like that.

Th. Do you know anything about homosexuality?

Pt. Well, after all, I've lived a little while, doctor, and I've heard things and that sort of thing, but I've never entered into anything like that.

Th. But you haven't any idea as to what the reasons for it are?

Pt. No . . . Is it ever normal, doctor?

Th. Well, in puberty and adolescence children of the same sex often experiment sexually with each other.

Pt. Until they don't . . . until they know better, is that it, doctor?

Th. Well, until they go to a relationship with a person of the opposite sex. Now, very often when a child is brought up so that she is afraid of the opposite sex, the only type of sexual activity that she can stand, because she is afraid of the other, is this early type of activity. A lot of homosexual people have never quite developed normally. They've sort of been arrested at a certain stage of their development. [*The purpose of this explanation is to attempt to allay a sense of guilt and to encourage associations to homosexuality, if this is a problem.*]

Pt. In other words, timid or bashful or something.

Th. Timid or bashful or frightened. Or very frequently what happens is that a person may have a bad experience with a person of the opposite sex, like being rejected. Then they may continue to be afraid of rejection, and they may prefer a person of the same sex.

Pt. Well, I've never had anything like that, so that as far as I can see there is nothing like that. [*The patient seems to repudiate the exploration of the area of homosexuality.*]

Th. To get back to the dream, do you have any other associations?

Pt. I don't know, doctor.

Th. What about the pocketbook?

Pt. Well, I had this pocketbook and I dropped it to save myself from falling into the water. (*pause*)

Th. What does the pocketbook remind you of?

Pt. Should it remind me of something?

Th. No, not necessarily. But what ideas come to your mind when you think of pocketbook? (*pause*)

Pt. Well . . . this is funny, you know, doctor, because . . . well, you know how people talk . . . they talk about a woman's private parts . . . some people do . . . as a pocketbook. Isn't that awful?

Th. A pocketbook is often a sexual organ in dreams.

Pt. Is that so? (*pause*)

Th. And in the process of jumping over and crossing a creek, the implication would be that you lost your femininity, and you're left like a sexless person. [*interpreting an aspect of the dream to encourage further associations*]

Pt. Well, that's something like it, isn't it? I mean with this last experience that I had, isn't it, doctor?

Th. So that your fear is that the only thing that is left is you as a sexless person.

Pt. You mean the pocketbook that I dropped?

Th. You dropped your pocketbook.

Pt. Yes, it's true, I dropped my pocketbook, and I was really quite disturbed about it, that I dropped it, because there was some money in it. But that's all that happened. And then that ugly looking red head on the top of it. She had to come along, and say that to me, that she and I would be wonderful together.

Th. Well, in the dream, if you are left with no femininity, your relations with men would be gone. The idea then might be that the next best thing is a relationship with a woman. [*Interpreting more deeply. It is possible that the patient feels that she has lost her sexual attractiveness and her femininity. This may symbolize a loss of self and account for some of her depression.*]

Pt. Well, I wouldn't do that in spite of it. I'd rather go in alone, 'cause that would be awful.

Th. Do you really feel that you've lost your capacity to establish a relationship with a man?

Pt. Well, it seems so, you know.

Th. Admittedly you've gone through something pretty terrible, with the experiences as you've reported them to me.

Pt. Well, I have, all the way down the line. And I think that's why I've been afraid to take a chance in many instances where I did have opportunities, don't you see? And I saw this friend of mine yesterday getting in a car. He lives just a block or two from me, and I saw him getting in his car, with one of these women that he's involved with.

Th. With *one* of them?

Pt. Well, there's two of them. I thought I told you there were two. I was walking, and I just happened to see it, so I stopped. I was on the other side of the street and I didn't want to pass. (*pause*)

Th. How did you feel about this?

Pt. I'm better off without him.

Th. Mm hmm.

Pt. Oh, I know I am, because it would only be worse.

Th. You'd get yourself into a bigger mess?

Pt. Possibly.

Th. Do you feel that you just don't want to get involved with *any* men?

Pt. No, I don't feel that way.

Th. You don't feel that way?

Pt. No, I do not. I mean, I'm game. I'll take a chance if there's a good prospect in view. Why not? It's the only way you can succeed. Isn't it? [*This verbalized determination is hopeful.*]

Th. It would seem so.

Pt. I hope I never . . . I don't keep on making mistakes, that's all. That's the thing I'd like to avoid, if it can be helped.

Th. Mm hmm.

Pt. Well, that would be fine if it happens. Of course, the way I'm going along now, I'm not going out with anybody. I don't really have a chance to meet anyone. But that's all right. That's all right. That'll take care of itself. (*pause*)

Th. Within a few months things may be different. [*said tentatively*]

Pt. Well, who knows; you never know anyway. (*pause*) At any rate I'm feeling better . . . Yes, I'm feeling better, and I'm happier, and I'd like to have a little more activity though. You see, I could do it; I feel well enough. I feel better since I've been coming to see you.

Th. Mm hmm.

Pt. One should be busy. (*pause*) [*Her desire to be busy is commendable and evidence of her having overcome some depression. I get a feeling at this point that the patient may not be motivated for deep therapy, involving exploration of the more repressed unconscious conflicts. She may be satisfied with a break-up of her neurotic character patterns which will lead to a more effective kind of life devoid of her former unhappiness. In view of her age, this may constitute an optimal goal.*]

Th. You should be busy?

Pt. Well, because I'm an active person. (*pause*)

Th. Can you, would you object to getting a job? [*At this point I decide to work on her finding some useful occupation or recreation to give her a purpose in living, greater than she has had.*]

Pt. Oh no, not one bit. You mean be ashamed?

Th. Do you feel that you just wouldn't want to work?

Pt. Oh, no, no. That doesn't matter to me, doctor. I like to.

Th. Is there any specific thing you're most interested in?

Pt. Well, you know I thought of taking up a course in antique furniture. I like antiques a great deal. And then my friends talked me out of that. I was going to enlist on the fourth of October, and they said, "Oh, you'll get up there with a lot of old women and you won't get any fun out of it." Well, I wanted to do that, but they talked me out of that. Now that's all over. There's several good schools in New York. But they're all closed now, and I can't get in. But I wanted to do that. I felt that it would be nice.

Th. Well, are you interested in antiques?

Pt. Yes, I would like to do that work. And I mean I could develop what taste I have. And I thought maybe I would go further with it, you know.

Th. How did you let them talk you out of it?

Pt. Well, because I just listen to everybody. I go around asking advice, you know. Well, that's how I get in trouble.

Th. I see.

Pt. Well, they felt that I wouldn't meet anybody that I'd be interested in or something like that. And I wasn't thinking about that. They said, "You'll meet a lot of old women up there."

Th. Well, the school is one thing. Your contacts with people outside are another thing.

Pt. Exactly, I mean, that's it.

Th. The study of antiques can be a very exciting thing.

Pt. Wonderful.

Th. You have to use your brain; you have to know what's in the field.

Pt. And every home presents a different problem. (*pause*)

Th. Every home has a different problem.

Pt. Don't you see. So I thought it would be nice. 'Cause I'm accustomed to all that, because every day in my business there were always different problems cropping up.

Th. When does the next term begin in this school?

Pt. I think in the Spring, you see, I missed that.

Th. Perhaps you can take specific courses without matriculating. [*This is a direct suggestion presented to her as a possibility for action.*]

Pt. Well, I'll find out. But, you see, I did want to go to a good school, naturally.

Th. Naturally.

Pt. 'Cause I felt if I'm going to learn something, I'll learn something from the people who have the best knowledge.

Th. But even though you can't get into a good school to matriculate, perhaps you can get your application in, and you can take scattered courses here and there, and also get some good books on the subject. Perhaps you can start getting into the field so that when you start taking the courses you'll have a pretty good background. [*I am pushing her a bit here to get involved in something that may turn out to be of value to her.*]

Pt. I think there is a school that has a few classes, you know. Let me find out what's going on around.

Th. Are you able to do it? [*challenging her as to her ability to follow through*]

Pt. Well, I'll tell you what I'll do. Vogue has about five or six pages of different schools, you know, on adult education. Supposing I look around. (*pause*) The trouble with me is that I haven't enough confidence in myself. I'll tell you why. My friends ask me to go shopping with them 'cause they like the things I select, you see. And I see very often people follow through on things that I've just talked about. I notice it, but they would never say to me that you gave us this idea or something, you know.

Th. Well, maybe you can make a different start. [*What I do here is get her off the track of beating herself with how badly she is treated by others, focusing on a positive course of action.*]

Pt. Well, that would be nice. You see, when I get in contact with people I'm accustomed to, I know how to talk with them, and I think I can sell somebody a bill of goods if it's necessary. I mean, if they would have enough confidence in me, doctor, that if I make suggestions they would feel that I could follow through on it. But everybody talks me out of everything I want to do, doctor. Really it's . . . but why do I let them?

Th. Why do you let them?

Pt. Because, well, I haven't enough confidence in myself.

Th. Precisely in what way?

Pt. Don't you see what I mean?

Th. You feel you make mistakes?

Pt. Well, everyone does.

Th. Everyone does, but your ability to feel that even though you made a mistake, you're all right, would be the liberating thing for you.

Pt. Why do I feel as if I amount to nothing?

Th. That's a good question.

Pt. As far back as I remember, as a child, because of the way I had been going from one place to another, I didn't feel loved. I just didn't feel that I had anything. I felt that I just sort, just had to push myself, and give in order to be liked and approved of.

Th. Now that wound seems to be carrying over to your present-day life, and it's necessary for you to evaluate yourself and see what you really are.

Pt. Yes, I think I have very excellent taste and can use my own judgment. (*pause*) Except, doctor, as you say, I haven't any confidence. You see, I feel that lack of education very, very much. It gives me, in the sense of the word, an inferiority complex.

Th. Can you explain that?

Pt. I really do, well, I'll tell you about it. I've worked hard for everything, for everything that I have. That is really working hard, you see. And very often I'm around people, and there are lots of things that I'd like to say, but I'm afraid to say them for fear that I will make a grammatical error, in the way that I express myself. Therefore, I just sit and listen, and never become, hardly ever become, a part of the conversation. It's true. And I thought when I'd sell the business, I was going to go and take up some language, and so forth, and I didn't do it, because I didn't have the ambition. Now that you've been talking to me, I feel entirely different. I felt lost.

Th. You felt lost, absolutely lost, and didn't know where to start.

Pt. Don't you see?

Th. If you take up antiques, you could also take up language and things to improve your vocabulary, if that's what you want. Antiques could give you valuable topics for discussion and develop you. [*I do not feel that it would be too fruitful to continue talking about her devaluated self-esteem and I focus on her doing something about herself.*]

Pt. Certainly, and I may have an office, and open a nice little office like you have here. And get some clients and give the work out to be done, and all of that.

Th. You've got enough contacts?

Pt. Oh, wonderful. I know some of the nicest people in New York, really, and they all like me.

Th. I see.

Pt. You see. (*pause*)

Th. And it's necessary to start right in then, if that's what you decide.

Pt. All right, no matter what.

Th. No matter what.

Pt. Just start in—all right.

Th. Start right in and get the ground laid. It might take you a little while to get into the field.

Pt. But, of course. It's what I want to do.

Th. After all, you've got to have something to do. Every person has to be involved in something he feels is important.

Pt. I see, to get some pleasure out of it. Doctor, then later I could go to Europe and study some of the furniture over there. I would really have a wonderful time.

Th. Mm hmm.

Pt. It's a tremendous outlook. I mean it could grow and grow to no end of things. [*Her enthusiasm means little unless she does something about her plans in reality. This we will have to wait for.*]

Th. The educational value of it alone, without even considering the practical value is important—the different periods and things.

Pt. That alone, too, is wonderful for the mind.

Th. Yes.

Pt. Well, those are the things I need, you see. I've never had any of it. The only thing I've ever known was to just work and work and worry, and that's all. But that's all over now. It's all over and I feel that that's a wonderful thing. (*pause*)

Th. Have you traveled through the museums and seen the period pieces?

Pt. No.

Th. You never have?

Pt. Never.

Th. Perhaps that's one thing you can put on your agenda before I see you again next week. Perhaps you could go to the Metropolitan Museum. [*again a positive suggestion to encourage action*]

Pt. All right. Is that up here on Fifth Avenue, doctor, on eighty . . .

Th. Yes, on 83rd Street.

Pt. I could just casually go around and see the old American, the various periods. It'll show all the different things . . .

Th. All right, now that's the first step. And also before I see you next time, perhaps you may want to start taking other steps in regard to getting the best training in antique furniture. [*I am being as positive in my suggestions as I can be without being too directive.*]

Pt. That's what I want, you see.

Th. Perhaps you can get matriculated, even if it's in the Spring.

Pt. Then I can look onward. (*pause*) Materials, designs, fabrics—all interesting.

Th. You may get a kick out of this.

Pt. Oh, I think it will be a wonderful thing for me. See, I could have been in it already if I went before.

Th. Of course, you were down in the dumps then.

Pt. Oh, but so low, you see, but so low.

Th. You were down in the dumps.

Pt. Yes, well it's all going to work out all right, isn't it, doctor?

Th. It has to if you really set your heart on it. [*implying her responsibility in making things turn out right*]

Pt. I must. I just must, that's all. It's ridiculous to just absolutely have no confidence in what you think, and what people who haven't nearly as much sense as I have say . . . I mean, I follow their advice. Do you understand?

Th. Why do you follow their advice?

Pt. Same old thing.

Th. Same old thing?

Pt. Well, now about my friends. Tell me doctor, something about that. I mustn't let them all go and neglect them. Well, now how do I go about it? (*pause*) [*The patient wants me to give her the answers here, which I must try to avoid.*]

Th. Well, now let's see if we can identify the problem. What is the problem?

Pt. Well, now, it's that I have nobody close.

Th. Do people call you?

Pt. Well, now they haven't called me. I have to call them, don't you see, call and say "hello." I can do that.

Th. What people, what friends do you have?

Pt. Well I have quite a few. Now a girl called me this morning. She's the girl that I always take out, you know, well, to lunch occasionally, and pay her checks and everything. She calls herself the perennial guest. Well, I mean, she never attempts to pay the check, so this morning she called me up and said, "Look, I'd love to go to the Horse Show tonight." She didn't say, "Would you like to go?" She said that she would like to go. So then I felt, well, now, Dr. Wolberg showed me that I shouldn't be taking everybody out, and all that and paying. [*The patient apparently has integrated the material we discussed in the last session.*]

Th. So what did you say?

Pt. So I said, "Well, I have an engagement this evening." Well, before I would have had to take her to dinner and the Horse Show.

Th. Did you want to go to the Horse Show?

Pt. Well, I don't want to keep taking her out.

Th. All right, but if you wanted to go to the Horse Show, mightn't you have said to her, "Fine, why don't *you* buy the tickets and take *me* out to dinner then."

Pt. I see.

Th. Well, that's what you *might* have said to her.

Pt. Well, she didn't ask me to go. She said that *she* would like to go. Why didn't she say would *I* like to go to the Horse Show tonight?

Th. Why do you think?

Pt. To pay her way somewhere, I know.

Th. To sponge on you?

Pt. Then I don't need her for this. I should ask her to take me out sometime.

Th. Put her on the spot this way. But it would be hard. [*challenging her determination*]

Pt. I know, but you have to do it.

Th. You have to do it to get these sponges off your neck.

Pt. She'll have more respect for me.

Th. She'll have more respect for you, and for herself, too.

Pt. And then I'll handle it that way. Yes.

Th. Now with your other friends?

Pt. Well, of course, there are a lot of married couples, the carry-overs from the time we all went out together. So I see them, and, of course, they entertain me in their homes, and then I entertain them. Now that's all right, isn't it?

Th. Who were the people who objected to your going ahead with your antique course? [*I dodge the question here by posing another.*]

Pt. This one girl that I know in Pennsylvania that's married. She's a very aggressive person.

Th. How often do you see her?

Pt. I don't see her very often.

Th. Do you have a desire to talk to her at all?

Pt. Not necessarily. Now that's another thing. I don't tell people what I do. That's another thing that's wrong with me. I keep all these things to myself.

Th. You're entitled to do what *you* want. [*encouraging her to think of herself*]

Pt. Yes, yes, and I'll do that. And that's true of a lot of other things too. But I'll cross my bridges when I come to them.

Th. You've got to repair your bridges now, but you've got to do it slowly and surely.

Pt. Surely. I'm glad I mentioned it to you, you see. I'm very glad I mentioned it to you, about the antiques.

Th. And it should open up many, many avenues to you.

Pt. Oh, it'll be wonderful. I'll meet people again. There's the contacts, you see, which will be nice for me. And it's creative too. It's nice to take a room and fix it and see that it looks so nice after you've worked on it, worked on it, you know.

Th. Mm hmm.

Pt. I think I'll enjoy it. Oh, I had thought of it, but they had talked me out of it, you see. That's probably why I don't tell about a lot of these things that I feel. I shouldn't listen.

Th. You apparently get yourself into a situation with people in which you're kind of—well, they feel that they've got to boss you around and tell you what to do.

Pt. Well, a lot of people call me and ask my opinion of things, too.

Th. (*It is time for the session to end.*) I see. All right, then I'll see you again next week.

Pt. Goodbye, doctor.

* * *

In this session the patient begins to make positive plans for the future. An attempt to deal with deeper unconscious material is revealed in a dream; however, the

patient resists this effort and seeks to keep the interview on her immediate environmental situation. I act more directive in suggesting a positive course of action.

SIXTH SESSION

This session is illustrative of sessions in which not much seems to be happening.
The working-through process may be going on nevertheless.

* * *

Pt. Hello, how are you. I'm sorry to be late. I couldn't get a taxi. The rain is
awful. How are you?

Th. Fine, and you? [*One might suspect resistance when a patient comes late,
but the weather is bad and her explanation is a reasonable one.*]

Pt. Very good. (*pause*) I've been really very quiet, thinking over the situation,
giving it a great deal of thought.

Th. Mm hmm.

Pt. Agreeing with you all along the line, that you have got it absolutely figured
out. And I feel very much better for it.

Th. You do?

Pt. Positively.

Th. The depression has left you?

Pt. Yes, I'm much happier. Things seem to be much easier for me to do, I mean,
that is, any little things that before, that I couldn't take care of, now I can get around
to it. And I enjoy doing some little things around the house, even, and writing letters
that I haven't been able to get around to in some time. These little things like that.
(*pause*)

Th. Did you do anything about the school? [*I am perhaps a little overanxious
to hear whether or not she did anything positive about the plans she made last week.*]

Pt. Well I tell you, doctor, I was going to go yesterday, but it was a miserable
day. It rained all day and my sister came in and I had her with me most of the day.
But I thought I'd go up there between this time now, when I leave you and when
I go to the art class. I did inquire about a school which may be adequate. I'll tell you,
I'll look into this one. It sounds interesting. I'll take care of that this afternoon. [*For
some reason she has not followed through. There seems to be resistance of some kind.*]

Th. Mm hmm.

Pt. Very nice.

Th. What else has been happening? (*pause*) Have you felt a little bit depressed? [*testing her professed improvement*]

Pt. No. No. I've been good. (*pause*)

Th. Anything happening on other levels, like at home?

Pt. Well, the maid, I've been giving her orders and she just doesn't know what's
happened to me. Poor girl, she seems to wonder what's happened to me. She looks
at me, you know. "What goes on here," I guess she thinks. Because I've been having
her do a lot of things that I've been doing, which had been perfectly ridiculous. I
mean, for instance, I like to have my things done nicely, and so sometimes I do them
myself, because she doesn't do them well. So I said to her the other day, "I want you
to do these things. I've been doing them and that's foolish for me to do them when
you're here." And I said, "I did them because I didn't like the way you were doing

them, but I want you to be more careful." She said, "Thank you." I said, "No. You were just a little careless, you can do them nicely, I'm sure." So she looked puzzled; she was wondering what's happened. [*This looks like a sign of returning assertiveness.*]

Th. Perhaps she'll have more respect for you.

Pt. Of course. (*pause*)

Th. And you may have more respect for yourself. (*pause*) Anything else?

Pt. I guess not. (*pause*)

Th. Any dreams since I saw you last? [*Since the patient seems to be blocking, an inkling of more unconscious happenings, such as revealed by dreams, may be helpful.*]

Pt. No, I haven't, I haven't, not since that last one. I guess that last one cured me. After me telling you what happened, and you asking what it meant, I guess I'll never dream again. That'll be the end of the dreams. I'm afraid now. (*laughs*) [*The levity displayed probably masks her fear of revealing unconscious conflicts. Even though great care was displayed in not interpreting, she seems to have been frightened by the implications of her last dream. Resistance is apt to become more intense.*]

Th. So the last dream really upset you?

Pt. Cured me. (*laughs*) [*What she means, perhaps, is "cured" her of going too deeply into herself.*]

Th. Cured you?

Pt. (*laughing*) That was quick.

Th. What was there in the last dream that upset you.

Pt. You mean the dream? Oh, I don't want to be that way, that's why.

Th. Be that way?

Pt. Well, I mean I don't want to be sexless. You said it might mean that I had no femininity, and I don't want that. [*This is a misinterpretation of what I said, but I decide to let it pass.*]

Th. That's a very healthy attitude on your part, not to want that.

Pt. Certainly.

Th. Because you don't want to cast sex out to the winds. It's important for you to envisage a life eventually with a man who's worthy and deserving. You don't want to live a solitary life.

Pt. No, certainly I want to live a normal life. And I'm not living a normal life now. (*pause*)

Th. What do you think the first step is to get yourself out of this groove you've been in, so that your estimate of yourself will gradually rise? You and I know how valueless and little you felt inside all these years.

Pt. Well, I think the reason for that was, doctor, that, you see, while I was capable of doing so many things, I wasn't recognized because John always kept me in the background. And that's really it. That's why I never gave myself the true estimate that was really, that I was really worthy of. He always, well, he was *it*, you see. With a capital "I," and I was out. And I thought, well, I just thought I'm not doing very well after all, and he's doing it, and these things are unimportant. And then by the time I did take over, well, that thing was so deep in me that I couldn't get over it, that I, you know, didn't have the ability. I mean, for so many years, he impressed me that I didn't have any brains, you see. [*This may be the dominant theme of the present session, that is, an exploration of feelings of having been, and of being undermined.*]

Th. Really?

Pt. Oh, yes, yes, yes.

Th. In what way did he do that?

Pt. Well, just that, oh, I could make suggestions, and he would say "Oh, what do you know?" and all this, and then I just wouldn't say anything. Then I would see that it would be done, but I just thought, well, all right then. And, I mean, it went on for so long that I thought, well, I guess maybe I don't know anything. And then, you see, when I was alone, I still didn't think that I had the capabilities. And that is really, I mean, that is the truth. I'm being absolutely honest about it. And that's what it is. That's what was done to me. That's a fact. And that goes all the way down the line, Dr. Wolberg.

Th. I see.

Pt. In business and in my own personality, well, it's too bad, but it is, it happened.

Th. It happened. And he kept undermining you?

Pt. Yes, undermining me, instead of building me up, you see. Which would have been a wonderful thing for me, because I had never had any opportunities, until I married him, that is to get out into this public work, and so forth, you see. And, well, he always . . . (*pause*)

Th. He always minimized . . .

Pt. Minimized my ability, my thinking capabilities.

Th. When you started in this career, when you started working with him, what aspect of the work did you handle?

Pt. Well, I'll tell you how it happened. You see this work, in this work, you're very confined, and you put in a good many hours a day. And when I married him, I was very much in love with him, and I felt, well, now if I don't become interested in this, I will hardly never see my husband, you see. So I said, well maybe I can be of some use, I could shop for supplies and things and supervise the details in the store, and see that it's kept immaculate—that sort of thing. Because I didn't have any experience along any other line, but I did know that I could buy these things that were needed. And then gradually I got into it more and more. If a saleslady was out ill for a day or two days, then I got in and took over her place, and, little by little, I began to learn everything about the business, you see, everything.

Th. Over how long a period was this?

Pt. Twenty years.

Th. Over a period of twenty years. When did he begin undermining you?

Pt. Oh, after I began to learn more of it, and, you see, then I took a course, then I used to express my ideas about certain things.

Th. And what did he do?

Pt. Oh, he pooh-poohed me out, you know. "What do *you* know?" and then walk away and light a cigarette. I'd be just left there and I'd say, "Well, maybe I don't know." So that's all right, I'll go along with it, and see what happens. (*pause*)

Th. That must have made you feel that you weren't respected.

Pt. Well, I'd feel that, I did, you know.

Th. That you weren't . . .

Pt. That I wasn't clever, capable of thinking of things, and so forth. But it did, over a period of time, it does something to you, Dr. Wolberg, you know that. Like somebody keeping on beating you down, and beating you down, and you . . . and that's why even today when I'm with people, I mean, I'm afraid to express myself or say what I think about things. You see what I mean?

Th. And you never felt that you contributed much?

Pt. No, after he died, then I still thought, well all of this is still what he built up, and it isn't mine. Do you understand, doctor, at no time did I ever get any credit for ever doing anything on my own.

Th. I see.

Pt. Exactly, you see. Oh, I've heard a lot of the customers say, "Oh, if it wasn't for you, the place wouldn't be the way it is, and we all know that you were the brains behind everything," and all that sort of thing. But I never took any stock in it because he never built me up, you see. And he was the one that I looked up to, to do that for me, and he never did, you see.

Th. And you needed that.

Pt. And I needed that so badly, because, I mean, that's all that there really was to it, you see. And gradually toward the end, that was very important when a lot of the other things were over. So I didn't get it, and it really, you know, Dr. Wolberg, it does, it sort of becomes a part of you, and you just don't have any confidence in yourself. It's a terrible thing, in spite of all the things that I know that I can do. But, however, I'm very glad I got out of the business. That was one thing that I never regretted, not for one instant, not an instant. I'm so glad I'm out of it. It was a tremendous responsibility, and it was getting worse and worse. (*pause*)

Th. You felt you were getting nothing out of working.

Pt. As if I couldn't do anything. He gave me that idea.

Th. He didn't really build you up.

Pt. A new estimate—I must get that.

Th. Perhaps you have a feeling that you are inferior because you didn't get a great deal of formal education? [*exploring material reasons she may give to explain her devaluated self-esteem*]

Pt. I haven't any of the, I mean, I never, I don't like to brag about things. And I know that some of my friends they brag, but to me it's sort of ridiculous because I see through the whole thing and it's so shallow. But, I mean, I haven't any of that, Dr. Wolberg, because to me it isn't important. I mean I don't brag about having done well financially in the business.

Th. Mm hmm.

Pt. You know, and I've . . . well, I mean, I don't brag about anything at all, and maybe that's another thing too. I don't know, maybe this is another inferiority I have. I don't know.

Th. You may feel that what you have isn't worth very much.

Pt. I do, I do. I don't place any importance on it at all.

Th. Well, there must be things that are important to you.

Pt. Well, I . . . a friendship to me is of great value and, of course, it starts me to thinking again of the good that I could ever do, and that to me means a great deal. And I like to live a nice clean life. But I don't want to do all the giving. (*pause*)

Th. You really feel you haven't been on the receiving end? You've been on the giving end.

Pt. All the way through.

Th. To be on the receiving end, you'll have to think enough of yourself so that you feel you deserve receiving. [*focusing on the need for better self-esteem before she can get a modicum of what she wants out of life*]

Pt. I feel I am lacking in personality. How can I build up my feeling about myself? (*pause*)

Th. The best way is through good relations with people. (*pause*) Perhaps you minimize a lot of things that you have about yourself.

Pt. Oh, I never think of it, you see.

Th. You feel it's all bad things you've got, no good things?

Pt. I never think of it, you see, I haven't any of those thoughts which I should really develop. It would be good to get some of these, because it would help me. (*pause*) Ever since I've been coming to see you, I've been giving more thought to myself than I've ever done in my whole life. Believe me, believe me. Because all through these years I just never think of myself, never, never, doctor. Nothing that *I* do ever amounts to anything, believe me, it was what everybody else did. That was the big thing with me. [*The patient doesn't yet see her own masochistic participation in, and need for tearing herself down.*]

Th. Other people were important to you then?

Pt. Oh, but definitely, definitely. No matter how small, no matter who they were, you see. And I never, never think of myself. Lately is the first time. Because as I've been going along, I've always thought about my mother, thought about John, and thought about the little girl, my brother and my sister. I've always helped. It's always all of those things that I had to think about, and do, you see. Before, I never had time to think about myself.

Th. Well, it isn't too late to change, if you're really fed up with that sort of thing.

Pt. It isn't too late.

Th. If you really thought it was too late, you'd just resign yourself and say there's no hope.

Pt. Well, I never will do that no matter how things are going to go. I'm never ever going to feel that way again because I want to live a normal life. If I'm lucky enough to, you know, really meet somebody nice, and that I'd be interested in, I think it would be wonderful.

Th. Maybe they'd be lucky to meet you. [*emphasizing how she undervalues herself*]

Pt. Well, that's the idea I should hold. It's really me. I know I should. Oh, I know I should. Yesterday, twice I had a call, and I said I wasn't home, and this chap is very, very wealthy, very wealthy. But he drinks, and I don't want that, that isn't for me, and I don't need his money.

Th. It's important for you to be discriminating, even if you wait. [*trying to put into words what the patient may feel, but has not yet verbalized*]

Pt. I don't care, doctor, I will not get in with somebody that's going to pull me down. I don't think that's good at all.

Th. No. (*shaking head*) [*reinforcing her conviction*]

Pt. I've struggled too hard.

Th. Another experience that tears you down will be very hard to bear. [*emphasizing the need to avoid another masochistic experience*]

Pt. Just one more will be too much.

Th. You've already gone through enough, except for that one interlude of your life.

Pt. With this man that did some good for me. That really pulled me out of all the other things; the only real relationship I had.

Th. Maybe you need another interlude.

Pt. Yes, like that, with someone nice. Well, of course, I was so much younger then, you see. I had more opportunities then. But it'll be a different thing, something different, if it comes again.

Th. If it comes again you have to be ready for it. You can't expect to be ready if you have a bad opinion of yourself. If you correct the bad opinion of yourself, when someone worthy comes along, you'll be able to accept the situation. [*linking her desire for a better life with the task to rectify her bad feelings about herself*]

Pt. Sure, no matter how good *they* were, if *I* felt good, it wouldn't matter.

Th. There is one thing you may have to watch for when you meet a worthwhile person. In the face of this man's apparent good qualities, you may say to yourself, "Well, gosh, he'll never see anything in *me*. Why should I get myself messed up over him? If he sees something in me, it's because he just wants sex, or because he wants to take advantage of me, or something like that; it isn't likely that he respects me for myself." And after that, you won't give him a chance; you'll just run like a deer. Now you've got to build up this estimate of yourself, if things are to be different. We have a fairly good idea of the origin of this bad estimate of yourself in your early upbringing. But this has produced in you an extremely insidious situation, in which you keep on despising yourself, in which you feel you have no inherent qualities, in which you feel that you can only be loved for what you can do for people, and not for yourself. Now these patterns keep messing you all up. [*This summation attempts to link up all the random bits of information we have. It also warns her that her problems still are with her even though she feels better. Anticipating her neurotic reactions when she relates to people, will give her the best opportunity to learn about her drives and to modify them. Another thing that an anticipatory comment does for the patient is to prevent him from becoming depressed and hopeless when his neurotic reactions reappear after he knows about them, and feels that therapy has annihilated them. Most patients want to rid themselves of symptoms so earnestly that they cannot accept the truism that time itself is necessary for the complete eradication of a neurotic pattern, even after insight into the pattern has been achieved.*]

Pt. Well, all right, now what will I do about this other thing?

Th. Which other thing?

Pt. Getting on with people.

Th. All right, now the first step is getting started on a program of building up your value in yourself. What do you think the first step might be?

Pt. Like going to school or meeting a new group of friends or a new group of people . . . like building an entirely new personality.

Th. A new personality and a new life for yourself. Does this mean you have to discharge all of your present friends?

Pt. No, but, I don't . . . not too much of them. Because that'll be all in that old type of thinking again, and surroundings and all the old ideas.

Th. Not that the old type of thinking isn't going to pop up again from time to time, even if your attitudes do change. [*again anticipating the old reactions*]

Pt. I know. I know what you mean.

Th. But it's starting with a new base, starting off with the idea that you're going to be frank with people that you meet, and by George, if they like you, fine, they like you for yourself.

Pt. It'll give me an entirely different outlook, and then I'll be surrounded with an entirely different environment.

Th. And the people . . .

Pt. Will like me as I am. [*How much she is voicing what she says to please me and how much is real insight and determination to react in a different way, the future will tell.*]

Th. Like you as you are, the way you are, not because you do things for people.

Pt. Well, that doesn't mean anything; they haven't anything to offer. They come to me to try to have me to give something of myself to them. Because most of these people are so, oh, just don't have any real interest to offer, you know.

Th. Yes.

Pt. They're a lot of negative people with a lot of money to spend and go around drinking every day, and live that way. Well, that's not of interest to me. I mean, I don't want anything like that. To me that's a waste of time. Now this last man . . . I decided to give him up. It was too much. [*The fact that the patient keeps bringing this man up shows that she has not resolved her problem with him, and probably wants to resume a relationship.*]

Th. Mm hmm.

Pt. One of my friends, she said, "You're foolish if you don't go with him." I said, "No, I'm not, I know what I'm doing." No, doctor, I couldn't go on with that.

Th. Why did she think you were foolish.

Pt. Well, because she thought he was good to me, see?

Th. Good?

Pt. I said he took too much out of me, he hurt me.

Th. You felt it wasn't worth what it did to your ego.

Pt. Oh, am I glad now that I'm rid of it. It's wonderful. At least now if I'm alone over weekends, it's my choice, at least.

Th. Yes.

Pt. Yes, and I don't feel like a dog for it, don't you know what I mean?

Th. Mm hmm.

Pt. The other way you think, well, gosh, here I am by myself. You see other people along the avenue with company, you know, men, and all of them together Saturdays and Sundays, and I'm alone. Well, what's the matter with me, I think. That's where all this trouble came, you see, when I saw this man. [*It is more apparent now that the rupture of her relationships with this man was a prime precipitating factor in her emotional illness.*]

Th. Torturing yourself with thoughts that you're not worthy.

Pt. That's right. And what is it worth?

Th. Mm hmm.

Pt. It's my fault.

Th. Your fault?

Pt. I'll get over it. (*pause*) I'll get over it. (*pause*) I'll get over this thing; I'll straighten myself out with your help, doctor.

Th. Mm hmm.

Pt. I need new surroundings. It'll be a nice type of people I'll be meeting.

Th. It'll be a nice type of people with whom you can establish the best kind of relationships. [*The question comes to my mind at this point as to whether the patient is "whistling in the dark," so to speak. Her capacity to put her insight into action will tell the story.*]

Pt. You see what I mean. It'll be nice. And then you see, doctor, before I was in a business where the people I met, they were forced on me 'cause I had to cater to them. And then I wasn't given any credit for it before, because John would never give me any credit for it, and then, you see, I was always in the background. He used to put me—make me do the most simple things, like assist in the cleaning.

Th. Why?

Pt. Well, when things were so bad during the depression, and I had to watch everything and work out where I was needed most.

Th. And you had to just keep this up all the time?

Pt. And it ran me down physically. (*pause*) Oh, I, well, I really got a bad break all the way through on this thing. Now I will come through it all right though, now I will.

Th. Well, are you worried about this all now?

Pt. Well, I'm not worried about it since I came to see you, 'cause I see it doesn't really matter. It's how I feel about myself that counts.

Th. How do you feel about yourself now?

Pt. You mean now? I thought I was different, you know, when I had that operation on my womb.

Th. Well, virtually there is a difference, but . . .

Pt. Of course there is.

Th. But it isn't so extensive a difference that would make it significant. I shouldn't think you have anything to worry about on that score.

Pt. Well, I haven't thought of it since I came to you. But I'm going to straighten myself out and I see that I have the right idea on it, and I'm thinking along the right lines with your help, and I'm going to get along fine. There's no question about it. I know that. [*This sounds good, but the future will tell whether she will or will not sustain her symptomatic improvement. There is also a possibility that she fears getting too deeply involved analyzing herself, and is showing a "flight into health" to get out of therapy. In the latter instance, a relapse in her symptoms will occur after leaving treatment.*]

Th. Good.

Pt. I know that Dr. Wolberg.

Th. You're making plans for yourself?

Pt. Oh, sure, there's no doubt about it.

Th. Well, let's make sure about next week's appointment.

Pt. O.K.

Th. (*checking my schedule*) So I'll see you the same time as last week.

*   *   *

This session was spent in listening to the patient express a more hopeful outlook on life. She has stopped beating herself with her inadequacies and with the wastefulness of her life. I get a feeling that she has broken up a neurotic pattern of allowing herself to be exploited in order to be loved. Feeling little value within herself, she has had to "give" to make up her imagined deficiencies. Genetically this is related to a shattered security and devaluated self-esteem originating in depriving childhood experiences. Her fear of rejection and the hostility mobilized by a feeling she is exploited by people may drive people from her, or may cause her to withdraw from relationships. She has started to assert herself with others and she is talking about leading a more active and independent life. That she has deeper unconscious conflicts which have not yet been explored, there is no doubt. Whether she will have the motivation to explore them, we do not know. A hunch I have at this point is that she will go into resistance and run from therapy if I push her into deeper anxiety material. We must remember that our goal may have to be a more abbreviated one than complete personality reconstruction, because of her age.

SEVENTH SESSION

In this session the patient seems to be moving out of her neurotic pattern into more constructive relationships with people. The old patterns, have, of course, not been completely resolved and we continue exploring them.

* * *

Pt. Hello.

Th. Hello.

Pt. Well . . . (*pause*)

Th. Well, what's happened since I saw you?

Pt. Oh, everything is all right.

Th. Everything?

Pt. Yes, fine. I went to two parties since I saw you—Friday evening and Saturday evening. Been stepping out, had a good time. (*laughs*)

Th. Did you?

Pt. Yes.

Th. You didn't have to force yourself?

Pt. No, no, I didn't think about it. Just got there and entered into the thing, didn't think about the people or anything, just had a good time, relaxed. (*smiles and pauses to light a cigarette*)

Th. You didn't think about having to do things for others? [*I say this almost as if I take it for granted.*]

Pt. Not having to do anything for anyone, no, no.

Th. Mm hmm. (*nodding*)

Pt. Certainly it makes all the difference in the world. (*pause*)

Th. How did the other people respond to this?

Pt. Better, better. I think they paid more attention to me, than they did before, I mean it. [*This, if true, is a real achievement, since she has not been allowing herself to give presents and to "knock herself out" to please others.*]

Th. Well, that's something we can talk about. [*The implication here is that she has accomplished a notable thing.*]

Pt. It was Friday night; this was a very lovely party. There were two married couples there and a professor from a University. This one couple are very old friends of mine, about ten years. I had introduced this girl to her husband, and, oh, we really had a wonderful time. All in all, it was very, very pleasant.

Th. What about the professor? [*I say this hopefully. Perhaps this man may be eligible and enable her to experiment with new attitudes.*]

Pt. The professor was all right. I would have liked to have had a talk with him, but another girl buttonholed him as soon as she got in the place, as soon as she got in the apartment. She got hold of him, and she had him all evening. He was a very pleasant fellow; he was a bachelor. As a matter of fact, I think they probably invited him there to have an extra man for me, but I didn't even get a chance to talk to him. (*pause*)

Th. Who was the girl?

Pt. Well, her husband was away. He had to go to Washington for that evening.

Th. Mm hmm.

Pt. He was very, very nice, but I didn't have very much chance to talk with him, or find out about him.

Th. Perhaps they might be able to arrange another meeting. [*My disappointment reflects itself in this statement.*]

Pt. Well that's just it; I wish they would.

Th. Do you know these people well enough to say, "How about arranging a party where I will be able to buttonhole him before anyone else does?"

Pt. Because that's really what happened, and he, let's see, I think I left . . . there's this couple that live at Park Avenue, and they took me home. They were going downtown, so naturally they said, "Come on and we'll give you a lift. And we'll all go down together." So he stayed on at the apartment.

Th. Did you feel that you should have stayed on?

Pt. Well not necessarily, I didn't. Same old thing.

Th. I wonder if you felt that you just couldn't get him interested. [*reflecting possible feelings*]

Pt. Same old thing.

Th. What same old thing?

Pt. Well, that I wasn't really interested enough.

Th. You weren't interested enough in him?

Pt. There was not enough there to appeal to me.

Th. Maybe you felt there was no sense in your even wasting your time. Unless you wanted to run away on the basis that he might reject you. [*opening up the possibility of a neurotic reaction*]

Pt. Well, you see, I didn't have a chance to find out whether he likes me or not.

Th. Yes.

Pt. That's very true. To enjoy each other's company you need a small group. You know when there's a big party—there were eight people altogether, you know that's quite a few people in an apartment—you never really get a chance to see very much of your hostess and host, for that matter. But it was pleasant and I enjoyed it; it was very nice. And Saturday night was a great big party too, twenty-four people. It was a birthday party. So we had a lot of fun, singing songs and dancing, and they had a lady there playing the piano. She was a school teacher and she came and played. We had a nice party.

Th. Did you go because you felt forced to go?

Pt. No, I wanted to; I enjoyed it. As a matter of fact, they wanted me to come back yesterday, and I did. I went back for dinner. That's something I never would have done before, but never. I mean, because I wouldn't even be interested enough. You know what I mean doctor? I want to do all those things that were hard for me to do before, you know. [*more encouraging signs*]

Th. You can sense that in your running away from people, there was something very neurotic in it? [*attempting to get her to talk about the meaning of her neurotic behavior*]

Pt. It was wrong. Isn't that right?

Th. What do you think?

Pt. Sure it was wrong, what it did to me.

Th. With all the resentment you must have carried around with you on the basis of being forced to do something that you didn't want to do, the feeling that you couldn't be accepted for yourself, but only for what you did for people, it's understandable that you'd want to drift away more and more from people. [*interpreting*]

Pt. Well, that's just exactly why I came to see you. Because I knew something bad was happening to me, you see. It was getting worse and worse, you see. I would be only happy when I was alone, and without anyone at all to disturb me. I mean just to sit there and think, you see. And really, I mean, I just . . . when anyone disturbed me I just hated it. It was just . . . to me it was a wonderful thing to be alone and just go over and over and over in my mind all these things. But it wasn't any good; it was just a waste of time. (*pause*)

Th. Mm hmm.

Pt. I had a dream last night. I dreamed that I was walking around in some strange place and I came into an auction room and there were some glass platters there and I stole one and ran and cut all around corners and everything to get away. Now isn't that a peculiar thing. A cheap glass platter, it wasn't anything, it was just an ordinary glass platter.

Th. What are your associations to the dream?

Pt. Why, I really don't know what it is.

Th. All right now, what do you associate with auction rooms?

Pt. Well, auction rooms—this one girl that was at the party Friday night said, "I was down in your neighborhood, I always like to go down there about once or twice a week and run into the auction rooms there. See what they have." They've got a lot of them all around, down there in that neighborhood. Well, that's the only thing I can think of.

Th. Which girl was this?

Pt. The one I had introduced to her husband.

Th. Oh, I see. And what about lifting a plate, a cheap platter?

Pt. Yes, it was nothing, doctor. It might be worth a quarter maybe. It was just a very inexpensive ordinary glass platter like a little glass . . .

Th. What are your associations to stealing the glass?

Pt. Terrible, why I think that's an awful thing to do, to steal anything. But imagine me doing that! And if I remember, I think I threw it away. I think I got frightened and I think I threw it away, or something like that—and ran.

Th. Have you ever stolen anything?

Pt. No!

Th. Never?

Pt. I might have when I was a kid, stolen a piece of cake from the ice box or something like that, if they didn't want me to have any more.

Th. But you never stole anything else?

Pt. Oh, no.

Th. And here you dream of being kind of a thief, and doing this thing and just running off. And in the other dream you dreamed about . . . [*I am trying to make a connection.*]

Pt. Jumping over a stream and dropping my pocketbook in the water.

Th. Dropping your pocketbook in the water. And this woman . . .

Pt. Making a pass at me, yes.

Th. Making a pass at you, and you feeling it was a terrible thing. All right, now in both the dreams the common denominator is being kind of a terrible person, isn't it? [*The connection that I make is that there is a deep feeling of being a terrible person in both dreams.*]

Pt. Well, yes.

Th. Now what does that suggest to you? Here in two dreams you dream about your doing something that's wrong or bad.

Pt. Yes.

Th. What does that suggest to you?

Pt. Well, it suggests to me that it's the same old thing, that I don't think I'm all right.

Th. Here you dream that you're a sneaky selfish person. Does this show the feeling that you have about yourself? That, if true, is in line with what we've been talking about, isn't it—a disparity about what you feel about yourself and what is actually so? Now again, what does this mean? Why do you have to keep teasing yourself with thoughts that you're a terrible person? [*She is aware of some reasons for her self-devaluation. What I am trying to do is get her to bring out more guilt feelings, inner fears and repulsive experiences, if there are any.*]

Pt. Well, I certainly don't get any pleasure out of it, because I'm not happy about it. And I don't know why I should even feel that way. I mean, I want to get over this feeling, but it isn't so easy, doctor. When you've been thinking a thing so long, you can't do it in just a few weeks, just throw it out the window. It isn't like taking a piece of furniture and saying I don't want that any more. I mean, that's a part of me. I've been thinking that way so long. It takes time. I can't do that so quickly. I'm doing it gradually. [*This is factual thinking; but is it also subtle resistance?*]

Th. These patterns and habits are so rigid—they go back so far into a person's life that it takes time. You know for instance, if you were going to break a cigarette habit . . .

Pt. Yes, I know. I did.

Th. You know how long it took you. You know that you craved smoking. Now, this is just a very simple little cigarette habit. Some people can't even break a cigarette habit. And that's a simple habit. Now just imagine how complex the habits of a personality are.

Pt. For years, for an accumulation of years and years and years.

Th. Yes, for years and years, your whole life seems to have been the same.

Pt. The same pattern.

Th. The same pattern, and it's a monumental thing to change now. But you can change, and the only way one can change is to find out why one has been just beating one's head against a stone wall. The only way you can change is to find out how the patterns you've been accepting as normal are abnormal.

Pt. Oh, the whole thing is that, I know it. Well, I have to work it out. I'm doing it now to the best of my ability, I mean the best I can. [*I get a feeling she is being defensive.*]

Th. You seem to feel that I'm impatient with you.

Pt. No I don't, no I don't.

Th. Well, I hope you don't, because I'm not.

Pt. No, I don't, I really don't feel that.

Th. I certainly understand how difficult it is for you, and how deep these trends are, and that it's going to take time—time, time, time.

Pt. Of course, and a lot of practice, doing things that are entirely different from what I've been doing, and thinking along an entirely different trend of thought. See, I'm alone so much you see. That's bad. And still I don't know of anybody that I could get any good from that I know, and that would be a good influence. You see, the people I know, they look to *me* to help *them* with their problems. Now you can imagine, I mean . . . they couldn't help *me*, could they? [*This may reflect her determination not to let people influence her toward exploiting herself.*]

Th. You feel you need a new set of companions.

Pt. Positively, you see—people that I would respect for their way of living, and their ideas of themselves, and so forth, you see.

Th. Mm hmm.

Pt. People who would give me stimulation in the right direction.

Th. Would any of your present friends be able to do that for you?

Pt. No, and not have a good influence.

Th. Mm hmm.

Pt. This man I went out with, well, I saw him yesterday. I was standing out in front of my house waiting for a taxi. He only lives three blocks from me, and he was over in front of his house.

Th. Did he see you?

Pt. I suppose he did. I didn't pretend that I saw him, because I don't want to pick that up, I don't want any part of that. (*pause*) [*Because she constantly brings the man up in her conversation, I get the feeling she dropped him because of a "sour grapes" attitude, that in not being able to command more of his attention, she concluded, he was no good in the first place. I decide to focus on him again to see if she has more ideas about the relationship.*]

Th. How'd you happen to meet him in the first place?

Pt. In my business.

Th. He came in and met you this way?

Pt. Oh, he'd been coming in for years, you know. No, I don't want any part of that any more. That is the best thing that happened to me in a long time, that getting rid of that situation. I'm very happy about it. [*The thought occurs that "the lady doth protest too much."*]

Th. You seem to miss him, however.

Pt. No, to the contrary, I mean I feel worse about him than I ever did. I almost hate him to a point, now.

Th. But even after all that time, it wasn't worth a row of pins?

Pt. No, no.

Th. Not worth emotionally what you went through?

Pt. It didn't help for three years to go through *that*. That certainly isn't living.

Th. Mm hmm.

Pt. There wasn't much to it, you see, as I got nothing. He used to expect everything from me, tell me all his troubles. (*pause*)

Th. He was the type of person that would make you the confessor, tell you about how he felt about things?

Pt. Oh, yes, yes, completely, everything—his daughters, his sons-in-law, and I was listening to all the troubles about everything.

Th. You were listening and acting understanding.

Pt. Oh yes, wonderful. (*said sarcastically*) He used to come out with all these things and get it off his chest and put it in my lap, you see. Yes . . . well, that's all over. I don't want any part of it. I don't want to even . . . if he would call me, I would tell him I don't want to have anything more to do with him. Just don't call me, I'd say. I don't like it. I wouldn't even go out and have dinner with him. I don't want to hear from him any more. I'm finished with it; that's the end of that. I'll go out to parties and things and have fun, like the last party. [*The explorative attempt I made was not too fruitful, so I decide to focus back onto the party she talked about.*]

Th. Well now, let's go back to this party. This woman that you introduced her husband to, what sort of a couple do they make?

Pt. They're very nice. She has entirely different ideas about things than I have. I mean, she's the sort of a person that likes to have an easy life, and definitely all for herself, you see. The fact that I would want to do anything again, you see, like when I said that I'm going to take up a course in antiques—oh, she thinks that's ridiculous. "You just got out of business, so you could play and have fun," she says, "why don't you go down to Florida and stay there for three or four months and have a good time." But I'm not in the mood for that. I wouldn't have a good time, I said, if I went to Florida. See, so that's her idea, just to have fun and play.

Th. What kind of a man did she marry?

Pt. Oh, a very nice fellow, very nice fellow. He's very good to her, and I think they're very compatible. They seem to be.

Th. Does he appeal to you at all? [*I am thinking of the dream in which she steals a platter. Her associations suggest a competitive attitude toward the woman. I am trying to bring this out, if present, through questioning.*]

Pt. To be married to? No.

Th. Not at all?

Pt. Well, he's nice, I like him, I respect him, but for marriage, no.

Th. There's no jealousy at all?

Pt. No, not at all.

Th. No envy of this woman?

Pt. No, no.. Why, did you feel that there might have been?

Th. Well, I don't know, I'm just thinking about that dream . . . the association of the auction, you see, and this woman. You going in and stealing something, might give us an inkling, but there is nothing definite.

Pt. Well, I . . . she went to Florida with me on this trip that one winter I was driving down, and I said for her to come on down. She was a widow. I said, "You've never been down, and I'd love to have the company. Come on down with me. It won't cost you anything in the car—come on down. We'll have a nice drive down together." I wanted to do something for her.

Th. Which is?

Pt. That same old thing. [*She does have good insight into her neurotic pattern in that she picks it out when simple cues are presented to her.*]

Th. Mm hmm.

Pt. And so she came down there with me, and I knew this fellow, and I introduced them, and they were married six months later. So that was one of those things, and it seems to be working out, so that's fine and I'm very glad of it. That was ten years ago. But I don't see an awful lot of her, and, as a matter of fact, she never mentions the fact that she's happy or ever says that that's the best thing that ever happened to her. She never mentions that I introduced her or anything like that. Never, never once has she ever said it. However, I'm not going to ask her if she's happy. She seems to be happy. I mean, I should think she'd say it to me, because I introduced her to him, and he certainly is good to her.

Th. And she never shows any gratitude at all to you.

Pt. She has never shown any appreciation, I mean, by way of doing anything for me. I don't want it, but I mean that's the way the picture is.

Th. I see.

Pt. And I wonder if she really is happy. She appears to be happy. He's been very, very good to her, like I said, and they live beautifully.

Th. Aren't you sort of . . . well, disgusted? [*The meaning of the dream may be that while this woman can go into auction rooms and pick out beautiful things, the patient must be contented with cheap things, and she has to steal them at that. This may refer to what she gets from life, or to her own feelings of self-worth. Resentment toward the woman may have sparked off the dream.*]

Pt. Yes, I mean, I'm sorry for her, because I'm sorry that she hasn't a little more . . . I don't know whether you should call it gratitude or a little more graciousness maybe, to sometime just express it to me, that she had a nice life with him, and it was so wonderful that I introduced her to him, something like that. But never ever, ever once, never. It's one of those things; but that isn't anything. Why are people like that doctor? They have no part of feeling for others.

Th. Some people are like that, others not. [*attempting to introduce reality into her thinking*]

Pt. Not everyone does that I suppose, but I get stuck with them that have no feeling.

Th. I know, but why should *you* get tangled up with those people?

Pt. Well, I won't. I don't have to now.

Th. You know there are some people who are sponges; their whole life is integrated around sponging on others.

Pt. Either in one way or another. Now, you see, this girl I told you I used to see a lot of, the one that lives with this doctor. He hasn't married her . . . why he hasn't married her, I don't know. He's free to do so; he's been divorced and she's divorced, and why should they live in sin when they don't have to, that's something I can't understand. It seems silly to me, because why not be married and have a perfectly normal life together; then if you disagree, all right, then get a divorce after ten years, but why do that? Well, any rate that's the picture. So I, so Saturday night they were at the party also, this doctor and the girl, and there's about a twenty-three year age difference there, and I just looked at her and I thought, "Oh, my, I should get into anything like that." This old man . . . old, I mean, real old—sixty-five, sixty-six—that's old, doctor, when you're fifty or something like that, don't you think so? [*Is the patient expressing a "sour grapes" attitude here too?*]

Th. Mm hmm.

Pt. That's a terrific difference.

Th. Of course, but it depends on the person too. There are individual differences. Some people at sixty-five can be still young; some people at forty-five can be awfully old. [*This statement of fact is intended again to introduce reality into her thinking.*]

Pt. Yes, but this man is—well, the fact that he doesn't marry her, he doesn't even think enough of her to marry her in spite of their age difference. He should be so happy to have her.

Th. Maybe *she* doesn't want to get married? [*Placing possible responsibility on the woman, in case the patient is trying to prove that all men are nefarious.*]

Pt. Well, she says so, but I wonder what woman wouldn't want to be married, instead of living that way.

Th. There are some.

Pt. Really?

Th. I believe so.

Pt. She says *this* way she can walk out whenever she feels like it. Well, that I can't understand.

Th. Could she just be holding on to him for security?

Pt. Well, then—this is what I really started to tell you—then this girl I introduced to this man who married her, said to me, when this girl and the doctor were quarrelling one time, she said, "Can't you introduce *her* to someone?" "Why," I said, "Why, I wouldn't think of it." I said, "What about the doctor?" I said, "I don't do—I wouldn't do things like that."

Th. Mm hmm.

Pt. "Well, but," she said, "can't you introduce her to someone else?" [*The implication is that the patient has a responsibility to introduce other women to nice men. People expect her to "give."*]

Th. Just like that. [*sympathizing with the patient's feeling*]

Pt. Just like that. So you see, that's the type of person this other one is.

Th. Apparently you size her up as a selfish person.

Pt. Well, that's the picture then; now you've got it, see?

Th. I certainly have the picture you've been used to following.

Pt. I guess you have.

Th. The defender of the rights of others, but not so much of your own.

Pt. (*indignantly*) Yes, almost to the extent that I would be a procurer if it comes to that. "Can't you introduce her to someone?" I said, "I don't do that," I said, "What about the doctor? She's with him, isn't she?" Now how do you like that? Well, now there it is. I get into awful—some awful kind of pictures.

Th. Apparently you've given people the impression that you are there to serve.

Pt. It's my fault.

Th. It's not a matter of fault or blame. You've given them that impression because you needed to have that kind of relationship with people. And you got yourself into spots where others . . . [*bringing up the matter of her "need" to do things for people, the satisfaction she gets from doing things for others*]

Pt. Take things for granted.

Th. And that must burn you up inside.

Pt. Well it does, it hurts.

Th. Of course, it hurts.

Pt. Every time I see this girl that married this fellow, it hurts. You say there may be a jealousy. No, there isn't any jealousy, because there isn't anything that she has that I haven't. I mean as far as that goes. While he is an awfully nice fellow, I wouldn't want to be married to him. And I mean he has no appeal for me. I like him as a person, and he's a very regular little fellow, you know, he's very nice, but . . . (*pause*)

Th. He's not the sort of a fellow that would really suit you.

Pt. No, no, that's right. He was a very good friend of my husband's, you see.

Th. I see.

Pt. And, so that's the picture, but still I don't think she has taken the right attitude toward me.

Th. Very obviously you don't think that.

Pt. That is a fact.

Th. Mm hmm.

Pt. Not once, as I say, has she ever given me a single thank you for that. Well, I just think it's a little abnormal, that's all. It's just something wrong about it. Because I know what I would do. I mean, I would mention it once in a while, just to make someone feel good about it. [*The patient is obviously fired with the indignation and resentment at how she has been exploited by others. Prior to therapy this suppressed resentment may have produced depression.*]

Th. That would be the . . .

Pt. The natural thing. But I would take up with people like that. As you say, I must have needed them, doctor, but they are hard on you, I mean they expect everything.

Th. It's natural for you to feel angry at people who like you only if you continue doing things for them. You know there's a story which explains that personality very well. It's about a man who had the same kind of problem that you have, always kept doing things for people. Now, on one occasion he was told by a friend that a person he had helped considerably in the recent past was hostile to him, spreading vicious and unfounded tales about his character. So he went over to see the man and said: "Look, why do you treat me this way? Why do you talk about me the way you do? Haven't I given you a car, found a job for you that pays you well, and even introduced you to several young women you've been dating." And the fellow replied: "Yes, that's true, but what have you done for me lately?" [*I passed up an opportunity to talk about her "need" to take up with the kind of people she detests. I was probably anxious to tell her a good story before it slipped my mind.*]

Pt. (*laughter*) That's good, he wanted him to keep on with the giving, and when he let down, well, then everything stopped, he didn't even act in any way grateful.

Th. The minute he let down on the giving, then he was his enemy.

Pt. That's right, doctor, that describes me all over. (*laughs*) [*The story apparently clicked.*]

Th. Could these attitudes on your part really be the things that are at fault, causing you to feel that people expect things from you, while you yourself secretly hope *they* will be the ones who will do things for *you*?

Pt. You know I take it too seriously. I should be a little more impersonal about these things. True, everyone's troubles are my troubles, and I get involved in these things. I should just mind my own business, in other words. How about it, doctor? [*The patient is unwilling to explore the provocative question I asked her.*]

Th. You find yourself drifting into things, not even wanting to?

Pt. Yes, and that's what I'll have to watch.

Th. You mean, you feel you'll have to watch yourself from wanting to take people over, do things for them, act the hostess, so to speak. [*again emphasizing her own responsibility in perpetuating the pattern*]

Pt. Yes, I can see, I can see how what you've told me is so true.

Th. Maybe you participate in this, encouraging them to depend on you more than you think.

Pt. I don't want to get involved, I don't, I don't.

Th. But you *do* get involved somehow.

Pt. Well, I tell you, you talk about those things—why, even my bookkeeper, when I was in business, don't you know, that he said, "Well, now I'd like to put a little money into this business." Now imagine, he wants to get in on an income from my business. Oh, that shows you, you're so right about it. Everybody has the impression that—well, I was theirs. [*The patient evades my implication.*]

Th. What I was saying was that by your manners and actions you may have encouraged their thinking you were theirs. [*This is a "perhaps" interpretation, but is given emphatically.*]

Pt. Well, whatever the reason was, it was all one-sided.

Th. One-sided, and then you stopped the supplies, they got mad at you.

Pt. Well now, I'm just going to . . . I've been doing that . . . and now I'm not going to do anything for anybody. [*This would, of course, be unhealthy, but I doubt that she means it. In resentment, a statement like this is apt to come out.*]

Th. You might feel if you didn't do anything for anybody, that they might not like you.

Pt. I'm through with it, honest and truly.

Th. Completely?

Pt. It's just something that will help me to build up a different impression of myself. I've got to do that, doctor, because things are no good the way they have been. That's why I thought I'd go ahead with studying, to build myself up to feel different.

Th. Have you thought any more about the course in antiques?

Pt. Yes, I'm going to go through with it. I am. I'm going to do it.

Th. Mm hmm. (*nodding*)

Pt. Now you see, doctor, if I wanted to really go ahead, I might go into the extended course which is eight months a year for two years, and that would give me time for vacations, you see. I might as well do it.

Th. Mm hmm. (*nodding*)

Pt. And do it right, and get a great deal of satisfaction out of it, the whole thing, you know. And then if I ever want to use it, I'll have it.

Th. You haven't had an opportunity to investigate yet when to register in the school?

Pt. Yes, I've done something about it. I have a catalogue there, and they have some of the dates there written. I'm sure I can get started on that. And I am going to. And then later, if I want to go in for myself, in business I mean, I can if I want to.

Th. Mm hmm.

Pt. You know what I mean?

Th. Not only for purposes of business, but better still, an education.

Pt. Everything, you see. The business angle is only part.

Th. Yes.

Pt. There are wonderful possibilities in this thing, too.

Th. And it's not only from the standpoint of having an interesting thing to do, but you can meet a lot of people in this way.

Th. Yes.

Pt. It's wonderful, it's certainly wonderful that I have the energy to do it. Go back to school, it'll be all so new.

Th. New and exciting.

Pt. Yes.

Th. All right, see you next week.

Pt. Yes, doctor, goodbye.

* * *

This session is characterized by greater hopefulness, and accounts of positive achievement. There is, however, reluctance to get into deeper, more unconscious, aspects of herself. In the seventh interview this could scarcely be expected, even if we desired to get into them. She seems to be moving along extremely well.

EIGHTH SESSION

This session is illustrative of some of the activity that occurs in the middle phase of treatment.

*   *   *

Pt. Hello, doctor.

Th. Hello.

Pt. Well, this man comes into it again. [*This is apparently the dominant theme today. It may give us an opportunity to explore her deepest feelings about the man.*]

Th. Well!

Pt. His sister passed away last week. I happened to hear of it very . . . it was quite an accident the way I heard of it. But at any rate I was tempted to write a letter and I was tempted to send a card, but I said, "Oh, no, don't start, don't let yourself in for that all over again." It would have been nice to write a letter to him, of sympathy or something, but I said it isn't the thing to do, so I just won't do it. Now I'm so glad I didn't, today I'm so glad I didn't. (*pause*)

Th. You were almost tempted to write. [*focusing on latent desires to see the man in question*]

Pt. Yes, and then I felt, well, Dr. Wolberg says no, that sort of thing is just poison for me, and why do I want anything that isn't good. [*The patient puts me in an authoritative position, as if I think it's wrong for her to make contact with the man.*]

Th. If I weren't around, what would *you* say?

Pt. The same.

Th. But after all, he's the last man in your life, and it is understandable that you would want to see him. [*This comment is intended to be both reassuring and provocative, stimulating her to associate more about her desire to renew the relationship.*]

Pt. You understand, it was no good for me.

Th. Is this because *I* implied he was no good for you? [*Attempting to bring patient to the realization that she is defining her values, not I.*]

Pt. You are right that he was no good for me. [*continues to put me in the authoritative role*]

Th. But there are still some memories about him.

Pt. Yes, but it wasn't the thing for me to, and this morning I was so glad I didn't do it, see? Because, I said, well now here I'll be right back where I started. If he should get the card or letter of sympathy, you know, he'll call me, and then it'll just be that hanging and dangling on, and what good will it do? [*This is the first time she has openly admitted a yearning to go back into the relationship. Her admitting the desire and her making a choice not to on the basis of intelligent judgment rather than resentment, will help her resolve her conflict. I might earlier have caused a verbalization of the desire by saying something like: "Most women would want to see their boy friend, and miss him, even if he was mean. You probably miss him too in some ways." Nevertheless, the patient did well with the tactics I employed.*]

Th. You may be tempted some more.

Pt. But I'm glad I didn't.

Th. Did you avoid doing it to please me? [*testing her use of me as an authority*]

Pt. (*laughs*) No, no, doctor, it would be bad for *me*.

Th. Do you think *I'd* disapprove if you did see him again?

Pt. No, but that is not what I want. Why, I feel so good today about that, that was such a lift, you know, that I thought, well, I did have enough common sense, and I wasn't swayed by my emotions of sympathy again, you know, to do something to help or be very obliging. [*This is a forthright, honest attempt to handle her feelings.*]

Th. Mm hmm. (*nodding*)

Pt. Oh, I'm so glad I did it, doctor, I just feel so good about it. That in itself is wonderful. Because I know just what would happen. See, he'd get the card, and he'd wait a few days to call. And, say I saw him, and then I'd be waiting again, you know, I don't want it. I'm so much better off without him. [*She seems finally to have made a choice.*]

Th. Mm hmm. (*nodding*)

Pt. Much better off.

Th. At least you feel independent, even though you may not have the pleasure of having him around once in a while.

Pt. Yes, but it wasn't worth it when I did have him.

Th. It actually undermined you in a lot of ways?

Pt. Breaking me down. So that's number one. And then I had a lovely Thanksgiving, it was a hen party, but it was fun. [*The patient shifts the topic, apparently having dealt with it to her satisfaction.*]

Th. That's good.

Pt. Well, it was at the house of this old friend of John's and me. We were about six girls and the old boy, he's about eighty-one.

Th. Well!

Pt. Well, he was just so happy; we really had a lovely evening. So I had a nice day. And then there's been a death in my brother's wife's family since I saw you, so I went over there, and helped my sister-in-law a little bit while she took care of some of the things for her father. That's really about all. And let's see now, and then last night I was to go to a cocktail party. I just went up for one drink to see this couple, and said "hello" to them and then left. About a half hour . . . I went up there. But I was glad I did that, because I want to take care of everything, don't you know, that I was afraid to do before. [*The patient diverts from the theme of her former boy friend, and her frustrations with him, to the constructive efforts she is making with life.*]

Th. It wasn't too hard?

Pt. No, no, it was all right. I'm glad I did go.—I want to do all the things that are hard for me to do, that I didn't do before. Isn't that right?

Th. Well?

Pt. Isn't it?

Th. Instead of just withdrawing, you do things, but more importantly, if you can get a little pleasure out of doing them, this would make it really worth while. [*Instead of answering "yes" to her question, I give her a possible reason for continuing in the path she is going.*]

Pt. Yes, well I am. I'm seeing things in a different way. I seem to, I seem to understand more about doing the things now than I did before. I mean, in a different way. I mean, before I thought, well, I *have* to do it, you see. Now I look forward to it with a little pleasure, you know?

Th. You were depressed before.

Pt. Terribly.

Th. And you didn't want to get out of the house. You wanted to stay within yourself. Anything you did outside the home was an effort.

Pt. Yes, that wasn't good. Now I want to talk to you about the going up to the Institution for the Blind and reading. I've been going there recently to read to this one man there, and he isn't completely blind. The way for him to read something, he has to look at it this way. (*brings hand approximately two inches from eyes*) I see that when he looks at his watch for the time, this way you see. So I've been reading to him for about three weeks. This isn't the young boy I read to before. I only substituted for a reader for this young boy. This chap is a different thing again. I've been reading to him about three weeks. So he's interested in psychiatry; so he had a book there. *Between Us and the Dark* is the name of it. I don't know if you know it. Well, it was about a woman that during the change of life, went all through all this emotional period, and was put away in a hospital, and so forth, and so on, and stayed there four years. Well, at any rate, I finished that book, reading it to him. It was very interesting. So now last week, last Tuesday, he has a book written by a Dr. Flanders Dunbar, *Mind and Body*.

Th. Yes.

Pt. Well, at any rate, he has a certain amount of it that isn't read, and then I come to the part almost immediately where it's marked off here. This is the chapter that I'm to read, and it's all about this girl that's having intercourse, that's being whipped, flogged, and all that. Oh, it's the worst, I mean, I never heard anything like it. First time I ever read anything like that. Well. . .

Th. Did he know that that was the material he wanted you to read?

Pt. Well, now wait. So then he said, in referring to that, he said, "Turn back to page 202, about the third chapter, and then there's more of this filthy stuff." He knew the book.

Th. Yes.

Pt. He must, he must have known the book, and he knew the page, you see. So now, how do you like that?

Th. And he wanted you to read that?

Pt. Oh, yes. So I don't think I'm going to go back there any more.

Th. It shocked you.

Pt. Yes, but isn't that awful. I mean, you go up to read and you want to do some good, and then here this thing is thrown at you. What is the idea with those people? [*The possibility crosses my mind that the patient may be employing this example to illustrate the uselessness of her making constructive efforts for herself.*]

Th. Well, again, doesn't it resolve itself to the fact that sometimes you feel taken in, taken advantage of?

Pt. But doctor, isn't that a shame?

Th. You want to do the best for people and they use you for their own selfish personal interests?

Pt. Yes, but well, isn't that a shame, doctor, now, really, I mean it. You go up there and you want to help somebody. And that's the reason I went up there. I felt that I would be doing some good, and I might get some, you know, pleasure out of it. And imagine to find this filth. I mean, I don't understand this.

Th. Well, if his interest is in something pornographic, he's not interested in the scientific attitude.

Pt. You don't think so? Why shouldn't he be?

Th. Should he be?

Pt. He's not a doctor.

Th. He's not a doctor.

Pt. Well, it's just that . . . (*pause*)

Th. Maybe all he wants is to be stimulated.

Pt. It's just filth.

Th. It disgusts you.

Pt. Reading these things, you see.

Th. These things are what sick people do, not healthy people. [*By emphasizing that constructive efforts may fail on sick people, but not necessarily on healthy people, I am hopeful that she will conclude that she need not seek out sick people to do things for.*]

Pt. Yes, I know it. And it's certainly for no one's pleasure to read to them. So then he said, "Well, you turn back to this page and there's a little of it on that 202 page." And he said, "Well, I'll have to return this book." He gets these books from the library, you see. He can't keep this book, but he wanted me to get all that old, all that filthy stuff out of it, you see, and read it to him. So I don't think I'm going to go back anymore. I don't, I don't like the fellow now, after that.

Th. Not all blind people are like that. [*introducing reality into the situation to forestall, if possible, retirement from further activity*]

Pt. Well, you know. So I'm going to forget that. I'll call it off.

Th. If that's what you want to do.

Pt. I will, I'll do that. Now that's that. Now isn't that something. I guess I just run in hard luck, because it looks like the other people go up there, and it seems to be all right.

Th. You do the best you can. The fact that people don't turn out to be the kind of people you imagine them to be is just unfortunate.

Pt. It is.

Th. But . . . this person, he's probably a very sick person emotionally. (*pause*)

Pt. Well, I don't know whether he's sick or not, doctor, but at any rate, he shouldn't be taking advantage of people who are coming up there, and with all good faith.

Th. Did you tell him you didn't want to read the material?

Pt. No I didn't. Do you think I should?

Th. You had a right to.

Pt. I can go there and ask if I can get someone else to read to. [*I was wrong in my thought that the patient seeks to run out of the situation. She does seem to be evaluating reality better.*]

Th. Mm hmm. Do you enjoy reading?

Pt. I would enjoy reading to the right type of person, and the right sort of thing, yes. I enjoy it very much.

Th. Well then, why don't you go up there and tell the people in charge what happened, and give them the reasons why you don't want to return. [*a suggestion for constructive action*]

Pt. All right. That's all right.

Th. Wouldn't that be better than not showing up at all, if you get any kind of pleasure out of reading?

Pt. Well I do, I do. I'd like it very much to be able to go there once or twice a week and read.

Th. There's no reason why you shouldn't.

Pt. I was enjoying it until this thing came along.

Th. You certainly owe it to the person in charge there to tell him what happened.

Maybe some people don't object to reading things of that sort, but you object very much. And you enjoy reading. Maybe they could get somebody else for you to read to.

Pt. Sure, I'll do it then. I certainly am not going back there to him. He's probably, as you say, a sick fellow, and he's sort of getting something out of this thing here, you know, probably something to have him believe, maybe, that he's all right, and he isn't.

Th. Mm hmm.

Pt. The book was all right you see, the book was interesting.

Th. Mm hmm.

Pt. It's good, but in its place, don't you know what I mean? I'm not interested about reading about some poor unfortunate that has to have those things. But the other book was an interesting novel. You know, it was a story that, well the woman that had written about the Snake Pit, it was her own experience. But this other thing, I don't want any part of it. And then he did say something very funny. He said, "I," he said, "I sell novocaine." He said, "Do you know anyone that has any use for it?" I said, "No, I don't."

Th. The man sounds like a dope peddler?

Pt. I said, "No, I don't know anyone at all."

Th. The man sounds as if he is a very sick man.

Pt. Well, I thought novocaine is only for dentist work, when they pull your teeth. It isn't like that other drug, heroin, or whatever you call it. Well, you see, he said, "Do you know anyone." And I said, "No, I don't know anybody."

Th. That sounds very suspicious.

Pt. I haven't any idea of going back there to read to him. As a matter of fact, I was going to forget the whole thing, but I think your suggestion is good. Let them know there, what kind of a man he is.

Th. They have a right to know, don't they?

Pt. Yes, only I wouldn't want to get involved in it. I wouldn't want to have anybody hurt you know.

Th. No.

Pt. You know what I mean?

Th. You don't want to get involved.

Pt. Exactly.

Th. But, they do have a right to know.

Pt. I'll do it.

Th. Do you think you can?

Pt. I'll do it.

Th. Good.

Pt. I enjoy reading, and I'd like to have them assign someone else to me, you understand. (*pause*) I think that it's the best thing. So that's been . . . that. (*laughs*) I certainly do get into things, don't I?

Th. Well?

Pt. I surely do. (*laughing still*)

Th. It involves you anyway. (*laughs*)

Pt. I certainly do. (*laughs*) The time will come, I suppose, when I won't have any of that stuff; it'll all disappear. I'll always have some, but I'll know how to take care of myself too, I mean.

Th. Now you sound more optimistic.

Pt. I am. I wouldn't be surprised if I met someone nice soon.

Th. Now if you did, you'd be tempted to act how? [*testing her insight*]

Pt. And that's another thing again. (*laughs*) Do things for him, I suppose, and then get mad at him for not liking me for myself.

Th. You can get yourself adjusted without that eventually, if the right sort of person comes along. [*presenting the possibility of a different way of reacting*]

Pt. I'll be attracted to them, and they'll be attracted to me, and it'll be so much better. Because what's the use, the way it is now. I suppose I'm not really ready completely, only partly. Really, I wouldn't know what I wanted, so what's the use of starting anything. [*This shows that she is not really "whistling in the dark." She seems to be assessing reality quite well.*]

Th. You feel there isn't any use?

Pt. Unless I was sure of the person. I'd only get in trouble, and that would just be another disappointment, then . . . oh, I'll just go along and I'll work it out. I know I will.

Th. On the other hand, you still just don't want to lose your faith in people, because there are still some very nice and decent people alive.

Pt. I know.

Th. And it's a matter of knowing where and how to find them. The people you've been most attracted to are the people who have needed help. They've been exploiting, they've used you. That type of relationship is a one way affair. And it's bound to explode, because you can't be adjusted in a situation of that type. [*repeating the same interpretation*]

Pt. Be giving all the time, you can't.

Th. You'll despise yourself too much, you'll feel as if you resent the time you put into it. And then such people become demanding and make you feel guilty because you don't do enough for them.

Pt. And then in the end, unless you keep on, and then when you do stop . . . well, then you find out that they don't really care anything about you. When you don't continue to keep giving of yourself, you know what I mean? That's really the way it works out. Because, I suppose people don't want you to be that way after all, do they?

Th. But if you have a *need* to be needed, you'll act that way in spite of everything —in spite of the kind of person you meet. [*again emphasizing her own need for participating in the pattern*]

Pt. But most of the people I met wanted mothering.

Th. Certainly there are some people who want to have a mother around that supplies things all the time. And they won't start any relationship except with a person of that type. You'll find them everywhere you go. There are always people wanting to sponge on you. They're always willing to give you their time, that is, unless they're busy doing something else that is more profitable for them.

Pt. That's right, then they don't even give you the time of day.

Th. Any time you spend with them, you'll have to be doing something for them, but the minute you stop doing something for them, they . . .

Pt. They don't want you anymore.

Th. I told you that story, "What have you done for me lately?"

Pt. Oh, yes, I love that story. It's cute.

Th. That's the type of person who saw in you a supplying mother. But on the other hand . . .

Pt. (*interrupting*) You don't have to be around them.

Th. They're sick people, immature, undeveloped. They're like children.

Pt. But don't you see, doctor, you learn all that, I mean just . . . well, I'll be on my guard, and I don't want to lose faith because that would be terrible to go through life like that, and I won't. But the way I feel now, it's been a letdown, the whole thing has been a letdown for me, and you don't get over it overnight.

Th. You still have the need for people, and still have the need for a nice relationship, but you're afraid to get involved again.

Pt. Well, not for long I hope.

Th. Because you've been hurt so much. And before you'll let yourself get involved with anybody, you may want to make sure he's the right person.

Pt. That's what I intend—and don't you think I'm thinking along the right lines?

Th. What do you mean?

Pt. 'Cause I could find any number of people that I could pick out that I could do things for.

Th. You probably could. Do you think you still have a need to get involved with sick people to whom you can give things? [*confronting her with responsibility for her pattern, which she had previously blamed on others.*]

Pt. Oh, listen, I told you I could, but I don't want to. Why should I just do things to make those other people—make other people happy? *I* want to be happy, I really do.

Th. You have a right to be happy.

Pt. Yes, I want a man to be attracted just to me, for myself.

Th. A reliable and a responsive person who's not a baby and who doesn't want a mother?

Pt. Fine.

Th. Fine, but until that time comes you've got to supplement your activities with some outside interests.

Pt. No matter what they may be, I must do that. (*pause*)

Th. To feel you are doing something constructive.

Pt. Yes, yes.

Th. But it may be very hard to do. [*challenging her determination*]

Pt. I know, I know, but I've got to do things, doctor, I know I can't just hang around the house. Yes, and I will. (*long pause*)

Th. What are you thinking about?

Pt. About a dream I had. It's not clear.

Th. Do you remember anything about it?

Pt. It was a dream with a fellow.

Th. Tell me about it.

Pt. Oh, that was it.

Th. Well, what?

Pt. Well we were . . . yes, that . . . yes . . . (*pause*)

Th. Well . . .

Pt. Intimate, having relations with him.

Th. Yes. What was your feeling about it?

Pt. Pleasant. (*pause*) There was another part. I gave him my pocketbook with valuables. He protected it, picked me up and carried me over a stream and kissed me. Then we walked hand in hand. Yes. Well that was all, that's that. [*My own associations to the dream are that it indicates a trust in a man, and a feeling that she has something valuable to offer. It sounds like a good dream, reflecting constructive tentative changes. It may also refer to the transference situation.*]

Th. Well, that dream is different from the other.

Pt. I should say it is. (*laughs*) It was a good dream.

Th. What do you think of it?

Pt. Nice, if it was true.

Th. Well?

Pt. Maybe it will come true.

Th. Do you think you would want it?

Pt. I think so.

Th. But it may not be for some time.

Pt. No, but as long as I know I am ready for it.

Th. It may not be forthcoming though, for some time—I mean in terms of you meeting someone worthwhile.

Pt. Will I be ready to accept it the right way when it comes?

Th. Do you really want to accept it? [*dodging the question and throwing it back to her*]

Pt. Surely, surely.

Th. You'd miss relations with a man.

Pt. Yes, yes. Well then, I can wait for the right one.

Th. Is it intense, I mean, do you miss it intensely?

Pt. Yes, well, ah, it just, it was one of those things, and I don't know, I suppose. It's been quite some time, you know, so I just had that dream, and that's all. I didn't have any others.

Th. Are you impatient for things to happen?

Pt. Well, I don't, I don't . . . no, and I'm not . . . I'm glad I'm not. I wouldn't think of starting anything over again, doctor. I haven't any idea of it, simply none, until I'm sure of the person and of myself. I don't want to get in with another one like the last man.

Th. He's too much involved.

Pt. Too involved, too much. He's too involved.

Th. If he could be free?

Pt. No, there's too much intrigue there. He's all tied up.

Th. He's all tied up.

Pt. Sure, what's the use?

Th. You may still want him. [*testing her*]

Pt. I doubt it very much. So that's over and that's that.

Th. If he were different.

Pt. Maybe that would be different.

Th. Mm hmm.

Pt. But he's too damn selfish.

Th. Mm hmm.

Pt. He doesn't want to give up anything.

Th. He wants everybody to come to him?

Pt. That's right. That's it.

Th. But you still sound as if you miss him. [*testing her again*]

Pt. No, I feel that he probably did me a great favor. (*pause*) Because eventually I know that I will meet someone worthwhile, and I wouldn't if I hung around with him. Waste my time! So it's all right then. That's a closed chapter, I'm just through with it, and I'm perfectly happy about it.

Th. You might meet a person who's worth twenty times more. [*I attempt here to reinforce her hopefulness.*]

Pt. Oh, sure, doctor. He wasn't for me. He was just a very conceited guy that just thought that money was everything and money could pay for anything he wanted. And you know, there's a lot of people that believe that. They think they can get what they want if they have money. And if they're that type of people, then it probably doesn't make any difference to them how they get it. Do you understand?

Th. It's no compliment to you to have a person like that around.

Pt. Well, it certainly is not. It certainly is not.

Th. It makes you feel cheap.

Pt. Sure, I don't need him.

Th. You don't need him?

Pt. I should say not. He didn't help me. I helped him. I mean, I was so far above him in every way, and I knew it and he knew it too.

Th. You were doing most of the giving?

Pt. And it didn't amount . . . and then always on the run, that wasn't anything, you know.

Th. He just popped in and out.

Pt. Yes, sure. I told you, one night a week.

Th. Mm hmm.

Pt. Silly. Well, it was my fault. However, I'm learning. I'll bet he expected a card or a letter from me this morning.

Th. Mm hmm.

Pt. Oh sure, and then he thought I'd be waiting again. No, no, oh I wouldn't go through that again, not for anything in the world. Now when I look back, I don't know how I did it. That's what happened to me.

Th. And then, when he didn't respond, when you got fed up finally and threw him out . . .

Pt. I did.

Th. You sort of hoped that he'd come back again. [*trying to get her to accept the fact that she secretly did want to get involved with the man until relatively recently*]

Pt. (*laughs*) I suppose I did. (*laughs*) But that's silly. I'd really be in a fix if he did. And now I'm so glad. And now, even if he did, I won't . . . I don't even, I wouldn't even see him. I wouldn't even go out with him for dinner. Because I know how aggressive he is, you know, he'd . . .

Th. Persist?

Pt. Oh, sure.

Th. And then you'd be right in it again.

Pt. Oh, certainly. What is it the fellow said? I need that like I need a something in the head?

Th. A hole in the head?

Pt. A hole in the head. (*laughs and then suddenly becomes very serious*) No, I'll just go along a little way, and then I'll get there just the same. (*long pause*)

Th. What are you thinking of?

Pt. I was wondering if I should find out about getting a job or something?

Th. Yes.

Pt. I was wondering if I should.

Th. Well, what were you thinking of?

Pt. Well, you remember I talked with you about it. I said that maybe I could get something part time.

Th. Mm hmm. And then you began to feel what?

Pt. Well, and then I was just wondering if I should. I don't know.

Th. You feel that maybe you're not up to it?

Pt. Well, you can't get over it overnight, so quickly, I mean, get well entirely, I mean.

Th. You won't get over it until you really start getting out of your shell, and begin to integrate and feel like a part of the world again. Perhaps a man will come along too—a good man.

Pt. I know, it's very important. I know it. But I will not get mixed up with any more of those married men, doctor, I mean I'm through with that. I mean it now, I mean it. No more. I don't want any part of it. Not any more. That's nothing. Waste all your time and you get nowhere, and it's a letdown for your pride.

Th. Your ego gets deflated.

Pt. Surely, you're playing second fiddle, or third, or whatever it is. Why should you? Find someone for yourself. Why not? And then you're somebody, and no matter who I mean, if he's a nice man, no matter if he doesn't have an awful lot. But as long as he is a really nice person, at least he's your husband or he's your sweetheart. There isn't all that other intrigue, and all that lying and conniving, and all that, that sort of thing.

Th. Mm hmm.

Pt. I do feel so much better, doctor. Really better than I've felt, as far back as I can remember. The cobwebs lifted. I'm sure I'm never going to fall back into that again, I mean. I'm very grateful to you, doctor, because I couldn't see what I was doing to myself, bringing this on myself, I mean, and blaming it on hard luck and things. Now I'm going to have people take me as I am, and not go doing, doing. No, no, that is no good, no good.

Th. No good at all.

Pt. Doctor, I may be leaving town. I got a letter from a friend in California. It will be a nice rest and a vacation. I'd like to go in a couple of weeks. It will be fun to go and see things.

Th. Mm hmm. We'll talk about that next week.

Pt. Goodbye, doctor.

*   *   *

This session is a good one and indicates that the patient is utilizing her insight in the direction of change. Life is opening up to her and she seeks to partake more of its joys. She does not yet trust herself, and recognizes that she may act-out her neurotic patterns in her relations with people. But she understands these patterns and she has a determination to rectify them. Her desire for a vacation is both a sign of her development and an indication that she may feel satisfied that she has achieved all she wants from therapy. If the latter is the case, I will have to decide on whether to deal with this as resistance, or to satisfy myself with the results of therapy; namely, a more reeducative than reconstructive effect, or, at most, a partial reconstructive result.

NINTH SESSION

This is the terminal session and illustrates some of the techniques employed in the terminal phase of treatment. The patient seems to have decided that she has achieved all she desires from therapy. I respect her conclusions and terminate treatment.

*   *   *

Pt. Hello, doctor.

Th. Hello.

Pt. Things have been so well, wonderful. I'm really feeling fine. (*laughs*) Like

I can do things again. I am being just matter-of-fact and not worrying that I hurt people by doing that, like I used to worry about before.

Th. Mm hmm.

Pt. Not worrying about that at all. (*pause*)

Th. Yes.

Pt. I told you how I would call people, you know, and wondered how they were, and think I was neglecting them if I wouldn't call them. But you know, I don't do that any more, and it's perfectly all right. Nobody seems to think anything of it. As a matter of fact, I might have been annoying them. It's very possible. (*laughing*)

Th. At any rate, you feel that it isn't necessary for you to make the rounds. You're not a postman to have to keep calling on them all the time. [*said facetiously*]

Pt. Exactly, I don't. (*laughs*)

Th. Do you find that they do come to *you,* if you don't come to them?

Pt. Oh, sure.

Th. Mm hmm.

Pt. Now, don't you see, going away for a vacation, like I mentioned last time, I made a few calls to my close friends and said I'm going away, and I want to wish you a Merry Christmas, and so forth. So a couple of them wanted to come to see me before I left, but I really haven't the time, I've got a lot of things to do. Why add all that confusion to it? [*The patient seems to have decided to go away. Also she is acting, perhaps for the first time, normally assertive.*]

Th. And you told them that?

Pt. I did, I said, "I'm sorry, but time is short, and I have so many things to do, so that I'll see you when I get back home."

Th. Mm hmm.

Pt. It all helps. You use so much up of yourself the other way, doctor, you do. You don't realize it. That's what I've been doing, you know.

Th. And it's been draining you.

Pt. Giving, giving, giving of myself.

Th. Mm hmm.

Pt. Giving, giving . . . things like that. The sponge is just being wrung out. No wonder I didn't want to mix with people. No wonder I didn't want to see anybody, because every new contact meant so much more . . . and the burden was just mighty miserable. Just terrible what I did to myself, just horrible.

Th. Yes.

Pt. I see it all now. (*pause*) And it's just a matter of being . . . getting a little horse sense in you to realize it that you've been going on wrong, the idea that people aren't going to like you, that people are going to reject . . . and that I'm a terrible person by not acting in this way they want. [*The patient says these things as if she really knows them and means them.*]

Th. I see.

Pt. And bend over backwards to try to get people to like you. (*pause*)

Th. Mm hmm. (*pause*) Have you had any dreams since I saw you last? [*I am trying to look under the surface for deep anxieties as a reaction to her present assertiveness.*]

Pt. Only about furniture. What does that mean?

Th. Well, let's see what the dream was.

Pt. Well, I was looking at all these books about furniture, and that's all. So what does that mean? Am I turning into a piece of wood or something like that? (*laughs*)

Th. What do you think it means?

Pt. Well, the feeling was good, I mean it was pleasant.

Th. What does looking at books of the furniture bring to your mind?

Pt. Well, it must have something to do with how I've been feeling lately.

Th. Mm hmm.

Pt. More action, more doing.

Th. Yes.

Pt. Yes . . . furniture, that's all; I mean, something new I want.

Th. You feel it indicates a new orientation? [*The dream sounds like a constructive one. At least no anxieties seem apparent.*]

Pt. Good.

Th. A new life?

Pt. Good, good, that's it, that's it.

Th. And?

Pt. I had two wonderful volumes sent to me from this lawyer, this old, old friend of the family's. It's all the pictures, of all the originals of individual owners, doctor.

Th. Of furniture?

Pt. Yes.

Th. Mm hmm.

Pt. Oh, beautiful—two volumes. Macmillan publishes it. It really is something.

Th. Real authentic antiques?

Pt. Yes, and the original owners, their names are down, people who possess these things. Even in their homes, 'cause they're so rare. They have the pictures in these two volumes. Wonderful, doctor . . . everything imaginable, even old clocks and beautiful old tables, and chests and . . . (*pause*)

Th. Mm hmm.

Pt. Of course its wonderful.

Th. This book made you feel well.

Pt. Sure, because they're real possessions, you know. They have beautiful things.

Th. All right, what does this have to do with *you,* now?

Pt. Well . . . (*pause*)

Th. Yes.

Pt. (*laughing*) Well, you see I'm planning for the future . . . a foundation that . . . (*pause*)

Th. A foundation that . . .

Pt. (*still laughing*) I don't know. I'll be careful though, I don't want to be too hasty.

Th. You have to be careful?

Pt. I've made arrangements to go to this school to study antiques. It starts after I get back from California. After that I'll go to school, and I was thinking I could go into business after that. But I will be careful.

Th. You've decided on going to California?

Pt. I'd like to, doctor. I believe I am ready, and I've been invited. Do you think I can do it?

Th. Do you feel you'd like to do it?

Pt. I would, doctor, I would. I feel so thankful to you . . . I don't know what to say . . . It's so hard to know how what happened, happened. It's hard to realize that a little while—a while ago, I mean, things were so hard, so hard for me. I gave up, things were no good for me. I felt that I never would be able to feel well again. I can see it . . . how it was, how it came, I mean . . . I mean, doctor, that is how I was before . . . feeling, feeling I was nothing and had nothing to give of me . . . so

I gave, gave of everything I could do for the person, doctor. And then hated myself and the person because you never know, this way, where you stand. (*pause*) [*This sounds like good insight.*]

Th. And how do you feel about that now?

Pt. Oh different, so different, doctor. I'm beginning to see that I placed no value on me . . . like I was no good. And that's silly, doctor, so silly, doctor, for me to feel that. The only way things will work out is for me to stop doing things, and be accepted for what I am. I have nothing to be ashamed of . . . I haven't done anything bad, you know. I'm as good as anybody. I really feel that, doctor.

Th. Good. And what about your going away? [*I decide here to explore what may be behind her going on vacation.*]

Pt. If you feel I shouldn't go, doctor, I'll stay.

Th. I'd rather have *you* decide that.

Pt. I'd like to go, doctor. It's an opportunity I'd like. It will be so much fun, you know.

Th. There is no reason why you shouldn't go, if you wish.

Pt. When I get back, doctor, can I see you if I need to come to do some more about me? I feel confident though now, as if the future had something for me.

Th. Of course, you can see me any time you want when you get back. You are likely to have ups and downs. People always do. In fact, you may still get yourself into the same position with people you were before, and then get infuriated and depressed. [*I am warning her here that a relapse of her neurotic reaction is quite possible. This is not too significant if she realizes her neurotic reaction for what it is and is capable of mastering it.*]

Pt. I don't think so, doctor. [*The patient hopefully believes she will have no relapses. Unless I warn her in advance of the possibility, she may react badly should a relapse occur.*]

Th. Well, after all, these old patterns are very deep, practically part of yourself, and the new patterns are of recent origin.

Pt. You mean the old way may come back if I don't watch myself?

Th. And even if you watch yourself. It takes time to overcome a problem that's been part of you all your life. If the old patterns return, you will better be able to correct them before they get you down.

Pt. Well, I won't let myself get into that same thing again, doctor.

Th. Maybe it won't happen, but if it does, at least you'll know better what's going on.

Pt. Yes, yes, I will, I won't be a fool if I can help it.

Th. Another thing, you may have some problems that still need further treatment, and you may later decide to get more treatment for them. [*It may be that the patient wishes to terminate therapy. Giving her a reason for returning is important.*]

Pt. I know that, I know that there are many things I can straighten out. I mean, I see what I did all my life, the damage of that early thing with my . . . that home situation. And it hurts.

Th. Yes, you may want to go further into yourself later on. As far as your present situation goes, do you feel you've got out of your treatment what you want?

Pt. Oh yes, yes. I have gotten more than I thought it was possible.

Th. Perhaps you may be able to avoid the patterns that get you into troubles with yourself; but the chances are they may try to repeat. [*I am reemphasizing a point I believe to be important.*]

Pt. You mean I might do that again, and get upset all over?

Th. Yes, the chances are you will. But the difference is that you will know what you are doing better, or catch yourself doing it. What will happen then is that you will learn again how automatic the pattern is, and not allow yourself to sink into it.

Pt. Catch yourself before it's too late.

Th. Yes.

Pt. Well, I can see that . . . you know it takes a long time to overcome this . . . but I know now I can . . . I will, I mean, because the other is just, just no good for me. And if they don't want me for myself, they can just go to blazes.

Th. Mm hmm.

Pt. Yes, they can. I mean that, doctor. Either they like me or they don't.

Th. Well, what about that? Do you believe you are likeable, and that there are people who can like you for yourself?

Pt. I know it now, with what's been happening in the past few weeks. People are very nice to me, and I don't do anything for them. It's funny I never thought of that before.

Th. Disappointments are apt to occur, however, you will still meet people who will want you for what they can get out of you. [*forewarning the patient again so she will alert herself to acting-out*]

Pt. Certainly, take it in slow easy doses, isn't that right, doctor?

Th. What do *you* think?

Pt. Absolutely, absolutely, and the person must accept me with my cards on the table.

Th. You have nothing to hide, nothing to conceal.

Pt. After a little while, after I feel that I'm interested, there is no reason why I can't tell them everything.

Th. Absolutely none. [*reinforcing her determination*]

Pt. You know that's so.

Th. Mm hmm.

Pt. Yes, after I know them real well, and I know that they're interested enough in me to really know what's what.

Th. But you're apt to have one old enemy—and that is you're likely to start saying, "Oh, I don't want to lose this person, I better not say anything about myself."

Pt. Well, that's the way I've always been, you see.

Th. Yes, that's the way it's been all along.

Pt. And like this other fellow, you know, that I went around with for three years, you know, I was always afraid that if I would ask him to be with me over the week-end, I'd never see him again. And well, now I don't see him anyways, even if I didn't ask him. I haven't heard a word from him, and I'm not sending him a Christmas card. I want to get rid of the whole thing.

Th. Mm hmm.

Pt. I want to get him out of my hair completely.

Th. You feel the sooner you get that thing out of your hair, the sooner you'll be able to concentrate on something else.

Pt. He just isn't . . . he isn't any good. That's all.

Th. There may be a lot of temptations still, to see him, because, after all, it's the last affair you had and he's around all the time. There's a lot of temptation to crawl back into that thing again. [*testing her resolution not to see the man*]

Pt. I won't do it.

Th. You may really want to.

Pt. It would be a waste of time.

Th. Maybe you feel you couldn't find another man?

Pt. No, doctor, it would take away all the good that I've gained so far, if I went back.

Th. And you'd be right back.

Pt. And I'd be right back where I started.

Th. But maybe you feel you couldn't find another man?

Pt. No, I don't think I will have trouble there.

Th. Suppose he happens to call you up or something, or insists you see him. [*continuing to test her*]

Pt. I wouldn't.

Th. If he did come back into your life, and crossed you up again?

Pt. I'd throw him right out.

Th. You'd throw him out.

Pt. But I wouldn't even want to do that. Why do it?

Th. Well, you may not have thrown him out of your thoughts.

Pt. Why do I need it for? He isn't any good for me. He's just a . . . he's really an awful person.

Th. Mm hmm.

Pt. Period. I could say a lot of other things. (*pause*)

Th. Well?

Pt. But what's the use? But he is, and I'm through with it. And I'm not going to bother with his daughter because he'll think that if I send her a card, all of that, he will want to try to get back in with me again, you know. Not a chance!

Th. You've given him plenty of opportunity.

Pt. Oh, to call me.

Th. And to come back again. And . . . (*pause*)

Pt. It's five months that I haven't even heard a word. Imagine! [*There seems to be an inkling of a desire to resume the relationship; however, she is resolute in her stand not to let her desires get the best of her better judgment.*]

Th. It must be terribly irritating.

Pt. Well, it shows me what a fool I was. It's irritating in that angle of the picture—that I was just a fool. (*pause*)

Th. Well?

Pt. He's too aggressive for me, doctor.

Th. He was very aggressive, he used you?

Pt. That's right. Just a fool.

Th. And you let yourself be carried away.

Pt. Well, of course.

Th. Maybe because you were afraid to lose him. Maybe you said to yourself, "Here's a nice man, maybe he'll be kinder to me, maybe he'll come to me eventually and I'll be the only one. I better not say anything to upset him."

Pt. Well, I thought in time, see, it would change. I thought he would get rid of this other girl, but . . . (*pause*)

Th. But?

Pt. He hasn't enough character to clean . . . to make a clean sheet of the whole thing, throw out the rest and start with something he really wants.

Th. Mm hmm.

Pt. Do you see? He will keep on dabbling with the women he has, and finish it that way. That's a lot of . . . that goes on in New York all the time. But do you know, another thing: I say, "Yes, all right, I'll be here; all right, I'll see you." And as soon as I say it, I *know* I shouldn't have said it. I know I'm wrong. I know I'm being too soft, too easy about things.

Th. Mm hmm.

Pt. Now, I . . . I don't know why I should do these things. I should think about it before I give an answer to something.

Th. There are reasons why you feel you have to do this.

Pt. Do you understand? (*pause*) You see? I say, "Yes," or "All right, I'll do it," and if I say I will, I'll do it, no matter what. But I shouldn't, I should be very careful of what I answer and say. I have to be . . . (*pause*)

Th. Yes. (*pause*)

Pt. See, I should think a little more. I should use my noodle.

Th. You have to be very careful about the situations that you can get yourself into?

Pt. Exactly.

Th. In other words, there'll be a lot of opportunities.

Pt. Exactly.

Th. So?

Pt. There'll be a lot of opportunities, but I must watch out not to start anything with someone—well, a man who isn't deserving, and I'm not going to get too involved, no matter what demands are made.

Th. Mm hmm.

Pt. No matter what people want from me. Because, if I do, there'll be some people who will just really wring. My big problem you showed me is what I do to myself because I feel I'm no good.

Th. It's not exactly what you want to do, because you really want to be liked for yourself. (*pause*)

Pt. Now you see, one of my people turned up that worked for me for about twelve years, a boy that I had a lot of trouble with. I knew he was stealing, but he was a good worker and I did the best I could to control it as much as I could, but I knew he was stealing from me every day. But at any rate, he took ill about three weeks ago, and he went to the hospital. So I had a Christmas card last week from his wife, and she said—on the card—Joe is very, very ill in the St. Francis Hospital, you see. Well, I know what that means, you know. Well, I called up—day before yesterday—to find out how he got through his operation. He was operated on two or three days ago, and they said he was doing nicely. So this morning I sent a little Christmas plant to him, and it said, "With all good wishes for a speedy recovery," but I'm not going to give him any money. I mean, I just did that, just with a little good feeling toward the fellow, because I knew he was wrong all the time he worked for me, too, see?

Th. Good.

Pt. See? You know?

Th. The moment you got that card you realized that it was just a touch?

Pt. I knew, sure. Sure she would have liked me to have gotten in touch with her and said, "Is there anything he needs?" Well, you know, she wouldn't say no, and I'd be right in for it, let myself in for the whole thing.

Th. You resisted it.

Pt. I mustn't do it.

Th. If you did, you would have resented it.

Pt. I know. Now you see, going back into the book shop now for the holidays, I'm not going to go in there. All those old help, they think I should give them something.

Th. Yes?

Pt. I'm just going to keep away from it. I really have nothing in common with these people. The only reason I saw them was because I felt I had to.

Th. Mm hmm.

Pt. I'm not going in at all. I'm not going to go in there.

Th. What do they think you are, Santa Claus?

Pt. Well, it's possible, you know. I have been to all of them. Around Christmas, I gave all of them a bonus, you know, Christmas money. (*long pause*) . . . (*laughs*) But that's all in the past. I won't do anything like that any more because I know it's wrong. And then it annoys me after, you see. See? It annoys me after I do it. I know it's the wrong thing for me to do. These people are using me, and I know it's not right.

Th. Mm hmm. And you are tired of being used.

Pt. Right.

Th. It's also the thing that it does to them. The most insidious thing is that this type of giving and this type of patronizing are bad for the people who accept it. And it's bad for them, and deep down they hate to have anybody just be in a position where they can give them presents. It makes them feel dependent and helpless.

Pt. I understand. Everyone likes independence. Everyone likes to do things for themselves. That's what they appreciate. (*pause*) The things that they can do for themselves.

Th. You can see the pattern, and the way it's working in you. All your lifetime you have had to give. All your lifetime you've had to give in order to feel accepted. You believed that this was the only thing left for you, that you couldn't possibly be accepted on your own terms, that you couldn't have things done for you, and still be loved and respected. Now this is one of the ways this thing started. But the more insidious thing was that it kept up. It kept up. When you see this clearly, you'll say, "Hey, stop this business." [*summarizing*]

Pt. Just cut it all out, that's all. And I'm doing it too. But I'm just going to keep away from the book shop—I'm not going to go in there at all. I don't have to go in. I'm not going.

Th. Your own guilt feelings inside may keep telling you, well, wouldn't it be nice to just go in there? People will think more of you, and they will like you better if you go in, and so on. [*challenging her*]

Pt. Well, I don't have to go in. I can just simply send them a Christmas card.

Th. Mm hmm.

Pt. One nice card.

Th. Mm hmm.

Pt. "Merry Christmas," it will say.

Th. Merry Christmas.

Pt. "And a Happy New Year," period.

Th. Mm hmm.

Pt. Good. I'll do that this afternoon, and I'll send it tomorrow, and that'll take care of the whole thing.

Th. Mm hmm.

Pt. That is good. (*pause*)

Th. And?

Pt. That takes care of that.

Th. That takes care of that.

Pt. Yes, and they'll have more respect for me.

Th. Mm hmm. (*long pause*) Well, what would you like to talk about now?

Pt. The thing that's on my mind now is about what I'll do when I get back from California.

Th. Mm hmm. [*Since she is leaving on a long trip, I decide not to stir up tension in this interview by provocative focusing on possible conflictual areas.*]

Pt. I don't like this being retired. I'm naturally very active.

Th. There are some people who are able to retire gracefully, and there are some people who are not.

Pt. Well, people that are very phlegmatic maybe.

Th. And you are not phlegmatic.

Pt. No, no.

Th. Well?

Pt. People who haven't any interest, and you just . . . it's a slow death. It really is.

Th. It's a slow death. That is not for you, is it? You're too active a person.

Pt. Yes, but still I always force that other part, you see. See, I have that drive, you know. I have, I mean I never give up, and I could just, well . . . the antiques thing interests me.

Th. The antiques interest could keep you occupied.

Pt. It'll be wonderful.

Th. If you really make a career out of it, then you'd feel accepted on a different level, not merely as John's wife.

Pt. Exactly.

Th. You'd be accepted for yourself.

Pt. Exactly. Yes, and if I do go in business, I can, I can just use my own name. It would be good.

Th. Mm hmm.

Pt. Yes, I have a different feeling about all that now.

Th. Mm hmm.

Pt. Not being afraid to face things.

Th. Fine.

Pt. Feeling real good.

Th. Mm hmm.

Pt. It makes me feel good that I could ever think of going ahead.

Th. Mm hmm.

Pt. You know.

Th. It may give you a better feeling of value, a feeling of worth.

Pt. Well, you know, doctor, one thing always leads to another. You know, when you do one thing, there's always so many other things that come out of it. You know what I mean? That through this thing, there are other happenings. It always works that way—in things you never realize.

Th. Yes.

Pt. You know, that you never think of. You can imagine what I mean.

Th. What?

Pt. Oh, everything—a lot of things.

Th. For instance.

Pt. Oh, (*laughs*) I did get involved so with the customers. (*laughs*) They had me run ragged.

Th. Doing things for them?

Pt. Oh, loved it. (*laughs*) When they let me do it, I would love to do it. There was politics in it too.

Th. Politics?

Pt. Oh yes, they used to bring me tickets. (*pause*)

Th. Tickets?

Pt. Yes, yes . . . Oh sure, there was one judge out in Connecticut. (*laughs*) He really was wonderful. I just took advantage of it because he was just so good about these tickets, you know, that he'd get. Put it in an envelope and send it to me. I made some good contacts.

Th. You've still got some good connections that you can utilize?

Pt. Oh, it'll be wonderful. I can use them too, later.

Th. You mean if you go into business?

Pt. Oh, it's a good contact with the good people—I really did know some wonderful people, I mean, and they all liked me, you know, and I can really, I can pick up some of those nice contacts when I get started, you see.

Th. When you get back from . . .

Pt. California, yes.

Th. I see.

Pt. Yes, when I get back from California I'll get in touch with a few people, the very nice ones.

Th. Mm hmm.

Pt. Yes, that would be good, sure. All you need really is a few good contacts, you know, a few good ones. And then they have guests that come in to see their homes, and they say, well, where did you get these antiques, you know. Here I go again, planning. (*laughs*)

Th. At least the planning is something constructive.

Pt. I've been thinking about that a lot, dreaming of a place I can set up, getting some people to work for me—real crackerjack people. (*pause*)

Th. Real crackerjack people.

Pt. Yes, workmen. (*pause*)

Th. Workmen.

Pt. That's the stuff, and that should be a big secret. No one should know who they are, either. Dig up someone that's very, very, very good.

Th. Your assistants.

Pt. That's right.

Th. Mm hmm.

Pt. They have to be very good, do excellent workmanship. You see, that's the secret of it all, because if you buy beautiful fabrics, and if it isn't done well, then the whole thing is lost. You know there's a big difference between good work and . . . shoemaker work, they call it, you know.

Th. This whole new field that you're exploring, it'll probably take quite a while.

Pt. Oh, of course, it will, of course it will.

Th. Yes.

Pt. In the meantime I will meet a lot of people, and I need to get out of myself.

Th. You do need people.

Pt. Here's another thing, doctor, you're going to like.

Th. Mm hmm.

Pt. I got new clothes, and a couple of new hats. Imagine? (*laughs*) [*This may be a reflection of better self-esteem.*]

Th. (*laughs*) That sounds like a revolution.

Pt. (*laughs*) For me it is, imagine, new hats that I thought I deserved for myself. And I used to feel I could only, only get things for another person.

Th. Is that one of the new hats you have on?

Pt. (*laughs*) Yes, it is.

Th. It's very attractive, becomes you well. [*This is a response which I believe I should express openly to her.*]

Pt. (*laughs*) Thank you, doctor.

Th. Do you think it's attractive? (*pause*)

Pt. Well . . . (*laughs*)

Th. Well?

Pt. Well, yes, I do. There I go boasting.

Th. Boasting?

Pt. (*laughs*) Yes, I do like it.

Th. Do you like the way *you* look in it?

Pt. You want me to say I like myself.

Th. Well?

Pt. I was looking in the mirror and I said I'm not bad looking at all, not hard on the eyes. (*laughs*)

Th. I should say not. Do you think men would find you attractive?

Pt. Wouldn't be surprised if they did. (*laughs*)

Th. If you gave them a chance.

Pt. Oh, I think everything will be all right there too.

Th. You'd give them a chance then?

Pt. Well, I wouldn't run if they came around, because, after all, I'm not so bad.

Th. Good. (*pause*) So I won't see you until you get back from the trip.

Pt. I'll drop you a line and call you when I get back. Doctor, I want to thank you ever so much for all you've done for me. It's wonderful, this work.

Th. (*laughs*) Thank yourself, too. After all, *you* did most of the work.

Pt. (*laughs*) Goodbye, doctor.

*   *   *

This was the last session I had with the patient. After a two months' stay in California she returned to New York. She telephoned me and cheerfully announced that she felt completely well and did not believe she needed further therapy. Periodically she communicated with me by letter, and, two years after therapy, she paid me a personal call. Her entire manner indicated a satisfactory adjustment. Five years after therapy, this adjustment was being maintained.

CONCLUSION

In evaluating what happened in the treatment of this patient, it must be remembered that rarely is treatment this short. In most instances, many more sessions are required to achieve a comparable result. The case was presented not to demonstrate short-term therapy, but merely to illustrate some of the essential processes that are involved in treatment.

One thing that will be apparent is that the patient did not get bogged down in too much resistance. Her motivation to get well was probably a great help here. Also, I did not let her get too dependent on me by giving her the answers to her questions; I let her, or I should say, forced her, to think things out for herself. We established a good working relationship, rapidly, and in relatively few sessions we were well into the middle phase of treatment. If the patient had developed resistances to the working relationship, especially transference resistances, we would probably have been involved in therapy for many, many months before we could have begun working constructively on her problems. Were there a strong secondary gain element to perpetuate her neurotic patterns, we would also have had to work through this resistance, which may have required many additional months. Had she established a transference neurosis with me, we also probably would have become involved in difficulties for a long time. Finally, had she become dependent on me, we would have had to resolve the trauma of separation, and this also would have required a considerable treatment period. While I was able to avoid these snags in this patient, I might not have been able to circumvent them in others.

Now I should like to say a few things about the quality of change achieved in this patient. We worked practically entirely on a characterologic level. She was able to recognize a prevailing pattern in her relations with people; she could see its repetitive and compulsive nature; and she realized how it was engendered by early feelings of insecurity and devaluated self-esteem. She did not reach levels of the deepest unconscious conflicts; namely, oral, anal and homosexual strivings, incestuous impulses and penis envy. She might have done so had therapy been more intensive and prolonged, and had we established a transference neurosis. Whether she would have responded with more reconstructive changes in her personality than she achieved in her present therapeutic effort, we cannot say.

Actually, in view of the fact that she was fifty years of age, and chiefly because she moved rapidly in treatment to a point of losing her symptoms and of relating herself better to people, the goals she achieved were probably optimal ones. Nevertheless, she might have progressed even further with more therapy.

The classification of the kind of therapy I used would fall into that of insight therapy with reeducative goals, even though I dealt with resistance, and, at least in several instances, with transference. Also, I employed dream analysis. I did not use free association, relying entirely on the focused interview. The effect was mostly of a reeducative nature.

A follow-up study of five years has shown that the gains the patient achieved from therapy were sustained, and that she has continued to grow in self-stature and in the kinds of relationships she establishes with people. There has not been any relapse of symptoms throughout the five year period. The patient could see how compulsive her patterns were, and she was, on a number of occasions, tempted to revert to her previous role with people. After a brief interlude of acting-out, however, she would interrupt her pattern, and enter into a different kind of relationship. She has developed outside interests along the lines planned in our talks, and she has, according to her own expression "never been so happy" in her life. These results are, under any standards, estimable ones.

References*

1. WATSON, G. (chm.): Areas of agreement in psychotherapy. Am. J. Ortho-psychiat. *10:*698–709, 1940.
2. ROSENZWEIG, S.: Some implicit common factors in diverse methods of psychotherapy. Am. J. Orthopsychiat. *6:*412–415, 1936.
3. SMITH, E. R., and TYLER, R.: Appraising and Recording Student Progress, in Adventures in American Education. Vol. III, New York, Harper & Bros., 1942, p. 18.
4. TRECKER, H. B.: Social Group Work, Principles and Practices. New York, New York Women's Press, 1946, pp. 16–18.
5. Towards Better Teaching. Washington, D.C., A.S.C.D., 1949.
6. GILES, H. H., McCUTCHEN, S. P., and ZECKIEL, A. N.: Exploring the Curriculum. New York, Harper & Bros., 1942, p. 5.
7. North Central Association of Colleges and Secondary Schools: General Education in the American High School. Chicago, Scott Foresman & Co., 1942, p. xii.
8. Commission on Preventive Psychiat. of the Group for the Advancement of Psychiat.: Promotion of Mental Health in the Primary and Secondary Schools: An Evaluation of Four Projects. Report No. 18, Topeka, Kansas, 1951.
9. SLAVIN, S.: Education, learning and group work. J. Educ. Sociology *24:*143, 1950.
10. CANTOR, N.: The Dynamics of Learning. Buffalo, Foster & Stewart, 1946.
11. WOODWARD, L. E.: Family Life Education, in Social Work Year Book. New York, American Association of Social Workers, 1951, pp. 181–182.
12. TOWLE, C.: Social Case Work, in Social Work Year Book. New York, American Association of Social Workers, 1947.
13. HODGES, M. B.: Social Work Year Book. New York, American Association of Social Workers, 1951.
14. United States Social Security Administration: Annual Report of the Federal Security Agency, 1949.
15. THORNE, F. C.: Principles of Personality Counseling. Brandon, Vermont, J. of Clin. Psychol., 1950.
16. ROGERS, C. R.: Counseling and Psychotherapy. Boston, Houghton-Mifflin, 1942.
17. SUPER, D. E.: Guidance and Counseling, in Social Work Year Book. New York, American Association of Social Workers, 1951, p. 220.
18. MATHEWSON, R. J.: The role of the counselor. Harvard Educational Review. *17:*10–27, 1947.
19. STRANG, R.: Educational Guidance: Its Principles and Practice. New York, Macmillan, 1947.
20. ROGERS, C. R.: Some implications of client-centered counseling for college personnel work. The Personal Counselor. *3:*94–102, 1948.
21. WOLBERG, L. R.: The spontaneous mental cure. Psychiatric Quart. *18:*105–117, 1944.
22. PAYOT, I.: The Education of the Will. New York, Funk & Wagnalls, 1909.

* See also page 5 for references toward a definition of psychotherapy, and page 579 for a list of books used in bibliotherapy.

23. BARRETT, E. B.: Strength of Will. New York, P. J. Kennedy, 1915.
24. ——: The New Psychology. New York, P. J. Kennedy, 1925.
25. VITOZ, R.: Treatment of Neurasthenia by Means of Brain Control, translated by H. B. Brooks. London, Longmans, Green, 1913.
26. EYMIEW, A.: Le Gouvernement de Soi-Même. Paris, Perrin, 1922.
27. WALSH, J. J.: Psychotherapy. New York, Appleton Century, 1913.
28. ——: Health Through Will Power. Boston, Stratford, 1913.
29. ERICKSON, C. E.: A Basic Text for Guidance Workers. New York, Prentice-Hall, Inc., 1947.
30. TRAXLER, A. E.: Techniques of Guidance. New York, Harper & Bros., 1945.
31. POOLE, N., and BLANTON, S.: The Art of Real Happiness. New York, Prentice-Hall, Inc., 1950.
32. BLANTON, S., and PEALE, N. V.: Faith Is the Answer. New York, Abington-Cokesbury, 1940.
33. HOLMAN, C. T.: The Care of Souls: A Socio-Psychological Approach. Chicago, University of Chicago Press, 1932.
34. BATES, E. S., and DITTEMORE, J. V.: Mary Baker Eddy. New York, Knopf, 1932.
35. Jewish Board of Guardians: Conditioned Environment in Case Work Treatment. New York, 1944.
36. BRUNO, F. J.: Trends in Social Work as Reflected in the Proceedings of the National Conference of Social Work. New York, Columbia University Press, 1948.
37. United States Children's Bureau: Trends and Developments in Public Child Welfare Services. Child Welfare Reports No. 4, 1949.
38. ATKINSON, R. C., and others: Public Employment Service in the United States. Chicago, Public Administration Service, 1938.
39. FRENCH, L. M.: Psychiatric Social Work. London, The Commonwealth Fund, 1940.
40. MENNINGER, W. C.: Psychiatric Social Work in the Army and Its Implications for Civilian Social Work. Proceedings of the National Conference of Social Work, 1945.
41. ROSS, H., and JOHNSON, A. M.: The growing science of case work. J. of Social Case Work. 27:273–278, 1946.
42. TOWLE, C.: Social case work in modern society. Social Service Review. 20:165–180, 1946.
43. VAN OPHUIJSEN, J. H. W.: Therapeutic criteria in social agencies. Am. J. Orthopsychiat. 9:410–420, 1939.
44. LOWREY, L. G.: Psychiatry for Social Workers. New York, Columbia University Press, 1946, pp. 342–366.
45. PRAY, K. L. M.: The place of social case work in the treatment of delinquency. The Social Service Review. 19:235–248, 1945.
46. HAAS, L. J.: Practical Occupational Therapy. Milwaukee, Bruce Publishing Co., 1946.
47. DUNTON, W. R.: Occupation Therapy. Philadelphia, Saunders, 1915.
48. ——: Prescribing Occupational Therapy, ed. 2, Springfield, Illinois, Thomas, 1945.

49. WILLARD, H., and SPACKMAN, C. S. (eds.): Principles of Occupational Therapy. Philadelphia, Lippincott, 1947.

50. SLAVSON, S. R.: Recreation and the Total Personality. New York, Assoc. Press, 1946.

51. DAVIS, J. E., and DUNTON, W. R.: Principles and Practice of Recreational Therapy for the Mentally Ill. New York, Barnes, 1946.

52. DAVIS, J. E.: Play and Mental Health. New York, Barnes, 1938.

53. SCHULLIAN, D., and SCHOEN, M. (eds.): Music and Medicine. New York, Schuman, 1948.

54. SOIBELMAN, D.: Therapeutic and Industrial Uses of Music. New York, Columbia University Press, 1948.

55. ANDREWS, J. S.: Directive Psychotherapy: Reassurance, in Readings in the Clinical Method in Psychology, ed. Robert I. Watson. New York, Harper and Bros., 1949, pp. 654–673.

56. THORNE, F. C.: Principles of personality counseling. Brandon, Vermont, J. Clin. Psychol., 1950, p. 270.

57. KRAINES, S. H.: The Therapy of The Neuroses and Psychoses. Philadelphia, Lea and Febiger, 1943, pp. 222–229.

58. COUÉ, E.: La Maîtresse de Soi-Même Par L'Autosuggestion Consciente. Paris, Oliven, 1936.

59. WOLBERG, L. R.: Medical Hypnosis. New York, Grune & Stratton, 1948, vol. 2, pp. 1–133.

60. THORNE, F. C.: op. cit. [56] pp. 317–335.

61. HERZBERG, A.: Active Psychotherapy. New York, Grune & Stratton, 1945, p. 49.

62. DuBOIS, P.: The Psychic Treatment of Mental Disorders. New York, Funk & Wagnalls, 1909.

63. ———: Education of Self. New York, Funk and Wagnalls, 1911.

64. DEJÈRINE, J., and GAUKLER, E.: Psychoneurosis and Psychotherapy. Philadelphia, Lippincott, 1913.

65. WOLBERG, L. R.: op. cit. [59] pp. 191–198.

66. HORSLEY, J. S.: Narco-Analysis. London, Oxford University Press, 1943.

67. GRINKER, R. R., and SPIEGEL, J. P.: Men Under Stress. Philadelphia, Blakiston, 1945.

68. HUBBARD, L. R.: Dianetics: The Modern Science of Mental Health. New York, Hermitage House, 1950.

69. CALL, A. P.: Power Through Repose. Boston, Little, Brown, 1891.

70. JACOBSON, EDMUND: Progressive Relaxation. Chicago, University of Chicago Press, 1938.

71. RIPPON, T. S., and FLETCHER, P.: Reassurance and Relaxation. London, George Routledge, 1940.

72. YATES, D. H.: Relaxation in psychotherapy. J. Genet. Psychol. 34:213–237, 1946.

73. NEUFELD, W.: Relaxation methods in United States Navy air schools. Am. J. Psychiat. 108:132–137, 1951.

74. JENSEN-NELSON, K.: Massage in Nursing Care, ed. 2, New York, Macmillan, 1941.

75. MENNELL, J. B.: Physical Treatment by Movement, Manipulation and Massage, ed. 5, Philadelphia, Blakiston, 1945.

76. WEIR-MITCHELL, S.: Fat and Blood, ed. 4, Philadelphia, Lippincott, 1885.

77. WRIGHT, R.: Hydrotherapy in Psychiatric Hospitals. Boston, Tudor Press, 1940.

78. DIETHELM, O.: Treatment in Psychiatry. Springfield, Illinois, Charles C. Thomas, 1950, p. 177.

79. SAKEL, M., The Pharmacological Shock Treatment of Schizophrenia, translated by J. Wortis. New York, Nervous & Mental Disease Monographs, 1938.

80. SARGANT, W., and SLATER, E.: An Introduction to Physical Methods of Treatment in Psychiatry. Baltimore, Williams & Wilkins Co., 1948.

81. KALINOWSKY, L. B., and HOCH, P. H.: Shock Treatments, Psychosurgery, and Other Somatic Treatments in Psychiatry, ed. 2, New York, Grune & Stratton, 1952.

82. CERLETTI, V., and BINI, L.: Electric shock treatment. Bull. Acad. Med. Rome. 64:36, 1938.

83. MYERSON, A.: Effect of benzedrine sulphate on mood and fatigue in normal and neurotic persons. Arch. Neurol. & Psychiat. 36:816, 1936.

84. PALMER, H. D., and BRACELAND, F. J.: Six years with narcosis therapy in psychiatry. Am. J. Psychiat. 94:35–37, 1937.

85. KLAESI, J.: Über die therapeutische Anwendung der "Dauernarkose" Mittels Somnifen bei Schizophrenen. Ztschr. f. d. ges. Psychiat. u. Neurol. 74:557, 1922.

86. WALSH, J.: Continuous narcosis: The advantages of oral somnifaine—a comparison. J. Ment. Sc. 93:255, 1947.

87. HALD, J., JACOBSON, E., and LARSEN, V.: Sensitizing effect of tetraethylthiuramdisulphide (antabuse) to ethyl alcohol. Acta. Pharmacol. et Toxicol. 4:285, 1948.

88. BOWMAN, K. M., SIMON, A., HINE, C. H., MACKLIN, E. A., CROOK, G. H., BURBRIDGE, N., and HANSON, K.: A clinical evaluation of tetraethylthiuramdisulphide (antabuse) in the treatment of problem drinkers. Am. J. Psychiat. 107:832–838, 1951.

89. CHILD, G. P., OSINSKI, W., BENNETT, R. E., and DAVIDOFF, E.: Therapeutic results and clinical manifestations following the use of tetraethylthiuramdisulphide (antabuse). Am. J. Psychiat. 107:774–780, 1951.

90. SACKLER, A. M., SACKLER, M. D., SACKLER, R. R., and VAN OPHUIJSEN, J. H. W.: Nonconvulsive biochemotherapy with histamine. A preliminary report on the treatment of hospitalized schizophrenic, manic-depressive and involutional psychotics. J. Nerv. and Ment. Dis. 110:149, 1949.

91. DIXON, H. H., DICKEL, H. K., COEN, R. A., and HANGEN, G. O.: Clinical observations on tolserol in handling anxiety tension states. Am. J. M. Sc. 220:23, 1950.

92. JENS, R.: Desoxycorticosterone in certain psychotic cases. Northwest Med. 48:609, 1949.

93. CRANSWICK, E. H., and HALL, T. C.: Desoxycortone with ascorbic acid in mental disorder. Lancet. 1:540, 1950.

94. FREEMAN, W. J., and WATTS, J. W.: Psychosurgery. Springfield, Illinois, Thomas, 1942.

95. BANCROFT, F. W., and PILCHER, COBB (eds.): Surgical Treatment of the Nervous System. Philadelphia, Lippincott, 1946.

96. PRATT, J. H.: The influence of emotions in the causation and cure of psychoneuroses. International Clinics, 1934, vol. 4, p. 1.

97. HARRIS, H. I.: Efficient psychotherapy for the large outpatient clinic. New England J. of Med. *221:*1–5, 1939.

98. RHOADES, W.: Group training in thought control for relieving nervous disorders. Ment. Hyg. *19:*373–386, 1935.

99. WENDER, L.: Group psychotherapy: a study of its application. Psychiatric Quart. *14:*708–718, 1940.

100. BLACKMAN, N.: Ward therapy—a new method of group psychotherapy. Psychiatric Quart. *16:*660–666, 1942.

101. LEVY, J.: Relationship therapy. Am. J. Orthopsychiat. *8:*64–69, 1938.

102. ALLEN, F. H.: Therapeutic work with children: a statement of a point of view. Am. J. Orthopsychiat. *4:*193–202, 1934.

103. TAFT, J.: The Dynamics of Therapy in a Controlled Relationship. New York, Macmillan, 1933.

104. LEVY, D.: Attitude therapy. Am. J. Orthopsychiat. *7:*103–113, 1937.

105. THORNE, F. C.: op. cit. [*56*] pp. 463–469.

106. MEYER, A.: Objective psychology and psychobiology. J.A.M.A. *65:*860–863, 1915.

107. ———: The Commonsense Psychiatry of Dr. Adolf Meyer. New York, McGraw-Hill, 1948.

108. MUNCIE, W.: Psychobiology and Psychiatry, ed. 2, St. Louis, Mosby, 1948.

109. BILLINGS, E. G.: A Handbook of Elementary Psychobiology and Psychiatry. New York, Macmillan, 1939.

110. KRAINES, S. H.: The Therapy of the Neuroses and Psychoses. Philadelphia, Lea & Febiger, 1943.

111. FINESINGER, J. E.: Psychiatric interviewing. I. Some principles and procedures in insight therapy. Am. J. Psychiat. *105:*187–195, 1948.

112. LAW, S. G.: Therapy Through Interview. New York, McGraw-Hill, 1948.

113. SNYDER, W. U.: The present status of psychotherapeutic counseling. Psychol. Bull. *44:*297–386, 1947.

114. ROGERS, C. R.: Therapy in guidance clinics. J. Abnorm. & Social Psychol. *38:*284–289, 1943.

115. WILLIAMSON, E. G.: How to Counsel Students. New York, McGraw-Hill, 1939.

116. ———, and DARLEY, J. G.: Student Personnel Work, An Outline of Clinical Procedure. New York, McGraw-Hill, 1937.

117. GOLDSTEIN, S. E.: Marriage and Family Counseling. New York, McGraw-Hill, 1945.

118. THORNE, F. C.: Principles of Personality Counseling. Brandon, Vermont, J. Clinical Psychol., 1950.

119. GARRETT, A.: Counseling Methods for Personnel Workers. New York, Family Welfare Association of America, 1945.

120. New York State Counselors Association: Practical Handbook for Counselors. Chicago, Science Research Associates, 1945.

121. ROGERS, C. R.: Counseling and Psychotherapy. Boston, Houghton Mifflin, 1942.

122. ———: The development of insight in a counseling relationship. J. Consult. Psychol. *8:*331–341, 1944.

123. ———: Significant aspects of client-centered therapy. Am. Psychologist. *1:*415–422, 1946.

124. ———: Client Centered Therapy. Boston, Houghton-Mifflin, 1951.

125. SNYDER, W. U.: A short-term nondirective treatment with an adult. J. Abnorm. & Social Psychol., Clin. Suppl. *38:*87–137, 1943.

126. ——: Casebook of Non-Directive Counseling. Boston, Houghton-Mifflin, 1947.

127. THORNE, F. C.: A critique of nondirective methods of psychotherapy. J. Abnorm. & Social Psychol. *39:*459–470, 1944.

128. ——: Directive psychotherapy. J. Clin. Psychol., in various issues from 1945–1950.

129. ——: Directive psychotherapy: VII. Imparting psychological information. J. Clin. Psychol. *2:*179–190, 1946.

130. ——: Directive psychotherapy: IV. The therapeutic implications of the case history. J. Clin. Psychol. *1:*318–330, 1945.

131. ——: Principles of Personality Counseling. Brandon, Vermont, J. Clin. Psychol. 1950, pp. 336–346.

132. HAMILTON, G.: Theory and Practice of Social Case Work. New York, Columbia University Press, 1940.

133. ——: Psychotherapy in Child Guidance. New York, Columbia University Press, 1947.

134. Psychotherapy and casework. Symposium of the Boston Psychoanalytic Society and Institute. J. Soc. Casework. June 1949, entire issue.

135. STERBA, R., LYNDON, B. H., and KATZ, A.: Transference in Casework. New York, Family Service Association of America, 1948.

136. Jewish Board of Guardians: The Case Worker in Psychotherapy, New York, 1946.

137. KASIUS, C. (ed.): A Comparison of Diagnostic and Functional Casework Concepts. New York, Family Service Association of America, 1950, pp. 78–169.

138. id. pp. 31–77.

139. JONES, M. C.: The case of Peter. Ped. Sem. *31:*308–318, 1924.

140. YATES, D. H.: An association set method in psychotherapy. Psychol. Bull. *36:*506, 1939.

141. MAX, L. M.: Conditioned reaction technique, a case study. Psychol. Bull. *32:*734, 1935.

142. MOWRER, O. H., and MOWRER, W. M.: Enuresis—a method for its study and treatment. Am. J. Orthopsychiat. *8:*436–457, 1938.

143. WOLBERG, L. R.: Medical Hypnosis. New York, Grune & Stratton, 1948, vol. 2, pp. 212–217.

144. THORNE, F. C.: Principles of personality counseling. J. Clin. Psychol. 1950, pp. 271–277.

145. SALTER, A.: Conditioned Reflex Therapy. New York, Creative Age Press, 1949.

146. KORZYBSKI, A.: Science and Society. An Introduction to Non-Aristotelian Systems and General Semantics, ed. 2, Lancaster, Pennsylvania, Science Press, 1941.

147. JOHNSON, W.: People in Quandaries. New York, Harper & Bros., 1946.

148. ROME, H. P.: Group psychotherapy. Dis. Nerv. System *6:*237–241, 1945.

149. LUCHINS, A. S.: Group structures in group psychotherapy. J. Clin. Psychol. *3:*269–273, 1947.

150. SOLOMON, J. C., and AXELROD, P. L.: Group psychotherapy for withdrawn adolescents. Am. J. Dis. Child. *68:*86–101, 1944.

151. SLAVSON, S. R.: The Field and Objectives of Personality Disorders, in Current Therapies of Personality Disorders, ed. B. Glueck, New York, Grune & Stratton, 1946, pp. 166–193.

152. ———: Current practices in group therapy. Ment. Hyg. July, 1944.

153. ———: The Practice of Group Therapy. New York, International Universities Press, 1947.

154. MORENO, J. L.: Who Shall Survive? Washington, D.C., Nerv. & Ment. Dis. Publ. 1934.

155. ———: Psychodrama. New York, Beacon House, 1946, vol. I.

156. GLATZER, H. T., and PEDERSON-KRAG, G.: Relationship Group Therapy With a Mother of a Problem Child, in The Practice of Group Therapy, ed. S. R. Slavson. New York, International Universities Press, 1947, p. 219.

157. SLAVSON, S. R.: An Introduction To Group Therapy. New York, Commonwealth Fund, 1943.

158. FREUD, S. On the History of the Psychoanalytic Movement. Collected Papers. London International Psychoanalytic Press, 1924, vol. I, p. 287.

159. BREUER, J., and FREUD, S.: Studies in Hysteria. Wash., D.C., Nerv. & Ment. Dis. Pub., 1936.

160. FREUD, S.: The Interpretation of Dreams, in The Basic Writings of Sigmund Freud. New York, Modern Library, 1938.

161. ———: Three Contributions To the Theory of Sex, in The Basic Writings of Sigmund Freud. New York, Modern Library, 1938.

162. ———: The Ego and the Id. London, Hogarth, 1930.

163. ———: The Problem of Anxiety. New York, Norton, 1936.

164. ———: A General Introduction to Psychoanalysis. New York, Boni & Liveright, Inc., 1920.

165. ———: New Introductory Lectures on Psychoanalysis. New York, W. W. Norton & Co., 1933.

166. ———: Papers on Technique, in Collected Papers. London, Hogarth Press, 1924, vol. II.

167. ———: Analysis terminable and interminable. Internat. J. Psycho-analysis 18:373–405, 1937.

168. GLOVER, E., FENICHEL, O., STRACHEY, J., BERGLER, E., NUNBERG, H., and BIBRING, E.: On the theory of therapeutic results of psychoanalysis. (Symposium.) Internat. J. Psycho-analysis 18:125–189, 1937.

169. LORAND, S.: Technique of Psychoanalytic Therapy. New York, International Universities Press, 1946.

170. SHARPE, E. F.: The technique of psychoanalysis. Internat. J. Psycho-analysis, vol. II, part 3 and 4, 1930; vol. 12, 1931.

171. STERBA, R.: The dynamics of the dissolution of the transference resistance. Psychiatric. Quart. vol. 9, 1940.

172. STERN, A.: On the counter-transference in psychoanalysis. Psychoanalyt. Rev. 9:166–174, 1924.

173. BERG, C.: Psychotherapy—Practice and Theory. New York, W. W. Norton & Co., 1948, pp. 349–457.

174. GLOVER, E.: Lectures on technique in psychoanalysis. Internat. J. Psycho-analysis, vols. 8, 9, 1927.

175. JONES, E.: The relation of technique to theory. Internat. J. Psycho-analysis 8:1–4, 1924.

176. LA FORGUE, R.: Exceptions to the fundamental rule of psychoanalysis. Internat. J. Psycho-analysis, vol. 18, 1937.

177. SCHMIDEBERG, M.: The mode of operation of psychoanalytic therapy. Internat. J. Psycho-analysis, vol. 19, 1938.

178. SEARL, M. N.: Some queries on principles of technique. Internat. J. Psycho-analysis, vol. 17, 1936.

179. ZILBOORG, G.: The fundamental conflict with psychoanalysis. Internat. J. Psycho-analysis 20:480–492, 1939.

180. KUBIE, L.: Practical and Theoretical Aspects of Psychoanalysis. New York, International Universities Press, 1950.

181. FENICHEL, O.: Problems of Psychoanalytic Technique. Albany, The Psychoanalytic Quarterly, Inc., 1941.

182. STRACHEY, J.: The nature of the therapeutic action of psychoanalysis. Internat. J. Psycho-analysis 15:127, 1934.

183. BALINT, M.: The final goal of psychoanalytic treatment. Internat. J. Psycho-analysis, vol. 17, 1936.

184. BIBRING-LEHNER, G.: A contribution to the subject of transference resistance. Internat. J. Psycho-analysis 17:181–189, 1936.

185. NUNBERG, H.: Practice and Theory of Psychoanalysis. Nerv. & Ment. Dis. Monog. No. 74, 1948.

186. GLOVER, E.: An Investigation of the Technique of Psychoanalysis. London, Baillière, Tindall and Cox, 1940.

187. ADLER, A.: Neurotic Constitution. New York, Moffat, Yard, 1917.

188. ———: Study of Organ Inferiority and Its Psychical Compensation. Washington, D.C., Nerv. & Ment. Dis. Pub., 1917.

189. ———: The Practice and Theory of Individual Psychology. New York, Harcourt, Brace, 1924.

190. ———: The Education of Children, New York, Greenberg, 1930.

191. ———: Social Interest: A Challenge to Mankind. London, Faber & Faber, 1938.

192. JUNG, C. G.: Psychology of the Unconscious. New York, Moffat, Yard, 1916.

193. ———: Psychological Types or the Psychology of Individuation. New York, Harcourt, Brace, 1923.

194. FERENCZI, S.: Technical Difficulties in the Analysis of a Case of Hysteria, in Further Contributions to the Theory and Technique of Psycho-Analysis. London, The Hogarth Press, Ltd., 1950, pp. 189–197. Also The Further Development of an Active Therapy in Psycho-Analysis, in Further Contributions to the Theory and Technique of Psycho-Analysis. London, The Hogarth Press, Ltd., 1950, pp. 198–217.

195. ———, and RANK, O.: The Development of Psychoanalysis. Washington, D.C., Nerv. & Ment. Dis. Pub., 1925.

196. RANK, O.: The Trauma of Birth. New York, Harcourt, Brace, 1929.

197. ———: Will Therapy and Truth and Reality. New York, Knopf, 1947.

198. STEKEL, W.: Technique of Analytical Psychotherapy. New York, Liveright, 1950.

199. REICH, W.: Zur Technik der Deutung und der Widerstandsanalyse. Int. Zeitschrift f. Psychoanal. vol. 13, 1927.

200. ———: Ueber Charakteranalyse. Int. Zeitschrift f. Psychoanal. vol. 14, 1928.

201. ———: Character-Analysis, ed. 3. New York, Orgone Institute Press, 1949.

202. ———: The Function of the Orgasm. New York, Orgone Institute Press, 1942.

203. RADO, S.: Developments in the psychoanalytic conception and treatment of the neuroses. Psychoanalyt. Quart. 8:427, 1939.

204. ——: Mind, unconscious mind, and brain. Psychosom. Med. *11*:165, 1949.

205. ——: Emergency Behavior: With an Introduction to the Dynamics of Conscience, in Anxiety, ed. Hoch & Zubin. New York, Grune & Stratton, 1950, pp. 150–175.

206. FROMM, E.: Ueber Methods und Aufgabe einer analytischen Sozialpsychologie. Z. Soz. I, 1932.

207. ——: Authorität und Familie, in Socialpsychologischen Teil, M. Horkheimer. Paris, Felix Alcan, 1936, pp. 77–135, 230–238.

208. FREUD, A.: The Ego and the Mechanisms of Defense. London, Hogarth Press, 1937.

209. THOMPSON, C.: Psychoanalysis: Evolution and Development. New York, Hermitage House, 1950.

210. FROMM, E.: Escape from Freedom. New York, Farrar & Rinehart, 1941.

211. ——: Man for Himself. New York, Rinehart, 1947.

212. HORNEY, K.: The Neurotic Personality of Our Time. New York, W. W. Norton & Co., 1937.

213. ——: New Ways in Psychoanalysis. New York, W. W. Norton & Co., 1939.

214. ——: Our Inner Conflicts. New York, W. W. Norton & Co., 1945.

215. SULLIVAN, H. S.: Conceptions in Modern Psychiatry. Washington, D.C., William Alanson White Psychiatric Foundation, 1947.

216. ——: The theory of anxiety and the nature of psychotherapy. Am. J. Psychiat. *12*:3–12, 1949.

217. ——: The Meaning of Anxiety in Psychiatry and in Life. Washington, D.C., William Alanson White Foundation, 1948.

218. ALEXANDER, F.: Psychoanalysis revised. Psychoanalyt. Quart. *9*:1–36, 1940.

219. ——, FRENCH, T. M., and others: Psychoanalytic Therapy. New York, Ronald, 1946.

220. DEUTSCH, F.: Applied Psychoanalysis. New York, Grune & Stratton, 1949.

221. ——: The associative anamnesis. Psychoanalyt. Quart. *8*:354, 1939.

222. KARPMAN, B.: Objective psychotherapy. J. Clin. Psychol. *5*:193–342, 1949.

223. ERICKSON, M. H.: The investigation of a specific amnesia. Brit. J. M. Psychol. *13*:143–50, 1933.

224. ——: A study of experimental neurosis hypnotically induced in a case of ejaculatio praecox. Brit. J. M. Psychol. *15*:34–50, 1935.

225. ——: Development of apparent unconsciousness during hypnotic reliving of a traumatic experience. Arch. Neurol. & Psychiat. *38*:1282–88, 1937.

226. ——: Hypnotic investigation of psychosomatic phenomena: a controlled experimental use of hypnotic regression in the therapy of an acquired food intolerance. Psychosom. Med. *5*:67–70, 1943.

227. ——, and HILL, L. B.: Unconscious mental activity in hypnosis—psychoanalytic implications. Psychoanalyt. Quart. *13*:60–78, 1944.

228. ——, and KUBIE, L. S.: The permanent relief of an obsessional phobia by means of communications with an unsuspected dual personality. Psychoanalyt. Quart. *8*:471–509, 1939.

229. ——, and ——: The successful treatment of a case of acute hysterical depression by a return under hypnosis to a critical phase of childhood. Psychoanalyt. Quart. *10*:583–609, 1941.

230. EISENBUD, J.: Psychology of headache. Psychiat. Quart. *11*:592–619, 1937.

231. KUBIE, L. S.: The use of hypnagogic reveries in the recovery of repressed amnesic data. Bull. Menninger Clin. 7:172–82, 1943.

232. LINDNER, R. M.: Hypnoanalysis as a Psychotherapeutic Technique, in Specialized Techniques in Psychotherapy, ed. Bychowski, G., and Despert, J. L. New York, Basic Books, 1952, pp. 25–39.

233. ——: Rebel without a Cause: The Hypnoanalysis of a Criminal Psychopath. New York, Grune & Stratton, 1944.

234. GILL, M. M., and BRENMAN, M.: Treatment of a case of anxiety hysteria by a hypnotic technique employing psychoanalytic principles. Bull. Menninger Clin. 7:163–71, 1943.

235. FISHER, C.: Hypnosis in treatment of neuroses due to war and to other causes. War Med. 4:565–76, 1943.

236. WOLBERG, L. R.: Medical Hypnosis. New York, Grune & Stratton, 1948, vols. 1 & 2.

237. ——: Hypnotic experiments in psychosomatic medicine. Psychosom. Med. 9:337–342, 1947.

238. BENDER, L.: Art and therapy in the mental disturbances of children. J. Nerv. Ment. Dis. 86:249–263, 1937.

239. BRICK, M.: Mental hygiene value of children's art work. Am. J. Orthopsychiat. 14:136–146, 1944.

240. NAUMBERG, M.: Studies of the "Free" Art Expression of Behavior Problem Children and Adolescents as a Means of Diagnosis and Therapy. Washington, D.C., Nerv. & Ment. Dis. Monogr. No. 71, 1947.

241. ——: Spontaneous art in therapy and diagnosis. Progress in Clinical Psychology 1:290–311, 1952.

242. NAPOLI, P. J.: Finger-painting and Personality Diagnosis. Genet. Psychol. Monogr. 34, No. 2, 1946.

243. ——: Interpretive aspects of finger-painting. J. Psychol. 23:93–132, 1947.

244. ARLOW, J. A., and KADIS, A.: Finger painting in the psychotherapy of children. Am. J. Orthopsychiat. 16:134–146, 1946.

245. FLEMING, J.: Observations on the use of finger painting in the treatment of adult patients with personality disorders. Character & Personality 8:301–310, 1940.

246. MOSSE, E. P.: Painting-analysis in the treatment of neuroses. Psychoanalyt. Rev. 27:65–82, 1940.

247. STERN, M. M.: Free Painting as an Auxiliary Technique in Psychoanalysis, in Specialized Techniques in Psychotherapy, ed. Bychowski, G. and Despert, J. L. New York, Basic Books, 1952, pp. 65–83.

248. LEWIS, N. D. C.: Graphic art productions in schizophrenia. A. Research Nerv. & Ment. Dis. Proc. 5:344–68, 1928.

249. FAIRBAIRN, W. R. D.: The ultimate basis of aesthetic experience. Brit. J. Psychol. 29:167–181, 1938.

250. ——: Prolegomena to a psychology of art. Brit. J. Psychol. 28:288–303, 1938.

251. PICKFORD, R. W.: Some interpretations of a painting called "abstraction." Brit. J. M. Psychol. 18:219–49, 1938.

252. McINTOSH, J. R., and PICKFORD, R. W.: Some clinical and artistic aspects of a child's drawings. Brit. J. M. Psychol. 19:342–62, 1943.

253. GRIFFITHS, R.: A Study of Imagination in Early Childhood and Its Function in Mental Development. London, Keegan Paul, 1935.

254. VERNONON, P. E.: The significance of the Rorschach test. Brit. J. M. Psychol. *15:*199–217, 1935.

255. JUNG, C. G.: Modern Man in Search of a Soul, translated by W. S. Dell, and C. F. Baynes. New York, Harcourt, 1934.

256. APPEL, K. E.: Drawings by children as aids to personality studies. Am. J. Orthopsychiat. *1:*129–44, 1931.

257. LISS, E.: The graphic arts. Am. J. Orthopsychiat. *8:*95–99, 1938.

258. HARMS, E.: The psychotherapeutical importance of the arts. Occupational Therapy *18:*235–39, 1939.

259. ———: Child art as an aid in the diagnosis of juvenile neuroses. Am. J. Orthopsychiat. *2:*191–209, 1941.

260. REITMAN, F.: Facial expression in schizophrenic drawings. J. Ment. Sc. *85:*264–72, 1939.

261. BAYNES, H. G.: Mythology of the Soul; a Research Into the Unconscious From Schizophrenic Dreams and Drawings. London, Baillière, Tindall & Cox, 1939.

262. MIRA, E.: Myokinetic psychodiagnosis: a new technique for exploring the conative trends of personality. Proc. Roy. Soc. Med. *33:*9–30, 1940.

263. NAUMBERG, M.: The drawings of an adolescent girl suffering from conversion hysteria with amnesia. Psychiatric Quart. *18:*197–224, 1944.

264. ———: Schizophrenic Art: Its Meaning in Psychotherapy. New York, Grune & Stratton, 1950.

265. KRIS, E.: Psychoanalytic Approaches to Art. New York, International Universities Press, 1952.

266. LEVY, J.: The use of art technique in treatment of children's behavior problems. Journal of Psycho-Asthenics. *39:*258, 1934.

267. CURRAN, F. J.: Art techniques for use in mental hospitals and correctional institutions. Ment. Hyg. *23:*371–78, 1939.

268. DESPERT, J. L.: Technical approaches used in the study and treatment of emotional problems in children. Psychiatric Quart. *2:*267–95, 1937.

269. BYCHOWSKI, G.: The rebirth of a woman: a psychoanalytic study of artistic expression and sublimation. Psychoanalyt. Rev. *34:*32–57, 1947.

270. MOSSE, E. P.: Painting-analysis in the treatment of neuroses. Psychoanalyt. Rev. *27:*65–82, 1940.

271. LOWENFELD, M.: The world pictures of children: a method of recording and studying them. Brit. J. M. Psychol. *18:*65–101, 1939.

272. WHILES, W. H.: Treatment of emotional problems in children. J. Ment. Sc. *87:*359–369, 1941.

273. TRAIL, P. M.: An account of Lowenfeld technique in a child guidance clinic, with a survey of therapeutic play technique in Great Britain and U.S.A. J. Ment. Sc. *91:*43–78, 1945.

274. BENDER, L., and WOLTMANN, A. G.: The use of puppet shows as a psychotherapeutic method for behavior problems in children. Am. J. Orthopsychiat. *6:*341–354, 1936.

275. WOLTMANN, A. G.: The use of puppets in understanding children. Ment. Hyg. *24:*445–458, 1940.

276. LYLE, J., and HOLLY, S. B.: The therapeutic value of puppets. Bull. Menninger Clin. *5:*223–226, 1941.

277. BENDER, L., and WOLTMANN, A. G.: The use of plastic material as a psychiatric

approach to emotional problems in children. Am. J. Orthopsychiat. 7:283–300, 1937.

278. AXLINE, V. M.: Play Therapy. Boston, Houghton Mifflin, 1947.

279. GITELSON, M.: Clinical experience with play therapy. Am. J. Orthopsychiat. 8:466, 1939.

280. FREUD, A.: Introduction to the Technique of Child Analysis. Washington, D.C.: Nerv. & Ment. Dis. Pub. Co., 1928.

281. KLEIN, M.: The Psychoanalysis of Children. New York, Norton, 1935.

282. CONN, J. H.: A psychiatric study of car sickness. Am. J. Orthopsychiat. 8:130–41, 1938.

283. LEVY, D.: Studies in Sibling Rivalry. Res. Monogr. 2, Am. Orthopsychiat. A., 1937.

284. SOLOMON, J.: Active play therapy. Am. J. Orthopsychiat. 8:479, 1938.

285. ———: Active play therapy: further experiences. Am. J. Orthopsychiat. 10:763–81, 1940.

286. HOCH, P. H., and POLATIN, P.: Narcodiagnosis and Narcotherapy, in Specialized Techniques in Psychotherapy, ed. Bychowski, G. and Despert, J. L., New York, Basic Books, 1952, pp. 1–23.

287. SCHILDER, P.: Results and problems of group psychotherapy in severe neuroses. Ment. Hyg. 23:87–98, 1939.

288. WENDER, L.: Group psychotherapy: a study of its application. Psychiatric Quart. 14:708–718, 1940.

289. SARLIN, C. N., and BEREZIN, M. A.: Group psychotherapy on a modified analytic basis. J. Nerv. Ment. Dis. 104:611–667, 1946.

290. SUTHERLAND, J. D.: Notes on psychoanalytic group therapy. I. Therapy and training. Psychiatry. 15:111–117, 1952.

291. FOULKES, S. H.: Introduction to Group-Analytic Psychotherapy. London, Heinemann, 1949.

292. SLAVSON, S. R.: Analytic Group Psychotherapy With Adults, Adolescents and Children. New York, Columbia University Press, 1950.

293. ACKERMAN, N. W.: Psychoanalysis and group psychotherapy. Group Psychotherapy. 3:204–215, 1950.

294. EZRIEL, H.: Notes on psychoanalytic group therapy: II. Interpretation and research. Psychiatry. 15:119–126, 1952.

295. ———: A psycho-analytic approach to group treatment. Brit. J. M. Psychol. 23:59–74, 1950.

296. SPOTNITZ, H.: Group Therapy as a Specialized Psychotherapeutic Technique, in Specialized Techniques in Psychotherapy, ed. Bychowski, G. and Despert, J. L., New York, Basic Books, 1952, pp. 85–101.

297. WOLF, A.: The psychoanalysis of groups. Am. J. Psychotherapy. 3:525–558, 1949, 4:16–50, 1950.

298. Proceedings of the Brief Psychotherapy Council, under the auspices of the Chicago Institute for Psychoanalysis, October 25–26, 1942.

299. Proceedings of the Second Brief Psychotherapy Council. (1. Psychosomatic Medicine. 2. Psychotherapy for Children, Group Psychotherapy. 3. War Psychiatry.), under the auspices of the Chicago Institute for Psychoanalysis, January, 1944.

300. Proceedings of the Third Psychotherapy Council, under the auspices of the Chicago Institute for Psychoanalysis, October 18–19, 1946.

301. REIDER, N.: Remarks on mechanisms of nonanalytic psychotherapy. Dis. Nerv. System, vol. V, no. 1, 1944.

302. CRANK, H. H.: The use of psychoanalytic principles in outpatient psychotherapy. Bull. Menninger Clinic. IV, 1940, p. 35.

303. DEUTSCH, F.: The associative anamnesis. Psychoanalyt. Quart. 8:354–381, 1939.

304. ———: Applied Psychoanalysis. Selected Objectives of Psychotherapy. New York, Grune & Stratton, 1949.

305. BELLAK, L.: The use of oral barbiturates in psychotherapy. Am. J. Psychiat. 105:849–850, 1949.

306. BENJAMIN, J. D.: Psychoanalysis and nonanalytic psychotherapy. Psychoanalyt. Quart. 16:169–176, 1947.

307. BERLINER, BERNHARD: Short psychoanalytic psychotherapy: its possibilities and its limitations. Bull. Menninger Clin. 5:204–213, 1941.

308. FUERST, R. A.: Problems of short time psychotherapy. Am. J. Orthopsychiat. 8:260, 1938.

309. GUTHEIL, E. A.: Psychoanalysis and brief psychotherapy. J. Clin. Psychopath. 6:207, 1945.

310. HERZBERG, A.: Short treatment of neurosis by graduated tasks. Brit. J. M. Psychol. 19:19, 1941.

311. GROTJAHN, M.: Brief psychotherapy on psychoanalytic principles. Illinois Psychiatric Journal. 2:1, 1942.

312. WOLBERG, L. R.: Hypnoanalysis, New York, Grune & Stratton, 1945.

313. ———: Medical Hypnosis, New York, Grune & Stratton, 1948.

314. ALEXANDER, F., FRENCH, T. M., and others: Psychoanalytic Therapy. New York, Ronald, 1946.

315. SAUL, LEON J.: On the value of one or two interviews. Psychoanalyt. Quart. 20:613–615, 1951.

316. FREUD, S.: On Psychotherapy. Collected Papers. London, Hogarth Press, 1924, vol. I, p. 249.

317. ———: An Outline of Psychoanalysis. New York, W. W. Norton & Co., 1949, pp. 63–64.

318. FENICHEL, O.: The Psychoanalytic Theory of Neurosis. New York, W. W. Norton Co., 1949, pp. 575–581.

319. STONE, L.: Psychoanalysis and brief psychotherapy. Psychoanalyt. Quart. 20:215–236, 1951.

320. OBERNDORF, C. P.: Consideration of results with psychoanalytic therapy. Am. J. Psychiat. 99:374–381, 1942.

321. JAMEISON, G. R., and McNIEL, E. E.: Some unsuccessful results with psychoanalytic therapy. Am. J. Psychiat. 95:1421–48, 1939.

322. HOWE, H. S.: Progress in neurology and psychiatry. N.Y.S.J. Med. 51:102, 1951.

323. KESSEL, L., and HYMAN, H. T.: The value of psychoanalysis as a therapeutic procedure. J.A.M.A. 101:1612–1615, 1933.

324. Editorial: An evaluation of psychoanalysis. J.A.M.A. 101:1643–1644, 1933.

325. FENICHEL, O.: The Psychoanalytic Theory of Neurosis. New York, Norton, 1945, p. 582.

326. GALDSTON, I.: The problem of medical and lay psychotherapy. The medical view. Am. J. Psychotherapy. 4:421, 1950.

327. DRAPER, G.: The concept of organic unity and psychosomatic medicine. J.A.M.A. *124:*767–771, 1944.

328. OVERHOLSER, W.: Physical medicine and psychiatry, some interrelationships. J.A.M.A. *138:*1221, 1948.

329. ALVAREZ, W. C.: Psychosomatic medicine that every physician should know. J.A.M.A. *135:*705, 1947.

330. GROOM, D.: Some applications of psychiatry in general medicine. J.A.M.A. *135:*403, 1947.

331. Psychiatry and Medical Education. Report of the 1951 Conference on Psychiatric Education. Wash., D.C., American Psychiatric Association, 1952.

332. STRAUSS, B. V.: The role of the physician's personality in medical practice (psychotherapeutic medicine). N.Y.S.J. Med., March 15, 1951, p. 753.

333. WHITEHORN, J. C.: Guide to interviewing and clinical personality study. Arch. Neurol. & Psychiat. *52:*197–216, 1944.

334. BARTEMEIER, L. H.: The attitude of the physician. J.A.M.A. *145:*1122–1125, 1951.

335. EBAUGH, F. G.: Evaluation of interviewing technics and principles of psychotherapy for the general practitioner. J. Omaha Mid-West Clin. Soc. *9:*29–35, 1948.

336. WATTS, M. S. M., and WILBUR, D. L.: Clinical management of "functional" disorders. J.A.M.A. *148:*704–708, 1952.

337. SMITH, G.: Psychotherapy in General Medicine. New York, Commonwealth Fund, 1946.

338. RENNIE, T. A. C.: What can the practitioner do in treating the neuroses? Bull. New York Acad. Med. Jan., 1946.

339. LEVINE, M.: Psychotherapy in Medical Practice. New York, The Macmillan Co., 1942.

340. LAW, S. G.: Therapy through Interview. New York, McGraw-Hill, 1948.

341. RENNIE, T. A. C. and WOODWARD, L. E.: Mental Health in Modern Society. New York, The Commonwealth Fund, 1948.

342. The Psychiatric Bulletin. Medical Arts Publishing Fundation, Houston, Texas, vol. I. no. 1, Summer Volume 1950–1951 and succeeding issues.

343. MOENCH, L. G.: Office Psychiatry. Chicago, The Year Book Pub., Inc., 1952.

344. WITMER, H. L. (ed.): Teaching Psychotherapeutic Medicine. New York, The Commonwealth Fund, 1947.

345. ZISKIND, E.: Training in psychotherapy for all physicians. J.A.M.A. *147:*1223–1225, 1951.

346. Committee on Training in Clinical Psychology of the American Psychological Association (David Shakow, Chairman): Recommended Graduate Training Program in Clinical Psychology. Am. Psychologist. *2:*548, 1947.

347. HARROWER, M. R.: The Evolution of a Clinical Psychologist. Transactions of the First Conference. New York, Josiah Macy, Jr. Foundation, 1947, p. 12.

348. ROGERS, CARL R.: op. cit. [*121*].

349. ——: op. cit. [*124*].

350. THORNE, F. C.: op. cit. [*118*].

351. RENNIE, T. A. C. and WOODWARD, L. E.: op. cit. [*341*], pp. 218–238.

352. JACOBSEN, C.: Preclinical Training of the Clinical Psychologist. Transactions of the First Conference. New York, Josiah Macy Jr. Foundation, 1947, pp. 16–21.

353. BINGER, C.: The Role of Training in Clinical Psychology in the Education of

the Psychiatrist. Transaction of the First Conference. New York, Josiah Macy, Jr. Foundation. 1947, pp. 57–58.

354. GALDSTON, I.: op. cit. [326], p. 422.

355. HAUN, P.: Psychiatry and the ancillary services. Am. J. Psychiat. 102–107, 1950.

356. SZUREK, S. A.: Remarks on training for psychotherapy. Am. J. Orthopsychiat. 19:36–51, 1949.

357. KUBIE, L. S.: Elements in the Medical Curriculum Which Are Essential in the Training for Psychotherapy—Training in Clinical Psychology. Transactions of the First Conference. New York, Josiah Macy, Jr. Foundation, 1947, pp. 46–51.

358. MILLER, J. G.: Elements in the Medical Curriculum Which Should Be Incorporated in the Training of the Clinical Psychologist. Transactions of the First Conference. New York, Josiah Macy, Jr. Foundation, 1947, pp. 41–46.

359. GARDNER, G. E.: Training of clinical psychologists. Round table, 1951. 4. The development of the clinical attitude. Am. J. Orthopsychiat. 22:162–169, 1952.

360. ELIASBERG, W. G.: Psychotherapy in cancer patients. J.A.M.A. 147:525, 1951.

361. KANT, O.: Deceptive psychoneurosis. Psychiatric Quart. 20:129, 1946.

362. HARROWER, M. R.: op. cit. [347] pp. 11–12.

363. YOUNG, R. A.: Treatment problems of the psychologist. Round table, 1949. I. The status of the clinical psychologist in therapy. Am. J. Orthopsychiat. 22:312, 1950.

364. MILLER, J. G.: op. cit. [358].

365. LINDNER, R. M.: Who shall practice psychotherapy? Am. J. Psychotherap. 4:432–442, 1950.

366. Committee on Clinical Psychology of the Group for the Advancement of Psychiatry: The Relation of Clinical Psychology to Psychiatry. Report No. 10, Topeka, Kansas, July 1949.

367. American Psychologist. 4:445, 1949.

368. American Psychiatric Association Newsletter. vol. 3, no. 9, May 15, 1951.

369. GERTY, F. J., HOLLOWAY, J. W. JR., and MACKAY, R. P.: Licensure or certification of clinical psychologists. J.A.M.A. 148:271–273, 1952.

370. Committee on Psychiatric Social Work of the Group for the Advancement of Psychiatry: Psychiatric Social Work in the Psychiatric Clinic. Report No. 16, Topeka, Kansas, Sept. 1950.

371. Committee on Psychiatric Social Work of the Group for the Advancement of Psychiatry (Marian E. Kenworthy, Chairman). The Psychiatric Social Worker in the Psychiatric Hospital. Report No. 2, Jan. 1948.

372. HAMILTON, G.: op. cit. [133].

373. DEUTSCH, F.: op. cit. [304] pp. 171–195.

374. TOWLE, C.: The Training of the Social Worker for Child Guidance. Handbook of Child Guidance, ed. E. Harms. New York, Child Care Publications, 1947, pp. 372–380.

375. GINSBURG, E. L.: The Training and Function of a Psychiatric Social Worker in a Clinical Setting. Transactions of the First Conference. New York, Josiah Macy, Jr. Foundation, 1947, pp. 31–40.

376. American Association of Schools of Social Work. Preprofessional Education for Social Work. New York, A.A.S.S.W., 130 E. 22nd St., N.Y.C., 1946.

377. Committee on Psychiatric Social Work of the Group for the Advancement of Psychiatry—Circular Letter No. 21, Topeka, Kansas, 1946.

378. ACKERMAN, N. W.: The training of case workers in psychotherapy. Am. J. Orthopsychiat. *19:*14–24, 1949.

379. LEMKAU, P. V.: What Can the Public Health Nurse Do in Mental Hygiene. Presented at a Mental Hygiene Conference for U. S. Public Health Service Nursing Consultants, Feb. 1948, Washington, D.C.

380. ——: Mental hygiene in public health. Public Health Reports. *62:*1151–1162, 1947.

381. Committee on Psychiatric Nursing and the Committee on Hospitals of the Group for the Advancement of Psychiatry: The Psychiatric Nurse in the Mental Hospital. Report No. 22, Topeka, Kansas, May 1952.

382. Committee on the Function of Nursing: A Program for the Nursing Profession. ed. Eli Ginzberg. New York, Macmillan, 1949.

383. MULLER, T. G.: The Nature and Direction of Psychiatric Nursing. Philadelphia, Lippincott, 1950.

384. CLAWSON, G., and PEASLEY, E.: Nursing care in insulin therapy. Am. J. Nursing *49:*621, 1949.

385. GAYLE, R., and NEALE, C.: Subshock insulin therapy. Dis. Nerv. System. *10:*231, 1949.

386. SHERMAN, C., and CHARBONNEAU, L.: Electric shock therapy. Am. J. Nursing. *48:*294, 1948.

387. FRIEDMAN, E.: Nursing aspects of the treatment of lobotomized patients. Bull. Menninger Clin. *14:*138, 1950.

388. BEHNKEN, P., and MERRILL, E.: Nursing care following prefrontal lobotomy. Am. J. Nursing *49:*431, 1949.

389. CAMERON, D. E.: General Psychotherapy. Dynamics and Procedures. New York, Grune & Stratton, 1950, pp. 270–288.

390. RENNIE, T. A. C., and WOODWARD, L. E.: op. cit., [*341*], pp. 188–190.

391. BENNETT, A. E., and EATON, J. T.: The role of the psychiatric nurse in the newer therapies. Am. J. Psychiat. *108:*169, 1951.

392. FOSTER, L. E.: Religion and psychiatry. Pastoral Psychology. *1:*7–13, 1950.

393. MENNINGER, W. C.: Psychiatry and religion. Pastoral Psychology. *1:*14–16, 1950.

394. KUBIE, L. S.: Psychoanalysis and healing by faith. Pastoral Psychology. *1:*13–18, 1950.

395. MENNINGER, K. A.: Religious applications of psychiatry. Pastoral Counseling. *1:*13–22, 1950.

396. HASTINGS, D. W.: The psychiatrist and the clergyman. Northwest Med. *47:*644–647, 1948.

397. ROBERTS, D. E.: Psychotherapy and a Christian View of Man. New York, Scribner's, 1940.

398. HILTNER, S.: Religion and Health. New York, Macmillan, 1943.

399. ——, and others: Clinical Pastoral Training. New York, Federal Council of Churches of Christ in America, 1945.

400. ——: Religion and pastoral counsel. Am. J. Orthopsychiat. *17:*21–26, 1947.

401. MORRIS, R. D.: The Essential Meaning of Clinical Pastoral Training, in Clinical Pastoral Training, ed. Hiltner, Seward. The Commission on Religion and Health, Federal Council of Churches of Christ in America, 1945.

402. WISE, C. A.: Pastoral Counseling: Its Theory and Practice. New York, Harper and Bros., 1951.

403. HILTNER, S.: Pastoral Counseling. New York, Abington-Cokesbury Press, 1949.

404. ROGERS, C. R., and BECKER, R. J.: A basic orientation for counseling. Pastoral Psychology. *1:*26–24, 1950.

405. HILTNER, S.: Hostility in counseling. Pastoral Psychology. *1:*35–42, 1950.

406. RENNIE, T. A. C., and WOODWARD, L. E.: op. cit. [*341*], p. 244.

407. *id.* p. 361.

408. WICKMAN, E. K.: Differences in the Attitudes of Teachers and Mental Hygienists, in Children's Behavior and Teacher's Attitude. New York, Commonwealth Fund, 1928.

409. RYAN, W. C.: Mental Health Through Education. New York, Commonwealth Fund, 1939.

410. PRESCOTT, D., and others: Helping teachers understand children. Understanding the Child. *14:*67–70, 1945.

411. BARUCH, D. W.: Procedures in training teachers to prevent and reduce mental hygiene problems. Pedagogical Seminary and J. Genet. Psychol. *67:*143–178, 1948.

412. MATHEWSON, R. H.: Guidance Policy and Practice. New York, Harper and Bros., 1949.

413. WATSON, G.: The Role of the Teacher, eds. Witty, P. A., and Skinner, C. E. in Mental Hygiene in Modern Education. New York, Farrar & Rinehart, 1939.

414. ZACHRY, C. B.: The psychotherapist and the school. Nervous Child. *3:*249–57, 1944. (The entire issue is devoted to psychotherapy and education.)

415. BERGER, D.: Guidance in the elementary school. Teachers College Record. *49:*44–50, 1947.

416. TRAGER, H.: The Primary Teacher, in Intercultural Attitudes in the Making. 9th Yearbook of the John Dewey Society, 1949.

417. ALLEN, W. Y., and CAMPBELL, D.: The Creative Nursery Center. New York, Family Service Association of America, 1949.

418. ALLEN, C. M.: Day Care Centers for School Children. New York, Child Welfare League of America, 1947.

419. CAMPBELL, D.: Counseling service in the day nursery. The Family, March, 1943.

420. BULLIS, H. E., and O'MALLEY, E. E.: Human Relations in the Classroom. Course I. Wilmington, Delaware, Delaware State Society for Mental Hygiene, 1947.

421. —— and ——: Human Relations in the Classroom. Course II. Wilmington, Delaware, Delaware State Society for Mental Hygiene, 1948.

422. TARUMIANZ, M. D., and BULLIS, H. E.: The human relations class; a preventive mental hygiene program for schools. Understanding the Child. *13:*3–10, 1944.

423. Commission on Teacher Education: Helping Teachers Understand Children. Washington, District of Columbia, American Council on Education, 1945.

424. Good Education for Young Children. Flushing, New York, New York State Council for Early Childhood Education, 1947.

425. ANDERSON, V. V. and KENNEDY, W. M.: Psychiatry in college—a discussion of a model personnel program. Ment. Hyg. *16:*353–383, 1932.

426. ANGELL, J. R.: Mental hygiene in colleges and universities. Ment. Hyg. *17:*543–547, 1933.

427. ANTHONISEN, M. R.: The practice of the college psychiatrist. Dis. Nerv. System. *3:*175–184, 1942.

428. BERNARD, H. W.: College mental hygiene—decade of growth. Ment. Hyg. *24:*413–418, 1940.

429. Association for Supervision and Curriculum Development. Fostering Mental Health In Our Schools. 1950 Yearbook. Washington, District of Columbia, National Education Association, 1950.

430. ZULLIGER, H.: Psychoanalytic experiences in public schools practice. Am. J. Orthopsychiat. *10:*37–85; 595–609, 1940, and *11:*151–171, 356–370, 1941.

431. AXLINE, V. M.: op cit. [*278*], pp. 414–470.

432. BARON, S.: Limitations of the teacher in guidance. Am. J. Psychotherapy. *6:*104–110, 1952.

433. LORAND, SANDER: op. cit., [*169*], p. 1.

434. THOMPSON, CLARA: Psychoanalysis: Evolution and Development. New York, Hermitage Press, 1950, pp. 241–242.

435. MEDUNA, L. J.: Physiological Background of Carbon Dioxide Treatment of the Neuroses. Paper read at the 109th annual meeting of the American Psychiatric Association, Los Angeles, May 7, 1953.

436. HARGROVE, E. A., BENNETT, A. E., and STEELE, MARION: An Investigational Study Using Carbon Dioxide as an Adjunct to Psychotherapy in Neuroses. Paper read at the 109th annual meeting of the American Psychiatric Association, Los Angeles, May 7, 1953.

437. GUTHEIL, E. A.: Music as an Adjunct to Psychotherapy. Paper read before the Association for the Advancement of Psychotherapy. New York, Feb. 27, 1953.

438. Committee on Nomenclature and Statistics of the American Psychiatric Association: Diagnostic and Statistical Manual. Mental Disorders. Washington, District of Columbia, American Psychiatric Association, 1952.

439. KNIGHT, R. P.: Evaluation of the results of psychoanalytic therapy. Am. J. Psychiat. *98:*434–446, 1941.

440. MILES, H., BARRABEE, E. L. and FINESINGER, J. E.: Evaluation of psychotherapy. Psychosom. Med. *113:*83–105, 1951.

441. DENKER, P. G.: Results of treatment of psychoneurosis by the general practitioner: A follow-up study of 500 cases. N. Y. S. J. Med. *46:*2164–2166, 1946.

442. BARTLETT, M. R.: A six month follow-up of the effects of personal adjustment counseling of veterans. J. Consult. Psychol. *14:*393–394, 1950.

443. LANDIS, C.: A Statistical Evaluation of Psychotherapeutic Methods, in Hinsie, L. E., Concepts and Problems of Psychotherapy. New York, Columbia University Press, 1937.

444. KLOPFER, B. and KELLY, D. M.: The Rorschach Technique. Yonkers, New York, World Book Co., 1942.

445. RORSCHACH, H.: Psychodiagnostics: A Diagnostic Test Based on Perception. Bern, H. Huber, 1942.

446. MURRAY, H. A.: Explorations in Personality. London, Oxford University Press, 1938, pp. 530–545.

447. TOMPKINS, S. S.: Thematic Apperception Test. The Theory and Technique of Interpretation. New York, Grune & Stratton, 1947.

448. DERI, S.: Introduction to the Szondi Test. New York, Grune & Stratton, 1949.

449. MACHOVER, K.: Personality Projection in the Drawing of the Human Figure. Springfield, Illinois, Thomas, 1948.

450. SONNEMAN, U.: Handwriting Analysis. New York, Grune & Stratton, 1951.

451. LEWINSON, T. S., and ZUBIN, J.: Handwriting Analysis. New York, King's Crown Press, 1942.

452. LEWIS, N. D. C.: The practical value of graphic art in personality studies. (I.

An introductory presentation of the possibilities.) Psychoanalyt. Rev. vol. XII, no. 3, 316–322, 1925.

453. ERIKSON, E. H.: Dramatics Production Test, in Explorations in Personality, H. A. Murray and others. New York, Oxford University Press, 1938, pp. 552–582.

454. JUNG, C. G.: Studies in Word Associations. New York, Heinemann, 1919.

455. PIOTROWSKI, Z. and SCHREIBER, M.: Rorschach, Perceptanalytic Measurement of Personality Changes During and After Intensive Psychoanalytically Oriented Psychotherapy, in Specialized Techniques in Psychotherapy. ed. Bychowski, Gustav, and Despert, J. Louise. New York, Basic Books, 1952, pp. 337–361.

456. FLUMERFELT, J. M.: Referring your patient to a psychiatrist. J.A.M.A. *146:* 1589–1591, 1951.

457. POWDERMAKER, F. B., FRANK, J. D. et al.: Group Psychotherapy. Studies in Methodology of Research and Therapy. Cambridge, Massachusetts, Harvard University Press, 1953.

458. WOLBERG, L. R.: Medical Hypnosis. New York, Grune & Stratton, 1948, vol. I, pp. 111–185.

459. MANN, N. M., CONWAY, E. J., GOTTESFELD, B. H., and LASSER, L. M.: Coordinated approach to antabuse therapy. J.A.M.A. *149:*40–46, 1952.

460. FOX, R.: Psychotherapeutics of Alcoholism, in Specialized Techniques in Psychotherapy. ed. Bychowski, G., and Despert, J. L. New York, Basic Books, 1952, pp. 239–260.

461. Council on Pharmacy and Chemistry: What to do with a drug addict. J.A.M.A. *149:*1220–1223, 1952.

462. GLAUBER, I. P.: Dynamic Therapy for the Stutterer, in Specialized Techniques in Psychotherapy, ed. Bychowski, Gustav, and Despert, J. Louise. New York, Basic Books, 1952, pp. 207–238.

463. WOLBERG, A.: The "borderline patient." Am. J. Psychotherapy. *6:*694–710, 1952.

464. EISENSTEIN, V. W.: Differential psychotherapy of borderline states. Psychiatric Quart. *25:*379–401, 1951.

465. FEDERN, P.: Principles of psychotherapy in latent schizophrenia. Am. J. Psychotherapy. *1:*129–145, 1947.

466. BYCHOWSKI, G.: Therapy of the weak ego. Am. J. Psychotherapy. *4:*407, 1950.

467. SULLIVAN, H. S.: The modified psychoanalytic treatment of schizophrenia. Am. J. Psychiat, *11:*No. 3, 1931.

468. ROSEN, J. M.: The treatment of schizophrenic psychosis by direct analytic therapy. Psychiatric Quart. *21:*3–37, 117–119, 1947.

469. FROMM-REICHMANN, F.: Transference problems in schizophrenia. Psychoanalyt. Quart. *8:*412, 1939.

470. FEDERN, P.: Psychoanalysis of psychosis. Psychiatric Quart. *17:*3–17, 470–487, 1943.

471. BYCHOWSKI, G.: Psychotherapy of Psychosis. New York, Grune & Stratton, 1952.

472. FROMM-REICHMANN, F.: Notes on the Development of the Treatment of Schizophrenics by Psychoanalytic Psychotherapy, in Specialized Techniques in Psychotherapy. ed. Bychowski, Gustav, and Despert, J. Louise. New York, Basic Books, 1952, pp. 159–179.

473. HADFIELD, J. A.: Functional Nerve Disease. ed. Crichton-Miller, London, 1920.

474. HORSLEY, J. S.: Narco-analysis. London, Oxford University Press, 1943, p. 12.

475. GROTJAHN, M.: The role of identification in psychiatric and psychoanalytic training. Psychiatry. *12:*141–151, 1949.

476. SZUREK, S. A.: Remarks on training for psychotherapy. Am. J. Orthopsychiat. *19:*36–51, 1949.

477. HASHAGEN, J. M.: Supervision. Journal of Psychiatric Social Work. *17:*94–99, 1947–1948.

478. LOWRY, F.: A philosophy of supervision in social case work. N.C.S.W., 1936, pp. 108–118.

479. REEVE, M.: The role of the supervisor in helping the student to a professional orientation, in F.S.S.A. Pamphlet, Some Emotional Elements In Supervision (Report of a Group Discussion), 1937.

480. HULSE, W. C. and LOWINGER, L.: Psychotherapy in general practice. Am. Practitioner and Digest of Treatment *1:*141–145, 588–598, 926–932, 1024–1030, 1950.

481. PFISTER, H. O.: Farbe und Bewegung in der Zeichnung Geisteskranken. Schweiz. Arch. f. Neurol. u. Psychiat. *34:*325–365, 1934.

Recommended Reading

PSYCHOSOCIAL DEVELOPMENT

1. JOSSELYN, IRENE M.: Psychosocial Development of Children. New York, Family Service Association of America, 1949.
2. Association for Supervision and Curriculum Development: Fostering Mental Health in Our Schools. Washington, District of Columbia, National Education Association, 1950.

PSYCHOPATHOLOGY AND PSYCHODYNAMICS

1. FENICHEL, OTTO: The Psychoanalytic Theory of Neurosis. New York, W. W. Norton & Co., 1945.
2. FREUD, SIGMUND: An Outline of Psychoanalysis. New York, W. W. Norton & Co., 1949.
3. FREUD, SIGMUND: A General Introduction to Psychoanalysis. New York, Liveright, 1935.
4. FREUD, SIGMUND: The Problem of Anxiety. New York, W. W. Norton & Co., 1936.
5. FREUD, ANNA: The Ego and the Mechanisms of Defense. New York, International Universities Press, 1946.
6. HOCH, PAUL H., and ZUBIN, PAUL (eds.): Anxiety. New York, Grune & Stratton, 1950.
7. WEISS, EDOARDO: Principles of Psychodynamics. New York, Grune & Stratton, 1950.
8. HORNEY, KAREN: The Neurotic Personality of Our Time. New York, W. W. Norton & Co., 1937.
9. HORNEY, KAREN: Our Inner Conflicts. New York, W. W. Norton & Co., 1945.
10. FROMM, ERICH: Escape From Freedom. New York, Farrar & Rinehart, 1941.
11. SULLIVAN, HARRY STACK: The Meaning of Anxiety in Psychiatry and in Life. Washington, D.C., Wm. Alanson White Foundation, 1948.
12. PEARSON, G. H. J.: Emotional Disorders of Children: A Case Book of Child Psychiatry. New York, W. W. Norton & Co., 1949.

ABNORMAL PSYCHOLOGY

1. MASLOW, A. H., and MITTLEMAN, BÉLA: Principles of Abnormal Psychology, New York, Harper & Bros., 1951.
2. HUNT, J. McV.: Personality and the Behavior Disorders. New York, Ronald Press, 1944. (2 vol.)

HISTORY OF PSYCHIATRY

1. ZILBOORG, G., and HENRY, G. W.: A History of Medical Psychology. New York, W. W. Norton & Co., 1941.

2. FREUD, SIGMUND: The History of the Psychoanalytic Movement, in The Basic Writings of Sigmund Freud. New York, Modern Library, 1938.
3. FERENCZI, S., and RANK, O.: The Development of Psychoanalysis. Washington, D.C., Nerv. and Ment. Dis. Publ., 1925.
4. THOMPSON, CLARA: Psychoanalysis, Its Evolution and Development. New York, Hermitage Press, 1950.

BASIC NEUROPSYCHIATRY

1. NOYES, ARTHUR P.: Modern Clinical Psychiatry. Philadelphia, W. B. Saunders Co., 1942.
2. LEWIS, NOLAN D. C.: Outlines for Psychiatric Examinations. New York, State Department of Mental Hygiene, 1943.
3. STRECKER, EDWARD: Fundamentals of Psychiatry. Philadelphia, J. B. Lippincott, 1942.
4. Diagnostic and Statistical Manual. Mental Disorders. Washington, District of Columbia, American Psychiatric Association, 1952.

GENERAL TEXTBOOKS ON TREATMENT IN PSYCHIATRY

1. DIETHELM, OSKAR: Treatment in Psychiatry. Springfield, Illinois, Thomas, 1950.
2. MOENCH, LOUIS G.: Office Psychiatry. Chicago, The Year Book, Inc., 1952.

TECHNIQUES OF INTERVIEWING

1. GARRETT, ANNETTE: Interviewing—Its Principles and Methods. New York, Family Welfare Association of America, 1942.
2. BINGHAM, W. V. D., and MOORE, B. V.: How To Interview. New York, Harper & Bros., 1941.

TECHNIQUES OF SUPPORTIVE THERAPY

1. LEVINE, MAURICE: Psychotherapy in Medical Practice. New York, Macmillan, 1942.
2. TRAXLER, ARTHUR E.: Techniques of Guidance. New York, Harper & Bros., 1945.
3. Jewish Board of Guardians: Conditioned Environment in Case Work Treatment. New York, 1944.

TECHNIQUES OF INSIGHT THERAPY
WITH REEDUCATIVE GOALS

1. General Insight Therapy

CAMERON, D. EWEN: General Psychotherapy. New York, Grune & Stratton, 1950.

2. Psychobiologic Therapy

   a. MUNCIE, WENDELL: Psychobiology and Psychiatry. ed. 2, St. Louis, C. V. Mosby Co., 1948.

   b. KRAINES, SAMUEL H.: The Therapy of the Neuroses and Psychoses. Philadelphia, Lea & Febiger, 1943.

3. Interview Psychotherapy

   LAW, STANLEY G.: Therapy Through Interview. New York, McGraw-Hill, 1948.

4. Casework Psychotherapy

   KASIUS, CORA (ed.): A Comparison of Diagnostic and Functional Casework Concepts. New York, Family Service Association of America, 1950.

5. Psychologic Therapy

   a. THORNE, FREDERICK C.: Principles of Personality Counseling. Brandon, Vermont, J. of Clin. Psychol., 1950.

   b. ROGERS, CARL R.: Counseling and Psychotherapy. Boston, Houghton-Mifflin, 1942.

   c. ROGERS, CARL R.: Client Centered Therapy. Boston, Houghton-Mifflin, 1951.

TECHNIQUES OF INSIGHT THERAPY
WITH RECONSTRUCTIVE GOALS

1. General Reconstructive Psychotherapy

   a. COLBY, KENNETH M.: A Primer for Psychotherapists. New York, Ronald Press, 1951.

   b. FROMM-REICHMANN, FRIEDA: Principles of Intensive Psychotherapy. Chicago, University of Chicago Press, 1950.

   c. DOLLARD, JOHN, and MILLER, NEAL D.: Personality and Psychotherapy. New York, McGraw-Hill, 1950.

   d. ALEXANDER, FRANZ: Fundamentals of Psychoanalysis. New York, W. W. Norton & Co., 1948.

2. Techniques of Freudian Psychoanalysis

   a. FENICHEL, OTTO: Problems of Psychoanalytic Technique. Albany, Psychoanalytic Quarterly, 1941.

   b. LORAND, SANDOR: Technique of Psychoanalytic Therapy. New York, International Universities Press, 1946.

   c. KUBIE, L.: Practical and Theoretical Aspects of Psychoanalysis. New York, International Universities Press, 1950.

   d. NUNBERG, H.: Practice and Theory of Psychoanalysis. Washington, D.C., Nerv. & Ment. Dis. Monog. No. 74, 1948.

   e. GLOVER, EDWARD: An Investigation of the Technique of Psychoanalysis. London, Baillière, Tindall and Cox, 1940.

   f. FREUD, SIGMUND: The Interpretation of Dreams, in The Basic Writings of Sigmund Freud. New York, Modern Library, 1938.

g. FREUD, SIGMUND: Papers on Technique, in Collected Papers. London, Hogarth Press, 1924, vol. II.

3. Techniques of Non-Freudian Psychoanalysis

a. ADLER, ALFRED: The Practice and Theory of Individual Psychology. New York, Harcourt, Brace, 1924.
b. JUNG, C. G.: Psychology of the Unconscious. Moffat, Yard, 1916.
c. FERENCZI, S.: Further Contributions to the Theory and Techniques of Psychoanalysis. London, The Hogarth Press, Ltd., 1950.
d. RANK, O.: Will Therapy and Truth and Reality. New York, Knopf, 1947.
e. STEKEL, WILHELM: Technique of Analytical Psychotherapy. New York, Liveright, 1950.
f. REICH, WILHELM: Character-Analysis, ed. 3. New York, Orgone Institute Press, 1949.
g. HORNEY, KAREN: New Ways in Psychoanalysis. New York, W. W. Norton & Co., 1939.
h. SULLIVAN, HARRY STACK: Conceptions in Modern Psychiatry. Washington, D.C., William Alanson White Psychiatric Foundation, 1948.

4. Techniques of Psychoanalytically Oriented Psychotherapy

a. ALEXANDER, FRANZ, FRENCH, T. M., et al.: Psychoanalytic Therapy: Principles and Application. New York, Ronald Press, 1946.
b. DEUTSCH, FELIX: Applied Psychoanalysis. New York, Grune & Stratton, 1949.

TECHNIQUE OF DREAM ANALYSIS

1. SHARPE, E. F.: Dream Analysis: A Practical Handbook In Psychoanalysis. New York, W. W. Norton & Co., 1938.
2. GUTHEIL, EMIL A.: The Handbook of Dream Analysis. New York, Liveright, 1951.

PSYCHOTHERAPY OF PSYCHOSES

BYCHOWSKI, GUSTAV: Psychotherapy of Psychosis. New York, Grune & Stratton, 1952.

ADJUNCTIVE AIDS IN PSYCHOTHERAPY

1. General Specialized Techniques

BYCHOWSKI, GUSTAV, and DESPERT, J. LOUISE (eds.): Specialized Techniques in Psychotherapy. New York, Basic Books, 1952.

2. Hypnotherapy

a. WOLBERG, LEWIS R.: Medical Hypnosis. New York, Grune & Stratton, 1948, 2 vol.
b. WOLBERG, LEWIS R.: Hypnoanalysis. New York, Grune & Stratton, 1945.

3. Narcotherapy

HORSELY, J. S.: Narco-Analysis. London, Oxford University Press, 1943.

4. Play Therapy

AXLINE, VIRGINIA MAE: Play Therapy. New York, Houghton Mifflin Co., 1947.

GROUP THERAPY

1. SLAVSON, S. R.: An Introduction To Group Therapy. New York, The Commonwealth Fund, 1943.
2. POWDERMAKER, FLORENCE B., FRANK, JEROME D., et al.: Group Psychotherapy. Studies in Methodology of Research and Therapy. Cambridge, Harvard University Press, 1953.

CHILD THERAPY

1. HAMILTON, GORDON: Psychotherapy in Child Guidance. New York, Columbia University Press, 1947.
2. FREUD, ANNA: Introduction To the Technique of Child Analysis. Washington, D.C., Nerv. & Ment. Disease Pub. Co., 1928.
3. ALLEN, FREDERICK H.: Psychotherapy With Children. New York, W. W. Norton, 1942.
4. WITMER, HELEN L.: Psychiatric Interviews with Children. New York, The Commonwealth Fund, 1946.

PSYCHOLOGIC TESTING

1. ROSENZWEIG, S., and KOGAN, K. L.: Psychodiagnosis: An Introduction To Tests In the Clinical Practice of Psychodynamics. New York, Grune & Stratton, 1949.
2. RAPAPORT, D., GILL, M., and SCHAFER, R.: Diagnostic Psychological Testing. Chicago, the Year Book, Inc., 1945, 2 vol.
3. SCHAFER, R.: The Clinical Application of Psychological Tests: Diagnostic Summaries and Case Studies. New York, International Universities Press, 1948.
4. HARROWER, MOLLY: Appraising Personality. New York, W. W. Norton, 1952.

PREVENTIVE MENTAL HEALTH

1. RENNIE, THOMAS A. C., and WOODWARD, LUTHER E.: Mental Health in Modern Society. New York, The Commonwealth Fund, 1948.
2. HILLMAN, ARTHUR: Community Organization and Planning. New York, Macmillan, 1950.
3. KING, CLARENCE: Organizing for Community Action. New York, Harper Bros., 1948.
4. BULLIS, H. EDMUND, and O'MALLEY, EMILY E.: Human Relations in the Classroom. Course I and II. Wilmington, Delaware, Delaware State Society for Mental Hygiene, 1947.
5. TIFFIN, JOSEPH: Industrial Psychology. New York, Prentice-Hall, 1947.

Appendices

The following forms include all the information which appears on the forms used in actual practice; in order to make these reproductions conform to the page size of the book, however, the layout has had to vary from the original in some instances, and occasionally spacing between items has been considerably reduced. For example, some forms which in reproduction here appear on one page, appear in practice on two pages, or two sides of one page. The actual forms are on standard 8½ x 11 inch sheets, with sufficient space between items to allow for complete entry of data.

Information regarding purchase of these forms may be had upon request to Grune & Stratton, Inc., 381 Fourth Avenue, New York City 16.

Appendix A*

(*To be filled out by therapist, initial interviewer, or intake worker in a clinic set-up*)

STATISTICAL DATA

(*short form*)

PATIENT'S NAME: Date:

ADDRESS: Interviewer:

TELEPHONE: BUSINESS PHONE: Referred by:

Informant (*if any*): Name and Address:

With whom is patient now living? (*list people.*)

Age of patient: Sex: Religion:

Education: Occupation: Salary:

If unemployed, sources of income:

Marital status: How long married?   Any previous marriages?

When?   Age of mate: Occupation of mate:

                                            Salary of mate:

Military record:

Miscellaneous:

---

* Information regarding purchase of the forms which follow may be had upon request to Grune & Stratton, Inc., 381 Fourth Ave., New York City 16.

Appendix B

(Complete statistical data outline to be filled out by therapist or social worker)

Patient's Name _____   Case No. _____

STATISTICAL DATA
(long form)

1. GENERAL DATA:

   a. Age: Date of birth: b. Sex (M,F)

   c. Race (W, B, Y, R):   d. Religion:

   e. Birthplace:

   f. If foreign born, date of arrival in U.S.A.:

   g. Naturalization dates: 1st Papers: 2nd Papers:

   h. Education:

   i. Occupation:

   j. Employed (yes, no):

   k. Salary:

   l. Yearly income, all sources:

   m. If unemployed, on what sources of income, or on what person is patient dependent, giving occupation and relationship to patient of this person:

   n. Military Service (yes, no); dates:

   o. Name and address of nearest relative or friend:

   p. With whom is patient living at present?

2. RESIDENTIAL DATA:

   a. Address:

   b. Character of residence: ( )house ( )apartment ( )room; ( )self-owned ( )rented, rental cost:

   c. Place of legal settlement:

d. Length of residence in this town or city:

e. Length of residence in state:

f. Home telephone no.:   Business telephone no.:

g. Previous addresses (*giving dates*):

3. MARITAL STATUS:

a. M., S., W., Div., Sep.:

b. Date of marriage:

c. Date termination of marriage:

d. Name of mate, if any:

e. Dates of previous marriages, if any:

f. Dates of termination of previous marriages and reasons:

g. Names and ages of children:

4. FAMILY IDENTIFICATION DATA:

a. Father's name: Living or dead?

Age at present, or, if dead, age at death and year of death:

Birthplace:

If foreign-born, date arrival U.S.A.:   Citizenship:

b. Mother's maiden name: Living or dead?

Age at present, or, if dead, age at death and year of death?

Birthplace:

If foreign-born, date arrival U.S.A.:   Citizenship:

c. Siblings (list names, ages and sex):

5. SOCIAL SERVICE EXCHANGE (*for clinic patients*):

Appendix C

(*To be filled out by initial interviewer*)

(1)

INITIAL INTERVIEW

PATIENT'S NAME: Date:

ADDRESS: Interviewer:

TELEPHONE: BUSINESS PHONE: Referred by:

Informant (*if any*): Name and Address:

With whom is patient now living? (*list people*)

Age of patient: Sex: Religion:

Education: Occupation: Salary:

In unemployed, sources of income:

Marital status: How long married?   Any previous marriages?

When?   Age of mate: Occupation of mate:

                                             Salary of mate:

Military record:

Miscellaneous:

(use additional blank sheets if necessary indicating item number)

1. CHIEF COMPLAINT (*patient's own words*):

2. HISTORY AND DEVELOPMENT OF COMPLAINT (*from onset to present*):

3. OTHER SYMPTOMS AND CLINICAL FINDINGS AT PRESENT:

☐ Tension	☐ Physical symptoms	☐ Phobias
☐ Depressed	☐ Fatigue	☐ Obsessions
☐ Severe depression	☐ Exhaustion	☐ Compulsions
☐ Suicidal	☐ Headaches	☐ Excessive sedatives
☐ Severe anxiety	☐ Dizziness	☐ Excess alcohol
☐ Hallucinations	☐ G. I. Symptoms	☐ Insomnia
☐ Delusions	☐ Sexual problem	☐ Nightmares
☐ Dangerous	☐ Impotency	☐ Other symptoms (*specify*)
☐ Excited	☐ Homosexuality	

Description of above:

4. DREAMS (*patient's own words*):

5. FAMILY DATA (*Health and personality of mother, father, siblings, spouse, children, and patient's attitudes toward them*):

6: PREVIOUS EMOTIONAL UPSETS (*from childhood to present illness*):

7. PREVIOUS TREATMENT (*including hospitalization*):

8. PSYCHOLOGIC TESTS:

(4)

9. TENTATIVE DIAGNOSIS:

10. TENTATIVE DYNAMICS:

11. TENTATIVE PROGNOSIS:

12. PATIENT'S RESPONSE TO INTERVIEWER: ( ) cooperative ( ) fearful
( ) suspicious ( ) hostile
13. INTERVIEWER'S RESPONSE TO PATIENT: ( ) positive ( ) ill-defined
( ) negative
14. PHYSICAL APPEARANCE: ( ) meticulous ( ) presentable ( ) untidy
( ) disheveled
15. PATIENTS ESTIMATE OF PRESENT PHYSICAL HEALTH: ( ) satisfactory ( ) poor
16. COMMUNICATIVENESS: ( ) garrulous ( ) satisfactory ( ) underproductive ( ) answers questions only
17. Insight and motivation:

( ) aware of a problem   ( ) desires to correct problem
( ) aware of emotional nature of problem ( ) willing to accept psychotherapy
( ) accepts present therapist   ( ) accepts conditions of therapy
( ) can arrange time for therapy   ( ) can afford treatment

18. DISPOSITION:

	Hours Patient Can Come for Treatment:	FEE:
( ) Case accepted		Initial interview
( ) Case referred		Testing
( ) Case closed		Therapy
( ) Emergency	( ) Appointment given patient	( ) Paid
( ) ℞ Urgent	( ) Notify patient of appointment	( ) Charge
( ) ℞ Not urgent	( ) Patient will call for appointment	( ) Send Bill

TYPE OF THERAPY:

CORRESPONDENCE REQUIRED:

RECOMMENDATIONS AND REMARKS:

Appendix D

(To be filled out by patient)

PERSONAL DATA SHEET

Please fill out the following blank as completely as possible. This will save time and make it unnecessary to ask you routine questions. All material is confidential and will not be released except on your written request.

Name _____

Address _____

(Will it be all right to write to you at the above address for billing, changes of appointment, etc? _____)

Telephone No. _____ Business Phone _____

(Can we call you at either of these? _____)

In the event of a change in appointment, at what time can we reach you at either of these phones? _____

_____

Age _____ Birthday _____ Sex (M,F) _____

Birthplace _____

If foreign born, date of arrival in U.S.A. _____

If foreign born, are you a citizen? _____

Approximately how long have you lived in this city? _____

Marital status (Single, Married, Separated, Divorced) _____

If married, how long ago? _____ If separated or divorced, when? _____

If married more than once list dates of marriage, length of time married, whether

marriage terminated by divorce, annulment, death: _____

Number and ages of children, if any _____

816

Occupation _____ Approximate gross yearly salary _____

How long have you been doing your present kind of work? _____

If unemployed, source of income at present: _____

How far through school did you go? _____

Name and address of nearest relative or friend: _____

_____

Any army service? _____

Whom are you living with at present? _____

Who referred you here? _____

How strongly do you want treatment for your problem? (*check*)

( )very much ( )much ( )moderately ( )could do without it, if

necessary ( )do not want treatment

What days and times can you come here for treatments? _____

If your answer to above is after 5 p.m., can you, if necessary, get away for an

hour once weekly during the day? _____

If psychologic or other tests are necessary to help your condition, would you

object to them for any reasons? _____

Do you know what psychotherapy is?

Appendix E

(To be filled out by patient)

NAME:

FAMILY DATA SHEET

Please fill out the following blank as completely as possible. This will save time and make it unnecessary to ask you routine questions. All material is confidential and will not be released except on your written request.

1. List the first names of your father, mother, brothers and sisters, in chronologic order, and supply the following information about each:

List first names.	Age.	Live in what city?	If dead, what year and cause?	Marital status— M,Div, Sep,Wid.	Do you see them often or write often to them? (Yes or no.)	Personality adjustment (good, fair or poor.)	How do (or did) you get along with them (good, fair, poor?)
Father:							
Mother:							
Sisters:							
Brothers:							

2. If married, age of mate: _____   Are you living with spouse now? _____
   Occupation of spouse: _____
   Personality adjustment of spouse (good, fair, poor) _____
   How are you getting along with spouse (good, fair, poor) _____

3. List all of your children of both present and previous marriages, by first names in chronologic order, giving the following information on each:

Name	Living or dead.	Ages	Living with whom at present	Check if by previous marriage.	Personality adjustment (good, fair, poor.)	How do you get along with child (good, fair, poor?)

Appendix F

PATIENT'S NAME

Examiner:	**DAILY PROGRESS NOTE**	Date:

At each visit enter: (1) present state of symptoms or complaints (absent, improved, the same, worse), (2) how does patient feel? (anxious, placid, depressed, happy), (3) important life situations and developments since last visit and how they were handled, (4) general content of session, (5) significant transference and resistance reactions, (6) dreams.

(On the standard form, this Daily Progress Note is given two full sides of an 8½ by 11 inch sheet, to allow for as complete a report as is required.)

Appendix G

(This form will be found helpful in clinics where there is routine supervision of the entire case load. It is turned over monthly to the supervisor)

Month covered in this report:

MONTHLY PROGRESS SUMMARY

(Fill out this side and on back of sheet* elaborate on any checked items as well as other items of importance, using additional sheets if necessary.)

NAME OF PATIENT: NAME OF THERAPIST:

NUMBER OF SESSIONS THIS   TOTAL NUMBER OF SESSIONS TO
MONTH: DATE:

NUMBER OF MISSED SESSIONS   *Reason for this:*
THIS MONTH:

PATIENT'S RESPONSE TO THERAPY:

  1. *General progress to date:* ( )excellent ( )satisfactory ( )poor
       Symptoms are: ( )better ( )the same ( )worse

  2. *Appointments:* ( )comes on time ( )comes early ( )comes late

  3. *Communicativeness:* ( )satisfactory ( )overproductive ( )incoherent
       ( )underproductive ( )responds only to questions
       ( )long periods of silence ( )other, describe:

* The original form is on one side of a sheet only.

4. *Relationship with therapist:* Working relationship: ( )good ( )fair ( )poor ( )intense dependency ( )sexual feelings ( )fear ( )detachment ( )negativism ( )hostility ( )other, describe:

5. *Resistance:* ( )low ( )moderate ( )strong ( )interferes with progress ( )"acting-out" tendencies

6. *Insight:* ( )achieving insight ( )curiosity about dynamics ( )intellectual, but no emotional insight ( )resists insight

7. *Translation of insight into action:* ( )excellent ( )satisfactory ( )poor

8. *Present symptoms:* (Describe any checked items on back.)

( )new physical symptoms or complaints	( )sexual disturbance	( )intense anxiety
	( )intense depression	( )hallucinations
	( )suicidal threats	( )delusions
( )exaggerated old physical symptoms	( )suicidal attempts	( )excess alcohol
	( )overactivity	( )excess sedatives or drugs
( )work disability	( )destructive tendencies	( )other, describe:
( )marked insomnia		

9. *Severe environmental problems:* ( )finances ( )work ( )family ( )other

REMARKS:

1. ( )Supervisory Conference Needed: ( )emergency foreseen
   ( )dynamics not clear ( )treatment going poorly
   ( )patient wants to discontinue
   ( )therapist considering closing ( )other, describe:

2. ( )Consultation Needed: ( )with caseworker ( )with psychologist
   ( )with medical consultant ( )with psychiatric consultant
   ( )other, describe:

3. *Other* (describe briefly on back of sheet what has been going on in treatment during the last month.)

Appendix H

TERMINAL NOTE

1. NAME OF PATIENT: _____

2. DATE OF INITIAL INTERVIEW: _____

3. DATE OF TERMINAL INTERVIEW: _____

4. TOTAL NUMBER OF SESSIONS: _____

5. REASON FOR TERMINATION: ( )planned termination
   ( )withdrawal by patient (explain)

6. CONDITION AT DISCHARGE:
   ( )a. *Recovered:* Asymptomatic with good insight
   ( )b. *Markedly Improved:*
       ( )Asymptomatic with some insight
       ( )Asymptomatic with no insight
   ( )c. *Moderately Improved:*
       ( )Partial reduction of symptoms with good insight
       ( )Partial reduction of symptoms with some insight
   ( )d. *Slightly Improved:* Partial reduction of symptoms with little or no insight
   ( )e. *Unimproved*
   ( )f. *Worse* (Describe)

7. AREAS OF IMPROVEMENT: (Use back of sheet, if necessary.)
   a. Symptoms:

   b. Adjustment to Environment: (work, community, etc.)

   c. Physical Functions: (appetite, sleep, sex, etc.)

   d. Relations with People:

8. PATIENT'S ATTITUDE TOWARD THERAPIST AT DISCHARGE: (Use back of sheet, if necessary.)
   ( )friendly ( )indifferent ( )unfriendly

9. Would patient object to a follow-up letter inquiring about progress?
   ( )Yes   ( )No

10. RECOMMENDATIONS TO PATIENT AT DISCHARGE: (if any. Use back of sheet, if necessary.)

11. DIAGNOSIS AT DISCHARGE:

12. ADDITIONAL COMMENTS: (Use back of sheet.)

Appendix I

PATIENT'S NAME:

Date of Summary:	**SUMMARY**	Therapist:
Prepared by:	Total Treatment Sessions:	Initial Interview Date:

(Type this form, if possible. Use and attach additional blank sheets in the event space for any item is not sufficient, carrying over the same item number. *Note:* This form has been condensed to two pages here; it is ordinarily in four pages, with considerable space between items.)

I. CHIEF COMPLAINT:

II. HISTORY AND DEVELOPMENT OF COMPLAINT:

III. OTHER COMPLAINTS AND SYMPTOMS:

IV. MEDICAL, SURGICAL AND GYNECOLOGIC HISTORY:

V. ENVIRONMENTAL DISTURBANCES (at onset of therapy):

VI. RELATIONSHIP DIFFICULTIES (at onset of therapy):

VII. HEREDITARY, CONSTITUTIONAL and EARLY DEVELOPMENTAL INFLUENCES:

VIII. FAMILY DATA:

IX. PREVIOUS ATTACKS OF EMOTIONAL ILLNESS:

X. INITIAL INTERVIEW (brief summary of condition of patient):

XI. LEVEL OF INSIGHT AND MOTIVATION (at onset of therapy):

XII. CLINICAL EXAMINATION (significant physical, neurologic, psychiatric and psychologic findings):

XIII. DIFFERENTIAL DIAGNOSIS:

XIV. ESTIMATE OF PROGNOSIS:

XV. PSYCHODYNAMICS AND PSYCHOPATHOLOGY:

XVI. COURSE OF TREATMENT (type of therapy employed, frequency, total sessions, significant events during therapy, nature of transference and resistance, progress in therapy, insight, change in symptoms, attitudes and relationships with people):

XVII. CONDITION ON DISCHARGE:

XVIII. RECOMMENDATIONS TO PATIENT:

XIX. STATISTICAL CLASSIFICATION:

Appendix J*

(*Case folder*)

NAME OF PATIENT: NAME OF THERAPIST:
(L-Late; B-Broken; C-Cancelled)

	DATE	L, B or C	BILLING
1			
2			
3			
4			
5			
6			
7			
8			
9			
10			
11			
12			
13			
14			
15			
16			
17			
18			
19			
20			
21			
22			
23			
24			
25			
26			
27			
28			
29			
30			
31			
32			
33			
34			
35			
36			
37			
38			
39			
40			
41			
42			
43			
44			
45			
46			
47			
48			
49			
50			
51			
52			
53			
54			

DATE	FORM
	Personal Data Sheet
	Family Data Sheet
	INITIAL INTERVIEW
	Personality Inventory
	Rorschach Responses
	Man-Woman Drawing
	Consultations:
	Psychiatric
	Medical
	Neurological
	Psychological
	Casework
	TERMINAL NOTE
	SUMMARY
	Transfer
	Follow-up 1 yr.
	Follow-up 2 yrs.
	Follow-up 5 yrs.
	Case Re-opened

MONTHLY NOTES

1	13	25
2	14	26
3	15	27
4	16	28
5	17	29
6	18	30
7	19	31
8	20	32
9	21	33
10	22	34
11	23	35
12	24	36

SUPERVISION

Date	Supervisor	Date	Supervisor
1		13	
2		14	
3		15	
4		16	
5		17	
6		18	
7		19	
8		20	
9		21	
10		22	
11		23	
12		24	

    * This form is printed on the front of a heavy manila correspondence folder, and the numbered record of appointments (left hand column) is continued in two columns on the back of the folder, provision being made for 165 appointments. (The above reproduction has been reduced in size from an original 9 × 11¾ inch folder.)

OUTLINE FOR CASE PRESENTATION

1. Age of patient.

2. Sex.

3. Marital status.

4. How long married?

5. Number and ages of children.

6. Age and occupation of mate.

7. Any previous marriages? When?

8. Religion.

9. Education.

10. Occupation.

11. Employed? Salary.

12. If unemployed, source of income.

13. CHIEF COMPLAINT (in patient's own words).

14. HISTORY AND DEVELOPMENT OF COMPLAINT (date of onset, circumstances under which complaint developed, progression from the onset to the time of the initial interview).

15. OTHER COMPLAINTS AND SYMPTOMS (physical, emotional, psychic and behavioral symptoms other than those of the complaint factor).

16. MEDICAL, SURGICAL, AND, IN WOMEN, GYNECOLOGIC HISTORY.

17. ENVIRONMENTAL DISTURBANCES AT ONSET OF THERAPY (economic, work, housing, neighborhood, and family difficulties).

18. RELATIONSHIP DIFFICULTIES AT ONSET OF THERAPY (disturbances in relationships with people, attitudes toward the world, toward authority and toward the self).

19. HEREDITARY, CONSTITUTIONAL AND EARLY DEVELOPMENTAL INFLUENCES (significant physical and psychiatric disorders in patient's family, socioeconomic status of family, important early traumatic experiences and relationships, neurotic traits in childhood and adolescence).

20. FAMILY DATA (mother, father, siblings, spouse, children—ages, state of health, personality adjustment, and patient's attitudes toward each).

21. PREVIOUS ATTACKS OF EMOTIONAL ILLNESS (as a child and later. When did patient feel himself to be completely free from emotional illness?).

22. INITIAL INTERVIEW (brief description of condition of patient at initial interview, including clinical findings).

23. LEVEL OF INSIGHT AND MOTIVATION AT ONSET OF THERAPY (How long ago did the patient feel that he needed treatment? For what? Awareness of emotional nature of problem, willingness to accept psychotherapy.)

24. PREVIOUS TREATMENTS (When did the patient first seek treatment? What treatment did he get? Any hospitalization?)

25. CLINICAL EXAMINATION (significant findings in physical, neurologic, psychiatric and psychologic examinations).

26. DIFFERENTIAL DIAGNOSIS (at time of initial interview).

27. ESTIMATE OF PROGNOSIS (at time of initial interview).

28. PSYCHODYNAMICS AND PSYCHOPATHOLOGY.

29. COURSE OF TREATMENT (up to time of presentation).
    (1) Type of therapy employed, frequency, total number of sessions, response to therapist.

    (2) Significant events during therapy, dynamics that were revealed, verbatim report of important dreams, nature of transference and resistance.

    (3) Progress in therapy, insight acquired, translation of insight into action, change in symptoms, attitudes and relationships with people.

    (4) Verbatim account of all or part of a typical session, if desired.

30. STATISTICAL CLASSIFICATION.

Appendix L

(This form is useful in determining the didactic and experiential equipment of an applicant for a clinic position)

APPLICATION BLANK FOR NEW STAFF MEMBERS

NAME   ADDRESS

AGE   MARITAL STATUS   TELEPHONE NO.

1. DEGREES *(where obtained and dates—undergraduate and postgraduate)*

2. DIDACTIC INSTRUCTION:

a. BASIC COURSES	WHERE TAKEN, YEAR, INSTRUCTOR
Psychosocial Development	
Psychopathology	
Psychodynamics	
Techniques of Interviewing	
Basic Neuropsychiatry	
Readings in Psychiatric Literature	
Techniques in Psychotherapy	
Clinical Conferences	
Continuous Case Seminars	
Child Psychiatry	
Group Psychotherapy	

b. What schools of psychotherapy or psychoanalysis have you attended as a matriculated student?

Dates:

Were you ever certified?
Have you been qualified by any Board?
Date of license, if any, to practice profession:
Membership in which professional societies?

3. PERSONAL PSYCHOANALYSIS OR PSYCHOTHERAPY

When started:

With whom:

Number of sessions per week:

Total number of sessions:

Additional therapy:

4. CLINICAL EXPERIENCE: (*Indicate names of therapeutic centers, clinics, institutions or agencies; date of affiliation; capacity in which you have functioned.*)

5. CASE EXPERIENCE:

When did you begin practicing psychotherapy?

Can you estimate the total number of patients treated?

Can you estimate the total number of patient sessions to date?

Underline the kinds of problems you have handled: character disorder

psychopathic personality   anxiety neurosis   anxiety hysteria

conversion hysteria   obsessive compulsive neurosis

psychosomatic problem   alcoholism   drug addiction

preschizophrenia   schizophrenia   psychoneurotic depression

manic-depressive psychosis   involutional melancholia

paranoid condition   marital problem   childhood behavior problem

childhood psychoneurosis   childhood psychosis   convulsive disorder

6. SUPERVISED CLINICAL EXPERIENCE: (*Give names of supervisors, place of supervision, dates, total number of sessions with each supervisor.*)

7. SUPERVISORY EXPERIENCE:

Have you ever supervised therapists in psychotherapy?

If yes, how many therapists?

Total number of supervisory sessions:

Have you ever had a course of instruction in psychotherapeutic supervision?

8. GROUP THERAPY:

Have you ever done group therapy?

If so, underline types: inspirational and supportive groups

educational groups   discussion groups   analytic groups

social and activity groups   psychodrama

Total number of group therapy sessions

9. PSYCHOTHERAPEUTIC TEACHING EXPERIENCE: (*Courses taught, dates, places*):

10. HAVE YOU EVER PUBLISHED ANY MATERIAL ON PSYCHO-THERAPY: (*Papers, pamphlets*) If so, list:

QUESTIONS YOU MAY HAVE ABOUT PSYCHOTHERAPY

1. DO I NEED PSYCHOTHERAPY?

If you have nervous symptoms such as tension, depression, fears, fatigue, and certain physical complaints for which your doctor finds no physical basis; if you find it difficult to get along in your work or in your relations with people; if you have a school, sex or marital problem; or if you merely feel irritable, unhappy and believe you are not getting the most out of life, psychotherapy will be of help to you.

2. HOW DOES PSYCHOTHERAPY WORK?

Nervous symptoms and unwarranted unhappiness are the product of inner emotional conflicts. In psychotherapy you are helped to understand your conflicts. In this way it is possible for you to do something constructive about solving them.

3. CAN PHYSICAL SYMPTOMS BE CAUSED BY EMOTION?

Many physical symptoms are psychosomatic in nature, which means that they have an emotional or nervous basis. When you come to think of it, it is not really so strange that emotional strain or worry should produce physical symptoms. After all, every organ in your body is connected with your brain by nerve channels; and so it is logical that when your nervous system is upset by some crisis or conflict, you may feel the effects in various organs of the body.

4. IF I CANNOT SOLVE MY PERSONAL PROBLEMS WITHOUT HELP DOES THAT MEAN THAT I HAVE A WEAK WILL OR AM ON THE WAY TO A MENTAL BREAKDOWN?

No. Even if you have no serious symptoms, it is difficult to work out emotional problems by yourself because you are too close to them and cannot see them clearly. More and more people, even those with a great deal of psychologic knowledge, are seeking help these days because they realize this. The fact that you desire aid is a compliment to your judgment and is no indication that you are approaching a mental breakdown. Psychotherapy has helped countless numbers of people to overcome serious emotional symptoms, and has enabled many others to increase their working capacities, and to better their relationships with people.

5. WHAT KIND OF TREATMENT WILL I NEED?

The kind of treatment best suited for you can be determined only by a careful evaluation of your problem by a psychiatrist.

6. WHAT HAPPENS TO THE INFORMATION ABOUT ME?

In scientific work, records are necessary, since they permit of a more thorough dealing with one's problems. It is understandable that you might be concerned about what happens to the information about you, because much or all of this information is highly personal. Case records are confidential. *No outsider, not even your closest relative or family physician, is permitted to see your case record without your written permission.*

7. HOW CAN I HELP TO COOPERATE WITH THE TREATMENT PLAN?

The general practitioner has his medications; the surgeon works with his instruments; the heart specialist has his x-rays and delicate recording apparatus. But for the most part, the psychotherapist has only one aid besides his knowledge—YOU. Your cooperation and trust in him are essential. You must feel free to take up with your therapist anything about the treatment process which disturbs you or puzzles you in any way. By doing this you have the best chance of shortening your treatment and of insuring its fullest success.

Appendix N

(To be filled out by the patient when indicated)

NAME_____   _____
         LAST   FIRST   DATE

PERSONAL HISTORY SHEET

This material is necessary for the completion of your records. In answering the questions use extra sheets if required, noting the number of the question that is being answered. This, as all other information, will be kept confidential. If you are particularly troubled by any question and do not desire to answer it, merely write in "Do not care to answer."

1. How would you describe your health (excellent, good, fair, poor)?

    a. Physical _____
    b. Emotional _____

2. What physical illnesses have you had? When?

3. When was your last examination by a physician? _____

    For what condition? _____

4. Have you in the last 2 years had

    a. Chest x-ray _____
    b. Urine examination _____

5. Have you ever been turned down for life insurance? _____

    If yes, why?

6. Have you ever been in a hospital? _____ If yes:

        Name of hospital _____
        Nature of illness _____
        Date and length of hospitalization _____

7. When was the last time you felt well both physically and emotionally for a sustained period? _____

8. Have you received treatment for "nervous" or emotional difficulties? _____
   If so:
       Date _____
       Frequency of visits _____
       Nature of treatment _____
       Whom treated by _____

9. Does your present job satisfy you?

   If not, in what ways are you dissatisfied?

10. Do you think you could handle a job more difficult than those you have held? _____

    If yes, describe.

11. What is your ambition?

12. Do you make friends easily? _____ Do you keep them? _____

13. Are most of your friends of one sex? _____ Which? _____

14. Can you confide in your friends? _____

15. How is most of your free time occupied?

Check any of the following that apply to you:

( )headaches
( )dizziness
( )fainting spells
( )palpitations
( )stomach trouble
( )no appetite
( )bowel disturbances
( )fatigue
( )insomnia
( )nightmares
( )take sedatives
( )alcoholism
( )feel tense
( )feel panicky
( )tremors

( )depressed
( )suicidal ideas
( )always worried about something
( )unable to relax
( )unable to have a good time
( )don't like weekends and vacations
( )over-ambitious
( )sexual problems
( )shy with people
( )can't make friends
( )can't make decisions
( )can't keep a job
( )inferiority feelings
( )home conditions bad
( )financial problems

Appendix O

MEDICAL FORM

RE: _____

DEAR DR. _____:

The above patient has given us permission to ask you for the results of his recent physical examination. I would appreciate your filling out this form and returning it in the enclosed envelope:

Head: E.E.N.T.

Neck:

Cardiovascular:

Pulmonary:

Genito-urinary:

Neurologic:

Additional:

Diagnosis:

From your findings is there any evidence of physical illness which requires treatment at this time? NO _____ YES _____

If, yes, what medical treatment do you recommend?

Sincerely yours,

_____ M.D.

Address _____

Telephone No. _____

Appendix P

PHYSICAL, NEUROLOGIC AND LABORATORY EXAMINATIONS

(Check items in which abnormality exists and explain below)

I. *Physical Examination:*

( )Stature   ( )Tongue   ( )Abdomen

( )Nutrition   ( )Gums and teeth ( )Hernia

( )Weight   ( )Pharynx   ( )Genitals

( )Skin   ( )Tonsils   ( )Muscles

( )Hair   ( )Neck   ( )Bones

( )Scalp   ( )Thyroid gland   ( )Joints

( )Eyes   ( )Chest   ( )Spine

( )Nose   ( )Breasts   ( )Extremities

( )Sinuses   ( )Lungs   ( )Nails

( )Ears   ( )Heart   ( )Lymphatic glands

( )Lips   ( )Blood vessels   ( )Other (explain

( )Mouth   ( )Blood pressure   below)

II. *Neurologic Examination:*

( )Station   ( )Oculomotor, trochlear and

( )Gait   abducens nerves

( )Tactile sense   ( )Trigeminal nerve

( )Pressure sense   ( )Facial nerve

( )Temperature   ( )Auditory nerve

( )Pain   ( )Glossopharyngeal nerve

( )Muscular sense

( )Stereognostic sense

( )Olfactory nerve

( )Optic nerve

( )Achilles reflex

( )Ankle clonus

( )Wrist, biceps, triceps

    reflexes

( )Babinski reflex

( )Oppenheim's reflex

( )Gordon reflex

( )Cremasteric reflex

( )Vagus nerve

( )Spiral accessory nerve

( )Hypoglossal nerve

( )Knee jerk

( )Abdominal and epigastric reflexes

( )Sphincteric reflexes

( )Motor disturbances

( )Paresis

( )Muscles weakness

( )Hypotonia

( )Tremors, tics, spasms

( )Other (explain below)

III. *Miscellaneous Examinations:*

( )Urinalysis

( )Blood analysis

( )Endocrine analysis

( )X-ray examination

( )Electrocardiogram

( )Electroencephalogram

( )Other (specify)

IV. SUMMARY OF PHYSICAL, NEUROLOGIC AND LABORATORY
EXAMINATIONS: (If examinations are essentially negative, check below.
Explain items which have been checked above.)

( )Physical examination negative

( )Neurologic examination negative

( )Miscellaneous examinations negative

Appendix Q

NAME OF PATIENT:

MENTAL EXAMINATION

(Check the following and elaborate below.)

I. *Attitude and General Behavior:*

    A. Physical appearance: ( )disheveled ( )untidy ( )unkempt

    B. Degree of cooperativeness: ( )fair ( )poor

    C. General manner: ( )mistrustful ( )suspicious ( )antagonistic

        ( )negativistic ( )defiant ( )preoccupied

    D. General activity: ( )motor retardation ( )hyperactivity ( )stereotypy

        ( )mannerisms ( )tics ( )echolalia ( )echopraxia

        ( )perseveration ( )compulsion

II. *Stream of Mental Activity:*

    A. Accessibility: ( )indifferent ( )self-absorbed ( )inaccessible

    B. Productivity: ( )voluble ( )circumstantial ( )flight of ideas

        ( )underproductive ( )retardated ( )mute

    C. Progression of thought: ( )illogical ( )irrelevant ( )incoherent

        ( )verbigeration ( )blocking

    D. Neologisms:

III. *Emotional Reactions:*

    A. Quality of affect: ( )elation ( )exhilaration ( )exaltation

        ( )euphoria ( )mild depression ( )moderate depression

        ( )severe depression ( )apprehension ( )fear ( )anxiety

        ( )irritability ( )morbid anger ( )apathy

        ( )emotional instability

    B. Appropriateness of affect: ( )incongruity with thought content

        ( )ambivalence ( )emotional deterioration

IV. *Mental Trend—Content of Thought:*
 A. Thinking disorders: ( )phobias ( )obsessive ideas
      ( )psychosomatic complaints ( )persecutory trend
      ( )ideas of reference ( )grandiose ideas
      ( )depressive delusions ( )nihilistic delusions
      ( )hypochondriac ideas ( )ideas of unreality
      ( )deprivation of thought ( )delusions of influence
      ( )autistic thinking
 B. Perceptive disorders: ( )auditory hallucinations
      ( )visual hallucinations ( )olfactory hallucinations
      ( )tactile hallucinations
      ( )reflex, microptic, hypnagogic or psychomotor hallucinations
      ( )illusions

V. *Sensorium, Mental Grasp and Capacity:*
 A. Disorders of consciousness: ( )confusion ( )clouding
      ( )dream state ( )delirium ( )stupor
 B. Disorders of apperception: ( )mild ( )severe
 C. Disorders of orientation: ( )time ( )place ( )person
 D. Disorders of personal identification and memory: ( )general amnesia
      ( )circumscribed amnesia ( )confabulation
      ( )retrospective falsification ( )hypermnesia
 E. Disorders of retention and immediate recall: ( )mild ( )severe
 F. Disorders of counting and calculation: ( )mild ( )severe
 G. Disorders of reading: ( )mild ( )severe
 H. Disorders of writing: ( )mild ( )severe
 I. Disorders in school and general knowledge: ( )mild ( )severe
 J. Disorders in attention, concentration and thinking capacity:
      ( )mild ( )severe
 K. Disorders in intelligence: ( )inconsistent with education ( )mild
      ( )severe
 L. Disorders in judgment: ( )mild ( )severe
 M. Disorders in insight: ( )mild ( )severe

VI. *Summary of Mental Examination:* (check and describe abnormality, if any)
 ( )Mental examination essentially negative
 ( )Disturbance in attitude and general behavior
 ( )Disturbance in stream of mental activity
 ( )Disturbance in emotional reaction
 ( )Disturbance in mental trend—content of thought
 ( )Disturbance in sensorium, mental grasp and capacity

Appendix R

AUTHORIZATION FOR RELEASE OF
MEDICAL RECORDS

TO: _____

ADDRESS: _____

I would appreciate your releasing to _____

all records or abstracts pertaining to my case. I herewith grant permission for this

release.

SIGNED: _____

Witness: _____

Date: _____

Appendix S

(This sheet may be given monthly to selected patients for a progress report.)

PROGRESS REPORT

NAME: DATE:

(At the beginning of each month, it would be helpful if you would write a brief report on how you feel and what you believe has been accomplished in the past month.)

Check the following:

The symptoms and complaints for which I sought treatment originally are:

( )the same   ( )better   ( )worse

My understanding of my condition is: ( )excellent ( )good ( )fair

( )poor

I believe my relationship with my therapist to be: ( )good   ( )fair

( )in need of improvement

I would consider my progress to be: ( )excellent ( )good ( )fair

( )poor

ADDITIONAL COMMENTS:

Author Index

Ackerman, N. W., 85, 124, 792, 796
Adler, A., 65–66, 788, 804
Aldrich, C. A., 581
Aldrich, W. M., 581
Alexander, F., 79, 80, 789, 793, 803, 804
Allen, C. M., 797
Allen, F. H., 37, 785, 805
Allen, W. Y., 797
Alvarez, W. C., 794
American Association of Schools of Social Work, 795
American Psychiatric Association Newsletter, 795
American Psychologist, 795
Anderson, V. V., 797
Andrews, J. S., 783
Angell, J. R., 797
Anthonisen, M. R., 797
Appel, K. E., 83, 791
Arlow, J. A., 790
Association for Supervision and Curriculum Development, 798, 801
Atkinson, R. C., 782
Axelrod, P. L., 786
Axline, V. M., 129, 792, 798, 805

Balint, M., 788
Bancroft, F. W., 784
Barker, R. G., 582
Baron, S., 129, 798
Barrabee, E. L., 230, 798
Barrett, E. B., 782
Bartemeier, L. H., 113, 794
Bartlett, M. R., 230, 798
Baruch, D. W., 580, 581, 797
Bates, E. S., 782
Bauer, W. W., 581
Baynes, H. G., 83, 791
Beck, L. F., 581
Becker, R. J., 797
Behnken, P., 796
Bellak, L., 793
Bender, L., 790, 791
Benedict, A., 580
Benjamin, J. D., 793
Bennett, A. E., 796, 798
Bennett, G. E., 33, 796
Bennett, R. E., 784

Berezin, M. A., 85, 792
Berg, C., 787
Berger, D., 797
Bergler, E., 787
Berliner, B., 793
Bernard, H. W., 797
Bibby, C., 581
Bibring, E., 787
Bibring-Lehner, G., 788
Billings, E. G., 785
Binger, C., 116, 579, 794
Bingham, W. V. D., 802
Bini, L., 32, 784
Blackman, N., 785
Blanton, S., 782
Bowers, S., 12
Bowman, K. M., 784
Braceland, F. J., 784
Brick, M., 790
Brenman, M., 82, 790
Breuer, J., 54, 787
Bruno, F. J., 782
Bullis, H. E., 582, 797, 805
Burbridge, N., 784
Bychowski, G., 83, 625, 637, 791, 799, 804

Call, A. P., 31, 783
Cameron, D. E., 126, 796, 802
Campbell, D., 797
Cantor, N., 781
Cerletti, V., 32, 784
Charbonneau, L., 796
Child, G. P., 784
Clawson, G., 796
Coen, R. A., 784
Colby, K. M., 803
Commission on Preventive Psychiatry of the Group for the Advancement of Psychiatry, 781
Commission on Teacher Education, 797
Committee on Clinical Psychology of the Group for the Advancement of Psychiatry, 795
Committee on Nomenclature and Statistics of the American Psychiatric Association, 798

Committee on Psychiatric Nursing and the Committee on Hospitals of the Group for the Advancement of Psychiatry, 796
Committee on Psychiatric Social Work of the Group for the Advancement of Psychiatry, 795
Committee on the Function of Nursing, 796
Committee on Training in Clinical Psychology of the American Psychological Association, 794
Conn, J. H., 84, 792
Conway, E. J., 799
Coué, E., 22, 783
Council on Pharmacy and Chemistry, 799
Crank, H. H., 793
Cranswick, E. H., 784
Crook, G. H., 784
Curran, F. J., 83, 791

Darley, J. G., 785
Davidoff, E., 784
Davis, J. E., 783
de Schweinitz, K., 581
Dejerine, J., 27, 783
Denker, P. G., 230, 798
Deri, S., 798
Despert, J. L., 83, 791, 804
Deutsch, A., 579
Deutsch, F., 5, 80–81, 789, 793, 795, 804
Dickel, H. K., 784
Diethelm, O., 5, 784, 802
Dittemore, J. V., 782
Dixon, H. H., 784
Dollard, J., 803
Draper, G., 794
Du Bois, P., 25–27, 783
Dunbar, H. F., 579
Dunton, W. R., 782, 783
Duvall, E. M., 580

Eastman, N., Jr., 580
Eaton, J. T., 796
Ebaugh, F. G., 113, 794
Eisenbud, J., 81, 789
Eisenstein, V. W., 625, 799
Eliasberg, W. G., 795

English, O. S., 580
Erickson, C. E., 782
Erickson, M. H., 81, 789
Erikson, E. H., 799
Eymiew, A., 782
Ezriel, H., 85, 792

Fairbairn, W. R. D., 790
Fedder, R., 581
Federn, P., 625, 633, 799
Fenichel, O., 109, 787, 788, 793, 801, 803
Ferenczi, S., 68–69, 788, 802, 804
Finesinger, J., 41, 230, 785, 798
Fisher, C., 82, 790
Fisher, V. E., 5
Fleming, J., 790
Fletcher, P., 31, 783
Flumerfelt, J. M., 799
Foster, L. E., 796
Foulkes, S. H., 85, 792
Fowle, H., 580
Fox, R., 620, 799
Frank, J. D., 799, 805
Frank, L. K., 581
Frank, M., 581
Franklin, A., 580
Freeman, L., 580
Freeman, W. J., 784
French, L. M., 782
French, T. M., 80, 789, 793, 804
Freud, A., 75, 84, 120, 789, 792, 801, 805
Freud, S., 11, 46, 53, 54–63, 75, 109, 137, 379, 423, 579, 582, 787, 793, 801, 802, 803, 804
Friedman, E., 796
Fromm, E., 75, 76, 120, 579, 789, 801
Fromm-Reichmann, F., 632, 637, 799, 803
Fuerst, R. A., 793

Gabe, S., 5
Galdston, I., 111, 117, 793, 795
Gardner, G. E., 118, 795
Garrett, A., 785, 802
Gaukler, E., 783
Gayle, R., 796
Gerty, F. J., 121, 795
Gesell, A., 581
Giles, H. H., 781
Gill, M., 81, 790, 805

Gilmore, J., 580
Ginsburg, E. L., 795
Gitelson, M., 84, 792
Glatzer, H. T., 51, 787
Glauber, I. P., 623, 799
Glover, E., 787, 803
Goldstein, S. E., 785
Gottesfeld, B. H., 799
Griffiths, R. A., 790
Grinker, R. R., 29, 783
Groom, D., 112, 784
Grossman, J. S., 580
Grotjahn, M., 5, 793, 800
Gruenberg, S. M., 581
Gutheil, E. A., 793, 798, 804

Haas, L. G., 782
Hadfield, J. A., 639, 799
Hald, J., 784
Hall, T. C., 784
Hamilton, G., 786, 795, 805
Hamilton, W., 582
Hangen, G. O., 784
Hanson, K., 784
Hargrove, E. A., 33, 798
Harms, E., 83, 791
Harris, H. I., 785
Harrower, M. R., 115, 119, 794, 795, 805
Harwood, E. C., 580
Hashagen, J. M., 800
Hastings, D. W., 796
Haun, P., 795
Henry, G. W., 801
Herzberg, A., 24, 783, 793
Hill, L. B., 81, 789
Hill, R., 580
Hillman, A., 805
Hiltner, S., 796, 797
Hine, C. H., 784
Hinsie, L. E., 580
Hoch, P. H., 85, 784, 792, 801
Hodges, M. B., 781
Hogue, H. G., 581
Holloway, G. W., Jr., 121, 795
Holly, S. B., 791
Holman, C. T., 782
Horney, K., 77–78, 580, 789, 801, 804
Horsley, J. S., 29, 640, 783, 800, 805
Howe, S. S., 793
Hubbard, L. R., 30, 783
Hulse, W. C., 113, 800
Hunt, J. McV., 801
Hyman, H. T., 793

Ilg, F. L., 581

Jacobsen, C., 115, 794
Jacobson, E., 31, 783
Jameison, G. R., 793
Jenkins, G. G., 581
Jens, R., 784
Jensen-Nelson, K., 783
Jewish Board of Guardians, 782, 786, 802
Johnson, A. M., 49, 782
Johnson, W., 786
Jones, E., 787
Jones, M. C., 47, 786
Josselyn, I. M., 801
Jung, C., 66–68, 83, 788, 791, 799, 804

Kadis, A., 790
Kalinowsky, L. B., 784
Kant, O., 795
Karpman, B., 81, 789
Kasius, C., 786, 803
Katz, A., 786
Kelly, D. M., 798
Kennedy, W. M., 797
Kessel, L., 793
Kilpatrick, W. H., 582
King, C., 805
Klaesi, J., 784
Klein, M., 84, 792
Knight, R., 230, 798
Kogan, K. L., 805
Korzybski, A., 786
Kraines, S. H., 783, 785, 803
Kris, E., 83, 120, 791
Kubie, L. S., 81, 117, 788, 789, 790, 795, 796, 803

La Forgue, R., 787
Landis, C., 230, 798
Larsen, V., 784
Lasser, L. M., 799
Law, S. G., 42, 113, 785, 794, 803
Lawton, G., 581, 582
Lemkau, P. V., 125, 796
Levine, M., 5, 113, 794, 802
Levy, D., 37, 84, 785, 792
Levy, J., 37, 83, 580, 785, 791
Lewin, S. A., 580
Lewinson, T. S., 798
Lewis, N. D. C., 790, 798, 802
Liebman, J. L., 581
Lighty, M., 581

Lindner, R., 81, 119, 120, 790, 795
Liss, E., 83, 791
Lorand, S., 555, 787, 798, 803
Lowenfeld, M., 791
Lowinger, L., 800
Lowrey, L. G., 5, 782
Lowry, F., 800
Luchins, A. S., 786
Lyle, J., 791
Lyndon, B. H., 786

McCutchen, S. P., 781
McHugh, G., 580
McIntosh, J. R., 790
McKown, H. C., 581
McNiel, E. E., 793
Machover, K., 798
Mackay, R. P., 121, 795
Macklin, E. A., 784
Makenzie, C., 581
Mann, N. M., 620, 799
Maslow, A. H., 5, 582, 801
Mathewson, R. H., 797
Mathewson, R. J., 781
Max, L. M., 47, 48, 786
Mead, M., 579
Meduna, L. J., 33, 798
Mennell, J. B., 783
Menninger, K. A., 579, 796
Menninger, W. C., 579, 782, 796
Merrill, E., 796
Meyer, A., 38, 785
Miles, H., 230, 798
Miller, J. G., 117, 119, 795
Miller, N. D., 803
Mira, E., 83, 791
Mittleman, B., 5, 582, 801
Moench, L. G., 113, 794, 802
Moore, B. V., 802
Moreno, J. L., 51, 787
Morris, R. D., 796
Mosse, E. P., 83, 790, 791
Mowrer, O. H., 47, 48, 786
Muller, T. G., 796
Muncie, W., 785, 803
Munroe, R., 580
Murphy, G., 582
Murray, H. A., 798
Myerson, A., 784

Napoli, P. J., 790
Naumberg, M., 83, 790, 791
Neale, C., 796
Neufeld, W., 31, 783

New York State Counselors Association, 785
North Central Association of College and Secondary Schools, 781
Noyes, A. P., 5, 802
Nunberg, H., 787, 788, 803

Oberndorf, C. P., 793
O'Malley, E. E., 582, 797, 805
Osinski, W., 784
Overholser, W., 794
Overstreet, H. A., 581

Palmer, H. D., 784
Payot, I., 781
Peale, N. V., 782
Pearson, G. H. J., 580, 801
Peasley, E., 796
Pederson-Krag, G., 51, 787
Pfister, H. O., 83, 800
Philtine, E. C., 5, 580
Pickford, R. W., 790
Pilcher, C., 784
Piotrowski, Z., 799
Plant, J. S., 579
Polatin, P., 5, 85, 580, 792
Poole, N., 782
Powdermaker, F. B., 569, 799, 805
Pratt, J. H., 784
Pray, K. L. M., 782
Prescott, D., 797
Preston, G. H., 579, 580
Proceedings of the Brief Psychotherapy Council, 792
Proceedings of the Second Brief Psychotherapy Council, 792
Proceedings of the Third Psychotherapy Council, 792
Psychiatric Bulletin, 794

Rado, S., 73–75, 788, 789
Rank, O., 11, 46, 69–70, 120, 788, 802, 804
Rapaport, D., 805
Rees, J. R., 580
Reeve, M., 800
Reich, W., 72–73, 75, 788, 804
Reider, N., 793
Reik, T., 116, 120
Reitman, F., 83, 791
Rennie, T. A. C., 113, 115, 126, 127, 128, 794, 796, 797, 805

Report of the 1951 Conference on Psychiatric Education, 794
Rhoades, W., 785
Rippon, T. S., 31, 783
Roberts, D. E., 796
Rogers, C., 5, 13, 42–44, 115, 116, 120, 781, 785, 794, 797, 803
Romano, J., 5
Rome, H. P., 786
Rorschach, H., 798
Rosen, J. M., 631, 799
Rosenzweig, S., 781, 805
Ross, H., 782
Ryan, W. C., 797

Sackler, A. M., 33, 784
Sackler, M. D., 784
Sackler, R. R., 784
Sakel, M., 784
Salter, A., 48, 786
Sargant, W., 784
Sarlin, C. N., 85, 792
Saul, L. J., 580, 793
Schacter, H., 581
Schafer, R., 805
Schilder, P., 85, 792
Schmideberg, M., 788
Schoen, M., 783
Schreiber, M., 799
Schullian, D., 783
Searl, M. N., 788
Sharpe, E. F., 787, 804
Sherman, C., 796
Simon, A., 784
Slater, E., 784
Slavin, S., 781
Slavson, S. R., 51, 85, 120, 569, 783, 786, 787, 792, 805
Smith, E. R., 113, 781, 794
Snyder, W. V., 785, 786
Soibelman, D., 783
Solomon, J. C., 84, 786, 792
Sonnemann, U., 798
Spackman, C. S., 783
Spiegel, J. P., 783
Spock, B., 581
Spotnitz, H., 86, 792
Steele, M., 33, 798
Stekel, W., 70–72, 788, 804
Sterba, R., 786, 787
Stern, A., 787
Stern, E. M., 582
Stern, M. M., 790
Stokes, W. R., 580
Stone, A., 109, 580

Stone, H., 580
Stone, L., 793
Strachey, J., 787, 788
Strang, R., 781
Strauss, B. V., 794
Strecker, E., 802
Sullivan, H. S., 631, 675, 789, 799, 801, 804
Super, D. E., 781
Symposium of the Boston Psychoanalytic Society and Institute, 786
Szurek, S. A., 795, 800

Taft, J., 37, 785
Tarumianz, M. D., 797
Taylor, K. W., 581
Thompson, C., 555, 579, 789, 802
Thorne, F. C., 44, 45, 48, 115, 781, 783, 785, 786, 803
Thorner, M. W., 5
Tiffin, J., 805
Tompkins, S. S., 798
Towle, C., 11, 781, 782, 795
Trager, H., 797
Trail, P. M., 791

Travis, L. E., 580
Traxler, A. E., 782, 802
Trecker, H. B., 781
Tyler, R., 781

United States Children's Bureau, 782
United States Social Security Administration, 781

Van de Velde, Th. H., 580
Van Ophuijsen, J. H. W., 782, 784
Vernonon, P. E., 791
Vitoz, R., 782

Walsh, J., 782, 784
Watson, G., 781, 797
Watts, J. W., 113, 784
Watts, M. S. M., 794
Weir-Mitchell, S., 784
Weiss, E., 801
Wender, L., 85, 785, 792
Whiles, W. H., 791
Whipple, D. V., 581
Whitehorn, J. C., 5, 113, 794
Whitman, H., 580

Wickman, E. K., 797
Wilbur, D. L., 113, 794
Willard, H., 783
Williams, V. T., 582
Williamson, E. G., 785
Wise, C. A., 796
Witmer, H. L., 794, 805
Wolberg, A., 625, 799
Wolberg, L. R., 82, 781, 783, 786, 790, 793, 799, 804
Wolf, A., 86, 792
Wolf, A. W. M., 581
Woltmann, A. G., 791
Woodward, L., 113, 115, 126, 127, 128, 781, 794, 796, 797, 805
Wright, R., 784

Yates, D. H., 31, 47–48, 783
Young, R. A., 119, 795

Zachry, C. B., 581, 797
Zeckiel, A. N., 781
Zilboorg, G., 579, 788, 801
Ziskind, E., 113, 794
Zubin, J., 798
Zubin, P., 801
Zulliger, H., 129, 798

Subject Index

Abbreviated goals, *see* Goals, abbreviated

Accenting (in interviewing), 176

Acceptance, need for, 319

Acting-out, 588–589, 473, 514, 523
  aggression as, 476
  in group therapy, 570, 571
  handling, 476–477
  as resistance, 466
  values in, 676

"Active psychoanalysis," 70–72

"Active therapy" of Ferenczi, 68

Activity
  building motivation for, 496–497
  employing, in reducing transference, 400
  stimulating, during session, case illustration,
    711–720
  of therapist, 93

"Activity group therapy," 52

Adjunctive aids, 569–582
  in psychoanalytically oriented psychotherapy,
    81–86
  in psychotherapy, (course), 141

Adjunctive therapies, 8

Adjuncts during therapy, 95

Adjustment, previous, in relation to prognosis,
  238

Adjustment problems and bibliotherapy, 578

Adler, Alexandra, 66

Adler, Alfred, school of, 65–66

Adler, Kurt, 66

Adlerian analysis
  interview focus in, 88
  See also Individual psychology

Adlerian Consultation Centers, 66

Adolescents
  books on understanding, in bibliotherapy,
    581
  books to be read by, in bibliotherapy, 581

Advice-giving, 93, 504, 527, 543, 625, 667

Age of patient, in relation to prognosis, 231

Age of therapist, 250
  answering questions about, 204

Aggression
  as "acting-out," 476
  permitting expression of, 668
  reeducative handling of, 545
  stimulation of, as a result of interpretation,
    450
  toward therapist, 514
  violent, hospitalization for, 588

Alcoholic intoxication
  acute, handling, 590
  apomorphine in, 109

Alcoholic, treatment of the (course), 140

Alcoholics
  acute intoxication in, 590
  inadequate motivation in, 275

Alcoholics Anonymous, 617, 620

Alcoholism, 615–620
  antabuse in, 33, 620
  benzedrine in, 33
  emergencies in, 264
  hypnosis in, 573
  prestige suggestion in, 22
  reconditioning in, 48
  supportive therapy for, 254, 523, 616

Ambition, compulsive, as resistance, 323

Ambition, neurotic, in therapist, 489–490

Ambivalence
  handling, 674–675
  in obsessive-compulsive reactions, 601, 602
  resolution of, 513–518

American Institute for Psychoanalysis, 78

American Medical Association, report on certification of psychologists, 121

American Psychiatric Association Council, 121

American Psychoanalytic Association, 63

American Psychological Association, Committee on Training in Clinical Psychology,
  115

Amnesia
  in conversion and dissociative reactions, 599
  effect of recovery of repressed memories on,
    425
  hypnosis in, 573
  See also Memories, forgotten

Amphetamine sulfate, in barbiturate poisoning,
  591

Anal personality patterns, 612–613

Analytical psychology, 66–68

Anesthesia, treatment of, 598

Anorexia, in depressed patients, 629

Antabuse therapy in alcoholism, 33, 620

Anthropology, contributions to psychotherapy
  in, 106

Anti-social behavior, handling, 588–589

Anxiety, 508, 512
  in detached personalities, 611–612
  environmental manipulation in, 589–590
  equivalents, 552
  increasing frequency of sessions for, 590
  stimulated by insight, 494
  handling of intense, 589–590
  stimulated by interpretation, 450–451
  and learning, 496
  myanesin therapy for, 33

Anxiety—*Continued*
  effect of narcosis on, 576
  narcotherapy in, 577
  in "schizoid" personalities, 610
  sub-coma insulin for, 590
  supportive therapy in, 589
  in therapist, 490
  in therapy of psychosomatic disorders, 605,
    606
Anxiety hysteria, *see* Phobic reactions
Anxiety neurosis, *see* Anxiety reactions
Anxiety reactions, 597–598
  hypnosis in, 573
  narcotherapy in, 85, 576
  prognosis in, 232
  reconstructive therapy for, 255
  sub-coma insulin treatment in, 32
  supportive therapy for, 254
  susceptibility to Freudian psychoanalysis of,
    109
Anxiety state, *see* Anxiety reactions
Aphonia, treatment of, 598
Application blank for new staff members, 827–
    829
Appointments
  breaking, 666
  lateness in, 666–667
Apomorphine for alcoholism, 109
Approaches in psychotherapy, 306–307
  blending, 662
Argumentativeness, handling, 665
Arguments, need for avoidance of, with pa-
    tient, 333
Art analysis, in the exploration of the uncon-
    scious, 429
Art creations, in psychologic testing, 268
Art therapy, 83–84, 8
  criticism of, 83–84
  problems susceptible to, 257
Aschner treatment for schizophrenia, 636
Assertiveness, fear of, in therapist, 490
Astasia-abasia, treatment of, 598
Atonia, hydrotherapy in, 31
"Attitude therapy," 8, 37
  problems susceptible to, 256
Attitudes
  change of, with bibliotherapy, 578
  interpretation of, 444
Authoritarianism in therapist, 489, 673
Authoritative approach, in conversion and dis-
    sociative reactions, 598
Authorization for release of medical records,
    form for, 839
Automatic writing, in hypnoanalysis, case illus-
    tration of, 433
Auto-suggestion, 22
  in phobic reactions, 600
Barbiturate addiction, 621

Barbiturate poisoning, treatment of, 590–591
Basic neuropsychiatry, (course), 138
Basic rule, *see* Free association
Battle exhaustion, *see* Stress reactions
Beginning phase of treatment, 195–358
  dreams in, 386
Behavior problems, inadequate motivation in,
    275
Belittling patient, need for avoidance of, 333–
    334
Benzedrine
  in alcoholism, 33
  in depressed patients, 629
"Best" kind of psychotherapy, 106–111, 307
Bias in psychiatric field, 106
Bibliotherapy, 578–582
Bills, non-payment of, 346
Blaming patient, need to avoid, 334
Boasting, need to avoid, 332
Borderline cases, 625
  abbreviated goals in, 563
  (course), 139
  supportive therapy for, 523
  transference in, 401
Borderline patients, *see* Borderline cases
Brain surgery, 34, 542
  in intractable pain, 595
  in obsessive-compulsive reactions, 604
  problems susceptible to, 256
  in schizophrenia, 34
Brain tumor, complicating therapy, 594
Breaking appointments, 666
"Brief" psychotherapy, *see* Short-term therapy
Broken appointments, charge for, 312
Business dealings with patients, avoiding, 352

Cancelled appointments, charge for, 312
Cancer, complicating therapy, 594
Carbon dioxide therapy, 33–34
Care of emotional problems by psychotherapy,
    305
Case folder, 686
  form, 824
Case history, *see* History-taking
Case illustrations
  activity during session, encouraging, 711–
    720
  attack on former therapist, handling, 274
  authoritative interpretations, making, 443–
    444
  choice of therapies, 251–254
  circumscribing the area of subject coverage,
    173–175
  clarifying misconceptions about therapy,
    286–287
  collating essential data, 209–215
  counter-transference, 492
  creating incentives for therapy, 281–282

defining therapist's role, 349–350

delineating patient's responsibilities, 347–348

diagnosis, making a, 221–226

dream interpretation, technique of, 383, 386, 388

dreams, 326–327, 381–382, 389–397, 452–461, 711–712, 734–736, 752–753, 766–767

explaining how psychotherapy works, 353–356

exploring trends and patterns, 412–416, 416–420

first inquiry, handling the, 199–200

focusing on, as a means of identifying patterns
feelings, 369–370, 370–371
interpersonal relations, 372–373
past history, 374
slips of speech, 374–375
symptoms, 366–368

free association, use of, as a means of identifying patterns, 377–378

guiding the theme of interview toward fruitful goal, 170–171

hostility toward therapist, 461–462

hypnoanalysis, 431–438

hysterical conversion symptom, relief of, 431–438

identifying an important theme, 166–167

initial interview, 293–302, 690–699

initial resistances, dealing with, 203, 204, 205, 206

insight, achieving, 720–733
through focused interviewing, 364–365
translating, into action, 500, 505–507, 733–742

interpretations
handling untoward effects of, 451–452
making, 179, 180–181, 452–462
tentative, making, 441–442

interruption of therapy, planned, 564–565

levels in focusing of interview, 168–169

middle phase of therapy, 720–733

misconceptions about psychotherapy, handling, 286–287

motivation, inadequate, 277–280, 288–291, 291–292

negative feelings, indicating acceptance of, 277–280

opening the interview, 161–162

parataxic distortions, self-interpretation of, 440–442

pauses, managing, 162–163

"primal scene," recovery of repressed memory of, 431–438

recognizing and reflecting negative feelings, 276–277

reeducative therapy, 688

referral for psychologic testing, 270

referring the patient, 264

resistance, handling of, 473–474, 474–475, 475, 475–476, 480–483
contempt for normality as, 468–469
intellectual inhibitions as, 465–466
to termination, 559–560

self-interpretation, 440–441

silence, managing, 164

structuring
of therapy, acceptance of, 356–358
the therapeutic situation, 700–709

termination of therapy, 769–779
discussing, with patient, 557–558

transference, 402–404, 404–405, 405–409, 430
break-through of, 401–402
negative, 519–520
neurosis, 409–410, 430–431
positive, 518–519
resistance, 480–483, 483–487

transferring the patient, 565

working relationship, signs of a, 337–339

working-through process, 509–510, 510–512, 518–522

Case presentation outline, 825–826

Case record, see Recording

Case summary, (recording), 684–685

Casework, 11–12
contributions to psychotherapy, 106
diagnostic, problems susceptible to, 256
functional, problems susceptible to, 256

Casework consultation, 267–268

Casework therapy, 8, 46–47

Caseworker, in teamwork functioning, 130–135
See also Psychiatric caseworker and Social worker

Castration desires and fears
as a sign of ego disintegration, 587
interpretation of, 449
as resistance, 473
symbolic significance of, 423

Cause of emotional illness, 304

Cerebral hemorrhage complicating therapy, 594, 595

Cerebral thombosis complicating therapy, 594

Certification of psychologists, 121

Character analysis, 72–73

Character disorder, definition of, 305
See also Personality disorders

Character
distortions, as a means of adjusting to conflict, 555
rigidity, supportive therapy in, 523
strivings, ego-syntonic nature of, 607
structure

Character—*Continued*
    analysis of, in group therapy, 571
    and cure, 678–679
    in obsessive compulsive reactions, 601
Child care, in bibliotherapy, books on, 581
Childhood origin of emotional problems, 304
Child psychiatry, (course), 139
Child-rearing and bibliotherapy, 578
Child Study Association of America, 581
Choice of therapist, 249–250
Choice of treatment method, 250–258
Christian Science, 19
Church facilities, in environmental adjustment, 502
Client-centered therapy, *see* Non-directive therapy
Clinical psychologist
    definition of, 306
    See also Psychologists
Clinical seminars, (courses), 139
Clinical team, *see* Teamwork functioning
Coercion, as supportive therapy, 24
Combat exhaustion, *see* Stress reactions
Combined therapy, 569, 572
Communicating
    acceptance, 328–329
    empathy, 329–330
    interest, 327–328
    objectivity, 329
    tolerance, 328–329
    understanding of problems, 325–326
Communication
    differences in, during supervision, 645
    explaining the manner of, 340–342
    need for free, 310–311
Communications of patient, 92–93
Communicativeness of patient, 247
Comparative study of psychotherapeutic approaches, (course), 138
Compensation and other medicolegal problems in psychiatry, (course), 141
Competitiveness with therapist, as resistance, 471
Compliance, excessive, reeducative handling of, 544–545
Compulsion neurosis, *see* Obsessive-compulsive reactions
Compulsions, 425
Compulsive symptoms, in psychosomatic disorders, 605
Compulsive talking, as a sign of ego disintegration, 587
Concentrative blocks as resistance, 465
"Conditioned reflex therapy," 48
Condonation, need for, in therapy, 319
Confession, *see* Emotional catharsis
Confessions of therapist to patient, 673

Confidential nature of communications, explaining, 343–344
Conflicts
    engendered by trends, 411
    exposure of unconscious, 421
    expressed in dreams, 385
    interpretation of, 444
    repressed memories as sources of, 423
Conscience, modification of, 516, 517
Constitution, in relation to prognosis, 234
Consultation with patient treated by another therapist, handling, 661–662
Consultations
    casework, 267–268
    with community workers, 681
    medical, 266
    neurologic, 266
    psychiatric, 266
    psychologic, 268–271
    securing essential, 266–271
Contempt
    for normality, as resistance, 468–469
    for therapist's values as resistance, 472
Continuous sleep treatment, 33
Contractures, hysterical, treatment of, 598
Control of obnoxious traits, best therapy for, 678
Controlling tendencies, as resistance, 472
Conversion hysteria
    narcotherapy in, 85
    reconstructive therapy for, 255
    susceptibility of, to Freudian psychoanalysis, 109
    See also Conversion and dissociative reactions
Conversion reactions, 598–599
    prognosis in, 232
Conversion symptoms, 425
    hypnosis in, 573
Convulsive therapy, 8, 31–32, 542
    problems susceptible to, 256
    role of nurse in, 126
    See also Electric convulsive therapy
Coronary attack complicating therapy, 594–595
Correspondence, essential, 265
Cortical undercutting, *see* Brain surgery
Couch position
    anxiety in, 669
    as a means of stirring up unconscious activity, 429
    avoiding of, to reduce transference, 400
    explaining use of, 344
    rationale of, 310
    use of, to accentuate transference, 401
Council for the Clinical Training of Theological Students, 127
Counseling, 12–13
    See also Therapeutic counseling

Counter-transference, 142–146, 488–493, 89, 184, 197, 320–322, 324–325, 328, 587, 673, 676
  case illustration of, 492
  as a deterrant to learning new patterns, 503
  effect of personal therapy on, 491
  insight as a deterrant to, 488
  interminable therapy and, 669–670
  need to analyze, in treating schizophrenics, 632
  sexual, 478
  during supervision, 654, 657–660
  transferring the patient, due to, 565
Creativity, loss of, in therapy, 309
Criminal, treatment of the, (course), 140
Criminality, hospitalization for, 588
Criminals, inadequate motivation in, 275
Criticism
  of another therapist, handling of, 274
  of patient, need to avoid, 331–332
Crucial decisions, making of, during therapy, 311
Crying in patient, handling of, 673
Cultural ideas of success in therapy, 552
Cultural standards, mediation of, in environmental manipulation, 528
Culture and personality, (course), 141
Cure, apparent and permanent, 678–679

Daily habits, correction of, in environmental manipulation, 528
Day-dreaming, excessive, as a sign of ego disintegration, 587
Decisions
  crucial, during therapy, 667–668
  important, avoiding, 348
Decorative scheme of office, 187
Defenses
  as revealed in dreams, 385
  characterologic, 513
  exposure of, 412
  interpretation of, 444, 463
  mechanisms of, effect of interpretation on, 450
Defiance as resistance, 471
Definitions of psychotherapy, 3–6
Delays
  in getting well, explaining, 343, 345
  in starting therapy, handling, 261
Delinquents, inadequate motivation in, 275
Delirium tremens, sub-coma insulin treatment in, 32
Delusions as a sign of ego disintegration, 587
Demands by patient, insistent, handling, 668–669
Dementia praecox, see Schizophrenic reactions
Demonstrativeness, limits of, 350–351

Dependency, 608–610
  activities of therapist that stimulate, 675–676
  analysis of, in termination, 558
  compulsive, consequences of, 512
  inadequate motivations for therapy in patients with, 472
  motivational lacks in, 608
  in obsessive-compulsive reactions, 601, 604
  in phobic reactions, 599
  reeducative handling of, 544
  as resistance, 322–323, 564
  supportive handling of, 608
  termination problems in, 558–560
  as transference, 470–471
Dependent needs, in therapy, 318–319
Dependent reactions, in alcoholics, 616, 618
Depersonalization, as a sign of ego disintegration, 587
Depression
  acute, group therapy in, 570
  due to hostile transference, 478
  effect of narcosis on, 576
  in narcissistic reactions, 614
  severe, supportive therapy for, 523
  severe, treatment of, (course), 141
  stimulation of, as a result of interpretation, 450
  suicidal attempts in, 585–586
  suicidal risks in, 583
  See also Depressive reactions
Depressive reactions, 605
  anticipating emergencies in, 264
  convulsive therapy in, 32, 605, 629
  See also Depression
Deprivations, imposing, 674
Desensitization, 28–30, 541–542, 8, 595
  in narcotherapy, 578
  in phobic reactions, 600
Destructive tendencies
  due to transference, 478
  supportive therapy for, 523
Detached patterns, dynamic significance of, 610–611
Detached personalities, 610–612
Detachment
  as a defense, 514
  inadequate motivations for therapy in patients with, 472
  in obsessive-compulsive reactions, 602
  reeducative handling of, 545
  as resistance, 323–324, 471–472
  in schizophrenia, 634
  in therapist, 489
  treatment of, by externalization of interests, 530
Detoxification therapy in alcoholism, 590, 616

Developmental history in relation to prognosis, 235–236

Diagnosis
  making a, 216–226
  in relation to prognosis, 231

Diagnostic casework, 46–47

Dianetics, 30, 308

Didactic analysis, see Personal therapy for therapist

Differences among the various psychotherapies, 87–95

Directive counseling, problems susceptible to, 256

Directive methodologies, choice of, in therapists, 491

"Directive therapy," 45–46

Directiveness in therapist, 489, 667

Disappointments in therapy, preparing patient for, 498

Disintegrative tendencies
  effect on therapeutic goals of, 555
  reappraisal of goals in, 578

Dissociating the treatment hour from life, as resistance, 467–468

Dissociation, 424

Dissociative reactions, 598–599
  hypnosis in, 573

Distributive analysis and synthesis, 38–41, 8
  problems susceptible to, 256

Distrust
  in depressed patients, 628
  as resistance, 323

Divorce, 667
  caution in advising, 502–503

Dogmatic utterances, need to avoid, 334

Dream interpretation, technique of, (course), 139

Dreams, 514
  anxiety, 670
  avoiding, to reduce transference, 400
  bizarreness of, 310
  case illustrations of, 326–327, 354, 356, 381–382, 383, 386–388, 389–397, 415, 452–461, 711–712, 734–736, 752–753, 766–767
  causes of, 310
  content of, 380
  dogmatic analysis of, need to avoid, 335
  excessive, 670
  explaining rationale of, 342–343
  focusing on
    to accentuate transference, 401
    as a means of identifying patterns, 379–397
    as a means of stirring up unconscious activity, 429
  instructing patient in, 342–343

interpreting, as a means of building a relationship, 326–327
  most important, 670
  observation of, as assigned task, 348
  possibility of interpretation of, 310
  repetitive, 670
  reporting of, 309–310
  resistance to working with, handled by bibliotherapy, 579
  as signs of potential suicidal risk, 583
  structure of, 379–380
  symbolism in, 422
  technique of interpretation, 382–389
  therapeutic use of, 94, 381–382
  use of
    in beginning phase of treatment, 386
    in exploratory phase of treatment, 386
    in phase of translating insight into action, 388–389
    in terminal phase of treatment, 389
  utility of, in interpreting sexual transference, 478
  as a vehicle toward insight, 324

Drug addict, treatment of the, (course), 140

Drug addiction, 620–621
  anticipating emergencies in, 264
  benzedrine in, 33
  inadequate motivation in, 275
  prognosis in, 232
  supportive therapy for, 254, 523

Drug therapy, 32, 8, 542
  problems susceptible to, 256

Drugs, tension-relieving effect of, 524

Duration of illness, in relation to prognosis, 231

Duration of therapy, 89, 312
  estimation of, 259–260

"Dynamic-cultural" school of psychoanalysis, 75–80
  criticisms of, 80

Dynamic interpretation of diagnosis, 216–220

Dynamics
  confusion as to, 667
  formulating the, 227–229
  of therapy, 645
  See also Psychodynamics

Eclecticism in psychotherapy, 38, 107, 677

Economic situation, adjustment of, in environmental manipulation, 528

Education, mental health in, 128

Educational approaches, 10–11

Educational background of the psychotherapist, 137–141

Educational disabilities, 271

Educational problems, guidance in, 255

Effect of psychotherapy, 108

Ego collapse, supportive techniques for, 524

Ego damage, effect on therapeutic goals, 554
Ego disintegration, signs of, during therapy, 587
Ego growth, 513
    catalyzing, during terminal phase, 560–561
Ego shattering
    during insight therapy, 586
    in transference, 586
Ego strength
    rebuilding of, 516–517
    as related to goals in therapy, 556
    as related to prognosis, 234–238
"Ego-syntonic" nature of character strivings, 607
Ego weakness in schizophrenia, 631, 632–633
Electric convulsive therapy, 588
    in depressive reactions, 32, 605, 629
    in involutional psychosis, 626
    in manic patients, 628
    in psychotic disorders, 626
    See also Convulsive therapy
Electrical recording, 686–687
Electroshock, see Convulsive therapy and Electric convulsive therapy
Emergencies
    anticipating, 264
    handling, 583–596
Emotional catharsis, 28–30, 541–542, 8, 524
    in "activity group therapy," 52
    and desensitization, problems susceptible to, 256
    effect of play therapy on, 84
    influence of narcosis on, 576
    interview focus in, 88
    need for, in therapy, 319
    promoting, with narcotherapy, 589
    in psychodrama, 51
Empathy, need for, 589
Encouragement of patient, indications for, 504, 543
Encouragement of positive aspects of adjustment, 676
Endocrine therapy, see Glandular therapy
Enthusiasms, unrestrained, handling of, 675
Environmental disturbance
    adjustment of, in translating insight into action, 501–503
    effect on therapeutic goals of, 554
    focusing on, as a means of identifying patterns, 370–371
    rectification of, in reeducative therapy, 544
    supportive measures in, 524, 543
Environmental factors
    early, in relation to prognosis, 234–235
    precipitation, in relation to prognosis, 237–238
Environmental manipulation, 19–20, 527–528, 8, 501–503

in acute anxiety, 589–590
in alcoholism, 618
in borderline cases, 625
in personality problems, 607
problems susceptible to, 255
in psychopathic personality, 614
in psychotic disorders, 625
in schizophrenia, 630–631, 637
in speech disorders, 622
Environmental situation, current, in relation to prognosis, 239–240
Environmental stress, severe, abbreviated goals in, 563
Equipment of the psychotherapist, 137–148
Erotic attitudes and feelings, interpretation of, 447
Erotic transference, 477–478
Errors, admitting, 673
Establishing connections (in interviewing), 177
Estrogenic hormones, in involutional psychosis, 626
Eukinetics, 623
Excited behavior, in acute alcoholic intoxication, 590
Excited states, hydrotherapy in, 31
Excitement
    drug therapy in, 32
    handling, 588–589
    in narcissistic reactions, 614
    sedation in, 588
Excretory activities, symbolic meaning of, 612
Exhibitionism, 621
Experience of therapist, answering questions about, 205
Experiences, forgotten, see Memories, forgotten
Experiential equipment of the psychotherapist, 146
Exploring patterns, 411–420
External life situation, effect of, on emotional problems, 303
Externalization of interests, 20–21, 529–530, 8
    in depressed patients, 628
    problems susceptible to, 255

Face-to-face interviewing, to reduce transference, 400
Factual understanding, need for, in therapy, 319–320
Failure judgments in therapy, 552
Failures, in reconstructive therapy, 554–555
Falling in love with therapist, 309
Family data sheet, 818
Family living, books on, in bibliotherapy, 580
Family
    members
        apprising, of patient's psychotic condition, 589
        conferences with, 670–672, 499–500

Family—*Continued*
  handling, 501–502
  handling attacks on, 273
  notifying, in psychotic attack, 587–588
  psychotherapy for, 672
  working with
    in borderline cases, 625
    in environmental manipulation, 20, 529
    in schizophrenia, 633–637
  problems
    environmental manipulation in, 255
    management of, (course), 141
  relations, mediation of, in environmental manipulation, 528
  standards, of success in therapy, 552
Fantasies, 514
  avoiding, to reduce transference, 400
  focusing on
    to accentuate transference, 401
    as a means of identifying patterns, 389
    as a means of stirring up unconscious activity, 429
  symbolism in, 422
Fatigue in therapist, 673
Fear
  activities of therapist that stimulate, 676
  of homosexuality, reassurance in, 532
  of impotence, reassurance in, 532
  of insanity, reassurance in, 531
  of killing, handling, 668
  of masturbation, reassurance in, 531–532
  of physical illness, reassurance in, 531
  of retaliation, symbolic expressions of, 442–443
  of therapist, as resistance, 471
Fears, simple conditioned, effect of recovery of repressed memories on, 425
Feces, symbolic significance of, 423
Feelings
  focusing on, as a means of identifying patterns, 368–370
  interpretation of, 444
  of unreality, as a sign of ego disintegration, 587
Fees, 312
  arranging, 260–261, 662
  handling neglect in payment of, 663
  overemphasis of, 490
  readjusting, 663
Ferenczi, Sandor, therapeutic modifications of, 68–69
Financial problems, environmental manipulation in, 255
Flattery, need to avoid, 335
"Flight into health," as resistance, 465
Focused interview, explaining rationale of, 340–342

Focusing
  as an aid to interpretation, 440
  in group therapy, 572
  relative importance of past and present, 664
  selective, in interviewing, 165–175
Follow up, 565–566
  notes, 685–686
Forgetting appointments, as resistance, 471, 514
Forgotten memories, *see* Memories, forgotten
Foster family placement, in environmental adjustment, 502
Free association, 55
  avoiding, to reduce transference, 400
  case illustration of, 377–378
  definition of, 310
  explaining rationale of, 342
  as a means of stirring up unconscious activity, 429
  rationale of, 376
  symbolism in, 422
  use of, as a means of identifying patterns, 376–378
  use of, to accentuate transference, 401
Frequency of sessions, 258, 92, 311–312
  decreasing, 667
    in dependency patterns, 610
    in terminal phase, 557
    to reduce transference, 400
  increasing, 589, 667
    to accentuate transference, 401
    in acute anxiety, 590
    as a means of stirring up unconscious activity, 429
Freudian psychoanalysis, 54–63, 8
  criticisms of, 63–64
  definition of, 307
  interview focus in, 88
  limitations of, 109–110
  problems susceptible to, 256
  versus non-Freudian psychoanalysis, 308
Friends of therapist, accepting, for therapy, 662
Frigidity, reassurance in, 532
Frustration tolerance
  building, in alcoholism, 619
  in power patterns, 613
Function of clinical team members, (course), 138
"Functional casework," 46
Furnishings of office, 187

General principles of psychotherapy, 149–156
Genetic origin
  of neurosis, 153
  of patterns, exploration of, in reeducative therapy, 544

Gift-giving
   limits in, 351–352
   as resistance, 472
Glandular substances, 33
Glandular therapy, in schizophrenia, 33, 636
Goal modification, need for, 555–556
Goals, abbreviated, 251, 563
   in alcoholism, 615
   in obsessive-compulsive reactions, 602–604
   practicality of, 555–556
   in psychotic reactions, 625
   in sexual deviations, 622
   terminating on basis of, 563–566
   See also Goals in therapy and Short-term
      therapy
Goals of the initial interview, 198
Goals in therapy, 551–556, 87, 96, 107, 361
   definition of, 196
   differences in, during supervision, 646
   minimal, in reeducative therapy, 679
   in "normal" and "neurotic" persons, 679
   practical, 554–556
   reappraisal of, in disintegrative tendencies,
      578
   reasonable, in reconstructive therapy, 679
   reconstructive, need for exploration of un-
      conscious in, 421
   in relation to dreams, 386
   in relation to prognosis, 230–231
   revision of, 563, 594
   See also Goals, abbreviated
Group affiliation, in dependency patterns, 610
Group contacts, as a social experience, 502
Group for the Advancement of Psychiatry, 120
Group psychotherapy, (course), 139
Group standards and mental health, 553
Group therapy, 569–572, 308
   acting-out in, 570–571
   "activity," 52
   analytic, 85–86
      criticism of, 86
      problems susceptible to, 257
   conduct of opening sessions in, 570–571
   content of discussions in, 571
   in detached personalities, 611
   handling of later sessions in, 571–572
   inspirational, 34–35, 8, 542
      in alcoholism, 617
      problems susceptible to, 256
   interaction encouraging in, 572
   in masochistic personality disorders, 570
   need for, 308
   organizing a group in, 569–570
   in personality problems, efficacy of, 569
   in psychopathic personalities, 570
   reconstructive, 85–86, 8, 257
      problems susceptible to, 257
   reeducative, 50–52, 8

   problems susceptible to, 256
   results in, as compared with individual
      therapy, 569
   in schizophrenia, 636
   selecting patients for, 569–570
   in speech disorders, 624
   in therapeutic stalemate, 669
   value of, 572
Growth process, normal, 424
Guidance, 17, 8, 526–527, 596
   in alcoholism, 616
   in conversion and dissociative reactions, 598
   in depressed patients, 628
   in group therapy, 571
   hypnosis in, 573
   interview focus in, 88
   in narcissistic reactions, 614
   passivity and submissiveness in therapist as
      a deterrant to, 489
   problems susceptible to, 255
   in psychopathic personality, 614
   in psychosomatic disorders, 606
   in psychotic reactions, 625
   in speech disorders, 622
Guilt feelings, symbolic expressions of, 422–
   423
Guilt in therapist, 490

Habit disorders
   prestige suggestion in, 22, 254
   supportive therapy for, 254
Hallucinating patients, group therapy in, 570
Hallucinations, as a sign of ego disintegration,
   587
Handwriting analysis, 268
Hatred toward patient, 673
Health factors, consideration of, in environ-
   mental manipulation, 528–529
Helping authority, therapist as, 320–321
Hereditary factors
   in neurosis, 305
   in relation to prognosis, 234
Histamine therapy, 33
History of psychiatry, (course), 137
History-taking, 207–208, 92
Hobbies, 529
   tension-relieving effects of, 525
Hodgkins' disease complicating therapy, 594
Home visits, 663–664
"Homework" assigning, to patient, 664
Homicidal behavior, in acute alcoholic intoxi-
   cation, 590
Homicidal tendencies
   hospitalization in, 588
   supportive therapy for, 523
Homosexual fears, reassurance in, 532
Homosexuality, 621
   acting-out in, 476

Homosexuality—*Continued*
  group therapy in, 570
  resistance in, 480–483
  significance of, 423, 612
Hormonal treatment, *see* Glandular therapy
Horney, Karen, school of, 77–78
"Horney analysis," interview focus in, 88
Hospitalization
  in alcoholism, 616
  in depressed patients, 629
  in drug addiction, 620–621
  indications for, 588
  in involutional psychosis, 626
  in psychotic disorders, 625
  in schizophrenia, 635–636
Hostile impulses, uncontrollable, as a sign of
    ego disintegration, 587
Hostile transference, 478
Hostility
  activities of therapist that stimulate, 676
  in alcoholism, 619
  as a defense, 480
  in dependency patterns, 609
  in detached personalities, 611
  fear of, in therapist, 490
  handling, by externalization of interests,
    529–530
  handling of, 330
  in obsessive-compulsive reactions, 601
  in psychosomatic disorders, 605
  permitting expression of, 668
  as resistance, 323, 471, 564
  resolution of, in supportive therapy, 525
  symbolic expressions of, 422
  tolerance of, 517
  toward therapist, 461–462, 514, 672
    interpretation of, 447–448
Housing problems, environmental manipula-
    tion in, 255, 528
Hydrotherapy, 31, 8, 542
  in depressed patients, 629
  in drug addiction, 621
  in involutional psychosis, 626
  in manic patients, 628
  problems susceptible to, 256
  relief of tension through, 524
  in schizophrenia, 636
Hypnoanalysis, 81–83, 8
  case illustration of, 431–438
  in the exploration of the unconscious, 429
  limitations of, 83
  in phobic reactions, 600
  problems susceptible to, 257
Hypnosis
  as catalyst in evoking forgotten memories,
    428–429
  in conversion and dissociative reactions, 598
  in depression, 629

effect in shortening therapy of, 308
in emergency relief of psychosomatic symp-
    toms, 591–594
in emotional catharsis and desensitization,
    29
indications for, 308
induction of, 574
  case illustration of, 434
influence of psyche, 572–573
in insight therapy, 573
in involutional psychosis, 626–627
limitations of, 573
narcosis in, 577
in psychopathic personality, 614
in reconditioning, 48
to reinforce prestige suggestion, 23
suggestive, 8
in therapeutic stalemate, 669
See also Hypnotherapy
Hypnotherapy, 572–576
  in stress reactions, 639–640
  symptom removal, 591–594
  See also Hypnosis
Hypochondriasis, brain surgery in, 34
Hypomania, *see* Manic-depressive reactions
Hysterical amnesias, effect of recovery of re-
    pressed memories on, 425
Hysterical conversion and dissociative reac-
    tions, as emergencies, 591
Hysterical personalities, suicidal attempts in,
    584
Hysterical reactions, narcotherapy in, 576
Hysterical symptoms in psychosomatic dis-
    orders, 605

Ideal objectives of mental health, 553–554
Idealized parental image, therapist as, 321
Ideas of reference, as a sign of ego disintegra-
    tion, 587
Identification with therapist, 516
Identifying important trends and patterns,
    361–410
Immorality and psychotherapy, 309
Impatience, displays of, need to avoid, 333
Impotence, reassurance in, 532
Impulses, interpretation of, 444
"Inadequate" personality patterns, 608–610
Inattention, as resistance, 465
Incentives for therapy, creating, 281–282
Incurable somatic disease complicating therapy,
    594–596
"Individual psychology," 65–66
Individual Psychology Association, 66
Industrial psychiatry, (course), 141
Infantile personality patterns, 608–610
Inferiority feelings, ineffectuality of reassur-
    ance in, 533

Infidelity of marital partner, reassurance in, 532–533
Information giving, 665
Informational sheet, 830–831
Initial interview, 198–302
  case illustrations in, 293, 690–699
  collating essential data in, 207–215
  (course), 138
  diagnosis in, making a, 216–226
  first contact with patient in, 198–206
  (form), 812–815
  handling verbal attacks in, 661
  inadequate motivation in, dealing with, 275–292
  patient's general condition during, estimating, 246–248
  practical arrangements for therapy in, making, 249–265
  prognosis in, estimating the, 230–245
  recording the, 683
  violent feelings following, 662
Insanity, definition of, 305
Insight
  achieving, case illustration, 720–733
  in allaying anxiety attacks, 589
  basic nature of, 677–678
  as a deterrant to counter-transference, 488
  difference in, in reeducative and reconstructive therapies, 678
  effect of, 508, 509
  inculcating, in interviewing, 175–182
  level of, 247
  rejection of, in relation to resistance, 479
  in relation to prognosis, 233
  as resistance, 467
  role of, 494
  signs of poor capacities for, 451
  translating, into action, 494–507
    case illustration of, 500, 505–507, 733–742
Insight therapy, 8
  in anxiety reactions, 597
  assumption of role by therapist in, 674
  bibliotherapy in, 579
  in conversion and dissociative reactions, 598
  in depressive reactions, 605
  ego shattering in, 586
  hypnosis in, 573
  in manic-depressive psychosis, 630
  in obsessive-compulsive reactions, 601
  in phobic reactions, 599
  with reconstructive goals, see Reconstructive therapy
  with reeducative goals, see Reeducative therapy
  role of therapist in, defining, 349–350
  in schizophrenia, 637
  supportive measures in, 542–543

translating insight into action during, 494–507
  case illustration, 500, 505–507, 733–742
  conferences with family members, 499–500
  psychodramatic techniques, 499
  uncovering of unconscious material in, 421
  See also Reeducative therapy and Reconstructive therapy
Insomnia, hypnosis in, 573
Institute of Pastoral Care, 127
Insulin in involutional psychosis, 626
Insulin shock treatment, 542, 588, 636
  in psychotic disorders, 626
  role of nurse in, 126
  See also Shock treatment
Insulin, sub-coma, in anxiety reactions, 598
Intellectual inhibitions as resistance, 465
Intellectuality as a defense in narcissistic, infantile character disorders, 480
Intellectualization of therapeutic process, 490
  in paranoid personalities, 613
  in personality disorders, 480, 606
Intelligence, in relation to prognosis, 232
Interaction, encouraging, in group therapy, 572
Interminable therapy, 669–670
Internist, cooperation with, in psychosomatic disorders, 606
Interpersonal climate of the interview, 183–185
Interpersonal relations, current
  focusing on, as a means of identifying patterns, 371–373
  mediation of, in environmental manipulation, 528
  in prognosis, 236
Interpretations, 178–182, 439–462, 430
  acceptance of, 450
  authoritative, 442–444
  content of, 444
  in dependency patterns, 609
  excessive, produced by counter-transference, 490
  of forgotten memories, 448
  handling untoward effects of, 451–452
  in hostile transference, 478
  of hostility, 447–448
  improper timing of, 451
  language of, 444
  need for rapport in, 445
  in paranoid personalities, 613
  in personality disorders, 607
  premature deep, need to avoid, 335
  premature, induced by counter-transference, 490
  presentation of, in forgotten memories, 430
  rejection of validity of, 451

Interpretations—*Continued*
  responses to, 449–452
  in schizophrenia, 637
  self-interpretation and, 439–441
  of sexual material, 447–449
  stimulation of anxiety by, 450–451
  as a supportive measure for anxiety, 451
  of symptoms, 447
  technique of presentation of, 446–447
  tentative, 441–442
  "terminal," 445
  in terms of past, 447
  in terms of present, 448
  timing of, 445
  of transference, 448–477
  of unconscious material, 448–449
  varieties of, 439–444
Interruption of therapy, planned, 564
Intervention in group therapy, 572
Interview
  clarifying purpose of, 336–337
  explaining time limits of, 343
Interview focus
  in Adlerian analysis, 88
  in emotional catharsis, 88
  environmental dissatisfactions as, 370–371
  feelings as, 368–370
  in Freudian psychoanalysis, 88
  in guidance, 88
  in Horney analysis, 88
  interpersonal relations as, 371–373
  intuitive feelings of therapist as, 375
  in Jungian analysis, 88
  in non-directive therapy, 88
  past history as, 373–374
  in persuasion, 88
  in Rankian analysis, 88
  in reassurance, 88
  in reeducative therapy, 88
  in semantic approaches, 88
  slips of speech as, 373–375
  in Sullivan analysis, 88
  symptoms as, 365–368
Interview psychotherapy, 41–42, 8
  problems susceptible to, 256
  See also Interviewing, Psychotherapeutic interview, and Psychiatric interviewing
Interviewing
  handling loquaciousness in, 663
  as a means of identifying patterns, 364–375
  rationale of, 314–315
  as a way of building a working relationship, 324–325
  written material in, 668
  See also Interview, Psychotherapeutic interview, and Psychiatric interviewing
Intolerance
  need to avoid, 334

toward patient, of therapist, 490
Introduction to psychotherapy (course), 138
Intuition in psychotherapy, 71
  use of, as a means of identifying patterns, 375
Involutional psychotic reactions, 626–628
  convulsive therapy in, 32, 626
  prognosis in, 232

Jung, Carl, school of, 66–68
Jungian analysis
  interview focus in, 88
  See also "Analytical psychology"

Kissing gestures, handling of, 352

Laboratory, physical and neurologic examination form, 835–836
Lateness in appointments, 666–667
  handling consistent, 345–346
Learning
  blocks, dissipation of, by interpretation, 440
  patterns, uniqueness of, 496
  problems in supervision, 650–651
  resistance to, in supervision, 658–659
  theory and psychotherapy, 495–496
Levels in focusing of interview, 167–170
Libido theory, *see* Freudian psychoanalysis
Licensure of psychologists, 121
Life history discussion, in reeducative therapy, 544
Loquaciousness, handling, 663
Love feelings for patient, 673
Love-making gestures toward therapist, 477
Lying to patient, 665–666

Manic patients, *see* Manic-depressive reactions
Manic states, excited, continuous sleep treatment in, 33
Manic-depressive psychosis
  convulsive therapy in, 32, 628, 629
  prognosis in, 232
  See also Manic-depressive reactions
Manic-depressive reactions, 628–630
  See also Manic-depressive psychosis
Man-woman drawing test, 229, 268
Marital partner, effect on, of improvement in patient, 500–501
Marital problems
  and bibliotherapy, 578
  environmental manipulation in, 255
Marriage
  books on, in bibliotherapy, 580
  effect of therapy on, 309
Masochism
  in obsessive-compulsive reactions, 603

as resistance, 323, 464
sexual, 621
Masochistic personality disorders, group therapy in, 570
Massage, 256, 542, 621, 629
Masturbation fears, reassurance in, 531–532
Mate, *see* Family members
Mechanics of psychotherapy, 306
Medical consultation, 266
Medical form, 834
Medicine, contributions of, to psychotherapy, 106–107
Medicines, in psychotherapy, 308
Memories
    in dreams, 380, 385
    repression of, *see* Memories, forgotten
Memories, forgotten, 423–429, 448
    in conversion and dissociative reactions, 599
    effect of narcosis on, 576
    effect of recall of, 427
    hypnotic recall in, 428–429
    liberation of, 515–516
    recollection of, effect on acceptance of repudiated aspects of psyche of, 430
    recovery of, case illustration of, 431–438
    in stress reactions, 639–640
Memory blocks, 465
Mental examination form, 837–838
Mental health
    "ideal" objectives of, 553–554
    preventive, 681
Mental Hygiene movement, 39
Mental Hygiene team, *see* Teamwork functioning
Metrazol, in acute alcoholic intoxication, 590
Meyer, Adolf, school of, 38–41
Middle phase of therapy, 361–547
    case illustration of, 720–733
Minister in psychotherapy, 126–127
Minnesota Experiment, 113
Misconceptions, about psychotherapy, 303–316, 195, 283, 287
    correction of, with bibliotherapy, 578
Mistakes in psychotherapy, 662, 689
Money, neurotic attitudes toward, in therapist, 490
Moralistic judgments, need to avoid, 331
Motivation, defective, 195
    in alcoholism, 616
    dealing with, 275–292
    in "inadequate," infantile and dependency patterns, 608
    supportive therapy for, 523
    termination of therapy due to, 563
Motivation for therapy, 247
    building, 496–497
    desire to fulfill neurotic demands as, 472
    influencing, with bibliotherapy, 578

in relation to prognosis, 232–233
Motor excitement, as a sign of ego disintegration, 587
Multiple sclerosis complicating therapy, 594
Muscular relaxation, 30–31, 8
    problems susceptible to, 256
Music therapy, 35, 8, 21
Mutism
    schizophrenic, 361, 631–632, 633–634
    during therapy, 514
Myanesin therapy, 33

Nail-biting, 22, 48, 573
Narcissism, in therapist, 490
Narcissistic reactions, 613–614
Narcoanalysis, 578
    in the exploration of the unconscious, 429
    See also Narcotherapy
Narcocatharsis, 576
Narcosis
    in conversion and dissociative reactions, 599
    prolonged, in involutional psychosis, 626
Narcosuggestion, 576, 578, 590
Narcosynthesis
    need for, 308
    See also Narcotherapy
Narcotherapy, 84–85, 576–578, 8
    in anxiety reactions, 598
    in emotional catharsis, 29
    induction of, 577–578
    problems susceptible to, 257
    relaxation with, 589
    in stress reactions, 639
    in therapeutic stalemate, 669
Narcotic sleep, prolonged, in panic states, 590
National Psychological Association for Psychoanalysis, 116
Need to be maltreated, as resistance, 471
Needs of patient, varying, 318–320
Negative feelings
    indicating acceptance of, 277–280
    recognizing and accepting, 276–277
"Negative therapeutic reaction," 480, 606
Negativism
    as resistance, 471
    during therapy, 514
Neighborhood situation, correction of, in environmental manipulation, 528
Neurologic consultation, 266
Neurologic, physical and laboratory examination form, 835–836
Neurologist, definition of, 306
Neurosis, ineffectuality of bibliotherapy in, 579
"Neurotic" person as differentiated from "normal," 679
Nomenclature, 220–221

Non-directive methodologies, choice of, in passive therapists, 491
Non-directive role, in dependency patterns, 610
"Non-directive therapy," 42–44
  interview focus in, 88
  problems susceptible to, 256
Non-directiveness, during terminal phase, 558–559
Non-Freudian psychoanalysis, 63–79, 8
  definition of, 308
  indications for, 254
  problems susceptible to, 257
Non-medical psychotherapy, 115–130
Non-motivated patients, treating, 291
"Normal" person as differentiated from "neurotic," 679
"Normality" in therapist, 680
Note-taking, explaining, 345
Nurse in psychotherapy, 125

Objectives in therapy, see Goals, therapeutic
Obsessional neurosis, narcotherapy in, 577
Obsessions, 425
Obsessive-compulsive reactions, 600–604
  brain surgery in, 34
  hypnosis in, 573
  and paranoid reactions, 613
  persuasion in, 255
  prognosis in, 232
  reconstructive therapy for, 255
  unfavorable reactions to transference in, 401
Obsessive neurosis, see Obsessive-compulsive reactions
Occupational therapy, 21, 529
  in alcoholism, 616
  in borderline cases, 625
  in involutional psychosis, 626
  in schizophrenia, 636
  tension-relieving effects of, 525
Oedipus complex, see Freudian psychoanalysis
  as explained by "dynamic-cultural" school, 75
Old age problems, books on, in bibliotherapy, 582
Omnipotence in therapist, desire for by patient, resistance, 470–471
Open-mindedness, need for, 336
Organ functions, symbolic expressions of, 422
Organic brain disorders, prognosis in, 232
Organization and operation of a mental hygiene clinic, (course), 140
"Orgone therapy," 73
Orientation, theoretic, differences in, during supervision, 644–645
Outline of psychotherapy, 189–191
Overactivity, handling, 588–589
Overanxious reactions, handling, 674–675

Overconcern, expressions of, need to avoid, 331
Overeating, hypnosis in, 573

Palliative psychotherapy, see Supportive therapy
Panic reactions
  handling, 589–590
  due to hostile transference, 478
  narcotherapy in, 577
  supportive therapy for, 523
Paraldehyde, in acute alcoholic intoxication, 590
Paralysis, functional, treatment of, 598
Paranoidal ideas, as a sign of ego disintegration, 587
Paranoidal personality patterns, 612–613
Paranoidal tendencies, group therapy in patients with, 570
Paranoidal traits, function of, 612
"Parataxic distortions," 78–79, 675
Parental representative, therapist as, 321
Parents, see Family members
Passivity in therapist, 489, 673–674
  accentuating transference by, 401
  stirring up unconscious activity by, 429
Past experience
  focusing on, as a means of identifying patterns, 373–374
  as a means of stirring up unconscious activity, 429
  to accentuate transference, 401
  interpretation of, 444
  minimization of, in the reduction of transference, 400
  overemphasis of, 426–427
Past and present, importance of, 664
Pastoral counseling, 127
Patient's responsibilities, delineating the, 346–348
Patterns
  challenging validity of, in utilizing insight, 496
  identification of, 361–410
Penis, symbolic significance of, 423
Penis envy
  interpretation of, 449
  as resistance, 473
Perfectionism
  inadequate motivation for therapy in patient with, 472
  reeducative handling of, 545, 546–547
  as resistance, 323
  supportive handling of, 607–608
Perfectionistic impulses in therapist, 490
Personal analysis for therapist, see Personal therapy for therapist
Personal data sheet, 816–817

Personal history sheet, 832–833
Personal references, need to avoid, 332
Personal therapy for therapist
  effect on counter-transference, 491
  effectiveness of, 680
  failures of, 680–681
  necessity for, 146–148
  resistance to, 148
Personality disorder, 606–625
  alcoholism as a, 615–620
  dependent, supportive therapy for, 523
  drug addiction as a, 620–621
  inability to recall repressed memories in, 428
  "inadequate," infantile, 608–610
  narcissistic, 613–614
  paranoid or "anal," 612–613
  power, 613
  prognosis in, 232
  psychopathic, 614–615
  reconstructive therapy for, 255
  "schizoid" and detached, 610–612
  sexual deviations as a, 621–622
  transference resistances in, 480
  unfavorable reactions to transference in, 401
Personality equipment of the therapist, 142–146
Personality of therapist, 108
  effect on patient of, 493
  influence on techniques of, 679–680
  in supportive therapy, 525
Personality patterns, interpretation of, 444
Personality problems
  books on, in bibliotherapy, 580
  dependency, use of insight as resistance in, 467
  efficacy of group therapy in, 569
  reeducative therapy in, 255
Personality structure
  contradictions in, 512
  in psychosomatic disorders, 605
Persuasion, 24–28, 533–540, 8, 595, 596
  in alcoholism, 616
  effect of narcosis on, 576
  hypnosis in, 573
  interview focus in, 88
  in involutional psychosis, 626, 627
  in narcotherapy, 578
  in obsessive-compulsive reactions, 603–604
  in paranoid personalities, 613
  in phobic reactions, 600
  in psychosomatic disorders, 606
  in speech disorders, 622, 623–624
  in stress reactions, 639, 640
  susceptibility to, 255
Perverse strivings, stimulating of, 514
Perversions
  prognosis in, 232

propensity for, as a sign of ego disintegration, 587
  See also Sexual perversions
Pets in therapist's office, 188
Phallic symbolism, 423
Phobic defenses, 424
Phobic reactions, 599–600
  desensitization techniques in, 542
  hypnosis in, 573
  need to face, 504
  prognosis in, 232
  reconditioning in, 48
  reconstructive therapy for, 255
  susceptibility to Freudian psychoanalysis of, 109
Physical appearance of patient, 246
Physical attacks on therapist, 477
Physical contacts with patient, avoiding, 352
Physical examinations, need for routine, 665
Physical exercises, tension-relieving effect of, 525
Physical health of patient, 246
Physical, neurologic and laboratory examination form, 835–836
Physical plan of office, 186–187
Physical position during therapy, 94
Physical surroundings of psychotherapy, 186–188
Physical symptoms
  disabling, supportive therapy for, 523
  emotional nature of, 305
Physician
  role in psychotherapy of, 112–115
  traits in, that may interfere with good psychotherapy, 114
Picrotoxin, in barbiturate poisoning, 591
Play analysis, in the exploration of the unconscious, 429
Play materials, manipulated, as psychologic tests, 268
Play therapy, 84, 8
  problems susceptible to, 257
Pleasure abandonment, during psychotherapy, 308
Pleasure values of treatment hour, reluctance to yield, as resistance, 469–470
Political discussions, need to avoid, 333
Pompousness in therapist, 489
Positive relationship, as differentiated from transference, 675
Postgraduate Center for Psychotherapy, v, vi, vii
Power impulse, supportive handling of, 608
Power patterns, 613
  inadequate motivation for therapy in patients with, 472
  reeducative handling of, 545
Praising patient, need to avoid, 335

Prejudice in schools of psychiatry and psychology, 680

Preoccupation with past, as resistance, 472

Present relationships
avoiding, to accentuate transference, 401
focusing on, to reduce transference, 400

Pressure and coercion, 24, 8
problems susceptible to, 255
in stress reactions, 638

Prestige suggestion, 21–24, 8
problems susceptible to, 255

Preventive mental health, 681
(courses), 140

"Primal scene," 424
recovery of, case illustration of, 431–438

Process recording, 647

Professional identification of therapist, answering questions about, 206

Prognosis
estimating the, 230–245
in obsessive-compulsive reactions, 604
psychological tests as indices of, 269

Progress in therapy, 512, 516

Progress, yardsticks of, in learning psychotherapy, 656

Progress notes
daily (form), 819
daily, recording, 683–684
monthly, (form), 840
monthly, recording, 684

Progress summary form, monthly, 819–820

Prohibitions, imposition of, relief of guilt in, 524

Projective psychological tests, see Psychological tests

Promises, false, need to avoid, 332

Pseudoneurotic schizophrenia, see Borderline cases

Psychiatric caseworker, definition of, 306

Psychiatric consultation, 266

Psychiatric interviewing, see Interview psychotherapy

Psychiatric supervision, see Supervision, psychiatric

Psychiatrist
definition of, 306
in teamwork functioning, 130–135

Psychiatry, books on, in bibliotherapy, 579–580

Psychoanalysis
"active," 70–72
contributions to psychotherapy of, 106
definition of, 306, 307
as differentiated from other types of therapy, 307
as differentiated from psychotherapy, 307
need for, 307
as preferred treatment, 307

see also Freudian psychoanalysis, Non-Freudian psychoanalysis, Psychoanalytically oriented psychotherapy, and Reconstructive therapy

Psychoanalytic Clinic for Training and Research at Coluumbia University, 75

Psychoanalytic training, need for, 680

Psychoanalytically oriented psychotherapy, 80–86, 8
criticisms of, 81
discouragement of transference neurosis in, 518
indications for, 254
problems susceptible to, 257

Psychobiologic therapy
definition of, 308
See also Distributive analysis and synthesis

Psychobiology, contributions of, to psychotherapy, 106

Psychodrama, 51

Psychodramatic techniques, in translating insight into action, 499

Psychodynamics, 216–220, 421–428, 644–645
of dreams, 379, 380, 383–385
general comments on, 361–362
role of past in, 373
See also Dynamics

Psychologic consultation, 268–271

Psychologic tests, 268–271, 92, 310
in formulating dynamics, 229
preparing patient for, 270
prognostic estimates on basis of, 269
value of, 269–270

Psychologic therapy, see Therapeutic counseling

Psychological testing, 699–700
art creations in, 268
case illustration of, 709–711

Psychologist, in teamwork functioning, 130–135

Psychologists
certification of, 121
functions of, 271
licensure of, 121
limitations in background and training of, 119
in psychotherapy, 115–122
traits in, that may interfere with good psychotherapy, 119
See also Clinical psychologist

Psychology
books on general, 579
contributions to psychotherapy of, 106

Psychoneurosis, definition of, 305

Psychoneurotic depression, see Depressive reaction

Psychoneurotic disorders, 597–605

Psychopathic personality, 614–615

acute alcoholic intoxication in, 590
anticipating emergencies in, 264
group therapy in, 570
hypnosis in, 573
inadequate motivation in, 275
suicidal attempts in, 584–585
Psychopathology and psychodynamics,
(course), 137–138
Psychophysiologic autonomic and visceral disorders, 605–606
See also Psychosomatic disorders, and Psychophysiologic reactions
Psychophysiologic reactions
hypnosis in, 573
prognosis in, 232
reconstructive therapy for, 255
unfavorable reactions to transference in, 401
See also Psychophysiologic autonomic and
visceral disorders, and Psychosomatic disorders
Psychosocial development, (course), 137
Psychosomatic disorders
inadequate motivation in, 275
narcotherapy in, 85
See also Psychophysiologic autonomic and
visceral disorders, and Psychophysiologic
reactions
Psychosomatic symptoms
effect of narcosis on, 576
as a means of preventing regression, 555
prestige suggestion in, 22
severe, handling, 591–594
stimulation of, as a result of interpretation,
450
due to transference, 478
Psychosurgery, see Brain surgery
Psychotherapeutic interviewing, 157–185
directing the flow of verbalizations in, 165
inculcating insight by, 175–182
interpersonal climate of, 183–185
language of, 159–160
maintaining the flow of verbalizations in,
162–164
managing pauses in, 162–163
managing silence in, 163–164
non-verbal communications in, 159–160
opening the interview in, 160–162
rationale of, 158
selective focusing in, 165–175
special problems in, 182–183
terminating the interview in, 182
verbal communications in, 159
See also Interview, Interview psychotherapy,
and Interviewing
Psychotherapeutic supervision, see Supervision,
psychotherapeutic
Psychotherapy
books on, in bibliotherapy, 580

definitions of, 3–6
operation of, explaining, 353–356
Psychotic attacks
during therapy, 586–588
hospitalization for, 588
self-injury in, 588
sodium amytal, intravenous, in, 588
suicidal tendencies in, 588
Psychotic disorders, 625–637
anticipating emergencies in, 264
inability to recall repressed memories in,
428
inadequate motivation in, 275
involutional, 626–628
manic-depressive, 628–630
schizophrenic, 630–637
supportive therapy for, 523
unfavorable reaction to transference in, 401
Punitive attitudes, need to avoid, 331

Qualifications of therapist, 306
Questioning, as an aid to interpretation, 440
Questions patients ask about therapy, answer-
ing, 303–316

Rado, Sandor, school of, 73–75
Rage, handling, 673
Rambling, as resistance, 471
Rank, Otto, school of, 69–70
Rankian analysis
interview focus in, 88
See also "Will therapy"
Rapport
developing, in schizophrenia, 631–632, 633
See also working relationship
Reactive depression, see Depressive reactions
Readings in psychoanalysis and allied fields,
(course), 137
Reading disabilities, 271
Reassurance, 530–533, 8, 504, 527, 543, 589
alleviation of guilt in, 524
through bibliotherapy, 578
in borderline cases, 625
effect of narcosis on, 576
extension of, 336
in frigidity, 532
futility of, 272
in homosexual fears, 532
hypnosis in, 573
in impotence, 532
in infidelity of marital partner, 532–533
in insanity, 531
in insight therapy, 668
interview focus in, 88
in involutional psychosis, 626
limitations of, 533
in masturbation, 531–532
measured, 330

Reassurance—*Continued*
  in narcotherapy, 578
  non-verbal, 530
  in obsessive-compulsive reactions, 603
  passivity and suubmissiveness as a deterrant
    to, 489
  in physical illness, 531
  problems susceptible to, 255
  in supportive therapy, 21
  unnecessary, need to avoid, 336
Recollection of early traumatic experiences,
    see Memories forgotten
Reconditioning, 47, 8
  in phobic reactions, 600
  problems susceptible to, 256
Reconstructive therapy, 53–86
  in alcoholism, 615
  in borderline cases, 625
  comparison with other therapies, (chart),
    90–91
  difficulty of working-through process in, 512
  failures in, 554–555
  formulating dynamics in, 228
  frequency of sessions in, 678
  goals in, 361, 362
  group therapy as an adjunct in, 569
  handling of the unconscious in, 429
  importance of handling transference in, 675
  importance of past and present in, 664
  indications for, 255
  insight in, 677–678
  interpretation in, 445–449
  interpretation of forgotten memories in, 448
  need for, in hysterical personalities, 598
  need to interpret transference in, 470
  persistence of unhealthy strivings in, 508
  the preferred treatment, 678–679
  recall of forgotten memories in, 423
  resistance in, 463
  in schizophrenia, 636, 637
  in sexual deviations, 622
  in speech disorders, 622
  theoretic basis for, 101
  transference in, 399
  use of, 100–102
  value of interpretation in, 439
  See also Freudian psychoanalysis, Non-
    Freudian psychoanalysis, and Psychoanalyt-
    ically oriented psychotherapy
Recording, 682–688
  electrical, 686–687
  problems in, during supervision, 646–648
  process, 647
  tape, 647–648, 686–687
  wire, 686–687
Recovery, apparent and permanent, 678–679
Recreational activities, 529
  in detached personalities, 611

encouraging, in environmental manipulation,
    528
  tension-relieving effects of, 525
Recreational facilities, in environmental ad-
    justment, 502
Recreational problems, environmental manip-
    ulation in, 255
Recreational therapy, 21
  in alcoholism, 618
Reeducative techniques, during middle treat-
    ment phases, 523–547
Reeducative therapy, 36–52, 543–547
  comparison with other therapies, (chart),
    90–91
  directive, transference in, 399
  discouragement of transference neurosis in,
    518
  formulating dynamics in, 228
  goals in, 361
  group therapy as an adjunct in, 569
  handling dependency in, 561
  handling of the unconscious in, 429
  indications for, 251, 255
  insight in, 677
  interview focus in, 88
  minimal goal in, 679
  in power patterns, 613
  repression of transference in, 470
  resistance in, 463
  in speech disorders, 622, 624
  technical aspects of, 543
  tenacity of maladaptive patterns in, 508
  transference in, 399, 470, 518
  uses of, 99–100
Referring the patient, 262–264
Reflecting (in interviewing), 177, 430
Regression and revivification in hypnoanalysis,
    case illustration, 434–437
Rehabilitation workers, use of, 271
Reich, Wilhelm, school of, 72–73
Rejection of patient by therapist, 490
Rejecting patient, need to avoid, 334
Relapses, after termination, 315, 561–562
Relationship
  building a, 324–325
  cooperative human, need for a, 320
  difficulties, in detached personalities, 611
  patient-therapist, 87–88, 94
  positive, as differentiated from transference,
    675
  "rules" for building a, 330–337
  with therapist, effect of memories on, 427
  time required to establish a, 337
  See also Working relationship
"Relationship group therapy," 51
"Relationship therapy," 37, 8
  problems susceptible to, 256
Relatives of patient

attacks on, handling, 273
handling, 501–502
See also Family members
Relaxation, 542
  promoting, with narcotherapy, 589
  tension-relieving effects in, 524
Religion of therapist, answering questions about, 205
Religious discussions, need to avoid, 333
Religious interests, cultivating, in fatal somatic illness, 596
Religious therapy, 19
  in alcoholism, 617
Remedial reading instructors, use of, 271
Reporting, problems in, during supervision, 646–648
Repression, 424
  bolstering, through bibliotherapy, 578
  circumvention of, through hypnosis, 438
  of conflicts, symptom relief due to, 552
  increasing, in schizophrenia, 635
  as resistance, 464
  resolution of, during working-through, 517
Repressive techniques, *see* Supportive therapy
Residence change in environmental adjustment, 502
Resistance, 463–487, 152, 196–197, 207, 411, 412, 508, 509, 513
  acting-out as, 466
  to action, resolution of, 504
  ambition, compulsive, as, 323
  amnesia as, 427
  analysis of, 445–446
  in anxiety reactions, 597
  broken appointments as, 346, 465
  case illustrations of, 465–466, 468–469, 480–483, 483–487, 559–560
  castration desires and fears as, 473
  competitiveness with therapist as, 471
  compulsive ambition as, 323
  concentrative blocks as, 465
  consistent lateness as, 346
  contempt for normality as, 468–469
  contempt for therapist's values as, 472
  controlling tendencies as, 472
  dealing with, at initial interview, 202–206
  defiance as, 471
  dependency as, 322–323, 564
  desire to terminate therapy as, 471
  detachment as, 323–324, 471–472
  dissociating the treatment hour from life as, 467–468
  distrust as, 323
  in dreams, 380, 385
  effect of narcosis on, 577
  fear of therapist as, 471
  "flight into health" as, 465
  forgetting appointments as, 471, 514

  forms of, 463–473
  to free association, 376
  frequent cancellations as, 346
  gift-giving as, 472
  in homosexuality, 480–483
  hostility as, 323, 471, 564
  hypnosis in dissipating, 573
  inattention as, 465
  influence on counter-transference of, 490
  insight as, 467
  intellectual inhibitions as, 465–466
  intensification of symptoms as, 464
  intensity of attack on, 446
  interpretation of, 444, 572
  to learning, 496
  to learning in supervision, 650–651, 658–659
  masochistic indulgence as, 323, 464
  memory blocks as, 465
  methods of handling, 473–478
  need for working-through of, 479–480
  need to be maltreated as, 471
  negativism as, 471
  non-payment of bills as, 346
  in obsessive-compulsion reactions, 601
  obstinacy as, 479
  omnipotence in therapist, desire for, as, 470–471
  penis envy as, 473
  perfectionism as, 323
  perseverence of, 446
  in personality disorders, 606, 607
  to personal therapy for therapists, 148
  preoccupation with past as, 472
  protective value of, 479
  in psychosomatic disorders, 605
  rambling as, 471
  to recall of forgotten memories, 427, 428
  recognition of derivatives of, 446
  in reconstructive therapy, 463
  in reeducative therapy, 463
  rejection of insight in relation to, 479
  reluctance to yield pleasure values of treatment hour as, 469–470
  repression as, 464
  ridiculing interpretations as, 471
  self-devaluation as, 464
  self-punishment as, 464
  to self-understanding
    dissipation of, by interpretation, 440
  sexual desires as, 472
  in sexual deviations, 622
  sexual feelings as, 323
  superficial talk as, 466–467
  in supervision, 658–659
  in supportive therapy, 463
  suppression as, 464
  suspicion of therapist as, 471

Resistance—*Continued*
  symptom intensification as, 464
  to terminating therapy, 518
  termination of therapy because of, 514, 563
  to termination, handling, 558–561
  to utilization of insight, 495
  to working with dreams, 579
  transference as, 470–473, 480–483, 483–487, 564
    handling, 477–478
    in personality disorders, 480
    resolution of, by hypnosis, 574
  transferring the patient due to, 565
  uncooperativeness as, 471
  unfavorable reactions due to, in patients with immature ego structures, 473
  use of educational materials as, 579
  to a working relationship, 318–320, 322–324
  working relationship as a means of resolving, 504
  working-through of, 479–480
Respecting rights of patient, 336
Responsibilities of patient, delineating, 346–348
Rest, 542
Restating (in interviewing), 177, 430
  as an aid to interpretation, 440
Returning to therapy after termination, 562–563
Rhythmics, 623
Ridiculing interpretations as resistance, 471
Ridiculing patient, need to avoid, 333
Rigidity in personality disorders, 607
Rogers, Carl, school of, 42–44
Role
  assumption of, by therapist, 525–526, 674
  defining, of therapist, 348, 352
  playing, 526
    in translating insight into action, 494
    to accentuate transference, 401
    to reduce transference, 400
  of therapist, 315
Roles of therapist, multiple, 320–322
Rorschach test, 229, 268
  case illustration of, 709–710
  in obsessive-compulsive reactions, 604
Routines in therapy, explanation of, 343–346

Sadism, sexual, 621
"Schizoid" personalities, 610–612
Schizophrenia, *see* Schizophrenic reactions
  latent, *see* Borderline cases
Schizophrenic reactions, 630–637
  Aschner treatment for, 636
  borderline, *see* Borderline cases

brain surgery in, 34
convulsive therapy in, 32
excited, continuous sleep treatment in, 33
and obsessive-compulsive reactions, 604
prognosis in, 232
shock treatment in, 31
suicidal attempts in, 585
supportive therapy for, 254
treatment of, 141, 632–637
School facilities, in environmental adjustment, 502
Schools of psychiatry and psychology, misunderstanding among, 680
Secondary gain
  in chronic stress reactions, 640
  effect of, on therapeutic goals, 554
  in narcissistic character disorders, 480
  in relation to prognosis, 233
"Sector therapy," 80
Sedation, 32
  in alcoholism, 616
  in anxiety reactions, 597
  in depressive reactions, 605, 629
  in drug addiction, 621
  in insomnia, 590
  in involutional psychosis, 626
  in manic patients, 628
  in psychotic disorders, 626
  in stress reactions, 638
Seductiveness of therapist, 490
Selective response to different therapies, 107
Self-devaluation
  in personality disorders, 606
  as resistance, 464
Self-esteem, devaluated, ineffectuality of reassurance in, 533
Self-help books, in bibliotherapy, 581
Self-hypnosis, 574, 624
Self-injury, hospitalization for, 588
Self-interpretations, 439–441
Self-punishment, as resistance, 464
Self-understanding in therapy, progressive steps of, 362–363
Semantic therapy, 49–50, 8
  interview focus in, 88
  problems susceptible to, 256
Separation, caution in advising, 502–503
Set-backs in therapy, 508–509
Sex
  explanatory books on, in bibliotherapy, 580–581
  of therapist, 205, 250
Sexual approaches to therapist, handling of, 352
Sexual attitudes and feelings, interpretation of, 447
Sexual desires, as resistance, 472
Sexual deviations, 621–622

Sexual fears in therapist, 490
Sexual feelings
    activities of therapist that stimulate, 675–676
    for patient, 673
    as resistance, 323
    stimulated by seductiveness of therapist, 490
Sexual impulses
    release of, 517
    released in therapy, 477–478
    sublimation of, by externalization of interests, 530
    uncontrollable, as a sign of ego disintegration, 587
Sexual indiscretions, in manic patients, 628
Sexual indulgence, as "acting-out," 476
Sexual material, interpretation of, 449
Sexual perversion
    acting-out in, 476
    anticipating emergencies in, 264
    inadequate motivation in, cases of, 275
    See also Perverse strivings and Perversions
Sexual problems, treatment of, 141
Sexual strivings, symbolic meaning of, 621
Sexual symbolism, 422–423
    in dreams, case illustration of, 452–461
Sexual tension, hydrotherapy in, 31
Sexual transference, 477–478
    case illustrations of, 480–483, 483–487
Sexual wishes, stimulation of, 514
Sexuality, symbolic significance of, 423
Shock therapy, 31–32, 8, 542
    need for, 308
    problems susceptible to, 256
    See also Convulsive therapy, Electric convulsive therapy, and Insulin shock therapy
Shortcuts in treatment, 308
Short-term therapy, 103–105
    chief use of, 679
    in conversion and dissociative reactions, 599
    criticism of, 103
    narcotherapy in, 576
Sickness in therapist, 673
Silence, management of, 163–164
Similarities among the various psychotherapies, 87–95
Sleep disturbances, hydrotherapy in, 31
Slips of speech, focusing on, as a means of identifying patterns, 374–375
Smoking
    excessive, prestige suggestion in, 22
    during the interview, 344–345
    reconditioning in, 48
Social activities, in detachment, 530
Social affairs, handling the meeting of patient and therapist at, 672

Social agencies, in environmental adjustment, 501
Social casework, see Casework, and Social work
Social contacts, with patient, 311, 352, 672
Social maturity, level of, in relation to prognosis, 238
Social standards, in determining goals, 552
Social work, in environmental manipulation, 19
    See also Casework
Social workers
    as adjunctive helpers, 501–502
    in psychotherapy, 122–125
    traits in, that may interfere with good psychotherapy, 124
    See also Caseworker
Sodium amytal
    interviews, see Narcotherapy
    intravenous, in excited psychotic attacks, 588
    in narcotherapy, 576, 577
Sodium pentothal, 576
    in narcotherapy, 577
Somatic illness, intercurrent incurable, 594–596
Somatic sensations, bizarre, as a sign of ego distintegration, 587
Special problems in therapy, (course), 139
Speech and voice disorders, 622–624, 140
Speech therapist, use of, 271
Speech training, 623
Spending, ruinous, hospitalization for, 588
Spontaneity of therapist, 674
Spontaneous cures and remissions, 14–16
Staff members, application blank for new, 827–829
Stalemate in therapy, handling a, 669
Stammering, see Speech disorders
Statistical data
    recording, 682–683
    sheet, long form, 810–811
    sheet, short form, 809
    Stekelian analysis, see "Active psychoanalysis"
Stimulants, 32–33
Stress handling, in relation to prognosis, 237
Stress reactions, 637–640
    hypnosis in, 573
    narcotherapy in, 576
    prevention of, 638
    prognosis in, 237
Stress sources, interpretation of, 444
Structuring
    in group therapy, 572
    purpose of initial interview, 201–202
    the therapeutic situation, 340–358, 196
        case illustration of, 700–709

Stuttering, *see* Speech disorders
Style of the psychotherapist, 149–150
Sub-coma insulin treatment, 32
  in acute anxiety, 590
Submissiveness
  as resistance, 323
  in therapist, 489
Success judgments in therapy, 551–554
Suggestion
  effect of narcosis on, 576
  in narcotherapy, 578
  in stress reactions, 639
Suggestive hypnosis, 8
Suggestive therapy, *see* Prestige suggestion
Suicidal attempts
  in acute alcoholic intoxication, 590
  in depression, 583
  dreams associated with, 583
  handling, 583–586
  in hysterical personalities, 584
  in miscellaneous conditions, 586
  in pathologic depression, 585–586
  in psychopathic personality, 584–585
  in schizophrenia, 585
Suicidal conditions, miscellaneous, 586
Suicidal tendencies
  hospitalization for, 588
  supportive therapy for, 523
Suicidal thoughts, fleeting, importance of, 668
Suicide in depression, 629
Sullivan analysis
  interview focus in, 88
  See also Sullivan, Harry Stack, school of
Sullivan, Harry Stack, school of, 78–79
Summarizing (in interviewing), 176
  as an aid to interpretation, 440
Summary form, 822–823
Superego, modification of, 516, 517
Superficial talk, as resistance, 466–467
Supervision
  as an interpersonal relationship, 657–660
  of community workers, 681
  functions of, 642–644
  medical, 135
  need for, 673
  psychiatric, 121, 122, 123, 134–135, 266–267
  psychotherapeutic, 641–660, 135, 689–690
    beginning stages of, 653
    counter-transference in, 657–660, 654
    differences in communication in, 645
    differences in goals in, 646
    differences in method in, 645–646
    differences in theoretic orientation in, 644–645
    evaluation of supervisee in, 655–656
    functions of, 642–644
    group, 655

"intensive" versus "technical," 655
    later phases of, 653–654
    preclinical training of therapist in, 652–653
    problems in learning in, 650–651
    problems in recording and reporting in, 646–648
    problems in technical performance in, 648–650
    problems in termination in, 651–652
    resistances in, 658–659
    transference in, 657–660, 647, 654
Supervisor
  administrative responsibilities of, 656–657
  qualifications of, 644
Support
  emotional, need for, 674
  extending measured, in the interview, 178
  measured, 330
Supportive measures
  for anxiety provoked by interpretation, 451
  in insight therapy, 543
Supportive psychotherapy, *see* Supportive therapy
Supportive techniques
  during middle treatment phases, 523–547
  in ego collapse, 524
Supportive therapy, 17–35, 8
  in acute anxiety, 589
  in alcoholism, 254, 523, 616
  in anxiety reactions, 597
  bibliotherapy in, 578
  for borderline cases, 523
  comparison to other therapies, chart, 90–91
  in crying or rage, 673
  in dependency patterns, 609
  in detached patients, 612
  difficulties of termination in, 558
  discouragement of transference neurosis in, 518
  formulating dynamics in, 227
  goals in, 330, 361
  group therapy as an adjunct in, 569
  handling dependence in, 561
  handling of the unconscious in, 429
  hypnosis in, 573
  indications for, 35, 523–524, 251, 254, 677
  limitations of, 98
  mode of action of, 524–525
  narcotherapy in, 576
  need for insight in, 677
  in phobic reactions, 600
  in psychosomatic disorders, 606
  in psychotic disorders, 625
  repression of transference in, 470
  resistance in, 463
  role of therapist in, 348
  in sexual deviations, 622

in speech disorders, 622
symptom removal in, 552
tenacity of symptoms in, 508
therapist-patient relationship in, 525–526
transference in, 399
use of, 96–98
Suppression, as resistance, 464
Suppressive techniques, see Supportive therapy
Surprise exclamations, need to avoid, 331
Suspicion of therapist, as resistance, 471
Symbiosis, desire for, as resistance, 470–471
Symbolic controls, acquisition of, 494
Symbolism, 612–613
in dreams, 380
of the unconscious, 422–423
Sympathetic remarks, making, 337, 504
Symptom relief
as a goal in therapy, 551–552
therapeutic measures leading to, 678
Symptom removal, 21–22
in conversion and dissociative reactions, 598
hypnosis in, 591–594, 573
Symptoms
as a means of adjusting to conflict, 555
effect of recovery of repressed memories on, 428
focusing on, as a means of identifying patterns, 365–368
historical origin of, 425
intensification of, during transference, 470
intensification of, as resistance, 464
interpretation of, 447
prognostic significance of, 237
severity of, in relation to prognosis, 231
symbolism in, 422
helped by psychotherapy, 303
Syndromes, therapeutic approaches in the different, 255–257
Szondi test, 229, 268

Tantrums, handling of, 674–675
Tape recording, 686–687, 647–648
Tapering-off of therapy, 557–558
Tasks, assigned, 348
Teacher in psychotherapy, 128–130
Teamwork
functioning, 130–136
in psychotherapy, 123
Technical performance, problems in, during supervision, 648–650
Technical procedures in psychotherapy, (course), 139
Technique of interviewing, (course), 138
Telephone in therapist's office, problem of, 188
Tension
drug therapy in, 32

maintaining of, in the interview, 178
muscular relaxation in, 30–31
myanesin therapy for, 33
Terminal note, 565
form, 821
recording of, 684
Terminal phase of treatment, 551–566
use of dreams in, 389
Termination of supervision, problems in, 651–652
Terminating therapy, 551–566
case illustration of, 769–779
desires for, as resistance, 471
on basis of transference resistance, 477
as resistance, 514
resistance to, 518
Thematic Apperception Test, 229, 268
case illustration of, 710–711
Theoretic basis for reconstructive therapy, 101
Theoretic constructs in psychotherapy, 87
Theories about psychiatry, 305
Therapeutic approaches in different syndromes, 255–257
Therapeutic change
dynamics of, 150
mechanics of, 155
Therapeutic counseling, 42–46, 8
Therapeutic failures, past prognostic significance of, 240
Therapeutic goals, see Goals therapeutic
Therapeutic interviewing, as a means of identifying patterns, 364–375
Therapeutic relationship
as a corrective experience, 503–504
as a means of ego growth, 513
managing deterioration of, 675
Therapeutic "ups-and-downs," 313–314
Therapist
conflictual feelings toward, 314
effect of personality of, on techniques, 689
projected attitudes toward, see Transference
responses of, variability of, 488
role of, 311
unsuitability of, for psychotherapy, 681
Therapy, choice of, 306
Threats, need to avoid, 332
Toilet activities, heightened interest in, as a sign of ego disintegration, 587
Tolerance of therapist, effect of, 515
Tolserol, see Myanesin
Topectomy, see Brain surgery
Toxic confusional states, sub-coma insulin treatment in, 32
Training of therapist
answering questions about, 205
pre-clinical, 652–653
Trance state, see Hypnosis and Hypnotherapy

Transference, 398–400, 55, 61–62, 89, 93–
    94, 151–153, 274, 309, 321, 322–324,
    525, 675
    activities of therapist that stimulate, 675–
        676
    analysis, avoidance of, in schizophrenia, 635
        in conversion and dissociative reactions,
            598
        in handling acting-out, 588–589
    arousal of forgotten memories in, 427
    in borderline cases, 401
    case illustrations of, 355, 401–402, 402–
        404, 404–405, 405–409, 430, 480–483,
        483–487, 519–520
    dependency reactions as, 470–471
    differentiating, from positive relationship,
        675
    in directive reeducative therapy, 399, 463,
        470
    divided, 271
    in dreams, 380, 385
    during supervision, 657–660, 647, 654
    effect on learning process, 515
    ego shattering due to, 586
    employing activity to reduce, 400
    encouraging, 401
    fear of therapist, 471
    focusing on, as a means of identifying
        patterns, 398–411
    handling, 675, 676
    handling negative, 664
    hostile, 478
    inability to tolerate, in patients with im-
        mature ego structures, 473
    initiation of acting-out in, 476
    interpretation of, 444, 447, 448
    in the learning of new patterns, 503
    mobilized by counter-transference, 490
    negative, avoidance of, in supportive ther-
        apy, 525
    reducing the severity of, 400, 477, 478
    relationship, need for, 320
    resistances, 470–473, 564
        handling, 477–478
    resolution of, 513–518
    role-playing and, 400–401
    sexual, 477–478
    stimulation of, 526
        in narcosis, 577
"Transference cure," 524, 330, 676
Transference neurosis, 514, 518, 675
    in anxiety reactions, 597
    case illustration of, 409–410, 430–431
    discouragement of, 518
    in conversion and dissociative reactions, 598
    in the exploration of the unconscious, 429
    in Freudian psychoanalysis, 109
    need for, 675

in obsessive-compulsive reactions, 602, 604
    in phobic reactions, 599
    therapeutic value of, 254
Transferring the patient, 565, 589
    due to deterioration of therapeutic relation-
        ship, 587
    in therapeutic stalemate, 669
    in unresolvable hostility, 672
Translating insight into action, 494–507
    See also Insight, translating into action
Transorbital lobotomy, see Brain surgery
Traumatic experiences, repressed, effect on
    symptoms, in recovery of, 425
    See also Memories, forgotten
Traumatic material, probing of, need to avoid,
    335
Traumatic memories, see Memories, forgotten
Traumatic neurosis
    narcotherapy in, 85
    See also Stress reactions
Tuberculosis complicating therapy, 595
Types of psychotherapy, 306

Ubiquity of neurosis, 304
Unconscious, symbolism of the, 422–423
Unconscious activity, sitrring up, 429
Unconscious material
    handling of, 429–430
    interpretation of, 448–449
    stirring up, dangers in, 429–430
    uncovering of, 421–438
Unconscious motivations in therapist, deter-
    mining choice of methodologies, 491
Uncooperativeness as resistance, 471
Understanding, need for, in therapy, 319
Unreasonable attitudes, handling, 674–675
U. S. Public Health Service Hospitals, 621

Vacation from therapy, in therapeutic stale-
    mate, 669
Vacations, planning for, 344
Value judgments of therapist, 503, 551, 552
    effect on patient of, 676–677
    ideal, 677
    in therapeutic goals, 553
Varieties of psychotherapy, 7–9
"Vegetotherapy," 73
Ventilation, see Emotional catharsis
Verbalizations
    directing the flow of, 165
    maintaining the flow of, 162–164
Visual disorders, treatment of, 598
Vocational problems, guidance in, 255
Vocational tests, 619
Voyeurism, 621
    "acting-out" in, 476

War neurosis
    narcotherapy in, 85

See also Stress reactions
Warmth, emotional, need for, 674
Weir-Mitchell "rest cure," 31
"Will therapy," 69–70
William Alanson White School for Psychiatry, Psychoanalysis and Psychology, 79
Word associations, 268
Work situation, mediation of, in environmental manipulation, 528
Working relationship, 317–339, 195
    as a means of resolving resistances to action, 504
    as a prototype of better interpersonal relations, 504
    counter-transference as a deterrant to a, 489

cruciality of, in working with weak egos, 586
development of, 672
hypnosis in expediting a, 573
need for, in therapy, 317–318
problems in, in personality disorders, 606
in psychosomatic disorders, 605, 607
resistances to a, 318–320
signs of a, 337–339
in supervision, 651
    See also Rapport and Relationship
Working-through, 508–522, 450, 576
    of resistance, 479–480
    of transference, 477
Written material, 668, 669

The Wells of
Memory

To the memory of my parents,
my father, Saleh Easa Al-Gurg,
and my dear mother, Maryam Al-Shirawi,
who gave me life and instilled in me
the principles by which to live it;

to my wife, Soraya Ali Kazim Al-Gurg,
who has so entirely changed my life for the better;

to my children and to the young people
of my country and of the Arab world,
that they may know the past
and, knowing it, may make a better future;

this book is dedicated.

Contents

Map of the Arabian Gulf   endpapers
Illustrations   ix
Introduction by Sir James Craig, GCMG   xiii
Preface   xvii

The Wells of Memory   1

Afterword   228
Bibliographical Sources   235
Index   241

Illustrations

(between pages 42 and 43)

1. Shaikh Mohammed bin Khalifa Al-Qasimi, the last Qasimi Ruler of Lingah
2. A letter from Shaikh Mohammed bin Khalifa Al-Qasimi
3. My father and I, *c.* 1940
4. Khansahib Dr Mohammed Ayyub
5. Dubai Creek when the flying boats first began to land
6. The Post Office in Bahrain, 1947
7. Dubai, 1947
8. My letter applying for a position with the Imperial Bank of Iran
9. The staff of the bank when it opened, October 1946
10. The buildings in which our first office was located
11. The bank's offices in Deira
12. Myself in Arab dress
13. Myself in European dress
14. In London during my first visit, 1956–7
15. The opening of the new BBME building in Dubai, 1964
16. With Kenneth Bradford and Shaikh Saqr bin Sultan Al-Qasimi

(between pages 106 and 107)

17. A Certificate of Manumission given to slaves in the Gulf states
18. A house similar to the one in which I was born
19. The interior of the Al Ahmediyya School

20. The inscription by my father which stands in my garden in Dubai
21. Ambassador of the UAE to the Court of St James
22. The mosque built by my grandfather in my family's home town of Lingah, *c.* 1890
23. The mosque that I built to replace my grandfather's mosque
24. The interior of the mosque at Al Khassab
25. The garden of my house in Dubai
26. The dining room
27. The courtyard
28. The presentation by Shaikh Zayed of the Order of Zayed II, 1997

(between pages 170 and 171)

29. With Shaikh Rashid and others at a Diwali dinner, *c.* 1950
30. With Shaikh Rashid and Harold Macmillan at 10 Downing Street, 1959
31. With Shaikh Rashid in his private *majlis* in Dubai
32. Shaikh Rashid with President Gamal Abdul Nasser, 1959
33. Silver salver presented to ESG by President Nasser
34. With Shaikh Rashid, Abdullah Al-Ghurair, Majid Al-Ghurair and Majid Al-Futaim
35. With Edward Heath during his visit to Dubai, 1961
36. With Shaikh Rashid at the proposed site for a landing strip in Deira
37. Dubai's new airport soon after its opening
38. The opening of the bank's new offices in Dubai, 1964
39. With Shaikh Rashid and Sir Humphrey Trevelyan
40. At a meeting of the Deliberative Committee of the Trucial States Development Office
41. With Shaikh Rashid and Shaikh Mohammed bin Rashid Al-Maktoum
42. Signing an Agreement with African and Eastern (Near East) Limited, 1965
43. With the then President of Ireland, Mrs Mary Robinson, and her husband

ألا إن أخلاق الفتى كزمانه   ✦   فمنهم بيض في العيون وسود

وتأكلنا أيامنا فكأنما   ✦   تمر بنا الساعات وهي أسود

وقد يخمل الإنسان في عنفوانه   ✦   وينبه من بعد النهي ويسود

" أبو العلاء المعري "

Man's ways are various,
Like man's days:
Some white, some black

We are devoured
by our days,
Those lions we call hours

He may be dull and lazy
When a man is at the peak of his youth;
But when the errors of his ways
Are shown to him,
He awakes to reason and excels

Abu Ala' Al-Ma'arri

Sweet to ride forth at evening from the wells
When shadows pass gigantic on the sand
And softly through the silence beat the bells
Along the Golden Road to Samarkand

James Elroy Flecker
'Hassan'

ما أحلى أن ترتحل في السماء من الينابيع حيث تمشي الظلال العملاقة على الرمل

وتقرع برفق في السكون الأجراس على الطريق الذهبي إلى سمرقند ....

جيمس إلروي فليكر "حـسّـان"

Introduction

PEOPLE SOMETIMES ASK ME who is the most remarkable man I have ever met. I have no doubt of the answer: Shaikh Rashid bin Saeed, the Ruler of Dubai for thirty years, a man of no formal education who taught himself to govern and whose judgement over a vast spectrum of subjects, political, economic, commercial and personal, was uncannily right.

Shaikh Rashid was the architect of his state's success. Easa Al-Gurg was the foremost of his lieutenants. Like the Shaikh, he is self-taught; like him, shrewd, pragmatic, energetic, hard working and successful through his own qualities and his own efforts. Banker, entrepreneur, politician, ambassador, his talents range widely and are matched by his vivid personality. What the reader misses from not seeing him in person is his hilarious story-telling. He acts out every character in every anecdote. He cavorts fluently from English to Arabic and back again. He is splendid company in every situation, serious and comic. I have known him for half my lifetime and I am proud to be his friend.

The story he tells is a remarkable one. Of course, the theme of rags to riches is neither new nor unique, particularly in the Gulf of his generation. What makes his life special is that his success is not simply the history of a seed of commercial talent, discovered in a land where there had been little or no commerce before, then nurtured and developed until it bore a luxuriant harvest. There are

xiii

plenty of splendid men in Arabia today who have gone through that process. But in Easa Al-Gurg it has been accompanied by an enthusiasm for other enterprises and the cultivation of other gifts: a political brain, a zeal for education, a mind open to new ideas and exotic influences, a generosity which is both material and spiritual, a gusto which beguiles and animates all who meet him and – perhaps the most enviable quality of all – an incessant and infectious energy.

The opinions he expresses in this book reflect that versatility. They are, as always, strongly held. They have, as always, made me think and made me want to argue. In the dichotomy which he describes between his love of the Arabs and his respect and affection for the British, he has been, it seems to me, over-kind to the one and over-harsh to the other, particularly to those British who worked, usually with benign intentions, in the Gulf states. But this is not the place for argument.

In any case there are wide areas of agreement between us. I recognize with regret that the West, and particularly the British, misunderstood and mishandled Gamal Abdul Nasser in his early days and turned a potential friend into an enemy (with a bit of help from Nasser himself). I accept that the colonialists' motives were not always altruistic. I believe that the Arabs as a whole have had a raw deal this century and that the people of Palestine have been the victims of a sad injustice.

I have spent almost all my adult life in the Arab society to which Easa was born. I have acquired by study and association the admiration for it which was bred in him by nature and nurture. I lament, as he does, the swamping of that society by the mass homogenizing culture of the West, the vulgarities of tourism, pop music, hamburger bars and pizza parlours. I do not regard that invasion as a conspiracy by the West to sell its products. The Arabs are free to reject it if they wish. The trouble is that too many of them do not.

So I share Easa's anxieties for the future. True to his nature, he believes that virtue will prevail. I am less sanguine; I remember that it was an Arab historian, Ibn Khaldun, who taught us that triumph and glory are often followed by a swift decline. Salvation now lies in the hands of the Arabs themselves, led (thank God) by men like Easa Al-Gurg, whose story is a cause for pride and hope.

James Craig
London, 1998

Preface

RITING THE ACCOUNT OF his life can often tell the writer as much about himself, in the inwardness of what it reveals, as it will, he hopes, inform the reader. Indeed, as I look again through the text of *The Wells of Memory*, I am struck by several elements in the story which I think may require some further word of explanation before the reader himself comes upon them.

Obviously, there are countless experiences which have conditioned the way I am, the way in which I have come to see things and the attitudes and cast of mind which have governed my life. I have tried, over the years, to remain true to certain ideals and principles which I formed when still young. These have provided the basis on which my life has developed and by which I would wish that life to be judged.

First, I see my commitment to the concept of Arab Nationalism as the single most important political ideal of my life. This came about in my teens, when I was living in Bahrain, where the political climate was far more bracing than in my home town of Dubai. Almost at the time that the creators of the Nationalist movement were formulating their ideas in Damascus, soon to see them spread throughout the Arab world, I was meeting men who became my friends and who introduced me, a very young and inexperienced youth from the southern Gulf, to the heady dream of the unity of the Arabs, which had been our heritage in the great days of the

Arab Empires. As I shall relate, the career of Gamal Abdul Nasser was crucial in making the expression of that dream something approaching a reality and was a profound inspiration to me; sadly, I have lived long enough to see that dream fade though I still believe that it is a true aspiration for all the Arab peoples, disunited though they may seem to be, once again.

This will make clear another aspect of my character which I have come to recognize – that my culture and my ways of thinking are firmly rooted in the Arab past, in that immense inheritance of which every Arab is the heir. My essential 'Arabness' has been supplemented – I would say strengthened and increased – by my apparently inbuilt ability to absorb influences from other cultures, too. In part, this may be because my ancestors lived on the Persian side of the Gulf for generations; in part, it may also be the result of being a citizen of the world as much as I am a citizen of the Arab lands.

This may lead some of my readers to find a paradox in the account of my life, for this ability to draw from and enjoy the fruits of more than one cultural stream, may sometimes seem to produce apparent contradictions. I have never wavered in my belief in the unity of the Arabs and I have been deeply critical of the involvement of foreign interests in our affairs. This situation has persisted into the very recent past; it has therefore been with me for all my adult life. Yet it will be evident that I have a great affinity with the culture of the West and, in particular, a deep and abiding affection for the British people; though, if one were to judge them solely by their political actions, it would be difficult to see them as other than having been amongst the more troublesome of foreign influences in our part of the world.

I have been told, from time to time, that I am too close to the British and I think it is true that I have more British friends than from any race apart from my own. I will leave the reader to decide whether this is indeed a contradiction or, as I like to think, the demonstration of a proper roundness of spirit. I have never been able to hate; but love and affection, for ideas as well as for individuals, have always come more readily to me.

I describe at some length one aspect of my rejection of foreign influence in the Arab world and in particular of the part which Britain played in our lives, which was, in my view, definitely not for the better. The result was the creation of the state of Israel and its implantation in our midst with the consequent suffering which it provoked. The reader will find that this is a theme which echoes through these pages.

I realize that this is a difficult issue for many people. After all, Christians and Moslems alike draw a part of their religious heritage from the writings of the Jewish scholars who assembled what Christians call the Old Testament, at the end of antiquity, in the period after the Babylonian captivity. Then, the grave wrongs which European countries did to the Jews, in Russia, Poland and, most especially, in the lands ruled by the Nazis, inculcated a deep sense of guilt in the European mind.

This guilt was to be overcome, it was believed, by the creation of a Jewish homeland in Palestine which was quickly transmuted into the idea of a national Jewish state. That it had nothing to do with Palestine or the Middle East was rapidly forgotten. But it cannot be forgotten by the people of Palestine or by those who shared their suffering and sense of dispossession.

To me it seems profoundly ironic that the Jews, who for many centuries have prayed 'Next year in Jerusalem', seek to deny the Arabs of Palestine the right to their occupation of the city which they have enjoyed since Jerusalem was a little hilltop settlement, long before the world had even heard of the Jews. They have treasured what they claim to be the memory of Jerusalem but they expect the Arabs to forget. If I return to this matter in my narrative it is certainly not because I am anti-Jewish but because, with the understanding which I have of our history, I know that a great wrong was done, whatever may have been the motives for it.

Finally (though this should perhaps be the first of the indelible influences that have shaped my life), there is my experience of Islam and of the family from which I have come. Although I have sometimes doubted that I have been as good a Moslem as I would have liked to be (but then, who is, I wonder?), I have never for a moment doubted my commitment to Islam and its teachings.

As far as my family is concerned, I have been driven all my life to restore its fortunes and its standing in the world. My family was noble in its way of life and in its dealing with its dependants and with those among whom we lived. My father, though these pages will show that he was an austere and sometimes formidable figure in my life, was a man of undoubted nobility of character, whose misfortunes, which were not of his making, never daunted his spirit. The harshness and disappointments of his life did not for an instant diminish his belief in the precepts of religion and the need for a man to live his life according to them.

I have been encouraged to tell the story of this life, to see if there is some order to it, perhaps a pattern which can be recognized, by a number of different motivations. I want to recall the past, my family and friends and those who have helped me to achieve whatever I have achieved. I want to remember the often important events in which I have participated, which had an influence on my homeland and on the lives of many, many people living in lands far away from it. In the course of my life I have often been a participant in, or an observer of, many such events, and I am probably one of the few witnesses now in a position to record some of them. I have also had the good fortune to experience many lives in living my own. I want to set down the memories which are important to me and which I would not wish to see lost.

More, perhaps, than anything else I want to offer my memories to my children, to their children and to all the others who will come after me, who may find some advantage in knowing what it was like to be alive during my lifetime; perhaps they may even understand better how the world which they will inherit came about. And, because I am also by nature a teller of stories, I want to relate some of the occasions and events which I look back on, not only with gratitude, happiness or pride, but also with laughter.

In preparing this book I have been greatly helped by the confidence and goodwill of my friends. I have been especially encouraged by many of my Arab friends, including members of the ruling families in Dubai and the other states in the United Arab Emirates, who have urged me to write my memoirs. In trying to respond to this encouragement I have sought always to rely on the facts of any situation or political issue which I describe; events in our part of the world have moved with such speed and with so many currents and influences affecting their outcome that I felt it right to set down my recollections as directly and as truthfully as I could. When I have dealt with political issues and particularly those concerned with our relations with Britain, I have supported my words by referring to the documents which have been made available by the Public Record Office in London. The relevant references will be found in the notes at the end of the book.

In addition to those many Arab friends (and many members of the Arab student community in the UAE and in Britain) who have urged me to set down what I know about the past, I would like to record here the names of some of my British friends who have been particularly helpful: Sir James Craig, who kindly agreed to write the Introduction, Sir Donald Hawley, Sir Terence Clark, Peter Mason, Brian Kendall, Ronald Codrai. I am also very grateful to the members of my family who have advised me and helped in so many ways. Finally, I wish to record my thanks to Michael Rice who has assisted me in the preparation of the text and in the editing of the book.

Easa Saleh Al-Gurg
Dubai and London, 1998

I

THE MAN IS SURELY fortunate who is able to live out his life within sight and sound of where he was born, no matter that it may have changed out of all recognition with the passage of the years. If he can remember his childhood as a time of happiness, he is doubly blessed. This is how it has seemed to be with me.

The place where I was born, in the period between the two world wars, when the British Empire still dominated the lives of countless millions of people all over the world, was a small fishing and pearling town in the southern part of the Arabian Gulf. It was called then, as it is still called, Dubai.

All the world now knows Dubai to be one of the centres of the oil industry and of finance and trading on an international scale, where great fortunes have been and are still to be made. That it was not always so I can testify: in my lifetime I have seen Dubai change, like a scene in a cleverly crafted film, from a place of extreme poverty to a metropolis of immense prosperity.

I will try and explain how this change came about and how it affected the lives of my family, my friends, the people with whom I grew up and the people of the town in which I was born. At the same time I will explain how those changes enabled me to have a life of wide diversity and to experience a range of activities which would have been unthinkable to anyone born in a generation before mine.

*

Where do I begin? Before I was born, certainly, because much of my early life was influenced by the fact that in my grandfather's time my family crossed the waters of the Gulf from the coastal plains of Iran, from the region known as Fars, and returned to our ancestral Arabia. The province of Fars, incidentally, was long ago celebrated, in the words of the fourth/tenth-century traveller Al-Muqaddasi, as 'the country where the people and the merchants are smartest and where there is the most vice'.[1]

If you come to know Dubai you will know that this crossing of the Gulf's often tricky and unpredictable waters has been the experience of many families living on this part of the Arabian coast. For a variety of reasons – including climate change, economic pressures, environmental decline, the ebb and flow of politics and war – people from the mainland of Arabia were often obliged to seek a livelihood or security for their families across the Gulf.

For some of us, particularly those families for whom the traditional ways of Islam and the way of life of the Arabs were of special importance and pride, there was another event which made the return to Arabia imperative. In the years after the end of the First European War, when the politics of much of the world were deeply disturbed, a revolution in Iran brought to power Reza Shah Pahlavi, the founder of the dynasty which ended with the overthrow of his son, Mohammed Reza Shah, by the Iranian revolution in 1979. Ironically, it was the first Reza Shah's attempts to reform aspects of Islamic custom which encouraged many of the Sunni Arab families, living like my own on the coast, to return to Arabia. Not least amongst the innovations to which the Arab families objected was the decision that women should go unveiled. In this the Shah was following the precedent set by Kemal Atatürk, who had deposed the last of the Ottoman sultans to rule in Istanbul. For the Arabs, on both sides of the Gulf, especially those from the old families of which mine was one, such proposals were wholly unacceptable.

At the time, the decision to return to Arabia must have represented a considerable surrender of much of what made life pleasant. Thus for my own family, life in Lingah, the town on the Iranian coast in which my forefathers had settled, was evidently good.

Though it was located on the Persian coast, Lingah was an Arab town, occupied and governed by Arabs, whose language and culture determined its character. My ancestors prospered there, with land, farms, animals and, above all, from harvesting the seas by sending out fleets to fish for the pearls which were the foundation of the Gulf's prosperity in the past. My immediate forebears were pearl merchants and landowners and enjoyed the products of that life abundantly; I still retain the title deeds to the lands which we owned in Dishgaan and Lingah. The distinctively Arab character of Lingah and of my own background is evidenced by the fact that every one of these deeds is written in Arabic, not Persian.

The British, who were to exercise a great influence on my life, came to the region as long ago as 1763, when they established the first British Political Agency at Bushire. In 1820 they signed the General Treaty of Peace with the shaikhs on the Arabian side of the Gulf and then, in 1853, the Perpetual Maritime Truce. These treaties were designed to bring peace to the area and to reduce the frequent tribal and dynastic disputes which had previously marred life here.

Lingah was a prosperous place and in the nineteenth century it was in line to become the location for the British Residency in the Gulf, when the British began to take an increasing interest in our region. This was in 1828[2] and although Bushire was eventually chosen, Lingah was the location of one of several 'Native Agencies' established by the British on both the Persian and the Arab shores of the Gulf in the 1820s; a British Residency Agent was appointed to Sharjah, next to Dubai, in 1829. Later still, in 1908, the British India Office proposed setting up a vice-consulate in Lingah but this idea was abandoned on grounds of cost.[3]

My family name, Al-Gurg, is unusual in the Arab world in that it is not derived from a word in familiar usage or from a given name, often of an important ancestor which then was adopted as the family name of his descendants. In the case of Al-Gurg the story is rather different.

According to the family legend I had an ancestor who was a powerful and fearless man. The place in which he was living was

3

menaced by a large and ferocious wolf, which preyed on the flocks, stealing goats and killing the people's chickens. The wolf was a cunning beast which had eluded the hunters who sought to kill him. Finally, the people came to my forebear and asked him to rid them of the wolf.

He devised a bold plan. In those days, the Arabs living on the Persian coast wore the *qraiat*, the turban which has become associated in particular with the people of Oman, in our own day; Oman had ruled that part of the coast in which Lingah is situated and no doubt adopted the characteristic turban from there. My ancestor took two of the very long cloths from which the turbans were made; these he wound round his hands and forearms. Taking a long knife, he set out one dark night and lay in wait for the wolf. Eventually he heard the wolf approaching; brandishing the knife, my forebear leapt out and grappled with the wolf. The animal flew at him and buried its teeth in his arm which was protected by the turban cloth wrapped around it. My ancestor then plunged the knife into the wolf's heart and it fell lifeless to the ground.

The villagers who had sought my ancestor's help were, naturally enough, delighted and ever afterwards called him 'Gurg' which in Persian, the language of the village people, meant 'Wolf'. The name stuck, in the Arabic form 'Al-Gurg', and became the name by which the family has been known ever since. There are people living in Syria who bear the name 'Al-Gurg', but whether they are connections of my family I cannot say.

Lingah experienced some moments of importance in the occasionally disputatious politics of the Gulf in earlier times. Thus one of the Imams of Muscat, a predecessor of the present Sultan, was killed in a battle near the town in the 1820s and was said to have been buried there. But in general life was tranquil in Lingah, the crops were abundant, the air was sweet and even the Arabic which the people spoke was somehow softer and more gentle than the harsher intonations of those who came from across the Gulf, from the eastern or southern shores of the Arabian peninsula.

There was always a degree of contact between the two shores of the Gulf. In the case of my own family, through a connection with the Al-Qasimi shaikhs who ruled parts of the Gulf coast on the Arabian side as well as ruling in Lingah where they had become established with the Arab families of the region in the 1720s, a tradition had been built up over the years that on Fridays during the winter-time when there was no pearling, members of the family, their friends and retainers together with people from Sharjah and Ras al-Khaimah, would cross the Gulf in a flotilla of boats, rowed by their sailors. They would arrive in Lingah in time for Friday prayers, after which they would be entertained by my family and other friends; then, when the evening prayer was concluded, they would return to the Arabian shore, reaching their homes at about midnight. The journey must have been quite a formidable one and that it was accomplished so regularly must be a tribute to the strength of the sailors whose strong arms drove the boats through the often unpredictable seas around the Gulf's shores. This crossing and recrossing of the Gulf showed, I think, how closely in contact the two sides, the Arabian and the Persian, always were.

Lingah appeared for a while on the stage of nineteenth-century international politics when, in 1887, Persia (as Iran was then still called) made a claim to several of the stategically sited islands in the approaches to the Straits of Hormuz, at the southern end of the Gulf, before it opens to the Indian Ocean.

Two of the islands were the Greater and Lesser Tunbs, which had been administered, certainly since the eighteenth century, by the Al-Qasimi Rulers of Lingah. The Shah of Persia of the day, Nasser Al-Din Shah, laid claim to the islands, and later to a third, Abu Moussa, on the pretext that as the Al-Qasimi ruled from Persian territory, the Ruler was in effect acting on behalf of the Persian Government. In fact, the Al-Qasimi shaikhs had controlled the Tunbs in their personal capacity and not as servants of the Persian administration. That the last Al-Qasimi Ruler of Lingah, Shaikh Mohammed bin Khalifa Al-Qasimi, was recognized by foreign powers as sovereign is demonstrated by the fact that in 1887 he wrote to an Ottoman official, assuring him that all Ottoman nationals who resided 'in our Emirate' were under his protection.

In the event, the Persians initially secured some degree of support for their claim from the British, though when they went deeper into the legal issues involved they recognized that the Ruler of Lingah had always maintained his allegiance to the Al-Qasimi Ruler of Ras al-Khaimah; the Tunbs, therefore, were unequivocally the territory of that Emirate. However, this did not discourage the Persians from attacking and occupying Lingah, expelling Shaikh Mohammed, obliging him to return to the Arabian homeland.

This action did not give credibility to the Shah's claim that the Al-Qasimi and their supporters were Persian subjects, but in fact made it clear that Lingah and its hinterland were ruled by Arabs and that the majority of the people living in it were Arabs. Subsequently, when the Shah laid claim to Abu Moussa, the British established to their satisfaction that the Ruler of Sharjah had always administered it directly and that therefore there was no basis for the Persian claim.

Not all the Arabs in Lingah left at once; my own family continued to live there until the 1920s when, as I shall describe, they returned to their home town, Dubai. Relations between the two sides of the Gulf continued amiably, despite the disagreement over the islands, and trade continued between the two coasts as it had always done. However, the time came when, for reasons which I will explain, the Arabs of Lingah and the Persian coast decided that they no longer wished to remain under Persian rule and most of the principal families, who were still there, returned.

The islands were to assume some importance in my lifetime, when, after the formation of the United Arab Emirates in 1971 and the final departure of the British from the Gulf, Iran, under the last Shah, Mohammed Reza Shah Pahlavi, invaded the islands and occupied them. A very complex legal case ensued, with the Rulers of Sharjah and Ras al-Khaimah asserting their historic rights to control of the islands; I will mention this again in Chapter 9.[4]

Trade was the mainstay of life in Lingah. People were free to get on with their own affairs, largely without interference from the authorities. Duties on the trade conducted through the port were minimal, though at one time the right to levy customs on trade through the town had been sold to Belgian interests, a form of tax-farming which was not entirely unheard of in Europe in earlier times. The pleasant circumstances of life in Lingah had begun to change in the early years of the present century when the Persian authorities succeeded in imposing Persian customs duties on Lingah's trade, which had otherwise been free of such imposts.[5] This provided an important stimulus to Dubai's early prosperity, which in no small part resulted from the migration back across the Gulf of merchants who had been established in Lingah for at least two centuries. It was the enlightened policy of the Dubai authorities to welcome the returning families, enabling them to re-establish their lives on the Arabian coast after their long sojourn on the Persian littoral. It was particularly Shaikh Saeed bin Maktoum, the father of Shaikh Rashid bin Saeed who was to influence my life so considerably, who invited the Arabs from the Persian coast to return. An entire area of the town, Bastakiyah, became identified with the houses of the Arabs of Persian origin.

One result of this transfer of people from the Persian to the Arabian shore was that amongst those who returned were builders skilled in the construction of wind-towers (in Persian '*badgir*', meaning 'wind-catcher', from which the Arabic word '*barjeel*' is derived). The wind-towers have become one of the most familiar features in all representations of 'Old Dubai'; they were wonder-fully effective in trapping any wind that there might be, coming from any direction, in the dreadful humid heat of summer which was one of the curses of life along the coast before the advent of air-conditioning. I suspect that few people, who lament their passing from the architectural landscape of Dubai and some of our other towns, realize that they were in fact an invention of the Arabs of the Persian coast.

Some families living in Lingah owned lands outside the town itself. Thus, my wife's grandfather, a rich and rather fierce patriar-chal figure, had farms outside Lingah worked by people who were little more than the poorest of peasants. Unusually for the time, he had sent his son to Europe to be educated, particularly in France and Belgium. In the first of these countries he had acquired a love of French culture and an admiration for the democratic system which he saw everywhere around him.

When his son was of an age to begin taking responsibility for the family's interests, his father dispatched him to the estates at

Dishgaan, the centre of Lingah's rich agricultural lands, which lay some distance outside the town. He was instructed to journey there to collect the produce which the farmers were required to hand over to him, as the representative of the proprietor of what today we might call their smallholdings. His son, who would eventually be my wife's father, was greatly distressed when he saw the poverty in which the farmers lived and the hardship which their children and womenfolk endured. They came to him humbly with the produce which they were accustomed to hand over to the landlord.

This my wife's father could not bring himself to take, insisting that they should keep it for themselves and their children. On returning to Lingah, he was greeted by his father who asked why he had not heard the familiar tinkling of the bells on the harness and fetlocks of the handsome white Bahraini donkeys which made up the caravan which carried the produce from the poor farmers' fields. My wife's father confessed that he had not brought anything back with him. In a towering rage my wife's grandfather flung his son into prison, from which, mercifully, he was eventually rescued by some of his friends. They smuggled him out of the place in which he was confined and helped him to flee to Bombay, where there was a substantial and prosperous Gulf community. There he prospered, joining Rosenthal, the famous firm of pearl dealers, where his European education was appreciated. When his father died he returned to Lingah where he was introduced to the carefully raised and educated girls of the leading Arab families, like our own. In the fullness of time he met and married my wife's mother, for which circumstance the thanks must be to God.

When my own family returned to Dubai they settled on the shores of the Creek; this was the little town's most distinctive feature and had even earned it the occasional reference in the reports of European and other travellers to our part of the world in times past. Dubai's Creek was not the only one on this part of the coast but it was certainly the most extensive, reaching deep into the desert. The town was sometimes called, perhaps rather fancifully, 'the Venice of the Gulf'.

My grandfather, my father, his brother and their families lived in a traditional merchant's house, a large and handsome building, with servants and all the modest luxuries of a family of our station of life; most people in the town still lived in the *barastis*, the very ancient dwellings built of palm fronds. The large central courtyard of the house, which is still standing, would have been full of the comings and goings of the family and of those who had business with them.

On one side of the courtyard was the '*Long Majlis*', the reception room in which the men of the family received their guests. The *majlis* was often used by Shaikh Saeed bin Maktoum Al-Maktoum, the father of Shaikh Rashid bin Saeed Al-Maktoum, with whose later career so much of my own life was to be bound up. Here Shaikh Saeed was accustomed to sit, to hear disputes and to settle the cases which were brought to him for judgement. The connection here was that the mother of one of my father's brothers (in the West, you would say 'half-brother', for they were by different wives of my grandfather) was from Qishim island where the Al-Qasimi family had been established since the 1760s,[6] from which a number of the shaikhs of this part of the Arabian coast had been drawn for many generations. Although my family were Arabs, they were not members of the Bani Yas tribe, from which the majority of the Dubai and Abu Dhabi Arabs derive their affiliations. My uncle was an important man in the town and much involved in its affairs. Life in Dubai was, so my father told me, good, with time to enjoy their world, small though it was, as well as time to pray. The lives of the people of Dubai at this time were bounded by the Creek, which marked, effectively, the limits of their world. Beyond the Creek lay 'the Big Sea', the Arabian Gulf itself. Beyond that? Who could tell?

The town was criss-crossed by a maze of little streets and alleys; at night the only light came from the oil lamps hissing in front of the more prosperous houses and the merchants' shops. After nightfall watchmen guarded the shops, each of them observing some ten or twelve and shaking the shutters to make sure that they were properly locked. Anyone walking in the streets at night might be challenged by the watchmen and asked to make themselves known. The sound of the lamps' hiss, their occasional splutter and the soft golden light which they diffused is a memory which everyone who grew up in Dubai in those days will recall, with all the comforting glow of childhood. Like me, they will still hear the cries of the watchmen as they went about their rounds.

Life in Dubai was generally tranquil but although the rate of crime was low, it was not entirely unknown. There were people of various nationalities living in the town and every so often there would be trouble. On one occasion which I remember, a man broke into a house one night. When he saw a woman inside suckling her baby, he went away. He was arrested, however, and then confessed to a number of crimes which had occurred in the town in the recent past. He was cast into the town gaol, there to await the inexorable workings of Islamic justice. On a Friday he was taken to a prominent site in the town and lashed to an ancient cannon which had been imported centuries before by the Portuguese, during the time when they were active in the Gulf. He was beaten and then his left hand was cut off. It was tied around his neck, the stump having been thrust into boiling pitch to cauterize it. For three days thereafter he was exposed in the *souq*.

Such measures were harsh but they did, without doubt, keep crime to a very low level in our towns. It was in the midst of this placid time, however, that a catastrophe happened which blighted the lives of all the generation to which my parents belonged, and which altered drastically the circumstances which awaited me when eventually I entered the world. I grew up during that ominous decade (according to the Gregorian calendar), the 1930s; it was then that the Japanese, that diligent and industrious nation, discovered the cultured pearl.

The introduction of cultured pearls on to the world market effectively destroyed the way of life of the fishermen, the owners and captains of the pearling fleets and the merchants like my father. They had made their living by selling to buyers who came to the Arabian Gulf towns from all over the world, in search of what were acknowledged to be the finest of all real pearls. Ports like Dubai numbered hundreds of boats which sailed in and out of their waters during the pearling season; at the turn of the century Lorimer, in his *Persian Gulf Pilot*, estimated that in Dubai alone 6,936 men were employed in the pearling fleets.

All along the Gulf, from Kuwait in the north to Ras al-Khaimah, close to the entry to the Arabian Sea which is part of the Indian Ocean, the situation was the same. Hundreds of families depended upon pearling and in a very short time their livelihood was entirely destroyed. The industry had been declining since the end of the First World War, but it was the coming of the cultured pearl which sounded the death-knell of a way of life which my friends who know about such matters tell me had survived for thousands of years, for the earliest evidence of the adaptation of pearls for jewellery comes from the Gulf, from before 3000 BC.[7]

The worst year was 1929, two years after I was born, which really saw the end of Dubai's trade. The previous years had been misleadingly prosperous, encouraging many people to speculate in new boats.[8] The consequence was that the trade was greatly over-equipped when the lean years came. Indian moneylenders had advanced loans with an annual interest as high as 36 per cent, and this crippled many families to the point of absolute ruin.

It may be difficult for people today to realize what devastation the collapse of the pearl trade caused in the communities of the Gulf. In my own family, my uncle, who had been such a figure in the life of Dubai, could not endure the change in fortune which the collapse of the pearling produced; he died tragically. Poverty, grinding hardship, malnutrition and still higher rates of infant mortality became the lot of all the people living in the little towns and villages, who had no other place to go. It was into such conditions that I was born.

My arrival in the world was hardly auspicious. My mother was suffering from malaria when she was carrying me; the disease at this time was endemic throughout the Gulf and much of western Asia. Consequently, I was a sickly child, about whose prospects of survival little confidence could be expressed. Not for me the simple childhood maladies which all children experience; in addition to the malaria which I inherited from my mother, I suffered from trachoma, asthma, diseases of the spleen and every intestinal condition known to man, these last the result of drinking tainted water from the well which was our only source and which was always liable to become infiltrated by salt. In the main, we had to rely on the supplies of drinking water carried into the town in BP four-gallon tins, borne on the backs of uncomplaining donkeys.

My body was covered with ulcers and my father used to take me to the Creek to clean them. This he did by excising them with the sharp end of a big hen's feather, rather like a quill which might have been used to illuminate some splendid manuscript. It was agonizing, and the pain was increased by the sulphur which he used to disinfect the wounds; I bear the scars to this day. But though the treatment was harsh, it was effective, and through the devotion of my parents I survived, although sometimes when I remember the sort of traditional remedies to which I was subjected I wonder how I managed to do so. Another therapy involved the branding of the patient with hot irons; I bear these scars also. More humane, and also more successful, was a treatment said to have been recommended by the Prophet himself, for conditions of the ear. This required applications of white honey to cure an infection and it worked very well for me.

Life was so harsh in our part of the Gulf when I was young that it may be wondered that any children survived at all. Certainly, the incidence of infant and child mortality was very high and the prospect for any child living to what would be considered, in the developed world, a normal life-span were poor indeed. My brothers and I, however, were cared for by my mother who, despite all the privations which the family experienced, always ensured that we had an adequate supply of fresh, nutritious food.

The mainstay of our diet as children was fresh milk from the two cows that were kept in the compound of the house and which were taken out to graze on the sparse vegetation. They were also fed a meal made from date stones and the dates which had become over-ripe for human consumption; to this was added a quantity of dried *doma*, the small, sardine-like fish plentiful in the Gulf's waters. Our servants milked the cows daily; my mother made ghee for her cooking from the milk, and yoghurt and butter, which she flavoured with herbs, creating in the process a delicious fragrance. The butter was also melted down and used as a salve which was rubbed over the bodies of us children when we had been bathed, to keep our skin soft and supple.

We also kept chickens and my mother was careful to control the supply of eggs, taking some from those birds which had too many and placing them under the birds which had none, thereby increasing her stock. Their eggs supplemented our diet admirably and on Fridays, as a special treat, we might sometimes actually have fresh chicken for our main meal of the day; for this purpose the cock birds were taken, the hens being preserved to provide more eggs and stock.

Living on the shores of the Gulf, we were mainly dependent on the fruits of the sea for most of the year; thus we had the benefit of what is probably the most nutritious of all foodstuffs, fish. We had a plentiful supply of fresh dates, and for vegetables, beans and peas; later on, we would occasionally have tomatoes from India and bananas, which were regarded so much as a luxury that if they were seen being taken into the house, the observer would politely ask whether anyone was sick.

Another item in our diet were the almonds which came from India and were pounded – skin, stones and all – into a highly nutritious and flavoursome mixture. All of these commodities meant that we children lived surprisingly well and none of us suffered from any notable deficiencies as we grew to maturity.

I suspect that children's instinct for survival ensured ours. I used to get into great trouble with my father when he discovered me eating the gypsum plaster which coated the walls of some of our rooms. Instinctively, I had realized that I needed calcium and somehow had discovered that the gypsum provided it for me.

Our living area was one large room, opening off the courtyard of the house. In the corner of the part where we slept was a small partitioned area, raised above the level of the rest of the room, which served as our bathroom. In it was located the *samowar* which heated the water with which we were bathed; the word is, I suspect, the same as the Persian *samovar*.

The society of the Arabian Gulf (then, of course, always referred to as the Persian Gulf) into which I was born was still deeply traditional, governed by the precepts of the Quran, and administered by traditional courts and the families of the Rulers who were

supported by the leading families of merchants, on whom the prosperity, such as it was, of the region depended. Our metropolis was
Bahrain, which was to become the Gulf's political centre when the
British moved their Residency, a sort of scaled-down viceregal
presence, from Bushire on the Persian side of the Gulf.

Britain was the self-proclaimed 'protecting power' of the southern Gulf states, which comprised what had for a century and more
been known as the Trucial coast, a term derived from the treaties
which determined the relations of the states with Britain and,
through Britain, with the rest of the world.[9] Strictly speaking, we
were not part of the British Empire; the states were considered to
be sovereign entities which had delegated some of their functions,
such as defence and their relations with foreign powers, to Britain
under the Exclusive Agreement of 1893.

As far as we in Dubai were concerned, the British presence was
not especially obtrusive. Dubai had been recognized as an independent shaikhdom since the early part of the previous century.
Generally speaking, relations with Britain were good. Occasionally
an official would come into the Creek to visit the shaikhs; more
frequently we were made aware of India, away to the east, from
where traders, more junior officials, soldiers and sometimes war-
ships would come into our field of vision.

It had not always been so, however. An incident from the years
when the British ruled India, which I suppose is recorded somewhere in the margins of Britain's imperial history, brought Dubai
and the might of the Empire into confrontation. The incident arose
from an allegation that the Rulers of Doha, up the coast in what is
today the state of Qatar, had appropriated some horses which were
being shipped to India.

Somehow, Dubai became involved. British ships moored in the
'Big Sea' were attacked, with armed men creeping on board, overpowering – in some cases, killing – the soldiers on watch and then
slipping over the side to swim away before their presence was
detected. As a consequence of these events, the British bombarded
Dubai, though the men who had attacked their ships had long since
melted away into the desert.

A settlement was reached; it was agreed that compensation

should be paid to the families of those who had been killed in the engagement. There was, however, a dispute over the number of deaths, with the British questioning the estimates of casualties provided by the local people. It was decided, finally, to count the number of coffins in which the dead had been placed. This was done, but the British did not realize that the coffins were being recycled, as it were, leaving the courtyard in which the British officials were sitting by one door and returning by another, each time covered in a cloth of a different colour. When it did dawn on them what was happening, it was judged to be too late to do anything about it and a figure of compensation was agreed.

This was not the only occasion when the British had intervened in the life of the Gulf coast towns. In much earlier times, in the 1820s, they had destroyed a number of forts in towns along the coast, including Dubai. My family's home town of Lingah was also shelled, but that turned out to be a mistake, for its people had taken no part in the events against which the British were reacting, and compensation was paid to them.[10] By the 1830s, Dubai was recognized as an independent shaikhdom, its relations with Britain and the outside world governed by the General Treaty of Peace.

The British prided themselves on ridding the coast of pirates. There are those who have suggested that the main concern of the British in those days was to preserve the field for themselves, but at all events, the political circumstances of those days brought them into the Gulf where they remained until 1971. But that belongs later in this story, a good deal of which is concerned with the latter days of British influence in what was to be one of the last vestiges of imperial history. The Ruler of Sharjah, HH Dr Shaikh Sultan bin Mohammed Al-Qasimi, B.Sc., Ph.D., has written compellingly of this period of the Gulf's history.[11]

An unquestionable achievement of the British, when they began seriously to involve themselves in our affairs, was their effort to eliminate slavery from the coast. In Islam, slaves had a quite different status from that to which they had been subjected in the Christian world. Slaves were protected by law, with clearly expressed rights; the Quran required slave owners to treat them humanely, and in my own family I know that those servants who were bound to us were treated as part of our family. When our fortunes were destroyed by the collapse of the pearl trade, the old servants, who would once have been regarded as slaves, had nowhere to go and they remained with us until their deaths, cared for by my parents.

The British could not perhaps be expected to comprehend the subtleties of Quranic law as it applied to slavery, and assumed that the same injustices which had been perpetrated in the British, American and Spanish colonies applied equally in the Moslem world. They regarded it as a duty to alleviate the condition of the slaves, particularly in the nineteenth century, and one means which they employed was that any slave who sought the protection of the British Crown would be granted his or her freedom. The act which symbolized this was that the slave would grasp the flagpole in the compound of the British Agency or Consulate, and by placing himself or herself under the flag's protection would be made free. Each slave so released was given a Certificate of Manumission, confirming that the British Government had effected the manumission of the person named on the document and that 'no one has a right to interfere with his/her liberty'.

From my boyhood, two incidents recalling this more troubled past stand out in my memory. First, in 1938–9 there was a movement to establish a separate centre of government in Deira.[12] It was widely believed that the British were behind the action which was taken to restore Dubai's control of Deira (which lay across the Creek and was Dubai's twin) for they evidently had fears about what they saw as the emergence of progressive tendencies demonstrated by the Deira separatists. In particular, they apparently disapproved of the establishment of a *majlis*, an assembly which was actually representative of the community; this was quite different from the Ruler's *majlis* and was indeed a return to a much earlier form of what was suspiciously like a democratic structure. It is interesting to reflect that an institution of this sort appeared in the Gulf more than half a century ago. For the British, as the imperial power, it was far more acceptable to deal with established, traditional social and tribal structures in the territories which they sought to control, than to have to cope with the more diffuse, less predictable activities of popular assemblies.

For boys like me it was an exciting time, as Shaikh Rashid, who exercised many of the responsibilities of Ruler on behalf of his father, Shaikh Saeed bin Maktoum Al-Maktoum, took over the house of Abdul Kader Abbas, which occupied the highest point in Dubai, to attack the separatists across the Creek; from the protection of the house Shaikh Rashid and his men were able to fire across the Creek into Deira. The bullets from their rifles cut directly across our house and courtyard and the sound of their passing was fairly alarming. The Abbas house was protected by sandbags into which the bullets from the Deira side struck harmlessly. We were captives in our house for a week and no supplies reached us; we had to make do with the very limited foodstuffs and drinking water which were available.

The second incident occurred two years later when there was a territorial dispute with Abu Dhabi, over an area called Khor Ghanadha.[13] An expedition set out from Dubai by sea with the object of enforcing what were considered to be Dubai's rights. It was believed at the time that the then British Residency Agent in Sharjah, Jasim Al-Kadhmawi (in those days the British representatives were often Arabs from other parts of the Middle East, or Indians), had encouraged Shaikh Rashid to attack Khor Ghanadha, which lay off the coast of Abu Dhabi, by sea. If this was the case then the British would appear to have misled Shaikh Rashid, for the fact that the 'invasion' was sea-borne gave them the excuse of intervening, effectively on Abu Dhabi's behalf, arguing that the action was illegal as their writ extended to all actions on the sea, as opposed to any on land, where the territory would be under the control of the shaikhs.

I mention these incidents only because they marked interruptions in the otherwise even tenor of our lives. Such events were characteristic of the Gulf in the past; mercifully, they have very largely disappeared today because of the wisdom of the governments of the region and, in the case of our particular part of the Gulf, of men like Shaikh Rashid bin Saeed Al-Maktoum and

Shaikh Zayed bin Sultan Al-Nahayan of Abu Dhabi. The creation of the United Arab Emirates and the Gulf Co-operation Council has further contributed to the stability of the area, for whilst disputes still exist and no doubt will continue to do so, the mechanism now is available to resolve them in a mature and equitable fashion. By one of those strange incidents of chance, many years later I found myself taking part in discussions between the Political Agency and Shaikh Rashid over the same disputed territory, after Julian Walker of the Foreign Office had demarcated a number of the Trucial States' frontiers.[14]

These events also demonstrated the growing antagonism in our part of the world, as in so many others, against the continued interference in our affairs by the colonial power. The equivocal role which the British played (or were alleged to have played, really much the same thing) in these two incidents contributed to the sense of grievance which many people began to feel about what was effectively a colonial presence in our land. The British did, of course, achieve much that was good in the territories which they ruled, but their readiness to intervene, in pursuit of their own ends, in the management of our societies, despite the fact that the states officially preserved their own identities, was greatly resented.

Such interruptions as these in the generally placid course of life on the coast were not frequent and the round of days continued much as it had always done. Apart from such occurrences, the Empire was remote from the general experience of our lives. However, India, the land from which all the trappings of Empire and the presence of the British in our small territory derived, was itself to have a decisive influence on my young life, wholly unexpected but nonetheless profound. It was an influence for which I have always been very grateful.

When I was old enough – I was probably about ten – I began to attend our local school, first at Al Falah, which provided teaching at primary or infant level, and which was located on the Dubai side of the Creek, and then at Al Ahmediyya in Deira. This school provided the equivalent of secondary education in a traditional Quranic background, where the emphasis of the teaching was on Islam and on what I came to realize were some fairly basic forms of mathematics at which I, as a future banker and businessman, showed remarkably little ability.

We were also taught history and I was fascinated and excited by the stories of the centuries when the Arabs were the rulers of a great Empire, stretching from the Euphrates to Spain. I loved the stories of the lost land of Andalusia, as the Arabs still call Spain. I have visited Granada on five separate occasions and each time I have wept, as did Abdullah, Granada's last Emir, as he turned to bid farewell to one of the most beautiful and civilized cities in the world at that time.

Next door to the school was a handsome Arab house, once the home of a prominent local merchant. It so happened that events in the world outside the Creek on which I was accustomed to spend my days had begun to make the British take a much enhanced interest in our part of the world. With the outbreak of war in Europe, Britain judged that it needed a more substantial operational base in the Gulf, which the military authorities realized would become an important staging post on the route to India – which was, after all, the reason for their having established their political presence there in the first place. The merchant's house was taken over and turned into a clinic. The doctor who looked after the RAF personnel in Sharjah, near Dubai, was Khansahib Dr Mohammed Ayyub and he lived over the clinic.

One day during our break, I was doing what I often did (for even then I was fascinated by the evidences of foreign ways), peering through the windows of the clinic and watching the doctor's assistants at work. I was particularly taken by the rows of different-coloured bottles which stood on the shelves in what I came later to know was the Dispensary. The people working there wore aprons, adding to their strangeness in my eyes.

On this occasion the doctor saw me and called me to him. I think he realized, for he was a shrewd as well as a kindly man, that I was keen to learn something of the world beyond the rather narrow horizons which bounded my existence.

Dr Ayyub had seven sons and he was anxious that they should not lose their English; a wise man, he did not want them to become isolated or bored and so he looked for some local Arab boys who could share their lessons with them. He decided that I should, if at all possible, be one of them.

Dr Mohammed Ayyub was, of course, a Moslem; it happened that he also spoke Persian and he first addressed me in that language, of which I had some knowledge though of course Arabic was the language spoken by my parents and family. Dr Ayyub recognized that I was quick to learn; he approached my parents and asked them to allow me to be educated with his sons and with the other Arab boys, who he thought showed potential to become worthwhile citizens of the world awaiting us. He realized that a grasp of English would be essential for any boy who sought to make his way in the world.

My father, for whom I had a deep and abiding respect, though it did not always prevent me from resisting his more determined efforts to discipline me, strongly disapproved of the doctor's proposal. He was a deeply pious Moslem to whom nothing was more important than the observance of the requirements of religion. He feared the effect that exposure to Western influences would have on what he evidently saw as my mercurial temperament. He refused to give his consent to the doctor's kindly suggestion.

However, at this point my mother intervened. She persuaded my father that my character was strong enough to withstand the temptations to which exposure to the English language might subject me. Reluctantly, and I am sure with every sort of misgiving, my father agreed, it being a condition of his consent that nothing should interfere with my attendance at the Quranic school to which I had already been admitted. Thus, in the mornings I sat at the feet of my Quranic teacher, learning the wonderful language of the Quran and the precepts of religion as well as mathematics and our history, whilst the afternoons were spent with Dr Ayyub and his sons studying the strange language of the English, concealed in the even stranger shapes of the writing which I also had to master. I devised a system of writing English words phonetically in Arabic, so that I could get an approximate sense of their pronounciation, and then, painfully, transcribing them into English. By this means I was able to expand my vocabulary each day by five or six words. This experience with Dr Ayyub was probably the most important in my young life, for which I have to thank my mother and the Indian doctor.

My education, though it was by modern standards pretty rudimentary, evidently did provide some sort of intellectual stimulus, for when I was about twelve years old, I decided to write a book. It was to be called *Life is a Passing Show: The History of our Part of the World*. Wherever did I find such a title?

I wrote it in one of my school books and it was progressing very well. One day I was sitting in one of the shops in the town where they made the fish oil which the fishermen used to waterproof the timbers of their boats. My father often deposited me there where I could be under the kindly eye of the shopkeeper, one of his friends, a cultured, rather eccentric man with boundless energy and enthusiasm. This was Sayed Hashim Al-Hashimi; he was what I suppose in English would be called a ship's chandler. He was keen to help me extend my education during the long summer period when the schools were closed for four months and, in particular, he made me practise my Arabic calligraphy; he himself had an especially fine hand and wanted me to write the language as beautifully as the characters deserved. I was sitting in the shop, a rather sickly small boy, wearing my little cap and reading what I had written, I hope with satisfaction, when he came over to me and asked what it was that I was writing with such diligence, as he suspected it was not always the texts which he had set me to copy. He took my book from me and began to read.

An expression of deep dismay came over his face. In my book I had written, critically it must be said, about the activities of the British Residency Agent in Sharjah, a Kuwaiti named Khan Bahadur Abdul Razzaq Razuqi, and of his dealings with the shaikhs. He was a man greatly disliked in the town and my writing evidently reflected this abundantly. Sayed Hashim read what I had written and immediately tore it to pieces. 'You will put us all in hell,' he cried. I did not realize that what I had written was so subversive or so sinful, but it was the end of my literary career until I began work on the book which you are now reading. Perhaps I was already becoming critical of British involvement in our affairs, an attitude of mind which was to remain with me for many years;

perhaps I simply did not like Khan Bahadur Abdul Razzaq Razuqi. Whatever the reason, a wider world than that which I had so far known was beginning to beckon.

At this point, I think that I should say something more about my parents. My father possessed to the full that most characteristic and most admired quality of the Arab, unreserved generosity. Even in the days of adversity, if he had 10 rupees in his pocket and encountered someone whose need he considered to be greater than his own or who simply appealed to his kindness, he would give his last coin away without another thought. My mother would sometimes reproach him, urging on him the needs of her children before the needs of strangers. But that was my father's way and nothing would change him. He was certainly not indifferent to the demands of his family, but the tradition of giving was too strong for him to do otherwise.

Later in life, when he who once had been a man of substance experienced real poverty, he wished to give a present to one of his friends, Khansahib Hussain bin Hassan Emad, on the occasion of his building a new house on the beach at Sharjah. He had no money with which to buy a present, so bleak had times become. Instead, he turned his hand to making a gift and carved a beautiful inscription, a verse from the Quran, which he gave to his friend. Now that gift has returned to me and I am proud to have set it up in the garden of my house in Dubai.

My father was admired in the Dubai of his day for two particular qualities, his unshakeable honesty and his skill as an arbitrator. He was often called on to write the agreements which were designed to record the sale of land; this was in the days before there was any sort of land registry. His standards were very high; sometimes, it seemed to us in the family, almost too high. His contemporaries valued his judgement and he was often asked to join in the negotiations for the sale of a consignment of pearls, for example. This he would do but if he were asked to tell an untruth, to praise the quality of pearls above their value or recommend a deal that he believed to be wrong, he would refuse to associate himself with the discussions.

He sometimes acted as a pearl broker, mediating between the buyer and the seller of pearls. For this service he earned a few rupees or a payment in kind; in the days of our family hardship such earnings, though they were meagre, were important to us. My father's probity, however, would not allow him to take any sort of payment from some of the merchants with whom he had dealings whose sense of honour and honesty were not as his. My mother, who had a loving concern for her family, would remonstrate with him but he would be unmoved because, as he said, he knew that one day he would stand before God and be required to account for his actions.

During the years of my family's greatest hardship my father constantly sought opportunities to provide some degree of income, no matter how modest, to support us. He was a man who loved books and the wisdom they contained. He took up bookbinding, a craft to which he brought the same determination and sense of purpose that he brought to all his endeavours.

I remember him so clearly, with the great press which he used to stamp the softened leather used for the bindings, impressing designs on them and their titles on their spines. He was very inventive and to provide some decorative elements in the designs he adapted the brass fittings on an old Indian safe which we had, turning the screw of the press to stamp their designs on the cover of the book on which he was working. For each book he might receive 10 rupees; not very much, it may seem, but it helped to feed his children.

My father was a man deeply learned in the Moslem sacred texts, the Holy Quran and the commentaries and other scholarly writings which had been compiled over the preceding 1,300 years. His study was not narrow, however, for he knew about the religious faiths of non-Moslems, though of course he regarded the followers of such faiths as irretrievably lost. I recall his advice to me once that, if I had to have dealings with Christians, I should choose the Roman Catholics. My father's reasoning was that, however misguided they might be, the Catholics were the true Christians. The Protestants and other sects had been formed as the result of human concerns, in the case of the Protestants because of Henry VIII's search for a woman who could bear him a son. In his eyes, the Catholics represented the authentic Christian tradition.

I was very close to my mother. She was a strong-minded person and like many Arab women she exercised a powerful influence on her family. She supported me whenever she judged that a development or an opportunity presented itself which would benefit me. Often she was at odds with my father on such occasions, but, as we have seen, she could always win him round.

My father sometimes found me a shade too independent for his taste; after all, in his time sons deferred absolutely to their fathers and I was not able to do this when I knew myself to be in the right. However, towards the end of his life he said of me to my mother, 'Listen to what this one says, for it will be he who will look after you.' I have always tried to fulfil my father's words. My mother, too, always treasured them, for when my brother wanted her to live with him and his family, she refused, preferring to remain in the house which I had provided for her, latterly in the grounds of my own house in Dubai. She said that she would go where I went, saying that her husband had told her always to depend upon me.

I recall at least three occasions during my childhood when I saw with, as they say, my own eyes, examples of the apparently strange powers which some people in small communities in the past often seemed to be able to exercise. I suspect that this has always been the case in relatively isolated societies like ours. In Moslem societies the role of such gifted people is well known; certainly I have encountered or heard of similar cases in North Africa, Egypt, Iraq and Iran. I suspect that the phenomenon was widespread though no doubt the onset of the modern world has eliminated all such out-of-the-ordinary events from people's lives.

Both my mother and my father possessed these abilities which, it should be stressed, were always employed for good and with the Quran's benediction. Let me try and give some examples.

One day some of his friends came to my father in great distress, for a substantial quantity of gold had been stolen from one of them. My father asked if they had suspects in the case; they mentioned the names of several. He took a china bowl and round the inner rim inscribed the names of seven powerful angels. Below the angels' names and between them he wrote the names of the suspects. Then he took his ring, tied it on a loosely plaited Indian silk thread, which for such purposes was always green in colour, and suspended it over the bowl, holding it very firmly. In a subdued voice he began to read from the Holy Book. After a while the ring began to move, its movements becoming more and more rapid until finally it stopped before one of the names. The gold was recovered. How it works, unless it be by the intervention of the angels whose names were invoked, I cannot say.

On another occasion I was in Medina on *Umra* (the small pilgrimage) with a group from Dubai, including one of the shaikhs from nearby Sharjah. By some mischance the man responsible for the organization of our passports, tickets and money exchange suddenly found, when we arrived at Medina airport, that all of them were missing. The police were told but offered little hope of their recovery. I telephoned my mother who, I knew, had the faculty sometimes of being able to 'see' the outcome of events. She told me that I would recover my passport but not the cash which had been stolen. The next morning the courier came to us in great excitement to say that the police had telephoned and that our passports were at a small hotel in the town. There they were but as my mother had predicted, the money had gone. We had our suspicions as to the identity of the thief but we were grateful to have recovered our passports. This process is called *Tahyoura*, meaning a reading from the Quran.

One of my maternal uncles suffered from epilepsy; I remember vividly the distressing attacks which he used to experience. It was decided to seek the help of a Yemeni Sayyed, who was reputed to be skilled in treating such conditions. The Sayyed agreed to undertake the cure and named a night when the moon was full on which he would carry out the necessary procedures.

The night came and the moon was riding high in the sky. All of the family were present and we children sat like little dogs on the white sand, brilliant in the moonlight, completely absorbed in this strange spectacle. The Sayyed (so called because he was recognized as a descendant of the Prophet) called for a bowl of boiling water and a dried lemon. He held my uncle's head and read from the

Quran. He began to sweat, both with the heat of the boiling water and with the concentration which he was obviously exerting over my uncle.

Suddenly, the lemon began to move. It became agitated, as if it had a life of its own, and then began to look as though it was itself boiling. All at once there was a great noise and the lemon was hurled upwards out of the bowl, as if by some immense force. It vanished and my uncle never again experienced an epileptic attack.

Sometimes my father would be asked to cure a toothache. He was no dentist but he would ask the sufferer to indicate which of his teeth was paining him. He then took a paper on which, he told me later, he inscribed the name of a powerful angel, Faqatata, who was said to stand close to the throne of God. My father wrote the name in his beautiful calligraphy and then gently began to hammer a nail into the loops and openings in the letters which made up the angel's name, whilst reading from the Quran. The toothache was cured. Sometimes, if the tooth had a particularly large cavity, my father would roll up the paper on which Faqatata's name was written and tell the 'patient' to insert it into the now dormant tooth.

Now this sort of procedure may well have been psychological in its effects and the confidence which the toothache sufferer had in my father's powers may have achieved his release from pain. But the other cases are less easy to explain; it may be that simple communities, living their lives close to nature and the world around them, did have access to knowledge or skills which we have lost. Yet these are true memories from my childhood and they are a part of the inheritance which I have drawn from my years in my father's house.

Another indelible memory, from the time when I was very young, is of the occasions when my father would take me with him on trips which, from time to time, he made to Ras al-Khaimah, to buy or sell pearls. This small shaikhdom lay up the coast, to the north and east of Dubai. In the days of my childhood it was perilous to attempt to reach Ras al-Khaimah by land because the desert route, which in those days consisted only of rough tracks across the sand, was frequently subject to attack by bands of marauding Bedu. It was safer, particularly for a child, to go by sea. My father would take one of his *shahuf* – the slim, sharp-prowed craft which he himself made and would sell to eke out our small income – and we would set out together on our voyage.

These journeys were magical for me because, although I suffered dreadfully from seasickness as our small craft pitched and rolled in the choppy waters along the coast, I was able to absorb the wonder of the sea and sky, the play of the waves and the clouds, to feel myself wholly part of nature and to look with amazement on the multiple works of God. During the voyage – for such it seemed to me – my father would recite verses from the Quran about the sea, the most majestic and the most mysterious of God's creations. It was sheer enchantment.

When we arrived at our destination on the first occasion, to my delight we were taken to the garden (in those days we did not have such things in Dubai) of the pearl merchant with whom my father had come to do business. Suddenly I found myself in a paradise of Indian almond trees, figs, tall palm trees and everywhere the scent of jasmine. My father's friend showed me a small pool which lay in the heart of the garden. While he and my father talked I was allowed to sit and play in the pool. Never before had I known fresh water on my body for in Dubai I was always bathed in the harsh salt water which was all that could be spared. Now I found myself in heaven, a foretaste of what it must surely be like for those fortunate enough to reach it.

The next morning we were awakened by another of the enduring sounds of my childhood, the bullocks plodding patiently and drawing the *mihale*, the device which in our part of the world was used to raise the water released into the irrigation channels to nurture the crops planted there. We heard the cocks calling us to prayer (this is one of the duties of those busy birds) and we began the day by praising God and His works in the wonderful language of the Quran. Then we breakfasted, surrounded by the beauty of the garden. According to custom, we would remain the guests of my father's friend for not more than three days; then we would begin the journey home.

I was fortunate that, despite the hardship which my family suffered in these years, I was able to experience our way of life as it had always been, in all its simplicity and dignity. Inevitably, I came to live between two worlds as I grew up and the ways of the West have come to dominate my life as they have for all the people who now live in the sort of society from which I came. But I treasure the memory of those times when life was lived closer to the roots from which our Islamic and Arab culture grew.

I do not want to sentimentalize my childhood. In many ways it was exceptionally harsh; sometimes, indeed, it was hateful. There was no sanitation, hygiene was minimal and medical attention was non-existent, at least until I was almost in my teens. Life was also exceedingly tedious, the more so for an alert and inquisitive child. There was simply nothing to do: endlessly we wandered in the streets or sat, watching the passing of the familiar traffic on the Creek. Then there was the perpetual round of prayer-times, when what little activity there was, ceased. Our education, outside Dr Ayyub's house, was entirely by rote with no opportunity to express an individual view or even to ask the questions which bubbled up in the mind of a boy who needed constantly to know the answers to all the mysteries of life. Yet the love and concern of my parents and the awakening realization of the wonders of the world around me, little though I saw of them then, impel me to recall those days with affection and gratitude.

When he judged that I was beginning to grow up my father began to take me with him when he called on the shaikhs or on his friends, the other merchants in the town. One day he announced that we were to join the Ruler, Shaikh Saeed bin Maktoum Al-Maktoum, when he called on a British Political Officer who was visiting Dubai.

As we walked along the shores of the Creek, passing the town's main burial ground, an area pitted with sand-dunes which now leads to the British Embassy compound, my father instructed me on my behaviour on such occasions. I was only to take a small amount of what was offered and I must certainly not reach out to grab whatever food or refreshments were available. I was rather alarmed by all this unfamiliar formality.

The British official on whom Shaikh Saeed was calling was a

Captain House, a tall, thin man with a small red beard. I recall that he had pitched three tents where the British Embassy now stands, one green, two white. He also had a little dog, to which he was much attached, called Wilhelmina.

'What sort of name is that?' asked one of the shaikhs.

'It is the name of the Queen of Holland,' replied Captain House, rather stiffly. There was a shocked and astonished silence amongst Shaikh Saeed's entourage. Were the British now so powerful that they called their dogs by the names of kings and queens?

Wilhelmina was obviously quite unimpressed by the occasion and ran cheerfully about amongst Captain House's guests. She came up to me, I suppose to be friendly, but I was nervous of her. She ran up to the son of one of the shaikhs and his father pushed her away with his foot.

Captain House was furious. He demanded that Shaikh Saeed should at once pay a fine to atone for so grave an insult to Wilhelmina. Shaikh Saeed was obliged to hand over two rifles and a payment of cash before Captain House was pacified.

As we walked away from the party, we came on two Persian 'coolies' who were fighting. Shaikh Saeed asked my father to find out what was the trouble and to quieten them. 'The Englishman will be sleeping,' he said, 'and if he wakes up it will mean more rifles and cash which we can't afford.'

My father spoke to the coolies and asked about the cause of their dispute, which was taking place in front of the BP depot, where the company stored its kerosene. The four-gallon tins, which when empty were also used for carrying Dubai's water supplies, were prominently marked 'BP'. One of the Persians insisted that this meant 'Blessed be Pahlavi', the name of the dynasty which some years before had come to power in Iran. The other Persian ridiculed this idea, knowing that BP meant British Petroleum.

My father gave them 5 rupees, telling them to be quiet and to let the Englishman sleep. Peace was restored. More than half a century later I recalled this incident when, in the same place, now the British Embassy in Dubai, I received from the British Ambassador the insignia of a Commander of the Order of the British Empire; a remarkable turn of the wheel of fortune for the little boy who had been sitting there so long before, hoping that Wilhelmina would leave him alone.

During the years when I was growing up, the larger world began to penetrate our smaller one. The outbreak of the Second World War had ramifications even in a place as distant from the centre of events as Dubai. In 1940 an agreement was reached with Imperial Airways, the foreunner of British Airways; as a result flying boats began to land on the Creek and Western visitors became familiar if fleeting figures in our lives. We now saw soldiers in strange uniforms and watched unusual degrees of activity, apart from the flying boats, in our otherwise normally tranquil harbour. In the *majlis*, the meeting place for the prominent members of our community, the talk, so my father reported, was of great changes in the world outside, even, it seemed, of threats to the stability of the apparently invincible British Empire.

For my part, I continued happily with my dual education, Islamic and Western. When the English soldiers – and especially the English air crews – started to appear on our streets and in the *souq* I realized that there would be occasions when my newly acquired English could be put to good use. The English forces seemed pleased to find a Dubai boy who could communicate with them. In particular, through helping Dr Ayyub, whose bag I often used to carry as he went about his duties, I became familiar with the RAF personnel who were stationed in the Gulf, providing services to aircraft flying to and from India. My ancestral merchant background soon came to the fore and I discovered that there were many opportunities for me to earn money from the foreigners, which made a welcome addition to my family's income.

With one of my friends I acquired suitcases and filled them with ties, watches and other merchandise which we bought in the *souq*. Often our customers would think that they had cheated us but we made a handsome profit. Thus I became a juvenile merchant and greatly enjoyed the experience.

It was not all plain sailing, however. My partner in this enterprise was my friend Ahmed bin Matter Albdoor, who shared in the newly found prosperity which came our way. One astute Indian trader saw our potential as merchants and advanced us 2,000 rupees of capital, a substantial sum for those days. We became more ambitious and despite some reservations on my part we began to 'export' goods across the Gulf to Iran. We brought back Persian carpets which we then sold to the RAF. Our profits swelled but as we did not find it necessary to worry too much about permits or the payment of duties we were eventually found out and our business was declared forfeit. I managed to save three shirts and two pairs of trousers from the wreck of our hopes; these humble garments were shortly to prove very useful.

My days of buying and selling in the *souq* perhaps laid the foundation for what was to be an important part of my career in manhood. But that was still far ahead in time. Though I was still very young, Dr Ayyub let me help him in his Dispensary, which had been established in 1939 and which had gone some way to demonstrate to the people of our town that sometimes the British imperial interest could bring positive benefits to those who lived in its shadow. At first I was only allowed to undertake small jobs, like washing the vessels and retorts in which he prepared the medicines which he prescribed for his patients. Gradually, however, he let me take on more responsibility until finally, after being examined by Colonel Rooney, the Chief Medical Officer from Bushire, I was able to qualify as a 'compounder', someone who was officially authorized to make up prescriptions to the doctor's instructions; the term nowadays would probably be 'dispenser'. This was, I think, in 1941; if, in my later life, I have not had much occasion to use this skill, acquiring it gave me a sense of Western science and of the value of such knowledge.

Another development occurred which was to have a profound effect on the future course of my life, though I could not have realized it at the time. The British had been keen to see a Post Office established in Dubai, mainly because of the presence of a sizeable Indian population who wished to communicate with their homeland. This was also in 1941 and the Post Office was to be the first in the Trucial States. Now it happened that at this time Dr Ayyub was about to be posted back to India. He was worried that without the opportunity for continuing my English language studies, my father would wish to take me into the family's remaining pearling business, very small though it now was. Despite all the calamities which the pearl trade had experienced, my father had kept one pearl boat and two of his old retainers who had nowhere else to go. They continued to fish a small pearl ground some distance from Dubai, known as Ghose Al Gahha, near Jebel Ali, but its output was meagre indeed.

Dr Ayyub knew that if I were to be drawn into the pearl trade I would have no occasion to use my English – which was already beginning to be quite fluent – and he suggested that I seek employment at the newly planned Post Office. Such an appointment would be made on the recommendation of British officials and from time to time such officials would visit Dubai, from the British administration in Bahrain. Dr Ayyub wanted to arrange for me to be around when the British official came to tea and for me to make a good impression. The fact that I could speak Persian, as well as Arabic and English, should count in my favour.

However, the Residency Agent in Sharjah, Sayed Abdul Razak Rezuki, dismissed the idea of my being appointed to the Post Office. He was, I suspect, prejudiced against me because of the Persian origin of my family and also because he had a candidate of his own whose interests he was anxious to advance. I knew that Dr Ayyub was determined that I should get the job; he and Sayed Abdul Razak Rezuki had a heated argument, to which I have to confess that I was eavesdropping, crouching under the window of the room in which they were; when I thought that I was about to be discovered I ran away like a little dog.

Sayed Abdul Razak Rezuki invited Dr Ayyub to his house for dinner; I think he may have been worried that Dr Ayyub would report him to the Imperial administration in Delhi. He also invited me to stay and eat with them at his house near the British Agency in Sharjah. I tucked myself away discreetly and ate with the most refined manners of which I was capable.

But Sayed Abdul Razak Rezuki was unimpressed and he refused to support my application for the job. Dr Ayyub and I left the house; we were both very depressed. 'Should I try on my own to change his mind?' I asked Dr Ayyub. He obviously felt that nothing could be lost by my doing so. I took a taxi from the old fort in Dubai where the taxis waited, shared with a group of Indians. I walked along the beach in Sharjah to the Agency. Sayed Abdul Razak Rezuki was not at home. I asked when he would return and was told that it would be at about 4 p.m., so I went back to the fort. It was very hot and although the people there kindly offered me food I declined and only took some water.

I waited until about 3 p.m. and then walked back to Sayed Abdul Razak Rezuki's house; my head was throbbing with the heat and the glare of the sun. Eventually he returned, in his large American car. He continued to dismiss my attempts to secure the position in the Post Office, saying that such an appointment was appropriate only for an Arab. I insisted that my ancestry was purely Arab but he remained adamant. I walked home, very unhappily.

Later Dr Ayyub saw me and realized what had happened. At the first opportunity he warned Sayed Abdul Razak Rezuki that if he persisted in this attitude he would report the matter to the Government of India, which should be aware of such racial prejudices being voiced in its dominions.

Now it happened that one of the officials from Bahrain arrived unexpectedly and came to Dr Ayyub's house for tea. Dr Ayyub arranged for me to be present and told the Englishman of my ambition to join the Post Office and of my suitability for the job. The Englishman enquired whether I knew the equivalent of my name, Easa, in English. When I assured him that it was Jesus I felt home and dry. However, he then expressed reservations on the grounds that I was too young and too small for such responsibilities. I realized it was time for some quick thinking, so I added two years to my age and declared that I had been born in 1925; in those days records were not kept of the births of children in traditional Moslem societies, so my deception could not be discovered. My date of birth still appears as 1925 in all official records but I am in fact two years younger than they assert.

Twenty-four hours after this meeting at Dr Ayyub's house I was offered an appointment at the Post Office for a salary of 25 rupees a month, approximately £2.00. Again, my father expressed considerable reservations; not only would I be involved with non-Moslems but it would be intolerable for a member of our family to be at the beck and call of the sort of people who were the Post Office's customers. Again, it was my mother who persuaded him and so I found myself an employee of the Dubai Post Office. This turned out to be a more fortunate circumstance than I could ever have expected. My career had begun.

Most of the people who made use of the Post Office were Indians and Persians, the merchants based in Dubai and their employees. My job included delivering the mail to the addressees, but I quickly decided that this was not at all appropriate for the son of a leading Dubai merchant family, despite the fact that our prosperity was not what it had once been. I let it be known, therefore, that I would stamp the incoming mail with such determination that it could be clearly heard in the *souq*, which was located under the Post Office building. At the sound of my energetic stamping the clerks from the merchant firms would gather and I would distribute the mail to them from the window of the Post Office, calling out the names of their employers from the letters addressed to them.

The Post Master was a man to whom the practice of religion was more absorbing than the everyday concerns of his office; most of his day was devoted to reading the Quran. I was therefore able to take over many of the responsibilities which would not have come to me so soon in the normal course of events, and I was quickly able to learn a great deal about the business of managing a Post Office.

Sometimes, however, my duties called for different skills. One day we received a brand-new but unpainted post box, sent to us by the Government of India with instructions that it should be fixed to the wall and painted red. I was deputed to arrange this. We had been given a pot of red paint and for the purpose I hired the services of an Indian painter. When the work was done, observing that something like half the paint still remained, I suggested we should give it to the painter, as a sort of reward. 'Certainly not,' said the Post Master, 'it is the property of the Government of India.' We decided then to paint the shelves in the office; still some paint remained and again I was instructed that it was undoubtedly the property of the Government of India and could not be lightly given away. I was running out of available surfaces to paint. I gave instructions for all the window frames to be enriched with the Government of India's remaining red paint. Still a little was left. Inspired, I decided to emblazon 'V for Victory', which I was aware was a code much favoured by the Allies, on the central leaf of the Post Office's door. When he saw it the Post Master was overjoyed. 'Oh, goodness me,' he said, 'the British soldiers will be very pleased.'

I made one final attempt to reward the painter. I suggested that we should give him the paint tin, which by now was entirely empty. 'Certainly not,' said the Post Master, once more, 'it is the property of the Government of India. We shall use it to hold the small change from the sale of stamps.' Thus was the property of the Government of India resolutely protected and put to full and rewarding use in one of its more distant outposts.

I did not find my work at the Post Office particularly demanding and I was able to make the best of any opportunities which presented themselves to increase my experience and knowledge. One such occasion presented itself when the British authorities sent an expedition to Sharjah and Dubai, staffed principally by Indian experts, to control the annual infestation by locusts, one of the scourges which afflicted the already meagre prospects of the farmers on the coast.

These appallingly destructive creatures can wreak havoc in a matter of minutes over a wide area. The statistics are enough to demonstrate how catastrophic a locust infestation can be. In a few weeks a swarm of locusts can multiply itself 900 times. A swarm can cover a distance of 100 miles a day; a locust eats its own weight each day and its potential devastation may be appreciated by the fact that a swarm can have a total weight of 100 tons.

The coast was known to be a potent breeding area and in 1944 the team was sent from Cairo and worked in a number of the towns and villages in our area, to attempt to control and destroy the swarms of insects. Accommodation was limited and the Post Master – on the instructions of the Political Agency in Sharjah –

invited the Indian staff of the locust team to stay on the floor of our building above the Post Office. This was divided into cubicles, where visiting, favoured merchants were accommodated, when they had business in the *souq* below. Of course I got to know them quickly. I was interested in the scientific methods which the team employed to control and eradicate the locusts; they used to take me with them on their expeditions into the desert and I bombarded them with questions.

I was their interpreter throughout their stay. I enjoyed my time with them greatly and I hope that I was of some help to them generally whilst they were in Dubai. I took them to the *souq* and arranged for them to be entertained in my father's house, which I think they enjoyed.

The recollection of these events was brought back to me when Mr B. G. Shabbir, one of the leaders of the expedition, came to see me in Dubai and we talked of these times. The last time that he had seen me, he remarked, I was a teenager, 'with a lean and thin body'. It was a long time ago.

By now I was handling virtually all the Post Office's affairs. Working there had also given me the chance to improve my English considerably; so much had it improved, indeed, that it was decided I should be transferred to our regional headquarters, in Bahrain. For this purpose I was interviewed by the Chief Inspector, a very distinguished gentleman who, though an Indian, seemed to me to be the very model of an Englishman.

To my disgust he appeared to be addressing me as 'lady'; naturally enough I refused to respond to this form of address. I was reassured by the Post Master that he was calling me 'laddie', presumably because he had heard British people using this rather patronizing term. My interview with this imposing official was successful, however; I was offered an appointment in Bahrain at the handsome salary of 140 rupees a month, vastly more than I had been paid in Dubai.

Once again, my father had to be persuaded to allow me to go. He not only had ideas of making me a pearl merchant, but he also had an extremely unfavourable view of Bahrain, towards which destiny seemed to be drawing me. Amongst my father's contemporaries Bahrain was considered to be a place of notorious licence and altogether deplorable freedom of behaviour. The omens were not good; it took my mother four months to persuade my father to allow me to go. 'Let him be thrown into the sea,' she said. 'Let him meet men that he may become a man. If he proves to be useless, let him be gone and then it will be he who will suffer all his life.' I have always remembered these words, which were spoken in my presence; I believe that they are the reason why I have been so keen to work hard all my life.

With what I am sure was every misgiving my father finally consented; he described me as 'the Ataturk of the Al-Gurg family', thus, however reluctantly, acknowledging my revolutionary spirit. But one final confrontation between father and son was still to be played out.

It was the custom in our part of the world for boys and men to have their heads shaved; my father shaved the heads of my brothers and myself every three weeks. I realized that I was going to look very strange if I arrived in Bahrain hairless, so I let my hair grow in the hope that my father would not humiliate me by insisting on shaving me. To my father, however, it was an article of faith that men shaved their heads and allowed their beards to grow. He discovered my plot and I was soundly beaten – for the last time, as it turned out.

At last I set off, leaving my family and my home town for the first time in my life; my father stood on the deck of the British India Steam Navigation Company's ship, the *Barala*, on which I was to sail up the Gulf to Bahrain, praying for my safe return. For the first time 'the Big Sea', which up to this point had marked the end of our world, became a reality. I was introduced to knives and forks and other wonders of Western culture and technology. In the confines of my second-class cabin I was setting out on a journey into the unknown.

2

THE BAHRAIN TO WHICH I was now heading was another world, strange, exotic and a thousand times more complex than my familiar Dubai which I had left behind. It was greatly exciting for one of my temperament, naturally inquisitive and quick to absorb new sensations. As soon as I arrived I began to take in an immense variety of impressions. I was fascinated by everything that I saw around me: the busy streets, the shops stocked with Western merchandise as well as an immense range of goods from India and the East, the British soldiers and airmen who wandered through the *souq* and everywhere a sense of bustle and activity on a scale which I had never known.

For the first time in my life I saw tarmac roads, with large American cars and huge lorries hurtling – as it seemed to me – in all directions; I can still hear the sound of their horns in my ears. Despite the clamour and bustle of Bahrain it soon became very sweet to me, an essential part of my life. I was delighted by the clean streets and the white houses, brilliant in the strong sunlight. I was delighted, too, by the sight of the young men, many of my own age, who wore beautiful white *thobes* and *aghal*, the long white outer garment that all Arab men wear and the black camel-hobble which secures the *ghutrah*, the cloth which covers the head; they were like toys, so smart and elegant were they. My father, after all, had accustomed me to the idea that men should be tough, just as it should be expected that life would be harsh. Men should be ready to walk unafraid in the darkness; it was considered effete, not to say effeminate, to carry a torch or lamp in the streets of Dubai. Bahrain could hardly have been a more complete contrast with my home town. It was all a great wonder and happiness to me.

The reason for all the activity and excitement that I saw around me as I stepped off the boat at the port in Manama in 1943 was because Bahrain was the centre of the British presence in the Gulf and Britain was locked into one of the most critical phases of the war which had begun in 1939. When I arrived in Bahrain, the course of the war was beginning to turn in the Allies' favour; America's entry into the conflict, prompted by the Japanese attack on Pearl Harbor in December 1941, had tilted the balance massively, bringing the vast industrial and material resources which America possessed to the support of her allies.

Bahrain was important to the British for a variety of reasons. First, it was the location of the Political Residency, the highest-ranking presence of the Imperial administration in the region, in charge of relations with all the Gulf shaikhdoms and with the Sultan in Muscat. The principal concern of the British authorities, then as in the past, was keeping the routes to India open; in this, the Gulf played a vital role.

Bahrain was also an important communications centre for the British. Its port was capable of handling quite large vessels which stopped there for victualling and routine maintenance. These functions contributed considerably to Bahrain's wartime prosperity. All of them contributed equally to my feeling of being overwhelmed by the modern world crowding in on me from every direction.

I began work at the Post Office's headquarters in Manama, Bahrain's capital. The Head Post Master was a Persian and he kindly sent his son to meet me from the ship and take me to where I was to stay, close to the famous Speedbird House, used first by Imperial Airways and then by BOAC, the forerunners of British Airways; for many years to come it was to be the only acceptable place to stay for visitors to Bahrain who valued their comfort. Speedbird House was owned by the family with whom I was to stay whilst I was in Bahrain and was let to the airline.

The Post Office was located in the Bab Al-Bahrain (the Gate of Bahrain) which then led from the waterfront into the principal *souq* area, where the merchants and traders had their businesses. The Bab was an imposing building (it still stands, much renovated) and was used by the Ruler of Bahrain's administration as its downtown offices. One of the sights connected with the Bab which was to become familiar to me was the figure of a tall, thin Englishman, mounted on a chestnut horse, who rode around the town early in the morning each day and then again in the evening, before dark.

This was Charles Belgrave (later Sir Charles), the Adviser to the Ruler of Bahrain, Shaikh Sulman bin Hamed Al-Khalifa. Belgrave was a somewhat enigmatic figure who later came to represent a particular element in my own developing political awareness. He had been recruited, as a very young man, to the service of Shaikh Sulman's father, Shaikh Hamed bin Isa, who wanted a young Englishman who was an Arabic speaker to help him introduce some of the reforms which he realized many of his people were beginning to expect.[1] Over the years the Bahrain Government had achieved much: in education, including the education of girls, then unheard of in the Gulf; in health care, including the establishment of the region's first general hospital; in transportation and the beginnings of an infrastructure which would eventually make Bahrain the most advanced state in the entire Gulf.

Bahrain's prosperity had been dramatically increased by its having been the first state in the Arabian Gulf to have discovered oil. The first exports of oil from Bahrain were made in 1932 and although the revenues which the state earned in the 1930s were tiny by the standards of today they enabled Shaikh Hamed and his son, Shaikh Sulman, when he succeeded his father in 1941, to accelerate the islands' development. When war in Europe broke out, Bahrain became even more important to Britain as a source of vital oil supplies. This importance was even signalled, a little while before I arrived, by the Italians' attempt, unsuccessful as it turned out, to bomb Bahrain's refinery.

By 1943, when I began my life in Bahrain, Belgrave was thought by many to be showing signs of wanting to hold back some – if not, indeed, most – of the influences of the modern world which he saw pouring into Bahrain and which he believed would change for ever the essential character of the country and its people. Shaikh Sulman, his employer, was hardly a radical figure but there is evidence that, later on, he began to realize that some degree of change was inevitable and that the important consideration, for traditional communities like those in the Gulf, was to ensure that change accorded with the traditions rather than collided with them.[2]

Belgrave was a rather lonely individual, distrusted by some of the British officials because of his unreserved loyalty to his employer, which they must often have wished to see replaced by a greater readiness to accept the British point of view in their not infrequent differences with the Ruler. Belgrave, in return, was often uncomfortable with his British contemporaries, especially those same officials with whom he had to deal and who he considered often lacked understanding or appreciation of his position.

But considerations of this sort were far from my mind at the time. Through connections of my father I was able to stay in the house of Shaikh Mustafa bin Abdul Latif, one of the prominent merchants of Manama. When I arrived, I was taken to their house and at once made welcome. I was exceptionally fortunate; Shaikh Ishaq, one of Shaikh Mustafa's sons-in-law, and his family accepted me as one of themselves and I discovered what family life could be like when material advantages, from which my own childhood had inevitably been so deprived, were added to the natural affection which bound the family together.

My family's connection with the family of Shaikh Mustafa bin Abdul Latif is a good example of the way in which prominent families in different parts of the Gulf kept in touch with each other and exchanged services and, when necessary, help. Shaikh Mustafa, a rich man by the standards of the time and a substantial merchant in the pearl trade, spent most of his time in Bombay where there was a large and prosperous Gulf community resident in the city. The family, which was Iranian in origin, maintained a large office in Dubai; my father used to assist members of the family in drafting agreements relating to the land deals with which they were frequently engaged.

For such help, acting often as a broker in the deals which were negotiated, my father was generally paid in kind.

One member of the family to whom my father was especially close was Shaikh Abdul Jalil, another of Shaikh Mustafa's sons-in-law. It was he who arranged my stay in Shaikh Ishaq's house. In common with many prosperous men, Shaikh Ishaq maintained an open house, to which all, rich and poor alike, were welcome. My years with his family were precious to me and I recall them now with gratitude. I still value the friendship of the younger members of the family who were my contemporaries.

I quickly came to realize the great opportunities for advancement which the wartime economy was bringing to Bahrain. The need for the British to develop some sort of infrastructure in the country meant that there were many different fields in which the Bahrainis themselves could make money. The country's prosperity, of course, was of long standing – the export of oil from the early years of the decade had meant that Bahraini merchants could benefit from supplying the needs of the Government, the oil company and the expatriate staff who began to work in the country. Land prices rocketed, one estimate suggesting that the price of a plot of land had increased thirty-five times by the latter war years.

In the early years of the war, Bahrain had actually experienced considerable shortages, for most of its foodstuffs had to be imported, but this situation changed once the Allies got the upper hand over the Axis powers in the war at sea. Nonetheless, it was the war years that saw the foundation of many of the merchant families' future wealth. The situation was notably different from that in my own home town, for Dubai, with little of the development which had taken place in Bahrain, suffered acutely from shortages in the early years of the war, adding to the people's already considerable privations. It was said that sometimes conditions of near-starvation persisted in Dubai and there were reports that there had actually been deaths from starvation among the inhabitants during the more critical days of the war.[3]

The situation changed considerably, however, when the British decided to establish a large camp for the RAF in Sharjah. A quota

1. Shaikh Mohammed bin Khalifa Al-Qasimi, the last Qasimi Ruler of Lingah

2. A letter from Shaikh Mohammed bin Khalifa Al-Qasimi to the captain of an Ottoman vessel, assuring the safety of all Ottoman nationals 'who reside in our Emirate'. This guarantee was given only a few months before Iranian troops captured Lingah in 1887

3. My father and I. According to a note on the original print this was taken in 1940 when I would have been about thirteen years old

4. Khansahib
Dr Mohammed Ayyub

5. Dubai Creek as it was when the flying boats first began to land

6. The Post Office in Bahrain in 1947, unchanged from when I started
to work there a few years before

7. Dubai in 1947, soon after I returned from Bahrain and started work at the bank

To,   DATED 22 April 1946.

The Manager Imperial Bank of Iran.

BAHRAIN.

Sir,

I most respectfully beg to write the following few lines for your kind consideration, and I anticipate that you will favour me with a reply.

It is heard that a branch of your Bank is expected to be organized very shortly at Dubai, and I believe that some clerks who are acquainted with the situation of Dubai are required by you. May I take the opportunity to offer myself for the above mentioned vacancy.

I am from a noble Muslim family, 20 years of age and a Dubai subject by birth, having good knowledge of English and Arabic, and moreover I have a fair knowledge of Persian. I am perfectly aware of the situation of Dubai and the people, regarding my experience, I beg to state that I have been working in the postel Department in the Capacity of a clerk for the past 3 years, at present I am in Bahrain, where I am posted in the Manama Post office, and I intend to resigne my present job for my future prospects.

Your early favourable reply will be very much appreciated.

I beg to remain Sir.
your most obedient servant.

8. My letter, written in my best English handwriting, applying for a position with the Imperial Bank of Iran, later the British Bank of the Middle East

9. The staff of the bank when it opened in October 1946. *Left to right*:
Yusef Al-Mahmoud; 'Chico'; the Manager, George Keast; the Chief Farash;
ESG; the Junior Farash; the Cashier, Abdullah Kamal Bulghari

10. The traditional buildings on the Creek in which our first office was located

11. The bank's offices in Deira (*on the left*), accommodated in two old warehouses

12. and 13. Myself at about the time that I joined the bank in (*left*) Arab
and (*right*) European dress

14. In London, during my first visit in 1956–7. I think that I was photographed
in Earls Court, where I used to lunch with friends from Dubai at the weekends,
who made sure that I was properly fed

15. The opening of the new BBME building in Dubai in 1964. I am on the far left, delivering the address of welcome to Shaikh Rashid bin Saeed Al-Maktoum, the Ruler of Dubai, on my left; and on his left Ross Hayder, Manager of BBME; Shaikh Ghulam Abbas Ansari, a leading merchant; Shaikh Hasher bin Maktoum Al-Maktoum; Saif bin Ahmed Al-Jarwan; and other leading merchants of the town

16. *Left to right*: Kenneth Bradford, BBME; ESG; and Shaikh Saqr bin Sultan Al-Qasimi, the Ruler of Sharjah, later deposed by the British authorities. Shaikh Saqr inscribed the photograph: 'To my dear brother, Easa Saleh Al-Gurg, for Remembrance'

system was in force which controlled the amount of essential supplies available to areas within the sphere of British influence. With the decision to expand the base at Sharjah, part of the Indian quota was diverted to the Gulf, to the benefit of both Sharjah and Dubai, with the latter serving as the principal distribution point for all the Trucial States, a consequence of the astute manoeuvring of Shaikh Rashid bin Saeed Al-Maktoum, the son of Dubai's Ruler. Dubai became more important as an administrative centre for the British than Sharjah, with consequent benefits for the town. This situation was enhanced by the silting up of the creek at Sharjah, an experience which was to prove a lesson for Dubai in the years ahead.

At once conditions in Dubai began to improve. There was a surplus of supplies which allowed the more enterprising Dubaians to export to Iran. A bag of sugar which would cost 100 rupees in Dubai would fetch 1,200 rupees in Bandar Abbas. Everyone benefited; it was even suggested that some senior British officials found the situation to their advantage.

Meanwhile, I worked through all the departments of the Post Office in Bahrain. In the evenings I attended night school where my English became still more fluent and I learnt practical qualifications like typing. A particularly fortunate circumstance was my being chosen for special tuition by a priest from the local Catholic church (I cannot imagine what my father would have said if he had known of it) who gave me more advanced lessons at the school attached to his church. These lessons lasted for nine months until, tragically, he was killed in a car crash in Saudi Arabia.

At the same time, I began to develop other skills and to gain new interests. For example, for the first time in my life I discovered the pleasures of dancing. I was encouraged in the acquisition of this new skill by the priest who recognized the need for me to be drawn out of myself. I found that I was now given the opportunity to take part in all manner of activities which gained me new friends and fresh experiences. Dancing was one of these which I took to with enthusiasm; another was girls, who I discovered for the first time could be friends whereas, before this, my knowledge of females had been confined to those of my immediate family. I lived in the knowledge that at some point my father would decide which of my cousins it would be appropriate for me to marry. With the model of my mother before me, I knew that women could exercise a profoundly important role within the family; Bahrain made me realize that they could participate in life at every level.

The cinema was another wonderful revelation to me. There were no cinemas in Dubai; in Bahrain there were several and they showed the latest Egyptian films. Some of these are today rightly recognized as classics and whenever I see one on television the memories of my youth come flooding back.

At weekends my friends and I would cycle out of Manama towards the north coast of the main Bahrain island to the site of the Portuguese Fort (as it was known then; today it is generally called 'Qala'at al-Bahrain', the Bahrain Fort). There we camped in the shadow of the most picturesque ruin in the Gulf. We did not know then that it would turn out to be one of the most important archaeological sites in the area, for it has proved to be the location for the main city of the Dilmun culture and its successors which dominated trade in the ancient world from four thousand years ago. Amongst my friends were some who were working at the new town of Al-Khobar in eastern Saudi Arabia, which was to become of importance when that country began to export oil in the late 1940s.

I began to adopt Western dress. Fortunately, I had retained the three shirts and two pairs of trousers which I had saved from the collapse of the business which my friend Ahmed Albdoor and I had run in Dubai. During this period, I made it a rule to write to my father every week. This I did conscientiously for the first months of my time in Bahrain. Gradually the interval began to extend and by the end of the first year my letters to my father were being written every three weeks; I suppose it was ever thus with sons and their fathers. The problem was simply that I was enjoying my new life so much and opening myself to so many new experiences that my duties to my father receded somewhat into the background. I hope that he understood.

My growing social life, the friends I made in the course of it and the constant widening of my awareness of the world around me now began to introduce me to what would become one of the most important influences in my life. This was my discovery of the political movement, then really for the first time sweeping through the Arabic-speaking world, which came to be known as Arab Nationalism and with which I was to be much identified in the coming years. Indeed, I was probably one of the first of my generation in the Gulf to become excited by the concepts which the Arab Nationalist movement expressed – the common identity and interests of all those peoples who spoke Arabic as their native tongue and their aspirations to the control of their own political destiny. This was to be a major preoccupation of mine in the years which now lay immediately before me, and I became increasingly conscious of influences which would be of profound importance in the world which I was beginning to enter.

I think that it may be appropriate here to turn aside from the more-or-less chronological recital of my life which I have so far written and to say a little more about the movement for Arab Nationalism and how it made its impact on me. The history of the movement reaches well back into the last century. At that time, foreign influences coming into the Arabic-speaking world made some of the intellectual and political leaders in the larger countries seek out their own past and question the often disadvantaged positions to which they found themselves relegated by the representatives of the colonial powers who were exercising more and more influence on their lives.

Much of the movement towards Arab Nationalism came from a sense of pride in the Arab heritage: first, in Islam and the recognition that the Revelation had been granted originally to the Arabs and, second, in the achievements of the Arab empires in the early centuries of Islam, in the sciences, medicine, the arts, music, law and the organization of society. At that time the Arabic-speaking world was far in advance of Western Europe, which was only beginning to emerge from its Dark Ages. The eastern, Byzantine Empire was powerful and highly organized but it did not display the same sense of excitement in experiment and the search for knowledge which so typified the Arab kingdoms. All of us, young men on the thresholds of our lives, looked back in particular to the splendour of the Moslem kingdoms in Spain, whose eventual

45

eclipse was so grave a blow, not only to Moslems but ultimately, I suspect, to the Christian world as well. The Moslem scholars (and, it should be said, the Jewish scholars also who lived peaceably amongst the Moslems and who were also fated to be driven out of Spain by the Christian kings soon after the Moslems were expelled) were the custodians of an immense treasury of scholarship and learning which had been accumulating over the previous seven centuries, including much of the scientific and technological heritage of the ancient world. It was only after the Renaissance in Europe, when a more liberal attitude began to flourish in the Christian West, that this well of knowledge began to flow once more, to the benefit of all mankind.

By my time, much of the thrust of the Nationalist movement was powered by something approaching hatred of the colonial regimes, amongst which Britain was the foremost influence in our part of the world. All too often British officials, employees of large companies, service personnel and miscellaneous travellers (and, particularly, it often seemed, their wives) came to the Arab world wholly unprepared, with no knowledge of our history and culture and, as often as not, with an unshakeable conviction that their way was the best. To a proud and ancient people such attitudes were intolerable and, sustained over many years, the resentment which they engendered became deeply engrained in our political consciousness. On countless occasions, particularly in the earlier years of this century in Egypt, Iraq and Palestine, the expression of Arab resistance or protest was ruthlessly suppressed, adding further fuel to the Arabs' discontent.

Often during my life I have found myself acting as a bridge between the two cultures represented by Islam and the West. This role was not one that I sought but it came about as the almost inevitable consequence of my business and political connections and I have tried to explain, as far as I am able, each to the other. It has not always been easy.

There is, sadly, a long history of distrust between Moslems and Westerners. There are many explanations as to why this should be so: the invasion of Europe during the early centuries of Islam, the Crusades, the Ottoman threat to the eastern European lands and the interventions of the colonial powers, all contributing to the decline of the influence of the Islamic states after so long and glorious a history. But the fact has to be faced that Moslems, Christians and Jews have all been taught to despise each other, to insist that their particular revelation is the purest expression of the will of God towards mankind.

In the case of the Moslems, although the states which were ruled by Islamic teaching tended to be more tolerant towards minorities than most Christian states, there is indeed deep distrust of non-Moslem influences which, in the minds of the more austere, corrupt the values of a Moslem society. When this distrust was allied to the evident technological superiority of Western societies in the recent past, the situation became explosive. At the same time, the West embarked on a course of colonialist expansion which brought to the fore all the elements and influences most particularly disliked by Moslems – government by non-Moslems, alcohol and drugs, a lack of respect for the family and for women. All these elements ran together in the twentieth century and produced a crisis of confrontation between the two cultures of which Arab Nationalism was the outward and visible expression.

The First World War, in this respect as in so many others, represented a turning point. Although the Arab world was still weak in almost every respect when compared with the West, the notion of 'the noble Arab' began to gain currency. This was to some extent, at least, the result of the exploits of figures like T. E. Lawrence, whose involvement in the campaigns against the Turks in Arabia was romanticized without much attention being given to the resentment which was bound to be created by turning one Moslem people, the inhabitants of the Arabian peninsula, against another Moslem people, the Turks, and which had not been forgotten by the time I grew to manhood. Indeed, some of the sympathy which some Arab and Moslem leaders showed towards Germany at the outset of the Second World War was the consequence of this still smouldering resentment.

The extent of the subjection of even those who were nominally leaders when appointed by the colonial powers is well demonstrated by a story which circulated about King Faisal I of Iraq, who had been put on his throne by the British after his expulsion from Damascus. The King had a friend, a well-known poet, who was especially close to him, and had immediate access to the King at all times. He was committed to the cause of Arab independence and was greatly admired by the young people of Baghdad. One day the students demonstrated, demanding the establishment of their own university; the government of the day had done nothing to meet their demands. The poet, using his right of access, went to the King and told him that unless he agreed to the creation of a university there would be a revolt.

'Listen, my friend,' said the King. 'You must understand this. I am an employee of the British Empire, in the grade of king. If you want to get them a university, go to the High Commissioner. If he says yes they'll get it; if not, not.'

The poet did as the King advised and the students indeed got their university. But the sort of dependence which the story reveals was deeply resented by Iraqis at all levels of society and was one of the factors which eventually led to the revolution which overthrew the monarchy.

After the end of the war in 1918, when the victorious Allies had imposed their ideas of nationhood on areas of the Arabic-speaking Middle East which had no previous experience of or desire for separation, it became evident to some of the more far-sighted of Arab leaders that Britain was considerably weakened, though many of the trappings of Imperial power were still in evidence. As the years passed, a new threat to the integrity of the Arab world appeared: the rise of political Zionism. This had first manifested itself in the latter part of the last century. With the persecution of the Jews in the Russian Empire, it was given new momentum as more and more European Jews made a home for themselves in Palestine.

This movement accelerated as a result very largely of the British giving expression and apparent support to the Zionist interest by the Balfour Declaration of 1917; and the rate of immigration into Palestine of people who were wholly alien to the Arabs increased alarmingly. The British, as the mandatory power with responsibility for the control of Palestine, seemed unable to stem the tide.

Violence broke out between the native Palestinian Arabs, Moslems and Christians alike, and the Jewish immigrants.

This situation was closely observed by Arab leaders, many of whom urged the British to limit the emigration of European Jews to Palestine; the British attempted to do so, but their efforts were generally feeble, certainly largely ineffective. By the latter part of the Second World War, just as I was growing to maturity, reports of the plight of the Jews in the lands under Nazi control gave fresh energy to their demands for the right to emigrate, and the Zionist movement began to secure powerful allies amongst the victorious powers as the war came to its end.

The events which led up to the proclamation of the Israeli state in 1948 gave an entirely new focus to the demand for the recognition of Arab aspirations. By the time that I became aware of the aims of the movement for Arab Nationalism, in Bahrain in the mid-forties and then when I was back in Dubai, the situation in Palestine and later the arrogant and repressive policies of the Israeli state, created the explosion of the anger which has dominated the politics of our region ever since.

In Bahrain itself, because of all the foreign influences which had poured into the islands as a result of the part which their economy was required to play in the operation of the war, vigorous and often outspoken debate was the rule wherever people met. Ideas began to circulate which, only a few years before, would have been unthinkable. The Bahrainis, who had always been an outward-looking people, the consequence of their age-old preoccupation with trade, now had more and more opportunities for travel and for meeting other Arabs from larger and politically more developed societies than their own, like Egypt, Iraq and Syria. Increasing numbers of them were being educated in centres such as Cairo, Damascus and Baghdad, where the levels of political awareness were higher by several orders of magnitude than was usually the case amongst their contemporaries at home.

Even in the early 1940s, Bahraini society was notable for the number of social and intellectual clubs where like-minded people could meet and debate the great issues of the day. This was a long-standing tradition in Bahrain, going back to the earlier years of the century. With the ideas which were abroad when I began to find my way around the clubs, they were exciting places for a young Dubaian to find himself.

The most outstanding of these places of discussion and association was undoubtedly the Bahrain Club in Muharraq, the sister to the main island of Bahrain. There the most lively local political activists had gravitated; there the most ambitious plans for the Gulf's future were explored. There I found myself, still in my teens, with men like AbdulAziz Al-Shemlan, Abdul Rahman Al-Bakir and Mahmoud Al-Meredi, all of whom were to be important figures in the development of the region's political awareness over the coming twenty years or so.

Political expression in Bahrain was not confined to debates in the clubs, however. From time to time there were demonstrations in the streets, largely directed against an oppressive foreign influence, particularly the British, on Bahraini affairs and on the free development of political expression. Such protest as there was, however, was generally well mannered. We rallied to hear the activists amongst us calling for change and urging the ruling authorities in Bahrain to allow some degree of free expression and, ultimately, participation. Long after I had left Bahrain, in the late 1950s, the leaders of the debates which we held at the Bahrain Club attained international celebrity when they were arrested and exiled to the remote island of St Helena, where Napoleon had been exiled and had eventually died. Curiously, at this time the British were accused by the Bahraini authorities of having been too supportive of the Committee which had been formed to press for political change in the country.

In the early 1960s, after the exiles had been released following an application to the Privy Council in London (and the payment of compensation to the one-time prisoners), AbdulAziz Al-Shemlan and AbdulAli Alowlaiwat, another of the activists, sought permission to move to Dubai with their families. However, the British authorities appear to have advised Shaikh Rashid not to give his consent, as to do so might offend Bahrain.[4]

The Bahrain Club had many attractions for a young man of my nature, anxious to extend himself and his knowledge of the world.

It had, for its time and place, a good library in which I immersed myself, continuing my self-directed education. It was in the Bahrain Club's library that I was first able to find books which told me of Arab history, of the contribution which the Arabs had made to the progress of humanity. I read deeply in Islamic studies also, thus augmenting both the groundwork of my earlier schooling in Dubai and my father's instruction.

It was also in Bahrain that I was first exposed to the influence of political writing, drawn from the magazines and journals, many of them of Egyptian origin, which were circulating in the Gulf, even in those comparatively early days. I recall magazines like *Al-Hilal*, *Al-Risaala* and *Al-Lataa'if al-Musawwara* (now called *Al-Musawwar*); these fed my increasing sense of common identity with all Arabs which I already recognized as the most significant aspect of the politics of my generation.

In particular, *Al-Musawwar* was to make a notable and quite unforeseen contribution to my future life. I was fascinated by the articles written by Fikri Abadha, praising the countryside of Britain, a land on which, of course, I had never laid eyes. He described the soft rains which fell, making the countryside green, in the sharpest of contrasts with the deserts with which I had grown up. Europe, he said, had ideas and secrets hidden, as it were, behind the curtain, which it would be in our interests to acquire. Politics apart, I could not have imagined then that forty years later I would buy a farm in that same green, rain-swept countryside.

My interests at the time were not only political, however. The Bahrain Club was also remarkable for producing plays which were performed in public. I took part in a number of these – an activity that I could never have anticipated undertaking in Dubai – which contributed much to my growing confidence and self-assurance; it also helped to increase my circle of friends, for I became known to more and more people as a result of my stage appearances. One quality I discovered that I possessed was an ability to mimic the manners and accents of the people around me, a faculty which has probably contributed to my ability to absorb languages quickly. I suspect that I have always retained something of the actor in my nature but nonetheless it was the Club's political dimension and the friends that I made there, who were themselves exploring such matters, that had the greatest effect on my life as it unfolded.

It was not long before I realized that I had absorbed all the knowledge and skills that the Post Office could give me. I had worked for it for about three and a half years and now I was getting restless; I also recognized that it was high time that I should think about returning home to my family whom I had not seen since leaving Dubai. One day, as I was sitting in the Post Office wondering what to do, one of the customers from a merchant firm who was collecting his mail, saw that I was preoccupied and, as if reading my thoughts, said that it looked as though it was time for me to go home. Why did I not think of applying for a job with the Imperial Bank of Iran, which he happened to know was planning to open a branch in Dubai? Thus I was introduced to an association which for me was to last for thirty-eight years.

It was clear that banking would become increasingly important in the post-war period which we were now entering. The Gulf states would need access to the most sophisticated sources of funding and investment which the international community had to offer, if they were to be able to undertake even the relatively modest levels of development which were beginning to be anticipated.

Despite its name, the Imperial Bank of Iran had become a thoroughly British institution. It had been founded in 1889 under the Qajar dynasty as the Imperial Bank of Persia; during one of the not infrequent financial crises which the Shah experienced, when the country's treasury was empty, the British acquired the bank's shares in return for a loan, thus putting themselves firmly in charge of Persia's economy. It became the Imperial Bank of Iran in 1935; in 1949, a while after I had joined the staff, it was renamed the British Bank of Iran and the Middle East and then, in 1952, the British Bank of the Middle East. Finally, in 1996 it assumed the marketing style of BritishBank.

It was suggested by my friends that, with my knowledge of English and the experience which working in Bahrain had given me, I would be of value to the bank and should apply for a position. In my best English handwriting (which even today I think to have been quite creditable for someone with my limited formal education) I wrote to the bank, seeking an appointment. I resigned from the Post Office though I had not yet received an offer from the bank. My friend AbdulAziz Al-Shemlan was an employee of the bank and had the job of recruiting staff for the planned Dubai branch; he promised to arrange for me to be taken on. I waited expectantly for a reply to my letter of application.

Three months went by and no offer was forthcoming; it appeared that despite Shemlan's assurances the complement of staff was filled. I used to spend part of my time in the shop of a Bahraini merchant, Yassin Mullah Ahmed, who was connected with the Kanoo family. He had a shop in the *souq* which sold haberdashery as well as perfumes and spices from India. He asked me why I seemed to have so much free time on my hands. I told him and he at once undertook to write to a friend of his, Jasim Khadmawi, who worked at the British Political Agency. At once things began to happen: Khadmawi spoke to George Keast, who was to be the Imperial Bank's manager in Dubai, and told him that there was this bright young Arab boy keen to join the bank and that they would be well advised to hire him, rather than some of the less appropriate candidates who were also seeking jobs there. My friend Mahmoud Meredi, telling me that at last my luck was rising, bought me a tie so that I would look my best for my interview; I met a Mr Burton, the manager of the bank in Bahrain, and received the offer of a six-month traineeship, at a salary of 145 rupees a month. I was now on the way to becoming a banker.

My period of training with the bank in Bahrain was not without its problems. My work in the Post Office had accustomed me to the organization and discipline of an office; I did not find the mechanics of banking, at least at the level at which I was working, especially demanding. My life was made miserable, however, by the person to whom I was attached for training. This was an Indian who, it appeared, was bitterly jealous of a Gulf national like me who, despite my youth, was obviously going to be favoured when the bank began operations in my homeland.

Matters came to a head when one day he deliberately pushed me as I was writing in one of the great ledgers which then formed the basis of the bank's records and accounting system. I was perched up on one of the high stools on which we sat. I had a pen of which I was particularly fond, an Eversharp which had been given to me as a present during the time when I was appearing on the stage of the Bahrain Club; on the same occasion I was given a length of rather vividly coloured suiting and two hundred Camel cigarettes. Many years later I was to remember this last gift when I found myself appointed agent by British American Tobacco Limited.

But it was the pen that I valued the most at that time. My Indian colleague's assault dislodged me from my perch, the pen fell to the ground and the nib broke. It was enough, I decided. I stormed in to see my superior, AbdulAziz Al-Shemlan, and protested at the manners and behaviour of the offending clerk. I could not go on, I said, if this was to be the way in which the affairs of the office would be conducted. AbdulAziz Al-Shemlan was evidently a wise man. 'Don't concern yourself about it,' he said. 'The time will come when you will rule over two thousand Indians.' In as much as my businesses today employ some two thousand people, mostly from the subcontinent, he was right.

As matters turned out, I was given the opportunity to open the branch in Dubai. I returned to my homeland – the first time since I had set out for Bahrain – by air, my first experience of flying. My time in Bahrain had fully accustomed me to wearing European dress; my wardrobe had expanded beyond the three shirts and two pairs of trousers and I had even acquired a hat. To my dismay, when the plane, a Sunderland Flying Boat, landed on the waters of the Creek, close to where the first bridge in the town was to be built, I saw my father waiting to greet me; I was so shaken by the sight of him that I left my hat, a very nice one, on board the aircraft. My father was horrified at my abandonment of Arab dress and, predictably, berated me with vigour; had I been wearing the hat, I hate to think what he might have done. As usual, it was my mother who eventually smoothed things over and my father, however reluctantly, accepted that I was not entirely lost to my origins.

3

THE ESTABLISHMENT OF THE Imperial Bank in Dubai is part of the region's background; it has been described in the official history of the British Bank of the Middle East, as it eventually became.[1] The bank had previously opened branches in Kuwait and Bahrain and in 1945 the directors in London heard that plans were afoot to set up a rival bank in the southern Gulf, backed by Indian and Iraqi interests, which would represent a serious degree of competition. Encouraged by the British representatives in the area (the bank always enjoyed close and frequently highly productive relations with the Foreign Office and its personnel on the ground), they moved quickly to establish a branch in Dubai.

An agreement was signed between the bank and the Ruler of Dubai, Shaikh Saeed bin Maktoum Al-Maktoum in January 1946. I arrived in October of the same year.

The first manager of the Imperial Bank was, as I have said, George Keast. He acquired a building – it was, in fact, two old warehouses – beside the Creek on the Deira side of the town. Conditions were pretty primitive but the atmosphere was good and we had the sense of pioneering a development which was to be of importance in the future prosperity of Dubai. As more staff were recruited to the branch, including expatriate British employees, a generally good atmosphere prevailed, something which evidently was not always the case in other branches of the bank in the region.

The bank's early days produced from time to time some surprising and amusing situations. When we first opened for business our premises were pretty simple, not to say, primitive. The two old warehouses which housed our offices were little more than large shops, with no services or facilities of any sort. Of course, there was no air-conditioning; our only relief from the appalling heat in the summer was provided by the *punkah* operated by a boy. Later on we were given a fan powered by kerosene; the *punkah* and the boy were more efficient.

The waters of the Creek came right up to the walls of our building. The only way of having a lavatory was for a platform with a seat to be slung on a sort of cantilever which was suspended over the water. It looked very much like the same sort of accommodation which could be seen mounted high in the stern of the old pearling boats.

The Post Office announced that it was introducing new letter-boxes with a slit into which mail could be dropped for collection. One day, a Persian merchant sent his son to post twelve letters. The young man rowed across the Creek to where he believed the new postal arrangements were located. He could find nothing that fitted his idea of a letter-box but he remembered that, when he found it, the box would have an opening into which the mail could be dropped. He continued to row, looking everywhere for it. Suddenly, he saw what he concluded was the object of his search: a structure suspended over the Creek with a conveniently placed opening in it. Without hesitation he posted his mail in our lavatory.

In the morning we arrived to open the bank. The entrance to the lavatory was secured with an iron bar to prevent anyone from making their way into the bank illicitly. When this was removed and the door opened, there was the merchant's mail, distributed on the floor. We asked him why he had posted his letters in our lavatory but he did not seem to find our question at all amusing.

My salary was 175 rupees a month when I took up my appointment at the bank; in Dubai in 1946 this was a substantial income. About six months after I had started working for the bank, my salary and the salaries of my Arab colleagues were increased by

10 rupees a month; even by the modest standards of Dubai at the time this was hardly princely and none of us, who came from families of some standing, regarded 10 rupees as an amount worth getting excited about.

One day George Keast, whose office was divided from the rest of us by a pink curtain, called me to him. He asked whether I had noticed any difference in my monthly pay. I had no idea what he was talking about and looked at him blankly. With some degree of exasperation he asked me whether I was not grateful for the 10-rupee increase which he had awarded me. Realizing now what was expected of me, I thanked him and returned to my desk.

My colleagues wanted to know why Keast had asked to see me. I decided that I was not going to be the only one singled out for this treatment, so I told them he was extremely hurt that none of us had thanked him for the increase and that any employee who failed to offer his thanks in the next ten minutes would be instantly dismissed. One by one, my colleagues trooped into the manager's office and with suitable humility, thanked him for his generosity. The significance of the procession was not, I suspect, lost on Keast.

When my colleagues returned I reminded them of the fable of the desert fox who, raiding a farmer's kitchen, was caught by the farmer's wife who cut off his tail. When he returned to his companions they all laughed at him for the loss of his tail. However, the fox extolled the riches of the farmer's kitchen and urged the other foxes to make the best of the opportunity to enjoy them. One by one the foxes went to the kitchen and, one by one, the farmer's wife cut off their tails. I felt that I did not need to labour the point for my colleagues to understand it.

Our life at the bank was full of incident, often the product of our customers' unfamiliarity with the ways of banks and bankers. Much of our work in the early days was concerned with the remittances and general business of the many merchants from the Indian subcontinent who were trading in Dubai. At this time all of our currency dealings were in coin; the rupees were bagged up in lots of 2,000, as I recall it, the responsibility for which was given to one of our few local employees. He, poor man, had some difficulty in understanding the instructions of the manager as to how he wanted the cash counted. So exasperated did the manager become that he struck the man across the face with the bag which had contained the coins; our poor member of staff accepted this brutal treatment without complaint, for the job was important to him and the support of his family.

Although many of our British colleagues were fine men, and many became my friends, there were some individuals who maintained what I might call a more 'colonial' attitude towards their work and the people with whom they had to deal. The incident with the bag of rupees was such an event. Another of our managers, though still quite young, was also very harsh and authoritarian in his manner to the bank's employees and even, on occasion, to some of its customers; this was demonstrated to me one day in a particularly alarming episode.

One of our customers amongst the subcontinental community was concerned with the residue of the once-rich pearl trade, which had shrunk to the movement of a few thousand pearls a year to India. The bank was responsible for sending the remittances for the pearls, paying them against invoices. It was my task to check all the documents relating to the letters of credit against the entries in the large, heavily bound ledgers in which our records were kept. On this occasion, about a third of the documents were missing. When I pointed this out to the merchant he became very agitated and insisted that it was of no importance and that the full amount should be paid forthwith. I, equally, refused for I knew that he was trying to persuade me to a wholly incorrect course of action.

Now it happened that the manager's office was adjacent to where I sat. He had had the intervening door removed, I suspect in order to make sure that I did not get up to any mischief. In consequence, he heard all of my exchange with the Indian merchant.

'Easa, bring me the ledger,' he said, rather grandly. I did so at once. He examined it carefully, ticking off each document as he identified it.

'Easa,' he said at last, 'send this man to me.' I indicated to the merchant that he should enter the manager's office. 'Mr Easa is entirely correct,' the manager announced. 'One-third of the documents are missing. We cannot complete the transaction.'

At once the merchant began to protest vehemently, his words tumbling over each other. The manager was unmoved. The merchant continued his protest, becoming more and more agitated. Suddenly the manager slammed the great ledger closed. To my horror he raised it high and brought it down firmly on the head of the still-arguing merchant. The manager turned to me. 'Easa,' he said, 'give instructions for this person to be removed from my office.' He returned to his papers.

I was, quite literally, speechless. I had a bell on my desk with which I used to summon the office's more lowly assistants. I rang it frantically and indeed kept on ringing it as the staff ran to my office. 'We're here, we're here,' they shouted to me. All that I could do was gesture, since I appeared to have lost all powers of speech by this time but, understanding the situation, the porters dragged the prostrate Indian from the manager's presence.

There were grave consequences of this action for the bank itself. The Indian merchant was, not surprisingly, incensed by the rough treatment and humiliation to which he had been subjected. He obtained the support of a number of his compatriots, also trading in the Trucial States at the time, and urged them to lobby for another bank to be invited into the region, whose managers might not be so handy with their ledgers. They secured the interest of the Eastern Bank, which was given a licence to operate by the Ruler of Sharjah, Dubai's immediate neighbour. In consequence, the monopoly which the British Bank of the Middle East had thus far enjoyed and by which its directors set much store, was broken. The Eastern Bank established itself in Sharjah and was soon to open a branch in Dubai. The British Bank was now obliged to face competition where previously it had had a clear field, an experience which did not please it at all.

The same manager was involved in another incident, this time with a junior member of our own staff who came, I believe, from Ceylon, as Sri Lanka was called in those days. This man was greatly impressed by the fact that the fishermen caught huge quantities of a small, sardine-like fish called *doma*, which were dried and exported in large quantities each year.[2] He decided that there was money to be made exporting dried *doma* to India.

He tried to interest the other employees in our office in this project, which he assured us would very quickly make a great deal of money for all involved. I was one of the first whom he approached but I was dubious about it and decided not to join in it. No doubt thinking that I was very unenterprising, he went ahead, having persuaded some other colleagues to invest.

Some time later, on entering the office early one morning, I was greeted by a strange sight. The office looked out directly on to the Creek. In front of its windows were iron bars and moored to the bars were six large fishing boats, piled high with *doma*. I did not know what had happened; perhaps our colleague from Ceylon had failed to pay the fishermen, but in any event they had evidently decided that they had grounds for some form of protest.

All day the boats and their cargo stood in the blazing sun. The next day they were still there and by this time the fish were in an advanced stage of decomposition; the stench was appalling. The manager must have been away when the boats first appeared, but now he returned. 'Easa!' he screamed. 'What in God's name is going on?' I did not want to betray my colleagues who had unwisely involved themselves with their Sri Lankan friend, and I tried to plead ignorance.

The manager persisted, however, and gradually the story came out. In the meantime, ever resourceful, he took a knife and slashed the mooring ropes which tied the boats to our windows. Slowly, majestically, they drifted into the Creek, taking with them their rotting cargo and the hopes for sudden riches of those who had invested in the scheme. Its principal instigator was swiftly dismissed and sent back to his homeland, a poorer but perhaps a wiser man.

I was one of seven employees and, in 1950, after a comparatively short time, I became a commercial assistant and was appointed an officer in the 'B' grade, then the highest status of any of the bank's Gulf employees. Although I was only twenty-two, this meant that I was empowered to sign on the bank's behalf; I prepared drafts of letters and documents and, of course, I often acted as interpreter with our Arab clients. No other Gulf national had, at this time, been given such responsibility. The official history of the bank contains some generous comments about the contribution to its

success made by the youthful Easa Saleh Al-Gurg.[3] I was appointed
to the 'A' grade in 1954.

For me, the next fifteen years represented a period of unremitting
dedication in my work for the bank. In this I was motivated both
by a strong sense of loyalty to the bank, from which I never
wavered, and by a determination to restore my family's fortunes at
least to what they had been in the days of their residence in Lingah.
I knew that I was the only one capable of achieving this, so I set
out resolutely to make money. I was determined, however, that
whatever I did would be honourable and honest; I knew well the
opportunities which there were for making a lot of money quickly
if you were not too scrupulous about your methods. I decided that
this was not for me and I never had any reason to regret that the
principles which my parents in particular had instilled into me
made me follow this course in the conduct of my life.

During the fifties and sixties life in Dubai was still very quiet,
compared even with Bahrain. We were much governed by routine,
working at the bank in the morning, returning home for lunch,
followed by a siesta; in the evening a few like-minded friends
would go down to the beach, to recite poetry and to talk, like
young men everywhere, of the future. It was a time which, as I have
said, had a quality of innocence about it; our pleasures were simple
and our lives relatively austere. We had many friends from the
expatriate Arab community as well as the Westerners who lived
amongst us. I used to visit the officers' mess in Sharjah where I was
made welcome; by and large we had few complaints about our
lives.

My work at the bank brought me into close contact with all sorts
and conditions of people who were beginning to appear in Dubai,
including merchants, entrepreneurs, officials, foreign businessmen;
not all of them were of the highest probity, and it was my job to
assess their creditworthiness. In this task I always pursued a cautious
policy, believing that I was not employed by the bank to take
unreasonable or unwise risks with their money.

This failed to make me very popular with the more dubious
types who sought the bank's services and help. I made enemies of

those who felt that I was too harsh in assessing their potentialities; but I knew that in many cases the bank would never have seen any of their loaned money again. Because I was seen to be a smart young man, who enjoyed life as well as maintaining a strict business and professional code, inevitably there were also those who were envious of me.

I became close to the British, both the business community, such as it was, and the officials at the Political Agency. To those who wanted to discredit me, this was evidence that I was a creature of the British, whose influence was often resented; a resentment which was not discouraged by the representatives of other nations who did not have the long-standing relationships which the British enjoyed.

Because of my English and perhaps because of my generally outgoing disposition, I was frequently invited to lunch with important foreign customers visiting the bank and to dinner at the Agency with the officials, politicians and journalists who came their way. I was grateful to my British friends for the opportunities such occasions gave me to meet new and often influential people, which helped to redress the sense of disadvantage I sometimes felt in my own community.

However, this access to the more sophisticated circles in our small society excited in particular the envy of one local employee of the Agency. He was a Persian but was possessed of few social graces. He was furious when, as I shall relate later, I was sent to England on a British Council bursary. I was being sent there, he told anyone in Dubai who would listen, 'to study spying'.

My father observed my growing prosperity and independence with what were, perhaps, predictable misgivings. He was aware of the life which I was leading and generally disapproved of it. One of his most deep-seated causes for anxiety was my failure to get myself married.

There was no special reason why I had so far failed to take this step, other than that as well as enjoying myself I was so thoroughly involved in my work. But the pressures on an elder son to marry are great and I was aware of my father's wishes.

I had an uncle, a wise and deeply religious man. He came to me one day and recited texts from the Quran which the devout believed would change the heart of the most recalcitrant sinner. Whether this was the case I cannot say, but one morning I awoke knowing that I would agree to my father's promptings and get myself married. I was equally certain that it would not work.

My father had chosen for me a girl in Kuwait, a relative and the daughter of a man with whom he had done business in the days of his prosperity. She was a nice, kindly girl but she did not have the same outlook on life that I had nor was she educated as I now was.

Matters were brought to a head by the death of my father; he died suddenly of a thrombosis. By this time I was engaged to the girl from Kuwait, though we had still not met. I could, of course, have called it all off but in our society the engagement is almost of the status of marriage and it would have gone hard with her had I done so. I suddenly became very ill with a paralysing condition known to us as *hagar bagar*. I feared that it was a judgement on my delay and so I decided the time had come. With my mother, brothers, some friends and a few of our remaining servants, I sailed to Kuwait and there was married, still feeling distinctly unwell. Shaikh Rashid had generously given me 2,000 rupees for the expenses of the wedding.

I returned to Dubai with my wife and settled down to married life. She was a good and diligent partner who gave me four children, whom I love very much. We remained married for the rest of her life, which sadly ended late in 1995.

However, I would not be entirely truthful if I did not relate that the idea of marriage had appealed to me long before. I had a cousin, from a prominent family at one time resident on the Persian coast like us, but who had for some time been living in India, where she was born. I have already related the harsh treatment which her father had received from his own father when he tried to deal in a kindly manner with the poor farmers who worked the family's land. My cousin had been educated in an entirely European manner, in a convent. To my father this indicated that she had fallen under the influence of infidels and that her children would no longer be Moslems. He adamantly opposed the idea of my marrying her and she was married by her family to a rich husband, somewhat older than herself.

They lived in Dubai and so we kept in touch, though we both observed the proprieties. However, the day came when she announced that she could no longer continue with a marriage which she believed was wholly wrong. She came to me and, as my cousin, asked for my help and protection. I tried to persuade her to change her mind, as I felt it my duty to do, but she was certain that it was the right course. In the fullness of time she and her husband were divorced and we married, with the approval and encouragement of my first wife who recognized that Soraya was destined for me, but with some reservation from Soraya's parents, who thought that she, who had been accustomed to the very best of standards, would find herself living in a mud house with a man who had no degree and, at that time at least, no wealth to speak of.

As matters turned out, her family's fears proved to be unfounded. We have lived happily ever after and my wife is my closest friend, most trusted adviser and my support in all that I do.

I have said that I was cautious in all the dealings which I undertook on the bank's behalf with our customers. There was one person at this time, however, who I was quite happy to allow to exploit my association with the bank, as indeed was the bank itself; this was the Ruler of Dubai, Shaikh Rashid bin Saeed Al-Maktoum. My growing contact and intimacy with Shaikh Rashid had its origins long before he became Ruler in 1958; he had, as I have noted already, assumed many of the responsibilities of the Rulership before his father's death and was set upon the development of his state. I was determined to do all that I could to help him realize this objective.[4]

Working with Shaikh Rashid in these early years was an exciting and rewarding experience. He had that ability, so vital in a political leader, of making men work for him for no other reason than that they wanted to do so and because they shared his ideals. At this time, working for the development of Dubai had about it a quality of comradeship amongst all of us, Shaikh Rashid included, which was especially happy. All of us felt that we were part of the same enterprise, that Shaikh Rashid was as much a part of us as we were of him. A request from Shaikh Rashid for advice or action would be responded to by all of us 'at the double'.

At this point in my career with the bank, an episode occurred which was to be a foretaste of the way in which it was to take shape in the future. Part of my duties involved from time to time travelling to Abu Dhabi, some six hours' rough journey by Land Rover up the coast; there were, of course, no tarmac roads at that time. I had often sailed along the coast to Abu Dhabi with my father in the course of his pearl business, small though it was by that time. Now the bank was keen to open a branch in Abu Dhabi for already it was known that oil in commercial quantities was to be found there.

I was on close and friendly terms with the sons of the Ruler of Abu Dhabi, Shaikh Shakhbut bin Sultan Al-Nahayan. Often his sons and I would slip away from the Ruler's eye and spend many happy hours talking about the future. Although overshadowed by his exceptional brother Shaikh Zayed bin Sultan Al-Nahayan who eventually succeeded him, Shaikh Shakhbut was a remarkable man, of shrewd perception with a type of primitive wisdom, the expression of which sometimes bewildered those who experienced it, for it was often couched in ways very much his own. I used to take our English manager to call on Shaikh Shakhbut in his *majlis* and it was the manager's devout hope that one day the Shaikh would give his consent to the founding of a branch bank.

Shaikh Shakhbut, unfortunately, had a profound distrust of banks, banking and bankers. However, I think it is true to say that he got on with me more easily than with many of the people whom he met. He would take me hunting into the desolate region called Abu-Muraikha, where it seemed that not even a rabbit was to be found. He always pronounced my name 'Al-Jerj'.

All of us, Shaikh Shakhbut's sons and the executives of the bank and the oil company which was exploring in the shaikhdom, were keen to see development of the little state begin. Shaikh Shakhbut, however, was very cautious in permitting anything which might disturb his people's traditional way of life. He knew that I carried with me a paper on which was drafted an agreement between himself and the bank, which would allow the bank to establish a presence in Abu Dhabi; he firmly refused to discuss it.

We spent many days in the desert among the sparse shrubs and plentiful scorpions; the Shaikh was amused that these creatures, which the others feared because they were constantly being stung by them, seemed never to sting me. I liked to think that it was because the scorpions were my friends.

When we went hunting, Shaikh Shakhbut had a little white tent in which he slept and which contained only his bed. The rest of us, his sons, his retainers and I, slept as best we could on the sands, each wrapped in his *bisht* (the finely woven cloak which all Arab men wear over the *thob*, the long outer garment that is the customary dress), having placed around us branches of the meagre shrubs to act as some sort of wind-break.

One one occasion Shaikh Shakhbut's cousin, Shaikh Hamdan bin Mohammed Al-Nahayan, joined us, bringing with him a large tarpaulin tent of a particularly bright shade of green. He saw us crouching on the ground and said that we were living like poor Bedu; he invited us into his tent. We were a great deal more comfortable than we had been.

On the third night a typhoon struck. The tent collapsed with us inside it, to Shaikh Hamdan's considerable amusement. In the morning, when the typhoon had blown itself out, we breakfasted as usual with Shaikh Shakhbut. He remarked that although my complexion was fair and my skin looked delicate, it was 'as thick as an elephant's'. Suddenly he asked, where was my paper? I produced it instantly and he signed it. The Abu Dhabi branch of BBME was eventually opened in February 1959.

Life with Shaikh Shakhbut was seldom dull. As it became apparent that the outside world was beginning to intrude on the placid life of the Trucial States, the British decided that it was time for a degree of modern organization to be adopted by what, up to this point, had been the most traditional of societies. I was asked by the Political Agency to persuade Shaikh Shakhbut's son, Shaikh Sultan, to establish an office for the Abu Dhabi Municipality of which he was the official head. Shaikh Sultan was much in awe of his father but he agreed and we set about creating the municipal office. This consisted of a deserted house on the beach which had belonged to one of the families who had left Abu Dhabi when the pearling collapsed. We placed a table, a chair and a filing cabinet in it and painted the exterior with Snowcem, a white cement-based liquid. On some empty oil drums, which we set up outside the office, we painted a sign which read 'Government of Abu Dhabi – Municipal Office'. All went well until one day I received a frantic message from Shaikh Sultan to come to him at once.

I drove to Abu Dhabi to find the young Shaikh in a state of panic. Shaikh Shakhbut had announced his intention of paying a visit to the municipal office the next day. I calmed Shaikh Sultan down and prepared him for his father's visitation. I told him to seat the Ruler in the chair as soon as he arrived and to take up his place behind him. I, as a humble bank employee, would stand some distance away.

Shaikh Shakhbut arrived and took his place in the chair. 'What is that cabinet?' he asked in his thin, reedy voice.

'It is for files,' said Shaikh Sultan, nervously.

'Bring me three of these files,' said the Shaikh; Shaikh Sultan did so. 'And what is that writing on the files?' Shaikh Shakhbut enquired.

'Government of Abu Dhabi – Municipal Office,' replied Shaikh Sultan.

'I see,' said Shaikh Shakhbut. 'Do you imagine that there is another government in Abu Dhabi, apart from your father? Get some kerosene and burn the files at once. I know,' he went on, 'it's that Al-Jerj who has put you up to this.'

I rushed into the *souq* and bought a half-drum of kerosene. We made a bonfire of the files on the beach. Shaikh Shakhbut waited until the flames rose high over the pile of files and then he drove away. I announced that I was returning immediately to Dubai and that I would not be coming back for some time.

Shaikh Shakhbut's consent for the opening of the branch was a great coup for the bank and a triumph for me. I was rewarded by being nominated for a British Council scholarship to England which was to prove another high point in my life. At the initiative of Peter Tripp, the Political Agent in Dubai at the time, I was fortunate enough to be given a six-month bursary from the British Council to go to London to take an advanced course in the English language. The bank also contributed to my support as obviously I now represented something of an investment to them.

I set out for London in the latter part of 1956, this time flying from Bahrain in, I think, a Britannia, on the long flight to London. The journey took some eighteen hours and we stopped constantly to refuel; it was a tremendous excitement for me. We arrived safely in London at Heathrow airport, which was small and poorly equipped by today's standards but which then represented the utmost sophistication in civil aviation.

I had no idea what I was supposed to do; somehow, no one in Dubai had thought to tell me what to expect or how to get myself from Heathrow into London. By another of those fortunate chances with which my life has been blessed, Mohammed Kanoo, from a prominent Bahraini family, was on the same aircraft and, knowing my father, he took me under his wing. I was driven into London in style in the Kanoo limousine, to Victoria station where Mohammed Kanoo had correctly judged that my escort would be waiting.

My escort turned out to be a tall, thin, retired official from the Admiralty, who performed this function for the British Council. We took the Underground – another amazing experience – and headed for Tavistock Square, near the British Museum. Here I was accommodated for the next two weeks in conditions of what were, for me, considerable luxury at the Tavistock Hotel.

My fortnight in the Tavistock was designed to introduce me to the refinements of British life. I survived the challenges of my first stay in London and at the end of the time we set out on a journey, by coach, to Scotland and the Lake District. This experience served to make me fall in love with the reality of the English countryside; up to this time I had only read about it.

On my return to London we set out again, this time for the mysterious-sounding Tooting Bec, which was to be my home for the next six months. There I was handed into the care of Mrs Anne Turner, who was to be my landlady whilst I was in Britain.

Mrs Turner was a rather fierce lady, so it seemed to me, though later she was to become a friend. She had rigid rules about the running of her house and the behaviour of the foreign students for whom she provided accommodation. These were set out in a 'Yellow Book', a guide to manners and what was expected of us, which had been compiled and produced by the British Council. Each of Mrs Turner's guests had been given a copy and was required to study it.

The house at Tooting Bec was 48 Drakefield Road. I was shown to the room which was to be mine. It was furnished with a very old sofa, a very old carpet and a bed which looked as uncomfortable as it proved to be. 'Do you like it?' I was asked.

'Fantastic,' I said. I have always believed that one of the Arabs' failings is the capacity to delude themselves as much as they delude others.

Each day I travelled by Underground to central London to attend lectures at the British Council. In Tooting I studied the 'Yellow Book'. This was full of instructions relating to the behaviour which was expected from us: no visitors in our rooms, High Tea punctually at five o'clock (later, and it was whisked away), helping with the washing-up. In this last duty I managed early on to break a cup and saucer, since washing-up was not a skill I had previously acquired. I was told that I was too clumsy to be allowed to do it again, a circumstance which my fellow guests thought revealed that I was craftier than I looked. We were not allowed in Mrs Turner's sitting room but were obliged to speak to her from the kitchen.

One important, if unwelcome, discovery that I made was that I was expected to do my own laundry. I found this very difficult as at home there was always a servant, even in our reduced circumstances, who fulfilled such tasks. I discovered from Mrs Turner that I should take my clothes to be washed at the launderette; what, I wondered, was that? She gave me instructions on how to find it. I crept out, carrying my clothes to be washed, thankful that no one would know who I was.

I found the launderette. Mrs Turner had indicated, with a circular motion of her hand, the basic principle of the operation of a washing machine. The assistant in charge told me that I should use number 5. I had not the least idea what she meant, and was totally paralysed with embarrassment and humiliation. A kindly woman, seeing my evident bewilderment, took pity on me and explained the workings of the machines.

It was clear that the time had come for some sharp Arabian thinking. I marched into Mrs Turner's sitting room, ignoring her protests, and demanded to know how much she was receiving from the British Council for my upkeep; reluctantly, she told me that it was £3.15s. a week. I offered her an extra £2.00 a week to look after my laundry and to relieve me of any responsibility for the washing-up. Mrs Turner made a proper show of reluctance, but when I returned that evening it was evident that she had accepted what she insisted on calling our 'deal'. We became great friends.

Life at Drakefield Road was pretty spartan for Mrs Turner's lodgers. Our five o'clock tea was not generously provisioned: fried eggs and chips, poached eggs and chips, and baked beans and chips seemed to be the limits of Mrs Turner's catering. However, she had two large dogs of which, in the way of the English as I discovered, she was extremely fond. The dogs were splendidly fed, dining each day on choice cuts of meat. One of our fellow boarders was an Iraqi, from Basra, a member of a rich family who had been sent by his father to learn English. Those of us who came from the Gulf were too polite to say anything about the discrepancy in our catering arrangements and those of the dogs. No such inhibitions restrained our Iraqi colleague, however. He demanded of Mrs Turner why the dogs should be fed better than us. 'Because,' she said firmly, 'they are poor dumb animals.'

Years later, I was talking with a friend who had become enthusiastic about the possibility of reincarnation, and he asked me how I would choose to return. I did not share his belief but the memory of my weeks at Mrs Turner's house came flooding back. 'I would choose,' I said, 'to be reincarnated and live as a dog in an English family's house.'

At the headquarters of the bank I was taken through all departments. It soon became evident that I had more than an average understanding of the way the bank operated and the nature of my work in Dubai. I attended lectures in the English language and literature; more horizons were opened up for me. If Bahrain had been a revelation, England, and London in particular, was full of amazing experiences. The scale of everything – the people in the streets, the traffic, the miles and miles of houses, the huge shops – created a sense of the great world as I had never been able to imagine it before. I was excited by the cinemas and the theatres, the like of which I had never seen. My addiction to the Arabic cinema, fostered in Bahrain, was now extended to American and British movies of which I found that I had a bewildering choice.

Looking back, I realize that my taste turned very much towards films which dealt with the historical past, films like Robert Bolt's *A Man for All Seasons*, which deeply impressed me with the character of Sir Thomas More whose principles eventually led him to the scaffold. I loved *The Wives of Henry VIII* and, on a less serious level, films like *My Fair Lady* and, from a slightly earlier time though I had not encountered it before, *Gone with the Wind*. It was a happy and fulfilling time for me.

Though I think I was by inclination a socialist, at least in matters relating to the protection of the disadvantaged and the equality of the individual, I was less captivated by the evidence of the creeping paralysis of socialism in Britain at the time; as I saw it, the growth of the power of the state and its capacity to interfere in the lives of ordinary people. I was asked by the British Council executive who was responsible for me how I had enjoyed my stay in Britain. Very much, I assured him, but then I could not contain the comment that everywhere I could see the evidence of socialist influences in British life and society but, nonetheless, as soon as the British came to our part of the world they became ardent capitalists. The British Council officials were much amused.

One of the places in London that I used to visit was the Institute of Dancing; I spent my last evening there before leaving London. I never thought that I would return, for how could I possibly afford the expense? We danced to the hit tunes of the day and I remember asking the band to play the popular number 'Bye-bye Love, Bye-bye Happiness'. It was my farewell to England; I did not know then that it would become my second home, the focus of much of my business life and, ultimately, the location of my post as the ambassador of my country. Only a year after my farewell to

England, I was back, and hardly a year has passed since then when I have not returned.

The experience of England was so great and I had so much to absorb, so many new impressions crowding in on me, that I had little time for political discussions or the opportunity for the pursuit of my political interests. However, the year of my visit to the United Kingdom was 1957 and the country was in something of a political turmoil, one of the principal causes of which was the invasion of Suez at the end of the previous year, and the consequences which stemmed from it. In our eyes, the architect of the Suez catastrophe was the British Prime Minister, Anthony Eden; he had resigned early in the year and had been succeeded by Harold Macmillan. We regarded Eden's departure from office as a victory for what Nasser and Arab Nationalism represented. I was shocked by the abuse of Nasser and the Arabs in which the British press of the day so readily engaged; I tried to persuade my English friends that the picture presented by the press was not at all how it really was. But mine was only one small voice and the interests which were supporting the attacks on Nasser and the Arabs were very great.

Macmillan, too, was often regarded as being hostile to the Arab world. I was interested to learn, therefore, many years later, that in a private conversation late one night with his intimates, with whom he used to sit and talk of all the issues of the day, rather in the manner of an Arab shaikh, the conversation turned to Abdul Nasser. 'You know,' Macmillan was reported as saying, 'we could work with that fellow Nasser; I think he's one of us.' As in his heart Nasser was deeply conservative, it was a perceptive statement; the comment was passed privately to the Egyptian Embassy, where it was received enthusiastically. Unhappily, however, the interests which were concerned to keep Egypt apart from Britain and the West intervened and ensured that nothing came of it. Perhaps nothing would have been done, but I wonder if yet another opportunity was not lost.

I went back to Dubai with my mind full of the opportunities for the improvement of social and economic conditions in the country which I had seen whilst I was in England. My usefulness as an interpreter meant that I attended all the important meetings between the bank's executives and its customers. These included meetings with Shaikh Rashid bin Saeed Al-Maktoum, who became the Ruler of Dubai in 1958. My father had always been close to the Ruler's family and from an early age he took me to the Ruler's *majlis* and those of other leading shaikhs. When I came to deal with them on the bank's behalf and to translate for them, I was readily accepted by them, despite my youth, as someone who could be trusted. I was to become very close to Shaikh Rashid as the years went on and he was to play a major part in my life as it unfolded.

My career with the bank prospered; I was promoted through successive grades until I became Assistant Manager. Eventually I became the bank's Representative in Dubai and, as such, its principal adviser.

Sadly, on the other hand, the bank's relationship with Shaikh Shakhbut of Abu Dhabi was not always to be a happy one. This was mainly the consequence, I believe, of his difficulty in understanding the role of bankers in the modern world and of his inherent resistance to change. The events which I am about to relate, though they belong, strictly speaking, to a later part of my narrative, and which were of great importance to our part of the world, came about in this way.

Shaikh Shakhbut wanted to buy some Holland and Holland rifles and a generator. He turned to the bank and asked for our help which of course we were happy to give, on normal banking terms. We ordered the rifles and the generator and they were delivered to Shaikh Shakhbut. He put the generator between the two forts which at that time stood by the Muqta bridge.

Time passed. The bank asked for payment but it became apparent that Shaikh Shakhbut had no intention of repaying what was owed, regarding the rifles and the generator as a form of gift made to the Ruler of the State by a company which was in his debt for having granted it a licence to trade.

We made representations to the Shaikh which served only to make him angry. He had in his employment a very decent and honest man, Darwish bin Karem, who had the unenviable task of managing the Ruler's finances; he led the prayers in the mosque and kept Shaikh Shakhbut's simple accounts. Shaikh Shakhbut now insisted that BBME had stolen from him money which the bank was holding for him on deposit. He tried to frighten poor Darwish bin Karem into agreeing that the bank was at fault; this he refused to do. Shaikh Shakhbut was furious and I was fearful for Darwish bin Karem's safety. Shaikh Shakhbut demanded of him, 'Has the bank stolen my money?'

Darwish bin Karem replied, 'I swear upon God that they have not done so.'

Shaikh Shakhbut became angrier still.

I felt that I had to intervene to protect Darwish bin Karem. I asked the Shaikh to attach any blame to me and not to his servant, who had done the best that he could, always to protect the Shaikh's interests. As a solution, I proposed that as the Egyptians were at the time the enemies of the British, he should commission a panel of three Egyptian accountants to examine the books and report on the bank's handling of his affairs; at least he could be sure that they would not unduly favour so British an institution as BBME. 'I don't need Egyptians to tell me that your bank has stolen my money,' was Shaikh Shakhbut's response.

By this time the issue between the Shaikh and the bank had become widely known. News of it had reached Whitehall, and the Foreign Office expressed considerable anxiety about the course of events, for they feared that if Shaikh Shakhbut expelled BBME, as indeed he was threatening to do, it could prejudice British interests in the state generally at the time when Abu Dhabi's oil revenues were becoming very considerable, with the promise of vast amounts more in the future. British companies had important interests at stake, both in the extraction of Abu Dhabi's oil and in the development of the state's infrastructure which, by the agreement of everyone except Shaikh Shakhbut, was long overdue.

The confrontation between the bank and the Shaikh was finally resolved by the intervention of Sir Alec Kirkbride, one of the bank's directors who understood the mentality of a traditional Ruler like Shaikh Shakhbut; by appealing to the ties of friendship, he restored relations between them. Shaikh Shakhbut, however reluctantly, accepted that BBME had not stolen his money and that the request for payment for the rifles and the generator was justified.

The episode had demonstrated how difficult it was becoming for the outside world to deal with Shaikh Shakhbut. As he grew older he became, if anything, more difficult and less reasonable. He bitterly resented the changes which he knew would come to his state and his people once the oil revenues began to flow; he also resisted change for its own sake. Later, in Chapter 7, I shall describe how Shaikh Shakhbut was deposed from the Rulership and succeeded by his brother, Shaikh Zayed bin Sultan Al-Nahayan, to the immeasurable benefit of the people of Abu Dhabi and of the Trucial coast as a whole.

My interests at this time, however, were primarily with Dubai and with the bank's fortunes in my native city which was beginning to develop rapidly under the enthusiastic rule of Shaikh Rashid. The bank prospered also, and became involved in a variety of activities, including providing support for the first hospital in the state, the Maktoum Hospital, which was opened in 1950; I sat on its management committee, as the nominee of the Dubai Government.

An important project for the future prosperity of Dubai was the dredging of the Creek. The experience of Sharjah which, prior to the silting-up of its Creek, had every advantage and might well have become the commercial centre of the southern Gulf, had shown how important it was to have unimpeded access to a port whose facilities allowed the direct unloading of merchandise without having to be dependent always on the use of tenders. The eventual establishment of modern port facilities for Dubai and the provision of deep water to permit modern seacraft to load and unload were among the most significant decisions taken by Shaikh Rashid and his advisers.

The project was initiated in 1954, before Shaikh Rashid actually became Ruler and was still acting for his father. With the support and encouragement of the British authorities, the bank guaranteed a loan which was secured from the Government of Kuwait for the work to be carried out, for which a leading firm of British consultants, Sir William Halcrow and Partners, was retained. I became a friend of their principal in Dubai, Neville Allen, whom I respected and who always impressed me by the sincerity of his concern for Dubai. The help which the Government of Kuwait gave to Dubai at this time was one of the first instances when one of the wealthier states in the Gulf had assisted one of the less fortunate – as, at least in financial terms, Dubai could then be said to be.[5]

Later, the bank also handled the share issue for the Dubai Electricity Company; after the visit of Shaikh Rashid to London in 1959, when I accompanied him, the bank's agreement with the Government of Dubai was further extended. As a result, it increased its own operations in the state. It came as something of a shock, therefore, to the directors when licences were granted for the establishment of what became the National Bank of Dubai and for a competitive American bank.[6] But these things happen and one has to live with them. In fact, BBME always enjoyed a special relationship with Dubai and its Government and shared fully in its development over the years to come.

Although he was a good deal older than I was, Shaikh Rashid liked me, I believe, because I had a quick mind and could usually see several moves ahead in any negotiation or deal that we might be discussing or undertaking. We also got on very well together at a purely personal level and I spent many hours each week in his *majlis*, often talking till midnight, discussing the events in the world outside Dubai and the plans which we were formulating for its future.

Shaikh Rashid himself, though he was deeply conservative, liked modern ideas. He was in many ways a remarkable man; though little educated in a conventional sense, he possessed legendary astuteness and faculties of judgement. At an early age he became actively involved in the Government of Dubai, often deputizing for his father, Shaikh Saeed. He realized that in order to survive, Dubai had to establish itself as the foremost commercial centre in the Gulf, and all his energies were directed towards this aim. This was long before there was any suggestion that Dubai would become oil rich; when the oil did come Shaikh Rashid still maintained the customs and attitudes of mind of a merchant prince. He would have been entirely at home in Venice or Florence in the fifteenth or sixteenth centuries, and his understanding of the importance to Dubai of creating the sort of conditions in which trade could flourish, provided a secure basis for Dubai's future when a finite resource like oil would be exhausted. Such was the wisdom of the man with whom I counted it a privilege to work for so long. I fear that when the oil is exhausted in some of the Gulf states, the inhabitants will be left stranded, like fish on the seashore when the tide has gone. That this will not happen to Dubai is a tribute to Shaikh Rashid's foresight as much as it is to Dubai's mercantile traditions.

Shaikh Rashid was totally sincere in his commitment to the furtherance of Dubai's position in the Gulf. He recognized, I think, that I too was dedicated to the same objectives. He could be aggressive when the occasion demanded it; he could also be ruthless, acknowledging that the role of a Ruler sometimes demanded harsh decisions in the public good. Sometimes he could seem timid in his dealings with others, shy even, yet he knew instinctively when to appear to concede a point, with the assurance of a greater victory two or three moves ahead. In his dealings with the British he could be very skilful, realizing that an apparent concession would often lead to them being drawn further into a commitment than they had originally envisaged. The British were past masters at manipulating the Rulers of the territories over which they exercised political control; Shaikh Rashid was at least their equal and, on occasions (one of which I will later relate) could beat them at their own game.

My knowledge of English and my work at the bank inevitably drew me into ever closer contact with the British Government representatives in Dubai and the Gulf as a whole. A number of these officials, often men of considerable ability who went on to achieve high rank in the British Foreign Service, became, and have remained, my friends.

The most senior British official resident in Dubai was the Political Agent. He exercised full powers over the areas of policy covered by the treaties, mostly dating from the nineteenth century, which governed Britain's relations with the shaikhs of the Gulf. By the fifties and sixties it was clear that the relationship would need to change; that it did so with such little disturbance is a tribute both to the skill and integrity of the Political Agents (and that of their immediate superiors, the Political Residents, stationed in Bahrain) as it was to the good sense and maturity of the societies in the Gulf themselves. With several of the Agents, whose post was raised to that of ambassador on the recognition of the full independence of the Gulf states in 1971, I worked in the closest collaboration in developing Dubai's governmental and social infrastructure. Together we were able to devise and carry into effect much of the early industrial and commercial development of the country.

My friends used to tease me by saying that although my heart belonged to Gamal Abdul Nasser, my brain belonged to the British. Certainly my affection for my English friends and my admiration for their dedication and efficiency did not for one instant diminish my belief in the destiny of the Arab world which Nasser seemed to have come closest to realizing. But I respected the British for their genius for order and administration and for their remarkable ability to appear to be assisting development of less advanced societies whilst resolutely pursuing their own objectives, a policy which I found altogether understandable since it was one which we ourselves always tried to follow. I admired their administrative competence and, in any case, I have always believed in the adage that it is better to have a wise enemy than a foolish friend; sooner or later those who were once enemies will find that, if their interests coincide, they have become friends.

My close relations with the British representatives in Dubai gave me an unrivalled opportunity to observe the workings of the colonial administration in its final days – at least in our part of the world. The British relied for much of their information on the intelligence which their officials, most of them very competent Arabists, were able to acquire, from a very wide range of sources. I have been surprised, however, when reading the records of these times, to find how often the British understanding of a given situation was at odds with what I knew to be the reality.

My advice was often sought by the British on matters relating to affairs in our part of the coast; sometimes I suspect that what I would tell them was not to their liking. My opinions and ideas were, I have no doubt, sometimes regarded as 'unsound' when they did not reflect the British officials' own preconceptions or the demands of a policy which was laid upon them from Bahrain or London, or when my declared Arab Nationalist beliefs informed the advice which I might give them. But I believed that it was important always to tell them the truth, even if it was uncomfortable for them, because, I told myself, since they were responsible to the extent that they were for the government of our country, the truth would enable them to run it better.

In those days I lived between the two important influences in my life, the bank and Shaikh Rashid's court, and provided a link between them. I was given unrestricted leave of absence from the bank whenever Shaikh Rashid needed me. I often found myself in the position of persuading the Shaikh to a course of action which I knew to be in Dubai's interest after I had discussed it and worked it out in detail with the Political Agent. This rather complex set of interrelationships was sometimes misunderstood – or misrepresented – by others of Shaikh Rashid's advisers but the wisdom of the policies which we then established can be seen today in the formidable international reputation and success which Dubai has enjoyed.

I have mentioned some of the projects which we introduced at this time and which I will describe further when I come to write about the work of the Trucial States Development Office, with which I was deeply involved and of which I was eventually to become the Executive Director. But before projects of this sort, primarily designed to promote Dubai's commercial standing, could be achieved, the governmental system had to be modernized and formed in a way that would be acceptable to the international interests which we sought to persuade of Dubai's potential.

With Donald Hawley (Political Agent 1955–8, now Sir Donald) we worked out the legislation governing the buying and selling of land and the registration of ownership, an essential consideration if foreign commercial interests were to be allowed into the country. It was an example of law-making which protected the rights of individuals and families to properties which they may have owned for generations but for which no formal documentation existed. This situation had always provided opportunities for abuse and the land reforms laid down a fair basis for land tenure, effectively for the first time. The registration of land also helped to stimulate the country's economy; for the first time it was possible for merchants and traders to raise mortgages from BBME on property which they could now prove that they owned. This provided a welcome encouragement to trade and to the growth of businesses which were to be among the foundation-stones of Dubai's future prosperity.

We drafted the plans for the establishment of the Dubai Municipality which set out the rules for the permits required for merchants to trade in the town. A Municipal Council was formed under the chairmanship of Ali Al-Uwais, a man similarly dedicated to Dubai's interests; when he died the British flags were flown at half-mast. I was appointed a member of the council.

Another of the successes of this time was the formation of the Dubai Port Committee, under Shaikh Rashid's chairmanship. Its members, in addition to myself, included John Colwell, J. Colville ('Col') Kelly, Alastair Macaskell, Ali Al-Uwais, Murshid Al-Usaimi, Ahmed bin Majid Al-Ghurair and Donald Hawley. The decision to develop a modern port facility in Dubai proved to be one of the most enlightened taken during Shaikh Rashid's reign, for Dubai's exceptional port facilities and the subsequent foundation of the Free Zone at Jebel Ali have contributed more, perhaps, than any other innovation to the present success which Dubai enjoys.

It is evident from their dispatches at this time (1961) that the British considered it appropriate, even at this relatively early stage in the realignment of their policy towards the Trucial States, that they should distance themselves from 'direct intervention' in Dubai's administration. 'Dubai,' it was said, 'is learning to stand on its own feet and its independence must be seen as a reality.'[7] Other views generally supported this policy, one urging that 'we [the British] must not try to be colonial administrators', an inclination which some of them all too readily displayed. However, the same dispatch observed, perhaps revealingly of the attitudes of at least some British officials, 'In any case, senior officials have probably better things to do than to absorb detailed briefs for a minor shaikh.'[8]

As our administration grew, though it was still only quite small, it was put to us that we needed to recruit experts from outside Dubai who could take over some of the newly defined responsibilities in the governmental organization. It was certainly true that there were few enough qualified local people to take on such roles but I wondered at the time, and I still wonder, whether it was necessary to recruit experts from as far away as, for example, the Sudan. I suspect that there may have been an element of the British wishing to maintain control of the emerging administration by ensuring that the key positions were filled by individuals whose loyalty was primarily to them. For the time being, it was necessary for such appointments to be made but it was regrettable that little attempt was made to train young, local people to take over the offices concerned. This was an aspect of our affairs which I tried – largely unsuccessfully – to correct when the time came to hand over the responsibility for development to the UAE authorities, when the Union Government was formed in 1972.

An important task which we carried out, also with Donald Hawley's help, was the drafting of a constitution for the Port Committee. This proved to be of great significance in the years to come and much of the work of drafting was carried out on a round table in the Customs office. I had had this made specially so that there would be fewer of the usual problems of those attending the meetings jockeying for position; with a round table no one, not even the Ruler, sits above the rest. I have often thought that the table should be preserved in the Dubai Museum, so much of the country's history did it witness at this time. It had a considerable psychological effect on those who attended our meetings and in its own small way contributed to giving Dubai some part of its open and relaxed character. It was also a small witness to the mechanisms of democracy.

Of course, not everything went smoothly. The situation in Dubai was such in these early days that it was bound to attract some who were driven by objectives which were clearly less scrupulous than were our own. There was one individual who infiltrated some of the centres of power, in the process establishing a most sinister influence which recalled that of Rasputin in pre-Revolutionary Russia. Sometimes Shaikh Rashid's need for revenue, to carry out the reforms and improvements to Dubai's infrastructure which he knew to be necessary, made him accept projects and proposals which some of us considered unwise. These were always related to raising revenue (they included the international marketing of issues of postage stamps and travel documents) and Shaikh Rashid knew that he had little choice but to accept them. However, he knew when I was unhappy about a proposal or a recommended project; I would remain silent, my eyes cast down. Then Shaikh Rashid would say, 'Easa looks at the carpet, and then tells me the truth.' It was a judgement that I was content to accept.

4

WHEN I HAD COME back to Dubai in October 1946 I had found that not only had I changed but Dubai was changing, too. By the sophisticated standards of Bahrain, Dubai was still a relatively simple community. I was instantly absorbed back into the family, from which it was as though I had never been parted. But I missed my friends with whom I had happily talked politics and whose concerns for the future independence of the Arab world I shared so completely. I was determined not to lose touch with the affairs of the world outside Dubai, despite the demands which my job made on my time and energies.

It was clear for all to see that the world in the post-war period was going to be a very different place from what it had been before. America had emerged as the most powerful nation on earth; Britain, though perhaps it was not yet so obvious to us, was exhausted and had been stripped of much of her treasure. Already there were rumblings of discontent in several of Britain's Imperial possessions.

Had we known it, events in one small part of the Arab world were about to change the character of many of the world's political alliances and priorities and to preoccupy us for many years to come. This, too, was one of the consequences of the war which had convulsed the European powers and which had dragged so many other peoples into misery as the result of actions which had nothing whatsoever to do with them.

I am not going to review the course of the Arab–Israeli conflict in these early years, for historians and commentators of all sorts have pored over every minute detail of the events of that unhappy confrontation. However, it did affect my life and my attitudes to the politics of my part of the world. The war of 1948 was a catastrophe for the Arabs, who tried to stem the tide of alien Jewish expansionism in Palestine.

To young Arabs like myself, the events of 1948 were of profound importance in the course of our lives. Although the idea of Arab Nationalism derived in part at least from the anti-colonialist movements of the last century, the evident impending decline of the colonial powers in the face of independence movements everywhere and the rise of world powers like the United States and Russia, meant that we could see the possibility of achieving the place in the world which we knew was ours by right.

All over the Arab world, but particularly in Egypt, Syria, Iraq and the recently independent Lebanon, an educated middle class was beginning to come to the forefront in education, business, journalism and government. In many cases, the army provided fertile soil for the growth of new, critical attitudes of mind no longer content to rely on colonial fostering (when it was not outright rule) which seemed still to determine the attitudes of the surviving colonial powers. From the more developed countries of the Arab world, influences began to spread even to its more distant corners such as the Gulf shaikhdoms. This was particularly the consequence of the importation of primary-school teachers from Egypt and Iraq and of the influence of what today would be called information media: the widely circulating newspapers from Cairo and Damascus and the increasingly penetrating coverage which radio stations from the northern states were giving to events in the Arab world and in the world at large. This aspect of modern living, the power of broadcasting, was one which was to prove of crucial importance in the future, in spreading the demand for political change.

The power of radio broadcasting was, incidentally, not entirely new to the Gulf. During the war I remember being taken by my father to listen to broadcasts from Germany on one of the very few radios in Dubai, belonging to the then Ruler, Shaikh Saeed bin Maktoum Al-Maktoum. We used to hear the violently anti-British broadcasts of Yunis Bahri from Berlin; I recall, in particular, the sound of the evident delight in Bahri's voice when he announced the sinking of the *Ark Royal*. Looking thoughtfully at his radio set, Shaikh Saeed observed, 'If the British had realized how much the radio would abuse them they would never have invented it.' Shaikh Saeed here was expressing the universally held belief in our part of the world that everything mechanical or technological had been invented by the British, despite the evident fact that the radio had been made in Holland. It is a belief which still lingers in certain quarters.

When the 'Iron Curtain' was said to have fallen across Europe, the Arab world received another set of signals for the future, this time from Russia which in the late forties and early fifties was testing its strength against the United States and the colonial powers remaining in Europe. Many of us, even in those days, doubted that communism could really enjoy a lasting influence in the Islamic world, but we could not calculate then the tensions which the two political blocs, represented by the United States and Russia, would arouse by their search for supporters in what was already coming to be spoken of as 'the Third World'. All around us was a ferment of political speculation, to which no one was immune.

The first, decisive moment for our region of the world came in 1952 when a group of young officers seized power in Egypt. All of us rejoiced that Egyptians, for the first time in centuries, were now in command of their country's destiny. We were proud, too, that the revolution was achieved without bloodshed and almost without recrimination. For us it was a moment of great hope which brought with it the belief that a new dawn, which would cast a new and kinder light on all our futures, was at last breaking.

We had not, at that point, calculated how profound was the anger and, as it now seems, the fear which the Egyptian revolution engendered in the minds of some politicians in the West, notably, it has to be said, in Britain and France. That it was Egypt which had thrown off the control of the colonialists was especially galling and although Gamal Abdul Nasser, who quickly emerged as the real genius of the revolution, tried to secure the understanding of the Western powers, he could not do so. When, therefore, he announced that Egypt proposed to nationalize its one substantial asset in foreign hands, the Suez Canal Company, all the demons of frustration and hatred seemed to be unleashed amongst politicians of all complexions in the West.

We know from the memoirs of politicians of the time how bitter were the attitudes towards Egypt in London and Paris. At the same time, the newly established Israeli state saw an opportunity, on the one hand, for flexing its muscles with the aid of powerful allies and, on the other, of creating the image of a powerful enemy bent on its destruction. Israel calculated, correctly as it turned out, that she would be able to win the support of the United States whose Secretary of State, Foster Dulles, in what must rank as one of the most disastrous decisions of the post-war period, decided to join in the coalition to overthrow Nasser and the revolution which he had led.

The story is almost wearisomely familiar. Britain, France and Israel attacked Egypt whose forces were no match for so powerful a line-up of antagonists. Only the intervention of President Eisenhower, in a show of decisive action not always typical of his presidency, obliged the antagonists to call a halt. But the damage had been done.

The Gulf was still dominated by the British. To most people, it appeared that they had done little to improve the lot of ordinary citizens. They did not seem very inclined to stimulate local business; they did not even search for new water wells, always the touchstone of enlightened rule in desert lands. Their attitude was well expressed by one Political Agent who let it be known that no complaint against a British subject would be tolerated by the Agency, no matter what was the nature of the complaint. I experienced something of this attitude myself when, during the time that I was involved with the Trucial States Development Office, I was invited to visit the Political Agency; there I was asked to drop my objections to the continued employment of a British officer, who I considered was incompetent and overpaid. Despite the pressure which was exerted on me, I persisted and the officer concerned was dismissed.

Sometimes British officials were extraordinarily insensitive. I have known of occasions when an official would summon the shaikhs to a meeting, to be held at the Agency. The shaikhs would arrive with their retainers at the appointed time. They would then be required to sit on the ground, in the blazing sun, awaiting the pleasure of whichever official had convened the meeting. After what might be hours waiting in these conditions, not only of dis-comfort but of humiliation – for it showed to all the lack of respect with which the leaders of the community were treated in front of their own servants – as often as not a lesser official would emerge to announce that it was no longer convenient for his superior to hold the meeting which he himself had called. It was inevitable that the impression given would be that the whole episode had been arranged to demonstrate where power resided. An episode of this sort occurred in Sharjah as late as the forties.

Against this sort of background and the atmosphere which such events created, Nasser's speeches were electrifying. Young people all over the peninsula were wild with excitement whenever he spoke and his words were broadcast across the Arabic-speaking world. Amongst the supporters of the new ideas which he was for-mulating were many of the younger shaikhs in the Gulf states and the princes of the same generation in Saudi Arabia. Later they may have become disillusioned but at this time Nasser's beacon burned bright.

The British became alarmed and tried to suppress as much as possible of what they considered Nasser's anti-British subversion throughout the areas in which British influence still lingered. To us he was the new Saladin; on one occasion my mother remarked that we did not remember the words of the Prophet in the way we remembered those of Gamal Abdul Nasser.

Through his words we had the sense of a nation being built. Throughout the Arab world there were demonstrations led by the students, with speeches of increasing violence raising the passions of the multitudes who gathered to hear them. It was a heady time.

In 1959, not long after Shaikh Rashid had succeeded his father as Ruler of Dubai, he received an invitation from the British Government to pay an official visit to Britain. At this time the British were attempting to develop the awareness of people and Rulers in the Gulf to the problems which the world beyond Arabia was facing. This was really a process of education designed to encourage the Rulers to extend their own administrations and, whilst not encouraging any sort of real independence from Britain, to begin to stand more on their own feet. British thinking was no doubt also influenced by the increasing evidence of the immense reserves of fossil hydrocarbons which were locked beneath the Gulf and the Arabian peninsula. There was also evidence of the first beginnings of the British Government's efforts to encourage the Shah of Iran in his aspirations for his country to become the dominant power in the region.

In the pursuit of this policy, the Shah had invited Shaikh Shakhbut of Abu Dhabi to Tehran on a state visit. A great banquet was held, to which some 2,000 guests were invited. Only the Shah, Shaikh Shakhbut and the most senior dignitaries present were seated at table; the other guests were served at a buffet. Shaikh Shakhbut would not eat any of the food placed in front of him, and when the Shah anxiously asked him if anything was wrong, Shaikh Shakhbut replied that he was waiting for all the other guests to be seated. The Shah explained that they would eat standing, as they were having a buffet. 'Strange,' said Shaikh Shakhbut, 'I thought only camels ate standing up.'

Shaikh Rashid decided that I should accompany him to London, to act as the party's interpreter. The others in the group were his sons, Shaikh Maktoum bin Rashid and Shaikh Hamdan bin Rashid; Major P. G. Lorimer; the Superintendent of Police; Shaikh Rashid's retainers and other members of his entourage.

When Shaikh Rashid and his party arrived in London, it became clear that no very demanding programme had been organized for us. Indeed, it seemed to us that our British hosts had no particular idea why we were there. We were taken to the Royal Tournament where we sat with the Queen and talked of horses and falconry; I acted as interpreter between the Queen and Shaikh Rashid. Later, at a football match to which Shaikh Rashid and his party were taken (I think it was at Wembley, the vast arena packed with spectators), the Foreign Office official escorting us, Terry (later Sir Terence) Clark, was worried because Shaikh Rashid was very quiet, gazing at the crowd and obviously deep in thought.

'Are you not enjoying the match?' he asked.

Shaikh Rashid smiled. 'Of course,' he said, 'but I was thinking that there are more people here in this stadium than in any of the towns which I rule.'

We were entertained to lunch by various companies and individuals interested in the prospects of Dubai's development. We were taken to Madame Tussaud's where our escorts seemed disappointed that we were apparently not frightened by the Chamber of Horrors. We felt that we knew enough of the horrors which had been perpetrated in the names of politics and imperial dominion. We visited the London County Council and were shown the wonders of the London Underground system; despite the publicity which was given by the newspapers, Shaikh Rashid did *not* say that he wanted to drive the train. I suppose that idea was the inspiration of someone who felt that simple people from the depths of Arabia would want to play trains.

We were received by John Profumo, the Minister of War in Harold Macmillan's cabinet. We exchanged pleasantries; again I was interpreting. At the conclusion of the visit, Shaikh Rashid presented Mr Profumo with a magnificent gold sword; Mr Profumo presented Shaikh Rashid with an umbrella.[1]

Mr Macmillan invited Shaikh Rashid to call on him at Number 10 Downing Street. The conversation was fairly bland, directed by the subjects listed on a paper which the Prime Minister kept on his knee and to which he referred throughout our meeting. We spoke of falconry and hunting and similar topics. When Mr Macmillan had exhausted his piece of paper, he muttered to the official attending the meeting that he could think of nothing else to say. I indicated to Shaikh Rashid that I thought it was time to go. As if he did not wish to impose more on the Prime Minister's time, Shaikh Rashid brought the meeting to a close, with great courtesy asking the Prime Minister's permission to withdraw.

We stayed at the Dorchester Hotel for the first days of our visit.

Then we were told that we would be moving to new quarters. These turned out to be the '21 Room' in Chesterfield Place, which in those days was notorious. I gather that the Foreign Office often used to put up visiting Arab dignitaries at this distinctly dubious address; it was one of London's few sophisticated night-clubs in those days and it was rumoured that the hostesses were very co-operative.

The reason for its selection was presumably a belief that there was only one other entertainment that appealed to Arabs, apart from driving Underground trains. Shaikh Rashid was an austere man of very simple habits; we moved the next morning to the Carlton Tower Hotel, where we insisted on staying at our own expense and not at that of the British Government. I gather that Shaikh Shakhbut of Abu Dhabi had a similar experience in London when he was given the hospitality of the 21 Room.

During our visit to London, Shaikh Rashid received an invitation to stop off in Egypt on our way back to Dubai. The British authorities were consulted but raised no objection and the invitation was accepted. Shaikh Rashid was by this time a skilled politician, who told the Foreign Office that he would like to visit the British Embassy in Cairo whilst he was in the city. The Foreign Office questioned the wisdom of this proposal, believing that such an open contact by a Gulf Ruler and the representative of the British Crown, when relations between Egypt and Britain had only just been restored after their suspension over the Suez crisis, might be provocative. Shaikh Rashid, however, was insistent and the Foreign Office's reservations did not prevail.

When we arrived in Egypt we were received with great cordiality and warmth. We stayed in Cairo at the Nile Hilton Hotel, on the corniche, looking out on to Egypt's glorious river. One of our first meetings with the President was in Alexandria and was, for me at least, a moment of great emotion and pride. Indeed, I was so thrilled at meeting Nasser that I became very emotional. I did not care. 'Long Live Nasser,' I cried and kissed him.

As we came out an Egyptian Intelligence officer gave me a cigarette. 'I think you'd better have this,' he said. 'It may help you to calm down.'

I never smoked but on this occasion I took the cigarette that was offered to me.

Nasser was a powerfully built man, quite tall, with a most charismatic personality, as potent when meeting him face to face as it was when he was in full flow in front of an audience of a million people. It is curious what one remembers from such encounters: I recall that Nasser carried his handkerchief thrust in his coat sleeve, a habit derived, I believe, from British Army officers who affected the same custom.

The President entertained us to tea at his house in the Manshit Albakri area of Cairo. It was an easy, simple occasion with his young son, Abdul Hakim, playing with a football in the corner of the room in which we sat. Nasser had very long ears which, when he sat down, touched the shoulders of his jacket.

He asked Shaikh Rashid about the administration of Dubai. Who, he enquired, ran the police, the health department, finance, water, the Post Office, electricity? In each case Shaikh Rashid replied with the name of the British official responsible, employed by the Dubai Government.

'Thank you,' said Nasser, 'for telling me the truth. I have files on all of them. Always keep the English with you. You can lean on their shoulders and you can use them to teach your boys and young men discipline. I am not against the English. Don't listen to all that Sout al-Arab says. We cannot fight them, for they are more numerous and better equipped than we will ever be. But we are like cats who can drive our opponents into a corner and there scratch their faces.'

On that same occasion Nasser said to me, 'Keep your English friends. We gave Europe much of its culture, through the Mediterranean and Spain. Now we have been bypassed and we should get back some of their culture and skill in return.'

I remember particularly clearly one of his speeches in which he said, 'I call on the Arab world to teach our children English. It is the language of science and no longer belongs only to the English.' Then, with the rather impish humour for which he was famous, he said, 'Bring the Irish to your country to teach the children English.'

One of our party, who was a Moslem activist, asked Nasser why he did not emphasize Islam more aggressively and why he had proscribed the Moslem Brotherhood movement.

'Look,' said Nasser, 'our world includes Africans, Copts who believe that they are the original Egyptians, and 60 per cent of the population of Lebanon is Christian; there are Christians in Syria, Iraq, Jordan – all over the Arab world. How can I ignore them? Believe me, if Arab Nationalism becomes powerful, Islam will become powerful too.'

We were invited to attend one of his rallies, on this occasion in Alexandria. We were given seats at the front of the audience. As a result, Nasser saw me when he came in; I had been filming him at our earlier meeting. 'Still taking photographs?' he asked.

'Who does not want to take pictures of you?' I replied.

On another occasion, at the Officers' Club, I was seated, by mistake, in front of Shaikh Rashid. He would not change his place, however, and motioned me to remain where I was. Nasser sat in the front row and I observed that when Mohammed Abdul Wahab and Umm Kalthoum, the two greatest entertainers in the Arab world, came in, he stood to receive them; he held them both in high regard, for their songs had swept the cause of Nationalism across the Arab world. To Abdul Halim Hafez, another popular singer, perhaps inclined to overindulgence, he said, rising only partially from his seat, 'Take care of yourself.'

Shaikh Rashid later related a conversation which he had with Abdul Nasser, to the then Political Agent in Dubai. The President had said that he wanted friendship with the British but that he was not prepared to be enslaved by them. This observation was reported in turn to the Foreign Office[2] but I doubt that it influenced British policy very much.

It will be clear that I was an unashamed enthusiast for all that Nasser represented. Arabs of my generation really did believe that all the ills of the Arab world – inequality, underdevelopment, lack of proper opportunities for our young people and, above all, the elimination of the affront with which the creation of the State of Israel by the West had faced the Arabs – would be overcome by the ideals of Arab Nationalism.

We believed that the capital of the Arab world was Cairo and that the Nile Valley would become the homeland of Arab development. I was an ardent activist and I was close to many of Nasser's officials in Egypt. The British, who were through all this time my friends, could not understand my dual loyalties. The officials amongst them became more and more alarmed about the spread of Nasserism amongst the young people in the Gulf states. They did everything in their considerable power to contain the spread of an influence which they rightly realized was wholly opposed to their own. Yet often their highly sophisticated intelligence network was defeated by quite simple devices.

Thus it was that young men and boys would be sent to Egypt for 'instruction' in the many dimensions of the struggle against an outmoded colonialist presence. This was, of course, wholly opposed by the British authorities and those who supported them. Those who were destined for Egypt would fly to Bombay, an entirely innocent destination, and there would visit the Egyptian Consulate. They would be provided with travel documents for Cairo. When their 'instruction' was completed they would fly back to Bombay, collect their passports and return to their homes.

Air transport, which was becoming increasingly important throughout the fifties and sixties, was an area of contention between those of us who supported the larger Arab interest and those who sided with the British. It seemed to me, for example, that it was wholly unreasonable for the British authorities to use their powers to prevent Arab airlines from using Gulf airports or to have landing rights in countries which were unquestionably part of the Arab world. I argued the case strongly with my friends at the British Political Agency, urging particularly that Egypt Air, the Arab world's most important carrier, should be granted rights enjoyed exclusively by BOAC (as British Airways was then called) but my arguments were met with fierce rejection by those who, otherwise, were my friends.

On occasion, the dilemma of those who supported Nasser in the Gulf states would be sharply brought into focus. After his death there was a proposal in the Dubai Municipality, of which I was a member, to erect a statue to his memory in the square which had been named in his honour. We got as far as installing the plinth on which the statue was to stand; then the project was scotched. Sir Humphrey Trevelyan, later Lord Trevelyan, perhaps the last of the great British proconsuls in our part of the world, one day attended a party in the offices of the BBME, of which he was a director and which looked out on to Nasser Square. He was talking to a group of young local men and was highly critical of Nasser, particularly in the light of the war in Yemen where, it was said, 50,000 Egyptian soldiers had died. What, he asked, had their deaths achieved? One of the party, a young man like the rest, confronted Trevelyan and said that for changing history and for the liberation of the Arabs, 50,000 deaths was nothing; did not Sir Humphrey realize that they could make 100,000 new Arabs in one night?

It is really not surprising that the British presence was so universally disliked. Nonetheless, for most of my adult life I have maintained these two apparently opposite loves, for Arab Nationalism on the one hand and for much of the British way of doing things on the other. One of my English friends summed up this apparent contradiction by relating how, on a trip to Cairo, I had welcomed the idea of a visit to the British Embassy, where I had been long before with Shaikh Rashid. I was fascinated then, as I had been earlier, by the proconsular splendour in which Britain maintained its senior officials, the portraits of many of whom still adorned the Embassy's walls. We recalled the episodes in the life of T. E. Lawrence which happened in the Embassy, when he embarked on what I have always believed to be his disastrous interference in the affairs of the Arabian peninsula. I enjoyed my visit greatly; at the same time my friend knew that whenever I am in Cairo I go to pray for the repose of his soul at the tomb of Gamal Abdul Nasser.

The death of Nasser in 1970 was a devastating loss to all of us who had grown up with the revolution which he had led. By the time of his death he was a saddened and disillusioned man; the smiling, laughing Nasser who had become so familiar a figure, both of love and of hate, throughout the world had grown into a taciturn, almost sombre man. The catastrophe of 1967, for which he accepted responsibility, was an immense blow to him; in a sense he never recovered from it. Yet his career, overall, was a triumph for he gave to the Arabs a sense of purpose and identity which, if it has not yet been fulfilled, nonetheless exists and will grow in strength.

There have been endless attempts to assess the course of Nasser's life. There are those who see him as a creature of American policy, unaware that he was being manipulated by its authors. According to this view Nasser and his followers were, from the outset of his career, encouraged by the Americans to overthrow the monarchy and disengage Egypt from British influence. Then, when they realized that he was a leader, a man of charismatic personality, they used him to head the anti-colonialist movement which was sweeping over the nations and peoples who had experienced Imperial rule; again, according to this view, their target was primarily Britain. The rise of Israel as a Western-oriented state in the Middle East provided the occasion for further manipulation of Nasser, to provide the 'enemy' which Israel needed to keep its Western supporters constantly ready to pour arms and money into the Jewish state.

There may be some truth in this analysis, though I doubt that even American foreign policy was quite so sophisticated in the fifties and sixties. There is no doubt that Nasser unwittingly sometimes served those interests to which he was most firmly opposed. I believe that he made one fundamental error of judgement, the result of political inexperience, I suspect, from which his career never wholly recovered. In 1956 President Eisenhower, as I noted earlier, intervened after the Suez invasion and required Britain, France and Israel to pull back. Egypt triumphed, at least morally, though at a high price. Eisenhower was no Zionist; indeed, no American President (with the exception perhaps of President Bush) was less moved by Zionist pressure than was Eisenhower. I believe that Nasser should have exerted all his legendary charm and diplomatic skills in winning over the United States to the Arab cause. At this time, Israel had not gained the influence over American foreign policy which it seemed to exert from the late fifties onwards, as Egypt was inexorably drawn into the Soviet sphere of influence, the most unnatural of all political alignments as the Russians were themselves eventually to realize. If Nasser had been able to capitalize on Eisenhower's one great decisive moment in his presidency, the history of the Middle East over the past decades might have been radically different. If the Arabs and the Americans had been partners and not enemies in the fifties, sixties and seventies, who knows what might not have been achieved?

At the time I urged this view on the Egyptian Intelligence personnel in Sharjah – mostly secondary schoolteachers attached to the Egyptian Educational Mission established in 1958–9 – whom I had made it my business to know. I begged them to alert Cairo to what I believed to be a policy which was so clearly in Egypt's interest, to try to work with the Americans rather than regard them as an implacable enemy. My voice, however, was a small one and already the influences were mounting which were to draw Nasser, and with him much of the Arab world, down a misguided path.

What is it that makes Egypt so important to all the Arabs? Of course, in part it is history, for the days of the Arabs' greatness will always be linked with Cairo and the Nile Valley. But there are other reasons: we sing Egyptian songs, we speak 'Egyptian' Arabic as though it were our native dialect. When we speak to an Egyptian friend we assume Egyptian speech, for the language and its expression are delicate and elegant. We respond joyfully to the poetry of Egypt, recalling that it was the King of Egypt who hailed Ahmed Shawki as 'Prince of Poets'. We delight in Egyptian songs, stories and legends and in its immemorial culture, aspects of which are the greatest the world has ever seen. And then there is the simple fact that the Egyptians are nice people, kind, gentle and generous – rather as we feel ourselves to be – and Egypt was always a refuge for Arabs who were politically persecuted in their own lands.

I have been asked why Iraq has never seemed to occupy the same place in the hearts of the Gulf people as Egypt has done, though geographically it is part of our region. Despite its noble history, Iraq has never had the same charisma as Egypt nor a culture which met the emotional and intellectual needs of our people to the same degree. Although the Tigris and the Euphrates flow into the Gulf, to us the river of the Arab world is the Nile; the cataracts at Aswan are the falls which to us symbolize sweet water.

Even modern politics has exerted its influence in not allowing

Iraq to enter more fully into the affairs of our region. The British resolutely prevented the Iraqis from acquiring a port on the Gulf, dearly though they wished for it. It must be remembered that it was the British who assembled the Kingdom of Iraq from three eastern *vilayats* of the Ottoman Empire which they and the other victorious allies dismantled at the end of the First World War. Until that time Iraq, like Italy before the unification of the peninsula, was more a geographical than a political expression, much as was the still more ancient term 'Mesopotamia'. It was created principally to provide Britain with the means to control Iraq's huge oil reserves and to provide a buffer against the uncertainties of the politics of countries still further east.

It was never Britain's purpose to create a democratic society; that a democracy of sorts did from time to time emerge in Iraq was a tribute more to the people of the country than it was to British Imperial interests. Similarly, Britain did not encourage Iraq to exercise any sort of role in the Arab world at large, until comparatively late in its history as a monarchy, nor, in particular, in the Arabian peninsula. No doubt they were influenced in this policy by the recognition of the long-standing tribal antagonisms which affected the relations of the leaders of the peninsular states like Saudi Arabia and Kuwait, the politicians in Baghdad and Iraqi tribal leaders.

Looking back, it is little short of extraordinary, for example, that the British did not encourage the export of Iraq's most abundant natural resource, water, to the peninsular states. In the thirties, the period of our greatest deprivation, Iraqi water would have transformed our lives, but it was not to be, any more than Britain was prepared to agree to the cutting of a canal between Iraq and Kuwait, though this was proposed several times and would have given Iraq the access to Gulf waters that she sought. Had Iraq had this access then, who knows, the recent history of our region might have been greatly different – though for better or for worse, who knows?

The British policy of excluding Iraq from its southern neighbours, though it may have had some historical justification, prevented the development of close ties or natural affiliation between us. This was in contrast to the attitude which was maintained towards Egypt, where Britain encouraged Egyptian involvement in the Arab world during the days of the monarchy.

Iraq has made it plain that it considers the system of government which prevails in the Gulf to be inappropriate to the times. No doubt Iraq would like to exercise far greater influence on our affairs than she does, but I cannot see the time when the Gulf people's fear of Iraq's intentions will be dissipated, at least whilst regimes like those which have ruled the country since 1959 remain in power.

The fact that Iraq was never really a nation in its own right until the present century has conditioned its world-view and deeply influenced the attitudes of its political leaders, even before the appearance of the present tyrannical regime. I am one of those who believe that history counts for something and that a country like Iraq, despite the majestic contributions which its constituent parts have made to human history, cannot suddenly create an identity and purpose for itself. It is still divided, the prisoner of too many conflicting sects and special interests.

5

I WENT ON MANY visits overseas with Shaikh Rashid during the early years after he became Ruler of Dubai. He had little money at his disposal from the state's revenues, which were then modest, and most of our expenses were financed by his son-in-law, the Ruler of Qatar. On one of our trips to Europe we went by way of Lebanon, Syria and Jerusalem. In the last named we sat in our hotel looking across the city, over the wall which divided it. Shaikh Rashid observed sadly, 'Jerusalem was really won by intrigue and cheating, not alone by war.' In his younger days Shaikh Rashid had been a warrior, fighting battles to secure his father's territory when opposition to his rule became dangerous to the welfare of the state, and to put down the lawless tribal groups which from time to time threatened the lives and prosperity of the people. As such he understood the nature of house-to-house fighting in confined settlements, when centuries of occupation had produced a honeycomb of little streets and alleys with the houses packed closely together. He knew that such an area could not be taken by simple force of arms but rather depended upon the sniper and the infiltrator who, from the safety of a building, could wreak havoc on attackers and defenders alike. To him, it was clear that Jerusalem was just such a case and he believed that only treachery and intrigue could have brought about its fall. I was fascinated to hear what to me was like a voice from a bygone age as he spoke.

Whenever we travelled abroad in those days I took the opportunity to expand my knowledge of the world and, in particular, the history and culture of the countries which we visited. In this I was driven, I suspect, by the consciousness of the deficiencies in my own education: my schooling had been fairly basic and I had not attended a university. But I was intensely curious, not only about the past of my own people but also about that of the lands around us and of those countries, such as the Western states, with whom it was clear that our future would be closely linked. Wherever we went I would be observing, taking in a flood of impressions and new ideas. It may sometimes be true that the self-educated man, if he is fortunate and keeps his eyes and ears open, has the best of teachers.

When we arrived in Jerusalem I was determined, as soon as possible, to visit the Haram al-Sherif, the Dome of the Rock, one of the most profoundly significant buildings in the Moslem world. I wanted especially to see the great stone which legend said hung in the air above the rock from which the Prophet Mohammed made his night journey. The stone was believed to be lowering itself slowly to the ground; when, in the fullness of time, it touched the earth, the Day of Judgement would dawn. Alas, I was disappointed to discover that there was no hanging stone, as I had been told in my childhood.

Later we went to Jerash, Dera'a and Jericho. At Khirbat al-Mafjar, in the valley of the Jordan River, north of the Dead Sea and near the very ancient city of Jericho, is a palatial building which contains an inscription dating to the reign of the great Umayyad Caliph, Hisham Abdul Malek (724–43 AD). The complex, which was never completed, consists of a palace, a mosque and a bath. I was fascinated by the great vaulted buildings which we were told were the stables of the princes who once had ruled there. Shaikh Rashid thought that I was mad, falling behind the main party and gazing at what he dismissed as 'a lot of broken stones'. This indeed is what they were, but I was so moved by them that I thought I could smell the dung of the horses which had been stabled there, so long ago. Who, I wondered, was the last man to mount his horse here and, perhaps looking back, ride away?

Khirbat al-Mafjar, despite its ruined condition, reveals that it was once very richly decorated and appointed, with lavish paintings and sculpture. I was particularly struck by a piece of elaborate window tracery, a five-pointed star made up of stonework carved in imitation of patterned cloth. The five-pointed star is, of course, a very ancient motif in Middle Eastern architecture, long predating its adoption by Jewish symbolism. In Khirbat al-Mafjar its use is probably derived from earlier, Roman precedents.

On another occasion, in Alexandria, we were entertained to dinner in the Muntazah Palace by Anwar Sadat. He had the rather distracting habit of making strange, smacking sounds with his lips but otherwise remaining entirely silent, sitting between Shaikh Rashid on his right hand and Shaikh Ahmed of Qatar on his left. Sadat confined himself entirely to the exchange of formal courtesies, first with one shaikh and then with the other. Since Shaikh Rashid, a rather shy and retiring man, did not have anything to say either, I felt that I should intervene and try to liven things up a little. I started a conversation, which soon became general, talking in particular of the new oil refinery at Alexandria. Afterwards Sadat said to me, evidently with some disbelief, 'Are you from these people?' I said I was. He said that he was sure that I must have had a Turkish mother. I remember that occasion, too, because of a particularly delicious water melon, which was so good that I forgot all my refined table manners and fell on it as I might have done in the desert at home.

Shaikh Rashid was, as I have said, a modest and austere man, who rejected all the customary entertainments and relaxations which Arabs are supposed always to enjoy when they are away from their homeland. On one occasion we were staying in the Hotel du Rhône in Geneva where we lunched in a room which had a large glass window from floor to ceiling. A group of very pretty Swiss girls passed by and were greatly intrigued by us; they had presumably never seen a group of Arabs in national dress before. A little to tease him, and also reverting to an earlier conversation, I asked Shaikh Rashid if he believed that these pretty girls would all go to Hell, since they were obviously not Moslems. 'Of course,' said Shaikh Rashid.

'In that case,' I asked him, 'why did God make all the people of
the world who are not Moslems if it was only to condemn them
all to Hell? How many millions are there in China, India, America,
Russia?' Each time one of his suite gave the figure. 'What,' I went
on, 'have the Arabs done for the past two hundred years except sit
in the desert, achieving little despite the splendour of our past?'

'Now I know you're a communist,' said Shaikh Rashid.

In fact, we had a very easy relationship and Shaikh Rashid
seldom showed any sign of resenting my direct way of speaking to
him.

We were staying at the Dorchester in London when the first
moon landings took place. Shaikh Rashid had denied that such an
event was possible. When I showed him the pictures from the
moon's surface on television he dismissed them, saying that they
had obviously been filmed in the mountains of Ras al-Khaimah,
specifically to delude fools like me.

A flight from Lebanon a while later enabled me to recover my
position. We were sitting together eating a delicious Lebanese meal,
served some 40,000 feet above the ground. Had he enjoyed his
meal, I enquired? He had. Could our fathers ever have imagined
eating such a delicious meal in such circumstances? He agreed that
of course they could not have done so. I grasped his arm and asked
him how he could explain the accomplishment of this miracle,
when he so firmly believed that the miracle of landing on the moon
was an illusion? Shaikh Rashid did not pursue the matter.

Sometimes we had difficulty reconciling the needs of Dubai as it
began to develop with the policies of Britain as the protecting
power. One such issue, which brought ourselves and the Political
Agency into something approaching a confrontation, was resolved
by Shaikh Rashid in a typically bold and subtle manner; it also
found me playing (in a literal sense) a distinctly complex part in the
small drama which resulted. These events took place long before
I became responsible for development in all the states, when
my principal concern was still for the improvement of Dubai in
whatever ways would best benefit the community.

The origin of this series of events was Dubai's long-standing wish to have its own airstrip. The British had established a civil airport at Sharjah, the shaikhdom next to Dubai, before the war; Dubai had given permission in 1937, before the outbreak of hostilities, for seaplanes to land on the Creek, but I do not recall any landings until after the war ended.

In 1939 the British decided to establish an RAF base in Sharjah, using the facilities originally intended for civil aviation. The British airbase was located close to the fort at Sharjah, which had been built of stone from a site on Abu Moussa island; the stone was rich in iron oxide and consequently the fort was a very distinctive red colour.

Among the most important contributions to the economies of the coastal shaikhdoms at this time were contraband shipments of gold to India. In the days before the oil began to flow, this was accepted as one of the few means available to the shaikhdoms to provide even a modest degree of revenue for their people. Dubai shared in this trade and as the Rulers followed a policy of allowing free and untaxed trading to take place, believing that such was beneficial to the economy of the state as a whole, the free movement of gold was crucial to Dubai's prosperity. Dubai was considerably disadvantaged by having to route its part of this trade through Sharjah, a situation made more acute when duty was imposed on all shipments arriving by air.

During Shaikh Rashid's official visit to London in 1959 he had held meetings with International Airadio Limited; the company confirmed its readiness to prepare plans for establishing facilities for a landing strip and air-traffic-control system in Dubai. One of the carriers of the gold shipments was flown by an ex-RAF pilot named Freddie Bosworth, who was later to be well known as a founding father of what was to become Gulf Air. Bosworth used to fly weekly shipments into Dubai, landing on a *sabkha* (impacted salt-and-sand) road in the middle of the town. This was near the old Deira graveyard, close to the present-day Hassani's supermarket.

When Bosworth landed on the *sabkha* road, the gold was unloaded and taken by Land Rover to the bank where it was stored. It was watched over by one elderly guard armed with an equally elderly, very rusty rifle. Sometimes I travelled with the shipment to make sure that it arrived safely at the bank; I wondered whether our security arrangements were really of the highest calibre but fortunately they were never put to the test. When the shipment reached the bank, Morgan Guaranty of New York, who acted as managers of the funds, would advise us of the payments due to the merchants. Shaikh Rashid realized that the informality of this system and the inadequacy of Dubai's landing arrangements could not continue, for if they did an important source of revenue to the Dubai merchants would be put at risk.

We approached the Political Agent and argued the case for Dubai's need for its own airport. An Englishman, Sydney Hodge, who was the General Manager of International Airadio Limited and of the base at the fort at Sharjah, wanted to see Dubai deprived of its own facilities, despite his headquarters' approval of the plan. He insisted that Sharjah would serve Dubai and the other shaikhdoms in its immediate vicinity: Abu Dhabi, Ras al-Khaimah and the rest. Like Dubai, Abu Dhabi had asked for its own facility and, like Dubai, had been refused; at least, we consoled ourselves, we were not alone the victims of discrimination.

It was clearly time for some creative thinking. Shaikh Rashid asked me to bring Freddie Bosworth to him; on this occasion he was asked to stay the night and I was to bring him to the *majlis* the next morning. Shaikh Rashid introduced the subject of the gold shipments and enquired whether Bosworth would be interested in supporting Dubai's proposal for its own airport. Now the Political Agent had always argued that there was no suitable location in Dubai for an airstrip, but Shaikh Rashid, however, knew every square inch of Dubai, literally like the back of his hand. He knew that there was solid, rock-based land under the sand-dunes at the region of Deira now known as Rashidiyya, and he directed Bosworth to it; he was sure that it was an ideal location for the airport of which he dreamt. Bosworth was asked to survey the site and to report on its suitability for the development of something more substantial than the *sabkha* strip which hitherto had provided him with his landing place.

Bosworth set off with a bulldozer and carried out his survey, spending two days examining the site. He returned full of enthusiasm, announcing that it was 'fantastic'. The bulldozer was employed to clear the site still further to make a basic landing strip and Bosworth was rewarded with 10,000 rupees for his trouble. We returned to the Political Agent with our report on the excellence of the Deira site for the building of Dubai's first airport; the answer was again an emphatic 'no'. We were greatly disappointed.

Shaikh Rashid next sent for me and instructed me to tell the leading merchants in the town to come to the Deira airstrip at 4.45 in the afternoon; Bosworth was also to be there with his aircraft ready for take-off. Finally, I was to ask the Political Agent to be there at 5.00 p.m. The merchants came and, with Shaikh Rashid and myself on board, Bosworth took off and flew down to the mouth of the Creek; as we returned to the airstrip, on the way circling the Political Agency, we saw the Political Agent standing at the end of the makeshift runway. We flew down along the strip, dipped as we reached the end and then soared off again, all in the sight of the Political Agent who, by this time, must have wondered what was going on.

As we landed Shaikh Rashid said to me, 'Easa, I am going to sacrifice you in the interests of Dubai. I shall say some very harsh things about you to the Political Agent when we land.'

'Highness,' I said, 'don't make them too harsh, please.'

We hurried to where the Political Agent was standing, looking rather cross. 'Excellency,' said Shaikh Rashid, 'we waited for you. Whatever happened to you? Why did you not come with us?'

Through clenched teeth the Political Agent explained that Easa Gurg had told him to come to the strip at 5.00 p.m.

'That fool Easa Gurg,' said Shaikh Rashid. 'He can't get even the simplest message right.' He apologized most profusely to the Political Agent, placing the entire blame for the incident on me. Later he explained to me that if we had told the Political Agent to come at 4.45, he would undoubtedly have instructed Bosworth not to take off and Bosworth could not have refused him. Shaikh Rashid would have lost face in front of the merchants, hence it was necessary to resort to a small subterfuge and tell the Political Agent to come fifteen minutes later. His time spent standing on the airstrip as we circled above him also served to impress on him the fact that the strip was perfectly safe for an aircraft to land.

However, the Political Agent was unmoved by Shaikh Rashid's explanation for the confusion; Dubai could still not have its own airport, despite the impressive display which he had witnessed and the enthusiasm of the merchants for the project. Shaikh Rashid called me to him and announced that we were to go to the desert to think, to try and find a solution.

We set out and sat in the desert thinking. Periodically Shaikh Rashid would ask me if I had found a solution; I had not. Finally Shaikh Rashid himself, as was so often the case, came up with an imaginative idea.

Once again I was asked to bring Bosworth to the *majlis*; Shaikh Rashid exerted all his charm which, when he wanted, could be considerable. Bosworth was also presented with a Rolex, a real one, not one of the counterfeit watches which circulated in the *souq*. Did he, Shaikh Rashid enquired, ever have occasion to see the Political Resident, the Political Agent's superior official, when he was in Bahrain? Bosworth acknowledged that he did; Shaikh Rashid smiled.

Bosworth went to Bahrain and saw the Resident, at that time Sir William Luce, a very senior British diplomat. Sir William was at first as firm in dismissing the idea of the airstrip as the Political Agent had been, until Bosworth made it clear, as Shaikh Rashid had instructed him, that Dubai would bear the cost of the development and would not look to Britain to fund it. Luce changed instantly. 'In that case,' he said, 'you may certainly have your damn airstrip. In fact you may have ten airstrips if you want them.'

Shaikh Rashid instructed me in what I was to say to the Political Agent when I next called upon him. He made me swear that I would deny absolutely that either he or I had had any contact with the Political Resident.

The Political Agent was, perhaps understandably, very annoyed. He did not invite me to sit. Who, he enquired as politely as possible, had contacted the Political Resident? I swore upon all that was holy that I had not done so and that Shaikh Rashid, equally, had had no contact with him.

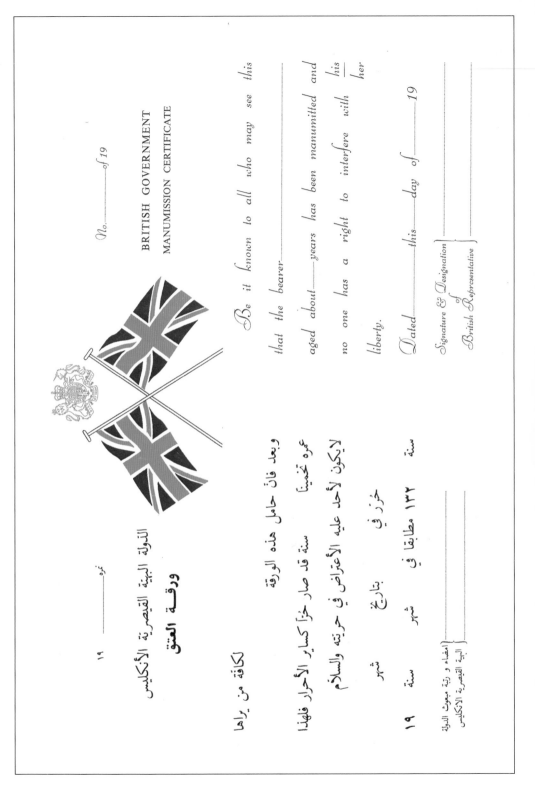

18. The house in which I was born was very like the one shown in this painting by M. Romesh. My family's house has now largely been rebuilt but originally it had a façade similar to this one, a courtyard behind it and rooms opening off the ground and first floors

19. The interior of the Al Ahmediyya School was a fine example of traditional Arab Islamic architecture. Fortunately, it still stands, having been preserved as part of Dubai's architectural heritage

20. The inscription, carved by my father, which he presented to his friend (see p. 22) and which now stands in my garden in Dubai. The inscription reads:
In the name of God, the Merciful, the Compassionate.
God is our Protector and is Most Generous in His Mercy towards us

21. On the occasion of the Presentation of Letters of Credence to Her Majesty the Queen on my appointment as Ambassador of the United Arab Emirates to the Court of St James. I am escorted by the Marshal of the Diplomatic Corps

22. My grandfather's mosque in my family's home town,
Lingah, built in about 1890

23. The mosque that I have built to replace my grandfather's

24. The interior of the mosque that I have built at Al Khassab in the Sultanate of Oman

25. The garden of my house in Dubai

26. The dining room

27. The courtyard

28. In August 1997, during one of His Highness Shaikh Zayed's visits to Britain, I was honoured by him with the Order of Zayed II, which he presented to me at his country house. Shaikh Zayed was kind enough to refer to my work as the UAE's Ambassador and to my activities among the Arab community in Britain. He remarked that my work as the UAE's representative expressed our country's policies and principles of peace, justice and co-operation amongst peoples. In thanking Shaikh Zayed for the honour which he had bestowed on me I undertook to continue to maintain his values and principles, in the interests of both countries

The Political Agent was now obliged to admit defeat; any objection to the development of the airstrip had been withdrawn. I returned to Shaikh Rashid who at once saw in my face that we had won. 'Has it given birth?' he asked, smiling.

'To a very big baby,' I replied.

This incident, which was to prove of great importance in the development of Dubai at that particular point, demonstrates the political skills which Shaikh Rashid had acquired. It also explains why those of us who worked closely with him loved him and why, despite all the problems and disappointments which sometimes arose, we enormously enjoyed our work. It is fitting, too, that such incidents should not be forgotten and that a record of them should exist to remind future generations of what life was like before our world changed so drastically.

Throughout this time my relationship with the bank continued to grow. I had been appointed Commercial Manager in 1964; I still interpreted for Shaikh Rashid, from time to time, and also for the shaikhs and the bank's directors and senior executives. On one occasion we went to call on Shaikh Saqr bin Sultan Al-Qasimi who, I have to say, was never an enthusiastic supporter of mine, although we had once been very close. At one point I was excluded from a meeting between a senior officer of the bank and the Shaikh, who insisted on using his cousin to interpret. Afterwards, I discovered that the Shaikh had delivered a long tirade against me, on the theme that I favoured Dubai at the expense of the other states. The bank, fortunately, knew otherwise.

In actual fact I was, if anything, over-meticulous in following instructions. The bank directed me and I did not have the courage to change their direction – except, sometimes, by persuasion.

My various assignments – to the bank, to Shaikh Rashid and increasingly to the demands of my own evolving businesses (which I shall describe later) – kept me very busy. I think that I put a great deal of the emotional side of my nature into my work, from which, at this time, I never really relaxed. After first visiting my businesses I would go to the bank and there discuss the issues of the day with the senior managers. I would brief them on the state of the market and, most important in a location where there was no published information about the health or otherwise of the businesses with which the bank was dealing day to day, on the standing and dependability of merchants and contractors.

The BBME was very alert to the changes which some of us saw coming in the Gulf. The bank's officials were sensitive to shifts in the market and, because they were located close to the *souq*, they were aware, often before others, of public opinion in our society. They had a considerable influence, I believe, on the opinions of the Political Agency, for whom they represented one of the more comprehensive and reliable sources of opinion and news. The influence of individual managers could be considerable; some of these were men of high character and ability, some, it must be said, much less so.

After I had dealt with my responsibilities to the bank I would move on to Shaikh Rashid's *majlis*. In European terms, I suppose the atmosphere was probably not unlike that of one of the Tudor courts or of pre-revolutionary France – except that it was on a decidedly more modest scale. It was all exceedingly informal, though everyone there knew, to a hair's breadth, his relative place. Shaikh Rashid was exceptionally skilled in a Ruler's most important accomplishment, listening carefully to conversations and arguments as they went on around him and from the general discussion extracting a consensus which would further the course of action which he favoured in any particular case. He would steer the discussions discreetly, seeking moderation and general acceptance; it was as though he were navigating a boat, seeking the more placid waters in the middle of the stream.

Shaikh Rashid was well known for driving round Dubai in his Land Rover, sitting beside the driver, with one foot drawn up on the dashboard. This was one of his favourite positions when he was thinking deeply, deciding on a course of action or on the introduction of a new initiative. He would return to his palace, really quite a modest building, and, at around seven o'clock in the evening, he would summon his advisers and anyone else whom he wanted to help with whatever scheme he was formulating. When we were together he would talk quietly, giving tasks to whomever he chose.

The few of us who were frequently called on in this way were like ministers, carrying out the instructions of the head of government, though we had no portfolios or administrations to support us in what we did. Inevitably, there were occasions when there were disagreements between us. Although I was quite a skilled advocate in arguing the case for any policy or development which I believed to be right, I did not always prevail – it would have been remarkable if I had. When it became apparent that Dubai was well set on a course to become the most important trading centre in our part of the Gulf, it was agreed that a trade centre would be needed to provide facilities and accommodation for the many trade fairs and exhibitions from abroad whose organizers wanted to promote their goods and services. The matter was discussed extensively in the *majlis* and in Shaikh Rashid's private office. I was keen to see a trade village built which would provide all the necessary facilities but which would also be an addition to our rather restricted urban landscape, and could be planted with trees and flowers. A village of the sort which I had in mind would enable exhibitions of local or international works of art to be held, and performances of music or theatre to take place. I also thought that a village would allow the *souq* to share something of the prosperity which it would bring, as the merchants would be able to open shops there and the owners of taxi-cabs would benefit from increased passenger trade.

The alternative proposal was for a high tower which would become a visible landmark, symbolizing the new Dubai and its place in international commerce. I was apprehensive about the idea, not least because I was not convinced that the lifts would always operate securely. I also had nightmares about what might happen in the event of a fire; in this I unknowingly anticipated the scenario of the film *Towering Inferno* by some years.

After long debate, the tower concept won the argument. What I believe clinched it was Shaikh Rashid being told that from the top he would be able to see three neighbouring shaikhdoms; though what that was expected to achieve I was never clear. In the event the Dubai Trade Centre became, as was intended, a statement of the city's international status; it has remained so to this day. I have no doubt that it has helped to give us the edge over the other states in the Gulf which also had ambitions to be recognized as centres of trade.

Not all the innovations of this time were uniformly fortunate. Frequently, ideas were sold to Shaikh Rashid which either had not been properly researched and costed or which were introduced to him more for the good of their promoters than for the good of Dubai. The Dubai Dry Dock was, I believe, such a project. It was built, at colossal expense, on the assumption that the supertankers, which were just then becoming fashionable in the international oil industry, would need repairing and servicing facilities between Europe and the Far East; Bahrain, however, was ahead of us in establishing *their* Dry Dock. The Dubai Dry Dock has also languished as a result of the decline in the use of supertankers, and its engineering, too, was badly planned and executed, requiring an inordinately high rate of expenditure in maintenance and servicing. Even our famed Jebel Ali Free Zone, though it has been vastly more successful, was originally conceived and constructed *ad hoc*, with very little real planning. However, as it transpired, the decision to build it was crucial and the credit for that decision must be given to Shaikh Rashid and to his exceptional far-sightedness. It is a tribute to its direction and subsequent management that it has become so important in Dubai's present prosperity.

When Shaikh Zayed became Ruler of Abu Dhabi and made increasingly generous funds available for development, the horizons of the less fortunate states began to widen; this was especially the case when the Development Office, which was to play a major part in my life, began operations. It is well known that Shaikh Zayed, even before the arrival of Abu Dhabi's oil revenues, was very generous, a man of great heart who loved people and sought always to help them.

On one occasion when Shaikh Zayed was *Wali* (Governor) of Buraimi, before the oil revenues began to flow into Abu Dhabi's treasury, he sent for me and told me that he had a project on which he had set his heart and which would greatly benefit the people of his governorate. After he had described it to me I was convinced that the bank should offer its support to bring the project to fulfilment. I knew that Shaikh Zayed's first concern was always for his people and it was agreed that I should go to London to put the case to the directors.

I was received with great courtesy in London and was invited to lunch with the board. They questioned me closely, especially about the influence which Egypt was exerting in the area. Was it, they wanted to know, going to be Aden all over again? I was able to reassure them but I was cross-examined by each director in turn; my proposal evidently stood up and after a week's deliberation, by which time I had returned to Dubai, the bank's support was agreed.

It only remains to be said that Shaikh Zayed always dealt generously with BBME, ensuring that the bank handled much of his business over the years; similarly, he was always ready to give opportunities to British companies seeking to do business in Abu Dhabi, in the times of its prosperity. Britain had cause to be grateful to him that when crisis came to Abu Dhabi, the tribes remained loyal to him, for they understood the depth of his care for them. Britain was repaid many times over for the confidence which was then shown in Shaikh Zayed and in his unassailable sense of honour.

6

UP TO THIS TIME my work for the bank and my responsibilities towards Shaikh Rashid had absorbed me totally. Now a new phase began, both for me and for Dubai and the Trucial States as a whole. The British, as the dominant power in the region, had not encouraged much co-operation between the different states; there were those who said indeed that, on the other hand, they encouraged dissent and division the better to obtain their own ends. Whatever was the truth of that belief, it was now apparent that the world was changing; Britain was feeling the strain of maintaining its colonial territories, and the coming of oil, especially in Saudi Arabia and Kuwait, was beginning to transform the view which the outside world, or at least those parts of it which were informed about such matters, took of the Gulf.

Whether the British had long anticipated their eventual withdrawal from the Gulf ten years later, is still disputed; I think there is good evidence that they were reviewing the possibility immediately after the Egyptian revolution, certainly before the Suez crisis. They were, as we know, acutely anxious to counter Egyptian influence in the region and they came to accept, however reluctantly, that the period of their involvement in the various states' affairs had done little to advance the prosperity or conditions of the people of the coastal towns. In 1952, by coincidence, I think, in the same year as the revolution which eventually brought Nasser to power in Egypt, the British had formed the Trucial States Council, comprising the Rulers of the states of the Trucial coast, in an attempt to begin to give the region's Rulers some involvement in the management of its affairs as a whole.[1]

I suspect that there were several reasons which prompted the British to create the Trucial States Council. It may be that there was a sense of guilt among the more enlightened British officials and politicians that so little, in real terms, had been done during the period when they had been in control. There was also, undoubtedly, the realization in later years that there were immense oil reserves, particularly in Abu Dhabi and to a lesser extent in some of the other shaikhdoms, awaiting exploitation. Then, some of our British friends began to recognize that it was uncomfortable for them to be ruling countries whose populations' per-capita income was likely to be substantially greater than their own.

But before any of these considerations came to pass, at an early stage in the history of the Council, a decision of lasting importance was taken which was to have ramifications over many years. In its beginnings, the Trucial States Council was seen to be an entirely British institution which was even presided over by the Political Agent resident in Dubai, who was accredited to all the shaikhdoms on the coast.

At a meeting of the Council in 1953 and on the initiative of Britain, it was decided to give the Council its own armed force. To this end the Trucial Oman Levies were formed, later to be called the Trucial Oman Scouts.[2]

The background to this decision deserves some consideration. In what might be called 'the old days', even as late as the forties, parts of the coast were still quite untamed; I have described how, when I was a boy, my father would not take me on long journeys overland for fear of the bands of Bedu who might be encountered there. The Awamir tribe was particularly powerful and virtually independent of any control. They would attack the small towns, stealing cattle, goats and produce from people who were already only subsisting. Dubai was too large to be affected and its then Ruler, Shaikh Saeed bin Maktoum Al-Maktoum, and more particularly still his son, Shaikh Rashid bin Saeed, were too determined for the Awamir or any other marauding group to make much headway.

Eventually Shaikh Rashid and Shaikh Zayed, the Governor of Buraimi in Abu Dhabi, decided that they would put a stop to the Awamirs' lawlessness. They met in Buraimi and agreed upon a strategy; they set out, roaming the desert and attacking the Awamir wherever they found them. The marauders were driven out of the region and peace restored.

It might have been expected that the British, as the protecting power, would have been pleased to see a peaceful solution to a conflict which, if it was not conducted on a very large scale, yet threatened the tranquillity of one of their spheres of influence. The British, however, seem to have seen the matter differently: if the Arabs of the coast could settle such matters for themselves, what role remained for Britain?

The creation of the Trucial Oman Levies introduced a military force into the region which discharged a very useful security function over the years. The Levies and later the Scouts were the army of the Trucial States and the Rulers were expected to contribute to their costs, to the extent of their various abilities. One of the smaller shaikhdoms provided an elderly Land Rover and two camels; others were able to be more generous. Some of the original members of the Scouts were from Jordan and the officer corps was largely British; the Commander was a Briton, too.

In time the Scouts provided a welcome source of employment for some of the young Bedu boys from the desert and countryside. Some of the young shaikhs also were recruited, to become officers in the force. The Bedu recruits were themselves keen to bring their friends into the service and this increased the local component significantly, to the point where it became possible to reduce the Scouts' dependence on the foreigners, including the other element in the contingents which had originally formed its rank and file, the Dhofaris.

One of the responsibilities with which the Trucial States Council was mandated was development.[3] In the early years of the Council's existence this did not rate a very high priority in its deliberations. Britain would be expected to provide a good deal of the funding for the sort of projects which it might initiate, particularly for the smaller and poorer shaikhdoms; although it did make some funds available from time to time, these, in the nature of things, were not very generous.

There was a proposal to open an Arab League office in the Gulf, which was to be located in Sharjah, of all the shaikhdoms at the time the most well-disposed towards Egypt and, from the British point of view, the most fractious. The threat of Egyptian and Arab League interest in the area, demonstrated not only by the attempts of the Arab League to establish a presence in the shaikhdoms but also by the alleged depositing by Egypt of £E 20 million in a Dubai bank, had the effect of sharply focusing the minds of the British authorities on the need for some sort of action. Abdul Khalek Hassouna, the Secretary General of the Arab League (who was still addressed by his title of Pasha despite the abolition of the Egyptian monarchy more than a decade earlier), visited Sharjah and was carried shoulder high by the excited youngsters who besieged his plane when it landed. He was borne through the streets with the crowds singing the songs which had come to be associated with the Nationalist movement.

Development suddenly became something of a priority, for the League had recognized that it could make an immediate impact on local opinion by offering money and skills to undertake the sort of development projects which were long overdue. This realization by the League was to have a considerable influence on my life over the next few years.

Sayed Nofal, the Deputy Secretary General of the League, made several visits to the Gulf to promote its policies. His intervention seems particularly to have alarmed the British, who saw him, not unreasonably, as an enemy. They were, in any case, in an invidious position for they had themselves been responsible for the creation of the Arab League, at the initiative of Anthony Eden, in 1945. Since 1948 the League had been the most outspoken opponent, other than Egypt herself in whose capital, Cairo, its headquarters were situated, of the policies of Israel, for whose existence as a state most Arabs blamed Britain. Nofal travelled backwards and forwards diligently, his movements being tracked with increasing dismay by the British officials in the area and by their superiors in the Foreign Office in London.[4]

The British alarm was understandable. Reading the dispatches exchanged between the Foreign Office in London, the Residency in Bahrain and the Political Agency in Dubai, with occasional interventions from the embassies in Cairo and Beirut, it is clear that the alarm which the 'interference' of Egypt and the League originally engendered was quickly approaching panic ('the most serious threat that we have yet had to face').[5] The officials realized that if the Arab League were able to introduce itself into the Gulf, Britain's hitherto exclusive position with the Rulers would become increasingly untenable. If the Rulers were prepared to admit the League to their territories it would be difficult, if not impossible, for the British to oppose an Arab organization, accepted throughout the world as representing the Arab states collectively, from taking over many of the functions which it had reserved for itself. The British saw the entire fabric of their presence in the Gulf unravelling.[6]

The officials responsible acknowledged – to each other if to no one else – that Britain's record in what had been done for the states under their tutelage was not especially commendable. They recognized that a formal structure would need to be set in place to take responsibility for development throughout all the states in the future.

Nofal was keen to persuade the Rulers of the desirability of signing a letter of commitment to the League, confirming that they would be prepared to accept Development aid from it; he offered them, one by one, what was described as 'A Plan for Arab Technical Co-operation'.[7] The Ruler of Sharjah, who had already welcomed an Egyptian educational mission to his state, agreed; a number of the other Rulers wavered, only Shaikh Rashid remaining firm. He told Nofal that he was bound to Britain by a treaty that precluded dealings with other foreign institutions. Nofal replied that 'treaties could be broken'.[8]

The situation became much complicated when King Faisal bin AbdulAziz of Saudi Arabia offered to put up £1 million for the development of the Gulf states. Some Rulers initially expressed reservations about the offer in the light of the continuing disputes over land boundaries which had adversely affected relations between Saudi Arabia and the southern Gulf states (including Oman) in the fairly recent past. However, King Faisal appeared to be motivated to help the people of the coast and, even more perhaps, to make sure that the Arab League and hence Egyptian influence, to which he was passionately opposed, should be excluded.[9]

He asked for assurances that the League would not be given the facilities which it sought. In May 1965 the British instructed their Embassy in Jeddah to inform the King that they would stand firm against the establishment of an Arab League Office in the Trucial States 'provided that the Saudi Arabian Government contribute £1 million to the Trucial States Development Fund'.[10]

A month later, the British themselves indicated that they would contribute £1 million. There was considerable uncertainty about the management of the Trucial States Development Office, which had been created by the Trucial States Council to discharge its own obligations in this area, and the British were very much concerned over the choice of director. A number of names were canvassed, Arab and British; originally they appeared to favour the appointment of an Arab, though not one from the Gulf. When they made their offer to provide funds to match Saudi Arabia's contribution, the British sought to establish whether 'the principal donors' would be prepared each to appoint a Deputy Director. They now indicated that they would welcome the appointment of an Arab League-nominated deputy, provided that all funds, including those from the Arab League, were channelled through the Development Office.[11] By early June, the British appeared to be ready to change their position once again, with the Political Resident recommending to the Foreign Office that they should 'abandon the policy of opposing the opening of an Arab League office although I recognize that this will probably mean the collapse of Rashid's resistance in Dubai'.[12]

The Rulers of the Trucial States, who were always divided in their attitudes to the idea of the League opening an office in their territories, became still more wary of supporting Britain. The

British Embassy in Jeddah warned the Foreign Office that it was 'very probable that the Saudis will wish to withdraw their offer of £1 million for the Trucial States Development Fund' on the grounds that 'the Saudis are not prepared to fatten the Trucial calf only to see it killed by Nasser'.[13]

Britain sent the Minister of State at the Foreign Office, George Thompson, MP (now Lord Thompson of Monifieth), to visit the shaikhs and to stiffen their resolve to resist the blandishments of the Arab League representatives. He had a number of frank exchanges with the Rulers but it was clear the damage had been done. As one dispatch later observed, 'the situation is rapidly passing out of our control',[14] and ominous warnings were given of the effect on Anglo–American relations if it became clear to Britain's American partners that Britain was no longer able to control the Gulf and its increasingly vital oil supplies. Sometimes a note of what must surely be exaggerated alarm is detectable, as when it was suggested that 'failure to keep the Arab League out of the Trucial States would be a turning point in the history of the Gulf and our position here . . . leaving a chaotic situation behind'.[15]

Although at one point the Foreign Office had appeared to be suggesting that the League should be invited to appoint a Deputy Director to the Development Office, the idea gained no support.[16] It had been decided that Nofal should be refused permission for any further visits and when it appeared that he was nonetheless planning another trip, the Political Residency closed the airspace at Dubai, Sharjah and Abu Dhabi airports.[17] The Arab League party was already in the air when they received the news of the closing of the Gulf's airspace and they were obliged to turn back, I believe to Baghdad.

It was the attitude of Shaikh Saqr of Sharjah which most upset the Foreign Office. They were dismayed that he had 'thrown down the first explicit challenge to Britain's position, in the presence of a visiting Minister of the Crown'.[18] So serious was the situation seen to be that the British Government even threatened to 'withdraw protection'[19] from the Ruler of Sharjah and his closest supporter, the Ruler of Ras al-Khaimah. Yet the fact was that even to a visitor to the region like the Minister of State, who had no special knowledge of Gulf affairs, it was obvious that the sort of aid which the League was proposing would lead to 'invidious comparisons' with British aid in the past. In a report which he wrote following his visit, he commented on 'the wretched conditions' of a number of the shaikhdoms and that Britain 'had given disgracefully little over the years in return for an exclusive position and facilities'.[20] It was little wonder that development, or even the prospect of it, should excite a political reaction as powerful as that which Britain now found herself facing.

Underlying this extraordinary sequence of events which, judged in the hindsight of history, must seem greatly out of proportion to the situation which Britain believed it was facing, was the fear of Egypt. The revolution was over twelve years old and Egypt and Abdul Nasser had become the principal focus for anti-colonial discontent throughout the world. Egypt was thought to be 'inciting' anti-British feeling wherever she found a sympathetic audience, which was not a difficult challenge. But if Britain had been more understanding of what the Egyptian revolution stood for in the minds of all Arabs, and had sought to make a friend of Abdul Nasser, the situation would have been very different. Abdul Nasser himself admired, as we have seen, much of what Britain stood for and what the British had achieved. It was said that he always wanted to know – and himself read – what the British papers were writing about him. He was often deeply hurt by what he saw as the deliberate distortion of Egypt's position and the attempts, by British media and politicians, to sour Egypt's relations with Britain and the West.

By June 1965 the situation had reached so critical a point that the Political Residency in Bahrain, as we have seen, urged consideration of actually abandoning British objections to the League's involvement in the affairs of the Trucial States. In this they were evidently influenced by the possibility of the treaties with Britain being denounced by 'four dissident shaikhs' as the Foreign Office described those they saw as particular troublemakers. In the event, this was avoided, and the crisis in the Gulf reached its climax and its resolution at the beginning of July 1965 when the Ruler of Sharjah was deposed and went into exile. The official version was that the deposition was the decision of a family council, the result of a loss of confidence in the Ruler's fitness to continue in office. The truth, as I understood it, was rather different.

The Shaikh was invited to a meeting with the Political Agent. He set out, attended by various of his retainers and two armoured cars. On his arrival at the Agency a paper was waved in front of him which was alleged to be the record of the family council's decision. The Shaikh asked to see the paper; this was refused. In fact, it bore only one signature, that of the Shaikh who was to succeed him as Ruler – and who was later to be murdered by the exiled Shaikh. He was led out of the back door of the Agency, avoiding his armed retainers at the front, driven to the airport and put on a flight to Bahrain. He was said to have wept as he saw his shaikhdom disappearing below him.

The British were not too concerned with ceremony when they felt that the time had come to remove a Ruler thought to be less co-operative than they would have wished. In Shaikh Saqr's case, it was his support of Gamal Abdul Nasser and Arab Nationalism which brought about his downfall. But his experience was not unique; the wonder is that the deposition of a Ruler, though it was a rare occurrence, was often carried out by British officials in the presence of heavily armed retainers, without any serious opposition being offered to them. This was one of the mysteries of the British colonial presence, the way in which the diktats of Whitehall (or, as in the case of the Gulf, of the Residency in Bahrain on Whitehall's behalf) were put into effect without a reaction from those who were supposed to be responsible for the Ruler's security. Never once was the action of the British resisted, so apparently powerful was the legend of Imperial might, even in its dying days.

Shortly before these events took place, a plan had been proposed for the formation of the League of the States of the Arabian Gulf,[21] but this was not to happen for some years and then under a different name. If the shaikhs had not been persuaded to maintain their traditional friendships with Britain, there is no knowing what Egypt's response might have been. It is unlikely that she would have sent troops to the states concerned, but undoubtedly there would have been a great upsurge in diplomatic activity which would certainly not have served Britain's remaining interests in the region.

Once the decision had been taken by the British to encourage the Trucial States Council to set up a development authority, the next decision was to determine its constitution and management. Their first thought, perhaps predictably, was that a Development Office, when it was established, should be under the control of a British director. An early candidate for this appointment seems to have been Brian Kendall, a friend of mine who was to be very much involved in the work of the Development Office, initially as its Acting Director. He was originally employed as Development Secretary in the Political Agency.[22]

The Rulers, and in particular Shaikh Rashid, felt that the appointment of a British director would send out quite the wrong signals. In the light of the British anxiety to counter Egyptian and Arab League influence, it seemed a little insensitive to propose that a non-Arab should head the board; certainly such an appointment would have played directly into the hands of those who were disposed to reduce, rather than increase, British influence on the coast.

The names of various Arab candidates were proposed though none of them was from the Gulf. Again, it was Shaikh Rashid who stood out for the appointment of a local man. Eventually two names were being discussed seriously: Sayyed Tariq bin Taimur Al-Busaid, a brother of the then Sultan of Oman, who was at that time virtually living in exile, and a Palestinian, Husni Abu Khalid.[23] Sayyed Tariq seems to have withdrawn from the discussion early on but Abu Khalid's name survived longer.

The process of the selection of the director was becoming unreasonably long-drawn-out and the British were increasingly apprehensive about the effects of the delay. In their dispatches to and from the Foreign Office and its Gulf posts, the officials made no attempt to disguise the fact that their anxiety to 'Arabize' the management of development in the Trucial States was their response to the Arab League's offer of development funds.[24] Equally they seem, perhaps rather optimistically, to have believed that an Arab director would 'increase the chances of getting aid from the sympathetic Arab states'.[25] Sometimes the advice was clearly confused; one suggestion was that 'a local dignitary (perhaps

on an annual rotating basis)'[26] should be appointed with 'contributing organizations', each having the right to appoint a deputy
director. It is not difficult to imagine the confusion which would
have resulted from such a course of action.

Kendall was still the Foreign Office's favoured choice; the
Ministry of Overseas Development, which was perhaps less
inclined to discretion than the diplomats, suggested that what was
needed was a 'figurehead' and that at all costs British influence
should be retained, especially over the distribution of funds. The
situation came to a head late in 1965 when, at a meeting of the
Council of the Trucial States, the Deliberative Committee, which
was to oversee the processes of development amongst the various
states, was actually formed; its members were nominated by the
Rulers and I represented Dubai as the nominee of Shaikh Rashid.

It was during these years, through the work of the Development
Office and the Deliberative Committee which directed its work,
that I became deeply involved with development in all the Trucial
States. I was wholly committed to the work and enthusiastic in
pushing through the projects which we sought to promote. I think
that I was able to help Kendall, for example, in obtaining funding
and logistical support for various of the programmes which we
introduced. I was not always popular, for I was so conscious of the
need for development schemes to be given priority that sometimes
I was intolerant of the special interests or entrenched positions of
individuals.

Brian Kendall continued in office as Acting Director during
these years. Finally it was decided that the time had come for a local
man to take over the responsibility. At a meeting of the Deliberative
Committee in 1971, attended by the British Political Agent,
various names were again discussed, this time in the open whereas
previously such discussion as there had been had taken place mainly
between the British officials responsible for the very uncertain
British policy in the Gulf. At the meeting to which I am referring,
the subject was reopened. Suddenly one of the shaikhs' representatives intervened and said, 'Why doesn't Easa take it on? He's
more experienced than anyone else, he gets on well with the
British and the fact that he's known for his sympathy with Arab

Nationalism won't be a disadvantage with the Egyptians or the Arab League.' The others at the meeting all agreed enthusiastically and so I found myself elected as Executive Director of the Trucial States Development Office.

I said that all those who were present were keen to see me take on the job. There may have been one reservation to this general enthusiasm; I suspect that the Political Agent of the day still had an alternative candidate whom he would have liked to put forward. In view of the unanimous adoption of the proposal to appoint me, however, he did not get the chance; in fact, we worked happily together when I took up my responsibilities as the Office's Director.

Some of the British officials were less generous in their response to my election; one of them, an architectural consultant, did not hide his dislike and mistrust, calling for my dismissal on the grounds that I was anti-British and a known Arab Nationalist. As many of my Arab friends thought that I was far too pro-British, I felt that I had probably got the balance about right. In any event my critic's attacks on me, which were in part motivated by the misguided concern that British contractors would lose out on contracts if I were appointed, were ignored.

Although there are aspects of this history of the Office's formation which I would find questionable and though I am quite sure that initially the British were concerned to advance their own strategies in the development of the area which they recognized must happen, I must acknowledge the remarkable skill and tactful diplomacy whereby British officials, in forming the Trucial States Council in the first place, managed to bring together a disparate group of individuals, many of whom had long-standing disputes with their neighbours. In the past, such disputes had frequently been resolved murderously, but the skill of individual British officials brought them together into a body which began to look at issues on a regional basis and not always in terms of clan or tribal advantage.

The formation of the Development Office, likewise, was a British initiative (whatever may have been its original motivation) and it was one of which they might reasonably be proud. Much of the credit for its creation must be attributed to my friend Donald

Hawley, who was Political Agent in Dubai from 1958 to 1961. His work was carried on by another friend, James Craig (now also knighted), Political Agent from 1961 to 1964, with whom I worked very closely, especially in development matters and their political implications.

I have described the process which went into the formation of the Development Office in some detail because it was a significant episode, for a number of reasons. First, it was a political response to a political situation, the fomenting of anti-British feeling in the Trucial States by the Arab League and Egypt and the consequent recognition by the British, however reluctantly, that their days were numbered. All the elements in the political situation contributed to their eventual withdrawal as 'Protecting Power' in 1971.

Then there was the acknowledgement that under British tutelage development had been very limited and, with the international attention which the League was focusing on the area, this was becoming embarrassing. The decision to promote development therefore came about partly as a result of the realization that their lack of action in the past was difficult to defend.

Above all, the entire process was important because it showed that, however difficult it might be, it was in fact possible to achieve a degree of co-operation amongst the states and a level of mutual participation in projects which had rarely, if ever, been the case in the past. In this respect the Development Office, like the Trucial States Council itself, anticipated the creation of the United Arab Emirates and, indeed, probably made it possible. The Council and the Office were also anticipations of the sort of institutions which are beginning to appear in the Gulf now, like the *majlis as-Shura* which, however limited they may at present be, are perhaps the forerunners of democratic institutions in the future.

For myself, the events which led up to the formation of the Development Office and my part in it were also important. I was now able to play a role in the development, not only of Dubai, as I had done since the accession of Shaikh Rashid, but in the states as a whole. From this experience my own business was ultimately to benefit when, on ceasing to be the director of the Development Office, I was able to resume *its* development. This was after the formation of the United Arab Emirates as an independent, sovereign state, whose various ministries succeeded to many of the responsibilities which the Office had undertaken.

I received only a nominal salary for my work in the Development Office. I retained my position at the bank which was happy to give me the freedom to undertake my tasks in the development of the economy and welfare of the societies throughout the Trucial States, which were included in the Office's responsibilities. This arrangement worked well enough and seemed to be in everyone's interest, since the bank was often able to facilitate the projects of the board, whose information and research facilities were valuable supports for the bank's work.

Shaikh Saqr bin Mohammed Al-Qasimi, the Ruler of Ras al-Khaimah, who was himself something of an intellectual, had become the Office's Chairman. I suggested earlier that the formation of the Office was significant in that it anticipated the introduction of the institutions which were to appear in later times. It was effectively the first open political institution formed in the southern Gulf. Young men from the various states were sent to Baghdad for training; a number of them have continued to this day to work for the prosperity of what is now the United Arab Emirates. They include Abdullah bin Humaid Al-Mzrouie, later the Minister of Labour and Minister of Justice, and Saif Al-Jawan, who, at the time of writing, is Minister of Labour, having held other ministerial appointments in the past.

It was clear to me, from the outset, that the Office should concern itself with the protection and advancement of traditional industries which had for generations provided a living for our people. This meant, in particular, fishing and agriculture and we concentrated our efforts on these two sectors and on the social infrastructures which were linked to them. The Office was provided with access to a helicopter to survey the land and as a result we were able to identify the lines of disused *aflaj* (the plural of *falaj*, the system of carrying water over long distances through channels both above and below ground, working by gravity) which could be reactivated and so bring water to gardens and plantations which had become arid.

We were given 150,000 rupees for this work, which was hardly sufficient. We had to be inventive in ways of saving money; these included delaying the payments of merchants' bills, even, sometimes in paying our employees' salaries late. However, the day came when the first of the *aflaj* for which we were responsible, at Hafra in Fujairah, was once more running with crystal-clear water. I was so overjoyed that I waded into it, up to my thighs, weeping tears of sheer happiness.

The work of the Office became known amongst the tribes in the desert interior who, naturally enough, wanted to share in the benefits of the development programme. We became involved in housing projects for the people, in reclaiming the *aflaj* and, with the access which this provided to additional supplies of water, to planting more trees and fruit gardens.

I have said that sometimes I found myself at odds with those whose priorities were different from my own. I was passionately convinced of the importance of bringing water to our people wherever this was possible. A contractor who was concerned to build houses argued strongly against my view. But I had a vision of trees, of birds nesting in them, of flowers and date plantations. Once water began to flow it could, if it were maintained properly, flow on for ever. Thus I believed that this aspect of our work would remain when the bones of all of us were long dry.

Often the wish to achieve results swiftly did not endear me to all of those with whom we worked, who sometimes failed to accomplish what they had undertaken. There was a plan to create some salt beds in an area between Ras al-Khaimah and Umm al-Qaiwain. Concrete beds were laid down where the incoming tide would flood them, the sunlight would evaporate the water and the salt, a highly valued commodity, would be left as a deposit. Time passed, one year, two years, more: no salt appeared. I became very angry; how was it, I asked, that man had been ten times to the moon and we could still not produce an ounce of salt?

I was ready always to cut through delays and the traditional arguments for postponing awkward or difficult decisions. I had become entirely accustomed to thinking in modern, technological terms, many of which I had absorbed from my contact with the British.

I persisted in these policies and I know that I was right to do so. But I would not want it thought that I am ignoring the value of the structures which the British had put in place, in the years before the Development Office was formed or when I became responsible for its management. We were greatly indebted to Donald Hawley, who campaigned vigorously for funds to enable a proper development programme to be introduced, and who never received the financial support from Whitehall that he had hoped for. After him, James Craig carried on and considerably extended many of the policies which Hawley had first introduced.

The programme of establishing medical clinics in the countryside, first introduced by the British, was vigorously extended in an attempt to look properly after the health of people who had never known such care. Doctors, recruited both before and after the formation of the Development Office, went into the countryside to bring the benefits of modern medical practice to the people. As there were few roads capable of accommodating a car, one of our intrepid doctors travelled around the states on a motorcycle, which, in the summer months, meant exposure to the region's terrible heat.

By herding cows and milking them mechanically we were able to provide clean milk, a great astonishment to the people. We made seeds available and provided instruction in agricultural and horticultural management. Tomatoes and cabbage were among our crops, adding considerably to the people's diet, in areas such as Digdaga in the territory of Ras al-Khaimah which had in the past been particularly deprived. We persuaded the shaikhs to provide land for cultivation and we began the replanting of date palm plantations, which in many parts of the Gulf had become seriously depleted. Two trade schools were launched, the first in Sharjah on Hawley's initiative and the second in Dubai on Craig's, under the direction of a British instructor, John Taylor. One of the trainees of the Sharjah school, Shaikh Sultan bin Mohammed Al-Qasimi, is now the Ruler of the state and the holder of a British Ph.D.

Programmes of development also continued in the more advanced centres, like Dubai itself, and gained pace as time went on. One of Dubai's achievements at this time was the introduction of electricity in our region. In this we were helped by Shaikh Rashid who provided us with 200,000 of the 500,000 rupees which the project demanded. With the help of International Airadio Limited, who had an involvement in air-traffic-control systems and were to design Dubai's airport, we introduced a telephone service, the ancestor of what is generally regarded today as one of the most comprehensive and efficient services in the world. We even inaugurated street lighting in some of the towns.

The Trucial States Development Office was fortunate in that Shaikh Zayed bin Sultan Al-Nahayan became Ruler of Abu Dhabi just as it came into being. He was a most generous benefactor and channelled many hundreds of thousands of pounds from Abu Dhabi's new-found oil revenues into providing all manner of services for all the people of the coast. Health care consumed a large part of our budget but we had an immense range of projects which we were able to carry through, from the building of the clinics to the roofing-over of the *souq* in a small town.

For us, development started from scratch. Every shop, every street, every hut on the beach for the fishermen for which the Development Office was responsible, was a small triumph. For the first time the people of the villages and small towns and the *badu* of the interior could begin to enjoy some of the benefits which the modern world had to bestow, for themselves and for their children. It was especially so in the case of the children, for the clinics which the Development Office funded began to make significant inroads into the appallingly high rates of infant mortality which had become accepted as part of the way of life on the coast.

As our work increased, so did public awareness of what we were doing. The public quickly accepted that we were a beneficent influence in their lives and readily co-operated with our staff working in the field, when their co-operation was needed. The shaikhs of the region, too, recognized that our work was changing the established order and began to put pressure on us to introduce schemes to benefit their people. Although such lobbying was fair enough and although sometimes it was difficult to achieve, we always maintained a policy of scrupulous fairness and honesty in all our dealings.

The work of the Office, especially in its early days, was discharged by a small, dedicated staff. My immediate assistant was Abdullah bin Humaid Al-Mzrouie, who was sent to Baghdad to further his training. The senior expatriate member of the organization was Brian Kendall, who directed the work of three British engineers. Broadcasting came into our portfolio and that was the charge of Riad Shuaibi, a Palestinian who set up and ran what ultimately became the United Arab Emirates radio and television service.

Our senior medical officer was Dr Asem Jamali. He had been recruited originally by Donald Hawley; James Craig later arranged for him to be sent to London for further training. He was responsible for the setting-up and management of the clinics which we established and, later, for the direction of the hospitals in the region. Our other colleagues, drawn from all the disciplines which were necessary to our work, included Palestinians, Zanzibaris, Indians and British. We all got along very well together. I look back on my involvement with the Trucial States Development Office with pride. I think I can say that, with my colleagues, I was one of those who helped to bring civilization to our coast.

The British authorities still represented a considerable influence in our affairs. Having taken only occasional interest in the welfare of our people in the past (they would argue, reasonably enough, that was not why they were there), the advent of the much-feared threat of 'Nasserism' made them realize that improved living conditions for the people would make the alternative claims of Nasserism less attractive. Such concerns often produced good effects, as when the British persuaded some of the richer states in the Gulf, notably Kuwait, to support us by making funds available, either by way of grants or by 'soft' loans. In this way, as I have already recorded, the Kuwaitis lent the money for the clearing of the Creek at Dubai, which transformed the state's economy.

Each of the states in the Trucial States Council had its own identity and character. As our work increased and it was observed that we were expending quite substantial amounts of money, jealousies were inevitably aroused. Dubai had always been the most advanced of the states in terms of its trading capacities; it could be said that Dubai's character was mercantile whilst that of Abu Dhabi was essentially traditionalist. When prosperity began to rise, as a consequence at least in part of what we were doing, fingers were pointed to the fact that I was a Dubaian and Dubai was becoming paramount in the trade of the region.

In fact, I did not favour Dubai above any of the other states but sometimes the British (with whom, as always, I was identified) did seem to put more benefits in the way of Dubai than they did some of the other states. The reason for this was, I believe, simple: in Shaikh Rashid they had found their man, one who understood what they were trying to achieve and, in so far as it might help his people, helped them to do so. Shaikh Rashid, incidentally, himself provided the funds for Dubai's principal development projects as well as contributing financially to the funds of the Development Office, for the benefit of the other states. Abu Dhabi, of course, did the same.

It was in the British interest to raise the level of sophistication in what, up to this time, had been one of the more backward of their spheres of influence. This was why they had begun to promote contact between the shaikhs, which led eventually to the creation of the Trucial States Council. I suspect that they originally had in mind the precedent of India and were inclined to turn the Rulers of the Gulf into maharajahs. If so, they miscalculated, for Arab culture and traditions were wholly different from those of the subcontinent; the Rulers, until the advent of oil, were very poor and could not maintain the sort of state that an Indian prince would take for granted. But I believe that the traditions of the Gulf, when they are properly understood, will make for the development of a more enduring society than that represented by the Indian states. Because of the essentially open and democratic nature of Islamic society, government has, in reality, always been closer to the people than in most other systems.

For ourselves, we were certainly not conscious of being so deeply involved in the politics of the region during the course of our work, but the various tensions and jealousies amongst the states meant that inevitably we were drawn into their disputes. In the same way, we were not aware that we were making history; yet, in the process of bringing health, education and material prosperity to people who had for so long been deprived, we were clearly as much changing the history of our part of the world as a conqueror might have done in the past – and, generally speaking, more benevolently.

7

B Y THE MID-SIXTIES IT was clear that the British would be forced to change their role in the affairs of the Gulf as a whole and in our part in particular. The war of 1967 between the State of Israel and the Arabs, led by Egypt, had been traumatic and had severely damaged the confidence of the Arab world in its future. Palestine was still a dominant issue but Egypt was now exhausted, an exhaustion which was to be seen in the face of Gamal Abdul Nasser himself. My own beliefs were unchanged though I had to admit that my priorities were altered by my involvement in the work of the Development Office and, later, by the demands of my own business.

During the sixties a number of discussions were conducted between the shaikhs and the British which explored the possibility of fundamental political change in the Gulf, with the Rulers assuming much more responsibility for the destiny of their own states and people. The most popular option which the British proposed vigorously was that of 'Federation'. This had been a favourite solution to the post-colonialist dilemma of the Imperial power but it had been singularly unsuccessful. Successive schemes had been hatched and applied in East Africa, the Caribbean, South Arabia and Malaya; only the last, based on an imaginative principle of a revolving kingship amongst the traditional (and, incidentally, Moslem) Rulers of the area, had shown any signs of lasting. All the others had ended, or were about to end, in disaster.

Nonetheless, the British pressed doggedly on, exploring the prospects of bringing the widely differing and often mutually suspicious Rulers and tribal groups of the Gulf into some sort of federal arrangement. The Rulers, understandably, saw the discussions, which never really reached the level of negotiations, as the opportunity for advancing their own interests and status. Only Shaikh Rashid in Dubai and Shaikh Zayed in Abu Dhabi when he became Ruler in 1966, brought sincere and thoughtful counsels to the meetings in which the future of the entire region and its people was being discussed.

From the outset, the problems which would act against the idea of federation could be recognized. The member states of the Trucial States Council were at least in the position of having had nearly twenty years of contact and interaction, even though it had often been slight. But states like Bahrain and Qatar, which would also be radically affected by any changes which the British might precipitate, were in a quite different situation, Bahrain with a developed administration and a recent history as the regional headquarters for the British administration, and Qatar which had aspirations to rival and to outdo Bahrain in everything. It was not likely that they would make easy partners in any grouping which the British might propose.

Once again, it was Shaikh Rashid who tried his hardest to promote the idea of a form of union amongst his fellow rulers, a fact which is clear from a reading of the British records of the time;[1] in this he was only partly successful. In particular, the Ruler of Sharjah, who had been the only one to accept the Egyptians into his territory when he had agreed to the setting-up of the Egyptian educational mission, opposed any sort of co-operation between the states; the British found him increasingly difficult to deal with and this was why he was eventually removed from the Rulership. After his departure, British suspicions tended to focus on the Ruler of Ras al-Khaimah; the Political Residency in Bahrain advised London that Ras al-Khaimah had become 'the new soft spot through which Nasser, under cover of the Arab League, is likely to renew his attempts to penetrate the Trucial States'.[2]

One of the crucial issues which had to be faced in the event of a change in the political structure of the Trucial States was the matter of a common currency. For some years, this question occupied the British, more specifically the Bank of England and all the financial institutions like BBME who had a concern with banking and the region's international trade.

For many years, Indian Imperial currency had been accepted throughout the states but, with Indian independence long established and the growing status of the Trucial States themselves, this was obviously no longer appropriate. There were also worrying rumours circulating in the early sixties that India was planning to devalue her currency, which indeed did eventually happen. To prepare for this eventuality and also to demonstrate the increasing economic importance of the Trucial States in the world, currency links were proposed between several of the states during these years. Amongst these proposals was one for the Dubai–Qatar Riyal, a unit of currency which underlined the relatively close ties which had developed between the two countries since the Ruler of Qatar had married Shaikh Rashid's daughter.

Shaikh Rashid early on appreciated that a common currency would do much to ensure that the several states would work together, moving inevitably towards some sort of federal structure. He realized that Abu Dhabi was certain to become an important member of any future grouping of the states and to this end decided to invite Shaikh Shakhbut to join in the proposed Dubai–Qatar currency. Shaikh Rashid prepared a letter[3] inviting Shaikh Shakhbut to participate. He asked me to go to Abu Dhabi to give Shaikh Shakhbut the letter and to discuss it with him. In the event, Shaikh Shakhbut did not comment on the letter but promised to read it and to reply to Shaikh Rashid in due course. From the dispatches sent to London by the Political Agency in Abu Dhabi at this time[4] it is clear that, unfortunately only too typically, Shaikh Shakhbut distrusted Shaikh Rashid's approach, suspecting that he was really concerned to lay hands on Abu Dhabi's future wealth. Shaikh Shakhbut was more inclined to join with Bahrain, although he was annoyed that the Bahrain Government had already taken the step of introducing its own currency. However, he admired the Bahrainis and regarded the state as being particularly well governed, so was prepared to drop reservations which he might otherwise have had. Coinage and banknotes issued by the Bahrain Currency Board had already begun to circulate in Abu Dhabi, reflecting the traditional ties which had for long connected the two shaikhdoms: there was also a plan to link the Gulf states' currencies with the Saudi Riyal after the devaluation of the Indian Rupee in June 1966. Shaikh Rashid's proposal would, I believe, have strengthened the economic basis of the Trucial States at this time, for if it had proceeded it would have meant that three of the states would have held their currencies in common, two of which, Abu Dhabi and Qatar, were well on the way to enjoying substantial revenues from oil; the third, Dubai, though at that time without comparable earnings from oil (this was to come later), would undoubtedly have been able to contribute to the prosperity of the association by the already demonstrable vigour of its economy.

The intricacies of the currency market were the occasion for the most important and most dramatic political change in the Trucial coast in the years immediately before the formation of the United Arab Emirates. I have described how everyone who had dealings with him, not least the British, found negotiations with Shaikh Shakhbut of Abu Dhabi increasingly difficult. He was as one lost in the new world which was opening for the people of the Middle East, with the development of the oil industry. He genuinely feared the onset of the modern world and of what its influences, all of them for the worse in his eyes, might do to his people.

However, Shaikh Shakhbut was an astute man. I have described how he sought to associate Abu Dhabi's currency with Bahrain's, the style of whose government he greatly admired. He was also a close friend of the Sultan of Oman, Sayyid Said bin Taimur Al-Busaid, whose policies and actions were often as unpredictable as Shaikh Shakhbut's. Shaikh Shakhbut showed signs of wanting to merge Abu Dhabi's currency with that of Oman, and as at this period Oman had very few revenues of its own, it was a situation which the British could not ignore. The stakes had become very high.

It was now evident to the British authorities that Shaikh

Shakhbut would have to be replaced. After Shaikh Zayed succeeded him, the British prepared a report containing a confidential assessment of the new Ruler's personality and of his history to date. The report makes clear what very great pressure Shaikh Zayed was under in the months preceding his brother's deposition. It comments that international opinion was anxious for a change, for 'Abu Dhabi had become a scandal'. Similarly, members of the Ruling Family recognized that the situation could not remain unchanged. When Shaikh Zayed returned from an overseas trip he found all of the arguments awaiting him, with added dissatisfaction being voiced by the tribal leaders.[5] Shaikh Shakhbut went into exile and Shaikh Zayed became the Ruler of Abu Dhabi.

One consequence of the deposition of Shaikh Shakhbut was the intense displeasure of Shaikh Rashid. To a very traditional Arab Ruler, as he was, the deposition of one of his peers was a most grievous matter. The British recorded what they described as Shaikh Rashid's 'recent outburst' to them, complaining that they were 'unseating Rulers right and left'.[6] It appears that Shaikh Rashid asked the British for an assurance of their continued protection. This they did not give, evidently being prepared only to confirm their obligation to protect the states against external aggression. Once again, Shaikh Rashid was said to be 'extremely upset' at the treatment of Shaikh Shakhbut.[7]

Shaikh Rashid's attitude began to cloud his hitherto very good relations with Shaikh Zayed, which went back at least until the forties. In the minds of the British, at least, were suspicions that he was 'stirring up trouble' amongst some of the other states, notably Sharjah and Ras al-Khaimah;[8] this last was likely to alarm the British in view of their fears that Ras al-Khaimah might become the successor to Sharjah as the likely point of the admission of Nasserite influences into the coast.

The Foreign Office records of the time contain a report from a senior official in the Political Agency in Dubai,[9] of a conversation with me in which I recounted a conversation with Shaikh Zayed, who expressed his concern at the evident deterioration of relations between himself and Shaikh Rashid and asked me why it should be so. I did not reply to Shaikh Zayed's question at once, for I had only just returned from a long leave. However, I emphasized that it was essential for the two leaders, the most important in the Trucial States, to be on the best possible terms with each other. Shaikh Zayed agreed and said that he would welcome a return to friendly relations.

Shaikh Zayed was apparently concerned that Shaikh Rashid nourished ambitions to become the dominant influence in the northern Trucial States. He suspected that Shaikh Rashid was planning to turn Ras al-Khaimah 'into a satellite state'; the Political Agent in turn was apprehensive that Qatar and Abu Dhabi 'might gang up' on Dubai.[10]

The Foreign Office report provides details of my subsequent conversation with Shaikh Rashid. On his repeating the misgivings which he had expressed at the manner of Shaikh Zayed's accession, I am said to have urged him to put such ideas out of his mind (the Foreign Office dispatch says that I 'told him to come off it'), as he must have known that the British would only intervene to remove a bad Ruler. Shaikh Rashid agreed that Shaikh Shakhbut's conduct had brought the situation on himself. On the issue of his relations with Shaikh Zayed, I asked that I might be allowed to act as an intermediary between the two of them. Happily, the good relations between the two were restored. The Political Agent in Abu Dhabi tells of a meeting with Shaikh Zayed, which included reference to 'a satisfactory letter from Issa [sic] Gurg.'[11]

The politics of the Trucial States Council in these years before the British withdrawal and the formation of the United Arab Emirates were complicated, as will be seen from these episodes which I have described. All of the arguments about the various proposals relating to currencies ultimately withered away at the introduction, in 1973, of the United Arab Emirates Dirham which is the unit of currency employed today by all the states.[12] However, whatever may have been the truth of his seeking to play off the various states which were Dubai's neighbours against each other, I believe that Shaikh Rashid's customary far-sightedness had realized at least seven years earlier the desirability of bringing as many of the principal states in the Trucial States Council as possible into an economic association.

The impending departure of the British from the Gulf pre-occupied the minds of most people who had any very substantial interests at stake, throughout the latter years of the sixties, long before any official announcement was made. Indeed, Shaikh Rashid told a British official of a conversation which he had had during an official visit to Iran with General Bakhtiar, the Iranian Deputy Prime Minister and head of the intelligence organization, Savak, in which the General told Shaikh Rashid that the British had given the Iranians 'a secret promise' to withdraw from the Gulf 'within fifteen years'.[13] This story may well have had its origins in the Iranians' optimism about their future role in the defence of the Gulf, and the likelihood of the British having given any such promise is remote; it is, however, perfectly possible that they 'planted' the idea with the Iranians, knowing that they would pass it on to the Gulf shaikhdoms, thus alerting them to the possibility of British withdrawal without the necessity of the British them-selves having to declare their hand directly. Nonetheless, the story does suggest the extent to which the possibility of a British with-drawal was being talked of, even in the late fifties when the conversation referred to took place.[14]

Most of us who were politically aware, especially those who shared the ideals of Arab Nationalism, fully expected to see the British remove themselves entirely from the Middle East. The idea of an ordered withdrawal, therefore, never really came into our calculations. When it became apparent that this was the way it was about to happen, our only course was to try to adjust to an entirely new situation. We had to recognize that although the British pres-ence was officially no more, the British themselves were still very much with us.

British apprehension at what they anticipated could be the deterioration of the situation in the Trucial States in the middle and late sixties is revealed by the preparation of a paper on the prospects of sabotage in Dubai by those who supported the ideals of Arab Nationalism. Shaikh Rashid was seen as a potential target for assassination, and the author of the report deplored Shaikh Rashid's refusal to take what he regarded as 'adequate precautions'. The report also proposed that 'Arabs sympathetic to the British presence' should be warned of the dangers to which they were exposed and that they should be supplied with arms and trained to use them. I am not aware that this recommendation was ever adopted.[15]

During the period that I was responsible for the Development Office I was exceptionally committed to my work, in addition to my other concerns. For this reason, I do not think that I was as taken up with the wider political issues as I had been in past times. The goal which all of us who believed in Arab Nationalism pursued was the union of the Arabic-speaking peoples and the restoration of the Arab nations' place in the world – a goal which mirrored my own personal determination to restore the standing and prestige of my family. In fact, so involved was I in development projects throughout the Trucial States and particularly in Dubai, that I did not follow my own business interests with the degree of single-mindedness which would otherwise have been the case. This continued to be the case throughout the period from 1965 to 1972; by the latter date, the United Arab Emirates had been formed and the responsibility for development and for all the departments which had been contained within our brief, had become federal responsibilities and the reason for the Development Office's separate existence had ended.

By this time, however, we had a great deal of experience and know-how; we also had a substantial database on conditions throughout the shaikhdoms which I felt would be of immense value to the new administration which would need to be established to run the UAE. I proposed, therefore, that the senior officials who were to be responsible for the various departments, constituted as ministries in the UAE, such as health, education, agriculture, fishing and housing, should spend, say, six months in each department familiarizing themselves with its problems and the information which it had at its disposal. They would be able to sit with our experts and, in an entirely methodical way, take over our work and integrate it into the new government structure which would emerge.

Sadly, the sort of jealousies and suspicions which seem always to accompany any attempt in our part of the world to offer simple, objective help, immediately became evident. I was accused of acting like a Prime Minister, of wanting, in the words of one authority, 'to form a government in the entrails of another'.

It really was not like that at all. I believed passionately, as I still do, in the virtues of law and order prevailing in all societies and that what is for the general good should determine the actions of all who are engaged in public life. I spoke earlier of Shaikh Rashid's court, in the early days, being like that which surrounded a Tudor monarch. To follow the same thought, inspired by *A Man for All Seasons*, the film by which I was so impressed with during my first visit to London, I saw myself as a very small Sir Thomas More, who believed in the supremacy of justice. Happily, unlike poor Sir Thomas, I managed to keep my head.

The largely unexpected return of the Conservative Party to power in Britain in 1970 encouraged some people in the Gulf to believe that the policy of withdrawal, which had been announced by the previous Labour Government, might be reversed, but by this time it was never really a possibility. The shaikhs offered to underwrite the costs of maintaining the British forces in the region but the offer was refused, the British insisting, in a rather hurt fashion, that they were not mercenaries.

The formal announcement came in the House of Commons on 14 February 1971, when the British Foreign Secretary, Sir Alec Douglas-Home, advised the House that British forces would be withdrawn by the end of December that year. The constitution which was adopted had been prepared by the British as a provisional, working draft. It was, however, taken over as the formal instrument determining the constitution of the new state. I confess that I regretted the adoption of the British model, which in some particulars has never really seemed to me to be adequate for a modern state in the modern world; in fact, I regarded it as little more than a 'Schedule of Work', a draft plan which had been produced by the then Political Agent, Julian Walker. It was, perhaps deliberately, vague and unspecific in parts and I would have been happier if the constitution prepared by the Egyptian constitutional expert, Dr Abdul Razak Sanhuri, had been adopted. He had drafted the Kuwaiti constitution which would, I think, have served as a much better model for our purposes. The British did not like it, however, and as they were still the dominant influence at the time of the discussions on constitutional issues, their wishes carried the day. The 'Temporary Constitution' proposed by the British remains in place to this day; the only significant change is that the word 'temporary' has been dropped. It is an intriguing thought, by the way, that the discarded constitution prepared for the Trucial States Council even provides for the protection of fundamental rights and freedoms of the individual.[16]

Undoubtedly, British officials helped significantly in bringing some of the reluctant shaikhs into the union, and their support internationally was of considerable help. The intricate and sensitive negotiations for the creation of the union required a sound diplomatic hand. Such a hand was found in Sir Geoffrey Arthur, the last British official to occupy the post of Political Resident in the Gulf. He it was who signed the various instruments founding the UAE and effecting the final confirmation of the sovereign independent status of the Emirates of Bahrain and Qatar. Arthur was a remarkable man and it was sad that he lived for only a comparatively short time after his retirement.

It was interesting for me to observe, at this time, the subtlety of Britain's handling of the various diverse and complicated elements which went to make up a political settlement as complex as the formation of the UAE. It is curious, to my mind, to compare the tactful consideration with which British officials managed this issue in their dealings with the shaikhs and other leaders of our societies, with the often harsh and insensitive way in which they had dealt with the same people in the past. I suppose that their priorities were different.

They managed always to handle each of the principal shaikhs in a quite different way, thus ensuring that they achieved the response which they sought. Sometimes one who had shown himself a friend to Britain might find that he was less generously treated than another on whose support the British felt less able to rely. The major foreign powers in the region all developed techniques for dealing with the shaikhs; when the Americans wanted to persuade one of a difficult course of action, they would arrange for their case first to be argued by a Saudi; with the British it was the Kuwaitis who fulfilled the same function.

It will be clear that, as the time for the formation of the Union approached, and as the nature of the British role in the Gulf began to change, Shaikh Rashid assumed a much greater regional influence and was of great help in bringing the Union into existence. His growing importance had been signalled some time before when one day I was asked to call on the Political Agent. It had been decided, he said, that it was no longer fitting for Shaikh Rashid to come to the Agency when there were matters of importance to discuss. Rather, for the future, the British officials would wait on him at his residence or at his office. I was asked to convey this proposal to Shaikh Rashid.

He rejected it out of hand. The British were bewildered, as they knew that Shaikh Rashid had wanted to have a Political Agent attached solely to Dubai, in a manner similar to Abu Dhabi; they obviously thought that their intention to call on him, rather than the other way about, would indicate a major change in his status in the eyes of the British Government and hence, would enhance his status in Dubai and the rest of the coast.

I represented their arguments to the Shaikh. He listened and then said to me, 'Don't you understand? If they call on me I have to receive them politely, listen to what they have to say, agree with whatever they want if I can. Our ways demand this; they know it and if they find that I agree to one request they will add another, and then another and another. But if I go to them and give them the opportunity to raise the issue which they want to discuss, I let them finish what they have to say. Then I will say to them, "Is this what you wanted to discuss?" When they reply, "Yes," I will answer, "Thank you very much," and leave at once.'

I came to admire Shaikh Rashid's political skills very much. He had become a superb political tactician who managed to keep good relations with all his neighbours; this, as anyone familiar with the Gulf in those days will know, was no small achievement. He could change his attitudes to suit whomever he was speaking to; it was necessary, he said, 'to wear a different shirt for different meetings'.

I have said that he was particularly close to the Sultan of Oman,

142

Sayyid Said bin Taimur, whom many people found difficult and complex in his dealings; Sayyid Said himself was later to be deposed. Shaikh Rashid also kept good relations with the Saudis despite the various boundary disputes which beset a number of the states and their largest neighbour, and he maintained the goodwill of the Shah, although he ruled the largest Shia nation and Shaikh Rashid was a devout Sunni Moslem. When Saddam Hussein attacked Iran after that country's revolution and demanded that Dubai should cease trading with Iraq's enemy, Shaikh Rashid was at his most Machiavellian and somehow managed both to mollify Saddam and to continue Dubai's highly profitable business with the Islamic Republic.

The British were helpful, in these last days, in a number of practical ways: for example, in the supply of experts to help with setting up the various departments of state which the UAE would require, particularly in the cases of the armed forces, the police and security. My earlier misgivings, that they might appoint people who would principally follow their own interests, remained, though many of the advisers whom they introduced have in fact been wholly committed to the various states which they served, and later to the UAE itself.

The British welcomed the formation of the UAE enthusiastically, both because they recognized the need for change and because it relieved them of a substantial part of the responsibility for the region's affairs, which Whitehall was finding distinctly burdensome. They also saw it providing a buffer in the future between Saudi Arabia and the Sultanate of Oman, with which Britain retained close relations, playing a major support and military role in the campaigns of Sultan Qabus bin Said to reunite his country and to eliminate the Communist-backed rebels who were active in the south.

Shaikh Rashid was worried that, as the prospect of the British withdrawal neared, the Rulers had still not resolved all their differences nor had they really made up their minds to make the union work. The problem of the status of Bahrain and Qatar remained, both of which, for their own reasons, had reservations about joining the UAE; and I think it was clear that the British did not wish them to do so. In the event, they did not join, and the United Arab Emirates, a uniquely constituted state consisting of a union of seven independent sovereign states governed by traditional Rulers and presided over by a President elected from among their number, was brought into being and formally proclaimed in December 1971, immediately before the British withdrawal.

That the UAE has survived and flourished to the extent which it undoubtedly has is a tribute in large part to the wisdom of Shaikh Rashid on the one hand, and on the other to the open-handed generosity and leadership of Shaikh Zayed of Abu Dhabi. Without these two men, there is no doubt that the Union would frequently have collapsed into the disputatious divisions which had marked our part of the world for so long.

It is in the nature of Islamic culture, and the Arab heritage, that the free and unrestricted access of the people to those who have responsibility for government has meant that many of the tensions and grievances which have affected larger, industrialized societies have been less corrosive in ours. That each state has been able to maintain its own identity and independence, permitting healthy competition between them, has also contributed to its success. This is not to suggest that everything is for the best or that no change is either desirable or necessary, but it is right to point to the success that the union has achieved, and to the prospects for the future prosperity and happiness of its people to which the very fact of its existence may eventually lead. My work with the Development Office had given me a vision of what a proper degree of co-operation between the states of the coast might achieve. From this experience I truly realized what the UAE might become.

The achievements of these years have been very great, greater by far than I could ever have dreamt. The extraordinary efforts of Shaikh Zayed and Shaikh Rashid to create the UAE cannot be overstated, nor can their accomplishments be adequately measured. Those who had the privilege of working with them in these years, in whatever capacity, were sharing in an experiment unique in the history of our region. The centuries of distrust and dissension, if they were not entirely excluded, were set aside. It was as if the 152 years of neglect and the exploitation of the Gulf ports as convenient stopping-off points for men and supplies on the routes to and from India, served now as an encouragement to make up for all the time which had been lost.

In all the responsibilities with which the Development Office had been charged and which were inherited by the central government, great advances have been made which have entirely changed the lives of our people. That the UAE can now count itself amongst the most favoured of nations is not only the consequence of oil wealth; it is also the result of a small number of men (of whom I believe I was one) who had a vision, and the capacity for making that vision reality. Of course there has been the downside: inevitably there has been waste, sometimes the priorities were wrong and not infrequently individuals have put their interests above the general good. But such is the way of the world and if there has been waste it has not been excessive; and as often as not it contributed, at least, to the prosperity of the *souq*.

Development, at all levels, speeded up enormously once the UAE became responsible for it, on a scale greater than we had ever imagined. With the formation of the UAE came a spirit of healthy competition amongst the Rulers of the various states over the development of their particular territory. As a result of this, the whole region began to develop very rapidly. The people of the UAE are strongly business-minded and industrious; if government in the region can be organized more directly on modern lines, the growth which could be anticipated over the next twenty years would be immense. It is remarkable that despite the extreme degree of change which the society experienced in these years it did not become destabilized; although the older among us no doubt deplore the passing of the ways with which we were familiar, the younger generation is balanced and now richly endowed with talented, highly educated people who should contribute much to the future growth of our country.

Much of what has been achieved is the result of the initiatives which Dubai took in the days before oil began to flow. The policies of Shaikh Rashid, although on a relatively small scale, had shown that it was possible for people of widely different cultures to live in harmony together. Dubai was, for its time, a sophisticated community and its example had an effect all along the coast. This, added to the capacity for absorbing change which I believe is one of the characteristics of an Islamic society, made what was done in Dubai and later in the other states so important. For me, one thing is certain. That I spent the years that I did in the early management of development projects in the territory which was to become the United Arab Emirates is a source of great and abiding pride to me.

I am convinced that the UAE will stand as an example of what an Arab state can achieve when it has the resources and the will to change its fortunes. Equally important is the fact that the UAE, though it has recruited the help and expertise of many nations, has been responsible for its own destinies during these past years. This, I am quite sure, is what has made the UAE's achievements, in so short a time span, so remarkable. It demonstrates what it is possible for the Arabs to achieve if they set out with clear objectives and the assurance which the control of their own destiny brings.

When I think of what countries like Iraq before the revolution would have been capable of, with their resources and the talents of a great and industrious people, I could weep that their place in the history of our region was so blighted by the interference of foreign powers concerned only for their own interests, who unwittingly created the situation in which the revolution of Abdul Karim Qassem was inevitable, as inevitable as was the martyrdom of Iraq under the Ba'ath Party. The notorious Baghdad Pact, engineered by Nuri Said and the British, was an example of how the involvement of foreign powers, as late as the fifties, was no longer acceptable in our part of the world. The pact was bitterly opposed by Nasser and was one of the principal causes of the revolution which destroyed the Iraqi monarchy in 1958.

What might Egypt not have done if the Egyptians themselves had been able to take command of their own affairs and not had to wait for Gamal Abdul Nasser? He restored pride and purpose in the Egyptians and in the Arabs but, because of the prevailing climate of international politics at the time and the distrust of the West, even he was not able to turn events successfully in a new direction. Though it is a small nation, it has been the UAE's unique destiny to show what still can be realized and that the Arabs can be great.

Of course, there is still much to be done; just as great opportunities remain for the citizens of the UAE, so there are still social inadequacies which will need the attention and understanding of the authorities in the states if the people, who are becoming increasingly aware, are able to realize their full potential and to play their part in taking the UAE even further ahead amongst the community of nations at large. Passports are still required for travel between the Gulf states, despite the existence of the Arab Gulf Co-operation Council, and customs duties are still levied on goods passing from one state to another; but I have no doubt that one day these will disappear.

8

THE YEARS WHICH NOW followed were busy and demanding for me. I was still involved in the unfolding political developments which led to the formation and early growth of the UAE but, sadly, the close relationship which I had enjoyed with Shaikh Rashid for so long came under strain and eventually fractured. The problem, I believe, was that as he grew older Shaikh Rashid became more dependent on the advice of some of those close to him who did not always present their recommendations to him entirely objectively. He had often said that my value to him was that I always told him the truth; later in his life perhaps this became less important to him than it once had been.

These years were often times of stress and anxiety for me. Sometimes I felt that I was swimming in a sea of darkness and I did not know what monsters I might encounter. Like all Arabs of my generation, I had lived through the catastrophe of the 1967 war with Israel and its outcome in the humiliation of the Arabs and the blighting of the prospects of an Arab union. But my own businesses, to which I was now able to give more attention, expanded and their variety of interests widened out from the largely consumer-oriented fields with which I had begun and which were still very important to me, to projects and products which were more industrial in scale and operation. I shall describe this aspect of my life further in Chapter 9.

I was now the senior consultant to the bank on Arab affairs and as such I was constantly asked to advise the directors on the rapidly changing situation in the Gulf and, in particular, in the Emirates which now formed the UAE. I travelled widely, visiting countries of which I had not even dreamt when I was young. These journeys also brought me more opportunities, for the expansion of my business and the introduction to Dubai of new products and services. I was always ready to seize an opportunity when it presented itself; I reacted to such occasions with enthusiasm and with the rather aggressive spirit which I have always brought to all my dealings, but I was still guided in all I did by the precepts which my father had taught me and by my determination to restore the honour and dignity of our family.

One way in which my changing status came early on to be recognized was in the field in which my business life had really begun: banking. I had gained an immense amount of experience during my years with BBME and as the Trucial States changed into the United Arab Emirates it was clear that banking would be an essential component of the local commercial scene for the future. With the Emirates' access to very substantial funds, a situation which increased each year after the rise in oil prices in 1973 which put the oil-producing countries on level terms with the oil companies and the consuming countries, a lively local banking industry was essential.

If I may be allowed a digression at this point, I have been greatly interested to discover in recent years, as a result of the work of historians and archaeologists working in the region, what a crucial part the Arabian Gulf has played in the history of banking and how very ancient our banking traditions are. Most people, if they have thought about it at all, will probably say that the roots of modern banking lie in the international houses formed in the eighteenth and nineteenth centuries in Europe, particularly by the great Jewish banking families. Others, with perhaps a deeper sense of history, may point to the immense power of the banking and trading businesses established by the Italian and French magnates in the Middle Ages; others may even consider that some of the orders of knighthood of the Christian West in Crusading times, notably the Knights Templar, who perhaps borrowed from financial institutions in the Moslem world, were the real ancestors of modern banking.

In fact, none of these is the earliest in the field. This distinction belongs to the organizations which were established at the end of the third millennium BC in the Arabian Gulf, to facilitate the trade which was conducted by merchants from Mesopotamia (now Iraq), down the Gulf and across the Indian Ocean to the great cities which flourished in the Indus Valley. This trade was even then of considerable antiquity, from early in the third millennium at least, when the Sumerians, the original inhabitants of southern Mesopotamia, voyaged up and down the Gulf in search particularly of copper which they bartered for goods manufactured in establishments very like modern factories.

Archaeologists working in Iraq and in all the Gulf states have found considerable evidence of this trade.[1] In the period from about 2300 to 1700 BC it was centred on Bahrain; however, much earlier settlements have been found in Oman and, particularly, in the UAE. From sites in Iraq a quantity of fascinating written evidence has been recovered, in the form of baked clay tablets on which the commercial records of the merchants trading throughout the area are preserved. From these we learn not only of the sort of products and goods which were traded, but also of the role of bankers in cities like Ur in southern Iraq (the home of the Prophet Abraham, the Friend of God) and the services which they provided to facilitate the activities of the traders.

These included the issuing of letters of credit, so that a merchant trading far from his home base could obtain the means to barter in a distant foreign land. Mortgages were held on property and goods against the provision of facilities; 'funds' were provided to the captains of vessels trading on their own account and a share of the profits agreed in advance. There were even 'Joint and Several Guarantees', committing all the partners in an enterprise collectively and individually to the repayment of advances made by the 'bankers'. The system was even more sophisticated when it is appreciated that this was in the days long before the invention of money (though there was something like a silver standard) and all loans and investments were expressed in terms of goods traded.

Altogether the facilities which these 'bankers' of four thousand years ago offered their clients, and the obligations which both sides undertook and which were confirmed by contracts, are remarkably similar to the basic mechanics of banking today. With my sense of the past, it was good to feel that I was sharing in so very ancient a tradition and that the concept of banking and bankers had originated on these shores.

But to return to the present day, my own bank, BBME, had been looking, rather tentatively, at expanding its operations as a whole in the Middle East. One of the markets which was of interest, though it was still controversial in the minds of some of our colleagues, was Egypt. After the war of 1973 and the consolidation of Anwar Sadat's authority, the commercial prospects in the Nile Valley began, slowly enough, to look more promising for foreign investment than they had done since the 1952 revolution. If, as seemed certain, Egypt was to begin seriously to tackle development, then investment from the Gulf would be one of the prime sources of funding for new projects.

My colleague in Dubai, Col Kelly, was keen for the BBME to set up a branch in Cairo; he prepared a careful study which was put before the board in London. By this time the bank had become part of the Hongkong and Shanghai Group and decision-making had largely shifted from the specialists in Middle Eastern banking and trade who had dominated the bank's affairs, to men who were skilled in the international markets but who did not claim the same degree of knowledge about our region.

One of the problems was that, at a political level, a number of the executives of the bank were highly sympathetic to Israel and, despite Sadat's policies, still regarded Egypt as Israel's principal enemy. I had no argument with those who adopted the side of that particular debate which was directly opposed to my own, but I regretted it when political attitudes began to colour business decisions in this way. The principal Egyptian banker whom it was intended to bring into the new bank was Dr Hamed Al-Sayeh, the governor of the Central Bank of Egypt during the era of Abdul Nasser; he was, I have to say, most deplorably treated by the bank's executives when he visited the new headquarters in Hong Kong. As I shall relate, I too fell victim to the changing attitudes which overcame BBME after the Hongkong and Shanghai Group management's own changes introduced executives who had very different priorities and ways of dealing with people from those with whom I had grown up and worked over so many years.

The attitudes towards Egypt which surfaced amongst members of the board in Hong Kong meant that Col Kelly's report, advocating the setting-up of a bank in Egypt, was suppressed. The subject was allowed to lapse. Eventually, however, it was revived and I was asked to advise on the desirability of proceeding with the bank's formation. It was decided to begin modestly; I was asked to speak to one of the bank's directors, the third in its hierarchy. He was clearly unenthusiastic and, despite all the arguments which I advanced, avoided any commitment about the Egyptian project.

We met in London, at the Carlton Tower Hotel. I found him arrogant and, frankly, not very congenial. I walked with him from the hotel, up Sloane Street, to Knightsbridge Underground station. Suddenly he stopped walking and, after a moment or two's silence, asked me if I would be prepared to take an interest in the bank in my own right. At once I said that I would. He relaxed and became a keen supporter of the bank's formation.

Our role was to encourage profitable investment in Egypt. We followed a generally cautious policy and our beginnings were quite modest. We were joined on the board of the bank, in time, by some distinguished British bankers and others whose careers in the Middle East, in business and diplomacy, were well known; they included Lord Denman, Sir James Craig, my old friend from Dubai, and John Hill.

Our board meetings in Cairo were always pleasant occasions but sometimes courtesy to foreigners got the better of some of our Egyptian colleagues. Intending, I suspect, to please the British members of the board who were present, some of the Egyptians began attacking Gamal Abdul Nasser and criticizing the building of the Aswan High Dam, the inception of which had created such a highly charged series of events in the mid-fifties, culminating in the Suez invasion. I kept quiet but finally I could not contain myself further, as my youthful support for the principles of Arab Nationalism with which Abdul Nasser had been so deeply identified and which I still believed, rose to the surface. I pointed to the gleaming tomatoes, the lush salad and delicious, fresh vegetables which had enriched our lunch. As politely as I could I said, 'All these have been brought to us by the existence of the High Dam. Without its waters you would have had nine years of drought and Egypt would have been as barren as Ethiopia.'

I have retained my interest in the Egyptian–British bank which today makes a substantial annual profit. I am very optimistic about the future of the Egyptian economy if the administration of President Mubarak can achieve two goals: the reduction of the Egyptian bureaucracy, which still puts to shame the practices of the Ottoman Empire at its height, and the containment of those who seek to wreck the society. The first of these objectives has perplexed the Egyptians since the days of the pharaohs, like the levels of corruption which always go along with an overblown government administration; the second demonstrates how dangerous it is when misguided or naïve activists invoke the name of religion to promote most irreligious objects, in this case employing means which are wholly alien to the Islam in whose name they claim to act.

For myself, I have no doubt that such people have laid themselves open, whether they realize it or not, to manipulation by those very men they claim to oppose. There are those who seek, for their own political purposes, to portray Islam as 'the enemy' and who lose no opportunity to disparage it. The supporters of the extremist settlers in Israel, for example, are foremost amongst these subtle and hence particularly dangerous voices. They contrive to encourage both the extremists in Islam and the media and political commentators, who are always seeking opportunities in report disaster and violence – or even simply the prospect of it. It is tragic that the name of Islam should be exploited in this way.

But life is coming back to Egypt, a fact which will make not only her friends in the Arab world rejoice. Egypt is too important a country ever to be allowed to fall under the burdens which she has had to bear.

It was not long after this that it became clear that my relationship with BBME, which had continued very happily for most of the preceding thirty-eight years, was now reaching something of a crisis. The problems began with a company which the bank had formed in Dubai and of which I was a director. This was the Middle East Finance Company which had been established to provide financing facilities for smaller projects, such as hire purchase for vehicles and the funding of building developments, particularly in the private sector.

Shaikh Rashid had invested 500,000 dirhams in the company, in partnership with the bank. Gradually, I became uneasy about some aspects of the company's management and the handling of its funds. I was doubtful about some of the decisions taken by the management on matters which seemed to me to be important, both in fact and in principle. I did not at all like the way things appeared to be going.

It then emerged that Hongkong and Shanghai wanted to absorb Middle East Finance Company into BBME; by doing so they would obviously strengthen BBME's balance sheet and make it more difficult to establish the true status of the finance company. I opposed this vigorously as I felt responsible, quite apart from other considerations, for Shaikh Rashid's investment. When I voiced my concerns to the bank's headquarters I was asked, in effect, 'Who pays you?' Such treatment was a new experience for me but I insisted and Middle East Finance Company retained its separate identity.

One of my tasks had for a long time been to advise the bank on opportunities for handling the increasingly important sources of funding represented by the shaikhs, who were growing richer as the result of the spectacular rise in the price of, and the demand for, oil. One of the bank's executives, with whom I did not have a happy relationship, and who was concerned with this aspect of our affairs, one day walked into my office – which was large and impressive, by the general standards of the bank – and asked me to agree to its partitioning, reducing its area by about half. I objected since this would certainly diminish my standing amongst the staff and amongst the customers with whom the bank was conducting its business. The writing was clearly on the wall.

The bank's merchant banking arm, Wardley Middle East, was approached by the Ruler of Sharjah for assistance in raising a loan. A meeting was arranged between the Ruler and the Chairman of Wardley Middle East; he was also the Area Manager of BBME. I was not informed of the meeting; it became evident that I was being kept away from it. One of my colleagues was very concerned when he discovered that I knew nothing about it, for it appeared that Sharjah was about to enter into an agreement with a French group which, of course, would result in the bank's exclusion from the business.

At the meeting which had been arranged between the Ruler and the chairman, for whatever reason the Ruler did not appear, to the chairman's considerable annoyance. He found it difficult to accept that arrangements for meetings in the Gulf, especially with Rulers, were often to be understood as an expression of an intention to meet rather than a firm commitment. As I had not been consulted, I did not feel that I could intervene. My colleague, however, went to the chairman and urged him to come to me, to seek my help. With as good a grace as he could muster, acknowledging that the bank was in trouble, he did so. I found the Ruler praying in an upstairs room and I was able to persuade him to give the business to BBME.

It was during this period that an event occurred which effectively removed one of the most important influences in my life up to that point. Shaikh Rashid bin Saeed, who had seemed so unshakeable a figure in our lives and in those of all the Gulf's affairs, was stricken. His spirit, however, was indomitable and despite his illness he still ruled and played a major role in Dubai's activities and in the affairs of the UAE; his strength of character was truly astounding. Inevitably his capacity for the long, intense working hours which he had devoted to his responsibilities had to be diminished; his sons assumed more and more of his work and my involvement in political matters was reduced. This suited me well at the time, though the challenge of life without day-to-day contact with Shaikh Rashid was much less exciting than it had been.

At about this time I was asked to attend a meeting of the board in Hong Kong. The UAE Currency Board had recently decreed that all foreign banks which had more than one branch in any of the states should close them. I had proposed that BBME should sell shares in its branches, reserving 51 per cent for the governments and the public, ensuring if possible that the offers would be structured in such a way as to allow ordinary people to become shareholders. The bank would retain 49 per cent itself.

Michael Sandberg, the Chairman of the Hongkong and Shanghai Banking Corporation, came into the boardroom and, rather obviously, did not greet me. His first remark was, 'I'm fed up with Arabs giving me advice,' hardly an auspicious or even a courteous opening. It turned out that he had been having problems with the Saudis over the Saudi–British bank and was obviously feeling rather jaundiced as a result.

The bleak atmosphere attending my reception continued. At lunch I was seated at a small table in a side room presided over by the bank's deputy chairman, instead of at my usual place beside the chairman himself. My assistant, a rather junior Persian, was, on the other hand, seated at the chairman's table. Such signals could not be ignored by anyone who came from my background or from my part of the world.

I was invited to meet the chairman later. He did not waste time with courtesies: he wanted me, he said, 'to step aside'; this would involve my becoming a director on the bank's London committee. He said something about 'horses for courses' and implied that now that Shaikh Rashid had, as he expressed it, 'disappeared', it was clear that some 'new, young faces were needed'. We agreed that I would think about the situation on my return to Dubai.

When I got home I consulted my friend and adviser Christopher Dixon, at that time a partner in the London firm of solicitors, Fox and Gibbons. His advice was for me to withdraw with dignity, which was wise and sensible counsel.

I will not pretend that I was not hurt by the way in which my thirty-eight years of service to the British Bank of the Middle East came to an end. I had dedicated myself to the bank as much as I had to working with the Ruler, a relationship which had been of immense profit to the bank. For fifteen years after the Hongkong and Shanghai takeover there was no interference in the day-to-day running of the bank's affairs; there was, as there had always been, a lovely spirit amongst us all, Arab and non-Arab alike, a real sense of comradeship. This had come to an end and, when I got over the first sense of loss which I experienced, I was relieved to be no longer part of an organization which, in my eyes at least, had changed so unhappily. As it turned out, my leaving the bank at this time proved to be of considerable advantage to the development of my other career.

The bank realized that it might not have handled my case with the greatest sensitivity. Knowing that I liked antiques, the chairman proposed that I should be given some worthy expression of their regard by adding to my collection. I thanked them for their proposal but I did not accept it.

The unhappy course of events attending my departure from BBME did not, however, curtail my involvement with banking; far from it indeed, for I have retained directorships in a number of the banks which were established in our part of the world after the states there achieved full independence. But whereas the Egyptian Hong Kong Bank grew out of an existing, long-established bank which had been trading in the region for many years, Emirates Bank International, the next organization which I shall describe, is the result of the amalgamation of a number of UAE banks, with originally what were much less distinguished histories.

Earlier, I made the point that when it became known that Dubai was, for the Gulf in its day, a relatively open society, in which businessmen with a contribution to make to its development would be welcome, a number of less scrupulous operators were drawn to the state. There were several examples of the class of bank which emerged particularly in the fifties and sixties; these could be immediately recognized by the lavishness of their presentation, the elegance of their offices and generally the well-concealed scarcity of their reserves. One of the best known of these was Intra Bank, a Lebanese institution which caused the National Bank of Dubai considerable embarrassment and substantial losses. Intra Bank was brought to Dubai by one of Shaikh Rashid's assistants, a fact which made its eventual if inevitable crash the more distressing.[2] The greatest banking scandal of the post-war period, the collapse of the Bank of Credit and Commerce International (BCCI), happily did not affect Dubai too much as I advised Shaikh Rashid against having any dealings with them and fortunately he took my advice to a large extent.

Those whose memories go back to the seventies will remember another, though lesser scandal, which attracted worldwide publicity. This was occasioned by the collapse of several Dubai-based banking operations which, up to that time, had earned themselves a good deal of generally favourable international attention. The banks concerned were associated with a well-known merchant family in Dubai, managed by a group of enterprising and adventurous brothers. The brothers were, it has to be said, unpredictable in their dealings and in the directions in which they sometimes seemed to be heading their businesses. They obtained permission from Shaikh Rashid to open a bank; they followed this by building a large hotel and then by establishing a publishing company which produced an English-language newspaper. The brothers maintained a very high style of living and were well known in the familiar entertainment centres of the Western world.

Then, as is so often the way, the brothers fell out. They parted and the departing brother then set up a mirror organization to that which he had left: a bank, a large hotel and a publishing corporation. In both cases their associates were not people of real substance and the management of their various enterprises, particularly the banks, was poor; almost inevitably the two empires collapsed and a serious crisis of confidence could have arisen, damaging Dubai's international reputation. However, the swift action which was taken began to set the matter to rights.

The Union Bank of the Middle East, the Dubai Bank, the Gulf Bank and the Middle East Bank were, as a result of the collapse which I have described, effectively bankrupt. Their state provoked a panic in the market and amongst the banking and commercial community, in Dubai in particular. Unfortunately, there had been no proper controls by the Central Bank to prevent the over-optimistic trading in which these banks had indulged.

Emirates Bank International was formed out of the remains of these four and I was asked to become a member of the board. US $1.2 billion was required to fund the bank initially; it was greatly to the credit of Shaikh Maktoum bin Rashid Al-Maktoum that Dubai's reputation was saved in this case, for it was he who provided the necessary funding. I joined the newly constituted board of the bank under the chairmanship of H. E. Ahmed Al-Tayer, a man for whose integrity and intelligence I have always had the greatest admiration; subsequently, I also became a member of the bank's Executive Committee.

Financial controls in operation in the period of the previous management had been hopelessly inadequate, likewise the reporting systems to keep the board informed of the bank's state of health and to signal any approaching crises. The bank's bad debts were appalling and something approaching US $1 billion had to be written off.

The Executive Committee took charge of all policy-making and imposed the sort of controls which had been so notably lacking. The new board brought in a number of senior staff who had retired from BBME and the situation was turned around at last.

We established the Dubai Investment Company and the Dubai Real Estate Company which has substantial property investments. Currently, the bank's profits are running at an annual rate of 500 million dirhams (US $137 million). The Government of Dubai has 80 per cent of the shares; the rest are held privately, including my own investment.

The formation of Emirates International Bank was one of the factors which contributed to Dubai's astonishing commercial success. Shaikh Maktoum bin Rashid Al-Maktoum's uncompromising and swift decision to underwrite the US $1.2 billion was the single action which guaranteed the bank's survival and its present success. Then, when the Iraqi invasion of Kuwait occurred and virtually all the expatriate companies and employees fled Dubai, it was the local airlines, banks and businesses which kept everything alive and, when conditions returned to normal, permitted the resumption of activities by the business community – including those who had run away. The stimulus which local businesses gave to Dubai's economy at this critical time recalled to my mind the practice which Shaikh Rashid used to adopt in the early days. If there was a recession in the market he would give instructions for the payment of outstanding accounts, starting with the smallest and rising to the largest amounts the Government owed. This way the market received an infusion both of cash and of confidence, buoying up the economy until times changed and conditions improved.

In my own case during the Kuwaiti crisis, I gave instructions that, contrary to my usual custom, my name should be displayed on the new buildings which I was erecting, work on which continued despite the anxieties of the political situation. I felt that if Easa Al-Gurg could be seen to be demonstrating confidence in the country, even in these circumstances, others would be encouraged to stay and to continue to manage their affairs as normally as possible. So it proved to be.

When I left BBME and was relaxing on holiday, I received a telephone call from the Ruler of the Emirate of Fujairah, who wanted to form a national bank and invited me to set it up. We met in his *majlis* in Dubai; present were three Franco–Lebanese executives who were, I gathered, to be part of the management. They seemed to me to have very limited ideas about the bank's potential and how it should be operated. They were keen to see as much of the bank's business as possible transferred to France and to French interests. I was not prepared to work in an arrangement in which I had no confidence. However, when it became plain to the Franco–Lebanese that I knew what I was talking about, they withdrew. I became the bank's Deputy Chairman and Chairman of the Executive Committee which I established to run it. The bank has made a significant contribution to the development of Fujairah, which has been one of the UAE's success stories; in 1996 it was making 62 million dirhams' profit (approximately US $17 million), a very satisfactory rate for a comparatively small enterprise.

The successes of the National Bank of Fujairah and Emirates International Bank demonstrate, I believe, an important principle, namely that local banks can succeed by their own efforts if their management is well trained, sincere and committed. They do not automatically require the importation of management services from international banks but can survive very well on their own.

My involvement in the banking industry in the region over the past fifty years, particularly in the period since the formation of the UAE and latterly of the Arabian Gulf Co-operation Council (GCC), has made me understand some of the fundamental realities about the role that banks, both the large international organizations and the locally financed and managed companies, will play in the future. To put what I have to say here into perspective, it is necessary to go back a little into recent history.

The politics of our region, and of much of the Middle East, changed profoundly after the death of Gamal Abdul Nasser and the establishment of the Presidency of Anwar Sadat. One immediate consequence of Sadat taking power in Egypt was the destruction of Nasser's associates and of the structures which he had set in place; eventually, this was to lead to the eclipse of the Arab Nationalist movement as a political force. Sadat's journey to Jerusalem, so widely promoted as an inspired gesture for peace was, in the minds of many of us, a betrayal of all that the Arab world had striven for since 1948. Yet the truth must be faced that the Arab world was tired and had lost, when it lost Nasser, the heart of its resistance to those foreign influences which the exploitation of its reserves of fossil fuels and the presence of expansionist, Western-backed interests had admitted to Arab lands. The disintegration of Russia and the Communist bloc meant the disappearance of the one power in the world which gave support, by whatever motivation, to patriotic Nationalist movements.

The discomfiture of the Western powers at the outcome of the Suez crisis made them change radically the nature and direction of their relations with the Arab world. Instead of the 'East of Suez' policy which had involved a substantial military and political commitment in the region, the Western powers, notably Britain and most particularly the United States, realized that their objectives, the principal one of which was the securing of access to the region's oil supplies and the manipulation of the wealth which accrued from them, could be achieved by the control of the mechanisms of international trade. These mechanisms were, supremely, banking and the international movement and management of money and the control of large-scale business, especially the sale of arms and security systems. It might be said that the Western powers left the region through the front door and came back in again through the window.

The penetration of the West into our societies since 1970 has been immeasurably greater than ever it was in the past. There is a saying in Arabic:

'What comes out of the West does not please the heart.'

When we were still locked in the sort of traditional societies which had persisted here for centuries, the foreign presence, notably that of the British in our case, made little general impact on our people's way of life; only the occasional rebel like me broke out of the mould. Now, our societies have become flimsy imitations of the Western way of life, with the cult of leisure, luxury and all the trappings of the consumer society. It requires no very profound understanding to see that the Arab world, which is commercially, strategically and politically valuable to the West (which, in political terms at least, now largely means the United States of America), can be kept docile by making sure that it receives its regular 'fix' of all the supposedly good things which the Western way of life has to offer. But the fundamental disparity between the oil producers and the consumers remains. Despite all the supposed benefits in goods and services which the oil-producing states are said to receive from the industrial world, the fact is too often forgotten that the governments of the industrial, oil-consuming nations exploit the producing countries' one natural resource by using it as a device to levy increasingly punitive taxes. It is fair to say that today the governments of the consuming nations receive as much as four times and more revenue from each barrel of oil as the countries which actually produce it.

Every Arab who knows the West and who has contacts with people from Western countries will be accustomed to receiving protestations of friendship towards the Arabs; every Arab, similarly, will know that the reality is not at all like that. The fact is that we in the Arab world fall over each other to be seen to be friends of the West, mainly because we are so astonished at the achievements of Western technology; the more thoughtful of us are also greatly impressed by the West's management of their affairs in an ordered and disciplined fashion. But as soon as there is an independent action on our part or the voicing of criticism which may seem to question the West's monopoly of righteousness, our Western friends suddenly change, their faces become dark and their declared affection for the Arabs is replaced by a steely determination to have their own way. I have even encountered this conflict of attitudes in my business life when a Western associate will suddenly demand wholly inequitable terms in the negotiations of a deal, no matter that the terms may already have been agreed. What is particularly galling is the assumption that the Arab partner to the discussion is expected to agree merely because the Western interest has required it. In my business life I am happy to say that they have seldom, if ever, succeeded.

Our societies are paying for this new colonialism through a veneer of education, without depth, as much as by the erosion of our traditional culture and the values which that culture represents. The consumer society is all-powerful and there is no real attempt to create a balanced infrastructure, since there is no need for us to create industries or manufacturing centres when we can order up anything that we require at the touch of a control on a fax machine.

Consumer goods, welfare and development, arms and security systems, all have to be paid for; this is where the banker achieves his principal role in recycling the funds which the oil-consuming nations pay to the oil-producing nations, thereby ensuring that a substantial part of those funds goes to fuel, in more senses than one, the economies of the consuming nations. It might be said that the oil consumers have resolved their dependence on the oil producers by promoting the excessive consumption of goods and services.

The moves towards globalization, of markets, distribution and the manipulation of demand, have all contributed to this situation. International trade and monetary agreements, promoted almost exclusively by the large industrial nations, have the effect of protecting their markets as effectively as did the control of colonial possessions and the administration of the empire for the imperial powers. The emphasis on 'the market', which has so typified much of the thinking of the governments of the industrialized nations in the recent past, has further served to ensure that consuming nations are kept alert and ready to respond to any new initiative, technology or product line which may be introduced to them. The countries of the Third World, many of them struggling to create viable economies to provide for their growing populations, find themselves under increasing pressure from the developed world to introduce legislation to give their workers protection and rights equivalent to those enjoyed in the West. By this means, the West ensures that the spending power of such countries, at least in the short term, is maintained so that Western consumer goods will be bought whilst, at the same time, higher wages will make the products of the countries concerned less competitive.

There are other instances of this inequitable treatment which the developed world adopts towards the rest. Raw materials and products imported from foreign suppliers are often punitively taxed by Western governments; oil is perhaps the most shameless example of this practice, as the principal natural resource of the oil producers, which is finite and diminishing, is used as a device for levying taxes by the governments of the developed world. The effect of these policies on the natural resources of Third World countries and the harm done to their environments are notorious; but if the countries concerned attempt to retaliate they are immediately subjected to the harshest economic and political measures.

The intervention of foreign interests in the economies of areas like the Gulf (and no doubt of others, in, for example, the Far East) is a very dangerous trend. The instruments for such intervention are various. In the belief that the existence of such institutions is one of the signs of a mature economy, there have been moves to establish stock exchanges in some of the centres which generate large capital surpluses, like the Gulf, but it is difficult to believe that these will ever really amount to very much. A viable stock market cannot be built on the buying and selling of a few hundred or a few thousand shares; none of the Gulf exchanges, actual or envisaged, remotely approaches the number of transactions which can make a market viable. The great centres of international finance will not permit the fragmentation of their interest by the creation of small, uncontrolled bourses; the markets are too small and the protection which the exchanges would require, even to survive, would be unacceptable in a free market environment.

The manipulation of even small local markets by the international financial institutions has a dangerous side. It enables foreign interests, often carefully concealed, to obtain control over local businesses, thus defeating all the expressions of the virtues of privatization which are constantly being urged on our communities.

The major international banks will grow more powerful, for it is they who will be responsible for the manipulation of the immense funds which will be both generated and required in the twenty-first century. The role of central banks will correspondingly diminish for they will be less able to impose controls in an environment where the one-time creditor nations become debtors, as will increasingly be the case in the Gulf states, whose wealth is based on one finite and diminishing resource. Governments will become more dependent on the goodwill of the banks for they will need to borrow to finance, probably on a permanent basis, the maintenance of the infrastructures which they have put in place over the past thirty years. Increasingly, development funds will be required from the private sector, both in the Gulf itself and from abroad, if any sort of progress is to be made.

Gulf businesses – and individuals – must be encouraged to invest in local enterprises where these can be viable and protected to the extent that they are not regarded as the preserve of a few individuals, who are free to take what they will. There will, therefore, continue to be important opportunities for foreign banks to operate in the Gulf and the peninsula at large. Local banks will tend more and more to find themselves handling the more dubious or risky enterprises and those which are subject to political leverage.

In the Gulf as a whole, I suspect that Dubai will continue to thrive, in whatever climate we find ourselves. Dubaians (or at least some of them) seem to be more industrious than many of their neighbours. They are more self-reliant and they have the advantage of a benevolent governmental structure which has understood the value of joining the free market economy. If the social and cultural consequences of this acceptance of the realities of the present world can be balanced with our past, then we shall be fortunate indeed.

9

THE DISCOVERY OF OIL in Persia in 1908 and then in Iraq soon prompted interest by the international oil companies in prospecting in Arabia and the Gulf. The first recovery of oil from the Gulf in commercial quantities was, as we have seen, in Bahrain from which the first exports were made in 1932. Ironically, and sadly for Bahrain, its reserves have always been modest, another example of the principle that it is not always a good thing to be first.

Saudi Arabia came on stream in the late forties and Kuwait at much the same time; both represented immense reserves of fossil hydrocarbons. The southern Gulf was longer in joining the ranks of the oil-rich nations; although it was known that the seismic formations were likely to be oil bearing, it was not until the fifties that serious exploration began. Concessions had been signed between some of the states and oil-prospecting companies before the Second World War but the war, and the disinclination of the British authorities to permit companies of other nationalities to become involved in any substantial way, meant that little was done until world demand required the opening-up of any and all available resources.

Dubai had received approaches from the Superior Oil Company, an American organization, in the late thirties and their interest was renewed after the war ended. Naturally, the bank was keenly interested in the development of the oil industry in the territories in which it was represented, and I followed events carefully as part of my overall responsibilities. I was not particularly involved, however, from the point of view of the Dubai Government's interest. The principal negotiations were ably conducted on the Government's behalf by Shaikh Rashid's trusted financial adviser, Bill Duff, though later others, not always as scrupulous as he, managed to involve themselves in the state's oil affairs.

Shaikh Rashid, however, still sought my advice and preferred to have me interpret for him whenever he needed to have direct dealings with oil company executives. Superior Oil had carried out an aerial survey of the marine areas of both Abu Dhabi and Dubai, using for the purpose a low-flying aircraft known as 'the Duck'. The company proposed agreements with the Rulers whereby they would receive varying amounts of cash in return for the prospecting concessions. I believe that Abu Dhabi received 10 million rupees; Shaikh Rashid was given 5 million. The Rulers of the smaller shaikhdoms were given amounts which diminished in scale depending upon the size and oil prospects of the shaikhdom concerned.

But then politics intervened. Because marine areas were involved and because all dealings with foreign powers and foreign interests were reserved to Britain and required British consent, the Government in London considered that its rights had been infringed by the negotiations between Superior Oil and the several states involved. The British Government sued Superior Oil in the International Court of Justice at the Hague and won.

One hot afternoon, when normally everyone would be sleeping before resuming work in the evening, I received an urgent message from Shaikh Rashid to come at once to the bank's office in Deira on the other side of the Creek. I hurried across and found him slumped in the manager's chair. With him were two executives from Superior Oil. Shaikh Rashid was ashen faced. 'Easa,' he said, 'the Americans are leaving; why is this?'

I asked the Americans what was going on.

'Tell him our chairman went mad and tore up the agreement,' one of them said.

I translated this for Shaikh Rashid. He was bewildered. 'But I still have my copy,' he said. 'They can make a copy of mine.'

At this time Shaikh Rashid was still relatively inexperienced in the ways of British diplomacy; later, of necessity, he was to become wiser in the ways of the world. On this occasion I pointed to a tall angular Englishman who was standing silently in a doorway some distance from the room where our meeting was taking place. 'I think that is the reason why their chairman went mad,' I said.

The tall figure standing in the doorway was that of the current Political Agent who would not permit Dubai to be responsible for its own affairs in this way. Dubai, like the other states, was not allowed to have contact with any interests which did not receive British approval in advance.

This unhappy experience with Superior Oil was rounded off by the fact that some three months after the meeting which I have described, after the Americans had left, an agreement, no doubt brokered by the British, was signed on virtually the same terms between Abu Dhabi and British Petroleum. Such is the way of the world; after all, BP is a British company. Dubai was, after the disappearance of Superior Oil, effectively an open market, and eventually Dubai signed an agreement with Continental Oil.

Another episode in what were the often convoluted dealings of the oil companies with the Gulf states, brought me a part in a more melodramatic event. I was asked by the Political Agency, which evidently continued to trust me despite my known commitment to Arab Nationalism, to go to Abu Dhabi, where I would find a pre-fabricated cabin, belonging to the Agency, at the end of the Creek. There I was to wait until three men arrived; they would knock on the door and I was to admit them. I was then to take them, as discreetly as possible, to call on the Ruler, Shaikh Shakhbut.

Everything happened as arranged; one of the three was Dutch, the others English. We made our way to the Palace, such as it then was, and were received by Shaikh Shakhbut. I was given a leather portfolio, in a beautiful rich burgundy colour, by the visitors and asked to hand it to the Shaikh. I did so; he opened it, glanced at its contents, closed it and handed it back to me to return it to the visitors. This I did and we withdrew.

For this service I received a fee of 21 guineas (which, in case anyone has forgotten, amounted to £22.1 shilling). To this day I have no idea what was in the portfolio that was so solemnly exchanged between the three men and the Ruler of Abu Dhabi.

The politics of the oil industry were complex enough as it was, without the intervention of the sort of bureaucratic muddle which often seems to attend the efforts of civil servants, of all nationalities, who involve themselves in commercial matters. This has always seemed to me to be one of the strongest arguments for private enterprise and my experience of the oil industry in the Gulf did nothing to alter this view.

In the sixties all the states of the region were anxious, reasonably enough, to share in the oil boom which, by that time, was clearly under way. A number of the smaller states wished to sign concession agreements with international companies, and the changing political climate made the British authorities less inclined to try and baulk such initiatives. One of these cases recalled the dispute over the islands in the Straits of Hormuz in the last century, when the then Shah of Persia laid claim to the Greater and Lesser Tunbs and Abu Moussa; these events, as I explained in Chapter 1, resulted in the deposition of the last Arab Ruler of my family's home town of Lingah and, eventually, in our return to the Arabian side of the Gulf. Now, more than seventy years later, the issue again became active in the politics of our part of the Gulf when it transpired that when the British had drawn up the territorial limits of the coastal states, indicating the extent of each state's jurisdiction offshore including the waters around the islands, they had allocated the same part of the seabed to two separate states. These states had, in turn, signed concessions in good faith with companies which were ready to carry out exploration and, if the presence of oil-bearing strata should be confirmed, the extraction of oil. The situation was compounded by the fact that part of the territory involved the several islands whose ownership was claimed both by members of the Trucial States Council and by Iran.

This had all the makings of a classic political confrontation and it did not disappoint those who expected it. Britain, in common

29. A Diwali dinner in about 1950. *Left to right*: ESG, Shaikh Rashid, Shaikh Khalifa bin Saeed Al-Maktoum and our host, an Indian merchant, Choitram

30. With the Prime Minister, Harold Macmillan, at Number 10 Downing Street, during Shaikh Rashid's visit in 1959

31. With Shaikh Rashid in his private *majlis* in Dubai

32. Shaikh Rashid with President Gamal Abdul Nasser, during our visit to Egypt in 1959

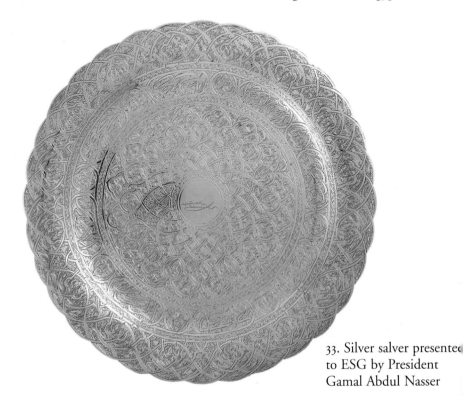

33. Silver salver presented to ESG by President Gamal Abdul Nasser

34. *Left to right*: ESG, Shaikh Rashid, Abdullah Al-Ghurair, Majid Al-Ghurair, Majid Al-Futaim

35. With Edward Heath, then Lord President of the Council, during his visit to Dubai in January 1961. The Political Agent Mr (later Sir) Donald Hawley introduces us

36. With Shaikh Rashid on the day when we landed in Deira,
on the other side of the Creek from Dubai, to demonstrate to the Political Agent
the suitability of the site for a landing strip

37. Dubai's new airport, soon after its official opening

38. The opening of the bank's new offices in Dubai in 1964. I am sitting next to Sir Dallas Bernard, Chairman of BBME; on the far left is B. W. J. S. Brisby, the Manager Designate, and next to him, J. C. Kelly. At this time I was the bank's Commercial Manager

39. Shaikh Rashid sits between Sir Humphrey Trevelyan (later Lord Trevelyan) and myself

40. At a meeting of the Deliberative Committee of the Trucial States Development Office, after my appointment as Executive Director. *Left to right*: Shaikh Hamdan bin Rashid Al-Maktoum; Ibrahim Mohammed Al-Midfa, representing the Ruler of Sharjah; Shaikh Saqr bin Mohammed Al-Qasimi, Ruler of Ras al-Khaimah and Chairman of the Committee; ESG; Shaikh Rashid; and Shaikh Zaid bin Sultan Al-Nahayan, Ruler of Abu Dhabi

41. *Left to right (front)*: ESG, Shaikh Rashid and Shaikh Mohammed bin Rashid Al-Maktoum

42. 1 March 1965: signing an Agreement with African and Eastern (Near East) Limited, part of Unilever – one of the first substantial contracts that I undertook in my career as an independent businessman

43. With the then President of Ireland, Mrs Mary Robinson, and Mr Robinson, on the occasion of my Presentation of Credentials on my appointment as Ambassador to the Republic

with all the Western powers, was at this time anxious to cultivate the Shah of Iran and to encourage his ambitions in the region, which were numerous. They were, however, also responsible for the welfare and protection of the states with which they were in treaty relations.

The lawyers, politicians and officials had a field day; only the oil companies and the states involved suffered. By this time I had met the celebrated American adventurer, Wendell Phillips, whose exploits in Oman and the Aden Protectorate were to become notorious. I was briefly involved in meetings with him in connection with oil concessions in Umm al-Qaiwain and Ras al-Khaimah, both of them involved in the issue which I have described.

I quickly realized what a liability Phillips was likely to be. On one occasion, we were queuing at the Passport Control at Dubai Airport as he was preparing to leave the country. Suddenly, I discovered that he had rushed to the head of the queue and was demanding special treatment and priority 'as he was writing the life of Shaikh Rashid'. This was simply untrue. I discovered that in any negotiation he would always raise his demands although a firm agreement had already been reached. He was simply not the sort that I wanted to see in Dubai and certainly not one with whom I wanted to be associated.

Phillips died when he was still quite young; he appeared to live on pills which he consumed throughout the day, on all occasions. He left behind him a mass of stories, most of them disreputable, about his exploits in Arabia. I know that it would have been more than his life was worth to return to some of the places through which he had passed, like a dark cloud.

Other characters with distinctly dubious reputations made their way to our territory, often with unforeseen outcomes. At one point, a libel action was started in the London courts by the board of an American company, Buttes Gas and Oil, on the one hand, and the somewhat sinister Dr Armand Hammer on the other, whom the Buttes' management accused of slander. Dr Hammer's company, Continental Oil, had signed an agreement with Dubai. The case was, I believe, only resolved by Dr Hammer's death many years later. I came to the conclusion that there were more agreeable – and often more honourable – ways to earn one's living than by trying to broker oil deals.

My years of working for the bank and my long involvement with the development of Dubai, as well as my close relationship with Shaikh Rashid, had naturally enough revealed to me the immense opportunities which now presented themselves to anyone who was prepared to work hard and to make use of all the new technologies which were appearing in the West; already they were beginning to reach our part of the world. However, so far I had not sought to involve myself directly in business, for I was convinced that my first loyalty was to the bank.

Those of us who constituted the intellectual élite of Dubai – which was not an especially numerous group – were accustomed to meet, as I have related earlier, in the late afternoons and on into the evening, to talk and to try to keep abreast of the fresh winds of speculation and change which were blowing around us and in the world beyond Dubai. We used to meet at the house owned by Rais Hasan Rais Saadi, near the bank; his house was like our club. It was entirely local in its 'membership'; for once there were not even any Englishmen who attended our gatherings, and certainly none of the more dubious individuals who were beginning to associate themselves with Dubai's future.

Now it happened that, by a series of chance connections, a leading German industrial company offered the agency for its products to the convenor of our leisure-time gatherings, Rais Abdul Rahim Saadi of Rais Hasan Rais Saadi. He was not really interested in business, preferring intellectual and artistic pursuits; however, he realized the importance of the approach and so he suggested that I should become his partner in the agreement which the Germans wanted to sign with him. The German company concerned was the large manufacturer of radios and communications equipment, Grundig. I was intrigued, flattered and not a little excited at the prospect of being handed, as it were on a plate, an industrial opportunity of great proportions. There was only one problem, in my mind.

My relationship with the bank was still very important to me, not only for the security which it gave me but also because I was always conscious of how much I owed BBME for having put so much trust in me over the years. By this time I was working as a Commercial Officer in the bank, a senior position for a Gulf national.

For some time past, I had considered the possibility of going into business on my own account; I could hardly have done otherwise, considering the opportunities which I saw around me every day. Nonetheless I hesitated; looking back now, it is a little difficult for me to believe it, but I was frankly scared of launching myself on my own. I think that I lacked confidence, but I also had a young and growing family to support and I was unsure what would be the response of the authorities around me when they saw me setting out to become an independent businessman. I was, as always, very aware of my family having come back across the water, and I knew that there would always be people who would be envious of any success that I might achieve.

All in all, I thought caution was called for, so in the terms of our first agreement with Grundig it was specified that although I was a partner my name should not appear in connection with it. This agreement was signed in April 1962. My relationship with Grundig has continued to this day and I shall have more to tell of it later in this narrative.

Very rapidly the Grundig business began to flourish; we handled the importation and sale of their radios, televisions and magnetic tapes. At this time one of their most popular products was the radiogram, which served both as a combined radio and record-player and as a handsome piece of furniture which would testify to the prosperity of anyone who owned one. The large Indian and Pakistani workforce in Dubai in particular admired the radiograms and they began to sell in significant numbers. As they were a relatively highly priced item, they returned correspondingly high profits. In a short time, Rais Hasan Rais Saadi and I were each receiving monthly profits of around US $7,000, a very considerable amount of money for those days in a small place like Dubai.

The next significant development in my infant business career was an approach from Georges Abiadh, the representative of the well-known Lebanese catering and trading organization, Albert Abela. This company had been quick to see the potential which the growing drilling and survey industries already appearing in and around the Gulf's oil installations would mean for business; Abela provided a range of catering services to the oil companies, thus reducing the companies' need to maintain their own catering stocks and staffs and so reduce their overheads.

Now Abela proposed to me that I should become the agent in Dubai for Kent. Again I was pleased that so important a company should have come to me, but what, I asked, was Kent? It was explained to me that it was a brand of American cigarettes, very popular amongst oil-company workers and local consumers alike. I said that I would think about it.

I still thought of myself as a committed socialist, an Arab Nationalist who had no time for the capitalist system and the wide variety of parasites who fed upon it. I was not enthusiastic about becoming a promoter of American cigarette brands. However, I took the agency for a year or so.

Now there occurred one of those fortunate events which have often happened at what turned out to be crucial points in my life. I was sitting in my office in the bank when a stranger walked in and enquired if I was Easa Gurg. I admitted that I was; he introduced himself as Lindsay Carter and told me that he had come to offer me the BAT agency. I decided to play cool; I said that I would think about it and that he should return the next day when we could discuss it further.

When he had left I hurried into the office of one of my colleagues in the bank, an Englishman, Christopher Reddington; he and I were friends and I frequently sought his advice. I told him of my meeting and asked him, what was BAT? Reddington was horrified that I did not recognize British American Tobacco Limited, one of the most important British companies, who were leaders in their field.

The approach from BAT came as a complete surprise to me; Christopher Reddington, however, praised the quality and integrity of the company and urged me to think seriously about their proposal. I met Lindsay Carter again and we immediately established a good relationship. This time I was more polite. I was drawn to the BAT proposal, rather than continuing the relationship with Abela, because I would deal directly with BAT whereas any connection with Kent would be through a Lebanese company which was itself the Kent agent. We came to an agreement which was signed on 25 May 1964.

Lindsay Carter introduced me to his district manager, Roger Barrett, who was based in Bahrain. They asked to come to my house and I invited them for a meal in the evening. Barrett asked me about my hobbies, a question which I was to recognize as very English; generally speaking, Arabs do not have hobbies but I played chess and so, it appeared, did he. Now it happened that I was rather a good player and Barrett really was not. However, I judged it well that he should win on this occasion; he did so and I was appointed the agent for BAT brands.

We encountered a problem at the outset of our association. BAT suggested, reasonably enough, that it would help them to establish a secure place in the market if I could persuade some of my influential friends to smoke their brands, and that to do this it would be more convincing if I were also seen to be smoking them. I was anxious to be as helpful as possible but there was one snag: I had never smoked in my life. I decided, however, that my new-found friends at BAT deserved my full co-operation and so I began to smoke.

At once I experienced a violent reaction: my eyes closed up and my face and neck swelled. I had revealed the classic symptoms of a nicotine allergy.

This presented me with a serious problem. One of my interests at this time was the stamp market, on which I worked with an American, Finbar Kenny; he had been brought to the Trucial coast on the initiative of James Craig, who encouraged his first agreement with Fujairah. We had formed agreements with the Governments of Ajman and Umm al-Qaiwain in addition to Fujairah, to design and print a range of stamps which would appeal to the international philatelic market, and at the same time produce some much-needed revenue for these states which were amongst the poorest on the coast. We had an international mailing list for the various issues which we produced and which were postmarked in Dubai. Sometimes we encountered unexpected problems. One day I learnt that one of the smaller states was proposing to issue a set of stamps, *the next day*, bearing the Queen's head; this represented every sort of infringement and would undoubtedly bring down on our heads the wrath of Britain and of the international postal authorities. I rushed round to the Political Agency and told them what was about to happen. With commendable decisiveness, the Assistant Political Agent, Terry Clark (whom I knew from the time when I had visited London with Shaikh Rashid in 1959), requisitioned a helicopter from the Scouts, flew to the state concerned and persuaded the Ruler to abandon the issue.

The philatelic business produced a regular monthly income for which I was required to send a weekly report to my American principal on our activities and sales. The consequence of my having taken up smoking meant that I could not see to write the report, because my eyes were so swollen; I used one of Grundig's recording machines to put my report on tape.

Carter and Barrett came to my shop one day as I was in the middle of dictating this report. They were horrified at my radically altered appearance and when I explained what had happened they urged me to stop smoking at once. I was worried that my allergy would disqualify me from holding the agency but, to my relief, they assured me that they would leave it with me. I stopped smoking and the symptoms receded.

From the outset of our working together BAT was very supportive, making warehouse space available and providing a Land Rover for our transportation. We began with an order for 60 cases; today we sell 9,000 every month, throughout Dubai and the northern Emirates. We also export to certain markets, some of which are surprising; quite often 40-foot containers are loaded up for shipment to more distant markets such as Somalia, Mogadishu, Sudan, Afghanistan and Sri Lanka. Such shipments have the considerable merit of being paid for in cash. These are really windfalls, unlooked for when we first began trading. We also supply the duty-free shops at the airports which, as everyone knows, is substantial business.

Meanwhile, as my interests were expanding and, in particular, my agreement with Grundig had begun to operate so successfully, I felt that I had to go to the bank and offer my resignation (this, of course, was before the disturbance of my relationship with the bank which I described in Chapter 8). I did not want the situation to arise whereby people in Dubai, which was already experiencing something of a boom, would accuse me of taking an unfair advantage or of looking into the business of people with whom, in another context, I might find myself competing. Equally, I did not want the bank, which, up to this time, had been so good to me, to be embarrassed by my exercising of two quite distinct roles, banker and merchant. I thought therefore that, however reluctantly, it was time to withdraw, for clearly I was going to become part of the new industrial and commercial infrastructure which was rapidly developing in Dubai.

The bank, however, took a different view. They trusted me and they valued my connection with Shaikh Rashid; they also believed that I could protect their interests and those of their customers whilst pursuing my own affairs. They knew, I think, that I was not likely to exploit the relationships which I enjoyed, to the disadvantage of any of them.

I was invited to go to London to meet the Chairman and the Chief Executive of the bank. As I arrived, I thought how different now was my situation compared with my earlier, first visit to the capital of the Empire, no matter that the Empire was no more and Britain was having to accustom itself to a much diminished role in the world.

The board of directors of the bank invited me to lunch with them in King William Street, in the City; they were courteous and cordial and questioned me closely about my plans. I was nervous about the outcome of our meeting but the directors insisted that they would refuse my resignation if I offered it. Instead I was promoted to the level of an 'A' officer in the bank, one of the first Gulf nationals to be assigned to this rank.

I now found myself in the interesting position of working for the bank, and being available to Shaikh Rashid whenever he needed my advice or help (I still interpreted for him from time to time); we also continued to discuss his plans for Dubai's development far into the night. At the same time, I was beginning to run my own businesses, which showed every sign of rapid growth. Each of the people with whom I was involved, the bank, Shaikh Rashid and the companies which I represented, knew of my connection with the others. Although such a combination of relationships could have been hazardous, the fact that it worked well and that no one felt disadvantaged by it is, I hope, an indication of an ability to keep the various interests with which I was concerned separate and, as far as possible, independent of each other.

All of my business accounts were conducted through BBME so the bank was fully aware of all that I was doing. My affairs became a sort of thermometer which indicated the health of local business; in this I think that the bank exercised considerable subtlety in encouraging me to maintain these various roles. Eventually I was appointed as consultant to the bank, for a monthly retainer which was almost the amount of the annual salary which I had been receiving not so long before.

My next important connection with foreign business came when I entered into an agreement, in March 1965, with African and Eastern, the overseas arm of the mighty Unilever. The introduction came from the British Political Agency, as did others during the years that I was building up my business. I suspect that the motivation for these expressions of goodwill was the thought that if they helped to make me rich I would be less inclined to pursue my belief in Arab Nationalism and my support for Gamal Abdul Nasser's policies. I am still an Arab Nationalist but I am now a rich one – to this extent at least the kindness of the Political Agency has achieved its purpose.

With African and Eastern I became responsible for the sale and distribution of all their products in Dubai and the northern Emirates; all their products, that is, with the exception of alcohol. I have always been very aware of the dangers which access to alcohol could have on a society which, after centuries of abstinence, suddenly was exposed to it in unlimited quantities. I did not want to become a connection between alcohol and the young, to have on my conscience the sort of harm which I knew could come to young and inexperienced people when suddenly they are able to drink without restraint. Sadly, the experience of what has happened in many Arabian societies over the past thirty years has only confirmed me in this view.

Like all Arabs, I have always believed in the value of land as an investment. When I began my independent business career in Dubai it was abundantly clear that the expansion of the city would quickly absorb the available land and I began to acquire property where I could. I acquired a piece of land near the Iranian hospital. A little while later, however, the land was expropriated by the Municipality, I believe as part of the planned development of the town.

This was a blow but I did not allow it to distress me; I did not panic, preferring to do nothing and to wait upon events. Two years passed and one day Shaikh Rashid asked me, 'Easa, have you lost anything? Has anything been taken from you, perhaps?'

I smiled and said, 'Whatever a man has belongs to his master.' Forty-eight hours later the Municipality informed me that I had been given a plot of land opposite the cement factory.

I had realized that after the Dubai Petroleum Company had been established to manage the state's oil affairs, the increasing numbers of expatriate personnel would require accommodation of a quality higher than was available in Dubai at the time. In partnership with the oil company I built forty-eight American-style villas on the site, the actual building costs being financed by the oil company. The rents of all the properties, which were leased to oil company personnel, were divided between the company and myself. The villas are still standing today and have certainly more than earned their keep.

Real estate was to become one of our group of companies' most important areas of investment, over the years which lay ahead. The group owns all its warehouses, showrooms, offices and factories, all of them built on our own land. This is one area of our business which we intend to expand in the future. There is a huge demand for high-quality accommodation in the UAE and, as the country continues its expansion – which we are convinced it will – that demand will increase.

*

In quite a short time, really only a few years after I had started working on my own account, I was by most standards a rich man. Many of my friends asked me why I did not relax and simply enjoy what I had already achieved. It was not an easy question to answer and the response was, in consequence, complicated.

I enjoyed what I did very much, in all the fields in which I was involved, and the way my businesses were growing gave me great satisfaction. My original motivation for becoming rich and establishing an honoured place for myself was to bring back the prosperity and respect which my family had once enjoyed. It was evident that I had achieved that, but there is more, for I believed that great wealth, if it is properly managed, with proper concern for others, should bring with it wisdom.

Chances do not return and in the process of sharing in the building of a nation I was given opportunities which it would have been foolish and improvident to ignore. I wanted my businesses to be models of their kind, well managed, profitable and efficient. To achieve such objectives it has been necessary to bring to them managers of quality and integrity; and in this world you have to be rich to be able to attract people of the quality which is required and which is sought after by every well-run enterprise.

It was not in my nature to ask for favours and, happily, the circumstances in which I found myself brought their own opportunities. I was very conscious of what was happening around me, in the Gulf and in the wider world. I have always been gifted with the ability to foresee events, whether in the development of business opportunities or in the larger issues of national and international politics. It is an ability which has been useful to me in my diplomatic and political work, and which I shall describe later in this narrative.

For someone like me, it has always been necessary to think three generations ahead. I confess that I am conscious of creating a dynasty on the success of my businesses; I want my children and their children's children to take them on into the future and to build on what I will leave behind me. For this reason alone have I wanted to die rich.

My business interests continued to expand, drawing me into

new fields of activity. I have mentioned that I was a director of the Dubai Electricity Company which was formed back in the 1950s; our first important installation was a modest 7½ kilowatt generator which was acquired from John Brown, one of the principal British manufacturers of such equipment. The consultants on the project were Kennedy and Donkin, who had been recommended by my friend Col Kelly of BBME.

The acquisition of the new generator was a success and the electricity company prospered. Its general manager was a pleasant, rather retiring Englishman named Roy York. His wife was a formidable lady who came to the view that her husband was too submissive to the board of directors and that he required protection at our meetings. She began the practice, therefore, of attending board meetings so that she could extend the protection to her husband which she judged necessary.

Arabs are, by custom, exceedingly polite, especially where women are concerned. Though the directors were somewhat taken aback by the lady's presence, none of us liked to voice any objection. This strange situation continued for some time until I could no longer tolerate the lady's interventions in our affairs. She was persuaded to retire from the proceedings.

A couple of years or so later, Roy York, perhaps out of gratitude for my management of his wife, recommended me to one of the many important companies which at that time were searching for reliable agents. Siemens, the German electrical giant, asked Roy's advice and he introduced me to them, when representatives of the company called on me in the Grundig showroom where we handled the radio business.

Despite my connection with Grundig, I think that I was still very much identified with British interests and British companies. My involvement with Siemens went some way towards changing this impression, though it still lingered as was shown when I visited Germany before signing the agreement with the company.

I decided that I needed to impress on the Germans that I was a serious and purposeful businessman and so I put on my most convincing appearance as a respectable banker, wearing my English three-piece suit for the occasion. I was received by Herr Schtole, one of Siemens' managing directors. He looked at me critically. 'Mr Gurg,' he said, 'you are an Englishman.' He then went on to tell me how during the war he had bombed Britain, piloting gliders and so ensuring that they could not be detected in the way that conventional aircraft could be. I listened to this with what I hope was polite interest.

We went to lunch. This was at the time that President de Gaulle of France was blocking Britain's entry to the Common Market. I found that my hosts largely agreed with this. They did not want Britain in the Common Market either and spoke disapprovingly of what they conceived as British business habits when contrasted with their own. They pointed out that their executives came to work at the time that a cleaner in a British bank arrived, whereas their British counterparts never came to their offices before ten o'clock.

'Should I pass this on to the British?' I enquired.

'By all means,' my German hosts replied.

No actual business was discussed on this occasion, only the shortcomings of the British. When I arrived in London I lunched with the bank's directors. I told them that the Germans were un-enthusiastic about British entry to the Common Market. I discovered, after a generously supplied lunch during which the tongues of my hosts were perhaps a little loosened, that they too were apprehensive about the prospect of Britain being linked to Europe when, as they put it, good British money would be wasted on poor Third World countries. In the event, Siemens and I got on very well together and today we turn over a very considerable amount of money annually, with a large stock of products which supports the orders generated by the business. We have also carried out a number of very large 'one-off' projects.

My relationship began with Siemens' electrical products, the agreement for which was signed on the last day of 1972. Then I took over the importation of their power engineering products and services, an aspect of their business which was of great potential in a country which was developing as rapidly as was Dubai; this agreement was signed exactly one year later on 31 December 1973. At the same time I became responsible for the whole of Siemens' electrical industry products, signing that agreement in January 1974.

As my businesses grew, so their demands on me increased. It was not easy; having come from a business environment, the bank, where I was part of a large, highly structured organization with systems, controls and colleagues who could be consulted whenever one might be in doubt, I was now the sole decision-maker. I kept the management of the businesses as tight as possible and ran them on the proverbial shoestring. I recruited several young men who I had noticed had talents which I could use, from the bank and from the business community in Dubai; they found working for me generally more demanding but I rewarded them more generously. When I took over the BAT agency I inherited a small group of staff who joined me. We worked well together for I always believed in dealing considerately with all whom I employed: we ate together and at weekends I invited them to my house and its gardens where we could relax in an atmosphere more casual than that of the working week.

Nonetheless, I came to realize the truth of the saying by Imam Shafei (3rd–4th century AH/8th–9th century AD):

بقدر الكدَ تَكْتَسَبْ ألمعَالي

ومنْ طَلبَ ألعلى سهرَ أللِيالي

The more effort you put in, the more you achieve.
Glory requires many sleepless nights.

*

I have to say again that I really enjoyed all that I did; I still do. As the businesses grew, so did my enjoyment of them. It quickly became apparent to me that I was playing a game, one for which I made the rules and the rewards for which were very high. I enjoyed the chase after contracts and the feeling of success which winning a new one brings, and I enjoyed the attention, in Dubai and far beyond it, which my business affairs brought to me. But the most important thing they brought me was that independence which had always been the objective of my life's endeavours.

As time went on, the scale of my business grew immeasurably greater than even I could have foreseen when I began. I deliberately sought to diversify and to become involved with as many areas of Dubai's business life as I could. I have been involved in contracts worth billions of dollars but considerations of size have never bothered me. I never see things as 'big' or 'small'; all the businesses, all their affairs and the deals which they make, require the same attention. I suspect that this attitude of mind is, like most other aspects of my personality, the product of my upbringing.

I think I can demonstrate this point by noting that one inheritance which I brought with me from my time in Bahrain was an interest in interior design and the furnishing of people's homes. This may seem relatively small in comparison with some of the very large public-works contracts with which I have been concerned, but it is an important side of our business today. I was very impressed, whilst I was in Bahrain, with the furniture showroom which was opened by the family of Shaikh Mustafa Abdul Latif, with whom I lived whilst I worked at the Post Office in Manama. I was, as I have always been, fascinated by Western ways. I was an addict of films which showed life in Europe and America; it is this enthusiasm, I am sure, which made me take part of my business in the direction of providing for people who wanted to equip their homes in an international fashion with the best available furnishings and materials.

When the opportunity seemed right I decided to open a furniture showroom in Dubai and invited two of the members of the Mustafa family to become my partners. The association did not last, however, because I worked in a quite different way from my friends; I was like a dog in the hot sun, looking for water or the cooling shade, and for me this meant getting up in the dark, visiting the various operations before the sun was up, hurrying to the bank, checking on the shops and the mood of the market, calling on the Ruler. My partners, however, followed more leisurely ways, preferring to come to the office at about 10.30, by which time I was setting out for my regular daily session with Shaikh Rashid. We were not destined to work together, I realized, and so we parted. For my part it was a busy and demanding life, but it was lived at speed because that was how I wanted it to be.

Year by year we have acquired new agencies when given the opportunity to do so. Currently we hold some three hundred agencies from many countries around the world, though 70 per cent of these are British. We have also expanded the various branches of the group's operations in areas other than trading. In 1974 we established the group of science-based companies which form the Scientific (Electrical and Electronics) Division of our group, which has played a major part in the development of Dubai and some of the other states. The projects which this part of the group has handled include the Ras al-Khaimah Earth Satellite Station, the Dubai Police Airwing, Ras al-Khaimah International Airport, gas turbines for the Jebel Ali 'G' Station, as well as contracts for the Dubai Electricity Company, the Dubai Municipality and the Dubai Port Authority. In recent years the value of these projects has amounted to billions of dirhams.

The huge rate of growth of Dubai City and the other centres of population in the UAE has required a similarly large-scale investment in building services, materials and supplies. Mac Al-Gurg, the product of the merging of several interests into one powerful unit, is one of the largest operators in the UAE. Mac Al-Gurg has handled many different projects over the years, in virtually every part of the UAE – housing and apartments in Liwa in Abu Dhabi, in Deira city centre, and hotels like the Bustan in Garhoud, Chicago Beach Hotel, Royal Abjar Hotel, J. W. Marriott and Holiday Inn Crown Plaza. Then there have been large public building and contracting projects, including Al Ain International Airport, the Al Ain Expressway, the Taweelah to Al Ain Pipeline, the Marfa Pipeline and many, many more.

The rapid growth of the UAE's economy in the latter part of the seventies meant that there was a hugely increased demand for, amongst other things, automotive products and services. This was largely the result of the influx of foreign workers, and to meet the demand we formed an association with Dunlop to distribute tyres, batteries and accessories; we also set up Target Auto Services, which provides auto repair services, and a petrol station. In 1990 we established Arabian Liquid Chemicals and in 1994 the Gulf Metal Foundry which will, I believe, lead to further investment directly in the industrial sector in our economy, something I am especially anxious to see developed.

In 1995, partly to remind my friends that I was still a merchant though half of my year was spent as the UAE's Ambassador in London, we expanded our operations still further. In that year we launched Al Mashrabia Furniture, Gulf Engineering, Al Samsam Building Materials, TTE Office Furniture, Technical and Trading and ID Design.

The years have brought with them immense opportunities. At first I was especially drawn to trading, to the sort of merchanting business, though now on a vastly greater scale, that my family had always undertaken. As the years have gone by, however, I have become more and more persuaded that the future of the UAE lies in industry, especially in manufacturing. One of the earliest manufacturing operations which we established in pursuit of this concept was Foseco Minsep. This was set up in 1974 and manufactures chemicals, sealants, additives and waterproofing compounds. It has now been taken over by Burma Castrol, to the great improvement of its management.

In 1976 we established the country's first steel-welded wire-mesh plant, for the manufacture of mesh which is used in concrete reinforcement. Our partners in this venture originally were GKN Nettlefords of the UK. In the 1980s the country experienced a slight recession; our partners reacted nervously and wanted to withdraw. We acquired the balance of the shares and thus own 100 per cent of the equity. Within a few years the profits of the company had multiplied fourfold.

An important development was the creation of the first industrial explosives plant in the UAE for quarrying, road-building and the like. The business was established in Ras al-Khaimah, as a joint venture with a French company, SAEPC.

Our involvement in steel was taken still further by the opening in 1994 of the first steel foundry in the UAE. This was a fascinating exercise, for we believed that we had detected an opportunity that no one else seemed to have appreciated. Experts in the industry were, frankly, incredulous; they could not believe that we could set up a steel foundry in, as they put it, 'the middle of the desert'. We invited them to come and see for themselves. They came, were impressed and at once placed orders for our products. We now export steel products to Europe, including the United Kingdom, France and Denmark, and to the United States.

In its first year of operation the foundry won an internationally competed tender for Dubal (Dubai Aluminium), for 1,600 tons of special steel castings for the smelter's expansion programme. In 1994 we also launched Gulf Engineering Industry, a plant for the medium fabrication of steel products and a fully fledged machine shop producing alloyed steels.

Other industrial projects in recent times have included the acquisition of 51 per cent of the equity of an industrial paint manufacturing company, in partnership with Leigh Paints of the UK, which owns the balance of the shares. We are now engaged in the expansion of the business, including building a new factory.

Our programme of expansion continues. We have set up a fully automated joinery, manufacturing furniture and shop interiors. We are certain that our policy is the correct one for the times; the future lies in the creation of medium-sized industrial plants for the market, for trading opportunities are now largely saturated. We export our products Gulf-wide and we have our own marketing and sales offices in most of the states.

Recently I was able to bring together all my senior employees who had been with me from the early days and reward them by giving them bonuses, according to their positions in the group. I was able thus to thank them for their dedication over the years – and to offer some form of apology for the often long and arduous hours which they were required to work when we were building the business together.

Our record of growth is one of which I think we can all be proud. The Easa Saleh Al-Gurg Group is now one of the largest merchant companies in the UAE, which means that it is one of the largest in the Gulf as a whole. When you consider that most of our group's real growth has been in the past twenty-five years, even I am surprised.

IO

THE DECADE OF THE seventies ended ominously for the Middle East and for many of the commercial and other foreign interests which depended on the uninterrupted supply of oil: in 1979 the revolution in Iran broke out. For more than ten years after this event, the whole region was to be profoundly destabilized as a consequence. As is always the way with such crises, what appears on the surface to be their cause is often found to be only part of the story. Where the West has been involved in the affairs of the Middle East this has tended to be doubly and triply true.

The Pahlavi regime in Iran had been kept in place by Western influence, from the days when the Shah, having fled ignominiously at the time of the Abadan crisis, was brought back and reinstated on his throne by the Americans and the British. In the Arab world there was much sympathy at the time for the movement which was led by Dr Mossadegh, the Prime Minister, but most thoughtful Arabs realized that a stable Iran was essential as a buffer against any ambitions which Russia might harbour towards the oil-producing states of the Arabian peninsula and the Gulf. Those of us who were living in the area were very aware, during the seventies, of the extent of the opposition to the Shah in Iran, and the disaffection caused by the extent of corruption, particularly in the exploitation of contracts by foreign and Iranian entrepreneurs. As Iran's oil revenues grew ever more immense, the Shah's ambitions grew proportionately. He was courted by the world's media and by the politicians of countries anxious to secure their portion of Iran's wealth. I recall a particularly shameful episode when the British Chancellor of the Exchequer, Anthony Barber, and one of his ministerial colleagues, Peter Walker, were kept waiting hour after hour whilst the Shah was out on the Swiss ski slopes.

Undoubtedly, much of what was done in these years benefited the Iranian people, or at least a proportion of them; poverty was rife and, out of Tehran's reach, all manner of exploitation took place. I have, however, never met anyone on our side of the Gulf who could with honesty say that they predicted the revolution or the form which it took. Ayatollah Khomeini was not an especially important member of the Shia hierarchy though he was well known by virtue of his tape-recorded sermons which circulated widely throughout the country, denouncing the Shah and his regime.

The sad and lonely travels of the Shah after he left Iran for the last time, seeking, as it turned out, a place to die, did not confer much credit on those countries which had supported him so firmly whilst he was in power. This fact alone made many people in our region convinced that the revolution, like the Shah's earlier re-instatement, had been engineered by the Western powers who had become angered by his pretensions and by his unrealistic belief that he could become 'the policeman of the Gulf', an ambition which he appeared to sustain. He had made it plain that if a threat occurred to the Gulf states (always the 'Persian Gulf', in his termi-nology), then Iran would see it as her duty to 'take over'. This was not the sort of language that the West wished to hear, any more than it wished to be told that the countries of the West had become soft and that they should adopt the sound, Aryan principles which were proving so beneficial to Iran. When the Shah announced that Iran would become the fifth largest industrial power in the world, a particularly absurd claim, the Western powers decided that enough was enough.

What those of us who followed affairs in the region did find difficult to believe was that neither the Americans nor the British had had any idea of the revolution's approach. Both countries had large embassies each with a considerable intelligence capability; in the case of the British, this went back for a hundred years. That such sophisticated intelligence-gathering failed to pick up any of the signs we simply found incredible. Our disbelief strengthened further our conviction that the whole affair had been encouraged by the Western powers and carried out, if not with their active involvement, then certainly with their foreknowledge.

Sometimes our friends accuse us of paranoia when we claim to see the West's hand in every misfortune that affects our area. Yet, from the collapse of the Ottoman Empire at the end of the First World War, through the years which saw the foundation of the State of Israel to the invasion of Kuwait, the involvement of the Western powers has always been there, however ambiguous its influence might prove to be for the people of our region. In the case of the Iranian revolution, it is clear that the effect of the Arab Nationalist movements in the earlier decades had disturbed the Western powers very greatly; the rise of the financial and commercial influence of the oil-producing states had made them realize that an independent Middle East could greatly harm their long-term interests. If, on the other hand, the region was kept in a mild state of instability, then the friendship and support of the West would always be seen as necessary, and highly lucrative markets for the sale of arms and security systems would be guaranteed.

There was another consideration which influenced the course of events in our region at this time; again, it harks back to the West's fear of the rise of Arab Nationalism. Iran had been regarded by the political strategists as the eastern 'bracket', to contain the spread of Nationalist movements in the area. When the Shah showed signs of developing his own form of Nationalistic intent, inflamed by his own particular *folie des grandeurs*, it was time to act. The eastern Middle East needed to be kept under control; it was no longer possible to bring this about with gunboats and troop emplacements (though indeed they were later to be brought into play, with great effect, protecting shipping in the Gulf and supporting the alliance against Iraq over the invasion of Kuwait), so other means had to be found.

It is easy to dismiss talk of 'economic colonialism' as a further example of small-nation paranoia, but for the Arab states of the Middle East it is a reality. The manipulation of oil wealth by the international community has, until relatively recently, benefited that community more consistently than it has improved the conditions of life for the majority of the peoples of the oil-producing states. The tension which it is obviously in the interest of the West to sustain, tended for many years to inhibit the growth and security of the area as a whole; in the case of some of the inhabitants of the countries involved, like Iran and Iraq, the suffering is real enough and I doubt that it is any longer sufficient to demand that the people of such unfortunate lands must do away with their Rulers before their plight can be relieved. Of course there was a positive aspect to the flow of money into the oil-producing states, especially in the eighties when countries such as Saudi Arabia, Kuwait and the UAE were able to use at least some of their wealth to help less fortunate countries in the Arab and Moslem worlds, and beyond.

The revolution in Iran was followed in 1981 by the outbreak of war between that country and Iraq. It was an act of madness for the Iraqis, whose political judgement, if it was ever present, seems entirely to have deserted them in this period of their history, to attack the Iranian revolution. This is surely one of the most frequently cited commonplaces of modern political theory; in the present case, it served to unite the Iranian people behind their rulers in a way that no other action could have achieved. The outcome was eight years of bloody and heartbreaking conflict, which destroyed the economies of both countries and the lives of countless thousands of young men. At the end of it, nothing had been achieved except the further destabilization of the eastern Middle East, and the commitment of substantial parts of the wealth of the neighbours of the two warring nations to the purchase, mainly from the West, of more and more costly arms equipment and systems.

The Iranian revolution had one immediate effect on the Gulf states, the formation of the Arab Gulf Co-operation Council, an alliance of all the peninsular states, comprising Saudi Arabia, Kuwait, Bahrain, Qatar, the UAE and Oman. The actual experience of the GCC has not been especially distinguished, thus far, though it did have a part to play in opposing the invasion of Kuwait by the Iraqis in August 1990. Certainly the determined coalition which defeated the invaders would not have been possible without the solid support of the GCC states in defence of one of their number.

Barely had the dust settled from the dreadful conflict with Iran than Iraq chose to launch another dangerous adventure. The invasion of Kuwait drew the Gulf states and Saudi Arabia directly to the edge of the abyss. Iraq was faced down and humiliated; the country was further wounded and, at America's insistence, left to bleed whilst its rulers were allowed to remain, apparently impregnable, in Baghdad.

It is often said in Iran, I have no doubt jokingly, that if you lifted a mullah's beard you would find written underneath: 'Made in England'. This may be to exaggerate Britain's influence in the latter part of the twentieth century, but it contains an element of truth and indicates how people often view such events in our part of the world. It may also explain the scepticism about British and American protestations over their ignorance of the impending revolution.

My friend Sir James Craig was sent by his government to report on the GCC's success and standing some time after the end of the Iraqi invasion. I gave a dinner for him in Dubai, in the course of which he remarked that, in the conversations which he had held with Rulers, government officials and citizens in the states during his tour, he had been unable to find much enthusiasm for the GCC. I suggested that most of the inhabitants of the Gulf states felt that the GCC had not been formed for them or for their protection. They were prepared to admit that there were some advantages as a result of its creation: when the military were involved it always seemed easier to obtain facilities and developments which otherwise would be postponed on grounds of cost, improved roads and communications generally being obvious examples. But as far as the interests of the people at large were concerned, the GCC had really made remarkably little contribution to their well-being.

I have summarized the events of this tumultuous period in the

Gulf's history both because it is important in understanding the underlying causes of the ebb and flow of international politics as they affect the region, but also because they formed the prelude to another transformation of my life. This was when I was called on to serve my country as its Ambassador to London.

It could be said that much of my earlier career was a training for diplomacy, though I never imagined then that I would be required to follow it as a professional. I did not think of myself as a diplomat – or even as a politician – when I was working for Shaikh Rashid on his becoming Ruler in 1958. My work as an interpreter brought me into touch with a wide range of important people and events; I found myself engaged with issues which were of importance not only to Dubai but also to the region as a whole. My close relations with the British Political Agency required me often to convey to Shaikh Rashid the 'inwardness' of a British proposal or comment; sometimes I was used as an unofficial channel for conveying information to him or from him to the British officials when neither side wanted directly to propose a course of action or seek a favour.

When I became a member of the Trucial States Deliberative Committee and later was responsible for development throughout the states which made up the Trucial coast, diplomacy, in the narrower sense of dealing sensitively with often difficult and overbearing people, persuading them to a course of action in the general good, became a high priority in my life. When, therefore, I was asked to become a diplomat full time, though it came as a great surprise as I shall relate, I was perhaps actually less unprepared for the task than I said I was. Certainly, I was always deeply aware of what was going on around me and I have also always believed that fate directs our actions and that we have no right of choice.

Before this happened and my life was changed again dramatically, Shaikh Rashid had been taken ill and was no longer able to carry out the role which he had so memorably discharged for so long. In consequence, my involvement in official affairs diminished and I was able to concentrate my energies entirely on my businesses. My life entered a tranquil period and, as I grew older, I became content, happy to enjoy my work, my family and the two to three months' holiday every year which I was able to spend with my wife, travelling to all the places it seemed we had never had the time to visit in the past. We came to London every summer and stayed in our flat in Cadogan Place; we cruised extensively, usually spending a month or so exploring one or more of the countries on our journey. I returned to Dubai each year by 10 October, when the milder weather generally begins.

I made it my practice to call on the principal shaikhs every two or three weeks to pay my respects and to catch up on the gossip of the *majlis*. I was much involved in the negotiations for a large, US $1.2 billion tender for my Siemens friends; in this I was greatly helped by Shaikh Maktoum bin Rashid, whose help and encouragement were invaluable and for which I am profoundly grateful.

One day, I received a call from the Municipality asking me when I intended to register my land. I had no idea what they were talking about; it transpired that Shaikh Rashid had given me a parcel of land but somehow forgotten to mention this to me. Before anyone might change their minds I registered my ownership and built a substantial centre for my Grundig business there.

On another occasion, I was sitting in my office – it was soon after the invasion of Kuwait – when Robert Hendrie, the British Consul General, called to see me. His was a post which had been created when the UAE became fully independent and exchanged ambassadors with the countries with which it had relations, including Britain; the Ambassador is resident in Abu Dhabi and the Consul General in Dubai. He told me that the Queen wished to offer me an important British decoration, designating me a Commander of the Order of the British Empire (CBE). As a committed anti-colonialist I was a little taken aback and asked what I had done to deserve it. The Consul General assured me that it was because of my long friendship with the British, my help to the Agency over the years, my involvement in the development of Dubai and of British participation in it, and my encouragement of Anglo-Dubaian trade. I said, of course, that I would be honoured to accept; after the end of the Iraqi invasion of Kuwait the British Ambassador, Graham Burton, came to Dubai and presented me with the decoration, at a party to mark the occasion. The event was widely reported in the UAE media and my friends seemed to be as pleased as I was.

During the holy month of Ramadan that year, I received a telephone call from Shaikh Maktoum's office informing me that he wanted me to take over the UAE Embassy in London, as the country's Ambassador to the Court of St James. I was frankly incredulous; I kept out of the way for as long as I could, hoping that the idea might be forgotten or that somebody more suitable might appear. However, when I next saw Shaikh Maktoum he made it clear that he was still very keen for me to take up the appointment. He would not listen to me when I said that I was too old and that I had my businesses to run. He said that arrangements could always be made to take care of that.

He told me to go to London and look at the situation on the ground. If, he said, I should decide that I did not wish to undertake the mission, it would make no difference whatsoever to the respect in which he held me. I could not refuse.

I expected to take the job on for three years. I assumed that I had been offered it because Shaikh Maktoum wished to honour me and also, perhaps, to reward me for some of the work which I had carried out during the lifetime of Shaikh Rashid. Obviously, I would be acceptable to the British, who had so recently conferred an honour on me. All in all, the omens seemed good.

I still had some misgivings, however. It was all very well to make arrangements for running my businesses whilst I was in London, but they represented a large part of my life and I was keen to see them grow. I knew that, in the nature of things, there were those at home who resented the success which I had been fortunate enough to have achieved so far. I did not want my absence in London either to put at risk what we already held or to limit the growth of the Group in the future.

Fortunately, Shaikh Maktoum was very understanding. It was agreed that I should spend nine months a year in London running the Embassy and three months in Dubai running the businesses; later this became six months in each location. Electronic communications make such a programme possible and mean that I can keep in touch, daily if necessary, with one interest whilst I am working at the other. I am greatly assisted by my daughter who manages the businesses on my behalf in Dubai, and by the management which I have set in place over the years. I have also been helped by the very understanding attitude of the Foreign and Commonwealth Office in London who have agreed to forgo my presence for half the year.

I set about introducing the sort of reforms and reorganizations which I would have brought to a business in which I might have become involved. I am profoundly grateful to my friend Ahmed Al-Tayer, the Under Secretary at the Ministry of Finance, who supported me in all that I wanted to do and who made sure that the money to do it was always available.

One of my first priorities was to create a new Commercial Department, for the Embassy has an important role to play in facilitating trade between the two countries. I brought in new staff and in quite a short time the commercial office was putting out more information about the UAE than the British Government's Department of Trade and Industry. I consolidated the Embassy's work with the Chamber of Commerce of the UAE constituent states and I obtained supplies of up-to-date material about all aspects of the UAE and its economy from the Ministry of Information in Abu Dhabi and Dubai.

I was keen to improve the Embassy's contact with the public in the United Kingdom. When I arrived, I insisted on seeing all the letters which the Embassy received and the replies which were sent to them. One day I saw a letter from a young boy asking if we would send him a reference for the country's flag, for a project which he was carrying out at his school. A week or so later I realized that I had not seen a reply: I sent for the official responsible, a locally recruited employee, and tackled her about it. To my amazement she told me that she had torn the boy's letter up as it was not worth bothering about. I pointed out that Britain was a democracy and that in fifty years' time that boy might be the Prime Minister of the United Kingdom; she was likely to be responsible for him having a grudge against the UAE all his life. She left the Embassy's employment. If the boy who wrote the letter ever reads this, I hope that he will forgive us for the Embassy's lack of consideration.

I introduced a range of state-of-the-art computers into the Embassy with the help of a young man from one of the Gulf states, who was an expert. I revised all the publications which the Embassy produced to ensure that information was readily available, attractive and accurate. I do not record these changes, necessary as they seemed to me to be, to show how dedicated I was to the task which I had been given, but rather to demonstrate the extent of what needed to be done and how a little determination and organization could bring about radical improvement. In time, I believe that our Embassy functioned as well as most European missions.

For every Ambassador to the Court of St James, the Presentation of Credentials to Her Majesty the Queen is a highlight of his experience in London. The drive in the horse-drawn carriage, escorted by the Marshal of the Diplomatic Corps, with my wife in a car behind us, followed by the ceremony of the presentation itself, are memorable.

To me the experience was even more, a rather moving example of how far a man can travel in his lifetime. I thought of my father and of the sickly little son whom he nurtured so well, riding in state to meet the sovereign of the power which had for so long dominated the lives of all of us who lived on the shores of the Arabian Gulf.

The Queen was gracious and kindly; I reminded her that we had met when she had visited Dubai and I was able to thank her for the award of the CBE, which I wore for the occasion. I remarked that God had brought me to her presence to allow me to thank her in person.

When I had settled into the post I found the day-to-day business of the Embassy very enjoyable. I met many old and new friends and, if you exercise a reasonable degree of caution, the business of being an ambassador, despite the number of lunches and dinners which you are required to eat, can be very pleasant.

One of the recurring duties of an ambassador in London is each year to attend the State Opening of Parliament. The Queen and her retinue come to the House of Lords where the members of the

House of Commons have been summoned to attend her. She reads the Speech from the Throne in which are set out the Government's proposals for legislation during the coming session of Parliament.

On one such occasion, I was sitting in the front row of the ambassadors present, and hence quite close to the Throne. The Queen was wearing the Imperial Crown as she does when she opens Parliament and my mind went back to an incident in my childhood.

One day, when I was quite small, my father took me with him when he called on one of his friends, Mustafa Abdul Latif (in whose house I was later to stay during my time in Bahrain), an important pearl merchant with whom my father sometimes did business. I was told to sit in the deep recess of one of the windows and, under my father's expert guidance, to practise my Arabic calligraphy, copying the beautiful flowing letters. There were bars over the window and sometimes my attention wandered and I watched the passing crowds in the street below.

As I watched, I saw a well-known Hyderabadi pearl merchant walk by; as he passed, he carried in his hand some of the pearls which he had been trading. The pearls were tied in small, linen bundles, the colour of milk chocolate, called *dimni*. As the merchant walked along he was fingering the wallet which held the *dimni*, as if he were counting the pearls or perhaps searching for a particular one; whilst I watched I saw that one of the bundles had fallen to the ground, though the merchant was unaware of its loss. I ran below and picked it up, then rushed upstairs and gave it to my father.

Later that day the Town Crier, as he might have been called in an English town in days past, went about the streets announcing the merchant's loss. My father at once went to him and returned his pearls. The merchant, naturally enough, was delighted and asked my father the circumstances of the bundle of pearls' recovery; my father told him that it was his son who had found it and secured its return to him. The merchant insisted that I should be brought to him, so that he could thank me. This he did; he also handed me a 10-rupee note as a reward.

I had never seen so much money; in today's terms it might be

199

worth fifty pence or so. I examined the note with wonder; I even smelt the paper on which it was printed. In particular, I was fascinated by the picture of an old man with a beard, wearing a strange object on his head.

More than half a century later I found myself sitting close to the old man's granddaughter, as she wore the same crown, or one very like it. I confess that my mind was happily at home and it is possible that I did not give Her Majesty's speech the close attention that I should have done. Again, I was moved to reflect how extraordinary are the workings of Providence, for no one could have imagined that the little boy in the window would one day have found himself in such exalted circumstances, with the Imperial Crown of England acting as the trigger for his memories.

Another of the pleasant experiences which come the way of an ambassador in London is that from time to time an invitation will be received to lunch or dine with the Queen and members of the Royal Family at Windsor Castle. These events are family affairs and very pleasing in their informality. Windsor is the place that the Queen and the Duke of Edinburgh regard as 'home' and the atmosphere in the Castle reflects this.

On one such occasion my wife and I were invited to dine; I found myself seated on the Queen's right hand, an honour for my country as much as it was for me. Before and after dinner the conversation is informal and the Queen will speak of her visits to the principal guests' countries – she must be by far the most widely travelled of all heads of state – and she augments her discussion of the countries concerned by reference to the albums of photographs of her visits which will surely form a unique archive for historians in the future. When my wife and I dined with her, she spoke with insight and perception about the problems of the Middle East. I suspect that I was not the first of her guests to be impressed by the extent of her knowledge and the depth of her feelings about some of the issues which were important to us.

I have been very conscious of the Royal Family's concern for the Queen's Moslem subjects and I have come especially to know and to admire Prince Charles's affection and respect for Islam. I know, too, that he shares a deep mutual respect with my own Head of State, Shaikh Zayed bin Sultan Al-Nahayan; they also share an interest in the planting and management of a herbal garden.

One of Prince Charles's enduring interests is the Oxford Centre for Islamic Studies. I have often seen him at work in the Centre and his dedication is apparent, a dedication which is borne out by the many public speeches he has delivered, seeking to strengthen the common ties between Islam and Christendom. I have been able to participate in the Centre's work by endowing in perpetuity the Easa Saleh Al-Gurg Scholarship. This scholarship is intended to support study in the area of the arts, humanities or social sciences (particularly in the fields of anthropology, economics, geography, history, international relations, law, literature, philosophy, politics, religion and sociology), contributing to a more informed understanding of Islam and the Moslem world. The scholarship supplements some of the other benefactions which I have been able to make to Islamic, Christian and non-sectarian causes throughout the world.

After the presentation of credentials, it is customary for the new Ambassador to hold a *vin d'honneur*, to which he will invite his close friends and colleagues; I decided to hold a luncheon. The main speech was given by my friend David (now Sir David) Gore-Booth, the scion of a great diplomatic family and firm friend of the Arabs, who was then Assistant Under Secretary for the Near and Middle East at the Foreign and Commonwealth Office. In the course of his speech, he emphasized how pleased he and his colleagues were that the UAE had chosen to appoint an ambassador from a business background. It was this comment, as much as any other consideration, which impelled me to place so much importance on the reorganization of the Embassy's commercial office.

As part of the London diplomatic family, I was able to renew many friendships with British officials whom I had known during their service in the Gulf. Not all of our contacts were so happy, however; in common with many of my Arab colleagues I was distressed to discover what seemed to us to be a singular lack of warmth – some might even have detected the appearance of deliberate discourtesy – in the manner of the then Foreign Secretary, Douglas Hurd (now Lord Hurd of Westwell) who was in office during the early years of my posting to London. Several of my Arab colleagues felt that the Secretary of State did not welcome contact with them and wished to keep any such contact as he was required to have, to the barest minimum. He had the peculiar habit, when obliged to shake hands with Arab ambassadors (whether it happened with others I cannot say), of seeming to push away the hand that he was apparently shaking. I know that this did not happen with European ambassadors; indeed, I took the trouble to watch the Foreign Secretary's behaviour with them, to make sure that I was not mistaken. However, when I enquired from other of my colleagues amongst the Arab ambassadors, they confirmed that they, too, had been exposed to what they all regarded as very odd behaviour. I also experienced this strange exercise in diplomacy.

My first official contact with him had not been encouraging. I called on him in the early days of my posting, a formality which all newly appointed ambassadors must fulfill. He was seated on a sofa, with beside him, placed rather obviously, though somewhat surprisingly it appeared to have been screwed up, a file which evidently contained the brief his officials had prepared about me. 'Tell me about yourself,' he said, I thought rather patronizingly. I said that I was quite sure I would not be able to tell him as much about myself as his file contained.

To my astonishment, at this point the Foreign Secretary slammed his hands down on his knees and said, 'The meeting is over!' It was, by any standards, a very extraordinary way for a senior politician to conduct himself towards the accredited representative of a friendly foreign country. I decided not to report the matter to my Government, as I knew that it would disappoint those at home who were Britain's friends, and embarrass those, on both sides, who were concerned to maintain good relations between us. Little would be gained, I felt, by drawing attention to the Foreign Secretary's rudeness and so I kept the matter to myself.

There was yet another occasion on which I was the witness to behaviour by the Foreign Secretary which seemed to me very far from diplomatic. I was invited to attend a discussion arranged by one of the British companies whose interests I represented in the UAE. The meeting took place in Bristol and the principal speaker was Douglas Hurd. It was at the time when Turkey was making one of its attempts to be accepted into the European Community. A young man present asked Hurd whether the Community would accept Turkey as a member. Again, with extraordinary vehemence, the Foreign Secretary retorted: 'No!' as though such an idea was unthinkable, despite the fact that part of Turkey is on the European mainland.

Let me say, to conclude the recital of these painful incidents, that I have never received anything but courtesy and consideration from other British ministers and officials. I can only conclude, sadly, that something prevented the Foreign Secretary from feeling at ease either in the context of Middle Eastern affairs or in the presence of Middle Eastern people.

I am also accredited as Ambassador of the United Arab Emirates to the Republic of Ireland. My Presentation of Credentials to President Mary Robinson was a good deal less formal, though certainly no less enjoyable, than my presentation to the Queen. It took place at Áras an Uachtaráin in the Phoenix Park, the official residence of the President and once the seat of the British Viceroy. We sat and chatted most pleasantly. Afterwards I found that a reception had been arranged for me to meet the members of the Irish–Arab Chamber of Commerce, an occasion of which I had had no notice whatsoever.

All passed off well, however. In my speech I said that the Irish and the Arabs had much in common and I addressed them, to their evident pleasure, as 'brothers and cousins'. Both peoples, I remarked, were eccentric, hot-blooded but quick to cool their anger, given to intrigue, hospitable and very polite. Since I have been Ambassador to Ireland the country's annual exports to the UAE have increased from around £5 million to £75 million in 1997.

*

As Ambassador of the UAE I am a member of the Council of Arab Ambassadors in London, which meets from time to time to discuss matters of common interest to the Arab world, such as the Palestinian question, as well as other political and cultural matters. We are concerned with those issues which affect both the Arab world and Britain and we are able to exercise some discreet influence on a number of issues, both public and, perhaps more so, private.

I am very grateful for the generous and kindly reception which my colleagues accorded me when I joined their number, the more so since I was not from their professional background. I have become very conscious of the challenges which face the representatives of the Arab states in a country like Britain, and sometimes I could wish that all of us had the opportunity of becoming more involved in the political and cultural life around us and of promoting the Arab interest, as a whole, more aggressively. As a group, the Arab corps of ambassadors tends to be seen as somewhat closed in upon itself; the problem really, I suspect, is that many of the Arab states have a different view of the role of an ambassador from that of, for example, a European country. Sometimes I wish that it were not so, but that, for the present at least, is how it is.

It is sometimes difficult for ambassadors from countries with authoritarian regimes to strike the right balance. I have noticed that in some of our meetings an ambassador will repeat almost word for word what has just been said by another. This, I gather, is known as 'registering a position', so that an appropriate report may be sent to the ambassador's Foreign Ministry. I understand the reasons but the practice does not make for a lively discussion.

Sometimes we find ourselves in strange situations. It was decided that groups of ambassadors should call on the Foreign Editors of leading British journals in an attempt to make them aware of the main preoccupations of the Arab world at the time. I elected to join the group visiting the *Guardian*.

In discussion, I ventured the view that it was a matter of regret that European countries, especially Britain, did not concern themselves more with the Palestine issue, given that it was a British action, the publication of the Balfour Declaration, which had started the tragedy of the Palestinian nation.

At this, one of the senior editors (who was said not to be a Zionist sympathizer), leapt up and shouted, 'This is nonsense; this is history. It's all past.' Some of his colleagues were clearly embarrassed. None of my colleagues intervened to support what I had said, so I judged that the best course was to remain silent.

My period of office in London and my observation of the workings of the different embassies and their ambassadors has made me reflect on the nature of modern diplomacy and the role of the ambassador in a world of instant electronic communication. I have heard it said that electronics have largely done away with the necessity for an ambassador to represent his country in any but a purely formal or ceremonial sense. Since I am not a professional diplomat but have come to diplomacy from the outside world, I can perhaps express a view which will not be dismissed simply as partisan.

It seems to me that the truth of the matter is quite different from that which argues that the embassy today is largely superfluous, and is useful only in the facilitation of visits to and from the home country, a sort of travel agency, and not a very glorified one. The very fact of the complexity of electronic and other media makes it important, in my view, to have skilled, professional people in the role of the representatives of their country to advise their governments, not so much on the broad sweep of policy as on the small print, the undercurrents which will determine the mood of a government, or the development of opinions which may begin to form the future policy of a country with whom relations are important. There is nothing to equal the value of being able to look into a minister's or an official's eyes when he is arguing or defending his government's policies; electronics are a poor substitute for an experienced, well-attuned faculty of judgement.

There are countless opportunities for an ambassador to advance the interests of his country if he is prepared to take them. With the pressure of all manner of interests, some competing, many obscure and requiring understanding and explanation, the alert ambassador can fulfill a valuable function for his government. But the first requirement is for his government to have a clear and explicit foreign policy of which he is aware and a modern machinery of government to support him and to ensure that decisions which affect the country's policy are taken thoughtfully and coherently.

One of the problems which the modern embassy faces today, especially if it represents a non-European country (either geographically or by cultural tradition) is that many Third World countries generally do not have traditions of diplomatic representation. This applies to much of Africa, south of the Sahara; to many, though not all, of the Far Eastern states and certainly to much of the Islamic world. This last point is the consequence of the course of international affairs over the past few centuries; in the great days of the Moslem empires, the exchange of diplomatic missions was part of the ordinary currency of government. The centuries of colonial rule, however, diminished the awareness in our societies of this aspect of our past as much as it deprived us of a proper understanding of our history.

It seems to me that governments need to examine carefully the role and function of embassies, and not simply to regard them as a part of the machinery of government inherited from the West that has to be accepted though not entirely welcomed. Generally speaking, my impression is that most of my colleagues are not sufficiently consulted about policy unlike, for example, their European counterparts, when government is formulating its view or its response to a given situation. I have come to believe, as the result of my experience in London, that ambassadors should be involved in all decisions relating to the countries to which they are accredited; at the present time it is all too obvious that, generally speaking, they are not. If the embassies are to discharge their responsibilities adequately, they should receive instant responses to their requests for information and guidance.

Unless the ambassador and his senior staff receive the sort of support they need, especially in terms of day-to-day information, they cannot properly or completely discharge even their routine functions.

I am conscious that I speak about these matters from the advantageous position of being largely independent; my future does not depend upon my qualities as an ambassador, nor do I sustain hopes of a career in diplomacy. I am not a career civil servant, and I think that there are occasions when it is to the country's advantage to appoint ambassadors from among the business community, as happened in my own case. This does not mean that it is not important for countries like ours to develop a professional, skilled diplomatic service; it is of the first importance and it is no easy matter to create such a service virtually from scratch. Some countries have done it, however, and it provides an acceptable and worthwhile career for both men and women. Our models should be some of the European embassies, particularly those from the smaller countries, which have established very sophisticated foreign services which perform a valuable function quite out of proportion to their cost. I believe that I have demonstrated the value of setting up an efficient administration in the Embassy, and in strengthening those areas which are obviously most relevant to relations with the United Kingdom: trade and commerce.

The relationship with Britain which I have enjoyed as the ambassador of my country has been greatly rewarding. But England had become my second home even before I was appointed to the Court of St James. I have mentioned our flat in Cadogan Place; after I had bought it, the agent who handled the sale for me suggested that I should buy a farm. I had not considered the idea before he mentioned it, but I agreed at least to look at the possibility of becoming a farmer.

We drove down from London to the east coast, near the seaside resort of Frinton. It was a bleak and very wet day. We arrived at our destination and my companion left me whilst he went to speak to the then owner of the farm; apparently he did not want to deal directly with any prospective buyer.

The farm was for sale as a result of a disagreement amongst the family to whom it belonged, a situation, I was to discover, not entirely unknown amongst English landowning families. The deluge of rain continued as I sat in the car waiting for my agent's return.

Eventually he did come back, bringing with him the owner's

price. A quick calculation showed me that it represented a price per square foot (the area in which I was accustomed to dealing at home) which was a fraction of the cost of land even out in the desert in Dubai. In addition, there was the rain, which continued to fall in sheets. To an Arab, the constant promise of rain is one of the most appealing aspects of life in England; here there was this sweet water falling from the heavens and costing nothing.

I bought the farm and set about improving it. During the war it had been an RAF base and Spitfires had been grounded there; there were still the remains of concrete runways, and bunkers in which the aircraft had been hidden from German reconnaissance planes and the bombers which came across the North Sea, which washes the perimeter of my land. Over the years, I have invested a considerable amount of money in improvements and modernization at the farm; it is now regarded as one of the best run in East Anglia and regularly wins awards at the county shows. It is a matter of some pleasure to me that I have been able to turn my youthful delight in the descriptions of the British countryside, which I enjoyed so much in the articles in *Al-Musawwar* when I lived as a young man in Bahrain, into the reality of owning a part of it.

I have also consolidated my ties with England further by buying a lease on a house in London's Regent's Park. We have only quite recently moved there but it is decorated to our taste and, whilst I use it as the official residence for the entertaining which is part of my job as an ambassador, it is also a family home for my wife and me. My children have the use of our other flat in Kensington, so it may be said that everyone is cared for.

My principal home remains the house and garden which I built for my wife and myself in Dubai in 1978. My mother had her own household there until her death and it is there that I feel most at peace. The inscription that my father carved for his friend occupies an important place in front of the house. The garden is now well established and, like all well-tended gardens in our part of the world, it has repaid generously the care which has been given to it.

To entertain one's friends has always been a duty to an Arab but for me it has also always been a great and rewarding pleasure. My house is designed for parties and for both informal and formal gatherings. I enjoy the presence of my friends greatly and I am pleased to think that they enjoy visiting my wife and me. I hope that they will long continue to do so.

I I

THE PROCESS OF COMPILING a record of one's life inevitably turns one's thoughts, not only to the past, but also towards the future. I am by nature optimistic and I want always to know what will happen tomorrow. Having led the sort of life which has been mine, with its mixture of business, politics and diplomacy, I would be at fault if I did not look to the future and set down what I see.

The fact that I am still in love with life and that each morning as I look at myself in the mirror I am pleased with what I see (I assure myself that I am still a nice-looking boy) makes me want to see the future as bright and hopeful; as for that part of the world with which I have mainly been concerned for all these years, I am not so sure. Let me say a few things about my present attitudes and beliefs.

I hope that anyone who reads these words will recognize that I have been deeply influenced by my Islamic birthright and by the character of my immediate forebears. I tell myself that I have not been a model Moslem, but I have always tried to follow the precepts and guidance which our religion provides. Islam urges its followers always to learn, to improve their knowledge and understanding, from the cradle to the grave. The culture of Islam which I have carried inside me colours my view of the future.

Islam is concerned always to help the less fortunate, the

dispossessed; this is why the misfortunes of the Palestinians have always evoked such deep-seated concern from all Moslems. Their fate is one of the key factors for the future, which I will consider further.

In my life, I have had to deal with many important men, those whom the world accounts as people of power. I have never found it difficult to sit as an equal with such men, for as a Moslem I know that all men are equal in God's estimation; I am also confident in the knowledge that my own family is a noble one, of dignity and attainment. If life is a stage then we are all players, with our parts set out for us to follow. For me, religion provides the framework for our lives; we have to live it as it is.

Islam teaches us that our actions and our future are determined; this indeed is one of the basic principles on which the faith is founded. The attitude of mind which this perception gives rise to has, in the recent past, led to an acceptance of the material supremacy of the West and, in consequence, of Western political domination. As a result, the belief has taken root that such domination is the expression of the will of God and is thus pre-ordained.

In our own time, those who, for whatever reason, wish to discredit Islam have invariably seized on what the modern mind will see as its negative aspects – for example fatalism, and the rejection of the modern world and of the validity of other systems of belief – and have encouraged all the emphasis of comment to be placed on them, inevitably resulting in the promotion of attitudes hostile to Islam. According to this view, Islam is condemned for ever to remain subservient to other systems and never to reach its true potential. To the Moslem, this requires the regulation of society according to the precepts of Islam, a situation which has not persisted since the earliest days of the faith, when it swept across much of the known world.

Then Islam was the repository of the most ardent search for knowledge and was responsible for laying down the foundations of modern scientific theory and understanding. The arts, too, gained immeasurably from the work of Arab architects, designers, poets and writers; no one should believe that Islam is simply a dry observance of rules, for in reality it is a vibrant expression of the richness of human life.

The creation of a truly Islamic society does not depend upon a narrow, 'fundamentalist' interpretation of the Quran, or upon the interpretations of the Prophet's Companions and the others who, over the centuries, have sought to explain the relevance of Islam to believers and non-believers alike. The Moslem world has, over the past half century, begun to make up for the centuries of atrophy and neglect; whether there is still time to build a truly Islamic society in the modern world I cannot say.

Despite my innate optimism, I must confess that sometimes the future looks very dark to me. Though I have no doubt of the absolute validity of Islam as a system of belief and as a means of managing human societies, I find myself questioning whether it is the peoples of the Middle East who will guard it and take it forward into its next contribution to the well-being of humanity. I suspect that the misfortunes which have lain upon the countries of the Middle East, at least since the end of the Arab Empires, have weakened the spirit of the people and turned their minds only to the acquisition of wealth and the external evidences of its possession. In fairness, I must record my recognition of the commitment which many young Moslems show to their faith and to their heritage. In my own family, I am impressed by the sincerity with which some of my nephews, for example, have combined successful professional careers with an Islamic way of life. They have demonstrated, I believe, that the two need not be mutually exclusive.

It may be that the future promotion of Islam as a living force will become the responsibility of non-Arabs. It may be that the responsibility will descend on people from the West (a paradox if ever there was one) for it is surely very significant how many people in the West are turning away from the values which their societies have elevated, to seek for other, more profound truths. It may be that the Moslem leaders of the future will come from Europe, the Far East and the fragments of the Russian Empire, where Islam survived despite all the attempts to destroy it.

Wherever the driving force for Islam in the future comes from I recall confidently the words of Surah Al-Hijr:

إِنَّا نَحْنُ نَزَّلْنَا الذِّكْرَ وَإِنَّا لَهُ لَحَافِظُونَ ﴿

﴿ سورة الحجر .. آيَةٌ

'Verily We: It is We who have sent you down the Zikr [i.e. the Quran] and surely, we will guard it [i.e. from corruption].'

This is the most certain assurance of the faith's survival. I remember, too, the story of the Prophet Mohammed's uncle, Abdul Mutaleb, during the attack on Makka by the King of Ethiopia during the Year of the Elephant, before the Prophet's birth. The King's soldiers attacked the Ka'aba, the sacred meteoric stone which stands at the heart of the Holy Mosque today, but at that time was enclosed in a heathen temple. The Ethiopians also seized some camels belonging to Abdul Mutaleb and held them as booty. The Prophet's uncle confronted the King and protested against the capture of his animals. The King, however, urged Abdul Mutaleb to protect the Ka'aba which his men were attacking; his camels, he suggested, were a small matter compared with ensuring that the shrine should remain inviolate. 'God will protect His house,' said Abdul Mutaleb, 'but no one except me will protect my camels.'

There are those who believe that the pressures within Western societies are mounting to the extent that they will become uncontrollable. They argue that the collapse of discipline, the decline of religion and the cult of materialism will, sooner rather than later, bring down the United States and the Western European states. For myself, I believe that the indulgence of every form of divergent eccentricity in a society, of the protection of the wrongdoer at the expense of the victim, the displacement of the family as the basic unit of society and the increasing dependence of the individual on the state for all the matters which have always been the responsibility of the individual or the family – education, health care, the care of the old and sick – is immensely harmful and, in some Western societies, have already achieved explosive proportions.

Yet I do not think that the prophecies of impending doom will come to pass. The experience of my life, and the experience of history in my part of the world and of others like it, suggest that the West will sacrifice everything and everyone to protect its interests. At the least they will contrive to keep much of the world in moral and economic subjection, to provide a cushion for the self-indulgent masses in their own societies. If you have read George Orwell's *1984*, you will be aware of the shape which such a future could take. Though Orwell envisaged a world dominated by extreme forms of Fascist or Marxist dictatorship, both political phenomena which have, for the time being at least, gone into the shadows, his vision of a world dominated by huge power blocs with the ordinary people of the state kept docile by access to unlimited pornography and drugs, is disturbingly close to the experiences of our lifetime.

There is, of course, no doubt that the Middle East will alter, not least because of the social changes which will come about when the oil ceases to flow in the quantities which have become accepted by the outside world as amounting to a fact of nature, despite all the evidence to the contrary. When the states of the Arabian Gulf, for example, have to earn their livings, rather than depend primarily on the benefits drawn from oil revenues, the experience of states like the UAE, to which I drew attention earlier, will, I trust, become accepted as the way in which such societies can manage their affairs, largely free from the intervention of others.

It is inevitable that there will be a movement towards a greater participation of the citizens in the running of even the most traditionalist states. This does not mean that any sort of confrontation is necessary; our societies in the Gulf have endured for a long time and it is in the interests of no one that this rich past should be discarded. It is well for reformers, whatever their motivations, to bear this point in mind, for if they do not they will merely bring more distress upon those whom they claim they would help.

I am certain that an acceptance of the democratic system of government would serve to strengthen the existing regimes in the Gulf, not threaten them. Participation is inevitable, and a wise Ruler will ensure that he encourages and guides its achievement, and in doing so, will make certain that the traditional values and practices of our societies remain in place. Democracy, the involvement of the community in decisions which affect the community as a whole, should not dismay any Moslem society; from the earliest days of Islam collective decision-making was the accepted way, though always with the acknowledgement of the role and prerogatives of the Ruler and, above all, the teachings of the Quran.

The movement towards a degree of participation is already apparent. In Kuwait, the experiment of elected assemblies seems to be working; the process will undoubtedly spread to other states. It may be that it is sensible to move cautiously and slowly towards this objective but it is not a prospect to be feared.

As the years go by, it is important that the members of the families which have provided our Rulers, and who have the respect and affection of many in our societies, understand the currents which are sweeping across the world. The world is becoming so small and the affairs of every nation (almost, it seems sometimes, of every individual) are instantly transmitted from one side of the globe to the other. It is not prudent to try to stand against these influences but rather to seek to manage them, to ensure that they do not undermine all our values from the past.

Hence, it seems to me to be most important that the younger members of the ruling families and of other families of influence in our communities should keep in touch with the people, not only to inform and persuade but to listen. This was something that their forefathers did very skilfully and it is perhaps the principal reason that the system with which they were identified survived for so long. There are liberal-minded men and women coming to the fore in the Gulf and they must be encouraged to bring a new world to birth. We shall need not only the understanding of our own people to bring this about, peaceably and constructively, but also the sympathy of the foreign interests which are now our partners, rather than simply the authors of so many of our misfortunes in the past and of our insecurities today. If the UAE, as the example of a brilliantly successful experiment in political management and growth, can be allowed another thirty years of uninterrupted development, there is no knowing what might not be achieved. If the Arabian peninsula as a whole, and the Arab world at large, could similarly

be left to find their own way, the entire region would be transformed. The changes, if they come, must come from within.

In our part of the world, there has always been a tendency to
favour certain tribal groups and clans over others; certain communities, like those which had moved away from the ancestral homeland, were considered somehow less deserving than those who
stayed. This is natural enough and its effect on the lives of those
who have experienced it should not be exaggerated. But in my case,
and that of others like me, the fact that my family came from the
Persian side of the Gulf and that my skin is very fair, probably made
it much more difficult to achieve what I have achieved than if I had
been from the dominant tribal group on our part of the coast.

From an early age, I tended to respond to all things and all ideas
which were modern, of the time in which we lived. I was not so
much in sympathy with many of the traditional forms of society
which lingered on, and which often seemed to dominate to an
unreasonable extent the life of our people. Seeing it as I did, I
became more and more apprehensive that it would restrict our
developing society from taking its place in the modern world,
which I knew to be our most urgent priority.

Perhaps the fact that we came originally from the Persian side of
the Gulf gave my family a rather different view of the world.[1] We
were proud of our Arab heritage − none more so − but we saw it
in terms different from those which our cousins on the Arabian
peninsular coast maintained. To us, Arabian culture and tradition,
the history of the great period of the Arab Empires, and the
contribution which those centuries had given to world culture,
owed little to a way of life rooted in an inward-looking system of
social organization which had its origins long before Islam. The
fact that we had lived in Iran for so long may have given us some
mental attitudes other than the exclusively Semitic cast of mind of
the Arabs of the peninsula. (I am using the term 'Semitic' in a lin-
guistic and cultural, not a racial, sense.) Much of my life has been
concerned with trying to reconcile these two quite distinct elements; I am still convinced that until we can reconcile our past with
the present day, our part of the world will never attain the place
which I know to be rightly its due.

The demands exerted by tribalism on the loyalties of tribal members, in the Arab world at least, have held our progress back. Although the traditions, coherence, loyalties and sense of community which have often typified tribal life throughout history are admirable qualities, I have always feared that unless they are reconciled to the very different circumstances which apply to all developed communities today, their admirable qualities will be lost, overwhelmed by pettiness and dissension.[2]

It must be remembered that most major societies go through a period of tribalization as they progress towards other, more complex social and political structures. This is particularly true of societies when they are undergoing change, when peoples, sometimes entire nations, are melting into each other. There are so many examples from history. Originally, the Greeks and the Romans were tribal: in the case of Rome, the division of the society into tribal and clan structures was retained theoretically, long after the actual tribal structures had disappeared. Before the Roman invasion, the British were divided into tribes, with each tribe occupying a specific part of the country, a situation which made it comparatively easy for the Romans to impose their rule on what was to become the most northernly and westerly province of the Roman Empire. The Germans, against whom the Romans also waged war, were tribal; so too were the Celts, though they managed to resist colonization until late, the Scots and the Welsh, for example, only falling victims to English domination in the course of the last thousand years.

We all of us know the horrors which are still being perpetrated in the name of tribal and ethnic superiority. In Afghanistan, an ancient society has been destroyed by it. The divisions which the British tried to ignore when they put the country together still prevent Iraq from becoming the important developed nation which it undoubtedly could be. But whilst it continues to be possible for influences inside and outside Iraq to promote the divisions between all the Sunni clans, the Shia, the Kurds, the Assyrian Christians, the Yezidi and the many other tribal and congregational groups which live uneasily with each other within Iraq's borders, the country will never achieve its real potential.

In the Arab world, we need to begin to free ourselves from these aspects of our past. This does not mean that we must necessarily lose touch with our traditions; far from it, and with the light of Islam before us we can hold on to the most important of the ties which bind us together, for it is the good fortune of Moslems that they are members of a community which transcends national or tribal allegiances.

I think that we must even question (as many other peoples have had the occasion to question already) whether we can, with any real truth, speak about the purity of races. Is there such a creature, for example, as a 'pure' Arab? If there is, how may he be recognized? All of us in the Middle East have cause to lament the raising of racial myths to the level of political programmes, when we see before us the example of the seizure of the land of Palestine by those who falsely claim 'rights', by virtue of a pretended descent from the very diverse tribal groups who lived there in the first millennium BC.

In one or two centuries, most populations undergo profound changes as the result of the incoming of new peoples or, as in the case of my own family's experience, of returning to a homeland. We have to accept that all people who live together in one place and who are citizens of that place have rights which should be respected.

I freely admit that, culturally, I have absorbed many influences in my lifetime. I am an Arab whose family spent many years on the eastern side of the Gulf, separated by a narrow strip of water, which also acted as the means of linking the two Arabic-speaking communities to each other. Nowadays, I think in English when the occasion requires it. But my loyalty to Dubai has never wavered and my life has been dedicated to its prosperity, within the capacity of my own modest abilities.

The divisions in the Arab world, of which our opponents make so much, are not real. We are, I am still convinced, one people driven by common goals, ideologies and customs. This is the message which the Arab world today receives from the early days of Islam and from the glorious centuries of the Arab Empires. Then it was possible for a man to be born in Baghdad, work as a lawyer in Cairo, practise medicine in Tunis and die as a respected government official in Damascus. Such a career would hardly be open to anyone today but the principle of the universality of the Islamic experience remains.

I commend the view of the world which the careers of the leaders of Moslem societies in the past demonstrate. Young people in the UAE today have opportunities for a richness and variety which have seldom, if ever, been set before a country's new generations in other days. It must be acknowledged, however, that, no doubt in common with all modern societies, 60 per cent of our young people can probably be 'written off', the consequence of the all-too-easy acceptance of the pleasures which will be handed out to them. Probably 20 per cent are worthwhile, undertaking their studies seriously, becoming the academics, the professionals and the political and commercial leaders of the future. They will keep our traditions and preserve our religion. They represent the future leaders of the UAE itself.

Of all the honours which I have received during my life, few have given me as much pleasure as the decision of the University of Al-Ain, one of the foremost centres of learning in the UAE, to teach the story of my life to its students, as part of the programme which they undertake to learn English. I am delighted that I am able in this way to help young people become proficient in a language which has meant much in my life, and which, I believe, is vital to anyone who wants to make their way in the world. I like particularly the final paragraph of the notes accompanying the schedule of questions which the students have to answer:

As a small boy, Easa stood on the shore of the Creek in Dubai, trying to imagine the countries across the sea. Since then, he has travelled to many countries and met many important people. His work has helped to make the UAE a part of the modern world.

In the future, I suspect that 10 per cent of our youth will follow the traditional paths of our society, becoming pious, unostentatious Moslems, the bookkeepers, clerks and artisans which our society will always require. The remaining 10 per cent will be those whom I would call 'harsh' Moslems, those who will seek to turn our societies back to an imagined past, who have no concern for the world in which the majority will have to live today.

I realize that it is in the way of things for a member of a previous generation always to have reservations about the sense of responsibility and preparedness to work hard of the following generation. It is certainly no new concern in our part of the world. More than four thousand years ago, in Sumer, the first literate society anywhere in the world, which emerged in what is now Southern Iraq, a scribe set down his anxieties about his son's conduct and his apprehensions about the future. A long cuneiform text[3] laments his many faults, though in the end it appears that the son prospers greatly – to the annoyance of his relations.

This book of mine appears at the time when the so-called 'Peace Process', brokered between Israel, the Palestinians and some of the Arab states, is still being promoted by its Western supporters as a solution to the confrontation between the Arabs and Israel. Whatever may be the conclusion to the hopes which the process has engendered, there is no doubt that for Israel the situation will change drastically, whatever the outcome. If the process endures and is accepted, then Israel, sooner rather than later, will become absorbed into the Middle East, and its increasingly secular population (it should be remembered that Zionism is as secular a political concept as Marxist–Leninism) will be absorbed into the generality of Middle Eastern populations. If the 'threat' to Israel, real or pretended, represented by the Arab states is withdrawn, then foreign support for Israel, provided by countries whose own economic problems are multiplying, will diminish, eventually to the point of invisibility.

As I come to the closing paragraphs of this book, I would express the hope that those who may read it will not think that the facts which I have recorded and the opinions which I have voiced are intended in any way to denigrate or to antagonize any race, nation or religious sect or any section of the societies with which I have been in touch in the course of my life. What I have sought to do is to show how the world seems to me, after a lifetime of involvement in its affairs. In thinking about the future of the type of society to which we have, for better or worse, become accustomed over the past two centuries, and in assessing whether it is likely to endure in any form which would be recognizable today, I am forced to the belief that colonialism is still at large, though it may have changed its form. I am certain that domination by a single superpower is profoundly dangerous unless that superpower is deeply convinced of its responsibilities to the world which it seeks to dominate. I am equally sure that, in the case of the Middle East, Zionism and the state to which it gave birth are substantial, perhaps absolute, impediments to the achievement of a just society, whether in Palestine or in the United States. It is necessary sometimes, I believe, to face up unflinchingly to unpalatable truths.

Despite my earlier pessimistic remarks, let me end this record of my life by expressing what seems to me to be the reality of the human condition; if we can accept that such is our place in the world we may be able to live more contentedly and less disputatiously. Ever since I discovered the delights of acting, so long ago in Bahrain and so wholly in opposition to all the ways in which I had been brought up, I have been an actor, playing many parts. I decided that 'life is a passing show' when I was about twelve years old; I have never seen any reason to change my view since then. Our world is a stage and we must make the best of the parts which we have been allocated.

Like all actors, I have always tended to stand back a little, to observe as much as to participate. I have never been inclined to rush decisions (rather, perhaps, to learn my lines carefully) and, when the occasion required it, to conceal my own emotions, like all good and conscientious actors. I think of myself as a creative man and my best creative effort has gone into the making of my life, but I hope that I have never lost the faculty of laughing at myself.

In common with everyone, I have had many disappointments and many occasions on which I think that I have been wronged. But I cannot hate; I am not vindictive and I am content with my life. Even if I have achieved what those around me judge as success, I am still anxious to do more, for no other reason than that it is in my nature to do so. I have been fortunate and I have enjoyed, and have been grateful for, my good fortune. I have been able to live much of my life with style; I have lived well, travelled much and learnt much, and I have been able to do some good for my fellow men. I have always believed that when a man has little money he should stay quiet in one place but once God bestows good fortune upon him, he should live as well as he may.

My father, though he experienced misfortune in his lifetime, used to say that you and your family should always dress as well as you could and eat the best food that you could afford. This is a principle that I have sought to follow. There is an Arab saying, 'Eat whatever you like, for yourself and your family, but dress as others like.'

As I look back on the record of my life, seeking to discover whether there is any discernible pattern in its course, I recognize that there are as many unanswered questions as ever there were. Our parents, in the springtime of their youth, come together, love one another and from that love we are created. We become Moses, Jesus, Mohammed, Alexander, Genghis Khan, Salahuddin, Napoleon, Hitler, Nasser or Saddam. We become writers, artists or perhaps humble people living their lives for others in their church or mosque.

The Moslem is taught to accept whatever may come as the will of God. The Quran says that we have been created to worship God and give thanks to him:

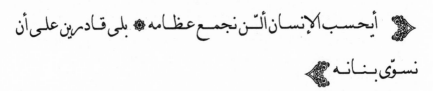

وما خلقنا الجنّ والإنس إلا ليعبدون

'And We (Allah) created not the Jinns and men except they should worship me (alone).'

أيحسب الإنسان ألّن نجمع عظامه ۞ بلى قادرين على أن

نسوّى بنانه

'Does man (a disbeliever) think that We (Allah) shall not assemble his bones?

222

Yes, We (Allah) are able to put together in perfect order the very extreme tips of his fingers.'

So you are created, handsome and strong when you are young; you grow old, die and are put into the ground. Where then is all the beauty, intelligence, affluence and achievement which has marked your life? What, for that matter, is the world around us – the air, water, fire, mountains, trees, flowers, fruits, the beautiful animals and birds with which we share the world, and the constant battle for all to survive – what is it all for?

Yet we surely must see that the entire universe is governed by a mathematical process which cannot simply be the consequence of chance. This fact alone leads me, as it has done so many others, to believe that there must be some directing intelligence, some order underlying the organization of the cosmos. I recall an occasion in St James's Palace when Prince Charles, speaking after a dinner there, said that if everything began with the 'Big Bang', it was certainly a very well controlled one. The Quran, as usual, has a comment to make which seems to me to be very pertinent:

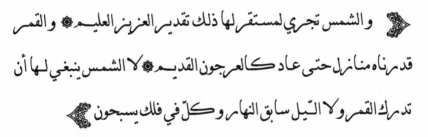

'And the Sun runs on its fixed course for a period determined to its resting place. That is the decree of the All Mighty, the All Knowing.'
'And the Moon, We (Allah) have measured for its mansions (to traverse) until it becomes like the old (withered) curved date stalk.'
'It is not permitted to the Sun to catch up the Moon, nor can the night outstrip the day. They all float (swim) along, each in its own orbit (according to law).'

*

Like every man who has ever lived, I am puzzled by the world I see around me and I wonder at it. Man has made astonishing progress in my lifetime, yet still there are great wrongs in the world, great suffering and sadness, despite the computers, the moon landings and the conquest of so many diseases which made the lives of men miserable in the past. As a Moslem, it is contrary to my faith to question these matters; as a man of the world, I admit that I am puzzled. The good Moslem thinks more of the next world, and of the rewards or punishments which we have been taught to anticipate. When I think of death I wonder, as Shakespeare did, will it be like a sleep, will we dream through our eternity?

My friend Sir James Craig told me of a conversation which he had had with a Christian friend from Egypt who told him that, as the result of intense study, he was convinced that the Quran was indeed the word of God and not man-made.[4] This, too, is my belief, for the more I read it the more convinced I become that it more perfectly describes the human condition and prescribes the best way in which our earthly life may be managed, than any other system of belief of which I know.

Yet as we find ourselves living in the world of today, it some-times seems that the noble concept of the resignation to the will of God is used to deflect decisions, to accept matters as they are and to resist the necessity for change. The time was when the Moslem nations, centuries after the lifetime of the Prophet, were the most advanced community in the world, foremost in science and learning yet wholly attuned to the message of the Quran. I find it difficult to accept, therefore, that it is Islam which is holding the Moslem world back from attaining a comparable place in the world today; the fault, I suspect, must lie with the Moslems themselves, some of whom make Islam the excuse for the failure to restore the Islamic world's historic status.

Islam does not require its followers to submit to the material and scientific superiority of others as a matter of doctrine; it is the Moslem's duty to make the most of the abilities and opportunities which God has given him. When I look back at the course of my life, having lived through a time of the most dramatic change for myself and my fellow countrymen, experienced on a scale which can rarely have been equalled in the past, I know something of what extraordinary feats of adjustment to circumstances humankind is capable. The record of my own country over the past quarter of a century and more is evidence of this. If this experience could only be repeated on the scale of the Middle East and the Moslem world as a whole, then the future would indeed be bright.

Soon after the completion of the text of this book, I flew with some of my colleagues, the Arab Ambassadors, to Dublin for the inauguration of the new President of the Republic of Ireland, Dr Mary McAleese. The ceremony took place in St Patrick's Hall in Dublin Castle and as I watched it I remembered well the occasion when I had presented my Letters of Credence to the President's predecessor, Mrs Mary Robinson.

Dr McAleese's election to the post of Head of State was historic, for she is the first President of the Republic to have been born in the North of Ireland. I listened carefully and with appreciation to her inaugural address. She spoke as one who is committed to the unity of Ireland, a Nationalist who believes also that the processes of democracy can bring about even so fundamental a change in the political structure of both North and South of that presently divided island.

As she spoke, I sat gazing at the deep blue carpet of the room in which the inauguration took place, just as long ago I used to sit considering what to say when Shaikh Rashid sought my advice or asked for my opinion on a proposed course of action. It seemed to me remarkable that here was I, an unashamed Arab Nationalist, attending the induction of the Head of State of a country which those who thought as I did, had always admired for having so early on freed itself from its colonial past. To us, the men who fought against the British in the early decades of this century to free Ireland were heroes, and I was proud now to find myself attending the happy outcome of their struggle.

As I thought about these things, I could not help but reflect that after all the efforts of so many noble-hearted men and women, during my lifetime and before it, the Arab world was still hopelessly divided, perhaps more so now than ever in the past. Arab Nationalism, which had itself inspired so many freedom movements in other parts of the world, especially in Gamal Abdul Nasser's day, had been defeated, not by force of arms or the ballot box but rather by the influence of material prosperity, by global markets and the acquisitiveness which now seems to be the guiding principle of our world.

But then, I reflected, perhaps there is another reason which, though it is difficult for me to accept it, may be why the Arabs are still disunited. Perhaps our dreams of an Arab nation, extending from Morocco to the Gulf, were illusions; perhaps the truth is that the peoples of what we call the Arab world are too diffuse, too different in their past histories and present objectives, ever to become one nation.

It may be that we have mistaken the elements which we have in common, particularly Islam and the Arabic language, as forces to bind us together. It has often been remarked that the fact that Britain and America share a common language has been the cause of more divisions and misunderstandings between them than any other single factor; we only have to think of the sort of tensions which erupt between brothers to recognize how even the closest family members can find themselves locked in the bitterest of disputes. Perhaps 1,400 years of a shared religion and a common tongue are not enough to eliminate self-interest and the demands of the smaller nationalisms which have dominated so much of mankind's history. In our own Middle Eastern world, perhaps we were too optimistic in believing that the millennia of strife between our peoples since the beginning of history could be swept aside by the acceptance of the Prophet's message.

Two developments in the recent history of the world also lead me to question whether it is possible to persuade men to live in accord with one another, guided by common beliefs, expressed in a common language. Marxism–Leninism, though it rapidly became a patently evil and tyrannous system which enslaved those people it claimed to liberate, began as an idealistic attempt to destroy the political and social systems which themselves deprived millions of the freedom to live their lives fully and happily. It collapsed in a moment of historic time and now its component parts are all asserting their individual Nationalisms, often in the most murderous fashion.

Then Europe, after fifty years of peace which were the product very largely of the fear which Russia represented in the minds of European politicians (in the early days of the 'Cold War', probably with every justification), is clearly having the greatest difficulty in overcoming the effects of centuries of the pursuit of self-interest by its constituent nations. Does Europe really exist, except as a geographical expression, as once was asked of Italy?

Towards the end of his life, Nasser evidently became discouraged, to the extent of questioning many of the ideals for which he had stood and fought in the days of his youth. Muammer Qadhafi, who admired him greatly, was shocked to find Nasser deeply despondent during one of their meetings. 'But Abu Khalid,' he said, 'you are the father of the Revolution, the first Arab Nationalist.'

'Yes,' said Nasser sadly, 'but I am also an old and tired Nationalist.'

Whilst I have not reached that stage of despondency, I think I understand what Abdul Nasser meant.

Afterword

THE WRITING OF *The Wells of Memory* was a collaborative effort in so far as Easa Saleh Al-Gurg (ESG), a man who by all standards is phenomenally busy, as a senior diplomat in London and as the head of a very substantial group of business enterprises in Dubai, discussed the form and contents of the book with me in detail and we worked out its final shape together. He had invited me, in the summer of 1995, to work with him on the book's preparation and I count myself distinctly fortunate that he did so. It is seldom that a writer, especially one whose concern has largely been with the ancient world and hence with the long-dead, is given the privilege of exposure to the workings of the mind of a living man like Easa Gurg and the pleasure of helping to bring those workings into the light of day. Then, with typical generosity, he asked me to write this note describing my part in the preparation of the book.

Despite the alarming schedule which appears to be ESG's normal working circumstance, the book was largely completed in little more than a year. That this was so is the consequence of his having a remarkably well-focused mind and a prodigious memory. This latter quality was especially important since he has never kept a diary or any continuing record of his lifetime's activities. This has had the effect, sometimes, of blurring the chronological sequence, but usually it has been possible to reconstruct dates and times, at least in broad terms, by reference to other events taking place at the same time. The book took shape during our many discussions, during which I saw my role as questioner, to draw out details which I felt might otherwise be obscure or which needed particular development.

My task was greatly eased by the fact that ESG's English is exceptionally fluent. He is one of those fortunate people with a facility for language; that he was able, as a small boy, to begin to teach himself English, in the deeply deprived circumstances of his childhood, is evidence enough. Despite this, he is diffident about his grasp of the language – a reserve which is entirely unwarranted.

The Wells of Memory is, I believe, important because it presents the inner dynamics of one part of the history of our times which has not been extensively recorded. ESG has lived through a time when the part of the world from which he comes, the Arabian Gulf, has gone through the most rapid and total transformation from the direst poverty (which he experienced bitterly) to the most abundant affluence experienced currently by any group of countries on earth. During his lifetime he has seen, and taken an active part in, the impact of Arab Nationalism on parts of the Arab world which were remote from that movement's centre but which represented the focus of the Western world's anxieties about the effects of the upsurge of Nationalist enthusiasms on their vital interests – on, indeed, the most vital of all, unimpeded access to cheap and abundant energy supplies.

It will be evident to anyone who reads *The Wells of Memory* that its author is a complex and multifaceted character. As he himself acknowledges in the Preface, this not infrequently results in apparent contradictions in his attitudes, especially in political matters, and in his response to events and to individuals. Nowhere is this more apparent than in his commitment to the ideals of Arab Nationalism, his rejection of the policies of the imperialist powers and his resentment at what he sees as the injustices which colonial regimes gave rise to, and, at the same time, his almost unbounded affection for the representatives of the most conspicuous of the colonial powers in the Gulf, the British. ESG has faced these apparent contradictions in the course of his narrative and by declaring them has gone some way to explaining why so many people of his generation have sustained what, in oversimplified terms, might be called a relationship with Britain of 'hating the sin but loving the sinner'. Having grown up myself in the time when the shadows were falling on the Empire and having spent all of my professional life working with countries which once were embraced within it, I can comprehend, I think, both the resentments of the once-governed and the bewilderment of the one-time governors, most of whom genuinely believed they were acting in the interests of those over whom they ruled as much as they were serving the interests of their own country. It is well for these conflicting views and emotions to be brought into the open where they can be acknowledged and, one hopes, set aside.

A corollary of the imperial heritage, at least as it has influenced ESG's life, is to be found in the record of the many years which he spent as one of the right-hand men of the Ruler of Dubai, Shaikh Rashid bin Saeed Al-Maktoum, when he participated in the early stages of the social and economic development of Dubai, culminating in his work for the Trucial States Development Office. The politics of this period, as revealed both by the papers in the Public Record Office in London and ESG's own recollections, present a picture of the events contingent on the British decision to withdraw from the Gulf and the anxieties which these engendered in the minds of the officials concerned. ESG was surely fortunate to be involved in this way in the development of his country, and it might be said that his country and the others in the Trucial States were fortunate in having his energy and commitment put to the task of bringing the common currency of civilized living to a part of the world which had been singularly deprived of even modest benefits of the modern world.

The progression from an involvement in the development of the states, particularly Dubai, as an unofficial and unpaid servant of the Government led, naturally enough, to a more direct and personal involvement in the development of Dubai's industrial and commercial infrastructure. This is not the least remarkable aspect of ESG's narrative, it seems to me, for he really did not set out exclusively on his business career until the early seventies, after the formation of the United Arab Emirates. Whilst he had begun trading on his own account before this, it was not until he could withdraw from the official development scene that he began seriously to pursue his own interests. The remarkable result of this has been the creation of one of the largest and most prosperous industrial and commercial groups in the UAE (which means also in the Gulf as a whole) in little more than twenty years and in the second half of ESG's own life.

Throughout these years ESG was employed, in increasingly senior positions, by one of the bulwarks of British commercial influence in the region, the British Bank of the Middle East. The vantage point which his connection with the bank gave him is one of the recurring themes of the book; it is also the occasion for one of the few episodes of disappointment which ESG experienced in his British associations, the ending of thirty-eight years with the bank in unfortunate circumstances, the memory of which obviously still pains him. But *The Wells of Memory* is remarkably free of one of the most typical indulgences of many memoirs, the settlement of old scores. Such wrongs as may have been done him do not seem worth recalling, his inclination seems always to have been to move on to the next positive opportunity which presented itself.

The group of enterprises which ESG has created and still directs is very large and diverse. Its extent and the variety of its interests have been outlined here, but it was decided not to devote as much to an analysis of their nature and activities as has been given to the book's political and social contents. The reason for this is that inevitably businesses change rapidly, from one year to the next. Had a detailed study of them been attempted here, it would have been out of date by the time the book was published. The Easa Saleh Al-Gurg Group is, however, a very remarkable phenomenon and one of which ESG is rightly proud. It does, other considerations apart, represent a direct line of descent from his merchant ancestors.

Easa Gurg comes from those remarkable people, the Arabs of Persian origin who, at some time in the relatively distant past, migrated from Arabia to the milder climes of the south-western Persian coast. There they flourished, especially as traders and pearl merchants. Communities of Persian Arabs are to be found in virtually every Gulf port where, over the past century, they have provided much of the commercial initiative which, when prosperity came to the peninsula in the second half of this century, so rapidly developed the towns along the coast to the extent that they enjoy today. The Arabs from southern Persia are known collectively as *holis*, 'migrants'; ESG is one of the first prominent members of this community to tell his story, and it may suggest that the part which the *holis* have played in the history of the Gulf deserves its own historian.

ESG is evidently much affected by his forebears; one of the driving forces of his life has been to restore his family's fortunes which, in his own lifetime, were shattered by the collapse of the pearl trade, after the introduction of the cultured pearl in the late twenties. His father, who plays an important part in the early pages of ESG's narrative, is often a tragic figure but one who is touched with nobility; he stands for a generation and an attitude to life fast fading from the Arabian peninsula. Although he does not talk of it here, ESG has endowed many charitable foundations in the Moslem world; one which must have given him especial satisfaction was the rebuilding of a mosque in his family's original home, Lingah, built by his father's father at the end of the last century.

The Arabian Gulf is, in so many ways, a very particular part of the world. It represents one of the oldest centres of civilization, contemporary with the great seminal cultures of Egypt and Mesopotamia. For two thousand years it was virtually forgotten by the world, only the occasional courageous or foolhardy traveller venturing among its fierce and disputatious inhabitants. Then came oil and the untold, unimagined prosperity of the twentieth century. The West has been, at best, deeply ambivalent in its attitudes to and its treatment of the states which have emerged to nationhood, with the paradox of small populations and great wealth. Perhaps inevitably, resentments and tensions have developed between the people of the region and the interests which are so dependent upon their sole resource; the very rich are seldom loved for themselves, still less if there are so many who depend upon their goodwill. It is often easier and more likely to secure applause from the envious, if the least attractive characteristics of societies such as those which have emerged in Arabia, are highlighted.

One of the themes of this book is that change must inevitably come within the societies of the peninsular states themselves. ESG argues that such changes should be allowed to occur naturally and by consent; it is in the interests of Rulers and citizens alike that it should be so. For this to come about peaceably, it will be essential for men of wisdom and goodwill to express themselves as thoughtfully as Easa Gurg has done.

The international media so often swings between flattery and abuse in its treatment of the peninsular states. Seldom is there an attempt to present a balanced exposition of the region and the circumstances which have brought it to its present ambivalent celebrity. *The Wells of Memory* belongs to a very select literary category, for there have as yet been very few books written by Gulf nationals from, as it were, the inside. It is surely fitting that one of the few should have been written by a man who, fortuitously, has in turn (and sometimes simultaneously) been banker, confidant of Rulers, politician, diplomat and businessman. His career has been crowned by his appointment as Ambassador for the country of which he is one of the architects. That he should be able to use his book, not only to document his life but also to explain, for those who wish to listen, how the Arabian peninsular states and in particular the group of independent shaikhdoms embraced by the United Arab Emirates, came to occupy their particular place in the world, with any luck will serve to encourage others to do the same.

Michael Rice
Cambridgeshire, 1998

Bibliographical Sources

As *The Wells of Memory* is essentially a personal memoir and not primarily a piece of historical research, I have relied mainly on my own recollections and my archives and memorabilia. However, when I have had occasion to refer to historical events, either before or during my own lifetime, I have made use of various sources available to me. In particular, I have made use of the admirable study of the origins of the United Arab Emirates by Dr Frauke Heard-Bey and the slightly earlier history of the Trucial States by Sir Donald Hawley. I have also had access to the relevant papers of the Foreign and Commonwealth Office relating to Dubai, the Trucial States and the UAE on its formation.

For anyone who may be interested I have listed the sources which I have consulted. Where I have made a direct quotation in the text it has been indicated by a reference number, the relevant details of which are set out below.

Amongst the works which have been consulted particularly are:

Belgrave, Sir Charles, *Personal Column*, Hutchinson, London, 1960
Hawley, Sir Donald, *The Trucial States*, George Allen and Unwin, London, 1970
Heard-Bey, Dr Frauke, *From Trucial States to United Arab Emirates*, Longman, London and New York, 1982 (Second enlarged edition 1996)

Jones, Geoffrey, *Banking and Oil: The History of the British Bank of the Middle East*, Cambridge University Press, 2 vols, 1987

Al-Qasimi, HH Dr Shaikh Sultan bin Mohammed, *The Myth of Gulf Piracy*, Croom Helm, London, 1986

Rice, Michael, *The Archaeology of the Arabian Gulf*, Routledge, London, 1994

Tuson, Penelope, *The Record of the British Residency and Agencies in the Persian Gulf*, India Office Records and Library, London, 1979

Chapter 1

1 Al-Muqaddasi, Shams al-Din Abu Abdullah Mohammad ibn Ahmed, *Ahsan al-Taqasim fi ma'rifat al-aqalim*, Descriptio Imperii Moslemici, Leiden, 1906
2 Tuson, pp. 10–15
3 Kelly, J. B., *Britain and the Persian Gulf 1705–1880*, Oxford, 1968, p. 378
4 Heard-Bey, pp. 364–6, 391–2; Ajami, Bassam T., 'Three Islands in a Sea of International Politics', *Gulf Daily News*, 30 May 1995
5 Heard-Bey, p. 244; Hawley, pp. 161–2, 199–200
6 Heard-Bey
7 Rice, p. 217
8 Heard-Bey, pp. 219–20
9 Hawley, passim; Heard-Bey, p. 271 ff.
10 Hawley, pp. 104, 113–4
11 Al-Qasimi
12 Heard-Bey, pp. 251–2, 255–7, 267
13 Hawley, p. 173
14 FO 371/15707–31723

Chapter 2

1 Belgrave
2 Wheatcroft, Andrew, *The Life and Times of Shaikh Sulman bin Hamed Al-Khalifa, Ruler of Bahrain*, Kegan Paul International, London, 1994, p. 199

3 Heard-Bey, p. 250
4 FO 371/15071–31723

Chapter 3

1 Jones
2 Heard-Bey
3 Jones, pp. 47, 125, 150–1
4 For Shaikh Rashid's early life see Abbas Abdullah Makki's *Rashid, The Man Behind Dubai*, Dubai, 1990 (Arabic and English)
5 Heard-Bey, p. 258
6 FO 371/168939–36, p. 381
7 FO 957/231: 31657
8 FO 371/15707: 317232

Chapter 4

1 FO 371/140293: FO to Political Residency, Bahrain
2 FO 1016/680

Chapter 6

1 Hawley, pp. 178–84; Heard-Bey, p. 342
2 Hawley, pp. 174–5, 190–1
3 Heard-Bey, pp. 319–34
4 FO 371/179916 31761: BT 1103/21
5 Ibid.
6 Bahrain to FO 371/179916: BT 1103/83
7 FO 371/179916 31761: BT 1103/84
8 FO 371/179916 31761: Bahrain telegram 354 to FO
9 FO 371/179917 31761: BT 1103/92
10 FO to Jeddah telegram 522, 24 May 1965
11 FO to Dubai telegram 226, 8 June 1965
12 FO 371/179918 31761: 1103/147
13 Jeddah to FO telegram 284 BT 1103/173
14 FO 371/179918 31761: BT 1103/177
15 FO 371/179918 31761
16 FO telegram to Dubai 226

17 FO371/179918 31761: BT 1103/178
18 FO 371/179916 31761
19 FO 371/179918 31761 telegram to Bahrain, 15 June 1965
20 FO 371/179916 31761 G. Thompson
21 Bahrain to FO telegram 555
22 FO 371/179916 31761: BT 1103/21
23 FO 371/179916 31761
24 FO 371/179916
25 FO 371/179916 31761: BT 1103/18
26 FO to Bahrain 212, 24 February 1965

Chapter 7

1 E.g. FO 371/157091, Foreign Office to the Political Residency quoting 'Shaikh Rashid speaking enthusiastically of federation' at the time of his visit to London in 1961
2 FO 371/185525–16
3 See the annex to FO 371/17450 1113/4 for a translation prepared by the Political Agency in Abu Dhabi
4 FO 371/17450 1113/64
5 FO 371/185529–97
6 FO 371/185525–22
7 FO 371/185529–44
8 FO 371/185525–53
9 FO 371/185525–30
10 FO 371/185525–53
11 FO 371/185525–40
12 See Naquib Abdullah Al-Shamsi's *An-Naqood* ('Currency'), Dubai, 1994 (in Arabic)
13 FO 1016/680
14 Ibid.
15 FO 371/185525 16915/66G
16 FO 371/185525–120

Chapter 8

1 Rice, pp. 264–99
2 FO 371/163038

Chapter 11

1 Heard-Bey, p. 245
2 Heard-Bey, chapter 2, pp. 27–77
3 See S. N. Kramer's *The Sumerians*, Chicago, 1963, pp. 244–6
4 *Asian Affairs*, Vol. XXVIII, part 1, February 1997, p. 42

Index

Abadha, Fikri, 51
Abbas, Abdul Kader, 17
Abdul Mutaleb, 213
Abdullah, Emir of Granada, 19
Abela, Albert, 174, 175
Abiadh, Georges, 173–4
Abu Dhabi, 65–7, 88, 104; Khor
    Ghanadha dispute, 17; BBME and,
    73–5; development of, 110–11; oil
    industry, 113, 168, 169–170; Trucial
    States Development Office projects,
    128, 129–130; common currency
    proposals, 134–5; Ruler deposed,
    136
Abu Dhabi airport, 118
Abu Moussa, 5, 6, 103, 170
Abu-Muraikha, 65
Admiralty (Britain), 68
Afghanistan, 176, 217
Africa, 206
African and Eastern, 178
Ahmed, Yassin Mullah, 53
air transport, 93, 102–7
Ajman, 175
Al Ahmediyya, 18–19
Al Ain Expressway, 185
Al Ain International Airport, 185
Al Falah, 18
Al-Khobar, 44

Al Mashrabia Furniture, 186
Al-Muqaddasi, 2
Al Samsam Building Materials, 186
Albdoor, Ahmed bin Matter, 30–1,
    44
alcohol, 178–9
Alexandria, 90, 92, 101
Allen, Neville, 76
Alowlaiwat, Abdul Ali, 50
Andalusia, 19
Arab League, 115–19, 121, 124
Arab Nationalism: ESG's belief in,
    xvii–xviii, 45–51, 92–4, 178, 229; in
    Egypt, xviii, 46, 84, 87, 92–5, 119,
    161; Suez crisis, 72, 86; spread of,
    84, 87; 1948 war, 84; goals, 139; and
    Iranian revolution, 192; defeat of,
    226–7
Arabian Gulf, 2, 5, 6, 9; pearl fisheries,
    10–11; in the 1930s, 13–14; British
    presence, 14–17, 18, 19, 86–7, 88,
    112–22, 129–30; Iraq seeks access to,
    97; British withdrawal from, 124,
    138–9, 140–1; Britain proposes
    federation, 132–6; banking history,
    149–50; Western influence over,
    161–3; oil industry, 167–8
Arabian Liquid Chemicals, 186
Arabian peninsula, 88, 97

Index

Arabian Sea, 11
Ark Royal, 85
Arthur, Sir Geoffrey, 141
Assyrians, 217
Aswan, 96
Aswan High Dam, 152–3
Atatürk, Kemal, 2
Awamir tribe, 113–14
Ayyub, Khansahib Dr Mohammed,
  19–21, 28, 30, 31–3

Ba'ath party, 146
Baghdad, 48, 49, 125, 218
Baghdad Pact, 146
Bahrain, xvii, 14, 184; ESG works in,
  36–7, 38–44; oil industry, 40, 42,
  167; Arab Nationalism, 49–51; and
  proposed Gulf federation, 133;
  currency, 134–5; independence, 141,
  143–4; prehistoric trade, 150
Bahrain Club, Muharraq, 50–2, 54
Bahrain Currency Board, 135
Bahrain Dry Dock, 110
Bahri, Yunis, 85
Bakhtiar, General, 138
Al-Bakir, Abdul Rahman, 50
Balfour Declaration (1917), 48, 204
Bandar Abbas, 43
Bani Yas tribe, 9
Bank of Credit and Commerce
  International (BCCI), 158
Bank of England, 134
Barala, 37
Barber, Rt. Hon. Anthony (Lord),
  190
Barrett, Roger, 175, 176
Bastakiyah, 7
Bedu, 26, 66, 113–14
Belgium, 6, 7
Belgrave, Sir Charles, 40–1
BOAC, 39, 93
Bolt, Robert, 71
Bombay, 8, 41, 93
Bosworth, Freddie, 103, 104–6
BP, 29, 169
Britain: Native Agencies, 3; and the
  Gulf states, 14–17, 18, 19, 86–7, 88,

112–22, 129–30; and Bahrain, 39,
  40–1, 42; Second World War, 39,
  42–3; and Arab Nationalism, 46, 48,
  87, 93–4; and Palestine, 48–9, 204;
  ESG awarded British Council
  bursary, 62, 67–72; Suez crisis, 72,
  86, 90, 95; negotiations with Shaikh
  Rashid, 77; and Dubai's
  development, 80–1; Shaikh Rashid
  visits, 88–90; and Iraq, 97–8; and
  Dubai's airstrip, 102–7; Trucial
  Oman Levies, 113–14; and Trucial
  States Development Fund, 117–18;
  withdrawal from Gulf, 124, 138–9,
  140–1; federal proposals for Gulf
  states, 132–6; deposes Ruler of Abu
  Dhabi, 136; formation of UAE,
  140–2, 143–4; Baghdad Pact, 146;
  Middle Eastern policy, 161–2; and
  Gulf oil industry, 168–70; and the
  Common Market, 182; ESG as UAE
  Ambassador to, 186, 194, 196–203,
  204–7; and Iranian revolution,
  190–1, 192; ESG's property in, 207–8
British Airways, 93
British American Tobacco (BAT), 54,
  174–5, 176, 183
British Army, 91
British Bank of Iran and the Middle
  East *see* British Bank of the Middle
  East
British Bank of the Middle East
  (BBME), 94, 159, 231; ESG's career
  with, 52–4, 55–62, 64, 72–3, 107–8,
  149; Dubai branch, 55–62, 64, 72–3,
  75–6, 80; Abu Dhabi branch, 65–6,
  67; loans to Abu Dhabi, 73–5,
  110–11; and ESG's directorship of
  Trucial States Development Office,
  125; common currency proposals,
  134; Egyptian investment, 151–3;
  ESG leaves, 154–7; and oil industry,
  167–8; and ESG's business interests,
  177–8
British Council, 62, 67–72
British India Steam Navigation
  Company, 37

British Political Agency, 18, 53, 62, 66, 77–9, 86–7, 93, 102, 104–7, 108, 113, 116, 136–7, 142, 178, 194
Brown, John, 181
Buraimi, 110, 115
Burma Castrol, 186
Burton, Graham, 195–6
Burton, Mr, 53
Al-Busaid, Sayyed Qabus bin Said, Sultan of Oman, 143
Al-Busaid, Sayyed Said bin Taimur, Sultan of Oman, 121, 135, 142–3
Al-Busaid, Sayyed Tariq bin Taimur, 121
Bush, George, 95
Bushire, 3, 14
Buttes Gas and Oil, 171
Byzantine Empire, 45

Cairo, 49, 84, 90, 91, 93, 94, 96, 115, 151, 152, 219
Caribbean, 132
Carter, Lindsay, 174–5, 176
Central Bank of Egypt, 152
Charles, HRH Prince of Wales, 201, 223
Christianity, xix, 23–4, 92
cigarettes, 174–5, 176
Clark, Sir Terence, 89, 176
Cold War, 85, 227
Colwell, John, 80
Common Market, 182
Communism, 85, 102, 161, 226
Conservative Party (Britain), 140
consumer society, 163, 164
Continental Oil, 169, 171
Copts, 92
Council of Arab Ambassadors in London, 204
Craig, Sir James, 124, 127, 129, 152, 175, 193, 224
Creek, Dubai, 8, 14, 17, 30, 54, 56, 60, 75–6, 103, 129
Crusades, 46
currency, 134–5, 137

Damascus, 49, 84, 219
de Gaulle, Charles, 182

Deira, 16–17, 18, 103, 104–5, 185
democracy, 214–15
Denman, Rt. Hon. Lord, 152
Department of Trade and Industry (Britain), 197
Dera'a, 100
Dhofaris, 114
Digdaga, 127
Dilmun culture, 44
Dishgaan, 3, 8
Dixon, Christopher, 156
Doha, 14
Douglas-Home, Rt. Hon. Sir Alec, 140
Dubai: economic success, 1, 7, 159–60; wind-towers, 7; Al-Gurg family in, 8–10; pearl fisheries, 10–11; Britain bombards, 14–15; British presence in, 14–15; independence, 15; control of Deira, 16–17; in Second World War, 30, 42, 43; British Bank of Middle East in, 54, 55–62, 64, 72–3, 75–6, 80; Creek dredged, 75–6, 129; development under Shaikh Rashid, 75–7, 80–2, 108–10, 145–6; oil industry, 76–7, 167–9, 171–2; British Political Agency, 77–9; land reforms, 79–80; gold trade, 103–4; Trucial States Development Office projects, 127–8, 129–30; currency, 134, 135; and British withdrawal from Gulf, 138; and Iran–Iraq war, 143; banks collapse, 157–9; future prospects, 166; ESG's business interests, 172–88
Dubai airport, 102–7, 118, 128
Dubai Bank, 158
Dubai Dry Dock, 110
Dubai Electricity Company, 76, 181, 185
Dubai Investment Company, 159
Dubai Municipality, 80, 93–4, 179, 185, 195
Dubai Museum, 81
Dubai Petroleum Company, 179
Dubai Police Airwing, 185
Dubai Port Authority, 185
Dubai Port Committee, 80, 81

Dubai Post Office, 31–5, 36
Dubai Real Estate Company, 159
Dubai Trade Centre, 109–10
Dubal (Dubai Aluminium), 187
Dublin, 225
Duff, Bill, 168
Dulles, Foster, 86
Dunlop, 186

Easa Saleh Al-Gurg Group, 183–8, 231
Easa Saleh Al-Gurg Scholarship, 201
East Africa, 132
East Anglia, 207–8
Eastern Bank, 59
'economic colonialism', 191–2
Eden, Rt. Hon. Anthony (*later* Earl of
    Avon), 72, 115
Edinburgh, HRH Duke of, 200
Egypt, 24, 146, 232; Arab Nationalism,
    46, 84, 87, 92–5, 119, 161; Suez
    crisis, 72, 86, 90, 95–6; 1952
    Revolution, 85–6, 119; Shaikh
    Rashid visits, 90–2, 101; importance
    to Arabs, 96; war of 1967, 132;
    BBME investment in, 151–3; under
    Sadat, 161
Egypt Air, 93
Egyptian-British Bank, 151–3
Egyptian Educational Mission, 96
Eisenhower, Dwight D., 86, 95–6
Elizabeth II, Queen of England, 88,
    176, 195, 198–200
Emad, Khansahib Hussain bin Hassan,
    22
Emirates Bank International, 157,
    159–61
Ethiopia, 213
Euphrates, River, 96
Europe, 227
European Community, 203
Exclusive Agreement (1893), 14

Faisal I, King of Iraq, 47–8
Faisal bin Abdul Aziz, King of Saudi
    Arabia, 116–17
Fars, 2
First World War, 47, 48, 97, 191

Foreign Office (Britain), 55, 74, 90,
    92, 116, 118, 119, 121, 136–7, 197,
    202
Foseco Minsep, 186
Fox and Gibbons, 156
France, 7, 86, 160
Frinton, 208
Fujairah, 126, 160–1, 175

Garhoud, 185
General Treaty of Peace (1820), 3, 15
Geneva, 101
Germany, 47, 84–5, 172, 182
Ghose Al Gahha, 32
Al-Ghurair, Ahmed bin Majid, 80
GKN Nettlefords, 186
gold trade, 103–4
Gore-Booth, Sir David, 201
Granada, 19
Grundig, 172–3, 176, 177, 181, 195
Guardian, 204
Gulf *see* Arabian Gulf
Gulf Air, 103
Gulf Bank, 158
Gulf Co-operation Council (GCC),
    18, 147, 161, 192–3
Gulf Engineering, 186
Gulf Metal Foundry, 186
Al-Gurg, Easa Saleh: Arab Nationalism,
    xvii–xviii, 45–51, 92–4, 178, 229;
    family background, 2–11, 216;
    childhood, 11–13, 16–17, 24–30;
    education, 18–22, 28, 30, 31–2, 51,
    100; honours, 29–30, 195–6, 198,
    219; in Second World War, 30–1,
    39, 84–5; works for Post Office,
    31–5, 36, 39–40, 43, 52; in Bahrain,
    38–44, 50–2; theatrical interests,
    51–2; works for British Bank of the
    Middle East, 52–4, 55–62, 64, 72–3,
    107–8, 149; British Council bursary,
    62, 67–72; marriages, 62–4;
    children, 63, 180, 208; works with
    Shaikh Rashid, 64, 76, 79, 108–9,
    177–8, 194; and British Political
    Agency in Dubai, 78–9; and Trucial
    States Development Office, 79,

Al-Gurg, Easa Saleh (*cont.*)
122–31, 139; overseas visits with
Shaikh Rashid, 88–90, 99–102;
business interests, 139, 148–9, 157,
172–88, 196–7, 230–1; relations
with Shaikh Rashid, 148; leaves
BBME, 154–7; and Egyptian-British
Bank, 151–3; and Emirates Bank
International, 159–61; nicotine
allergy, 175–6; as UAE Ambassador,
186, 194, 196–207, 225; East
Anglian farm, 208; homes, 208–9;
importance of Islam to, 210–13
Al-Gurg, Saleh Easa (ESG's father), xx,
12, 13, 20, 21, 22–5, 26–9, 32, 33–4,
36–7, 41–2, 44, 54, 62–3, 199, 208,
222, 232
Al-Gurg, Soraya Ali Kazim (ESG's wife),
64, 196, 208–9

Hafez, Abdul Halim, 92
Hafra, 126
Halcrow, Sir William and Partners, 76
Hammer, Dr Armand, 171
Al-Hashimi, Sayed Hashim, 21
Hassouna, Abdul Khalek, 115
Hawley, Sir Donald, 79, 80, 81, 123–4,
127, 129
Heathrow airport, 68
Hendrie, Robert, 195
Henry VIII, King of England, 23–4
Al-Hijr, Surah, 212–13
Al-Hilal, 51
Hill, John, 152
Hisham Abdul Malek, Caliph, 100
Hodge, Sydney, 104
Holland and Holland, 73
Hongkong & Shanghai Banking
Corporation, 151–2, 154, 156, 157
Hormuz, Straits of, 5–6, 170
hotels, 185
House, Captain, 29
House of Commons (Britain), 140,
199
House of Lords (Britain), 198
Hurd, Rt. Hon. Douglas, 202–3
Hussein, Saddam, 143

Ibn Khaldun, xiv
ID Design, 186
Imperial Airways, 30, 39
Imperial Bank of Iran *see* British Bank
of the Middle East
India, 13, 14, 18, 19, 130; Gulf
community, 8; and Dubai Post
Office, 31, 34–5; gold imports, 103;
currency, 134, 135
India Office (Britain), 3
Indian Ocean, 5, 11, 150
Indus Valley, 150
Institute of Dancing, London, 71
International Airadio, 103, 104, 128
International Court of Justice, 168
Intra Bank, 158
Iran (Persia), 24; al-Gurg family in,
2–8; and Straits of Hormuz, 5–6;
Imperial Bank of Iran, 52; aims to
become dominant power, 88; and
British withdrawal from Gulf, 138;
Iran–Iraq war, 143, 192; relations
with Shaikh Rashid, 143; oil
industry, 170–1, 189; revolution,
189, 190–1, 192
Iraq, 24, 92; Arab Nationalism, 46,
47–8, 84; Gulf Arab attitudes to,
96–7, 98; creation of, 97; seeks Gulf
access, 97; Iran–Iraq war, 143, 192;
Baghdad Pact, 146; revolution, 146;
prehistoric trade, 150; invasion of
Kuwait, 159–60, 191, 193; tribalism,
217
Ireland: ESG as UAE Ambassador to,
203, 225
Irish-Arab Chamber of Commerce,
203
Iron Curtain, 85
Ishaq, Shaikh, 41, 42
Islam, xix, 2; slavery, 15–16; education,
18; Arab Nationalism, 45–7, 92;
Prince Charles's interest in, 201;
importance to ESG, 210–13; future
of, 224
Israel: creation of, 49, 191; 1948 war,
xix, 84; Suez crisis, 86; Western
support, 95; war of 1967, 132, 148;

Israel (*cont.*)
   extremists, 153; 'Peace Process',
   220–1; Zionism, 221; *see also*
   Palestine

Jalil, Shaikh Abdul, 42
Jamali, Dr Asem, 129
Japan, 10, 39
Al-Jawan, Saif, 125
Jebel Ali, 32, 80
Jebel Ali Free Zone, 110
Jebel Ali power station, 185
Jerash, 100
Jericho, 100
Jerusalem, xix, 99, 100, 161
Jews: in Spain, 46; Zionism, 48–9;
   creation of Israel, 49; 1948 war,
   xix, 84
Jordan, 92, 114; Shaikh Rashid visits,
   99, 100
Jordan River, 100

Ka'aba, 213
Al-Kadhmawi, Jasim, 17, 53
Kanoo, Mohammed, 68
Kanoo family, 53
Karem, Darwish bin, 73–4
Keast, George, 53, 55, 57
Kelly, J. Colville ('Col'), 80, 151, 152,
   181
Kendall, Brian, 121, 122, 129
Kennedy and Donkin, 181
Kenny, Finbar, 175
Kent cigarettes, 174, 175
Khalid, Husni Abu, 121
Al-Khalifa, Shaikh Hamed bin Isa,
   Ruler of Bahrain, 40
Al-Khalifa, Shaikh Sulman bin Hamed,
   Ruler of Bahrain, 40, 41
Khirbat al-Mafjar, 100–1
Khomeini, Ayatollah, 190
Khor Ghanadha, 17
Kirkbride, Sir Alec, 74
Knights Templar, 150
Kurds, 217
Kuwait, 55, 63, 97, 142; pearl fisheries,
   11; aid to Dubai, 75–6; oil industry,

112, 167, 192; and the Trucial
States Development Office projects,
129; constitution, 140–1; Iraqi
invasion, 159–60, 191, 193;
democracy, 215

Labour Party (Britain), 140
Lake District, 68
land ownership, 179–80, 195
Al-Lataa'if al-Musawwara, 51
Lawrence, T. E., 47, 94
League of the States of the Arabian
   Gulf (proposed), 120
Lebanon, 84, 92, 99, 102
Leigh Paints, 187
Life is a Passing Show, 21
Lingah, 2–3, 4–8, 15, 61, 170, 232
Liwa, 185
locusts, 35–6
London, 67–8, 69, 71, 88–90, 102,
   152, 177, 186, 194, 195, 196–203,
   207–8
Lorimer, *Persian Gulf Pilot*, 10
Lorimer, Major P. G., 88
Luce, Sir William, 106

Mac Al-Gurg, 185–6
McAleese, Dr Mary, 225
Macaskell, Alastair, 80
Macmillan, Harold, 72, 89
majlis as-Shura, 124
Makka, 213
Al-Maktoum, Shaikh Hamdan bin
   Rashid, 88
Al-Maktoum, Shaikh Maktoum bin
   Rashid, 88, 159, 195, 196
Al-Maktoum, Shaikh Rashid bin
   Saeed, Ruler of Dubai, xiii, 9, 73;
   and Deira separatists, 17; Khor
   Ghanadha dispute, 17; in Second
   World War, 43; and ESG's marriage,
   63; ESG works with, 64, 76, 79,
   108–9, 177–8, 194; development of
   Dubai, 75–7, 80, 82, 108–10;
   character, 76–7, 101–2; overseas
   visits, 87–92, 99–102; and Dubai's
   airstrip, 102–7; political skills, 107,

Al-Maktoum, Shaikh Rashid bin
  Saeed, Ruler of Dubai (*cont.*)
  142–3; and the Awamir tribe,
  113–14; and the Arab League, 116;
  and Trucial States Development
  Office, 121, 128, 130; British
  support for, 130; and proposed Gulf
  federation, 133; common currency
  proposals, 134–5, 137; relations with
  Shaikh Zayed, 136–7; Shaikh
  Shakhbut deposed, 136; and British
  withdrawal from Gulf, 138;
  formation of UAE, 142, 144;
  relations with ESG, 148; invests in
  Middle East Finance Company, 154;
  ill-health, 155–6, 194; economic
  policy, 160; and oil industry, 168–9
Al-Maktoum, Shaikh Saeed bin
  Maktoum, Ruler of Dubai, 7, 17,
  28–9, 55, 76, 85, 113
Maktoum Hospital, 75
Malaya, 132
Manama, 39, 41
Marfa Pipeline, 186
Marxism-Leninism, 227
Medina, 25
Al-Meredi, Mahmoud, 50, 53
Mesopotamia, 97, 150, 232
Middle East Bank, 158
Middle East Finance Company, 154
Ministry of Information (UAE), 197
Ministry of Overseas Development
  (Britain), 122
Mogadishu, 176
Mohammed, Prophet, 87, 100
moon landings, 102
More, Sir Thomas, 140
Morgan Guaranty, 104
Moslem Brotherhood, 92
Mossadegh, Dr, 189
Mubarak, President Husni, 153
Muharraq, 50
Muqta bridge, 73
Al-Musawwar, 51, 208
Muscat, 4, 39
Mustafa bin Abdul Latif, Shaikh, 41–2,
  185, 199

Mustafa family, 184
Al-Mzrouie, Abdullah bin Humaid,
  125, 129

Al-Nahayan, Shaikh Hamdan bin
  Mohammed, 66
Al-Nahayan, Shaikh Shakhbut bin
  Sultan, Ruler of Abu Dhabi, 65–6,
  67, 73–5, 88, 90, 134–6, 169–70
Al-Nahayan, Shaikh Sultan bin
  Shakhbut, 66–7
Al-Nahayan, Shaikh Zayed bin Sultan,
  Ruler of Abu Dhabi, 18, 65, 75,
  110–11, 114, 128, 133, 136–7, 144,
  201
Nasser, Abdul Hakim, 91
Nasser, Gamal Abdul, xiv, 78, 178;
  Arab Nationalism, xviii, 87, 92–5,
  227; Suez crisis, 72, 86, 95–6; 1952
  revolution, 85–6, 119; Shaikh
  Rashid visits, 90–2; 1967 war, 94–5,
  132; opposes Baghdad Pact, 146;
  criticism of, 152–3; death, 93–5, 161
Nasser Al-Din, Shah of Persia, 5, 170
Nasserism, 129, 136
National Bank of Dubai, 76, 158, 159
National Bank of Fujairah, 160–1
'Native Agencies', 3
Nazis, xix, 49
Nile, River, 96
Nofal, Sayed, 115–16, 118
North Africa, 24

oil, 112, 113, 135, 149; taxation, 162,
  164; in Dubai, 167–9, 171–2; Iran,
  190–1; 'economic colonialism', 192
Old Testament, xix
Oman, 4, 117, 135, 143, 150
Orwell, George, 214
Ottoman Empire, 5, 46, 97, 153, 191
Oxford Centre for Islamic Studies,
  201

Pahlavi, Mohammed Reza, Shah of
  Iran, 2, 6, 88, 143, 171, 189–90, 191
Pahlavi, Reza, Shah of Iran, 2, 189
Pahlavi dynasty, 29

Palestine: Arab Nationalism, 46; creation of Israel, xix, 49; Zionism, 48–9; *see also* Israel
Palestinians, 204, 211, 220
Pearl Harbor, 39
pearl trade, 10–11, 32, 199–200, 232
Perpetual Maritime Truce (1853), 3
Persia *see* Iran
Persian Arabs, 2–8, 231–2
Persian Gulf *see* Arabian Gulf
Phillips, Wendell, 171
Portuguese Fort, Bahrain, 44
Post Office (Bahrain), 39–40, 43, 52, 53
Post Office (Dubai), 31–5, 36, 56
postage stamps, 175–6
Privy Council (Britain), 50
Profumo, John, 89
Protestants, 23–4

Qadhafi, Muammer, 227
Qajar dynasty, 52
Qala'at al-Bahrain, 44
Al-Qasimi, Shaikh Mohammed bin Khalifa, Ruler of Lingah, 5–6
Al-Qasimi, Shaikh Saqr bin Mohammed, Ruler of Ras al-Khaimah, 125
Al-Qasimi, Shaikh Saqr bin Sultan, 107, 118, 119–20
Al-Qasimi, Dr Shaikh Sultan bin Mohammed, Ruler of Sharjah, 15
Al-Qasimi family, 5–6, 9
Qassem, Abdul Karim, 146
Qatar, 99, 101; Doha incident, 14; and proposed Gulf federation, 133; currency, 134, 135; independence, 141, 143–4
Qishim island, 9
Quran, 13, 15–16, 20, 22, 23, 24–6, 27, 62–3, 212, 215, 223, 224

Ras al-Khaimah, 5, 102, 104, 126; Tunbs dispute, 6; pearl trade, 11, 26–7; and the Arab League, 118; and proposed Gulf federation, 133; Nasserism, 136; oil industry, 171

Ras al-Khaimah Earth Satellite Station, 185
Ras al-Khaimah International Airport, 185
Rashid, Shaikh *see* Al-Maktoum, Shaikh Rashid bin Saeed
Rashidiyya, 104–5
Razuqi, Khan Bahadur Abdul Razzaq, 21–2, 32–3
real estate, 179
Reddington, Christopher, 174
Renaissance, 46
Al-Risaala, 51
Robinson, Mary, 203, 225
Roman Catholic Church, 23–4, 43
Roman Empire, 217
Rooney, Colonel, 31
Rosenthal (pearl dealers), 8
Royal Air Force (RAF), 19, 30, 31, 42–3, 103, 208
Russia, 84, 85, 95, 161, 189, 212

Saadi, Rais Abdul Rahim, 172
Saadi, Rais Hasan Rais, 172, 173
Sadat, Anwar, 101, 151, 161
SAEPC, 187
Said, Nuri, 146
St Helena, 50
Sandberg, Michael, 156
Sanhuri, Dr Abdul Razak, 140–1
Saudi Arabia, 44, 97, 142; Arab Nationalism, 87; oil industry, 112, 167, 192; and development of Gulf states, 116–17; and Trucial States Development Fund, 117–18; currency, 135; relations with Shaikh Rashid, 143; and Iraqi invasion of Kuwait, 193
Savak, 138
Al-Sayeh, Dr Hamed, 151–2
Schtole, Herr, 181–2
Scotland, 68
Second World War, 19, 30–1, 39, 42–3, 49, 84–5, 167, 182, 208
Shabbir, B. G., 36
Shakhbut, Shaikh *see* Al-Nahayan, Shaikh Shakhbut bin Sultan

Sharjah, 5, 6, 19, 22, 32–3, 61, 87, 96, 179; British Residency Agent, 3; locusts, 35; in Second World War, 42–3; Creek silts up, 75; airport, 103, 104, 118; and the Arab League, 115, 116, 118; Ruler deposed, 119–20; Trucial States Development Office projects, 127; and BBME, 155; and proposed Gulf federation, 163

Shawki, Ahmed, 96

Al-Shemlan, Abdul Aziz, 50, 53, 54

Shia Moslems, 143, 191, 217

Al-Shirawi, Maryam (ESG's mother), 11, 12–13, 20–1, 22, 23, 24, 25, 34, 37, 54, 208

Shuaibi, Riad, 129

Siemens, 181–3, 195

slavery, 15–16

socialism, 71

Somalia, 176

South Arabia, 132

Spain, 19, 45–6

Sri Lanka, 176

steel industry, 187

stock exchanges, 164–5

Sudan, 176

Suez Canal Company, 86

Suez crisis (1956), 72, 86, 90, 95–6, 161

Sumerians, 150, 220

Sunni Moslems, 2, 143, 217

Superior Oil Company, 167–9

Switzerland, 101

Syria, 84, 92, 99

Tahyoura (reading from the Quran), 25

Target Auto Services, 186

Taweelah to Al Ain Pipeline, 185

taxation, oil, 162, 164

Al-Tayer, H. E. Ahmed, 159, 197

Taylor, John, 127

Technical and Trading, 186

Tehran, 88

Al-Thami, Shaikh Ahmed, Ruler of Qatar, 101

Thompson, Rt. Hon. George (Lord Thompson of Monifieth), 118

Tigris, River, 96

Tooting Bec, 68–9

Trevelyan, Sir Humphrey (Lord Trevelyan), 94

tribalism, 217–18

Tripp, Peter, 67

Trucial Oman Levies, 113–14

Trucial Oman Scouts, 113, 114

Trucial States Council, 113, 114–15, 117, 121, 122, 123, 124, 130, 133–4, 137, 141, 170

Trucial States Deliberative Committee, 122, 194

Trucial States Development Fund, 117–18

Trucial States Development Office, 79, 86–7, 110, 139, 145; formation of, 117, 118, 123–4; choice of director, 121–2; ESG as director, 122–5; projects, 125–31

TTE Office Furniture, 186

Tunbs, Greater and Lesser, 5–6, 170

Tunis, 219

Turkey, 203

Turner, Anne, 68–70

'21 Room', London, 90

UAE Currency Board, 156

Umayyad Caliphate, 100

Umm al-Qaiwain, 126, 171, 175

Umm Kalthoum, 92

Unilever, 178

Union Bank of the Middle East, 158

United Arab Emirates (UAE), 6, 135; creation of, 18, 81, 124, 125, 139–46; radio and television service, 129; currency, 137; constitution, 140–1; success of, 144–7; banking industry, 149; prehistoric trade, 150; economic growth, 186–8; ESG as Ambassador of, 186, 194, 196–207, 226; oil industry, 192

United States of America, 83, 84; Second World War, 39; Cold War, 85; Suez crisis, 86, 95–6; and Nasser,

United States of America (*cont.*)
95; formation of UAE, 141–2; and
Iranian revolution, 190–1, 193; and
Iraqi invasion of Kuwait, 193
University of Al-Ain, 219
Ur, 150
Al-Usaimi, Murshid, 80
Al-Uwais, Ali, 80

Wahab, Mohammed Abdul, 92
Walker, Julian, 18, 140
Walker, Rt. Hon. Peter (Lord), 190
war of 1948, 84

war of 1967, 94–5, 132, 148
Wardley Middle East, 155
Western lifestyle, 162–3
Windsor Castle, 200

Yemen, 94
Yezidi tribe, 217
York, Roy, 181

Zayed, Shaikh *see* Al-Nahayan, Shaikh
    Zayed bin Sultan
Zionism, 48–9, 95, 221